"Hush, hush! for God's sake. Here he comes. Make way—make way, I—I must let him pass. For God's sake, sir, don't stop him."—"But I will."—"No, no; you would not stand in the way of——."—"Who, who?"—"The—the *king!*" I shrank back for a moment amazed, and *George the Fourth* passed across the hall, stepped into his carriage, and drove off.

MANUSCRIPTS

FROM

THE DIARY OF A PHYSICIAN.

> Life, as it is, adorns the page.
> Of human smiles and tears
> We paint the record—all the joys,
> The hopes, the raptures, and the fears
> Of sparkling youth and bending age.
>
> SHENSTONE.

VOL. I.

LONDON:

PRINTED AND PUBLISHED BY E. LLOYD, AT THE OFFICE OF "LLOYD'S WEEKLY LONDON NEWSPAPER," 12, SALISBURY-SQUARE, FLEET-STREET.

1844.

PREFACE.

The Publisher of the tales from the "DIARY OF A PHYSICIAN" feels himself now called upon to say a few words concerning that work, and the new form in which it has been presented to the public.

It will be in the knowledge of a number of the readers of these most unprecedentedly popular tales, in this their integral form, that they were originally produced by their Author in "LLOYD'S PENNY SUNDAY TIMES,"—a journal which has for years past catered so successfully for the public.

The tales comprised in this volume have been reprinted from that periodical at the request of a large number of its readers, and the extensive patronage they have received in this, their new form, has been such as to meet the warmest expectations of their Publisher.

Notwithstanding the great outlay which was necessary to secure these highly popular tales to "LLOYD'S PENNY SUNDAY TIMES," an arrangement has been entered into with their author, by which they are still continued in that journal.

Since, however, the "PENNY SUNDAY TIMES" is a journal of a miscellaneous character—comprising every branch of literature—it was not possible to insert so much matter weekly as each number of this work contains.

The consequence of this has been that although these most interesting tales are continued in the "PENNY SUNDAY TIMES" with a vigour and a sparkling reality, that bring the pictures they present home to every breast, this volume has reached the same point with regard to the "DIARY OF A PHYSICIAN" as the journal above-named.

Some short period must, therefore, necessarily elapse before there can be sufficient material in hand in the "PENNY SUNDAY TIMES" to reprint in this form.

In the meantime, those of our readers who have honoured this volume by a perusal, may continue these lively and interesting tales in the "PENNY SUNDAY TIMES," and afterwards have them in this extracted form.

LONDON, 1845.

MANUSCRIPTS

FROM

THE DIARY OF A PHYSICIAN.

INTRODUCTION.

During a long, and I hope not unuseful professional career, it has been a pleasing, although at times a melancholy occupation to me to record all those "moving incidents" and closely cherished family histories which are unfolded to none more freely than to the physician. Many of the characters that will move, speak, and have their new being in these scattered leaves from my Diary, have long since mingled with the dust; for I am now myself in the " sere and yellow leaf." Their crimes and their virtues,—their ambitions,—their plans, and hopes, and dearest projects,—their hot tears and their merry ringing laughter,—all have alike faded away in the dim vista of the past, and I, the old physician, am left, the sole depository of more tales of deep, heartfelt agony,—more episodes of human existence as it is in its fearful yet beautiful reality, than are to be found in the laboured pages of the wildest romance.

Those who still live, and would feel a heart-pang at some of the pages of my Diary, need have no fears. I will only speak of the past. The leaves of my Diary which would wound the feelings of the living must, for a time, still remain sealed. Among the earliest records of my life is an adventure as singular as it is interesting, and one which indeed proves that truth is stranger, far stranger, than fiction. If it awaken a feeling sigh, or perchance a tear, from my readers, the old physician will be amply repaid for his tale of woe.

THE DEAD RESTORED;

OR, THE YOUNG STUDENT.

Early in the year 18—, when I was still but a young man and studying hard for my degree at the University of Edinburgh, a fellow-student and myself were indulging in a quiet stroll in the neighbourhood of the city in which we pursued our studies. As we passed the end of a lane which was inhabited by the very poorest of the population, a loud voice broke upon our ears,—broken, though loud and harsh; and it required but little skill to discover in its tones that it was the voice of some one battling with a mighty grief.

"Dead!" cried the voice,—"dead! God of Heaven, no! It cannot be,—it is impossible. Let me see her,—oh! let me see her! She is my child, woman; she is not dead!"

We paused in the hope of hearing more, and the snuffling tones of an old woman replied to the deep dejected voice of the man.

"Na, na, sir; bide ye frae the bairn. She's no that canny to glower o'er. Deed, and she is dead."

Without another moment's hesitation we, with one accord, turned down the lane, and, directed by the bustle, we paused at the open door of a miserable-looking habitation, from the interior of which came sounds of expostulation and lamentation.

"Let us go in," said my companion.

I hesitated a moment, for there was ever to me something sacred about grief which repressed all curiosity.

"Pho! pho!" said my young companion, "our profession is our passport to such scenes. We may be of some service."

I no longer hesitated, but followed him into the house of mourning.

The staircase, narrow and dilapidated, was exceedingly dark, and it was only by the sounds of deep grief and convulsive sobs that smote our ears as we ascended, that we were enabled to guide our steps in the right direction.

"Hush! Musgrove," said I to my companion, (for such was his name,)—" hush! The sounds come from this room to our left. Shall we knock?"

"Certainly," said Musgrove, applying his knuckles to the door.

"Who now?—who now?" said a voice from within. "Has death returned to give me back my child?"

"Eh! what awfu' talk," said the voice of a woman, and at the same moment an old crone opened the door.

We walked into the room, which presented an appearance of the most abject poverty. The walls were bare, and dripping with unwholesome moisture. A miserable truckle bed was in one corner, and that, together with a table and two invalid chairs, completed the appointments of the place.

Scarcely had we time to make the most cursory observation when we were confronted by a tall, soldierly-looking man, in whose countenance anger was struggling with deep dejection. His eyes were blood-shot and swollen, his dress disordered, and his pale haggard face showed that either grief or want, or perhaps both, had rioted upon the springs of life.

"Well, sirs," he said, after a moment's pause, during which he evidently made a strong effort to suppress his feelings; "well, sirs, you are come at last."

We stared at him and at each other in mute astonishment, and he continued:—

"You are too late. Death has been here—an earlier visiter. God forgive you,—God forgive you!"

"Sir," said I, "there must be some mistake."

"Mistake!" he repeated,—"mistake! Oh, Heaven! if there were,—but, no,—no."

PUBLISHER'S NOTE

PP.5-6 ARE MISSING.

He turned his eye to the miserable couch, and shuddered.

"That is too terrible a truth,—too real,—too real. Away, away, sirs; you are not wanted now, and my heart is too bruised to quarrel with you. There was a time,—but no matter. Away,—away!"

He sank upon a chair, and, covering his face with his hands, sobbed audibly.

We were thoroughly astonished, and looked at the old woman, who was rocking herself to and fro upon a crazy chair by the bedside, to see if she looked at all inclined to give us an explanation.

"We are medical men," said Musgrove.

"No doubt—no doubt," said the old woman.

This was not at all explanatory, so I said,—

"If we can be of any assistance, either professionally or otherwise, we should be very much pleased."

"Pleased!" cried the man, starting up so suddenly that we involuntarily made for the door. "Pleased, say you? Can you talk of pleasure here? Fiends! fiends! When—when can I know pleasure more? Look on that silent form—look!—look!"

He pointed to the bed, and we saw what we had before surmised, that beneath the sheet which lay completely over it was a body.

We neither of us spoke, and, after a pause, the man resumed:—

"You are in danger here. There is something struggling within my breast which tells me so. In my poverty and bitter destitution, while—while my child—my Mary still lived, I sent for ye, and ye came not."

"Indeed you are wrong," said I; "we were taking a walk, and hearing the sounds of lamentation from the end of the lane, curiosity first, and a better motive afterwards, led us to the house."

He looked in my face for a moment, and then turning to the woman he said:—

"Neighbour, is not this Mr. Dalrymple?"

"Deed na, major," said the woman. "When I cam to tak a gude glour at the lads, they are no just either o' them Dalrymple, the docterer."

"Pardon me, gentlemen, pardon me," said the man. "Grief has blinded me. I—I sent for aid to my dying child, and it came not—now, now it is too late."

We neither of us knew very well what to say, and merely bowed.

"Come, come," he continued, "I—I will shew her to you, or—or you would never believe how beautiful she was."

He then took me by the arm, and led me towards the bed; then, gently turning down from off the face of the dead the sheet, he pointed to the calm features of a young girl of apparently seven or eight years of age. The beauty even of that face in death exceeded anything I had ever beheld. There was still a faint tinge of colour on the cheeks, the beautiful lips were slightly apart, and through the long silken eyelashes a glimpse of the clear blue eyes could be obtained: a flood of golden hair hung over her breast and the pillow on which she lay.

I was quite fascinated by the still picture before me. She looked like some beautifully executed piece of wax work.

For two or three minutes there was a deathlike silence in the room; then Musgrove said, in a low whisper,—

"I can hardly believe her dead."

The father's feelings were overcome, and he fell heavily upon the floor in a swoon.

Musgrove raised him from the ground, and with the assistance of the old woman took the necessary means to restore him. In the meantime I laid my ear to the heart of the dead child to assure myself by that test that all vital action had ceased. Alas! it had—she was dead.

"What was the matter with the child?" I said to the woman.

"Deed, sir," she replied, "I canna say. The poor bairn was ailing and moping, and then she went off ye see."

This was not a very satisfactory medical report, but I saw that no better was to be obtained, and to question the father would be unjustifiable cruelty.

"Eh, sirs!" continued the old woman, "she was winsome and boney, and noo there's a superscription going aboot."

"A what?"

"A superscription."

"A superscription, my good woman."

"'Deed yes. It's to place the poor bairn decently in the kirkyard, ye ken."

"Oh, a subscription you mean."

"Weel, weel, a superscription or a superstition, just as you like, sirs."

"And when will she be buried?"

"Just the in-coming Sabbath."

"And where?"

"I' the kirk-yard by the Caulknows."

"He's coming round now," said Musgrove.

"Then we had better go," I said; and I whispered to my young companion about what the old woman called the "superscription."

We were neither of us very rich; but we managed to leave behind us a couple of sovereigns, and taking another look at the calm still face of the beautiful child, we left the house of mourning with our minds full of our strange adventure.

* * * * *

It was on Wednesday that our visit to the dwelling in the lane had been made, and I did not see much of my friend Musgrove for the next two or three days, as he was not studying at the same hospital as myself. On the Sunday morning, however, he came to me, and, with an air half confident and half perplexed, he said,—

"Do you know when that child we saw in the lane was to be buried?"

"Yes," said I.

"When?"

"To-day."

"To-day! Hem!"

"Why, what are you driving at, Musgrove?"

"Do you know where she is to be buried?"

"Yes, at Caulknows."

"Caulknows? Oh, that is ——"

"To the left of the Leith road."

"Yes, yes, I know it. To-day—at Caulknows."

"Well, what then, Musgrove?"

"I should like vastly to know what she died of."

"Some disease of the heart, you may depend."

"Hardly in so young a subject; but ——"

"But what?"

"We might know."

"How?"

"By getting—the body."

I must own I was not much shocked at the proposition. My professional education had rubbed off the rust of a good many of my prejudices; but still I shrunk from disturbing the repose of that young creature.

"Leave her alone, Musgrove," I said. "It's hazardous, and, besides, I really shrink from the undertaking."

"I tell you what," said Musgrove, earnestly, "I must do it."

"Must, Musgrove?"

"Yes; the idea has haunted me, sleeping or waking, at home or abroad. I believe I shall never know peace till I find out what that child died of."

"Why, Musgrove, are you mad?"

"It almost amounts to a monomania," said Musgrove, smiling; "but call it what you will, I am resolved, with you or without you, to possess myself of that girl's body to-night."

"Reflect, Musgrove; be persuaded."

"I'm fixed."

"Nay, now ——"

"It's of no use to try to dissuade me from it. Will you come with me, or will you not?"

"Rather than anybody else should, I will."

"You will?"

"Yes."

"Then come away now to Caulknows, and find exactly the spot, so that we may know it again at midnight."

Reluctantly, although such adventures were nothing new to medical students at that time, I allowed Musgrove to link his arm in mine, and conduct me to the ancient graveyard of the kirk of Caulknows.

As we arrived at the wicket gate leading to the humble churchyard, a throng of persons were just issuing from it, and we stood aside to allow them to pass.

"We are too late," whispered Musgrove. "There's the old dame whom we saw at the house in the lane. They are all coming away from the funeral."

"Hush!" said I, "the father is not here. Can you not guess where he is to be found?"

"At the grave of his child," said Musgrove.

"Now once more," I whispered—"once more let me im-

"Martlett's-court, young man," said Mrs. Green. "If so be as you goes down Bow-street, it's the second turning as you ——"

The carriage was in motion before Mrs. Green had finished her elaborate direction, for the servants of a popular physician know all parts of the town alike.

In order that the reader may be able fully to comprehend my feelings upon the reception of the note, I will, during the drive to Martlett's-court, recount so much of Emily Beauclerc's story as is necessary to connect the incidents of my mournful and affecting narrative.

Emily Beauclerc was the only child of Major Beauclerc, a soldier, who had married, late in life, a lady possessing every domestic virtue which could render a happy home a terrestrial paradise; and when the major clasped to his heart for the first time, his little Emily, he thanked Heaven, in the fulness of his joy, for making him so blessed.

It was when Emily was nearly ten years of age, and beautiful as a little Hebe, that I became acquainted with the happy and united family of the Beauclercs. During a temporary residence at the Isle of Wight, after a fatiguing professional year, I made a friendship with the major, and myself and wife rarely passed happier hours anywhere than in the beautiful and picturesque marine villa of the Beauclercs.

Emily, as she grew in stature, expanded into the loveliest girl I think I ever saw. She was rather above the ordinary standard of fifteen, and her blue eyes and long silken tresses were the most beautiful that could be conceived.

Among the occasional guests at the villa of Major Beauclerc was a Mr. Willoughby, who, as well as being presumptive heir to an old baronetcy, was certainly a most prepossessing individual. He united all the charms of good sense with a lively and polished exterior, and no one for a moment who looked into his fresh, candid-looking countenance, could have suspected that his heart was so hollow as it afterwards proved.

It is strange that those persons who are most interested in what is passing around them, are commonly the last properly to comprehend it; and so it was with the Beauclercs. They did *not* see that Mr. Willoughby was paying the most assiduous homage to their beautiful child, but I did; and while I saw it I likewise saw an air and a manner about Willoughby that I did not think at all consistent with truth and honour. Yet, what could I do? It is very difficult to convict a man of harbouring bad intentions in his heart from the tones of his voice or the glances of his eyes!

I did, however, suspect Mr. Willoughby; and before leaving the Beauclercs, one radiant summer, I earnestly desired my wife to make an opportunity of speaking to Mrs. Beauclerc upon the subject. She did so speak, and got for answer that Mr. Willoughby was a most estimable man, and, moreover, affianced to his cousin, a young lady of large fortune and expectations.

My wife likewise told me that she fancied she discovered after that conversation, an air of coldness about the Beauclercs towards us, and as I had fancied it too, we gradually withdrew ourselves, and felt how hard a thing it is to give advice to people.

Emily, as I have stated, was then in her sixteenth year, and a paragon of loveliness; and on the quay at Ryde, as myself and wife were about embarking for Southampton, we met the Beauclercs with their constant attendant—Mr. Willoughby.

I could see in the manner of the major that he wanted to say something, but did not know exactly how to begin, and I said,—

"Well, major, we may not meet again for some time. Believe me I wish you every happiness the world can afford."

"I thank you, Dr. ——," he replied, "and from my soul I believe you mean well; but let an old soldier tell you, that gratuitous advice is always unwelcome."

I understood him, and replied:—

"What my wife said to Mrs. Beauclerc I instructed her to say, and I regret it has been ill received. I valued my friend's honour."

"A soldier and a gentleman," he replied stiffly, "knows how to take care of his honour. My child, sir, must be like Cæsar's wife, not only innocent, but above suspicion."

"You have greatly mistaken me," I said.

"Good day, sir," he replied.

I bowed coldly, and so we separated from the Beauclercs.

"Now, after that," said I to my wife, "who would stop his best friend from going to destruction?"

"Oh, never mind," replied my wife, "they will come round again."

However, for a long time they did not come round, or square, or any shape whatever, as regarded us, and we had ceased to talk of them, except occasionally to wonder how Emily looked, and if she was married or not.

It was full two years after the little bit of irritable conversation I have recorded, that I was passing through Finsbury-square one day, when suddenly somebody laid hold of my arm with a grip, positively painful. I turned quickly, and saw a haggard, pale, care-worn face before me, and a pair of deeply-sunk bloodshot eyes glaring in my face in a most unpleasant manner.

The strange-looking man still held me, and in a hoarse, discordant voice, he said—,

"You were right—you were right."

I knew him by his voice; it was Major Beauclerc.

"Good Heavens, Major Beauclerc!" I exclaimed, "what has occurred?"

"You were right," he repeated, "you were right, Dr. ——"

"What do you mean?" I said, in some alarm, for I fancied he must be mad.

For a moment he appeared choking, and gasped for breath; then he pronounced the name of Willoughby.

The truth flashed upon me, and drawing his arm within mine, I said:—

"Hush—hush!—Be calm, now, be calm,—and walk home with me."

"You were right," he replied. "I tell you, doctor, that man was a villain!"

"Come, come, we will talk over this matter more calmly. Come home with me, Major Beauclerc."

He looked in my face a moment, and then, linking his arm in mine, he walked with me some minutes—neither of us spoke; I knew that his heart was too full for utterance, and I preferred allowing his freshly awakened feelings to calm a little before I made any inquiries.

We at length reached my house, and, before I would allow him to speak, I insisted upon his taking a stimulant and sedative, which I recommended to him.

He then laid his hand upon my arm, and said, in a voice of deep anguish,—

"Doctor, you guess all?"

"Nay," said I, "I cannot presume to do so. That some domestic calamity has befallen you, I cannot doubt, but ——"

"Yes, yes," he cried, "a domestic calamity indeed, sir. If death had stalked into my house, armed with all his terrors, real and imaginary, I—I could have smiled in resignation; but—but ——"

"But what?"

"You ask me what?"

"I needs must, my dear major."

"Dishonour!" he screamed. "Reproach!—contumely —disgrace!"

"Disgrace?"

"Yes, am I not disgraced when my child—my—my— Emily! There, sir—there, doctor—I have mentioned a name that has not passed my lips for many a weary year."

"Be as calm, Major Beauclerc, as you can," I said, mildly, but firmly. "If I can be of service to you, you know I will; but in order that I may be so, you must tell me all, and tell it to me mildly and rationally."

"Rationally!" he repeated.

"Certainly. You are a father, but still you are a man, and have, I hope, both sense and patience."

For a moment he seemed annoyed at my affected calmness, and then he said,—

"You are right,—you are right. I will be calm; but my heart bleeds, doctor."

I said nothing, and he continued,—

"About four months after you and I last parted, we were assembling for breakfast, when a note was placed in my hands. Here it is."

He produced a soiled and crumpled piece of paper from his pocket, and handed it to me. I read as follows:—

"FATHER,—Forgive me, and dear mother, too, plead for me. He whom you knew I loved has persuaded me to a private marriage,—I believe merely to avoid the écles of a public one. Father, dear father, I am happy. In a short week you will hear again from your own   "EMILY."

I returned him the note, and crunching it up in his hand, he looked me steadily in the face.

"Then," I said, "Emily eloped with ——"

"Hush!" he cried; "name him not,—you will drive me mad if you do. "No one names *him* to me."

"Well, but,' I continued, "it was certainly a strange proceeding; but.——"

"But—but,—oh! you know not what followed. No, no, no,—this," striking the note with his hand, "this was nothing,—a mere passing pang,—but,—but, ——"

"But what?"

"I did hear again from her in a week."

"And ——",

"Can you not guess?"

"I cannot."

"No! How could you guess at such monstrous villany? How could you? Read that,—read that."

Thrusting his hand into his breast, he produced another note, and handed it to me.

Its contents shocked me, although I was, in some measure, prepared for them.

The note ran thus:—

"FATHER, — I am betrayed—my marriage was a hideous mockery—I am ruined and abandoned. Forget, oh, forget your lost, lost   "EMILY."

"What did you do, Major Beauclerc, upon receipt of this?" I asked.

"Do?" he cried; "do? I—I flew to London,—I sought my child, but she was gone!—gone!"

"You could not find her?"

"I could not. Then I sought her betrayer. He had left the country. He had told an acquaintance that he would come back when the old man was dead, meaning me."

"The heartless scoundrel!"

"No, no, doctor; call him nothing yet. We—we must coin some new word to call such a man."

"And what has happened since?"

"I—I scarcely know," he replied. "I have wandered many months in search of my—my Emily, but I have not found her. Oh, doctor, look for her!—look for her!" He leant his head upon the table, and sobbed like an infant.

I was much affected, but I mastered my emotions, and said,—

"My old friend, all that I can do I will do to aid you. Are you staying in London?"

"Yes," he gasped.

"Come to me, then, every day, and let us consult what can be done to find your child, if—if——"

"If she still lives, you would say, Doctor? Nay, never fear me. I am familiar with the idea of her death."

He shortly afterwards left me; but although I made every inquiry, I could hear no tidings of the beautiful Emily Beauclerc. In a few months the major left London, fancying he had found some clue to his child in an inland county, and I had not seen him for a considerable time, when I was surprised by the call of my vulgar, but most welcome visitor, with whom the reader will recollect he left me seated, in my carriage, and driving to Martlett-s-court, Covent-garden.

* * * * * *

We made a rapid progress towards the locality for which we were bound, and I had barely time to ask a few necessary questions of my companion, when the carriage turned down Little Russell-street, and stopped opposite a narrow archway, by the side of a public-house.

"Now, madam," I said, "if you will alight and lead the way, I shall be happy to follow you."

"Lauks me!" exclaimed the lady, "is we here a-ready? what an unkimmon comfortable coach, to be sure. Show you the way? Oh, dear, yes, Mr. Thingummy, with a vast deal of pleasure."

"If you please, ma'am, and as quickly as convenient."

I sprang out of the carriage after her, and followed her into Martlett's-court. She stopped at the door of a mean, dirty-looking house, and after pausing to cuff some half dozen dirty children, who were playing upon the steps, she invited me to walk in. "What an abode," thought I, "for Emily Beauclerc. She, the child of love and luxury, the petted and caressed."

I stumbled through the dark, dirty passage, full of melancholy thoughts.

"Walk up, Doctor Whatdoyecallum," cried the lady, "and mind the broken stair, it's the thirdest from the top."

Coming fresh out of the light, the place seemed to me as dark as night, but by degrees, as I slowly ascended the rickety staircase, my eyes became more accustomed to the place, and could see pretty well to steer my course among cracked pitchers, flat-irons, mops, brooms, and all sorts of litter.

"Here's her door," suddenly cried the lady.

I entered a small back room, and, accustomed as I was to all sorts of misery, I sunk into a broken chair with a deep sigh, and my eyes were in a moment rivetted to a squalid couch, on which lay what had once been the admired, the worshipped Emily Beauclerc. Yes, pale and wan, on that miserable couch lay Emily Beauclerc. She slept, or seemed to sleep; one arm lay outside the clothes, and so white and thin was it, that I can compare it to nothing but a narrow strip of moonlight resting on the squalid, miserable couch. Her long fair hair streamed over the pillow and bed, and hung down nearly to the floor. Good Heavens! what a picture of desolation did she present!

Could the villain who had brought her, the child of love and luxury, to such a pass have seen her at that moment, it must have broken his heart, if he had such an article to break.

Mrs. Green saw by my face, I suppose, how deeply I was interested, and she said:—

"Ah, deary me, it's melancholic! Poor young thing!"

"I'm sure, though I say it as shouldn't, I've been up early and late with her. Oh, deary ——!"

"Hush!" said I, "Hush! I do not wish her to be awakened just new. Here, take this to the nearest chemist's, and bring what they will make up for you as quickly as you can."

I tore a leaf from my pocket-book, and wrote a prescription for an anodyne.

"Lauks me!" said Mrs. Green, "what will it come to, sir?"

"What does this lady owe you, madam?"

"Three blessed pounds and sixteen and fourpence."

I gave her a five pound note, saying:—

"Take this, pay yourself, and get the medicine. If you are back in ten minutes you can keep the change."

Mrs. Green immediately vanished, and I was alone with Emily Beauclerc.

I sat down by the side of the wretched couch, and determined to wait until she was awakened.

Her breathing was irregular, and heavy, and from the general aspect of the face I feared that she was not long for this world.

Mrs. Green returned in an incredibly short time, and taking the medicine from her, I placed my finger on my lips and pointed to the door.

I was by the bedside in a moment, and said softly:—

"I hope you are better, Miss Beauclerc? I am Dr. ——; you know me?"

"Who speaks?" she cried, "Beauclerc? Who calls me—Beauclerc?—No—no—Willoughby—Willoughby—not—not Beauclerc—no—no—no!"

She sunk on the pillow and burst into tears.

I said nothing, but let her weep on for some moments; then stooping close to her ear, I said,—

"Emily, I think you may still be happy."

"Happy?" she cried, turning her face to me, "oh! you are Dr. ——."

"Yes, and you must take this immediately."

I offered her the medicine which I had poured into a cracked cup I had found on the table.

"Yes—yes, certainly," she said, and she took it at a draught.

"Is it poison?"

"Poison, Emily?"

"Yes."

"Nonsense, Emily, doctors don't poison, you know, or they would lose their patients too soon," I said, with a smile. "Are you strong enough to tell me briefly how you came to be here?"

She raised herself in the bed, and said with a look which I shall not forget to my dying day,—

"Doctor, I am Willoughby's wife,—in the sight of God I am his wife. We were so happy for one week,—'twas like a summer's day. Then, Doctor, one morning I found a note on my pillow, and he was gone."

"Have you that note?" I asked.

"They have tried to get it from me," she whispered.

"Who?"

"Don't you see them?"

DIARY OF A PHYSICIAN.

"See what?—who?"—" The gibbering fiends;—look—look—there's a struggle;—now the good angel conquers—pity—pity!"

I had not suspected till now that her mind was affected, and I was much shocked.

"Hush, hush," I said; "will you let me read the note?"

"Who are you?" she said.—" Why, Dr. ——; you know me."

"Ah!—indeed—I knew you in the other world—the bright world. How happy we all were. Yes, you shall read it; here it is."

She drew a crumpled note from under her pillow, and handed to me. I read it as follows:—

"EMILY,—You cannot be such a little simpleton as to fancy yourself my wife. Our marriage was a mock one, and a friend of mine acted the clergyman. I shall make you a handsome allowance—keep your heart up. "Yours,
"YOU KNOW WHO."

It required but little skill fully to comprehend the story of the innocent and unfortunate Emily Beauclerc, the victim of a forced marriage, that diabolical refinement on ordinary seduction which triumphs over virtue, not weakness.

I was now most anxious that the opiate I had given her should take effect, so as to leave me at liberty to take some immediate steps to remove her from her present uncongenial situation.

"Well, Emily," I repeated, "I do not see why you should not yet see many happy days."—She shook her head despairingly.—" Not, certainly," I added, "if you give way to despondency and are determined to be miserable."

She looked fixedly in my face as she said, in a voice of unnatural calmness,

"Doctor, you know well ——"—" What, Emily?"

"That I am dying."—" Indeed, I know no such thing."

She sunk back upon the pillow, and I saw that the opiate was taking effect. Her eyes gently closed, and murmuring some words indistinctly, she relapsed into a deep sleep.

I gently rose and left the room, closing the door behind me. On the staircase was Mrs. Green, and I more than suspected that the "lady" had had her ear in very close proximity to the key-hole of the door.

"Dear me, sir, so you are a going," she said, with an affectation of deep deference.—" Yes," I said, "but I shall return soon, and in the meantime do not, on any account, allow Mrs. Willoughby to be disturbed."

"Disturbed!" cried Mrs. Green; "lauks a mussy, sir, we never has no disturbance here. There's Mr. Lee, as has the one pair front, he's as quiet a gentleman as ever darkened a door; and then there's the Miss Migginses, as is *figurantoes*."

"What?"—" *Figurantoes*."

"What do you mean?"—" Why, they dances and does *nympheses* in the *ballots*."

"Oh, I understand; they belong to the theatre."—" Yes, sir, to Common Garden."

"Well, Mrs. Green, keep your house as quiet as you can, and you may find it to your advantage."

So saying, I, for a short time, bid adieu to the elegant locality of Martlett's-court. On my road homewards, I discussed with myself upon what I had better do with regard to Emily Beauclerc. That she was in a most critical and dangerous state I firmly believed, but still it was impossible to say how much rest, comfort, and serenity of mind might do for her.

After reflection upon the subject, I thought my first steps should be cautiously to apprise poor Major Beauclerc, who had left me his address, of what had occurred. He had requested me to forward all letters to him through an army agent, at Charing Cross, and, in order to lose no time, I directed my coachman to drive there at once, intending to write a note from their office.

When I arrived and explained my errand, I was informed that Major Beauclerc was expected in town that very day, so I merely left my card, after writing on it that I wished to see him immediately.

After making my necessary morning visits, which I rendered as short as possible, I hurried home, and related to my wife my adventures in Martlett's-court.

"Let the poor girl be brought here at once," was her immediate suggestion.—" I confess," I replied, "that you have anticipated my wishes."

"Then go back and bring her: or, stay, I will go with you. Poor Emily, what she must have suffered!"

In five minutes more all were in the carriage, and *en route* for Martlett's-court.—Mrs. Green was all smiles and sweetness, and we soon found ourselves by the bed-side of the deserted Emily.

"She will awaken soon," I said; "let us wait. She had better awaken naturally than be roused by us."

I had scarcely spoken when the sleeper moved, and opening her still beautiful and expressive eyes, she fixed them upon my wife.

"Where am I now?" she said.—"Emily, you know me; I am Mrs. ——."

"Are you dead too?"—"Dead?"

"Yes; I have passed the gates which separate the living from the dead. All here are spirits. I—I am waiting for *him*. Oh, God, it was not much pain to die!"

My wife looked at me inconceivably shocked.—"She is mad," she whispered.—"Her mind certainly wanders," I replied; "but there is no distinct mania. Do not be alarmed. Her present mental aberration is only the result of temporary excitement acting on a weakened system."

"Why do you whisper?" said Emily, suddenly.—I sat down by the side of the bed, and looking her fully in the face, I said,—"Emily Beauclerc."

She was silent for a moment, and then said softly,—

"Emily Beauclerc! I was that."—"And are still," I continued. "Come, you have been dreaming. I mean you to come home with us, and be reconciled to your father."

"My father?"—"Yes; your poor disconsolate father."

I had touched the right chord, and was glad to see her burst into tears.—My wife would now have interposed, but I motioned her to be silent.

"My poor father," sobbed Emily, "disconsolate?"—"Yes, Emily; but he wishes you to comfort his old age."

"Me? Can he, will he, forgive his erring child?"—"Certainly he will."

"Oh, doctor, and you, my dear Mrs. ——, how can I thank you?"—"You know us, then," said my wife.—"Know you, my kind old friends?—oh, yes, yes."

"Well, then, Emily," I said, "let us fully understand each other. Willoughby deceived you by a mock marriage, and then deserted you. Your father shall know all from me, and will joyfully receive again his child. I will see Willoughby, and if he have a heart at all, he shall make honourable reparation. I have been thus explicit, because, as you are coming home with us, I wished you to have nothing on your mind in the way of fancying that we did not know all your story. Now you can consult with us freely. Mrs. —— will assist you to rise, and I will wait in the carriage."

So saying, without waiting for a reply, I left the room.—In about ten minutes my wife appeared with Emily's arm linked in her's, and before another half hour had elapsed, we were in sight of my door.—When I entered the hall of my house, with Emily upon my arm, my servant said,—

"Sir, there is a gentleman waiting for you."

"Who is it?" I said.—"I, doctor," cried Major Beauclerc, suddenly opening the parlour door exactly facing his daughter. He stood, transfixed, as if suddenly turned to stone, and Emily, with a piercing shriek, fainted in my arms.

* * * * *

Feb. 20th.—Emily Beauclerc has been in my house a week. She has never recovered the shock of suddenly meeting her father. She is sinking rapidly.

* * * * *

Such is the entry I found in my Diary; and on the evening of the day that I made it we all met in the dying girl's chamber,—that is, myself and wife, and her heart-stricken father.—We were silent, for we knew not what to say, and the dying girl—for dying she was—looked from one to the other of us, and could not fail to read the fatal truth in our countenances.

"Dear father," she faintly cried, "and you, dear friends, I shall leave you soon."—The major could not speak, but turned to the window to conceal his deep emotion.—Emily continued,—"I have but one wish now on this side of the grave."

"Name it, Emily," I said, "and if it is in human power it shall be complied with."

"Willoughby ——"—"Curses," cried her father.—"Hush—hush," said I. "You wish to see him once more, Emily?"—"Thank you, doctor," she replied.

I took the major by the arm, and led him to the window, saying,—

"She must be indulged in this. The present moment is not one to curse in, but to weep."

"But how?" he asked,—"how—the——"—"I know what you mean. You think Willoughby has left the country?"—"I do."

"He did, but has, I have ascertained, returned recently, and is now Sir Montague Willoughby. Will you baulk the last wish of your dying child?"—He sunk on a chair, saying,—"Do as you like—as you like, doctor. I—I shall soon follow her."

"Then I must candidly tell you she cannot survive the night."—"God help me!" he cried.

I went to Emily, and said,—

"Your father consents. You shall see him."—"Within an hour?" she said, earnestly.

"So soon?"—"Yes, doctor; for the next hour will be my last."—I believed her, and was silent, while she continued,—"Go—go at once. Bring him, and recollect I must see him *alone*."

"You shall," I replied; and I immediately left the room.

I had ascertained the address of the seducer, and not waiting for my carriage, I stepped into a cab and drove off to the lordly residence of Sir Montague Willoughby.

My card was a passport to his presence: but he received me coldly and haughtily. I had no time for set phrases or courtly harangues.

"Emily Beauclerc is dying," I said. "Within the hour she will be no more. Her last wish is to see you."—He was moved—he trembled, and in another ten minutes we were alighting at my door.

"Go in there," I said, as I opened the door of my visiting room. "I will come for you in a moment."

I rushed up the staircase, and into Emily's room. She rose in her bed when she saw me.

"He—he," she gasped.—"Is here," I said. "Compose yourself. I will send him to you."

I then beckoned my wife and the major from the room, and having earnestly requested them to remain in the drawing-room till Willoughby was gone, I went down stairs to the parlour. The unhappy man—for unhappy he was—stood by the window, looking as pale as death.

"Where—where is she?" he faltered.—"Alone on the second floor," I said. "Go up. You will see a door partially open—that is her chamber."

I saw him stagger as he left the room, and he walked slowly up the stairs. The house was as still as the grave, and a strange feeling came across me as I stood in the hall and heard the measured tread of that miserable man slowly ascending the stone staircase of my house. Once I heard him sob—then came a dead silence. He had reached the room. My heart beat tumultuously—each moment seemed an age.

Suddenly a shriek, so awful that even it now seems to ring in my ears, filled the house with its dreadful echoes. I could not move, but stood rooted to the spot. Then came a heavy plunging noise down the staircase, and before I could resolve thought to action, Sir Montague Willoughby fell upon the marble floor of the hall, with a hideous, sickening crash.

The whole house was then in commotion. Servants ran here and there in consternation. I flew to the baronet, and an instant examination told me he was dead. His skull was fractured by his fall. I then sought the chamber of Emily. The door was wide open, and she lay exactly in the same position I had last seen her, but she was *dead*.

We never knew the exact truth of how it all happened; but my opinion is, that Emily died before Willoughby reached her room, and that he must have flown from it in such horror that he fell down the staircase, and so met his death.

Major Beauclerc still lives; but, alas! reason has fled.

THE GHOST-SEEKER.

Perhaps one of the most singular stories in my Diary turns upon an event which happened to me in the early part of my professional life, and it is the more remarkable, in consequence of being the only case of mania presenting so many curious symptoms and contrary manifestations which I ever encountered.

I was waited upon one morning by a lady who appeared in very deep affliction, and who in broken accents asked me if I would meet Dr. ——, an eminent physician, who I well knew by name, to consult concerning her husband's case.

I, of course, professed my readiness to do so, and at the same time said,—

"If quite consistent with your feelings, madam, I should be glad to know the nature of your husband's disease."—"It's dreadful, sir," she replied, "most dreadful."—"Indeed? I trust you deceive yourself, madam. There are many diseases that appear dreadful to a patient and his friends, but which present no extraordinary difficulties to the physician or the surgeon."—"Oh, doctor," she said, "I wish it were so, but I am worn out."

"Worn out?"—"Yes, with watching and anxiety; my supplications, my entreaties, my prayers and tears, have been of no avail,—he will not give up the mad pursuit."

"Mad pursuit, madam?"—"Yes, a horrible conceit."

"Pray explain yourself. I presume some species of dementia afflicts your husband?"—"Yes; I can bear it no longer; my health is sinking; want of rest is killing me."

"Pray, madam, be more explicit," said I, my curiosity being strongly awakened by what she had said.—"I will, doctor; my husband in every other respect is all that an attached wife could wish, but he is a Ghost Seeker."

"A what?" cried I, in astonishment.—"I use his own words. He calls himself the Ghost Seeker, and says he never shall be satisfied till he has seen a ghost."

"I should not be at all surprised at his being very soon gratified," said I.

"Gracious Heavens, doctor, what do you mean?"—"I mean," said I, smiling, "that if his imagination be so strongly acted upon on that subject, I am surprised it does not create visions enough for him."

"Can anything be done, sir?"—"I can scarcely say at present. Dr. ——, you tell me, has attended him?"—"Yes."

"I apprehend the case, then, comes within the sphere of medical influence. The principal difficulty in all these brain diseases, whether general or local, is to manage the patient so as to induce him to adopt the necessary remedies."

"But you will come, doctor."—"Certainly, if you wish it; but perhaps it would be better to leave him alone. Does he run into any violent excesses, in pursuit of that mania?"

"Oh, yes—yes. He is always making incantations; then he brings home human bones from churchyards; and at twelve o'clock he rises from his bed, and calls and taunts the ghosts of their owners to come for them."

"That is sufficiently disagreeable," I replied. "And now tell me one other thing. Is your husband willing to see medical men?"

"Yes, doctor, quite so. He will talk quite rationally to you except on that one point. Nay, he will argue with you as to whether it is a disease or not."

"Well, I will attend any appointment you may make with Dr. ——"

The lady then left me her address as Mrs. Harrington, St. John's Wood, and it was arranged that I should meet Dr. —— the next morning at eleven o'clock at her residence.

I must confess I was a little anxious to see the singular Mr. Harrington, and during the day I made some inquiries concerning him, the result of which was that he was a retired merchant of considerable wealth, and had always been esteemed a most sensible and acute man.

Had my time been at my own disposal, I should have called on Dr. —— previously, but as it was I had no resource but to meet him at St. John's Wood, and there gleam what I could of the nature of the case.

* * * * *

I was punctual to the hour, and found a house replete with every comfort. I was ushered into a handsome and spacious drawing-room, and there found Dr. ——, who had been waiting for me about five minutes.

Mrs. Harrington joined us in a moment, and now that she was divested of her walking attire, I could plainly see that want of rest and anxiety had made great ravages on her health.

"Madam," I said, "something must be done for your health, if we should fail in giving a more healthy tone to your husband's mind."

Before she could reply, the door opened, and a tall, gentlemanly man, of apparently about fifty years of age, entered the room.—He bowed, and we both returned the salutation.

"Mr. Harrington," said the wife to me; then turning to her husband—"Henry, this is Doctor ——."

"Sir, I am delighted to see you," said Mr. Harrington. "Gentlemen, will you take any refreshment?"—"Do," said Doctor —— to me—"Thank you," I said.

"Mary," said Mr. Harrington, in the most rational manner in the world, "tell William to bring a tray and some wine."

While he was giving this order, Doctor —— whispered to me,—

"Don't allude to the mania. Let him come round to it himself."

I nodded acquiescence.

The tray was brought, and we all three sat down to an excellent, though somewhat early, luncheon. Mrs. Harrington had left the room, and we certainly looked as rational a party as could well be supposed.

"You have a charming abode here, Mr. Harrington," said I.—"Yes," he replied; "to me, who have lived pent up in the City the greater part of my life, it appears, indeed, most delightful."

"These suburban villas," remarked Dr. ——, "always had a charm for me."

Mr. Harrington seemed thoughtful for a moment, and then, looking me hard in the face, he said,—

"I beg your pardon for the abrupt question I am going to ask you."

Doctor —— gave me a nudge with his elbow, and Mr. Harrington continued,—

"Did you ever find a ghost?"—"A ghost?" I repeated.

"Yes, sir, a ghost. Did you ever find a ghost, sir?—that's what I ask. Because you know Dr. Johnson says that many persons who deny their existence with their tongues, confess it by their fears, and the Rosicrucians could raise spirits. The world is teeming with invisible life, sir. We are surrounded—hemmed in. At our table,—in our chambers we have them—everywhere. Now, what I ask you is, did you ever see one?"—"I certainly have not," I said.

"Nor have I," he replied, "and that's what vexes me and nearly drives me mad."

He gave a thump on the table that made the glasses jump again.

"Sometimes," he continued, "I catch a glimpse of one, and then he's off again. A hand—a foot—the side glimpse of a face—the flash of an eye. I have seen all that; but they torment me, and won't let me see a *whole ghost*. So I'm a ghost seeker, you see, naturally. Look here."

He suddenly drew from his pocket a human thigh bone, and laid it with a dab upon the table.

"Look here," he continued. "Here's the thigh bone of some fellow. I've been taunting him for a week about it, but he won't come!"

Again he gave the table a thump. Then suddenly fixing his eyes on one part of the room, he cried,—

"There!—now there's one there! but he won't show himself—no, not he. There's just a dim shadow of something. Don't you see? Look!—there—there! It goes along by the wall. See! see! Curse you."

So saying, he caught up the bone, and threw it with great force against the wall.—During all this paroxysm one circumstance struck me as confirmatory of his insanity. He carefully avoided meeting my eye.—When he had thrown the bone, however, he turned to me, and I fixed his gaze, and saw him cower, immediately, as all insane people will do.

"Mr. Harrington," said I, "you can't expect people to call upon you if you behave so strangely."—"I—I," he muttered—"I was provoked, you see."—"Provoked!—nonsense!"—

"I'm the ghost seeker, you know," he said, calmly, "and people know how annoyed I am."

"That may be," said I, "but you ought to know better than to behave so ridiculously. I'll place you in the way of seeing as many ghosts as you like. Why, you are making a fuss about the commonest thing to men of science that can be."

Mr. Harrington looked at me with an air of profound astonishment.

"You shall be gratified," I continued. "Good day for the present. To-morrow we will again meet and arrange the particulars."

I saw his cheek grow pale, and I congratulated myself that I had frightened him a little.—We said nothing particular to Mrs. Harrington, except that we had hopes of a cure, and we then took our leave.

"What do you think of our plan?" I said to Doctor ——. —"It is the only one that presents any chance of success," he said. "He may be frightened out of his ghost mania."

"So I think," I replied; "although we may find some difficulty in carrying out the scheme. The only chance is to bring him to your or my house, and if needs be we must make a ghost for him. I think that the shock to the nervous system will prove beneficial. As it is he is a pest to his whole household."

"That he certainly is, and unless this crotchet of his is checked by some stronger feeling, he will become an unmanageable lunatic."

"Well," I said, "I will call upon you to-morrow at ten, and we can take a quiet drive to the villa, and consult upon a plan of operations on the road. I pity his poor wife from my soul."

So we parted, and I flattered myself I had made a step towards the cure of Mr. Harrington.

* * * *

The next morning I was true to my appointment with Doctor ——, whom I found waiting anxiously for me.

"I like the idea of humouring this mania of Harrington's," he said. "Have you arranged any means of carrying it out?"

"Yes," I replied. "We must get him to my house, and I think I can then manage it pretty well. I have a very dark room in the back of my house, and I think if we could get him there and make him believe that we can easily gratify his whim of seeing a ghost, that he will give it up because it is no longer unattainable."

"I think that nothing is more probable," said Doctor ——. "Now let us see our patient."

We were conducted to the room in which Mr. Harrington sat, and were welcomed by him in the same courteous manner as on the preceding day.—I inquired after his health, and he replied,—

"I am very well, thank you. Really, you are very kind. Will you take lunch?"—"Why," said I, "the fact is, I made you a promise yesterday, Mr. Harrington, which I am bound to fulfil."

"Well," he said, quickly, "I should not have mentioned it if you had not. What I want is to see a ghost. You know that?"

Bang went his hand on the table, and I assented, saying,—

"Certainly, and you shall be gratified."

"Gratified?"—"Yes."

"You mean I shall see a ghost?"—"Certainly."

"Along with you?"—"No, I can't say that. I have no liking for such company. Every one to his taste, you know, Mr. Harrington. You shall see a ghost; but it must be alone."

"Alone!"—"Yes, to be sure. You will be gratified. Are you not the Ghost Seeker?"

"True—very true. Then you believe in—in ghosts?"

"You do likewise," I replied.

"Yes—yes; but it's so strange you are the only person I've found who didn't argue me mad about what they called my delusion."

I shook my head in a very disparaging manner of everybody else, and I saw that the monomaniac began to look upon me with fear.

"You must come to my house," I continued.—"Oh, very well," he said. "Here, Mary, my dear, this gentleman is going to show me a ghost at last. Just take care of these for me till I come back."

So saying, he disencumbered his coat pockets of several human bones, and laid them upon the table. I saw a tear in Mrs. Harrington's eye, and her voice faltered as she whispered to me,—

"Should you succeed in scaring from his mind this terrible mania, you will have restored me to a new life."—"It is only an experiment, my dear madam, we are trying," I said; "but from what I can observe of the state of your husband's mind, I am, I own, sanguine of success."

Mr. Harrington, although with a little nervousness of manner, stepped willingly enough into my chariot, and he, I, and Doctor —— proceeded to town very amicably.

* * * *

The room that I have mentioned in my house was admirably adapted for the purpose I had in view of alarming Mr. Harrington, so as to give him a thorough sickness of ghost seeking. I could see he was in a nervous, fidgetty state as we proceeded, and he looked almost as if he would gladly run away when my carriage stopped at the door of my residence.

I took him by the arm, and at once led him to the room I have mentioned, and which, I ought to have stated, was a dark room, having no window whatever, so that I had been compelled to have gas laid on in it for my own convenience.

Mr. Harrington looked a little scared when he saw the dark den into which I requested him to walk.

"Sit down, sir," I said. "I trust we shall not be obliged to detain you long here."

"It's—it's very dark," he remarked.

"Yes," said I, "and we must keep it so to a certain extent, or we shall not succeed in our endeavours."

I then lighted a small chemical lamp, which burned pyroligneous ether, and which only sufficed to impart an additional air of gloom to the various objects in the room.

The light from such lamps robs the complexion of every particle of colour; and if the face be placed near to the flame, it acquires the ghastly hue of death.—Doctor —— purposely placed himself close to the lamp, and he being a man of florid complexion, the pallid hue that the flame gave to his face was all the more remarkable, and I took care that Mr. Harrington should notice it.

"Doctor ——," I said, "you look very ill; perhaps you would rather not go any further in this matter yourself. Mr. Harrington and I can manage, I think, without you."

"No—no," replied Doctor ——, "I'll stay. But the real fact is, I do feel a strange nervousness creeping over me." —"So—so do I," said Mr. Harrington.

"Then," said I, solemnly, "the lamp is beginning to act."

"The lamp?" cried Harrington.—"Yes; it's very singular, but that lamp, if it be continued burning for any length of time, attracts round it the inhabitants of another world."

"Indeed. I—I wasn't aware you had begun," stammered Harrington.

"What was that, Doctor ——?" I said suddenly, pretending to hear something. "Eh?—what?" said Harrington.

"Hush—hush!" replied Doctor ——, "I am sure one is here."—"One!—eh?" cried Harrington, giving a start. "You don't really mean ——"—"Now I smell it," I remarked.

"Smell it?"—"Hush—hush!" I said, laying my hand upon Harrington's arm. "Say as little as possible. Don't you smell a strange odour?"—"Yes."

"As if from some long pent up vault?"—"Ye—yes."

"Where the dead have lain rotting for centuries in all the ghastly corruption of the silent tomb?"—"Yes; I—I smell just that. It's—it's rather awful."

The fact is, that the pyroligneous ether has a peculiar charnel-house kind of smell, and approaches nearer to the peculiar odour from graves than anything else I am aware of.

"There, again!" suddenly cried Doctor ——, "did you hear?"—"Yes," said I, "a rushing sound."—"Ye—yes," faltered Harrington, "I heard it too."

"My dear sir," I said, "you will soon be gratified. I hope you will not again ask for such an exhibition, for I know it will be days before the impression leaves my mind."—"Yes; it's certainly rather dreadful," said Harrington.

I was beginning to be disappointed that our patient did not back out of the experiment before this, for I was scarcely prepared to go any further; and how to show him anything that would do for a ghost I could not conceive on the spur of the moment.—I pretended to be busy about the room, and as I passed Doctor ——, I whispered,—

"When I say, 'now it's coming,' put out the light, Doctor ——."

He nodded assent, and I went to a drawer in which were some osteological specimens, and selected a finely whitened and well articulated arm, with all the fingers very perfect.

"Now it's coming," said I, and at that moment Doctor —— put out the light.

"The light's gone out," cried Harrington. "Hilloa! Light—light."— I gave a deep groan.—"What's that?" he cried—"eh? Doctor ——, where are you? I don't like this. God bless me! how very dark—eh? What? Didn't you speak? What an odd smell! Really, now, I—eh?"— Another groan.—" Somebody in pain, Doctor ——. I say, Doctor ——, upon second thoughts, do you know, I think you—you need not trouble yourself. After all, it's better to —to leave ghosts alone."—Here I made a most unearthly noise, which nearly threw Doctor —— into fits of laughter, which he was nearly smothered in suppressing.—"There— there," cried Harrington, "I don't want to see one.—That'll do. Let them go, I say. I'm done with them. Hilloa, there!—Help!—Murder!—Good God!—Murder!"

I glided behind Doctor ——'s chair, and giving him a lucifer match, I said:—

"Light the lamp again."

He did so, and I having the skeleton arm in my hand, placed the long bony fingers over Doctor ——'s shoulder.

Mr. Harrington turned his eyes towards the light, and the first thing he saw was the seeming hand of a skeleton grasping the shoulder of Doctor ——.

"The Lord help us!" he cried, making a spring to the door. "There's one!—There's one!"

Now, it never struck me that Doctor —— was a nervous man himself, and did not know what I was doing at all, and when Harrington, with horror depicted on his countenance, called out "There's one! there's one!" he thought it merely the effect of an excited imagination, and he said:—

"Where, Mr. Harrington,—where?"

"Help!" cried Harrington trying to open the door which I had locked, "on your shoulder ——"

Doctor—— turned his eyes to his shoulder and saw the hand apparently playing with his collar, upon which, to my surprise, he gave a great jump, and upset the table, lamp, and everything else, coming down in the midst of the ruins himself with a great crash.

I ran and unlocked the door, dragging Harrington out with me, who seemed petrified with terror. * * *

In a quarter of an hour afterwards, I bade Mr. Harrington good-bye at my door, when I said to him,—

"Now, my dear sir, I think you have had enough of ghosts. I should advise you to take a trip to the Continent, and amuse yourself. * * * * * *

I find entered in my Diary about six months after:—

Oct. 10th. — Note from Harrington, the Ghost Seeker, dated Florence, running thus:—

"MY DEAR SIR.—I promised to write to you, and I do so with great pleasure, to say that we shall be in England by Christmas. By-the-bye, I begin to think I was a little cracked about that ghost business. I am quite ashamed of it."

THE SURGEON'S DAUGHTER.

AMONG my earliest acquaintances was a young man of the name of Stretton. He was a surgeon, and his whole dependence in life was upon the uncertain proceeds of that overstocked profession. He had married, at the early age of nineteen, a beautiful but portionless girl; and when I first made his acquaintance, he was twenty-eight, very poor, rather desponding, and the father of four children.

There seemed to be some spell against poor Stretton's welldoing. From neighbourhood to neighbourhood he removed, —from house to house,—and then from lodging to lodging. He was on the inclined plane of ruin, and down, down he went, lower and lower, without a hope of saving himself and family from absolute beggary. Yet Stretton was a clever man, and a well educated and industrious one; but, alas! he wanted that most valuable of all mental gifts,—*method*. Everything he did was done in a desultory way. He was always too late at an appointment, in fact, he was one of that large class who are not to be depended upon, although no vice could be laid to his charge, and everybody declared that poor Stretton was one of the best hearted fellows in the whole world.

Time wore on, and Stretton had six children, and less to keep them on.

Occasionally I had recommended him employment, for I knew he was skilful; but he never, by any accident, kept his time, and I was in a perpetual worry when I had anything to do with him. Still I believe I was his only friend, for, one by one, all had deserted the fallen man, and many a time I believe that Stretton and his family would have starved had it not been for my wife, who, from our abundance, gave them something.

Thus affairs went on for some years, until the young children were growing up, and the eldest daughter, Mary, was about sixteen.

Oh, how my heart bled for Mary Stretton. Imagine a young creature, just at that period of life, when, if the world have any romance and beauty, it should then be seen, condemned to hopeless drudgery, want, and degradation.

Mary was a tall, delicate girl, with light flaxen hair and mild blue eyes. There was an infantine beauty about her prettily rounded chin and small pouting mouth. She was at once the pride and the anguish of her poor mother; for while she gazed with delight upon the growing beauties of her darling child, she could not check the rising sigh, as she thought that in their situation in life those charms might prove, instead of a blessing, the bitterest cause of woe and anguish.

But to my tale.

I had not seen the Strettons for nearly a fortnight, when one morning, at breakfast time, my servant announced to me that a young lady wished to see me.

I immediately went down stairs, and in the waiting-room I found Mary Stretton.

"Mary?" I said.—"Oh, sir," she cried, "Dr ——"

"What is the matter? You are agitated."—"Father."

"What of your father?"—Here she burst into tears.— "They ——" —"Who are they, Mary? Come with me. You shall explain to Mrs. —— as well as to me how this has happened?"

I led her to our breakfast-room, and after some crossexamining, discovered that her father had at last found his way into a debtors' prison, at which my only wonder was, how he had contrived to get sufficiently into debt.

This, however, Mary explained in her simple way.

"Oh! Mrs.——," she said, addressing my wife, "I don't understand it; but some one got father to sign his name to a bill, I think they call it."

"Oh!" I said, "that's enough. I understand it now completely. And so your father is arrested, Mary?"—"Yes— yes," sobbed Mary.

"My dear," I said, "you are too young to understand these things, but this is the worst predicament your father could have placed himself in. I will see him, and know better if anything can be done for him."

Mary named a well known metropolitan debtors' prison, and after my wife had given her something for present exigencies, she departed.

"Well," I said, "I will go and see Stretton; but really it almost amounts to criminality in such a man, to get into so disgraceful a scrape. Were it not for his poor wife and family, I should leave him to his fate."

"But let us do what we can," said my wife, "for the sake of those poor helpless children."

"I will," said I; "and now I will drive to where Stretton is at once, and at least know the particulars of the affair."

* * * *

In the course of an hour, I found myself at the gates of one of those receptacles of human misery—vice—tears—recklessness and debauchery, called debtors' prisons.

After being scrutinisingly looked at through a little grating, by a man with a very inflamed face, I was asked,—

"What do you want?"—"To see a prisoner," I replied.

"Are you a solicitor?"—"No."

The man then walked calmly away from the grating, and, setting his back against a wall, began to whistle a tune.

"I want admittance," said I.—"Can't," said the man.

"Why?"—"Not time."

"When, then, is the time?"—"Ten."

I looked at my watch. I saw that it wanted but five minutes to that hour, so I determined to wait; and, before the great man opened the door, the steps on which I stood were thronged with a motley assemblage of persons.

Ten o'clock at length sounded from a neighbouring steeple, and, the door being opened, we entered a small vestibule, and I hesitated as to how I was to proceed.

"Vell!" cried a man, with a bunch of keys in his hand.—To this I made no reply, and he again repeated,—"Vell!"—I was still silent, and he then cried.—"Foller yer nose, can't yer?"—"I wish to see a prisoner," said I.

"You vants im called, does yer?"—"Yes."

"Valk in there, then. Vot's the name?"—"Stretton," said I, as I entered a little dingy room, which the man pointed out to me.

Presently I heard reverberating, in faint echoes, through the building,—

"Stretton!—Stretton! Gate, Stretton!"—and then a great cry of, "Doctor!—Doctor!" and in a few minutes Stretton entered the room.

He got up a faint smile as he came in, and perpetrated the prisoner's stale joke of being "always at home." I shook my head, and he was serious in a moment.

"It's very kind of you, Doctor ——," he said, "to come to such a place as this to see a poor fellow in his misfortunes."—"Stretton," I said, "you know this is not a misfortune."

"Not a misfortune, Doctor——?"—"No."

"Why, really ——"—"It is your own act, Stretton, and personally you deserve neither pity nor help."

He looked abashed, and replied,

"It's hard to refuse a friend——"—"What?"—"Why, just to put one's name, you know ——"

"To a bill?" – "Yes."

"Which you can't pay."—"Why, yes, to be sure."

"Now, Stretton, is that not remarkably like swindling?"—"Swindling, Doctor ——?"

"Yes, swindling!"—"Why, I can't exactly ——"

"It is," I said, "a covert robbery, and somewhat worse than a highway one, inasmuch as it is not done so boldly, or so openly."—"But when a fellow is hard up, you know, Doctor ——, of course, you know—why, you see ——"

"You mean he must rob somebody."—"Why, I'll tell you how it was. Lambton, who is a good fellow, every inch of him, asked me to sign a bill."

"And you did it?"—"I couldn't refuse him."

"No, Stretton; it was easier to leave your children to starve than to refuse to aid a dissolute acquaintance in a transaction savouring very much of dishonesty. But enough of this—what is the amount?"—"Twenty seven pounds, thirteen, and twopence."

"So much?"—"Yes, you see, Doctor ——, Lambton thought the thirteen and twopence would make the bill look so natural and genuine. He's rather a clever fellow, is Lambton."

"Well, and what do you mean to do?"—"I haven't really thought of that."

"Well, then," I said, "I tell you what I mean to do. Your poor children shall not want; but, as for yourself, you must just remain here, and taste the bitter consequences of your own folly."

So saying, I left the prison, certainly very much annoyed and provoked.

* * * * *

Notwithstanding my manner to Stretton I was much grieved at the thoughts of the destitute state to which his young and helpless children must be reduced by his palpable indiscretion. I say destitute state as regards his little ones, because, although they might subsist upon my charity, they were none the more independent, nor did subsistence from such a source in any way increase their own resources.

But most of all, myself and wife grieved for the young and beautiful Mary Stretton, gentle creature as she was,—

"Just in the spring time of her beauty,"

and at a time of life when the sensibilities are alive to every endearing feeling.

"Let us," said my wife, as we were talking about the Strettons, "let us offer Mary a home with us."

I caught at the idea, and the next morning I found time, between two of my professional calls, to drive to the miserable lodging in Somer's Town, occupied by Mrs. Stretton and her poor, helpless, and unoffending children.

My wife had taken care previously to send to them some of the actual necessaries of life, and I was, therefore, with the hope of finding them as comfortable as, under the circumstances, they could fairly expect to be.

The back room, on an attic floor, which was tenanted by the family of the young surgeon, was the picture of squalid wretchedness. Mrs. Stretton had apparently lost all hope of well doing, and, as is too often the case under similar circumstances, by want of spirits to do better, hastened the consummation of that downfall and misery which might have been robbed of some, at least, of their terrors.

"Mrs. Stretton," I said, "my wife will do all that she can for you, rest assured, and she commissions me to say that she will take Mary home with her."

I saw the tears start into Mrs. Stretton's eyes as she thanked me, and I at once asked where Mary was.

"She goes every morning to see her father."

"What," I said, "to that place so unfitted ——"—"She will go, sir. I go as often as I can; but you know, doctor, I cannot frequently leave these little ones."

"He should not allow Mary to see such a place," I said. "Poor girl."—"But she will go, sir."

The door at this moment opened, and Mary herself entered the room. She looked fatigued and flushed with her walk, but I fancied there was an air of exultation in her countenance, which, to my mind, but ill accorded with her own or her father's situation. However, I made her the offer of coming to live with us as companion to my wife.

She shook her head as she said,—

"You are very good to me, doctor; but ——"

"But what, Mary?"—"I—I cannot ——"

"You cannot come to us?"—"Indeed, do not think me ungrateful; but I cannot. There are—that is, there is a circumstance —but I can say no more. Time will show you, sir, how deeply I feel your kindness."

"Some mystery, Mary?" I said, gravely.— She blushed and hung down her head.—"Do you know, Mary?" I continued, "that a wise man was asked once what was the most dangerous thing in the world, and he answered—a secret."—"Did he," said Mary, in a tone which seemed to say, "but my secret is worth having."

"He did, Mary," I replied; "but it is not for me to urge you."—"Oh, sir!" cried her mother, "do urge her; for these last few days she has dealt in mysterious words. She kisses the young children, and tells them they shall soon see their father and be so happy. Oh, Mary, Mary! now that Doctor —— is here, explain what you really mean."

"Mother—mother, I cannot," said Mary.

Verbatim from my Diary:—

"August 3rd. Letter from Stretton, to the following effect:—

"DOCTOR ——,—You, and you only, have been kind to my wife and children. For God's sake come to me—Mary is lost! "G. STRETTON."

I perfectly reeled when I read this note. The truth flashed across my mind like lightning. Mary's unsuspecting nature had surely been played upon by some villain, who, by inducing her to believe that she would save her father, her mother, and her infant brothers and sisters from misery, had torn her from home, friends, and virtue.

I hesitated not a moment, but hastening to the prison, asked for Stretton. As I was luckily within the prescribed hours, I was at once ushered into the little dingy room I have before described. In a few moments the wretched father appeared. His apparel was disordered, his eyes were bloodshot, and his whole appearance bespoke an agony of mind which it was truly pitiable to behold.

"My child!" he cried, "my child! Have you found my Mary, doctor?"—"Stretton," I said, "from my heart I feel for you now. Tell me all about this sad affair."

"Yes—yes—it should be told. You know my child—my beautiful Mary, with her mild blue eyes, and cherub face?—Well, sir, you nod.—You knew her well?—She is gone—gone— and I am here behind bolts and bars a prisoner; and —God of Heaven, I am denied the right to search for my own lost child! Is it not dreadful, doctor?—dreadful—dreadful!"

He sat down, and rocking to and fro, he repeated the word "dreadful" in a tone of such exquisite anguish that my heart melted, and I at once resolved to pay the debt, and liberate the unhappy father. With this view I accosted a man who was in the passage; but judge of my surprise when I was told that there were detainers against Stretton upon old debts and liabilities to the amount of nearly two hundred pounds. This was a sum with which I could not conveniently part, and I returned to the wretched prisoner.

"Stretton," said I, "be patient, on this consideration, that everything which can be done shall be done to discover your daughter. Now tell me when she was missed."—"Let me think," he said; "she did not come when—when did she not come?"

"Recollect yourself," I said.—"I—I am only slightly mad," he replied, " and I can recollect things sometimes. Yesterday;—aye, it was yesterday. She should have come yesterday.

Then they came and told me she had kissed her mother and all the little ones, and they heard her sobbing as she went down the stairs. Then they thought she was coming to me, but she never came;—never!—never!"

"That was yesterday? You are sure?"—" It was. I waited, but she came not; I hung against the bars of the prison-house, but she came not!"

" Well, Stretton," I said, "let me leave you now; I will return to-morrow to report progress. Be of good cheer. All may yet be well."

He shook his head despondingly, and shortly afterwards I left the prison, revolving in my mind what steps I should take to redeem my promise to the heart-stricken father. * * *

I immediately repaired to a magistrate, with whom I was partially acquainted, and related to him the whole of the circumstances connected with the Stretton family, terminating with the mysterious disappearance of Mary.—He heard me with gentlemanly attention until I had concluded; then he said:—

" This girl, you say, was very handsome?"—"She was."

" Her fate, then, can be easily guessed at. Some of our rich ' men of pleasure,' as they are called, have decoyed her on some pretence or another away from her home. We know a great deal of these things. Leave the affair to me for four-and-twenty hours, and if I can get no information by then, you can adopt any course you think proper."

I, of course, thanked the magistrate, and adopted the course he recommended, returning home with some sort of hope that before long I should hear something of poor Mary. Alas! how little I then thought how soon I was to hear of her.

* * * *

At a quarter past one in the morning I was called up to attend a patient who resided on the Surrey side of the water. I dressed myself in haste, and as the air was very cold and chilling, I set off at a good round pace from my home. My nearest road, as well, as the most pleasant, lay across Waterloo Bridge, and, paying my toll, I with hasty steps entered upon the silent, and, to all appearance, deserted thoroughfare.

The night was beautifully clear, and myriads of stars spangled the heavens. Not a breath of air stirred the slumbering river, in the bosom of which were reflected, in faithful beauty,

"The starry host that twinkled over head."

The sensation of cold I had experienced upon leaving my home had gone off, and by the time I reached the centre of the bridge, 1 was delighted that I had been called, so calm —so beautiful,—so refreshing, both to mind and body, was the scene around. There was something awfully grand and impressive in the slumbering city, and the deep stream flowing through it, while the lights of heaven looked down in such rare beauty on the world, which might be so happy a one if mankind chose.

I paused for one moment at the centre of the bridge, and scarcely had I done so when a stifled sob met my ears. I started, when from one of the stone seats there sprung a figure that had escaped my notice. I was so taken by surprise that I involuntarily recoiled a few steps. With a loud shriek, the figure—which was that of a female—clambered upon the parapet of the bridge, and before I could reach out my hand, it was gone into the rush of waters below.

A sickening sensation came over me, and for about the time that a person might have counted four, I could neither move nor speak; then I sprang forward, and called " Help! help!" A letter lay on the stone seat;—I seized it, and rushed back to the toll house.

I gave an alarm, and several boats put off. I was dreadfully shocked; but judge of my feeling, when, upon glancing at the letter, which I still held, I read the address:—

" To Doctor ———"

I tore it open; —it was as follows:—

" Doctor ———, —I have been betrayed—I am lost. The waters of the river will be kinder to me than has been ———. Oh, comfort my poor father and mother.

"Mary Stretton."

The name, which I have left blank in the letter, was that of a foreign prince; but that is all I can say, for there is a law which makes truth a libel in England * * * *

The full particulars of Mary's story I never could learn. Her body was not found, but who can doubt the facts? The innocent girl had been watched going backwards and forwards to the prison, and some panderers to the vices of the "noble and illustrious personage" I have alluded to, had, by some insidious means, worked her moral destruction.

* * * *

Stretton died by his own hand a few months afterwards. He had always accused himself of being the indirect cause of Mary's death. The thought worked upon his brain till it induced insanity, and the wretched father sought relief in the uncertainty of the grave

MR. AUGUSTUS BROWN'S METAMORPHOSES;

OR, THE NERVOUS GENTLEMAN.

The most troublesome patient which a medical man can possibly have is a nervous, fidgetty, hypochondriacal gentleman, and were it not that such patients are rather profitable, the members of the medical profession would raise a great outcry upon the subject, and nerves and nervousness would be rated bores instead of being attended to with great gravity and prescribed for with great regularity, the ordinary "medicine" given consisting usually of bread pills rolled in magnesia, and effervescing draughts, *ad libitum*, according to the strength of the patient's credulity and purse. I am a retired physician now, so I can afford to be a *little candid* now and then.

Nearly twenty years ago, there lived in Bloomsbury-square one of my best patients, by name Mr. Augustus Brown.

Mr. Brown was a gentleman of competent independence, and of a literary and virtuoso turn of mind. At about forty years of age he began to study medicine a little, and to take care of his health a great deal. He bought medical books, prowled about the wards of hospitals, and made himself as unhappy as any comfortable, middle-aged, single gentleman could wish to be.—I learnt these particulars of him from a friend who recommended him to me.

When I was first called to attend him, not knowing that his diseases were all imaginary, I was quite taken in for about a quarter of an hour or so.

I found him lying on his back on the sofa; the room was darkened, and he was groaning in an extremity of anguish.— I turned to his housekeeper, who had marshalled me in, and said,—

" What is the matter with Mr. Brown?"—He heard me, and called out,

" What is the matter—the matter? Oh! oh! oh!"

I advanced towards him, and said,—" I am sorry to find you so indisposed, sir."

" Oh! oh! oh!" was his only answer.

"Perhaps," I continued, " you will have the kindness to describe your symptoms."

After a few preparatory groans, he commenced.—"I—oh! oh!—ah! you'll scarcely believe it, but look at my leg, down by my ankle, I mean. Oh! oh! oh!—horrible, horrible."

I cast my eyes down to his ankle, and, to my surprise, saw that it was tied fast by a silk handkerchief to the leg of the sofa.

"What is this for?" I said.—" You may well ask—oh! oh!"

" Whatever may be the matter with your ankle, I shall undo this most unsurgical and very improper bandage."—

" Wretch!" he cried, " would you destroy me?"

" Destroy you?"—" Yes. What dependance have I if I am not tied—what hold upon the the world have I?"

" What do you mean?" said I.—" Listen," he said.

" Well."—"I am *too light!*"

" Too light?"—" Yes."

" Pray, sir, explain yourself."

" You know why a balloon goes up?"—"Yes, surely."

" Why?"—" Because it is lighter than an equal bulk of air."

" Very good."—" Well—but, sir, how does that ———"

" Apply to me, you would say, Doctor———."—"Exactly."

"This way. I am lighter than an equal bulk of air; and if I was not tied down, whiff I should go up—up—up! Oh! it's dreadful!—oh! oh! oh! ah!"

He always put in the ah! as if he had been suddenly seized with some dreadful pain, and it really had a most comical effect.

I now saw through the case in a moment, and I said,—

"Are you sure you are not mistaken?"—"Mistaken?" he cried.

"Yes."—"You ought to know better. A friend of mine told me you were a very clever man."

"What! suppose, now," I said, "you were to allow me to undo this handkerchief."—"Up I should go!" he roared; "and if the window was open, out I should sail."

"Indeed," I said.—"Yes," he continued; "I have a very slight hold upon the earth. For some days I found myself getting lighter, until at last you see I am forced to tie myself down,—oh! oh! ah!"

"Suppose I hold your collar," said I, "while the handkerchief is taken off."—"I don't mind," he replied, "just to convince you."

I therefore held his collar with one hand, and unbound the handkerchief with the other.

"There, you see," he said, "look at my leg," and he poked his leg up as high as he could.

"But you could put it down," said I.—"No, no."

"Oh! yes, you could. There, you see, I've let go your collar."—"But I'm holding on, you perceive, and it's no little exertion. I begin to think you don't understand my case."

"Oh, yes, I do," said I; "you must have a course of *preponderating* pills."

"What!" he cried, suddenly dropping his leg.—"Preponderating pills!"—"I never heard of them."—"Very likely."

"But, my dear sir," he exclaimed, bolting suddenly upright.—"Dear me, Mr. Brown," I said, "you are better."

"No, I ain't,—oh! oh! ah!"—"Well, I can remedy your disease."

"You can?"—"Yes, by the preponderating pill."

"They will increase my density, I suppose, by contracting the—the absorbents, and so on."—"Exactly."

"Astonishing! My dear sir, you are the only medical man that ever understood my case; and last year when I was gradually *vitrifying* ——"

"Gradually what?" — "Turning into a kind of porcelain ——."—"Oh!"

"Well, I went to Abernethy, and what do you think he did?—the fool!"—I shook my head.—" Why, he told me to squat down like a Chinese, and try and have some odd colours burnt into me, so that by the time I was finished, I should be a respectable mandarin for an old China closet."

"Indeed."— "Yes; and when I remonstrated he actually turned me out!—oh! oh! ah!"

I flattered myself that I had made a great hit in Mr. Augustus Brown's case, by my mention of preponderating pills, and I was only astonished at the amount of his credulity upon the subject. I sent him some extremely mild pills, composed of a common harmless drug, and waited the result with some degree of patience and a considerable degree of expectation.

In a few days a message came to me to go to Mr. Brown immediately, for that he feared he was *sinking fast*.

"Sinking fast?" said I.—"Yes, sir."

"Is he so weak?"—"Weak, sir?"

"Yes; you say he is sinking."—"Oh, it's cos he's *too heavy!*"

"Too what?"—"Too heavy, sir."

"Ridiculous!"—"Master says, sir, as he's got so heavy, he's forced to be on the ground floor."

"Tell him I'll be with him immediately."

The boy, who had come from Mr. Brown's, departed, and I felt myself thoroughly posed by this second extraordinary fancy of Mr. Augustus Brown.

"So much," thought I, "for my extreme cleverness in inventing preponderating pills."

I, however, lost no time in going to my most eccentric patient. I found him in the kitchen, lying on his back, in the middle of the floor, and groaning, as usual.

"Oh,—ah!" he cried, when he saw me, "you are come. Oh,—oh,—ah!"

"Yes," I said, with difficulty repressing a smile; "I am sorry to hear you are not quite well, Mr. Brown."—"Quite well! Oh,—oh,—ah!"

"What is the matter now, sir?"—"Oh, doctor, those preponderating pills. Oh,—oh,—ah!"

"What of them, sir?"—"They are too powerful. Much too strong, sir,—awfully strong."

"Too strong?"—"Yes, doctor; they have driven me to the other extreme."

"Indeed."—"Yes. You know how dreadfully light I was; you had, you recollect, to hold me from shooting out of the window."

"Hem!" said I.—"Well, do you know," he continued, "I'm now altogether as dreadfully dense and heavy. You see, I'm forced to be on a ground floor, or else I should go through the boards. Oh,—oh,—ah!"

"You must leave off the pills," said I.—"Ah, that's all very well, doctor; but you see the mischief is done. Here's a weight."

So saying, up went his leg, and down again with a heavy dab.

"What do you think of my case now?" he said. "Here is a dreadful situation to be placed in. Heavier than lead,— horrible,—horrible! If I once begin, from my extreme weight, to break through the crust of the earth, where shall I stop? Oh,—oh,—ah!"—"It's rather a serious case," said I; "but there are remedies."

"Remedies! you bring me new life."—"Yes. You must take some anti-ponderous draughts, and be careful of your diet."

"My diet?"—"Yes."

"What must I eat?"—"Mutton, principally."

"Very good. Oh, doctor, you are a clever practitioner. I find you understand my case. You are the only medical man who ever took a sensible view of my terrible constitution. Oh,—oh,—ah!"

* * * * *

"Now," thought I, as I made up a draught of distilled water with some vegetable colouring matter, for Mr. Augustus Brown; "now I think I have managed this troublesome patient pretty well."

Alas! how vain are human anticipations. Just three nights after, I was rung up in the middle of my first sleep, so violently, that I thought for a moment that the house must be on fire. I popped my head out of the window, and asked,

"Who's there?"—"Me," was the reply; a very usual one, by the way, under such circumstances.

"Who's *me*? said I, with a laudable contempt, at the moment, for grammar.—"Please, sir, Mr. Brown's boy."

"Oh! Mr. Augustus Brown?"—"Yes, sir."

"Well, what's the matter?"—"Oh! please, sir, master's very uncommon bad."

"Indeed?"—"Yes, sir."

"Is he light or heavy this time?"— "That's gone off, sir."

"What," cried I, 'some new freak?"—" Please, sir, yes."

"What is it?"—"Master, sir, says as you must come directly, cos he's a going to be *merrymopussed*."

"Eh?"—" *Merrymopussed*, please, sir."

"Merry—what?"—" That's what he called it, sir."

"Just try and explain yourself, will you, my boy?"— "Why, sir, I thinks as he means he's a going to be turned into *somethink* else."

"Oh! metamorphosed."—"Something like that, sir, or some other wild animal."

"Tell your master, I'll be with him soon."

The boy departed, and with great vexation, which even the prospect of my fee could not subdue, I put on my clothes, and sallied out to see Mr. Brown's metamorphoses.

"What can have put such a thing into his head?" said I to myself; "at least my medicine is innocent this time."

When I arrived at Bloomsbury-square, I found the whole house in confusion, and I was at once shown into the drawing-room, where sat Mr. Brown in a night-gown and slippers.

"Good night, Mr. Brown," said I.

He only replied by a wave of his hand towards a seat. I sat down and said,—" Well, sir, you are looking very well."

He shook his head.

"Doctor, oh,—oh,—ah!—" Well, sir?"—"You *have* done it at last."

"Done what?"—" Me, sir, me,—Augustus Brown, Esq."

"As how, sir?"—"What directions did you give me when you were last here?"

"Directions?"—"Yes; now don't cavil."

"Certainly not. I told you to take the pills I would send to you."

"Well, sir? and what else, sir?"—"I told you to attend to your diet."

"But what did you tell me to eat?"—"Mutton."—"Ah!"

"Well, Mr. Brown, what of all that?"

"Mutton?"—"Yes, mutton."—"Well, doctor, I have eaten mutton. I have taken mutton for breakfast, mutton for luncheon, mutton for dinner, mutton for tea, and, d—n it, sir, I took mutton for supper."

I could not, for my life, suppress a smile, and it put Mr. Brown quite in a rage.

"So," he cried, "you laugh do you?"—"Nay, my good sir——"

"Don't good sir me,—you laughed, sir."—"Very well."

"Oh! it's very well, is it? Well, doctor, what do you suppose has been the result of all this mutton, eh, sir? I wait your answer."—"A great demand for sheep," said I, smiling.

"Don't smile," he cried.—"Well, then, seriously speaking, Mr. Brown, I don't apprehend any particular result."

"You don't?"—"I don't."

"Then I do."—"So I presume. But may I ask what, Mr. Brown?"—"You may."

"Well, what, sir?"—"Ma—a—a—a."

What?'—"Ma—a—a—a."

"Are you mad or joking?"—"Neither, doctor; but I've eaten so much mutton, that you see, as a natural result, I am in process of becoming a sheep."

"Oh, ridiculous!"—"Ma—a—a—a," was his answer, in a voice which was really a good imitation of the bleating of a sheep.

"Mr. Brown," said I.—"Ma—a—a—a," he replied.

"Sir!"—"Ma—a—a—a."

"Let me tell you once for all ——"—"Ma—a—a—a."

"You are the unhappy victim——"—"I know it. Ma—a—a—a."—"Of self delusion."

"Eh?"—"Self delusion, I repeat, Mr. Brown."

"What, sir?"—"You are a nervous hypochondriac, sir."

"I am no such thing, sir."—"You are, Mr. Brown. Your complaints are all delusions,—the creatures of your own fancy."

"You don't understand my case, sir."—"Perfectly I do."

"You are a fool!"—I smiled.—"An idiot, sir. Delusion, indeed! Ma—a—a—a,—oh,—oh,—ah!"—I laughed outright. "Leave my house, ignoramus," he roared.

"With pleasure," said I, taking my hat.

Thus ended my first connexion with Mr. Augustus Brown, the nervous gentleman, whom, however, I attended for years after that.

THE MISER'S DEATH-BED.

The physician sees many strange death-bed scenes. Woe may render him, to a certain extent, callous to those sights which would appal the stoutest heart; but still, in the course of a long practice, even he must encounter some death-bed scenes, the recollection of which will cling to him like a night-mare, and which he may be years in shaking from his imagination. Such an one was that which I am about to describe to my readers.

For ten or eleven years a bent and miserable old man had been in the habit of clinging each morning to my area rails, to beg of my servants broken victuals. His appearance was so haggard, and his tone and manner bespoke such a depth of misery, that I gave orders never to refuse him anything that had come from the table; so that, at last, he grew into a regular pensioner upon us, and we used to expect him regularly every morning as our own breakfast.

The name of the old mendicant we never knew, nor where he resided. In fact he seldom spoke a word to my servants; but he would come, in the heat of summer, when the warm genial sunshine lit even the worn flag stones into beauty, and cling to the iron rails, looking the only miserable, or at least the most miserable, object in creation. In the depth of winter, too, when the bleak north east wind blew fiercely and the blinding snow drifted through the air, he would come, and, still clinging to the rails, while his rags fluttered round him, wait for his daily dole.

This had gone on so long, that one morning, when he did not come, I felt quite uneasy, and there was a general inquiry through the house as to whether any one had seen the old man. The next morning passed away, and still he came not. I began to think that he must be ill or dead, and, after wondering at the usual hour for about another week, we began to forget the old beggar who had visited us so long. One morning, however, he was brought to my recollection again somewhat singularly.

I was told that a young girl was waiting in my hall to see me, and going out to her, she told me that a Mr. Temple wanted me as soon as I could go to him.

"Where does he reside?" I said.—She named a low wretched street in Soho, and, wondering at the address, I said,—"Who is Mr. Temple?"

"I don't know, sir," said the girl. "He lodges with my mother, sir."

"You are quite sure he sent for me?"—"Yes, sir. We didn't know his name till this morning, and he's lived with us since I was born."

"Indeed! that's odd enough. Is he very ill?"—"Oh! very; he's a groaning so."

"Well, run back, and tell him I'll call as early as I can in the course of the morning."

The girl departed, and about half-past eleven I found myself sufficiently disengaged to call upon my new patient in —— street, Soho. The house was miserable and dirty in the extreme, and, upon asking for Mr. Temple, a slip-shod, grinning looking woman screamed up the kitchen stairs,—

"It's the three pair back!"

"The what?" I said.—"The three pair back, to be sure, replied the woman, just showing her head on a level with the passage.

"Can't you show me his room?" said I.—"Who are you, I wonder?" screamed the woman. "Hoity-toity, old mealy mouth! Show you up indeed! Perhaps you'd like a mould candle too?"

Positively declining the candle, I ascended the staircase, surmising that the three pair back must be up three flights of stairs, and a back room somewhere.—When I arrived at the landing-place at the very top-most story of the house, I heard a low moaning sound proceeding from a room to my left, and pushing open a low black door I entered one of the most miserable rooms that I had ever seen.

Furniture it had none. A cracked water jug was upon the floor, and by its side an earthenware saucer, such as are used for garden pots. In one corner lay what at first appeared to be a mass of old rags, but the groans that proceeded from amongst them told me that a human being was there.

"Has he come? Has he come?" cried a thin voice, as if struggling with pain.

"Did you send for me?" said I.—"Thieves, murder, help," suddenly cried the same voice, and from among the mass of rags and filth a long, skinny arm protruded, grasping a pistol.

I own I was a little alarmed, and said hastily,—"I am Dr. ——."

"You—you have not come to rob me, then?"—"Rob you! Certainly not."

"But—but—you know if you had, I—I have nothing. Mind, nothing,—nothing!"

"Is your name Temple?" I said.—"Ha!" he screamed; "how do you know that? No, no,—I am a beggar!"

"A Mr. Temple sent for me."—"Stay, stay! Fasten the door; place the jug against it. We,—we shall be robbed else. Not that I have anything to lose. No, no; I am miserably poor,—wretchedly poor."

"Then you should apply for assistance," said I, "where you have a right to demand it. If I were to give you a prescription, you could not get it made up for nothing, you know."—"No, no," he replied. "I—I know. Look at me, —look, doctor, look."

He raised himself on his arm, and in the thin and horribly emaciated face of my strange patient, I recognized the old beggar who used to cling to my area rails.

"I do recollect you," I said.—"You do now?"

"And your name is Temple, is it not?"—"Temple!" he screamed;—"who says my name is Temple?"

"Your own messenger."—"Then,—then,—I must have raved."

"What complaint have you?" said I.

Slowly he drew his hand from under the rags, and letting an old tarnished guinea drop from his clenched fist, he said, with a deep sigh,—

"There,—there's your fee."—"I do not require it of you," said I.

"You,—you are sure?"—"Quite sure."

"Then, I—I—then I will keep it. Don't tell anybody you saw it, or I shall be robbed!"

He clenched the coin again, and withdrew his ghastly attenuated hand and arm. I could see by his whole appearance, that he was suffering from want of nourishing diet, and I said,—

"You must spend that guinea to-day in some wine and arrow-root."—"Guinea!" he cried, "what guinea? I have no gold. Do you want to rob me? I am ill,—I know I am ill. Tell me what's the matter with me; but mind one thing—"

"What is that?"—"I,—I am not dy—dying. Mind that, —I am not dying. No, no,—not dying!"

"You will, though," said I, "if you do not take some nourishing drinks."

He fixed his ghastly eyes upon my face as he muttered,

"Do you think half a pint of porter is really necessary for me?"— I laughed, and said,—"A bottle of good port wine, you mean."

"Wine!" he cried. "Good God! and I so wretchedly poor,—so miserably poor!"

"Do you know," said I, "I begin to suspect ——"—"What—what?" he cried.

"That you are not so poor as you affect to be. Have you not some secret hoard, now, that, freely used, would make the remainder of your days comfortable?"

"What! gold!" he shrieked; "you do not think I have gold?"—"Yes, I do. You are a miser."

"A miser!"—"Yes."

He fell back on the bed with a gasp; then, suddenly springing up, he screamed,—

"Thieves! thieves!—help! help!—robbers!"—"I shall leave you," said I, "if you make such a noise."

The door now opened, and a coarse man put his head into the room, with the polite inquiry of,—

"What's the row?"—"Nothing," said I; "the old man is ill, and raves."

"Oh! that's the ticket, is it? He's a going all for to assault the bucket, at last, is he? There'll be a spicy nut for Old Nick,—crikey!"

Having delivered himself of this elegant opinion, the man withdrew his head, and shut the door. When I turned again to the old man, he lay in a swoon on his miserable bed.

* * * *

I am never without restoratives about me, and I very soon succeeded in restoring my patient to at least his former state. With a long drawn sigh he opened his eyes, and fixed them upon my face with an expression of mournful intensity.

"How are you now?" I said.—"Better—better," he murmured.

I saw that it was not so, for an awful change had come across his face, and there was a peculiar gaze about his eyes, that told me he was dying. Impressed as I was with the conviction that he had money secreted somewhere, which might be of the utmost service to some one claiming kindred with him, I did not hesitate to tell him his real condition.

"Do not deceive yourself," said I, "you are dying."

He sprung up in the bed with a shriek as if he had been galvanized.

"Dying!" he cried; "no, no, not dying. Let me live— live on, though it be in torture. Why should I die? No— no, I cannot—I dare not die!"

It was dreadful to see the agitation of his features. Hot, scalding tears poured down his cheeks; he clutched the scanty covering which was upon him till the blood started from his nails, and still he shrieked,—

"I cannot—dare not die!"—Then he suddenly turned to me, and clutching my arm, he cried, in the most supplicating tones,—"Save me! save me!—for the love of Heaven, save me. Hold me to the world. You are skilful; save me by your art. Look at me, a miserable poor old man. I will kneel to you,—bless you—be your slave, but give me life— life—life!"

I knew that a few hours must end the scene of his mortal agony, and I seized the opportunity of leaving the room, and getting somebody in the house to fetch some wine and brandy, for I knew that by stimulants alone could the flickering flame of life be kept alive for the next few hours.

When I returned, I started, for he had risen from his pallet, and was kneeling before the wretched little skeleton grate, which, by its rust, had evidently not seen a fire for years. He did not hear me, and I paused to observe him.

With feeble efforts he wrenched from its place the little grate, and then I saw him eagerly clutch at something. I advanced, and laid my hand on his shoulder. With a scream, he sprung to his feet, and, as he did so, a heavy bag fell from his relaxed hold, with a loud clash, upon the floor.

"Wretched man!" I said, pointing to the bag, "is it for this you cling to life?"

He tried to speak, but could not. His hand clutched the air wildly. Inarticulate sounds came from his throat, and I had just time to catch him when he fainted again. I carried him to the bed, if bed it could be called, and then carefully replacing the grate, I lifted the bag he had dropped, and concealed it under some musty apparel which lay in a rotting heap in one corner of the room.

I was most anxious that he should live to make some bequest of his money to some good purpose, and I, with some anxiety, felt his pulse; it was beating feebly, but there was a tolerably regular action. I left the room again, and was glad to meet on the staircase a dirty girl with the wine and brandy. I took them from her, and returning, poured a little of the former into the miser's mouth.

In a few moments returning animation began to shew itself, but I feared he was delirious, for he talked strangely.

"They are all dead, now," he muttered;—"dead, I tell you; they don't want my gold; it's twelve years ago. They are dead—dead!"

"Who are dead?" I said.—"Ha!" he cried. "Who speaks to me in the dark?"

"The dark!" said I.—"Yes; the night is very dark, so very dark."

I looked at his eyes, and my medical skill enabled me to see at once that the sight had gone. He was stone blind. I feared that his other perceptive faculties would quickly follow, and I said,—

"Tell me truly. Have you any kindred?"—"Kindred!" he repeated.

"Yes; have you a child or a child's child?"—"A child—a child?" he said, falteringly, "have I a child's child? Did my own little blue-eyed Emma ever fondle a darling of her own, because—because, God have mercy upon me—that would be my child's child."

While I live I never shall forget the burst of frantic grief which followed these words. His sobs were terrible. Such an agony of sorrow I never before saw, and hope never to see again. I was deeply affected. Grief in the young is distressing, but there was something awful in the heartfelt anguish of that white-haired old man.

"Calm yourself," I said, though my own voice was broken with emotion; "there may be still time to repair, in some measure, the past. Confide all to me, and I promise, before Heaven, to do what I can in furtherance of, I hope, your newly awakened kind feelings."—"God bless and prosper you," he said, faintly. "I will tell all—all."

His voice was very faint, and I stooped over him to listen. Mingled with broken sobs and many tears, he thus addressed me :—

"I had a wife, whom I loved, and—and a little blue-eyed thing, with a sweet laugh, who was as happy as the day is long, and we called her Emma. My wife, the companion of my young days, wasted away before my eyes, and died. Then I was alone with my child, my little one; but there came a chilling shadow across my heart, and I was unhappy.

At last it shaped itself into form, and avarice—avarice became my passion—gold my god! I hoarded—hoarded all, but still in want, in misery, and privation, my little child clung to me, and loved me. The pleasures of childhood she never knew; playmates she had none; yet she clung to me, and she grew in beauty, too, till she was sixteen, then one day she hung upon my neck, and told me she was loved by a mere youth. I knew him. His genius was his only possession, and I scorned him. Then one day he came to me; and he and my child, my Emma—it was her mother's name—they knelt at my feet, and asked for my blessing."

He paused, for his tears choked his utterance, and the scene he had conjured up was too much for his feelings. I gave him some wine, and he proceeded.

"I turned them from my door—and—and saved my gold."

"And what became of them?" said I.—"I left the place, and came to London; but a man met me in the streets, and told me——"

"What?"—"That—my child—my little Emma—you know——"

"Take time," I said.—"He—he told me she was dead,—the little thing who used to nestle in my breast; he said she had *died of want* in giving birth to a child. *Absolute want.*"

"Good God!" I said.—"Hush!" he cried, "hear all—hear all. Her young husband—he, too, they said, had *kissed his child, and then sought a grave in the river*, and I had saved my gold!"

"When did you hear this?"—"The last time I clung to the railings of your house. Since then I have not tasted food."

"The child?" I said; "your Emma's child; did it live?" —"I know not."

"Where did all this happen?"—"At ——."

"That is a small place near ——."—"It is."

"And your daughter's husband's name?"—"Was Durham."

I immediately formed a resolve, and rising, I said,—

"Be calm till I return. Take a little wine occasionally, and I will send you a nurse and other refreshments."—"Take with you the dross which has been my destruction," he moaned; "take the gold."

"I will return soon," said I.

I hurried from the room. Medical men know plenty of nurses, and in half an hour I sent one to the old man with medicine and food; then I hurried home to my wife.

"Mary," said I, "I am going to ——."—"To where?"

"Don't ask me any questions, but come with me. I have ordered post horses, and we shall be there within three hours they tell me. I'll tell you everything on the road."

* * * * *

Good fast horses and a well paid postillion do wonders. As we neared ——, I called to the driver.

"Is there a workhouse at ——?"—"A workus?" he cried. "Lor! I thinks as there isn't; but there is at ——. A workus!—Lor!"

I had told the whole story to my wife, and she had at once suggested an inquiry at the workhouse, to ascertain if the child had lived or died, as the parish must have been cognizant of the whole affair. We soon rattled up to the workhouse door and I was ushered into the master's room.

"I am, Dr. ——," I said. "Have you a child here of the name of Durham?"—"Yes, sir," was the immediate answer.

"Thank God," said I. "What is it, a boy?"—"No, sir, a girl."

"Its age?"—"About eleven, sir. You see, we had to bury the mother, and the father drowned himself."

"Will you trust the child to me?"—"I dare not, sir," said the man.

"I will hold you harmless," said I. "You know me by name."—The master hesitated a moment, and then said,—

"I will, sir. Will you please to take a seat a moment?"

He was scarcely two minutes gone, when he returned, leading by the hand a little girl dressed in a blue stuff gown of five centuries ago, and a little pinched up white cap. She was a beautiful little thing, with mild blue eyes, and a look of earnest simplicity upon her face, which I admired very much.

"Thank you, sir," said I to the master. "You shall hear from me to-morrow."

He bowed, and I took the little orphan by the hand, and led her to the chaise. The moment I appeared at the workhouse door, a great crowd that had there assembled, greeted me with a loud hurrah.

I handed the child into the chaise, and followed myself.

"To London," said I.—"Hurrah!" shouted the crowd, and away we went.

* * * * *

I had been away five hours exactly when I entered the miser's room with his daughter's child. He was asleep, and the nurse told me he had been quite delirious. I felt certain it was his last sleep, and I motioned the child, who was a sweet-tempered, tractable little thing, to stand quietly by the bed-side, while I waited for his awakening. There was a dead silence for about a quarter of an hour, and then he muttered in his sleep,—

"Yes, darling—yes; kiss me, dear. My little Emma! Bless you—bless—bless ——"—"Are you better?" I said, softly.

"That's Dr. ——," he said.—"Yes," I replied.

"I am much better, thank you," he said: "in fact, quite strong and well. I had a pain, but it's gone; and it's still night."

I saw by some infallible sign that he was dying.

"If," I said, "your daughter had a child, it would inherit all you have?"—"Dr. ——," he said, "I could die happy if some one could assure me that my poor Emma's child was alive; but—but ——"

He burst into tears. The little girl, who was very tender-hearted, was so much affected, that she wept audibly. I shall never forget the expression of the old man's face as he heard her.

"Who is that?" he cried; "who weeps? Who—who weeps for me?"

"Listen," I said. "*It is your own Emma's child.*"

He clasped his hands, and his face for a moment was lit up with heavenly joy; then opening his arms, he said,

"Come! come to my heart!—to my heart!"

I placed the child in his arms, saying,

"Kiss your mother's father."

She twined her little arms round his neck, and kissed his furrowed cheek.

Slowly the old man's arms relaxed their hold. He fell back on the pillow. There was a smile of joy on his face, but he was dead.

* * * * *

Property to the amount of five thousand pounds was found belonging to him, which the poor parish child came into undisputed possession of; and I can only say for myself, that no event of my life has given me greater pleasure to think of than THE MISER'S DEATH-BED.

THE DUEL;

OR, THE CAPTAIN'S WIFE.

THERE is no life so harassing as that of a popular physician. People take care that he shall not eat the bread of idleness, and it generally happened, in the course of my professional career, that my most troublesome and fatiguing engagements came when I should have been glad of a little rest. Thus it was with the case I am about to draw the attention of my courteous readers to.

I had sat down comfortably by my own fireside, after a long day, and my wife had just remarked:—"My dear, you have not met with anything remarkable for your Diary lately," when a furious ring came at the door.—"There!" cried I, "you can put that down as a remarkably loud ring."

"I dare say it's a runaway ring," said my wife; but it was not, for my servant came in to tell me I was wanted immediately at No. —, Devonshire-street, Portland-place, for a lady was dying.

It is astonishing how the sense of the necessity for exertion banishes fatigue. I had drawn on my boots, and was half way towards Devonshire-street on foot,—for I had dismissed my carraige,—before I again thought how tired I was. I soon found No. —; it was a large, handsome house, and, as I knocked, I could guess, by the hurrying backwards and forwards of lights past the windows, that there was a great deal of confusion within the mansion. The door was opened to me by a female domestic, who was in tears.

"I am Dr. ——," said I.—"Oh! sir, walk in," she replied; "I am so glad you're come. My poor mistress is so bad."—"Let me see your mistress directly," said I.

She took a lamp from off a slab in the passage, and preceded me up stairs. The bed-room I was ushered into was a very handsome one, and replete with every convenience that the most refined luxury could wish. My attention, however, was at once directed to its principal occupant. Surrounded by several alarmed servants, a lady, in an evening dress of great splendour, lay across the foot of the bed. They made way for me, and I immediately approached, saying:—

"Is this the lady for whom I was sent?"—"Yes, sir," said a respectable looking servant.

"Assist me," I said, as I raised her to a sitting posture.

Several of the servants lent their aid, and I saw that the lady, who was young and beautiful, was in a deep swoon.

"You are easily alarmed, all of you," I said. "Your mistress has only fainted. Bring me some cold water."

The water was brought me, and some one likewise handed me some pungent salts.

"How did this fainting fit come on?" said I. The servants looked at each other, and shook their heads.

"Are you all dumb?" I said.—"Please, sir," said a little girl, with her apron to her eyes, "I am the under nursemaid."

"Well, but you being the under nursemaid surely did not make your mistress faint away?"—"Oh, lauk-a-mussy! no, sir; but a letter comes, and, as John wasn't no way tidy,—leastways, he was in his thingumy sleeves only, without his coat, you know, sir——"

"Well, go on."—"Well, sir, then I brings the letter up to missus; cos, thinks I to myself——"

"Well, never mind what you thought to yourself. How did this letter affect your mistress?"—"Why, sir, she just read it, guved a scream, and fainted away clean."

"Oh, then, it's easily accounted for,—an agitating letter, and a consequent fainting fit. See, she is recovering."

My beautiful patient—for I think I never saw a lovelier woman—now slowly opened her eyes, and stared vacantly around her.

"Are you better, madam?" said I.—"Rather better," she repeated. "What—what has happened? Good heavens! what has happened?"

"Don't alarm yourself," said I; "you have only fainted, and will be quite well again soon."—"Fainted!" she repeated; "why did I faint?"

"Why, mum," said the little under nursemaid, "when I brought you the letter——"

A scream burst from the lips of the lady, which took me so unawares that I jumped again, and the servants set up a general screech in sympathy.

"Silence!" I roared; "silence, all of you."—"The letter, the letter!" screamed the lady, springing from the bed. "Where is the letter?"

"Here, here," cried several voices, as they pointed it out on the floor.

She seized it, and devoured with straining eyes its contents; then, thrusting it on one side, she cried, in a frantic voice,—

"My bonnet!—a shawl!—a coach! God of Heaven, take me away."

I was amazed at all this, and still more so when she snatched up a magnificent Spanish hat, with a white plume, that lay upon the bed, and darted from the room like lightning.

"Why didn't you tell me she was mad?" said I.—"Mad, sir!" echoed the servants.

"Yes, mad."—"She never was mad before, sir."—"Then run after her directly, and bring her back."

Bang went the street door at this moment, and I had just time to run to the window and see the flutter of the lady's garments, as she turned the corner of the street. I was completely puzzled, and turning to the servants, I said,—

"Can any of you explain all this?"

A prim, starched-looking female approached me, and I saw she had the letter in her hand that had produced such a riot. Pursing up her mouth with a look of severe virtue, she said,

"Are you a married man, sir?"—"Yes," said I.

"Then you can *foller* me, sir; for I'm the most fittestest to explain all in a private interview, which your being a married man don't make improper."

So saying, with a glance at the assembled servants as much as to say, "Did you ever hear of such propriety and virtue?" she sailed from the room, and I followed her. She conducted me to another little room, and then turning towards me her prim countenance, said,—

"You are quite sure you are a married man?"—"Oh! quite," said I.

"Then I—I may venture to say something."—"Just whatever you like," said I; "I shall not be shocked in the least."

"Then, sir, missus is no better than she should be."—"You mean she's not quite so good?" said I.

"*Preceesely.* Master is Captain Hargrave. He's been at sea for a year. Hem—hem—hem!"—"Oh!" said I.

"He's expected back. This letter says so. Master's friend, Sir Phillip Rawston, *has* been here *too* often. Hem—hem—hem! You are sure you are a married man? Because if you ain't—good gracious!"

The extremely particular housekeeper, for such I learnt afterwards she was, then placed in my hands the letter which, it appeared, had had such an effect upon the guilty Mrs. Hargrave. It ran thus:—

"My Dear Marian,

"I am at Portsmouth, and am forced to stay on official business some hours; so this note will reach you, as the post is just going off, before I can possibly be in London. Dear, dear Marian, I shall be at 'my own fireside' within the next twenty-four hours. God bless you and the little ones. From, my dear Marian, your affectionate husband,
"Robert Hargrave."

"How dreadful," said I, "that a letter like this should scare a wife from her home."—"Uncommon dreadful, sir," replied the housekeeper, "and, in my opinion, it's worse a vast deal than dreadful."

"Worse, madam? It can't be much worse."—"Yes, it is, Dr. ——; it's positively improper. I don't mind dreadful things; but impropriety nearly kills me."

"It's a pity your feelings are so sensitive," said I. "However, I can be of no further use here, so ——"

While I was speaking there came at the street door a peal that awakened every echo in the house.

Directly afterwards I heard somebody coming up the stairs at frantic speed, and in a moment the door of the room was flung open, and there entered a gentlemanly looking man, in the undress uniform of a naval officer. The glow of health was upon his cheek, and in the expression of his face there was a certain manly air of good feeling and generous emotions that was very pleasing.

"Marian! Marian!" he cried, as he entered the room. "Where's Marian and the children? Where are they? Not in the drawing-room,—not in the nursery,—not in bed?"—

"Why, Captain Hargrave," said the housekeeper, pursing up her lips into so small a space that her words could hardly escape them, "you don't mean to say you've been in all these rooms in this minute?"

"Yes, I do though," he cried. "I've only just arrived, so I gave a kick at all the doors as I passed them. Come, Mrs., make as much headway as you can; I half forget the navigation of the house. You know, however, all the staircases and closets; ferret them out, and bring them here. Yet,—yet, where can Marian be? My voice she must hear. Marian! Marian! I say—my girl, where are you? Surely I can make myself heard here in a calm, when I piped to the loudest wind that ever blew. He went to the landing-place of the staircase, and in a loud voice, called—"Marian! hilloa! don't hide, Marian,—don't hide, for God's sake. Answer me, Marian,—I—I'm your husband. Marian,—my Marian!"

All save his own voice was as still as the tomb in the house, and when he turned into the room again, I saw that he was getting very much alarmed.

"Who are you?" he said, apparently only just then noticing my presence; then he quickly added,—"I beg your pardon, sir; I see you are a gentleman."

I bowed, and said,—

"I am Doctor ——."—"Dr. ——?—Dr. ——?"—"Yes, Captain Hargrave, for that I perceive is your name."

He stepped up to me, and, laying his hand on my arm, his lips quivered, and the colour left his cheeks, as he gasped,—

"You say you are a physician. Then my Marian is—is ill,—perhaps dead!"—He sank upon a chair, and continued,—"Tell me,—tell me all."—"Your wife, sir," said I, "is alive for aught that I know to the contrary."

In an instant he was on his feet.

"Alive and—and well?"—"Most certainly."

"Bless your heart! so am I, then. I don't care what brought you here, unless it was about my little ones."—"I have never seen your children, sir."

"Then d—n me, if you have come in at the window, you are welcome. Here, let's have some wine,—wine here,—wine, I say. But,—but, where's Marian?"—"It's my delicate duty, Captain Hargrave, R. N., to inform you——" said the housekeeper.

"Don't put R. N. to the stern of my name," warned the captain.—"I see it in the newspaper," remarked the housekeeper.

"Hang the newspaper! come, out with your log book, old stiff and steady, and let's hear what you have got to say."

The expression of horror at the captain's highly improper mode of speaking which sat upon the countenance of the prim housekeeper was highly ludicrous, and I believe, out of sheer revenge, she said at once,—

"Mrs. Hargrave has left the house."—"What?"

"Left the house," repeated the housekeeper.—"Left—left the house! My wife—my Marian,—the mother of my children? She who—who—what an infernal lie it is!"

With a faint shriek the housekeeper dropped upon a chair as she cried,—

"Can my poor nerves stand this?"

"Tell me again," cried Captain Hargrave, "again, I say, what do you mean, woman?"

The housekeeper did not answer immediately, and the captain, taking her by the arm, gave her what he, I dare say, considered a very gentle shake, but which, in the opinion of the lady, was so exceedingly "improper," that she forthwith became hysterical, and, after gasping out,—"Heavens! look down. To be shook by a he man! Oh, oh! oh!" she commenced a series of screams, which I only put an end to by saying, "I'll bleed her in a moment;" upon which she immediately recovered, and only groaned.

The door now was slowly opened, and the young girl who had previously announced herself to me as the under nurserymaid, made her appearance with one child in her arms, and a little toddling thing, about three years old, by the hand.

The captain sprang forward, with pleasure beaming in his countenance. He caught up both the children, and pressed them to his heart. He covered them with kisses.

"So,—so," he said, "you are all right, my little ones,—my little Marian, and you, Bobby. Ah! you have both grown like your dear mother. Her eyes,—her mouth,—pretty rogues. Bless you both. Where is mamma? Hilloa, there, my girl! you are a good-tempered looking little lass. What do you do in the ship, eh?—no, the house, I mean."

"Please, sir, I minds Miss Marian and Master Robert. Please, sir, my name's Mary, please, sir."

"And a very nice little girl you are, too, Mary," said the captain. "I can see you've been good to the children, or they wouldn't smile at you so, the rogues. So, Mary, we must all of us be good to you. What are you piping your eye about, eh? Don't cry."—"Oh! Captain Hargrave, R. N.," sobbed the girl.

"What the deuce possesses you all to put R. N. to my name?"—"Please, sir, the housekeeper told us as you was a R. N."

"Oh! this old fool?"—"Yes, please, sir."

The housekeeper darted a withering look at Mary, which spoke plainly of a month's notice and no character.

"Why, how you have grown, both of you," continued Captain Hargrave, fondling his children; "but once more let me ask where is my wife? You may go and tell her I am here."—Mary began crying bitterly.—"God of Heaven! there is some mystery here," cried Hargrave. "Doctor, can you tell me?"—"Sir," said I, "I am a stranger here. I was certainly called in to attend a lady who had fainted ——"

"Was that my Marian?"—"I was told the lady was Mrs. Hargrave. There was no serious illness."

"No serious illness?"—"Certainly not."

"Oh! then I see it all. She fainted, and is now sleeping, perhaps. Why didn't you tell me before, some of you?"

I thought it was no business of mine to interfere in family affairs, so I merely said to him,—"I will bid you a good night, sir, or rather, a good morning."

He bowed, and, with the children still in his arms, followed me from the room which led into the drawing-room. He was upon the point of saying something, when the street door slammed, and I heard a rapid footstep ascending the stairs.

The door was opened without the least ceremony, and there entered, with an easy, assured air, a fashionably dressed man. He was in an opera costume, and a crush hat was placed jauntily under his arm.

The moment, however, that his eyes fell upon Captain Hargrave, he gave a start as if he had been suddenly electrified.

"Hilloa!" cried the captain; "why, my dear fellow, how did you hear of my arrival? Well, this is kind. You've run away from the opera too, I see. Give me your hand. I—why—what's the matter? Well—by G—d, he has gone mad."

The captain might well look surprised, for no sooner had the smartly attired gentleman recovered his first shock of meeting Captain Hargrave, than, dropping his opera hat, he turned round, and rushing down the stairs with frantic speed, he flew from the house, banging the street-door behind so as to shake the building to its foundations.

Captain Hargrave lost all patience, and, rushing to the bell, he rang a peal which presently brought up several servants half dressed.

"You sir," he roared to a footman, who was adjusting his cravat, "what is the meaning of this strange reception in my own house?"—"A low man, sir, has just left this here note," said the footman.

The captain snatched the note from his hands, and tore it open.

I saw him breathing hard as he read it; I saw his cheek grow pale.

"A lie,—a base lie!" he gasped, and I had just time to take the children from him, when he fell to the floor as if shot.

* * * * *

From my soul I pitied poor Captain Hargrave. He was evidently of a frank, candid disposition. I saw that his feelings were warm and affectionate. Alas! how sad it was that such a man should be subjected to so heart-rending a domestic calamity as the defection from her duty of her upon whose faith he had relied, and upon whose love he had

"Built up an air structure of pure happiness."

I shall never forget his look of utter, hopeless despair when he recovered sufficiently to be fully conscious of his situation. His eyes fell on the weeping children.

"Take,—take," he faltered, "these away!"

A servant led the eldest to the door, and carried the little one in her arms. He followed them with his eyes, and when another moment would have shut them from his view, he cried,—

"No, no, come back,—come back. You have not deceived me, my own little ones!"

He clasped them in his arms, and tears coursed each other down his manly cheeks. "Oh, God!" he cried, "that ever I should weep for shame to think of your mother, my little ones. Now take them; this is no hour for them to be up. To bed with them, and leave me to think. Ha! a horrible suspicion crosses my brain,—Sir Phillip Rawston,—why did he fly from my presence with such guilty precipitation?"

He rose, and I saw that he was making the most desperate efforts to control his feelings, as he said,—

"Is my own man, Henry, in?"—"Yes, sir," said a servant.

"Send him to me, then."

In a few moments, a respectable looking fellow of a servant made his appearance.

"Henry," said Captain Hargrave, "you know where — where Sir Phillip Rawston resides?"—"He is still at the Albany," replied the servant.

"Go to him, then, and—and—if your mistress ——"— "Don't say any more, sir; I understand, please, sir," said the servant.

"I—I must say it, Henry; if *she* is there, then, on your return, call on my old friend, Mr Seaton. You know his house?"—"I do, sir."

"Bring him here with you, if you can."

The servant bowed, and went on his errand, and I thought it high time that I, too, should go; so, turning to the captain, I said,—

"Sir, I beg you accept my best wishes; I will now leave you."—"Oh! I beg your pardon," he said; "you are Dr. ——; pray excuse my inattention."

I bowed myself out and went home, and glad I was to get to bed again, although it was then past three o'clock in the morning.

* * * * *

Half past seven o'clock. Awakened again by a violent ringing at my bell.

"Who would be a physician?" cried my wife. "There you are called up again."—"I am really very tired," said I; "but I can't say nay to these applications. A physician has always too much or too little to do."

Half asleep I huddled on my clothes again, and opening my bed room door, asked my servant who wanted me.

"Somebody, sir, from Captain Hargrave's," was the girl's reply.

"Indeed," thought I; "what's amiss now, I wonder."

Out I sallied, and was soon again rapping at the unfortunate captain's door. When I was admitted, I saw that the place was one scene of confusion. Servants were running here and there, some crying, some directing, and, in fact, there appeared "confusion worse confounded."

"This way, sir; for God's sake, this way, doctor," cried the young man who was called Henry. "Oh! my poor master,—my poor master."—"What has happened?" cried I.

He did not answer, but ran up the stairs, like a madman, and I had no resource but to follow him at once.

"This way, this way," he kept saying; and I followed him into the same room in which I had found the guilty Mrs. Hargrave upon my first visit to the house.

On the bed lay Captain Hargrave, soaked in blood, and moaning faintly.

I darted forward exclaiming,—

"How is this? Has he shot himself?"—"No, sir; master and Sir Phillip Rawston fought a duel this morning at half-past six."

"Good God!" said I, "why don't you run for a surgeon directly?"—"Sir," stammered the young man, "ain't you a—a doctor, please, sir?"

"Yes, but I am a physician. This is a surgeon's business. Go directly to Mr. ——, at No. —, Queen Anne-street, and tell him to come immediately to attend a bad wound from a duel. He will know then what instruments to bring with him. Don't lose a moment, and I will do what I can for your master in the meantime."

With consternation in his looks, the servant left the room, and I immediately turned my attention to the unhappy Captain Hargrave.

He was moaning feebly, and occasionally he spoke in a low incoherent strain. That he was badly hurt about the head I could see, but I preferred waiting till Mr. —— should arrive with proper aids, before making a minuter examination.

"Now,—now, my lads," he muttered, "we'll weather this gale. Think of ; our wives and little ones. Now,—now,—there again. Helm a port! Stand to your guns! Give way now! Yes,—you see I've come home, my Marian. God bless you, and my dear little ones! It will soon be light. Oh, God!—oh, God!" He groaned in mortal agony.

In an incredibly short space of time Mr. ——, the really eminent surgeon, entered the room. He walked at once up to the bed.

"A bad accident, I fear, doctor," he said, as he glanced at the groaning captain. "When did this happen?"—"At half-past six, sir," said Henry.

"A duel?"—"Yes, sir."

"Pistols, of course?"—"Yes, sir."

"Draw up those blinds, and fetch me some tepid water, a sponge, and some vinegar."

"I am afraid, sir," said I, "it's a very bad case."—"So am I," replied Mr. ——, "here seems to have been great loss of blood."

Without entering into professional details, it is enough to state, that everything which skill and humanity could suggest, was done for the wounded man. The ball from his antagonist's pistol had struck him in the face, and had inflicted a wound, from the consequences of which Mr. ——, the surgeon, thought it would be a miracle if he recovered.

The ball was with difficulty extracted, and, having procured a nurse for our patient, we both left the house, promising to call again in two hours time.

I made my usual morning calls, and then directed my coachman to drive homewards. The moment I entered my own house, I was told that a lady was waiting to see me, and, judge of my surprise when I saw, upon entering my visiters' parlour, Mrs. Hargrave.

"You here, madam?" I said.—"Yes," she replied, in a voice hoarse with emotion; "look on me with the contempt—the loathing I merit; but oh! grant my prayer."

She threw herself at my feet and burst into an agony of tears.

"Explain yourself madam," said I, "and pray rise from that posture."—"No, no," she replied, "I have killed him! I have killed him!"

"There are certainly but faint hopes of your husband's recovery," said I.—"Sir," she said, with clasped hands, and in a voice of awful agony, "will you carry to him my repentance? Will you tell him that I ask not forgiveness either from him or from Heaven; but oh! implore him, for the sake of one who will soon follow him to the grave, that he will permit me, guilty as I am, to tend his couch of pain. Tell him I wish but that, and—and then to die! I will not ask to see my children; I will not ask forgiveness, nor even a word of kindness. Let him loathe—reproach me, but, oh! let me night and day, sit by him, and tend him. I—I ——"

The violence of her feelings overcame her, and she sank insensible at my feet. I soon recovered her, and I confess, that I was stricken to the heart by the evidently deep and sincere repentance of the unhappy woman. What strange hallucination of mind, thought I, must have come over such a woman to induce her to act as she has done! When she was sufficiently recovered to speak, I said to her :—"

"Mrs. Hargrave, do you know the real state of your husband? He is perfectly insensible. He knows no one, and I am compelled to add, that there is great doubt of his ultimate recovery. Under the present circumstances I will not deprive you of the melancholy satisfaction of tending what I really fear is your poor husband's death-bed. There is a nurse already there, but you can assist her. I pity you from my soul, but God forbid that I should add one pang to a repentant heart."

She rose from the chair, in which I had placed her, and for a moment could not speak. Then she said faintly, "God bless you!" and leaning heavily upon my arm, we left the house together, to seek the mansion of suffering,—perhaps of death.

The evening was fast approaching as we entered Captain Hargrave's house. There was an awful stillness in the mansion. The servants walked about on tip-toe. They knew their mistress, but none spoke. The children's maid was sitting on the staircase, crying. Onwards we went to the sick chamber. A dim lamp was burning on the table, and the nurse was sitting with professional apathy, reading some book.

"This lady," said I, to the nurse, "will assist you."

The nurse looked very ill humoured, but dropped a curtsey, and replied by an equivocal kind of cough only. When I asked, did Mr. —— say he would come again, she replied,—

"He says, sir, that if so be as when the poor gentleman wakes, he keeps better for about ten minutes, I am to send for him; and if so be as he just wakes, and dies off clean away, I isn't; and he rather thinks as he'll do that same last thing."

"Oh, Heaven help him!" sobbed Mrs. Hargrave.

"Madam," I said to her, "you have heard the whole truth as regards your husband. I beg you to control your own feelings."—"I will,—I will," she said; and there she stood by the bed-side of her murdered (for I can call it nothing else) husband, and I saw the tears drop from her eyes upon the bed.

I looked narrowly at the face of the sleeper, and I felt no doubt of the result; there were certain indications of approaching dissolution.

"How long has he slept?" I whispered to the nurse, "About half an hour," she replied.

A long drawn sigh from the wounded man now attracted my attention, and I laid my hand upon Mrs. Hargrave's arm, saying,—

"Don't let him see you the moment he awakens."

I drew her behind the curtain, and scarcely had I done so, when the captain spoke.

"What is the time?" he said.—"Don't move or exert yourself, Captain Hargrave," I said gently.

"You are Dr. ——?"—"I am."

"Rawston hit me, you see, Docter. Where are we now?"

I saw by the restless expression of his eyes that his mind was a little affected.

"I'm in no pain now," he continued. "What a strange colour everything is. Who is that sobbing?"

It was his unhappy wife.

"Captain Hargrave," I said, "I ought not to conceal from you your real situation."

He looked fixedly in my face for a moment, and then said, firmly,—

"I am dying."—I was silent, and he continued,—"I would rather have fallen on the deck of my gallant ship; but now that my—my Marian has left me, I am willing to die anywhere; and if it were not for my poor little children,—I—I should feel that the pangs of living now were far greater than the one pang of dying."

I whispered to the nurse to fetch the children.

"Doctor," he continued, "'twas very hard for her—you know who I mean—to leave me. God knows how I loved her, and she knew it too. Oh! how I thought of her when far, far away; and now I die desolate, and—and—alone!—If you ever see her, doctor, tell her I forgive her, and if she can be happy when poor Hargrave, who loved her too well, is gone, tell her to be so, and forget him!"

"No no," gasped the wife, tottering to the bed-side; "leave me your curse,—kill me,—anything. Oh, God! oh, God! anything I could bear but *kindness*."

He looked at her as she spoke, and a fearful change came over his face. A cold perspiration settled on his brow.

"Go,—go!" he said, faintly.

The nurse at this moment brought in the children, and led them to the bed.

"Here are your children," I said.—"Where?" he replied. "You have put out the lamp. All is dark."

I placed the youngest close to him, and he passed his hand over the soft face, and burst into tears.—His wife stood like a statue; she neither moved, spoke, or wept.

"Marian," said the dying man, "are *you* here?"—"I am," she said, in a startlingly unnatural voice.

"I will leave you ——"—"A curse! a curse!" she shrieked.

He rose half in the bed, and opened his arms, saying,—

"No, my forgiveness,—my blessing,—and,—and,—my children!"

With a sob of mortal agony she threw herself into his arms. There was a dead silence for a moment, and then I lifted Mrs. Hargrave from the body of her husband.

"Find serenity," said I, "if not joy, in the recollection of this scene."

I spoke to a corpse! She was dead!

THE BARONET'S DAUGHTER;

OR, THE HEIR AT LAW.

VERY early one morning a note was brought to request my immediate attendance upon a well known baronet, whose name I do not like to mention, although he has been dead now many years, because an exemplary member of his family, whose feelings I greatly respect, is still living. He resided in a costly mansion in St. James's-square, and the request for my attendance was so urgent, that I lost no time in complying with it. When I got to the house and gave my name, I was at once ushered into a spacious and handsome library, and I was scarcely in the room a minute when a young lady of, as I guessed, about sixteen years of age, came hurriedly into the apartment.

"You are Dr. ——?" she said, in a nervous, agitated manner.—"I am," I replied.

"My father is very ill," she said, "and,—and——"—"And what?" said I; "pray confide in me."

"You will be secret? That is, as yet; because right *shall* be done, if all is not a delusion."

I looked at the young lady in momentary doubt as to her sanity; but that feeling was quickly dispelled, and I was certain that her incoherent speech arose from genuine, heartfelt emotion of some kind.

"Whatever you wish me to do or promise," I said, "I am willing"——"I know it," she cried. "Physicians hear many family secrets."

"They do, indeed," I replied.—"It is for you, then, sir," she continued, "to see my poor father, and to judge of what he says. That is, should he make to you any strange communications, if they be really true, or merely the result of what I dread still more,—a disordered mind."

"I will use my utmost skill," said I. "Does my patient expect me, or have you only sent for me?"—"I have persuaded him to see you," she replied.

I saw that she was struggling with some painful feelings which I could not assuage, because the whole affair was as yet to me enveloped in the greatest mystery.

"Will you be pleased to accompany me, sir?" said the young lady, "and I will take you to my father."

I followed her, and she tapped at the door of a room on the first floor; then, turning the handle, she said,—

"Go in, sir; I—I will wait for you in the library."

I saw that her eyes were full of tears, and being anxious if possible, to unravel the mystery in which the whole affair appeared to be entangled, I at once entered the room.

Leaning back on an easy arm-chair was a gentleman, past the prime of life, but presenting the wreck of what had once been a remarkably fine frame. He looked at me very languidly as I approached him, and said,—

"You are Doctor ——?"—"I am," said I.

"Well," he said hurriedly, "you see I am ill, very ill; I wish for your opinion of me."

I looked at him, and by the peculiar appearance of his eyes, I fancied he must be suffering from the effects of some narcotic.

"What have you been taking?" I said.—"Taking?" he repeated, and I saw a flush of colour for one moment visit his pale face. "Shall,—shall I die, do you think?"—"Sir," I said, "you have made an attempt to poison yourself."

He half rose from the chair, and, catching me by the arm, said,—"Hush! hush! I had a dream,—an awful dream. You fancy me Sir ——, but I am not."—"Before you say anything else," interrupted I, "tell me at once what you have taken."

He glared at me for a few moments, and then, in a faint voice, said,—"Laudanum!"—"How much?" said I, quickly.

He did not answer me, and I saw that a frightful change was coming over his countenance, and he was settling into a lethargic state. I immediately rang the bell, and a servant appeared, closely followed by the young lady.

"He has taken poison," said I. "Run to the nearest chemist's, and get what I have written."

I wrote for the best antidote we have for narcotic poisons, namely, citric acid; and then I endeavoured to rouse my patient.—The moment the daughter heard me say that her father had poisoned himself, she clasped her hands and fainted away.

"Leave the young lady," I said to the servant, "and go on my errand at once."

The man looked bewildered, but he laid his young mistress on a couch, and scampered off. Again I rang the bell loudly, and I suppose the servant I had sent off had given the alarm, for the ring was answered by at least half a dozen members of the establishment.

"You females," I cried, "see to your young lady; and here, some of you men, raise up your master, and walk him up and down the room. Keep him in action whatever you do."

They did as I desired them, and the motion seemed to shake off the drowsiness that was before momentarily gaining strength upon him. The man soon returned with the antidote, and Sir —— was just sensible enough to drink it copiously. Suffice it to say, that in the course of a couple of hours I was under no apprehension concerning the laudanum, of which he could have taken but a small quantity; and although I was somewhat curious to know what he meant by not being Sir ——, when it was perfectly well known that he was, I did not think myself authorised to ask any questions; so, after ordering him proper medicines, and hearing that the daughter was better, and in her own room, I left the house.

* * * * *

I had that day a great many professional calls to make, and I returned home later than usual, very much fatigued, and I was quite grateful that the whole evening passed over without my being called upon to go from home. I went to bed early, and it might have been about one or half-past one in the morning, that I was awakened by a violent ringing at my bell, and presently my servant tapped at my room door, and said,—"Sir, you are wanted at Sir ——'s, in St. James's-square, directly."

"There is something the matter with that crazy baronet again," said I to my wife, as I hurried on my clothes"—"I wish" said my wife, "people would sleep quietly at night, and only get ill in the day time."

I certainly agreed with the wish; but it was no use wishing, so I hurried off as quickly as I could, and soon reached St. James's-square from my house, which was not then a quarter of a mile distant from it.

The hall porter was standing with the door in his hand to let me in the moment I appeared. He cried out in a voice of alarm,—

"The drawing room; Sir —— is in the drawing room."—"Very well," said I, as I ascended the staircase. A door was half open, and upon entering the room, I saw that it was crowded with half dressed domestics, carrying all sorts of lights, from an Argand lamp to a rushlight.

"Here's Dr. ——," they all cried, as they made way for me, and, advancing to the middle of the throng, I saw the baronet himself, seated in a chair, with nothing on but his night-clothes and a dressing-gown, shaking so violently that it was painful to see him.

"Oh! doctor," cried the daughter, springing to me, "what is the matter with my poor father? This is too horrible,—too dreadful!"—"My dear young lady," I said, "don't alarm yourself. You would be much better in bed. Get some brandy directly, some of you."

The baronet looked at me, but he did not speak. There was great anxiety in his countenance, and his eye was continually roving all over the apartment; added to which symptoms, he shook in every limb, and his teeth chattered against each other.

The brandy was brought, and, without asking any more questions till I had done something for my patient, I got him to take some, as well as sopping his temples and the palms of his hands with it. The trembling soon partially subsided, and I turned to the servants, saying,—

"Can any of you tell me when and how your master was taken this way?"—"I—I will tell you," he gasped.—"Go—go, all of you,—go. Light the lamps first."

"My dear sir," I said, "you had much better go to bed."—"No, no," he cried, "never again,—never again! No rest,—no rest for me!"

He said this in a tone of such bitter anguish, that my curiosity was more than ever awakened, and I turned to the servants, saying,—"Do as you are bid; but be within call."

They then lighted several lamps which were in the room, and left me alone with the baronet.

"I will tell,—I will tell all," muttered the baronet. "Perhaps, oh, God! perhaps I may then have ease.'

The lamplight shed a brilliant colour upon his ghastly face, and the gilding and rich ornaments of that luxurious apartment were sadly at variance with the expression of anguish in the face of the master of so much wealth and refinement.

My curiosity was strongly excited, and I prepared myself either to listen to the ravings of a madman, or some tale of iniquity, which thus late in life had jarred strangely on the nerves of the rich and prosperous man.

"I do not know," he commenced, "even now if we are alone. The thought is horrible;—but I will not anticipate. Some powerful feeling urges me to tell you what I have hitherto concealed in the inmost recesses of my heart. I have now enjoyed the title and estates of the family from which I spring for more than eighteen years. The—the young creature whom you saw here is not my daughter."

—"Not your daughter, sir?" said I.

"Hush!" he cried, "let me finish my story. I wish to do tardy justice. You may have heard that I am the second son of the late baronet, my father; and you may likewise be aware of the mode and manner of my eldest brother's death?"—"He was killed from a fall in riding, I think I heard," said I.

"He was," continued the baronet. "He was in good health, under thirty years of age, and I had then about as much prospect of succeeding to the title and estates I now enjoy, as—as you have."

He here paused, and an universal tremor shook his frame. Deep sighs rose from his breast.

"Enjoy!" he repeated; "alas! have I ever enjoyed or known one moment's peace since I stepped into this lordly mansion as its owner?"—"Calm yourself, sir," I said; "anything that you wish me to do, either professional or otherwise, to give you ease of mind, I am willing to perform. I do not ask your confidence, but I am ready to listen to all you are willing to impart."

"Yes," he faltered, "I will tell all, and then,—then I will try to sleep. My father, doctor, was a proud, stern man, and I and my elder brother well knew that he would never forgive either of us if we contracted any matrimonial alliance beneath what he called our *caste* in life. This was a truth in connexion with my father's character which we were made aware of in so many ways from early life, that we never could forget it. Well, sir, it happened that during a temporary visit my brother and I paid to Vienna, my brother became very passionately enamoured of a young orphan girl of that city, who had nothing to recommend her but her beauty and amiability of mind, which I never saw equalled. This passion grew to such a height in my brother's heart, that he declared to me that his future happiness in life all depended upon making the young and beautiful Genevieve his wife In vain I painted to him the injury he would do himself with his father; in vain I conjured him to try and smother a passion which, must, in the end, I thought, produce misery to all parties.

He would not, or could not, control his heart, and he was married to Genevieve in the Roman Catholic faith, at Vienna.

"The day after the ceremony he told me of it, and as the mischief was done, I seriously set myself about repairing it, as much as possible, and advised that he should bring his wife immediately to London, and there solemnize his nuptials in the Protestant faith. This plan was adopted, and we all three came to London together.

"The first news that met us was of the serious indisposition of my father, and the declaration of my brother's love for the fair orphan, and its result, was kept secret between us three until my father's health should be restored. At an obscure country church my brother again went through the marriage ceremony with his matchless wife. I was the only person present at the ceremony, and at its termination my brother handed me the certificate of the marriage, with these words:—

"'Brother, I confide this to you; it will be the proof of the legitimacy of my children, should I be blessed with any.'

"He and his wife then lived together in a cottage, some distance from town, and happy in each other's society. Their only pain was the necessity of carefully concealing their union, lest it should come to the ears of my father, and from any other source than themselves, and they feared, in his state of precarious health, the effect which such a communication might have upon him.

"Thus a year passed away, and my brother's wife gave birth to a boy. This was a death blow to my hopes of ever succeeding to the title and estates, and I banished the idea from my thoughts of ever being other than what I then was, —a younger son, with eight hundred a-year.

"Well, doctor, my brother was carried off in the prime of life by the accident you have mentioned. He was riding a high-spirited horse in Hyde Park; he was thrown, and never spoke again. I was likewise in the park, and seeing a crowd collecting, I rode to the spot, when the first object that presented itself to me was the lifeless body of my brother.

"My first thought was of his wife and child, and, after giving proper directions with regard to his remains, I clapped spurs to my horse, and galloped to the cottage, where was the gentle and affectionate Genevieve awaiting his return.

"Her situation was at once calculated to inspire any one with the tenderest sympathy. Her boy was nearly eighteen months old, and she was, as I knew, in daily expectation of adding another heir to the barony.

"I declare to you, doctor, that a thought of self-interest never crossed my mind as I galloped to the cottage. My heart bled for the young mother, and my only anxiety was how best to frame the dreadful tidings of which I was a messenger. I was, however, spared the task, for my brother's groom, who, I believe, thought Genevieve a mistress merely, had preceded me, and bluntly told the melancholy truth.

"When I arrived, the house was a scene of confusion. A medical man was there, who prognosticated the worst results. Alas! they were realized. In an hour Genevieve gave birth to a female child, and died!

"I was so confounded by the rapidity of all these events, that I knew not what to do or think. I merely charged the servants and the nurse to look properly to the children, and then retired to the little parlour, where I had so often sat with my brother and his wife, to reflect upon the awful incidents of the last two hours.

"The medical man entered the room, and he said a few words which awakened a train of ideas in my mind which might otherwise never have come across it.

"'I presume, sir,' he said, 'you would not wish this matter talked about, as the lady was, I understand, not your brother's wife?'

"I started, and felt the blood rush to my face, as the new idea of concealing the marriage darted across my mind.

"'Yes, certainly,' I stammered, 'send me your bill, and say nothing.'

"Then, in the solitude of the next hour, it occurred to me how easily I could suppress all evidence of my brother's marriage. The more I reflected upon it, the more feasible appeared the scheme. Doctor, I yielded to the temptation. I —I proclaimed the children illegitimate."

"And is the young lady," said I, "who called upon me your brother's child?"

"She is his second child. But listen,—you have not heard all. The shock of my brother's death produced a crisis in the disease of my father. He died likewise within a week after, and I became Sir ———, and the unquestioned possessor of a fortune of princely amount."

He paused for a few minutes, and then continued in a broken voice,—

"My poor brother's children grew up in health and beauty. I married, but was childless, and my wife wasted away before my eyes, and died a lingering death. Then I took home my brother's daughter to live in my house."

"And what became of the son?"

"*I killed him!*"

"*You killed him?*" said I, looking with horror at the man who could commit such a crime.

"I—I did not steep my hands in his blood," he said, "I did not pour poison in his young veins; and yet, oh, God! oh, God! I killed the boy."

I was silent, and in no enviable state of mind as to what I ought to do.

"I will tell you how it was," he continued. "I lavished wealth upon him; I made him, in education and in station, a gentleman. At as early an age as I could,—that is last year,—I purchased for him a commission in one of the best regiments in the army. Some brother officer, in the heat of a mess-room argument, taunted him with his illegitimacy, which was currently understood and believed. They fought the next morning, and my poor nephew received his death wound. Then was it not I that truly killed him?"

"It was a most unhappy circumstance," said I; "who can calculate the consequences which may spring from one error?"

"They are fearful,—frightful," he cried. "Now hear me further:—I have written all this down at length. The paper is in a bureau in my chamber. Should I die suddenly, you will know what to do."

"Then this niece of yours is the heiress of all the family property?"

"She is, and she will have it soon. Perhaps now I may get a night's repose."

"What has hitherto spoilt your rest?" said I.

"I have scarcely slept," he said, "for some months, because of my brother."

"Your brother? Your thoughts of him, you mean?"

"No, no. He has been in the house for a long time. I meet him on the stairs, in my chamber; at my meals he glides past me. Go where I will, he follows; and when I lie down to rest he sits by my bed-side, and looks at me with eyes of such deep grief and reproach, that,—that, God of Heaven! I am nearly mad! To-night he came again, and — and—*his son with him!*"

"His son?"

"Yes. They stood hand in hand by my bed-side, and looked at me. The young man's hand was pressed to his heart; it was where the bullet had entered that took his life. I could see the blood coming through his fingers. Oh, horrible! horrible! Can you wonder that I am as I am?"

"I think," said I, "you will get rid of these visions if you allow yourself to adopt the remedies I suggest. You have it still in your power to do justice to your niece."

"Yes," he said, "I have enclosed the certificate of my brother's marriage in my confession."

"Well, then," said I, "I advise you to go to bed now, and, if you please, I will call to-morrow, or rather, later to-day, and we can talk more upon the subject."

"To bed," he muttered; "they are there!"

"Oh! you must not think that."

"I know they are waiting for me," he replied; "the father and son. I cannot bear their looks."

"Your imagination deceives you. I will accompany you to your room, if you please."

He hesitated for a moment, and then said,—

"Yes, yes, you shall, and,—and I can show you the drawer in the bureau where the papers are."

I immediately rang the bell, and when a footman answered the summons, I desired him to precede us with lights, and then turning to the trembling baronet, I offered him my arm, and we thus followed the man up a flight of handsome marble steps to the baronet's bed-room.

He said nothing, but I could tell by his manner that he was in a dreadful state of excitement; and when we arrived at the door of the room, he trembled so as scarcely to be able to stand.

"Come in with me," I said, "I will stay with you a little time."

He did not speak, but allowed me to lead him into the spacious chamber, which was well lighted by a lamp from the ceiling.

"You see," I said, when the servant had left, "the room is empty."

He glared wildly round him, and said, in a whisper,

"That is the bureau; the,—the papers and marriage certificate are there; and—look here,—look here!"

He took me by the arm, and leading me to the side of the bed, pointed to the floor.

"What is that?" said I, as I remarked some dark spots.

"Blood," he whispered; "I saw it drop from the wound in,—in my nephew's breast."

"You must be mistaken," said I.

"No, no; I saw it drop."

His eyes were incessantly wandering round the room, as if in search of something; and although I am far from being nervous now, and was then twenty years younger, I could not help feeling a certain vague uneasiness creeping over me.

"I must leave you now," I said. "Depend upon seeing me to-morrow. You had better go to bed."

I had taken one step towards the door, when it slowly opened without any visible agency, that I saw, and my heart leaped to my mouth with the surprise of the moment.

A stifled shriek burst from the baronet, and pointing the fore fingers of each hand in an awful manner at the door, while his eyes seemed starting from their sockets, he cried,—

"There,—there,—there!"

I saw nothing, although I certainly felt a little flurried, and I followed with my eyes the direction of his fingers, as he continued to point from the door, slowly moving towards the bureau.

The whole occurrence was scarcely the work of a minute, and while my eyes were off the unhappy man, I heard him convulsively gasp, and turning to him, I saw him tearing his shirt-collar. In another instant, he fell with a heavy lump on the floor.

I rang the bell violently. The room was soon filled with domestics. We raised the baronet from the floor, and found him *a corpse!*

* * * * *

My tale is over. The young lady, who had always been believed the baronet's own illegitimate daughter, was proved to be his legitimate niece, and she is now the wife of one of England's noblest nobles.

THE OUTCAST;

OR, THE DISCARDED CHILD.

It was my custom, after sunset, provided I had no professional calls to make, to dismiss my carriage for the day, and trust to my good fortune in being alone till the next morning, or, should I be called upon in an emergency, I had still considerable reliance left upon what they term in Scotland "shank's naggy," and in England "the ten-toed machine," which, in my early career, had safely transported me to all parts of the town.

One rainy evening in October, when everybody remained indoors, that could command so much felicity, I was summoned to attend a rich but eccentric old lady, who resided near Vauxhall. This was a formidable journey to undertake on foot on such a night; but I sallied forth, however, without delay, trusting, as a matter of course, to meet with refuge in a hackney coach. But such was not my fortune; I was doomed to

"Bide the pelting of the pitiless storm,"

and after repairing to several well-known stands, and not finding even the ghost of a conveyance on any of them, I reluctantly came to the conclusion that I must rely upon my own physical resources to convey me through Westminster, Millbank, and across that most gloomy of bridges,—Vauxhall. Having, then, quite convinced myself that I had no resource but walking, I turned up the collar of my coat, pulled my hat down nearly to the bridge of my nose, and with a feeling of great desperation, paddled onwards,—paddled is the proper word, for the rain was coming down in torrents, and the streets were complete pools of water. It was a most provoking kind of rain, for it came down so quietly and calmly, soaking one without any blustering or noise. If the wind had howled, and there had been a little thunder and lightning, I could have put up with it a great deal better; but there is nothing, to my mind, so provoking as those steady, quiet rains, which soak one to the skin quite calmly, and as a matter of course. I felt my hat getting limp on my head, and I had not a dry thread upon me.

"Pleasant this," thought I, "for a man who keeps a carriage; but then he's a physician, and of course must turn out in all weathers." Here, I am afraid, I wound up my reflections with something resembling an oath.

On I went, however, and on went the rain. I passed the frowning Penitentiary, crossed the bridge, and stood at my patient's door without, I believe, meeting six persons on my road.

There was but slight occasion to have sent for me, but I prescribed, pocketed a handsome fee, and, having stayed till my coat and hat had been well dried, I again started for home.

Upon leaving the house of my patient I was agreeably surprised to find that the rain had entirely ceased, the dun clouds in the sky had dispersed, and a full, clear moon was sailing in all its majesty in a sky that I had rarely seen equalled for clearness and purity of colour.

"Well, this is an improvement," I thought. "I dare say hackney-coaches will now be plenty; but I won't have one. I walked through the rain, and I won't ride through the beautiful moonlight."

I stepped briskly forward, and was soon on the bridge. The moonbeams fell sweetly on the water, as it took its lazy way through the arches, and I involuntarily paused to gaze on its sparkling lustre, and to cast a glance at the huge, slumbering city, which stretched its mighty masses of bricks and mortar as far as the eye could reach. I leaned upon the balustrade, and I know not how long I was lost in contemplation of the varied scene before me, when my meditations were abruptly broken in upon by a voice, the faint tones of which, as they struck upon my ear, I never shall forget.

There was an awful solemnity in its tones which, combined with the peculiarities of time and place, affected me most powerfully.

The words were these:—

"They have cast me from them; but, oh, God! may they never be cast away from Thee. They would not forgive me, but, just Heaven, forgive thou them! Bless him,—my father,—though,—though he turned me from the door to die;—and—and my mother,—my dear mother! Oh, God! oh, God!"

A burst of wild hysterical weeping smote my ears, and I stood as one turned to stone, so great was the effect produced upon me; not so much by the words themselves, as by the heart-rending tone in which they were uttered.

The frantic grief subsided into deep sobs and moans; then they ceased, and in another moment a figure rushed from one of the covered alcoves of the bridge, and clung to the parapet close by me.

"Forgive me, oh, God!" cried the same voice, and rapid as thought the figure began clambering over the rails. I started as if a spell had suddenly taken possession of my faculties.

"Hold!" I cried, in a voice which echoed from one end of the bridge to the other.

I sprang forward, and laid a firm clutch on the figure that, in another instant, would have been far down in the flowing stream.

"Hold! what, in Heaven's name, would you do?"

Slowly the female (for such she was) turned her face towards me. The bonnet was off her head, and hung to her neck by its strings. A quantity of light silky hair floated idly in the breeze that blew from the water, and long, long after that night were my slumbers haunted by the vision of that beautiful, pale, cherub face which met my gaze, wearing an expression of such deep,—oh, such agonizing woe.

The moon fell upon the small and exquisitely chiselled features, and the blue eyes, which were bent down with a gaze of such awful dejection, looked more than earthly by that silver light.

"What do you mean?" I repeated; "for God's sake, what was your fearful object?"—"To die!" she replied, clasping her hands.

"Reflect—reflect," I said, in great agitation of manner: "you are young. What could drive you unbidden to the throne of the Almighty?"

"I reflected," she murmured, "till thought and reflection have been the parents of madness. God will forgive me. Yes,—yes; He—He will forgive me that I seek refuge with him. Sir, stay me not. Take your hands off. Now,—now I should have been calm,—so calm and happy *there*."

She pointed to the water, and strove to disengage herself from my grasp.

"I cannot let you go," I said; "I should be myself answerable to my conscience and to Heaven for your destruction. My poor girl, I pity you, and——"

"Stop, stop," she cried; "oh, don't speak to me in that voice; I cannot bear it."

"Wherefore?"—"Because it—it is—the voice of kindness."

"I mean it as such," I replied, "and if I can be kind to you, I will."—"Oh, cease,—cease," she cried, wringing her hands; "you know not *who* and *what* I am."

"You may have erred," I said; "but who shall stand up before his God and say, 'I have sinned not.' I care not who you are. You are one of God's creatures, and that is enough; *what* you are can never stint the hand of pity."—"And yet,—yet you are not my father," she gasped.

"You have a father?" said I.—"I,—I had."

"He is dead?"—"No, no; he spurned me from his door. I did seek him in repentance of heart, sir I did indeed. I sat down on his threshold, and wept as I said, 'Father, your repentant child has come to you again;' and,—and he would not take me in."

"Is this possible?"—"It is,—it is. Oh, sir, then I found myself alone indeed, and I came here to die!"

There was an artlessness of manner about the young creature that won upon my heart and powerfully affected my feelings. I felt the tears crowding to my eyes as I said—

"My poor girl, if you say to God what you said to your father, *He* will not renounce you. I bless the opportunity that has enabled me to save you from destruction. You are too young to have become lost in error, whatever may have been your history. If I say to you I will become your friend, provided you are truly repentant, and have told me the truth as regards yourself, will you be more happy? I am a physician, a husband, and a father. What is your answer? Dare you stand the test of rigid inquiry?"

She clasped her hands, and sank on her knees at my feet. Sobs of grateful feeling choked her utterance.

"I am so unused to kindness," she said, "that,—that it is too much for——"

Her head sank, and upon stooping to raise her, I found that she had fainted at my feet. I immediately took her in my arms, and she was as light as a child of eight or ten years of age. Without giving a thought as to the singularity of the thing, I carried her into the toll-house, to the great surprise of the toll collector, who stood gaping with astonishment first at me and then at the girl, with his hands in the two canvass pockets of halfpence that hung before him. At length his intense dismay vented itself in the elegant expression of,—

"Well, I'm blowed!"

"I am Dr. ——," said I, with an air of authority, laying my card on the table; "get me some water immediately."

My name and manner produced a magical effect upon the man, and he became perfectly respectful, and hoped "as the young lady vasent wery bad."

In a few moments the young creature recovered, and she immediately started and looked wildly around her, till she saw me, when she suddenly stretched out her little hand, and catching mine, pressed it to her lips, with an expression on her face of such intense gratitude, that I was much affected.

"Can you get me a coach?" said I, to the toll man.—" In course, sir," he said; "there's a stand o' t'other side o' the bridge. If any vun comes, gist be so good as to take a penny."

"I will," said I, and off set the man, leaving me in the most unexpected appointment of toll collector to Vauxhall Bridge!

I did not long retain my enviable situation, for the man quickly re-appeared, with a hackney-coach rumbling after him.

"The coach, sir," he said; "nobody bin, I s'poses?"—"No one," I replied. "Take this for your trouble," giving him half-a-crown.

The coachman rolled off his box, enveloped in all his great

coats, and stood with the door of the crazy vehicle in his hand, when it all at once occurred to me that I was not quite clear about where I was going. Home! certainly did not like to go until I knew something more of my new acquaintance. I turned to her, and said, in a low voice,—

"Have you a home?"—She shook her head, saying, "I am destitute."

"I must lodge her somewhere, that's clear," thought I, and all at once I recollected a poor but honest family that had been pensioners on my wife for a long time, who, I thought, would cordially receive my unfortunate *protege*. The worst of it was, that they lived as far off as Islington; but, after a moment's reflection, I gave the coachman their address, and, assisting my companion into the vehicle, off we set.

The poor girl shrank up into one corner of the coach, and covering her face with her hands, I could hear her crying as if her heart would break.

"Come," said I, "you should not cry now, for I will keep my word, and be a real friend to you, if I find you deserving."—"How,—how can I thank you?" she sobbed. "When I was happy at home, I thought little of these things; but now I know what it is to be hungry and houseless."

"Well, well," said I, "don't talk of that now; tell me your name."—"Florence Seabright," she replied.

"Florence?" I said, wishing to amuse her, "that is rather a remarkable name. And how old are you?"—"Sixteen," she faltered.

"How long, then, Florence have you been from your father's house?"—"Eight weary months," she replied; "oh, what an age it has seemed!"

"I will not pain you," I said, by asking you why you left your home; but you can tell me if you please. I am getting an old man now, and have seen so much of the world, that you need fear no harsh judgment from me. 'Judge not lest ye be judged,' has always crossed my mind when I have heard of errors, or even the crimes, of my fellow creatures; so, Florence, you may speak to me without fear."

She was silent for some moments; then, in a low, suffocating voice, she said :—

"You,—you ought to know me, sir. Under a solemn promise of marriage,—a promise which the name of God was used to sanction,—I left my father's home. I,—I was betrayed and deserted!"—"Then your first step was to return to your father?"

"It was, sir. Many a weary mile I travelled on foot before I reached the well-known spot. Then,—then I sank on the threshold, and prayed for forgiveness."—"And is it possible he received you not?"—"He,—he cursed me! Oh! God! my father cursed me."

"Well," said I, "say no more about it at present. I will call upon you with my wife to-morrow, at three o-clock. I am taking you now to a poor but honest and respectable home. They who keep it need know nothing further of you at present than that you are Florence Seabright and a patient of mine."

"God bless you, sir," she cried; "let me work, slave for you,—die for you, sir, and,—and give me but a kind word now and then to make me happy."

Again she burst into tears, and sobbed like a child.

We were now near our place of destination, which was in a little street near the Angel Inn, at Islington, and by the time the coach, with a great deal of swagging backwards and forwards, stopped at the door, I found that it was half-past eleven o'clock.

Some of the family were still up by good fortune, and my visit was very graciously received by the good lady herself, who was a kind-hearted, ignorant woman.

"This young lady is a patient of mine, and I wish you to let her be here at my cost."—"Oh, dear yes, in course," exclaimed the good woman. "Come in my dear. Bless us, how poorly she does look, to be sure."

"She has been, and is very ill," I said. Then, taking the woman aside, I gave her some money, with directions to purchase some wine and arrowroot for Florence, and that I would call with my wife on the morrow.

I then turned to the poor girl herself, who followed me with her eyes all round the room.

"I will see you to-morrow, Florence," I said; "and I hope to see you refreshed by a good night's sleep."

I saw she could not speak, for her heart was full, and without another word, I left the house, and ordered the coachman to drive me home.

My wife was very much annoyed at my being so long gone from home, and I deferred my communication about Florence Seabright till the morning, because my wife always, when she is a little out of temper, calls me "doctor," and this night she kept doctoring me at every other word; so I thought it better to wait till the breakfast things were on the table in the morning before I said a word of my adventure.

Not that I for a moment doubted my wife's goodness of heart in the matter; but married men know very well that there is a proper time for all things; and, if they don't know it, they will find it out some day.

So, when we were very cosily sitting at breakfast in the morning, I said,—

"My dear, I met with quite an adventure last night; but you kept on calling me 'doctor' at such a rate, that I could not tell it to you."

"Well, tell me now," she replied, with a smile; "but, you know, I shouldn't have called you 'doctor,' at all, if I hadn't been afraid you had caught your death of cold."

"Oh!" said I, "that's quite reason enough, and conclusive."

So I told her then all I knew of Florence Seabright. She was silent for a few moments, and then she said,—

"Women feel more strongly on these subjects than men, and I think, my dear, you did quite right; just as I would expect and wish you to do."

I saw she was affected, and a tear trickled down her cheek, as I said gaily,—

"I knew you would say so. Now I will go and pay my morning calls, and we will go together to see poor Florence."

"You are a great deal too good for——"

"Nonsense," said I; "I see you are going to praise me, and that always ends in a cry; so I'll go away at once."

* * * * *

I hurried my visits as much as I could, so as to keep faith with poor Florence, and by three o'clock I and my wife were at the door of the place of refuge I had found for her.

We were welcomed by the good woman with a profusion of apron smoothings and smiles, and in reply to my question of,—"Well, how is my patient, Mrs. Martin?" she lifted up her hands and eyes, and exclaimed:—"She's a angel out o' *eaven*."

"Indeed," said I.—"Oh! lauks me, yes. She's the *genteelest* creature as was ever known,—that she is. Poor dear thing. Oh! that cough!"

"Cough," said I; "I,—I didn't know she had a cough."—"It's a *churchyarder*," exclaimed Mrs. Martin.—"A what?" cried I.—"A *churchyarder*," repeated the good lady. "Oh! she's a-going, she is. Poor dear thing!"

I felt very much shocked at this information, and proportionally anxious to see Florence.

"Where is she?" I said.—"Poor thing!" cried Mrs. Martin, "we can't get her to come down stairs."—"Come with me," I said to my wife; "we will go up to her, Mrs. Martin."

The house was not so extensive that we could go very much astray upon ascending the narrow staircase; so, declining the escort of Mrs. Martin, we ascended and knocked at the first door we came to. It was immediately opened by Florence, and I saw that her eyes were red with weeping.

My wife stepped forward and took her by the hand, saying kindly,—

"My dear, I have come to see you, and hope you will receive me as an old friend; I am Dr. ——'s wife."—"You are too good to me,—much too good," said the poor girl, struggling with her tears. "Oh, madam, can you condescend to speak kindly to a poor unfortunate girl like me?"

"There lies your claim to kindness, Florence," said my wife; "you are poor and unfortunate."

I saw the face of Florence Seabright now in the clear daylight much better than I had done on the preceding evening; and I think I scarcely ever saw so much gentle beauty in one countenance. Still I could not but regard the poor girl with a painful feeling, for I saw, by the transparent blue veins that streaked her temples, and the unusual purity of the colour that just tinged her pale cheeks, that she was one of those beings, so fragile and beautiful, who fall before the first rude breath of sickness into an early grave.

"Have you a cough, Florence?" I said,—"Yes, sir; lately I have had a cough," she replied.

"Come, now, my dear," said my wife to me, "Florence and I will have a chat by ourselves."—"Very well," said I; "I will go down stairs and talk to the Martins."

I turned to the door, and just as I reached it, I heard Florence cough. I paused; again a dry hollow cough met my ears.

"Poor girl!" I thought; "she will not be long a burthen to anybody. Too well I know the sound of that consumptive cough. By my soul's safety, I would not have been her father, and acted as he has done, for the crown of England!"

In about a quarter of an hour my wife came down the stairs, and I saw in a moment by her eyes that she had been weeping.

"Come home," she said to me; "I have persuaded her to lie down. Come home."

We bade adieu to the Martins, leaving strict injunctions to pay every attention, at our cost, to Florence, and we were soon in our carriage rattling homewards.

"If ever," said my wife, "there was such a thing as a fallen angel, that poor girl is one. She has been betrayed in the most shocking manner by a person who enjoyed all the confidence of her father's house, and then was deserted with a taunting advice to procure a livelihood by infamy."—"And her father?" said I.

"Her father, Dr. ———," cried my wife—"father, indeed! I've no patience."—"Well, don't call me Dr. ———," said I. "I am not her father, you know."

"But, my dear, that man is not fit to be called a father. *If his child had erred ten times, and come again to him for forgiveness, he should have opened to her his arms, and said 'Welcome.'*"—"That," said I, "is a sentiment which should be engraven on tablets of gold. But who is this father?"

"He is a Mr. Seabright, residing, she tells me, in Suffolk, at a place called Fairfield."—"And what rank in life does he fill?"

"He is an independent gentleman."—"Independent, but not a gentleman," replied I.

"A very religious man."—"A religious man, and a bad, unforgiving father."—"No, my dear, that cannot be. There is no religion on the face of the earth, from paganism to the pure and holy precepts of Christianity, that would not have taught him better."

"Then he's a wretch," said my wife; "his daughter is an angel, and you are the best ———"—"That will do," said I. "Here we are at home, and I have some medicines to send to poor Florence, after which we will consult what is to be done for her."

"She shall never want."—"We are quite agreed," said I, "upon that point. God has blessed us with a superfluity, and 'out of our abundance she shall be fed.'"

My wife pressed my hand, and we entered our happy home.

"Now tell me your real opinion," said my wife, after we had conversed some time concerning Florence Seabright; "do you consider the poor girl in immediate danger?"—"No, I do not," I replied, "if by immediate you mean that she may live a few weeks. My candid opinion is, that care and serenity of mind would preserve her for perhaps years; but she is certainly in a very delicate state, and suffering of any sort now would convey her to an early grave."

"Poor thing," said my wife; "that father of her's surely, my dear, cannot be deaf to all appeals in favour of a young thing whose guilt, if guilt it can be called, should rather be pitied than condemned."—"My time, you know," said I, "is very precious."

"And why so?" urged my wife; "only because it is well employed."—"Why, that's true enough," said I; "what do you want me to do?"

"What you are going to do, I'm quite sure; and that is, to go to this poor girl's father, and tell him what an unchristian wretch he is."

I smiled as I replied,—

"It won't do to tell him that. I must persuade him to be a Christian wretch; and about my going to him, why, I confess you have pretty well guessed what I was just thinking about."—"Of course," replied my wife, and, as she spoke, I saw a tear glistening in her eye; "it's easy to say beforehand what you'll do. One has only to think what would be the best and kindest course."

"There now," cried I, "you have some design upon me by your outrageous compliments. To-morrow, at the same hour as to-day, we will again visit Florence, and I shall then be better able to judge of her real state of health; and on the next day, if possible, I will go to the place where her father lives, although I believe it is nearly a day's journey."

My wife was quite pleased with this arrangement, and we both were anxious to see the beautiful and unfortunate Florence Seabright again.

At three o'clock we were at Mrs. Martin's door, and welcomed as before, with a series of outrageous curtseys.

"How is Miss Seabright?" said my wife.—"Ah, poor thing!" said Mrs. Martin, "she's a going. Bless her! I always says as the good goes first, and leaves the bad behind."

"Go up to her room," I whispered to my wife, "and tell her I am here."

My wife ascended the staircase, and in a few minutes she called me to come up.

Oh! what a deceitful glow was upon the face of the unfortunate Florence. A medical man might almost have been deceived by the colour in her cheeks into a doubt of her real state of health. How beautiful she looked! Her long fair hair was parted and plaited in the simplest manner, and a plain morning frock, which my wife had sent her, set off her exquisitely moulded figure to the greatest advantage.

I was silent for a moment when I entered the room, for I was really struck with the loveliness of that young creature, who, I sincerely believed, was hovering on the verge of the tomb. I thought of the description by Rousseau of the evanescent nature of the most beautiful objects:—

"Even while we smile with gladness at the advent of so much beauty and goodness, the tears with which we shall mourn its departure are swiftly gathering."

"Florence," said I, "you are better to-day?"—"Yes, dear friend," she replied, "I think I am."

Even as she spoke the colour faded away from her cheeks, and left them as pale as alabaster; then, with a flashing glow, it came back again. Alas! too well I knew what such rapid changes portended. I saw her before me in all her beauty,— on the threshold of existence, marked, by the unerring hand of Providence, as a victim to that insidious disease which ever comes clothed in beauty, and lays its heavy blight upon the youngest, and purest, and the most lovely. Consumption! thou caterer for the grave! thou that, like the pagan priests of old, decked thy victims with fair flowers—alas! how many of England's best and fairest daughters have fallen from thy fell influence!

"Florence," I said, "your mother still lives?"—"Yes, yes, she does."

"Well, my dear, I don't wish to distress you with questions," said my wife; "but will you tell us in confidence the name of him who ———"—"I know who you mean," faltered Florence; "yes, I ought to tell you. His name is, — is ———"

She was here interrupted by the recurrence of the cough, which I considered so alarming a symptom in her case, and it was several minutes before she could continue. Then she told us that it was a Mr. Western, a gentleman of large property, in her father's neighbourhood, who had wrought her so much woe.

"But, sir," she said, when she had told us, "and you, too, dear madam, do not seek him. I loved him because I thought him great and good,—now, oh, Heavens! I shudder at his name. You know not, and I cannot tell, what he said to me when he cast me upon the wide world, a desolate and friendless being. It was a horrible suggestion, and from the moment it passed his lips, I was cured of my blind passion. I—I do not love him now."

She burst into tears, and hiding her face with her hands, sobbed bitterly for several minutes.

"I promise you, Florence," said I, "that no appeal shall be made through me to Mr. Western. Appeals based upon justice and right feeling to such men are completely thrown away. That I know from experience."—"But if," continued Florence,—"oh! if my father would but say one word of kindness to me, I could die in peace."

"Don't talk of dying, Florence," said I, assuming a gaiety which I did not feel; "you know I am a doctor, and what's to become of my reputation if I let you die?"

She smiled faintly, and again the colour on her cheeks went and came with flashing quickness.

After some few minutes' more conversation, we left the house, and scarcely was I seated in the carriage, when, with impressive earnestness, my wife asked me my opinion again of Florence's state of health. "I think," said I, "there are all the evidences of incipient consumption; but, without very great weakness should quickly ensue, she may live till—"
—"Till when?"

"Till the spring."—"Poor Florence!" said my wife. "Let us make her brief sojourn in this world as happy as it can be made."—"That is a duty now from which you will not find me shrink," said I, "and to-morrow I will go to Fairfield, and do what can be done to move the better feelings of this poor girl's father."

* * * *

I found, upon inquiry, that by starting tolerably early in the morning, I could reach the neighbourhood in which Florence's parent resided in time to transact all the business which took me there, and get home again shortly after nightfall.

Full of expectation, therefore, of finding but little difficulty in reconciling the repentant child to her parents, I started for Fairfield. I had then a better opinion of human nature than I have now, and I could not believe it possible that any circumstances could occur to extinguish totally the natural affection between a parent and child. * * *

I need not fatigue my reader with an account of my journey, but suffice it to say, that by about mid-day I was set down by a coach that was going further on, at the corner of a beautiful green lane, which, they told me, led direct to Fairfield; the guard of the coach adding, in an under tone, as the vehicle drove off, that I had nothing to do but to "follow my nose," which certainly is a very good guide, always providing it is set in the right direction.

The green lane was very beautiful, for it was that season of the year when vegetation is gently changing from its vernal bloom to the rich and varied tints which conduct it gradually and beautifully to decay and death.

I did follow my nose, and in about ten minutes I saw through the trees a cluster of houses, with antique gable ends, and some with old thatched roofs, which, I presumed, indicated my arrival at my place of destination. I quickened my pace, and in a few moments more, upon emerging from the green lane, I found myself upon the margin of a pond, in which were disporting a colony of ducks. A boy was leaning idly across a gate,

"Whistling for want of thought,"

and, going up to him, I asked him if I was in Fairfield.

He merely nodded, and went on with his whistling, without vouchsafing to make me any audible reply.

"Do you know where Mr. Seabright lives?" I said. He pointed to a house at some distance. "That house with the cropped trees?" said I.

Again the boy nodded, and, rather amused than annoyed at his taciturnity, I walked onwards towards the house he indicated.

When I arrived close to the dwelling, its external appearance certainly did not prepossess me in favour of its inhabitants. Not a tree was allowed to retain its natural shape, some were cropped so as to resemble a great green dumpling; others again presented a long spire at the top; in fact, nature was outraged in every possible manner in the garden of Mr. Seabright.

In front of the house was a lawn, and curling round it, like a very clean yellow snake, was a prim-looking gravelled walk, upon which, by its appearance, I doubted if any one had ventured to tread for a long time. The gate leading to this lawn was painted a dull lead colour, and upon the gate post, on one side, was painted in black letters the word "Sion," and on the other, the continuation of "House," which incontestibly meant that that was "Sion House."

I confess I felt, when I noted all these little particulars that my task of reconcilement might not be so easy as I had fondly anticipated, and hoped,—for I began to suspect that Mr. Seabright was one of the over virtuous, who are so good themselves, that they cannot possibly forgive the slightest dereliction in others.

In vain I tried to open the gate; it was fast locked, and, after some searching, I discovered a bell, at which I gave a vigorous pull,—so vigorous, indeed, not knowing its delicate constitution, that I heard it tolling some five minutes, at least, before any one appeared to answer the summons.

At length I descried a prim-looking woman approaching, the gate with slow and measured steps.

"Is this Mr. Seabright's? I said, when she came sufficiently near to hear me.—"Yes," she replied, rubbing her hands together in a very disagreeable manner, but making no sort of effort to let me in.

"Well," said I, "I want to see him."—"He is at prayers," was the answer.

"How long will he be at prayers?" I asked.

She shook her head as much as to say, "Here's a wretch!" and then, in a drawling, canting voice, such as I especially detest, she said,—

"The key of the gate is in Mr. Seabright's pocket, and until he removes from his Maker, I cannot ask him for it."—"So, when a visiter comes to your master, he must sit on the gate, I suppose, till he has done praying? Here, take my card and, whenever your master can be spoken to, give it to him. In the meantime, I suppose I can wait in some room of the house for him. The gate is no great obstacle; I can climb that ——"

"What!" shrieked the woman, as if I had proposed some dreadful sacrilege, "climb the gate of Sion House!"—"Exactly," said I, commencing operations.

"I never in my life heard of such a thing."—"You see we live and learn," said I, clearing the gate, and making a great disturbance in the gravel by my jump.

The astonished domestic then retreated before me to the house, muttering some prayer, but whether it was a petition for grace to me or otherwise, I could not tell. Still mumbling, or grumbling, to herself, she ascended three white steps, and opening a glass door, ushered me, or rather I followed her, into a small apartment, which was cold looking and gloomy in every respect.

I sat down without any ceremony, merely saying,—

"Give that card to your master, and tell him that Dr. —— wants to see him, on urgent and particular business, as soon as possible."

I saw by the manner of the female as she left the room, that if she gave any opinion of me before I saw her master, there was no danger of its being too favourable a one. However, I did not see that anything could alter the real circumstances of the case I came to lay before the godly Mr. Seabright; and I thought to myself, "if this man has been really praying, and not, as is too frequent under that name, blaspheming the Almighty and damning his fellow creatures, he must yield to what I will say to him concerning his child."

I had scarcely arrived at this conclusion when the door opened, and a tall, thin man entered the room, with a book in his hand. The vanity of plainness was most manifest in his attire, and he wore round his neck a white cloth, which gave a most disagreeable look to his cadaverous complexion.

I rose and bowed. He stiffly returned my salutation, and said in an affected voice,—

"May I inquire on what errand thou comest here?"—"Certainly," said I; "you have a daughter ——"

"I—I," he shrieked —"Yes; you are Mr. Seabright?"

"No; I am his godly counsellor and staff through the wilderness."—"My business, then, is with Mr. Seabright, and not with any godly counsellor but his own heart."

The man gave a deep groan before he replied, which, I suppose, was meant to imply his own great superiority and my unworthiness.

"I repeat to you," he then said, "that I, unworthy as I am, must hear what you have to say before it reaches the ears of that great sinner reclaimed, John Seabright."—"And I repeat to you," said I, rather warmly, "that I will not confide to you my business."

He seemed alarmed at my speaking so loud, and looking anxiously at the door, he said,—

"You speak of the daughter—is — is" — "Is what!" I cried. "Is she dead?"

There was a peculiar look upon the scoundrel's face as he asked this question, which at once settled the point in my mind as to whether he was a fool or knave, and I immediately replied in a loud voice,—

"I am glad I have seen you, for, from my soul, I believe your object is to separate the father and his repentant and dying child."—"Dying!" he repeated, with an expression of triumph.

At this moment the door opened, and there entered a man of apparently about fifty years of age, whom I immediately guessed, and guessed rightly, to be Mr. Seabright.

I saw by the expression of his face that he had heard my last words, for he seemed to be fortifying himself against his own feelings.

"Are you Mr. Seabright?" I said.—"Yes," he replied; "what do you want with me?"

"I am Dr ——," said I, "and I came to speak to you about your daughter Florence."—"She who departed from the path of glory and righteousness, snuffled the godly counsellor, "and went forth among the sons and daughters of iniquity. She who——"

"Peace, sir!" cried I, in indignation; "I speak to a father of his child, and not to a saintly hypocrite, who, if he believes

e tithe of what he preaches, must, sooner or later, dread the
stice of that Providence he is continually profaning."

The godly counsellor looked aghast, and, without giving
m time to reply, I continued—

"Mr. Seabright I am come here as a man and a Christian to
eak to you of the dear child that God gave to your care.
ou cannot refuse to listen to me!"—"What—what would
u say?" he faltered.

"She has erred, sir," I replied, "but she repents of her
ror, and she asks her father to forgive her—"

He shook his head ——

"As he hopes to be forgiven himself."

"Brother Seabright's of the elect, " said the godly counsel-
r.—"And therefore," said I, " independent of Heaven's
ercy. Is that what you mean by elect?"

"Scoffer!" cried the wretch, reddening with anger.

"Sir," I said to Mr. Seabright, "this scoundrel has evi-
ntly steeled your heart against your child."—"No, no" said
abright, "he—he is a man of grace,—of wondrous grace."

"And preaches resentment and unforgiveness. Oh, sir! if
er you loved your child, whom God made so beautiful and
od, think more charitably of her now. Do not embitter
ur death-bed by the horrible thought that you are going
ask forgiveness and have not forgiven."—"I did love
r," he said; " as the apple of my eye I loved her."

The godly counsellor caught at the simile, and ex-
aimed :—

"If thine eye offend thee, cast it from thee."—"The devil
an quote scripture," replied I.

"I will hear no more," said Mr. Seabright.—"You cannot
ean what you say. Your child fell a victim from her very
irtues."

"Her virtues!" sneered the counsellor.—"Yes," I conti-
ued, "her virtues. She was innocent of guile herself, and,
erefore, suspected it not in others. She knew nothing but
uthfulness in her own heart, and, therefore, never suspected
eceit. She is not wicked—in the eye of Heaven she is not
icked, and you know it."

"She left me for a stranger," said Seabright.

"Aye," I cried, "even as your wife left her home for you.
he utmost that can be said of her is, that she has been
eak; but is that a reason for trampling on her? I implore
ou to receive her, and be kind to her again."

"I cannot," he replied. "She is an outcast; I discard her
or ever !"

"Where is her mother?" I cried.—"On a sick bed; you
cannot see her."

"Mr. Seabright," I said, "let me make one more appeal,
—your daughter is dying."

He started, but the godly counsellor immediately added,—

"Such is the judgment of the wicked."—"Yes, yes,"
aid Seabright; "leave my house, sir; I have no daughter,—
renounce ——"

"Hold! hold!" I cried, "Heaven hears you. Can you
xpect mercy hereafter, who will not even accord justice here
o your own child?"

"Away, sir,—away!" he cried, "I will hear no more!"—

"Let us go and pray," said the other.—"Pray!" I cried;
'you pray!"

He glanced at me with a look of fiendish malice, as he
ook the arm of Seabright, and led him to the door.

"Sir," I cried, "reflect again,—your own child ——"

The canting hypocrite pushed him through the doorway,
and then, protruding his yellow visage towards me, he said,—

"A pleasant journey back again. We will pray for you."

* * * * *

I think I was never in such a rage in my life, as when the
door closed upon the triumphant visage of Mr. Seabright's
pious friend, and I had a great deal of difficulty to control
my feelings sufficiently to prevent my rushing after him and
giving him a hearty kicking.

I stood for some minutes in Mr. Seabright's gloomy parlour wondering what I should do, when the same disagreeable
looking female, who had been so shocked at my scaling the
gate of so pious a mansion as Sion House, appeared, and intimated an intention of immediately clearing me off the premises.

I made no resistance, but quietly followed, and this time she
produced the key of the leaden coloured gate, which she opened, and seemed very much relieved when I passed through it.

Here, then, was an end of all my hopes for poor Florence.
I strolled slowly up the lane in a deep reverie upon the fate
of that poor girl, and I thought of a thousand things that,
now it was too late, I wished to have said to her father, for
the purpose of awakening in his breast whatever traces of
past affection for his child might still be lingering there.

"Too late! too late!" I repeated; "alas, poor Florence!
strangers must supply the place to thee now of those who
should have soothed and comforted thee in thy affliction."

My whole anxiety now was to get to town, and I was
pleased, upon consulting my watch, to find that it wanted
but half an hour to the time when I had been told a mail-
coach passed the end of the lane. I sat down on a verdant
bank, studded with sweet wild flowers, and gave myself up
to a reverie on fanaticism, until the distant sound of wheels
smote my ears, and far down the dusty road I saw the coach
approaching.

I was soon on its roof, and by nine in the evening I once
more stood on the step of my own door.

* * * * *

"You have been unsuccessful?" said my wife, looking at
me scrutinizingly in the face.

"I have been unsuccessful," I replied; "poor Florence
Seabright must look to us for the future; and, alas! poor
girl, I fear that will not be long."

"Well," cried my wife, "if anybody had told me beforehand, that a father could behave in such a manner towards
a child, I should have thought it a libel upon human nature."

"Say no more about it," said I, "I never had so sickening a journey in my life. Let us now only think how to
make the poor girl as happy as possible under existing circumstances."

* * * *

The month of September had just commenced, and I
dreaded the effect of the winter season upon the delicate
frame of Florence. I thought if by any means I could get
her over the winter, and then remove her to a mild situation
on the coast, there might be a chance of her ultimate recovery;
but, while I admitted to myself, that there might be such a
chance, I could not conceal from my own mind the conviction
that it was a slender one, indeed. I resolved, however, to
make a point of seeing her once a day, if possible.

LITERAL EXTRACTS FROM MY DIARY.

Sept. 5th.—My wife and I called upon Florence. She is
evidently much weaker. She has ascertained from Mrs. ——
the unsuccessful issue of my visit to her father's. It seemed
to affect her very much.

Sept. 6th.—No change.

Sept. 8th.—Upon going this day, I was shocked, although
not surprised, to hear that Florence had fainted, and remained
insensible for nearly two hours.

Sept. 9th.—Florence can scarcely walk across the room.
She weeps incessantly, and appears to take to heart her being
a burthen to us. Alas! she will be a burthen no one for
long.

Thus affairs went on for another week, and each day Florence's health was rapidly declining. Her appetite was gone,
and she seemed but the shadow of her former self. I
told those around her, that the gentle girl would not be long
with us, and that they were now to deny her nothing, but to
wear cheerful aspects, and try to amuse her mind. My wife
sobbed as if her heart would break, when I told her that even
I had ceased to hope for a change in Florence's state, and the
poor young thing herself was so grateful for all that was done
for her, and spoke so affectionately, that she was endeared
to all hearts, and there was not one of Mrs. Martin's family
who would not have made any sacrifice for her benefit. But
the dread fiat had gone forth. Florence Seabright was to
pass away like a bright exhalation of the morning, and be
seen no more.

Sept. 19th.—Upon my calling this morning, I found Florence had changed materially for the worse. She could not
rise from her bed, and I felt a presentiment, as I looked at
her, that she never would rise from it again. She called me
in a weak voice, and said, while she fixed her mild blue eyes
upon me, that seemed to shine with a preternatural lustre,—

"Dr. ——, I am dying."—

"Dying, Florence," I replied; " what put that into your
head?"—" Because I hear such strange sounds," she replied.—" Strange sounds? Of what nature are they?"—
"Sometimes, Dr. ——, there are many voices round my
bed, holding murmuring discourse together; the voices are
very sweet; and then sweet and solemn music joins faintly
to them, and when I long to hear more, the whole will fade
away—dying off in the distance, like a long-drawn sigh."

"Oh! that is all imagination," said I; "when you get better and stronger, these fancies will all leave you."—"I ought to wear black," she suddenly said.

"Wear black?—what for?"—"Because my mother is dead," she replied, solemnly.

"How do you know that?" I said.—"I don't know how I heard it; but I know she is dead!"

Here she burst into a passion of hysterical weeping, which I knew it was useless to interrupt, and it of itself gradually subsided into deep sobs.

I thought she was going to sleep then, and I was gently stepping towards the door to leave the room, when she suddenly said, in a firm voice, that quite startled me,—

"Dr. ——"—I immediately turned, and replied,—"Well, Florence, what would you say?"—"I am so much better that I shall get up. Will you ask Mrs. Martin to come to me?"

"Don't get up, Florence," I said.—"But I am better—a great deal better," she reiterated. "Yes, I must get up. What a fog there is; but still I must get up."

I saw that she was dying, and I made a great effort to command my voice as I said,—

"Lay still, Florence, till I send Mrs. Martin to help you."

She smiled, and lay down and I hurried down the stairs. Poor Mrs. Martin burst into tears when I told her that I wished she would send one of her children to my house to tell my wife to come, for that Florence would not live till sunset. I begged of her, then, to go and stay with the dying girl, and I told her I would return myself in a few minutes.

I then went to the next chemist's, and procured a medicine, which I knew would soothe and alleviate any pangs that might arise at the last. When I returned, I walked at once up to the chamber of Florence.

Mrs. Martin was, with tears in her eyes, trying to persuade her against rising, and when I entered the room I saw that even in the few minutes I had been gone from the bed-side, a rapid change had taken place in the countenance of Florence. She was sitting up in bed, and fixing her melancholy eyes upon me, she said, in a voice of deep feeling,—

"You have been very good to poor Florence. God bless you! I shall live long to thank you."

I was silent; I did not wish to tell her she was dying, and yet, in that awful hour, I could not bring my mind to deceive her with a prospect of life.

I sat down by her bed-side in silent sorrow, determining to wait till all was over.

Florence continued to talk, but it was in a rambling and incoherent manner. Her mind was evidently wandering to the sunny days of her happy childhood.

"Yes," she said, "I know the dear summer is coming; I have been so careful of my flowers; they will all bloom again, oh! so beautiful, and we shall all be so very happy."

I heard a step on the stairs; it was my wife, who had just arrived. I walked to the door and whispered to her,—

"Don't alarm Florence. Speak to her cheerfully."

My wife walked gently to her bed-side.

"Florence," she said, how are you now?"—"Ah! that is Mrs. ——," cried Florence. "I am better, so much better, and when the white mist clears away I shall see you, though I cannot now."

The sun was streaming in at the window, and there was not a cloud in the sky; it was the sight of the dying girl which was gently leaving her.

My wife could not help crying, and Florence suddenly started, and listened attentively.

"Who is that crying?" she said.—"No one, Florence, I replied. "Do you not feel fatigued?"

"I think I could sleep a little," she said. "I will try, and when I again awaken I will get up and go for a walk in the green lane, and bring home some wild flowers."

She lay calmly down as she spoke, and her breathing was so gentle and regular that I believed she slept.

My wife whispered to me anxiously,—

"Oh! will she ever waken again?"—"Most probably," I replied. "Hush! she stirs."

Suddenly she sat up in the bed, and grasped my arm, while she pointed with her attenuated hand towards the other end of the room.

"Can you tell me who that is?" she said. "The face is divinely beautiful. See, now, there are more of them. Hark! hark!—their voices are like Eolian harps. What a throng there is, and such dear music. Dr. —— and Mr. ——, God bless you both."

She sunk back upon the pillow, with a radiant smile upon her face.

I turned to the window to endeavour to control my feelings. My wife came to me, and touching my arm, said,—

"She sleeps again."

I shook my head, and walked to the bed-side; then turning to my wife, I could just find breath to say,—

"My love, she sleeps the sleep that knows no waking. The discarded child is now with God."

My wife burst into tears, and leaned upon my shoulder in great grief. Florence lay in the repose of death, with the smile still lingering on her pale face. I pointed to her as I said,—

"*Do not weep for her. Let us rather pray for the father who could make an outcast of his repentant child!*"

THE CERTIFICATE OF LUNACY;

OR, THE YOUNG WIFE.

THE various iniquities and awful cruelties practised some years since in lunatic asylums have lately attracted so much attention from the humane and charitable, that I conscientiously believe now the greater number of those establishments are conducted with the greatest probity and humanity. Such, however, was far from being the case when I was a young man. Then there could not be very well devised a more snug method of getting rid of a troublesome connexion than by a certificate of lunacy.

The story which I have given the above title to, came under my cognizance professionally, and, as I was the fortunate means of righting the wronged and succouring the oppressed, I, of course, tell it with all the self-satisfaction which an old man feels in recounting the exploits of his youth.

The circumstances occurred in the neighbourhood of Bath, and all the parties connected with it have, I believe, gone to their "long account;" but some of the old inhabitants of that city will recollect some of the circumstances, probably, although in my diary only is to be found "the whole truth, and nothing but the truth."

I had just entered upon my medical career, and thought myself very fortunate in being offered, by a wealthy old gentleman, a handsome sum to attend him to Bath as his medical adviser; and as I had no fear then of being very much missed in London, I thankfully accepted the temporary post of family and travelling physician to Sir Felix Meriton, which was the name of the old fidgetty mortal with whom I was condemned to associate (for my sins, I suppose,) for some months.

If ever there was a fidget of forty-horse tantalizing power, that same, as they say in Ireland, was Sir Felix Meriton. Every day he had some fresh ailment to direct my attention to, and my life was a continual worry from morning till night, and not unfrequently from night till morning likewise.

We used to take a walk every morning to the Pump Room, and there Sir Felix picked up several old acquaintances, among whom there was one he was very much delighted with, although he was not an old acquaintance either of Sir Felix's, but only the son of one. His name was Hetton, and he was a good-humoured looking, jovial young man, of about six-and-twenty years of age. Still, to my thinking, there was a peculiarity of expression about him sometimes, which looked very much as if his good-humour and frankness were all assumed to hide darker passions. Moreover, I caught my gentleman in several awful lies,—awful, I mean, on account of their barefaced effrontery, but relating to trivial matters; and as my father used to say, when he found out any one in a lie, "Don't trust that man, the truth is not in him," I did not trust Mr. Hetton, for I believed the truth was not in him.

He, however, paid great attention and court to me, as it will be seen hereafter, for a particular purpose of his own, and

the old Sir Felix was so delighted with his stories and his drolleries, that he used to look for him every morning; and, at last, an evening seldom passed without Hetton dropping in at our hotel, and consuming some bottles of old wine at the expense of Sir Felix.

It was some time before I knew his station in society, or what he was; but one evening, after he had gone, Sir Felix turned to me, and said,—

"Doctor, that is the most estimable young man I know."—"Indeed, sir," said I.

"Yes," he continued; "he has confided to me a matter which shows his heart to be in the right place."—"I am very glad of it," said I.

"You must know, doctor, that his brother, Charles Hetton, is one of the largest landed proprietors about here. He is believed to be worth upwards of forty thousand pounds per annum."—"That is a large sum, sir."

"It is; but you must know," (old Sir Felix generally prefaced everything with, "you must know,") "that it's very unjust indeed that he, Charles Hetton, should have so much, and this Robert Hetton so little. I knew the father so well years ago, and I couldn't have believed it possible he would have made no better provision for his second son than a thousand pounds a-year. You must know it's very wrong."—"Ah!" said I, not knowing whether it was wrong or right.

"Well," continued Sir Felix, "they are the only children of their father, and here's one with forty thousand a-year, and the other with only one thousand."—"Were there no special reasons, sir," I said, "for so unequal a provision?"

"Oh! nothing to signify. You must know, Robert Hetton was, as he tells me quite candidly, a little wild in early life; but I was wild—even I—and you, doctor, were wild."—"I beg your pardon," said I, laughing; "I am not aware of any particular wildness about me. But was there any specific act committed by this Robert Hetton to induce his father to make so great a difference in circumstances between the brothers?"

"'Pon my soul, I don't know," replied Sir Felix; "but you must know, doctor, that Robert Hetton is a capital fellow, a first-rate fellow."—"Is he?" said I.

"Oh, dear, yes! Now I'll tell you, quite in confidence, a trait in his character which is noble in the extreme."—"Believe me, then," said I, "I shall hear it with pleasure."

"Poor Robert!" continued Sir Felix, "he—he shed tears when he told me. You must know, doctor, that Charles, his eldest brother, you know, who had all the property, you must know,—eh!—well—he—what do you think, eh, doctor?"—"How can I think?" said I, with difficulty suppressing a laugh at Sir Felix's singular and original manner of telling a story.

"Ah! well, you must know Charles Hetton is mad."—"Mad!" I cried.

"Yes, quite mad. Don't mention it. Poor Robert—his heart's in the right place. He cried, you must know, when he told me. Eh! what do you think of that? Poor fellow, his heart is in the right place."—"Did he add anything else, sir, to this confidence respecting the madness of his brother?"

"Anything else? Oh, yes. He cried like a bewildered babby, and he said he knew he ought,—it was his duty to take care of his brother."—"And his property?" said I.

"Eh? dear me!—So he did say his property, doctor; you are old witch—no, a young witch, I mean. Well, he said, you must know, that he couldn't bring his mind to have his poor mad brother popped into a lunatic asylum, you see."—"I do see," said I.

"Well, that's all right. You must know I argued with him, and when he said, 'Sir Felix, I know it's my duty to take care of him——'"—"And his property," added I.

"Very true,—he did say his property. 'Still,' says he, crying all the while, 'I can't bring my heart to do it;' and you see—eh, doctor—that's how I came to find out that his heart is in the right place, you must know."—"And what did you advise him to do, sir?"

"Advise him! Oh, why, you must know, I advised him to get some medical man to see his brother; and then he asked me, quite confidentially, what I thought of you, you must know, and I told him I had the very highest opinion of you."—"You are very kind, Sir Felix," said I.

"Then he said, he 'supposed you were very well off?' you must know; and I said, 'No, you were not.'"—"Which is strictly true, Sir Felix. What did he say then?"

"Oh, let me see,—then he cried again, poor young man, and said something about neglected merit, and all that kind of thing, you know."—"Yes, pretty well," said I.

"So he said then, doctor—eh—you must know, he said, if

he did get a medical opinion about his poor brother, and a certificate of his lunacy——eh——you understand?"——"Perfectly."

"Well, if he did, he would have him under the care of some medical man, who should visit him once a-week as long as he remained in a mad-house, you know; and, upon my strong recommendation of you, you know, I think you'll get the job, you see—eh? Five hundred a-year he says he'll give."—"As long as his brother is in the mad-house, Sir Felix?"

"Exactly; that's it."—"Did he say anything more, sir?"

"No; I think he cried again, and I saw, you understand, that his heart was in the right place."

I reflected for a moment, and then I merely said,—

"I thank you from my heart, Sir Felix, for your kind mention of me, and to-morrow I will endeavour to make up my mind on the subject."—"Do, do," said Sir Felix. "Good night, doctor, good night."

* * * * *

"Is this affair a piece of monstrous villany or not?" I said to myself, as I sat down in my bed-room, after I had bidden Sir Felix Meriton good night; "does this Robert Hetton speak the truth, or is this a deep plan to force his brother into a mad-house, and take possession of his property? I must be cautious; but, at all events, I feel it to be my duty to ascertain the truth."

I then sat for full an hour reflecting upon what would be the best plan I could pursue to foil the villany, if villany it was, of Robert Hetton, and place the elder brother upon his guard against the frightful conspiracy that the other was endeavouring to hatch against his peace.

Fidget as Sir Felix was, I knew, as he himself would have expressed it, that *his* heart was in the right place, and I felt quite certain of his cordial support in the right cause, always provided I could convince his peculiar mind which was that cause.

I at length determined that I would converse with Robert Hetton upon the matter, and try to come to some positive opinion regarding his intentions, and that at the same time I would make inquiry in the city concerning both him and his elder brother, and learn all the particulars I could in order to form an accurate judgment of the affair.

With this resolve I went to bed and to sleep. My first thoughts, however, upon waking in the morning were directed towards the best means of commencing my inquiries concerning the family of the Hettons.

* * * * *

I learned with satisfaction from Sir Felix at the breakfast-table that he would not go from home until after luncheon time, and I congratulated myself upon having all the morning to pursue my inquiries; but then arose the puzzling question of where and how to begin them? I thought and thought until my brain was fairly tired, and at last I determined to go to the Pump Room, and see if chance would throw any casual acquaintance in my way who might aid me.

I accordingly sallied forth, and, as good fortune would have it, almost the first person I met was a gentleman with whom I had frequently exchanged civilities, and who always seemed to know something of everybody in Bath.

After some trifling chit-chat, I said,—

"Can you tell me anything of a family of the name of Hetton, residing here?"—"What, do you mean the Hettons of the Grange?" he replied.

"Very likely I do," said I; "there are two brothers."—"Charles and Robert?"

"Exactly; the one is rich, and the other but moderately so."—"And you might add," said my acquaintance, "that the one is a gentleman, and the other—a-hem!"

"I heard that Robert Hetton had been a little wild in early life, and had so angered his father."—"Wild!" cried my acquaintance; "bless your innocence! It's kept very close by the family, but I happen to know that it cost his father ten thousand pounds to save Master Robert from hanging."

"Is that possible?"—"It's true if it isn't possible, as the man in the play says. The fact is, Robert Hetton, who I am really sorry to see so intimate with your friend, Sir Felix Meriton, has run through a career of extraordinary crimes; his escapes have been wonderful. His father left him but one hundred a-year to live upon, which, however, his brother Charles generously increased to a thousand, with a further intimation of an annual increase if he behaved himself with common propriety. I heard all this from the professional adviser of the family, and can depend upon its truth. I would not tell it to you, but I can see by your manner that you have some cause for your inquiries, and I know sufficient of you to feel sure it is a good motive that prompts your curiosity.

"I am extremely obliged to you," said I, as, indeed, I truly felt. "Will you answer me two more questions?"—"Certainly; as many as you like."

"Well, then, what sort of man is Mr. Charles Hetton?"—"A scholar and a gentleman. One of the best hearted men that ever breathed, but nervous and rather irritable, and a little eccentric through want of intercourse with the world."

"You never heard," said I, "any doubts of his sanity?"—"Certainly not."

"Now will you tell me where the professional gentleman lives, who acts for Mr. Charles Hetton?"—"Yes, his name is Steel, and he lives in Princes-street."

"I thank you," said I; "you guess rightly when you think me much interested in this matter. At present I cannot tell you why, because my suspicions only are aroused, and I have no certainty to go upon; but when next I see you, I think I can tell you a bit of news."—"Well, take your own time," said my friend. "Adieu!"

We parted, and I hastened home again, having, by good luck, fully accomplished the object of my morning's peregrinations.

"Well, doctor,—eh," said Sir Felix, as we sat at luncheon, "have you considered about Robert Hetton's exceedingly handsome proposal, eh? You must know such things don't turn up every day—eh?"—"But are you quite sure, sir," I said, "that Mr. Charles Hetton is insane?"

"Sure—sure! how should I be sure? I don't know anything about it, you know, further than Robert Hetton said. He cried a great deal. Dear me, you know his heart is in the right place— eh?"—"I hope it is, sir."

"You hope! Ellow, doctor, you don't doubt, do you? God bless me! you must know I thought of asking him to dinner,—eh?"—"I am very glad of it, sir," said I, "because if you will be so kind as to say you have mentioned the matter to me, he will talk about it, and I shall be able to come, perhaps, to some understanding with him."

"Very good," said Sir Felix, "so I will. You must know, doctor, he's a capital fellow."

I shifted the conversation, for I was anxious to have Mr. Robert Hetton to dinner, and get him to expose as much of his goodly plot as he would, before attempting to open the eyes of poor Sir Felix, who would have spoiled everything by his honest precipitancy,—for at bottom a better man never breathed than the eccentric old knight. So to dinner Mr. Hetton was invited, and to dinner he accordingly came. We were exceedingly jolly; the cloth being removed, Sir Felix ordered the best of wine, and we sat at a small table with every appearance of extreme cordiality towards each other.

"Well," said Sir Felix, when the second glass of wine had gone round, "you must know, Hetton, my good fellow, I just mentioned to the doctor our little conversation—eh—about the clanking of chains and all that kind of thing."—"The what, sir?" said Hetton.

"Oh, you know,—the mad business. You know, whenever there's anybody mad in a play,—eh—it's done with a wisp of straw and a chain, you know—eh?"—"Consider, sir, the feelings of a brother," said Hetton, covering his eyes for a moment with his handkerchief.

"Oh, dear me, beg your pardon, really."—"Don't say another word, my good friend," said Hetton; "it's—it's my weakness. Never mind me, sir."

The old man gave me a nudge with his elbow, and making his hand up into a trumpet, he said,—

"Doctor—eh--you see—heart in right place!"

"Sir Felix has mentioned to me, Mr. Hetton," said I, "something concerning a conversation he had with you about your brother."—"Oh, doctor," said Hetton, "what an awful calamity is insanity!"

"It is indeed," I said, "the most awful calamity to which the human race is subject without doubt."—"I am placed," he continued, "as you see, in a most painful situation. My poor brother might have indulged his insane eccentricities unheeded by the world, and I could have palliated and softened them all; but now he is actually going to marry a young woman, who must know his real condition, and therefore is, without doubt, actuated by sordid motives."

"Indeed!" said I; "about to marry is he?"—"Yes; it is truly shocking—dreadful—awful."

"So it is," cried Sir Felix; "it must be put a stop to.

Why, good gracious! in—in nine months, you know, doctor, —eh—there would be a mad baby—eh?"

"There would—of course, there would," said Hetton, again covering his face with his handkerchief, as I strongly suspected, to smother a laugh.—"That's viewing the subject in a very serious light indeed," continued Sir Felix. "You must know I think that is a dreadful supposition."

"Certainly," I said, "viewing the matter in that light, it does present itself in disagreeable colours."

I saw the sharp, small, twinkling eyes of Hetton fixed on me as I spoke, in order evidently to judge, if possible, by my countenance what I really thought upon the subject. I flatter myself, however, that I completely baffled his penetration, for I felt the urgent necessity of getting as much of his intentions out of him as possible, in order the more effectually to defeat them.

After a pause, he said, turning towards me,—

"If you, doctor, would consent to see my poor brother, and give me your candid opinion as to whether you consider it necessary to remove him to an asylum on your certificate of his lunacy, and for you to visit him there once a week for an annual stipend of three hundred pounds, I should esteem it a great favour, although it cuts me to the heart to be under the necessity of asking such an one."

This speech was a tolerable home thrust, and oh! how I thanked God in my inmost soul, at that moment that I was free from the contagion of that common opinion, that money, however obtained, is the source of happiness! young, inexperienced, and poor, as I then was, what a treasure three hundred pounds a-year would have been to me, if I could have, for an instant, contemplated the deep, damning crime to the commission of which this man, or rather this fiend in the shape of man, would have tempted me.

The meaning of Hetton's speech was so clear to me; it was so evident to my mind, that he wanted to bribe me, as a young and poor physician, to write a certificate of his brother's lunacy, which he could then have got backed by a magistrate, and used as a legal authority for removing him to a lunatic asylum, that I looked at Sir Felix Meriton in amazement that he, too, did not clearly perceive the drift of Hetton's discourse.

I saw, "in my mind's eye," in a moment how artfully the scoundrel had arranged his scheme and calculated upon its results. His brother was going to marry, and should he have children, there was an end of the hopes and speculations of Mr. Robert Hetton. Now, if he could succeed in placing poor Charles in a lunatic asylum, he could then petition the Lord Chancellor for leave, as the next heir, to hold the property in trust, and even should the most rigorous inquiry be instituted, the probability would be that Charles Hetton would have been long enough subject to the horrors of a lunatic asylum to be driven really insane, *as has frequently been the case!* Of my fidelity, too, had I entered into the scandalous plot, he made himself sure by offering an annual sum of money instead of a heavy bribe all at once.

All this passed through my mind much more rapidly than I could tell it, and, fearing that Hetton might, by a possibility, find some medical man who would be bribed—for I knew such things had been—I feigned to understand him and to receive his proposition as he wished, in order the more effectually to defeat it.

"I will see your brother whenever you wish," I said; "shall it be to-morrow?"—"If you please," he said, "it is a melancholy duty, but it must be done."

"You do visit your brother, eh, Robert?" said Sir Felix; "because, you must know, I thought you were not on visiting terms—eh? You know he has not used you well about money matters—eh? Only to think—one brother forty thousand, and the other only one!"—"We need not bear malice, Sir Felix," said Hetton.

"Malice! Oh, dear, no! Certainly not; I honour your feelings. Your heart, my dear Hetton, is exactly in the right place—eh, doctor?"—"Exactly," said I.

We sat for a considerable time longer, and, before we separated, Sir Felix, I saw, had taken just about one glass more than it was strictly prudent for an old gentleman to take. Hetton saw it likewise, and he took occasion to whisper to me,

"At what hour to-morrow would it be convenient for you to meet me?"—"In the morning," said I; "I will be at the Pump Room at ten precisely."

"Thank you," said he; "I feel very much pleased at having met you, and I assure you that you will find me liberal in the extreme."

I merely bowed my head to this, and, after Sir Felix had tried to sing "Alice Gray" and the "Fine Old English Gentleman" to the most extraordinary tunes that can be conceived, we separated for the night.

* * * * *

I rose early the next morning, in order to give myself some time for reflection before I met Hetton, according to appointment. After considering the matter in every point of view, I came to the conclusion that I had better see Mr. Charles Hetton, in order to be able, on oath, if necessary, to depose to his perfect sane state of mind on that particular date, being, at the same time, of course, aware that his worthy and affectionate brother declared him insane.

With this idea in my mind I left the hotel to proceed to the Pump Room. The clocks were striking the appointed hour as I entered it, and I had not taken two turns up and down its extent, when Hetton stepped up to me with a

"How do you do, doctor? You are very punctual."— "Yes," I replied, "I have great habits of punctuality."

"One of the cardinal virtues," he added.

Then drawing my arm within his, he said, in a confidential tone as we left the room,—

"Doctor, I hope we understand each other?"—"I hope we do," said I, determined to make him speak out.

"I can take you to my brother's house," he continued; "of course he need not know who you are, or what is your errand."—"Of course not," said I.

"Three hundred a-year, you know, doctor, to a young man, and all his time at his own disposal besides, is no joke."—"If it is," said I, "it's an exceedingly pleasant joke."

"Very well. Then I think we have no difficulties before us."—"I don't see any," said I.

"Well then, we thoroughly understand each other? My brother Charles is mad."—"Madness," said I, "is an awful calamity!"

"Oh! very," he added. "The idea, now, of his thinking of marrying a young girl."—"Mad people should certainly not be allowed to marry," I remarked; "I consider it wickedness."

"I see we shall get on very well together, doctor. You are just the sort of sensible medical man I wished to meet with. You understand me quite?"—"Oh! yes," said I. "How can I mistake?"

"Upon your certificate of my brother's insanity, I can have him conveyed to an asylum?"—"Certainly you can. By-the-by, who is this young person he was going to marry?"

"Oh! it's a most ridiculous affair. Some poor devil's daughter or other whom he has taken a fancy to, and for what, think you?"—"I can't guess—is she beautiful?"

"Why, yes, pretty well; but that isn't it. He is going to marry her because of some ridiculous nonsense about her kindness to her father, who was blind, and all that sort of thing."—"Oh! indeed," said I.

"You may well say, 'indeed.' Now just see how I am situated, a young man of seven-and-twenty—my brother Charles is thirty-two, and this young girl is nineteen. A fine joke truly! Why, she may have a large family, and where are my expectations then?"—"Ah! where?" echoed I; "and your brother mad, too."

"Ha! ha!" he laughed; "upon my soul, doctor, you are a droll fellow. But come, here we are on the road to my brother's seat. It's three miles out of the town, so we had better take a fly."

I agreed, and we took a fly, which soon rattled and jolted us over the three miles. We stopped at the gates of a handsome park, and in the distance I saw a noble mansion, surrounded, except to the west and south, by old and magnificent trees, that lent an air of grandeur to the landscape.

"This is my brother's place," said Hetton; "as far as your eye can reach is all freehold and belonging to him, and fifty of the best houses in Bath are likewise his property; in addition to all which, he has landed property in some of the richest counties in the kingdom. Now, you see, by G—, doctor, all this is a stake worth playing for."—"It really seems a fine estate," said I.

In such discourse we proceeded towards the house, and when we came close to it Hetton said to me,—

"What shall I call you? What name, I mean?"—"I decidedly object to an alias," said I. "If you don't call me by my right name, I shall certainly decline going in at all."

"You are right," he cried; "by Jove, you are a deep one, doctor."—"Oh, you are flattering me," said I.

He laughed, and rang the bell. The summons was immediately answered by a grey-headed domestic, who, in answer to Hetton's inquiry if his brother was at home, answered in the affirmative, and we were ushered into a spacious and handsome parlour.

"You see," said Hetton, "everything is in good style here, eh, doctor?"—"Indeed, I seldom have seen a handsomer mansion," I replied. "What a pity its proprietor should be insane."

"You funny fellow," cried Hetton; "by Jove! you have a wonderful face. You beat me hollow."

A servant now appeared, and said that Mr. Hetton would see us in the drawing-room if we would follow him. We did so, and were conducted into a magnificent apartment, in which was seated, reading, a tall, gentlemanly man, of a pale and studious cast of countenance, but with one of the most intellectual expressions I ever saw.

He bowed gracefully to me, and then turning to his brother, he said, —

"Well, Robert, how are you? This gentleman is some friend of yours, I presume?"—"Yes," replied Robert, "Mr. ——, my brother Charles."

I bowed, and Mr. Charles Hetton kindly invited me to be seated.

"You have a beautiful place here, sir," I said.—"Yes," he replied; "to me it is very beautiful, because it is full of family associations."

"That, indeed, sir, must lend it an additional charm."—"Yes," he continued, "I do love the old house and the majestic oaks. Every spot is dear to me. Even my love of science cannot compete with my love of the beauties of scenery and association which surround my dear, ancient house—the house of my father!"

"And this is the man," thought I, "that would be consigned to the gloom and despair of a lunatic asylum, if I were as unscrupulous as his brother."

"You see," said Robert, "I just brought up my friend to have a look at the old house."—"Any *respectable* friend of yours," said Charles Hetton, "is most welcome."

I saw Robert wince a little at this speech, and I could not but feel myself that I was liable to be suspected of being no better than I should be in consequence of coming in the questionable character of a friend of Mr. Robert's.

However, I had a duty to do, and I was determined to carry it through.

We did not stop many minutes longer, and after partaking of a glass of excellent old wine, we left the house.

"It's a very fine day," said Hetton; "shall we walk back to Bath, doctor?"—"As you please," said I.

So we started at an easy pace towards the city.

"Do you know the exact form of such certificates?" said Hetton, after a moment's silence.—"What certificates?" said I, with an innocent look, and beginning, in my own mind, to enjoy my situation amazingly.

"What certificate?" he repeated, "why a certificate of lunacy, to be sure."—"Oh! yes," said I, "I have seen several. I could show you the form any day."

"What *do* you mean?" he said, looking hard at me.—"Mean? What do *you* mean?" said I; "you don't look at all anxious, as I expected to find you."

"Anxious about what?" he roared.—"Why, your brother's state of mind, to be sure. You did me the honour of calling me in to decide as to his sanity or insanity, and I have the pleasure to inform you, that he is *not only quite sane, but exceedingly sensible!*"

I never shall forget the look of dismay that Hetton cast on me as he stammered,—

"But—you—know, you consented to ——."—"To see your brother as a professional man, and give you my opinion as to the state of his mind," said I; "and that opinion is, that your fears are groundless, for he is perfectly sane."

"You are joking, doctor?"—"Joking! Why should I joke upon so serious a subject? Upon my word, Mr. Hetton, *one would think you really wished your brother to be mad!*"

"Curse you!" he cried, losing all patience at having so completely failed.—"Oh!" said I, "if that's your conduct, I shall trouble you for my fee, and cut your acquaintance."

He looked at me for a moment with such a demoniac expression of countenance, that I really thought he meditated some mischief. His face was perfectly livid with rage. He seemed nearly choked with passion, and clenching his hand, he shook it at me, saying, between his clenched teeth,—

"You have made an enemy. Beware! Curses on you—beware of me!"

So saying, he darted from me, and left me to pursue my walk by myself.

* * * *

My feelings, as I walked towards Bath, were of the most agreeable nature, for I felt that I had signally defeated a plot of the vilest and most wicked description.

I repaired directly to the hotel, and when I saw Sir Felix I immediately said,—

"Sir, I have been with Mr. Hetton to see his brother."—"Eh—oh, the mad fellow?" cried Sir Felix. "He that's going to have a mad babby, eh? You must know I don't approve of that at all, doctor, eh?"

"Nor I either," said I, "if he had been mad; but I have the extreme pleasure of stating, that he is in his perfect senses, and a more quiet, intellectual, gentlemanly man I never saw."—"Indeed!" cried Sir Felix; "I am glad to hear it, on my life I am."

"I know you are," said I; "for, permit me to say, without flattery, that *your* heart *is* in the right place. But Mr. Robert Hetton was *not* glad to hear it, and has threatened me with his vengeance, because I would not write a certificate of his brother's insanity."—"Eh, what?" gasped Sir Felix.

"The truth is as I tell it to you, sir."—"The—the infernal rascal—the villain! God bless us all! You must know, doctor, my eyes are open now, and I see it all. Oh, the thief! And you, my dear sir, have acted nobly."

"I beg your pardon, Sir Felix. I should have been an unmitigated scoundrel if I had acted otherwise than I have. Surely a man is not entitled to any great credit for refusing a bribe to commit a great crime."—"You may say what you like," cried Sir Felix, "but you acted well, and you know it. Eh, you rogue of a doctor! You must know I won't forget it. Oh, that rascal, Hetton. Who would have thought it? And he cried, too, so much,—the vagabond!"

I was greatly amused at the indignation of poor Sir Felix, and I said,—

"Sir, I don't think we shall see any more of Hetton. His design against his brother was monstrous in the extreme, and, after feeling, as he must do, that I know his villanous intentions, the probability is, that he will leave Bath."—"Ah, you know that's all very well, doctor," said Sir Felix; "but I'll write to Mr. Charles Hetton, or call upon him; I will put him on his guard."

"Recollect, sir, that we can say nothing positive," said I. "All we can assert for a certainty is, that Hetton employed me to visit his brother professionally, and then was very angry because I would not say he was mad."

"All!" cried Sir Felix; "d—n it, doctor, ain't that enough, eh? You must know that Hetton ought to be hung."—"I believe, sir, many a better man has been hung," said I; "and you may depend, that he is making pain and misery for himself in the long run."

"Of course he is, doctor,—of course; and you have made for yourself a pleasant reflection while you live, eh? So now we'll have a bottle of champagne, and drink confusion to that d—d rascal!"

"Mr. Hetton, sir!" said a waiter, at this moment popping his head into the room.—"Eh—eh?" gasped Sir Felix, his face assuming a purple hue from excessive rage.

"Mr. Hetton, sir!" repeated the man.

With all the impudence imaginable, Hetton was about to walk into the room with a smile upon his face, when Sir Felix suddenly caught up a decanter of water that was on the table, and, to my dismay and astonishment, discharged it like a cannon shot at Hetton's head.

It missed him, and hit the door with such a crash, that it smashed into a thousand pieces, and deluged the waiter with water and bits of glass. Hetton, I fancy, saw that the game was up as regarded Sir Felix, for, without a word, he turned from the door, and disappeared, while the waiter rushed down the staircase in a very frantic manner, screaming "Murder,—murder!"

I could keep my countenance no longer, but burst into such a roar of laughter, that the room rang again with my boisterous mirth.

Affairs soon assumed their usual aspect in the hotel. The price of the decanter satisfied the landlord, and a guinea perfectly satisfied the waiter, while the champagne satisfied Sir Felix and myself, in which we duly drank confusion to all hypocrites and scoundrels, more especially to Robert Hetton.

* * *

The sequel, however, will show that Sir Felix Meriton

and I were no match for Master Robert Hetton; but, not to anticipate them, I will relate the events as they occurred.

After Sir Felix and myself had returned to London, and I had fulfilled the term of my engagement with him, I "committed matrimony," and took a respectable house with a determination of pushing my fortune, if possible. It was long, however, before I procured sufficient professional employment to "keep the wolf from the door," as the saying is; and many were the privations we were compelled to endure.

My house being near the parks, I used very often to amuse myself by a stroll in the Mall, and, upon one of these occasions, after tiring myself by walking up and down upon the disagreeable little stones which are there placed, I sat down on one of the wooden seats for rest.

I had not sat long when a lady, for such she evidently was, likewise sat down upon the seat. A black veil closely covered her face, and, as she leaned upon the rough arm of the wooden bench, I was surprised to hear her sobbing bitterly. I debated with myself for some time whether I should say anything or not; and at last the grief of the lady became so excessive, that I gave up all scruples, and determined to say something to her.

"Madam," I said, "I trust you will give me credit for better intentions than rudeness or curiosity, when I venture to inquire if I can be of any service to you in your affliction?"

She started, and clung to the seat, as she said, in a sweet but faltering voice,—

"No, no, I thank you, sir; no, no."—"Perhaps," I continued, "when I tell you I am a physician, you may feel more inclined to trust to the civility of a stranger."

"A physician?" she repeated, as if grasping with her mind some idea that gave her relief; "a physician are you, sir?" —"Yes," I said, "here is my card, and if I can be of any service to you, pray command me?"

She took my card and read the name; and then, as if communing with herself, she said,—

"Perhaps Heaven, in its mercy, has ordained this. A physician? Sir, I—I am poor."—"So am I," said I.

"But I cannot compensate."—"Oh!" said I, interrupting her; "we often give advice gratis. You know it costs us nothing, so don't let any thoughts about fees hinder you from making me useful professionally."

She lifted her veil from before her face, and looked earnestly at me; then, as if satisfied with my physiognomy, she said gently,—

"I have a dear friend who is ill."

The tears were standing in her eyes as she spoke, and there was a look of interesting simplicity upon her pale face that greatly pleased me. She could not be above nineteen or twenty years of age, and although not what would be commonly called a beauty, there was evident, in her general manner and appearance, so much refinement, and intellect combined with innocence, that I was delighted at the chance which had given me the opportunity of being of any service to her.

"I am married," she said, showing me, with a blush, the wedding-ring on her finger.—"So am I," said I, cheerfully.

"I will tell you, sir," she added, "my melancholy errand in London; but perhaps you will best gather it from that paper."

She handed me a written paper, and opening it, judge of my intense surprise when the first words that met my eyes were these,—

"EMILIA HETTON, the wife of Mr. Charles Hetton, implores that the Lord Chancellor would be pleased to hear her, on behalf of her much injured and dear husband, who has been torn from her and his happy home by authority of a certificate of lunacy."

The paper nearly dropped from my hands; I positively gasped for breath.

"Thank God!" I exclaimed fervently.—"Sir?" cried Emilia Hetton, in surprise.

"I thank God," said I, "that I have met with you. You are the young wife of Mr. Charles Hetton, of the Grange, near Bath. His brother Robert has bribed some unprincipled medical man to write a certificate of insanity in order to rob him and you of your property; but he won't succeed, for I'll foil him yet. Now take my arm, and come home with me, and we will hold a council of three, consisting of you, I, and my wife."

She looked at me quite bewildered as I spoke, and then clasping her hands, said,—

"In Heaven's name, sir, who are you?"—"I am the physician," said I, "who was first attempted to be bribed by Robert Hetton. That will give you a key to everything and show you what effect my evidence is likely to produce."

She strove to give utterance to her thanks, but I cut them short, and, taking her arm within mine, I, to the surprise of my wife, took her home, and introduced her as Mrs. Charles Hetton.

Emilia's story was very soon told. It appeared that Charles Hetton had a great aversion to the *eclat* of a public marriage, and had privately married Emilia, who was the young lady to whom Robert Hetton had alluded with such indignation a few weeks after my visit to his house: and, as she related to me, the very day after, five men came to the house, accompanied by a constable, and producing a certificate of lunacy from a Bath physician, which was likewise backed by a magistrate, they insisted upon removing him from his home. All the dormant passions of Charles Hetton's nature were roused by this proceeding, and, unhappily, he by force resisted the men. The consequence was, that he was dragged away in a straight waistcoat, leaving his servants completely paralyzed by surprise and grief, and his young wife in a state nearly bordering on distraction.

Robert Hetton, it appears, had planned everything so artfully, that he procured within three days, authority, as the next of kin, to take possession of the property, in trust, and had actually the effrontery to deny Emilia's marriage being valid, and to turn her from the house with insult and menace.

I certainly was amazed at the unparalleled audacity of these proceedings, and for a time was perfectly at a loss thoroughly to comprehend them.

"Did you," said I to Mrs. Hetton, "go to Mr. Steele, who is, I am told, Mr. Hetton's attorney?"—"I did, sir," she replied, "and they evidently doubted the fact of my marriage being legal, and, at all events, said all that they could do would be to petition the Lord Chancellor to issue a commission of inquiry, and that, they said, as the courts were not now sitting, could not be done for months to come. So I determined to make a personal application, and came up from Bath with a few pounds that Charles had given me, to call upon the Lord Chancellor. I took with me the written paper I showed to you, but I was refused admittance at the house, and was returning to my humble lodging nearly heartbroken, when I met with you."

"Very well," said I; "we will now see what can be done. I am only at a loss what should be the first step in the business."—"The first step," said my wife, who knew all the previous history, "should be to call upon Sir Felix Meriton."

"You are right," cried I; "he is rich and influential, and, what is more, he is really a just and kind-hearted man, notwithstanding all his eccentricities."—"And in the meantime," added my wife, "will Mrs. Hetton honour us by becoming our guest?"

"How can I sufficiently thank you?" cried the young wife. "You have given me new life."—"I will leave you two together," said I, "and go to Sir Felix at once; for I am so shocked and irritated at this most iniquitous business, that I am sure I shall never rest easy till I see you and your husband righted."

Mrs. Hetton thanked me with an eloquent look of gratitude, which said a great deal more than words could express—and seizing my hat, I started immediately to call on Sir Felix Meriton. Luckily I found him at home, and at once explained to him the whole affair, ending with an exhortation to him to do what he could to right the oppressed and punish the oppressor.

When I had done, the old man immediately rose, and rang the bell, and when a servant appeared, he screamed out,—

"The carriage—the carriage!"—"It's at the door, sir," said the man with alarm.

"All right, eh?" cried Sir Felix. "Come along, doctor, come along. You must know, I'm in a great rage—an infernal rage, eh?—you know; and I—I won't eat, nor drink, nor—nor sleep,— d—n me, come along, doctor. You must know I'll see justice done, or my name ain't Meriton, you know. Oh, the villain! The—the thundering thief!"

So saying, he dragged me to the carriage without my being able to say another word, and when we were fairly seated, and the footman touched his hat in an inquiring manner to know where his master would be driven to, Sir Felix thundered out in a tone that made the man jump again,—

"To the Lord Chancellor's!"—"Dear me," said I, "that is active."

"I know it is, sir," he roared; "you must know, eh?—

the Lord Chancellor and I are old college friends, and I happen to know that his heart's in the right place, you know, and—and d—n me, I'll make him—make him eat his wig if he don't do what's right in this business, you must know, eh?"

The carriage soon stopped at the residence of Lord L—— the then chancellor, and Sir Felix Meriton's card, on which he scribbled,—" Dear L——, I want to speak to you particularly and privately," procured us instant admission, and in five minutes more I found myself in the presence of the Lord Chancellor of Great Britain.

Sir Felix Meriton always carried with him a yellow bamboo stick, and upon this occasion he was not without it; and I was not a little astonished to see him bring it down with a thump upon Lord L——'s table, and exclaim at the same time,—

"All lunatics are under your jurisdiction, eh?"—"I believe so," said the chancellor, with a smile; "have you come, Sir Felix, to place yourself under my care?"

"No, I haven't, cried Sir Felix, laughing, in spite of his excitement; " all I want you to do is, to listen to what this gentleman has to say."

He then formally introduced me, and I all at once found myself in the embarrassing situation of making a speech to one of the first orators of the age.

I suppose I managed to get on pretty well, for when I had quite done, and fairly related all the circumstances of the case, how Robert Hetton had attempted to bribe me in the first instance, down to what his young wife had related to me, he said,—

"This appears to be a very bad transaction. I will instantly grant a commission to try the question of lunacy, and appoint medical men upon it of unquestionable integrity. You, sir, I would advise should be a witness merely. Mr. Charles Hetton must be produced upon my order, and should he prove sane, I shall then advise a prosecution against his brother, and the medical man who gave the certificate, for conspiracy, which will, without doubt, end in their transportation. Robert Hetton shall have immediate notice to produce his brother here, at my house on the morning of the third day from this."

This was quite satisfactory. No one could expect more, and Sir Felix and I left with a conviction that all would end well for Charles Hetton and his young and interesting wife.

I returned home, and communicated the success of my intercession, and Amelia strove to wait with patience until she could once more behold her husband, who had been so cruelly torn from her, and of whose place of confinement even she was ignorant.

* * * * *

The three tedious days at length passed away, and I on the third day had received a notice to attend the inquiry at the chancellor's house, which he had promised to institute.

The hour named was an early one, but my impatience would not allow me to wait for it, and I was the first arrival in the large parlour at his lordship's which was set apart for the investigation. Soon Sir —— and Mr. ——, the eminent physicians, arrived, and precisely at ten o'clock his lordship entered the room and took his seat.

Several of the old servants of Mr. Charles Hetton had been sent for, and they gave their eager and affecting testimony of the sanity and kindness of their master. Then I gave my evidence in full, and when it was concluded Robert Hetton was called in, for he had not thought fit to disregard the chancellor's summons.

He deposed, with unblushing effrontery, that his brother was insane, and that he called in the medical man who gave the certificate. He denied entirely all my statement about what passed after he and I had left his brother's house, and concluded by saying, that in obedience to his lordship's summons, he had brought his brother Charles, who was below with a keeper.

"Very well," said the chancellor; " let the alleged lunatic be brought in."

That was a moment of terrible suspense to me. The door opened, and Charles Hetton walked slowly into the room. He was greatly altered. His face was ghastly pale, and he seemed to be suffering from extreme weakness and exhaustion.

There was a dead silence for a moment, and then the lord chancellor said, kindly,—

"Do you know why you are brought here, sir ?"

Charles Hetton cast an anxious glance round the room before he replied; then he said,—

"I hope, sir, that this is an impartial inquiry into my state of mind?"—"It is," said the chancellor, evidently gratified with the answer; " I am the lord chancellor."

A flush of colour came across the pale face of Charles Hetton, and his whole frame seemed to dilate, as he said emphatically,—

"Thank God! Hear me, sir. I was torn from my happy home on a plea of lunacy. It was hoped that cruelty, solitary confinement, and obloquy of all kinds, even to blows, would really drive me mad, and then who should take upon him to say when my insanity commenced? Sir, to avoid actual cruelty, I have now for a whole week feigned to be mad. I doubt not but I have been brought here with a conviction that the hellish plot had succeeded. Thank God it has not. Solitude did not affect me, for I am used to it. I claim inquiry; bring hither my servants,—my few private friends, —my wife,—and ask them all what I have been, then judge for yourself, sir, what I am. There, sir, stands my enemy, my own brother! There, cowering beneath my gaze, he trembles. God be thanked he has grace even to tremble."

Every one was powerfully interested and affected by this address, and the chancellor, turning to Sir ——, the eminent physician, said,

"Will you ask any questions, sir?"

"You a e married sir?" said the physician to Hetton.

"I am," he replied; " I married privately a young lady whom I admired for her virtues."

"What is the amount of your property?"—" Rather over forty thousand pounds a-year."

"You are fond of science?"—"Passionately."

"Ask him," cried Robert Hetton, " if he has made any remarkable scientific discoveries?"

Charles turned to him with a look of contempt, and then said,—

"Gentlemen, and you, my lord, in order to deceive my brutal keepers into a notion that they had driven me distracted, I told them that I knew how to turn the moon round, so as to produce a full moon at my pleasure."

"What is your opinion, gentlemen?" said the chancellor. —" Mr. Hetton is as sane as I am," said Sir ——.

"I quash the certificate of lunacy," said the chancellor; " Mr. Hetton, you are free!"

"My wife?" were Hetton's first words.—" She is below," said I.

"Show Mrs. Hetton up instantly," said the chancellor.

Emilia was the next minute in her husband's arms. Robert Hetton saw that the game was up with him, and he crept towards the door.

"Stay, sir," cried the chancellor, " I commit you to the Fleet for contempt of court in not reporting the asylum in which your brother was confined; and, you, sir," he said to the medical man who gave the certificate, " I shall likewise commit. An indictment for conspiracy shall be drawn up against you immediately, and you will, in all probability, be both committed to Newgate this evening. Officers, take them away."

* * * * *

Mr. Hetton and his Emilia started that day in a carriage and four for the Grange, and a happier couple never enjoyed the blessings of mutual affection. From this adventure I may date my success in my profession; for not only did Mr. and Mrs. Charles Hetton do a great deal for me, but Lord L——, the chancellor, recommended me to many first-rate patients. So Sir Felix was quite right when he gave me a poke in the ribs the next day with his bamboo, and said,—

"Doctor,—doctor, eh? You must know that affair will do you no harm, eh? You know you have won golden opinions, eh? By-the-by, what an infernal, thundering rogue that Robert Hetton was; and you must know, he used to cry too, eh? I thought *his* heart was in the right place, but you know I turned out to be a ld fool, eh?—and it's your heart, after all, you know, doctor, eh?"

At Charles Hetton's intercession, Robert and the medical man who had signed the certificate, escaped being transported, but they were each imprisoned for two years, while the lunatic asylum in which Charles had been confined was completely broken up and ruined by the very proper prosecution he instituted against it.

And thus ends my tale of the Certificate of Lunacy, and a more satisfactory passage I can scarcely find in my Diary.

THE MERCHANT'S WIFE;

OR, THE LOVE CHILD.

AT a period towards the close of my professional career, a domestic tragedy occurred, with the persons concerned in which I was, in some measure, mixed up,—a tragedy of so dreadful a nature, involving, as it did, destruction to several, and unhappiness to many, that for a long time I have hesitated whether or not to give it a record in these pages. And yet so true a picture of human nature do the events pourtray, and so much is there that may be learned from this recital, that, suppressing the real names of the actors in the melancholy drama, I am at last tempted to lay before my readers one of the most secret, if not the most secret, passages of my Diary.

Although I did not become acquainted with the facts in the order in which I shall relate them, still, from diligent and patient inquiry, I was enabled to collect the fragmental pieces of the family history which from time to time I heard, into one perfect whole in my Diary, and then, and not till then, was I fairly enabled to judge of what appeared to me at first, and without perfect and complete information, the most extraordinary and contradictory circumstances.

I was not called upon to interfere in the calamitous affairs which my story will comprehend until a frightful catastrophe had occurred : but I will begin earlier, so that my reader shall have the advantage, which I had not, of really beginning at the beginning.

One of the most opulent and respected merchants which London ever produced was a Mr. Markham. What he exactly called himself, or dealt in, I don't know, but he had many ships, and it was well known that his commercial transactions extended to all quarters of the habitable globe. He was a man of considerable ability, and possessed great tact in his commercial undertakings. His only fault was a petulant irritability of temper, which always tempted him into disputes and contentions about trifles which were really undeserving of notice.

It was late in life before Mr. Markham thought that his accumulated thousands would, with the addition of an amiable woman as his domestic partner, make an exceedingly valuable and happy home ; and when once possessed with this idea, he was unceasing in his endeavours to discover some young person possessed of the necessary qualifications which he looked for and expected in a wife. Fortune he sought not, for he had enough himself to satisfy his wildest wants. He wished for a loving, kind, amiable companion ; nor was he long in fixing his choice upon one who he considered, and who really was, in every respect, qualified to make any home happy.

This young lady's name was Emma Dorrington. She was the youngest child of a poor gentleman who had been for years struggling with a large family to preserve the station in life to which, in the earlier part of his career, he had been accustomed. Beneath that struggle, he sank into an early grave, leaving a widow and five children to the tender mercies of a tender and merciful (Qy.) world, and the scanty comforts obtainable from an annuity of sixty pounds per annum.

Emma, at the time of her father's death, was but ten years of age, and it was seven years after this event that Mr. Markham saw her, and at once felt that she was the person destined to meet his wishes in every respect. His age was then forty ; but this disparity of years did not strike him as any particular objection, seeing that his great wealth enabled him to settle at once a handsome competence upon his young wife, who, in the natural order of events, would outlive him.

Now Mr. Markham, although a man of unblemished integrity and a kind heart, was by no means a very sensitive or romantic individual ; and when he had once made up his mind that he should like Emma Dorrington to become Mrs. Markham, he set about the affair in a business-like manner, that is to say, he made an offer at once, which, although not couched in the usual manner of such epistles, yet showed so much real sense and goodness of heart, that it was impossible to give it other than a respectful reception.

At the time this offer was made, there was one circumstance which Emma Dorrington did know, but which Mr. Markham did not, and that was, that the gentle and affectionate heart of the young girl had been struck by the estimable qualities and good looks of a young gentleman of the name of George Grant, who, although distantly connected with a noble family, and a far-off heir to estates and a baronetcy, was, notwithstanding, about as poor as any gentlemanly young man could very well be.

Now what made the business more complicated and unhappy for all parties, was the circumstance that Mr. Markham had owed his introduction to the family of the Dorringtons to this very George Grant, whose family was well known to the rich merchant, and for whom he had always, from a boy, ever had the greatest affection.

Had George Grant, when he introduced Mr. Markham at the humble home of the Dorringtons, mentioned that he loved Emma, what heaps of future misery and wretchedness might have been spared ; but with the natural sensitiveness of a young man, he shrunk from such a confidence, and Mr. Markham was the last man in the world ever, of his own accord, to find out, or even suspect, an affair of the heart.

The motive of George Grant in introducing Mr. Markham to the poor family is easily explained. He wished him to become acquainted with their worth, and then he knew well that the kind-hearted merchant would soon find some means of bettering their condition in his own way.

The reader then, being cognizant of all these circumstances, may imagine the dismay of poor George Grant, when, upon calling one day at the Dorringtons, the mother of Emma placed Mr. Markham's letter in his hands, which ran thus :—

"TO MRS. DORRINGTON."

"MY DEAR MADAM,

"I trust you will believe me sincere in every word which this letter contains, and from a conviction of that sincerity, pardon the bluntness of the language ; and I think—nay, I am sure—your daughter Emma would, as my wife, merit my esteem and affection ; and in here proposing marriage to her, I say it shall be my earnest endeavour to promote her happiness. Should she accept me for a husband, I will settle upon her five thousand pounds per annum, which shall be entirely at her own disposal, because I know that the use she would make of such a sum would be gratifying both to me and herself. Awaiting your and her answer, believe me, madam, your obedient servant,

"JOHN MARKHAM."

George Grant was perfectly confounded at this letter, and sat with it in his hand glaring at Mrs. Dorrington without being able to say a word.

It must be presumed that Emma's mother was quite ignorant of the existence of any attachment between her youngest child and George, when she said earnestly,—

"Now, Mr. Grant, you know more of Mr. Markham than we do. What is really your opinion as to his principles and disposition ?"

"He is the best and kindest of men," said George, who scorned any other than the truth, even of his rival ; "his acts of private benevolence, which have through accident only occasionally been heard of, are munificent."

Mrs. Dorrington heard this with evident pleasure, and she replied in an animated manner,—

"I am glad to hear that, Mr. Grant ; and I, who know too much, alas ! of the world and its miseries, would wish my darling child no better fate than to be married to such a man."

This was enough for poor George. He rose trembling, and took his leave. Hurrying home to his obscure lodgings, he leaned his head upon his hands, and wept bitterly. Then sober reason came to his aid, and he began to think what he ought to do, which thought ended in one of the most heroic acts of self-devotion which it is possible to conceive, and which the following note to Emma will explain. I have the original now before me. It is discoloured by tears, and the trembling hand in which it is written would never be supposed to be that of a young man in the prime and vigour of his life.

"MY DEAR EMMA,

" Mr. Markham has just made, through your mother, an offer for your hand. Accept him, for the sake of yourself and all you love. Accept him, for your mother's sake, who now, in the decline of life, requires its comforts and its luxuries. Accept him for the sake of your brothers and sisters, who will live to bless you as the architect of their fortunes. Accept him for his own sake, for he is kind, generous, and good, and forget that you ever knew or heard of

"GEORGE GRANT."

Oh! what a bitter agony it was to write this to her he loved so fondly. But it was done. He had made the sacrifice, and, composing his convulsed features as much as he could, he sealed his note, and packing up all the valuables he possessed, he went forth from his humble abode. The first letter-box received the note to Emma, and then he took his course to the London Docks.

To the first lounger he saw, he said,—

"What ships sail to-day?"—"There's one just dropping down with the tide now," replied the man.

"Where is she going?"—"To Hamburgh."

"Do they take passengers?"—"Yes. Shall I give your honour a cast on board her? I have a wherry here."

"Yes," said George Grant; and in an hour he had settled for a passage, and was off for Hamburgh.

* * * * *

We will not pause to depict Emma's feelings at the receipt of George's note. At first she thought it most unkind—then she wept to think what a noble heart she had gained in gaining the love of one who was capable of making such a sacrifice.

She wrote him an answer—an answer full of clinging affection, offering to be his in poverty rather than another's with the world's wealth at command. Her letter came back to her unopened, for George was gone. Then did a feeling of desolation creep over the young girl's heart, and, deserted by her lover, she yielded to the solicitations of her mother, and became the wife of Mr. Markham.

And now, had no previous passion lingered in her heart, she might, she must have loved her husband, for he idolized her. He anticipated her slightest wish, and there was not one word or act of his towards her that did not spring from and indicate the purest and most unbounded affection.

Emma knew all this. She felt it fully, and was deeply grateful. Her husband possessed all her esteem—her unbounded gratitude, and she felt it to be a sacred duty to promote the happiness of one who did so much for her. Here, then, were good grounds for steadfast and enduring happiness and contentment.

If there were none of the sweets of passion, there were none of its doubts and fears—if there was no ecstacy, there was no disappointment. Thus passed two months of Emma's wedded life. She saw all around her happy and provided for munificently, and had it not been that occasionally the thought would cross her mind that what a paradise upon earth she should be dwelling in if George Grant had been her husband, with the same means of doing good that Mr. Markham possessed, she, too, would have in vain searched her heart for one cankering care.

They (Mr. and Mrs. Markham) were sitting together at breakfast, when, for the first time since their marriage, the name of young Grant was mentioned between them.

"I wonder," said Mr. Markham, "we have not had a visit from my young friend, Grant."

Emma started at the mention of that familiar name, and for a moment or two she could scarcely command her feelings.

"He is a most estimable young man," continued Mr. Markham; "I have a high esteem for him, and I have been casting about in my mind, Emma, for some means of doing him some permanent and lasting good."—"Yes, yes; certainly," said Emma, faintly.

"I would take him into partnership directly," added Mr. Markham, "and then he would be constantly with us, were it not for Mr. Colleti, my partner, who will not consent to having any one else in the business besides ourselves, and he has brought such very large sums from time to time into the business, that I cannot in any decency force a junior partner upon him merely to gratify my own feelings of partiality towards a young man whom I esteem so much as I do George Grant."

"Yes, yes, certainly;" was all that Emma could muster strength and ability to say.

"By-the-bye," continued her husband, "Colleti will be back from the continent in a day or two now, and I wish him to dine here, Emma, immediately on his arrival, in order that I may formally introduce him to you."

Emma was glad to change the conversation from George Grant to Colleti, and she said,—

"What kind of person is this Colleti, your partner, of whom I have heard so much?"—"Why, to tell the honest truth," replied Mr. Markham, "he is not a very loveable or agreeable personage. His appearance is rather against him, inasmuch as he squints awfully."

"Indeed."—"Yes, and his manners are a trifle uncouth or so; but I always found him upright in all his dealings, and I believe him to be a strictly honest man."

"That is a cloak which does, and ought to, cover a multitude of sins," said Emma.—"I shall have no fear of your falling in love with Colleti," added Mr. Markham, with a smile as he rose from his breakfast, "however much you may admire him as a curiosity."

"You expect him soon?" said Emma.—"Yes; possibly to-day, although not very likely so soon."

"It's very strange," said Emma to herself, when she was left alone, "I never saw this man Colleti, but a shudder comes over me and my heart feels chilled whenever I hear his name mentioned. It seems, too, as if the shadow of some awful event, connected in some way with him, preceded his coming, and warned me of him. How childish are such fancies!" she then added, after a pause; "I must combat with such silly sensations. What can Colleti be to me, or I to Colleti?"

Notwithstanding all her efforts, the same dark foreboding came across Emma's mind whenever she thought of her husband's partner; and when Mr. Markham returned from his counting-house to spend the remainder of the day in the society of his wife, and announced that Mr. Colleti had returned, and would dine with them on the morrow, a feeling of apprehension came across her mind which was absolutely sickening.

The morrow came, and Emma had succeeded in reasoning herself into comparative calmness with regard to Colleti, whom she longed to see, in-order to judge if his personal appearance coincided with her preconceived notion of him.

The dinner hour was close at hand when a servant announced Mr. Colleti, and in another moment her husband's partner stood before her.

Mr. Markham formally introduced him, and, after a few moments, Emma ventured upon a closer scrutiny of his face and general appearance.

He was very tall, but his limbs seemed none of them to belong to him. He looked as if, like the monster in Frankenstein, he had been made from odds and ends, picked up in some popular churchyard. His complexion was more that of a corpse than a living being, and the squint which Mr. Markham had mentioned gave a peculiarity to his face that at times was perfectly awful.

Emma shuddered as she looked at this man, and the undefinable feeling of dread connected with him came more strongly than ever across her agitated mind.

One circumstance, too, contributed greatly to annoy Mrs. Markham, which was, that in consequence of the peculiar obliquity of vision of Colleti, she never could tell whether he was looking at her or at some other object quite in another direction; and, once, when she felt perfectly sure that he was examining very critically a painting at the other end of the room, and she took the opportunity of, as she thought unobserved, studying his singular physiognomy, he suddenly bowed to her with an amorous expression, as much as to say,—

"You do me a great deal of honour, madam, by your distinguished notice."

After this circumstance, Mrs. Markham scarcely dared to trust her eyes in the direction where Colleti sat, and it was quite a relief to her when the cloth was removed, and she felt herself at liberty to retire from the table.

The moment, however, she rose, Colleti sprang from his seat, and with obsequious politeness handed her to the door, and, as she was passing out, he squeezed her hand and assumed such an awful leering expression of admiration, that Emma was thoroughly alarmed, and when she reached her own room, was very nearly in a fainting state.

Her first thought was to take the earliest opportunity of telling her husband of Colleti's singular conduct; but, upon maturer reflection, she justly thought how very slight a subject of complaint she had, for the pressure of her hand might have been accidental, and, indeed, with many persons, is quite a thing of habit; and she could not very well complain to her husband because his partner was an exceedingly ugly man, and squinted awfully.

With this kind of reasoning Emma strove to laugh away her fears of Colleti; but yet there was a something lurking

DIARY OF A PHYSICIAN.

at the bottom of her heart which assured her that some evil would arise in which he would be the prime agent and mover, but what that evil was particularly to consist of, or what precise shape it was to assume, she had no possible means of judging.

Colleti at length left the house, and Mr. Markham asked his young wife, in a jocular manner, what she thought of his "handsome" partner.

"He is the most alarmingly ugly man I ever saw," replied Emma.—"Well," said Mr. Markham, "Colleti is not an Adonis certainly; but I believe he is a good-hearted man. Over our wine to-day he gave his consent to something which I know will give you a great deal of pleasure and make us all much happier."

"What is that?" asked Emma.—"Why, he agrees that I should offer George Grant a small share in the business."

A sudden faintness came over Emma, and she felt as if she was involved in some combination of horrors of which this was the commencement.

Mr. Markham could not but see the changing colour of his wife, and he rung the bell in great alarm for her maid.

By a great effort of mind, however, Emma recovered, and attributing her illness to the heat of the room, she begged to be left alone for a time, in order that she might lie down.

"What will become of me," she thought, "if I am to see, and be constantly seen by, George Grant? Alas! alas! my own heart tells me that I respect and honour my husband; but I—I—God of Heaven! what was I about to say? That I love George? Oh! Heaven protect me—save me—save me from myself. He must not come. No, no; it would be misery to both. I must see him, and beg, implore him to accept of a provision abroad, and never to set foot within this house."

In these and such like reflections Mrs. Markham passed several hours, until, exhausted by the tumult of her own feelings, she sank into a troubled and uneasy slumber, in which she was haunted by fearful visions, Colleti being, with the horrible leer upon his face, ever present to her excited imagination.

Mr. Markham was quite in despair at the indisposition of his young wife, and urged her tenderly, in the morning, to have medical advice. She, however, rallied herself as much as possible, and persisted in declining it, saying she was quite sure she would be better when he returned from business in the afternoon. With this assurance the merchant reluctantly left his home; but scarcely had he been gone ten minutes, when, to the surprise of Emma, Mr. Colleti was announced, and before she could decide upon whether to deny herself to him, or admit him, he walked into the drawing room with an easy familiarity of manner, which was especially disagreeable to Emma, who immediately rose, resolved to cut the interview as short as possible, and to show him that she did not contemplate his becoming so intimate as to call whenever he pleased.

"I find, charming Mrs. Markham," he said, with one of his peculiar looks, "that I have missed my good friend Markham; I intended to walk with him to business this morning."—"He has been gone but a short time since," replied Emma; "you may yet overtake him, Mr. Colleti."

"Oh! it don't matter in the least," said Colleti, seating himself as if he was quite at home.

Emma was confounded at his assurance, and remained standing, which he observing, said,—

"Pray be seated, Mrs. Markham: I wish, if you please, to ask you a question."—"Sir," said Emma, "you can have no question to ask me which may not be asked with greater propriety of my husband."

"There, now, you mistake," said Colleti, "most charming of women."—"I must request, sir," said Emma, her face flushing with indignation, "that you will not address such expressions to me. I am Mr. Markham's wife."

"Ah!" replied Colleti, giving a horrible leer, "that is true; but it is so difficult to repress one's intense and overwhelming admiration. However, I will be discreet; you may depend, no one but yourself shall ever hear me give utterance to an admiration which will be, if possible, the more intense in proportion as it is concealed."

Emma was confounded at the cool insolence of Colleti, that for some moments she had not the power to speak or act. The instant, however, that she could command herself sufficiently, she at once walked to the door, and was upon the point of leaving the room, when Colleti said,—

"It was of Mr. George Grant I came to speak."

Emma paused, and said faintly,—

"George Grant?"—"Yes," replied Colleti; "but I, who am not so very intimate with him, add 'Mr.' to his name."

"What do you mean?" said Emma.—" Mean!" said Colleti; " why, I have consented to take this young man into an old established and lucrative business on Mr. Markham's representation that it would very much oblige you, and I merely wished to hear, from your own lips, a character of this young man."

"I—I do not wish," stammered Emma. — " Do not wish what?"

Emma tried to speak, but every object swam before her, and she had the agony of just retaining consciousness enough to know that she was fainting in the arms of Colleti.

She felt his horrid face touch hers—his breath came across her cheek—he pressed his lips upon her very mouth in a kiss of fire.

That pollution would have roused Emma from death. She felt renovated with new strength and with great energy she pushed him from her so violently, that he reeled again.

"Monster — wretch!" she cried; " my husband shall know——" — " *That you love George Grant!*" whispered Colleti; " keep my secret, charming woman, and I will keep yours. Adieu, for the present!"

So saying, he left the room, and Emma, exhausted by her feelings, sank upon her seat in a torrent of tears.

Emma wept on for many minutes, and her tears certainly relieved her burning heart.

"What have I done," she exclaimed, " that I should be thus tortured? Is this man, Colleti, my evil genius? And yet, what have I done? I am innocent—ay, innocent even in thought. Have I not suppressed the beatings of my heart—stifled my first love, because it was my duty, and still must this strange and inexplicable man triumph over my weakness and make me shudder because I might be guilty, but am not? I must tell my husband all but — but, that all must comprehend something of George Grant. Then I must tell him that I was sold to him for his wealth, at a moment when my admiration of him I really loved was deepened into veneration by a generosity of behaviour unexampled. Oh! Heaven, direct me. What a tangled web is woven around me! How shall I escape—how free myself from the awful meshes in which I am caught—how rid my shrinking soul from the horror of that bad man, Colleti?"

Covering her face with her hands, she again burst into a passion of hysterical weeping, after the subsidence of which she made a resolution which, dangerous although it was, she thought more prudent than commiting to writing, or employing an agent in the transaction—that resolution was, to offer no obstruction to George Grant coming to London, provided he was prevailed upon to do so, which she doubted; but when he came, to get a private interview with him, and then and there urge him, as he valued her, himself, and honour, to go away again, and never let her see him more.

With this determination in her mind, Emma met her husband with more calmness than could be expected, and even controlled her feelings sufficiently to inquire if he had written to George Grant, making the offer of the junior partnership.

"You may be sure I have, Emma," replied Mr. Markham, " and you don't know how happy I feel at Mr. Colleti giving his consent. You are sure you are quite recovered from your indisposition of this morning?"

Emma assured him that she was, and made every effort to assume her usual cheerfulness of manner. The evening, therefore, passed away more happily than Emma, under the circumstances could have supposed. She felt certain, that if, in a moment of weakness, George should consent to come to London, she could induce him, for her sake, again to leave it; and this thought brought her consolation. Alas! how ready we are always to blame the weakness of others without at all speculating upon what would be our own conduct under similar, or perhaps far less temptations.

Emma intended to represent to George Grant how wrong he was in coming from where he was too distant to be dangerous, and she never for a moment suspected that she herself might not be able to sustain the trial of the presence of one who was dearer to her heart, and who had obtained a firmer hold upon her best affections than she herself at any time suspected.

* * * * *

The next day came, and after Mr. Markham's departure, poor Emma was in an agony of apprehension lest she should again be subjected to the horrors of a visit from Colleti. To her great relief, however, the morning passed away, and he came not, and Emma passed the time in duly weighing and considering what she should say to George Grant in her interview with him, should such ever take place.

She flew to welcome her husband home at his usual hour, and she longed to say, "Have you heard from George Grant?" yet lacked the courage to do so.

Her mind was, however, quickly relieved from this suspense, for not many minutes elapsed when Mr. Markham said gaily,—

"Well, Emma, I have had a very gratifying letter from George Grant."—"And—and," stammered Emma, " he—he accepts——"

"Of course he does," replied Mr. Markham; " he could not possibly do better, you know. He accepts my offer with many thanks, and his letter altogether says a great deal both for his head and his heart, Emma."

"Have you the letter with you?" asked Emma.—"In truth, I have not," answered her husband; " I showed it to Colleti as a matter of course, and he took it from me, saying, " You must permit me the pleasure of showing this letter to Mrs. Markham, as this young man is her *protege*, and the pleasure it will give her will repay me for my consent to admit him into the business."

"Colleti!" repeated Emma.—"Yes,"continued Mr. Markham. " I think it showed a great deal of delicate consideration upon his part, don't you? Ah! you will find that beneath a rough exterior, Colleti hides a generous heart and a kind disposition, Emma."

"I—I hope so," said Emma.—" You hope so, Emma? I assure you that such is the case. He is certainly odd and eccentric in his way, but that's all."

"I—I am glad to hear it."—"Why, now, Emma, I shall think you prejudiced against poor Colleti on account of his looks."

"His looks are, indeed, against him," said Emma.—" But then, you know, he can't help them," suggested Mr. Markham.

"Very true," replied Emma; " but you would scarcely believe that I have quite a dread of him."—" A dread—pho! pho! I am sure, in this affair of George Grant, he has quite deferred to your feelings."

"And—and," faltered Emma, " when is George expected?" —" To-morrow, or the next day, at the farthest."

"Let me, then, make one request of you," said Emma.—"A request of me?" cried Mr. Markham " you know, Emma, there is no occasion to shape any of your wishes into a request; for there is nothing that you would ask, I am quite sure, that I would refuse you."

"Will you," said Emma, faintly, " prevent Colleti from giving me the letter, and give it to me yourself?"

"Of course, if you wish it, Emma; but it will be depriving poor Colleti of a great pleasure, I am quite sure."

Emma was silent, and Mr. Markham added,—

"Come, now, Emma, I promise you I will do as you wish, although I wish you would think better of it."

Emma, however, persisted, as she had good reason to do, and Mr. Markham promised that he would comply with her desire, and get Colleti to give up the letter of George Grant.

Twenty times Emma was on the point of communicating to her husband the audacious behaviour of Colleti in the drawing-room, but she as often shrank from the recital, fearful of the consequences which might ensue; and she had such an awful notion of the malignant power and machinations of Colleti, that she did not feel at all quite certain, but in the event of her enraging her husband against him, he would find some means of involving her, Mr. Markham, and George Grant in one common destruction.

It is true, that Emma's reasoning was not very just upon this point, and that she commited the capital error of supposing that anything was to be gained by concealment which would not be much better gained by open ingenuousness; but then every allowance must be made for the peculiar situation in which she was placed. The wife of a man she could not really love, and loving him whom she could never be aught to but an acquaintance, and even less than that.

* * * * *

Another morning dawned upon the unhappy and agitated Mrs. Markham, and she reminded her husband before he departed to his office of his promise concerning the letter.

Scarcely, however, as it had happened before, had he left the house, when a knock at the street-door threw Emma into an agony of alarm lest it should be Colleti. She immediately rose to desire her servants to deny her to him in the most positive terms. She had not patience to ring the bell, but flew to the door of the room just in time to encounter

Colleti. For a moment neither spoke. Emma was completely paralyzed and panic-stricken by his sudden appearance, and he stood silently regarding her with that abominable leer upon his face, than which nothing could be more hideous and offensive.

"Charming Mrs. Markham," he said, "allow me to congratulate you upon your good looks."—"Let me pass!" cried Emma, "I will not talk with you. Let me pass!"

"One question," said Colleti, "and you are free," at the same time closing the door. "Have you told your husband what passed between us at my last visit?"—"No—no!" cried Emma; "let me pass, sir, or I will alarm the household."

"Indeed!" said Colleti; "I know Markham better than you do. It is too late."—"What is too late?" cried Emma.

"To tell him," cried Colleti. "I was in danger. You might have told him at once. Now you *dare* not."—"Dare not!" echoed Emma.

"Ay, dare not,—because he will ask you why you did not take the *first* opportunity of acquainting him that Colleti, his partner, had dared to love his wife."—"Wretch!" screamed Emma.

"As you please. Woman is never so beautiful to me as when in heat or in anger," said Colleti. "Hear me, Mrs. Markham—I do love you! I avow it; but I am a patient man, unless goaded to excess. I can ruin your husband when I please—I can ruin your lover, George Grant, or perchance kill him."

Emma shuddered.

"Come, now," continued Colleti, "we understand each other. I will be generous. Just now and then give me one kiss from those pouting, tempting lips—twine those arms of snowy whiteness round my neck, and say, 'Colleti, I love you——' "—"Monstrous!" cried Emma.

"Yes," resumed Colleti, "love me monstrously, and George Grant shall make his fortune, while your husband enjoys his unmolested, and still continues to you the means of supporting all those that are dear to you in comfort and luxury."

"Villain!" cried Emma; "I—I have not words to speak my scorn."—"Exactly," said Colleti, calmly.

"I loathe you."—"Yes."

"Detest——"—"Ay."

"My husband shall know all."—"There you are wrong, charming, delightful creature, because, if you tell him but one word of what passes between us in our delicious little private conversations, I will breed such a quarrel between George Grant and him, founded on jealousy, that they shall fight, and one or the other, if not both, shall lie a corpse at your feet."

"No! no! you have not such fearful power?"—"I have sworn it."

"Are you human?"—"Scarcely," cried Colleti, advancing towards her.

"Hold off!" cried Emma. "Oh, if you have one spark of better nature in you, let me fan it to a flame of virtue! Relent, fiend!"—"Delightful creature," said Colleti, "how these little charming difficulties enhance my passion! By-the-bye, I promised our good friend Markham to give you George Grant's letter."

"I will not take it from you. It is polluted by your touch," said Emma.—"As you please," coolly remarked Colleti. "I fear we must now part. Ah! send me not away without another pressure of those divine lips."

"You were villain enough to take advantage of a moment of insensibility to insult me," cried Emma; "and I was weak enough not to tell my husband. Now beware, Colleti, approach me not, or you will make me desperate."—"Well, well," said Colleti, "another time—another time will do."

"My husband shall know all," said Emma.—"Ha! ha!" laughed Colleti, "so he shall—so he shall; I will tell him."

* * * * *

Bewildered and confounded, Emma stood in the centre of the apartment which Colleti had just left, quite incapable of rational thought. In vain she strove to collect her scattered faculties and decide upon some immediate method of freeing herself from the horrible and hateful persecution of the villain Colleti.

At length she made her decision—she would tell her husband. He should know all, and at once forgiving her for the past, rid her of the annoyance of Colleti's visits.

After she had made this resolution, she became more easy in her mind, and her only impatience was for Mr. Markham's return from his counting-house.

The day wore on, and the hour at length arrived. She heard his well-known knock at the door, and her heart beat violently at the thought of the interview that she had to go through.

Mr. Markham walked gaily into the room, and to Emma's surprise his first words were,—

"So you and Colleti have had a little quarrel!"

"Little quarrel?" gasped Emma.

"Pho! pho!" cried Mr. Markham. "Don't look so serious about it. Colleti told me the whole particulars. Come, come, don't be put out about a trifle."—"Trifle!" echoed Emma.

"Oh, to be sure; it is only Colleti's manner. He is afraid, poor fellow, that he has offended you past forgiveness; but I told him I would make his peace."

Emma was too thunderstricken for a moment to reply. Then she said,—

"Will you tell me what Colleti said?"—"Oh! nonsense," cried Mr. Markham. "Say no more about it. You should make allowances, Emma, for a man with a continental education. A little harmless gallantry, you know, is thought nothing of abroad. Not that I approve of it by any means myself,—no, no. Had Colleti really been rude to you, instead of your merely fancying it, I—I would break with him, though it brought me to want!"—"To want?" cried Emma.

"What—what?" said Mr. Markham; "what did I say?"

A cold shudder passed through Emma's frame. "Colleti's words were true, then," she thought. "He can ruin my husband. God of Heaven! what a hideous train of circumstances are around me."

"You look ill," cried Mr. Markham, himself looking very much confused at the slip of the tongue he had made.—"No, no," said Emma; "it's only a trifling passing faintness; it's over now."

"You had better take some restorative," said Mr. Markham, kindly, "and think no more of Colleti's awkward gallantry. Depend upon it he meant nothing. I know him well, Emma."—"Will—will—he——" gasped Emma.

"Will he what, my dear Emma?"—"Will he come here again?"

Mr. Markham looked perplexed a moment. Then he said,—

"Certainly not, if you make a point that he should not; but it will be very difficult and awkward for me to forbid my partner my house, you see, Emma."

"I—I see," she said faintly.

"But if you will have it so——" "No, no," said Emma; "at least, I will think of it. I am not very well, and,——"

She could no longer control her feelings, but, sinking into her husband's arms, burst into such a passion of hysterical sobs, that the alarmed merchant would have rung for all the servants in the house, had it not been that Emma clung to him so convulsively that he had not the power to move.

Suddenly she looked up in his face, and dashing away the tears from her eyes, she said imploringly,—

"Will you answer me two questions, as you love me?" —"Certainly, I will," replied Mr. Markham; "for Heaven's sake, sit down and be calm."

Emma still hung upon his arm as she said,—

"Firstly, tell me exactly what Colleti said."

"He said he snatched a flower from your waist in a moment of thoughtlessness, and kissed it."

"That was all?"—"All he told me, Emma."

"Now then, my dear husband, answer me another question. It is a great confidence I ask."—"I will answer it," said Mr. Markham, "for I know I can trust you."

"Indeed you may. *Are you in this Colleti's power?*"

Mr. Markham's lips turned pale as, bending down close to his wife's ear, he whispered,—

"*Emma, I am.*"

Emma shuddered.

"Remember," said Mr Markham, "that a husband's honour — —"—"Is safe," cried Emma, "in a wife's heart!"

* * * * *

It was in the silence and solitude of her own chamber that Emma wept long and bitterly over the singular and, to her, dreadful events of the last few days.

"Shall I," she asked herself, "bring to ruin—to despair—perhaps to death—the man who has loved me so tenderly, who has done so much for me and mine? I cannot—I cannot! and yet can I in silence endure the insults of this Colleti? Oh, horrible alternative!"

Thus was the unfortunate Emma's mind racked by contending emotions; and the only thought that cast now a gleam of comfort upon the wretchedness of her condition was a vague, indistinct hope that George Grant might be able to do something to ward off the threatened miseries that surrounded her, and possibly protect her against Colleti, without compromising her husband's safety or reputation.

As if by mutual consent, although no such agreement was entered into, the merchant and his young wife avoided any allusion to the subject of their agitating conversation, and the morning again came, bringing with it the usual hour of Mr. Markham's departure. Emma saw him go with trembling apprehension, for she dreaded another visit from the now ten times more dreadful Colleti.

An hour passed in the utmost anxiety, and, as no one came to announce the dreaded name, Emma began to breathe a little more freely, when, just as she was congratulating herself on an escape for that morning at least, she heard a knock at the street-door. which renewed all her alarms.

She heard the door opened—some murmured inquiry—and then the domestic's foot upon the stairs, she doubted not to announce the, object of at once her dread and abhorrence. The door was opened, and the servant announced Mr. George Grant.

Oh! what a relief to Emma was the sound of that name! How sweetly and musically did it ring in her ears when contrasted with that of Colleti, which was foremost but a moment before in her imagination so strongly, that she almost doubted her own senses, and made the servant repeat "Mr. George Grant," before she could fully believe in the reality of the relief it afforded her.

She remembered not all her prudent resolves concerning her former lover. She forgot that she intended to meet him with coldness, and by argument force him from her presence for ever, but, with a heightened colour, she stood, after giving the order to admit him, in a flutter of delight awaiting his arrival. She knew his very step upon the stairs; she could have sworn to his shadow as it darkened the entrance. In another moment he stood before her—the door closed behind him, and they were alone.

"Emma," said George.

That name recalled her to herself. For one half instant she placed her hand upon her heart, as if to still its anxious beating, then in a low, faltering voice, she said,—

"Mr. Grant, my name is now Markham."

He was silent, and she looked for the first time in his face.

"Emma," said George Grant, in a low voice of deep emotion, "while I remain here, which will not be long, permit me to call you by that dear, remembered name. It was not Mr. Markham's letter, offering me golden advantages, that brought me back to the shores of England. No; I was compelled to visit London in order to take possession of a small legacy which has been left me by the only person that I could claim kindred with. I am now the last of my race; I have no kindred; I call none by the same name as myself; all those dear, social ties, which disarm the rude shocks of the world of half their terrors, exist not for me; I am lonely, Emma, and desolate!"—"No, no," sobbed Emma "there are still those who esteem and—and—love you, George."

"I believe it—I know it," he replied; "and those even my cruel destiny forces me to leave for ever. Emma; I have come here to bid you a last farewell, for we may never meet again in this world."—"Do not say so," sobbed Emma, and, in her tumultuous feelings, she forgot all but the agony of parting with him she loved.

"Could you imagine me," he continued, "so inconsistent as, after making a sacrifice which rent my heart asunder, to come to you now to be your evil spirit, Emma—to haunt you now with my unhallowed presence, when—when —in honour, I might have clung to you and dared to love you in the face of the whole world?"

Emma looked up in his face. The paleness was gone—it had given way to the flush of excited feelings and generous emotions.

"Then—then—you have not consented, George, to become a partner of my husband's?"—"I have not, Emma. The two letters came by the same post, the one announcing the death of my relative, and the other from Mr. Markham, making me the generous offer of future competency, if not wealth. I wrote him an answer, saying I should be in London immediately, and thanking him for his offer. This he has imagined to be an acceptance of it; but I meant it not as such, knowing, that in London, I could not avoid him and his friendly hospitality; I intended—with many kind thanks —more than I could put in a letter—to refuse the offer, see you once more, and leave my native shores for ever!"

"For ever, George!" echoed Emma,—"Ay, Emma, for ever. You would not think me so base, so cowardly, as to make a virtue of resigning you to another, and stand in the way of your serenity, at least, if not of your happiness?"

"I ought to have known you better," said Emma, stretching out her hand; "George, forgive me!"

His hand trembled as he took the delicate small fingers of her he loved so fondly and with such self-sacrificing devotion in his own.

"Farewell!" he said, in choking accents, "farewell, Emma. God bless you!"—"No, no, George, you must not, cannot go, for ever. You will come again, when time has quenched all youthful passion and age has dulled the feelings? Oh, George, I cannot—cannot say farewell?"

"Emma," said George, and his voice was deeply shaken, "Emma, for your own sake—for mine—for your husband's, let us now and at once part as though we had never met." —"God of Heaven!" cried Emma, throwing herself upon a sofa, "sustain me in this hour of trial."

George leaned close down to her ear, and whispered,—

"There will come a day when we shall both thank Heaven that gave us strength thus to part."—"Go, go!" said Emma. "Once more then, farewell!"

George stepped to the door. His hand was upon the lock. Emma raised her head from the sofa and called frantically on him by name—

"George! George! I shall die."

With one bound he was by her side.

"Once thus and let *me* die," he cried as he folded her in his arms. She clung convulsively around him—her warm breath fanned his cheek—"You—you will not go?" she whispered.

"I cannot," he cried.

He clasped her gentle heart to his own. Burning kisses fell like rain upon her lips.

At this moment a shadow darkened the window. Emma glanced in the direction whence it came. Colleti stood outside the casement, with a smile of derision on his lips. His long, bony fingers pointed into the room, and his hideous obliquity of vision made him look like some fiend come to glory in the destruction of the young and good.

Emma gave one loud shriek, and dropped a lifeless burthen in the arms of her first and last love!

* * * *

Emma's shriek alarmed a female domestic who instantly hastened to the room.

"Do not be alarmed," cried George; "bring some water, say nothing to any one. Stay, she moves."

Emma slowly opened her eyes, and seeing the face of George bending over her, she smiled faintly, and holding his hand clasped in hers, she said—

"George, dear—dear George, I have had such a dream. I thought I was married to another."—"Hush! hush!" cried George; "recollect yourself, Emma. Look around you."

She sat upon the couch and pressed her hands to her temples, then as recollection returned she trembled violently, and looking at George, said,—

"George the struggle is over!"—"What struggle?" said George.

"The struggle of passion with principle!" replied Emma. "I am yours! Take me—oh! take me away!"

The servant girl looked amazed and terrified, and was about to rush from the room, when George seized her by the arm, exclaiming,—

"What would you do? Your mistress is innocent yet. You can destroy her by relating this scene, and you may save her by keeping it a secret."

The girl trembled.

"Rosa," said Emma, "is that you?"—"Ye—yes, madam," replied the girl; "I will say nothing—not a word."

"Stay with me now," cried Emma, seizing the girl's hand. "George, I shall see you again ——"

George clasped his hands and groaned.

"To-morrow," said Emma—" To-morrow!" repeated George, and rushed like one distracted from the house.

When Mr. Markham came home, he found his wife in bed, and very unwell. Tenderly attached to her, his grief at her indisposition was excessive, and if any one circumstance more than another could have added acutely to Emma's mental sufferings, that circumstance would be the tender and devoted affection of her husband. She was really ill, for the agitation of her feelings had exhausted her frame, and the medical man, who was immediately called in by the anxious Mr. Markham, declared himself puzzled to account for the nervous agitation of her system, and evidently was incredulous when he was assured by Mr. Markham that nothing had or could possibly happen to give her mind a shock.

The merchant watched by her bed-side the whole night, and oh! what agony it gave to Emma's feelings to receive such marks of affection from him whom she could not love, although it was her duty to do so. Her slumbers were short and troubled, and it was not until the grey light of morning began to render objects in her room visible, that the fever of her frame somewhat abated, and she implored her husband to leave her for awhile, and endeavour to take some repose. Upon her repeated assurances that she was much better, Mr. Markham consented to go and lie down on a sofa in the drawing-room—that very sofa on which Emma had sunk, in the excess of her wild emotion, during her interview with George.

Then, when once more left alone with her own thoughts, the unhappy wife strove to think of some means of rescuing herself from the brink of the fearful abyss upon which she felt she was standing, and once more she resolved, if George should come to seek another interview, that it should be the last, let it cost her what effort it might. With a shudder, and nearly a shriek, she recalled to mind the appearance of Colleti as he stood outside the window, pointing at her and her lover. She felt now that she too, as well as her husband, was in the power of that dreadful man, and she felt, too, that her only hope of safety from his persecutions was in the immediate departure of George Grant from England.

"Yes, yes," she whispered to herself, "I will urge him to go. Then, when he has left me for ever, I will, on my knees, tell my husband all. I will tell him that I honour, respect, and hold him dear, and ask him to forgive the past, and trust to the future for calm happiness."

A gentle slumber now stole over her exhausted frame, and when she again awakened the sun was shining brightly in the heavens, and she saw Mr. Markham bending tenderly over her, watching her slumbers.

"Emma," he said, "thank God you have had a long and, I hope, refreshing sleep."

Emma started.

"What is the time?" she cried.—"'Tis past eleven."

"Then you have stayed away from business this morning?"—"Could I leave you, so unwell as you were?" said Mr. Markham kindly. "I have sent a note to Colleti not to expect me, and I shall pass the day with you, Emma. Ah! you know not what I have suffered on account of your indisposition. Emma, we never know the real value of anything till we are apprehensive of losing it."

"How true that is," said Emma, with a shudder, as she thought of George.

A low knock at the chamber door summoned Mr. Markham to it, and Emma heard the servant say,—

"Mr. Grant, sir, has called."—"Mr. Grant?" cried Mr. Markham. "I trust he has not gone again."

"No, sir; he is in the drawing-room."—"I am very glad of it," said the merchant. "Emma, I will persuade Grant to stay with us the whole day; it will amuse you more than anything else, I am sure, to talk with him over old occurrences and old friends."

Emma could not speak. The unsuspecting fondness of Mr. Markham sensibly touched her heart. She strove to rouse herself to say something, but the utmost she could produce was a faint and sickly smile.

"Get up as soon as you can, Emma, if you feel well enough," continued Mr. Markham, "while I go and at once secure George for the day."

So saying, the merchant left the room to welcome George Grant, and to inflict unknown pangs upon his generous heart by his professions of esteem.

Emma, left again to herself, strove to decide what she had better do. Then she resolved it was better as it was. Her husband's presence would act as a safeguard upon any outbreak of feeling either upon her part or on George's; and some opportunity might occur in the course of the day for her to tell him that she desired to see him no more, and to make that his last interview.

With this feeling Emma rose, and made a hasty toilette, which she had scarcely completed when Mr. Markham returned.

"My dear," he said, "George has consented to stay, but I had a great deal of trouble to persuade him. I don't know what can be the matter with him. He looks the very picture of wretchedness."—"Indeed!" gasped Emma, and she would not have uttered another word for kingdoms.

"Yes," continued Mr. Markham; "he positively rejects the share in the business, and really I don't know what to make of him. He is wonderfully altered. I feel quite sure that there is something upon his mind which gives him great uneasiness."—"You—you think so?" said Emma.

"Indeed, I do; and I tell you what will be the best plan, Emma. He won't tell me what affects him, but I dare say he would not refuse to confide it to you. Now, after dinner, I will run down to the counting house, and see what is doing, and while I am gone, you may, perhaps, find out what weighs so heavily upon his spirits. I dare say it is something about money matters, and that makes me anxious to know, because he shall be at once relieved and accommodated."

This speech fairly overcame Emma, and she felt that if she attempted to speak she should betray her feelings; so placing her arm within her husband's, she allowed him to lead her to the drawing room.

* * * * *

Her first glance at George Grant showed her that he, too, had suffered. He was very pale and his voice trembled as he paid the usual compliments of the morning.

"My dear Grant," said Mr. Markham, "you don't look at all like yourself, as I have been telling Emma. Why, I remember when you were full of life and health."—"That," said George, attempting to rally his spirits, "was before I went to Hamburgh."

"Ah, Hamburgh don't agree with everybody," continued Mr. Markham; "it is damp."—"It is," replied George.

"And yet you talk of going there again? You will make me suspect, George, that you have fallen in love with some Dutch damsel. Come, now, confess you have left your heart among the dikes and porcelain of Holland."—"My heart!" echoed George.

"Ah! now I am sure of it. You are in love, Grant,—madly, desperately in love, or you never could have said 'my heart!' in that tone. But here is luncheon, and I hope you are not so far gone as to lose your appetite."

George endeavoured to smile, and Emma combatted with her feelings somewhat successfully, so that the little party sat down to luncheon with tolerable harmony. Mr. Markham, however, had almost all the talk to himself. That Emma should be so silent and abstracted, he accounted for by her recent illness; and nothing could persuade him but that George had fallen in love since he left England, and his present evident depression was on account of his want of means of marrying the object of his affection. When luncheon was over, the merchant looked at his watch, and said gaily,—

"It wants now two hours and a half of dinner time, and I will walk down to the counting-house, and be back in time. I will leave you, George, in Mrs. Markham's care; only mind, you don't, in a fit of absence of mind, mistake her for your Dutch beauty, and make a declaration of love—eh, George?"

So saying, and without waiting for a reply, Mr. Markham left his home with as pure and as perfect a confidence in the virtue and integrity of the two beings he thus left together, as he had in the mercy and justice of Heaven. Emma heard the retreating footsteps of her husband upon the staircase; she heard the street door close behind him, and then she felt that the moment was come to put in practice all that she, in the silence and solitude of her chamber, projected.

She raised her eyes towards her lover, and, in a low, faltering voice, half-choked with emotion, she said,—

"George, go now,—go for ever—without a word, go."

Slowly he rose from his chair, and she saw him totter towards the door. There was a death-like paleness upon his face, and such was his agony of mind, that he was compelled to pause and lean against a table for support.

"George," said Emma, "you—you are very ill."—"No; it will pass away."—"I think, dear Emma, I am dying. I have heard of the mind, by its intense action, wearing out the body in a few short days, so that a young man may die of premature old age."

Emma wept bitterly.

"Before," continued George, "I go for ever, say, Emma, that you forgive me. My life has been a mistake. When I thought I was acting nobly and rightly in resigning you, Emma, as I did, it was but a false pride I was consulting, although the great God of Heaven knows I thought it for the best."—" It was noble," said Emma.

George shook his head.

"No, Emma, it was foolish only. I have involved you and myself in much unhappiness. We—we loved each other, Emma, and upon that love we ought to have built our hopes of happiness alone. The mistake I made was that the dear love glowing in our hearts, required wealth to gild it."

Emma looked in his face; through her tears she saw it beaming with tenderness, and she clasped her hands, saying,—

"George,—George, if you love me,—go."—"If I love you, Emma!" he repeated.

"Speak not again," she cried, frantically; "in every look, in every tone, there is *temptation*."—"I—I am going," he faltered; "but when far off, let me not tell my heart that we parted thus. Let us, for one brief moment, Emma, trust ourselves. One look, one pressure of the hand, to think of when my heart is lone and sad, and I am gone for ever!"

She covered her face with her hands, and wept with a bitterness of anguish that was awful to hear and look upon. Slowly George advanced, and took one of her hands in his. He pressed it to his lips—his manly heart was nearly broken! Unbidden tears came to his eyes, and with one deep sob of anguish, a sob which smote upon Emma's ears with more awful intensity than would the crack of doom, he tore himself from her, and reached the door.

"No, George," she cried, "not thus, not thus. That sob would haunt me, and I should go mad. I—I dare not, Geoge, part with you thus."

He sprang towards her, and opened his arms.

"Emma!" he said.

A radiant smile lit up h's face. It came upon the heart of the agonized girl like a gleam of sunlight. In that moment all was forgotten.

"George,—dear George," she whispered.—"My heart's treasure!" was his reply, as he clasped her gentle form to his breast; "mine—mine!"

"Yours only!" she gasped.

* * * * *

Husband, home, honour, all were forgotten. Emma had plunged into an abyss from whence there was no return. She awakened from that dream of joy an adulteress!

* * * * *

A loud knock at the street door announced the return of Mr. Markham—that knock seemed to strike upon Emma's heart. She sprang from her seat, exclaiming wildly,—

"Hide me—hide me! I cannot see him. No, no. Oh, George, kill me—I cannot meet my husband's eyes. Oh, God—oh, God! what *was* I, and what am I now?"—"Go to your chamber, Emma," cried George, "and recover yourself. Quick—oh, fly! I—I will make some excuse for you. God help us, Emma. We have erred, but, oh! for the love of peace, happiness, and life, compose yourself."

"Hark—hark!" cried Emma, "I hear his foot upon the stairs. He comes to upbraid me with my guilt. Oh, how shall I meet his eye?"—"For Heaven's sake, go," urged George; "Emma, if you would save bloodshed, if you would avert destruction from all you hold dear and sacred, go now, and do not see your husband until you can command your feelings."

"Yes, yes, I—I am going," gasped Emma, hysterically; "I am guilty, and must fly. I am going,—I am going."

With an unsteady step she crossed the room, and passed out at an opposite door to that at which Mr. Markham was upon the point of entering. Scarcely had the last flutter of her garments left the sight of George, when Mr. Markham, followed by Colleti, entered the room. "What," said the merchant, "all alone, George?—Well, now that is too bad of Emma."—"She—she," stammered George, "that is, sir, —Mrs. Markham is not very well."

"I'm afraid she's delicate," remarked Colleti.—"You are right, she is delicate," said Mr. Markham, who did not remark the sneering tone in which Colleti spoke.

"You don't look well, Mr. Grant," said Colleti, casting one of his strange glances at George.—"Not well, sir?" replied George; "I beg your pardon, I am very well."

"He is pale," said Mr. Markham. "Come, now, confess, George; Emma has been persuading you to stay in London, and you are agitated by the passion of love."—"Love!" echoed George.

"Yes; do you think me blind or stupid, that I cannot guess your situation?"—"Guess—my—sit—u—ation," gasped George, the colour forsaking his very lips, as he gazed in surprise at Mr. Markham, who immediately added—

"Yes, to be sure. Come now, George, make a clear breast."

George groaned.

"You have left your heart with some Dutch Venus, at Hamburgh,—eh, George?"—"Left my heart, sir!"

"Why, what's the matter with you? You can do nothing but repeat my words. Really you look ill, George."—"Perhaps," said Colleti, "Mr. Grant has some secret on his mind of fearful importance, and a stray word of yours, Mr. Markham, may have touched closer than you think."

George was saved from the necessity of a reply to this sarcastic speech by the sudden entrance of Emma by the door at which she had passed from the room. She was pale, but composed, and her voice was firm and unbroken, as she said,—

"I trust I have kept no one waiting."—"My dear," said Mr. Markham, "here is Colleti come to apologise to you for any unintentional offence he may have given you."

"Yes," said Colleti, assuming a horrible leer, "I most humbly apologise."—"I am willing to accept of Mr. Colleti's apologies," said Emma, coldly, but firmly.

"What unheard-of condescension!" cried Colleti, giving his features a horrible twist.—"Well, now," cried Mr. Markham, "that's all settled. Let us go to dinner."

Colleti immediately rose, and taking two gigantic strides across the room, offered his arm to Emma, to escort her to the dining-room.

There was an insolent familiarity in his manner, which made Emma shudder, at the same time that it aroused her indignation; but she had lost the one safeguard against impertinence. The high prerogative of virtue was no longer hers, and she dared not now refuse the arm of Colleti, for his words had been significant of an awful meaning, and a sickness of the heart came over Emma at the extreme possibility of Colleti, by some mysterious means, being acquainted with her guilt.

Mr. Markham was in high spirits during the dinner, and Colleti plied him with wine, and took a fiendish pleasure in turning the conversation always upon George Grant, and the supposed reasons he might have for remaining in London or leaving it. The longest day, however will have an end, and to the great relief of Emma the hour of rest came at last.

Mr. Markham attributed her subdued and nervous manner to him to ill-health, and was unremitting in his kind attentions to her, which, of course, to a mind constituted as Emma's was, was a greater punishment than coldness or neglect—a keener torture than the most bitter reproaches could have inflicted.

She lay the whole of that night in sleepless anxiety and misery, and it was not until the morning sun was stealing gently into the chamber that exhausted nature sunk into repose.

Mr. Markham, finding Emma in a deep sleep when he rose, would not disturb her, but leaving orders to say that he had gone to his counting-house, and would not be back till dinner-time, left his house, full of regret at the apparently delicate state of his wife's health.

It was nearly eleven o'clock when Emma awoke, and, having summoned her maid, she learnt the message that Mr. Markham had left. It was a relief to her to find that he had gone, and that she had the day before her to decide upon some course of action.

"Mary," said Emma to her maid, who was assisting her to dress, "let me be denied to all visitors this morning."—"I am sure, madam," replied the servant pertly, "that will seem very odd."

Emma looked at the girl in surprise, for she had always been remarkable for the excessive humility of her manner, and the submissiveness with which she spoke.

"Mary," said Emma to her maid, "what possesses you to answer me so strangely?"—"Oh!" replied the girl, "I only thought it odd."

"Odd, Mary?"—"Yes, madam; I know master don't like his friends sent from the door."

"What do you mean?" said Emma.—"Perhaps what I mean is a secret," said the girl, pertly.

"A—a—secret, Mary?"—"Yes, madam; may not I have a secret as well as my betters, if so be as they is my betters?"

Emma was silent, for in a moment the dreadful suspicion crossed her mind that she was in the power of this girl. Oh, what a terrible thing is guilt! Emma trembled before her own servant—a servant that she had taken from poverty and want, and treated kindly; now, she shook like an aspen leaf, as she said, in low, choking accents,—

"Mary, explain yourself fully. You wish to do so, or you would have said nothing. Go, on girl; never heed me. Say all you know."—"Then I know all, madam."

"All—all!"—"Oh! you may trust me. Mister Grant is a very handsome young man, to be sure, though I do pity my poor master."

"Cease—cease, girl!" shrieked Emma; "another word, and—and—I will kill you. How dare you! Leave my sight instantly. Is it for you to—to—yet, stay—stay—I have been kind to you—oh, God! you will not, cannot betray me? You see, Mary, the consequences of guilt; I was yesterday your mistress—I am now your suppliant."

Emma dropped her head on the dressing-table, and wept bitterly.

"I'm sure," said the girl, "I don't want to betray nobody —not I; only I don't like to know things and not be trusted. You may have as many lovers as you like, I'm sure, for all I care."—"Peace, girl,—peace," said Emma. "Listen to me; in a moment of weakness, when Heaven surely forgot and deserted me, I sinned. The weakness is past; a life of bitter repentance shall henceforward be my lot. I will never see George Grant again—never—never!"

"Oh, as to that," replied Mary, "I'm sure I wouldn't think of such a thing. Now, there's Mr. Colleti."—"Colleti, girl; what of him?"

"I'm quite sure he loves you."—"He—he love! Name him not; I do abhor that man. Attend to me, now, Mary, and do my bidding. You know my awful secret, and you shall see my repentance. Here is a note to Mr. Grant; take it, unopened as it is, and seal it yourself after reading it. You will see by it that I renounce his sight for ever."

"As you please, madam," said the girl, taking the open note; "but I'm sure you'll think better of it."—"No—no— no!" cried Emma; "a thousand times no. Go, Mary, at once. The address is on the note. Now go, and let me feel that I have at least taken one step that is correct."

The girl left the room, and in the course of another half hour Emma, for change of scene, descended to the drawing room. She entered it without perceiving that it was not empty, and what was her horror when, turning, after closing the door, she beheld, lying negligently on a sofa, and leering at her with his horrible eyes—Colleti!

She was for a moment too much paralyzed with terror and amazement to move, and before she could recover, to her astonishment, he said, in a tone of hideous and insolent familiarity,—

"Emma, how are you this morning? And yet why do I ask? You are as you always are—divine."

Emma replied not, but turned at once to the door, and would have left the room, but Colleti called out in a loud tone,—

"Hold! Go, now, from me, and you go at the price of your honour, your husband's disgrace, and George Grant's life!"

Emma stood as if suddenly turned to stone.

"Oh!" sneered Colleti, "you will not go; I have stated weighty reasons."—"Man!" cried Emma, "or devil, if you be one, what mean you by these words?"

"You know," replied Colleti.—"This is some hideous dream," cried Emma; "a phantom of the imagination."—"No," said Colleti, "it is real and life-like. Mrs. Markham, I know everything; I can tell all—prove all."

Emma staggered to a seat. "But, then," continued Colleti, "what matters? I love you—adore you."

Emma wrung her hands in deep agony of heart.

"Be comforted, most charming of women," said Colleti; "your secret, serious one as it is, is safe with me—on conditions!"—"Lost—lost! I am lost!" cried Emma.

"By no means," interposed Colleti, bringing his hideous face close to hers; "you are saved instead of lost—saved, on conditions!"—"Conditions!" gasped Emma, "conditions!"

"Yes, can you not guess!"—"Guess! I—I will consent to banish him for ever. I have done so. I will lead a life of tears and bitter repentance. I will pray for pardon."

"Pho! pho!" cried Colleti, "no such thing. Leave prayers to the saints, and tears to children; I never shed one in my life. As for banishing your lover, that's all very well. All I ask of you is, to replace him with a richer, a more powerful, and quite as devoted a one."

Emma gazed at him as if scarcely understanding the import of his words, and, emboldened by her silence, he continued —

"All you have to do, my charming Emma, in order to ensure to yourself the twin blessings of concealment and love, is, to transfer to me the delicious kisses that you gave yesterday to another."—"Monster!" cried Emma, shuddering.

"As you please," said Colleti; "just cast those snowy arms around my neck, and press those dear, pouting lips to mine, while you breathe in my ear the fervent words 'Colleti, I love you.'"

Emma sprang to her feet, and with more force than it could be supposed she was capable of exerting, pushed him from her, crying,—

"Wretch—hated and abhorred wretch! dishonour, death, —all were preferable to thee. Proclaim my crime—crush me beneath the weight of my deep sin—tell my husband that I am a perjured wife—tell all the world—kill me—anything but thy base, polluting touch!"

Colleti's sallow face became of a livid purple with suppressed rage as he said,—

"The passion is well acted—now for the kisses!"

"Hark ye, sir," cried Emma; "you think I have no escape from the coil that is around me. I have, though. I can fly for refuge to death, leaving the task of retribution to him before whom your coward nature would shrink."

"Coward!" howled Colleti.—"Yes, coward," cried Emma; "if there be on God's earth one coward more contemptible and base than another, 'tis he who, having the power to blast the virtue of a woman, comes to make *conditions* for his silence. Coward—base coward!"

"Now, then, hear me," said Colleti. "If by to-morrow I find you in no more complying a mood, Mr. Markham shall know all; and when you are turned, as a guilty wretch, from your home, you will, perhaps, be glad to take refuge in the arms of him you now treat with so much scorn."— "Never—never!" gasped Emma; "I can still die."

"No," sneered Colleti, "women are hard to kill. You will not die. I will leave you now. Think on my words— reflect on my power. Your husband and your lover are both in my hands; you may destroy them, or you may save them. I know *all*."

Colleti departed, leaving the wretched Emma a prey to every agonizing feeling that can rend the human heart.

* * * * *

The morrow came, and Emma saw its bright sunlight with a shuddering horror. Again and again she asked herself the fearful questions,—"What horrors may occur before yon sun again sinks in the west? Shall I see it rise to-morrow, or is this day to be my last?"

Mr. Markham saw with a deep anxiety, that he did not attempt to conceal, the deep depression under which Emma was labouring. He endeavoured by every possible kindness and attention to render her more cheerful, and to such a mind as Emma's, what agony it was to receive from him she had so much injured such affection and solicitude. But one idea possessed her mind, and that was that George would act upon her letter, and fly for ever from England, and then she would seek in death oblivion from the memory of the past.

With a calm and awful resolution she arranged all this in her mind, and although her face was ghastly pale, and there was a look upon her countenance of unutterable woe, she did not betray, by even a stray word, the deep anguish of her soul.

In vain Mr. Markham earnestly entreated her to allow him to send for a physician. She replied to all his solicitations in the negative.

"No, I shall be better," she would say. "Do not heed my looks; they are fallacious—I am not ill."—"My dear," said Mr Markham, "I am afraid you don't see enough cheerful company. When I am away all the day upon business, you are too much alone. I am very glad we shall have some visiters again to-day."

"Visiters to-day?" said Emma.—"Yes; Colleti has quite invited himself, and you know I could not very well say, 'you shall not come;' so I pressed George Grant to come, in order to keep you company, and as a relief from Colleti, who is certainly not quite what is usually considered good company."

Emma could only reply to this news with a look so nearly approaching to despair, that, had Mr. Markham observed it, which he did not, it would have seriously alarmed him. Fortunately, however, his attention was called off at the moment by his letters being brought to him from the counting-house, and before he had done perusing them, Emma had, with great effort, succeeded in subduing her feelings so as to present no appearance of extraordinary agitation.

"I must leave you for a few hours," said Mr. Markham, after attentively perusing his letters.—"Do not—go," faltered

Emma, for the dreaded visit promised, or rather threatened, by Colleti, rose up before her mind in all its horrors.

"I will return as quickly as possible," said Mr. Markham; "but among these letters there is one which must be attended to by myself. At twelve o'clock I will be back. Keep up your spirits, and take care of yourself, for my sake, Emma."

Mr. Markham departed, and Emma, with a shuddering horror, awaited the visit of that awful man, who, she began to think, was appointed by fate to be her evil genius.

Ten - eleven o'clock came, and Emma was still alone. A gleam of hope stole across her heart that Colleti's last words were only idle threats, and that he was really convinced of the fruitlessness of further persecution. Every minute this idea strengthened in her mind, and a feeling of relief came over her.

"George," she thought, "shall go for ever! Then years of devotion to my husband may, in some measure, expiate my deep sin."

So absorbed was Emma in these reflections, that she did not observe the room door open, nor was she aware of the presence of any one, till the voice of George Grant recalled her to herself by pronouncing her name.

Emma started, and hastily withdrew the hand he would have clasped in his own.

"George," she said, "this is ungenerous,—unkind. Why, oh, why do you come here? Why did you not act upon the letter I sent to you?"—"The letter!" said George; "I have received no letter from you, Emma."

"You—you are sure?"—"As sure as that I exist."

"Then," cried Emma, clasping her hands with a despairing look, "we are lost! My suspicions of my servant have now resolved themselves to certainty."

"If," said George, "you mean the girl who attends upon you, I saw her in earnest conversation with Colleti."

Emma shuddered and sank upon a chair.

"George," she said, "all is over,—we are lost—lost!—Colleti, then, knows all."—"But—but—he is a man," gasped George; "he has some feeling."

"No, no; he has no feeling," cried Emma; "he is a fiend in human shape. Hear me, George; I feel convinced that some dreadful calamity will overwhelm us all, and it will be through the malice of that man."—"He dare not," said George.

Emma shook her head.

"Indeed, he dare do any evil, George. I doubt not but he is in possession of the letter I wrote for your eye alone. That would of itself be condemnation."—"Condemnation, Emma?"

"Yes, George; by bitter experience, we shall find that the ways of guilt are tortuous and intricate. That letter, which, if faithfully delivered, might have released us both from much suffering, may now prove our utter destruction."—"This Colleti," cried George, "shall not be the man you have to fear. Before another hour elapses I will see him; I will tax him with all he knows. I will wring from him his intentions, and I will dare him, for very fear of personal injury, to so much as utter a word against you."

"Alas! alas!" cried Emma, "you do not know the man you talk of, George. He is wild and revengeful. He has the art and the cunning of a demon. Honour he knows not. There is nothing in the shape of sympathy or feeling that he will allow to stand between him and any object his bad heart is set upon. George, George, all is vain. We may struggle, like birds in the net of the fowler, but the struggle is in vain. We are lost—lost—lost."—"No, no," vociferated George; "dear—dear, Emma, do not give way thus to despair. This man, this Colleti, is mortal."

"George," cried Emma, "what mean you? You would not kill him?"—"I have a fair quarrel with him," said George, "and he shall meet me face to face to decide that quarrel. If I fall, then his hatred, or whatever passion it is that thus stirs him against us, ought to be satisfied; if he fall, then there is one bad man the less in the world, and our mortal foe no more."

"Oh! this is wild talking," cried Emma; "Colleti is a man who will place himself on an equality with no one. His whole life is a series of underhand schemes to obtain false advantages. George, he will crush us both before he will give you the faintest chance of fairly coping with him."—"We shall see," cried George; "but first let us be assured that he has this letter. Ring for the girl you entrusted it to, Emma, and I will ask her for it."

With a trembling hand Emma rang the bell, and desired Mary might come to her. When the girl entered the room, it was at once evident, from her pert manner, that she guessed what she was sent for, and knew her own power.

"Mary," said Emma, "I gave you a letter for Mr. Grant." —"Very well, ma'am," said the girl, carelessly.

"Why did you not obey your mistress in the delivery to me?" said George, indignantly.—"Perhaps you'd like to strike me, Mister Grant?" said the girl.

"Answer me," cried George.—"That's as I please."

"Insolent menial!"—"Don't speak to me in that way," cried the girl, tossing her head affectedly; "I know what I know. I sha'n't answer any of your questions."

"Girl," said George, "look at your mistress. Have you no feeling for one who has rescued you from poverty and want, as I know she has?—Have you no gratitude?"—"Oh! that's all very fine," said Mary pertly, "but it don't make any difference to me."

"I believe it don't," said George; "you heartless, abandoned creature. Leave the room instantly. Were you a man, I would provide you a quicker passage through the window." —"Indeed," sneered the girl, as she left the room with an insolent air.

"You see, George," said Emma, mournfully, "how low guilt sinks us."

George was silent for several moments. He was evidently quite at a loss what to say or do. Perplexity and chagrin were stamped on his face, and he could only regard Emma with a look of deep compassion and agonizing tenderness.

"Oh! Emma,—Emma," he cried at length, "are there any means—by the sacrifice of my life even—of extricating you from the awful circumstances that surround you?"— "None—none," sighed Emma.

"Emma," he continued in a voice broken by the anguish of his feelings, "I—I foresee much evil—much misery. Your husband loves you, and may, in the course of time, forgive the past, if I, by the absence of hundreds of miles, show the sincerity of my deep repentance; or, if I thought my death would move him to forgive you, and even to think of me with pity instead of anger, I would not live!"—"Oh! speak not thus—speak not thus," cried Emma; "pursue your first thought of leaving England. Go this very day."

"I will—I will."—"Your absence may calm the passion which your presence might inflame to madness."

"And yet—yet, Emma, it looks so like cowardice to leave you."—"Heed not that, oh! heed not that," she cried. "What can you do to save me from my husband's most just reproaches? Would not any word of yours add fuel to the fire of his awakened resentment?"

"'Tis too true—too true!" gasped George; "but I cannot, will not, leave you at the mercy of this Colleti. Him I will seek, and wring from his fears a solemn promise of secrecy. The man who would wantonly betray a woman must be an abject coward. I will seek him at once; I fear him not." —"Then you won't have far to go," said Colleti, at this moment entering the room, and fixing one of his hideous glances upon George.

Emma was thunderstruck at this sudden appearance of Colleti, and for a few moments even George Grant seemed paralyzed by the appearance of that most singular man.

"Well," said Colleti, "are you dumb? You were but just now in great haste to see me. Here I am. What have you to say to me?"—"Much," cried George; "you have threatened this lady; those threats you shall retract."

"Shall!" sneered Colleti, "that is a bold word."—"I meant it as such," replied George; "digest it as you may. You are a coward—you know you are a coward. The fears of such men as you can always be successfully appealed to, for they know none of the more noble feelings of the mind. Now, Colleti, I threaten you, if you dare, by word or action, to insult or injure this lady, I will take ample and personal vengeance."

"Now, if I were a passionate fool, like yourself," said Colleti, calmly, "I should storm and rage until I exhausted my fury; but I know better. You cannot move me. Come, now, I will offer you both easy terms. You, George Grant, shall leave this country for ever."

"That I am most willing to do," said George.

"Exactly," sneered Colleti; "and in your absence this charming lady will console herself——"—"Yes," said George, "she will console herself with the conviction that she is doing right."

"Humph! exactly," said Colleti; "but there is another source of consolation, which I shall make more particular

mention of shortly. First, then, George Grant, let me tell you that I look over your boyish insolence, because I despise you too much to resent it."—"Or else dare not," said George; "is not that nearer the truth?"

"I may remark," said Colleti, throwing himself into a seat, "that time to you is rather precious; Mr. Markham returns at twelve o'clock: it now wants twenty minutes to that hour. Unless we come to some amicable and pleasant arrangement before that time, I shall communicate to him *all* I know, and bring forward as evidence the girl Mary, and your letter, madam, addressed to this silly young man, urging him to leave this country, for reasons which cannot for a moment be mistaken."

Emma could not speak. She covered her face with her hands, and sobbed bitterly. Her tears, however, did not appear to have the least effect upon Colleti, who, with a countenance quite unmoved, awaited George's reply.

"How dared you appropriate a letter addressed to me?" cried Grant.—"Oh!" said Colleti, "I am quite above making petty mysteries; they only confuse affairs. I gave the girl Mary twenty guineas for that letter; so, you see, I bought her over thoroughly to my interests. You had no chance with her, unless you could have outbidden me. You see how frank and candid I am."

"Man or devil," cried George, "for I know not which you are, can it pleasure you to spread death and despair into a peaceful family?"

"Ay," cried Emma, suddenly, "Colleti, you have, you must have, some human feelings. At the bottom of your heart there must be some kindly emotion. Have mercy."—"How beautiful she looks," said Colleti, as if appealing to George's judgment about some quite indifferent matter.

"Infamous scoundrel!" cried George, losing all patience, "I defy thee."—"Do you, indeed," sneered Colleti.

"Ay, do your worst. Monster of vice—villain as you are, we may yet escape you."—"My worst?" said Colleti; "my worst, young man, you can have no notion of in your puny mind. I could destroy you, Markham, and this female here, who will in time be taught to love me as easily—ay, as easily as I could save you all."

"This must be some hideous dream," cried Emma; "there can be no human heart so utterly devoid of common humanity."—"It may be a dream," said Colleti; "only think of awakening in my arms."

"I can bear this insolence no longer," said George Grant.

As he spoke he rose, and dealt Colleti such a blow in the face that his gaunt frame swerved under it, and he nearly lost his balance. Then for an instant a storm of passion seemed to be kindling in his eyes; but that again dissipated, and although blood was upon his face, and a large contused wound betokened the force of the blow, he laughed, actually laughed, and rising from a chair into which he had staggered under the influence of the sudden attack upon him, he rang the bell as calmly as if nothing had happened.

The summons was answered in a moment by Mary, who, from the quickness of her entrance, could not have been far from the key-hole of the room door.

Colleti took a letter from his pocket, and handed it to the girl.

"Mary," he said, "stand in the hall, and when your master comes in, do you give him this letter, and beg him to read it at once."—"Certainly, sir," replied the girl, and she immediately left the room.

At that moment Mr. Markham's well known knock sounded on the street door.

"There is yet time," cried Colleti; "say you will love me." He darted towards Emma, and seized her arm.

"No, no," she cried; "death is preferable."—"Another moment, and all is lost!"

"Let all be lost, then!"

Colleti, through his clenched teeth, uttered a bitter—an appalling curse, and walked to the window.

George stood motionless, with his hands clasped in mute despair. He could not move—he could not speak—he could not even think. It seemed to him as if the world was coming that moment to an end.

Again Mr. Markham's knock sounded on the street door, and it would seem as if Mary suspected she might be called back; but such was not the case. Colleti never looked from the window at the second knock, and Emma and George kept a profound silence. They heard the door opened—they heard it closed. There was an awful stillness in the house. They could almost hear the beating of each other's hearts. Suddenly there was a rushing sound of footsteps. George instinctively flew to Emma's side. She threw her arm around him, and with a piercing shriek fainted on his breast.

"The time has passed," said Colleti.

George heard him not. His eyes were riveted on the door, and his whole attention was absorbed in the expectation of the immediate appearance of Mr. Markham. Still he came not. Nay, if it were he, he had evidently rushed past the door to the upper part of the house.

A look of surprise even began to creep over the countenance of Colleti, when again the hurried step was heard descending the flight of stairs leading to the rooms above, and the next moment the room door was dashed open, and Mr. Markham appeared, pale, ghastly, and dreadfully excited, with the open letter in his one hand, and a brace of pistols in the other which he had been to his bed room to procure.

"Villain," cried Markham, fixing his flashing eyes upon George,—"villain—false hearted wretch—I have nourished a serpent in my bosom and it has stung me!"—"Mr. Markham," said George. "I am here. Take my life, if it so please you. You cannot reproach me more than I do myself. Say to me what you please, and then kill me."

"No!" shrieked Markham. "I—I will not die on the scaffold for a wretch like you. Mr. Colleti, you are here a witness. Here are pistols; take your choice, black-hearted villain! One or both of us shall perish here, in this room."—"You are certainly a very injured man, my dear Markham," said Colleti.

"Take your weapon, sir. Quick—quick!" screamed Markham, thrusting the pistols close to George, who took one of them with the abstracted air of a man in a dream.

Mr. Markham turned and retreated several steps; then, facing George, who held the pistol listlessly in his hand, he cried,—

"Fire!—fire!—revenge!"

A deafening report immediately followed, and when the smoke cleared away, George Grant was still standing like one in a trance, and Mr. Markham was lying on the floor with a ghastly wound in his face.

The report of the pistols acting so suddenly upon the nervous system of Emma, recovered her from her state of insensibility. She started up with a shrill scream that filled the house with its awful echo, and, ere that echo had ceased to reverberate, Emma was an *idiot!*

Her reason had fled for ever! She sat down by the still breathing body of her husband, and drew fantastic figures on the carpet.

Colleti slid across the room like the father of all evil, and whispered in George Grant's ear,—

"Well, are you ready for the gibbet?"—"Are you really the arch enemy of mankind?" gasped George.

"No, I am Colleti, the *respectable* merchant."—"Then I can kill you!" cried George, in a voice of thunder, and he fastened his hands about the throat of Colleti with a power lent him by despair.

* * * * *

The girl Mary, hearing, it appears, the report of the pistols, was alarmed at what she had been instrumental in doing, and my residence being close at hand, she rushed from Mr. Markham's house to mine, and with frantic gestures implored my professional assistance, exclaiming that some one was murdered.

I made what haste I could, and my first introduction to the whole affair was being shown into the drawing-room just at the crisis at which I have left off my narrative, the particulars of which I collected afterwards.

Colleti was bent backwards over the arm of a sofa. He was quite dead. His neck was mangled and broken, and George had fled no one knew whither. He had mysteriously disappeared, and to this day his fate is as complete a mystery as ever.

Mr. Markham must have expired almost immediately, for his wound was most awful. The unhappy Emma—once the pride of all, the true hearted, the beloved, but alas! weak Emma—lived a few years in a lunatic asylum; and perhaps it was a great mercy from Heaven that she did not recover her reason till a few moments before her death, and then she merely said,—

"God bless me! I have dreamt. Now let me sleep again; it is not yet morning."

She left a child to mourn the death of its parents—it was the child of love.

THE MAD BRIDEGROOM;

OR, THE CROTCHET.

One morning, among my poor patients, there came to my house a respectable-looking widow woman, who, with much shaking of the head and some tears, begged to know if I could do anything for her son.

"He should have come here instead of you, madam," said I.—"Ah! sir," she replied, "he won't come. He'd murder both you and me if he thought we were at all consulting about him."

"Indeed," said I; "you are certainly very kind to draw me into so dangerous a piece of business. Your son must be mad."—"No, no," said the poor woman, with a sigh, "he's only got a *crotchet*——"

"A what, madam?"—"In his head, sir."—"Something in his head? No wonder he's mad."

"You misunderstand me, sir. I mean, by crotchet, that he is only a little cracked about one thing—that's what is called a crotchet."

"Really," said I, "you quite instruct me. We medical men, in our conceit, call that disease monomania; but crotchet, I dare say, will do quite as well."—"But you must know, doctor, that a lady that I know was cured by you—oh! cured completely."

"From monomania," said I, "or a crotchet?"—"No, not exactly, but something very similar."

"Indeed! Who was the lady?"—"Mrs. Angerstein. Knowing what a deal of good you had done to her, I thought of coming to you, you see, doctor."

"But, my good lady," said I, "Mrs. Angerstein had no crotchet, as you call it. Her disease was a complaint on the lungs."—"Well, as I always say," replied the widow, "a complaint is a complaint, and a doctor is a doctor."

She looked at me quite triumphantly after this piece of logic, which certainly I had no ready means of controverting; so I merely said,—

"Well, madam, I am not prepared to assert that a doctor is not a doctor; but as my time is rather precious, will you be so good as to tell me at once what your son's crotchet happens to be?"—"Why, sir, my son Tom is a Universal Bridegroom."

"A what?"—"A Universal Bridegroom, sir."

"Can you be a little more explanatory, madam?"—"Certainly, sir; for as I often says, who's to understand a thing all at once? Seeing's believing, says, you, however."

"As quick as you conveniently can, madam," said I fidgetting dreadfully.—"Then you shall hear, sir. Jemima Jenkins——"

"Why, what's Jemima Jenkins? Has she a crotchet too?"

"No, sir, but she's a hussy, that's what she is! Oh, if I had her here."

"Madam," said I, "I cannot waste any more time upon you. Good morning."—"I'll tell you in a moment, doctor," she cried. "Jemima Jenkins gave my Tom every encouragement."

"Did she?" said I; "then Jemima Jenkins ought to have known better."—"She flirted with him here,—flirted with him there,—walked with him to so and so,—talked with him."

I was fairly beaten by the woman's perseverance, and sat down on my chair again with the grace of a martyr.

"I thought you'd be interested," said the widow, with a complacent smile; "well, as I was saying, Jemima Jenkins was quite set down to be my son Tom's wife, you see, doctor, and the day was fixed for the wedding.—You may guess what a *cumflustration* I was in."—"A what?"—"A cumflustration."

"Oh! very well. Pray go on."—"Well, what do you think that hussy did?"

"Jemima Jenkins?"—"Yes, to be sure."

"How can I tell you, madam, what she did?"—"Can't you guess?"

"Certainly not."—"Just try, now. I'm sure you won't guess right."

"So am I, quite sure."—"But do try, now, doctor."

"Why, she—she married your son Tom."—"No, she didn't."

"She went mad—died—hung herself—ran away?"—"No, no, no."

"Then I don't know what she did."—"I'll tell you, then, and you'll be quite taken by surprise—she married the baker."

"Oh!" said I.—"What do you think of her now, doctor?"

"Why, really, I—I don't know what to think. The circumstance is of that astonishing and romantic character."—"You are a sensible man, doctor," said the widow.

"Thank you, ma'am," said I; "but when it's quite convenient for you to go on with your story, I shall be materially obliged."—"Certainly doctor. Well, my son, from that very day as Jemima Jenkins married the baker, took his crotchet. He went to the church they were going to be married at. He dressed like a bridegroom."

"Indeed!"—"Yes, he did; white trousers, pumps, ribbed silk stockings, and yellow waistcoat,—it's enough to break a heart o' hard flint to think on it. Blue coat—excuse my tears—brass buttons. Think, doctor, of a mother's feelings—no, I mean the best double gilt. Oh, dear! oh, dear!—a fancy cravat! Couldn't you give me a glass of water? Fawn colour, with blue sprigs on it—oh, oh, oh, oh—straw coloured Berlins. I shall faint, I am sure I shall faint away—and his father's watch. Don't you feel for me?—and a white satin bow, pinned on his breast, a bunch of flowers in his hand, and—my head swims round and round!"

I had the greatest difficulty to suppress a roar of laughter at this descriptive speech; but gravity is part of the physician's trade, so I merely said,—

"Dear me, that was all very shocking indeed. What happened next?"—"He—he went to the church, doctor," continued the widow, blowing her nose with excess of feeling, "and in the middle of the ceremony he gives the baker a push, and says,—'I'm the bridegroom!'"

"And what did the baker do?"—"Why, made bread, and cheese, and so on."

"But I mean what did he do when your son gave him the push?"—"Oh! my son was too many for the baker, a low wretch! But Jemima Jenkins, she fainted away, and the beadle was called."

"Well, ma'am, what then?"—"Why, doctor, my Tom he laid hold o' the rails of the communion table, and away they all came, so that's how they conquered him, you see, sir."

"And the baker married Jemima Jenkins?"—"Oh! the hussy, she did marry the baker, and ever since then my—my poor Tom goes to all the weddings in that very identical beautiful dress, and he always fancies it's his own wedding, and when—when—when—"

The widow seemed quite overcome by her feelings, and I really pitied the poor, simple-hearted woman, although there was much of the ludicrous in her story.

"When what?" I said. "If I can do anything for your son you may depend it will give me great pleasure."—"When the dear clergyman, white sleeves and all, says, 'Will you take this man?'—oh, oh, oh!"

"Compose yourself," said I.—"My Tom, he—he rushes forward, and he says with a scream, 'I—I'm the bridegroom!' and he really thinks he is."

"A decided case of monomania," said I.—"Then, doctor, the clergyman sometimes drops his book, and sometimes—oh, dear! oh, dear!— he calls out murder! and the bride always faints away."

"I can imagine all that," said I.—"And the bridegroom always swears, except one nervous gentleman, and he ran out of the church, calling, fire!"

"Upon my word," said I, "it's quite distressing to you, I dare say."—"And it's all owing to Jemima Jenkins as was—Mrs. Luckydaddle as is. Oh, oh, oh!"

"What an odd name! That's the baker's singular cognomen, I suppose?"—"Yes, yes. There she is to be seen any morning with a blond cap,—only imagine my feelings—and pink ribbons!—serving the first batch of rolls, while my heart's breaking—with black silk mittens!"

"I really feel for you," said I.

The poor woman wrung her hands, and became deeply affected. The tears coursed each other down her cheeks, and, in spite of the ridiculousness of the whole affair, I could not but commiserate with the feelings of the mother.

"Let me advise you," said I, "to apply to the parish authorities. They will take care of your son until this monomania is gone. I dare say it is curable; but it is quite out of my power to apply any immediate remedy. In these cases medicine is of no avail whatever."—"My—my poor Tom!" sobbed the widow; "oh, oh! that odious Jemima Jenkins!"

Here the poor creature showed such unequivocal symptoms of hysterics, that I hastily quitted the room and ran up stairs to my bed-room, to get some camphorated ammonia that I knew was there, to restore her.

I was not gone above three or four minutes, but when I returned my widow was gone!

I rang the bell hastily, and when the footman answered the summons, I said,—

"Has that widow woman left the house?"—"Yes, sir."

"When?"—"Just as you went up stairs, sir."

I cast my eyes on the table, and in one moment the whole truth flashed across my mind—my gold watch was gone! I glanced to the sideboard—a silver cup, worth twenty guineas, was likewise gone!

My servant ran out into the street after the widow, but she was fairly off.

I never was so taken in in my life.

THE STEP-MOTHER;

OR, THE EARL'S CHILD.

I was upon the point of stepping into my carriage in order to pay my usual round of calls, when a footman arrived breathless and heated at my door, and inquired if I was within. Hearing the question, I returned to door of my hall, and asked him his business.

"The Earl of Broughton, sir," he said, "presents his compliments, and would be glad to see you immediately."

Now, the Earl of Broughton was very well known to me by name and reputation, but I had never even been in his company, and I said,—"Are you quite sure there is no mistake? I am Dr. ——; were you desired to come to me?"—"Yes, sir, I am quite right; I am sure I am right."

"Is it a case of illness?"—"Yes, sir; young Lord Ratcliffe is very ill."

"Who is he?"—"The earl's eldest son, sir."

"Very well. You can ride with my coachman, and direct him. I will go to the earl's first."

All this was very quickly settled, and the carriage stopped at a very handsome house in a fashionable square westward.

I was evidently expected, and upon alighting was at once shown into a small, but exquisitely fitted and furnished boudoir. That it was a private and favourite room of a lady, I could easily perceive, by the number of little costly nicknacks that were strewn about, as well as by several ornaments connected with feminine costume, which were upon a couch of pale green satin, that stood between two windows.

I was kept about ten minutes before any one appeared, and then the door suddenly opened, and a lady entered the room. She was certainly very handsome. Her age I guessed was about twenty-two, and the elegant and exceedingly tasteful morning dress in which she was attired conduced to show her fine figure to the greatest possible advantage. Altogether she was a fine finished specimen of an English lady belonging to a very high class of society.

There was a hurried manner about her as she entered, and, there was a particular anxious look upon her beautiful face, which struck me directly as being something very different from mere uneasiness, or even grief at the illness of one near or dear.

I rose, and handed her a chair, which she accepted with the air of an empress.

"Pray, sir, be seated," she said; "I presume you are Dr. ——?"—"Yes, madam."

"Yes, yes," she repeated nervously: "you know me?"—"I have not that honour, madam."

"Oh, I beg your pardon; I ought to have announced myself. I am the Countess Broughton."—"I certainly did not know your ladyship," said I, "as I have not, to my knowledge, ever had the honour of seeing you before."

"The earl, doctor, is—is so wrapped up, heart and soul, as I may say, in Lord Ratcliffe, that he thinks him very ill, when such is not the case."—"That is too common an occurrence," said I, "to surprise a physician. I may be more candid than prudent, perhaps, when I say that our imaginary patients are more numerous than our real ones."

"Yes, indeed. Oh, certainly, by all means," said the countess, with an abstracted air, that convinced me she had paid no attention whatever to what I had said.

"What can be the meaning of all this?" thought I; "there is some mystery here."

She interrupted my meditations by suddenly saying,—

"So you understand, doctor? You must not suppose that Lord Ratcliffe is really seriously ill; I assure you it is no such thing."—"I am not an alarmist, your ladyship," I replied, "and rest assured I should think it most unwarrantable on my part to exaggerate the case of any patient."

"Oh! of course; yes, yes," she replied; "but, you know, children are deceptive. You might fancy Lord Ratcliffe ill, when he is not."

I bowed to this equivocal compliment, and she added, with an earnest pertinacity that quite puzzled me,—

"I again assure you, he is not very ill. A slight cold,—perhaps a little fever,—but that is all. I am certain you will agree with me, that he is but very slightly indisposed."—"It will give me great pleasure to do so," said I.

"Yes, yes; you see I am right."—"Your ladyship forgets that I have not yet seen my patient."

"No, true; I am forgetful. Pray pardon me, doctor, if I give you your fee beforehand, while I recollect it."—"As your ladyship pleases," said I, rather amazed at the whole affair.

She took out her purse, and placing in my hand two ten pound notes, she looked fixedly in my face, and said,—

"You will find that Lord Ratcliffe is only slightly indisposed by a cold."—"I hope so," said I.

"And does not require medical advice," she added.—"I hope so, likewise," said I.

She, however, accompanied her words with so peculiar a manner, that I felt no doubt but the unusually large fee was meant as a bribe to me to sanction her own opinion, and her manner altogether was so extraordinary, that I almost began to doubt her sanity.

"Your ladyship has, I dare say, taken a correct view of the case, but it is impossible I can give an opinion as yet, for not only have I never seen Lord Ratcliffe, but I was not aware of the existence of such a person, as I had no knowledge whatever of your ladyship or the earl."

"Oh! the earl is terribly nervous and anxious," she said. "He thinks Ratcliffe is very bad indeed, and I don't, so, you see, we are quite at issue about it."

"How long has Lord Ratcliffe been ill?" said I.

She stammered, and turned pale and red by turn as she said,—

"About—about—a month."—"A month?"

"Yes, very slightly—a little indisposition only."—"May I ask how old is the young lord?"

"Eight," she replied.—"Eight," thought I; "you cannot be his mother."

She seemed to read my thoughts, and said, with an air of great confusion,—

"Lord Ratcliffe is the earl's only son by his first countess."

I merely bowed to this piece of information.

"His only son," replied the countess, "heir to his earldom, his honours, and his estates."

A wild kind of expression came over her face as she spoke, and fire seemed to flash actually from her eyes as she bent them upon me with a glance that made me wink again. Physicians may say anything, so I asked, quite in a calm, off-hand manner,—

"Has your ladyship any children?"—"One," she said, with a tone of voice that quite startled me.

"A girl?" said I.—"No, a boy."

"Oh!" I involuntarily cried; but before we could say any more, the door opened, and a gentlemanly-looking man walked in. I immediately rose, and the countess said,—

"My dear, this is Dr. ——: and this," turning to me, "is the Earl of Broughton."—"Sir," said the earl, "I sent for you quite in opposition to the wishes of the countess. She thinks that my boy has only a slight cold, but really I ——"

"Now, my dear Broughton," said the countess, "I have told Dr. —— all that, and how fidgetty you are, and so on."—"Oh! very well; then that's enough," said the good-tempered earl, who, I soon saw, was one of those easy men who are led by anybody who chooses to take the control of them.

"I have told Dr. ——," continued the countess, "that poor Ratcliffe has only a slight cold."—"Well, I hope so, I'm sure," said the earl, in a submissive kind of tone; "but you know, my dear, I could not feel satisfied without sending for somebody. Sir ——, our medical friend," he added, turning to me, "is at Windsor, and so I did myself the pleasure of sending for you, doctor, having heard so much of your skill."

"Your lordship is very kind," said I: "you and her ladyship may depend upon my paying every attention."—"Well, now, you see, my dear," said the earl, "that's all very satisfactory indeed. Will you ring for Ratcliffe?"

"I think we had better take Dr. —— to him," said the countess; "he really is so well, that I don't like to drag him from his own room, with all his playthings and amusement."—"Very true," said the earl; "besides, his sickness might come on again."

"Sickness?" said I.—"Oh! nonsense," interposed the countess; "sickness, indeed! A little too much marmalade at dessert merely."

"Well, my dear," said the earl, "I know it's very kind and amiable of you to make Ratcliffe out as well as possible, but I really think he looks very delicate."

I began to despair of ever seeing my patient, between them both, and I suppose I showed some little impatience in my looks, for the earl said,—

"We are detaining Dr. —— very much. He must have a great many calls to make."—"Indeed I have," said I.

"Then, my dear, let us go at once."—"Stay a moment," said the countess, as she rang a hand-bell.

A servant immediately appeared.

"Where is Lord Ratcliffe?" said the countess.—"In the dining-room, my lady."

"Not alone?" said the earl.—"Miss Atkins is with him, your lordshi.."

"Oh, very well. Miss Atkins, doctor, is the most attentive and kind nurse to a sick child I ever heard of. She constantly attends Ratcliffe, who, in my opinion, is very delicate—very delicate indeed."—"That is your imagination," said the countess.

"Well, come, my dear, let us proceed."

* * * * *

Lying on a sofa, in a spacious, handsome dining-room, was the object of all this solicitude and apparent anxiety. In age the child did not look above six, although he was, as the countess had told me, eight. He was a fair-haired, delicate-looking boy, and there was the appearance of great languor and distress about him, which I was rather puzzled to account for.

"You see, doctor," said the countess, "that there is really nothing the matter."—"Nothing whatever, my lady," said a prim, disagreeable-looking woman, who stood by the head of the sofa; "I assure your ladyship, that just before you came in his lordship was quite in high spirits."

The child turned his large, intelligent-looking dark blue eyes towards her, and if ever a look conveyed the lie direct to an assertion, that look did, and Miss Atkins, who, I afterwards found, was the prim-looking female, absolutely quailed beneath it.

"No doubt, no doubt," said the countess.—"Well, I'm very glad to hear it," cried the earl.

"Father," said the boy, and he stretched out his hand, and took that of the earl with an appearance of intense affection, which interested me greatly in the young sufferer.

I sat down by the side of the sofa, and took his other hand, saying,—

"Are you well?"

He turned his large, melancholy eyes to me, and for a few

minutes seemed to be intently studying my countenance, then, as the investigation seemed satisfactory, he smiled faintly, and shaking his head, replied,—

"No, no, not well."—"My dear Ratcliffe," interposed the countess, "don't say you are not well."

"Indeed it's quite wicked," chimed in Miss Atkins.

The boy did not condescend a reply, or even look at either of them, and the earl himself evidently did not know what to say. "Are you in pain?" said I.—"Not now," he replied; "oh, no; not now."

I felt his pulse; it was very feeble, and there was evidently great debility from some cause. I looked at his eyes; they were languid, and presented a peculiar appearance of lassitude and want of bodily energy.

"Are you sick?" said I.—"Yes; oh, so often," he replied.

"How can you say so?" cried Miss Atkins.—"Because it is true," said the boy. "Wicked Miss Atkins, how can you tell stories?"

Miss Atkins looked absolutely petrified at this bold accusation from a mere child, and I saw the colour fly from the cheek of the countess, leaving her very lips quite white.

"This is all very strange," thought I. "What can it all mean?"

I rose from the sofa, and intimated that I had done with my examination of my patient. The earl and countess immediately left the room with me, and as soon as we were in the lady's boudoir again, before I or the earl could say a word, the countess remarked—

"You see, doctor, that there is really nothing the matter, although I shall be glad to see you professionally whenever you think proper to favour us with a call."

"Pardon me, your ladyship," I said, gravely; "I cannot just yet take upon myself to say specifically what is amiss with Lord Ratcliffe; but there is a degree of weakness which is to me alarming."

"Alarming!" echoed the earl. "Good God!"

The countess I thought, for a moment, would have thrown something at me; she glared at me like an enraged tigress.

"Pho! pho!" she cried, making an effort to assume an unconcern, which I saw she was far from really feeling, "pho! pho! the child has a cold, and is naturally languid and sickly-looking."—"I must differ from your ladyship," said I, in as grave and firm a tone as I could assume.

"Do you then really, doctor," said the earl, "think my boy is very ill?"—"He is in a bad state of health."

"Which might be dangerous."—"Most certainly."

"That is your candid opinion?"—"It is."

"Do you hear, my dear? You are wrong; Dr. —— says Ratcliffe is really ill."

I was taken by surprise at the countess's reply. She completely altered her former tone, and bursting into tears, she cried,—

"Oh, no; can it be so? My poor dear Ratcliffe!"

The earl seemed completely taken in by this emotion of his lady, but I was not, for I fairly believed her tears were wrung from her in consequence of sheer vexation with me for not coinciding with her in opinion—an opinion which she had evidently some strong reason for endeavouring to propagate.

"Now be pacified," said the earl. "There is no positive danger just now, and, please God, my poor boy may be spared to me."—"No," I said, "I can see no positive and immediate danger now; but there is in the child, I repeat, an extraordinary debility, which must arise from some cause, however hidden that may be."

The countess dropped her head upon her hands, and was, or pretended to be, weeping, so that I could not see the expression of her face.

"What can be done?" said the earl.—"Not much in the way of medicine," I replied; "we must endeavour, by repeated trials, to find out what food agrees with him the best; that, then, he must have, and I should recommend gentle exercise in the open air."

"Yes, certainly," cried the earl.—"The country would do him a world of good," said the countess, suddenly looking up; "or suppose we go to Italy?"

I shook my head very gravely, as I replied to this remark,—

"Madam, I cannot recommend a warm climate in a case of such extreme debility as Lord Ratcliffe's. I should recommend rather his remaining in England, under careful treatment, the first object of which should be to discover the *cause* of the weakness."

I laid some emphasis on the word "cause," and I could see, as I did so, that the countess caught her breath convulsively, as if the word had given her a sudden twinge.

"That is very reasonable," said the earl; "I must remark, doctor, although you have greatly increased my anxiety regarding my poor boy, that you alleviate it at the same time, by your exceedingly rational view of the case."—"Of course we had everything to expect from the known skill of Dr. ——," said the countess, with the slightest possible sneer; "at the same time, my feelings will not permit me quite to agree with him regarding the state of our dear Ratcliffe."

"Ah!" said the earl, "you are so wrapped up in that dear child's health and welfare, that you cannot permit yourself to confess that you think him ill."—"What does Lord Ratcliffe principally take?" said I; "that is, does he take solids or liquids most?"

"Latterly," said the earl, "he can scarcely touch meat. His appetite used to be very good indeed, and he never had an ailment, except such as are incidental to children."—"Then it is only lately that this extraordinary weakness has come over him?"

"Within a very short time," said the earl.—"My dear Broughton," said the countess, "how can you say so? You know Ratcliffe was always delicate, and I had apprehensions two years ago with regard to his health."

"But if he were delicate," said the earl, "you know he was not in his present state."—"If you will permit me," said I, "I will leave a prescription which will embrace merely a medicine calculated to improve the digestion, and I will do myself the pleasure of calling again to-morrow. I should say, Lord Ratcliffe should be very carefully attended, and his diet should not be too liquid."

I wrote the prescription, and, as I had already lost more time than I could very well spare, I made haste to leave the residence of the Earl of Broughton.

* * * * *

For the whole of the day I could not get out of my mind the pallid, sickly appearance of the really handsome boy about whose health there appeared to hang so much mystery. The countess's manner puzzled me amazingly. Her nervous fidgettiness concerning the young heir to the earldom and estates of Broughton—the wild fire that flashed from her eyes when she declared him to be so highly born—her anxiety to make him out only slightly indisposed, when he was really very ill—and last, although not least, her barefaced attempt, as I considered it, to bribe me by an unusually large fee, into backing her out in her opinion—all combined to raise in my mind unpleasant feelings and suspicions, which I was ashamed and afraid even to own to myself.

It happened that one of my calls was at the house of a Mrs. Michaelson, who belonged to that class of persons who know something of everybody and everything in London.

"I have been this morning," said I to this lady, "to make a call at Earl Broughton's."—"Indeed," she replied; "how very ridiculous Earl Broughton has made himself, to be sure. I suppose you know all about it, doctor. You physicians know everything."

"I believe, then, I am an exception," said I, "for when you mention it, I don't know even to what you allude."—"Is it possible? Why, you must know, then, that Earl Broughton married a governess."

"Then that is the young lady I saw this morning. She is very handsome?"—"Yes, and accomplished. But still it is a very ill-assorted match for an earl."

"She has a child, I understand?"—"Yes, but you know the the earl has a son by his first countess, and consequently my new lady's children will be very properly cut out of the inheritance; and when Lord Ratcliffe comes to his title and estates, it is to be hoped he will look upon the governess's family in the proper light."

"Certainly," said I; "everything should be looked upon in the proper light—families and pictures included."—"Now, doctor, you know very well what I mean; but who did you visit at Earl Broughton's?"

"Why, this very Lord Ratcliffe."—"Indeed! Gracious goodness! you don't think he is going to die?"

"I really can't tell," said I; "he is weak and unwell."—"I declare," said Mrs. Michaelson, "I don't know just now anything that would vex me so much as Lord Ratcliffe dying and making way for that odious governess's brats."

"He is a handsome and intelligent boy," said I, "and I should be sorry, for his own sake, to see him fall into an early grave."

* * * * *

At several other houses that I called at, I took occasion to mention incidentally my call at the earl's, and from every one I obtained the same information I had been favoured with by Mrs. Michaelson, although varying in manner according to the disposition of the different parties.

All this convinced me that it was certainly for the advantage of the present Countess Broughton that Lord Ratcliffe should die; but I am not one who is disposed to judge hastily and harshly of human nature, and I did not immediately conclude that because his death would be advantageous to the countess and her offspring, she wished him dead. Before I came to such a conclusion as that, I was resolved to see a great deal more of my interesting young patient and his stepmother.

It was, therefore, with a degree of interest much greater than a physician usually feels in a patient, that I the next day drove up to the Earl of Broughton's, making his house my first visit.

I was shown, as before, into the countess's private room, and I had scarcely been there a minute, when she entered the room, with an empressment of manner, and a confidential kind of air and expression towards me, that looked very like, to my mind, another attempt to coax me over to her own views and opinions, not to say projects, as regarded the young lord.

"I am very glad to see you, doctor," she said; "your prescription has done Ratcliffe a great deal of good. He seems decidedly better this morning."—"I am very glad to hear it," I replied; "but in his state of weakness we cannot expect any very rapid results from even the most judicious treatment."

"Certainly," she said; "that is quite true; but it is a great pleasure to see improvement, however slow it may be proceeding."

I bowed merely to this, and she added,—

"Shall I have the pleasure of showing you to your patient?"
—"If you please, madam," said I, opening the door for her.

She paused a moment, and then said in a confidential tone,

"Do you know, doctor, myself and the earl have the very highest opinion of your skill."—"You do me much honour, madam," said I

"But you know—you must have observed—how nervous and—and—I may say rather weak, the earl is. If he thought anything really serious was the matter with Ratcliffe, I should not wonder at his becoming very ill himself. So, between you and I, doctor, we will not frighten him, whatever may be our own opinions."

I was about to make some reply to this speech, which would probably not have been very pleasing to her ladyship, but a moment's reflection convinced me that it was better unsaid, and I took refuge in that most convenient of all subterfuges, —a very polite bow.

She seemed satisfied that she had made some progress with me, and then preceded me to the same room where I had before seen the young Lord Ratcliffe.

He was sitting on the sofa, with a table drawn close to him, on which were several books, one of which lay open before him. As I entered the room, he looked up languidly, and his eye brightened as he saw me.

"Good morning, sir," he said.—"Good morning," I replied. "I am glad to hear you are better."—"Oh, he's getting quite round again," said Miss Atkins, who I had not noticed to be in the room; "his cold will soon leave him."

"Lord Ratcliffe has no cold," said I, in a tone that at once put a stop to the loquacity of the woman, and I seated myself by the side of the child, who made room for me with an air of pleasure and satisfaction.

"Have you been sick again?" said I.—"No," he replied. "It's that nasty broth that makes sick."

"What broth?"—"Really, Ratcliffe," said the countess, in a voice that had something very strained and strange in its tones, "you pay me a very bad compliment indeed, by calling the broth by such a name."—"Yes, my lady," chimed in Miss Atkins, "I am sure nicer broth couldn't be. How can you call it nasty, sir?"

"Madam," said I, to the countess, "you would be doing me a favour if you would prevent this person from interfering between me and my patient.?"

I pointed to Miss Atkins as I spoke, although I intended the rebuke to apply to the countess as well. I saw the colour rush to the very brow of the countess, and she replied, after a moment's pause, "Oh, certainly; you can leave the room, Atkins."

Miss Atkins, after a look of venom at me, that, if looks could kill, would have at once snapped the thread of my professional career, walked out of the room.

I turned my attention again to the boy, and he looked up, in my face with so much earnest attention and confidence that I felt assured Miss Atkins occupied no very high place in his esteem.

"The broth is nasty" he said.—"Indeed?" said I. "Then you must not have any more of it."—"No more?" he cried. "I am so glad."

"I think, madam," said I, turning to the countess, "it is injudicious to give a weak stomach anything that it seems so much to loathe and reject. Imagination will convert really wholesome food into an emetic in some cases. I should advise by all means a discontinuance of the broth."—"Oh, certainly," said the countess.

"There," said I, "you hear, Ratcliffe, you are to have no more of the broth."—"I am so glad," said the boy; "but Miss Atkins will make me drink it."

"No, she will not now," said I. "You may depend she will not."

The boy shook his head, and by a side glance at the countess, I saw she was biting her lips with rage and vexation.

"Have you any pain?" I asked.—"Yes, a little."

"Where is it?"—"Here," he said, pointing to his throat. "Something burns me."

"Burns you?—in your throat?"—"Yes, it's that broth—I know it is."

"Nonsense," cried the countess, unable any longer to preserve her imposed silence. "Broth create such a sensation!— You know, doctor, that is impossible—quite ridiculous."— "It may as well be discontinued," said I.

The door at this moment opened, and the earl, in his dressing-gown and slippers, entered the room. I rose to receive him, and after shaking hands cordially with me, he said,—

"Well, doctor, you find your patient better?"—"Certainly I do," I replied. "He complains of disliking some broths that have been given him, and I have ordered her ladyship to discontinue it."

"Broth!" said the earl—"what broth?"—"Mutton broth," said the countess. "I thought it the best possible thing for him; but as Dr. —— objects to it, of course he shall have no more."

"Certainly not," said the earl. "I really did not know exactly what he had. The countess, doctor, is so very careful of his diet. I have actually known her to be what I call messing about in her own room for hours, preparing something or another for poor Ratcliffe."

"I should think, my lord, that the plainer and simpler the food he takes, the more good it will do him. Give him twice a day a moderate quantity of roast mutton and bread. Do not, on any account, let him be drenched with slops—medicine he does not require. Give him no sauces. Let him take gentle exercise. If he is fond of riding, get him a pony, and let him be in the parks every day, no matter how cold it is."

"A pony!" said the boy; "oh, papa, you will let me have the pony again?"—"Again?" said I.

"Why, he had a pony, and was very fond of it," said the earl; "but the countess was so decidedly of opinion that the exercise was too violent for him, that she would not allow him to ride it for the last two months."

"He always came home exhausted," said the countess. "I am quite sure that hard exercise is much too violent for such a delicate child."

"I would rather agree with you, madam," said I, "than differ; but I certainly vote for the pony."—"My pony, and no broth," cried the boy, rising from the sofa with renewed energy.

"There," said I, "he is better now."—"My dear Ratcliffe," said the earl, kissing him affectionately, while I could see the tears starting from the fond but weak father's eyes.

The countess looked very pale, and said nothing.

"Will you allow me," said I, "to give you no prescription to-day, as I am quite satisfied with no broth and the pony?"

"My dear sir," said the earl, "you shall just do as you like, only let us see you every day."

The young lord shook me heartily by the hand, and evidently looked upon me as the best friend in the world. The earl presented me with a five pound note as my fee, and I went away very well satisfied with my visit, although still terribly puzzled to satisfactorily account for the strange conduct of the countess.   *   *   *   *   *

LITERAL EXTRACTS FROM MY DIARY.

Aug. 21.—The young Lord Ratcliffe is much better; tells me he has had no broth.

Aug. 22.—The change in Lord Ratcliffe's appearance is astonishing in two days merely. The countess did not see me to-day, but the earl scarcely seems to know how to express his gratitude towards me, and the young lord welcomes me with unalloyed pleasure.

* * * *

Sept. 18.—Lord Ratcliffe is quite recovered. The Earl of Broughton has presented me with a hundred pounds, and the countess begs me to rely upon her eternal gratitude. What was the matter with him I cannot even dare tell, but certainly a change of diet, from something pernicious to real nutritious food, has rescued him from an alarming state of debility.

* * * *

After the above entry in my Diary, I find nothing concerning the Broughton family for at least two months, and then what occurred in relation to them I had better place before my readers in a more finished and connected form than it appears in the mere rough notes of my Diary.

One morning, then, towards the latter end of November, a hasty knock at my street door, immediately followed by a ring at the bell, that threatened dislocation to the wire, easily conveyed the impression to my mind that I was wanted immediately for some case of real or imagined danger—I say imagined, because the physician is far oftener sent for in a violent hurry, when he is not wanted at all, than when he really might be of most essential service.

I was sitting in a parlour close to the passage, and the moment the door was opened I heard a man say, as well as his want of breath would permit him,—

"The Earl of Broughton wishes to see Dr. —— immediately."

I instantly caught up my hat, and, to the surprise of the messenger, I darted past him, saying, "I am going to the earl's."

I fancy the messenger must have thought me next to a necromancer, for, glancing back to my door, after I had left it but a few paces, I saw him gaping after me in mute astonishment, with his hat lying at his feet, and his mouth so wide open, that it seemed questionable whether it would ever shut again.

I hailed the first hackney coach I saw, and directed the driver to make what expedition he could to the earl's house, in —— Square, the consequence of which was, that I was transported there at the extraordinary pace of at least five miles an hour, and after being half shaken to death, was deposited, with what is vulgarly called "pins and needles" in my feet, at the earl's door. From the lights which were hurrying to and fro in the windows, and the time I was kept at the door, I guessed that considerable confusion reigned within the mansion.

After knocking twice I was admitted, and upon giving in my name as Dr. ——, I was immediately shown into a small room, and before I had time to look about me, the countess appeared in the doorway.

The appearance of the Countess of Broughton was quite sufficient to have appalled any man of ordinary nerves, and, used as I was to scenes of all kinds, I confess that for a moment I was completely staggered by the strange, and I may almost say demoniac, expression of her countenance. Her hair hung nearly down to her waist in the wildest disorder, and, being of jet black, it contrasted quite painfully with the deathly white of her complexion—her very lips were colourless—her hands were clasped tightly, the knuckles standing out rigid and white, like those of a person in some fearful fit. Her eyes positively blazed; they looked like two burning coals set in her head, and as she thus confronted me I could see her make many convulsive, gasping efforts to speak, without being able to utter one intelligible sound.

I was both shocked and astonished at the extraordinary spectacle before me, and I exclaimed,—

"Good God! Lady Broughton, what is the matter?—what has happened?"— "No—nothing," she gasped. "Happened? Nothing, nothing. W—w—what could happen? What do *you* mean? You don't suspect me?"

I took her hand as I said,—

"Lady Broughton, you are excited and ill. Pray sit down, and calm yourself. Where is the earl?"—"With him," she said, "with him."

"With who?"—"Ratcliffe. It is nothing. He would send for you, but you see it is nothing."

"I think you had better retire to your own chamber, madam," said I. "Will you allow me to ring for assistance?" —"No, no, no!" she exclaimed, and she clutched me so tightly by the arm as to be absolutely painful. "No, I say, no; there's no danger, none whatever. 'Tis a delusion—all imagination. There is no danger, I say, none, none!"

"But I beg of you ——"—"Hush! hush!" she said. "Here is your fee. Why don't you call every day? I should be glad to see you. Your fee shall always be paid."

She with trembling hands took from the breast of her dress several bank notes, and held them towards me.

"No, Lady Broughton," said I. "I cannot thus impose upon you."— "Yes, yes, take them,—take them," she said.

I took the notes from her hand, and placed them on the table.

"Now," said I, "as your physician, I must insist upon your retiring to bed."— "I cannot," she replied; "I am quite well. Who says I am ill? Who dare say I am ill? I am only grieved—naturally grieved."

"Grieved at what?"—"At what! Why, do you think me destitute of all feeling? Because I am a stepmother, do you imagine me brutal?"

"By no means," said I. "Allow me to ring."— "No, no; I wanted, you see, to talk to you first. 'Tis quite a false alarm; but the earl is nervous, as you know."

"I certainly cannot say the alarm is altogether false," said I; "I am only surprised to see you out of your chamber."— "See me—me? I am not ill."

"I must say I think you are; and I am quite sure the earl must think so too."

The fact was I began to fancy that the countess's mind was affected, and her strange, incoherent remarks each moment strengthened that supposition. I expected to see the door open, and the earl or her attendants enter, for I doubted not but she had given them the slip in some way.

"Who said I was ill—or—or agitated?" she cried.—"No one." I replied. "Pray compose yourself."

My object now was to temporize with her, and amuse her mind till assistance should arrive to conduct her to her chamber, from whence, by the disordered state of her apparel, I had no doubt she had escaped.

"You will be much better if you will sit down and talk to me calmly," I said.—"Yes, quite, quite calmly," she repeated. "I will tell you first how it commenced, and then you will be better able to judge."

"How what commenced?"—"The illness, to be sure," she cried.

"Oh, yes, certainly," said I, looking anxiously to the door, and wondering no one appeared. "We retired to bed early last night," she said, "after a very slight supper. This morning there were some symptoms of uneasiness and feverish disposition; but no notice was taken of it, as we thought it might be merely accidental, and would wear off as the day proceeded. You quite understand me, doctor?"

"Oh, quite," said I, although I thought it very odd all the time for a sick person to be giving so curious and circumstantial an account of her own illness and its gradual approaches.—"I persuaded the earl that nothing was the matter," she continued, "although, to tell the truth, my own anxieties were awakened, and I watched every symptom very change of colour, with the greatest solicitude."

"Yes, yes," said I.—"The day then wore on much as usual, till about two hours ago, when there were evident signs of great mental restlessness."—"No doubt," thought I; "this is the strangest shape that insanity ever in my practice assumed."

"Then I advised the earl to send for you," she continued, "if in the course of another hour no favourable change took place."—"Exactly," said I.

"You may guess my state of mind, doctor?"—"Oh, yes, quite well."

"The harrowing nature of my feelings?— the throbbings of my pulse?"— "Of course. Pray be calm, my dear madam; do not agitate yourself by a description which must be distressing to you."

"And placed too," she added, after a moment's pause,— "placed in the peculiar position I am, with every eye watching me, every idle tongue ready to make comments upon my slightest and most innocent actions, my very maternal love and solicitude liable to be construed by a suspicious mind against me, you may guess, doctor, what a difficult, what a most ungracious task is mine."

For the life of me I could not make out what she meant,

and referring every word she uttered to mental aberration, I replied,—

"Certainly, madam, I feel for you very much."—"I knew—I was sure you would," she cried; "and, let what may happen, allow me the sweet consolation of knowing that I have made a stanch friend of Dr. ———."

"Certainly, madam."—"One who will put the best, the most charitable construction upon all—one who will not cause, by surmises and suspicions, grief and sorrow to pervade a whole family?"

"How could you suspect me to be capable of such things?" said I.—"Hush! hush! We understand each other — I may rely upon you?"

"You may, madam."

At this moment the door was opened so very suddenly that the countess gave a scream, and I, although not very nervous, could scarcely forbear an exclamation of surprise.

The Earl of Broughton, pale, anxious, and with the traces of deep grief upon his countenance, entered the room, exclaiming,—

"Good God! has he not come?" Then seeing me, he added,—

"Doctor, doctor, why waste precious moments here? Save my boy—my dear son—my boy—my poor boy. Oh, save him; doctor, save him!"

I stood transfixed with astonishment, looking from the earl to the countess, and from the countess to the earl, doubtful whether they were not both a little insane.

"My lord," I gasped, "w—what do you mean?"—"Mean?" he replied, wringing his hands; "are you mad, doctor?"

"Mad? No; are you?"—"I tell you he is dying."

"Who?" cried I, recovering all my faculties in a moment.—"My son, my dear boy!"

"Lord Ratcliffe?"—"Yes."

"Why, good God! madam, you have been detaining me here this quarter of an hour, and never so much as hinted at such a thing."—"False! false!" shrieked the countess; "it is false!"

She fell upon the floor in a swoon as she uttered these words, and Earl Broughton stood glaring around him like one possessed, or a man just awakened from some awful dream, the shadow of which still held his reason in bondage.

"Follow me," he suddenly cried, and darted from the room.

I followed, and although I soon lost sight of him, I continued to keep in his track, guided by the sound of his footsteps. Then a door opened, and I heard a sound of voices and lamentations. I darted forward, and entered a small bedchamber. It was full of people, but they all made way for me, and the first object that presented itself to my eyes was the Earl of Broughton standing at the foot of the bed, with his hands clasped in an attitude of inexpressible grief.

My eyes then fell upon the bed instantly, and pale, haggard, and convulsed, there lay the young Lord Ratcliffe.

I immediately laid my hand on the boy's heart; it still beat feebly. A cold perspiration was on his brow, and his features were fixed and livid.

"How has all this happened?" I said; "tell me, some of you, how and when all this occurred."—"Two hours ago, sir," cried several.

"Oh! save him,—save him!" groaned the earl.

I raised the boy in my arms; I examined his eyes, his mouth, and the feeble pulse, that scarcely could be noted.

"I will do what I can," said I, solemnly; "but this boy is poisoned."—"Poisoned!" shrieked the earl, and immediately fell down upon the floor like one struck with lightning.

"Poisoned!" echoed the servants, and they looked at each other pale and aghast.

From the symptoms I judged that some mineral poison had worked all the mischief.

"Bring me some warm water and soap directly," I cried

Several of the servants immediately rushed from the room to execute my orders, and in a few minutes I was supplied with what I required.

"Some of you remove the earl," I said; "he has only fainted."

While they lifted their unhappy master from the floor, I mixed the soap rapidly with the warm water, and taking some up in a glass, I raised the boy, and called to him loudly to drink.

He groaned deeply, and slightly opening his eyes, cried, in a voice of excruciating anguish,—

"Pain,—pain,—burning pain!—oh, such pain!"

Then an awful sickness came over him, and I thought as I held him that his fragile form could never stand that dreadful convulsion of the system.

"Ratcliffe," I cried, "look at me. I am your friend; I am Dr. ———. "Drink this, and you will not suffer so much pain. Drink it, Ratcliffe,—drink it."

He seemed to comprehend me, for he clutched my arm convulsively, and while I repeated in a loud tone,—

"Drink, Ratcliffe,—drink," he took a quantity of the soap and water I had prepared for him.

The good effects of the antidote soon became apparent. He was still dreadfully sick, but it was unattended with the burning pain and convulsive action which it had presented before. I plied him incessantly with the warm soap and water until he sank back upon the bed quite exhausted, and could take no more.

While all this was going on my thoughts were so much engrossed by my patient, that I forgot the very existence of the Earl of Broughton; but now that I had done all I could for the boy, and I saw that sleep was stealing over him, I bethought me to inquire for his father.

"Has the earl recovered?" I said, in a low tone.—"No, sir," was the reply.

"Where is the countess?"—"In her own room, sir."

"What are you?"—"The footman, sir."

"And you?" pointing to another.—"Coachman, sir," was the reply.

"Well, then," said I, "I leave you two in charge of this boy for a little time, while I go and speak to the earl. Do not disturb him, and on no account suffer any one but myself or the earl to enter this room."

The men stared, and one said,—

"Miss Atkins, please, sir, attends on my young master always."—"Listen to me," I said, solemnly; "if you permit Miss Atkins or the countess to come into this room, you will have the death of your young master to account for. Ask no questions, but do as I tell you. Now every one else leave the room, and some of you show me to the earl directly."

I saw the footman and coachman look at each other in amazement, but I was satisfied that they would obey my orders, and I followed another servant, who volunteered to show me to the chamber of the earl.

The unhappy nobleman was still insensible when I reached his room, but by the use of restoratives, which I always carry about with me, I soon restored him to a consciousness his situation.

When his eyes opened and met mine, I never shall forget the mournful earnestness of the gaze he cast on me. That look spoke more eloquently of the father's broken heart than the most glowing and impassioned language.

"Ratcliffe,—Ratcliffe!" he said, in a hasty whisper, "is—is ———."—"Spare yourself," said I, "Ratcliffe still lives."

With a cry of joy he clasped his hands, and uttered a fervent—

Thank God! you have saved him, doctor,—you have saved my poor boy"—"I think him better," said I, "but I cannot pronounce him out of danger. It is my duty to tell you, that I consider his situation as most precarious."

"But—but he lives?"—"Certainly he does."

"Let me see him; let me go to him."—"Pray do not," said I; "he has, from complete exhaustion, dropped into a slumber. The slightest excitement now would snap the slender thread that holds him to existence."

"Doctor!" almost shrieked the earl, suddenly, and so suddenly, too, that I started back several paces.—"Doctor, I recollect now; you—you said a word."—"What word?"

"You, in the excitement of the moment perhaps uttered an opinion."—"Earl Broughton," said I, slowly, "I cannot pretend to misunderstand you. I have no hesitation at all in saying, that Lord Ratcliffe has been poisoned."

The earl covered his face with his hands, and while he trembled excessively, he said,—

"Go on—go on."

"Months since," I continued, "a vague suspicion of this crossed my mind; but it was so awful, so fearful a thought, and involved such mighty consequences, that I strove to banish it from my mind, like a hideous spectre, as it was, haunting my brain and whispering to my fancy the most horrible suggestions."—"I—I can imagine all—all you thought," he gasped; "go on, doctor, go on."

"I declare to you, Earl Broughton, that when your son recovered, and grew strong and healthy, I felt a sensation as

truly delightful as you, his fond, doting father, could feel; for then I got fairly rid of my horrible suspicion, and I thanked Heaven many times that I had had the firmness to keep the dreadful thought locked up in my own breast."—"But—but now?" he said; "now?"

"Now suspicion has become certainty."—"Oh, God—oh, God!"

"The once fancied chimera of the imagination has shaped itself into an undoubted, unmistakeable reality. Your son has been poisoned!"—"Hush! hush!" he said; "oh, hush!" and he trembled to that excess that he could scarcely stand.

"I have done," said I.

With a painful emotion visible in every movement, he crept to the door, and with difficulty, on account of his shivering, turned the key in the lock; then, coming back to me, he laid hold of my arm with desperate energy, and placing his mouth close to my ear, he said, in a strange, hissing, unnatural whisper,—

"Do—you—think—*she* did it?"—"I would much rather give no opinion," said I; "in fact, I think I am quite unauthorized to attempt to criminate anybody."

"I—I am answered," he said.—"Answered, my lord?"

"Yes; I named no name, and yet you knew *who* I meant. God help me! And I lavished such love and tenderness upon her—no wish ungratified, no taste unindulged. God of Heaven! can it be possible that such crimes can have a place in such a form? She might have ruined my fortune or been false to my love, but—but to practice against my poor boy,—my dear Ratcliffe,—oh, horrible! horrible!"

I was silent, for I felt myself placed in an exceedingly awkward situation. I had no wish to become the accuser of the Countess of Broughton in a matter of life and death; and besides, as yet I had not a shadow of legal proof of her guilt, although I would have staked my eternal salvation upon the fact that the countess had endeavoured to get rid of the young Lord Ratcliffe by poison, in order to make way for her own progeny; and yet I felt that as a man, a father, and a Christian, I would not leave the earl and his child to the mercy of that unnatural stepmother. How to protect them, what to say, or what to do, puzzled me amazingly.

While these thoughts were passing in my mind, the earl continued to groan and rock himself to and fro, speaking occasionally in such an incoherent manner, that I felt convinced he was quite incapable of taking any rational step in the affair.

Before I could come to any conclusion on the subject, a tap at the door announced some one, and, the earl taking no notice, I opened it myself, and saw that the person demanding admittance was one of the servants I had left with young Lord Ratcliffe.

"If you please, sir," he said, "young master is awake."—"Awake! I will go to him."

With a rapid step I then sought the boy's chamber, and there, true enough, he was awake.

I looked into his face. I saw the restless movement of his little hands. *He was dying!*

He turned his unnaturally bright eyes upon me, and stretching out one of his little hands, he said,—

"Will you take it away?"—"Take what away, Ratcliffe?" said I; "don't you know me, my boy?"

"They are bees," he added, flinging his arms about him, and trying to brush away some imaginary objects that went flitting across his fast fading vision. I turned to the man who remained, and said in a low tone,—

"Fetch the earl instantly."

The man immediately left the room.

"Yes," said the boy, "fetch the earl; that's my own father —my own father."—"Ratcliffe," said I, "what have you had to eat?"

"Jelly—jelly," he said, hastily.

As he spoke he pointed to a green hock glass that stood upon a table near the bed. I immediately reached it.

"You had jelly in this?"—"Yes—yes."

I looked in the glass. There was something in it, and without a moment's hesitation I wrapped it up in my handkerchief, and put it in my pocket.

"It was my new mother," said the boy; "but she don't love me—she don't love me."

The earl at this moment entered the room, and staggered like a drunken man.

"Papa," said Ratcliffe.—"My boy—my own boy—God bless you, my Ratcliffe—God bless you!"

He folded the boy in his arms, and for several minutes nothing was heard in that chamber but the deep, agonising sobs of the unhappy father. Then he slowly unwound his arms from around his child, muttering,—

"God bless and preserve you, my Ratcliffe! God bless you, my boy!"

The earl's child was dead! He had breathed his last sigh upon his father's breast.

* * * *

For several minutes the earl did not seem to be aware of the death of his much-loved and murdered boy, and, for the life of me, I could not muster resolution to tell him. At length he started, and I saw an awful change come over his face.

Several times he dashed the tears from his eyes, and gazed wildly and fixedly upon the calm face of the boy. Then, in piercing accents, he exclaimed,—

"Doctor—doctor, he moves not! See how still my Ratcliffe is. He don't speak. God of Heaven! look at him. He is not dead!—no, no, Ratcliffe, my child—my beautiful boy, speak to your father! Why is this frightful, rigid look, doctor, upon his face? Tell me he is asleep, and take all I possess! Tell me—assure me this is but sleep!"

"It is the sleep of death!" said I.

"Death—death?" he repeated, as if the word scarcely conveyed a meaning to his mind.—"Yes," I added, "your child is dead."

He sank into a chair by the bed-side, and it was fortunate that tears came to his aid. I was very glad to see them flow, for I knew that they would relieve greatly his excited and overwrought feelings. I said nothing to him; I made no movement to attract his attention; I let him weep on, and it was not until I saw, or rather heard, that the storm of feeling was passing away, that I touched his arm, and said gently,—

"Earl Broughton, come with me."

He started to his feet, and I was much pleased to hear his first words.

"Doctor," he said, "my dear child is with his God in Heaven. I have now a duty to perform. My boy has been murdered!"

"He has been poisoned, I can aver," said I; "your whole household has heard me say as much. It is the truth, and I cannot now flinch from proclaiming it."

The earl walked to the door, saying,—

"Come, come, we will seek her."—"The countess?"

"Yes, the countess and the murderess.—She is the wife of my bosom—I loved her—but look there" (pointing to the bed). "Is that sight not enough to turn my heart to stone?" —"'Tis very sad," said I; "but what do you propose doing, my lord?"—"Come, come," was his only reply, and snatching a night lamp that was in the room, he walked out, and left me to follow him or not, as I pleased. I chose the former, and shutting the door of the chamber of death, I followed the earl in silence, wondering what he meant to do if he found the countess.

I said nothing, nor did the earl address me until we came to a door, which he opened, and, holding it in his hand, he said,—

"Doctor, I loved her; but you know I must have justice for my murdered boy."

He then entered the room, and I followed him. It was a large, handsome apartment, furnished in the most costly and luxurious style. It was surrounded by handsome couches, and the walls were resplendent with looking-glasses.

He paused but for a moment to cast his eyes around this room, and then, passing onwards, opened a door opposite the one we had entered, which at once conducted us into a bed-room. A costly bed stood in the middle of the gorgeous apartment, surmounted by a coronet, richly gilt.

The earl placed the lamp he carried upon the dressing-table, and turning to me, he pointed with a trembling hand to a door, saying in a low, agitated voice,—

"Doctor, she is there."

"The countess," said I, "should be judged either by the laws of her country, or left to the accusations of her own conscience. I deprecate all violence, my lord, and I trust you mean none."—"None, none," he said; "I wish to see her once again, that I may note if she be still human."

He laid his hand on the handle of the door he had pointed out to me, and strove to open it, but it resisted all his efforts.

"She has locked herself in," he said.

Then, raising his voice, he cried loudly,—

"Harriet! Harriet! open the door; I must and will see you. Open the door instantly."

No answer was returned, and he rattled furiously at the lock.—I was really afraid he meant to murder the countess.—"What is your intention?" said I; "tell me what it is you intend to do?"—"I know not," he cried. "Open the door, I say!"—Still there was no answer.

"Doctor," he said, "do you speak to her."

I approached the door, and cried aloud,—

"Countess Broughton, I am desired to call you by the earl. You need fear no violence; I am here, and will see that no harm is done."

Still there was no reply, and what immediately then occurred made me thankful that we were not successful in luring the countess from the room, if she were really there.

Apparently in an instant losing all control over himself, the earl, with a cry of rage that sounded more like the wild yell of a savage than a sound produced by a civilized being, drew from his pockets a pair of long duelling pistols, and, before I could raise my arm to prevent him, or even utter an exclamation to divert him from his purpose, he fired them both through the door, the balls with which they were loaded splitting and crashing the gilt panels in an extraordinary manner.

"Now," he shrieked, "now, fiend in human shape, may Heaven in its justice have guided the bullets to your heart." I sprang forward, and exclaimed,—

"Good God! sir, you are not justified in this violence. Earl Broughton, are you mad?"—"Yes, yes," he said, turning round upon me so suddenly as to make me jump again,— "yes, I am mad—raving mad!"

He made a rush at the door of the room he had fired into, and came with such force against it, that it gave way with a loud crash, and precipitated him into the room.

At the same moment I seized the bell-rope, and rang a peal that soon brought every servant in the house to my assistance.

"Follow me," I cried, and snatching up the lamp, which the earl had placed upon the dressing-table, I dashed into the room, followed closely by the servants, several of whom carried lights.

It was a small apartment, fitted up as a dressing-room, and at the end opposite the door was a very large couch. At my first hasty glance around the room I did not see the earl, but a second look showed me where he was.

Crouched up, like a wild animal ready for a deadly spring, upon the sofa, was the Earl of Broughton. His eyes were glaring like coals of fire; his face wore an awfully strange expression. My first glance was enough. I felt that he had become a dangerous lunatic! The servants all shrank back in horror. They would have fled from the room, for the pistols were in the hands of the earl, had I not stopped them by saying,—

"For God's sake, remain here. Those pistols are not now loaded."

Thus encouraged the domestics lingered close to the door, and fixing my eyes upon those of the earl, I said, in as bold a tone as I could assume, for I felt anything but comfortable,—

"Earl Broughton, do you not know me?"

A low growl was his only answer.

"I am Dr ——," I added; "come, will you go to bed now!" —"I'll kill you all," he cried, "every one of you; I'll drink your blood,—blood is the richest wine! I'll kill you all!"

Slowly he uncoiled himself from his crouching position on the sofa, and began crawling along with his eyes fixed upon me one moment, and on the trembling servants another, with an expression easier to be imagined than described.

It did not take the servants long to decide upon their course of action. With one accord they turned and fled from the room with the greatest precipitation, leaving me singly to encounter the wild fury of the mad earl; for if I had felt inclined to make my escape likewise at that moment, I could not have done so, owing to my position in the room, for the earl made a sudden spring, by which he nearly succeeded in catching the hindmost of the servants, but quite succeeded in placing himself between me and the door.

I felt now that firmness and an apparent absence of all fear was my only chance of escape from death at the hands of the dangerous lunatic I was alone with.

He surveyed me for some moments with a smile of triumph on his face, and it seemed to me that he was considering what manner he would be best pleased in putting me out of the world.

"Earl Broughton," I cried, in a haughty, commanding tone, "what do you mean by this conduct?"—"To to kill!" he muttered, and he spread out his fingers like

"Nonsense!" said I, "I will have no killing to-night. Come, walk with me, I have got something to tell you."—"Do you think you could tell it with your throat cut?" said he. "I will not be spoken to in this manner," said I; "you have offered me no refreshments yet. Cannot we go into the drawing-room, and have something?"

"Wait a bit, and I'll carry you," he said.

He then produced from his pocket a case of razors, and deliberately taking out two of them, he began sharpening them against each other, as people do sometimes with dinner-knives. My sensations at this moment may be imagined, but I am quite sure I could not describe them. I felt that I had no more chance in his hands, if it came to a personal struggle, than an infant; and the uncomfortable idea of being slashed with the razors made my blood run cold again. I slowly retreated behind a round table as my only means of avoiding his spring.

What a desperate chance, too, it was to think of dodging a madman, with a razor in each of his hands, round a small table!

Still he sharpened away with the razors, and although he kept cutting his fingers every moment, he paid not the least attention to that, and in fact was, I make no doubt, unconscious of the pain.

When he had, as he thought, sharpened the blades up to the pitch he wanted them, he tried them steadily and carefully on his thumb-nail, and then expressed his satisfaction with a "Ah! beautiful—these will do."

He fixed his wild, rolling eyes upon me, and I really thought my last hour was come. I held the table with a desperate clutch, I tried to fix him with my eyes, which will sometimes subdue madmen when they are otherwise ungovernable; but he seemed proof against that, or else I did not show sufficient firmness, for he slowly advanced, and at every step or two he replied, "Ah!" which always made me give a great start, in consequence of the nervous state I was in, and my visible alarm appeared to amuse him greatly.

Now he was within arm's length of the table, and he reached towards it with one of his razors, and tapped its edge.

"Earl Broughton," I cried, in despair, "what do you mean? Keep off—keep off!"—"Ho! ho! ho!" he laughed, and coming close up to the table, he made a slash at me across, which came within an inch of my nose.

This made me desperate, and I resolved to sell my life as dearly as possible. I caught up the lamp, which was upon the table, and by a sudden impulse dashed it in his face.

The glass smashed, and I saw him reel with the blow. In the next instant all was darkness. I had forgotten that the lamp was the only light in the room; and there was I, in a dark small room, with a howling, infuriated madman, armed with two razors.

All this came across me in a moment, and without moving my feet, I crouched down, so as to be below the level of the table.

The earl now commenced a series of frightful cries and yells, which were terrible to hear, and I was perfectly aware he was cutting and slashing about with his razors in the most frantic manner imaginable.

Further and further I cautiously crept under the table, and I scarcely dared to breathe for fear of letting him know where I was concealed.

"Good God!" I thought to myself, "what will be the end of this frightful adventure?"

"Kill! kill!" shrieked the earl, and I felt by the pressure on one side that he was leaning over the table with the hope of reaching me. Then he began scrambling on the top of it, and I expected every moment it would break down beneath his weight, and I should have both him and the table upon me.

I could hear him scrambling to his feet, and I was quite sure he was standing on the table. Then he commenced another series of frightful yells, that were dreadful to hear, and must have attracted the attention of even passengers in the street.

In the midst of all this a sudden gleam of light came through the broken doorway. Oh! how welcome was that single ray to me! It was like a reprieve from execution. Some help was surely coming. The madman saw the light, and ceased his screaming, commencing in its stead a low hissing, which he increased in intensity as the light approached.

Whoever was coming seemed aware of the danger, for they came very slowly and cautiously indeed. I did not move a muscle, and looked out from under the table with the greatest anxiety.

How tardily whoever was coming seemed to me to approach. Each moment was an hour of agony and suffering enough to shatter the nerves for a whole life.

"Hiss—hiss—hiss!" continued the earl, and exceedingly thankful was I now that by his standing on the table he could not see me, and even my shadow was cast the contrary way to which he was looking.

A strong blaze of light now streamed into the room, and I saw standing, ready to run away, two policemen, with their truncheons in their hands, and fear, curiosity, and amazement, upon their countenances.

"Hiss!" cried the earl, and the two guardians of the peace gave a simultaneous start backwards.

"Hiss!" again cried the earl, and another jump was the consequence.

I dared not say a word for my life's sake, and my only change of circumstances now seemed that I might still be murdered, with two policemen to look on as evidence; and yet, after all, what could they fear? If anything could be considered as quite extra duty, this was.

"Jenkins!" said one of the policemen, rubbing the side of his nose with his truncheon, "here's a go!"—"You may say that," replied Jenkins; "I thinks myself as ——"

"Hiss!" cried the earl, and another jump from the policemen seemed to amuse him very much, for he began sharpening his razors again, and roaring with frantic delight.

Suddenly now I saw the head of another man appear at the open door, adorned with a fur cap. He took a long penetrating look at the earl, who hissed at him ineffectually several times, and then he cried in a loud voice,—

"Hilloa, there!"—"Hiss!" said the earl.

"Fetch me a large thick blanket," said the man with the fur cap, quite coolly, to some one behind him.

"A—a—what?" said one of the policemen.—"Hold your tongue, and get out of the way, will you?" said the man with the fur cap.

The policeman looked astonished, and commenced a careful examination of his truncheon from the handle to the tip, and from the tip to the handle again, as if some flaw in that emblem of authority, which a close scrutiny would discover, could only account for the man with the fur cap presuming so to address B 202.

"Fiends! devils! kill—kill!" shrieked the earl, and the two policemen immediately made a precipitate retreat.

In another moment a blanket was handed to the man with the fur cap, who, throwing it over his arm in a peculiar manner, fixed his eyes upon the earl, and, with a slow, measured step, walked into the room.

"Hiss! hiss!" went the earl, but the man with the fur cap would not be hissed away.

I thought now I might possibly be of some assistance, and suddenly rising up, with my back against the table, I gave such a lurch, that down went the madman, razors and all, with a thundering noise, on the floor. I then immediately scrambled to my feet, and was about to rush from the room at the top of my speed, when the bold and mysterious man with the fur cap shouted,—

"I've got him, sir; there's no fear now."—"Indeed, but there is," said I, "whatever may be the amount of danger."

I paused, however, and saw that the earl was so much enveloped with the blanket as to be completely harmless. The man cautiously allowed first one and then the other of the madman's arms to be at liberty, and with great dexterity and strength disarmed him of his razors.

"Who are you?" said I.—"I am from Dr. Martin's Asylum, sir," replied the man.

"Oh! you are a keeper?"—"Yes; I takes care o' most o' the *hobstropulous* patients— *impatients*, I calls 'em!"—"How came you here?"

"One o' the servants, I supposes, sir, as had some gumption in him, sent for me."—"Gumption, indeed," said I; "my friend, I feel pretty well assured, if you had not come, I should have lost my life."

"Very likely," said the man, quite calmly.

All this while he was fitting rapidly a strait waistcoat on the earl; after he had done which, he looked him full in the face till he shrank again under the steady and practised gaze of the keeper; then, lifting up his finger in a menacing attitude, he said, in a voice that astonished me,—

"Quiet!"

The madman shrank and cowered before the keeper, and allowed himself to be assisted to rise as passively as an infant.

"You have extraordinary power over the insane," said I.—"You may say that," said the man; "I always get the better on 'em. They soon gets afeard o' me."

"Well," said I, taking out my purse, and handing him the contents, "I feel very much indebted to your skill and courage."—"Thank you, sir," he said.

"I am Doctor ——," I continued, "and I will accompany you to Dr. Martin's. He knows me, and I will explain to him the circumstances which have driven the unhappy nobleman to his present state of mental aberration."—"Isn't none o' the family here, sir?" said the man.

"I fear not," said I; "there have been some strange things happening in this house."

I rang the bell as I spoke, for when I upset the table all the servants had rushed screaming away, and not a soul, except the mad earl, the keeper, and myself, was now in the suite of rooms.

It was several minutes before any one answered my summons, although I went into the outer room of the three, justly imagining that whoever did come would venture no further than that apartment.

The first indication that my ring had been heard consisted in the door opening two inches, and a policeman's staff being poked through the aperture, and shaken in a most ludicrously threatening manner.

At any other time I should have laughed, but as it was I was in no merry mood, and I called out loudly,—

"Come in, there is no danger now."

The door was opened a little wider, and a face appeared.

"Come in," I again cried; "the earl is secured."

This announcement seemed sufficiently satisfactory, and, the door opening wide, disclosed to me the whole household, headed by the two policemen, with their truncheons, in attitudes of defence.

"Where is the Countess of Broughton?" said I; "it is proper she should know what has occurred."—"The countess has left the house, sir," said a footman.

"Left the house?" I cried.— "Yes, sir; the hall porter let her out more than an hour ago."

"You are quite sure of that?"—"Yes, sir; I went and told her you said my young master was poisoned, and in five minutes after she left the house, sir."

"Indeed! Well, I have nothing to do with the countess's movements. Grief for the death of his son has driven your poor master mad. Who is the nearest relative of the family?"—"Viscount Manningtree, sir," replied the footman; "his lady is my lord's sister."

"Where do they live?"—"In Berkeley-square, sir."

"That will do. Where is the housekeeper or butler?"—"Here, sir," said a little punchy man, rolling forward.

"You are the butler?"—"Yes, doctor."

"Then take care of everything till you hear from Viscount Manningtree. I will go to him at once. Your master must be removed; he is not in a fit state to remain at home. Fetch a coach somebody, or get the earl's own carriage ready, for he must be removed at once, for his own sake as well as for the sake of everybody else."

* * * * *

The unfortunate Earl Broughton was conveyed in his own carriage, in care of the keeper, to the asylum of Dr. Martin, and that intelligent physician gratified me very much by giving it as his decided opinion that the insanity of the earl would be but very temporary, and was not at all likely to settle into any confirmed mania.

I did not consider myself called upon to say anything concerning the countess to any one but a member of the family, and Dr. Martin imagined that intense grief at the sudden death of his beloved son and heir was the cause of the earl's insanity. The real facts might have modified the opinion of Dr. Martin with regard to the duration of the earl's state of mind; but still I did not think myself at liberty to disclose them, and, at all events, I felt satisfied that I had done all that humanity could suggest for the unfortunate nobleman.

* * * * *

I resolved that as early as possible in the morning I would pay a visit to the earl's near relatives in Berkeley-square, and put them in possession of all I knew concerning the melancholy death of Lord Ratcliffe, the disappearance of the countess, and the truly lamentable state of the unhappy earl himself. I further determined to be entirely guided by them as to my future conduct in the business, which I a thousand times wished myself well out of; for, exclusive of the great personal danger I had encountered, I foresaw a host of troubles in perspective, should the relatives of the earl choose to discover the retreat of the (in my mind) criminal countess, and prosecute her on my evidence and that of the earl, should he shortly become convalescent.

However, I had a duty to perform, and I felt fully the necessity of doing it quickly, for the evils I might expose myself to by secrecy were stupendous in comparison with those which even a public prosecution of the Countess of Broughton might inflict. However, as my wife urged—why should this murderess escape the just penalty of her crime? Did not the very circumstances of rank and splendour by which she was surrounded make her deep criminality ten times worse than if she had been driven by misery, or urged by injury, to commit the dreadful crime?

I rose earlier than usual, and making a hasty breakfast, I set out for the residence of Viscount Manningtree, in Berkeley-square, which I reached before nine o'clock. I sent in my card, on which I wrote under my name these words:—

"On urgent and particular business."

The servant told me that his lordship was not up, but very politely took my card to him, and in a few moments brought me back word that he would see me in ten minutes, if I would do him the favour of waiting for that time in his dressing-room, whither I was accordingly conducted.

In less than the time mentioned Viscount Manningtree entered the room and announced himself.

"Under any other circumstances than those I shall detail, my lord," said I, "this visit would be a great intrusion."—"I am quite sure, doctor," he said, "that you have something important to say; I only hope it is not of a melancholy character."

"I am sorry to say it is, my lord, of a very melancholy character. It concerns your lady, however, more particularly, although I doubt not but your lordship's sympathies will be much affected."—"It is something about the Broughtons, then," he cried, hastily. "Good God! what has happened? What has that woman done?"—"My lord?"

"I beg your pardon, doctor," he hastily added; "forget what I have said; but neither Lady Manningtree nor myself admire Lady Broughton."—"I fear what I have to say, then, will not tend to raise her in your estimation, my lord," said I, solemnly.

I then related to him distinctly all that I knew, from my first acquaintance with the family to the awful and calamitous proceeding of the previous night.

"Good Heavens!" he exclaimed, when I had done; "poor Broughton! We never thought such horrors as you have described could occur; but we have long since detected the countess's aversion to the unfortunate Lord Ratcliffe. Excuse me, my dear sir."

He rang the bell hastily, and, when a servant appeared, he said,—

"Go quickly to my solicitor, Mr. Hart, in Lincoln's Inn, and tell him I want him instantly, on a matter that will admit of no delay."—"May I ask what are your lordship's intentions?" said I, when the servant had left the room.

"My dear sir," he replied, "if you can spare half an hour, we will consult upon what should be done when my solicitor arrives; and if you will excuse me for a few minutes, I will break this matter to Lady Manningtree."—"Certainly," I said, and he left the room.

"Well," I thought, "here will be a prosecution for a certainty." * * * *

In about a quarter of an hour a servant came to request my attendance upon his lordship in the breakfast parlour.

There I found Lord Manningtree in earnest conversation with his lady, who was weeping bitterly. He introduced me to her, and she endeavoured to apologize for her emotion.

"Madam," I said, "the only consolation I can offer you is, that Earl Broughton will most probably soon be restored to health."—"Doctor," said the viscount, "the Countess of Broughton became such, to our knowledge, by the most artful and vile tricks. My wife and I are of opinion that we should sink every other feeling in bringing her to justice. That she is guilty of poisoning the boy, there can be no doubt."—"My lord," I replied, "what I have told you, I can swear to, and should you decide upon a prosecution, I cannot conscientiously withhold my evidence."

"Mr. Hart," announced a servant at this instant.—"Show him here," said the viscount. "My dear," turning to his wife, "use your own discretion in staying with us or retiring."

"I will stay," she said. "Alas! my poor brother."

She burst into tears, and continued weeping for several minutes after Mr. Hart, the solicitor, had entered the room, and been introduced to me by the viscount.

The attorney looked at us with a face of no little surprise, for we certainly presented a most mysterious appearance.

"I have sent to you, Mr. Hart," said the viscount, "to give your advice upon a most disagreeable piece of business."

The lawyer bowed, as much as to say, "Disagreeable pieces of business are quite in my line," and the viscount proceeded to detail to him all that I had related.

Mr. Hart listened attentively, and at the end of the narrative he said,—

"Why, really, my lord, this is a disagreeable affair. There will be a coroner's inquest."—"By Heaven! I never thought of that," cried the viscount; "all will come out then, in spite of us. Lady Broughton will assuredly be apprehended."

"Of course," said Mr. Hart, "we are talking now in confidence; but the proof appears so strong against her ladyship, that you would be quite justified in placing her in custody."—"My dear," said the viscount, turning to his wife, "what do you say about this affair? Your feelings ought, I think, to be especially consulted, considering your near relationship to the Earl of Broughton."

"He is my brother," said the lady, "and the poor boy was my nephew,—I cannot forgive his murderess."— "Then you are quite willing that Mr. Hart should take this matter up professionally?"

"I am," said the lady.—"Then we ought to get a warrant, and apprehend Lady Broughton at once," said Mr. Hart. "If we are to do anything, we should do it quickly. Perhaps, doctor, you will accompany me and his lordship to a police office?"—"Certainly," I said; "unpleasant as this business is to me, I do not feel justified in hanging back."

* * * * *

It was nearly eleven o'clock before we procured a warrant, on my testimony, for the apprehension of Lady Broughton, on the charge of administering poison to her step-child, and, accompanied by an experienced officer, we all proceeded in the viscount's coach to the residence of Earl Broughton.

We found the house in much confusion, and, in answer to our inquiries, we were told that the countess had never returned, or been heard of, since she had left the house so suddenly and mysteriously the preceding evening.

Here, then, was a complete stop to our further proceedings. Where to seek the runaway criminal we had not the least idea, and all that Mr. Hart could advise was, to leave the officer in the house to take her into custody in case she returned to it, and then await the verdict of the inquest, when stringent steps could be taken to discover the retreat of her ladyship.

This being agreed upon, I felt myself at liberty to make my morning calls, after which I called upon Mr. ——, the eminent chemist, and requested him to do me the favour of analyzing with me the contents of the glass which I had taken from Lord Ratcliffe's bed-room. We spent some hours in a careful analyzation, and discovered such clear proofs of the presence of arsenic, that the mode by which the unfortunate boy had been hurried to the grave was quite apparent; and I wrote to the coroner to summon Mr. —— upon the inquest, in order to give his evidence as corroborative of my own professional opinion that Lord Ratcliffe had been shattered in constitution for a long time by minute doses of arsenic, and then suddenly carried off by a larger portion of that mineral poison.

The inquest was held two days after the death of the young and interesting boy, and the evidence was so clear and conclusive, that a verdict of "wilful murder" against the Countess of Broughton was returned without a shadow of hesitation.

A hundred pounds reward were immediately offered by the viscount for her apprehension, and, as might be expected, the whole affair created an extraordinary sensation in the public mind, and particularly in the higher class of society, in which the parties moved.

The feature of the business, however, which seemed to give the greatest annoyance and dissatisfaction to the family of the Earl of Broughton, was the fact that the criminality of the countess by no means vitiated her son's claim to the peerage after the earl should die. This child of hers was over two years of age, and although by no means a robust one, was more than likely to live and really enjoy the fruits of his mother's wickedness. The relations of the family were inexpressibly vexed and annoyed at this state of things, because they fairly enough argued that it was a lamentable thing a crime of immense magnitude could be committed, with a certainty of legally attaining the object of its commission. Grumble, however, as they might, such was the fact, and the son of the murderess was, to all intents and purposes, presumptive heir to the earldom and estates of Broughton, with all appertaining thereto.

This singularly circumstanced child was placed, immediately after the inquest, at nurse with a respectable family in the Isle of Wight, while no exertion or expense was spared to bring to justice his guilty mother.

The Earl of Broughton, from the judicious treatment he was subjected to, slowly but surely recovered from his mental aberration, and although a deep melancholy settled upon him, he was quite restored to society and his home.

The child of the murderess, however, he could not bring his mind to see, and it was evident that his heart was in the coffin of his murdered child. Every engine was set at work to discover the hiding-place of the countess; but in vain. The government offered a reward of five hundred pounds, but it produced no effect; and two years passed away without anything occurring to throw a light upon the mysterious circumstances connected with her disappearance.

What I am now going to relate may sound like fiction, but there is not a more true saying than that truth and real life abound with more strangeness and romantic incidents than the most imaginative brain could invent.

About two years, then, after the events I have recorded, and when people had long ceased to talk or think of the singular fate of Lord Ratcliffe, and the disappearance of the Countess of Broughton, a visitor was announced to me one evening of the name of King.

"Mr. King," said I; "I don't know him; but show him into the patient's room, and say I shall be with him directly."

It was what is called just between lights, that is to say, scarcely dark enough to light candles, and yet not light enough to see well without them, and before going to my visitor I ordered lights, and then entered the room.

A tall man was standing on the middle of the floor. He wore a cloak, and his back being to the window, combined with the very insufficient light, quite prevented me from seeing anything but the mere dusky outline of his form.

"Mr. King, I believe?" said I.—"Yes," he replied, in an evidently assumed voice; "you are Dr. ——?"

"I am," said I; "we shall have lights directly, and then you can state your business."—"I beg your pardon," he said, "but, if you bring lights here, I shall go directly. If I had wanted lights at our interview, I could have come earlier."

"Indeed," said I; "I don't know you, and you must excuse me for positively refusing to have an interview with a perfect stranger in the dark."

"You positively refuse?" he said.—"I do," said I, and made a step towards the bell, for I concluded neither more nor less than that my visiter was a thief.

He stepped forward, and caught my arm.

"One moment," he said; "what I have to say I can easily carry elsewhere."

There was something earnest in his manner that made me pause, and I said,—"Give me a reason for your conduct, and I may humour you."—"I bring you news of Lady Broughton," he whispered in my ear.

"What, the—the ——"—"Murderess of Lord Ratcliffe," he added; "now, doctor, I do not choose to be known to you just yet, until I see what arrangements we can make. Order in your lights, and I'm off. You can't stop me,—I'm *armed and desperate!*"

These last words he pronounced in a tone that left no doubt on my mind of their genuineness. Even as he spoke, the flash of lights from the passage came in at the half open door, as my servant was bringing them.

"Stop them!" cried the man.

I immediately went to the door, and countermanded the lights, to the great astonishment of my footman, and then, returning and closing the door, I said,—

"Now, sir, I am at your service; but recollect, I can receive no confidential communication. Whatever you say to me, I must again repeat to the Earl of Broughton."—"I am prepared for all that," said the stranger.—"The rewards for the apprehension of the Countess of Broughton amount altogether to seven hundred pounds."

"I believe so," said I, ——— instinctively from the man, who, I immediately ——— to betray the unhappy woman for gold.—"Well," he proceeded, "I know where she is."

"I would much rather you would make this communication to the proper authorities," said I; "I do not wish to have anything more to do with the business."

"The authorities be d——d!" said the man; "it isn't at all convenient for me to come in contact with them. I will tell you, if the reward is handed to me; I will show the Countess of Broughton to you or the earl, or anybody but an officer."

"I repeat," said I, "that all this is nothing to me. Go to Bow-street with your information."—"Doctor," said the man, after the pause of a moment, "if you reject my offer, you will never hear of me again."

I felt myself placed in a very awkward position indeed. I did not like to bid the fellow go without hearing more, for I might have been blamed afterwards for such a step, and I had certainly a great and increasing reluctance to have anything to do with him.

"Whoever you are," I said, "let me tell you, that I have no interest in this affair further than the common public one, which all men have, that crime should meet its just punishment. The Earl of Broughton and his family may have feelings and wishes upon this subject which cannot influence me. All, therefore, that I can say is, if you like to come here again, I will in the interim communicate with them, and their answer will of course be mine."—"Give me your word, doctor, "that I shall come and go harmless, and I consent," he said.

"I might arrest you now," I said.—"No such thing," he replied; "I am strong enough for you and all your household. Besides, see what a loss you would be to society, doctor, if I were to blow your brains out. I tell you I am a desperate man, and have no food; it has come to that even. Likewise, you have no charge against me. I know something of the law, however, and the next visit I make you, a magistrate's warrant might be in waiting for me. Promise, then, that I shall come and go harmless, and you will see me again —not else, you may depend."

"This fellow," thought I, "is a great scoundrel; but what he says is so far reasonable, that I have no particular grounds for refusing his request;" and I accordingly said,—

"I will promise."—"Very well," he replied; "I will be here this time to-morrow."

So saying, without another word he walked out of my parlour, and opening the street-door as if he had been used to it all his lifetime, was gone before I could recover from the general surprise that his visit to me had occasioned.

I lost no time in surmises or useless conjectures, but went at once to the Earl of Broughton, determined to be guided entirely by him in the affair.

The earl turned very pale, and trembled when I related to him the object of my visit.

"Doctor," he said, in a voice of deep emotion, "whatever resentment once filled my breast against the being who deprived me of my poor boy, has now long since departed, leaving in its place no feeling but one of grief. If this unhappy, guilty woman be still living, I have no wish to bring her to a shameful and ignominious end. Let her live, and in the solitude of her own conscience repent of her grievous sin."—"I think," said I, "you take the wisest as well as the most Christian view of this distressing affair: but your lordship must be aware that such a man as my visitor of this evening will not be satisfied with our rejection of his offer. He will, I fear, go elsewhere, where the mercy you are inclined to show will not be found."—"That is true," said the earl; "I must see this man myself."

"Such a course would be most satisfactory to me," said I. "If you will do me the honour of coming to my house at the appointed hour, your lordship can make your own terms with this man, who, I dare say, will do anything in the world for money."—"I will do so," said the earl. "We must be quite certain that this man really is in the possession of the secret he boasts of, and in that case I will give him the reward to leave the unhappy woman to the justice of Heaven."

With this understanding the earl and myself separated, and I must own that my curiosity was very strongly excited to know how this singular affair would end.

* * * *

A little before the appointed time the Earl of Broughton came on foot to my residence, and we both sat in the parlour, waiting the arrival of Mr. King, with his promised communication. The earl was dreadfully dejected in spirits, and I wished Mr. King and his officiousness at the bottom of the sea rather than he should have recalled all the painful and afflicting circumstances, which were now evidently pressing with nearly their original intensity upon the mind of the unfortunate nobleman.

A heavy single knock at length announced the mysterious stranger, and as I had previously given orders to my servant to admit him at once without ceremony, remark, or question, he was quickly with us in the parlour, placing his back to the light, in the same manner as before, so that we could not see a single feature of his face.

There was rather a disagreeable silence for a minute or so, and Mr. King appeared to be waiting to be spoken to, like a ghost, before he could utter a word.

"This is the Earl of Broughton," said I.—"What have you to say to me?" inquired the earl, in a low voice.

"Only what I have already said to Dr. ——," replied the stranger; "I know where the Countess of Broughton is concealed."—"And you will give her up for the reward?" said the earl.

"Yes, I will; this night, if requisite,—only show me the money."—"Has she trusted you?"

"What do you mean?"—"I mean has she confided in your secrecy as to her identity and place of concealment?"

"You may call it so, if you like."—"Then I am to understand that you betray her confidence in you, and are willing to sell her to the scaffold for seven hundred pounds?"

"Understand what you like," said the man; "I can give her up."—"Exactly," said the earl; "now we fully comprehend each other. You are willing to betray her who has trusted you for the sum of seven hundred pounds. Now, in what manner do you intend to prove to us that this tale of yours is not a rank lie from beginning to end?"

"You are plain in your language, my lord," said the man, bitterly.—"I mean it to be so," said the earl; "I apply coarse and opprobrious epithets to you because you are likely to understand them."

"I don't want you to trust me," said the man. "I didn't expect you would. I'll trust you, though. Promise me the reward if I show her to you, and you shall stand within arm's length of her first."

"You are aware that the bulk of this reward is only to be paid on conviction?" said the earl.—"I know that," cried King; "but I want it before, you understand. I can't wait."

"I don't wish a prosecution," said the earl.—"Oh! you don't," said King. "Well, it's all one to me. D——n prosecutions!" say I.

"Then, provided you get the money, you are quite indifferent whether she is prosecuted or not."—"Quite,—quite. What matters it to me? Don't try to get me into a line, though. I have already told the doctor that it ain't convenient for me to be seen or known in this affair; but I can set the officers on her, you understand, and not at all endanger myself. Bilk me out of the reward by saying you don't intend to prosecute, and, mark me! you shall be called upon to do so before you are twenty-four hours older, my lord. I can give her up, and, by G——d! I will, if you don't pay me one way or another. It's all the same to me. Hang her or save her, I want the money!"

"I accept your conditions," said the earl. "Show the unhappy woman to Dr. —— and myself, and I give you my honour you shall have the money. But, mark me, sir. If you should then, from any motive of revenge, let loose the law upon her, I will have you hunted down, if it cost me my whole possessions."—"I shouldn't interfere with her," said the man. "Come, now, business is business; I can take you to her in half an hour."

"Where is she!"—"Why, as we understand each other now, and are quite confidential, she's lodging in a court in St. Giles's."

"Doctor, will you do me the favour of accompanying me?" said the earl.—"Certainly," I replied.

The earl then turned to King, and said,—

"Beware, sir, of any treachery. I have taken steps for my own protection and that of this gentleman."—"Oh, you have, have you?" said King.

"Yes, steps that will do you no harm whatever, if you are acting candidly; but if this is any scheme of robbery, be assured you are quite surrounded, and cannot escape."— "You are very careful, my lord."

"I am. Now lead on. We will follow you with perfect confidence."

* * * * *

I was quite struck with astonishment at the change which had taken place in the manners and character of the Earl of Broughton. He seemed now to be endowed with a vigour and precision of thought which was quite foreign to his former state of mind. Grief makes some men and mars others. It appeared as if the hidden stores of reflection, which were really existent in the mind of the Earl of Broughton, had only required some extraordinary stimulus to bring them into active operation. Before the calamitous death of his son, his life had glided on so smoothly and calmly, that his mind had become slothful and indolent. Since then, however, how great had been the change! Thought, like a slumbering giant, had roused itself within the chambers of his brain, and, aided by all the knowledge which his station in society had forced him to become a recipient of in early life, he became an intellectual and high minded man.

The stranger walked on a few paces in advance, and the earl and I conversed in low tones as we followed his dusky figure.

"You talk of precautions, my lord," said I. "May I ask what steps you have taken?"—"Certainly, doctor. While I knew that this man could trust to our honours, I was not quite so certain that we might trust to his. I have accordingly taken such measures, as will guard against any planned robbery or treachery on his part. We shall be followed wherever we go to-night by persons who, at a signal from me, would make their immediate appearance."

"I own your precaution is just and reasonable," said I, "for there is no knowing where this rascal may lead us. May I now ask if you have decided upon your course of conduct should he really lead us to—to ——."—"The countess, you would say, doctor," interrupted the earl, seeing my embarrassment: "yes, I have decided; I will tell her to fly from this land for ever, and furnish her with the means."

"We are approaching a delightful locality," said I, as our guide turned up one of the lowest streets in St. Giles's.— "Has she sunk so low!" murmured the earl, rather to himself than to me.

The man now slackened his pace, so that we might approach nearer to him, and when we were within a few steps, of him he beckoned to us, and dived down the arched entrance of a dirty, squalid-looking court.

We did not hesitate, but followed him closely.

"This way," he said, and, guided by his voice we entered an open doorway. "The stairs are to the left," said the man again, in a low voice; "all's safe; you will see a light almost directly."

We groped along the passage, which was in total darkness, till we stumbled against the stairs, and scarcely had we done so, when a faint light gleamed across our eyes, and we saw our guide standing some distance up, shading with his hand the flickering flame of a rushlight from the wind that blew in from the open door. He merely beckoned us, and we followed him up the staircase till we reached the landing-place of the second floor. Here the man paused, and taking a key from his pocket, unlocked the door, and showed us into a dirty room, in which were several articles of wretched furniture.

"You see, my lord, I'm rather down on my luck," said the stranger. "It was time for me to think of something."— "Perform your promise," said the earl, sternly.

"I'm a going," said the man; "but first I'll tell you how she come to be so queerly off. When the countess left your house, she took with her all her own jewels."—"She did,— she did!"

"Well, they are all gone now!"—"Sold?"

"No—popped."—"What do you mean?"

"Pawned, I suppose you'd call it. And now, my lord, —honour bright,—afore I go a step further, give me the reward."—"What! before you have earned it?"

"Yes, my lord; you can take it away again if I deceive you. Give me the money now, and in five minutes I'll show you the countess."—"You are in my power," said the earl, "and I can do so with safety."

"I know it," replied the man; "some of the oldest of the Bow-street traps have been on our heels all the way. Do you think I didn't see 'em?"—"I made no secret of my caution," said the earl; "a word from me would cause your instant apprehension; but you have my promise of safety, and that, you know, you can rely upon. Here's the money; I give it to you now to save time, but if you deceive me, it can and will be wrested from you before you are ten minutes older."

As he spoke, the earl handed some notes to the man, who, after examining them, thrust them into his pocket, and taking up the light, said,—

"Now, that's a respectable way of doing business. This way, please, gentlemen."

He walked to the further end of the room, and opened a door, which, by the dim light, I had not before observed.

We followed him into a smaller room, in which was a low, dirty couch. The earl advanced quickly; I heard him groan, and was by his side in a moment.

By the dim uncertain light of the candle I saw, lying pale and haggard upon that couch, the Countess of Broughton!

"There she is!" said the man.

The sound of his voice aroused the countess, who seemed to be sleeping. She opened her eyes, and they met those of the earl. A scream burst from her lips, and her features assumed a fixed and ghastly hue. I sprang forward and laid my hand on her wrist. One pulsation answered to the pressure,—then a gentle flutter, and the guilty woman was dead!

The earl stood as still as a statue, and for several minutes not a sound was heard in that room. Even the coarse wretch who had guided us there seemed shocked by the spectacle of death before him.

"My lord," I said, touching the earl's arm, "the countess is dead."—"Thank God!" said the earl.

"Well," said the man, "who'd a thought of her slipping off so soon. You're a physician, howsomdever, and that accounts for it. My old father died very soon after they fetched a physician."—"Peace," cried the earl; "you have got your reward. Guilty though she was, recollect, sir, who she was."

The man laughed, and placing the candle on the floor, he said,—

"You are rich, my lord, and can afford to purchase secrets."—"Well, sir, what then?"

"Why, I've got one to sell."—"It concerns not me."

"It does, though. Look, my lord,—London,—nay England,—is rather too hot to hold me now. Give me a couple of hundred more, and I'll tell you a secret which shall be worth the money, as well as giving you the duplicates of all the jewels my lady took away from your house."—"What is the nature of your communication?" said the earl.

"Ah!" replied the man, "there's the very thing. One word tells it you."—"Some of these jewels you mention," said the earl, "have been long in our family,—so long that I scarcely consider them the individual property of any one member of it. Give me the tickets you mention, and depend upon me sending you the two hundred pounds to-morrow."

"I'll trust you my lord," said the man. "Here's the tickets,—and now for the secret. Who's that lying there?"

He pointed to the body.

"The Countess of Broughton," said the earl.—"You are wrong, my lord."

"Wrong!" said the earl, snatching up the light and viewing the face closely; "I cannot be deceived,—it is she!"— "You are wrong," added the man.

"What do you mean? Explain yourself instantly."— "That's Mrs. King, then," said the man.

"Mrs. who?"—"Mrs. King! She was married to me afore she saw you, and there's the secret. Now she's dead, where's the odds? They can't lag her for bigamy now."

"Can you prove this?" said I.—"Yes, I can, doctor. We were married at Stepney church. She had a edication, —I hadn't. Well, we couldn't manage together no how, and she took a situation as governess, where my lord first saw her. He married her, as is very well known, and, to keep my tongue quiet, she sent me as much money as I wanted."

"Go on,—go on," said the earl.—"She was mad to have her child by you, a nobleman, so she took the life of the other; but mind you, by G—d, I knew nothing of that piece of business till it was done. She left your house and came to me. That was the first I heard of it. Then she told me all about it, and said the doctor had found her out."

"This passes belief," exclaimed the earl.—"It is true, though," exclaimed the man; "she's no more your wife an she's your daughter."

The earl looked thunderstruck. He turned to me and said,—

"Doctor, I know not whether to be pleased or afflicted at this information. Can it be true?"—"Its truth or falsehood can very easily be ascertained," I said.—"Exactly," cried the man; "you are right doctor. In the register at Stepney church you will find the entry, my lord. Now good bye to you both, for I've no more to say, but that I'll call to-morrow morning for the two hundred, and in the meantime you can search the marriage register at Stepney."—"Be it so," said the earl; "I will send persons to-morrow to perform the last offices for this erring creature."

"You'll bury her, and all that kind of thing, my lord?"—"I will."

"Well, then, I shall be off to-morrow morning, and no mistake. You see I might have waited till the young 'un as would have comed to the title after you really had it or come of age, and he might have paid well to have the secret kept; but I ain't so young as I once was, and I might be under ground myself long afore all that comes to pass."—"Never mind your motives," said the earl.

He then cast one look upon the corpse, and hurried from the room.
                    *   *   *
The next day the truth of the man King's statement was substantiated, and the earl was convinced that his only living child was illegitimate. He provided for it, however, most handsomely in his will immediately.

King called for his money, and was never more heard of. The guilty woman was decently and privately buried and no one guessed that "Mrs King" was the quondam Countess of Broughton.

THE MURDERER'S DEATH-BED.

I HAVE stood by the death-bed of the innocent and young, and seen the pure spirit wing its homeward flight with scarcely a sigh, on leaving its earthly tenement; I have seen the weak babe fall beneath the breath of disease; I have seen the strong man wrestle, as it were, with death, and yield, but with much pain and difficulty, his life to the grim destroyer; I have heard the shrieks and lamentations of the living while the warm breath still lingered around the lips which were no more to part to utter sounds of life and love. All this have I seen, and beyond the passing sympathy of human nature for its kindred in affliction, I have felt no pang: but the scene to which I am about to introduce the reader was one that haunted me for many months, and sleeping or waking it was long before I could rid my seared imagination of the horrors of the murderer's death-bed!

I was but a young man, and had not been long in practice, when I was summoned to attend a Mr. Nicholson, who resided upon a handsome property of his own some two miles westward of the metropolis.

I thought it a great piece of good luck to be called to Mr. Nicholson, and although the night was far advanced and the weather was very far from being inviting, I started in very good spirits to make my professional visit.

Mr. Nicholson's house was called Meriton Villa, and was situated some distance from the high road, after passing through the little bustling village of Bayswater.

It was past ten o'clock before I reached the gate entering upon the pleasant little lawn in front of his house, and there was then every indication of an exceedingly stormy night.

I rang several times before any one came to admit me, and at last, when a trembling man servant came with a key, and opened the gate, I was positively alarmed for a moment at his scared and ghastly appearance.

"What is the matter with you?" I said; "you look frightened out of your wits."—"And well I may be, sir," he replied; "master does go on so, it's quite enough to congeleate a person's blood."—"Do what to your blood?"

"Congeleate, sir."—"Well, I never heard of such a process. I am Dr. ———, so take me to your master at once."

"I guessed, sir, as you was Dr. ———," said the man, "and that was why I ventured to use a scientific term as I learnt at our Patent Royal Mutual Literary Scientific and Artful Society for the Amelioration of the Human Race, and more particularly Bayswater!"

"Oh!" said I; "well, you have certainly profited as such societies generally profit their members; and now, if you please, without any more science, I will see your master."

"The atmospheric current has blown out the hall lamp, you see, sir," said the learned footman; "I'll just produce vivid combustion again, and show you to master in a minute."

The hall lamp was again lighted, and scientific John proceeded to show me to his master's room.

He conducted me up stairs, and pointing to a door which stood partially open, he said—

"That's master's room, sir; he's quiet now."—"Quiet?" said I.

"Yes, he's been making all sorts of sounds, and it strikes me that the inerd apparatus of his cranium is in a state of derangification."—"Well, well, I see there's a light. That will do," I said, and pushing the door open, I entered the chamber of Mr. Nicholson.

There was a light burning on the dressing-table, and it cast a bright light into every corner of the apartment. A handsome bed, with massive silk hangings, met my eyes, and advancing towards it, I drew aside the curtains, expecting to see my patient lying between the sheets, with his head upon the pillow, in due order; but such was not the case. The pillow was quite vacant, and I could only judge that the bed was tenanted, by the clothes being heaped up in the middle, as if some one lay there coiled up like a ball.

I waited several minutes patiently, and then I cried,—

"Sir,—Mr. Nicholson!"—"Off—off!" shrieked a smothered voice from beneath the bed-clothes; "off, I say! Go away, Sinclair. I am dying — oh, leave me for a moment!"

"Mr. Nicholson," I again cried, "I am Doctor ———; I beg of you to come from under the clothes."—"Who—who?" he cried.

"You sent for me; I am Doctor ———."

There was a movement of the clothes, and presently I saw from amid the mass a wild, bright, glaring eye fixed upon me.

"You are alone?" said my patient.—"Perfectly," I replied. "Allow me to ask you who you are?"

"Stop," he cried, "look around the room. There's no one here. He is not hiding?"—"Who?" I said.

"Never mind who. Look well. Assure me that we are alone, and then close the door. Place a chair against it, and on the chair put that lamp. No, no, not the lamp,—the dressing-glass; then, if he should come, its fall would give the alarm, and we needn't strain our eyes to watch the door so incessantly."—"I will see that no one comes here, Mr. Nicholson. You have sent for me professionally. May I now ask what ails you?"

"What ails me?" he repeated; "what's o'clock?"—"Twenty minutes to eleven."

"I shall die at twelve, then."—"Nonsense," said I; "you make yourself ill by such fancies."

"Did you know Mr. George Richmond?" he said, suddenly.—"Yes," I replied, "I know him and his family well."

"It was in consequence of hearing him talk of you that I have sent for you," he added; "what do you think of my state?"

I felt his pulse; it was extremely irregular.

"How long have you been ill?" I asked.—"A week now, doctor. Are you religious?"—"I hope so," said I.

"Did you ever commit a murder?"—"A murder! Certainly not, Mr. Nicholson. Allow me to say, that is a very strange question."

"What's to-day?" he cried.—"Thursday."

"Ah! yes, yes," he groaned, "Thursday night at twelve; oh, God,—oh, God!"

"What do you mean? You will really produce a serious illness if you go on in this way, Mr. Nicholson. This incoherent conduct is quite beneath a man of sense. You are feverish, but I don't see any bad symptoms about you, and as yet you have made me acquainted with none."—"There,—there," he suddenly shrieked,—"oh, save me! save me!"

He sat up in bed, and pointed with both hands to the door.

"What is it?" I cried; "be calm. What is it?"

His lips moved without producing any sound; a low gurgling proceeded from his throat, and then, while the clammy perspiration of intense fear rolled from his brow, he continued to gasp in a husky whisper,—

"He—he is knocking again?"

In the death-like silence that followed I own I heard, or thought I heard, a low tapping at the chamber door; and that, combined with the awful terror depicted on the distorted countenance of Mr. Nicholson, I confess gave me what people call "rather a turn."

He turned his eyes upon me, and then shrieked,—

DIARY OF A PHYSICIAN.

"You hear all,—you hear it; it is no delusion!"

Whatever had produced the sound, or whether it was merely my own imagination, it, at all events, ceased.

"I hear nothing," I said; "nay, to satisfy you, I will look," which I instantly did, as much to satisfy myself as my patient. The lamp, when the door was opened wide, threw a bright light into the corridor, and nothing was to be seen. I closed the door again, and returned.

"This is all imagination," said I; "there is no one there." —"But there was," said he.

It was very difficult to meet this assertion, so I said nothing, and, in the temporary pause that followed, I could hear that the wind was increasing, for it howled round the villa like a living thing.

"Hark,—hark!" cried Nicholson; "do you hear nothing?" —"I hear the wind," said I; "it will be a stormy night, I dare say. There were indications of it when I arrived here."

"I am dying,—I know I'm dying," groaned my patient. "Doctor, on your soul, tell me one thing."—"What is it?"

"Do you think that the—the vengeance of Heaven is in any way appeased by a confession of crimes on a death-bed?" —"Repentance of evil," said I, "even at the last, we are told, shall avail us. Inasmuch as all true religionists must believe that it is more pleasing to God to pardon than to punish, I should answer your question most decidedly in the affirmative."

Mr. Nicholson was silent for several minutes; then he said, in a low tone of great anguish,—

"Tell me the time now."—"Ten minutes to eleven," said I consulting my watch.

"There is time,—there is time," he groaned; "oh! doctor, I—I will tell you. For thirty years now I have been haunted. There is time, and I will make my confession to you."—"Your confession," said I; "I trust you have nothing very particular to confess, Mr. Nicholson."

"Hush,—hush!" he cried.

Then suddenly lifting up his arms, he added,—

"The stain of blood is upon these hands!"—"Blood?"

"Yes; I am—a murderer!"

There was an awful sincerity in his manner that shocked me exceedingly, and although I was more than willing to set down all that he was saying to aberration of intellect, yet a doubt that it might be true crept over me, and chained me to the spot in breathless attention.

"Do not interrupt me," he said, "and I will tell you a tale which may prove through life a lesson to you, and possibly move the mercy of Heaven to me; for oh! I have suffered much. My life now for many years has been a hell!"

I said nothing, and, after another pause, he proceeded to to mutter to himself unintelligible sounds. Sometimes he would weep, then groan, and strike his breast.

The wind kept increasing in fury, and swept round the house, howling and moaning as if in unison with the bitter and awful thoughts of the soul-harrowed man before me.

After a time he became more composed, and, turning his wild and bright eyes full upon me, he said,—

"Listen, listen. Do not shrink from me in horror; do not curse me, but listen to the end."

I bowed my head in assent, and he continued thus, in a voice occasionally broken by deep sobs, but, upon the whole, clear and distinct :—

"I am the second son of Sir George Nicholson, who was knighted about five-and-fifty years ago. My elder brother was named Sinclair Nicholson.

"He was not absolutely a bad man, but he was haughty and distrustful in temper. My father, after his knighthood, became quite ridiculous about his kinghthood or rank, his family influence, and so on, and he made no scruple of letting me know that my brother must inherit all he had to leave, while I was to endeavour to work my way onwards, with an annuity of one hundred pounds a year, in any profession I might choose.

"This oppression rankled in my mind. I knew that my father's annual income was above two thousand pounds, and I thought it monstrous that because by accident I was his second born, (and there were but two of us,) I was to be punished by being condemned to a life of drudgery, while my brother, merely because he was the elder, was to riot in luxury.

"I represented this to my father. He heard me out, and then told me that I wanted to ruin the respectability of his family by cutting up his property. In vain I urged the injustice of the course he was pursuing. He got angry and commanded me never to mention the subject again, or he would take care that the hundred pounds annuity should not be mine.

"I went to my mother, and told her all. I implored her to see justice done between her children. Her reply was, that she thought my father's conduct quite natural.

"'What for?' I asked her.

"'Because your brother is the eldest,' was the reply.

"I laughed in her face, and from that moment she hated me, a hatred which I returned with interest; for, doctor, I argued that when a mother forgets her sacred duty to her child, the child was not bound to remember his to a mother.

"Well, another year passed away; I was told by the family solicitor that my father had perfected his arrangements, and left all to his eldest son, and I cursed him in my heart.

"It then happened that my mind became diverted from every other consideration by that master passion of the human mind, love. In the immediate neighbourhood of a country-house that my father passed half the year in, lived a family of the name of Renshaw. The second girl of that family, Lucy Renshaw, was all that my imagination had ever painted as beautiful and loveable in woman.

"I loved,—adored, worshipped her. I have kissed the ground she trod on,—my passion became a mad worship. She was my divinity.

"I think she loved me. I will think so till my last breath. Yes, she loved me,—Lucy Renshaw loved me!

"One day we met, and, with all the ardour of youth and fervent passion, I poured forth my love. She wept,—I pressed her to my heart. I implored her to tell me the cause of her tears, for there was no mistaking them,—they were tears of sorrow and bitterness.

"At length, doctor, she told me that she was sure that her parents would never consent to our union, because my elder brother had proposed for her through his mother, and they thought it so much more eligible a match.

"I thought at that moment that my reason was going, but I replied calmly, and bade her adieu for the night. I watched her to the house, and saw her go in, and then I waited an hour; after which I knocked at the door of Mr. Renshaw's house. An old servant answered my summons. 'Is your master in?' I said.—'Yes, sir,' he replied; 'walk in.'

"I was shown into the parlour, and, turning to the servant, I said,—

"'Your master is out of business now, but I wish to talk to him about a most important sale of goods.'

"The servant stared at me, and I believe there was something very wild about my manner. He made no remark, however, but left the room, and presently Mr. Renshaw entered it.

"Mr. Renshaw was a polite man, with a small collection of brains. He had an enormous dislike to anything like fancy, imagination, or excitement, all of which he considered, to use his own cursed phrase, 'as not at all respectable.'

"I could see he was annoyed at my appearance at that time of the evening, and his bow and polite inquiries after my health were very frigid.

"I believe I was half mad, and I addressed him thus:—

"'Renshaw, do you love your daughter? Come, now, for once in a way, defy respectability, man, and let your little grovelling soul avow one intense feeling.'

"He looked at me perfectly aghast, and muttered something about 'exceeding impropriety.'

"'D—n it, man,' I cried, 'can't you answer a plain question? Do you feel any affection for your daughter Lucy, or are you too respectable to stoop to the vulgarity of any feelings whatever?'

"'Love my daughter Lucy!' he stammered; 'I feel, of course, that proper parent's love for—for a child, which is implanted in so exceedingly proper a manner by the Great Author of all things, and which, in its sober and decent manifestation, is so very respectable.'

"'Exactly, Mr. Renshaw,' I said, with a sneer; 'I understand you perfectly. What is the lowest price, now, you put upon your child? A respectable price, of course,—but tell me the lowest now.'

"'What do you mean?' said Renshaw, getting up a faint imitation of indignation.

"'You know very well what I mean,' replied I; 'you would sell your daughter to my brother Sinclair, because he is the eldest, and will have the family property.'—'Sell, sir?'

"'Yes,' I thundered; 'sell is the word, however you may try to gloss it over. You know my brother has two thousand pounds a year, or he will have it when his father dies; therefore he has the preference over me. Now, Renshaw, I love your daughter, and I think she would be happy with me. If I had the two thousand pounds instead of my brother, I suppose you could have no objection in the world to me,—eh, Renshaw?'

"'You come here to insult me, sir, I am quite sure,' was his reply.

"'No such thing,' I cried; 'I thought you would say so, because respectable people always take refuge in indignation at any disagreeable home truth. Answer my question, sir.'

"'It would be the height of impropriety in me,' he said, 'to say that I had any personal objection to you, Mr. Nicholson; but, you see, your brother is the oldest, and your exemplary mother——'

"'Stop there, sir,' cried I; 'no mother can be exemplary whose mind is so narrow and vicious as to think it *natural* to prefer one of her children to another.'

"'Well, Mr. Nicholson,' resumed Renshaw, 'I really, you see, have a duty to do——'

"'Exactly,' interrupted I, 'and that is, to sell your child to the highest bidder.'

"He muttered something now about propriety and respectability, which I had not patience to hear, and I said calmly and firmly,—

"'Let me thoroughly understand you, Mr. Renshaw. You refuse your consent to my marriage with your daughter because I am the younger son, and cannot become possessed of the family property?'

"'Why, a—a—yes.'

"'Good night, sir,' said I, and I abruptly left the house.

"I went home immediately, and inquired for my brother. He had gone to his room. I ascended the stairs and tapped at his door.

"'What now?' he cried, in his usual surly voice.

"'Tis I,' I replied; 'I want to speak to you very particularly'

"'Wait till morning, then,' he growled.

"'I'll see you d—d first!' said I, as with one kick I smashed in the door and entered the room.

"He scowled at me, and knit his brows: but that was so usual with him that I thought nothing of it.

"'Brother,' said I, 'I know you are a surly, cross-tempered brute, and that it's exceedingly difficult, for me especially, even to get a civil word from you; but I have now come to have some talk with you, and will have it.'

"'What do you mean?' he growled, his sallow countenance becoming pale with rage.

"'I mean to have some talk with you,' I said; 'and if you give me any of your insolence, I'll thrash you within an inch of your life, for I am the stronger of the two. I know you are surly and ferocious as a wild beast, and fair words are thrown away upon you; so I speak to you in your own way.'

"'Be off with you,' he cried.

"'No, I will not be off. You know well that there is only one person in this house who will put up with your savage insolence, and that is your foolish mother. Now hear me. Do you know that you are to have all when your father dies?'

"'Well, what then?'—'Do you know it?' I thundered. —'I do.'

"'Do you think it just—honest?'—'Go to the devil!' was his elegant reply.

"I immediately gave him a blow on the head that sent him to the other end of the room.

"At that moment my mother rushed into the room: I think she had been listening at the door, for she burst into a torrent of invectives against me.

"'Madam,' I said, 'there's your pet cub; I have just given him a little practical lesson in common civility.'

"'Oh, you wretch!' screamed my mother. 'My dear Sinclair,' turning to my brother, 'are you hurt?'

"'Don't bother me,' he cried, roughly shaking off her hand.

"'Oh, you monster!' said my mother, turning to me.

"'Madam,' I said, 'you have made a mistake; it was dear Sinclair who gave you that amiable shake and growl.'

"My mother looked as spiteful as possible, and I laughed in her face and walked out of the room."

* * * * *

The wind blew a perfect hurricane, and the windows of Mr. Nicholson's villa rattled and creaked as if they would inevitably be dashed in by the blast, as he paused in his wild, strange narrative, about which there was, to my mind, a great air of truth, although tinctured by his excited imagination.

Perhaps I felt a greater degree of sympathy in his story than I should have otherwise done on account of the fact that in my own family there had been ruin and degradation, arising from my mother having favourites among her children, and making marked distinctions in her conduct towards them.

"What's o'clock?" murmured my patient, after a long pause.—"More than half-past eleven."

"Then I must be brief," he said; "I have not a great deal more to tell."

"The day after this fracas with my brother, the affair was detailed to my father by my mother in this fashion.

"She was passing the chamber door, she said, when she was alarmed to see it broken, and, stopping to listen, she heard Sinclair say,—

"'My dear brother, retire to rest now, and in the morning command me in any way.'

"Then she heard me, with shocking imprecations, violently assault him, because he was the eldest and the cleverest, upon which she rushed in, and was abused dreadfully by me, to all of which my brother said,—

"'Dear mother, never mind it; don't distress and bother me,—I forgive him.'

"This was my mother's usual method of dressing up a story, and my father sent for me to ask how I could think of behaving so very badly.

"'What must your mother think of you?' he said, after I had got from him her version of the story.

"'I know she hates me,' said I, 'and I'll tell you what I think of her.'

"'What?' he said.

"'That if she were ten times my mother, she's a liar.'

"My father got into a great passion, and I left him with a laugh. Then I went to my own room, and shut myself up for many hours, brooding over all that happened.

"Awful thoughts passed through my brain as I there sat, with my head resting on my hands, and my whole frame quivering with emotion. Some species of insanity then came over me, and I then thought how glorious it would be to disappoint them all by compassing the death of my brother. Ay, you may start, doctor, but I laughed aloud as I thought over the deed. How very much shocked would the 'respectable' Mr. Renshaw be!—What a blow it would be to my mother! How annoyed my father would be! Again and again I laughed at the idea. I felt quite happy, and went to the window to look out upon the sunshine in quite a delighted mood.

"As I stood there I saw Sinclair leave the house with a fishing-rod in his hand.

"Till that moment I had not given a thought as to the means of accomplishing his death, but now, like a flash of electricity, it crossed my mind that I would follow him, and throw him into the stream that he was taking his road to.

"I went hastily down stairs, and ordered my horse to be saddled.

"'I am going to ——' said I, naming a village some miles off, in the directly opposite direction to that in which the stream lay that my brother was proceeding to. 'If anything is wanted there, I can order it.'

"'If you wouldn't mind putting in a letter,' said the man, 'it will save me a long walk, sir. It's missus's letter, sir.'

"'Oh, my exemplary mother's letter,' said I, taking the letter. 'It shall be posted, John.'

"I mounted my horse, and then, calling to the man, said,—

"'John, tell me exactly the time by the hall clock.'— "'It's a quarter past ten, sir.'

"'How long, I wonder, will it take me to ride to the village?'—'You can't very well get there, sir, nohow, in less than half an hour.'

"'That will be a quarter to eleven?'—'Yes, sir.'

"'Very well.'

"Away I went at an easy canter. Leading to the high road was a green lane, thickly wooded on each side, and across a couple of meadows to the right of this lane, the house lying to the left, was the stream where I felt sure Sinclair was going to fish.

"I cantered to the middle of the lane, then threw myself from the horse, and tied the animal to a tree. The lane was very little frequented, as it only led from the high road to some farm-houses and mansions, so I did not anticipate any one finding my horse.

"I clambered the bank and burst through the hedge. Stooping low, I scoured across the meadows like a hunted hare. A bank only separated me now from the stream. I ascended it slowly. Just on the declivity of the other side, which was sloped down to the stream, sat my brother fishing. With a bound I was by his side, and I roared with laughter as I cried,—

"'Well, Sinclair, any sport?'—I saw him shrink and tremble, for, like all brutal people, he had no true courage. He answered me not a word, but bit his lips in a manner usual with him.

"'Don't you think your dear mamma would miss you, sweet, kind Sinclair, if you were to die suddenly?' said I. 'Pray answer, if it's only one of your amiable growls.'— 'Bah!' he cried.

"This was a favourite expletive of his, and he always clenched all arguments with, 'bah!'

"'Well,' said I, 'I have no time to lose, for I've got a letter to put in the post for mamma, and I dare say she won't like it delayed.'

"'What do you mean now?' he growled.—'I'm going to throw you into the stream,' said I, with perfect calmness.

"He was going to say 'bah!' but he looked in my face, and saw something there that alarmed him. He made a movement to rise, but I sprang upon him like a tiger. The strength of ten men seemed to be in my sinews. I lifted him up as if he had been a child, and threw him with a heavy plash into the stream. There was one stifled scream, and down he went. I knew the stream was deep, and that he could not swim, so I folded my arms, and looked on to see him rise again.

"Once—twice he rose! The second time I saw his face, turned towards me. His eyes were starting from their sockets, and the whole expression of his countenance was one of intense agony.

"I shouted—laughed with joy, and, as the water slowly closed again over his sallow, distorted countenance, I cried,— 'Bah!' and laughed till the tears ran down my cheeks.

* * * * *

"Three miles were done under the quarter of an hour, so I had the eight or nine minutes to spare for the next mile, and it was scarcely one. I dismounted, and wiped the horse carefully down with my handkerchief. I plucked some grass, and cleaned his mouth thoroughly from the foam that hung about it. When this was done he did not look so distressed, and at an easy canter I went the other mile, getting to the door of the post house just two minutes before the quarter to eleven.

"'Hilloa, Mr. Martin!' I cried, to the postmaster, 'here's a letter for your care.'

"He came out and took it from me.

"'What's o'clock?' said I.—'Just on the stroke of the three quarter chimes to eleven, Mr. Nicholson,' he said.

"Even as he spoke the village church clock struck the three quarters to eleven.

"'How far do you call it from our house to this place?' said I, carelessly.—'It's under the four miles, sir.'

"'I've come it in half an hour.'—'It's a good half-hour's canter, sir.'

"'Yet I came easy.'—'Oh! I mean easy, sir.'

"'Good day, Mr Martin.'—'Good day, sir.'

"I took the road home again. I had no motive for hurrying now, and, after having gone half way, I dismounted and let the horse get cool a little; then, mounting again, I reached the hall-door a few minutes after the quarter past eleven.

"'John,' said I, 'how long have I been gone?'—'Just an hour, sir.'

"'Oh! I thought I'd been longer. It's a long canter, John.'—'Yes, sir.'

* * * * *

"I walked into the common sitting-room, and there was my mother at work. She was always muddling over something, and I saw now that she was sewing some splendid black fur on the wrists and collar of a coat belonging to my brother.

"'Dear me,' said I, 'that will be very warm and comfortable when it's done. I wonder if it would keep out a great deal of damp?'—My mother put on as dignified a look as she could, and said nothing. Oh, how I chuckled to myself!

"'Have you got any more of that fur?' I said.—'No, I—have—not,' said my mother, fancying she was being very grand with her two negatives.

"'Oh, dear! what a pity,' said I; 'I should so have liked some on my green frock.'—My mother only gave a sort of snuffle in reply to this, and blew her nose.

"Oh! I could have shouted and roared again, I was so delighted. I had the prudence, however, to be quiet, and I left the room, I dare say to the satisfaction of my mother.

"How the idea of that fur coat pleased me! I ran up stairs to my own room; I bolted the door, and then lay on the bed, and kicked and laughed for half an hour. I never had enjoyed anything half so much in all my life.

"'No, I—have—not,' I repeated to myself over and over again, in imitation of my mother, and then I blew my nose with a snuffle, and nearly laughed myself into hysterics."

* * * * *

There was an awful, shrieking laugh which my patient indulged in occasionally, which, taking into consideration his situation, and the subject matter of his confession, sent a cold chill to my heart every time I heard it.

"For the love of Heaven, sir," I said, "do not speak in such a strain of those you are bound to love and honour."—"Doctor," he said, "you are right so far; I did love and honour my father and my mother, but they turned the love to hate,—the honour to scorn!"

"Can you," said I, "at this hour, when you are fully impressed with a belief of your approaching end, attempt to justify so awful a crime as murder, and that the murder of your own brother?"—"Hush! hush!" he cried; "don't speak of him just now. What noise was that?"

"I heard no noise."—"I did—I did," he whispered. "Look about. Do you see nothing?"

"We are the only animate forms here," said I; "your imagination tortures you, Mr. Nicholson."—"Yes; torture," he exclaimed; "torture is the right word,—torture—torture!"

"Were you never suspected of the deed you had committed?" said I, wishing to lead him back to his strange narrative.—"True—true," he said; "I have not told you all. Listen, doctor; that day was one of unmixed joy to me."

"Joy?"—"Yes, joy. I revelled in delight; but do not interrupt me. Hour after hour passed, and my brother came not home. The dinner was delayed—oh, how I laughed!—delayed for the swollen body that was at the bottom of the stream. My father at length lost all patience, and would wait no longer; so we sat down to dinner. My mother pricked up her ears at the least sound indicative, as she thought, of the approach of her sulky darling. Twice or thrice I made her jump, by suddenly exclaiming,—

"'There he is!' and when she cried, 'Where,—where?' I laughed in her face, and filled her with rage.

"Well, the dinner passed off, and my mother sent for the gardener, and said to him, with her usual hypocritical snuffle,—

"'Simon, be so good as to go to your young master, and tell him to come home. He went to fish, Simon.'

"'Yes, ma'am,' said Simon.

"'Mind you bring him home, Simon,' said I.

"My mother cast at me an indignant look, and rose to leave the room. I sprang from my seat and opened the door for her. She turned up her nose as she passed me, and looked as disagreeable as she could, which, in her case, was very disagreeable indeed. Oh! how much mortified would I have been that day had my mother shown any degree of kindness or gentle consideration for me! It would have killed me! And yet I was continually tempting her to do it.

"She passed out of the room, and I followed her into the passage.

"'Mother,' I said, 'if you will speak kindly to me, and think as much of me as you do of my brother, henceforward, I will forget all that has passed, and love you very much.'

"She blew her nose, and said,—

"'I am sure (snuffle) it's very natural I should like the eldest best; I have no ill will (snuffle) against you, I'm sure.'

"'Thank you,' said I; 'you are very kind indeed. Really you overpower me.'

"She passed on, and I went back to the dinner parlour, quite in an ecstasy of delight. In about half an hour the man Simon, who had been sent for my brother, returned with the fishing implements he had found on the banks of the stream, but with no tidings of the missing favourite. I ran up stairs to my mother's room, and tapped at her door.

"'Come in,' she cried.

"I walked into the room, when her brow was immediately covered with wrinkles, as she said pettishly,—

"'What *do* you want now? Really, I must speak to your father; you are quite an annoyance.'—'Pray excuse me,' said I.

"'What *do* you want!' she cried again.—'Simon has returned,' said I, half choking myself in efforts to smother my laughter.

"'Well, well, that will do,' she said; 'now do go away.'—'But he has not brought the dear, courteous, delightful favourite with him.'

"'What!'—'It's just as I tell you, dear, exemplary mother; it seems to be Simon's impression that the sweet, persuasive darling has fallen into the river, and got drowned—bless him!'

"My mother gave a loud scream, and fainted away, falling flat upon the floor. I then put my hands in my pockets, and walked down stairs quite happy. At the door of the dining-room I met my father.

"'What noise was that?' he said.—'Up stairs!' said I.

"'Yes, a scream.'—'Oh! that was dear mamma.'

"'None of your ribaldry, sir,' he cried, shaking his fist in my face. 'What do you mean, you scoundrel?'—'Go and see,' said I.

"He immediately struck me, and I returned the blow with interest." * * * * *

"Mr. Nicholson, you cannot mean to tell me that you struck your own father?" I said to my patient, with horror.—"I did," he replied.

"Good God!" I said, "I cannot believe you. Such a crime is awful. Had you never heard the divine commandment to 'honour thy father and mother, that thy days might be long in the land?'"

He made no reply, but I think my words made some impression on him, and that he at that moment felt that a child, in its intercourse with its parents, let them behave how they may, ought to have no passions, no frailties, no errors of impulse whatever; but love, honour and obey, everlastingly, according to the creed of all good and just men.

"Doctor," he said, "you are right; I know you are right now, although I thought very differently then. I thought at that time, in my ignorance and presumption, that the duty and love between a father and a child should descend from the parent to the child, and not ascend from the child to the parent. I used to think, in my folly, that parents ought, from their maturer age, to keep their temper, and show examples of forbearance to the children, instead of the young, erring, inexperienced things being called upon to rid themselves of all human frailties, and have consideration for their parents. I now see my error."—"I trust you do," said I; "but if it will ease your mind, pray go on with your awful confession.

"I have not much more to tell, doctor. The stream of water was dragged, and the ghastly, swollen body of my brother was found. My mother was frantic, and my father raved, while I used to lock myself up in my own room to laugh undisturbed. Well, doctor, my father died; in his last moments he sent for me and my mother, and turning to her, he said, in a very solemn, affecting voice,—

"'We have been punished by Heaven for our great sin in preferring one child to another. I now ask, before I meet my justly offended God, the forgiveness of my second son.'

"'You have it freely,' said I.

"My mother said nothing, but with a great blowing of her nose left the room. My father died that night. The next morning my mother was insane, and talked incessantly of a supernatural visit from my father to upbraid her with unjust favouritism among her children."

Here my patient paused for several minutes, and his hard breathing betrayed how much he suffered on account of his deep sinfulness. The wind had dropped, and no longer moaned around the murderer's dwelling. There was an awful and death-like stillness over Nature, which seemed to affect him more than the partial storm which had before howled around his home. In a much weaker voice he continued his awful narrative:—

"I stepped into undisturbed possession of the whole of the family property on the same day that my father was consigned to the tomb, and my mother to a lunatic asylum."—"But you were not happy?" said I.

"Happy,—happy!" he shrieked; "listen! On that night, for the first time since his death, I saw my brother!"—"Your brother!"

"Yes; he came with his swollen face and saturated clothes, and sat down at my bed-side."—"A dream," said I.

"No, not a dream. There he sat till morning, when he rose and walked away. I could see him in the dark, for there was an awful white light upon the ghastly face as he sat, pale, passionless, and immovable, gazing upon me for hours."—"How did you support such an awful fancy?" said I.

"You will call it a fancy," he replied.—"Certainly I do."

"It was real,—too real. When any one sat up with me, the figure would wait outside the chamber door."—"How could you know that?" said I.

"I *felt* it in my mind," he said; "I was sure of it. Doctor! doctor!"—"Well, what?"

"*It is there now!*"

I gave an involuntary start as Mr. Nicholson said this, for there was an impressiveness in his manner which cannot be described, but which thrilled through my whole system, and made my blood creep coldly in my veins.

"You know it is there," he added; "you feel as I do."—

"I will convince you that you are mistaken," said I, rallying from my first sudden surprise, and hastily walking to the door.

He partially rose from his bed, and followed me with his eyes. I opened the door, I own not without some degree of nervousness, which, under the circumstances, every one would have felt. The moment I did so, I gave a start back. There was some one there!

"There,—there!" said Nicholson; "oh, God! oh, God!"

He fell back upon his pillow with a deep groan, while I made a rush into the corridor, and caught the learned footman by the tail of his coat.

"Oh! sir, sir," he bellowed, "I only placed my *auricular* organ against the *inert* matter forming the door."—"How dare you listen to your master's private conversations?" said I.

"Knowledge is power, sir; it—it—says so on the admission cards to the Patent Mutual——"—"Pshaw!" said I; "you have most probably frightened your master to death with your absurd folly."

I gave him a shake, and hastily returned to the sick chamber, leaving him muttering something about the march of mind and the diffusion of useful knowledge.

Mr. Nicholson was quite insensible, but I soon restored him to consciousness; and he looked in my face with an expression scarcely human. He slowly extended his long, attenuated finger towards the window, and in a hoarse guttural voice he said,—

"Hark,—hark!"—"To what?" said I.

Then again he added,—

"Oh! save me from him,—save me. Let me die, at least, in peace. There,—there! His nails have grown after death, as many people's do, and,—he is tapping against the glass of the window to be let in. Oh! horrible—horrible!"

He covered his head now completely over with the bed-clothes, and trembled so violently that he shook the whole bed.

I looked towards the window, and it gave me a little shock to hear a distinct tapping against the glass, which it required no very great stretch of imagination to convert into the precise sound named by the guilty conscience of the murderer of his own brother.

A second thought told me how the sound was really produced. It was the pattering of rain against the glass!

I immediately walked to the window and ascertained that such was the case. The casement had a south-easterly aspect, and the rain, now that the high wind had abated, was beating thickly against it, producing exactly a sound similar to the awful one which the dying man had imagined.

"Mr. Nicholson," I said, shaking him by the shoulder, "it is the rain against the glass of the window, that your imagination has transformed into the sound you have mentioned."—"No, no," he shrieked from beneath the bed-clothes; "the curse of Cain is upon me; I am a murderer! Hell is at my feet; I am stepping into an abyss of fire! Help, help!"

He then commenced screaming in so dreadful a manner, that I was thankful the sounds were partially smothered by the bed-clothes, that he would not let me remove from his face.

"Mr. Nicholson, silence," I cried; "silence!"

He ceased screaming, and peered at me with one eye, which looked like a coal of fire, from beneath the clothes.

"What's o'clock!" he said suddenly.—"Never mind what's o'clock," said I; "be calm, and I will send for some medicine for you that will enable you to sleep."

"Are we alone?" he said, and his eye flashed with the wild fire of insanity.—"Quite alone," said I, fancying he alluded to the supposed presence of his murdered brother.

"Will you fetch me a paper you will find in yonder table drawer?" he said.—"Certainly," I replied, and I at once walked to the table drawer.

I thought then I heard a slight noise behind me, and turning my head quickly, I saw, to my horror and alarm, my patient creeping out of bed, with his eyes fixed upon me with an expression at once convincing to me that I was in the power of a dangerous madman. I involuntarily made a movement towards the door. He saw it, and with a spring flew towards it, and locked it, drawing out the key, and flinging it to the other end of the chamber, with a cry of exultation.

"Ha, ha, ha!" he shrieked, "I have you now,—I have you now!"—"Mr. Nicholson, what do you mean, sir?" said I, with as much courage as I could, on the spur of the moment, assume.

"So, so," he continued, "you are the favourite, are you? You want to drive me mad, too, with your dead face and clammy hands; but I'll kill you,—I'll kill you a second time! You shall haunt me no more. I threw you in the water whole, and that is the reason why you have got back; but now I will tear you to pieces. Ha, ha, ha! a rare plan, —a rare plan. You can't haunt me then."

"You mistake me," I shouted, with the hope that my voice might alarm the house; "I am Dr. ——."

He answered me by a yell, and at the same moment made a rush towards me; I avoided him, however, by dodging behind the table.

"I am your murdered brother's spirit," I said, as solemnly as my rather flurried nerves would permit me.—"I know it, —I know it," he roared; "you shall torment me no more."

"I will forgive you, and go to my grave in peace," I added, "if you will go to bed now."—"Who the h—l is to trust you?" he replied; "you are your mother's favourite, and a liar of course."

"The only way I have of convincing you," said I, "is by jumping from the garden in at the window of this room."—
"Ah!" he said; "then, indeed; but I'll have you jump out first."

"Oh," said I, "that's nothing. Anybody could jump out; but jumping in again is the thing."—"So it is," he said. "Be quick."

"You have locked the door," said I.—"There's the key," he replied; "mind and be quick. I'll stand here."

With a feeling as if I had been reprieved from execution, I picked up the key and went leisurely to the door. I was afraid of causing the madman's suspicions by hurrying, and I will say, that the few moments it took me to reach the door were perfectly agonizing and terrible.

"Are you going?" he cried.—"Yes," said I, with a jump, as I unlocked the door.

"Stay!" he roared.

Some such thought as "don't you wish you may get it," crossed my mind, and I fell at full length just outside the door, over the abominable learned footman, who was on his knees, listening at the key-hole.

* * * *

John screamed, and cried "murder!" the mad Mr. Nicholson yelled, and I won't, at this distance of time, say that I did not swear roundly. Such a confusion of sounds, perhaps, never was heard. What happened for the next few moments I can scarcely say, save that I gave and received a number of hard knocks, and then John and I rolled down the staircase together.

I scrambled up in the passage, half stunned, just as I saw an easy chair thrown down upon us by Mr. Nicholson, as if it had been a feather. He seemed to be possessed with the idea of pelting us. Bang came the dressing-glass; smash came a great water-jug: then the argand lamp came with a grand crash, just as I had scrambled to the street door.

"Murder,—murder!" roared John.—"Curse you!" said I; "your curiosity is as bad as Blue Beard's wife's,—quite fatal."

"Fire!" roared John, when he saw the lamp come swinging through the air, burning.

I opened the street door, and ran into the garden. The rain was coming down in torrents, and I was without my hat, so I paused a moment to consider what I should do, when out rushed John, and banged the door after him.

"Oh! sir," he groaned, "are you really *corporcally* here, or is you a false image on the *optic nerve?*"—"You have nearly been my destruction and your own," said I, "by your impertinent curiosity, and here we are, exposed to this rain, all in consequence of you."

"Why, certainly," he replied, "in consequence of the *attenuation* of the atmospheric atmosphere, the clouds is a discharging of their *aqueous* contents."—"Don't be a fool," I cried, for John's philosophy was just then sadly out of place, as far as I was concerned.

"You see, sir," he added, "the *porous natur* of human garments admits of *fluid fluidities* to get *insinivatingly* through the blessed *interstices*."—"I tell you what, John," said I, "if you give me any more of your science, I'll knock you down."

"Prostrate me, sir?"—"Yes."

"Reduce me from the *perpendicular* to the *horizontal* by the effect of *percussion?*"—"Now tell me, did your master come down stairs?"

"He was just a-going to remove *hisself* from the upper to the lower *stratum* of the house, when I bounced out with a great acquired *momentum*, and closed the outward *aperture* of the house with a great *concussion* of the air."—"Get me my hat," I cried.

"Supposes as we both wentures in at the scullery window?" suggested John; "it's at a *right angle* from the *washus*." —"I think we had better," said I, amused, in spite of myself, by John's scientific method of explaining everything.

He led me to the other side of the house, and, scrambling on the top of a water-butt, not without some risk, as he would have said, of being submerged in the aqueous mass, he opened the scullery window, and, with the assistance of a push from me, entered the house.

The moment he jumped on to the floor I heard a loud shriek. "It's only the cook and housemaid," cried John; "they have shut *theirselves* in the front kitchen, and are agitating of the atmosphere by screams and *highstericks*."— "Oh!" said I.

John then helped me in, and I tapped at the kitchen, crying,—"Silence!"

Whether or not my voice was taken to be of a supernatural character, I don't know, but the screams were stopped; and John, procuring a light, he and I cautiously, and very slowly, ascended the kitchen staircase, expecting each moment to be pounced upon by Mr. Nicholson. We, however, proceeded quite to the hall without any interruption or indication of the presence of the madman. There lay the chair, the lamp, and a heap of smaller articles which he had thrown after us; but there was no noise, nor could we see any signs of him, either in the hall, on the staircase, or in the rooms on that floor.

"Well, now, John," said I, "your master is a little mad, and would be more than a match for one sane man; but I think you and I may manage him, and it is your duty, as his servant, and mine, as his physician, not to desert him in this extremity."

John looked rather nonplused at this, and said,—

"Why, sir, I—I—that is, the doctrine of *utility*, and the —the———"—"If you have been taught any doctrine," cried I, "that will enable you with a clear conscience to refuse me your assistance, I am very sorry for you, John."

He looked rather posed at that, and, after a moment's hesitation, replied,—

"I—I will come, sir; but suppose as we goes in together, 'Union is strength, as well as knowledge is power,' as the schoolmaster said when he tied the two birch rods together to flog a young gentleman."—"Come on, then," said I, not a little amused at John's original and striking illustration of his moral aphorisms.

We took some time in creeping up to Mr. Nicholson's bedroom, and when we came near it, John, by my direction, placed his light upon a window sill, that he might not be encumbered in case of a sudden attack.

We heard nothing and saw nothing, however, until we reached the door of my patient's chamber; and then we did not see much, for the said door was close shut.

"Hush!" said John.—"Hush!" said I, and, treading upon our toes, while we scarcely breathed, we arrived on the landing close to the door.

I then listened attentively. All was still as the grave.

"He's a-waiting for a spring," suggested John, in a whisper.—"I hope not," I replied, in the same tone.

Then I put my ear close to the door, but heard nothing. I jammed my eye against the key-hole, but all was darkness in the chamber of the maniac.

"What shall we do?" whispered John.—"Why, we will stand out of the way of the door, and then knock," said I.

"The *very* thing," remarked John.

We accordingly posted ourselves quite clear of the doorway, so that if Mr. Nicholson should take it into his head to make a sudden bolt out, he would, perhaps, tumble down stairs, but would, at all events, miss us.

John then, after some search, took from his pocket a piece of lead pencil, and reaching out his hand, he tapped very gently at the door, immediately springing backwards several paces to see the result; but result there was none.

"He's very artful, sir," remarked John, in a whisper.— "Very; knock again."

John knocked again without any success.

"Louder," said I, and John hammered away at the door with great energy.

Still no notice was taken.

"He don't mind it a bit," remarked John.—"Mr. Nicholson!" I cried, in a loud voice, "will you open the door?"

No answer was returned.

"Bring the light, John," I said; "we must go in, since he will not come out."

John brought the light with a trembling hand, and I turned the lock of the door with some trepidation. There was no movement within the chamber. I flung the door wide open; the light fell in a stream upon the floor of the room.

The murderer lay *dead*, with a look of horror upon his face that I shall never forget! *   *   *   *

A distant relative laid claim to Mr. Nicholson's property, and I said nothing, at the time, of his strange confession. By inquiry, however, I quite satisfied myself of the truth of his story. His brother had been accidentally drowned, I was told; no one knew how or when. I asked if the younger brother was ever suspected of the crime. I was told, "Yes; but it was proved he was at another place at the time, and could not have had time to do it."

As for John, I found, by a little judicious pumping, that he had not heard enough at the key-hole to understand what his master was talking about.

The family are now extinct, and, therefore, I have felt no hesitation in bringing forward this passage from my Diary.

THE FRIGHT.

THE imaginary maladies of the human race afford more employment to physcians, surgeons, and apothecaries, than all their real complaints, and I honestly say, now that I have retired from practice, that I am more indebted for the little independence which is now my own, and which it gives me pleasure to think will save my children from the struggle their father had in early life, to my imaginary patients than my real ones.

Imagination will, however, react, as it were, upon the physical structure, and produce not unfrequently more fatal results than disease in the first instance, as the curious case I am about to relate will sufficiently testify to my readers.

As I have remarked somewhere before, it was my custom to receive my poor patients, who could not afford to pay anything, before nine o'clock in the morning, and after that hour even. I conscienciously say I never refused my advice to any one for any fee that was tendered to me, along with the assurance that it was all the party could conveniently give; and I will here say, for my professional brethren, that I never met with but two instances in the course of forty-eight years of a physician refusing his advice on account of the inadequacy of a fee tendered by a poor person; and I have known, to the honour of the medical profession, hundreds of instances in which the physician has not only given his advice gratis, but money out of his own pocket to purchase the medicines he prescribed for the case.

But to my story.

As early as eight o'clock there came to me one morning a young man of gentlemanly exterior, although a second glance convinced me that he and good fortune were by no means intimate, and in a tremulous voice requested to know if I would accept a very small sum for my advice.

"What," said I, good-humouredly, "do you call a very small sum?"

He coloured a little and named a sum under half my usual fee.

"I am sure," I replied, "if you can afford no more than that, you can afford nothing at all; so I shall take nothing from you. Just state to me your case, and I will do all I can for you."

He thanked me, and I could see that he trembled violently, and kept fidgetting about, and casting the most troubled and anxious glances around him. "Compose yourself," I said. "There is no particular hurry. Pray take your own time."

"Sir," he said, "I—I have had a fright."

"A what?" said I, in surprise.

"A fright, sir; and I thought, perhaps, that it might have arisen from some affection of the brain, as I have read of such things."

"Pray be a little more explicit," said I. "What has alarmed you?"

He was now seized with such a fit of trembling, that for several seconds he could not speak, and I was quite lost in conjecture as to what could have produced so terrible an effect upon the nervous system.

"Take your time—take your time," I said; "I dare say we shall find a cure for your fright. Your imagination has deceived you in some way. Pray be composed; nothing, I assure you, is more common."

"Did—you," he faltered, "ever have a patient such as I?"

"I have had patients more frightened than you are," replied I, smiling, "and, I dare say, with quite as little cause. You look well enough; but I suppose you fancy something very dreadful is the matter with you?"

"No, sir," he said, "I am well enough, if it was not for the fright."

"Well, I am all attention," I said.

"Sir," he began, "I am clerk to a barrister in Lincoln's Inn, and was very intimate with a fellow clerk of the name of Montrose. We almost lived together, and better friends could not be. Well, sir, Montrose died very suddenly."

"When?" said I.

"About a year since. I regretted his loss very much; in fact, it quite preyed upon my mind for some months; but after that time I began gradually to forget him, and recovered entirely from the shock his decease had given me. I should tell you that he died in the week in which it was my birthday, and I had contemplated giving a little party at my mother's, which the death of my bosom friend entirely put off, for I was then in no spirits for such a thing.

"This week, however, my birthday came round again, and as poor Montrose had been dead a year, and I had got over my excessive grief, I determined upon having the party which had been usual for so many years, with the exception of the last.

"We met, then, sir, at my mother's humble house, and about twelve young persons were as happy as could possibly be. The thought of my lost friend never once crossed my mind all the evening, and in fact it was remarked by every one that I was in unusual spirits, and was quite the life of the party. Then, sir, some one proposed a game at cards."

Here my patient paused, and glanced uneasily around him again, his colour going and coming almost with every breath he drew, and his eyes starting in a very wild and incomprehensible manner.

"Go on," I said, for I confess that I was becoming interested in his story, which I was quite convinced would terminate in something curious.

"Some one proposed cards," he repeated, "and I immediately seconded the proposition, and gaily asked my sister for the cards.

"'They are in the cheffonier,' she said; but upon my searching there they were not to be found.

"'Now I recollect,' suddenly said my mother, 'I put them up-stairs in the cupboard on the staircase.'

"'Did you?' said I; 'then I will get them in a moment if you will lend me one of the candles.'

"I then snatched a candle from the table, and full of gaiety of heart, humming an air as I went, I ascended the staircase to seek the cards, which I understood were in a cupboard that was situated on the landing of the second floor.

"I found them easily, and with the same lightness of heart turned to descend again to the room from whence I could distinctly hear the sounds of laughter and merriment. I don't know, then, sir, how it was, but a strange sensation came over me as I was descending the staircase, and I trembled violently. I reached the landing of the first floor, and had my foot upon the second stair of the next flight, when, *standing two steps below me, in the very centre of the staircase, stood Montrose.*"

"What," said I, "your deceased friend?"

"Yes, doctor. There he stood, motionless, in the middle of the staircase. I saw his pale face as plainly as I now see yours. An awful chillness crept over my heart, and my blood seemed to pause in its current through my veins. I stood for several awful minutes petrified with intense horror, with the light in my hand, stretched out before me, and wanting power to move or scream. Oh, those moments were horrible! horrible! horrible!"

"This might have been mere fancy," said I. "You ought to have reason enough to battle against such a freak of the imagination."

"I—I wish I could think it imagination," he said. "I have come to you, sir, to be assured it was nothing else."

"But what happened next?" said I. "How did this affair end?"

"I don't know how long I confronted the vision, but by a powerful effort I at last succeeded in turning my eyes from the pale, horrible, immovable face, and then, like one awakening from a frightful dream, I found strength to scream, and uttered a loud cry, that it appears alarmed the assembled party below. I suppose I then fainted, for I knew nothing more till I found myself in the parlour, and my mother bending over me with restoratives."

"And what account did your friends give of the transaction?"

"They told me that I was gone an unusual time, and they were upon the point of calling to me, when they heard me scream, and rushing out of the parlour, they found me lying in the passage in a state of insensibility, and the cards all strewed about, while the candlestick was firmly clutched in my hand."

"But did they see or hear anything of this extraordinary vision of yours?"

"Nothing, sir. They could not divine the cause of my fainting and alarm until I related to them what I had seen."

"All this was last night?"—"Yes, sir."

"How have you slept?"

"Slept?—I have not slept at all, sir. I shall never sleep again, because I shall be afraid of being alone."

"Oh," said I, "you must not allow yourself to be scared in this way. Your health will suffer, and your existence will become a burden to you."

"It is now," he exclaimed. "What shall I do?—What will become of me? I shall have no peace till I am in the grave, now, for I shall ever in my hours of pleasure expect again to see that horrible vision, with its ghastly pale face, which will, I am certain, drive me mad."

"You must be aware," said I, "that it is scarcely within the province of a medical man to be of any service to you in this dilemma; but speaking to you now merely as one man to another, I should say you ought to endeavour to reason yourself out of this fright."

"How, sir?" he said; "it overcomes all reason."

"Why, in this way," I replied; "this appearance of your friend was either real or imaginary."

"Granted, sir; oh, of course."

"Well," continued I, "if real, it is highly and monstrously inconsistent with the general designs, as we know them, of a beneficent Diety to allow one class of his creation to torment another; and you should look upon this visitation with some degree of philosophical interest, as merely one of the various and complicated phenomena of nature."

"Yes, yes," he said; "but it is so fearful, so awful a phenomena, that it shakes our very natures, doctor."

"But on the other hand," said I, "the strongest probability exists that this appearance was merely a coinage of your own brain. Such cases are common in medical practice, and we are unprovided with remedies for them when they do occur."

"I wish I could think it was imagination," he said.

"You may depend it is."

"It will, notwithstanding, be my ruin," he said.

"Your ruin? In what way?"

"To tell the truth, sir," he said, trembling, and his teeth chattering with nervousness, "I dare not go to the chambers of my employer in the evening, for fear of being confronted, when alone some time, by that horrible spectre."

"If you torture yourself that way," I said, "you will become a burthen to yourself and every one else. Endeavour, to the extent of your means, to take as much amusement as possible, and come to me whenever you please; but above all things attend to your business as usual, and do not permit yourself to be scared merely because you are alone."

"But I cannot sleep, sir."

"Well, if you should get no sleep to-night, come to me in the morning, and I will write you a prescription that will obviate that evil."

He thanked me with pale, quivering lips, and moved trembling to the door of the room, out of which he looked cautiously before he would venture into the passage. Then he hurried out of the house in great perturbation of manner.

I considered this young man's a most melancholy case, and I felt quite certain, from the state of mind he was in, that if he did not speedily rally from his fright, he would inevitably become insane. I should have mentioned that he left his address with me, and I resolved, if I could spare time, to call upon his mother, and talk with her upon the subject of her son's singular delusion, although it was certainly one of the best authenticated ghost stories that I had ever met with in the course of my life.

His family lived in Carey-street, near to Lincoln's Inn, and it happened that it was very little out of my way to make a call, which I accordingly did; and upon stating who I was, and my errand, I was favoured with the particulars of the scream being heard upon the staircase, and the fainting,—just as my patient had himself described them to me, to all of which, however, was added a firm opinion of the reality of the vision; and I could see that the family were in a state of alarm very little inferior to the young man himself.

I reasoned with them upon the absurdity of their conduct, and more particularly pointed out the necessity of treating the matter lightly to the young man, as a contrary course must necessarily greatly aggravate the case.

This they promised me, but I could easily see that it was not from conviction of the imaginary character of the alarm. I left my card, and requested them to make no scruple in sending for me should anything happen of an alarming character.

For two days now I heard nothing of my patient in Carey-street, whose name, by the bye, was Booth; but after dark on the evening of the second day, as I was sitting at tea, my servant told me that a lady wished to see me, and I accordingly at once repaired to my reception-room, where sat a young lady.

I bowed, and made some casual remark, as my visiter was a stranger to me, when she said,—

"You don't recollect me, sir? I am Miss Booth."

"I beg your pardon," said I; "indeed, I did not recollect you. You are the sister of Mr. Booth, who imagined he saw a ghost, I believe? I hope he is recovered from his fright."

"I think, sir, my brother is better—a little,—but,—but, sir,——"

Here she paused, and, I waited for some moments in expectation that she would proceed; but she only shook and sobbed.

"What is the matter with you?" I said; "what is the meaning of this emotion?"

"Oh! sir," she said, "you will scarcely believe it, but,—but——"

"But what?"—"I have seen Montrose."

"Seen who?" said I, for at that moment I quite forgot that was the name of the ghost who was making himself so common in Carey-street.—"The apparition, sir; the same that my brother saw upon the staircase."

"Now my dear girl," I said, "how can you be so very absurd? You have allowed your fancy to brood over this matter until you have quite disordered your brain about it. Surely you cannot for one moment be so foolish as to think you have seen such a thing, except in imagination, or in a dream?"

"It was no dream, sir," she said; "oh! I shall never forget it."—"Well, tell me all about it," said I; "where did you see Mr. Montrose?"

"This afternoon, sir, I went up stairs to my bed-room, as I usually do, to make some change in my dress, and I am sure I was not thinking at all of Montrose, although I knew him very well, as being a frequent visiter of my brother's. It was quite light enough to see everything, although very near sunset, and I walked into my bed-room, as free from any superstitious fears as any one could possibly be, when, to my horror and surprise, I saw, as plainly as I now see you, sir, a figure seated in a chair, with its face towards the door, the first glance at which assured me that it was Montrose."

"What did you do?" said I.

"I should have screamed, I am sure, if I could; but my tongue seemed to cleave to the roof of my mouth, and I suppose I fainted, for I found myself lying on the floor after a time, and I heard my mother's voice calling, 'Mary,' from the bottom of the stairs. I had presence of mind enough then to feel the necessity of not alarming her, and I cried, 'I am coming,' in as composed a tone as I could assume."

"Then you have said nothing about this at home?"

"Nothing, sir," she replied; "I rose as hastily as I could, and you may be sure my first glance was at the chair, and it was a great relief to me to find it no longer occupied by that spectre. I then made some trifling alteration in my dress, and went down stairs to my mother."

"Your story is very strange," said I. "You are quite certain there were no clothes or other articles on the chair that could in the dim of the evening light deceive you by accidentally assuming the shape of a human being?"

"Quite, sir," she said; "the chair was vacant, I am sure."

* * * * * *

I own I felt myself completely at a loss what to say to Miss Booth. She told her tale so clearly and distinctly, and moreover had shown so much sense and discretion in keeping the visitation of the spectre to herself, and saving her mother the alarm and her brother the great additional shock of the second appearance of his deceased friend, that to laugh at her was quite out of the question.

"Miss Booth," said I, "you do not believe in supernatural appearances?"

"I never did, sir," she replied; "but what would be your feelings if you felt confident you had seen what I feel confident I have seen?"

This was rather a home question; but I replied gravely,—

"There have been so very many well-authenticated affairs of this kind, Miss Booth, that have been afterwards explained quite in a rational manner, that however singular this one may seem at present, I cannot but think that something or another will turn up to deprive it of its supernatural complexion."

"I hope so, sir," said my visiter; "but—but I really cannot help thinking there is something in it of an awful character, sir."

"Well," said I, "my time, you must be quite aware, Miss Booth, is rather valuable, and I cannot waste a great deal of it watching at your house for the ghost: but should it come again, I certainly will do my best to obtain a sight of it. I beg, therefore, you will send for me directly anything of an alarming character happens."

The young lady, having then thanked me for my politeness, left me, and I could not but be surprised at the singular delusion under which the family were labouring, and, in fact, I fully expected to hear much more of the ghostly appearances at Carey-street.

Two days now elapsed, and I heard nothing from the Booths; in fact, I began really to think that the ghost was laid for ever in the Red Sea, or some such comfortable locality.

On the morning, however, of the third day, a note came from Miss Booth, earnestly requesting I would favour her and her mother with a call. This request I complied with as soon as I had leisure so to do, and when I arrived I found the family in a state of consternation and alarm that surprised me.

"What has happened?" said I.—"Oh! sir," exclaimed the mother, "we have a lease of the house."

"Have you?" said I; "I hope it's a valuable one."

"But that's what torments me."

"Indeed! I thought it was the ghost that tormented you. Has the lease of the house taken to walking?"

"Ah! sir," she said, "don't you see we can't conveniently move, in consequence of having a lease? Who would take a dreadful haunted house?—and we can't give notice to quit."

"Why, certainly," said I, "that is rather a disagreeable dilemma to be placed in: but you have not been annoyed, I hope, since I saw you?"

"Annoyed!" screamed Mrs. Booth.

"Annoyed!" exclaimed Miss Booth.

"Yes, by the ghost?" said I.—"Sir, we haven't a whole piece of crockery in the house. All is broken."

"Broken?"—"Yes, smashed."

"By the ghost?"—"Yes, sir, we suppose so. There again."

Bang,—crash went something at this moment, apparently in a room over head, and while the mother and daughter looked at each other with blanched faces, and looks of terror and consternation, I, without any ceremony, rushed up stairs as quickly as I could to the scene of the noise.

I ran into the first room that presented itself, and there I saw a tolerably handsome looking-glass lying on the floor in fragments. One glance round the room was sufficient to assure me there was no one there, and I hastily walked down about three of the stairs, and called to Mrs. Booth in the parlour.

She answered me from the passage.

"Madam," said I, "is there any one up here?"—"Not that I know of," she replied; "Mary, where are you?"

"Here, mum," said a voice from the lower regions.

"Will you come up stairs," said I, "while I watch this room door, and thoroughly ascertain that there is no one here?"

After a few moments' delay, the mother and daughter crept up the staircase.

"I will search," said I, "if you will permit me, provided you two stand at this door, and see that no one passes."

They both stood trembling on the landing, while I explored the remainder of the house, and quite satisfied myself there was no one in it. I returned with a feeling of disappointment to the landing-place.

"You have seen no one?" I said.—"No, sir."—"Nor have I."

"What was the noise?"—"Something broken, we suppose?"

"Yes, a looking-glass. Here it lies."

We entered the room together, where lay the fragments of the glass.

"Ah!" said Mrs. Booth, "that's the way all day long. We shan't have a whole thing left presently."

"That may have been quite accidental, you know," said I.

"Yes," said Mrs. Booth, "but everything is going in the same way."

Smash at this moment went something below stairs.

For a moment we all three stood staring at each other, and then down I rushed into the front parlour, where the first object that presented itself to me was a broken pane of glass in the window.

In a moment the mother and daughter followed me, trembling.

"The window is broken," said I.

"Where will all this end?" exclaimed poor Mrs. Booth, sitting down and weeping bitterly, in which Miss Booth soon joined company.

"Come, come," I said, "don't give way to this affair in this way. Call up the girl, and let me question her. Servants have been known to play these tricks."

The girl was summoned, and appeared, looking very much scared. She was a simple-looking-girl, with rather a prepossessing appearance.

"Well, Mary," I said, "what do you know of all these breakages?"—"I know, sir?"

"Yes, you."—"I've guved missus warning, sir."

"Oh! have you? But what do you think of the ghosts, that break the things?"

"I wouldn't stay on no account, sir, and I'm afeard I shan't get another place. Oh, oh, oh, oh!"

Here she covered her face with her dirty apron, and set up a howling that I was glad to stop, by saying,—

"Hush,—hush! why shouldn't you get another place?"

"Be—be—because people will—will say I—I—I—I—came from the ghostess's house. Oh! lor! There's a char—char—character to have. Oh, oh, oh!"

"Nonsense," said I, "go along with you."

She curtseyed and left the room.

"Well, madam," I said, turning to Mrs. Booth, "I cannot offer you an explanation of what is going on; but that some explanation, not at all, of an alarming or supernatural nature, will turn up very shortly, you may depend."

"They can't break much more," said Miss Booth, "for we have not such a thing as a whole plate in the house."

A knock now announced a visiter, and I rose to go; but Mrs. Booth begged me to stay, saying that it was her son's knock, who was returned from his office.

In a moment afterwards he came, and saluted me with a sickly smile. He looked pale, emaciated, and care-worn.

"Well, mother," he said, "Mr. —— says I must leave him if I cannot attend chambers in the evening."

The mother sighed.

"My dear young man," said I, "you will surely not give up your means of livelihood for such a thing as that?"

"Doctor," he said, "I cannot go into those dark rooms alone at night."—"Why not?"

"I have a presentiment that if I do I shall never come out a living man."—"Oh! nonsense," said I; "that is sheer nervousness and imagination."

"Mr. ——," he said, naming his employer, "is quite right. Evening attendance is absolutely necessary for the business."—"How is that?"

"I am with a barrister," he said, "and the attorneys many of them make a practice of not sending out briefs and papers until they close their own offices."—"When is that?"

"At eight."

"So you barristers' clerks are compelled to remain later?"

"Yes; we must be at the chambers till nine, to give the attorneys' clerks time to bring us papers."

"But why do they not send them earlier?"

"Because the clerk's time would be occupied, whereas now these papers are given them to deliver at over hours."

"Oh, I see," I said; "well, you, as an individual, cannot hold out against a system, however bad it may be."—"I cannot go," he said.

"But what resource have you?"

"I must starve," he cried, despondingly, "or try to get into a solicitor's office, where I shall not be alone."

"When ought you to go back,—to-day?"—"At about seven."

"Well, then, if you will promise me that in future you will go by yourself, should there be no alarm to-night, I will go with you for this once."—"You, sir?"

"Yes."—"I sincerely thank you, sir. I did promise to attend to-night, but fear I should have shrunk from it."

"Well, well," I said, "we will go together. It's half-past four nearly, now. I will come here for you at seven."

The whole family were profuse in their thanks to me, and I went home to settle some affairs for the evening, before accompanying my young friend to his lonely chambers.

It wanted ten minutes to seven when I again knocked at the door of my patient. I was admitted by Mary, who looked more frightened than ever, and when I reached the parlour I found the family assembled, looking at each other in a most unhappy frame of mind.

"Well," I said, "nothing else has happened, I hope, since I was here?"

"Only all the windows up stairs broken," said Mrs. Booth, with a desponding look.—"Indeed."

"Yes; and how we know not, for we heard no noise."

"I cannot deny that it is very strange," said I; "but still I adhere to my opinion that the thing will explain itself some day or another."

The young man now rose to accompany me to his office, and I saw that he trembled, and was in a state of nervous excitement, so much so, indeed, that I hesitated in my own mind upon the propriety of letting him go to his office: but then I reflected that any shrinking on my part would do him more injury than the little excitement of going, and I was sure that after he had been, he would be a great deal better, and recover his equanimity.

"Well, are you ready," I said, in a cheerful voice.—"Quite, quite," he replied, nervously.

"Come along, then," said I, "and for once in my life I will become an assistant barrister's clerk."

He smiled faintly, and I saw him cast a sad and dejected look round the room before we left it.

"You will be home by nine?" said his mother.—"At a quarter past," he said.

We then left the house, and when we were in the street he said,—

"Doctor, I am sure if I were to see anything in these chambers, the shock would kill me,"—"Nonsense," I replied; "why should it? You do not take a rational view of this matter at all. You may depend that the best way to get over a dread of supernatural appearances is to admit the possibility of them, and then reason yourself out of any fear of them. You may be assured that when you have once reached that point of philosophy, you will never see, or fancy you see, a ghost."

"Yes," he said; "but,—but it requires a strong mind.—"A strong fiddlestick!" said I; "you are weak just now and nervous, but if I were you, I should feel some curiosity to see the inhabitant of another world. Only fancy, if there were but one solitary instance, that was beyond a doubt, of the appearance of a person after death, how many religious and other doubts it would solve."

"Yes, that is true."

"The misfortune is," continued I, "that ghosts never will settle that question, since they always choose to appear so mysteriously as to leave ample room for doubting if they ever appear at all. Now, if some benevolent ghost, who was fond of demonstration, would but appear at Charing Cross some day at noon, and settle the question, what an admirable thing it would be."

"You are not a believer, doctor."—"But I should be, then."

"Well, I will tell you what alarms me in my office at night."—"What is it?"

"The room in which I sit is large and lofty. One corner of it, distant from my desk, is railed off by a partition and little rails, as you see in counting-houses, just high enough for a person to look through."

"I understand," said I.—"Well, I can never get rid of the idea that a face is looking at me through these rails."

"What face?"—"The face of Montrose, for he used to sit there often."

"Your desk is at the other end of the room, I presume?"—"It is."

"And that railed in space is dark?"—"Yes."

"Then I will tell you of a simple remedy for what you mention."—"Indeed! How, sir?"

"Go you and sit there yourself. Make it your place."—"I never thought of that."

"You will then deprive it of its gloom and its terrors. You shall sit there to-night."—"I certainly will," he said; "but,—but you will stay with me?"

"If you wish it, I certainly will; but I only contemplated —seeing you comfortable, and then coming away."—"I think after to-night," said he, "I shall do very well, doctor."—"I am sure you will."

"Here we are," he said, diving into a dark doorway in ——'s Inn.

"Where are your chambers?"—"On the ground floor. We have three rooms. One is a waiting-room; the other is the private room of Mr. ——, and the third is the one I occupy."

"How do you get a light?" said I.—"From the lamp on the staircase," said he; "I left a candle just within the door."

He now produced the key of the outer door, and although I could not see, I felt sure, from the time he was in opening it, that his hand shook. Moreover, I could hear him catching his breath in a singular manner.

"I will walk in," said I, "while you get the light."

The outer door was now opened, and a latch key which he produced opened the inner one, leading into the waiting-room he had mentioned. Into that I stepped, and he said,—

"I have the candle, and will bring a light in a moment."

So saying, he left me in darkness in the haunted chambers. In about a minute he returned with a light, and then I saw that he looked very pale and haggard. Again I hesitated whether it would not be better, even now, to take him home; but again the thought came across me, that as nothing would happen to alarm him in the chamber, I had far better proceed with him.

"Which is the door of your room?" I said, gaily, — "the ghost room, I mean?"

There were two doors, and he pointed to the farthest, saying,—

"That is it."—"Very well," said I; "come along."

I opened the door and walked in, he following with the light. I gave a glance round the room—it was spacious and dismal, but before I could utter a remark I was stunned by a piercing shriek from Booth, and he instantly exclaimed,—

"The face!—the face!—oh, God, the face!"

I instinctively looked towards the railed-in corner of the room, and at the moment that my patient fell to the ground with the light, I did see a strange, unearthly-looking face peering between the wooden rails.

For a moment my heart leaped to my mouth, and I started back. All was then darkness, for the candle had gone out, and there I was in a pretty predicament.

In a moment I heard a low rustling sound. I was standing close to the door, and I stretched out my arms till I found it.

The slight noise continued, and I heard a cautious step in the room. I held my breath to listen, and planted myself exactly in the doorway.

Cautiously the step approached me, and I strove to convince myself that the whole affair was either some heartless trick or a projected robbery.

I stretched out my arms so as to fill up all the doorway, and felt satisfied no one could pass out without striking against me, if it was a form of flesh and blood. I own the few minutes of suspense that ensued were especially disagreeable, but nevertheless I kept my position.

The footsteps cautiously advanced, and before the lapse of another moment something touched my left arm. With my right I immediately made a plunge forward, and got hold of some one, who, I felt convinced, belonged to this world, and was of earth, earthy.

"The devil!" cried a voice.

In an instant I grappled my opponent, and with my left hand commenced hitting out as rapidly as I could, and had the satisfaction of feeling that every one of my blows told well upon some one, who now began to roar lustily,—

"Murder,—murder,—murder!"

This did not stop me, however, and I only at length desisted from striking out with one hand and holding fast with the other, when several people carrying lights rushed into the room.

"What's the matter?" cried at least half a dozen voices in chorus.

"Murder,—murder!" bellowed the ghost.

For a moment the lights dazzled me, and then I saw, sitting on the ground, whereon he had dropped upon my releasing my hold, the person I had been battering away at, adorned with a face full of contusions and a bleeding nose.

"What's the matter?" again cried everybody in a breath.

"Murder,—fire!" shrieked the ghost, who, I imagine, could scarcely see out of his eyes.

"I can scarcely tell you what's the matter," said I; "can any of you tell me who that person is?"

"Why," said one, "that is Nikel, Mr. ——'s clerk."

"And who is Mr. ——?" said I.

"He has the next chambers."

"Murder!" again shrieked Mr. Nikel.

"Silence!" said I; "cease your bellowing, and explain, if you can, how you came here, will you?"

"I—I came here for a piece of fun," groaned the punished Nikel.

"Fun?" I said.

"Yes, I wanted to frighten Booth. My key fits his door. Oh, my nose!"

"You are rightly punished," said I, in a tone of great disgust. "As yet, I am ignorant of the amount of mischief you have done by your heartless jest."

I stooped, and raised Booth from the floor, and with the assistance of those who had entered the chambers, alarmed by the cries of murder, placed him in a large arm-chair. I laid my hand on his pulse, then on his heart,—*He was dead!*

I suppose those around me saw, by the expression of my face, what had occurred, for they looked at each other in mute terror and astonishment.

"Fetch a constable," said I, "some of you. We shall want one."

"I am a constable, sir," said one who was present; "I am the gate-keeper, and a sworn constable."

"Then," said I, "I give that man," pointing to Nikel, "in charge for murder!"

"Murder!"

"Yes, I distinctly charge him with causing the death of this young man."

"Me,—me!" exclaimed the sham ghost, "I never touched him. I—I only came here for fun. He told me that he was afraid of a face behind those rails, and I hid there just for a lark. I didn't kill him."

"Constable," I said, "I am Doctor ——."

The constable made a low bow.

"You will take charge of this man. You are now answerable for his safe keeping. You had better take him to the watch-house at once, and in the morning I will attend at the police-office, to prefer a charge of murder against him."

"Certainly, sir," said the constable; "come, Mr. Nikel, this here's a ugly job. Come, get up, and *foller* peaceably."

"You,—you don't mean it?" exclaimed the terrified sham ghost; "take me up, and I haven't done anything!"

"Not done anything?" said I; "look there, at that mute but solemn and eloquent witness against you. Look, sir, there lies the dead victim of your 'piece of fun.'"

He gazed at the dead body of Booth, perfectly aghast.

"I,—I never touched him," he said.

"But yet you killed him. Constable, take him away."

"No, no,—mercy!" cried Nikel; "I—I didn't mean to do it. I only meant to frighten him by showing him the face he was so much afraid of."

I took hold of Nikel by the arm, and led him to the corpse.

"There," I said,—"there is a face that, I were in your situation, would haunt me for ever."

He screamed, and covered his face with his hands.

"Take him away,—take him away, and may this be an awful warning to all who indulge themselves in heartless jests against their more susceptible fellow-creatures."

He made no further remark, and the constable took him off, asking me to follow, and substantiate the charge at the station-house.

After ascertaining the residence of Mr. ——, the employer of Booth, I myself locked up the chambers, leaving the body laid on the chairs, and hurried after the constable and his prisoner.

The business was very soon concluded. I formally charged Joseph Nikel with murder, and he was as formally conducted to a cell, there to ruminate on his condition.

* * * *

Half an hour more found me in Russell-square, at the house of Mr. ——, the barrister, in whose service poor Booth had been. I was received by that gentleman with all the courtesy which distinguishes his profession; and when I related to him the particulars of the evening, and their fatal termination, he voluntarily offered to attend at the investigation on the morrow, and likewise to go with me to Booth's mother, to break to her, with as much gentleness as possible, the affecting tidings of the sudden death of her son.

This we did as well as it could be done, although what can soften the shock of such news to a mother's heart?

On the road to Carey-street I related to Mr. —— all that had occurred as to the mysterious breakings in the house inhabited by the Booths, to which he seemed to pay very great attention.

When Mrs. Booth had heard all we had to say, and was assisted by her daughter and myself to her chamber, I returned to Mr. ——, who was waiting in the parlour.

"Doctor," he said, "all these breakages must be contrived by some one in the house."

"So I think," said I; "but who?"—"The servant of course."

"You can question her," said I; "but she seems innocence itself."

"I knew a case similar to this," said he, "when a little stratagem succeeded in finding out the guilty party, at the same time that it inflicted no needless alarm upon the innocent."

"Indeed!"—"Yes; let us go into the kitchen; and do you take your cue from me."

Without further ceremony we descended to the lower regions of the house, and, to the intense astonishment of Mary, we walked into the kitchen.

"Well, my lass," said Mr. ——, "so all your crockery is broken by the ghost?"—"Yes, if you plase, sir."—

"We don't believe in ghosts."—"Don't you, sir?"

"No; and we fancy some one concealed in the house has done all the mischief."—"Lor, sir?"

"Yes; we feel sure of it; and now what's your name?"—"Mary, sir."

"Mary what?"—"Mary Brown, sir."

"Very well. Just light us a fire in the copper."—"The copper, sir?"

"Yes; and lend us a carving-knife, a large frying-pan, and the rolling-pin."

Mary opened her eyes so wide at this, that I thought she would never get them shut again.

"Please, sir, w—w—what for?"

"To find out who broke the things."—"How sir?"

"Oh, that's a secret known only to doctors and lawyers.—We don't mind telling you a little, in case you should be frightened."—"Ye—ye—yes, sir."

"Have you an old leaden spoon?"—"Ye—yes, sir."

"That will do to melt," cried Mr. ——, turning to me.

"Exactly," said I.

"We had better use a tea-spoon, because a quantity of molten lead might produce instant death if poured incautiously down anybody's throat."

"I rather think it might," said I, with difficulty suppressing a smile.

"A tea-spoon, then, Mary."

"M—m—melted lead, sir? W—w—what for?"

"Why, when we have completed the *habeus corpus*, eh, doctor?"

"Yes," said I, "and the *lunatico inquirendo*."

"Exactly. The melted lead will go in one continuous stream down the throat of he or she who broke the crockery."

"Of course."

Mary looked from one to the other of us as we spoke, until she gasped again.

"Light the fire," said Mr. ——.

"And get the frying-pan," said I.

Mary hesitated a moment, and then, falling on her knees with a dab that shook the kitchen, she cried,—

"Oh, let me go,—let me go; it was me!"

"You!" cried Mr. ——.

"You!" said I.

"Yes. I—I thought as—as it would be a—a piece of fun to—to frighten missus, partikler as she—she only gives seven pound wages, and—and stops break—breakages."

"Oh," said Mr. ——, "so that mystery is exploded. You see, doctor, what a passion there is for practical joking."

"There is, indeed.",

"Mary Brown, you will be hung."

"Hung!" screamed Mary; "hung by—by my neck?"

"Why, you don't want to be hung by your heels, do you?"

Mary now executed a fit of hysterics, and Miss Booth came running down stairs to know what the uproar was about, to whom we explained the discovery we had made, and in whose care we left the simple, innocent, quiet-looking Mary Brown, the ghost of Carey-street.

"I will meet you to-morrow morning at the police-office," said Mr. ——, as we parted, "for I am determined to make an example of this fellow Nikel, and to give a heavy blow and a great discouragement to all dangerous practical jests."

* * * * *

I had given my card at the station-house, accompanied by a request that I might be informed in the morning at what hour it was probable my attendance would be required at Bow-street on the examination of the facetious Mr. Nikel.

At about ten o'clock, accordingly, a messenger came to my house to say that I must not make it later than eleven before I made my appearance before "his worship."

This was a very awkward hour for a physician, but there was no resource, and as I had begun the business, I felt bound to go through with it.

When I arrived at the police-office I had to wait until a gentleman was fined twenty shillings for what the magistrate declared to be a ruffianly assault; and had I been in such a humour I might have derived considerable amusement from the variety of countenances around me.

Mr. Nikel, however, was next brought up, and it was evident, from the sudden influx of persons into the small and incommodious room, which from courtesy is called a court of justice, that a case of some consequence and interest was expected.

I was not, however, so unskilled in the human physiognomy as not at one glance to perceive that Mr. Joseph Nikel intended to brave the matter out if he could, and that his night's meditations had induced a spirit of resistance to the consequences of his act, rather than contrition for its committal.

At this moment Mr. A——, the barrister, entered the court in his wig and gown, and for a moment Mr. Nikel turned pale, for well he knew that the employer of his victim was more likely to come there to assist in prosecuting than defending him.

The prisoner's emotion, however, was but transitory, and in a minute, or less, he assumed the same air of insolent defiance which had characterized his first appearance in the court.

After the first compliments of the morning had passed between me and Mr. ——, I said to him,—

"What do you think of the prisoner?"—He glanced at me, and shook his head.

"He will be his own ruin," he whispered to me. "I have heard something early this morning from his employer, and I am told he has a wonderful notion of his own importance and dignity, in consequence of being Heaven knows what at one of these societies, or institutions, for turning the heads of silly young men."

"Indeed," said I; "then that accounts for his peculiar looks, and likewise for the strange assemblage in the court."

In truth there was a strange assemblage in the court; and when I looked round me I saw that they were chiefly boys between the ages of fourteen and eighteen or nineteen, and upon their countenances sat that indescribable expression of self-conceit which makes the human animal at that period of life so especially disagreeable.

The magistrate now bowed to Mr. ——, and invited both him and myself to a seat on the bench, a proceeding which produced so many looks of scorn and indignation from the prisoner's friends, and such loud murmuring, that the crier cried "Silence! silence!" repeatedly, before silence could be procured.

The magistrate now examined the charge-sheet, and turning to the prisoner, said mildly, but firmly,—

"What is your name?"—"Mr. Joseph Nikel," replied he.

"What are you?"—"Perpetual chairman of the class for the Study of Elocution and the Enlightenment of Society at large in the Institution for ——"

"I mean, how do you get your living?" said the magistrate.

"I am, then, a barrister's assistant."

There was a laugh in the court from the reporters and others, while the friends of Mr. Nikel winked at each other, as much as to say, "Bravo, our chairman!"

"Prisoner," said the magistrate, in a kind tone of voice, "allow me to step out of my way to give you a word of advice. You are a young man, and have fallen into a disagreeable position, through, most probably, a great error of judgment. By the course you are now pursuing you are doing yourself great injury. Humility and repentance would suit your situation much better."

"Humility, sir?" said Mr. Nikel.—"Yes, humility. Believe me, I advise you well, and as a friend."

"I am not aware that you are my legal adviser," said Mr. Nikel.—"I have done," said the magistrate, glancing at Mr. —— and me.

I was then sworn, and deposed to all that had passed, which, being a very straightforward tale, did not take long in the telling.

Mr. —— then rose, and said he appeared for the prosecution, and wished to ask me a question.

I bowed, and the magistrate said, "Certainly."

"What is your opinion of the cause of the death of the deceased?"—"A sudden shock to the nervous system," I replied, "which acted fatally upon the brain or upon the heart."

"What did the prisoner say when Booth fell with the light?"—"Nothing; he only attempted to leave the room as I have described."

"What did he say when given in charge?" said the magistrate.—"He begged for mercy."

A general look of indignant astonishment pervaded the learned society at the bare idea of their perpetual chairman begging for mercy.

"Prisoner," said the magistrate, "have you any question to ask Dr. ——?"—"A—a—a—hem!" cried Mr. Nikel, clearing his voice, and giving his hand an oratorical flourish,—"I have."

"Very well; go on."—"Where were you born?" he said to me.

"Ridiculous!" cried the magistrate. "Prisoner, you are under an error. You have no right, because you are charged with a serious offence, to ask irrelevant questions of the witnesses. Your questions must relate to the evidence."

"Oh!" said Mr. Nikel, "it is as I thought. The freedom of speech,—the birthright of an Englishman,—the unsullied palladium of the British constitution, which was cemented together by the blood, the bones, and the brains of our never-to-be-forgotten and glorious ancestors,—is denied to me!"

The prisoner's friends cried, "Hear,—hear!" and the magistrate, with a pardonable pun, said,—

"If you say that again, you shall not be here any longer, for I will clear the court of all you boys; and mind I don't fine some of you. Have you any questions to the purpose, prisoner, to put to Dr. ——?"

"I have only," said Mr. Nikel, "only to apply for a warrant against him."

"A warrant?"—"Yes, for an outrageous assault and battery."
"Prisoner,—are you mad?"—"No,—are you?"

This stroke of wit threw many of the boys into convulsions, and several blue cotton handkerchiefs I saw crammed into as many mouths, to prevent an explosion of laughter.

The magistrate shook his head, and Mr. Nikel then continued :—

"Upon the deposition of this medical witness I asked for a warrant against him. He has admitted the assault."

"But does not your legal knowledge carry you so far," said the magistrate, "as to know that you were trespassing at the time, and had likewise laid yourself open to a criminal prosecution, any one being at liberty to arrest you? Young man, let me again warn you."

"I shall bring an action against you in the Queen's Bench," said Mr. Nikel, "and I shall bring an action against this doctor for an assault. You had better mind what you are about, all of you."

"Very well," said the magistrate; "in the meantime, however, I commit you Joseph Nikel, to Newgate, for manslaughter."

"Manslaughter, sir?"—"Yes; make out his committal."
"I suppose heavy bail would be taken?" said the prisoner.—
"Heavy nonsense," said Mr ——.

"Ah! Mr. ——," cried Nikel, "take care what you say, or I will bring an action against you for words slanderously spoken, and defamation of character,—so mind."

"The prisoner is committed," said the magistrate, "and I dare say the verdict of the coroner's jury will be manslaughter likewise."

"Stop!" cried the prisoner.—"Wherefore?"

"I have a right to speak. I believe it is usual to ask the gentleman who is the victim of a vile prosecution what he has to say?"

"Well, what have you to say?"—"A great deal."
"I hope not."—"But I have."
"Pray be brief."—"I cannot be brief."

The magistrate looked at me and Mr. ——, as much as to say, "Here's an infliction!"

"Oratory," continued Mr. Joseph Nikel, "oratory has, since the palmy days of a Demosthenes and a Cicero, rather declined, and, I may say, retrograded, than, in a manner of speaking, advanced and gone on. Still, when, in the profundity of the human intellect, we look backward, and forward, and obliquely, through the vistas of ages gone away, and turning the mental vision inwards, with a —a— kind of moral and philosophical—a—a—look, we cannot help, while we soar aloft upon the wings ——"

"Prisoner," interrupted the magistrate, "I cannot sit here to listen to your bombastic rubbish. You may reserve all that for a jury."

"But I will speak," cried Mr. Nikel, with a furious look.
"Officers, remove him," said the magistrate.
"Liberty," shouted Mr. Nikel,—"liberty—down with tyranny, down with magistrates, down with everything!"

At this climax Mr. Joseph Nikel was forcibly removed from court by a Herculean officer, who very kindly whispered in his ear a few words of practical advice, couched in the sentence, "don't be a fool."

Thus ended the examination of the practical joker at the police-office.

A coroner's inquest was held on the body of poor Booth, and a verdict of manslaughter against Joseph Nikel, as the magistrate had prophesied, was duly returned.

The sessions did not commence for some time, and in the interim Booth was buried, and I became a frequent visitor at his mother's. I should, however, inform my readers of a scene which the next day Mr. ——, the barrister, and I had with the innocent and simple Mary. When we called in Carey-street to tell Mrs. Booth the result of the examination at Bow-street, we naturally asked her how she and Mary Brown got on together, after the delinquencies of which the latter had been guilty, and she replied,—

"Mary is going from us this evening, on my promise of forgiving the past."

"Have you ascertained," I said, "how she contrived to do so much mischief without being detected in it?"

"She only cries when I ask her," replied Mrs. Booth, "and I can get no particulars from her upon the subject."

"Then allow me," said Mr.——, "to talk to her, for I am really curious to know how she could manage so well."

"Certainly," said Mrs. Booth, and forthwith Mary was summoned. She gave a start of surprise and trepidation at seeing Mr. —— and me, who, no doubt, she thought were two of the mightiest conjurors she had ever, in all her life, heard of.

"Before you go," said Mr. ——, "you owe it to your mistress, as the price of forgiveness, to relate how you contrived to do all the mischief you have done, without being caught in the fact."

Mary looked down, and muttered something that was unintelligible.

"Come, come, we must know," said Mr. ——. "What has been broken, Mrs Booth, that you can particularize?"— "A looking-glass up stairs, for one thing," replied the lady.

"Well, now, Mary, about the looking-glass?" said Mr. ——; "how was that managed?"

"Ay," said I, "and I am certain she was in the kitchen all the time."

"I—I loosened the nails," confessed Mary.—"Well?"
"Then I knew that when a heavy cart passed the house, it would shake it, and down would come the glass."

"Well, that's ended," said Mr. ——. "So the heavy cart came, I suppose?"

"Yes, it happened to come while the doctor was here."
"What next, Mrs. Booth?"

"The parlour windows,—they are all smashed, and to all appearances from outside, when there was scarcely a soul in the street."

"Well, Mary, how do you account for the parlour windows?" —"I broke them from the kitchen."

"From the kitchen?"—"Yes."
"How?" "I leaned out of the kitchen window with the long broom.

"Oh! you did, did you? I hope that is satisfactory, Mrs. Booth?"

Mrs. Booth sighed, and said,—

"But how could she break all the crockery in the kitchen while she was up stairs, as I well know, making the beds? How could she do that?"

"Well, Mary," said Mr.——, in a jocular sort of tone, "that's a puzzler, I should think. How did you smash the crockery?"—"I—I did it ——"

"We know you did it, but we want to know how."—"I made 'em fall."

"Exactly; but you are no conjuror, Mary, we know, although Dr. —— and I are, without a doubt."

"Well, then, sir, I went up stairs with Miss Booth to make the beds ——"—"Very well."

"And I left missus in the parlour."—"Very good."

"I knew missus would ring for some coals in a little while, because I could hear the bell up stairs."

"Go on, Mary."—"Well, sir; before I went up stairs I placed the great tray on the very *cornerest* edge of the dresser, next the fire-place."

"Indeed!"—"Yes sir; and then I puts the soup tureen a top 'o that ere."

"Yes."—"Well, then, a top o' the soup tureen, as turned undermost side toppermost, I puts the beer jug and the roasting jack."

"The roasting jack?—Well."—"A top o' them then I puts the dozen and a half o' cheese plates, and at top o' them the dozen and a half and one odd *un* o' dinner plates."

"Why, you must have had quite a pyramid of crockery!"
"The pie dishes you mean, sir?"—"Oh! exactly."

"I puts them a top o' the dinners, and then I crowns 'em all with missuses riveted punchbowl, and the vegetable dishes as is odd, and as missus couldn't match nohow."

"Your mistress will never match you no how," said Mr. ——.

"Well, sir, then I thinks as I've done it pretty well, sir."
"I think so too. But how did you manage to make them all come down while you were up stairs making the beds?"

"Very easy, sir."

"Doubtless, when we know. Did you trust, as before, to a heavy cart?"

"Oh, dear, no, sir!—that wouldn't do. *Leastways* the kitchen never shakes, *cos* of its being, as one may say, *undergrounded.*"

"Very well; how was it done, then?"—"I told you missus was in the parlour?"

"You did?"—"And wanted coals, 'cos she's chilly?"
"The coals you mentioned, and the chilliness we assumed."
Mary turned to the bewildered Mrs. Booth, and said,—
"Please, ma'am, when did you hear the great smash?"

"Directly I rang for coals."—"I knowed it."

"You know it,—how?"—"I heard the smash, and I says to myself, says I,—'Missus has rung, and done it now.'"

"What do you mean?"—"Why, I tied a bit o' fiddle-string to the bell wire—leastways one end on it, and the other end to the tea-tray, as was undermost; so, when missus pulled the bell, in course that pulls the fiddle-string, and that pulls the tray, and that pulls down everything, with never such a smash as never was seen."

"You abominable hussey!" cried Mrs. Booth, unable to control her rage.—"Please, mum, you forgived me," said Mary with a demure aspect.

"Mary, Mary," cried Mr. ——, "what could induce you to act in this manner to a kind and indulgent mistress? Are you not ashamed of your wickedness and ingratitude?"

"Yes, sir."

"Then what induced you to behave so?"—"The devil, sir!"

"The what?"—"The devil, sir."

*   *   *   *   *

The Old Bailey Sessions duly came on, and a true bill was duly found by the grand jury against Joseph Nikel for manslaughter. I was subpœned, of course, on the trial, and my evidence was given to the same effect as I had given in the police-court.

The prisoner pleaded Not Guilty, and, during the progress of his case, injured himself greatly in the minds of the jury by his silly and uncalled-for remarks.

In summing up, the judge said, that it was necessary, for the well-being of society, that the prisoner should not escape punishment for his heartless joke, and that it was high time silly persons should be made aware that they could not with impunity tamper with the nerves and lives of others, even by way of jest, and that the excuse of "They didn't mean it," would not avail them in a court of law. He likewise added, that the prisoner was evidently one of those unhappy young men, calling themselves the benefactors of the lower classes, and great philanthropists, and who fill the minds of their dupes with chimerical notions of their own importance, which they forget can only exist in the small circle in which they move, and which did them irreparable injury when attempted to be asserted in the great world: and he considered that if the institutions and societies for teaching everything would, among other studies, teach a little modesty, they would be much to be commended.

Mr. Joseph Nikel, to his consternation, got twelve months' imprisonment for his joke, and was led from the dock blubbering like a great booby!

Miss Booth never saw any more ghosts.

THE ASSASSIN;

OR, THE MURDER AT THE INN.

When first I commenced practice in London I occupied apartments in Old Broad-street, near the Bank; and I must say, although I finished my professional career in the more aristocratic vicinity of Portman-square, I never experienced greater liberality and kindness than I received when quite a young man, and unknown as a physician, from the hospitable citizens of London.

The singular tale which I am about to relate I have no doubt I should have placed before my readers in an earlier part of my Diary, for it is one which is sure to interest all parties; but the truth is, that I did not feel myself at liberty to publish the extraordinary narrative without the permission of a gentleman still living, whose feelings, for aught I knew, might have been wounded by the recital of events which had been allowed to slumber now for more than forty years.

That permission, however, has now been freely acceded to me; and although I shall adopt fictitious names, I shall suppress no facts connected with this striking and singular portion of my Diary.

Those who are conversant with the City know that there are still to be found, down narrow winding streets, and in odd corners, some of those old inns, with large court-yards, and extensive galleries around them, of a peculiar antique appearance.

There was one of these in the immediate vicinity of my residence, for they were then much more plentiful than they are now, and this was called the Old Rose Inn, probably taking its sign from as far back as the wars between the rival houses of York and Lancaster.

A number of old swaggering coaches, such as are now quite extinct, used to come and go from this inn, at various stated hours, one of which in particular used to amuse me mightily, by being called the Rocket, when I am quite sure eight miles an hour would have been a killing pace for both steeds and coach.

Be this as it may, however, I used to see the Rocket pass my window every day going to some place, the name of which I forget, and return in the evening of the next day, covered with dust in summer, and mud in winter weather.

I had no great deal of practice, and used to sit in my solitary rooms of an evening amusing myself by writing or reading, or making fancy calculations upon little scraps of paper until bedtime; and it was upon one of the evenings so occupied that the first event connected with my tale occurred.

I had sat until I heard twelve o'clock struck by the neighbouring churches, and then was upon the point of retiring to bed, when a loud ring, which was repeated in about a moment, pretty clearly indicated to me that I, the lodger of the second floor, was required.

I was partially undressed, but not sufficiently so to prevent me going down to the door. When I got there and opened it, a man was standing on the outside, who said, in a coarse gruff voice,—

"Are you Mr. ——?"—"I am Dr. ——," said I, for a young physician never forgets his dignity.

"Oh, then, Mr. Saunders wants you."

Now I knew a very respectable chemist in the neighbourhood of the name of Saunders, and said,—

"Do you mean Mr. Saunders, the surgeon?"—"Yes," he replied.

"Very well; tell him I'll come soon," said I, of course supposing that some one was ill, who he wanted me to attend to.—"Oh! soon won't' do," said the man.

"Why?"—"There's been a gentleman killed at the Rose."

"The Rose Inn—a murder?"—"Yes, yes;—that is, a gentleman killed."

It struck me afterwards how very much averse this man was to pronounce the word "murder," although I did not pay much attention to it at the time.

"Why did you not say so at once," cried I, "instead of standing parleying with me here? A moment may be precious."

I did not wait for his reply, but bounding up stairs I thrust on my coat, and seizing my hat, I was out in the street in a few moments, and hurrying towards the Old Rose Inn, which was not three minute's walk from my own door.

When I arrived I could see in a moment that the whole place was in commotion. Lights were flashing to and fro, and there seemed to be a general consternation throughout the entire establishment.

"Where is Mr. Saunders?" I said, to the first person that I could lay hold of.—"In the murdered gentleman's room," was the reply.

"And where is that?"—"The second door in the gallery."

I sprung up the stairs, and guided the hum of voices, I pushed open the door, and entered a bed-room, which was nearly full of men and women.

"Mr. Saunders," cried I.—"For God's sake clear on one side," I heard the voice of Mr. Saunders say, "that is Dr. ——; let him in."

The people made a sort of lane for me to approach through, and there was the surgeon supporting on the edge of the bed a pallid figure dabbled in blood, and partly wrapped up in the quilt of the bed.

"What is this?" I said.—"This gentleman is stabbed," said he; "I have been trying to rally him, but cannot at all."

"Where?"—"In the breast."

I immediately looked in the wounded man's eyes. He was dying! I shook my head.

"I fear it's all over," said Mr. Saunders.—"There is no hope," said I.

Even as I spake the wounded man seemed to rally a little, and made a convulsive effort to speak. With great pain and labour he uttered the words,—

"*Red—red—cloak*," and then, with a shiver, instantly expired.

"This is a bad business, doctor," said Mr. Saunders, as he laid the body upon the bed; "but we have secured the murderer."

"Ah! and if these words don't hang him, my name ain't Jenkins," said a voice that I recognized as belonging to the man who had called upon me.

"What words?" said I.—"Red cloak," he replied.

"There's truth in what he says," remarked Mr. Saunders.

"How?"—"The murderer has a cloak lined with bright red."

"Indeed!"—"And you will allow that the dying words of this murdered man could have no other signification."

"There is something in that," said I; "but where is the murderer?"—"There!"

Mr. Saunders pointed to the farther end of the room, where I saw, to my surprise, tied to a chair, a young man in his night-clothes.

"Yes, yes, that's the murderer!" cried everybody in a breath.—"No, no, no!" cried he who was bound; "I am innocent,—I am innocent, or else I am mad,—mad or dreaming! Will nobody kill me? I am innocent!"

"How do you know that this is the criminal?" said I.— "He was caught here in the room."

"Well," I said, turning to Mr. Saunders, "will you walk home with me, and tell me all about it, or shall I walk home with you, Mr. Saunders?"—"You come with me," he said.

A bustle now announced the arrival of an officer, who had been sent for. He was one of that race of red-waistcoated gentlemen now extinct, and he had small, keen, ferret-looking eyes.

"Where is my man?" he said, immediately upon entering the room.—"There! there!" said he who had called me, pointing to the unfortunate wretch pinioned in the chair, who glared about with an appearance of bewilderment that, if it was not real, I remarked to Mr. Saunders, was the best piece of acting I had ever seen in my life, or ever expected to see.

The officer went up to him, and looking him in the face, said, with an air of disappointment and surprise,—

"I don't know him."—"Did you expect to see an acquaintance?" said I.

"Why, sir," he replied, after a tolerably keen look at me, "we generally find, in affairs of this kind, that we stumble upon an old friend. People don't generally begin with such an out-and-out murder as this."

"Murder!" shrieked the prisoner; "what do you all mean? I am innocent,—God knows that I am innocent!"

"Who'll fetch his clothes?" said the officer, with the most unconcerned look that was possible.

The clothes were soon brought and handed to the prisoner, who dressed himself with a mechanical kind of movement, that looked to me as if he did not know what he was doing.

When he was attired he presented the appearance of a respectable young man belonging to the middle, or probably rather better class of some country town.

"What have I done,—what have I done?" he muttered incoherently.

The officer produced a pair of handcuffs, and locked them on the wrists of the prisoner; then, with a wink at us, he said,—

"Deep, deep, and down as a hammer. Don't know where he learned it, though. You'd better leave the body where it is for the inquest. Come on, my cove."

This was addressed to the prisoner, who, still muttering, "What have I done,—what have I done?" was taken off by the police officer from the inn.

In another quarter of an hour Mr. Saunders and I were seated in his snug little parlour, when he gave me the following particulars of the murder, that he had been told at the inn before I came.

* * * * *

It appeared that both the murderer and his victim had come up that day by the Rocket coach to London, and had been very sociable together on the road.

The murderer's name was Berridge, and what he was was unknown, as he had been picked up by the coach on the road.

The gentleman lying dead at the inn was well known. He was a Mr. Franklin, and reputed to be wealthy, being agent to several gentlemen in London, who entrusted the management of their estates to him; and it was believed that he had in his possession a very large sum of money, with which he was coming to London to pay into the hands of various bankers on behalf of his employers, when he met his death at the Old Rose Inn.

Mr. Franklin had appeared amused by the country simplicity of Berridge, and they had taken a glass together in the coffee-room of the inn before retiring to rest for the night.

To Berridge belonged a large cloak lined with red serge, and this he took with him across his arm from the coffee-room, he and Mr. Franklin being shown up to their rooms by a man of the name of Jenkins, who acted as boots, messenger, &c. to the Old Rose Inn.

It appears, then, that every body had retired to rest, except the guard of the coach, who states that he was crossing the inn yard, when he heard a cry of "murder!" from one of the bed-rooms in the gallery, and being alarmed himself, he awakened the man Jenkins, and with him ascended the stairs to see what was the matter.

The first thing they saw was the door of Berridge's room open, which was next to Mr. Franklin's, and then, hearing a cry from the room of the latter, they burst it open, and caught Berridge in the act of getting out of the window, while Mr. Franklin lay weltering in his blood. An alarm was instantly given, and the whole inn was aroused. Mr. Saunders sent for me, and the rest the reader is already aware of.

All this seemed very conclusive against Berridge, and I retired to rest with a firm conviction of his guilt.

The next morning we all attended before the magistrate, and these various facts were sworn to by Mr. Jenkins and the guard, whose name was Moore.

Berridge, when called upon to state what he had to say why he should not be at once committed for trial, spoke as follows, and produced some sensation by his earnestness of manner:—

"I know no more of this awful business than the child unborn. I am the son of poor but respectable parents in Worcester; I never was guilty of a crime; I appeal to God for my innocence of this murder. Mr. Franklin was kind and civil to me on the road to London, and upon my telling him I came with letters of recommendation to some gentlemen who might procure me a situation, he promised to give me one himself, which, he said, he thought I should find of very great service. I knew not if he had any money or not. If I have murdered this gentleman I am a monster,—a thing for man to shudder at, and Heaven to forsake. Yet you see I can, with an unblanched cheek, call on God to witness my innocence! I am guiltless of this crime, and Heaven may yet point out the hidden perpetrators of it. Mr. Franklin had a small portmanteau with him when he went to bed, and we bade each other good night at my door. Then I turned to the man Jenkins, and gave him my cloak, with a promise of a shilling if he would brush it well, and bring it to me in the morning. He took it and went away; I went then to bed. How I came to be in Mr. Franklin's bed-room, as Heaven is my judge, I know not. I did no murder,—I had no weapon. I am innocent. My life may be sacrificed, but I am indeed innocent. God help me,—God help me!"

There was a death-like silence in the court when the prisoner had done speaking for several seconds, and the spectators looked at each other, apparently in doubt and surprise, at his earnest and simple words.

"Where is Jenkins?" said the magistrate.

There was a little bustle in the justice-room, and Jenkins was brought again before the bench.

"On your oath," said the magistrate, "did the prisoner, or did he not, hand you his cloak, and promise you a shilling for brushing it, as he says?"—"He did not."

"On your solemn oath?"—"God forgive you!" said Berridge.

"You say that Moore, the guard, called you?" said the magistrate.—"He did."

"Did you see the little portmanteau the prisoner mentions?"—"Yes."

"When?"—"When Mr. Franklin went up to bed."

"Have you seen it since?"—"No."

"What can have become of this portmanteau?" said the magistrate.

No one spoke, and he then added,—"Was no knife or

weapon discovered with which the wound on the unfortunate Mr. Franklin could have been committed?"

There was no answer.

"Prisoner," said the magistrate, "this case is involved in some mystery, by the absence of your supposed temptations to commit the murder, namely, the portmanteau, and the not finding the weapon with which Mr. Franklin was stabbed. I do not see how you could have found time to conceal these things, seeing how and where you were taken; but it is my duty to commit you for trial. The dying words of your victim concerning the cloak are against you. You are fully committed for trial on the capital charge."

Berridge clasped his hands and fainted away, falling heavily upon the ground. The sessions did not come on for a month, and during that time an inquest had been held upon the body of Mr. Franklin and Mr. Saunders and I had made a *post mortem* examination of the remains.

We found that his heart had been pierced by some sharp weapon, and the only wonder was, that death had not ensued more quickly than it did.

The verdict was "wilful murder," of course, and everything appeared in a fair way for hanging Berridge. I don't know how it was, however, but as the day of trial came nearer, a conviction of the innocence of the accused man came more and more strongly upon my mind, till at last I became quite uncomfortable upon the subject.

The trial was now to come on in about four days, and Mr. Saunders and I sat in my room talking over the matter.

"Saunders," said I, "I can't believe that poor fellow, Berridge, murdered Franklin."

"Can't you?" said Mr. Saunders; "then you did, doctor."
—"I know you think him guilty, but ——"

"Hang it, doctor, how can you have a doubt upon the subject? Was he not found in the murdered man's room?"
—"Granted ; but where's the knife."

"How should I know?"—"And the little portmanteau?"

"Granted in my turn, doctor : but the unaccountable disappearance of a knife and a little portmanteau forms surely no sufficient reason for letting off a man who has manifestly murdered another."

"Certainly not; but has he?"—"Who has, if he has not?"

"You have the best of the argument, Saunders," said I ; "but will you assist me to do a good deed?"—"What is it?"

"This poor fellow, Berridge, may be innocent."—"He may be. I have heard of rain in Egypt."

"Will you put a couple of guineas and a half to a couple of guineas and a half of mine for him?"—"What for!"

"To see Mr. Sinclair, the eminent counsel, in his behalf."
—"Well, doctor, I'll do that, and I don't think the worse of you for the proposal. Extraordinary things do happen, and something may turn up for a man who was certainly as nearly seen in the act of murder as possible."

"Something may, Saunders. His few words before the magistrate I have never been able to forget."—"They were impressive, and, for so young a man, astonishing."

"Astonishing, if guilty."—"Exactly; but when I speak of him, I candidly confess I cannot help assuming his guilt from all the circumstances. But I should tell you that I know something of Mr. Sinclair, and, indeed, can take the liberty of calling upon him."

"Can you?"—"Yes."

"What's o'clock?"—"About seven."

"Where does he live?"—"In Finsbury."

"My dear Saunders, let us go at once, then, to him."—
"With all my heart," said Saunders, and in a few moments we were walking arm in arm to Finsbury-square.

Mr. Sinclair, who was then the most eminent counsel as well as the most conscientious counsel at the bar, was fortunately at home, and from our reception I was inclined to think that Mr. Saunders had allowed his modesty to underrate his degree of an acquaintanceship with Mr. Sinclair.

I was introduced, and then Mr. Sinclair said,—

"We have come to you on a strange errand, Mr. Sinclair."

"I believe," said Mr. Sinclair, "lawyers, like doctors, have a great many strange errands brought to their doors; but what is it?"—"About Berridge."

"Berridge,—the presumed murderer? That is a very strange affair indeed. I should really like to hold a brief for the prisoner."—"Should you?" said I.

"Yes, indeed."—"Then our strange business is to offer you one, Mr. Sinclair."

"Is it possible?"—"Yes; the prisoner's friends are poor, and as yet have not, I believe, retained any counsel, while the prosecutors—that is, the family of Mr. Franklin—indefatigable in their efforts to convict the prisoner."

"I know who they have retained," said Mr. Sinclair, "a brief was offered me for the prosecutor, but I declined it."

"You will, however, accept of one for the defence?"
"I will."

"We ought, then, to tell you its amount," said Mr. Saunders.—"Oh! I must have a shilling," said Mr. Sinclair.

"A what, sir?" said I. "A shilling. Counsel cannot act without a fee. Get the consent of the prisoner to name some attorney on his behalf, and give me a shilling, and we will do our best in this most strange case."

"Perhaps it would be unfair, Mr. Sinclair," said Mr. Saunders, "to ask you your candid opinion upon the case?"

"Why, you know," said Mr. Sinclair, with a smile, "lawyers never do give a candid opinion about anything; but unless I extract something out of the evidence favourable to the prisoner, he will be hung."

"I fear so," said Saunders.

"And further I will say," continued Mr. Sinclair, "that from what I know of the case, either Berridge, or Jenkins, or Moore, or Jenkins and Moore together, committed the murder of Mr. Franklin."

"My very thought," I exclaimed; "I consider your guess much nearer the truth than my friend Saunders's, who wants to hang me if he couldn't hang Berridge."

"Hang you, doctor?" said Saunders.—"Yes; did you not say that Berridge or I must have committed the murder?"

Mr. Saunders laughed, and handed a shilling to Mr. Sinclair, who took it with great gravity from him, and after a little more conversation, we left the house.

The next morning my first care was to find out where the parents of Berridge lodged; for, poor people, they had come to London in an agony of grief and apprehension for their son. Their place of abode was easily found, for they visited the prison every day in which their unfortunate son was confined. From one of the turnkeys I got their address, which directed me to a little court in the immediate vicinity of Newgate.

When I arrived at the humble abode of these poor people, I encountered a scene of suffering such as I had seldom witnessed. The father was a man who had evidently seen better days, and the situation of his son appeared to have prostrated within his breast all hope for the future. I never saw such a picture of utter despair.

The mother was apparently a kind-hearted woman, such as would have made an admirable and exemplary mistress of a farm-house; and between grief concerning her son and solicitude for the state of her husband, her sufferings were evidently deep and painful.

I had some difficulty to persuade them to listen to me, for, in their minds, all who had given evidence that told against their son, were counted among his enemies. I made every allowance for such feelings in their minds, and after a time succeeded in convincing them that I had only spoken the truth, without favour or prejudice, which I was bound by my oath to do.

"Well, well," said old Mr. Berridge, "hang him among you, I know you will, but he never did the murder. I tell you my boy was quite incapable of it; if you were to swear you saw him do it, I wouldn't believe it. He is innocent."
—"Believe me," said I, "that my visit here to you is in consequence of my always having had strange doubts of your son's guilt."

"You do not think he did it, sir?"—"I do not."

"God bless you, sir," cried the old man, fervently; "you are the first who has said so many words of comfort to me since I have been in London."

"Circumstances," I said, "are very strongly against your son, you must yourself admit; but still there is a mystery connected with the whole affair, which, if it could be solved might clear your son. If he did this murder, it amounts almost to a miracle what could have become of the weapon."

"It does, sir."—"Moreover, the portmanteau belonging to Mr. Franklin has never been found."

"I assure you, sir, my boy is innocent," cried the father.—"I am willing to think so," I replied; "and I think, likewise, that the mere doubt on such a subject should induce every one to do what he can for your son."

"I thank you, sir; but what can be done?"—"Mr. Sinclair, the eminent counsel, is willing to undertake his defence."

The old man shook his head.

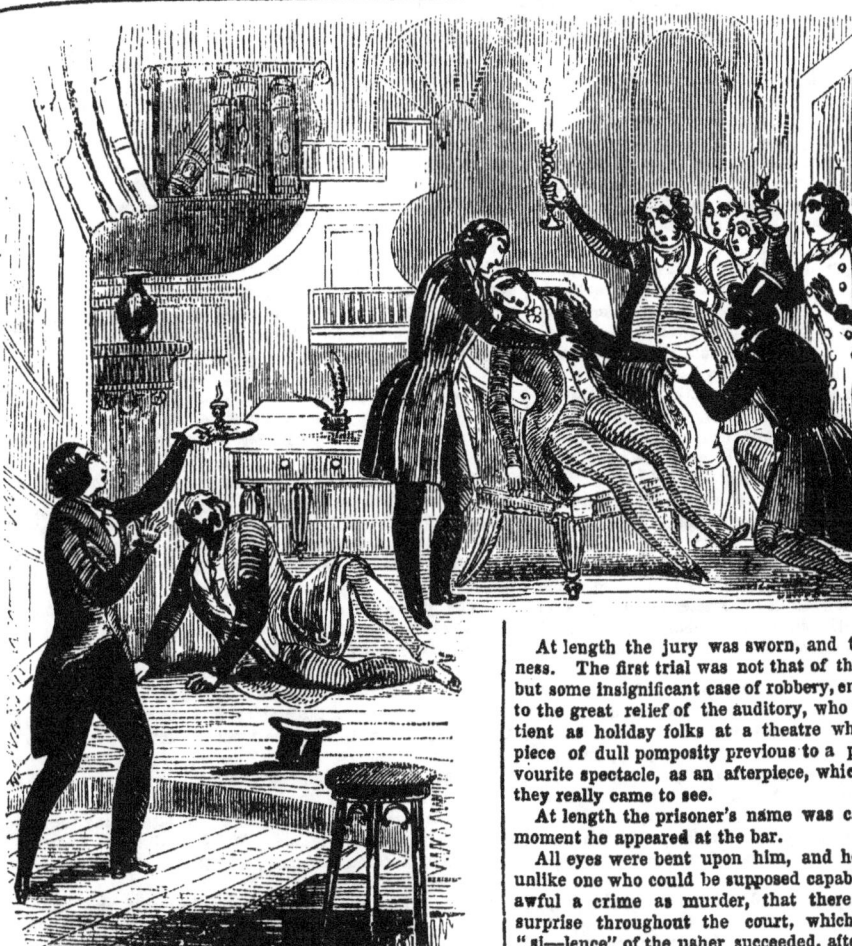

"Alas!" he said, "we have not the means of employing him."—"He is already employed," said I; and then I related the particulars of my interview with Mr. Sinclair, together with his opinion upon the unhappy young man's case.

"He is right," said the father, after expressing his gratitude in suitable terms; "he is right. I am as certain as that I am a living man that those two men, Moore and Jenkins, know more about the matter than my poor son."

"Let us hope for the best," said I; "you may depend that your son is in good hands now, and that Mr. Sinclair will not be satisfied without this affair is sifted to the very bottom. Hope for the best."

"I will, sir," he said; "you have given me new life by your visit, and when I see my poor boy to-morrow, I will tell him not to despair, for even at the last Heaven has found him a friend."

* * * *

The morning for the trial of Berridge for the murder of Mr. Franklin at length arrived, and the greatest interest appeared to be excited by the event. The doors of the court were thronged at an early hour, and it was remarked by the officials connected with the Old Bailey that they had not for many years seen so much public excitement as upon the occasion of this trial. As for myself, I felt so exceedingly nervous and fidgetty, that I scarcely knew what to do.

Mr. Saunders and I breakfasted with Mr. Sinclair on the morning of the trial, and we proceeded together to the court, which was quite crowded by the time we arrived, although the business would not commence for half an hour. The ushers and officers had the greatest difficulty in preserving order, and it was full ten minutes after the judge had taken his seat before quiet was obtained in the densely crowded court.

At length the jury was sworn, and the court began business. The first trial was not that of the accused murderer, but some insignificant case of robbery, ending in an acquittal, to the great relief of the auditory, who were quite as impatient as holiday folks at a theatre when listening to some piece of dull pomposity previous to a pantomime, or a favourite spectacle, as an afterpiece, which, and which only, they really came to see.

At length the prisoner's name was called, and in another moment he appeared at the bar.

All eyes were bent upon him, and he looked so entirely unlike one who could be supposed capable of committing so awful a crime as murder, that there was a murmur of surprise throughout the court, which only the sonorous "si—lence" of the usher succeeded, after a few moments, in suppressing.

He was much paler than when I last saw him, which rather added to the pleasing and candid expression on his countenance than detracted from it. He was neatly and plainly dressed, and altogether his appearance was very much in his favour, considering that the evidence against him, although very strong, was still only circumstantial.

There was a dead silence while the indictment was being read, which charged the prisoner with the wilful murder of George Franklin; and when he was asked to plead guilty or not guilty, all eyes were turned anxiously upon him. There was a moment's pause, and then he lifted up his hands as if in an appeal to Heaven, and said,—

"Not guilty, as God is my judge!"

These words produced an extraordinary sensation in the court. A murmur of approbation arose, and one cried out aloud—" He is innocent !"

The judge then spoke, saying,—" Officers, bring me the person who spoke, and I will commit him."

The person, however, could not be found, and, after a deal of bustle, order was once more restored. The counsel for the prosecution then rose and spoke as follows :—

"My Lord, and Gentlemen of the Jury,—The prisoner at the bar stands charged with one of the most heinous crimes that can defame human nature, but God forbid that I should attempt to prejudge that prisoner at the bar, and say that he is guilty. My duty here, gentlemen, is to elicit truth, not to exert myself to convict a fellow-creature of a crime, which, if you should pronounce him guiltless of, will enable me this night to lie down to rest with a lighter heart and far pleasanter feelings than would be mine should you pronounce him guilty.

"Gentlemen, my duty here is merely to see that all the circumstances which have conspired to induce a suspicion—a well-grounded suspicion, of the guilt of the prisoner, should be laid before you without concealment, without evasion, and in a clear and ungarbled state. That is my duty on this occasion, and should any circumstance occur that is favourable to the prisoner at the bar, I should not be doing my duty to my fellow-creatures, nor an acceptable act in the sight of Heaven, were I to attempt to hide, detract from, or stutify that favourable occurrence.

"Gentlemen, the object of the prosecutors in this case is not vengeance against the young man at the bar; it is to discover who murdered their unfortunate relative; and the feelings of my learned friend who will conduct the prisoner's defence could not possibly be of a more gratifying nature at the acquittal of the prisoner, should that be the result of this trial, than would be my own!

"I pray you, gentlemen of the jury, to dismiss from your minds all that you may have heard or read upon this subject, and particularly what the newspapers have said, for what they say consists generally of some pure invention, and not of facts. Always recollect, gentleman, that there are newspaper reporters who would be glad to hang anybody for one penny per line; and when the death of Sir Robert Angerstein was once reported, and he wrote to his nephew contradicting it, in case he should feel distressed, his nephew wrote word back to him, that he never believed it for one moment, for he had seen it in the 'Times.'

"With these few preliminary observations, gentlemen of the jury, I come at once to the particulars of the charge against the prisoner at the bar.

"You will be told, most probably, by my learned friend who will stand up in his defence, that he is the son of parents who have borne an unsullied character for many years in the place of their birth, and I unfeignedly rejoice that I have it in my power to corroborate that statement. At the same time, gentlemen of the jury, in an inquiry of this exceedingly grave and important nature, the question is, what has the prisoner done, and not what he has not done; for until a crime be committed by an individual, that individual must possess a good character, and, therefore, in my humble opinion, my lord and gentlemen of the jury, the good characters that are given to prisoners at this bar, seem to me to amount to nothing more, even if they be quite correct and true, than a satisfactory piece of information that the prisoner, to the best of his friends' belief, had not previously made himself amenable to justice.

"It appears, then, my lord, and gentlemen of the jury, that this murdered gentleman, Mr. Franklin, had been to various large towns for the purpose of receiving money on account of several noblemen and gentlemen, by whom he was employed in the capacity of agent for the collection of the proceeds of their estates.

"This money, you will be told in evidence, amounted to no less a sum than three thousand five hundred pounds, or thereabouts, and was deposited by Mr. Franklin in a small leather portmanteau, which has never been seen by any one since the time of the decease of its most unfortunate owner.

"Mr. Franklin, then, having received this money, and concluded his business, supped at the house of a friend at a market town called Higham, and then proceeded by a foot-path across some fields, in company with that friend, for the purpose of meeting the coach called the Rocket, which was known to pass by a certain high road at a particular hour.

"Gentlemen of the jury, we have no difficulty in tracing the proceedings of Mr. Franklin. The coach was met,— the unfortunate gentleman got inside, with his portmanteau in his hand,—a fact which will be sworn to by the guard.

"About five miles from that part of the road at which Mr. Franklin met the coach, it was hailed by some one, and the fare to London was made a subject of inquiry. The coachman replied, that he had no outside place, but said, that if the gentleman who was inside—meaning Mr. Franklin—had no objection, he would allow the traveller who had hailed him to ride inside for the outside fare. Mr. Franklin made no objection, and the traveller was very soon comfortably bestowed inside the coach.

"Gentlemen of the jury, that traveller, thus kindly and considerately treated, was the prisoner now at the bar of this court, charged with the wilful murder of Mr. Franklin.

"As the coach now rolled on towards London, a conversation ensued between the prisoner and the deceased, by his own admission. What that conversation was, what it consisted of, and what revelations Mr. Franklin may have made concerning the property he had with him, we cannot know but through the medium of the prisoner at the bar, and he is, of course, no evidence in his own cause.

"In due time, then, the coach arrived at its place of destination in London, called the Rose Inn, and it was evident that a very good feeling subsisted on the part of the deceased Mr. Franklin towards his young fellow-traveller. They took some refreshment together, in the coffee-room of this Rose Inn, and then, as will be shown in evidence, a man, named Jenkins, who has long been connected with this Rose Inn, and who acts there in a humble but useful capacity, lighted Mr. Franklin and the prisoner at the bar to their respective chambers.

"These chambers, gentlemen of the jury, were very close to each other, and were respectively numbered, as chambers are in inns, 17 and 18.

"Now, there is one important fact in the train of circumstantial and presumptive evidence which has led to this inquiry, and that is, that the prisoner was possessed of a large cloak, with a bright red lining, which made the garment an exceedingly conspicuous one to behold.

"You will be informed, then, gentlemen, that the prisoner ascended the staircase with this cloak lying across his arm, and that he took it with him into his bedroom. This, I am instructed, will be distinctly sworn to by the man Jenkins, who lighted both him and Mr. Franklin to bed.

"This was nearly twelve o'clock at night, and it appears that very soon afterwards there were no persons up in the Rose Inn but the night-porter and the guard of the Rocket coach, and they continued talking together upon indifferent subjects for several minutes in a small room adjoining the booking-office.

"The guard then bade the night-porter 'good night,' and was crossing the inn-yard towards his own bed-chamber, when he heard a cry of 'murder!' proceeding from the direction of the bed-rooms on the gallery.

"The guard then awakened the man Jenkins, who was asleep in the loft over the stables, and the two proceeded up the gallery, when the cry was repeated, and Jenkins at once said,—

"'That cry comes from Mr. Franklin's room.'

"They forced open the door, and the first sight that presented itself was the prisoner at the bar attempting to escape from the room by window. Mr. Franklin was lying half out of bed, bleeding profusely, and the cloak with the red lining was upon the floor.

"The first act of these two men, the guard and Jenkins, was to secure the prisoner, and raise an alarm. The whole inn soon became a scene of commotion, and in the course of ten minutes two medical gentlemen were in attendance. In spite of this care, however, the unfortunate gentleman expired, his last words being, 'Red cloak,' which bore a strong signification, as attaching to the cloak of the prisoner at the bar. Mr. Franklin, then, gentlemen of the jury, instantly expired, and the prisoner looked on, half stupified at the scene around him.

"An officer then was sent for, and the prisoner given into custody. It seems he protested his innocence, but could give no account of his appearance in the chamber of the deceased gentleman, Mr. Franklin.

"These facts, gentlemen of the jury, which I have thus briefly related to you, will come out more fully in the evidence, and I shall, therefore, leave the case in your hands, convinced that it will receive from you a patient examination, and fervently hoping that the truth, and the truth only, may, on this unhappy occasion, prevail."

* * * * *

There was now a pause of several moments after the counsel for the prosecution had concluded his address: and certainly the facts appeared to be so conclusive against the prisoner, that no one could imagine him otherwise that guilty of the dreadful crime with which he stood charged. He alone, of all the court, looked unmoved, and presented a look of calm and lofty innocence.

* * * * *

The first witness now called was the friend at whose house Mr. Franklin had supped previous to proceeding to meet the coach, and he deposed to the sum of money which Mr. Franklin had about him.

The next person put into the witness-box was the man Jenkins, and the contrast that he offered to the prisoner was indeed most striking.

If ever a man was cursed with a villanous physiognomy, that man was Jenkins; and as he cast around him an uneasy scowl, it was evident that there was a strong feeling against him in the court.

The examination proceeded as follows on behalf of the prosecution :—

COUNSEL: What is your name?—WITNESS: Ephraim Jenkins.

COUNSEL: What are you?—WITNESS: Boots and messenger to the Old Rose Inn.

COUNSEL: Tell us, then, as distinctly as you can, and in their proper order, the events of the night of the arrival at the Rose Inn, and the death of Mr. Franklin.—WITNESS: I —I don't know much about it,— not much.

He here cast a glance behind him.

COUNSEL: What are you looking for?—MR. SINCLAIR: He exchanged glances with the witness Moore. My lord, I request that Moore be ordered to leave the court while the witness Jenkins undergoes his examination.

The judge granted the application, and Moore was taken from the court.

COUNSEL: Now, then, Ephraim Jenkins, proceed with your evidence.—WITNESS: I was called to light Mr. Franklin and the prisoner to their rooms. Mr. Franklin had his little portmanteau in his hand, and the prisoner had his cloak on his arm.

COUNSEL: Well, what then?—WITNESS: I was tired, and went to bed.

COUNSEL: Where?—WITNESS: In the hayloft.

COUNSEL: Go on.—WITNESS: I was nearly asleep, when Moore called to me. I rose, and then he told me he had heard some one cry "murder!" from one of the rooms on the gallery. He asked me to go with him and see what was the matter. We went, and heard the cry again, and as it seemed to come from the bed-room of Mr. Franklin, we went in there, when we saw him bleeding, and the prisoner at the bar getting out at the window.

This was the gist of Jenkins's evidence, and when the counsel for the prosecution sat down, Mr. Sinclair rose to cross-examine him.

MR. SINCLAIR: What kind of fastenings are there to the doors of the bed-chambers on the gallery at the Rose Inn?—WITNESS: There are locks.

MR. SINCLAIR: So that a person might lock his own chamber.—WITNESS: Yes.

MR. SINCLAIR: Do you ever call early travellers?—WITNESS: Sometimes.

MR. SINCLAIR: You bring them their boots?—WITNESS: I do.

MR. SINCLAIR: I suppose they give you a shilling sometimes?—WITNESS: Yes.

MR. SINCLAIR: Now, for a shilling, which should you think the best job, to clean a pair of boots, or brush a cloak?—WITNESS: A—a—cloak?

MR. SINCLAIR: Yes,— a cloak with a red lining. Speak, sir, at once!—Jenkins turned very pale, and held fast by the railing.—WITNESS: I—I never had a cloak with a red lining to brush.

MR. SINCLAIR: Now, on your oath, did or did not the prisoner at the bar, when you three,—that is, he, Mr. Franklin, and yourself,—arrived at the top of the gallery staircase, hand you his cloak, saying, "Brush it well for me, and I will give you a shilling?"—WITNESS: He did not.

MR. SINCLAIR: You swear that?—WITNESS: I do.

MR. SINCLAIR: Very well. Now, tell me what Moore, the guard, said, when he came to awaken you in consequence of the cries he had heard.—WITNESS (hesitatingly): He said, "Get up; there's murder doing."

MR. SINCLAIR: You swear to those words?—WITNESS: Yes.

MR. SINCLAIR: Now, you state, that when you entered the room of Mr. Franklin, you saw the prisoner at the bar getting out at the window?—WITNESS: Yes.

MR. SINCLAIR: Where does that window look to?—WITNESS: The inn-yard.

MR. SINCLAIR: How deep from the window is the inn yard?—WITNESS: I don't know.

MR. SINCLAIR: Is it forty feet?—WITNESS: May be.

MR. SINCLAIR: Very well; you may go down.

The next witness was Moore, the guard, who was called in from outside the court. He gave evidence of hearing a cry of murder, and going to rouse Jenkins, and then described how they entered Mr. Franklin's room, and found Berridge at the window. This man gave his evidence with great self-possession, and the counsel for the prosecution cast a glance at Mr. Sinclair, as much as to say "You will not shake his testimony." Mr. Sinclair then rose and said,—

"How long have you been guard to the Rocket coach?"—WITNESS: Six years.

MR. SINCLAIR: You have often seen Mr. Franklin?—WITNESS: Yes, often.

MR. SINCLAIR: Had he always a little portmanteau?—WITNESS: Always.

MR. SINCLAIR: You state that you were talking to the night-porter before this murder took place?—WITNESS: I was.

MR. SINCLAIR: What is the night-porter engaged for?—WITNESS: To look after the premises, I believe, in case of robbery.

MR. SINCLAIR: That is to say, I suppose, it is considered proper to have some one whose duty it is to be awake in so large an establishment, while every body else is supposed to be asleep?—WITNESS: Yes, exactly.

MR. SINCLAIR: In case of any alarm, I presume, occurring?—WITNESS: Yes.

MR. SINCLAIR: Then, when you heard an alarm, of a very serious nature, why did you not apprise this night-porter of it, whose special duty it was to see to such things, instead of crossing the yard to awaken a man who swears he was asleep in a hay-loft?

The witness looked terribly puzzled at this home question, and for several moments was unable to reply. It was not, however, Mr. Sinclair's tactics to allow him to recover from his confusion, and he repeated the question in a tone of voice calculated to bewilder the witness's faculties completely. After a time he spoke:—"I—I don't know," he said.

MR. SINCLAIR: You don't know? Do you mean you won't know?—WITNESS: I—I don't know. You—you see Jenkins is my cousin.

MR. SINCLAIR: Oh! he is your cousin, is he? You row in the same boat together, do you? Perhaps you have an agreement between you, that when you are alarmed, you run to Jenkins, and when Jenkins is alarmed he runs to you?—WITNESS: No, no, we have no agreement.

MR. SINCLAIR: And you never thought of the night-porter, even after you had succeeded in rousing Jenkins, at the expense of a delay which, for all you know, might have, and most likely did, cost Mr. Franklin his life? Eh,—you never thought of the porter?—WITNESS: No, no.

MR. SINCLAIR: Although you had just been speaking to him?—WITNESS: Yes.

MR. SINCLAIR: You are an extraordinary guard, Mr. Moore. I presume, if your coach was to be attacked, you would never think of your blunderbuss?—WITNESS: I don't know.

MR. SINCLAIR: Well, then, after all that, tell me what you said when you awakened Jenkins; and before you do so, let us have Mr. Jenkins out of court.

Pale and trembling, Jenkins was led from the court, and Mr. Sinclair repeated his question to Moore, who replied,—"I asked him if he heard anything."

MR. SINCLAIR: Can you recollect the exact words you used?—WITNESS: I said, "Jenkins, do you hear anything?"

MR. SINCLAIR: You swear that?—WITNESS: I do.

MR. SINCLAIR: Then I trust the jury will see the remarkable discrepancy between this man and Jenkins. Here Moore swears he asked Jenkins if he heard anything, and Jenkins swears Moore alarmed him by crying, "There's murder doing," &c. One or both of these men are perjured!

COUNSEL FOR THE PROSECUTION: The point is of very small importance.—MR. SINCLAIR: My lord, and gentlemen of the jury, a feather will show which way the wind blows.

Mr. Sinclair then sat down, having evidently made an impression on the minds of the jury in the prisoner's favour.

My friend, Mr. Saunders, gave his evidence next, and deposed as to finding the wounded man upon the edge of the bed, at the point of death. He then described the nature of the injury received by Mr. Franklin, which he and I had ascertained, upon a *post mortem* examination, to have been a deep stab, of more than seven inches in depth, and which divided the lungs and perforated the heart, our only wonder being, from the nature of the injury, that Mr. Franklin had lived long enough to say what he did concerning the cloak.

I was next placed in the witness-box, and deposed to being sent for to the Rose Inn, and what happened subsequent to my arrival there. Our evidence being purely medical, no questions were asked us, and we volunteered no opinions on the subject.

This was the case for the prosecution, and there was a little bustle in the court from the entrance on to the bench of some of the civic authorities. When that was over, Mr.

Sinclair rose, and silence was at length restored, as his sonorous voice echoed through the court.

"My Lord, and Gentlemen of the Jury," he commenced, "on my conscience, as a man and a Christian, I believe I stand here to speak for the falsely-accused young man now before you at the bar of this court.

"This, gentlemen of the jury, is a case of strong circumstantial evidence against the prisoner; but I do say, that the stronger circumstantial evidence is, the more carefully it should be sifted, and there are some remarkable and most extraordinary defects in the case as it is put forth against the prisoner, which it behoves you most carefully to consider, and most tenderly to weigh.

"When a fellow-creature is accused of a crime, and especially so rank and so awful a crime as murder, we always endeavour to seek for some motive on which the mind may rest, and imagine all that followed to be within the range of possibility; but here we have the monstrous anomaly of a monstrous crime committed without any probability of benefiting by it. My learned friend who conducts the case for the prosecution may tell me that Mr Franklin's little portmanteau and its precious contents form a sufficient motive; but I have asked again and again, where is that little portmanteau? No one knows. Mr. Franklin himself took this precious depository of three thousand five hundred pounds into his bed-room, and, lo! it disappears, as if by magic, and is seen no more.

"Gentlemen of the jury, what has become of this portmanteau, the only probable motive the prisoner could have had to commit the terrible crime of which he here stands accused?

"Did Mr. Franklin himself hide it in his room? No, gentlemen, that is impossible. The room affords no facilities for such a course, and, moreover, it has been searched almost to its demolition since this most awful murder.

"Could the prisoner have hidden it is the next question? And if any body should think he has, I would ask them where? In the room? No. Did he throw it into the yard? He would have been seen directly. What, then, became of it? Can we invent any probable hypothesis of some one else having plundered and murdered Mr. Franklin, and then throwing the onus of the crime on the prisoner at the bar?

"It is true, gentlemen of the jury, that the prisoner was caught in the act of throwing himself out of a window forty feet in height. His death must have been the consequence. Surely that was no attempt at escape? Then, again, gentlemen, if the deed of blood was committed by the prisoner at the bar, where is the weapon with which he did it? How did he contrive to dispose of that, as well as the portmanteau, with such consummate art as to defy hitherto the vigilance of experienced police officers, who, up to this hour, are unable to hazard a conjecture upon the subject.

"Here we have a wound, deposed to by respectable medical men and surgical evidence as being so deep as to be within a trifle of passing right through the body; and I would ask, then, where is the long knife necessary to produce such a wound?

"That knife, I presume, has gone after the portmanteau, or the portmanteau after the knife.

"You have heard there was a cry of murder, and you have heard that there was a night-porter, who was not summoned by the man Moore, who heard that cry; and likewise it will be very odd if that night-porter should swear to you, gentlemen, that he never heard that cry; and I am instructed that if he be put into the witness-box, he will so swear, gentlemen.

"Then, I say, that you have nothing against the prisoner but the barren fact that he was found in the chamber of the murdered man, as presumptive evidence that he is the murderer. Against that presumption you have a multitude of facts and probabilities.

"The evidence,—the whole evidence for the prosecution, comes from the mouths of the two men, Jenkins and Moore, —two men who have grossly prevaricated, and, as you have seen, contradicted each other most fully and completely. That is the evidence for the prosecution,—two men, one of whom would be indicted for perjury, if we knew which to lay hands upon.

"My lord, and gentlemen of the jury, I do assert, as and advocate of some experience at this bar, that if my client, the prisoner at the bar, had chosen to say that he, hearing a cry, ran into Mr. Franklin's room, and found him wounded, before the arrival of Jenkins and Moore, and that he opened the window to call for help, he never would have been at this bar, and the testimony of these two precious witnesses could never have affected him.

"But, my lord, and gentlemen of the jury, my client could not stoop to the degradation of a falsehood, even to save his life! It was not so. He did not hear the cry of 'murder!' and then fly to the bed-chamber of Mr. Franklin; not but, what he would have so flown, had he heard that cry. How he came in that room, he knows not. Whether or not he sought it half asleep, hearing some cry amid the phantasmas of a dream, or whether or not he was, when in a deep slumber, dragged from his bed, and thrown into that chamber, he cannot tell. He only knows that he is innocent of the crime laid to his charge, and you, gentlemen of the jury, know that those who have borne testimony against him are not to be believed upon their oaths, for they give widely different accounts of one and the same transacton.

"But, gentlemen, lest you should imagine that the discrepancy in the statement of these two men is not important, inasmuch as it does not relate to any vital fact connected with this business, it shall be my duty to place a witness in that box who will, upon oath, invalidate one of their statements upon an exceedingly vital question, and one upon which the presumed guilt of the prisoner is supposed greatly to rest,—I mean, concerning that cloak that has been so often mentioned, with the remarkable red lining."

At this stage of Mr. Sinclair's speech Jenkins tried to leave the court, but the judge said directly,—

"Detain that man; we may want him again."

The officers directly placed themselves in the way of Mr. Jenkins, and Mr. Sinclair called aloud the name of Hannah Smith.

"Hannah Smith!" shouted the crier.

In a moment a young girl was placed in the witness box, whom I had never seen before, and whose evidence I had never heard of.

"Relate," said Mr. Sinclair, "what occurred on the night of the murder of Mr. Franklin."

The witness was duly sworn, and, amid a death-like stillness in the court, spoke to the following effect:—

"I remember well the night of the murder at the Rose Inn. I am under-housemaid there, and it is my turn every other week to light all the fires; I was to begin on the morning after the very night the poor gentleman was killed.

"I went to bed at a quarter before twelve; but I don't know how it was, I couldn't sleep a wink, and I lay very restless and uncomfortable until a quarter past twelve; I heard it strike; all of a sudden the thought came into my head that I would get up."

At this juncture of the witness's statement Jenkins suddenly exclaimed,—

"It's a lie! it's a lie! She's been paid to get me into trouble."

"You!" cried Mr. Sinclair, with a voice that rang again through the court; "she never mentioned you! Does your conscience forestall her evidence?"

A murmur of intense surprise and interest pervaded the court, and the judge leaned forward with his eyes fixed on the pale, working face of Jenkins.

"Where are you, Moore?" he exclaimed,—"where are you? They are all against us,—all,—all, you see!"—"Idiot!" shrieked Moore.

"I cannot allow this," said the judge; "officers, take both these men into custody, but keep them in court."

Mr. Sinclair now turned to the witness, and said,—

"Hannah Smith, go on with your testimony, and fear nothing; the court will protect you amply."

The young girl then continued as follows:—

"As soon as it came into my head to rise and lay the fires ready for morning, I became more and more restless and uneasy, and at last I got up; I had to cross the yard to get to the scullery, and as soon as I opened the door leading out, I saw Jenkins cross the yard from the stables, *with the gentleman's cloak with the red lining on his arm!*"

MR. SINCLAIR: You are quite sure it was Jenkins you saw?—WITNESS: Quite.

MR. SINCLAIR: You have no hesitation whatever in swearing to it?—WITNESS: None.

MR. SINCLAIR: What light was there?—WITNESS: There is a lamp always hanging from underneath the gallery stairs.

MR. SINCLAIR: And by that you saw him?—WITNESS: I did.

MR. SINCLAIR: What did you do then?—WITNESS: I went back to bed directly.

THE JUDGE: Without laying your fires? — WITNESS: Yes.

THE JUDGE: And what made you give up your intention of doing so?—WITNESS: I was afraid of Jenkins.

THE JUDGE: Why?—WITNESS (hesitatingly): He is always teasing me to marry him.

THE JUDGE: Oh! that will do.

MR. SINCLAIR: Now, tell us why you did not mention this circumstance before?—WITNESS: I was not aware till yesterday that Jenkins denied having the cloak; but as soon as I knew it, I made up my mind to tell what I had seen.

THE JUDGE: And very proper too. You have given your evidence very creditably, and, reviewing all the circumstances of this case, I cannot help saying, that it is the most perplexing one I ever witnessed.

"My lord," said Mr. Sinclair, "there is another important witness for the defence that I cannot make available to-day. I have to request your lordship, as the hour is now late, to adjourn this trial until ten o'clock to-morrow."—"If the counsel for the prosecution makes no objection," said the judge, "I shall accede to your wish."

"Not in the least, my lord," said the counsel, energetically.

"The trial, then, shall be postponed," said the judge, "and until to-morrow I shall not allow any of the witnesses to leave the building. Let them be carefully provided for, except Jenkins; he is to be considered in custody."

At this moment Berridge fainted away upon the floor of the dock.

* * * *

The postponement of the trial produced a degree of excitement such as I rarely recollect to have seen in any criminal case. Mr. Saunders and myself attended to the prisoner professionally, and we found him in a very weak, nervous state, from the events of the day.

We recommended that he should be at once removed to bed, and the governor of Newgate, who had been present at the trial, was so convinced that there was some mystery in the affair, and that Berridge was innocent of the crime imputed to him, that he said he should have a bed in his own private apartments, taking upon himself any blame that might be visited upon him for giving a prisoner such an indulgence. We saw Berridge to bed, and Mr. Saunders and I remained for some time talking to the kind and humane governor, when Mr. Sinclair's name was announced, and in a few moments that gentleman joined us.

"Well, gentlemen," he said, "what do you think of Berridge's case now?"—"It is materially bettered," said the governor.—"Certainly," said I.

"Well," added Mr. Sinclair, "I am glad to hear you say so; but I have a suggestion to make to the judge and the jury to-morrow that will, I think, have some effect."

"What is it?" we all said.—"Why, gentlemen, as we are all inclined to think well of the prisoner, I shall endeavour rationally to account for his being in the chamber of Mr. Franklin on the night of the murder."

"If that can be done, he must be acquitted," said the governor; "for the evidence of those two men, Jenkins and Moore, is not worth a rush."—"It can be done."

"I am all impatience," said I.—"Then, gentlemen," said Mr. Sinclair, "solemnly I declare to you my firm conviction that this persecuted young man *walked into Mr. Franklin's chamber in his sleep!*"

"I could swear it," exclaimed Mr. Saunders; energetically. "By Heavens! that accounts for everything."—"It does indeed," said I; "and, Mr. Saunders, you or I ought to have thought of that."

"It is an admirable suggestion," said the governor; "and if any one who has known the prisoner intimately can depose to his ever having walked in his sleep before, he must be acquitted."

At this moment a loud scream came upon our ears, and the door was flung open by a female servant of the governor's, who rushed into the room in an extremity of terror.

"What is the matter?" we all cried.

"A ghost—a ghost!" shrieked the girl; "oh! it's a ghost."

"Nonsense," said the governor; "how dare you make this silly alarm?"—"Good God! what's that?" suddenly exclaimed Mr. Saunders, pointing with a suprised look to the open doorway.

All our eyes were immediately turned in that direction, and we saw, slowly advancing, a figure attired only in night clothes, and wearing a solemn and afflicted look upon his face!

"Good Heavens!" whispered Mr. Sinclair, "it is Berridge!"—"Hush!" said I! "he is in a state of somnambulism. Do not wake him."

"This is surely the doing of Providence," said Mr. Saunders. With his eyes wide open, fixed and glassy, Berridge slowly advanced into the room. His step was light and cautious, and his hands were folded across his breast. We all made way for him in mute wonder as to what he would do. Still he advanced to a sofa, which he touched gently. Then he spoke in a low tone, saying,—

"Sir,—sir,—sir, I have had a dream. Sir, are you awake?"—Then he paused for some moments, after which he added,—"You have spoken kindly to me to-day, sir, and, could not rest while I thought you were in danger, sir. I have had a dream; I thought two men came to murder you. Pardon me, sir, for disturbing you; it was but a dream,—only a dream,—only a dream. I will go back—yes, back."

I made a sign to Mr. Sinclair, and he closed the door of the room. Berridge now turned and walked slowly away from the sofa. When he came to the door, he tried it, and exclaimed,—

"Fast, fast. What noise—what noise!—Ah! the murder! I will cry for help; the window,—the window!"

"It is enough," said I; "catch him in your arms; I will awaken him."

Mr. Saunders and Mr. Sinclair laid hold of him, and he immediately awoke with a cry of surprise.

"God of Heaven! where am I?" he exclaimed.

We led him to a seat, and he looked about him perfectly bewildered.

"Berridge," said I, "you have been walking in your sleep."

"In my sleep," he said.—"Yes," added Mr. Sinclair, "and it's the best walk ever you took in your life."

"What—what is all this?" he exclaimed; "for God's sake tell me what has happened to me."—"In the morning you shall know all," said I; "you must go to bed now. Here, take this."

I handed him a composing draught that had been prepared for him after the trial. He took it, and after a little time we got him to bed again, and he fell into a deep slumber.

When we were once more together, that is, myself, Mr. Saunders, the governor, and Mr. Sinclair, the latter said, "I think we can have no doubt now of the innocence of poor Berridge. The murder must have been committed in my opinion, by Jenkins or Moore, or possibly both assisted at the deed."

"I agree with you," said the governor; "it is quite clear that this young man, sleeping, as he did, in the next chamber to the unfortunate Mr. Franklin, must have heard in his sleep the cries of the unhappy gentleman, and risen, as we saw him now, to warn him."

"Your supposition, I would lay my life, is a correct one," said Mr Sinclair; "whoever committed the murder most probably shut Berridge in the room, thinking it a fair opportunity of shifting the onus of the crime on to his shoulders."

"Exactly," said I; "there can be no doubt but that Berridge acted over the scene here precisely as it occurred in Mr. Franklin's bed-room. His going to the window, when he found the door fast, tallies with what has been stated."

"Well, then, we have now two things to do," said Mr. Sinclair; "the one is, to clear, to-morrow morning, the prisoner Berridge of the charge, and see if we cannot bring it home to Moore and Jenkins, who I consider to be the real criminals."

"How can you do the latter?" said the governor; "there is no direct evidence against these two men. That a jury will acquit poor Berridge there can be very little doubt; and even should they convict him,—for it is very difficult to know what juries will or will not do,—the judge will forward a recommendation to the Secretary of State that will save him."

"Leave all to me," said Mr. Sinclair; "I have a plan which may succeed. At all events, I will try it to-morrow."

* * * *

If possible, the court on the following morning was more densely crowded than before, and long ere the judge took his seat on the bench, there was not standing room to be found for any extra person.

I was there, with my mind prepared for something of a novel and extraordinary nature, and I was greatly assured by the confident look of Mr. Sinclair when he came into court.

Precisely at ten the judge took his seat, and the prisoner

was brought into court. He was very pale, and altogether looked so ill, that by the direction of the judge, he was accommodated with a chair in the dock.

The jury took their seats, and the business of the day was about to commence, when Mr. Sinclair rose and said,—

"My lord, I have to request permission, at this stage of the trial, to examine the witness Jenkins touching some new points that have come out favourable to the prisoner at the bar, since this court last met."

THE JUDGE: I should scarcely imagine that any evidence coming from Jenkins can now be of the slightest importance.

MR. SINCLAIR: I quite agree with your lordship, and trust that the jury will take a similar view of that man's extremely prevaricated statement concerning this transaction. But when I assure your lordship, that in consequence of events that have transpired during the night,—events which it would have been highly indecorous to have acquainted your lordship with privately,—it is absolutely necessary, for the furtherance of the ends of public justice, that I should have the man Jenkins again at that bar,—I am sure your lordship will not refuse this application."

"Certainly not," said the judge; "I have no hesitation, likewise, in saying, that a jury can scarcely commit any one upon such evidence as is offered against the prisoner at the bar. In my opinion, the men Jenkins and Moore are not to be believed on their oaths. I will grant your application."

"Call Jenkins," said Mr. Sinclair.

Jenkins was immediately brought forward and placed in the witness-box.

The awful, ghastly look of this man was perfectly dreadful. He seemed in a state of the most abject terror, and his eye wandered restlessly about the court, as if with a hope of catching some friendly or assuring glance from among the many persons there assembled.

Mr. Sinclair again rose, and said,—

"My lord, may I request that the officers shall be directed to keep all the doors closed against any one leaving while I make the extraordinary statement I am about to deliver?"

"I cannot do that," said the judge; "but, after what you have said, I dare say no one will attempt to leave the court."

"Very well, my lord," said Mr. Sinclair.

The crier called "silence!" several times, and I could see Jenkins draw his breath hard between his clenched teeth, while a heavy, bead-like perspiration stood upon his brow, as he clutched the brass rail of the witness box.

"My lord, and gentlemen of the jury," commenced Mr. Sinclair, "the extraordinary circumstances that have transpired since last we met in this court, relating to the murder of Mr. Franklin, are of so startling a nature, that, were they not supplied by unimpeachable evidence, you might well be pardoned for not giving credence to them.

"My lord, and gentlemen of the jury, you will scarcely believe that within the few short hours that have intervened since last we met in this court to conduct this most extraordinary inquiry,—extraordinary on account of its complexity and strangely varying facts,—I say, gentlemen, you will scarcely believe that within that short space of time it has pleased Heaven to clear up all that was mysterious in this case,—to afford a key to every circumstance that was before perplexing and unaccountable,—to prove the innocence of the prisoner at the bar, and to fix the load of guilt on other shoulders!"

Jenkins fixed his eyes upon Mr. Sinclair's face, and seemed not to have any power to withdraw them, and it was evident he must have fallen but for the aid of the railing, to which he clung with desperate and fearful energy.

Mr. Sinclair continued, in a clear, solemn voice, that brought conviction to every heart:—

"There is an infirmity inflicted by the hand of God upon His creatures which causes them sometimes, when the body has been harassed by travelling, or the mind strongly acted upon by some vision of sleep, to rise up in a state, as it were, between life and death, and walk forth unconsciously."

While Mr. Sinclair was speaking, Jenkins trembled fearfully, and made several gasping efforts to say something; but he seemed quite unable to command the power of uttering a word.

"The prisoner now at the bar," continued Mr. Sinclair, "is a somnambulist. He rose in his sleep, and sought the chamber of the murdered Mr. Franklin, while he ——"

Mr. Sinclair turned and pointed in the face of Jenkins, who broke into a wild cry, that horrified every one.

"Spare my life,—spare my life!" he shrieked, and I will tell all. "Spare me,—spare me! I did it! I did it! but Moore tempted me. Oh, God! spare my life!"

* * * * *

The effect which this had upon the crowded court was perfectly electrical. Every one rose to his feet, and it was some few moments before the venerable judge, who himself rose, could command a hearing. When he did so, his first words were,—

"Officers, secure the man Moore."

He was immediately handcuffed, while he exclaimed,—

"Jenkins did it—Jenkins killed the man! I had nothing to do with it. I turn evidence! Jenkins did it."

The judge waived his hand, and when all was still, he said, addressing Jenkins,—

"Unhappy man! If your sorely burthened conscience prompts you to confess yourself the murderer of Mr. Franklin, I will hear you, at the same time that I warn you you act upon your own responsibility. I ask you not; I give you no hopes; I am only willing to hear you."

* * * * *

After a pause, Jenkins spoke.

"It's a relief now it's all found out," he said; "I have been in hell since that night; I have never once slept; never,—never once."

"I turn king's evidence," said Moore.

"Take that man away," said the judge, and the officers immediately removed him from the court.

Jenkins continued,—

"It was Moore; I tell you all it was Moore that tempted me. When the coach came in that night, he spoke to me of Mr. Franklin, saying, 'he has been one of his money-collecting journeys, and there is no reason why we should not have it.'

"I shrunk from the job, but he continued to persuade me, and said that if any one was suspected, it would be the young man Berridge, and not us. I refused for a long while; indeed I had not made up my mind to it until Mr. Berridge gave me his cloak to brush."

A murmur of indignation passed through the court as Jenkins made this avowal concerning the cloak.

"Then," he continued, "then I thought it would be easy to fix the—the murder on him, by leaving his cloak in the room. So Moore and I went up the staircase together, and —and he gave me his clasp-knife, and told me to silence all opposition with that. Moore stood just at the door, while I went into the room. Mr. Franklin directly cried 'Who's there?'—I answered nothing, and he jumped out of bed. I wanted to get away, but he took hold of me, and then turned and run the knife into him!—Moore had a lantern, and I saw him take up the portmanteau, when, just as we had got out of the room, the young man Berridge met us. *He was walking in his sleep!* He passed us and went into the room. Then Moore said, 'He is in for it now, by God!'

"We fastened the door on the outside, and ran down the gallery stairs."

Jenkins here paused, and groaned bitterly, while every one in the court seemed transfixed with horror.

The judge then said,—

"Where is the portmanteau?"—"Buried in the stable," replied Jenkins.

"And the knife?"—"With it."

An officer was directed to go and search, and while he was absent, the counsel for the prosecution rose and said,—

"My lord, and gentlemen of the jury, no one in this court can rejoice more than I do at the issue of this trial. The indictment against the prisoner is abandoned."

The judge then said,—"Let the acquittal be formal."

—"Not guilty!" cried the foreman of the jury in a moment.

Berridge was, by direction of the judge, immediately taken from the prisoner's bar, and shook hands with Mr. Sinclair, Mr. Saunders, and myself.

But who shall describe the joy of the parents of the liberated prisoner upon this occasion? They laughed and wept by turns, and their feelings of thankfulness brought tears into many eyes. * * * *

In about twenty-five minutes the officer who had been dispatched for the knife and the portmanteau returned with both those articles. On the haft of the knife, which was one of those that open with a spring, was the name of Moore, and in the portmanteau there were found upwards of three thousand four hundred and seventy pounds.

But little more remains now to tell. Jenkins and Moore were tried during the week for the wilful murder of Mr.

Franklin, and, after a patient investigation,—for Jenkins after all pleaded not guilty,—they were fully convicted. An immense crowd attended the execution, and not one pitying expression accompanied them to

"That bourne from whence no traveller returns."

As for Berridge, the whole affair was the making of him, for Mr. Franklin's relatives and friends, who were really good and respectable people, thought they could never make sufficient amends for the imminent danger they had placed him in by the prosecution.

He was placed in a situation very far above his utmost expectations, and it was long before the murder at the Old Rose Inn ceased to be a subject of prolific gossip throughout the neighbourhood in which the occurrence took place.

THE DUEL;

OR, MISCHIEF-MAKING.

DURING a period of many years I was acquainted with a very amiable gentleman, named Palgrave, for whom I always entertained the highest respect and consideration. He was noble-minded and generous to a fault, and there was about his manner a winning candour that won him the good opinion of every one who had an opportunity of forming his acquaintance or of even being in his company.—From acquaintances merely Mr. Palgrave and I became very firm and good friends,—a friendship which rather increased than diminished as time wore on. We were both young men at the commencement of our intimacy, and one morning Palgrave came to me as I was sitting at breakfast with a countenance of the most animated and joyful cast, exclaiming,—

"Well, doctor, I am going to be married."—"At last," said I, for I was aware that he had been engaged in an affair of the heart for some time.

"Yes, at last," he repeated; "a domestic calamity to my dear Aurelia has hastened the period of my happiness."—"Indeed!"

"Yes; her mother, who has been long in an infirm state of health, is now no more. Aurelia is an orphan, and you cannot conceive what an exquisite pleasure it is to me, under such circumstances, to be able to offer her a comfortable, and, I hope, a happy home."

"I can conceive it very well," said I, "and I am quite sure that it will be her own fault if she is not happy with you, Palgrave."

"Thank you, doctor,—thank you. Only it's quite the other, for, without exception, Aurelia is the most charming, the most——"

"There,—there," said I; "that will do. Now, will you take a cup of coffee?"—"Well, I don't care if I do; but, as I was just saying, Aurelia, you know, doctor, happens to be the most——"

"Exactly. Help yourself, Palgrave."

"Ah! you will fall in love yourself some day," he said "and then I will cut short your transports in the same manner you do mine, which is really abominable of you."

He then poured, in a fit of abstraction, the coffee into the sugar-basin, and the milk into the coffee-urn, all the while looking so grave, that I was ready to burst with laughing.

"Palgrave, Palgrave," I said, "don't come here any more till you have been married five weeks."

"Five weeks! Why?"—"Because then the honeymoon will be fairly over, as well as your first week's repentance. You have spoiled all my sugar, and wasted the milk in your raptures."

"My dear doctor," he cried, covered with confusion, when he saw how matters stood, "I really beg your pardon."—"Don't mention it," said I; "I only hope you are not marrying in a fit of abstraction."

"Oh, no," he said; "you may depend upon that. The virtues of Aurelia are resplendent as the sun."—"Then I suppose, when you look at them, you have a beam in your eye?"

"Now really that's too bad," he cried; "an abominable pun is bad at the best, but when Aurelia is the subject of it, it becomes atrocious."—"Very."

"I should scarcely have likened her to the sun; she is more like the silver orb of night in chaste, calm beauty, among myriads of clouds."—"That is to say, you consider her virtues and beauties all moonshine."

"You will make me do something desperate," said Palgrave, "if you go on that way. It's really past all endurance."—"You will make me do something desperate," said I, "without my making you."—"What is that?"—"Why, marry, to be sure."

"I won't stay with you another minute," he cried, jumping up and seizing his hat. "You are quite incorrigible. I was going to ask you to be a father to the bride."—"Heaven forbid!" said I.

"Then you won't give her away?"

"Yes, I will, and wish you all sorts of happiness. Besides Palgrave, I have expended all my jokes, and have not th' ghost of one left. May your week of repentance never come but a perpetual honeymoon hold Time by the leg."—"Confound you, doctor, I never know when you are jesting, and when you are in earnest."

"I am in earnest when I wish you joy, and I will give away the bride."—"All's right then. Dear Aurelia's mother——"

"Who is a saint in Heaven," interrupted I.—"Poh—poh!"

"Well, you know, Palgrave, whenever a deceased mother is mentioned on the stage, she is always a saint."—"Yes, but this is real life."

"All the world's a stage."—"Very, well, then; the old lady, who may be a saint for all I know to the contrary, is to be buried the next week, and the week after, oh——"

"What! bury her two weeks in succession?"—"No, no; I was only a little overcome by the blissful thought of calling Aurelia mine. The week after we marry."

"And then my services will be required?"—"Yes; she has no living relative in England, doctor. Poor girl! if some one did not love her for her own sake,—she has no natural ties to cling to,—her lot in life would be most desolate."

This was past a joke, and I replied,—"Palgrave, I rejoice that she has found such a protector as you. She must, I am convinced, have been an amiable girl to have attracted you, for, imaginative as you are, I believe your judgment never sleeps. From my heart I wish you every happiness."

"Thank you, doctor, thank you," he said, with emotion. "We shall have many pleasant evenings by my fireside, for my wife is one who will esteem her husband's best friend."

* * * * *

That day fortnight saw me at a little suburban church, officiating in the novel character of father to the bride.

Sceptical as I then was in such matters, I could not but confess, when I saw Palgrave's choice, that she came as nearly as possible to his very flattering description of her. She was certainly a very beautiful girl, and her manners were of that gentle, amiable character which almost always bespeaks a well-regulated and quiet mind.

She was attired in deep mourning for her mother, and she seemed to behold Palgrave as something above ordinary mortals, so entirely did she appear to love him.

Palgrave himself, I should tell the reader, was studying for the bar, and had a small patrimony, which, although not sufficient to procure the more expensive luxuries of life, was still ample enough for domestic happiness.

The ceremony went off as such ceremonies usually do, with a great deal of nervousness on the part of the bride, and a great deal of screwed up courage on the part of the bridegroom, who, were he not ashamed to do so, would not unfrequently betray more weakness than his fair intended; but at marriages it is the fashion for the lady to be nervous, while the gentleman must be as bold as brass.

A very few minutes sufficed to make Aurelia Mrs. Palgrave, and then we merely—(for no other guests were at the wedding)—adjourned to a pretty quiet-looking inn in the village, to take a slight repast, previous to the newly-married couple starting to spend the honeymoon at Cowes, in the Isle of

Wight, where, Palgrave told me, he had made arrangements for a most pleasant and delightful sojourn of one month.

I own that when they dorve off and left me alone at the inn-door, I never did feel so thoroughly lonely in all my life before, and a strong matrimonial disposition arose in my mind.

"Well, it may be my turn some of these days. I shall meet with some one who in herself can picture—deuce take it! I am growing quite romantic," I cried.

I soon started for London, and in a few days the decidedly melancholy impression which a wedding always produces on my mind wore off, amid the bustle of my professional duties, for I was then physician to a dispensary, and had plenty to do, although the proceeds were lamentably small.

In about a week I received a letter from my friend Palgrave, who spoke in the most enthusiastic terms of his happiness, and ended with taunting me to marry, if I could by hook or by crook get anybody to venture upon having me.

I transcribe the epistle, as it is rather a curiosity in its way, and may amuse some of my readers, who have been placed in similar circumstances to my enthusiastic friend at the Isle of Wight, or who expect to be so situated.

"Cowes.

"MY DEAR DOCTOR,—I positively could not write to you before, for my mind was never so occupied as it is at present. Here in this delightful locality I am surrounded with the greatest beauties of nature which a temperate climate can afford, and around this splendid coast we have some views and some objects which approach, if they do not absolutely reach, the sublime.

"And then—and then, my dear doctor, I have my dear Aurelia to participate in every feeling of wonder or admiration. It is a most delightful thing to have, in the true sense of the word, a companion, one who really participates in every thought, and can understand one's feelings; such a companion to me is Aurelia. I never found half the graces of her mind, which have now flashed across my delighted and truly happy senses.

"She is, indeed, all, and more than I had ever pictured her, and I have only to say to you, before you grow musty —marry!—Marry, doctor—marry, if by hook or by crook you can possibly find anybody to venture upon having you.

"Marry, and take all your meals with an angel; marry, and wish to live to the age of Metheuseleah, for your days will fly like minutes! Marry, and be a happy dog!

"Yours ever, CHARLES PALGRAVE.

"P. S.—We shall be in town on the 26th instant, when we expect a visit from you that evening. Don't forget, and go to sleep in your dreary and uncomfortable single man's lodgings."

* * * * *

Now all this was amazingly satisfactory concerning my friend's happiness in the marriage, and I quite forgave his bantering me on my position of solitary bachelorism, if I may be allowed the expression, in the real pleasure I felt in the conviction that two exceedingly amiable and worthy persons, such as Palgrave and his wife, had been so fortunate as to meet with such very congenial dispositions in each other.

The 26th, when they were to return to town, duly came, and I did not fail to present myself at the pretty little suburban house in which they had fixed their residence.

I was received with the utmost cordiality and friendliness by Palgrave, who said,—

"My dear doctor, you cannot imagine how very happy I am. Aurelia and myself were surely created for each other. Before my marriage, I used to be occasionally dull, and have fits of melancholy, but now such is never the case. I am, indeed, quite an altered man, so don't begin any of your horrid jokes about matrimony, because I assure you they will not tell."—"Well," said I, "allow me only one."

"What is that?"—"You say you are a married man!"

"Certainly."—"Then I suppose you allude to the martrimonial *noose* when you talk of being *haltered*."

"Abominable—vile—wretched!" cried Palgrave.—"I know that," said I; "but you know we long ago settled that there were but two descriptions of puns worth anything, and those were the very bad and the very good."

"Well, well, you have now had what I may call your matrimonial snarl. I will go and tell Aurelia that her papa is here."—"Thank you."

In a few moments the young married lady made her appearance; she was attired in a very plain, but becoming and tasteful evening dress, and looked perfectly charming. We passed a most agreeable hour in chatting over the wedding, and so on, and the only thing that at all annoyed me, was the innumerable little fidgetty attentions which Palgrave and his wife paid each other, and which newly-married people are always indulging in before other people.

If she rose to ring the bell, he would spring to his feet as if a pin had been in the cushion of his chair, and a charming little pretty contest would take place, he saying,—

"Now, really my dear, I cannot think of giving you the trouble," and she replying,—"Yes, I will. Now sit down, my dear."

"Nay, now, my love."—"I insist, my dear."

Finally they would both get hold of the bell-rope and give it a simultaneous pull, when she would give him a playful tap on the shoulder, &c.

Then if Aurelia wished for an additional lump of sugar in her tea, they would be quite sure to upset the sugar-basin between them, and then knock their heads together to pick up the pieces.

I was in two minds to scream suddenly when they did anything of that kind, by way of showing my due appreciation of it, but upon second thoughts, as they might both have gone into hysterics, I abstained.

Notwithstanding all this, however, I passed a very agreeable evening, and went home with a strong conviction that Palgrave was a very happy fellow, and his wife just some such a person as would grace a fire-side of my own.

In a few days I had a visit from my friend, and after we had talked for some time upon indifferent topics, he said,—

"You know I am absent at chambers a good part of the day, doctor, and consequently Aurelia is left rather lonely." —"Yes," said I. "But when you have a large family, you know, that will be obviated."

"A large fiddlestick," he exclaimed. "I am thinking of getting my aunt Deborah to live with us."

"What?"—"My aunt Deborah to live with us. She is a clever, agreeable woman, and has a small independence of her own, so I think it would be a very good arrangement."

"You do?"—"I do."

"Now, listen to me. I never saw your aunt, and know nothing whatever about her; but don't be a fool, Palgrave." —"Thank you, I don't mean."

"Don't have her to live with you. Since the beginning of the world the experiment of taking relations to live with you has been repeatedly tried, and always failed. It never has succeeded, and it never will. There have been more quarrels, more unhappiness, more separations, between man and wife from that one cause, namely, the meddlings of relatives, than any other circumstance that could ever —"
—"Pho! pho!"

"You may pho! pho! as much as you like, Palgrave, but it won't do. If your wife was a female cherubim, and your aunt a ministering angel, it wouldn't do."—"Really you are going to extremes, doctor."

"I know it, and as a friend I implore you never to allow a relative of any kind or description, near or remote, to make your house a home. You will bitterly repent if you do. Perhaps, when too late, and if not too late, you will find it a very uncomfortable job to repair your error, and turn a person out of doors whom you have invited in."—"But," he replied, "no general rule of that kind can possibly apply to all cases. Surely there may be some few exceptions."

"None—not one. Try it, if you like, Palgrave; I have warned you. A wilful man must have his way."—"You are always so violent, doctor, in anything you take into your head. You used, you know, to abuse matrimony. Now you see I am happy and contented, and you cannot but confess that I have cause to be so."

"Agreed."—"Well, now you are violent against my taking a relative to live with me, and you will, in the same manner, be forced to confess that another exception to your general rule has occurred."—"Try it—try it," said I.

"I mean to do so. Aurelia is all amiability, and would win anybody's affection. I am quite sure, too, that my aunt is far—very far from being likely to become disagreeable, and my firm impression is, that we shall make a very agreeable little family party."

"Try it," I repeated.

* * * * *

The next time I visited the Palgraves, there, sure enough, was the maiden aunt with the small independence. She was one of those rather frigid-looking women, who seem to

be, or affect to seem to be, so full of sensibility and refined humanity, that they weep and make awful faces at anything and everything.

I was formally introduced and received with a low curtsey, and I was not long without setting down the aunt, in my mind, as a bore of the very first magnitude.

"My dear," she said to Aurelia, "you must really change your place. Go to the other side of the fire-place, I implore you."

"Why, aunt?"—"There's a draught here enough to turn a mill. Look now—there—don't you see the fringe of your scarf moving?"

"I don't feel it," said Mrs. Palgrave. "I rather prefer this side, because it faces the window, do you see."

The aunt here showed a strong disposition to cry, and Palgrave said,—

"Move, my dear, to please your aunt. You know she will be quite unhappy, in her kind solicitude for you, if you don't."

Thus urged, Aurelia shifted her place, and it gave me a very high opinion of her temper, that she betrayed no irritation on the occasion, when I was ready to snap the aunt's nose off, I was in such a passion.

"Do you think, doctor," said Palgrave, "that fellow, Jones, will be hung?" alluding to the perpetrator of a murder, which was then occupying a good deal of the public attention.

"I should say yes," replied I, "and he surely, in my opinion, deserves it."

The aunt immediately rose and quitted the room very abruptly. Palgrave winked at me, as much as to say, there, did you notice that? I looked as calmly inquisitive as I could, for I neither admired the lady, nor the mode of her exit.

"You notice, she couldn't stay," he said.

I only replied by a grunt which produced just the ghost of a smile from the corners of Mrs. Palgrave's mouth.

"She is absolutely so tender-hearted," continued my friend, "and so feeling, that she cannot bear the slightest allusion to human suffering of any description."

"Indeed?"—"Yes. The mere allusion to the probability of a man being hung has quite overcome her."

"Dear me."—"I very much fear, too, that you are utterly lost in her good opinion, by what you said just now."

"That's very afflicting. But I must beg to say, in addition, that I think such overdrawn sympathy and exceeding sensitiveness is rather ridiculous than otherwise. Can't she break herself of it, poor lady?"

"Break herself of it?"—"Yes. I consider it a kind of moral disease."

"You surprise me, doctor. I really consider myself that it shows a very amiable disposition."—"Then I don't—I only consider it shows a very weak one."

"Well, you are a very unaccountable man; I thought you would have admired my aunt very much."

"Not so," said I; "but I hope she will get the better of her affliction."

"She is very humane," added Palgrave; "she would not hurt a fly."

"I knew a lady once," said I, "who would not hurt a fly. She weighed thirteen stone, and one hot day at Ramsgate rode a poor little tottering donkey to death. Besides, she worried her husband into his grave, and sent her daughter into the world an outcast, when the shelter of a parent's home would have saved her from utter destruction. Oh! I hate your exceeding sensitive people, who stop at straws, and leap over mountains."

Mrs. Palgrave said nothing, but she raised her eyes and gave me a look which it required very little skill to translate into "I cordially agree with every word of that."

"Well, well," cried my friend, "I am ready to agree with you that over-sensitiveness is certainly an evil, and perhaps an error; but then you know it is one on the right side."

To this I could not reasonably object, and shortly the conversation shifted to other topics. Upon the whole, I passed an agreeable evening, for the aunt kept coming into the room only occasionally, and making long absences as her nerves were now and then affected by some shocking remark of mine. After this had gone on for some time, I began to find a very great amusement in tormenting her, for I found that it was far from a difficult matter to say something which made her think it necessary to leave the room, either from excessive delicacy or fine-drawn humanity.

Nevertheless I did pity Mrs. Palgrave, for what was an

amusement to me as an occasional visiter, must have been a very great torment to her for a constancy. However, affairs went on tolerably smoothly for about four months, when one day Palgrave came to visit me at my lodgings, and I could not but observe that there was something disagreeable upon his mind.

I was upon the point of asking him what it was, but, upon second thoughts, I determined upon not doing so, and waited patiently for him to make the communication which I was quite sure, by his manner, he had come on purpose to make.

After he had poked my fire several times, he suddenly said, "Doctor, I want you to advise me what to do."

"In what?" said I.—"Why, the fact is," he continued, "Aurelia don't seem thoroughly to appreciate my aunt."

"Oh," said I.—"No. There does not appear that similarity of sentiment between them that I had really hoped to see."

"Indeed!"—"Sometimes Aurelia laughs at what my aunt cries at; and, in fact, Aurelia treats her feelings with a kind of levity ———"

"Stop there, if you please, Palgrave," cried I, "and recollect that there are two sides to every question, and more particularly to domestic ones."

"What do you mean, doctor?"—"I mean this, that it is much more likely that your aunt's feelings are absurd, ridiculous, and really laughable, than that your wife, who is sensible and amiable, should laugh at them, if they were reasonable and proper."

"Upon my word," he said, "you are quite a champion of Mrs. Palgrave's."—"I am a champion of every one who I think in the right," said I; "I see no reason in the fact of an amiable woman being your wife, which should make me shrink from expressing my opinion of her."

"Oh! that's all very well," he said; "but from the first you know you were prejudiced against my aunt."—"No, no, that I deny. I should have wished to like her, but having seen her, and gone a little way into a study of her character, I must candidly say I don't."

"Ah! there it is—there it is. Now, I think it's very wrong of Aurelia."

"What's very wrong?"—"To laugh at my aunt's feelings."

"You don't want your wife to be a hypocrite, Palgrave, do you?"

"No; but ———"—"Oh, nonsense, there's no buts in the case; I think your aunt's feelings are supremely ridiculous. She always reminds me of the very humane lady who was shocked at the practice that existed somewhere in the country of sweeping chimnies by putting a live goose down the flue, and in an agony of sensitive feeling for the goose, urgently recommended the use of a couple of ducks."

"There you go again, doctor," he cried, "with your jokes. What I want to ask you is, if I should give way to Aurelia's ridiculous whims of telling my aunt that we should be much happier without her company."

"Does your wife recommend that course?"—"Indeed she does, as plainly as possible, and she seems to think herself quite justified in it, I can assure you."—"And so she is."

"She is?"—"Yes. Surely she is a judge of her own happiness, Palgrave."

"Then you would ———"—"Send your aunt to the right-about, and politely request her to carry her fine feelings somewhere else."

"But, consider, after offering her a home; you know it would look so very strange."

"True, you offered her a home; but you did not wish to make your house an asylum for destitute feelings. Your aunt is quite independent, is she not?"—"She is."

"Then there can be no possible impropriety in politely putting a period to her residence in your house. Your wife is a reasonable and an amiable, feeling woman, I have heard you say, and if she thinks it necessary to ask you to get rid of your relative for her happiness with you, you may depend she has most ample cause."

"I don't know what to think," said Palgrave; "but I suppose I must hint it to my aunt, and trust she may go."
—"Now, my dear Palgrave," said I, "we are very nearly of an age; but I have learnt one piece of real, sound, practical wisdom, which I wish to instil into you."—"What is that?"

"*There was never anything hinted that had not far better have been said.* A hint is, in my opinion, an insult. If you are ashamed of saying anything, drop it altogether; but never try to smuggle it in by the despicable means of a hint."

"Really, doctor, you are quite oracular," he said; "but I cannot do otherwise than agree with you, and I will tell my aunt, and not hint, that Aurelia does not desire her to prolong her visit."

"That's right," said I. "You will have a happier home for it."—"And yet," he cried, with a sigh, "my aunt is a most amiable and admirable woman. If she sees any little fault in Aurelia, she mentions it to me so quietly and considerately."

"What! Does she have the unparalleled impertinence to find fault with your wife to you? Now, by the infernal Styx, Palgrave, I would have shown her the outside of the door, if she had been the most wonderful specimen of the female sex, and ten times my aunt."

"Oh! you are violent."—"Of course I am."

"Well, well; good morning. You never can, and never will, appreciate my aunt. All day yesterday a tear was glistening in her eye."

"What for?"—"Why, there's a charming little boy, who lives opposite to us, and he's got an iron hoop. Well, you see, a ruffian was coming by on horseback, and the little innocent, in one of those frolicksome moods so common to childhood, bowled the hoop between the horse's legs."

"Well, well?"—"Why, down came horse and man; the animal on his knees, and the man on the flat of his back in a moment."

"What then?"—"The savage jumped up, and just caught the engaging infant as he was getting the area gate open to take refuge in the kitchen, and in the most barbarous manner he laid into him behind with his horse-whip."

"Serve him right," cried I. "Curse his engaging innocence. Why, I would have made an impression on his mind that would have converted an iron hoop into a bugbear for life to him. How can you be such a fool, Palgrave?"

"There you go again, doctor, off like an effervescing draught. My aunt saw the monster belabouring the innocent, and she has wept ever since, I assure you. Nevertheless I will take your advice, and tell her to go. Good morning."

"Good morning," I growled, for I was in a rage with Palgrave and his aunt. * * * *

Two days elapsed, during which I saw nothing of my friend; but on the morning of the third, as I was sitting at my breakfast, there came the following very extraordinary epistle:—

"MY DEAR DOCTOR,—Distraction has seized upon my brain; I am going mad—mad—mad! Oh! Aurelia, that it should come to this! My blood foams like liquid lava through my brain; it bubbles through each starting artery with fiery vehemence; I am lost—lost—lost! Come to me, my friend, as soon as possible, and tell me, from your medical knowledge, the shortest method of leaving a world that is now to me a desolate waste. Oh! horror—horror! My aunt has unfolded to me a secret that freezes my marrow, and has toppled my reason from its throne. Come soon to your despairing, horribly sacrificed, and bewildered friend,

"CHARLES PALGRAVE.

"P.S.—Ask for me, not for—I cannot name her, but you know who I mean."

I read this epistle twice before I could believe the evidence of my own senses that it was really in the handwriting of my friend, Palgrave, and not a joke of some one's. But there it was; I could have sworn to the writing, although the first line began at the top of the paper, and ended in the middle.

"What has happened now?" I asked myself. "What devilish lie has the fine feelings of that infernal aunt hatched up now?"

As may be supposed, however, I did not waste a long time in deliberation, but hastily finishing my breakfast, I was in the act of putting on an outer coat, when my room door was suddenly opened, and there stood Palgrave.

His hair stood on end in the most ludicrous manner, and he wore a long cravat, which was buttoned in front, leaving the ends dangling behind him. A boot was upon one foot, and a red Morocco slipper upon the other. His waistcoat was buttoned all the way up upon the wrong buttons, and his face had evidently been untouched that morning by a razor, or soap and water.

"Good Heavens! Palgrave," I cried, "what is the matter with you?"—"Look at me?" he said.

"I am staring at you with all my might," I replied. "Come in and tell me what has happened?"—"Happened! Ha! ha! happened?" he repeated, with some such a laugh as is used by Mr. O. Smith, when he is representing a melodramatic hero of no common order.

"Yes, happened," I said. "Don't make those d——e faces, but explain yourself."

He walked into my room, and sat down on the sofa, after which he gave his head a thump, and then his chest several others.

"Well, what now?" said I.—"There is a hell within me!" he said

"Is there; but how came it there?"—"Aurelia is false."

"False!"—"Yes! false as fair. Her embrace is like the deadly coil of a serpent. False—false!"

"Oh! indeed; are you quite sure?"—"Sure—sure? Do you want to mock me, or drive me mad?"

"I thought you were mad," said I, rather impatiently, for I had a suspicion that the whole affair would turn out to be a mare's nest. "What made me ask if you were sure, was, for fear it was only some infernal nonsense of your aunt's."

"Profane not the name of that excellent and most observant woman She it is who has opened my eyes, and made me know myself the wretch I am."

"Upon my word that's very kind of her. I should not be much obliged to anybody who was to show me I was a wretch."—"I am wounded!" he said.

"Where?"—"My honour; my life!"

"Oh! your honour. Well, I suppose, Palgrave, it really comes to this—that your aunt has told you something against your wife."

"Against her!" he shrieked. "She is a monster, and I a wretched, deceived husband. The brightness of my life has passed away, and all will be gloom, suspicion, and despair. My faith in human nature is shaken to its foundation. Oh! doctor, you have seen, you have heard her speak, and could you imagine that wickedness could dwell in such a form? Oh! what a mansion have those vices got that for their habitation chose out her! You, I am sure, could never have imagined that she should be—bad—bad —bad!"—"Certainly not, nor do I imagine so now," I replied, with great calmness.

"Don't you?"—"No, nor will I, without probably more evidence than your aunt can produce."

"Doctor, I am a miserable man," he said. "My dream of happiness has fled."

"Well, let it fly, provided it leaves a substantial reality behind. Beware, Palgrave, how you lightly compromise the happiness of your wife and the comfort of your fire-side. Whatever has been told to you, I beg you to weigh well, before founding anything upon it. Above all, too, I beg of you, let the circumstances be what they may, not to rave and storm, but to conduct yourself like a rational being. If you are injured, do not allow yourself to be laughed at, in addition, by the extravagant manner in which you take it. If you, on the contrary, should find that you are mistaken, and that your wife is all that you would wish her, and I believe her to be, you will be exceedingly mortified to have made a great tumult and fuss about nothing."

He seemed rather struck with my words; and after a pause, he said,—

"You must be in the position of an injured husband, before you can appreciate the agony and feelings of one. A heavy sadness is pressing on my heart, doctor, and although it may have assumed some extravagant shapes, yet it is not the less sincere."

"I believe you," said I; "and now, if you came here to tell me all about it, tell me at once; and if not, only remember I have no desire to pry into your affairs."

"I have come to tell you," he replied. "After I had written to you, I could not control my impatience, and have followed my own letter, which you have doubtless received by this time."

"I have; but I confess it has not enlightened me much."

"Listen to me, then, and I will tell you all. Agreeably to your advice, I determined upon speaking openly and candidly to my aunt, and telling her that I feared her continued presence was incompatible with the harmony of my house, without going at all into any subjects of complaint."

"And what did she say?"—"She heard me out with perfect composure, and then as nearly as possible in these words addressed me,—

"'Your wife, my dear Charles, has put you upon getting me out of the house?'

"'Mrs. Palgrave fears she cannot assimilate sufficiently with your habits,' I said, 'to make you comfortable here, and certainly desires your departure.'

"'I thought as much,' she then said. 'Oh! Charles, I have a dreadful secret to communicate to you.'

"As you may suppose, I was naturally alarmed, and begged her to explain, when she informed me that for the last five mornings my wife had, after I had left home for chambers, been in the habit of going out alone for upwards of an hour, in a most mysterious way, and getting rather angry when rigidly questioned as to where she had been, as well as positively refusing to allow my aunt to accompany her on any one of these morning excursions, which were quite a surprise to me.

"My aunt further added, that, alarmed and very much shocked as she was by such very mysterious conduct, she resolved one morning upon following and watching her. She did so, but was baffled by my wife getting into a hackney-coach at the first stand, and driving off in the direction of the west-end of the town. Now, doctor, what am I to think of all this?"

"I cannot tell you that," said I; "but I tell you what I would do."

"What?"—"I would ask my wife at once where she went of a morning."

"And bespeak some fabrication!"—"That does not necessarily follow; but tell me what you have done."

"Nothing,—nothing. Of course my wife's motives for trying to get rid of my aunt are sufficiently transparent now. She was in the way, and I am a miserable man for life."

"What do you mean to do?"

"I cannot tell; my mind is bordering on distraction. Advise me what to do, my dear doctor, for I am incapable myself of thought. I have but one feeling, and that is, that there can be no more domestic happiness for me. You will admit, with all your partizanship in favour of Mrs. Palgrave, that her conduct is suspicious in the extreme. Why should she make these mysterious visits when my back is turned? Why get into cabs and coaches, and drive Heaven knows where, without saying anything about it?"

"Well," said I, "if you will be guided by me, you will adopt yourself a course widely differing from that you complain of in your wife."

"How,—what do you mean, doctor?"—"Simply this, that you should do nothing secretly, but go home at once, and say to her, 'Aurelia, where do you go in the mornings alone, after I have left home?'"

"That would indeed be absurd," he cried; "why, what answer do you expect I should get to such an application?" —"Most probably the truth."

"Most probably quite the reverse. Suppose she chooses to say she went to the milliner's or the dressmaker's, or merely for a walk or a ride?"

"Well, then, at least you would have more evidence to go upon, if, upon proper inquiry, which you could found upon her answer, you discovered she had deceived you in any way."

"No, no," he cried, "that plan will not do; my feelings are too much harrowed up to permit me to do so."

"What will you do, then?"—"To-morrow morning I will watch her."

"I hope you will do no such thing, Palgrave. It is the very worst course you could possibly adopt. By so doing you will expose yourself to a thousand disagreeables, and run the chance of being seen by her, which, if she be quite innocent, would expose you to her contempt, and, if guilty, merely put her more effectually upon her guard."

"I must do so, doctor. It is the only plan I can carry out. All I have to say is, that if you will not assist me, and countenance me in it, I must seek some other, perhaps far less judicious, friend."

This last remark of Palgrave made some impression upon me, and caused me to waver in my previously determined resolve to have nothing personally to do with this affair. I thought now to myself that it became a kind of duty in me to see the affair perfectly investigated, and considered that I might be doing essential service to Mrs. Palgrave, if innocent, by stepping between her and any mad-brained intemperance on the part of her husband; and if she was really guilty of any indiscretion, I might save the honour and feelings of Palgrave by acting as a moderator to his wrath, which otherwise would assuredly drive him into indiscreet excesses, which all the after calm reflection in the world would not suffice to efface.

Hastily running these considerations over in my mind, I began to think it would be a species of moral cowardice in me to shuffle out of the affair.

"Palgrave," I said, "if you are determined to act foolishly in this matter, I will not abandon you; but, for the object of seeing that justice is done to your suspected wife, who from my soul I believe to be innocent, I will accompany you on the expedition you propose."

"I thank you, doctor," said Palgrave, "from my heart I thank you There is but one other friend to whom I could have applied, and that is Captain O'Leary."

"For Heaven's sake," I cried, "do not apply to him in any emergency. He is a very good-hearted man, I believe, but the sheerest blunderer in anything that requires nice discrimination that can be found."

"He is certainly hasty," remarked Palgrave; "very hasty, I may say. But now, doctor, do me the favour of writing a note to my wife, to say that I shall be engaged with you on some important business which will detain me till dinner-time to-morrow."

"Indeed," said I, "I shall do no such thing."

"Why not?"—"Why not! How can you ask me? A pretty figure I should cut in the transaction, if, at the outset of it, I commenced with a thumping lie."

"It is necessary, however," he cried, impatiently, "that something of the kind should be done, and if you won't, I must, however unwillingly, take up my pen to write to her myself."

"You can write home, of course, whatever you like," said I; "but don't show it to me, or make me a party to it. Once more I warn you, Palgrave, you are going on a wrong course, and fighting against your own peace of mind."

A knock at my door now announced a visitor, and upon my opening it, who should make a wild kind of rush into the room but Palgrave's detestable, meddling, sentimental aunt.

"Oh, nephew!" she exclaimed, "I have found you at last!" and then, drawing out her handkerchief, she commenced a disagreeable kind of snivelling, for which I would gladly have thrown her out of the window.

Palgrave stood staring at her, and caught hold of a handful of his hair on the top of his head, as if he was only waiting for some awful, stunning piece of information from his aunt to induce him to tear it out by the roots, and fling it on the floor, like C. J. Smith in the pantomime.

"Oh—oh—oh!" sobbed the aunt, until I lost all my patience, and bellowed out to her,—

"Would you like a stiff glass of hot brandy-and-water, ma'am, to compose your delicate and susceptible feelings?" —"I—I shouldn't mind a small drop neat," she replied, to my astonishment, for I looked upon my offer as a joke upon her, tinctured with a little gall.

I looked at Palgrave, and he said,—

"My aunt is compelled by the state of her nerves to take a little spirits occasionally, notwithstanding her extreme aversion to it."

"As a medical man," said I, very gravely, "I should most decidedly say that spirits are the worst things you can take, madam; and you need never do your feelings so much violence as to force you to take any brandy. I should strongly recommend a blue pill and a black draught, instead of brandy, whenever you feel yourself so very much overcome by your feelings."

I took care not to suffer the ghost of a smile to appear on my face as I said this, and she was forced to forego the small drop of brandy, saying,—

"Dear me, do you think so, doctor—a-hem! Really, I have always been told to support myself with stimulants."

"The worst thing you can do, ma'am," I replied; "a cold bath would agree with you."—"How very odd," she said.

Then turning to Palgrave, who stood glancing first at me and then at her during this little dialogue, she said,—

"My dear Charles, she's gone again."—"Again—again! Oh, powers above!" he cried, and then stalked up and down my room like a melodramatic hero.

"No sooner had you gone out this morning," continued the aunt, interrupting her narrative with many tears and woful shakes of the head, "than she went up stairs and put on her blue satin bonnet, with the straw coloured ostriches ——"
—"Oh, horror—horror!" cried Palgrave.

"Then she rang for Susan to settle her scarf, and, without saying anything to me, she came down with her parasol and a pair of violet gloves ——"

"Yes, yes; what then?" cried Palgrave.—"Then, my dear Charles, she walked into the parlour, laid her black net mittens on the table, and, with all the effrontery in the world, she said to me, 'Good morning.'"

"Did she? Oh, falsehood! thy name is woman!" cried Palgrave.—"Aurelia," corrected the aunt.

"Go on—go on," he groaned.—"Then I said to her, 'Where are you going?' and what do you think she replied to me, and with as much calmness as if she had said nothing at all?"

"What—what?"—"'On private business,' says she, and out she went without another word of explanation."

"You hear, doctor; you hear," said Palgrave. "Did you ever dream of such strange, awful, perfidious conduct in your life?"—"I must confess," said I, "that I cannot perceive anything so particularly dreadful in Mrs. Palgrave's conduct."

"Not see it!" shrieked the aunt.—"Not see it!" exclaimed Palgrave.

"Certainly not. Mrs. Palgrave goes out, previous to which she declines giving information to one totally unauthorized to demand it, of whither she is going."

"Oh, dear me!" exclaimed the aunt, with a toss of her head, "you are a very great friend of Mrs. Palgrave's, doctor. I was not aware of that, doctor."—"Doctor," cried Palgrave, "you are a very prejudiced and obstinate man. You are indeed."

"I beg to deny that," said I. "Recollect, Palgrave, who you are fighting against. You are, I again warn you, fighting against your own peace of mind. Beware, Palgrave—beware."

He looked a little scared as I spoke; but the aunt immediately chimed in,—

"My dear Charles, you really must not allow yourself to be sacrificed by your wife. You are an ill-used man."—"I am—I am," he cried; "I will not, I must not be sacrificed. My dear aunt, I owe a great obligation to you. Now tell me what steps you took after my—I cannot call her wife—left the house."—"I flew up-stairs and put on my best plaid and beaver bonnet."

"Yes, yes."

"Then I ran after her as fast as I could, and was just in time to see her get into a hackney-coach, numbered 5076."

"Confusion!" cried Palgrave, giving his forehead a great slap; "there is a liquid fire in my brain."—"I wish," said I, "there was a little more solid sense."

"To-morrow—to-morrow," he cried, "I will have damning, blasting proofs—to-morrow I will watch her, and follow her wheresoever she may go. To-night I will press a restless couch at the Hummums Hotel. I cannot go home. No, no; that would be too severe a trial."—"I'll tell her you have to go out of town, my dear, on business," said the aunt.

"Do, do," he cried; "and now, doctor, once more, after what you have heard, will you accompany me to-morrow on my sorrowing expedition?"—"Yes," said I; "and I can only say that, from what this lady has reported, I am more than ever convinced of Mrs. Palgrave's entire innocence, and be assured that the time will come when you will feel the bitterest and most poignant regret for your present suspicions."

"Impossible!—impossible!" he cried; "I am not a jealous man, but here are circumstances enough to rouse the demon in the heart of the most confiding. To-morrow, doctor, I will come here for you, unless you will take breakfast with me at the Hummums."

"I will prefer that," said I, "for I am much more likely to be punctual than you are. So now good morning."

* * * * *

By an early hour I was at the Hummums in Covent-garden, where I found Palgrave, who, from his heavy, listless appearance, I guessed had not been in bed all night. After the morning salutation, we commenced breakfast very nearly in silence. He seemed to avoid purposely the disagreeable theme which was of course uppermost in his mind, and it was not for me to begin a conversation upon his private affairs. At length he rose, and looking nervously at his watch, he said,—

"It is time; she—she always goes at eleven, and it is now a quarter after ten."

"How do you mean to proceed?" said I.—"I have been thinking about that," he replied. "My street is a very quiet one; but there is a public-house in it that commands a good view right and left. That has a back entrance, so I propose that we go and sit at one of the windows of it until we see her pass."

"Very well," said I; "come along, then, for it's a tolerable walk, I know."

We left the hotel arm in arm, and half an hour's brisk walking brought us to the next street to that in which Palgrave resided. We entered the Sir Somebody's Head, and proceeded up stairs to a room on the first floor, which at that time of the morning, as may well be supposed, we had all to ourselves. In fact, so odd did it appear, apparently, to the pot-boy who answered Palgrave's ring, that two persons should come there and order brandy-and-water at such an hour, that he carried out the poker in triumph, as if he suspected our intention might be to appropriate it.

The window commanded a view of the house of Palgrave, and as we sat at it we could not fail to perceive whoever went in or out. We had not waited long, when an upper window of the house opened, and a yellow silk pocket-handkerchief was waved at it in a very mysterious manner.

"What's the meaning of that?" said I.—"That's my aunt," said Palgrave; "it's an agreed-upon signal between us to let me know that my wife has not yet left the house."

"Oh!" said I, "you and your aunt have arranged all that, have you?"

"Yes; she is to show a red handkerchief when she thinks my wife is putting on her bonnet to go out."

"There it is," I cried, as at that moment a red handkerchief, like a flaming banner, was shaken out of the window.—"Gracious powers! it is too true," exclaimed Palgrave; "she must now be tying her bonnet strings."

The red handkerchief was now quickly withdrawn, and the two arms of the aunt appeared at the window instead, flourishing about like those of some maniac. Then she pointed downwards, which Palgrave informed me intimated that Mrs. Palgrave was in the room below attiring herself for her mysterious morning peregrination.

"Oh! this is horrible," said Palgrave. "Do you not pity me, doctor? Only fancy my dreadful state of mind at this present moment."—"You have yourself to thank for that," said I; "if you will take my advice, you will cross the road now, and knock at your own door, and when you see your wife, ask her at once where she is going."

"No, no, I cannot—I cannot."

At this moment the door of Palgrave's house opened, and out came his wife, sure enough, in the blue satin bonnet, the scarf, the parasol, and the violet-coloured gloves.

"There she is,—there she is!" he suddenly cried, in a frantic manner.—"Where,—where? What is it?" exclaimed the pot-boy, who had just, on some pretence, entered the room, and now made a rush to the window, with a face beaming with the most intense curiosity. This was too much for my gravity, and I laughed outright, while Palgrave pushed the boy's head against the window-sill with a savage vehemence.

"Take that," he said, "you infernal villain!"—"Murder!" cried the boy,—"murder!"

Palgrave then rushed down stairs and into the next street, leaving me in pawn for the brandy-and-water, which I paid for as speedily as I could, with the accompaniment of a shilling to silence the clamours of the boy, and then ran down the street after Palgrave, leaving, I have no doubt, a strong impression at the Sir Somebody's Head that we were two madmen.

When I arrived at the corner of the street, I found Palgrave screwed up into a doorway, and making gesticulations to me.

"What's the matter now?" I said.—"Hush—hush!" he replied; "she has just turned the corner. Let her get on a bit, and then we can take a run to the next corner. Don't you see that's the way to follow without being seen by her. Always let her turn a corner, and then run after her and watch her to another."

"It's both unpleasant and fatiguing," said I; "but as I am here, I suppose I must go through with it."

He then peered round the corner in the most ridiculous manner imaginable, and when his wife was nearly out of sight, he set off running again as if for a wager.

I was by no means charmed with the idea of scampering along the streets in such a frantic manner, but I saw no remedy for it but to follow him, so long as I proposed to myself to be of any service to his wife, who I verily believed to be the calumniated victim of the detestable aunt. Off I set, therefore, and, at the bottom of that street, there was Palgrave again, ensconced in the doorway, as before.

This kind of game was continued until we reached a coach-stand, which, by hiding in the doorway of a shop, we could just see conveniently. Palgrave absolutely danced in an agony as he saw his wife beckon to one of the vehicles, into which she got, and it immediately drove off. Palgrave directly rushed from the doorway, and bounding into the road like a madman, he scampered after the coach with a speed that I could not dream of attempting to equal or imitate. I, therefore, contented myself by watching him as I walked on at rather a rapid pace. I saw him overtake the lumbering vehicle and jump up behind, to the great amusement of the chance passengers. Then a boy shouted the old cry, which is so seldom heard now in London streets, of "Cut, cut behind!"

The coachman immediately began slashing away with his whip at the back of the vehicle, and presently the whole affair turned a corner, amid the cries, hoots, shouts, and laughter of the populace.

Here was a pretty climax to the morning's adventures! I stood for some moments ruminating with myself as to what I should or could do in the affair, and at last came to the very unsatisfactory but rational conclusion, that I had better go home again, being, as I was, perfectly distanced and thrown out in the chase.

I was upon the point of carrying this resolve into effect, when who should I see rushing towards me, with but one skirt to his coat, and a lot of mud upon his face, but Palgrave himself.

"A coach!—a coach!—a coach!" he shouted, and on the instant no less than three wheeled from the stand.

"Who can go fastest?" he cried.—"Here you are, your honour," cried one of the jarvies; "my osses is the runners. That ere off oss has wonned never so many cups and plates."

"None o' yer gammon," interposed another; "you know yer can't get out o' two mile a hour. Mine's the *hanimals*, yer know."—"You be bothered!" screamed the third; "jist step in and see how these ere sleek 'uns go, yer washup."—"You knows, Joe," screamed the first, "that one o' your bags o' bones, as you calls osses, is called Grief and Skin, and the other Skin and Grief."

"Villains! wretches!" roared Palgrave, struggling among them, for he was surrounded by the rival jarvies; "let me go, or I'll murder some of you." He then made a dart into the first coach, and I followed him. "Drive on!" he shouted to the coachman; "take the first turning to the right, and the first to the right again. Overtake 5072, and I'll give you a sovereign."

This was an inducement with a vengeance, and off we went at a very tidy pace indeed, considering all things. We doubled the corners according to the direction of Palgrave, and then the coachman inclined his head towards the front glasses, and cried,—

"I see him, sir, he's only a little ahead."—"Keep behind him," roared Palgrave, "but don't pass him for your life. Curse that villain! he lashed me so I was forced to get down, leaving one of the tails of my coat on the spikes behind."

"Oh, indeed," said I, scarcely able to suppress my laughter.—"Yes, doctor; but I will track her now. I am a desperate man, and I will have revenge."

"I shall have to bleed you, and then drive you to Bethlehem," said I, "if you go on in that extraordinary manner. Recollect you know nothing yet, but that your wife got into a hackney coach."—"We shall see. We shall see," he grumbled, moodily; "I will have a blighted heart's revenge."

"A blighted fiddlestick," said I. "You will some day or another be ready to gnaw your head off for all this folly."

On we went, following 5072, until we came to the corner of Fitzroy-square, when our driver slackened his speed, and cried through the glass,—

"He's a drawing up, your honour."—"Stop, then! stop!" roared Palgrave, and he thrust his head out of the coach window.

"There—there! Now she's getting out," he cried. "There she goes! Look—look!"

"I can't look," said I, "for your head."

"There—there! Oh! Heaven—she descends the steps

—she pays the coachman—she knocks—she—she rings. My brain reels—my blood boils! Oh! agony! Horror unspeakable! She's gone into No. 1."

This was too ridiculous, and I fell back in the coach in a paroxysm of laughter. Palgrave was exceedingly indignant at my mirth, and abused me roundly for my want of feeling, hinting that what was a joke to me was death to him.

"Well, my dear fellow," I replied, "it was very wrong of me to laugh; but I could not help it. Now tell me what you mean to do?"—"To do! Exterminate her. Have unexampled and awful vengeance!"

He tossed his arms about in a very wild and maniac kind of manner as he spoke, and called to the coachman to open the door of the vehicle, and let him out.

When we alighted I took good care to keep close to him, for I was really afraid he would commit some extravagance; and, at all events, I wished that some further information as regarded the proceedings of Mrs. Palgrave should be obtained previous to the enraged husband making a public exhibition of his real or supposed wrongs.

"Now, Palgrave," I said, "I beg of you to be guided by me in this business, and not to give way to impulse in the manner you are so much inclined to do."

"What would you have?" he cried. "I am a deeply injured man, and I must have revenge."—"So you shall, and justice, too, Palgrave; but, that you may have both, you must be calm."

"I am calm—I am calm," he cried "Ha! ha! ha! I am cool—quite cool. Never was cooler and calmer in my life. Oh! ten thousand devils!"—"That's a large number," said I. "But, at all events, permit me to go and inquire for Mrs. Palgrave at the house you saw her enter."

"You? Why you?"—"Because I am really calm and collected, and you are not. You are too precipitate, and might do or say something that you would be very sorry for some time hence, supposing your wife to be innocent."

"Innocent! innocent!" he shrieked. "Impossible! You jest. Innocent she cannot be. I will tear down the house—I will burn London. I—I don't know what I won't do; but my name shall become a terror and sound of horror to all faithless women for generations to come."—"That's very sanguinary. But will you wait here while I knock and make inquiries?"

"I will, if you will promise to arrange a hostile meeting for me with the wretch who inhabits that house."—"I will take care of your honour, you may depend," said I.

"Go, then—go. I will walk up and down here till you return. You see how calm I am—how cool and collected. Any other man in my situation would tear up the paving-stones, he would."

Palgrave accompanied these observations with such maniacal gestures, and stamped so violently on the pavement, that several people crossed to the other side of the way rather than pass him, and an old lady ran half-a-dozen steps down an area, the gate of which had been left open.

"I shall not keep you long," cried I, and immediately walked up to the door indicated by Palgrave as the one at which his wife knocked and entered.

Upon one of the panels was a brass plate, on which was the name of Mr. Burn, and when I knocked I made up my mind to ask for that individual.

The door was opened to me by a boy in livery, to whom I said,—

"Is Mr. Burn at home?"—"Yes, sir," he replied; "but he is engaged just now."

"Cool that, rather," thought I, as I said—

"Is it a lady who is with him?"—"Yes, sir. Mrs. Palgrave, sir."—"Oh!" said I. "Just go to your master, and say that a gentleman wishes to see him on most particular business, which will not detain him many moments."

I was ushered now into a handsome parlour, where I waited for about ten minutes, after which the door opened, and a little, elderly, prim-looking gentleman, with a very shining bald head, came in.

"I am sorry to have kept you waiting, sir," said he, "but I have a lady with me. Pray be seated, sir."

"Your name is Burn, sir, I presume?" I said.

"Yes, sir, it is," he replied, and I was rather amazed at the peculiar manner in which he noticed me. Sometimes he would open his eyes very wide, and give me a good stare—then he would nearly shut them up, and twinkle them at me in the most comical manner; all of a sudden he shut one eye, and fixed the other one, which seemed preternaturally wide open, upon me. Then he shaded his eyes with his hand, and took a survey of me as I stood in astonishment, and his last manœuvre was to make up his two hands into an imitation telescope, and take a look at me that way.

I really thought Mr. Burn was a madman, and began to feel very uncomfortable.

"A very good subject," he suddenly said, "very good, indeed. I have seldom, sir, met with one more to my taste."

"Bless me," thought I, "does he want to eat me?"

"Just take a seat," he then said, "and I'll fetch some canvass."—"Really, sir," I said, "I don't understand you."

"A—not understand me?"—"Not at all, sir."

"Why, you came for a three-quarter."—"Came for a what?"

"A three-quarter—your name is Twisselton, I believe?"—"Indeed it is not."

"Bless me, there's some mistake then. Mr. Twisselton was to come at this hour to give me his first sitting for his portrait, and I made sure you were the gentleman."

"Mr. Burn," said I, "what are you?"—"A portrait and enamel painter, sir," he replied.

"Do you know a Mrs. Palgrave?"

"Yes, I do. Did she recommend you?"—"No, she did not; but, in one word, Mrs. Palgrave has been traced secretly to your house."

"Has she?"—"Yes, sir; and I must say you take the matter very coolly indeed."

"Of course, it ain't much matter to me; but still, for her sake, I hope her husband has not traced her here."

Of all pieces of impudence that ever I came near, or heard of, this, in my mind, was the greatest; and I looked at Mr. Burn's little, prim, shining face for some moments, in too much real astonishment to say anything, and he actually had the impertinence again to make his hands up into a telescope, and take another look at me in a very extraordinary manner.

"Sir," I said, "you have the most unblushing effrontery of any one I ever met with."—"Sir, you are insolent," he said.

This fired me, and I exclaimed, in no gentle voice,—

"You are an old scoundrel, sir. What do you mean by encouraging the visits here of a young married lady?"—"Because it is my business, sir."

"Your business, you old goat!"—"Yes, sir. I have many of them come here, sir, and I can tell you they recommend one another, because they know I keep the affair secret, and can be depended on, sir. They admire my colour, sir—and my tone, sir—and my manner, sir; and I can only add, you are a vagabond, sir."

The little man's face assumed a purple hue with rage, and we stood stamping at each other for some moments in the most ridiculous manner imaginable.

"Is the unfortunate woman here?" I cried.

"Who the devil do you mean, sir?" he bellowed.—"Mrs. Palgrave."

"And what makes her unfortunate?"—"Why, in intriguing with such a lump of ill-looking carrion as you. She must be insane."

"Intriguing?"—"Yes—intriguing."

"Good God! there's some mistake. I never intrigued in the whole course of my life."—"Explain your conduct then, sir."

"Why, she comes here to have her miniature painted on an enamel brooch, which she intends to surprise her husband with as a present upon his birth-day, to-morrow."

In one moment the whole truth flashed across my mind, and I felt a degree of delight, which, I am sure, would not have been greater had Mrs. Palgrave been my own wife.

After all, the affair had turned out merely to be a little stratagem of affection on her part for her husband. This was the cause of the mysterious morning visits—all to give him pleasure.

"My dear Mr. Burn," said I, "I beg you thousands of pardons—I do, indeed; you have made me quite happy."

"Upon my soul, sir," said the artist, "you are a very extraordinary man, sir, and I don't understand you a bit, sir."

"My dear sir, don't be angry," I cried; "the fact is, that Mrs. Palgrave's husband is a very jealous man, and, having been informed that his wife had left her home on some mysterious expedition for several mornings, he determined to watch her, and, with all the wild fury of a jealous man, he this day dogged her to your door, Mr. Burn."

"Indeed! you don't say so, sir?"—"It is the fact, and I

DIARY OF A PHYSICIAN.

assure you I had the very greatest difficulty in persuading him to allow me to call here instead of himself, which I am, however, rejoiced he did at length consent to."

"What a dilemma!" cried Mr. Burn; "why, sir, I am fifty-eight, and Mrs. Palgrave, I suppose, is about twenty." —"She is," I replied, "and the most amiable of women, Mr. Burn. I can never, sir, sufficiently apologize to you for my intemperate warmth."

"Don't say a word about that," he cried; "I was as bad as you. I am very irritable, I assure you, and was to the full in as great a rage as yourself."—"Well, sir, you shall paint my portrait, if you will do me that honour," said I.

"With pleasure," he replied.

I laid my card before him, and he was pleased to say he had heard of my very great skill from many persons, and expressed much pleasure in making my acquaintance.

"Now, doctor," he said, "don't let me go in fear of my life from this jealous husband."—"I have been thinking of that," said I, "and have a very great favour to ask of you, Mr. Burn."

"What is it, sir?"—"Why, that you will assist me in converting this affair into a matter of permanent benefit to the amiable Mrs. Palgrave, by curing her husband of his absurd disposition to jealousy."

"I will do anything with pleasure for that object," replied the good-hearted man; "put me to any trouble you like,—I will go through it cheerfully."

"Has Mrs. Palgrave left here?"—"She has, and taken with her the finished enamel brooch."

"Very good. Then all I wish you to do, Mr. Burn, is this—to see Mr. Palgrave, and decline offering any explanation as to his wife's conduct, merely declaring her innocence and virtue, and referring him to herself for explanation."

"I see—I see," he cried, "that will do him good, and show him that if he had spoken to her at first, he would have saved himself both pain and trouble."

"Exactly," said I; "but that is the very last thing he will do in his present state of mind. He will most probably storm and rave, and only be pacified by the prospect of fighting a duel with you."

"A duel with me!"—"Yes; and I beg of you to accept the challenge, Mr. Burn. Our object should be now to draw Mr. Palgrave into every excess we can, so that when he learns the real truth, it will make such an impression on him that he will never again yield himself to a ready belief in circumstantial evidence, however strong."

"Yes, I see all that," said Mr. Burn; "but how is the duel business to be arranged?"—"I want you to fight him, and be shot dead in the encounter."

"Do you—you are very kind, doctor."—"Rely upon me," I said, with a laugh; "the duel shall be a harmless one: I must be Palgrave's second, and if you are asked to name a friend, mention Mr. Sinclair, of 24, Moorgate; he is a friend of mine, and between us three we can manage to completely hoodwink the jealous husband."

"I'll do it—I'll do it," he said.—"Very well, Mr. Burn. Palgrave is now waiting in the street; I will go and tell him you refuse all explanation, and refer him to his wife."

"Exactly."—"I will then bring him back here, and you must manage him as well as you can. I will be here to prevent any evil consequences from arising."

"So do. Mind you keep him from violence. I cannot contend with a desperate, jealous man, you know."—"Certainly not; I will manage him."

* * * * *

I went out into the street, and there was Palgrave, with his hat drawn down upon the bridge of his nose, and his whole appearance indicating agitation and passion.

"Well, doctor,—well," he cried, "what have you heard? Have you seen her? Shall I have a horrible revenge?"—"Hush! hush!" I said; "the gentleman who keeps the house is a Mr. Burn, and he distinctly refuses all explanation. The house has a door round the corner, and by that it appears your wife has left and gone home."

"The monster! Oh—oh—oh!"—"Well, hear me out. Burn avers solemnly that your wife is as pure as possible, and perfectly innocent."

"Psha!"—"He refers you to her for an explanation of her apparently ambiguous conduct, but declines all explanation himself."

"A paltry subterfuge!" cried Palgrave. "The villain thinks to get me away by such means."—"Well, Palgrave," said I, "as your friend—and speaking in all sincerity—I strongly advise you to take Mr. Burn's advice, and go home and question your wife."

"Wife! home!" he bellowed. "I have no wife—no home! I will have Burn's blood."—"Very well; as a friend, I will stay by you, but blame only your own intemperate passions if evil be the result of your conduct. Once more, will you go home and ask an explanation of Mrs. Palgrave?"

"I'd rather go to hell!" he said, "and ask an explanation of the devil."—"Very well; if such is your determination, you had better see this Burn; he does not shrink from encountering you."

"I will see him—I will annihilate him," cried Palgrave. "Come on—come on!"

He rushed up to Mr. Burn's door, and knocked a furious knock, that instantly brought the alarmed boy in livery.

"Burn! Burn!" cried Palgrave. "I want to see the monster, Burn!"—"Hilloa!" cried little Mr. Burn, popping his head out of the parlour door, "what madman is that? I think we shall want a strait jacket here."

"Are you Burn?" cried Palgrave, rushing into the parlour. —"Yes, I am Burn."

"Then you are a villain, and thus——"—"Hold! Palgrave," said I, as he was upon the point of making a rush at poor Mr. Burn, who looked rather alarmed. "Hold! no violence here."

"No violence—no violence! I must have blood!"—"You shall; but it must be in the manner of gentlemen. Say what you have to say to Mr. Burn, and hear his answer."

"I will hear nothing," roared Palgrave. "I am as calm as—an oyster, and yet, with a sense of my deep wrongs, I will hear nothing. Mr. Burn, look upon yourself as a dead man, sir. My friend here stands between us, or I would spread your brains, sir, upon yonder wall."

Poor Mr. Burn looked quite alarmed at the threat, and made a movement towards the door, upon which I said, —

"Stay, Mr. Burn. Since my friend cannot command himself sufficiently to question you upon the very disagreeable subject of this visit, perhaps both he and you will allow me to ask you categorically a few pertinent questions."

"Go on, sir," said little Mr. Burn, with a wink at me.

"Wretch—villain!" shrieked Palgrave, throwing himself upon a sofa, when he saw that I was resolutely bent upon preventing him from executing what he considered summary justice.

"Mr. Burn," said I, "has Mrs. Palgrave paid you a visit this morning?"—"Yes, she has."

"Very well, sir. Is it her first visit?"—"Not by half a dozen."

"Those visits were clandestine?"—"I understood they were unknown to her husband."

"What explanation have you to offer as regards the transaction, Mr. Burn?"

"I have only this much to say; that, as far as my knowledge extends, the conduct of Mrs. Palgrave is irreproachable, and characterised by the greatest attachment to her husband; that there is a secret, I admit, but delicacy to a lady forbids me entering into any explanation of it. I advise Mr. Palgrave to go home and ask his wife."

"Death and the devil!" resumed Mr. Palgrave; "do you want to drive me mad among you? You old bald-headed sinner—you shiny old wretch, listen to me. I will fight you if you had as many doubles and shifts as a hunted fox. Fight you shall, sir."

"If I must fight, I must fight," said Mr. Burn. "I stand upon a point of honour towards a lady, and if it cost me my life, I must forfeit it. I promised Mrs. Palgrave to keep her secret, and I will keep it, let it cost me what it may."

"Name a friend," cried Palgrave. "My revenge brooks no delay."—"I name Mr. Sinclair, of 24, Moorgate," said Mr. Burn, according to my instructions; and, before Mr. Palgrave could make any remark, I chimed in,—

"If you are determined upon fighting, Palgrave, I will second you, much as I think you are hasty in not seeing your wife before you take another step."—"See my wife? curse her! I'll never see her again," he exclaimed.

"She may be innocent."—"No—no—no—no! she is false as hell. An ignis fatuus—a quagmire—a serpent—a crocodile!"

"Then, if you will hurry on this affair," I added, "let the responsibility of it be upon your own head, Palgrave. I have a strong presentiment it will turn out unhappily."—"I will have my revenge," he cried; "doctor, go directly and see this man's second. I will wait for you wherever you like."

"Very well. If you won't go home, you had better go back to the Hummums, and I will come to you as soon as possible."—"As you please, gentlemen," said Mr. Burn, putting on a pair of blue spectacles, and glaring through them at Palgrave, who glanced back defiance upon the little portrait-painter.

We were soon in the street, and then Palgrave exclaimed,—

"Oh, doctor, who would have thought that she would have stooped to such a wretch as that?"—"You are, perhaps, jumping at a conclusion," said I; "once for all, will you go home and ask your wife why she visited Mr. Burn so secretly?"

"No, no; I will fight—I will fight. You will find me at the Hummums. Revenge—revenge!"

So saying, he stalked down Charlotte-street, to my great amusement, and I got into a coach, desiring to be driven to the city with all convenient speed. My friend Sinclair was a young medical student, and when I explained the affair to him, he was in raptures at the idea of what an excellent joke it would be.

"Capital—capital!" he exclaimed; "I have pistols; we can put in a good charge of powder and plenty of wadding. By Jove! it's the likeliest piece of fun I've heard of for a year past."

"Come along, then," said I; "you are to be Mr. Burn's second; and recollect that he is to be killed."

"Exactly. Oh! it will be prime. He shall be shot. Come on, come on."

We drove back to Mr. Burn's, where we found that gentleman anxiously expecting us, and, after about ten minutes' chat, we agreed that the duel should come off in the fields between Hampstead and Highgate, and that Mr. Burn was to be shot. The time of meeting, it was further determined, should be early on the morrow morning, which was Palgrave's birthday, when his wife had pictured to herself the pleasure she would have in presenting him the enamel picture.

My next step was to hasten to the Hummums, where my principal was sitting with the "*Times*" newspaper before him upside down, pretending to read.

"Well, well," he cried, when I entered, "have you settled all, doctor?"—"I have."

"Oh! he don't want to sneak out of it, then?"—"Not in the least. The time is arranged between Mr. Burn's friend and myself to be seven to-morrow morning, and place Hampstead Fields."

"Very well; so be it. I will have that old wretch's blood. I will ——"

"Is not to-morrow your birth-day, Palgrave?"—"So it is; it is. That false one used to make me some pretty present on my birth-day? Oh, woman, woman, what awful hearts you must have!"

"You still think her guilty?" said I.—"Guilty, doctor, you are perfectly silly in your opinion of that woman."

"Well, I consider that she *may* be innocent."—"The stars *may* fall," he cried, "and the sun *may* go out. I have no more moral doubt of the guilt of—of—Aurelia, than I have that I am sitting here in the Hummums Hotel."

"Well, things must take their course, then," said I; "good day to you now—I have some patients to attend to, but I shall take care to be here in time to-morrow morning." —"Good day," he said, "good day. I am obliged to you for becoming my second, but I think you quite infatuated to form a shadow of an excuse for my wife."

* * * * *

When I left Palgrave, I went directly to his house, and, sending my card to his wife, I requested to see her. In a few moments she came into the little parlour into which I had been shown, and received me kindly as her husband's friend.

"Mrs. Palgrave," I said, "excuse my visit; but I have something to tell you which will, I hope, immediately conduce to your happiness."—"Indeed, sir!"

"Yes, madam. In the first place your husband is dreadfully jealous of you."—"Jealous of me?"

"Yes; instigated by his aunt, he has watched you to an assignation with that immoral but handsome young scamp, Burn, the portrait painter."

Mrs. Palgrave looked at me so intensely bewildered, that I could not help laughing, as I added,—

"The honest truth is, Mrs Palgrave, your husband is nearly beside himself, at your secret morning journies."

"Alas!" she cried, "they were undertaken to give him pleasure. I was recommended to go to Mr. Burn by Charles's own sister, who had agreeably surprised her husband by a present on his birthday."

"Mrs. Palgrave," I interrupted, "I know all. You have acted from the best of motives; and, unless I am very much mistaken, this little affair will accomplish two important results."

"And what are they?"—"One will be to make your husband ashamed of ever being jealous of you again; and the other will be to release you from a dragon."

"A dragon, doctor?"—"Yes, in the shape of aunt Dorothea."

Mrs. Palgrave laughed, as she said, —"I have endured much more from Palgrave's aunt than I should like to tell him."

"Well, Mrs. Palgrave, will you be guided by me in this little affair?"—"Yes," she said frankly, "I will."

"Then never mind your husband not coming home to-day, but do you come to-morrow morning to my place, unless I send—your husband will be there."

"I will do so," she replied; "but you have made me very unhappy; I have not seen Charles now for a day and a night."

"Never mind—all will be right. He is in the hands of friends, you may depend, Mrs. Palgrave; and to-morrow you shall see him, give him the miniature, and hear him ask you to forgive him for his absurd jealousy."

The morning was anything but a pleasant one. There was a raw air, and a strong indication to rain, when, at a quarter past six, I arrived at the Hummums to take Palgrave to the duel. I found him expecting me. There was, however, a nervousness in his manner, and a general appearance of uneasiness about him, which showed how very restless he was in his mind. I quite pitied him, and, far advanced as matters were, I gave him yet another chance of redeeming himself, and saving himself much useless suffering and anxiety.

"Palgrave," I said, "will you even now, before you attempt the life of a fellow-creature, go to your wife, and ask an explanation of her conduct?"

"No," he muttered—"no. She who could so treat an indulgent husband, would not scruple to raise fabrications to save herself from the consequences of her guilt. I will not now take one receding step."

"Have you arranged your affairs?"—"I have—and, bad as Aurelia is, I have placed her above want, should the encounter prove fatal to me."

"I think you have in that acted properly," said I. "Now come on, for we have very little time to lose indeed."

We drove to Camden Town, and then, dismissing the coach, we turned to the right; after proceeding some distance up the Hampstead-road, we entered the fields, which were much more solitary and unfrequented than they are now.

Sinclair and I had agreed upon the spot, which was on the side of a hill, then called Traitor's Hill, on account of its being said that one of Guy Fawkes' conspirators stood upon it to see the blowing up of the Parliament.

The grass was damp and the ground was wet and heavy, so that by the time we arrived at the place of meeting we were tolerably dirty, and intolerably tired.

"There they are," suddenly exclaimed Palgrave, as we came near the appointed spot; and there, sure enough, was Mr. Burn, seated upon a folding stool, making a sketch of an old oak tree that is still there to be seen, and by the side of which is a stile. Sinclair was smoking a cigar, and leaning his back against the oak.

"You wait," said I, keeping Palgrave back; "I will advance and settle the preliminaries."—"They seem to be taking it easy," remarked Palgrave.

"Very," said I. "That Burn has iron nerves. The idea of sketching at such a moment as this!"—"Curse him and his nerves too," said Palgrave.

I now advanced, and Sinclair met me with a great deal of mock ceremony. He pretended to converse with me for a few moments, and then I went back to my principal, and said,—

"They wish to know if you still insist upon the duel?" —"Insist!—Certainly I do."

"Very well. Mr. Burn only wishes, he says, again explicitly to state, that you force the quarrel upon him, and that your wife is innocent."—"He is a coward—he wants to creep out of the consequences of his villany," remarked Palgrave, with vehemence.

"Well, well—then I am to say that you refuse all ac-

DIARY OF A PHYSICIAN.

commodation?"—"Yes; I must and will have my revenge," he added.

I now returned to Sinclair, and we measured out twelve paces; after which we loaded the pistols with a good charge of powder, and placed our principals opposite to each other.

Mr. Burn had on his blue spectacles, and a more ridiculous figure for a duel could not well be conceived. Sinclair and I had the greatest difficulty to keep our countenances; but it was imperative that we should do so, and we managed pretty well.

The signal to fire was to be given by my throwing up my glove; and now all being prepared, I stood with it in my hand ready to give the signal.

Away went my glove, and bang went the pistols; when the smoke had cleared away, Mr. Burn, by previous arrangement, was lying on the flat of his back.

I marched forward, and stooping down to the pretended defunct little portrait painter, I smeared his face with some crimson paint, which he had himself provided me with.

Palgrave stood like one paralysed, and when I walked up to him, and said,—

"Well, Palgrave, you have had your revenge, for you have killed Mr. Burn," he seemed scarcely to comprehend me.

"Killed him?" he cried—"killed him?"—"Yes; the bullet has entered the brain."

"Good God!—I—I didn't mean that."—"Oh, that's nonsense, Mr. Palgrave," said Sinclair. "Mr. Burn is dead, and I advise you to look to your own safety, as his friends will most assuredly procure a warrant."

"Dead—dead!" he cried; "surely you jest."—"Come and look at him," said I.

He advanced about two paces; but the moment he saw the red paint upon Mr. Burn's face, he started back, exclaiming,—

"Horrible! horrible! I am a murderer."—"Mr. Sinclair," said I, "it is my duty now to see to the safety of my friend. I leave you to take what steps you think advisable in this most unhappy piece of business."

Palgrave wrung his hands, and appeared lost in despair.

"Come," I cried, taking him by the arm, "you must take refuge in my chamber until night, when you must start for the Continent, or America, or Australia."

He made no answer, but looking the very picture of wretchedness, suffered me to lead him away. He walked rapidly across the fields, till we came again to Camden Town, where we met a stage running to Hendon, upon which we climbed, and in less than half an hour more were in my lodgings.

The morning's proceedings seemed quite to have stupefied Palgrave, and he was evidently incapable of thinking for himself.

"Where do you propose taking refuge," said I; "for tomorrow the pursuit will be hot for you, and my apartments will of course not escape? In fact, I shall be taken up myself, most likely."

"Heaven only knows what will become of me," he replied; "I am a miserable, blighted man. Oh! would that I had fallen instead of him."

"It is now too late for such regrets," said I.—"Did he speak after ——"

"After he was shot?" — "Yes; did he say anything, doctor?"

"He murmured something about the innocence of your wife, and his forgiving you."—"Alas! alas! if after all I should be wrong, what will become of me?"

"Palgrave, you should have thought of that before," said I. "You have shot Mr. Burn now, and all your after thoughts cannot bring a man to life again, with an ounce of lead in his brain. I have no wish to aggravate your unpleasant condition; but certainly by your, perhaps after all, ill-founded jealousy of your wife, you have taken the life of a fellow creature, made yourself an exile from your country, ruined your prospects, and, perhaps, got me into serious trouble, and separated yourself for ever from an amiable and virtuous woman."

"Lend me a razor and I'll cut my throat," he cried; "lend me a razor."

"No, Palgrave. If you had the courage to suspect your wife, and murder a man upon that mean suspicion, do not be such a coward as by suicide to fly from the consequence of your acts."

"But what shall I do—oh, what shall I do?"—"Let me send for your wife, and, at all events, now satisfy your mind of her innocence or guilt by asking her the questions I wished you yesterday to speak to her, of why she went secretly to Mr. Burn's."

"As you please—as you please," he said. "Send for her, doctor, and let me see her for the last time."

I immediately procured a messenger in my landlady's son, who I sent to Mr. Palgrave's. Just as he was going out at the door, Sinclair and Mr. Burn arrived, and I took them up stairs cautiously, and placed them in my bedroom, which opened by folding-doors to my sitting-room, where Palgrave was, and had likewise a door communicating with the landing of the staircase.

"Now, Mr. Burn," I said, "you can hear all that passes in the next room, and when I say rather loud, 'Things may turn out better than you expect,' come in."

"I will," said Mr. Burn. "Upon my word I was a little nervous when the pistols went off."

"Don't speak a word," said I, "or he will hear; remember how very wrong it is for a man who has been so recently shot to be talking."

I then rejoined Palgrave, who was leaning his head upon the table, immersed in painful reflections.

"Doctor," he said, "I begin to see my conduct in a different light now. If Amelia should really turn out to be innocent, there will not be such a wretch on earth as I. Death will be my only hope—my only consolation."

"We shall see," said I; "you are a jealous man, and that is a passion that tinctures every trifling circumstance with suspicion. I should recommend you to go to some of the islands in the Pacific Ocean, and lead a quiet life for the remainder of your days."

I continued tormenting him for a full hour, and then a knock at the street-door announced an arrival, which I ascertained from the window to be Mrs. Palgrave.

I hurried down stairs and intercepted the servant who was going to open the door, which service I performed myself.

"Is Charles here?" cried Mrs. Palgrave.—"Yes," I replied; "don't mind what he says; there has nothing happened, I assure you, and within a quarter of an hour he will be a happier man than ever he was in his life."

Mrs. Palgrave looked perfectly satisfied with my assurance, and showed me the brooch which Mr. Burn had painted. It was a small, elegant article, and in the centre was certainly an exquisite miniature of herself. She then accompanied me up stairs, and I threw the door open, and announced her.

Palgrave started up and confronted her with so pale and distracted a countenance, that she became alarmed lest he was seriously ill.

"Charles!" she exclaimed, making towards him, and taking his hand, "you have been ill."—"Amelia," he replied, "I—I have been, and am nearly mad."

"Mad, my dear, and your birth-day!"—"My birth—I wish to Heaven I had never been born!"

"Oh fie, Charles. You pay a poor compliment to me by speaking so."—"Amelia, this is idle talk. I have a serious—an important question to ask you."

"Before you put it, Charles, you must take my birth-day present," she cried; "shall I wish you many, many happy birth-days, Charles? Here is a brooch; you see it is a tiny thing, and can be worn. It contains a miniature of myself—much flattered, I think—but it was not for vanity I had it painted, but with a hope that you would take the hint, and let me have to contemplate when you are from home some likeness of yourself which I can talk to, though it cannot answer me. Look at it, Charles. Do you think it well done? Oh, I have had such trouble to surprise you with this little trinket. Your sister recommended me to old Mr. Burn, the miniature painter, and I made him promise that he would keep my secret. Then of a morning, when you had left home to go to your chambers, I stole out mysteriously to give the good old man a sitting for the picture. Yesterday only the last few touches were put to it. Charles, dear Charles, you do not look at it. Are you not pleased with my simple plot to give you pleasure?"

During this speech it was worth while to watch the countenance of Palgrave. As his wife proceeded, and so artlessly unfolded the little plot connected with her mysterious visits to Mr. Burn, he looked like one awakening from a dream, and when she had concluded, he sunk into a chair with a deep groan.

"Palgrave," I said, solemnly, "what would you give now to recall the last four-and-twenty hours?"—"Give? give?" he cried; "I—I would give worlds—my life—my life!"

"What a dreadful lesson is this," I added, "to the jealous, who, upon suspicion merely, take the terrible steps you have."—"Lesson—lesson," he cried. "No—no; lessons are for our future benefit. This is my utter destruction. I am lost—lost for ever!"

"Perhaps not," said I. "Things may turn out better than you expect after all."

No sooner had I uttered these words, than little Mr. Burn opened one of the folding-doors, and popping in his head with the blue spectacles, he cried,—

"I'll forgive you, Mr. Palgrave; never mind, I'll forgive you."
 * * * * *

The reader may imagine Palgrave's astonishment, and the sudden revulsion of feeling from the depths of misery to a sense of lighthearted joy, such as he had never known before. He was most effectually cured of his jealousy, and that evening the aunt took her departure in a fly from his house, after prophecying all sorts of miseries, and shedding abundance of tears.

THE LOST WILL;

OR, THE ORPHAN.

There is a narrow thoroughfare close to Doctors' Commons, called Paul's Chain, and in that narrow thoroughfare dwelt a Mr. Anthony Marshall. He was reputed to be a misanthrope, in the fullest sense of the word, and universally shunned and disliked from his snarling, sarcastic manner of speaking, and the hatred which he seemed to bear to all and every one who came near him. Some thought he had money, but by degrees this opinion gradually went out, if one may be allowed the expression, and then Mr. Anthony Marshall became a greater wretch than ever; for, as the public remarked, "What right has a man to make himself disagreeable who is not rich?"

He inhabited the attic floor of the house he lived in, and his sole cook, housekeeper, &c., was a girl of about fifteen years of age, but whether she was his daughter, or his granddaughter, or his niece, or any relation, or no relation, puzzled, worried, and sorely troubled all the ladies in and about Paul's Chain. So much for the *status* in society of Mr. Anthony Marshall; and now for the peculiar circumstances which brought me acquainted with him.

It happened that I had been examined as a witness upon a case of considerable medical as well as general interest that occurred in one of our law courts, and I gave my evidence at great length, which was reported by the *Times* newspaper, with only the usual trifling errors of altering my name to something else, and making me give a different opinion to that I generally gave upon every point of importance.

This was to be expected; but, notwithstanding the affair gave me much notoriety, and procured me several patients, among whom I may reckon Mr. Anthony Marshall.

I was at breakfast when my landlady came to me to say that a young lady wanted to see me, and, having desired that she might be shown into my visiter's room, I, in a few moments, which were spent in exchanging my dressing-gown for a proper professional black coat, repaired to the young lady who had honoured me with so early a visit.

When I entered the parlour, I found standing by the window, a young girl, of about fifteen or sixteen, habited with exceeding neatness, although her clothing was of the plainest description.

"Pray sit down," said I.

She took a seat, timidly, and looking in my face with great earnestness. said,—

"Are you Dr. ——?"—"I am," said I.

"Then, sir, I am sent to know if you will attend upon Mr. Marshall?"—"Certainly," I replied; "where does he live?"—"In Paul's Chain."

"Do you mean Mr. Anthony Marshall?"—"Yes, sir—he is very ill."

"I will go back with you if such is the case. I presume you are the young person who attends upon him?"—"I am, sir; he has been ill now a whole week, and it's only this morning I have at last persuaded him to send for a doctor; when he consented, he named you."—"Very well, my dear; we will walk back together. Just wait a moment while I get my hat."

I ran up stairs, and hastily putting on my hat and gloves, I soon rejoined my young guide, for I had heard a good deal of gossip about Anthony Marshall, and was rather curious to see the interior of his abode, and desirous to know what manner of man he was.

We soon went the distance between my place of abode and Paul's Chain, and my guide stopped at the door of the low, mean house, entirely let in lodgings, in which my new patient had, for so many years, resided. She went before, and I, as well as I could, followed her up the dingy, dirty staircase, which I thought was endless, until we came to the very topmost story; then she paused, and said to me in a whisper—

"I will tell him you are come."—"Very well," said I, and she cautiously opened a door and disappeared.

In a very few moments she again appeared, and beckoning me to enter the room, I did so, and found myself in a strange apartment, where there was the greatest struggle between cleanliness and discomfort that could possibly be imagined by any person.

There was no carpet on the floor; but then the boards, although old and rotten, were as white as milk, so clean were they; two old broken chairs, a table, and at one end of the room a low couch, constituted all the furniture; but poor and miserable as the place was, I could not see a speck of dirt anywhere. On the couch lay the form of old Anthony Marshall, partially dressed and but scantily supplied with clothing upon him.

The little girl—for she scarcely looked her age—went up to him and whispered something in his ear, to which he replied in a weak tremulous voice,—

"Yes, yes, Mary—yes. I—I see him; did you speak of —the—guinea?"

The girl shook her head. I fancied he was regretting the usual fee to me, and stepping up to the bed side, I said,—

"Don't disturb yourself about my fee, Mr. Marshall. Anything that I can do for you, I am sure I shall have much pleasure in doing, independent of any pecuniary ——"

"Hush, hush!" he cried, impatiently interrupting me. "Don't be silly, young man; you fancy I don't want to pay you your fee, but you are mistaken; you are like the rest of the world, you fancy old Anthony Marshall a miser!"

I was rather nonplussed at this speech, which was so very different from what I expected, and I rather stammered as I replied,—

"I beg your pardon, Mr. Marshall, but indeed I understood you ——"

"There, there," he cried, "that will do. Of course you thought old Anthony a miser—of course you did; but when I spoke of the guinea it was to ask my young friend here if she had assured you you were to have it. Now Mary, my dear, give the doctor his fee—give it to him, my darling."

Mary went to a cupboard, and unlocking it, presently brought me a guinea, which she handed to me with a low curtsey.

"I hope, Mr. Marshall," I said, "that you will believe me when I assure you I would have waited upon you willingly without thinking of any payment."

"I believe you would—I believe you would," he cried, "which is one reason why those who can should always pay you. But now tell me—you were examined on a trial some time ago, about large property left away from relatives by one Murchison?"—I was."

"Did you say this?"

As he spoke, he took from under his pillow a newspaper, and read as follows:—

"Dr. ——— (naming me), differed from the other medical testimony as to Mr. Murchison's state of mind, and did not consider the mere fact of a man leaving his property to other persons than his near relations a proof of insanity, neither did he consider that Mr. Murchison during life preferring a contempt for certain members of his family, presumptive evidence of an unsound state of mind, as such might arise in the highest orders of intellect, since the fact of relationship was merely accidental, and the conduct of relations quite their own acts."

"Did you really say that, Dr. ———?" he said, after he had read this passage in my evidence.—"Yes, I did."

"And you think with it from the bottom of your heart?"— "I do, most certainly."

"Then I will trust you, most implicitly, for you are the only reasonable man ever I met with in my life."

I was quite puzzled to know what Mr. Marshall meant by all this, for I had been much abused for the opinion which he seemed to admire, because it was opposed to the prevailing prejudices of society, one of which inculcates, that if by accident of birth, or force of custom, a man or woman can call themselves by the name of any term signifying relationship to you, that such accident or custom at once gives him or her a full and free licence to abuse and rob you without any fear of the usual consequence of such acts.

To Mr. Marshall's intention of trusting me, I merely bowed assent, and waited what he would next say.

After a pause of some minutes, he turned to Mary, and said,—

"My darling Mary, go into the next room, and don't come back till I knock on the wall, for the doctor and I have some great secrets to talk about."

This was said so kindly, that I much admired the old man for it, and Mary at once entered through a narrow doorway, opening into her own little chamber.

When she was gone and had closed the door, Mr. Marshall fixed his eyes upon me, and said, calmly and solemnly,—

"Doctor, you are a stranger to me; but I am, notwithstanding, about to repose a great trust in you."

"I am sure," said I, "you may depend upon me fulfilling, to the best of my means, any trust you charge me with; but had I not better first ascertain the state of your health?"

"As you please," he replied; "but I know that I am dying, although not so hurriedly as to make a few hours of consequence."

"You may be mistaken in your estimate of your condition," said I, "and I trust you are. What symptoms have you to induce you to think yourself so near death?"

"None, in particular," he replied; "but I feel myself sinking fast."

I took his hand, and felt his pulse; it was certainly very languid; but that I attributed to a want of nourishing, and partially stimulating diet, probably, and I remarked,—

"You are rather in a low state, Mr. Marshall; but 'tis probable that you do not take enough nourishment to keep you up."

He shook his head as he said,—

"You are wrong, there; over-feeding does not agree with me. I am sinking from an actual decay of nature; not that I am very old; but early in life my constitution was much tried and wasted, so that now I am older as a living thing than my actual years would lead any one to suspect. There is a great difference in the manner in which different men live. Some work vitality in the same manner as a machine may be over-worked, and come to pieces by the mere wear and tear of its material."

"There is a great deal of truth in your remark," said I; "people are, from the very causes you mention, sometimes old at thirty years of age."

"I know it—I know it," he cried; "in early life I was pushed about very much by the mob of society."

"Indeed!"

"Yes. My mother was a silly woman, who thought more of her son's personal vanity than anything else. My father was a gentleman, and——but it is needless to look back to the circumstances that threw me, at an early age, upon the world friendless, and nearly destitute."

"Was such, indeed, the fact?"

"It was, although I had near, very near relatives. I might have been a little wayward; but I was never vicious and unruly; they had no occasion to turn their backs upon me. They did, however. One reviled me for one thing, another for another; but it all came to one grand point, and that was, that I might go anywhere, or do anything, so long as there was no danger of my becoming a burthen upon them.

"About the age of seventeen I was destitute, absolutely in want of food, and then I appealed to them. I applied to my brothers—they would do nothing for me, because they were saving money to set up in business with, and would not take a shilling from their hoard on any account.

"'Listen to me,' I said to them. 'I have energy and some talent. If ever the family, to which we all belong, is to rise from the obscurity it has sunk to for now so many years, it will be through me. Help me on as you love yourselves.'

"They laughed at me, and I saw in a moment that such was their selfishness and envy, that they would rather have their names ungilt, than that the gold should come from me. They jeered at my assertions, condemned everything I had done or professed to do, and finally told me they would do nothing for me.

"One of them then had the kindness to suggest, that as I was very poor, and likely to remain so, I should do them a favour, and myself much honour, if I changed my name."

"That was a heartless suggestion," said I.

"So it was," replied Mr. Marshall; "but strange as you may think it, I accepted it, and did change my name.

"'Listen to me now,' I said. 'You are my brothers, and from you I expected relief, comfort, and such assistance as you had it in your power to bestow.'

"Then one replied in these remarkable words, which I have never forgotten:—

"'*Relations are mere accidents.*'

"'Then,' said I, 'as an acquaintance merely, and a private friend, will you assist me now in my distress?'

"'We don't want your acquaintance,' was the answer.

"'Very well,' said I, and away I went.

"A stranger who did value my acquaintance soon afforded me temporary shelter and timely assistance. I changed my name to what it is at present."—"And what is your real name?" said I.—"Henry Ogilvie."

"You have for many years now passed by the name of Marshall?"—"Yes; I am now nearly sixty. I have one elder brother, four younger, and a legion of other relatives who have lost sight of me long ago."

"They probably think you dead?"—"Most probably they do. However, about ten years ago, I made my appearance among them, to see which would help me in my extreme need; but at that time I had in the public securities a sum of upwards of a hundred thousand pounds."

"Is it possible?"—"It is."

"How could you have acquired so large a fortune?"—"When I was cast out by those who should have aided me, I turned my whole energies to one object, and that was the making of money. It is astonishing what progress a human being, in thirty or forty years, can make in any one pursuit."

"I can well believe it."—"Before I was thirty, I had worked hard, and saved a hundred pounds. That was the first step to fortune. I was successful in several speculations, and by the time I was thirty years of age, I had several thousands of pounds."

"You must have made the remainder very quickly," said I.—"I did," he replied; "with my money I took a share in a privateer. It was then the height of a war, and I sailed in the vessel that was partly mine. We had not been a week at sea, when, off Dungeness, we rescued from the clutches of a French frigate, an East Indiaman, with a cargo valued at nearly half a million sterling. We brought her safe into an English port, and my share of the salvage came to forty thousand pounds."

"That was, indeed, brilliant success," said I.—"It was," he continued; "with my large fortune I came to London. I invested it profitably, for money was scarce, and I then sat down to bethink me what I should do, for I was a lonely man.

"My heart then yearned towards those very relatives who had turned their backs upon me in my hour of distress, and after much thought, I wished to give them one more chance of benefiting by my industry and good fortune. I took a mean and miserable lodging, and then bought some shabby, wretched-looking clothing. I allowed my beard to grow, and in every respect I made myself appear like a poor man who had been much buffetted by ill-fortune.

"In this guise, then, I sought out my relatives. The first I called upon was my elder brother, who kept a handsome shop, and was reported to be a prosperous tradesman. I knocked at the private door of his house, and sent in word that a stranger wanted to see him.

"In a few minutes he came half-way down stairs, and wrinkling up his brow, he cried in an imperious voice:—

"'Who is it?'—''Tis I, Charles,' said I, in a humble tone.

"He knew my voice, and exclaimed:—

"'Henry!'—'Yes,' said I; 'I am as poor as ever.'

"'D—n it, of course you are,' said he. 'Now, once for all, don't come here plaguing. I can't be disgraced by you.'—"'Pray assist me,' said I.

"'Well,' he replied, putting his finger and thumb into his waistcoat pocket; 'I don't mind giving you a shilling, if you will give me your solemn promise never to come here again.'—'I will take an oath of it, if you like,' said I.

"'Well, well, there's a shilling.'

"He threw the coin at my feet, and I took it up and walked away.

"The next I called upon was a younger brother, and he muttered something about some people always turning up again like a bad penny, and forbade me his house peremptorily.

"Thus I went from one to another of my relatives, with the hope that some one out of all would give me an excuse to heap my wealth upon them; but no! They all shunned me as if I were infected with the plague, and I returned from my visit to the last one with a heavy and oppressed heart.

"I was weary and disgusted with human nature, when a circumstance occurred to me, that relieved me from my painful feelings, and has been ever since a source of the most delightful reflections.'"

"What was that?"—"You shall hear. As I turned from a wide thoroughfare into the miserable court where I had fixed my temporary abode, in case any one of my relatives should really make inquiries about me, I met an aged and poor looking woman. She evidently belonged to a poor and industrious class, and it seemed as if hard work and deprivations had done, or was doing its work upon her bent form.

"She stopped immediately in front of me, and laying her trembling hand upon my arm, she said,—

"'Excuse me, sir; but is not your name Ogilvie?'—'It is,' said I.

"'Then you are Master Henry.'—'My name is Henry.'

"'God bless you, Master Henry; don't you recollect me?'—"No.'

"'Why, I used to wash for your mother for a many years. Don't you recollect me, Master Henry!'

"I looked earnestly at her, and then her features called up to my mind a faithful, honest creature, who was a washerwoman, and for years had attended our family, becoming a patient nurse when any of us were sick, and, in fact, behaving as kindly as she could under all circumstances.

"My heart leaped within me as I thought 'Here is a chance, thank Heaven, of finding one honest heart.'

'Your name is Meadows?' I said.—"'Yes, yes. You recollect me now, Master Henry. Don't you remember I nursed you when you had a bad fever once, bless you! It's like old times to see you again.'

l 'How are getting on?' said I.—"'Oh!' she replied, with a sigh, 'but poorly, Master Henry. I begin to feel the hard work now, and yet am obliged to do it. I've got a little grand-daughter to keep at home, and she and I have to make little enough do sometimes.'

"'Then you are very poor?'—'Heaven knows I am.'

"Oh, how I rejoiced to hear her say so? I had much difficulty to act my part, but I did it, and thank Heaven for it.

"'Mrs. Meadows,' said I, 'I am destitute, and all the family turn their backs upon me. Where to go to-night, to get a morsel of food, or a place to lay my head in, I know not.'

"I shall never forget the look she gave me; as if doubting the evidence of her own sense of hearing, she exclaimed—

"'Master Henry Ogilvie!'—'It is true,' said I.

"She shook her head, and a tear stood in her eye as she spoke—

"'We are very poor, but what we have, Master Henry, you shall share. Come home with your poor old nurse, and never say again that you do not know where to get a crust or a place of shelter. Come, Master Henry, we will all share alike.'

"'But,' said I, 'you surely would not work for me?'—'Why not—why not? Bless you, Master Henry, I am poor? but still I can share what little I have, and perhaps Heaven will bless it, and make it more—who knows?'

"I could not speak; but placing her arm within mine, I and the old woman went to her humble abode together.

"When we reached it she made me as welcome as sh

could, and Mary, who called upon you this morning, bustled about and did all she could to add to my comforts."

"This Mary is your grand-daughter?"—"She is, bless her, and a better, kinder heart than her's never beat in human bosom."

"Pray, proceed, sir," said I; for I had become deeply interested in the old man's simple story.

Mr. Ogilvie, as I shall now call him, continued—

"I saw little Mary go with a few pence, it was all they had, for coals to warm me by; and I am convinced that night in the old woman left herself without one farthing that night in attending to my comforts; and I—oh, what a joy it was to me to know that I possessed the means of converting, as if with the word of an enchanter, her humble, poor home into a palace.

"After I had been about an hour in the poor woman's room, I said—

"'Mrs. Meadows, what are you going to do to-morrow?'— 'I have a hard day's work to-morrow,' she replied, 'a very hard day's work.'

"'Then,' said I, half choking with emotion, 'you sha'n't do it.'

"'Not do it?'—'No.'

"'I must, my dear Master Henry.'—'Mrs. Meadows,' said I, taking her hand in mind, 'will you forgive me for deceiving you?'

"'Deceiving me!—How?'—'I am not poor, but rich beyond your utmost notions, Mrs. Meadows. While you live, you shall be surrounded with every comfort this world can afford you, and your little Mary shall be my heiress.'

"The old woman burst into tears, and cried—

"'Say what you said about Mary again, dear Master Henry.'

"I was much touched with the utter generous disregard of self in Mrs. Meadows. It was my promise as to her grand-child that affected her honest heart.

"'Mary shall be my heiress,' I repeated."

* * * * *

Mr. Ogilvie seemed rather exhausted, and he lay back upon his pillow for many minutes in silence, a silence which I would not on any account interrupt.

At length he resumed—

"Doctor, you can imagine all that followed. The next morning I removed Mrs. Meadows to a handsome lodging, and surrounded her with every comfort and luxury that her age required. Although very old, she lived five years to reward my care, and died blessing me, and leaving the little Mary to my care.

"As my income far exceeded my expenses, my property continued to accumulate year after year, and when Mrs. Meadows died, I still retained the name of Marshall, and Mary and I came here to live; for I wished her, in early life, to know the value of money, as well as having a strange conceit to leave her the sum of one hundred thousand pounds."

"'Tis a large sum."

"It is. But I have it; and what I want of you is to assist me in making a more ample will than I have hitherto done, as well as by your medical skill, to keep me alive if you can, until I can see Mary surrounded by all that her wealth can bring about her, and perfectly happy."

"I will assist in carrying out your wishes with pleasure," said I; "but permit me to say it would be much better to employ some respectable attorney."

"No—no," he cried, "not one of them shall come near me. You may get the will drawn if you please, doctor, by a barrister, and then I will sign it; but do not tell him any of my history, if you please."—"I shall obey your wishes," said I.

"Thank you—thank you. Will you take my instructions now, doctor?"—"If you please."

He knocked on the wall, and Mary appeared instantly.

"Mary, my darling," he said, "bring the doctor writing materials."

The girl obeyed with alacrity, and I was soon in possession of paper, pens, and ink.

"Now, Mary, my dear, go into your own room again," he said, and she left us alone.

"Now," said I, "if you will dictate to me, I will write."

"Thank you. I wish to be tombed in the vaults of St. Paul's."

I made a memorandum to that effect, and Mr. Ogilvie continued:—

"I bequeath the whole of my property to the Lord Chancellor, in trust, for my dear young friend and companion, Mary Swanston, who is an orphan, subject to the following legacies:—

"Item—One shilling to my brother Charles Ogilvie.—
"Item—One bad penny to my brother Adolphus Ogilvie.—
"Item—One thousand pounds to Mr. George Stevens, of St. Paul's Church-yard."

"Who is he?" said I.—"He invited me in one day in a storm of snow, and gave me a chair with much kindness."
"Item—One thousand pounds to Mrs. Bainbrigs, residing in this house."

"Who is she?" said I.—"She came up once when I was very ill, and did some little acts of kindness."

"Oh!"—"That is all," he said. "I cannot leave you a legacy, because I wish you to witness the will; but I will not forget you."

"Never mind me," said I.—"But I will mind you. We will talk of that when I see you again; and now I can only say, that the sooner this will is completed, the sooner will a great weight be off my mind."

"Before I do so," said I, "permit me to assume the duty of a physician, and to advise with you regarding your own health, Mr. Ogilvie."—"Thank you," he said, "I will do or take whatever you may please to direct."

"Then, Mr. Ogilvie, you ought to remove from here, and surround yourself with all those comforts so essential to your time of life."—"I will do so, doctor. My object is accomplished. I have full a hundred thousand pounds for Mary; the interest of that sum, while I live, will supply every want of my life. Although at present I live in this poor seclusion, I know how to spend the income of a gentleman; and, indeed, I should be glad to see Mary established in a line of life more suited to her ample means before I leave her."

He knocked on the wall, and Mary appeared. The old man took her small, delicate hand affectionately, and said,—

"Mary, my dear, we are going to make a great change in our mode of life."

"What change, dear friend?" said Mary. "We will remove from here to where we shall be surrounded with light and beauty, Mary."

The girl looked thoughtful for a moment, then she said,—

"We must take Dash and Flora with us then?"—"So we will," said the old man; "so we will, my dear; for they have both been very kind to us in their way."

"Who are they?"—"A cat and dog," replied Mr. Ogilvie.

At this moment I was rather startled by a strange noise outside the door of the humble apartment.

"There she is!" said Mary, and springing to the door she let in a handsome cat, who, with all the ease and confidence in the world, uttered a short peculiar cry of pleasure, and then sprang upon the couch.

"Well, Flora," said Mr. Ogilvie.

The cat immediately uttered a sound in answer to him, and then standing on her hind feet, she rubbed her head against Mary's face as she stood by the bedside.

"Dash has gone out," remarked Mary.

"Well, doctor," said Mr. Ogilvie, "take a good look around you, so that you may know this place again, and tell me what I shall take, and when shall I see you again?"

"You must take the best and most nourishing diet by small quantities often during the day," said I, "and drink about two glasses in twenty-four hours of good port wine. Not the thin sour fluid, called fine by pretended connoisseurs, but good new wine, with a full flavour of the grape."

"Very well," he said; "when will you come to me again?"
—"Suppose we say the day after to-morrow."

"Very well, be it so; unless I am able to call upon you in the meantime.'—"I think you might," said I; "for I really don't think anything is the matter with you, excepting debility."

"I will try. Mary, show Dr. —— down stairs; we must do the honours ourselves until we can get up a proper establishment."

* * * * *

I went home, very much amused and not a little surprised at my interview with Mr. Ogilvie, and my only fear was, that the great singularity of his legacies to his heartless brothers, and his strange mode of life altogether, would afford them a chance of attempting to set aside his will on the plea of insanity. This, however, I was resolved to prevent, if possible, by taking some medical men of my acquaintance to see him, whose evidence, afterwards, if his will was ever called in question, would be conclusive and satisfactory, as to his perfect sanity.

My first step, however, was to take the memoranda connected with his will, to an eminent counsel in the Temple, and desire him to have it drawn with perspicuity, in such a manner as to leave no loop-holes for litigation on the part of Mr. Ogilvie's relatives. I said to the barrister,—

"I hope the will does not contain anything illegal, or at all calculated to affect its legality?"

"Nothing of the sort," he replied; "we have every day much more singular wills to draw than this. Mr. Ogilvie has a right to bestow his acquired property upon whoever he may choose."

"Then his relatives have no chance of upsetting the will?"

"I should say not. You must be careful of it, as a document, and when the testator dies, mind you act under good advice in all the steps you take, if you are going to mix yourself up in the transaction."

"The Lord Chancellor is appointed trustee."

"Well, that is all right. He will accept the trust as a matter of course. In fact, in his peculiar position, he cannot very well avoid it."

"When will you have the will ready for me?" said I.

"I am busy," he replied; "and, although this is to all appearance a simple matter, I cannot let you have it until Thursday."

With that assurance, I was forced to be satisfied, although it involved a delay of three days, and I returned home, congratulating myself that at least I had succeeded in putting matters in a proper train for carrying out the wishes of Mr. Ogilvie.

* * * * *

Notwithstanding the barrister in the Temple could not let me have the will by the time I had next promised to visit my sick patient, I resolved to go, in case he should think me neglectful of what I had undertaken to see performed. On the morning of the second day, therefore, after my first visit, I made up my mind to call in Paul's Chain, and I was sitting at my solitary breakfast ruminating upon that and other matters, when I heard a great rush and dash of wheels at my door, and, in a moment after, the knocker was plied with a lusty hand, awakening all the echoes in the neighbourhood.

I never for a moment suspected that I was the object sought out by so much noise and clamour; but, in a very few moments, my landlady came into my room with a look of importance, not unmingled with flurry and alarm, bearing in her hand a gentleman's card.

"Sir—sir," she cried, "here's such a carriage come to see you, sir; a green and silver gentleman, drawn by two such grey horses!"

"A what?" cried I, for my landlady's transposition of the carriage and the gentleman, in her hurry, rather staggered me. "I mean the gentleman is in the carriage, sir—oh, dear me!"

"That's more likely," said I. "Is that the card of the gentleman?"—"Yes, sir, it is. It was given to me by the old gentleman hisself, and he has got a *postylion!*"

"A what?"—"A *postylion.*"

"Do you mean a postillion?"—"I supposes I do; and I am sure there ain't much difference in your way of calling it and mine, with all your larning, doctor."

"Very likely—give me the card."

She handed me a very plain card, on which was the name of Mr. Henry Ogilvie, and the address No. 2, Cumberland-terrace.

I rubbed my eyes, and looked again, but there it was, sure enough; and turning to the landlady, I said,—

"Has he a young lady with him?"—"Yes, he has; and a more sweeterer young lady I never seed."

"Show him up."

The landlady disappeared, and I said to myself, "It must be my patient, and if so, he has indeed lost no time in altering the general aspect of his condition and style of life."

I had not long time for reflection, for in a very few minutes my door was flung open by my landlady, and I saw before me Mr. Ogilvie and Mary.

They both advanced towards me with smiling faces and extended hands.

"Mr. Ogilvie," said I, "this is an unexpected pleasure, indeed."—"I hope our visit is a welcome one," he said. "Mary and I have taken your advice, and changed our quarters."

"So soon!"—"Yes; I have a talisman for effecting rapid changes; I have but to show it and convince people I really possess it, and nothing becomes impossible."

"I understand you—you mean gold?"—"I do."

"Well, Mr. Ogilvie, how do you feel in your health?"—"Better—much better," he said.

I looked at him fixedly, and my opinion by no means agreed with his own; for there was a false shifting colour in his face, and, to my eyes, an appearance of overwrought excitement that in a man of his age was far from safe.

"You had better not exert yourself too much," I said.—"No, certainly not. How can I? I have a carriage now."

"Exactly. But mental exertion is worse than bodily fatigue."—"Depend upon it I will be careful," he said. "And now, what do you think of my adopted child—my Mary?"

The young girl was dressed with rich simplicity. A tightly fitting satin vest set off her shape to the best advantage, and her long dark hair showed in admirable relief upon it. Altogether, she was as lovely a girl, now that she was surrounded with the advantages so well becoming her, as ever I saw, and she would have done credit to any noble family of the land.

Mr. Ogilvie saw my look of admiration with evident pleasure. Then he said,—

"You were coming to see me this morning—were you not?"—"I was," said I.

"Well, then, carry out your intentions, and come with us now. The carriage is at the door."—"With pleasure," I said, and, to tell the truth, I was not a little curious to know in what kind of style my patient now lived.

He preceded me, and I was soon in a very handsome carriage. The footman touched his hat at the door.

"Home," said Ogilvie, and off we dashed, at a rattling pace.

"Depend upon it, Mr. Ogilvie," said I, "you will find all the benefit in the world from this change."—"No, no," he replied, "not I; it is for my dear Mary's sake."

I saw the young girl's eyes fill with tears as he spoke, and she looked from the window of the carriage to hide her emotions; for, if ever any one was sincerely attached to another, I believe she was to him, who had acted the part of a father to her.

At the pace we were going, the town was soon traversed; and, before I thought we had got far, the carriage drew up shortly and cleanly at the door of a handsome house westward. We all then alighted, and passed through an entrance-hall, in which were several obsequious domestics, one of whom preceded us, and threw open, with a low bow, the doors of a drawing-room, furnished with every kind of costly luxury that the most fastidious mind could suggest.

"Sit down, doctor," said Mr. Ogilvie; "pray sit down. Do you think this place is good enough for my Mary?"

The young girl rose, and, giving Mr. Ogilvie a look, half of reproach, and half of tenderness, she left the room.

"There goes as kind a heart as ever lived in human bosom," said Ogilvie. "Mary is eminently worthy of all I can leave her—all I can do to make her happy."

"From my heart I believe she is," said I; "to me she appears amiable and beautiful, and well fitted to adorn the station you have raised her to."

His eyes sparkled with pleasure as I spoke, and he was about to say something, when a hectic flush came over his face, and for a moment he drew his breath with pain and difficulty.

"You are not quite well, Mr. Ogilvie, yet," I said.

"Well," he replied,—"doctor, I am dying—but yet I shall have time to do all that I wish. My will—my will—when can you get it ready for me?"

"It is promised me to-morrow," said I, "and you may depend upon my hurrying it."

"Good, good," he said; "I should never rest in my grave in peace, if any of my money were to find its way into ungrateful and bad hands."

"I cannot but approve of your making Mary your heir," I said, "however I may censure the causes which have led you to such an act."

"Yes, yes," he replied, "we may censure—we may censure, but that is all. I have told you how I was treated—how I was scorned in my poverty—and now shall I, when I have, by my own courage, prudence, and the many privations I have undergone, accumulated a large fortune, turn round to my oppressors—those who would have seen me starve in the public streets, and say, 'My good fellows, here is a fortune for you to act the churls with; here are thousands for you to hoard or spend merely for your own selfish purposes.' No, no; they shall have nothing but the bequests I have promised them in my will."

"The shilling and the bad penny," said I.—"Yes, yes—the shilling and the bad penny. Good. I can imagine their looks—when—when ——"

He suddenly turned deathly pale, and placed his hand over his heart. I was in some alarm, and, approaching him, said,—

"You are not well, sir."—"Not—very—well," he replied.

"Are you in pain?"—"Oh, God! yes. A spasm at my heart. Heed it not, though—heed it not—it will go again even as it came. I am dying; but not yet—not till I have signed my will."

I rang the bell, and, hastily writing a prescription, I gave it to the footman, saying,—

"Get that made up at the nearest chemist's. See you be quick."

The man immediately hurried off; but, before he got back, Mr. Ogilvie was nearly recovered from his indisposition.

"There," he said, "it is over now; I shall be better—much better. You will stay with us, I hope, to dinner?"—"That, I fear, I cannot," said I, "for I have an engagement at four o'clock."

"Then we will have luncheon whenever you like."—"That I will be happy to partake of," said I.

Mary soon after re-appeared in an elegant morning-dress, looking, to my eyes, more lovely than ever, and the conversation became more general.

At one o'clock luncheon was served, and a most ample and magnificent meal the old man made it. As I looked upon the costly service—the plate, the rich dazzling cut glass, and the rooms, I smiled to myself as I thought—"Who would recognise old Anthony Marshall in the possessor of all this wealth?"

I certainly enjoyed my luncheon very much, and at a quarter past two I rose to go, when the footman brought in a card, upon a silver waiter, to his master, Mr. Ogilvie.

He looked at the card a moment, and then said, calmly,—

"Where is the person?"—"In the hall, sir."

"Tell him I will not see him."

The footman went on his errand, but presently returned, and said,—

"Beg pardon, sir, but he says he must see you."—"Turn him out, then," said Mr. Ogilvie.

The footman again departed, and returned no more. Who it was that had thus broken in upon the old man's privacy, I knew not; and, as he made no further remarks upon the matter, of course I could not say anything.

After bidding Mary and Mr. Ogilvie good day, and promising to dine with them on the morrow, I left the house, having declined an offer of the carriage to take me home. I had not got many paces from the door, when I was accosted by a stranger, who said, in a sneaking kind of a voice,—

"I beg pardon, sir; but you came out of Mr. Ogilvie's, I think?"—"Yes," said I; "what then?"

"I—I suppose you are a friend of his?"—"I am."

"Oh—well; have you known him long?"—"My good sir," said I, "I don't know you at all, so you must excuse me from answering any questions."

"Mr. Henry Ogilvie, sir, is my brother."—"Oh, indeed, is he?"

"Yes, sir, and I wish to take care of him myself, and see that he is not imposed upon."—"Then probably you are the gentleman who was turned out of the hall by the footman just now?"

He looked very angry as he replied,—

"That is neither here nor there, sir; I wish to ascertain the state of my brother's mind, and—and his affairs."

"I can answer you as to the state of his mind," said I, "for I am a physician; and I am sure you will be much gratified when I tell you that he is perfectly clear headed, and rational; being highly capable of disposing of his large fortune."

"Great God, sir, where did he get it?—what—what is he going to do with it?"—"I have nothing to do with all that, sir," said I, "and I never interfere in family affairs. Good day, sir."

"But—but stop a moment," he cried; "really it is very extraordinary. I only heard of him by accident at the coachmaker's. He surely requires some relative about him."

"People of large property," said I, "find many friends,—now, if he had been poor and destitute, your anxiety about him would have been most kind and proper; but, as it is, I think he is managing very well."

He could hardly speak for rage; so he growled out,—

"Oh! very well, sir—very well, indeed! We shall see. People, of course, are always interested in keeping rich people to themselves. Perhaps you understand me, sir?"

"No," said I; "and I think you scarcely well understand yourself."

"You are a physician, sir?"—"Well, sir ——"

"And you attend my brother professionally, sir?"—"I attend Mr. Henry Ogilvie professionally, as well as calling upon him in the capacity of a private friend."

"Oh! very good—very good—all very fine, sir; but are you a reasonable man?"—"I think I really am."

"Then, sir, there have been some unfortunate differences in the family, and, as you know, it would be a thousand pities for us not all to be friendly. I can only say, that if you will bring about a reconciliation with my brother, I shall take care to see you substantially gratified."—"I never interfere in family affairs," repeated I, coldly.

"You refuse?"—"Unhesitatingly I do refuse."

"Then, sir, you're—you're—I look upon you as artful, sir; and ——"—"Beware!" said I; "if you call me by any hard names, I shall kick you."

"Kick—kick me?"—"Yes, most unquestionably. Your motive for seeking your brother is most clear and transparent—he is rich now."

"By G—d! sir, how much has he really got?" he cried, forgetting his indignation at me in his eagerness to know what money was at stake.

I made him no answer, but walked away, leaving him foaming with rage, and muttering curses against me as long as I was within ear-shot of him.

* * * * *

I was somewhat anxious about the will of Mr. Ogilvie, for two reasons. Firstly, I had a suspicion in my mind that his present sudden restoration to health and comparative strength was merely the result of animal excitement; and, secondly, I was anxious to see the document completed, for poor Mary's sake, in such a manner, that there could be no cavilling by the disappointed relatives of the rich old gentleman.

It gave me great pleasure, therefore, on the next day, to be assured by the professional gentleman, that although Mr. Ogilvie's will might be called an eccentric one, there was nothing in it that could invalidate it in a court of law or equity.

"You must be careful," he said, "to get it properly attested, and then you are all safe, but use a little caution with regard to your attesting witnesses; whenever you have the least suspicion that a will may be disputed, always get persons to witness the will who, from their age, are likely to outlive him who makes it, and never allow servants, unless you know their honesty and faithfulness, to act as witnesses."

"I shall be much better pleased," said I, "if you will come yourself, and see that everything is properly done."

"Certainly, if you wish it I will," he said; "only I hope Mr. Ogilvie will not consider my presence an intrusion."

"I am sure he won't," said I.

"Very well, then, name your own hour, and I will be at the new house you tell me he has taken with the will."

"At six," said I, "in the afternoon;" and that hour was finally agreed upon.

The next day I did not fail to keep my dinner appointment with Mr. Ogilvie and Mary Levenston. I thought he looked very pale and strange; and I certainly began to entertain serious apprehensions with regard to his health.

"When this excitement has all passed away," said I to myself, "he will die."

The dinner was admirably got up, and he seemed to revive a little as Mary talked and smiled in evident happiness; for she was deceived by the hectic flush on the old man's cheek, and thought him getting quite well.

We had dessert on the table when the professional gentleman I had employed in the matter of the will arrived, and Mr. Ogilvie received him with the greatest cordiality and gentlemanly courtesy.

The document was carefully read over to Mr. Ogilvie in the next room, while Mary and I discoursed on various matters; and she surprised me much by the justness of her remarks, and the varied nature of her knowledge; for she had evidently read much in her long solitude with Mr. Ogilvie.

In about half an hour they returned.

"Everything is quite to my satisfaction," said Mr. Ogilvie; "and I am very much pleased with the services of this gentleman."

"We must now conclude our business by having the will witnessed," said the attorney.

"You can be our witness?" said I.

"I can," he replied; "but you cannot be the other, sir."

"Why?" said I, in momentary surprise.

"I should be sorry to do you so much injury," he added, glancing at Mr. Ogilvie, who smiled faintly. "Those who are mentioned in a will cannot become witnesses."

I was quite for the moment astonished, and was about to stammer out something, when Mr. Ogilvie said,—

"Well, well, never mind about that. It is far better, at any rate, to have some absolute stranger."

"Certainly it is, sir," said the attorney. "It is a small favour for anybody to do; and I dare say any respectable tradesman about the neighbourhood will come at once."

"Will you so far oblige me as to get me a witness?" said Mr. Ogilvie.

"With pleasure, sir."

The attorney left the house, and soon brought back with him a very respectable man, a baker, who lived in the next street, and was quite willing to sign what he called the "wull;" for he was a Scotchman, and had managed to retain his native dialect during a residence of more than eight years in London, in all its original perfection.

Writing materials were brought, and Mr. Ogilvie wrote his name freely and boldly, saying, as he did so,—

"This is my last will and testament."

Then the baker signed his name as a witness, and then the attorney, and the document so important to Mary Levenston was at length duly completed.

"Now, sir, at any future time," said the attorney, "you can add one or more codicils to this will."

"I shall have no occasion to do that," said Mr. Ogilvie; "my mind is now at peace."

"Will you take the custody of the will yourself, sir?" said I.

"Yes, yes," he replied. "But you shall know where I put it by and by."

He rose and left the room with the will in his hand, and we remained taking a glass of wine with the baker.

"The auld gentleman does no look ower strang," remarked the Scotchman.

"And yet he may last all of us out yet," said the attorney. "It's astonishing, doctor, how life lingers."

"Yes," said I, "it is not always the robust and the strong that live the longest."

"Ah, weel, ah, weel," said the baker, tossing off a glass of port, and smacking his lips. "I had an auld wife who was a second cousin, and she was deeing—deeing for mair than forty year."

"Your wife died, you say?" remarked the attorney, interrogatively.

"Eh, na, man, we just call auld women auld wives in Scotland. Na, na, I can do vera weel without an incumbrance as a wife."

"On," said the lawyer.

"Weel, as I was telling you about this cousin o' mine; about three years ago, or it may be three and a-half; I was just sitting in my back parlour, thinking all to mysel', aboot a great many auld matters in the family, and don't ken to this day what put such thachts intil my heed just then, but so it was. I began to think o' all those that were deed and gone, lang, lang ago."

"Indeed," said I; "such melancholy thoughts will often come across the mind without our being able to account for them."

"Just so, sir; but, as I was saying, I got quite in the melancholies, when just as I got up to go into the shop, and, by bustling abot abit, get up my spirits, the parlour-door unlatched itself."

"Did what?"—"Cam open by itself, sir."

"Indeed!"—"Yes; it was fairly shut, for a great draught used to come from the bakehouse, and I was particularly careful."

"And it opened without human agency?"

"Indeed, sir, it did. It cam very gently aboot half open, and then a strange sort o' sensation cam over me, as if something no canny was in the room."

"No what, sir?" said the attorney.

"Oh, we just call any supernatural thing no canny," said the baker.

What I was going to say, I cannot at this time, nor ever could, remember, for it went out of my memory in the subsequent flurry; but I had just opened my mouth to speak, when the door of the room in which we were sitting slowly and deliberately came unlatched, and opened wide. We all looked towards it, expecting to see a servant or Mr. Ogilvie returned, but there was no one there; and for about half a moment a strange sensation came over me, which I could neither account for nor define. Mary was the first who spoke, and, clasping her hands, she exclaimed,—

"Oh, something dreadful has happened."

Her words broke the spell which seemed upon us, and we simultaneously rose, and moved a step or two towards the mysterious door.

"Ring the bell," said the attorney.—"The ould man's dead!" said the baker, solemnly.

The bell was rung, and, when the footman came, I said, with as much calmness as I could command,—

"Where's Mr. Ogilvie?"—"In his bed-room, sir."

"Tell him we wait for him, if you please."—"Yes, sir."

The man retired.

"Come, come," said I; "in Mr. Ogilvie's state of health such an alarm as this ——"

I had just said so much, when we heard a great shuffling of feet upon the stairs, and in a moment the footman appeared pale and aghast at the door.

"Master—master," he stammered.—"What of him?" said I. "Speak, man."—"He is dead."

Mary uttered a loud scream, and fainted away, while I, followed by the attorney, ran up the staircase three steps at a time.

I no more knew which room was the chamber of Mr. Ogilvie, than as if I had suddenly dropped from the clouds; but, when I reached the second floor, I opened every door I could see, and my third attempt led me into a large and spacious chamber.

At first I saw nothing alarming; but, when I rounded the bed, I saw Mr. Ogilvie lying lifeless, to all appearance, on the floor, between the dressing-table and the foot of the bed.

* * * * *

For perhaps about the duration of half a moment, I was staggered and deprived of the power of action. Then I lifted Mr. Ogilvie, heavy as he was, and laid him on the bed. Without a word, I laid my hand flat upon his heart. It had ceased to beat—he was indeed no more.

I would not, however, notwithstanding my own firm conviction that he was past all human aid, neglect anything that presented the smallest hope of his restoration, and I bled him, or, rather, tried to bleed him, in the temporal artery, with a lancet I always had with me. One drop of sanguinous blood I did perceive, but that was all. Mr. Henry Ogilvie, with all his faults and all his virtues, was a corpse.

The attorney and I, and the Scotch baker, looked at each other for some moments in silence—then I heard a sob from the landing-place of the staircase. I guessed it was Mary, and went to her immediately.

She clasped my hands, as she exclaimed,—

"Oh, sir, is he very ill?"—"No, Mary," said I. "We must bear with fortitude the dispensations of Heaven. Your old friend will be ill no more." She burst into tears. "You had better go to your own room, Mary," I added, "and try to compose your spirits; I will see you again before I leave the house."

Weeping bitterly, she turned away, and entered a room on the same floor, while I returned to Mr. Ogilvie.

"This is a strange chance, doctor," said the attorney.—"It is indeed," said I; "but something all day seemed to warn me of it."

"Ah, weel—ah, weel," said the baker; "poor auld man. He just looks as if he was taking a bit of sleep. Weel, weel, these are just the mysterious ways o' Providence, and we maun a' some day bake our last batch, and be rasped off, in a manner o' speaking."

"Well, sir," said I, turning to him, "you have witnessed Mr. Ogilvie's will, and nearly witnessed his decease. There will be a coroner's inquest, of course."

"I was just wondering," said the baker, "if he was ony relation to the Ogilvies, of Maclanan's-place, here."—"Upon my word, I don't know," said I; "but we must now take some immediate steps in this business."

"Ah, weel, that reminds me that I must gang awa' home.

You can let me know if I am wanted, ye ken."—"Thank you," said I, "you will sure to be wanted, both on the inquest, and at Doctors' Commons, about the will."

"Weel, I'm always at home. Gude day to you booth, gentlemen."

The Scotch baker walked down the stairs, and the attorney and I heard the door slam after him as he went out.

"Well, doctor," he then said, "as this thing has happened, I don't know that it could have happened at any time better, for here are we—his medical man and his lawyer, to see that everything is properly attended to."—"The signing of the will," said I, "is little short of providential."

"You are right there, doctor. Mary Levenston comes, indeed, into an enormous property, and he has added a codicil, leaving you two thousand pounds."

"Indeed?"—"Yes. And nothing gave me so much pleasure, I assure you, as writing those words."

"You are very kind," said I; "but really I don't deserve a tithe of such a sum, at Mr. Ogilvie's hands."—"Nor did I what he gave me."

"What was that?"—"Why, he said, 'sir, I am very much obliged to you for your trouble in this matter, and I will prefer paying you in my own way, to your sending in a bill.' Then he gave me a fifty pound note."

"I am very glad to hear that, too," said I. "Poor gentleman, all his best feelings were crushed and subdued by the harshness and selfishness of his relations."

"The next thing then we have to do, is to seal up all papers and documents, and I think, as a non-interested party, I had better take possession of the will, and produce it when it is wanted after the funeral."—"Do so," said I.

"It must be in this room, somewhere."—"Oh, of course."

"Well, we must not leave without it. I have, perhaps, less repugnance than you to the dead, and I will see if he has it in any of his pockets."

I could see that the attorney would as soon have touched a bomb-shell as the dead man, but I had been early broken in to such things, and made a careful search in Mr. Ogilvie's pocket.

There was a considerable sum of money, but no will.

"He has placed it away somewhere," said I, "and the question is, where?"—"In this cabinet, of course, I should say," responded the attorney. "It's the most natural place of all."

As he spoke, he pointed to an old cabinet that stood in one corner of the room, and which I recognised as having seen at his lodgings in Paul's Chain.

"It is no doubt there," said I. "I recollect, now, his telling me that cabinet had been his father's, and that it was the only article he had to remind him of him."

He approached the cabinet, and saw that a small key was in the lock.

"Ah, here is presumptive proof indeed," said the lawyer; "we shall find it here, doctor."

We opened the cabinet, and searched for about a quarter of an hour; but, contrary to our expectations, we did not find it there.

"Well, this is odd," said the attorney. "I certainly expected to find it here," said he; "let us pull out all the drawers and have a more careful search."

There were twelve small drawers in the cabinet, and those we pulled out and placed on the floor, so that we had it quite empty; and then we were forced reluctantly to come to the conclusion that the new made will was not there. I began to get a little anxious, and in the next few minutes had opened every drawer in the room. But no will was to be found, or vestige of one.

"This is strange," said the attorney; "he must have come direct up here."—"I could swear he did," said I.

"How can we account, then, for the mysterious disappearance of the will?"—"He took it up with him."

"He did. Let us see if he has dropped it on the stairs."

We walked carefully down, examining every step, but no will was to be found, and we stood in the drawing-room looking at each other in mute dismay.

"What's to be done?" said I.—"I don't know, really," replied the attorney; "it fairly bothers me."

"The will must be in this house."—"Unquestionably, but where?"

"Let us have another hunt."

We had another hunt, and another after that, but we might as well have left it alone, and spared ourselves the trouble, for we found no will.

"The baker," said I, "cannot have taken it surely?"—"He could have no motive," said the attorney; "and, besides, strange and uncouth as he is, you may depend upon him as to honesty; I know him well."

For another hour we searched, but without any success, and then I went to Mary, who I found still weeping.

"Mary," I said, "you will be very dull here, don't you think?"—"Oh, never mind me, sir. He was so good to me always, that I'm sure my heart will break."

"She had better not be left here," thought I. "Mr. ———, the attorney, is a married man, and I am not; she had better stay at his house until everything is arranged some way. By degrees I broke this proposal to Mary, who at first resisted it, and then consented. As for the attorney, on whom I knew I could well rely—for a better-hearted man never breathed—he accepted the charge with the greatest kindness.

We then sealed up the key-hole of Mr. Ogilvie's door where he lay now so calm and still, and past all worldly troubles. In a few minutes more the house was left securely in care of the servants; and, with mingled feelings of awe, wonder, and vexation, I took my way homewards, resolved to be punctual the next morning in meeting the attorney at the house of death, as we had made an appointment to do.

* * * *

I could not get a wink of sleep all night in thinking of the strange occurrences of the day, and it was not till towards morning that I fell into a feverish slumber, haunted by all sorts of strange visions and distressing fancies.

At one time I fancied myself reading the will of Mr. Ogilvie, and then some unseen hand would snatch it away from me, and the face of the brother of Mr. Ogilvie, whom I had encountered in the street, would jeer and mock at me. The words "Heir at law," "Mary Levenston a beggar!" would appear before me in characters of flame, dancing and tumbling about like so many fiery snakes. Over and over again I fancied myself searching the cabinet, and by one of those singular anomalies of dreams I was assisted by the dead Mr. Ogilvie himself, who suddenly, I thought said,—

"You won't find it here. It's of no use trying," and then I thought he went and lay down dead on his bed again.

Such visions as these in endless variations, but the will always forming a part of them, came across my slumbering fancy until I awoke, far from refreshed by such a dreamy slumber.

All my breakfast time I could not get the yesterday's proceedings out of my head, and I was quite impatient for the time to come when I should meet the attorney once more to renew the search for the lost but all-important document.

I walked down to his house before the time we had agreed upon, for my state of nervous fidget would not allow me to wait any longer; besides, I was exceedingly anxious to have some conversation with Mary Levenston upon the subject, to endeavour to extract from her any information she might casually possess with regard to where Mr. Ogilvie was likely to have placed so important a paper as the one upon which all her fortunes turned.

Although I arrived before I was expected at the attorney's, I was not the less cordially welcomed, and my first inquiry was,—

"How is Mary?"—"Poor girl," he replied, "she seems to take terribly to heart the death of Mr. Ogilvie; but time, you know, doctor, accomplishes wonders as regards human griefs."

"It does, indeed," said I; "but has anything turned up in your mind with relation to the lost will?"—"No, nothing—although I have been dreaming about it all the night."

"So have I, and no wonder too."—"Well, whenever you please, I am willing to renew the search."

"As soon as possible; but if Mary is up I should like to see her."—"Come with me," said the attorney; "she is with my wife, no doubt."

He led me into a pretty little breakfast-room, and there sure enough was Mary, pale, thoughtful, and with the traces of recent tears upon her cheeks. After the first salutations were over, I said to her very seriously,—

"Mary, have you, were the question put to you of where would Mr. Ogilvie be most like to put by anything for extreme safety, any idea where he would put it?"

I saw the tears ready to start to her eyes at the mention of his name, and she replied with some difficulty,—

"I should guess the old cabinet."—"That in his bed-room?"—"Yes."—"Has it any secret drawers?"—"Not that I know of. It was an article he was much attached to, and has often told me that during all his wanderings abroad he took care to leave it in the hands of some one whom he could rely to preserve it for him."

"The fact is, Mary," I added, "we cannot find Mr. Ogilvie's will."—"His will, sir?" said Mary, innocently.

"Yes, he made a will, by which he left you very large property, and we cannot find it anywhere."

She burst into tears as she said,—

"Oh, sir, never mind it—never mind it for my sake."

"Well, we must do our best," said the attorney; "so come along, doctor, and let us have another turn out at the old cabinet."

We soon left the house and proceeded to Mr. Ogilvie's. No one had called, and taking the seal off the chamber-door we entered the melancholy room.

Mr. ——— evidently shrunk from going near the bed on which lay the lifeless remains of the man he had cheerfully conversed with not four-and-twenty hours since; and, I must confess, that, professionally hardened as I necessarily have been, I never yet could go into a room where lay a corpse without a strange nervous feeling creeping over me, which I can neither fight against nor define.

There is something so solemnly awful in death, under any circumstances, that it seems a principle of human nature to shudder at contact with it in any shape or form whatever.

We went directly to the cabinet, and deliberately pulled out all the drawers, and hunted and poked about in every corner with the same ill-success that had attended our attempts on the previous day. The will was not to be found. Then we had another hunt among all the drawers we could find in the room, with the like ill success.

"It is no use pursuing this inquiry any further here," said I. "Let us summon the servants, and ascertain if Mr. Ogilvie went into any other room but this when he left us down stairs yesterday."

We did so, but could get no information, further than that they heard his step going up stairs."

"Well, we must search the house," said the attorney.

We did so, and not an improbable hole or corner did we leave unransacked. In fact, we had nothing but disappointments.

"Well," said the attorney to me, when we sat down tolerably tired in the dining-room, "we have several things to do now. We must apprise the coroner of the matter, for an inquest must be held. Then we must see to the funeral, I suppose; although it's all very awkward, having no will to act upon; because, under the circumstances, the heir-at-law could come in, and, politely or unpolitely, as the humour suited him, turn us out."

"The devil he could," said I. "Then, after all, one of those odious brothers will come in for the hard earned wealth of poor Ogilvie, that he had been pleasing himself was destined to make Mary Levenston so happy."

"It looks very like it, doctor, and I am not a little vexed on your account, too."

"Oh, what I never had," said I, "I shall never miss, so don't mention that, although I will not deny that the sum left to me in the mysterious will by Mr. Ogilvie, would put me singularly forward in my profession."

At the moment I thought of the poor dog and cat who had been provided for in the will, and I could scarcely repress a smile, as I thought how, in a moment, all of us, Mary, myself, the dog, the cat, and others, to whom small sums had been left in Paul's Chain, were completely thrown overboard, as it were.

While we were conversing on these matters, the undertaker's men, to whom I had given the order on the preceding morning, brought a shell, in which to place the body, and with much loitering proceeded up stairs to this, in my mind, loathsome and horrible business.

We soon afterwards left the house, after charging the servants to hunt for the will, and promising a reward of twenty pounds among them if it was found.

Undoubtedly Mr. Ogilvie's brother, had he known of the circumstances, could, and doubtless would have come down upon us pretty quickly, but we determined to give ourselves as many chances as possible, and kept the whole affair quiet until the morning of the inquest; after which we well knew the newspapers would take care to make it known.

Myself and Sir—, the eminent surgeon, opened the body and found an organic disease of the heart of long standing, which fully accounted for his sudden death; so that when the inquest was held, there was no difficulty in the case, which did not altogether occupy twenty minutes, when a verdict of "Died by the visitation of God," was returned—a phrase which I perceive now by the reports in *Lloyd's Weekly London Newspaper*, is, in most cases, altered to the more understandable and rational one of natural death.

* * * * *

Here we were, then, all in a nice position. No will to be found, and poor Mary destitute—no, she was not destitute, for I was resolved, come what may, I would see that she was taken care of, poor girl, until she could do something for herself.

There was, as may be supposed, not fifty pounds' worth of property in the house belonging to Mr. Ogilvie, as in fact there had not been time for him to purchase anything, with a few exceptions in favour of Mary, who, after much pressing, told us that he had bought her a gold watch and a necklace of brilliants on the same morning he had called upon me in the carriage, and had given more than a hundred pounds for the two.

The moment we learned that, I and the solicitor hurried off to the house to possess ourselves of the articles, for they at all events were Mary's own property. Judge, however, of our chagrin and astonishment to be informed when we entered the passage that Mr. Ogilvie's brother was there.

"His brother!" cried I.—"Yes, his brother," said the same person who had accosted me in the street, popping his head out the parlour door. "What have you to say against that?"—"Nothing," said I, "only your presence here is father——"

I really did not know what to say, and I have no doubt, looked rather foolish than otherwise.

"You are an intruder, sir," he cried, "unless you come for your bill. You are a doctor, I suppose?"—"I am the medical attendant of the late Mr. Ogilvie."

"Very well, sir; that's—Eh? Oh—nothing to me, I am —Eh?—Oh—the heir-at-law, and—Eh?—Oh, I hold possession."

I could not for a moment imagine what he meant by turning his head round every minute, and saying—Eh?—Oh! but I soon saw that some one was prompting him from the parlour.

"Are you the next brother of Mr. Ogilvie?" said I, almost sick at the turn affairs had so unfortunately taken.—"I am, sir."

"Mr. Ogilvie left a will."—"A—a—will!—Eh? eh?"

A small cunning-looking faced man appeared from the parlour, and his little piggish eyes twinkling upon us for a moment before the owner spoke, we had some slight opportunity for arranging ourselves.

"Let me answer all questions," said the lawyer to me in whisper. I of course nodded assent. "Well, gentlemen," said the person who had been prompting Mr. Ogilvie, "may I ask, as the solicitor of the heir-at-law to the late Mr. Ogilvie's property, what may be your business here?"

"Mr. Ogilvie left a will, sir," was the reply.—"Then, sir, you ought to have advertised the relations of the deceased of the fact, proved your will, and proceeded regularly."

"This day week, we, as the most intimate friends of the deceased gentleman, appoint as the day on which to read the will," said the attorney.

The brother's face blanched as he spoke, and he whispered something to the lawyer he had brought with him, to which the other made no reply; but turning to us, he said,—

"On condition that we affix our joint seals to all locks, we agree."—"Nothing shall be touched," said I, "but what belongs to Miss Levenston."

"And who may she be?" cried Ogilvie.—"A young lady to whom your brother has left the bulk of his property," I replied.

"For what, I should like to know?"—"Because she and her mother, people in the most humble situation of life, were kind to him in his supposed distress."

"Oh, yes—a young lady, indeed," sneered Ogilvie; "we can guess what kind of a young lady she is."—"If you say one word to the prejudice of that young lady," said I, "I will knock you down."

The cowardly calumniator made a precipitate retreat into the parlour as I spoke, and his lawyer called out—

"We'll have a warrant against you. You are using words, sir, calculated to provoke a breach of the peace."—"We claim to take from this house freely," said my friend, "all that belongs to Miss Levenston; including a gold watch and a brilliant necklace."

"Oh!" cried Ogilvie, "I think I see you. Call a policeman—she sha'n't have a thing."—"We must not take anything by force," said my friend to me in a whisper. "I fear Miss Levenston will lose these things unless we can get some other evidence than her own to prove they were given to her by the deceased."

"That is very hard," said I.—"We can do nothing now but affix our seals to everything."

"Well," said I, with a sigh, "we can't help it. Where can that infernal will be?"—"Gentlemen," said my solicitor, turning to our opponents, "we adopt your suggestion of fixing our seals along with yours on the doors and cabinets, until this day week, if you please. Mr. Ogilvie will be buried before then; and, in compliance with his wishes, such burial must take place in the vaults of St. Paul's."

"The vaults of St. Paul's!" exclaimed his brother; "what an odd wish."—"As you please, gentlemen," said the cunning looking lawyer with the piggish eyes. "All expenses, of course, will come out of the estate, whoever gets it."—"Certainly," said my friend.

We then proceeded upstairs in a body, and sealed up everything, so that I was quite certain none of Mr. Ogilvie's papers, or Miss Mary's property could be removed; but as we went up the stairs I heard Ogilvie's lawyer say to him in a careless whisper,—

"They have no more a will than I have."

We were glad to leave the house in order that we might hold a consultation upon the circumstances of the case, and repairing to a neighbouring hotel, we sat down to fully consider it in all its bearings; but consider what we would, the only question that it all came to in the end was, where is the will? and that being one that we could not answer, we found ourselves not much forwarder after our consultation.

"There is now no resource," said the attorney, "but on the day the will is to be read to make another vigilant search, or before, if you don't mind telling the other party we have lost the document,"

"It will look very ridiculous," said I, "to summon a parcel of people to hear a will read, and then have none to read."— "It will; and the only way to get over that is, to declare at the funeral that the will is mislaid."

"Then let that be done."—"And, moreover, we can have another hunt for it on that day. They cannot refuse us leave to try and find it."

"Alas, poor Mary, you are, indeed, misfortune's child."— "I regret very much her ill luck," said the solicitor; "she is as amiable as she is beautiful, and, come what may, she shall never want while I have the means to save her from it."

"My dear friend," said I, "I have made the same determination, and it will go hard with a doctor and a lawyer, if between them they cannot do something for an orphan."

"It will, indeed," he said. "Let us, however, have better hopes for Mary; something may turn up when we least expect it, to throw a light upon this mysterious affair."

* * * * *

The time soon ran round, and the morning of the funeral of Mr. Ogilvie came at length. I was early at the house, where my friend soon joined me; and from east, west, north, and south, had come eager relations of the deceased gentleman, to see if anything was to be got.

People who would not have given sixpence to save him from starvation, pretended to weep at his death; and there was the brother, too, who claimed all, and another brother who kept cursing and swearing, and saying he ought to have half of it; altogether, such a set as the relations of Mr. Ogilvie I never met.

On a table in the dining-room were placed cakes, wine, and spirits, and the funeral guests certainly did not allow their grief to interfere with their appetite, for the room was quite a fair with their going in and out constantly gulping down wine, and munching cake.

At length, when we were nearly all assembled in the drawing-room, after everybody had eat and drank to repletion, the undertaker came in to say that if any one wished to take a last look at the deceased, now was the time, for the coffin must be screwed up immediately.

Every one went up stairs; and such being the case, my friend and I thought we had better follow the example, so we went up with the throng.

There lay poor Mr. Ogilvie, exposed for the last time to the gaze of his fellow-men; the countenance had sunk, and turned of a ghastly yellow, with rings of blue round his eyes; decomposition was commencing, and the room was far from pleasant.

"You will not have a better opportunity than this of making the statement concerning the will," said the solicitor to me; "or shall I make it for you?"—"Yes, do you," said I.—"Very well. Gentlemen."

All eyes were turned upon my friend, as he spoke in a clear, earnest tone,—

"I here declare to all present, that Mr. Ogilvie, who now lies dead, made and executed a will, by which he bequeathed the bulk of his property to Mary Levenston. I am the solicitor who drew up that will. I saw him sign it."

"Then, pray, sir, produce it," said the brother's attorney.—"It must be in this house."

"Where, sir?"—"Mr. Ogilvie, in my presence, and in the presence of this gentleman, Doctor ——, and a neighbouring tradesman, who was called in as a witness, took the will from the drawing-room in his hand, to place it somewhere in safety, and we never saw him alive again."

"But the will, sir—the will," said the lawyer of the brother.—"We cannot find it."

"Hem! It is very difficult to find things that were never lost."—"Cease you insinuations, sir," said I. "It may please Heaven yet to produce that will, in which case you will look essentially ridiculous."

"Not more ridiculous than you look now, sir," he replied. —"This kind of conversation," interrupted my friend, "is as indiscreet, considering the presence in which we now are, as it is useless on every account. Our impression was, that Mr. Ogilvie had placed his will in that old cabinet in the corner."

All eyes were immediately turned upon the cabinet, and the brother turned a death-like paleness.

"You have searched it?" he gasped.—"We have."

"And—and—you—you—"—"We are satisfied the will is not there."

"Time is up, gentlemen," said the undertaker, now coming into the room.

At that moment the solemn deep-toned bell of the neighbouring church began tolling. There was a general movement among the funeral guests, and the undertaker said,—

"This way, those gentlemen who are mourners; we have no time to lose."

Suddenly, then, the brother of the deceased Mr. Ogilvie cried,—

"No, no, not yet. My poor brother and I unhappily were not good friends when he died. Leave me with him alone, if it is but for five minutes, to pray."

He pretended to be much affected, and sank into a chair.

"If you are over five minutes, sir, we shall have to go at a quick rate," said the undertaker, shaking his head.—"I will not be longer. Leave me alone with him—leave me."

This was one of those requests coming from so near a relation as a brother, that, under any circumstances, no one would have liked to say nay to; and, under the present circumstances, when he was master, in the absence of a will, of all in the house, as heir-at-law, no one could interfere, so in a few moments the room was evacuated.

I was the last to go out, and as I did so, I remarked a strange look on the face of the brother; but whether it was exultation, or intense grief, or contrition, I could not take upon myself then to say.

The moment I was clear of the room he rose and shut the door. Then I heard him lock it, and double lock it; after which there was an intense stillness for about two minutes.

I thought then I heard a strange creaking sound come from the chamber, and then there was a loud snap, as if some hard-springed pistol or gun-lock had been moved.

"What on earth can he be doing?" whispered the solicitor to me.—"I can't imagine," said I.

"He is surely not committing suicide?"—"He is not the subject," I replied; "you may depend no such thing will occur."

While we were speaking the door was suddenly unlocked, and Ogilvie appeared. His face was as white as a sheet, and he trembled in every limb.

"I am ready," he said.

I looked hard in his face, and he turned on one side to avoid my scrutiny altogether. I could not, for the life of me, make out what he meant.

The undertaker's man now came in to screw up the body, and he walked in with them and superintended the work. I saw him draw a long breath when the coffin-lid was fairly screwed on, as if he had experienced a great relief.

In a few moments more all was ready; and at a slow pace the magnificent black horses dragged the mournful cavalcade towards St. Paul's.

* * * * * *

The vaults of St. Paul's, as all know who have, when visiting that stupendous structure, penetrated beneath its pavement, are of vast extent, and seem almost a second church below the upper one. But very few persons were, at the period I write, buried in those long dreary vaults, and I believe still fewer now; but whatever may be the rules and regulations now adopted, at the period of the death of Mr. Ogilvie, by payment of a tolerable sum, any one might be placed on a shelf in the vaults.

It is doubtful if the brother of the deceased would have permitted that respect to his remains to be shown, of ever placing them where he had expressed a wish for them to repose; but the reader will recollect that we, that is, myself and the kind-hearted solicitor, had ordered all that before the brother took affairs in hand, or supposed himself entitled so to do.

Mr. Ogilvie was therefore peacefully conveyed to the vaults, and there deposited in their gloomy precincts, to await undisturbed that great day when all shall rise again, and behold the light of a brighter day than ever dawned upon their mortal career.

I was in anything but a pleasant state of mind when I returned from the funeral, and my reflections were of the most painful character. "What is to become of Mary?" was my constant thought, and I own that once a sort of idea of marrying her came across my mind, but I had the prudence to repress it; for then I was in no condition to support a wife. I will make one effort, thought I at length, upon the generosity of the brother who steps into the property so comfortably as heir-at-law. Surely he cannot refuse to do something for her who was the cherished friend and companion of his deceased brother, and who had really been so amply provided for, but for the strange and most unaccountable disappearance of the will so immediately after its execution.

But although I much suspected, I by no means knew the selfish character I had to deal with in Mr. Ogilvie that was now. When we arrived home, and the undertaker's man had left, I turned to him, and said,—

"Sir, as far as circumstances at present go, you are the master by lineal descent of all that was the property of your deceased brother; but, upon my sacred honour, there was a will."

"Produce it," said he.

"That I cannot; but what I implore of you now is, from the wealth unexpectedly thrown into your hands, to make some provision in the shape of a small sum yearly for Miss Mary Levenston."

"I'll see her and you d—d first," he cried; "my brother and I were never friends, and it's a great triumph for me to get his money now he's dead, whether he likes it or not. Say your worst, and do your worst. Go to the devil all of you, and carry Mary Levenston with you. I won't part with one farthing, nor wouldn't to save you all from being hung."

"You are a brute and a scoundrel, sir," said I, "and before I go, I'll kick you round this room."

"No, no," cried the solicitor, laying his hands upon me, "no, no. Leave him alone. Come away now—I will proceed against him instantly for the recovery of what really belongs to Mary. Come away, doctor, you are too hasty."

"Ah, take him away—take him away. He's a madman," cried Ogilvie, who had rushed behind a couch. "A mad doctor. Off with him; and hark ye, if either of you ever darken my doors again, I'll send for a constable and have you lodged in the watch-house."

I was in such a rage I could have thrashed him well, but upon after reflection, I was, of course, glad that the solicitor had dragged me away, for violence never benefits a good cause, and I should have done no service to Mary by thumping the possessor of what ought to have been her's of right.

"What is to become of Mary?" I said, when we were fairly in the street.

"Oh, she will, perhaps, be as happy without the money as she would have been with it, doctor; but come and take a biscuit at our friend's, the baker's. He lives only round the corner here. We ought to tell him what has occurred."

I followed the lawyer quite in a fever from my recent quarrel with the selfish man who had unexpectedly become so rich, and yet refused to part with any of his wealth for an object so dear to his deceased brother's heart as Mary.

The baker was in his shop, and when he saw us, he asked us very hospitably and cordially to walk into his back parlour.

"Weel, weel," he said, "so the auld man's just buried, is he? Ah, weel, it's what we must a' come till."—"Indeed it is," said the solicitor; "and it's a most provoking thing that we can't find his will."

"Not find his weel?"—"No. The will that you witnessed has most unaccountably disappeared."

"Ye dinna say so? That's extraordinary. It minds me o' an auld Scotch story—but ye'l tak a dram?"

We both declined, but the baker wanting, probably, an excuse for a dram himself, went to a corner cupboard, and produced some dreadfully strong Highland whiskey, which, he assured us confidentially, had never paid one farthing to his Majesty's revenue, and was the real Glenlivit. We each took a glass at the risk of choking, for it was a perfect liquid fire.

"A weel," said the Scotchman, smacking his lips, "I just confess it's rather strong."—"You don't mean to say they drink such awful fiery liquor as this in Scotland?" said the lawyer.

"'Deed but I do, mun; and what for, no? But ye war saying you had lost the will quite entirely. I made sure ye had laid your hands upon it before now, and a' was right."

"I am sorry to say all is wrong," replied I. "The young lady you saw is deprived of everything, and it really is a hard case that all the money Mr. Ogilvie denied himself almost the common necessaries of life for many years to be enabled to hoard, should after all be diverted from its proper destination."

"Gude gracious! it's too bad," cried the Scotchman. "It minds me o' a bailey we had at Edenbro', and he had a wild scamp o' a nephew that had nearly broke the old man's heart, who was himself childless. Weel, the bailey died, ye ken. Will ye take another glass?"—"No," we both replied.

"A weel," continued the baker, pouring himself out another. "Where was I?"—"The bailey was dead," said I.

"So he was. Weel, he had left a will that had been made a year before, in which he had left his graceless nephew only fifty pounds a-year, and all the rest of his property to good, honest people, that would make a good use o' it."

"The nephew then, was next of kin, was he?" said the lawyer.—"'Deed was he. Just so. Weel, on the day of the funeral he came to the house ——"

"The nephew?"—"Yes. He walked about just where he liked, and in and out the room where the corpse lay."

"Yes, yes."—"Well, after the funeral there was a grand hunt for the will, but it could not be found, and everybody believed the nephew had come upon it in some drawer, and put it in his own pocket."

"Like enough."—"But that's not all, sir. The nephew took a grievous illness, and died himself within the same year; and just before he went he sent for a minister, and confessed that on the day of the funeral he had found the will in a cupboard in the room where the corpse lay, and fearing to be detected before he could go home and destroy it, he just lifted up the dead man's head, and laid it underneath him in the coffin, where it was buried with him in the Grey Friar's kirkyard."

* * * * *

The lawyer looked at me, and I looked at the lawyer, when we both exclaimed at once, "How singular!"

"'Deed it was," said the baker.

My friend then rose, and giving me a significant look, moved to the door, saying,—

"Good morning. Come along, doctor."—The moment we were in the street, he called out,—"Coach! coach! coach!"

"Good God!" said I, "are you mad?"—"Coach! coach!"

A coach soon drove to the curb-stone, for we were opposite to a stand.

"Where are you going?" I cried.—"Get in—get in."

He bundled me in without any ceremony, and when the waterman touched his hat, saying,—

"Where to, your honours?"—"St. Paul's," he cried.

The coach moved on, and then he laid his hand upon my arm, and said,—

"Doctor, I feel a presentiment that Mr. Ogilvie's will is in his coffin."

"You do?"—"On my soul I do. His brother was left alone in the room. He found the will, you may depend."

"Then," said I, "it must have been in some secret drawer of that old cabinet."

The lawyer doubled his fist, and, to my dismay, gave himself a punch on the side of the head, crying,—

"Oh, that I should have been such an ass! I ought to have had that cabinet broken into small pieces. There is some secret drawer in it of course. The brother knew it, and had but to lay his hand upon the spring. The will is either in his pocket or in the coffin, I could take my oath."

"Upon my word it appears probable."

"Probable? Of course it does. Did you mark his anxiety till the coffin was secured up—did you mark his look of relief and exultation when it was so? As I'm a living man I do believe we shall find the will at St. Paul's, and if we don't we'll go to Ogilvie, and you shall hold him while I search all his pockets, let the legal consequences be what they may."

In due time we reached St. Paul's, and upon asking for leave to descend the vaults, we were told that we could not do so that day—without an order from the dean.

"Well, then, doctor, we had better," said the lawyer, "go to the dean at once, especially as we want to open a coffin."

"Do what, sir?" said the man we were speaking to.—"Oh, nothing particular. Come along, doctor."

The solicitor was in such a state of excitement that it was of no use for me to say anything to him, and I therefore suffered him to drag me about wheresoever he pleased, and to the dean's house we accordingly drove.

We explained the whole particulars to him, and after a pause, he said,—

"It is very unlikely, I should think, that the will is with the dead body; but under the very strange circumstances, I have no great objection to grant your request, but I shall accompany you myself, for your sakes, in case you really find the will there—my testimony may be important."

"A thousand thanks, sir," said I; "you may be the means of restoring to the orphan, Mary Levenston, what of right belongs to her."—"I am quite ready to attend you, gentlemen—I will order my carriage."

* * * * *

In another half hour we were all three alighting from the dean's carriage at the door of St. Paul's, and were obsequiously ushered into a private room.

"Bring the keys of the vaults," said the dean, "and send for a respectable undertaker. Tell him to bring tools for opening a coffin."

The order was received with respectful bows, and the excitement among all the officials of the cathedral appeared to be immense.

We had not to wait long, when everything was ready, and we proceeded, accompanied by the verger, an undertaker, and several of the usual attendants in the sacred building.

My feelings were very much excited by this time, and I began to be almost as enthusiastic in the matter as the lawyer, who seemed for once to have resigned himself completely to the sway of his imagination. The low gloomy portal leading to the vaults was opened, and, one by one, we descended the dark staircase.

"This will be a surprise to poor Mary," whispered the lawyer to me.—"My dear friend, wait till we have found the will before you calculate upon its effects," said I, in reply.

"Doctor," he said, solemnly, "if we are now in St. Paul's,—if this is my right hand, the will is in Mr. Ogilvie's coffin. I never felt so strong an assurance of anything in all my life. The finger of Providence is manifest in this affair."

"Let us hope and trust so," said the dean, who had overheard the last observation. "Heaven works for us always, and if the will you mention be found where you anticipate, I shall look upon the circumstance as a direct interposition of Providence, whose humble instruments we all are."

"We are much indebted to your promptness and liberality, sir," said I, "in acceding to our very strange request."

"It is, under the circumstances, my duty," said the dean. "Is there any one here who can take us direct to the spot?"—"I think I can," said I.

"Tell me where you wish to go, sir," said the verger, "and I will guide you."—"We wish to open the gentleman's coffin who was buried here this day."

"Mr. Ogilvie?"—"The same."

"This way, then, gentlemen, if you please."

The verger led the way now, and we all followed him in anxious expectation of what the next ten minutes might produce. Every one present seemed impressed with the solemnity of the place, and when we were at length collected around the coffin of Mr. Ogilvie, not a word was spoken for some moments, and a pin might have been heard drop in the solemn silence that reigned around.

"This is the coffin that was placed here to-day," said the verger.

The undertaker advanced and took out a small screw-driver from his pocket.

"Remove the lid," said the dean, "as quickly as you can."

We all crowded round, and the man commenced taking out the screws with great rapidity.

"Now," whispered the solicitor to me, "another moment will make Mary Levenston wealthy, or leave her a poor dependant orphan."—"True," I replied, "for if the will be not here, you may depend that by this time it has been destroyed."
—"I fear so, and yet that it is here ——"

"Shall I take off the lid now, gentlemen?" interrupted the undertaker.—"Yes," said the dean.

The cold white face of the corpse was the next moment exposed to our view.

"Are you satisfied?" said the dean. "Allow me," said I, "to turn the body."

They all drew back a pace as I advanced, and although my profession had rubbed off a great deal of the natural prejudice we all have at handling the dead, I must own I did not half like the job of dragging the dull heavy mass out of the coffin. A strong sense of duty, however, urged me on, and sliding my arm under the head, I lifted the corpse into a sitting posture.

* * * * *

Exactly beneath lay the will, tied round with red tape, and looking damp and mouldy from contact with the body.

* * * * *

Although we had all of us come there expressly to look for the will where we found it, and of course with some hope of success, yet we were really, when we saw it, all so confounded that we looked at each other like so many idiots for some moments.

The dean it was who first spoke,—

"The finger of Heaven," he said, "is in this. Gentlemen, I never knew or heard of so extraordinary an occurrence."

"It is most wonderful," said the solicitor as he took the will in his hand. "Here, gentlemen, is the document uninjured. I will trouble every person here present to put his name at the back of this most important document, and then there can be no cavilling about it."

One of the men was despatched for pens and ink, and there beside the dead we all solemnly put our names to the recovered will, in order that, if litigated, we might swear to it as the same found in our presence in the coffin.

"Now, sir," said I to the dean, "the innocent and the fatherless is righted, and we have to thank you warmly for your prompt and kind attention."

"Nay, sir, no thanks to me," said the dean, "I have but done my duty, and I do rejoice that your errand here has not been a fruitless one."

The coffin lid was replaced over the face of the dead, and the dean said a short prayer, which was heard by all with feelings of gratitude and reverence.

In a few minutes more we stood in the daylight, beneath the ample dome of the cathedral, and the transition from the close damp atmosphere of the vaults to the cool refreshing air that was in the church was exceedingly agreeable.

I saw that my friend the solicitor was all impatience to leave, so after paying the undertaker, and being liberal to the officials of the cathedral, we took a courteous leave of the dean, and left St Paul's together.

"Doctor," said the lawyer to me, as we walked through St. Paul's Churchyard, "where are you going now?"—"Home," said I.

"Nonsense; I am going to pay a visit to Mr. Ogilvie's brother. You must come too." "Had you not better wait till to-morrow?"

"Certainly not. Why should I? That would be giving him another pleasant night's repose at the idea of his successful villany. So come on; I am determined to see him to-night, and show him the will."—"Well," said I, "if you are determined, I had better go with you than not."

We walked rapidly, and as we now had pleasant matter of conversation, we reached the late Mr. Ogilvie's house in what appeared to me an incredibly short space of time.

The gloomy hatchment cast its shadow upon the window over which it hung, and we could see no lights in the building.

"You may depend there is no one here," said I.—"We will knock and see," was the reply, and the lawyer plied the knocker like half-a-dozen footmen rolled into one.

We waited some few moments, but no answer was returned. Then, just as the lawyer was going to ply the knocker again, the door was opened by an old woman, who appeared to be half asleep or half stupid.

"What do you want?" was her not very courteous salutation, as she held the door nearly closed.—"I want Mr. Ogilvie," said the lawyer.

"Then he's dead."—"Yes, one Mr. Ogilvie is, but I want his brother."—"Oh! do you? Well, he ain't here."

"When will he be here?"—"Not till to-morrow. You are sure to find him here to-morrow; there's to be a grand party here of never so many people."

"Indeed?"—"Yes—a very grand party, indeed. Ah, there will be lots of trouble, I'll be bound. I am only put in to-night to mind the house, as all the other servants are sent away."

"To-morrow?"—"Yes. A grand evening party."

"Thank you; good evening."—"Won't you leave your names?"—"Tell him two gentlemen from below called," said the lawyer.

We walked away laughing, and then he said to me,—

"Doctor, this brother has no more feeling for the death of an old friend, whose will I have in my pocket, than an arm chair. Suppose we go to-morrow night and disturb him and his grand party a little."—"He deserves it."

"We cannot have too many witnesses, you know, doctor; besides, we must do nothing rude to his unoffending guests, you know."—"Agreed then," said I, for I confess I was rather tickled with the *coup de theatre*, which such a proceeding partook of.

"Now, then, come home with me, doctor, and you and I, and Mary and my wife, will pass a pleasant evening."—"You forget that we have been to a funeral to-day," said I.

"Oh, hang it, so I did; but our friend Ogilvie, who is gone, I am sure would not wish us to feel more than a gentle regret on his account. He was an old man, and Heaven, in his case, was kind enough to spare him a painful illness. So come home, and without being callous to what we have seen this day, we can enjoy ourselves with quietness and moderation."

We were fatigued now, and getting into a hackney-coach, we were in that oscillating vehicle transported to the lawyer's house.

If ever a man was blessed with a happy home, he was, for he had had the good fortune to meet with a partner in every way as warm-hearted and affectionate as himself. A person, likewise, she was of considerable judgment, which does not always accompany the most amiable disposition.

She and Mary were sitting by the fireside when we arrived, and from the recent tears on Mary's cheek, I guessed she had been talking in her usual kind way of Mr. Ogilvie.

"My dear," said the lawyer's wife, "where have you been?"—"Been?—been?" he said.

"Yes. Your coat is all over clay, or mould, or something of the kind."—"Ah, my dear, the doctor and I have been on an expedition. Mary, can you stand surprise well, do you think?"

"I think I can, sir," said Mary.—"Then I am going to kiss you," said the lawyer, a threat which he immediately put into execution, and in which he instantly did succeed in surprising Mary and his wife both.

"My dear, are you mad, or—or—bless me," said his wife.
—"Drunk, you mean, hurra! hurra!" cried the lawyer.—
"Mary, my dear, God bless you."

Mary looked perfectly astounded; what with the sudden and unexpected salute from a professional gentleman in the presence of his wife, and the hurrahs that followed, I could see she thought him rather mad than otherwise, and looked at me for an explanation, when a wild spirit I have sometimes tempted me to enjoy the surprise of Mrs. Sinclair, whose looks were inimitable; so without more ado, I (being single then) of course walked over to Mary and kissed her.

"You too, doctor!" cried the lawyer's wife. "The men are lunatics."—"No—no—no, my dear. Come now, sit still—don't scream or ring the bell, and you shall know all."

"All what?"—"Something has happened that has made the doctor, as you see, a little excited."

"Me excited!" cried I.—"You mean yourself; I have had the greatest difficulty, I assure you, madam, to control his buoyant spirits."—"In Heaven's name, explain yourselves if you can," said Mrs. Sinclair.

As for poor Mary, she looked the greatest picture of astonishment that ever I saw in my life.

"Explain, doctor, explain," cried the lawyer.—"Then, Mary Levenston," said I, "and you, madam, will be somewhat surprised to hear from me that we ——"—"Have found the will," roared the lawyer, interrupting me, and pulling the document from his pocket with a triumphant look.

"The will!"—"Yes, Mr. Ogilvie's will, wherein he leaves Mary a princely fortune."

Mary clasped her hands together, and burst into tears.

"No crying," said the lawyer. "Come, come, Mary, excuse my boisterous behaviour to you; I was really so pleased upon your account, that I could not, especially after the very outrageous manner of the doctor, remain so quiet as I ought to have done."

"Well," said I, "that is well of you, when I only made myself a little ridiculous to keep you in countenance."

"Do you forgive us, Mary?"—"Forgive—my best—only friends?"

"Now don't you plague her any more," said the lawyer's wife, taking Mary's hand. "You two may stay by yourselves till supper time, and Mary and I will talk it over by ourselves. Come, my dear."—"That's as good a girl as ever lived," said the lawyer, when she had left the room. "You are quite frantic not to marry her."—"Oh, I couldn't think of such a thing," said I—"I—besides—I—you know ——"

"What are you stammering about?"—"I'm engaged!"

* * * *

I dreamt all that night of vaults, and wills, and graves, and brilliant parties, mingling them together in most admired and picturesque confusion.

I was quite thankful when the morning dawned, and I had some excuse for getting up, for sleep of a sound, refreshing character, was quite out of the question.

We all assembled—the lawyer, his wife, Mary and I—to breakfast, when we thought over our plan of operations, and, not, however, without some gentle remonstrance from Mary, determined upon having some amusement from the present possessor of Mr. Ogilvie's property.

The best of the joke was, too, that, as far as things had already gone, the brother was spending his own money in all his jollifications, for the necessary legal proceedings of administration, &c., were not to be got through so quickly as to enable him to finger any of Mr. Ogilvie's cash yet.

Our plan then was to go in the evening, when we supposed his gaiety to be at its height, and ask an interview with him, when, after a little angling, we meant to astound him with our news, and turn him out of the house, and in this last measure we did not consider ourselves as acting harshly, because he had a home of his own to go to.

We were all impatience, until, as the novel writers say, night put on his sable mantle, and the dim watching stars shone forth in the blue vault of Heaven.

In other and plainer words, we waited till ten o'clock, and then we started for the house in which in so brief a space so many strange occurrences had taken place.

When we reached the street we found it almost blocked up with cabs and hackney-coaches, in which the guests of Ogilvie had come from their various homes, and through which, after much difficulty, we succeeded in pushing our way up to the house itself. The continued thump-thump and shuffle-shuffle within told us that a dance was in progress. A crowd of idle boys and others were collected round the doors, and the whole neighbourhood was in an uproar.

How sadly at variance was all this with the hatchment the undertaker had put up by our orders above the windows of the first floor in which this scene of riot and confusion was going on.

It was with the greatest difficulty that the lawyer and myself could push our way through the throng, and reach the door; and when we did we had to wait until a cab with three fat women inside, and a boy on the box with the driver, had discharged its motley cargo.

The street-door was wide open, and we ascended the steps in a twinkling.

An occasional waiter—one of those beings who are so easily recognisable—demanded our name.

We gave our real names, and the man, thinking I was "somebody," with doctor before my name, ushered us very politely into the drawing room.

Never shall I forget the scene that presented itself. The really magnificent apartment was crammed to excess by as strange an assemblage of people as could very well find standing room. To save time, I presume, they were all talking at once, and the laughter, coarse jests, and horrible voices came upon my ears like a sudden whirl of sound from the infernal regions. Moreover, what a villanous smell of tobacco was there—what a reeking odour of gin-and-water;—even now I think of the shock my system received as I walked into the room.

"Good God!" I said to my friend, "I really did think that Mr. Ogilvie's brother was a step or two above all this."

"Ah, doctor," he replied, "money always exalts or lowers its possessor—it never leaves him where he was. With his own means this man might only have been a callous, hard-hearted rogue, but now the sudden possession of a fortune has brought out all the strong points of his character in full relief, and you would find that he would kill himself by excess."

"This atmosphere is enough to kill the devil," said I; "so let us transact our business as quickly as possible, and be done with it."

The groom of the chambers—which, I suppose, we had better call the occasional waiter—announced our names in a voice that sounded above the general din, and which he gave great effect to by placing his hand by the side of his mouth, as gentlemen who perambulate with a donkey and a truck do when they cry greens.

In a few moments there was an unusual bustle, and, having pushed his way from the further end of the room, Ogilvie, his face inflamed with liquor, and his general appearance bespeaking passion and intemperance, stood before us.

"How do you do Mr. Ogilvie?" said I.—"How do you do, Mr. Ogilvie?" said my friend.

"And pray, gentlemen," he said, trying to balance himself well, by setting his legs far apart, "to what circumstance am I to attribute the honour of this visit?"—"We thought we would just call," said the lawyer, "to see how you were."

"D—n your impudence, then," cried Ogilvie.—"Oh, Mr. Ogilvie," said I, "really now, you ought to be civil."

"Civil!" he cried; "civil to two vagabonds who would have deprived me of my property!"—"But you know ——"

"I know nothing, sir."—"Oh, indeed; well, I suppose you will make us welcome?"

"Welcome!"—"Yes; you will ask us to stay?"

"I ask you to stay—I make you welcome!" he cried. "You two thieves—you vagabonds—you housebreakers!"—"Hard names, Mr. Ogilvie," said I.

"What you deserve, sir," said he. "Hilloa, everybody come here!"

His guests being used, I suppose, to such a polite mode of address, all crowded to the door, within a few paces of which we stood, and regarded us with looks of defiance.

"Here's a pretty pair of fellows!" cried Ogilvie—"a doctor and a lawyer. They have both been trying to keep me out of my property, and now, when I have succeeded in spite of them, they have the impudence to come here to my party uninvited."

"Kick 'em down stairs," said one.—"Throw them out o' window," said another.—"Indict them for a trespass and conspiracy," suggested Ogilvie's lawyer, who was one of the most favoured guests.

"Ah, now, Mr. Ogilvie, this is cruel," said my friend, in a bantering tone.—"Cruel be d—d, sir!" cried Ogilvie.

"Ah, ah!" exclaimed a gentleman with exceedingly wide trousers, a coat cut in the most out-of-the-way burlesque upon the fashion, and a glass stuck by muscular contraction in his eye. "Ah, ah! permit me to—ah, ah!—kick these—ah, ah! —individuals down—the ah!—stairs—ah!"—"Hurrah, hurrah!" cried the guests.

"May I—ah, ah!—take that liberty in your house, Mr. Ogilvie—ah!"—"Kick him, doctor," said my friend.

I accordingly took the gentleman by the collar with one hand; and bestowed half a dozen hearty kicks upon the hinder part of his person, which seemed quite to astonish him, and produced a confusion of ideas.

"Now, sir," said the lawyer to the discomfited bully, "I know you. You are junior clerk, with fifteen shillings a week, to Messrs. Wright and Kemp, in Gray's Inn. Do you know me now, sir?"

"I—I—humbly beg pardon, sir. I—I—know you now. You—you are Mr. ———, of—of—Basinghall-street. Mercy, sir!"

"It would serve you right if I were to mention this little affair to your employers."—"Oh, sir, don't!"

"I won't this time, but mind you don't give yourself such

ridiculous airs for the future."—"Oh, you villain!" exclaimed a very corpulent lady, tearing a handful of hair right out of the lawyer's clerk's head; "you told my dartar as you was Captain Fitznoodle, you abominable wretch!"

There was a general laugh at this, and Ogilvie, turning nearly frantic with rage, although he kept a cautious distance from us, said, in a loud voice,—

"Am I to be insulted in my own house? Am I to be master here, or those wretches, I should like to know?"— "Mr Ogilvie," said my friend, "we came on business to see you."

"Business be d—d! I have a fortune, and I am going out of business."—"But this is business of importance."

"Oh! some more nonsense about the property of the young lady, I presume," he said, with a sneer.—"Yes, that's it; but it's quite of a private nature," said I.

"Is it, indeed?"—"Yes, and we request the favour of your company in another room for five minutes."

"Then you won't get the favour. If you've anything to say to me, say it here."—"Are you serious, Mr. Ogilvie?"

"I am. Out with it, and be hanged to you. When you're done, I'll pretty soon clear the house of you."—"Well, then, we come from the vaults of St. Paul's."

He changed colour, and stepped back a pace, and then recovering himself, he said,—

"Have you? Well, well—I don't care if you come from hell, provided you soon go back again."

"Shall we go on?" said I.—"Go on! What do I care whether you go on or off? What is it to me?"

"Nothing to you," said the lawyer, "but a great deal to some one else. Will you just tell Mr. Ogilvie, doctor, your dream?"—"With pleasure," said I.

"Dreams be hanged! Be off with you!" he cried. "Here, police! police!"—"I had a dream," began I, "and I fancied I was looking through the keyhole of Mr. Ogilvie's chamber, where he lay dead."

"Well, sir! Curse your dream! What is it to me?"— "You shall hear. I thought I saw you approach an old carved cabinet, and press upon a secret spring."

"It's a lie—a lie!" he cried. "I never saw the will; it was not there; I didn't take it; I would not have touched the corpse or the coffin for a thousand pounds."—"I never said anything about a will," said I. "How true it is a guilty conscience needs no accuser? No one mentioned the will but yourself."

"I—I never mentioned it," he cried; "what do you mean? This is an attempt to entrap me. Friends all, you see these two men—this doctor and this lawyer—they want to ruin me."—"Shame! shame!" cried the guests.

I stepped up to Mr. Ogilvie, and said in his ear,—

"We have found the will in your brother's coffin, where you put it." His knees trembled, and a ghastly paleness came over his face—"where you put it," I repeated.

"Spare me—I—I. Oh, have mercy!" he gasped; "don't —don't prosecute!"—"We don't mean," said I; "the will shall be read in this house at twelve to-morrow. Do you come and hear it, for your own satisfaction. We will now leave you, convinced that your own reflections must be a greater punishment to you than anything we can say or do."

"Then—then you will have mercy!" he gasped.—"We will," said my friend the lawyer, who had advanced; "but it will be upon one condition."

"What is it? Anything—anything you like, gentlemen." —"This—this; that you tell your guests, that in respect for the memory of your deceased brother, whose house you are now in, you cannot entertain them any longer."

"Yes—yes—I will make them go."—"Do so at once."

With a dreadful wry face Ogilvie turned to his guests; but when he saw all their eyes bent upon him, his courage failed him, and he turned again to us, saying,—

"No—no—I can't."—"Transported for stealing a will," said the lawyer, composedly.

Ogilvie groaned, and turning to his guests, said,—

"Ladies and gentlemen, I—I—you see. Some most afflicting intelligence has—in a manner of speaking—reached me, and I am—in a manner of speaking—ladies and gentlemen, under the painful necessity of—of—requesting you to go."

A murmur of dissatisfaction arose among the guests, and Ogilvie groaned again.

"Tell them they must go," said I.—"Ladies and gentlemen, you—you—must go."

The guests upon this became indignant; and epithets of "shabby,"—"wretch,"—"beggar on horseback,"—"low fellow," became very rife, being all directed against the unfortunate Ogilvie, who groaned and wrung his hands in despair.

The house was now getting rapidly cleared of its motley inmates, and when the last two or three were leaving, Ogilvie turned to the lawyer, and said, in a whining tone,—

"You will allow me all the expense I have been at?"— "Not one farthing. The Lord Chancellor must pass all the accounts; but there is a legacy mentioned in the will for you, and one for your younger brother."

"A legacy?"—"Yes."

"Money?"—"Certainly."

"How much!"—"That you will learn to-morrow, on the reading of the will."

"My dear sir, I will attend, of course. Bless me, a legacy! Well, things are not quite so bad, after all, as I thought they were."—"No," said I.

"I—I will attend, most certainly. You have quite relieved my mind, gentlemen. Good night to you—a very good night, indeed."

* * * * *

The next morning at twelve the lawyer read the will to both of Mr. Ogilvie's brothers. To one, as the reader will recollect, was left a shilling, to the other a bad penny!

Their rage knew no bounds, and we had to threaten them with legal proceedings, before we could get them from the house, which they at length left, cursing us all, and vowing bitter revenge, which, however, they have not yet been able to execute.

* * * * *

Mary Levenston is married, and the mother of four as fine children as ever I saw. Her eldest boy is fourteen, and destined for the church.

THE PRISON DUEL;

OR, THE ESCAPE.

During the time that I was occupied in walking the medical wards of one of the London hospitals, I became acquainted with a very agreeable young man, who was house-surgeon to the same hospital. His name was Meadows, and his agreeable manners, and thorough good-fellowship, made him a general favourite with the students, whether of medicine or surgery.

It was the duty of Meadows to be ready all night in case of any accident being brought into the hospital; and not unfrequently on those occasions we used to make up a little party far removed from any of the wards, so that we were no annoyance to the patients, and keep up all sorts of fun until the morning's dawn.

These were not drunken orgies, but rather feasts of wit and repartee, although we certainly did not debar ourselves occasionally from a few choice stimulants to the imagination in the shape of whiskey punch, &c. Meadows was about one-and-twenty then, and skilful, considering his opportunities, in his profession; but the spirit of conviviality soon deepened into something worse, and occasionally Meadows in the morning would present the lack-lustre eye and pale face of one who, over night, had sacrificed too freely to the rosy god.

These occasions became more and more frequent; but at length a great change came over him, and all at once he became sober, steady, and exceedingly neat in his appearance. His time at the hospital was nearly out, and at length, about a week before he was to leave, he invited me, and several others with whom he had been on terms of intimacy, to take a farewell supper in his snuggery at the hospital.

We met according to appointment, and were as merry as a parcel of crickets. To my great satisfaction, too, I observed that Meadows was very moderate in his potations.

"Well, Meadows, my boy," said one, when we had our cigars, and had drawn round the fire for a comfortable chat, "I suppose you are going to set up at once when you leave here?"—"Yes," said Meadows, "and have chalked out my future line of life. I am now twenty-one; I shall set up in business, marry ——"

"Marry!" cried one. "Marry!" shrieked another.—"Ah, to be sure. You know that a medical man must marry, or he never can get into good practice."

"Ah, well," said one, putting one foot on the hob, "everything has its drawbacks. What a d——d shame it is that a fellow is obliged to marry in this profession."—"I am quite certain," said Meadows, "that the company of a lovely and amiable woman—one who ——"

We immediately all rose and drunk the health of Mrs. Meadows, for, from the words of our host, we had no doubt but he was either actually at that present time married or engaged.

"Come now," said I, "speak the truth. There is a Mrs. Meadows?"—"There are three," said he.

"How do you make that out, old boy?" cried he who had possession of the hob.—"There's my grandmother," said Meadows.

"Oh, ah! a dear old lady—takes snuff—wears a snuff-coloured gown—ear-trumpet—calls you little Jackey, &c., &c."—"No, she don't."

"Bed-ridden — sciatica — oh, my back?" — "Nonsense. Well, then, there's my mother, and—ahem!"

"His wife, said I."—"My wife, gentlemen."

"Now the murder's out," cried we all at once. "Meadows is a Benedict. No more suppers—farewell to the steaming grog ——"—"The dreamy, mild cigar—the dance—the opera—the station ——"

"Well, well," cried Meadows; "such things are all very well sometimes; but they have their day. Now, I tell you what I mean to do. I shall fag hard, not only in my profession, but in literature, to which you know I am much attached, for twenty years, and then I believe, according to Cocker, I shall be of the ripe and mellow age of forty-one."

"Well, what then?"—"Why, I hope by then to have secured, not a fortune, but a competence, for myself, my wife, and family."

"Eleven dear pledges of affection," cried one.—"About

fifteen confinements in twenty years, at the very least," suggested another. "Why, Meadows, you might as well set up a lying-in hospital at once, and be cried up to the skies for your noble philanthropy, and all that kind of thing. There will be nothing but squall, squall, from morning till night: five of the dear innocents with the hooping-cough, four with the measles, and the others with the scarlatina. Upon my word, Meadows, you have sketched out for yourself a comfortable twenty years."

"Ah, that's all very well given in its way," said Meadows; "but let me paint a picture with a little more sunshine in it than you have bestowed upon yours." — "Paint away, Meadows."

"Then, in the first place, people don't have eleven or fifteen babbies all at once."—"That's true."

"Very well, then—the lying-in hospital falls to the ground. Imagine an elegant and accomplished woman, one who concentrates in herself all the young heart in its——"

We all set up a simultaneous mewing like so many cats, and Meadows said—

"Well, well, I will not trouble you with my raptures. You are quite right to object to them—like a dose of salts and senna, they are only very interesting to one party. But consider the pleasure of seeing growing up around you those whom you love, and who reciprocate your affection in the tenderest manner."

"One boy runs away to sea," cried Job's comforter, with his foot on the hob. "Another 'lists for a soldier—a third runs away with the chambermaid. One girl marries the footman; another omits the ceremony, and increases the population with the assistance of the groom; a third ——"

"Monstrous! monstrous!" cried Meadows. "Now you are out of all character. Recollect, I am a married man now, and bound to stick to my order."

"Stick to it, then, manfully," said I, "and be happy, Meadows, with your wife, in spite of all that carping, disappointed bachelors can say against matrimony."

"Yes, yes," cried they all; "but then Meadows has so often sworn that he never would tie himself to the finest woman on the face of the earth."

"Nor has he," said Meadows. "I swore never to wed a

woman—I have kept my word, for Mrs. Meadows is an angel."

"Gammon!"—"Gammon!"—"A dead shuffle."

"Now I tell you what I mean to do to get practice," said Meadows."

"Advice gratis, and physic for nothing?"—"No."

"A pill and a penny to any poor person who likes to apply?"—"I shall look out for some respectable tavern, or better sort of public-house, in the neighbourhood in which I commence business—some place where the respectable tradesmen congregate of an evening. I shall go among them, make myself sociable, and pick up practice."

"Meadows," said I gravely, "that won't do. You have just chalked out the road to ruin. You have a few hundreds, I understand, to begin business with; but if you have any notion of picking up a medical practice at taverns, you are most wofully mistaken. It will never answer. You will lose the respect of the whole neighbourhood, and the less they think of you the less they will think of your professional skill."

"Oh, I think it a good plan."—"It is a destructive one—it will ruin you."

"Well, I cannot help differing from you. I shall certainly try it."—"Then you will certainly fail, and I am sorry for your poor wife."

"My poor wife?"—"Yes. You will get into a habit of attending public-houses in preference to your home. It never will answer, Meadows."

"Ah, well, that's your opinion."—"It is my firm one—my unalterable one—I implore you not to descend to such a vile, fallacious scheme."

When the others saw I was so much in earnest, they became serious, and joined me in endeavouring to dissuade Meadows from his mad scheme, but I could see the idea was too firmly seated on his mind to be easily dislodged, and we all separated, much less merry than when we met.

* * * * * * *

My readers will recollect that I have before stated in other pages of my Diary, that, at my outset in life, I accepted several situations as travelling physician to noblemen and gentlemen, and hence it was that after one more interview with Meadows, I never saw him for nearly sixteen years. Not that I was away from London all that time, but when I came back I could hear nothing of him, and he was evidently not in business, or I would easily have discovered his place of abode.

I conjectured, therefore, that he had either left the metropolis, or was dead, as the only news I could get of him was, that he had removed no one knew whither.

Sixteen years, then, as I say, passed away, and I knew nothing of Meadows, or his wife. The very recollection of him was beginning to fade away in new connexions, and in the pleasure I experienced in my own small domestic circle.

I had taken a house in Old Broad-street, and was in good practice, when one night I was awakened by a ring at my night bell, and upon looking out of my window, and demanding who was there—a practice I had when any one rang my night-bell, because I had been "done" occasionally, as all medical men are by small wits who think it fun to ring a man's bell and then run away, for fear of being kicked, I was told that a sudden death had happened in Whitecross-street prison for debtors, and that Mr. ——, the governor, sent his compliments, and begged I would come.

"Very well," said I, for I knew Mr. —— very well as a worthy and humane man. "Say I will be there very soon."

I dressed myself rapidly, and was soon on my road to the gloomy building, which then contained so many broken hearts, so much reckless profligacy, and altogether such a picture of human nature, as was not to be found within any other walls.

After being scrutinized by the turnkey through a small grating, I was admitted, and at once conducted to the governor, who was but partially dressed.

"Doctor," he said, "we have had a sudden death in the prison, and the first during my administration here—you will, I am sure, excuse my sending for you, as there is considerable excitement among the prisoners upon the subject."

"I am quite at your service," said I.

He then led me along some gloomy lonesome passages, into the great yard of the prison, which we crossed to a ward situated in the extreme corner of the right hand. A turnkey preceded us with a ponderous bunch of keys, with one of which he opened a grating that blocked up the staircase, and then we ascended to one of the sleeping rooms of the place in which was collected one of the strangest assemblages of human beings that ever I saw in my life.

Most of them were wrapped up in the coarse woollen rugs which were the counterpanes of the beds, and their unshaven faces, lank, disordered hair, and gaunt visages, gave them altogether a most extraordinary appearance.

"Now, gentlemen," said the governor, "here is Dr. ——. Pray, permit him to view the body."

The throng opened and allowed me to pass on to one of the miserable beds, where, stretched in death, lay a tall man, of apparently some fifty or fifty-five years of age.

I soon satisfied myself that he was quite dead, and the surgeon of the gaol, who at that moment arrived, said to me—

"I quite expected him to go off this way some day. He has had all he could desire here, and voluntarily left the infirmary."

"What was the matter with him?"—"A heart disease of long standing."

"Well," said I, "we can do nothing."

"Can't you bleed him?" said one of the prisoners.

"Nonsense," said the surgeon.

"My good friend," said I, "bleeding is of no use whatever. The man is dead, and no earthly power can restore him to life."

"Good night to you, gentlemen," said the governor. "The body shall be removed directly."

"Ah," said one, "it's all very well. But we are put in here to die—we shall die on these d———n beds and breathe our last. Its murder! murder! murder!"

"That's the way some of them go on," whispered the governor to me. "Imprisonment drives many of them mad, I am convinced."

"There must come a day," said I, "when it will be found out, that if a man cannot pay his debts when he is at liberty, that he will never pay them within the walls of a prison."

"I think so, too," said the governor. "the system is quite absurd."

We moved towards the door of the sleeping room, and when the governor had passed out, a haggard, gaunt-looking man, with a beard of at least a month's growth, and a rug from his bed huddled round him, stepped up to me, and laid his hand upon my arm.

"Well, sir," said I, as he did not speak.—"You are Doctor ——," he then said in a hollow voice.

"I am."—"Do you know me?"

I looked hard at him, but I had no sort of recollection of the wan features—the sunken eyes, and the wild, bearded and moustached face before me.

"Do you know me?" he repeated.—"No," said I.

"No—no," he repeated. "How should you know me now? I am, indeed, altered, while you are much the same, but that you are stouter and stronger-looking than you were."

"Indeed; I don't recollect you," said I; "but if I once knew you I am very sorry to see you thus situated."—"I have been here fifteen months, now."

"That is a long time."—"You foretold it."

"I?"—"Yes—virtually. My name is Meadows."

"Meadows? John Meadows of —— Hospital?"—"The same. I am what was once Meadows—house surgeon of —— Hospital—look at me now. I am Jenkins here. My profession is unknown, and I am only waiting to lie down like he has."

He pointed to the corpse as he spoke. It was some moments before I could reply to him, I was so thoroughly astonished at his most unexpected appearance. Then I said—

"You shall see or hear from me to-morrow."—"No—no," he said.

"Do you doubt me?"—"Yes."

"And wherefore?"—"From long practice. So many have said they would come here and see me to-morrow, until the word is one of despair. I have lost confidence in human nature; we are all savages—monsters."

"You misjudge me," said I. "I will assuredly visit you some time to-morrow; till when take this."

I put a guinea into his hand. He looked down at the coin, and I saw a tear drop on it with a dull sound. I hastened down the staircase, and with a suffocating feeling at my heart, I left the place.

* * * * * *

When I was alone with the governor, I asked him if he knew Meadows.

"Meadows, Meadows!" he said. "We have no such person here."

"I was speaking to him."

"Oh, Jenkins, you mean?"

"Ah, he told me he was known by that name, but his real name is Meadows, and he is a surgeon."

"Indeed!"

"Yes, and a clever one, too."

"He is a very intemperate man here."

"Well, he is an old acquaintance of mine, and I wish to have some talk with him to-morrow."

"Very well; you can come at any time you like, and have him into a private room. I will leave orders to that effect."

"Thank you," said I; "I will be here about three, if that time will be convenient."

"Perfectly," said the governor.

* * * * *

At a little after three on the following day, I applied for admittance at the door of the prison, and was ushered into a little gloomy room, within a few paces of the portal, where I was told Jenkins would be sent to me, and presently I heard the name—Jenkins, Jenkins! resounded through the building and passages in all sorts of intonations.

In about five minutes he came, and now that he was dressed, I knew him far better than before, although there was no change in his bearded face.

"Well, Meadows," I said, "so you see I have come, in spite of your suspicions to the contrary."

"Pardon me for what I said so foolishly," replied Meadows; "I ought to have known you better, but the mind gets soured and vitiated in this place, till we scarcely know right from wrong, or friend from foe."

"Now, then," said I, "won't you sit down and tell me what has brought you to this plight?"

"Yes, yes, doctor. Hilloa! there—a pint of half-in-half here directly."

"Very well," said the turnkey; "you needn't make such a noise about it."

"You must have it all to yourself," said I, "for I must decline drinking so early."

"Ah, it may be early out of doors," he said, "but time has nothing to do with us in here."

The half-in-half was brought him, and after emptying one half of it at a draught, he said,

"Well, doctor, you were right; I set up in business, and tried the tavern scheme."

"Which utterly failed?"

"It did. I was sold up in twelvemonths, and everybody then abused me, and most of all those spoke ill of me who had drunk continually at my expense. Then I took another shop out by Hornsey, but that didn't last above a week. Then I came down to a lodging, and then to a much worse one, and so on, accumulating little debts and bills"

"What do you mean?"

"Bills of exchange. I have put my name to stamps to the amount of some sixty thousand pounds, I dare say."

"Good Heavens! Meadows, you must have been mad."

"No; a Jew gave me sixpence in the pound for doing it; at last my name got too common."

"Why, then, you can never hope to extricate yourself from your difficulties?"—"Never."

"Nor from this place?"—"Never."

There was a silence of some minutes' duration, and then, for want of anything else to say, I said,

"What—what are your notions of what is to come of all this, Meadows?"—"Drinking and fighting, swearing and singing."

I shook my head.

"Are you so lost?"—"Quite—quite," he said.

"And—and your wife?"—"Is starving!"

"Have you children?"—"Yes—five."

"And they?"—"Starving too."

"Meadows! Meadows!" I said, "This humour, I am sure, suits not with your real feelings. This recklessness is assumed."

I saw a slight quivering of his lips, and I continued,

"You long for the fresh air of Heaven—the green fields and the sunny skies, the society of your wife, and your dear children. Meadows, you are not quite hardened yet—I am sure you are not."

He made several attempts to speak, and then he gasped rather than said,

"I—I am," and burst into tears.

"That will do," thought I; "I have moved him, and got rid of that frightful feeling of apathy that was upon his soul. He will be much better now."

For some minutes I let him weep on undisturbed, and then I said,

"Come, now, Meadows, we will talk a little rationally. All that I can do to assist you I will. Hope for the best, for you shall find in me an indefatigable friend, if not a very effective one."

He looked up at me, and I was struck with the remarkable change in his countenance. It had lost much of its wild expression, and he looked more like himself.

"Why, if you were shaved," said I, "you would not be so much altered."

"I have lost the heart to shave," he said.

"Oh, nonsense."

"What is the use here? We all get reckless, and care for nothing."

"But that must not be the case with you. That very reckless spirit that you tell me you all get here is the thing that deprives you of one half the sympathy you would otherwise get. Now, Meadows, listen to me. I will go to all your creditors, and endeavour to convince them that there can be nothing got by keeping you here. Those who are vindictive, I think ought to be satisfied with the punishment you have already received, and those who have the least hope of getting any money from you in such a position, I can surely reason out of their absurdity."

He shook his head, and was about to say something, when a low knock came upon the outer door of the prison, and I heard from the little room in which we were the harsh voice of the turnkey exclaim,

"Well—what now?"

"I wish to speak to my husband, sir," said a timid female voice.

"Good God!" exclaimed Meadows, springing to the door, "that is my wife."

"Hilloa, hilloa! young fellow," cried the turnkey, "not so fast here; it's past the time, and she can't come in. You must come to-morrow."

"Oh, Meadows, Meadows," cried the wife from the outer side, "Margaret is dying."

"Dying?"

"Yes, our dear little Margaret is dying; she has taken a fever, and the parish doctor will not come to her."

"Dying!" gasped Meadows. "Parish doctor—my child—I in prison, and could perhaps save her."

I saw him clinch his hands, and turn upon the turnkey, and was just in time to rush forward and hold him before he involved himself in inextricable trouble by an attack upon the authorities of the prison.

"Meadows—Meadows!" I cried, "are you mad?—what would you do?"

"Let me go—let me go!" he cried; "a hundred of them should not keep me from my child."

"This is madness, Meadows," cried I; "your child shall want for no medical attention. You can place confidence in my medical skill, surely, and I give you my solemn word that I will pay every attention."

The wife was sobbing bitterly outside the grating, and Meadows now sank upon a stone bench in the hall in a fit of shivering which quite astonished me. I immediately sent for the governor, and had some brandy administered to him.

When he was recovered, I again assured him that I would go that instant to his child, and bring him on the following morning a report of her health.

It would have been now cruelty to protract my stay, so I departed at once, and making myself known to his wife, she and I walked arm-in-arm to a miserable court in the immediate neighbourhood of the prison, where she lived in order to be near her unhappy husband.

The room into which I was shown was the picture of wretchedness, and the wife's account of how they had become reduced to such a state was affecting in the extreme. With tears in her eyes, she told me that no reasoning could lead Meadows out of the idea, that by frequenting taverns and public-houses he should get up a good connexion, and business in his profession would follow.

"It is true, sir," she said, "that he got patients in abundance, but no money. All the professional employment he procured through such a source was gratuitous; and no one of his boon companions thought of paying him for his advice, whom they were in the daily habit of drinking with, and being on the most familiar terms."

"Certainly," said I, "your view of the subject is most correct. As soon as a man loses caste he loses everything."

The child I had volunteered to attend was a sweet little girl of about five years of age, and in a moment I saw there was but slender hope of her recovery. She was suffering from a fever peculiar to the low, mean, dirty, localities of the metropolis; and when once it takes a firm hold of the child, it is almost impossible to eradicate it. It was affecting to hear the little thing, in her disturbed slumber, calling upon her papa to come to her; and I could see poor Mrs. Meadows trying to stop the tears which would each moment fill her eyes.

"I will send you," I said, "such medicines as are necessary, and in the meantime you must make her some broth. Now, as I consider the broth as quite medicinal, you must permit me to furnish it. So, if you please, take this, and use it at your discretion."

I handed her two sovereigns as I spoke, but they dropped from her hands, and staggering to a seat, she burst into tears. I knew that she would recover much sooner by herself than with me in the room, so picking up the money, and placing it in her lap, I said,—

"Good day, Mrs. Meadows, I will call again before to-morrow, but I may be late."

I thus left the scene of misery with a heavy heart, thinking deeply what must have been the sufferings of that delicately-nurtured young female, in being yoked to a man who in the outset of his career in life had made so great an error.

*   *   *   *   *

When I mentioned to Mrs. Meadows that it might be late when I called again, I knew I had to go as far as Windsor to a consultation respecting a case of a gentleman residing in that town. It so happened that I was detained later than I expected, and having to cross the whole length of the city, in order to reach the lodging of Mrs. Meadows, it was nearly twelve o'clock at night before I made my solitary way down the little court, and sought for No. 5, which was the house where they lived.

The medicines I had promised I had sent, and I was not without a hope, although a very faint one, that the child might have derived some benefit from them.

The room was at the very top of the house, and with some difficulty I groped my way up the creaking, ricketty staircase, when, seeing a dim ray of light streaming from one of the seams under the ill-fitting door, I gently tapped, and was answered at once by Mrs. Meadows, who said,—

"She is sleeping, sir."

"Then she will recover," said I; "but she must not be awakened, or it might prove fatal to her."

"Thank God for my child!" sobbed Mrs. Meadows.

"Hush—hush!" said I. "Do not give way to your feelings. Recollect that each moment now that she sleeps gives her an increased hold upon existence. Be careful not to awaken her, but watch until she arouses from her sleep quietly, and then give her some meat broth, and persuade her to try to go to sleep again. By pursuing that system the fever will be overcome."

"How can we thank you, sir?" she cried.

"Never mind me," said I. "I will call again to-morrow morning by ten o'clock."

As I spoke there was a strange noise upon the staircase, as if some one was ascending it upon one leg, for the sound was a steady tread, tread, at intervals, such as could not have been well or easily produced by any one ordinarily coming up.

"What is that?" said I.

"I do not know," replied Mrs. Meadows, with an alarmed look.

"Remain here while I go and see," I said, as I took the rushlight which was burning on the table, and walked to the door.

When I got to the landing I heard a heavy blow apparently given against some door, and then a voice cried,—

"I want my child?"

"You and your child be d—d!" screamed some one from the room which had been assaulted.

"Not there—not there," said the first voice, and then the same strange tread ascended to the second flight of stairs.

I was confident the voice was not that of Meadows, although the suspicion did at first cross my mind that he had escaped in some curious manner, and had come to seek his dying child, and was knocking at the various doors, knowing the house, but not the room his poor family occupied in it.

The mysterious footstep now come nearer and nearer, and I leaned over the banisters to catch a glimpse of who it might be who was coming at such an hour, with so strange a sound upon the staircase. Judge of my horror and surprise when I saw Meadows, half clothed, and with but one boot on, which had caused the strange sound as if only one foot was ascending the stairs, and a look of awful wildness in his eyes, which at once convinced me he was insane.

In his hand he had a long walking-stick, to which, at its extreme end, was tied the blade of a razor, making a formidable weapon. I sickened as I saw the blade and the stick; both were reeking with blood. He fixed his eyes upon me as he came up, and smiling, only as a lunatic can smile, he said,—

"Ah, doctor, how are you? I've come home, you see—you have not heard of my duel."

"Your duel, Meadows," said I; "good God! what do you mean?"

"My husband," screamed Mrs. Meadows, as he reached the landing.

"Hush, for Heaven's sake!" said I; "if you awaken the child, it will die."

A low wail from the sick child praclaimed that the noise had awakened it.

"What cry is that?" said Meadows, trembling.

I took him by the arm, and led him into the room—his child was dead.

"Look here," said I.

With a deep groan he fell backwards quite insensible.

Mrs. Meadows began screaming and wringing her hands.

"Hush! hush! madam," said I, "do not make bad worse by useless lamentations. Bring me some cold water instantly."

She obeyed me mechanically, and brought me a pitcher with water. I immediately dashed some of it in the face of Meadows, and with a deep sigh he recovered.

"Good God! what has happened?" he said; "where am I? Oh, tell me, am I dead?"

"Meadows," I said, "do you know me?"

He looked me in the face as he replied,—"Yes, yes—you are my best friend; you advised me well, but I would not follow your counsel. Is Freeman dead?—is he quite dead?"

"Who do you mean?"

He pressed his hand upon his brow for a moment, and then said,—

"Doctor, listen to me; and you, dear," to his wife. "I will tell you how I came here. I have fought a duel in prison."

"A duel in prison!"

"Yes; strange as it may appear, a duel has taken place within those walls. If my memory serves me, I will tell you all; let me think—I am Meadows. Is Freeman dead?"

"He wanders in his mind," whispered I to his wife.

"No, no," he cried, with the quick sense of hearing so often allied to insanity; "I do not wander—you think me mad, but I am not—I will tell you. There was some quarrel in the long dormitory in which many sleep—ah, now I have it. Some woman brought in liquor secretly, and many of us partook of it—then we sang, shouted, and laughed, till a quarrel arose between me and Freeman, and we agreed to fight. Here is my weapon."

He gave the stick, at the end of which was the razor, a sweeping flourish round his head.

"We had nothing but razors, and those we fastened, as you see, to the end of sticks. Then the squalid, half-mad prisoners yelled and shouted around us, and the fight began. Oh, what joy was that—we cut and slashed like fiends. Then, as the blood flowed, some flew to the window, and cried for help. 'Murder! murder!' they shrieked, but none came near us, nor dared. We kept them all at bay, until at length I gave him a hideous gash—you should have seen it. It was in his neck, and the blood flew out like water from a conduit. He staggered, and fell in his own gore. I was the victor. I know not what followed next, but some tried to seize me, and I walked away thus, like the destroying fiend, death, himself. They fell mangled before me; they opened doors to let me pass out, for I should have killed them all. Who could cope with me then? I was mad—my brain was on fire—yes—I was mad—mad!"

These last words he shrieked out at the top of his voice, and I feared each moment that he would commit some act of frantic violence, and kept as close to him as possible, deeming it safer than being at a convenient distance for him to slash at me with the horrible weapon he was armed with, should he take it into his head to use it.

"Meadows," said I, mildly, "do you know me?"

"Don't glare at me," he cried, "I know your tricks; you think I'm mad, and you want to catch my eye that you may awe me into submission; but it won't do—no—no—you shall not—you dare not."

"You mistake me, Meadows," said I; "I have no such intention as that you impute to me. You are not mad, I'm sure. Come, now, will you lend me that razor to shave with?"

"When?"

"Oh, now, I mean; it seems a good one."

"Yes; shall I try it on your throat?"

"Not at present," said I, trying to assume a calmness which I was far from feeling; "but, if you will give it me, you shall come and see me try it to-morrow."

"No—that won't do—ha! what noise is that?"

I listened attentively, and heard the sound of footsteps coming slowly and cautiously up the stairs. "Now," thought I, "they are coming to take him, and in his rage I am very likely to be sacrificed."

"Hist! hist! not a word, not a word," he said, in a low tone; "not a word, and they sha'n't take you. You are poor drunken Meadows, the half-mad surgeon, and I am Doctor ———. Very well, you have escaped from prison, and they want to drag you back again, but I won't let them."

"Very good," said I; "but I will defend myself if you will lend me that razor."

"No, I will defend you—hush! hush! hush!"

He crept to the door with the noiseless tread of a cat, and stood exactly behind it, with the razor and stick uplifted, ready to bring them down upon the head of the first man who ventured to enter.

"This must not be," thought I; "there will be murder done if I don't give some alarm."

He was watching my countenance, and seemed to divine my thoughts, for he suddenly lowered the razor, and made a sweeping cut at my legs, which only missed me by a hair's breadth, saying, at the same time,—

"If you speak I'll chop you in two."

I was now regularly terrified, and expected every moment another cut to be made at me, for he appeared amused at the consternation that I suppose was visible in my face. Then his ear again caught the sounds of the ascending footsteps, and he laughed quietly as he held the razor in its former attitude. I could hear a whispering on the landing of the staircase, and then I heard one voice say,—"Knock; if he is there, he will probably answer." A knock immediately came upon the panel of the door, but Meadows was as still as the grave, and every moment he glanced at me with a terrible meaning in his eye, so that for my life's sake I dared not say a word.

His wife had thrown herself upon her knees by the bed-side, and had either fainted, with her head upon the bed, or was praying silently. My state of mind was exquisitely painful; each moment seemed an hour, and with death staring me in the face, for my life depended upon the wayward fancy of the madman, I felt unutterable anguish. Since then I have been in quite as perilous, if not more perilous situations; but that was my first encounter with a dangerous lunatic, and all my feelings were in the most feverish state that can be imagined.

The knock at the door was, after a few moments, repeated, and Meadows laughed silently with a sort of devilish glee, as he held the dreadful weapon ready poised to descend upon the head of the unfortunate wight who should summon courage to protrude that part of his person into the room. Then I saw the handle of the door slowly turn, as if some one meant cautiously to peep in; the door was opened about three inches, and a police staff was poked in, while a voice from the outer side said,—

"Hilloa, there. Come, come, no nonsense."

Meadows made no reply, but he stood as still as a statue. Then the door opened a little wider, until, by degrees, the opening was wide enough to admit a man's head. To my horror, a head slowly appeared, and, with a cry that sounded through the house like the yell of a wild beast, Meadows brought down the razor upon it. I heard the blow, and in the next moment he sprang upon the bed, trampling upon the dead body of his child, and collecting all his strength, in one terrible spring he went through the window, crashing, as he went, glass and framework in one mass of splinters. I placed my hands over my ears involuntarily, that I might not hear his fall.

In a moment the room was full of police officers.

"Who was hurt by the razor?" said I.

"This ere hat," replied a man. "I poked it on the end of my staff, for I heard him a breathing. I'm up to them ere mad fellows."

I immediately rushed down the stairs to the yard of the house. There lay Meadows a mangled corpse.

* * * * *

The tale he told of the events of the prison was substantially correct. The man Freeman was dead, and some half dozen others had received fearful gashes from the razor. Such, then, was the end of the man who fancied drinking and business such as his could ever assimilate. His poor wife and surviving children found refuge from the storms of fate in a charitable institution for some time, and then a subscription, which I set on foot, enabled her to set up a school; but a weight of melancholy hung upon her, and she lingered but two years after her unhappy husband.

THE CHANGELING;

OR, THE DREAM OF RETRIBUTION.

In glancing over the pages of my diary, memory conjures up scenes, events, and people, which have long been forgotten, although in many cases I believe that the various, strange, and eventful circumstances that flit before my mind's eye, as I trace the records made by me at the time of this occurrence, have exercised a powerful influence upon my career of life, and, by giving me a more ample and enlarged knowledge of human nature, have softened down many of the harsher feelings of humanity which people are apt to start with early in life.

I was about thirty years of age when the events I am about to record happened, and I am quite sure that I saw forty dawning upon me before I got rid of some of the impressions made upon my mind by the train of horrors which one single act of crime in a person, from a false motive, gave rise to. But to my story.

A day of intense professional labour was drawing to its close, and I was congratulating myself that I should get some uninterrupted repose, when the tingle, tingle of my bell made me give a responsive groan, as I conjectured it might portend a summons to some distant part of the town.

In a few moments the servant made her appearance to tell me I was wanted.

"Who is it?" said I.

"Goodness, gracious, sir, I don't know," said Martha, who was of a romantic turn; "but it may be some captain of banditti. The drawbridge fell with a clinkum, clankum, and the spectre nodded its ghostly head, while ———"

"Why, Martha, what are you mumbling about?"

"Sir?—eh! Oh, I forgot, sir. I was a reading when the ring comed, sir; and—and—you see, sir, I can't get out of my head the ' Phantom of Despair; or, the Ghost of the Grey-eyed Nun.' The *light* struck twelve, sir, and the *clock* went out with a dreadful smell."

"Well, well," I said, "that will do, Martha. If you've got a phantom of despair in your head, I've got one in mine, for I'm dreadfully afraid I shall get no sleep again to-night."

"Lor! sir—you don't say so," exclaimed Martha, as she took up my slippers, which I had just thrown off, to drag on again my unwelcome boots. "The young and accomplished Medora Juliana Fedorina never slept for twenty-one days and nights, while she was a hexploring of the vaults of Dunderbluster Castle."

"Didn't she?"

"No, sir; and the skeleton forms shook, and the wind, with a sing'ler sound, carried on its bosom ———"

"Thank you; I'll hear the rest some other time," said I, as I walked down stairs to my visitor, who, when I came to see him, presented himself in the very unromantic character of a footboy, with a blue jacket, and an unlimited quantity of little sugar-loaf buttons upon it.

"Oh, please, sir," he said, "you are wanted at Grove Villa, Hampstead-road."

"Immediately?"

"Yes, sir; missus says as I was to bring you with me, sir, if so be as I found you at home."

"Very well; go and get a coach, my boy, and as you know the way, and I don't, you can go with me."

It was a considerable distance from the city, where I lived, to the Hampstead-road, but by the time the clocks were proclaiming eleven, I entered a handsome cottage residence, with a garden in the front, and replete with all those little prettinesses which make our suburban villas such desirable abodes.

The boy opened the door with a latch-key, and directly we got into the house, a female servant said, in a tone almost as low as a whisper,—

"This way, sir, if you please;" and preceded me up stairs.

"Ah!" I thought, "here's somebody very bad, I suppose, as all this quiet is considered necessary;" and yet there was rather an air of mystery and secrecy than quiet; but I had not much time for conjecture, being shown into a room at the top of the first flight of stairs, in which, by the dim light that was there, I could perceive a female figure leaning her head upon the table.

"Here's the doctor, ma'am," said the servant.

There was no reply, and the words were twice again repeated before the female betrayed consciousness of them. Then, however, she started up so suddenly, that she alarmed me for the moment, and I stepped to the door. She sunk back into her seat in a moment, and said, in a tone of exquisite anguish,—

"Leave the room, Sarah; I will ring for you when the doctor is going."

The servant left us, and I turned to the lady, saying,—

"I hope, madam, no serious indisposition?"

I had got just so far, when she interrupted me by exclaiming,—

"Doctor, tax your skill. Think of some drug—some potent means of banishing sleep for ever from my eyes. I must not—dare not—sleep again."

She spoke in a hollow, low tone, as she replied, "The reason is a simple one." Then she shuddered again, as she pronounced the words, "I dream!"—"Oh, is that all?" said I. "We will get rid of the dreams, madam, without depriving you of your sleep."

"Never—never!" she cried frantically. "Oh, God, never—never—never! Too well I know that dreadful vision will ever come to me. Oh, spare me—spare me, Heaven. 'Tis too horrible! My brain must sink, and then—then madness will ensue, and in the wild delusion I shall tell all, and while I blast the happiness of many others, bring upon myself disgrace and infamy. Oh, God—oh, God! what awful sufferings do not some of Thy creatures undergo. Spare me—spare me! Mercy—mercy! The dream—the dream!"

All this was uttered with such a wild vehemence of tone and manner, that I was perfectly astonished, and said, hastily,—

"Pray be calm, my dear madam. Some freak of the imagination in a dream has distressed you, but you will soon forget it."

She fixed her eyes upon me as she said, slowly and distinctly,—

"This morning a beggar came to the gate—she was trembling with cold, fainting with hunger—her face was perished and wan with want and misery—the scanty rags that covered her were shaken by the slightest wind—tears streamed down her sallow cheeks, and she prayed for the hardest crust, the merest offal, to allay the pangs of hunger. Doctor—I envied her."

"You envied her?" said I, as I glanced round the apartment, which was replete with every luxury.

"Oh, Heavens, how I envied her!" she repeated. "But time is flying. There—there, sir, is your fee. Write me a prescription that will banish sleep for ever. I must never sleep again."

I shook my head, as I said,—

"Madam, you ask an impossibility. We have no means of banishing sleep except by producing the sleep of death. All our energies are frequently directed to procure sleep for our patients, and even had I a means of making you wakeful, I must use my own discretion, upon a careful consideration of your case, and not yours."

Her eyes flashed with resentment, as she cried,—

"You are an impostor, sir."

"I am very sorry you sent for me, madam."

She then clasped her hands convulsively together, and cried,—

"Sir, I implore you to save me. I cannot endure existence. 'Tis too frightful. Have mercy on me!"

"I really, at present, cannot comprehend you," said I. "You send for me as a physician, and yet complain of no tangible indisposition."

"For five nights now in succession I have had a dream," she said, in a voice of plaintive misery,—"a dream which has made me start raving from my slumbers. Oh, how I have striven to keep awake—but all is vain."

"You have allowed this dream to take too strong a hold of your imagination," said I. "I will write you a prescription, not to keep you awake, but to make you sleep sounder."

"No—no—no; sleep is horrible. Oh, sir, do you think there is any mercy for—for ——"

She paused, and I said, "For who?"

"No—no matter—not now. There may come a time, but not yet. The dream will come again, and then I shall go mad. I know it too well—too well."

"May I ask if you are married, madam?" said I, for I was anxious to speak to some one concerning her who would be a little more rational than herself.

"Married?" she repeated; "I am—I am, and, as you see, childless. You know my child died—died in its infancy, and I put up with the dispensations of Providence; but now I am tormented by dreams—dreadful dreams—that drive me mad. What do you suspect?"

"Suspect!"

"Aye; you look so suspicious, man. What do you suspect?"

This was so strange a question, that it was a moment or two before I could reply to it, and then all I said was,—

"Madam, I must leave you, for I fear our further conversation is not likely to benefit you. I will write you a prescription which cannot harm you, although I must say I know too little of the case to fancy it will do you much good."

She rose suddenly, and before I could be aware of her intention, she caught up a small phial which was upon the table, and applied its mouth to her lips.

In a moment I had wrested it from her.

"Are you mad," I cried; "and if so, why send for me to be your keeper? I will call assistance."

She threw herself on her knees at my feet as she spoke, and looked up in my face with such an expression of abject fear that I was much moved, and said to her in a kinder voice,—

"Will you confide in me, and tell me frankly the cause of your evident great mental perturbation?"

The same shudder I had noticed before came over her, and she rose from her knees, saying, in a voice but little above a whisper,—

"No—no, I dare not—I cannot. Go now—go now at once. You have been here too long."

A ring at the gate now sounded clearly through the house, and it was echoed by a scream from my strange patient, who, then sinking into a chair, exclaimed hysterically,—

"My husband—my husband! All is lost."

"Your husband?" said I. "Upon my word I am very glad it is your husband, for he may be able to give me some explanation of the strange scene we have had together."

"No—no—not a word. If you would avoid the curse of a dying woman, breathe to him not a word. Go in peace as you came; but, oh! speak not to him."

"I don't see how I can avoid him," said I.

"Yes—yes—you can hide."

"I beg your pardon, but I shall do no such thing."

"This closet," she muttered, not heeding what I said, and opening the door of a large cupboard, which was at one end of the room.

"But," said I, "madam ——"

"Silence, sir," she said, suddenly turning from the closet, and presenting at my head a large pistol.

For the moment I was so taken by surprise that I was perfectly speechless, and we made a very interesting tableau between us.

"Choose, sir," she said, while her dark eyes flashed again. "Choose between a few minutes' concealment in that closet until I can get you out of the house without my husband's knowledge, or instant death. This weapon is loaded."

I felt myself in a pretty predicament, and like most persons so situated, I began to prevaricate and endeavour to cast about for some mode of escape.

"That closet?" I said; "why really, madam, your conduct is altogether so extraordinary."

"Keep off, sir," she cried, as she deliberately presented the pistol; "the slightest attempt on your part to take this weapon from me will cost you your life."

At this moment a step upon the staircase broke upon my ears, and the lady immediately said, with frantic eagerness—

"The closet, or death."

There was something in her looks and tone that was not to be despised, and really, ridiculous as I may appear for so so doing, I popped into the closet to avoid a worse fate.

She immediately closed the door, and to my great trepidation fastened it on the outer side. In a moment I heard some one enter the room, and a man's voice said,—

"My dear, you should not have sat up for me in your very delicate health," and the lady, in quite an altered tone from that she had used to me, said,—

"I could not sleep; you know that I am afflicted with terrible dreams."

"What dream is it that troubles you so?" said the husband; "you never would tell me."

"An idle fanciful dream, not worth the relation," replied the wife, in a high hysterical tone of voice. "Some day you shall know all."

"All what?"

"Nothing—nothing, a mere nothing. I am much better now. Go you to bed, and I will come very soon. I have some of my things to put to rights in this room."

"Then leave them till to-morrow," said the husband, in a kind tone of voice; "you look feverish and unwell, and had better retire to rest. I declare I will, in spite of all you can say to the contrary, send for a physician to-morrow."

"No—no," she replied; "physicians can do nothing for me. Time may obliterate."

"Ah! you have ever been unhappy since our great loss. If our dear child had lived."

"Hush—hush! you will drive me mad," cried the wife; "never—oh, never allude to her unless you wish to see me, some day, drop a corpse at your feet. I cannot bear it; she is lost—lost to us for ever; there is—there can be not the least hope."

"Hope!" echoed the husband; "of course there is no hope on this side of the grave. I live myself but with the consolation of seeing my beloved child in heaven."

The wife gave a loud scream, and then shrieked, rather than said,—

"There I shall never see her—never—never—unless God has more mercy upon me than 'tis possible to conceive."

"What do you mean?" said the husband; "you alarm and afflict me by those strange hints. Oh, wife—wife! If there be anything pressing on your mind, let me know it, and what consolation one human being can afford to another, you shall have. If it be only that you continue to grieve for the loss of our dear child, believe me I feel as acutely as you do, although I will not allow myself to be entirely beaten down by a domestic calamity, however terrible it may be."

She only replied by an agonizing burst of hysterical weeping; her deep sobs were dreadful to hear; and I never in my life found myself in so awkward and uncomfortable a position.

"Good God!" said the husband, suddenly; "why have you this pistol on the table? My dear, you should not meddle with these things, for you may pinch your fingers, although they are not loaded."

"Not loaded!" thought I; "here's a fool I've been—frightened into a cupboard for nothing."

"Leave me—leave me!" cried the wife; "I shall be better soon—leave me."

"No, indeed, I shall not leave you any more to-night," was the reply, "you need comfort and society, so come away now to your chamber; I have some letters to write, which I will do at the dressing-table, while you endeavour to get some sound refreshing sleep."

"Sleep—sleep!" she cried; "I shall never sleep again,—I would not sleep for worlds; no—no—such another dream would kill me."

"Always harping upon that dream," muttered the husband; "it's very strange—very strange, indeed."

"It is—it is—awfully strange! but leave me, now—oh, leave me, I pray you."

"Well—well," said the husband, "I will write my letters in my own study, if you wish it, but I shall send Martha to stay with you. Bless me, whose gloves are these?"

They were mine.

"Here's a pretty piece of business," thought I; "oh, what an ass I have been ever to consent to get into this confounded closet."

"Whose gloves are these?" repeated the husband.

There was no reply; and he again said, with a tone of some asperity—"Whose gloves are these?"

"Gloves!" repeated the wife; "I told you they were thrown in at the window, and I took the pistol out of the closet to defend myself."

"You never told me anything of the sort," said the husband, suspiciously; "this is the first I have heard of it, Mrs. Bennet."

"Oh, their names are Bennet," thought I; "confound you, Mrs. Bennet; you are getting me into a nice scrape."

"I care not whether you heard of it before or not," she replied, carelessly.

"I have my suspicions, ma'am," he replied.

"You are welcome to them."

"Woman!" he said, after a pause; "there is guilt upon your soul. Your manner, your trepidation, and your dread of sleep, all tend to prove that some secret cause of disquietude is ever present to you."

"God of Heaven!" she said; "there wanted but this to fill my cup of misery to the brim."

"In Heaven's name, explain yourself!" cried the husband.

"Will you kill me?" she said.

"Kill you?"

"Yes—will you, will you do me so much grace as to take my life? Oh, I could worship the hand that would take my life!"

"I cannot understand you. To-morrow we will talk more at large concerning this affair, but for the present I will keep these gloves, with the hope of finding an owner for them."

With these words I heard him leave the room, and he had scarcely been gone a moment, when the wife opened the closet door, and clasping her hands, she said, in a tone of wild entreaty,—

"Fly—fly! you will easily find your way—leave this house instantly."

"Upon my word, madam," said I, "you are complimentary as well as considerate, but I will not fly."

"You will not?"

"Certainly not. Why should I?"

"To save one who is innocent from despair; to light up for the remainder of a life the flame of joy; to restore the parent to his child. Meet me to-morrow night at eight o'clock, by the corner of Spring-gardens, and you shall hear a tale which in the telling may kill me."

"Thank you, I'd rather not," said I.

"Then hear me now swear, as I believe there is a Heaven above us, I will destroy myself this night, without repairing the evil I have done."

"You had better tell your husband."

"No—no—no. Some stranger alone can act in such a manner as to restore what is lost."

"You speak in riddles," said I; "but I promise to meet you as you propose, with this promise, that I do not bind myself to keep any secrets."

"I do not wish you," she said; "when I tell you it is with the wish that you should be the medium of divulging what has been kept locked in my own heart for five years now. The other one who knew it is dead—gone to that dreadful account which I shall soon go to. Oh, horror—horror! Is there no hope? Oh, Heaven, have mercy!"

Something remarkably like "I'll be d——d if I stay here any longer," came across my mind; and as Mrs. Bennet flung herself into a chair, quite exhausted by her feelings, I went down the stairs as softly as I could, intending to get out of the house without a row, if possible.

The fates would have it, though, that just as I got to the stairs, a door immediately opposite opened, and a gentlemanly-looking man appeared with a light in his hand.

We stood for a moment or more opposite to each other without speaking, and then I was so confounded that all I could say was,—

"How do you do, Mr. Bennet?"

He seemed to be so astounded at what he considered my cool

impudence, that he said nothing for another moment, when he darted into the parlour, and before I could get past the door, he returned with a poker in his hand.

"Mr. Bennet, you are labouring under an error," said I, "pray be calm."

"I think it is you, you scoundrel, that are labouring under an error," he replied, with a face as white as a sheet from passion, "and you shall very soon be labouring under this poker. Pray, sir, may I so far presume in my own house as to ask you if these are your gloves?"

"They are, sir, but ——"

"None of your buts, sir."

"I will explain."

"I want no explanation," he cried, and aimed a blow at my head with the poker, which, as I stepped on one side, took effect upon a plaster cast in the hall, which it smashed to pieces. I took the opportunity immediately to close upon the infuriated husband, and being the stronger man of the two, I soon bundled him, poker and all, into the parlour, and the key luckily being in the outside of the lock, I fastened him in, and then rushed from the house, pursued by a little yelping terrier, who got hold of the leg of my trousers, and would not leave go, until I kicked him off with a great piece of cloth in his mouth.

I ran across the garden, clambered over the gate, and found myself in the Hampstead-road, minus my hat and gloves, in a mizzling shower of rain.

"Well," cried I, "of all the fiends on earth, that Mrs. Bennet is the worst. If I don't have satisfaction for all this, I'll be hanged. Wait till to-morrow, Mr. and Mrs. Bennet, and we shall see how you can then carry it off. Hang it, I shall get wet to the skin."

* * * * *

I was scarcely ever out in so persevering a rain. It came down in perfect lumps of water, as it were, and ran into one's neck, splashing and dashing a trickling stream down one's back of an intense coldness; however, I was by no means attired in befitting garments to "stand the pelting of the pitiless storm," and I shrank under the friendly archway of a neighbouring stable-door, with an intention of waiting until either the weather should moderate, or some vehicle should come past which would give me a lift to town.

But it was something like waiting for a legacy, to wait until that diabolical rain should cease;—on—on it went with a provoking calmness, that looked mightily as if it had made up its mind to continue for an indefinite period. There was no bullying—no blustering about the weather, as in the case of a thunder-storm, when the mere noise there is, and the more bluster—like human passions—we know it will the sooner be over. But this was a steady, easy going, cautious rain—one of those rains that go steadily pelting on, as if they knew they had lots to come.

After waiting about twenty minutes, I began to get very cold, for I had been in the rain quite long enough to get very damp, although not wet through, and I reluctantly thought of moving.

"I must walk on," thought I. "There is no other resource; and I must ring them up at the first public-house I come to."

It was far from pleasant to be without a hat; and all I could do was to wind my handkerchief round my head, in the manner that old women do in Paris, which, however, was far from an effectual repulse to the rain. I was then upon the point of leaving my shelter, when the welcome sound of wheels came upon my ears. Some vehicle was evidently coming from Hampstead towards London, and that at a pretty smart pace too.

"Here's a chance, at all events," I thought; and I sallied out into the road, and cried hilloa!

"Well, what now?" said a man in a chaise-cart, drawing up very quick.

"I have lost my hat, and will pay you for a drive on to London."

"Lost your hat?"—"Yes."

"Was it a beaver?"—"Yes."

"Eat it then," said the fellow, and he drove on, leaving me looking despairingly after him.

"Oh," I thought to myself, "I might have known I should meet with such a reception. This is a highly civilized and religious country, and of course it's every one for himself."

With this splenetic speech I walked on; and my indignation was so much aroused by the conduct of the man with the chaise-cart, that I soon got into quite a glow of heat, and I dare say, after all, saved myself from catching a very severe cold, which might have been the result of riding in an open vehicle through the rain, in my unprotected state.

When I reached Camden-town, I wisely procured a coach, and easily arrived at my house, wet, tired, and in not a very amiable temper, at the delightful hour of sunrise in the morning.

* * * * *

The next morning, when I came to consider all the circumstances connected with the affair, I was more than ever bothered to come to any conclusion with respect to the mysterious conduct of Mrs. Bennet. Upon a careful review of all the affairs, I came very closely to the opinion that she was not mad, but that some circumstance, probably, of a very guilty character, was preying upon her imagination, and inducing the state of mind in which I had found her. What that circumstance was, I had not the slightest clue to discover; but nevertheless I determined upon recovering my hat and my gloves, even if it were necessary to apply to the police for assistance in the business.

While I was sitting at my breakfast making these reflections, a gentleman was announced, and I desired he might be desired to walk in, when, to my surprise, Mr. Bennet, who I knew in a moment, from a singular twist of his nose, entered my room.

"You are doctor ——?" he said.—"I am."

"Then, sir, I have one question to put to you."—"Have you?" said I. "Now you are here, Mr. Bennet, I have a great many to put to you."

"Are these your gloves, sir?" he said, throwing my gloves on the table.—"Yes, sir, they are."

"Then, sir, I have come to horsewhip you, in case you refuse me the satisfaction of a gentleman."—"Mr. Bennet," said I, "you are a fool!"

"What, sir!"—"A fool, sir; for you don't look before you leap. You want me to fight a duel, without asking the least explanation of my appearance at your house."

"I want no explanation, sir. The circumstances explain themselves."

"But, nevertheless, I am willing to look over your very intemperate manner, and to explain to you the cause of my appearance at your house, if you will take a chair."

"D—n your chair, sir," said he. "Answer me in one word. Will you meet me when and where our respective friends may point out?"—"No."

"You will not!"—"I am happy to say I am far better engaged."

"Then you must take the consequences."

So saying, he pulled a horsewhip from under his coat; but I was young, and tolerably strong, so I sprang upon him on the instant, and brought him to the floor, where I easily wrested the whip from him, and threw it on the fire.

"Mr. Bennet," I said, "you are making yourself very ridiculous, and I am sorry to see you in this situation. I can satisfactorily, so far as your honour and my own is concerned, explain to you the cause of my presence in your house."

I then hastily related to him all the circumstances, of which the reader is aware, and concluded by saying,—

"Now, sir, all I have to request of you is, to leave my house, and send me my hat."

"Sir," he said, "I beg your pardon."—"Granted," said I.

"Will you allow me your acquaintance?"—"Certainly, Mr. Bennet; sit down."

He sat down with a deep sigh, and said,—

"Sir, I am the unhappiest of men. Fourteen years ago, I married the woman of my choice, and one in every way worthy of such a choice. We lived a life of uninterrupted happiness together. My wife bore one child—a girl—and then, as she fell into a very bad state of health indeed, we were, much against our inclination, compelled to send it to nurse with my wife's sister—a woman I never liked. Well, sir, the child seemed to thrive and do well for some time; when one day I found my wife in tears. The reason was soon told—our child had died suddenly, in some of those spasmodic complaints incidental to teething.

"I was inconsolable. For a week I scarcely eat or drank; but time at length assuaged the violence of my grief, and I began once again to mingle with my fellow-creatures, and to feel an interest in the affairs of the world.

"My grief, however, remained, although it had calmed down to a more sober feeling. But the most remarkable circumstance connected with the whole affair, was the conduct of my wife, who seemed to forget the loss of her child completely, and with the exception of occasional fits of gloomy despondency, she was ever in good spirits.

"I often spoke to her about our loss; but she always answered in such words of resignation as I never yet heard come from the lips of a mother, however unreasonable they may be. Well, sir, time wore on; we had no more children; and it seemed, as I recovered from my grief at the death of my child, and resumed my usual habits, my wife gradually sank beneath the pressure of some hidden grief. She scarcely ever sleeps; and when she does, she is sure to start awake with cries for mercy. She remains for whole hours together weeping; and as yet I have not been able to induce her to tell me the reason of her strange conduct."

"Your situation is a distressing one, Mr. Bennet," said I, "but it may arise from some incipient mental disease, which might yield to medical treatment, if taken soon enough."

"I do not think she is insane," he replied. "I have a dreadful fear, from her muttering in her sleep the name of her sister, that she has been induced by her to engage in some transactions which now, in her stings of conscience, is bringing with it its own punishment."

"Have you any idea of what that transaction can be?"

"None."

"What is her sister?"

"She has a small property, which she ekes out by taking a child to nurse. At the time she had ours, she likewise had a very weakly little thing, who was the heiress to an earldom."

"Indeed."

"Yes. The Earl and Countess of Barrowcliff were advised to send their child to some cottage in the country, in preference to the costly nursery they would have provided for it. They let my sister, at a very high salary, have the care of the infant, which was the same age as our own little one, within a week or so."

"And both the children died?"

"No; ours, the healthy child, died. The weak young scion of nobility lived to bless her parents."

"That frequently happens," said I. "There is no counting upon the lives or constitutions of infants for a day."

"What would you advise me to do, doctor?"

"Why, the best thing would be, if you could, to get a clear statement from your wife as to what troubles her, and then take some measures thereupon. It may be, after all, some mere trifle acting upon a nervous system, and dressed up in imaginary horrors merely by a diseased fancy."

"Heaven send it may be so," he said. "But I fear she will not confide in me. Will you do me the favour to call again?"

"I—don't much mind," said I.

"You may depend upon nothing disagreeable occurring, because I look upon all that ensued before as arising from her extreme nervous terror at my finding you. Now, if you will call when I am out, as if you had made the visit from your own thought, she may possibly be induced to put confidence in you."

"Very well," said I. "You can tell me what hour you will not be at home, and I will call upon Mrs. Bennet."

"This afternoon," he said. "Any time before six o'clock."

"I will call then," said I, "at three, and meet you where you please afterwards."

"If you walk down the road," he said, "I will meet you between Grove Villa and Camden Town."

With this understanding we separated, Mr. Bennet leaving me with a great deal of curiosity concerning what could cause the mysterious and inexplicable conduct of Mrs. Bennet.

* * * * *

For the remainder of the day I could not get out of my head the mysterious Mrs. Bennet, and I teased myself with a thousand conjectures as to what could be the cause of her singular conduct. Three o'clock, however, was at length near at hand, and I walked to the Hampstead-road, to keep my appointment with Mr. Bennet.

A little distance beyond the turning which leads up to Chalk-farm I met him, and could see by his countenance that he had no good news to tell me concerning his wife.

After we had exchanged civilities, he said,—

"Mrs. Bennet remains shut up in her own room, and will scarcely speak to any one. I fear much that her mind is affected."

"Well, well," I said, "do not torture yourself by conjectures. I will do my best to get the secret cause of her deep melancholy from her, and I think I am likely to succeed. I intend to prescribe for some harmless medicines, which, I dare say, assisted by her own imagination, will compose her mind considerably; and then, for the sake of further relief, she will, perhaps, confide in me."

"My mind misgives me very much," said Mr. Bennet, "that something terrible will arise from all this; she has occasionally repeated the name of her sister and of our lost child, evidently with so much mental agony that I cannot but think the key to the mystery will be found in connexion with them."

"When shall I see you?" said I. "My visit cannot be a very long one, because I must be in town again by six o'clock; but if you will wait anywhere about here for me, I will call for you as I come back."

He pointed to a house of entertainment in the vicinity, and saying that he would take a private room there and leave his name at the bar, we parted, on the understanding that I should call on my return from my visit.

I must own that I did not feel very comfortable when I rang at the garden-gate of Mr. Bennet's little villa, but as I had promised, I resolved to go through with the adventure.

The same servant who had admitted me on the former occasion now answered my summons, and upon my telling her that I had called to see her mistress, she showed me into the parlour while she went to acquaint her with my visit.

In a few minutes she returned to say that her mistress would be glad to see me, and I was conducted up stairs to the same room in which my former interview with Mrs. Bennet had taken place.

"I have called, madam," said I, "to make a friendly visit, and hope I find you better."

"Better—better," she repeated, with a wailing voice that bespoke the utter abandonment of her heart. "How can I ever hope to be better? No—no. Have you brought me some drug that will make me sleep?"

"Yes," said I, for I was prepared for her then, and had made up some bread pills rolled in magnesia, in order to see if her imagination would make her sleep after taking them, supposing them to contain an opiate.

"Then I may know some peace; but, tell me, will they make me dream, because, you know, that would be dreadful?"

"They will not, Mrs. Bennet; but even should they, why cannot you expect pleasant dreams?"

She shuddered as she said:—

"I expect pleasant dreams! Do the damned enjoy pleasant dreams? No—no!—There are no dreams but those of horror to me. All I hope for is a temporary oblivion for thought."

"Now, Mrs. Bennet," said I, solemnly and seriously, "listen to me. We physicians can do a great deal, when we know what really affects our patients. We can restore the mind to its healthy functions frequently as well as the body, but there is one condition with which we are as likely, and, in fact, more likely to do good than harm, and that is unreserved confidence on the part of our patients."

She was silent, for some moments, and sat with her hands clasped before her, glaring at me in a truly fearful manner. Then she spoke in a low hollow voice, saying,—

"You would have my secret, but I dare not tell you. No, no, no. God have mercy on me, but man can have none. I am nearly mad now, but to tell that fearful tale would unsettle my reason for ever—for ever!"

"I think you are wrong," said I. "Confidence in any one relieves the mind, and you must be assured that what is told to a physician is kept sacredly secret."

"No—no!" she shrieked. "Tempt me not to my ruin—to shame—to disgrace—to—the scaffold!"

I was unprepared for this, and started as I repeated the word—

"Scaffold? Surely I misunderstand, Mrs. Bennet. You cannot mean that ——"

"Hush," she cried, "hush! Another word of suspicion, and I will take your life or my own! Am I not sufficiently punished? Oh, Heavens! am I not punished enough? Where is my child that now would have been so great a joy to me? Oh, save me—save me from the fiend that even now is gnawing at my heart!"

"It is my duty to tell you," said I, "that you will make yourself seriously ill if you go on in this way."

"Man, man," she shrieked; "you know not what you say."

"No physician can visit you, madam, if you give way to these paroxysms; I must really at once take my leave of you if you do not become calmer."

I rose as I spoke, and with a grave air walked to the door; she saw me place my hand upon the lock before she spoke again, and then called me back, saying—

"I will be calm, sir. Do not desert me now, or I shall do myself some violence. If you have one spark of pity for the most miserable creature that ever drew the breath of life, aid me to procure some trifling forgetfulness of my sorrows."

I returned, as in fact I had quite intended to do upon the least possible excuse, or none at all, for my only object was to alarm her, if possible, into a confession of what was the secret cause of grief that preyed upon her spirits, and drove her to the wretched mental state she was in.

"Well, Mrs. Bennet," I said, "I trust you will confide to me then fully your grief. By so doing you will make a confidential friend, who will not only advise you to the best of his power, but keep your secret, if it be necessary, inviolate."

"I dare not—I dare not," she moaned. "Doctor, did you ever commit a crime, which in the ignorance of your heart you fancied would contribute to your happiness, and then found in its results nought but misery?"

"I cannot, thank Heaven, charge myself with any serious offence," said I.

She sighed deeply, as she muttered,

"Then die soon and be happy—die soon—die soon."

"You will confide in me?" said I.

"Not now—not now," she replied. "I will think—let me sleep first—let me know the dear comfort of rest, and then in my thankfulness to you I may tell all. Give me first the means of rest."

"Well," I said, "these are the pills which I believe will produce that effect, and I will call again upon you as early as I can spare time to-morrow."

"Thank you, thank you," she said. "For Heaven's sake avoid my husband."

"Be at rest upon that head," said I. "Good day to you, and remember your promise of communicating all to morrow."

"I will think—I will think," she muttered.

I then left the villa, and made the best of my way to Mr. Bennet, who was very anxiously expecting me. To him I related the particulars of the very unsatisfactory interview I had had with his wife, and when I concluded, he said,—

"Now doctor, that you have had a second interview with her, what is your real opinion as to the cause of mental inquietude?"

"Why, Mr. Bennet," said I, "my opinion may not please you, but I cannot help thinking that your wife has really something on her mind of a serious character; and from a review of her past life, I should say you were much more able than I to come to some guess, at all events, with regard to the nature of it."

"There is nothing in her past life," he replied, "that I am at all aware of which could induce any criminality. Her sister was a scheming immoral woman, and at one time, to my regret, had a considerable share of influence over my wife's mind; but that was years ago, and I never knew of any circumstance which could have embroiled Mrs. Bennet in anything disagreeable."

"She is not insane," said I; "there are peculiar symptoms in connexion with insanity, which cannot be mistaken."

"I should have said she was from one reason only," replied Mr. Bennet, "and that is her very strange and anomalous conduct on the occasion of the death of our child."

"What conduct was that?"

"Why, sometimes when open to observation, she would appear involved in the deepest grief, and at others I have entered the room suddenly unawares in which she was, and found her capitally amused by some trivial thing, which would have passed by a mind really with grief oppressed quite unheeded."

"Well, that certainly does look symptomatic of insanity, but still I adhere to my opinion, and at all events as the case is a curious one, I will attend to it with attention if you think proper."

"I feel much beholden to you, doctor," he said, "and when you visit her to-morrow, I hope you will not think it too much trouble to meet me, as you have done to-day, here in the same place."

"I certainly will meet you," said I, "and am not a little anxious to know whether her imagination will really cause her to sleep to-night, under the impression that she has taken a powerful narcotic."

With this Mr. Bennet and I parted, my mind being very much engrossed with the really singular case, and anticipating my visit on the morrow to my strange patient with considerable interest.

*　　*　　*　　*　　*

I did not know how long I had been asleep, or what the hour was, but some time during the night that followed the day on which I had the interview with Mr. Bennet, which I have just recorded, I was awakened by a knocking at my chamber door, which at first I thought must be a continuation of some dream, and paid no attention to; but the voice of Martha, the romantic maid of all-work, convinced me I was awake.

"Sir, sir," she cried; "sir, here's a adventure."

"A what?"

"A adventure, sir. It's raining uncommon."

"Hang the rain," cried I. "What do you mean by awakening me, by telling me it's raining?"

"But she won't go, sir."

"Who are you talking about?"

"Why, didn't I tell you, sir, it's a lady, sir, as says she must see you, and won't go away nohow. She's dreadful mysterious, sir, and 'minds me of the 'Spirit of the Haunted Hogshead; or, the Wet Spectre of Wimbledon.'"

"What are you muttering about," I cried, as I jumped out of bed; "I suppose a patient wants me?"—"Oh, dear! no, sir."—"Who then?"—"It's a dreadful impatient, sir."

I knew perfectly well that Martha was quite incapable of punning, or I should have rushed out, and almost knocked her down for perpetrating so atrocious a one as that she had unconsciously given utterance to. As it was, I commenced getting into my clothes as quickly as possible, not over well pleased at being called up, more especially as I was frequently dragged from my bed in the same manner, and got no fee after all. However, I called out to Martha, that I should be down stairs in a few moments, and while I was dressing, I heard the rain pattering away at a great rate, which did not tend to ameliorate my feelings, as I thought of the possibility of a long trudge through it.

In less than five minutes I opened my chamber-door, and descended to my parlour. A dim bed-room candle was burning on the table, and with her head leaning upon her hands, was sitting a female figure. She looked up at my entrance, and regarded me with a glance of awful dejection. It was Mrs. Bennet.

I started back in amazement, for certainly of all the unexpected visitors I could have thought of, she was the most unexpected.

"You are surprised to see me here," she said, in a low, hollow voice.

"I am, madam," said I; "but pray do not mind that. Can I be of any service to you?"

She saw that I wished to soothe her, and with an impatient gesture, she said,

"Peace, peace. I am not a child or a maniac, although how soon I may be the latter, I know not. Tell me what fiend put it in your head to bring me that medicine?"

"The sleeping medicine?"

"Aye," she exclaimed, with sudden vehemence. "I did sleep, but what awful drug was there, to drive me mad with dreams of blood? Oh, God! such dreams that I would not sleep again for the universe. No, not for my salvation. I am nearly mad—nearly mad."

"Madam," said I, "it is out of our power to produce such an effect. On my conscience, I swear to you there was nothing in the pills to lay hold of the imagination in the manner you speak of. Mrs. Bennet, you are, I assure you, much mistaken."

"No, no!" she screamed, with vehemence. "Even now the images of the dream haunt me. It was a dream of retribution. I saw the blackened face of the corpse. Plainly I saw it, as I now see you. Oh, spare me such another awful dream. Let medicine work its utmost now to save me from ever again closing an eye in slumber. No more sleep—no more sleep."

"I will get you something," said I, "that will do you good."

I was anxious to get out of the room to send for her husband, and when I reached the passage I called to Martha, who answered me from the regions below, and told her to go to the door and promise any one five shillings to go to Grove Villa, Hampstead-road, and tell Mr. Bennet to come to me directly, for Mrs. Bennet had found her way to my house.

"Dare to send for him," exclaimed Mrs. Bennet, suddenly seizing my arm, for she had followed me unknown from the parlour, "and I will do more murder!"

I was, I confess, alarmed at her vehemence; but I felt that my only chance of subduing her was by an exhibition of firmness; so turning to her I said, in a voice of assumed anger,—

"Madam, I will send for whom I like, and if you talk in that outrageous manner I will have you placed immediately under restraint. Do you imagine that I am to have my actions controlled by you?"

My manner seemed to awe her, for she went back to the parlour, muttering to herself, in a low wretched tone,—

"The dream—the dream; the awful dream of retribution! Oh, save me from sleep!"

"Now, Mrs. Bennet," I said, "listen to me as calmly as you can. You sent for me as a physician, and I have nothing to do with you or your past life. It is, however, quite evident to me that there is something on your mind which will always be more than sufficient to baffle the utmost exertions of your medical advisers. From this moment, therefore, I beg to decline, most distinctly, attending upon you any more."

She looked in my face with a strange expression, and then clasping her hands, she said, in a hoarse whisper,—

"I will tell you all. I will place my life in your hands, and tell you all."

"Your life, Mrs. Bennet?"—"Yes—oh, God! yes! Do not interrupt me. I seem just as if I was compelled to tell you My child, my beautiful child! how I doated on it! I was sinful in my love, for it made me forget Heaven. My sister had it to wean at the same time that she was nursing young Lady Borrowcliffe, the infant heir to the earldom of that name. My child was healthy, but the young lady was a weak sickly thing, and its noble parents never thought to rear it. Oh, Heaven! it was my sister who started the dreadful idea. It appears she had been promised a large gratuity in case she succeeded in weaning the young noble. The eyes and general appearance of the children were alike. Can you not guess the awful truth—oh, can you not spare me the dreadful recital, and guess my dreadful crime?"

"Indeed," said I, "I would not think of hazarding guesses in such a case; I might do you some grievous injustice."

"No—no—no," she shuddered, "that were impossible. I am a murderess!"

I made no reply, and after a moment's pause, she continued,—

"One day when I went to see my child I found that young Lady Borrowcliffe was dying, or appeared to be so. Her parents were to visit her that day, although her severe illness had come on so suddenly they did not know of it. Then my sister whispered an awful suggestion in my ear, to the effect that if the scion of nobility was dead, and my child could be passed off upon the parents as their own, it would reap all the benefit of its noble and wealthy connexion, while she, as its nurse, would be amply provided for. She painted to me in glowing colours what a delight it would be to me to know that my child, upon whom I doated so fondly, was one of England's richest ladies, loaded with honour—the theme, perhaps, of a nation's adoration! She pointed out the likeness between the children—a likeness which dress would perfect; and I was cruel enough to listen."

"Pray go on, Mrs. Bennet," said I; "depend upon it you will not repent your confession."

"You do not guess all," she said. "We—we placed a pillow over the face of the sick child—we murdered it!"

I rose from my chair and looked at the woman with perfect horror; for I thought, from the tenor of her story, that after all it would turn out that she was merely guilty of making an exchange of the children.

"Aye," she cried, "shrink from me—loathe me, for I am indeed a wretch to be detested. I tell you we killed the child—its rich apparel was placed upon my infant. The earl and countess came; they were overjoyed to see their child, as they supposed it, looking so well. The countess said that, but for the eyes she should not have known it, and I was for a time foolish enough to be pleased."

"Your husband knows nothing of this?" said I.

"Nothing—nothing!" she replied. "He was imposed upon by being told that the child was dead. I knew he never for one moment would have sanctioned the fraud. Time passed on, and then conscience, that horrible monitor, began to strike to my affrighted ears, my crime. I became restless —unhappy—agonised; I could not sleep; my solitude was peopled ever with frightful shapes. Then what I had never once thought of occurred—my child was taken away by the earl and countess, and I have never since seen it. You now know all. Heaven help me—Heaven help me!"

I felt quite at a loss to know what to do, and when Mrs. Bennet had finished her frightful narrative, I continued gazing at her for some moments in silence thoroughly astonished and bewildered.

She trembled now so excessively, that I became seriously alarmed at the condition she was in.

"Mrs. Bennet," I said, "repentance may yet open for you the gates of that Heaven whose mercy is boundless."

"Heaven for me!" she shrieked. "No, no, my crime is too terrible for hope; I am damned—lost for ever! Oh, what agony is mine!"

"Tell me," said I, "is your sister alive?"

"She is—she is! Heaven help her! She tempted me to do the horrible deed. Can I make any reparation? Oh, tell me how to fly from my own affrighted soul!"

There came at that moment a loud ring at my night bell, and I moved to the door.

"Stop! stop!" she cried; "that may be my husband. Swear to me, by all your dearest hopes of a hereafter, that what I have told you shall remain locked in your own breast!"

"I cannot take such an oath," said I. "I pray you be calm. Your story has so amazed me that I know not what to say to you."

I heard now the door opened, and Mr. Bennet's voice in anxious accents inquiring for me.

"'Tis he! 'tis he!" she gasped. "Oh, save me from him!—one word will kill me. Save me! save me!"

"Hush, hush, for Heaven's sake hush!" said I. "I will return to you in a few moments. Remain here quietly."

I with some difficulty released myself from her hold and went into the passage just in time to take Mr. Bennet by the hand and lead him into the back parlour.

"My wife," he said, "is she here?"

"She is. Be calm and you shall know all."

"Good Heaven, she is dead!" he cried, alarmed by my tone and manner. "Suspense is terrible. Tell me at once, doctor."

"You are wrong, Mr. Bennet; but —— "

Bang went the street door at this moment, and I flew into the passage and thence into the front room—Mrs. Bennet was gone.

"Good God! what has happened?" cried the distracted husband; "give me some explanation."

"Your wife was here, and has now left for home," said I. "You can follow her or remain here and listen to what I have to tell you, just as you please."

"I will return—I will return," he cried, as he rushed from the house.

* * * * *

What to do, or how to act, in the peculiar situation in which I now found myself, quite puzzled me, and I wished over and over again, now that it was too late, that I had never attempted to gain the confidence of Mrs. Bennet, but had rather have been ignorant of so uncomfortable a secret as that I was now burthened with.

The remainder of the night I passed in anxious thought; finally, the only conclusion I could come to was to shift as far as I could the onus of the future proceedings off my shoulders, by communicating the affair to Mr. Bennet, and leaving him to take what steps in it he might think proper.

I rose by the first streak of daylight, determining to see him before the business of the day commenced, if possible; and swallowing a hasty breakfast, I was upon the point of sallying forth, when my servant, as she brought me my boots, said,—

"If you please, sir, the milkman says as there's been a body picked up at London Bridge."

"I suppose he said so, whether I please or not," said I. "When was it?"

The words were scarcely out of my lips when a hurried knock at the street door made me, in my nervousness after the proceedings of the night, drop the egg I was eating and start up from my chair with a suddenness that produced a scream from the girl.

The knock was immediately repeated.

"Open the door directly," cried I, and she flew to obey the summons.

Pale, haggard, and exhausted, Mr. Bennet staggered into my room, and sank with a deep groan into the first vacant chair.

"She is dead—she is dead!" he cried.

"Mr. Bennet," exclaimed I.

"Yes, yes—she is dead!"

"Mr. Bennet," I said, slowly and calmly, "you are, I see, full of grief at the loss of your wife. Be consoled. I have that to tell you which will make you thank Heaven she is no more."

"Her body was picked up at London Bridge," he said. "In some frantic moment she has drowned herself. Oh, Heavens! that it should come to this."

I saw that he did not heed what I said, so I resolved to proceed with the story his wife had told me, never doubting but it would soon attract his utmost attention. He listened at first listlessly; then, with growing interest, and by the time I had concluded, his feelings were wrought up to the highest pitch of intense interest and excitement.

"Can this be true?" he exclaimed.

"I believe every word of it," said I; "you may now do just what you please."

"My child!—my child!" he cried; "my child lives—my beautiful child." * * * * *

Little more remains to be told. The sister, who had tempted Mrs. Bennet to the commission of the dreadful crime of murder, suffered the penalty of her guilt on her own confession,—she was executed. The grief and consternation of the Earl and Countess of Borrowcliffe were excessive when they learnt the truth; but they would not part with their adopted daughter, although she changed her name to Miss Bennet, and visited her father frequently, who did not long survive the shock he had sustained by a knowledge of his wife's guilt.

ELLEN HARGRAVE;

OR, THE ELOPEMENT.

How truly pitiable it is when talent and genius are arrayed against the simplicity of innocence—when those rare qualities—given to their much favoured possessors for noble purposes, are diverted from their proper channels, and made to pander to vice and iniquity.

I was sitting one morning in my study, culling from my notes some of the most interesting records of my diary, when my servant came to tell me that a young lady wished to see me.

"She seems, sir, very ill," he said, "and in great pain."

"Indeed," said I; "where is she?"

"In the patient's room, sir. She is as pale as death."

I immediately rose, and hastened to the room where she was, and there, half lying on a sofa, with her face hidden in her hands, I saw a young and apparently delicately-formed female. She was sobbing piteously, and scarcely heeded my entrance.

I went up to her, and said,—

"My name is ——. You wished to see me?"

"Oh, help me—help me!" she cried, vehemently, falling on her knees at my feet. "Save me, for the love of God—oh, save me from eternal perdition. I—I have taken poison!"

"Poison?"

"Yes—yes. Even now 'tis burning through my veins like liquid fire. Oh! save me, doctor—save me! I thought to end all my miseries, and to rush to the oblivion of the grave; but now, now—oh, God! my guilty soul shrinks in horror from death. Give me life—life—life."

"For Heaven's sake," said I, "waste no words in explanation now, but tell me what you have taken?"

"Arsenic—arsenic," she gasped.

"I immediately rang the bell, and when my servant appeared, I said,—

"Bring me eggs, and soap and water here immediately."

Accustomed to obey me promptly, the man instantly left the room, when there came such a thundering knock at my street-door, that I thought it must have broken in.

"Never mind the door," cried I, "bring me what I have ordered you."

"Yes, sir," said my man, and away he ran; at the instant that another appeal, more loud than the former one, was made upon my knocker.

"Save me, save me!" the young lady kept crying, "I dare not die now. Oh, I cannot die!"

"Everything shall be done for you," said I, "that the skill of man can suggest. Wait one moment."

In no very patient mood I ran to the street-door to open it myself, and scold the person who knocked so furiously, and just succeeded in opening it as another knock was about being administered.

"How dare you?" cried I, and then I paused, for the death-like paleness of the young man who staggered into my passage stopped me from saying more.

"Good God!" I cried, "what's the matter?"

"She—is here?" he gasped.

"Who?—who?"

"A young person—I saw her go in. She has taken poison."

"George!" shrieked the young lady, as she rushed from my parlour, and fell into the arms of the young man.

"Ellen—Ellen!" he cried frantically, "is it true that you still live?"

"I—am dying—dying!" she gasped. "Tell—tell my father and mother ——"

She would have fallen on the floor if I had not caught her in my arms. I carried her at once into the parlour, and there was my servant with the remedies I had directed him to procure; but they were of no avail in her present state, and with my utmost exertions it was full ten minutes before I could restore her to consciousness.

"As you value your life," said I, handing to her the antidote I had now thoroughly prepared, "take this draught—drink—drink."

"I burn—I burn!" she cried; "oh, heavens, I burn! George, forgive me—say you forgive me."

"Ellen—Ellen, you will kill me," he cried.—"Drink—drink," said I.

She gave a convulsive shudder, and fell back upon the sofa. I saw that there was no hope—she was dying. My looks, I suppose, told the melancholy truth, for the young man she called George burst into tears, crying,—

"Save her—save her, sir—oh, surely something can be done?"

"While poison is in the stomach we can do much," said I; "but this case has gone too far."

With a deep groan she now drew up her limbs as if in great agony, then a damp cold dew came upon her brow; she gasped convulsively for breath, and then all was over.

There was an awful silence of a moment or two. The young man seemed stupified by the suddenness of the event. He glanced wildly around him like a maniac; then clutching his hands above his head, he shouted in a tone that made me shrink from him—

"Vengeance! vengeance! I will have his life!"

"My good sir," said I, trying to stop him, "allow me, if you please. I ——"

"A thousand arms should not stay me," he cried; "I will have his life. I will have his life!"

"But, sir, before you go, permit me to ask who you are, and who this young person is?"

"Ellen, Ellen, I will revenge you," he shrieked, not at all heeding my question. "I will crush him to the earth, were he ten times what he is. Oh, Heavens! have we thus met? Is this the end of the bright dream that lit my youthful fancy? Save me from madness!"

I stood between him and the door, as I said,—

"Compose yourself, sir, and tell me who you are. What am I to do with the body of this young lady?"

He rushed to the corpse, and seizing one of the cold, lifeless hands, he called upon her frantically to speak to him. He conjured her by every tender epithet to say but one word—to tell him she lived, and would live for him. He kissed the pale lips, and then, with a cry of despair, he rushed past me, and was out of the house before I could interpose to prevent him from going.

* * * * *

My position was anything but an agreeable one. Here was a poisoned young lady lying upon my sofa, and without the least means of ascertaining who she was. I rang the bell hastily, and when my servant came, I said,—

"Thomas, run down the street, and see if you can catch the young man who was here. If you do, detain him anyhow, till I get my hat and follow you."

Thomas ran out, and in a few moments I ran after him, but the young man was gone, and we were compelled to come back as wise as we went.

"Upon my word," said I, "this is as awkward a predicament as any man could well be placed in."

There lay the body—a hideous spectacle—upon my sofa, and the hour was close at hand when my usual patients would arrive.

"Thomas," said I, "you must assist me to carry this body somewhere else."

"The—the body, sir?" said Thomas. "I—I—oh, yes."

While Thomas said, "Oh, yes," he backed towards the door, with an evident repugnance to the job.

"Come, come," said I, "you must not have any of these foolish scruples; I cannot carry it by myself. It must be removed somewhere till I can see the parish authorities, and have it taken from the house, so do you take the feet; between us we must carry it into the back parlour."

"I—I—never took hold o' the feet of a *corpses* in all my life," stammered Thomas.

"But you must now; so come, be quick."

Thomas with great reluctance assisted me to lift the corpse from my sofa, and we got comfortably enough into the passage with it, when a knock at the street-door so startled Thomas, that he immediately dropped his end of the burthen, exclaiming,—

"Oh, lord, sir, what's that?"

"Why a knock at the door, to be sure," said I; "what a foolish fellow you are."

By dragging the body along, I now got it myself into the back parlour, just as Thomas opened the door. I heard a voice ask for me, and the visitor was shown into the parlour so recently occupied by the ghastly object I had removed.

In a moment my servant brought me a card, on which was written Lord Mandelholme, and informed me that it was given him by the gentleman in the parlour.

I went at once, expecting his lordship had come to me for professional advice; but when I entered the room, I was struck by the peculiar paleness of his face, and the agitation that seemed to pervade every limb of him.

"Doctor," he said, "although unknown to you, I have heard your name very frequently."

"I trust I may be of service to your lordship," said I; "let me beg of you to be seated."

"My visit," he continued, speaking evidently with difficulty, "is not a professional one. Do you know a family named Sarsfield?"

"Sarsfield," said I. "Yes. Some years ago—at least seven, I should think—I knew intimately a family of that name. They went to settle at Boulogne permanently, since which, my professional engagements have prevented me seeing them. I know them very well indeed."

"At that time," he continued, "there were two young children—the one a little over ten years of age, and the other younger."

"There were, and Ellen, the elder, was as beautiful a child as ever ——"

He sank into a chair with a deep groan,

"What is the matter, sir," said I; "are you ill?"

He looked up at me with an expression of face I shall never forget, and, in a hollow tone, he said,—

"Doctor, you have read Shakspere, no doubt, often attentively, and I may say in the words of one of his bright creations, 'Who can minister to a mind diseased?' I am ill, but it is a sickness of the soul. I have come to say, that should a young lady come here, and announce herself as Ellen Hargrave, that is Ellen Sarsfield."

"Indeed, sir, and under what circumstances do you expect her to come here?"

"She recollects your address as a friend of her father, and might come to you as a mediator. She was seduced by—by —one who ——"

"What!" cried I, "Ellen Sarsfield, the beautiful creature who a few short years ago was the darling and the pet of a large circle—she, torn from her fond father's heart by a villain? Why—why, sir, she must still be quite a girl. Good Heavens! you do, indeed, both surprise and afflict me."

"Let me have some water, sir," he said, faintly.

I rang the bell, and he was soon accommodated with some, into which I dropped a little ammonia, which recovered him from the faintness which seemed to be coming over him.

"Doctor," he continued, "if you have five minutes' time to spare I will tell you all; but should she come here, you shall know her by her long hair; it is worn low, and wound up in it is a small thread of silver."

I started from my seat as at once the conviction came across me that poor Ellen Sarsfield's corpse lay even now in my back parlour. He saw my emotion, and likewise rose with a face of alarm.

"Whoever tore her from her home," cried I, "has a fearful account to settle."

"'Twas I—'twas I," cried Mandelholme; "say what you will to me. Upbraid me as you will, my spirit is now broken, and I can bear all. I took her from her happy home—I tore her from the encircling arms of those who loved her."

"Good Heavens! what inducement could you offer to her to lead so horrible a life?"

"Marriage; I offered her marriage; but spare me. She swore this morning she would take poison, but that first she would come to you to leave a message for her parents. Since she left me, my heart has been wrung by fiends. I am a man of sorrow. Oh! should she come here, tell her I will fulfil all promises; tell her she shall be mine, and that the mock marriage which deceived her shall be succeeded by a real one, and she shall smile again."

"A mock marriage, sir!" said I; "so it was by that most vile stratagem that poor Ellen was undone. No wonder, sir, your heart is full of bitterness; but you do not know the worst. Heaven extend its mercy to you. But were I Ellen's father I should have to pray for patience. Ellen Sarsfield is now ——"

A tremendous knock at my door at this moment startled me, and made Lord Mandelholme fall back in his seat, looking like an apparition. In a moment I flew to the window, and saw what I did not know before, namely, that a carriage of Lord Mendelholme's was at my door.

As I was looking from the window, Thomas opened the door, and in an instant the young man who had ran off so suddenly, and whom the dying girl had called George, came into my room.

"Where is he?" he cried; "where is the seducer—suborner of justice—the foe of the innocent, the virtuous, and the beautiful. Ha, the villain!"

He strode towards Lord Mandelholme, who rose with a cry of terror, while I threw myself in between them, crying,—

"Hold—hold, gentlemen! I cannot have my house converted into an arena for your quarrels. Peace, sir, peace!"

"Nay, sir," cried the last arrival, "come not between me and this man. You know him not. By arts as base as villain ever imagined, he tore from the arms of those who loved her as fair a piece of nature's workmanship as ever blessed the world. You have seen her, sir—you know her. Let me get at the villain. I will tear his black heart from his breast!"

"Keep him off—keep him off!" said Lord Mandelholme: "I would not have his blood upon my hands, but I will defend my own life."

"You may well do so," cried his opponent; "for no man should be more afraid to die."

"Gentlemen," said I, "I will not have violence here. Go both of you into the street, if you must fight, but it is most unseemly here."

Lord Mandelholme drew a pistol from his pocket, as he said,—

"I will defend my life—I will defend my life."

"Fiend," cried he, whom the unhappy girl had called George; "fiend—monster in human form! you have made many hearts desolate, and I will not now be baulked in my revenge. Nay, it is justice—a more sacred name. I too am armed. Here are weapons."

He struggled so much with me, that I saw there was no chance of holding him much longer; therefore, as a last resource to stop bloodshed, I suddenly let him go, and in a moment throwing open the folding doors which divided my two parlours, I cried,—

"Behold! let that sight disarm you both in this house. Profane not death by a contest in its awful presence."

On the table lay the corpse, as I had placed it, and, for a moment, they both stood as if paralysed. Then Lord Mandelholme, with a loud cry, strove to leave the parlour by the door leading from the passage, but his opponent darted after him, and, ere he could accomplish his purpose, dragged him back again. Before I could interfere, Mandelholme fired his pistol; in an instant there was another report—a loud terrific shriek, and the noble seducer lay weltering in his blood.

"Good Heavens! young man," I cried, "what have you done?"

"Taken wild justice," he cried—"revenge! The betrayer of gentle innocence and virtue will betray no more; let him die. Touch him not—I am the avenger; let him die—let him die!"

I hurried to the side of the wounded man, and, raising his head, I saw that the shot had entered somewhere near his ear, and most probably lodged about the back of the neck. His eye, though, told me he was dying; there was no hope.

"Is he dead?" asked the other.

"No," said I; "but he soon will be; he is dying."

The young man then dropped the pistol which he held in his hand, and walking into the next room, he, with a deep sob, approached the corpse of the unhappy girl. He kissed convulsively the pale face.

"Helen, Helen," he said, "you are avenged! Rest, rest, pure spirit. He who turned your gaze from the light of Heaven is no more."

I was so bewildered that I could take no steps to prevent him from leaving the house, although, as I was told afterwards, it was unquestionably my duty to detain him. He, however, made good his escape, my servants, who had been startled at the shots, and were collected round the parlour door, fancying that he had gone for assistance. When I heard the street door shut, I somewhat recovered from my mental stupor.

"Fetch the police," I cried; "stop that young man."

Before any one could stir, Mandelholme uttered a faint groan, and then, in weak, painful accents, said,—

"No, no, let him go; I am dying."

"Tell me, sir, for God's sake, where your friends may be communicated with," said I.

He shook his head, and then, after a pause, said,—

"Listen. I think Heaven will give me strength for one purpose, if for no other—to confess my wickedness, and pray even now for pardon—for mercy."

He paused, and a quantity of blood in his mouth evidently stopped his utterance. I beckoned to the servants to assist me, and we raised his head, placing under it a sofa cushion, when, after a few moments, he again spoke,—

"That still form, which even in death is so very beautiful, was my victim. Look on her now that she is robbed of the intelligence of vitality, and you may guess what she was by what she now is. When I first saw her, she was young, virtuous, lovely, and I coveted to make her miserable. I sought her destruction, but her virtues rose ever before me like a battlement, which there was no surmounting, and—and—as I could not woo her to sin, I turned her best feelings into weapons against her, and told her I would marry her secretly, and then, as her father's circumstances were indifferent, that she should have the pleasure of relieving him, by the agreeable surprise of telling him she was the wife of a nobleman, and possessed of unbounded means. She refused for a long time, but I had won enough of her affections to blind her judgment, and she at length consented."

He paused now again, and was evidently suffering the most acute pain. It was several minutes before he proceeded, and then his voice was much weaker, as he said,—

"She consented. A note was left with her father, and she eloped with me. We were married in London ——"

"Married!" said I.

"Yes, yes, a mock marriage. My valet was the mock priest; she believed herself my wife, and then she claimed my promise of returning the following day to her parents. By one excuse and another I put her off, and then I wrote a note to her parents as if from her, bidding them adieu for ever. The reply came. It did not suit me, for it was full of love and expostulations. I wrote an answer myself, imitating the handwriting as well as I could, and that plunged her in despair, for it harshly discarded her for ever. Well, she insisted upon going to throw herself at her father's feet. I entreated, I commanded, and finally I told her all. She rushed from my house, and—and there—she is, dead—dead! Oh, Heavens, have mercy upon me!"

He tossed his arms wildly in the air for some moments,

and then lay perfectly still, the only indication of life being an occasional low moan.

"Go to the next street," whispered I to my man, "and fetch M——, the surgeon."

Thomas ran off, and in less than ten minutes came back with the eminent practitioner I had named to him.

"A bad accident have you here, doctor?" he said.

"Yes; look at him, I fear——"

Mr.—— shook his head, after carefully examining the eyes of the dying man.

"No hope?" said I.

"None," was the reply.

Suddenly Mandelholme sat upright, and, stretching his arms up towards the ceiling, he cried,—

"Help, help! Helen, save me—save me!"

He gasped for utterance; a dull, rattling sound in his throat succeeded, and the seducer lay a corpse!

* * * *

Lord Mandelholme's friends took away his body, and Helen was interred in the nearest churchyard. The young avenger was never, to my knowledge, heard of again.

THE RESTORATION;

OR, INNOCENCE AND GUILT.

It does sometimes happen that, contrary to the dictum of Shakspere, the physician can "minister to a mind diseased," as well as administering such remedies for bodily ailment as lie within the province of his art.

The circumstance with which I am about to please myself, and I hope my readers, will show how from evil sometimes springs the greatest good, and how much we are mistaken occasionally in our estimate of human mischances, and what we call misfortunes.

During the early period of my professional career, I was compelled, as I have before hinted to my readers, to reside in lodgings, in consequence of my circumstances being rather straitened; and many scenes of mirth and sorrow, gaiety and gravity, smiles and tears, passed before my observation in the different places where, from time to time, I fixed my abode.

Among the most striking of these chequered passages of human life, if not the most striking of all, was the one which I have entitled as above.

It was in the year 17— that I went to lodge and partially board in the house of a widow, who, with three daughters, the eldest of whom was a very beautiful girl of seventeen, eked out a very precarious existence by letting her house to single gentlemen. Her name was Meriton; and certainly Mary Meriton, the daughter, was as amiable and lovely a girl as it was possible to imagine. I often now think of her as I used to see her, with her gentle, downcast eyes, and plain but simply becoming attire, gliding about the house like some benignant spirit, filling the widow's home with serenity and quiet joy. She was admired and respected by all who knew her, and her life was like a peaceful streamlet, wending its way along some smooth channel, with scarce a ripple to disturb the serenity of its onward march.

In an evil hour, however, there came to reside at the widow's a young man of flighty and frivolous habits—one of those beings who are more thoughtless than vicious, but who produce as much, if not more real mischief, than the really bad-hearted, because the latter are very soon found out, and people get upon their guard against their machinations; whereas, your good-hearted, thoughtless, devil-may-care people, are continually being trusted, and as continually behaving as badly as the vicious, with the best intentions in the world.

Such an one as I have described was Charles Langton. There was an air of open frankness and sincerity about him which was very taking, and irresistibly impressed you with a belief that he was a very good fellow indeed; and so he was in intention, and, if I may be excused for perpetrating a very old pun, I should say Charles Langton was a very *promising* young man, but his *performances* were quite different things.

It is said that people are fond of their opposites, and I am inclined to believe the saying is founded in truth—at least Mary Meriton was an example of it; for nothing could be well more opposite to her mild, quiet, truthful manner, than the rattling, rollicking, heedless, hand-over-head kind of ways of Charles Langton. Yet she loved him; and as quiet waters are ever the deepest, she loved him with a purity and intensity of affection that I often and often wished had been devoted to a more congenial object; for although from the first moment of his coming to the house he had evidently set his heart upon Mary—that is, as far as he could set his heart upon any one object—and regarded her with the greatest admiration, I thought, and so did Mary's mother, that he was very far from being calculated to become a domesticated husband, such as would have made a happy home for the gentle Mary.

With pain I watched the growing intimacy of the young people. I saw Mary hang, as it were, upon every word he spoke; and in the course of six months it was clear that she had irrevocably fixed her affections upon him.

At the request of Mrs. Meriton I made many and close inquiries concerning Mr. Langton, and the result was of a mixed character. He had good friends and wealthy connexions, was able to support a wife in quiet respectability; nobody said any ill of him, but several shook their heads, and hoped he would some day get a little steadier, and so on.

Now, to request a young lady violently in love to discard her lover because he is not steady enough to please elderly people, would be something like trying to coax a little pat of butter out of a dog's throat; so Mrs. Meriton was not so foolish as to attempt anything of the sort, but tried to make the best of a bad bargain.

Time passed on, until Charles and Mary's acquaintance had continued nearly twelve months, when one morning Mrs. Meriton came to my room with a face that had the marks of recent tears on it.

"Mr.——," she said, "Mary is married."

"Married!" cried I, with a jump.

"Yes; she has just now confessed to me that yesterday she was married to Mr. Langton."

"Oh! well," said I, for I confess I was rather puzzled to know what to say, "I wish you all joy, I'm sure. You know it was expected, Mrs. Meriton."

"Yes, but not in this manner. You may depend, sir, that these clandestine matches seldom come to any good; but now that Mary is a wife, I shall insist upon it being acknowledged freely."

"You are quite right there, Mrs. Meriton," said I. "You should insist upon Mr. Langton, since he has taken Mary to be his wife, placing her in society as a married woman."

"That is just what I wish," said Mrs. Meriton; "but it appears that Mr. Langton has been persuading Mary how much better it would be for her to remain here with me, and let everything go on as usual, than to make what he calls a fuss and botheration about the marriage."

"Don't you consent to any such thing, Mrs. Meriton," said I. "You can always keep a good watch over your daughter's happiness; but do you by all means make as much noise about the wedding as you possibly can. Do not allow Mr. Langton to have merely a holiday wife, as it were."

"I certainly will adopt your advice," said Mrs. Meriton, "and I will have Mary called now by her proper name; there shall be no secret about it."

Mrs. Meriton then left me, and in a few minutes I descended from my own room to the breakfast-table, where were assembled Mrs. Meriton, the two younger children, and the newly married couple.

To the confusion of Mary, and the annoyance of her husband, I said immediately,—

"Good morning, Mrs. Langton. I beg to congratulate you upon your change of condition, and to wish you all sorts of happiness."

Mary only looked down and blushed; but Langton, in his rattling manner, said,—

"Oh, that's all very well, but you must remember the whole affair is a secret."

"A secret?" said I.—"Yes; mum's the word, you know."

"Upon my word," said I, "I don't know any such thing. I never heard that your marriage was a secret, or that mum was the word."—"Nor I," said Mrs. Meriton.

"Oh! well, just as you please," said Charles; "only I thought it would be so devilish convenient—that's all, you know."

"I should think," said I, gravely, "it might become very inconvenient for a married lady to keep her change of name a secret."

"Yes; but Mary could have gone on so comfortably, just as usual, I thought; but I don't care, you know, a bit."

"Have you put the marriage in the papers, Mr. Langton?" said Mrs. Meriton.—"The papers!"

"Yes; I mean, have you advertised your marriage, so that all your connexions and friends may know of it properly?"

"Advertised be d—d! I beg your pardon, but I don't want my friends and connexions to know anything about the affair."—"Then I do," said Mrs. Meriton.

"Well—well," cried I; "I am going to the city, Mrs. Meriton, and I shall be happy to leave the advertisement. Where do you mean to live, Mrs. Langton?"

Mary looked rather confounded at all this, and I could see Charles Langton bite his lips with vexation, as he said,—

"If we can't live here, we shall find a home, I dare say, somewhere."

"You will excuse me, Mr. Langton," said the mother, "but I cannot help saying the home should have been found first. My child is very dear to me; but she ought to be still dearer to her husband. I certainly had hoped that all those arrangements had been properly entered into."

"No; hang it," cried Langton, "I never thought of anything of the sort. I really imagined Mary would be much more comfortable at home here; because now, for instance, if I was out late, or anything of that kind, you would be with her."

"Any time that you intend being out so late that Mary would require companionship," said Mrs. Meriton, "if you will send me a note a day or two before, letting me know, I will make arrangements to come to her."

"A day or two before," cried Langton—"why d—n it"—the d—n came this time without the apology—"how can I tell when I am going to stop out? It's impossible."

"As a married man," chimed in I, "your own home must ever be your first consideration."

"Certainly, as a married man," said Mrs. Meriton.

"A married man!" said the youngest child, scarcely comprehending the meaning of the words.

Langton looked from one to the other of us, and seemed half inclined to get into a passion; but he controlled his temper, and rising, said, with a laugh—

"Well, Mary, we shall be turned out, it appears. I must go and look for some home for us."

I saw a tear in Mrs. Meriton's eye as he made this harsh remark, and rising likewise, I said to him firmly and gravely—

"Mr. Langton, you have married Mrs. Meriton's daughter, and placed her in the entirely new social position of your wife. What you mean by turned out, neither I nor Mrs. Meriton can possibly conceive. She may, I think, very properly ask you to provide a home for your wife."

"Do you all want to quarrel with me?" he said. "Because if you do, say so."

"No," said I; "but we all want to convince you of your change of position. Your marriage is not the same pleasant little adventure you seemed to think it. Love and respect your wife, Mr. Langton, and do not try to ingraft the wayward manners and desultory life of a single man upon the more staid and steady life of a married one."

Mary now burst into tears; and it was pretty clear that she thought we were rather ill-using her husband than otherwise, who said—

"It's quite clear I've no friends here. Never mind, Mary; I'll take a lodging for us, and will leave before dinner-time."

Then with a look as if he had been the most injured piece of innocence in the world, he put on his hat and left the room, banging the street door after him—and all because he was expected to keep his wife.

"Now, Mary, my dear," said Mrs. Meriton, "I dare say you think I am very unkind to your husband, but time will show you that I am not. It was absolutely necessary to force him to a proper appreciation of you. What he wanted was evidently to keep you here just as you have been, for him to come home to whenever he pleased, or was tired of out-door enjoyments; that is to say, you would have filled the not very dignified situation of nurse to him in sickness, and companion of his ennui."

"I dare say you are right, mother," said Mary; "but it does afflict me to leave home."

"My dear, you mistake," said the mother. "By leaving here, now that you are married, you should consider yourself as going home."

I now left the room, satisfied that Mr. Charles had been made to view his matrimonial freak in a somewhat different light; for I was quite sure he had not looked upon it as any way serious or calculated to give him the least trouble. What he wished was to be still the fine and easy single young man, with his latch key, and his full liberty as to time and absence, with only the small difference of having a beautiful girl to welcome him home when his other amusements had become tiresome to him. I certainly took quite a malicious pleasure in disappointing him; and I took care that an advertisement should appear in the morning papers setting forth the marriage.

It was close upon dinner-time when Mr. Charles came home, and then he evidently looked wearied and vexed. Lodging hunting is not the pleasantest pursuit in the world; and I could have laughed outright in his face, I was so amused.

"Have you found a lodging?" said Mrs. Meriton, with provoking calmness.—"Yes," was the brief reply.

"Oblige me with the address"—"No. 2, Felix-place."

"Oh, that is not far off; and when do you remove to it?" —"Now," he said, standing up.

"I have invited Mary to dinner," said Mrs. Meriton; "and I hope you will favour us with your company."

Mary cast an imploring look at him, and he said—

"Oh, very well. Just as you like, Mary."

We certainly were not the most sociable party in the world on that occasion, and Charles looked very much provoked that Mary was not as short in her manner, and as full of indignation as himself; but the fact was, Mrs. Langton did not want for sense, and during the morning her mother had quite convinced her that the steps she was taking were those most likely to insure her happiness, and that, together with the assurance that she would see her every day, and would always be at hand to counsel, assist, and protect her from any formidable disagreeables, enabled Mary to see matters in a different light altogether, so that her serenity was restored; and much to the evident aggravation of her husband, she would not consider herself as the deeply injured creature he would fain have had her.

The dinner passed off, and then Charles rose, saying—

"Come, Mary, let us go to our own home," laying an emphasis on the word "home."

In a few minutes the young couple had left the house, and then the mother's feelings overcame her, and sitting down, she wept aloud, while the younger children looked on in wondering awe.

"Mrs. Meriton," I said, "your feelings are very natural; but depend upon it you have pursued the right course as regards your daughter, and a more weak course of action might have seriously compromised her happiness. Now, when of course Mr. Langton's feelings are in all their freshness, he may get into regular domesticated habits—nay, even his present indignation may assist him in behaving with propriety to Mary."

"I am quite sure what you say is true," said the widow; "but still I cannot help feeling, and that too more acutely than I would allow Mary to see, the loss of my dear child."

"Well—well, never mind, Mrs. Meriton. You will be consoled by being a grandmother yet some of these days."

Mrs. Meriton smiled as she said—

"If Charles Langton would but be more steady, I could have no objection to him; but I have been told by more than one person, that he thinks nothing of playing at bagatelle for hours together."

My life was one of many vicissitudes in the early part of it, and it was strange that on the evening of the very day which had witnessed the departure of Mary to her new home, I was compelled to leave Mrs. Meriton's for the purpose of accompanying an invalid gentleman to Rome. My journey necessarily caused a long absence, and even when I returned, so many new objects called my attention, and so many new opportunities for the practice of my profession had presented themselves to me, that I was nearly twelve months in London before I one day started up from my chair, and said to myself,—

DIARY OF A PHYSICIAN.

"I will call upon Mrs. Meriton, my old landlady, and see how her daughter Mary gets on with her rather unpromising husband."

I accordingly at once started for the little street which was so well known to me, but only appeared as much smaller and meaner than when I last visited it. Have not all my readers felt the same sensation upon revisiting some well known spot after an absence of some time?

I knocked at the door, and as I did so a full tide of recollection rushed across my brain, and I wondered if Mary Meriton, or rather Mrs. Langton, as I ought to call her, had been happy in her lot.

A woman opened the door; she was a stranger to me, and upon my inquiring for Mrs. Meriton, she replied with the usual exaggeration of her class,—"Lor—sir—she's been dead long ago."

"Dead!" said I.—"Yes, sir—she's dead and gone."

"But not long ago," said I, "for I was talking to her in this very house within the last two years."—"Oh! well, at any rate she's dead."

"And what has become of the rest of the family?"—"I don't know."

I saw there was no information to be got from the woman, and I turned away disappointed, it is true, but satisfied that it was quite useless to trouble myself any further about the affair.

Another three months passed away, and I accepted an engagement with a chemist in the city, to be at his house between eleven and one three times each week in order to give gratuitous advice to poor patients, he finding his account in supplying the medicines which were indispensible in their various cases, and which I believe I ordered by far too scanty to please my employer, for I did not retain my situation long. But that has nothing to do with my story.

I had not been above a fortnight attending to my professional duties in the way I have intimated, when, one morning, a thin, wretched, sickly-looking female presented herself. She had a veil over her face, and her whole appearance bespoke faded gentility. She trembled as I offered her a chair, and spoke some inarticulate words. Then, to my surprise, she pronounced my name, and burst into tears.

"My dear madam," said I, "compose yourself. Pray let me remove your veil."

"Do you not know me?" she said, in a low, faint voice, struggling with emotion.

"Indeed I do not," said I.

"Do you now?" she sobbed, as she removed her veil. I confess that even then I looked at the thin, pale face before me, bearing, as it did, traces of much beauty, for some moments, before a vision of Mary Meriton rose up in my mind, and I exclaimed—

"Good God! you are Mary—I mean Mrs. Langton!"

"I am," she said; "I do not wonder, Doctor ——, at your not knowing me. I sometimes scarcely know myself; sorrow and misery change the features, and make us prematurely old."

"Indeed, Mrs. Langton," said I, "those two things are great enemies to health and beauty. I am very much grieved to hear you talk as if you had experienced them."

"I have indeed," she replied; "and now I think I am dying, doctor; but I am content to die. It is for another's sake that I came to you."

"Your husband?"

"No—my only child. The one tie that binds me to existence. The only gleam of light that illumes the darkness of my destiny. I think that if it had not been for that young thing looking up to me for that love and protection which there was no one to render it, I should have sought rather the mercy of Heaven as a suicide than have lived on enduring what I have endured."

"Believe me," said I, "it grieves me very much to hear you speak in that way. If you will give me your address I will call upon you the moment I can leave here."

"Will you—can you really be so kind?" she sobbed.

"Oh, never mind that, Mary—I beg your pardon—Mrs. Langton."

"Call me Mary. It is a dearer name, I was happy then. But now—oh, Heaven help me! Heaven help me!"

"Now do not give way to such feelings," said I. "Give me your address, and go home yourself at once. I will follow you as soon as I can, you may depend, and mind, never despair—who knows but from this day your prospects may mend, and your griefs begin to disappear, presenting to you a brighter future."

She seemed quite overcome by my words, and for some moments could scarcely speak. I saw her agitation, and went into the shop to procure her a stimulant, which, at my pressing solicitation, she partook of, and then rising, she looked at me with tears in her eyes, saying, with a voice broken by emotion,—

"Your words are the only ones of kindness and hope that I have heard for many a day. I will write my address."

I gave her a slip of paper, and she wrote with a trembling hand her name and address.

I have that small slip of paper now before me. It is an interesting memento of Mary Meriton to me. Here and there the letters are nearly illegible, for her tears dropped fast as she wrote. The address was in a part of the town by no means notorious for its gentility, but I immediately placed the scrap of paper in my pocket-book, saying,—

"Before two o'clock you will see me without fail, Mary. Till then, be of good cheer, for you shall have a friend in me, as well as a physician."

I shook hands with her, and the small delicate fingers, as they rested upon my hand for a moment, struck me as being dreadfully thin—they were nearly transparent—alas! poor Mary—what a change was there in her, since first I saw her —radiant in the spring-tide of her beauty.

I was dreadfully impatient after she was gone, but I was compelled to wait till one o'clock, and even some time afterwards; for although no more patients were received in the waiting-room after that hour, we were compelled to dispose of those who had been, perhaps, an hour waiting for their turn.

At length, however, the last had come and gone, and I hastened towards the abode of Mary.

On my road my mind was filled with conjectures concerning the various occurrences which had possibly or probably reduced the beautiful Mary Meriton to her present miserable state; she had not said one word in her interview with me about her husband, and I came to the conclusion that the worst fears of Mrs. Meriton and myself had been verified, and that his conduct had not been what was proper towards the unhappy Mary.

Half an hour's smart walking brought me to the neighbourhood in which was situated the miserable street, the name of which Mary had written down to me; after many inquiries I found it, and proceeded to the number to which I was directed.

It was a wretched-looking house. The cellar was in the possession of a sweep; the parlour belonged to a cobbler who worked at the open window, and exposed for sale, at prices varying from fourpence to eighteenpence, dilapidated boots and shoes on the window-sill, while he hammered away within.

The door was wide open, so there was no necessity whatever for announcing one's approach. This circumstance, however, presented rather a difficulty than otherwise in such a densely populated house, and I was fain, after entering the passage, to walk out again and address the cobbler through his open window, inquiring for Mrs. Langton.

"One pair back," was the brief response, and I accordingly ascended to that locality, and tapped at the door indicated to me by the cobbler.

It was opened by Mary herself, and now that she was divested of the shawl she had worn in her visit to me, I was more than ever struck with the ravages bad living and sorrow had made upon her frame; I was careful, however, to avoid any expression of my feelings, and merely said,—

"You see I am tolerably punctual."

"Heaven reward you," said Mary. "Come in, doctor. This is a wretched home to ask you to."

"Never mind that," said I, anxious to put her at her ease; "you should recollect the man whose friend remarked to him,—

"'My dear so-and-so, you have a very bad cold,' and who replied, 'I know it, but it's the best I could get, and it does quite well enough for me.'"

Mary smiled faintly, and taking me by the hand, she led me to a corner of the room, where, upon a very small bed, lay a young infant sleeping.

"That is my child, doctor," she said. "Oh, save him to me, and I shall bless you."

"What is the matter with him?" said I.

"I know not, but he wastes away daily, and sometimes he is very sick. He is now sleeping from exhaustion, induced by a violent fit of sickness."

"Well, but Mary, there may not be much harm in all that, you know."

I took the child's hand in mine, and the touch awakened him, as I wished it should, for I wished to look in his eyes. The little thing looked terrified at me, but in a moment his eyes met his mother's; he stretched out his arms to her, and she lifted him from his bed. I could see she was crying, and she strove to hide her tears by kissing the child.

"Oh, doctor," she exclaimed, "do you think?"

"Yes, as far as human judgment can go."

A smile crossed her face, and clasping her hands, she said, "Thank God for that!" then she kissed the little fellow with the most frantic eagerness. A new life seemed to have been given her by my assuring words,

"He is delicate just now," I said, "but with proper food and purer air he would be quite well, and, I have no doubt, would become robust and hearty. There is not the least indication of disease about him."

"Proper food—purer air," faltered Mary, and in a moment all her short-lived joy vanished, and she burst into tears.

"Come now," said I, "this is too bad for you, for if you make yourself ill what is to become of your little one?"

"That is true," she said; "but what am I to do? My babe will be killed, and I am not able to help it. I am a most miserable mother! Heaven help me—Heaven help me!"

"Where is your husband?" said I.

"I know not," was the reply.

"He has not left you?"

"No; only deserted me. He comes home sometimes, when—when he is tired of out of doors."

"Tell me now, Mary, as a friend, who, although his power is limited as regards pecuniary means, still has a good will to serve you, and may, perhaps, do so more effectually than were he richer,—how have you passed the time since your marriage? There must have been much fault somewhere to reduce you to your present state."

"I will tell you," said Mary. "The story is not long, and I have been told there is but little new in it. For a few months after my marriage all was well, and I was very happy, but then Charles began to yearn after his old associates, and his old habits. Home became distasteful to him, and when he found those resources going in the regular routine of domestic expenses with which he had been accustomed to indulge in out-of-door enjoyments, he grew angry; then whole days and nights would pass away without my seeing him; I did not upbraid him, and he made it a fault with me that I did not. He could not bear the reproaches of his own heart when I met him with a welcome home; to avoid the disagreeable feeling that assailed him, then he stayed away more than ever, and the demon intoxication set its ban upon him. My poor mother died in the midst of all this, and I became a mother one week after that event. I had fondly hoped that the birth of a child would rouse the love of my husband, but on the contrary he avoided home more than ever, and I could but get from him the smallest pittance to support me and my babe.

"A situation that he had procured he lost through his intemperance; another was recklessly thrown away from the same cause. How he now lives I know not, but I have been told it is by frequenting public-houses and playing games of chance and skill, and betting upon others' play. Now and then only I can wring from him a few shillings, which he gives me with oaths and execrations. Oh, doctor, can you wonder that were it not for my little one I should deprive myself of life, and rather trust to Heaven's mercy to forgive me that great sin than to the lost love of my husband? I am very— very wretched."

That poor Mary was, indeed, under such circumstances, very—very wretched, I could easily believe, and when she had done speaking, I own I was as completely puzzled to know what to say or do as ever I was in my life. What consolation could I offer to the sorrowing woman? Could I say your husband will reform, his affections will return, and you will be happy? Alas, no! that would have been poor, impossible consolation.

Meanwhile she continued kissing her child, and weeping in a manner which it made my heart bleed to witness. At length I said,—

"Mary, I can offer you but little assistance. Such medicines, however, as I think will bring round the constitution of your child I will send to you."

"No—no," she said, "I have not the means."

"Never mind that," said I; "you know we doctors always charge well, at least the public say so, and we can afford to wait, now and then, for our money."

"I understand you," said Mary; "but I will not pain you, which I know it would, by rejecting your proffered kindness."

"That is the right view of the case," said I; "you must likewise let me send you some strengthening medicine, for I am sure you stand much in need of it, and the only other thing I can do at present, is to seek out your husband, and endeavour to reason him into a better line of conduct."

"How can I thank you?" she sobbed; "surely Heaven has not deserted me while such a friend still lives."

"Heaven never deserts anybody," said I, "if they do not desert themselves. Now, good-day to you; I will send the medicines and call again to-morrow, but you must tell me where I can most likely find your husband, Mary."

"Alas, I cannot," she replied, "I have not seen him now since yesterday morning."

"Hilloa! hilloa! fal de ral de rido!" cried a hoarse lusty voice at this moment, and the door was thrown wide open by Charles Langton, who reeled into the room with his hat on one side, and his apparel generally disarranged, evidently in a state of maudlin intoxication.

"What—what's the row?" he exclaimed, as he tried to balance himself with his hands in his pockets, and looked round him with drunken gravity.

"Oh, Charles, Charles," said his wife.—"Don't speak to me, don't—female woman avaunt—d—d—don't speak to me."

"Mr. Langton," said I.—"Don't be impertinent. I—I'm not the—the character you take me for. I—I'm an injured individual. It's enough to make anybody weep, and all I can say is—Fal de ral de rido."

"You hear him, doctor," said Mary.—"Indeed I do," said I.

"Female woman," continued Charles Langton, "don't presume to address me.

"Merry and free are a bachelor's revelries,
So happy and cheerily proves his life;
He don't care a d—n for domestic devilries,
Troublesome children and—and—

Hang me if I remember—I forget the rest—but it's something about one's cursed wife. What shall we say, gentlemen, after that? 'Here's to all unfortunate monarchs.'

"Here's a *smile* for those that love me,
A *tear* for those who hate,
And whatever sky's above me,
Give me a pot of half and half.

How do you do, old brick—I didn't see you before," taking my hand.

"Do you know me, Mr. Langton?" said I.

"No, if I do may I be d—d; but I'll tell you how to commit genteel suicide. Get married, and live in the country—that's the way, my boy. That's a wrinkle I can tell you. You can retail it, you know, I won't split; honour bright, honour bright."

To attempt any reasoning with Langton in his then state would have been quite absurd, so I rose to go, saying to his wife,—

"Will he remain here long, think you?"

"I don't know," she replied; "he is always thus when he is in this state, but when he has slept off the drunkenness, his temper becomes sullen and ferocious. Then his anger blazes forth until I am glad to see him go out again to imbibe that liquor which has been his destruction and my ruin."

"You ain't going?" said Langton; "Mary, what have you got to drink?"

"Nothing, nothing," she said, in a tone of sorrow.

"Good day, Mr. Langton," said I, "you don't seem to recollect me at all."

"Oh, I dare say you are a good fellow," he replied, "that's enough for me. You take your glass like another, that's the thing."

"Keep him here, if you can," said I, "and I will call in a few hours, when I am in hopes to find him sober."

Mary nodded her acquiescence, and just as Charles Langton commenced a new song, the particulars of which consisted of a great many allusions to goblets and sparkling wine, I left the room.

I then called upon a medical friend in the vicinity, for the purpose of waiting until there was a probability of Charles Langton being sufficiently sober, either to listen to reason, or at once put an end to all hopes of making him behave better than he was doing. Of course the conversation of myself and my friend turned upon the subject of intemperance, and among other opinions, my friend said,—

"You may depend upon it that intemperance is so strong a feeling of the mind when once it takes root, that no reasoning will ever dislodge it. Nothing but some severe shock to the whole mental structure will suffice to effect a radical cure, and it commonly happens that when a drunkard survives such a shock, his amendment comes too late to be of any benefit, for the circumstance which has cured it, is in all probability some great calamity, produced by his previous bad habits."

"I am indeed afraid," said I, "that I shall have but little chance of doing any good by reasoning with Charles Langton."

"The probability is that you will do harm, notwithstanding all your good intentions; such men generally become much irritated at any advice, because in their own hearts they know they are wrong, and then they make anger stand in the place of argument."

"I have found that the case," remarked I, "but too often; nevertheless, I cannot help making some attempt to rescue poor Mary from her miseries."

"I tell you what," said my friend, "that poor girl is as likely, some of these days, to destroy herself as not—that would be a shock which, while it sobered her husband, probably, you see, would be too late. Such a catastrophe you should quite look forward to—I should."

"I sincerely hope not," said I; "but there is one thing I wish you to do, and that is, to make up some medicines for Mrs. Langton and child."

My friend kept a chemist's shop, which he now bustled into from his back parlour.

He rather stared at me when I wrote one prescription for Mary and another for her child, in neither of which was any medicine mentioned.

"Bless me," said he, "this is physicing people with a vengeance—Port wine, sago, arrow root, &c., &c. I think your patients had better go to the butcher and the wine-merchant's."

"Yes; but they can't afford it; and unless I give this poor, unfortunate girl nourishment under the guise of medicine, I know she would shrink from accepting it at all."

"I understand you," said my friend. "I will do all these things up in medical bottles and packets, properly labelling them, and so on."

"Do," said I. "You can tell me what they come to when I see you again; and now I shall go and make the experiment with, I hope, the by this time sobered Charles Langton."

"I wish you success," he said, "with all my heart; but I very much doubt it."

* * * * *

Notwithstanding the gloomy prognostications of my friend, I was determined to try what I could do by as mildly and feelingly as possible representing to him the eventual misery he was entailing upon himself by his intemperance, as well as the present injustice he was doing to his innocent wife and helpless child.

Full of these thoughts, I once more reached Mary's abode, and this time needing no direction, I walked up at once to the door, and knocked.

Mary immediately opened it. She was in tears, and had the child in her arms.

"Come in," she said; "he is sleeping."

I stepped into the room; and there upon the bed which the poor child had been dispossessed of, lay the slumbering man—sleeping off some of the hilarious effects of his intoxication, but to awaken to the miseries and sufferings of life.

My entrance into the room seemed to disturb him, for he opened his eyes, and stared at me with stupid amazement for some moments. Then he half sat up in the bed, and said,—

"Who the devil are you?"

"I am your friend, Mr. Langton," said I, "if you choose that I should be so."

"But who the devil are you?"

"My name is ———. I used to live in the same house with you before you married."

"What brings you here?" he roared, as he tore off his cravat, for he was dressed just as he had come in, and threw it on the floor. "Be off with you! Because I'm poor now, you come here to crow over me, I suppose?"

"No, Mr. Langton, I do no such thing. I came here to

reason with you, and to persuade you, if I can, to your own welfare."

"Bah!" he cried, "I've heard enough of that trash. I tell you what, I've an old grudge against you, and if you don't turn out of here directly, I will see who is the strongest."

"That would be very soon seen," said I, "for you are a drunkard, and I am not."

"Do you want to insult me?" he cried, springing from the bed.—"No," said I, firmly; "I want to do you a favour."

"Curse your favour; get out, get out, I say; I know well enough what brings you here. My wife ain't so good looking as she was, but she has some amount of beauty yet."

"Charles," cried Mary, while her eyes flashed fire with indignation, "your insinuation, which I will not affect to misunderstand, is false, and well you know it, Charles."

"Go on, go on," he cried, "this is all very fine, mighty fine; is there anything else you would like to back each other out in?"

"Mr. Langton," said I, sternly, "in your present state of mind it is demeaning to me to converse with you. There is my card, and, for the sake of your helpless child, I do hope that you will see your own folly, and amend your life ere it be too late."

I pronounced the words "too late" emphatically, for I thought of the opinion of my friend, and then, turning to Mary, I added,—

"Good day, Mrs. Langton; Heaven help you." After which, waiting for no reply, I instantly left the room, and was in the street in a few moments, much grieved at the non success of my interference.

* * * * *

All the remainder of that day I could not get rid of the painful thoughts which poor Mary's situation engendered in my mind. I resolved only upon one thing, and that was, as far as my means allowed, sending her, in the shape of medicine for herself and child, wine and nourishing mixtures, which would tend to preserve her from sinking under bodily exertion; but to the mind I felt that I could minister no relief, and I could only commend the unfortunate young thing to the care of that providence which watches over the fall of a sparrow.

I called upon Mary only once the next week, for I was much hurt at the groundless and insulting insinuation of Langton, which, to a physician, was out of all character. I found her in much the same state of suffering as when I had last seen her, with the exception that I thought there was a flightiness about her manner, and a restlessness in her eyes which alarmed me much, but which I had not noticed at our first interview.

She spoke of Heaven protecting her child, and then kissed it with a frantic eagerness, and asked me what I thought would be a mother's feeling if she were going a long journey without the darling of her heart? I scarcely knew what to say to her, but I infused as much hope as I could into her mind, assuring her that some day her husband must see his errors, and they would yet be happy.

She shook her head and smiled feebly, as she replied, "That it was not much matter *now*," and many such expressions, which annoyed, perplexed, and alarmed me much to hear.

Finally, after in vain trying to reason her out of her depression of spirits, I left her in much the same strange and fantastical mood, feeling myself the greatest concern for her, and anxiety concerning her safety. It is not to be, therefore, wondered at that I should go to bed so full of my anxious thoughts as to weave them up into dreams; and the fact was, that I had no sooner got to sleep, than Mary Meriton became the presiding genius of my slumbers.

I fancied that I stood upon some steps, which appeared to lead to some water, for the sound of it came with a sullen flow every now and then close to my feet. Then I thought I looked down and saw the pale face of Mary Meriton just above the black surface of some stream, and her long fair hair floating behind her. I thought I saw her go slowly down, and I had not the power to move hand or foot to save her; my tongue was glued to the roof of my mouth—I was, to all useful purposes, a mere breathing statue. The struggle I made to call out, I suppose, awakened me, for I sprung out of my bed, crying,—

"Save her! save her!"

The truth of my position in a moment flashed across my waking intellect, and, hoping I had not disturbed the house, I jumped into bed again, feeling very nervous and uncomfortable.

It was some time before I could get to sleep again, but, when I did, there I was upon the same steps again, and the sound of the flowing water.

I thought I then cried out in my dream,—"Good God! where am I?" I dreamt this once, and some one said,— "These are the steps by the left of Blackfriars Bridge."

Then the pale face of Mary Meriton appeared to me, and again I saw the long hair floating on the surface of the river. That was too much for moral endurance. I tried to shout, to scream, to rush into the water to help her, but, as before, my limbs refused their office—my voice was gone.

Then I was suddenly awakened by a loud knocking at my chamber door, and starting up in bed, I cried loudly,—

"What's the matter? what's the matter?"

"Are you ill, sir?" said the voice of my landlady; "I've been quite terrified by hearing you moan so in your sleep, sir."—"Oh, yes, I am well," said I, feeling very much confused, "quite well."

"I am very glad to hear it, sir; good night."—"Good night—good night."

I heard my landlady shuffle away, and then, by a sudden impulse of mind that I could not at all resist, I sprang from my bed, and, procuring a light, the means of which I had always ready at hand, I began mechanically dressing myself with great speed.

To this day I cannot recollect having any particular thought of what I was about. I felt what I should suppose a somnambulist must feel during his involuntary actions and peregrinations. I, however, dressed myself completely, and, taking my hat and the candle I had lighted, I slowly and rapidly descended the stairs. When I reached the passage I put out the light, and, pulling my hat firmly over my brows, I repeated to myself,—

"These are the steps by the left hand of Blackfriars Bridge." I then opened the door, and shutting it carefully behind me, I started off at a rapid pace towards Blackfriars.

* * * * *

The night was dark, cold, and disagreeable, but I pushed on without heeding the aspect of the weather, and the only thing I recollect distinctly is, repeating to myself at every corner I came to,—

"These are the steps by the left of Blackfriars Bridge."

On—on I went, till I descended Ludgate Hill, and turned into Bridge-street. Then I quickened my speed, and almost flew up the left hand side of the way. A very few minutes sufficed for me to reach the bridge. Everything seemed as still as the very grave. I turned to the left, the steps were before me. In a moment I descended them, and there I stood, precisely as I had stood in my dream, with the water almost laving my feet.

A cold chill shot across my heart, and I gazed around me for a moment or two in a kind of surprise to find myself there at all.

"My dream, my dream," I muttered; "am I still dreaming? or have I been so foolish as to come all this way on the faith of a night vision?"

The words had scarcely escaped my mouth, when I heard a sound behind me on the stairs. I mechanically slunk on one side, and the blood retreated to my heart with a frightful gush. A female figure glided down; she passed me. I felt quite paralysed. I saw her clasp her hands,—I heard a sob, such as might well have come from a broken heart.

"God forgive me," she said, and then plunged with a sudden dash into the stream.

I knew the voice—it was Mary Meriton's.

* * * * *

I usually had sufficient presence of mind for any kind of emergency, but the circumstances of that night had been altogether so peculiar, that for some moments I was quite unequal to the task of giving even an alarm. My dreams— my sudden rising from my bed—my walk to the bridge— and then the sudden confirmation of the awful vision of my slumber, by the appearance of Mary, confounded me. I knew not whether I was asleep or awake. This state, however, could not have lasted very long, for I rushed down the steps until I felt the cold water about my waist. I could not swim, and it was with the greatest difficulty I now preserved my footing. My energies were, however, restored to me, and with a voice such as I never thought I before possessed till then, I shouted,—

"Help! help! help!"

Scarcely had the echoes of my voice been awakened among the arches of the old bridge, than I saw almost within arm's length of me, something floating in the water. A wash of the tide moved it, and there was Mary's face the same as I had seen it in my dream, with her long fair hair floating on the surface of the water like some beautiful sea-weed.

At the same moment, several boats shot out from under the bridge, and various voices cried,—

"Hilloa, there! who cries help there?"

"Save her! save her!" I shouted.

A man from behind me on the stone steps threw a broad glare of light upon the water, by means of a lanthorn he had.

"Pull away!" I heard a man cry; "it's a woman in the river."

A boat, in which were a man and a boy, dashed forward, and Mary was lifted by the man from the stream in a moment.

"This way," I cried, with frantic eagerness; "bring her ashore this way."

The keel of the boat grated against the steps, and in a moment I took the insensible form of Mary in my arms, and not feeling her weight any more than as if she had been an infant, I walked up the steps with her, and was in Bridge-street in a moment.

I flew rather than walked with her, and coming to an hotel I knocked, and very loudly.

The door was instantly opened by an alarmed night porter, who cried out,—

"Bless us, and save us, is it fire?"

"No, it ain't," said I; "it's water. A bed directly, and a warm bath—run and knock up, likewise, the nearest medical man, and tell him Dr. —— sends his compliments and wants him to come and assist in the restoration of one apparently drowned."

By the time I had said this much the whole house was alarmed, and, I must say, that more considerate kindness than was instantly shown by every resident in the hotel, could not be found. A lady gave up her bed on the instant, and there was not a female, high or low, staying in the place, who did not eagerly offer every assistance.

Mr. ——, a surgeon in the neighbourhood, soon arrived, and he and I, with the assistance I have mentioned, tried for some hours to restore the vital spark. I was beginning to despair, and Mr. —— shook his head, when a slight move-ment of one hand gave us new hope. With renewed alacrity we tried every means for the accomplishment of our object, and by five o'clock in the morning Mary opened her eyes, saying, faintly,—

"Oh, God, where am I?"

The chamber I had immediately darkened, and leaving the strictest injunctions to keep her warm and quiet, I went out with the surgeon to get her some medicines. He promised to attend upon her unremittingly until he saw me again, and, as wearied and exhausted as ever I was in my life, I got into a hackney coach and went home.

So astounding to me had been the events of the night, that when I was fairly in my own room again, I was in half a mind to go back to the hotel in Bridge-street, to assure my-self that all was not a dream. I, however, threw myself on my bed bewildered as I was, and soon dropped into a sound sleep unvisited by any visions, a sleep which lasted till I was awakened by a boy who came usually of a morning to clean knives and boots, and who, I presume, had been sent into my chamber with instructions to thoroughly wake me, for, when I opened my eyes he was shaking my arm as if it had been a pump handle.

"Well, Jim," said I, "what now?"—"You're wanted," said Jim.

"Who is it?"—"St. Luke."

"Who?"—"St. Luke, I tell you."

"Why, what on earth have you been drinking so early in the morning, Jim?"—"Nothink; but doesn't the mad people go to St. Luke?"

"To St. Luke's they go, certainly."—"Well then I sposes as that's oos St. Luke is more madder nor us, and if so be as that's the ticket and no mistake, why it's St. Luke as is down stairs, any how."

"A madman, Jim," I said, as I hastily prepared to go down.—"Yes—he's been a screaming and tearing his hair out by the roots—he's now a laying all over missis's best kiddy."

"Best what?"—"Oh, the kiddyminster I mean, in course—the blessed carpet, you know."

"Upon my word, Jim, you have quite a language of your own; but are you sure this mad fellow asked for me?"—"Quite," said Jim, as he shuffled down the stairs before me.

"This is an awkward interruption," thought I. "I was in hopes of being left alone this morning, in order to attend upon Mary."

I opened the parlour door and walked in, when who should I see lying on the floor, apparently fainted, but Charles Langton, the dissolute husband of poor Mary.

I instantly rang the bell for assistance, and raising him up, I found that he was in a deep swoon. There was an expres-sion of terror and pain upon his face, and as Jim had said, he had actually dragged some of his hair out by the roots, for his hands were full.

When I had lifted him from the floor and laid him upon the sofa, I saw a letter lying on the carpet, which, upon picking it up, I saw was addressed in the hand-writing of Mary to her husband. Under the circumstances, especially as it was open, I thought myself justified in reading it. It is before me now, for I kept it—it ran thus:—

"CHARLES,—When I am gone do not reproach yourself. Think that it is for the best, and be kind to our child. If my death will have so much effect upon you as to make you an altered man, and a good father to our little one, I am content to die. Live as I have lived, I cannot. You have struck me, Charles—God forgive you, as I do. Before, perhaps many hours before you receive this, I shall be no more. You will find our child with Mrs. Mathew in the parlour.—Farewell, Charles.—God bless you, farewill.

"MARY."

The mystery of Charles Langton's agony of mind was now sufficiently clear. I put the letter in my pocket, and at that moment I made a resolution that he should not know of his wife's miraculous recovery, unless he should show such de-cided symptoms of amendment as to warrant her in again trusting her happiness to his keeping.

"No," I thought, "among my friends I will find some employment for her, which will support her and her child in comfort far away from her unkind husband."

Having made this resolution, I turned all my attention to the restoration of Langton from his fainting fit in which he still lay.

It was long before I could procure from him any signs of life, and when at length, with a deep sigh, he opened his eyes, he glared around him with an expression of such utter despair, that my heart bled for him, even although I knew how much he deserved to suffer.

"Are you better?" said I. "How do you feel now, Mr. Langton?" He answered me by a deep groan.

"Come, come," said I, "you retard your recovery very much. Cheer up, now."

"Oh, God! oh, God!" he cried, and clasped his hands with such an appearance of intense mental suffering, that I was almost tempted to tell him Mary lived, but I checked the impulse, and merely said,—

"In this world, Mr. Langton, we have all our grievous trials, and those are the happiest who can say that they are guiltless of bringing on their heads the misfortunes which they mourn."

"Guiltless—guiltless," he moaned. "Oh, how guilty am I! Mary—Mary—I am—your murderer! 'Tis I who have hurried you to the throne of your Maker, with the sin of self-murder on your soul! Oh, kill me! kill me? Will no one take a life which will henceforth be a hell of remorse and black despair—despair!"

"Mr. Langton," I said, solemnly, "it is needless for any one to reproach you for what is past. If you can from this moment live an altered man, and strive, for your child's sake, to make up for—for—the misery—I cannot call it by any other name—you brought upon its poor, fond, affectionate, innocent mother, you will, believe me, do much to appease the just wrath of Heaven against you. Be repentant, Mr. Langton, but not despairing."

"Can I," he moaned, "do aught but despair—can I have any hope—oh! Heaven, help me, was there ever one so guilty as I am?"

"Many—many, Mr. Langton, I grieve to say—it is dreadful to think of, but there are many fond trusting hearts, such as was your Mary's, that are broken by clinging to one in whom they had centered all their earthly hopes, but who

—ted the glorious treasure they possessed, and awoke to a sense of what they had done for their own misery too late."

"Too late—too late!" he gasped.

"Yes," I continued, "even you now, I'm sure, would give the world to see your Mary once again in the sweet bloom of health and beauty, as you have seen ——"

"The world—the world," he cried—"just Heaven! I would give a universe. I would barter every hope I have in this world, or in that which is to come, but to hear the words of forgiveness from her lips. But it is too late—too late—I am lost—my heart will break—my heart will break!"

"Think of your little one," said I.

He burst into tears, and sobbed for many minutes in the most agonised manner. I own I was very much moved by his deep distress, but I said to myself, "be firm—be firm. This penitence may not last, and then what new chance for poor Mary could possibly arise—be firm, and test the sincerity of his present feelings more fully." I did not interrupt his tears, but allowed him to weep on till the full tide of feeling somewhat abated, and his deep-drawn sighs came at greater intervals. Then I said to him,—

"Mr. Langton, the worst of us can do as much as the best of us in the sight of Heaven, after we have done that which is wrong. We can but be sincerely penitent, and for the time to come, amend our lives. May I hope that you, learning a practical lesson from this sad and solemn occurrence, will become sober and kind to your child—avoid all those associates who drew you from your home, in which you might have been so very happy with her who loved you?"

"Hear me, doctor," he said in choking accents; "the remainder of my days—and God grant they may be few—shall be spent in prayer. I will keep Heaven constantly in my thoughts, and mankind shall point at me as the once drunken, dissolute Charles Langton, who has become a humble penitent and a devotee."

"For Heaven's sake, don't go to extremes," said I. "If there is anything more disagreeable than another, it is one great jump from licentiousness to piety. You can alter your mode of life, and become a practical Christian without being always in tears, and praying from morning till night. There is no gloom in true religion, although your pious people will sometimes have it that a smile is a heinous crime in the eyes of Heaven. Believe me, Mr. Langton, you have more habits to leave off than acquire; and you will have taken a great step towards happiness, both here and hereafter, if you abstain from idleness and drunkenness, and endeavour to make a happy home for your child, now left solely to your care."

"Oh, doctor! if we could but recall sometimes a few short, fleeting hours!" he said. "If I now could obliterate the short time that has passed since the sun last set, and go to my—my Mary, and tell her that she should be happy for the future—pray her forgiveness for the past, and promise an amended life. If, doctor, I could do that, I might know what peace was—but now—now all is over—and I have hurried from the world the best, the kindest, gentlest heart, that ever beat in human breast."

He dropped his head upon his hands, and I could hear his sobs of frantic grief, and see the tears trickling through his fingers.

"Mr. Langton," I said, "we cannot undo what is done, nor would the riches of the earth recall one fleeting moment that is gone. The future, however, is before us. There is a sphere of action all our own, for, although we cannot command success in the usual pursuits of man, yet there is one thing we can command—it is virtue! No one can wrest from us that dear possession. In the midst of distress, difficulty, terror, we can, if we please, still retain the integrity of our own hearts, and interpose that as a shield between us and all misfortunes. Look, then, to that future, and despairing, even as you are, there may be greater happiness yet in store for you than you in your wildest imagination can think possible."

"Happiness for me!"

"Yes. Heaven's mercy is boundless. How often is it that when we consider we are at the bottom of an abyss, from which there is no return, we find that we are much mistaken, and that the very circumstances we believed to be without hope and flushed with misery, are those which lead from all our miseries to a heaven of joy we never supposed ourselves capable of approaching in this world."

"No—no—no!" he said, faintly. "Will Heaven restore he dead?"

"Even that has been done," said I.

"You mock me, doctor—you mock me! I am a poor heart-stricken man, but I am not quite mad—not quite. It would be happier for me if I were."

"Well, now, Mr. Langton," said I, "you must bethink yourself what you mean to do to provide for your child. I have great faith in your promises of reformation, and the only way you can show that it is sincere is by your attention to the welfare of the little one who is now solely committed to your care. It seems to me as if Heaven had in its goodness left you that one chance of redeeming the past."

"Do you? Can you really think so?" he said.—"On my conscience, I do!"

He clasped his hands, and in a tremulous voice, he said,—

"My Mary—my poor sacrificed Mary! if from the pure realms of Heaven you can hear my words—listen to me now, as I promise, by the faint hope I yet cling to of pardon for all that I have done, that henceforth I will devote my life to the comfort and happiness of our dear child."

"I am sure, Mr. Langton," I said, "that you feel some peace in your heart, even from the mere fact of making such a resolution."

"I do," he replied—"I do. Oh, how besotted I have been! It seems to me as if I had been mad, and only now recovered my senses. When I had at home such a one as Mary to welcome me, with her quiet smile, and to talk to me with her gentle voice, I could not appreciate such blessings—must needs haunt the taverns and low pot-houses of London, destroying my health, and stultifying my intellect with drink, listening to coarse language, frightful oaths, and neglecting all which would have made my life glide onwards happily, to cultivate every habit and bad association, which was sure to end, as it has done, in an awful catastrophe. Oh, doctor! doctor! I do, indeed, see my folly now. I have returned to my home, sometimes maddened with drink and excitement; then, because poor Mary would not wrangle with me, I have felt the bitterest feelings towards her, and blamed her for the very gentle virtues which should have won my admiration. But tell me—where is she? I must look upon her once again, although the sight kill me. Tell me, tell me—where is she?"

"That, at present, Mr. Langton, you must excuse my telling you. In a few days you shall have the melancholy gratification of looking in her face, poor thing! But now, tell me what situation you were last in."

"I was collecting clerk to Messrs. Andrews and Miller, the coal merchants."

"And they discharged you for drunkenness?"

"They did, and justly too."

"Now, if I were to call upon them, and induce them to employ you again, would you do your duty faithfully?"

"For my dear child's sake, doctor, I would. By the memory of her who is gone!"

"Very well, then. The experiment shall be tried. Now, go home to your child, and get some person to attend to it. Here is some money for present exigencies, and, remember, even now you stand upon the brink of a precipice. The slightest slip, and you fall for ever."

"I feel it," he said. "You are very kind to me. May the prayers of a heart-broken man avail you!"

With an expression of such terrible grief that it quite pained me to look upon his face, he now left me, and in a few moments I started off to see Mary, and inform her of the change which had taken place in her husband.

Beyond mere debility and a cold, Mary had received no injury from her terrible adventure at Blackfriars'-bridge, and she was quite well enough to be conversed with, although I would not allow her to leave her chamber at the hotel.

Her first inquiry was after her child, and I said,—

"Now, Mary, you may make your mind quite easy on that score; and as we may truly say 'out of evil springeth good,' you must know that I am firmly of opinion that very much happiness is in store for you."

The tears gushed to her eyes as she said,—

"Happiness for me! Alas! alas!—where am I to find even peace except in the grave?"

"Listen to me, Mary; Charles Langton thinks you dead!"

"Dead!"

"Yes. I have impressed him with an idea that you were successful in your attempt at self-destruction, and the shock it has given his mind has had the happiest effect. He now fully sees all his former errors in their proper light, and is full of remorse and tenderness towards you. I do honestly believe he would cheerfully lay down his life could he but restore you, who he believes dead."

Mary's tears now fairly mastered her, and she could not speak for weeping, but I could see that they were tears of joy, and would not check them. When she had recovered a little, she said,—

"And does he still love me, doctor?"

"He does. The scenes he has gone through will be a terrible lesson to him. You are both of you very young indeed, and it will, I think, be your own faults, if, for the future, you do not live as happily as any couple need to live."

"Oh, what joyous words are these!" said Mary. "How could I have believed such happiness possible this time yesterday, when my heart was as cold as a stone with despair?"

"When things are at the worst, you know, they mend," said I, "and my belief in the reformation of Langton is sincere; yet I counsel a little delay."

"Delay!" said Mary, with a disappointed air. "May I not see him now?"—"Certainly not now, Mary. But I promise you, if nothing happens to alter my views, within three days that I will bring him to you. During that time I beg of you to remain here, and make yourself happy with the thought that all is going on as you would wish, as regards both your husband and your child."

"Three days," she repeated, "'tis a long time."

"Not so long, Mary," said I solemnly, "as you contemplated separating yourself from those you loved last night."

"Forgive me doctor," she said; "I was very wrong to murmur. I will leave all to you, and be thankful that Heaven has given me such a friend in my affliction."

"I am but too happy," said I, "if I can but be the humble instrument of restoring both you and your husband to domestic comfort."

I then told her of my scheme for restoring Charles to his employment, and painted to her such a picture of the domestic happiness which I thought was in store for her, that I had the pleasure to see the colour revisit her cheeks before I left, and she looked more like what she was when first I knew her than I thought it possible.

"Now, Mary," I said, as I rose, "for these three days you must take all the nourishing matters that I shall leave orders for you to have, for I wish to present you to your husband a very different looking person to what you have been while suffering from his bad conduct."

She promised to comply with my directions, and I left her, very much pleased with the train in which I had put the whole affair. When my next anxiety was to see Charles Langton's late employers, and induce them to take him back again, and I confess I felt some little diffidence in calling upon perfect strangers with such a request; but it had to be done, and, like a disagreeable operation, the sooner it was over the better; so I walked at once down Thames-street until I came to the extensive establishment of Messrs. Andrews and Miller. I entered the counting-house, and asked the first person I saw if either of the partners were within.

"Mr. Miller is here, sir," said a clerk; "I will take your name to him, if you please."

I gave my card, and after waiting some few minutes in no very agreeable state of suspense, I was ushered into a small private counting-house, where was a little elderly-looking man with a shining bald head, and a screwed-up, irritable-looking countenance, that did not look very promising to my hopes.

"Mr. Miller, I presume," said I.—"I—am—Mr. Miller," said the old gentleman with the bald head, sententiously.

"I am afraid, sir," said I, "that you will consider my visit an intrusion."—"A-hem!" said Mr. Miller.

This was not very pleasant, and in fact I scarcely thought it courteous, so that I dare say there was a little asperity in my tone, as I said,—

"Sir, I have come to you with the most disinterested feelings, on a subject of humanity, and I expect to be received with courtesy, if not with consideration."

"Then why the devil, sir," said Mr. Miller, "didn't you say so at once? I thought you had come about some nonsense or another that would annoy me."

"Mr. Miller, I have come with the hope that you will be instrumental in making a fond, faithful heart happier than it has been."

"What do you mean?"—"You had once in your employ a young man named Charles Langton?"—"A scamp, sir—a scamp."

"Granted, but now reformed, and the sole hope in this world of a most amiable and gentle woman, and a helpless child."

"You—you don't mean that?"—"I do, though, Mr. Miller."

I then related to him the whole circumstances connected with poor Mary's attempt at self-destruction, and he heard me without interruption, although with a great deal of fidgetting about. When I had concluded, he said,—

"I tell you what it is, sir. You—you—confound you, sir; give me your hand. I am proud to see you here, and be hanged to you. Excuse me—you're an honest man, sir, and I respect you. Charles Langton shall behave well to his poor wife, and I will give him a permanent salary, the villain —I will."

"Mr. Miller," said I, with a smile, "I perceive your heart is in the right place."—"No it aint," said the irascible but really good-hearted man. "I've been teased to death, sir, by ungrateful wretches, I have; and I had made up my mind that I would never relent, or do a good-natured thing again. No more I won't—only this once. That's all, hang me if it aint."

"Mr. Miller," said I, with a smile, "you cannot help being what you are."

"What am I, sir?"—"A kind, good creature."

"I ain't. How can you think of calling me such names, sir? I—I'm a good mind, only I won't—to say that Charles Langton shall have no employment from me."

"Very well, Mr. Miller. Good morning, sir. When shall he come to you?"—"On Monday morning, the vagabond."

I was very much amused indeed with Mr. Miller, and when I got into Thames-street I could not forbear from laughing to myself at the strange mixture of misanthropy and affected harshness, with all the kindly feelings of human nature, which evidently formed his character. This would be a happier world if there were more of such men in it.

* * * *

I lost no time now in communicating to Charles Langton the success of my mission to the eccentric Mr. Miller. I found him with his child, and a more remarkable alteration than had taken place in him I never saw depicted on the countenance of a human being. The careless, half wild expression, that his almost habitual intemperance had given him, was completely gone, and he wore a look of calm, steady thought, which, while it made him look much older, by no means detracted from his appearance, rather, in fact, improving it in my eyes.

When he saw me, a gush of feeling seemed to come across his heart, and for some moments he could not speak I was sure. Then he said, in a broken voice,—

"Doctor, you will keep your word with me, and let me see poor Mary's remains before—before they are consigned to their last home?"—"Certainly I will," said I. "The day after to-morrow, if you think you can bear the sight, you shall go with me to see her, Mr. Langton."

"Yes, yes," he said, "and I will take with me this little one,—this babe, who has been rendered motherless by my deep sinfulness. In its presence, and in the presence of Heaven, I will pray for forgiveness. Oh, doctor, there surely can be no hope for such as I. I shall never—never behold my poor murdered Mary again! Oh, if she had but lived a year, a month, aye, but a week, that I might assure her of my changed heart, and breathe to her some words of fondness, such as she has not heard from my lips for many a day!"

He wept bitterly, and such was the extent of his anguish, and bitter self-upbraidings, that I was shocked and affected to see him, and fervently wished the three days had elapsed, that I might restore him to his wife.

"You must not," I said, "give way to this unavailing sorrow. For your child's sake you must mingle with the world, and perform your allotted part in life. I have seen Mr. Miller, who has kindly consented to receive you again into his establishment. You are to go on Monday, and I hope that you will remain there permanently, and with credit to yourself."

"I am much, very much beholden to you, doctor," he said. "I cannot tell you how much I feel and appreciate your kindness; but the best return I can make for it is to show you that it has not been in vain—I shall carry with me to the grave a saddened heart, but while I live I will do my duty by my child."

"Do so, Mr. Langton, and we may find some means of lightening your load of grief. Perhaps, if you were to marry again, you know ——"

"Marry again!"—"Yes; why not? I hope some day to see you in a happy, comfortable house, with a wife by your side."

"Never—never!" he cried. "If ever you hear me call a woman by the name of wife, shut me for ever from your friendship."—"Well, well, we shall see. Strange things come to pass in this world, Mr. Langton. The day after to-morrow, remember, I will call here for you."

He changed colour as he said,—

"Yes. Though the sight of her shall madden me, I will look upon her once again. My poor—poor Mary!"

"You shall see her, and remember that the worst of our anticipations more frequently turn out quite the reverse than a realization of our fears."

He shook his head hopelessly, and after settling with him the particular hour that I would call upon him, I took my leave, and went to see how my patient, Mary, was getting on. I found her very much better. In fact, beyond the cold she had caught,—and that even was yielding rapidly to medical treatment—she was quite well. I own that I had some difficulty with her, as well as with Charles Langton, for when she heard how penitent he was, and how much remorse he suffered upon her account, she was as anxious to see him as he could possibly have been to see her, had he known she was still among the living.

"Cannot you bring him to-morrow, doctor?" she said, while the tears filled her eyes.—"Now, Mary," said I, "that is too bad of you, after promising me that you would wait."

"But—but—well, I will wait. Heaven knows how much we owe you. Your word should be law to us, for I am sure you have saved us both from destruction."

"One day and two nights," said I, "will soon pass away, and then you will be quite happy. It is but a short probation your husband has to go through."

* * * *

"Well," I thought to myself when I got home, "I am nearly impatient for the day after to-morrow as Mary can be; but I am resolved to wait, for Charles deserves his punishment; and Mary's health would suffer from the emotion consequent on an earlier restoration to her repentant husband."

Fortifying myself with these and similar reasons, I wandered about like one who did not know what to do with himself, and had it not been that my attention was distracted from Mary and her husband by my duties the next day at the chemist's, in Holborn, I think I should almost have broken through my resolve, and gone to Charles, saying,—

"My good fellow, come along, and I will take you to your wife, who, like Jack Robinson in the ballad, has never been dead at all."

However, the morning of the third day came at last, and I hailed it with no small degree of satisfaction. It was one of those clear, delightful mornings when all nature seems more full of life and energy than usual, and the world looks more than commonly rare and beautiful. It was a fit morning for the restoration of two fond, loving hearts that had been long estranged.

I called upon Mary first, and told her an hour later than I thought I should be at the hotel, in order to prevent her from being nervous and impatient as the time drew near. She was looking extremely well. Indeed, I had never seen her look so beautiful, for upon her cheek was the flush of expectation which just gave her the bloom that so finely contrasted with the pure whiteness of her brow, and the soft beauty of her eyes.

"Now be patient," said I, "and this will be the happiest day you ever saw."

I then hurried off to Charles Langton's lodgings, which he had taken in the house of a decent, homely widow, who agreed to take charge of his child. He was flushed, nervous, and agitated, and I could guess had passed a sleepless night. The moment he saw me, he said,—

"Oh, doctor, I shall thank Heaven when to day is past. Take me at once to see my poor Mary, or suspense and anxiety will kill me."

"Come along, then," I said, "I do not wish to delay you. She was taken to a hotel in Bridge-street, Blackfriars."

"Has there been no inquest?"—"Not yet, to my knowledge. But never trouble yourself about such things—come along."

"My landlady has promised to bring the child," he said; "I wish it to be with me when I look upon the cold corpse of its poor mother."

In a few minutes Charles and I were walking arm in arm towards Bridge-street, while the landlady followed with the child, assuming a sympathetic aspect, for she, of course, thought as Charles did, that his wife was no more, and that his present visit was to the dead. I could feel his arm tremble in mine as we went along, and I was almost fearful that his feelings would overpower him before I could get him to the hotel.

"Come now," I said, "rouse yourself, and be more calm and resigned. We must all submit to such things as these, and when anything is quite immutable, we should endeavour always to put up with it with so much philosophy as to rob it of most of its terrors. Believe me, you will see many happy days yet, Mr. Langton."

"'Tis kind of you," he said, "to try to cheer me, but philosophy makes but a poor impression upon real grief."

"Ah, well, well," said I, "here we are in Bridge-street, Charles, so your interview will soon be over."

"Which—which is the house?" he gasped.—"Yon large white house opposite."

We crossed to the hotel, and having taken Charles Langton into the coffee-room, I whispered to him,—

"Remain here a few moments until I go and tell the landlord you have come. I will not detain you long."

He merely nodded, and with trembling hands took up a newspaper, which I observed he held upside down, while I proceeded up stairs to Mary. She was surprised to see me so soon, and her colour went and came, as she said,—

"Is—is he here?"—"He is, Mary," said I.

She moved towards the door, but I gently detained her, saying,—

"For Heaven's sake, do not be precipitate, and all will be well. Pray be guided by me."

She sank into a seat, and seemed much affected, while I closed the shutters of the room, leaving it in total darkness.

"Now, Mary," said I, "oblige me by not speaking, whatever you may hear, until I open one of these shutters. Do you promise me that?"—"I do."

"Very well, then; I will not keep you long silent."

I then went down stairs to the coffee-room, and touching Charles Langton upon the arm, I said,—

"Come. All is ready."

He rose, and leaning heavily upon my arm, ascended the stairs. When he reached the top, he said in a hoarse, husky whisper,—

"The—the child?"—"It shall come up directly," said I. "This is the room."

I pushed the door of the darkened room open, only sufficiently wide to admit us, and then closed it again so suddenly, that he had no opportunity of catching a glimpse of his wife. Then, as we stood in the dark, I said,—

"Charles Langton, you are now in the presence of your wife."

"Oh, let me look at her," he moaned.—"You shall; but now, in the bitterness of your heart, what would you not give to see her once again in life, and tell her how much you repent of the past. How you would love and cherish her for the future."

"Oh, torture, torture!" said Charles. "If, doctor, by years of prayer—ages of suffering—I could procure the blessed boon of hearing the voice of my much injured Mary once again, to say that she forgave me, I could be happy yet. Yes —yes—oh, God, I could be happy yet!"

A deep sob burst from Mary.

"What—what was that?" cried George. "Oh, Heaven, what sound was that?"—"Charles, Charles," said Mary, "all is forgotten—all forgiven—my husband—my husband!"

A cry burst from Charles Langton, and he shouted,—

"It is her voice. It is my Mary's voice. My prayer is granted!"

On the instant I flung the shutters of one of the windows wide open. A broad stream of glorious daylight came into the room; Charles Langton stood like one transfixed, gazing into the beaming countenance of his beautiful wife.

"Your Mary lives," cried I, "to bless your reformation."

"Lives! lives!" he shrieked.—"Yes, Charles—yes," said Mary, as she threw herself into his arms, "and may this be the happiest day we have yet seen."

* * * * * *

From that time Charles and Mary lived together as happily as man and wife could do. She became the mother of as charming a family as ever I saw, and many a time, as I have sat by their fireside, we have talked over the merits of The Restoration.

THE MILLINER'S APPRENTICE;

OR, THE ORPHAN CHILD.

I HAVE before had occasion to inform my readers that for some time I attended at the shop of a chemist in Holborn for the purpose of giving gratuitous advice to poor patients, and the chemist found it to his advantage in so employing and paying me by selling to them the various medicinal preparations which I found necessary for their different complaints.

It was on one of these occasions that a young and very interesting female was introduced to me, whose extreme timidity and embarrassment interested me very much, the more especially as I could see she was in a very weakly state of health.

"Pray, sit down," said I, "and tell me freely what advice you want from me."

She burst into tears as she exclaimed,—

"They are killing me!—they are killing me!"

"Who—what do you mean?" said I, in no little surprise at this commencement of our conference.

"Ah, sir!" she added, "forgive me for troubling you; but I have overheard, accidentally, a conversation in which you were named, and it was said you were kind to those who sought you for advice, making no distinction between the poor and the rich, but equally to all doing what good you can."

"It is my duty," said I, "to do my best, without regard to the circumstances of my patient; but what is the matter with you that you seem so much affected?"—"I—I want something to give me strength to bear up against much—much work, and ——"

Here she paused, and I said,—

"Come, you must be explicit to me; and what?"—"Ill usage," was her reply.

"Hard work and ill usage!" I exclaimed: "who can have the heart to behave so to you? Why, how old are you?"—"Sixteen, sir."

"Have you no friends?"—"None! none! I am a lone thing in this world. There is no one to love me,—no one to speak a kind word to me,—no one to take my part. Oh, God! I wish that I was dead."

"Come, come, you must not despond in this way," said I.

"If you are not ill now, you will make yourself seriously so by giving way to such feelings as those you are now expressing to me."

"I cannot help it—I cannot help it," she sobbed. "Oh, sir, if you can give me something to deaden the sensation of pain—to enable me to endure fatigue more, though I die in a short time, I will bless you for it."

"This will not do at all," I replied. "We cannot give medicines to enable the oppressed to bear their evils; but if, as you say, you are so ill used, pray tell me circumstantially how it is, and by whom this ill-usage is inflicted?"

"I will—I will," she said; and I could see her small hand tremble as she spoke, and her colour come and go like the sunshine of an April day. "About a year and a half ago I was left an orphan by my mother; my father died far away when I was an infant. The parish workhouse was my home for some weeks, till one day I was apprenticed to a milliner."

"What is her name?"—"She calls herself Madame Rendell, but her real name, I have been told, is Gibbs."

"Then she is an Englishwoman?"—"Yes, sir. It is the custom of the parish officers to make a formal inquiry of any child apprenticed from the poor-house seven days after it has gone to its master or mistress to know if it has been well treated. For that seven days I had no complaint to make against Madame Rendell, but after that time she commenced, I am sure, aiming at my death."

"In what way?"—"I am at work from four in the morning until half-past twelve at night, and if I fall asleep she strikes me dreadfully."

"Well, but you should have applied to the parish officers who apprenticed you."

"I have done so once, sir; but they only took me back to her and remonstrated with her a little, leaving me to be worse treated than before, for she was revengeful against me for telling any one of her ill-treatment of me."

She trembled then so excessively that I had to give her a glass of wine to restore her to anything like composure.

"My good girl," I said, "you take a most erroneous view of your situation; your mistress will not be allowed to ill-treat you, although you are her apprentice. Your notion of coming to me for medicine in order to enable you to bear ill-usage is a very erroneous one, indeed. We must put a stop to the ill usage itself."

"Oh, if that could be done," she said; "if I could but be taken from her and given to some one else, I would cheerfully work where I received a kind word in return; but I cannot—cannot stand the dreadful persecution I endure with her."

"Has she any other apprentice but yourself?"—"Yes, one other."

"And is she ill-used in the same way?"—"Oh, no. I don't know how it is, but she is very well treated. I have to do her work and my own too, and then I am kicked and cuffed about because since—since—since——"

"Since what?"

She was silent for a moment, and then said,—

"Since I refused to let Madame Rendell's rich cousin kiss me."

"Oh, indeed! and when was that?"—"About eight months ago she came to me one day and said, 'Well, Emma, there's my cousin, who is a great deal too good-tempered, he says that he thinks you work too hard, and has begged me to let you have a holiday whenever he asks for it.' I replied, with tears in my eyes, that I was much obliged to him, indeed, and then she brought in with her to the room a gentleman whom she introduced as her cousin; but he—he wanted to kiss me, and I screamed and repulsed him, since when I have been treated worse than ever; and Madame Rendell often says that over-scrupulous people are fit for nothing but hard work. She is killing me, I know she is,—I know she is."

"But you forget," said I, "that Madame Rendell is not to be allowed to have all her own way in this world. Have you seen this cousin since?"

"Yes, twice. I have each time been offered holidays and money if I would go out with him in his carriage; but I dreaded his very looks and would not, threatening to scream if he came near to me. The terror of him—the little sleep I get, and the rough usage my mistress gives me, have altogether broken my heart."

"What is your name?"—"Emma Moorsam."

"Where does this Madame Rendell live?"—"In Hemingham-street."

"Very well. Now, Emma, you must go home, and I give you my word of honour that you shall hear from me within four-and-twenty hours from now."

She thanked me with tears in her eyes, and as I watched her pretty sylph-like figure leave the room, I entertained no doubt in my own mind as to the motives of Madame Rendell and her fine cousin. I had heard of such frightful iniquities as this young girl in her artless tale hinted at, being perpetrated in London, and I was resolved that in this case I would do my utmost to unmask the hidden designs of the pretended Madame Rendell. Too many young, fair beings, whose lives would have glided on in peace and innocence, are forced into a course of life that one shudders to contemplate, by either the deliberate villany of their task mistresses, or the suffering they endure from the frightful avarice which strains human nature to its utmost stretch of endurance; and then the fine fabric of the mind, becoming enervated by physical suffering, ceases to cast the shield of virtue over the misery which seems to know no hope, and the poor victims sink into that abyss from whence, alas! there is no return.

Before I left the chemist's, I related to him the case, with the hope of interesting him to become a coadjutor in the work of rescuing Emma Moorsam; but he was one of those cautious men who shrink from embroiling themselves in such matters, and he in reply to me only answered something about it being no part of a physician's duty to interfere with such things, and wondered at the girl coming to me at all.

"Sir," said I, "at the same time that I always remember I am a physician, I see no occasion that I should forget I am a man; and if I can save this poor, friendless girl from the plot which has been laid for her destruction, I shall think myself as well, if not better employed, than ever I was in my life."

"Very well—very well, sir," he replied; "I, of course, don't mean to depreciate your exertions—I only must decline having anything to do with the affair myself, being fully engaged in my professional pursuits."

"That is quite sufficient," I said; "I shall not trouble you any more upon the subject."

The street that Emma Moorsam had mentioned to me was in a parish, the name of which, although the occurrence I am relating happened many years ago, I would rather not mention; but suffice to say, it was some mile or so from Holborn. When my labours for the day were concluded, and I had likewise made an end of the unsatisfactory little bit of conversation I had had with the chemist, I resolved upon calling, in the very first instance, upon the parish officers, for the purpose of endeavouring to interest them, which I had no doubt I should easily do, in the case.

Not knowing where any of those parish magnates resided, I went direct to the workhouse, and ringing the bell, inquired of the deaf porter (there is generally a deaf man as porter to a workhouse) if he could give me the address of any of the overseers.

When he comprehended my wishes, he replied, that I had better see the beadle, who managed everything.

"Does he," said I. "Well, I will see the beadle then."—"Come on, then; he's in the house," said the porter, and then he hobbled before me to a kind of office, in which was the functionary he had named.

Before, however, he ventured to knock at the door with his knuckles, he motioned with his hands for me to take off my hat, adding, in one of those loud whispers peculiar to deaf people, who think everybody as deaf as themselves,—

"He's *wery pertikler* is Muster Swabsly; oh, wery."—"Is he, indeed," said I; "then I am particular likewise, and prefer keeping my hat on my head."

"What! and go into the wery presence?"—"Yes, even into the very presence."

The porter made a movement of his head, as much as to say, well, an obstinate man must have his way, and I wash my hands of the consequences of his terrible rashness. He then knocked in a very submissive and gentle manner at the door of the room, which produced a series of sounds as if somebody was nearly choking and making great efforts to clear his throat.

"What noise is that?" said I.—"It's Mister Swabsly a showing of us who he is and who he isn't."

"Indeed."—"A—a—a-hem!" said the beadle from within the room; "a—a-hem. Come in."

Without any further ceremony I opened the door, and entered the awful presence of the parish factotum, who was sitting in his shirt-sleeves before a table, on which were spread some documents, which appeared sadly to have puzzled him, for he was gnawing the end of a pen, while the perspiration was pouring down, like grease from a candle, his fat face. He stared at me out of a pair of grey goggle eyes for some minutes in silence; then he condescended to utter the word,—

"Well!"—"I want the address of some of the parish authorities, that I may communicate with them concerning a pauper child who has been ill-used in a place they have sent her to."

"A—a—pauper?"—"Yes; a pauper."

"A female pauper?"—"Exactly."

"Oh! we never listens to no complaints. We orders 'em all to lay on the table, and there they lays. What's her name?—who are you?—where is she?—how comed you to interfere? I dare say she's one o' our *incourageables*."

"Are you the beadle?" said I.—"I is—I is."

"Then I'll pull your nose if you are impertinent, for I never allow a beadle to be other than respectful to me. Do you understand me?"

The organ that I had threatened to pull became of a purplish hue as the blood rushed from the beadle's heart into that promontory, and he gasped a moment for breath. Then he looked up to the ceiling, as if he expected some great avalanche of mortar to fall upon his head, in consequence of my unheard-of presumption.

"The address of one of the overseers, directly!" cried I, giving the table purposely a terrible blow.

The beadle's nose immediately became supernaturally white, as he gasped out in reply,—

"Muster Bellamy, No. 3, Ge—Ge—George-street. Spare my life!"

"Who threatened your life?" said I. "It is not worth the taking. You are a great deal more amusing as a buffoon while you life, that your carcase would be useful to dissect after death."

DIARY OF A PHYSICIAN.

"I a *buffon*! Me a buffon? *Biscet*, a beadle. Oh, oh!—here's a *evolution*; workuses is a standin' on their heads, and beadles is flummuxed."

* * * * *

I did not wait to hear what further expressions of horror would burst from the lips of the astonished great man, but, having obtained the address I wanted, namely, that of one of the overseers, I at once left the workhouse, and proceeded to George-street, which was in the immediate vicinity.

I found No. 3 to be a handsome house, on the door of which was a plate, with the name of Bellamy on it, and underneath that again was a still smaller plate, on which were the words, "ring also;" an injunction which I obeyed by, after I had knocked, pulling a bell, which presented its handsome bronzed handle invitingly through the door-post. My summons for admission was answered by a smart footman, to whom I handed my card, saying,—

"If Mr. Bellamy is within, say that I would be happy to have a short interview with him on some business connected with his office in the parish."

"Mr. Bellamy is dressing for dinner, sir," said the footman, "but I will hand your card up to him."

He then called another servant out of livery, who having placed my card upon a richly-chased silver salver, trotted up stairs to Mr. Bellamy, while I was shown into a room, which, from the cursory examination I was enabled to give it, impressed me with a notion of the piety of Mr. Bellamy, and induced me to believe that at his hands I should surely receive every assistance in the prosecution of my attempt to rescue the unfortunate Emma Moorsam from the snares that were spread around her for her destruction.

On the walls of the apartment were engravings of the most evangelical nature, such as the ascent of meek, stupid-looking people through clouds, attended by angels, and the descent of others of a more restless looking disposition, through smoke, to that region which is not to be mentioned to ears polite. Then, there was open upon the table an immense family bible, and upon a chair was a pocket bible, with silver clasps, and there were prayer-books, too, about, of every size and shape, from a tolerable sized octavo volume to a diamond edition.

"Well," I thought, "Mr. Bellamy is evidently a religious man, and I hope that that will teach him his duty to the poor and the fatherless."

Scarcely had this thought passed through my mind, when the door opened, and a staid, middle-aged, exceedingly gentlemanly-looking man, came into the room.

We mutually bowed, and I said—

"I presume I have the honour of speaking to Mr. Bellamy?" With something between a groan and a conventicle whine, he said,—

"My name is Bellamy; but let us give honour to him only,

'Who sits upon a throne of grace,
    As pious volumes tell,
Frowning on sinners great and small,
    And hurling them to ——.'"

"My business, Mr. Bellamy," said I, "is not of an evangelical tendency, and I don't approve at all of the atrocious verse you have used as a quotation."

The fact was, I was thoroughly disgusted, as I always am with canting hypocrisy, and my manner as much as my words must have at once convinced him he was mistaken in me. He was silent for a moment and then said, in a tone of slight embarrassment,—

"Are you not the Reverend Mr. Elias Mudpoke?"—"Indeed, I am very happy to say I am not," said I. "There has been some mistake. I am Dr. ——," I added, "and my business with you is concerning some alleged ill-treatment of a young girl who has been apprenticed by the parish of which you are an overseer."

"A—a—young—young girl?"—"Yes; by her account she has been very badly treated, and I can likewise gather from her that there is a scheme on foot for her seduction, although, poor thing, she does not seem herself to be aware of the extent of that villany."

"Why—why—really," stammered Mr. Bellamy, "this is scarcely a time to enter upon such business, sir. I am about to dine, and expect some company."—"But this case I consider urgent, sir."

"To-morrow must do for its consideration, when, with the assistance of the Lord, something shall be done. Can you tell me the girl's name?"—"Yes; Emma Moorsam is her name, and she is apprenticed to a woman, calling herself Madame Rendell."

I thought he looked very odd as I spoke, and he was some moments before he said, in something of the whine he had adopted when he thought me the Reverend Mr. Mudpoke.

"The orphan shall be protected, and right shall be done—woe to the seducer—woe to the harlot—woe—woe—woe! There shall be gnashing of teeth and howling!"

"My good sir," said I, "if nothing can be done in this business till to-morrow, I hope something will then be done effectually."

"Upon that you may build your faith as upon a rock," he said. "Have you yet seen the way to grace?"—"I don't understand you, Mr. Bellamy?"

"I mean, how do you do, inwardly?"—"Sometimes better and sometimes worse; but it won't do for doctors to complain often, you know."

He gave a deep groan as he saw that I would not understand his questions, and added,—

"I will have prayers put up for you to the throne of grace, that the new light may break upon you, and you may become even as one who walketh on the edge of a pit, and falleth not in. Even as one ——"

"I beg your pardon," I interrupted: "but I really hope you will not give yourself any such trouble on my account. Pray tell me at what hour to-morrow I shall wait upon you concerning this business?"—"Leave it to me—leave it to me!" he replied, "and the innocent shall be righted!"

"Indeed, Mr. Bellamy, without at all doubting that you will do all that I wish you in this matter, permit to say, that I never leave anything to anybody when once I interest myself about it. Therefore I cannot rest contented until I see something done to rescue this young girl from her great peril."

"But surely you have done all that was required of you. Here you have called my attention to the circumstance; and when I assure you that I will interfere and see the affair thoroughly investigated, you will be satisfied?"

"Quite, as far as you are concerned, sir, and as far as poor Emma is concerned, but not in my own mind. I beg that you will allow me to know what is done in the matter as it is doing, and not after it is done."

"Are you," he asked, "a parishioner of this parish?"—"No," replied I.

"Ah, well. I cannot undertake to meet you to-morrow; but some time during the day I will either call upon or send for Madame Rendell, and have this matter put thoroughly to rights. You can, if you please, call upon me to-morrow, and I shall be very happy, the lord being always willing, to let you know what has been done in the matter."

I did not wish to injure poor Emma's chance of being righted by over precipitancy, or quarrelling with so very pious a character as Mr. Bellamy, so I was obliged to be content with this information and arrangement, merely saying—

"Very well, sir, I will call upon you the day after to-morrow, when I hope to hear that Emma Moorsam is taken away from the infamous woman who is evidently endeavouring to bring her to sin and shame."

"Ah," said Mr. Bellamy, with a groan, "our immortal welfare is what should be looked to. What is life but a vain tinkle, a shadow, a mote, a ——"

"Very true, sir; but while we are here, it strikes me we ought to make the best of it. Now, I am a physician, and I think I should look like a very great fool, and deserve to be kicked out, if, when called to a patient, I was, with a disagreeable snuffle in my nose, to take upon myself to say—'Oh, what is life, &c.'"

To this his only reply was to cast up his eyes with a moan, and say—

"The wicked triumph for an hour,
    And then are singed in heaps,
In that great range that's down below,
    An awful Satan keeps."

I was out of all patience, and, rather than come to an open quarrel with him, I bowed and said,—

"Good day, sir; I shall be here about this time the day after to-morrow."

He accompanied me to the street door, and I passed out on to the step before I recollected I had left my walking-stick in the hall. The door was not closed quite, and I pushed it open just in time to hear Mr. Bellamy say, in the most natural manner in the world, to the footman,—

"D—n you, which room did you put the Rev. Elias Mudpoke in?"

* * * * *

I was not unmindful of my promise to see Emma within four-and-twenty hours, and, on the afternoon of the day after that on which she had come to me at the chemist's in Holborn, I went to Hemmingham-street, and sought out the abode of Madame Rendell. I certainly had serious doubts in my own mind as to receiving any assistance whatever beyond some weak remonstrance to the cruel and abandoned woman, from the hypocritical Mr. Bellamy; but, at all events, I was bound to let the time he had mentioned pass quietly over before I made any further stir in the matter.

I found that the establishment of Madame Rendell in Hemmingham-street was a very fashionable one, and a large brass plate upon an inner door bore upon it, with many flourishes, the words "Madame Rendell, court dress-maker and milliner." A neat brass knocker was upon this door, and, seeing no other medium of communication with the house, I gave a rat-tat with it, which was immediately answered by a page in livery, who demanded to know my business.

"I wish to see a young person here of the name of Emma Moorsam."

The page look bothered as he said,—

"I'll tell missus."

"Take my card," said I, "and say that I wish to see the young person I have mentioned for a few minutes."

After a moment's hesitation the page allowed me to pass the door-way, and, opening the door of a room to the right, he said,—

"Take a seat there, sir, if you please, and I will carry your card to Madame Rendell directly."

The room was a kind of waiting-room, and very nicely furnished indeed. I had not waited in it many minutes when a door at the further end from that I had entered was opened, and a female presented herself, whom I shall endeavour, although, I fear, but faintly, to describe.

She was on the shady side of forty, and, if she did not indulge in ardent spirits, her nose libelled her most desperately. Upon her head she wore one of those monstrosities called turbans—huge ear-rings hung pendant from her large ears, and her double chin bobbed about like the dew-lap of a cow. She was a great, masculine-looking female, and carried herself with that air, to me, so specially disgusting, which seems to say, "Look at me—I'm a fine woman;" and so she was, and so would have been called by hundreds of men who pretend to taste.

As she entered the room, there was that expression upon her face which at once convinced me I had to deal with an unprincipled character, and that, in all human probability, I should have some trouble in obtaining an interview with Emma Moorsam.

She made what I dare say she considered a very elaborate and petrifying curtsey to me, and then, with a toss of her head, which kept up a quiver and a "nodification" of a bird of paradise feather that was stuck on the top of the turban, she waited for me to open the conversation.

"Are you Madame Rendell?" said I.—"I am Madame Rendell," she replied, with another quiver of the turban, which seemed to say, "what have you got to say against that?"

"Then, I have to request you will allow me to see Miss Emma Moorsam."

She drew in a very long breath, as if she meant to blow me out of the house upon respiring it in again, and then said, while the turban and the bird of paradise feather shook tremendously,—

"And pray, sir, may I ask you what you want with Miss Emma Moorsam?"—"I am her physician," said I.

"Her physician—her physician?"—"Exactly."

"Pho—pho—pho!"—"Will you have the goodness to translate me, 'pho—pho?'" said I.

For a moment Madame Rendell looked as if she would make an attack upon me, and I kept on the alert to push a chair between us, should such be the case. But she apparently thought better of it, and in that cool manner which people strive to assume sometimes, when they are in a tremendous rage, she said,—

"Perhaps, sir—you may not be aware, sir, that Miss Emma Moorsam, sir, is my apprentice, sir—my parish pauper apprentice, sir?"—"Oh, yes, perfectly."

"In—deed; then, sir, it does strike me as just a little odd, that my parish pauper—horrid—wretched apprentice, should have a physician calling upon her, sir!"—"Yes," said I, calmly, "it is odd."

"I should say very odd."—"You are right, madam; but there is no fighting against facts, you see. Here I am."

The calm manner in which I replied to her seemed perfectly to infuriate Madame Rendell, and, trembling with passion, she cried,—

"Then, sir, you shall not see her."—"I will," said I.

"You tell me you will—me—me———"—"Ay, you. The young girl I come to see may be your apprentice, madam; but she is not your prisoner, nor shall she be your slave. I repeat, that I will see her, or———"

"Or what?"—"I will go at once to a magistrate."

Madame Rendell grasped the back of a chair for support, as she said,—

"Get out of my house. Wretch—villain!"

"Madam, how dare you speak to me in this manner?" I said, in a loud, firm voice. "I come professionally to attend upon the young girl, whom you, by your avarice and cruelty, have reduced to an exceedingly delicate state of health. You dare not refuse to let me see her!"

She was completely cowed by my bold manner, as all your fine, insolent women very readily may be subdued, and, sinking into a chair, she said,—

"I hav'n't ill-used her; she wants to ruin me—I know she does. I have been quite a mother to that girl."—"As a physician, having undertaken to visit her professionally, and attend to her health, I have no hesitation in saying, she is suffering from exhaustion, in consequence of late hours, and over work.?'

"It's false—it's false!" cried Madame Rendell. "She is an odious hussy, and wants to take away my character."—"I am quite sure she wants no such thing," said I; "she would say nothing that was untrue, and surely, Madame Rendell, you can have nothing to fear from the truth."

She saw that I was bantering her, and, rising from the chair into which she had thrown herself, she said,—

"Sir, however you have been misled by that artful hussy's tales about me, I can tell you that my character will bear stricter scrutiny than perhaps some people's not a hundred miles off."

The bird of paradise feather gave a grand nod at this speech, and continued to vibrate in great glorification at its termination.

"I have no doubt, Madame Rendell," said I, in the calm, ironical tone in which I had conducted the principal part of the conversation, "that within a mile of a hundred miles from here, might be found a great many persons whose characters would bear even a less scrutiny than yours. There is an amazing deal of iniquity in the world indeed."

"No doubt, sir," she cried with a sneer, "it's a very convenient thing to be a physician."—"Yes, very."

"A-hem! because he can call upon girls *professionally*—a—a—a-hem!"

"You have a very bad cough, madam," said I.—"Wretch!" I smiled.

"Villain—vagabond!"

"Pray, madam, have you a husband?" said I.—"What's that to you?"

"Only this much, that if he will back you out in all your vulgarity and low abuse, you odious, disgusting woman, I shall have very great pleasure in horsewhipping him on your account."

Madame Rendell upon this flourished her arms in the air like a maniac for a few moments, during which she hit the bird of paradise such a side blow, that it fell from the turban on to the floor, and then in her rage trampling over it, and ruining its capacity for nodding for ever, she rushed from the apartment, leaving me alone.

"What now?" I thought, as I found myself left by the enraged Madame Rendell to my own reflections. I waited and waited for some time, in expectation of her return, but she came not. At length I got impatient, and rang the bell tolerably smartly. In a few moments a servant appeared, of the most slatternly order, and stared at me some time without speaking.

"Where is Madame Rendell?" said I.—"She's got the 'historics,' and can't see nobody."

"Got the what?"—"The kicking 'historics.'"

"Do you mean hysterics?"—"Very likely. I ain't no scholard."

"Oh, indeed. What's your name?"—"My name's Kit."

"Well, then, Kit, just find out Emma Moorsam, and tell her the physician is here, and wants to see her."

"You've seen missus?"—"Oh, yes; it's all right. I will wait here, and do you send Emma Moorsam to me as soon as you can."

The girl left the room, after giving me another very hard stare; but she performed her message, for in a very few minutes my patient entered the room, and, rushing up to me, she clasped my hand, saying,—

"Oh, sir, have you come to take me away from here? I am so happy."—"No, Emma," I said, "I have not come to take you away—that I cannot do; but I am attempting to better your condition as quickly as I can, and my object in now calling upon you was to convince you that I had not forgotten you."

"How can I thank you, sir?"—"Don't try to do so at all, Emma. I have forced a promise from the parish authorities to interfere in your behalf, and we must wait to see what they will do, before taking any steps in defiance of them."

"Yes," she said, "I will be guided by you, sir, in everything; but I am afraid that they will use me worse if they find you have been here."

"Nay," said I, "I don't think so, for I have seen Madame Rendell, and, I believe, alarmed her a little. Be patient, Emma, for a day or two, and trust in my seeing you righted as soon as possible. Now, tell me, has this cousin of Madame Rendell's been here lately?"—"Not for some days, sir. Oh, I dread him more than all."

"You shall be freed from his importunities, never fear," said I. "Keep up a good heart, and all will be well."

The door burst open at this moment, with a bang that nearly wrenched it off its hinges, and Madame Rendell appeared with her hair hanging wildly about her ears, and a general appearance of disorder, which, I suppose, the "historics," as the servant called them, sufficiently accounted for.

There could be no manner of doubt, likewise, that the remedy she had used was not one to be found in the list of accredited drugs in use by physicians, for she brought in with her such a strong odour of gin that it filled the room completely.

"Oh, you vile, good-for-nothing hussy!" said she, as she made an attempt to fly at Emma, like an enraged tigress; "how dare you see your fellows in my house?"

"Madame Rendell, or Mrs. Gibbs," said I, as I interposed between her and the object of her wrath, "I will give you in custody to a constable, if you dare to lay hands on this girl. Know that I have resolved to protect her—that I have the means as well as the inclination, and if you attempt to vilify her character or mine, I will drag you into a court of law, when we will perhaps find out who your cousin is."

She looked perfectly petrified at this speech, and for some moments was incapable of answering me; then she gasped out, in a curious, spasmodic manner,—

"What—what do you know about my cousin?"—"More, perhaps, than you are aware of," said I, "Be careful, madam, and do not let me hear when I come again—which will be to-morrow—that you have aggravated your case by additional ill-usage of this young person, who will be protected, you may depend."

Then turning to Emma, I said,—

"Should the slightest attempt be made to ill-use you, Emma, do you make your way out of the house, and come to me; you will find me at No. 11, Broad-street, in the City; and should I not be at home, you will be taken care of there till I return."

"She—she is my apprentice," said Madame Rendell.

"I know she is," said I: "but that gives you no license or authority to ill-use her, and it shall not be done. Were she your daughter, the law would step between you and her, if you exceeded the proper bounds of a parent's authority. Beware, madam, what you do, or this affair may assume a more serious aspect than you imagine. Now, Emma, good day to you—keep up your spirits, and rely on me."

I then left the place, feeling tolerably assured that I had made a sufficient impression upon Madame Rendell's fears to prevent her from perpetrating any ill-usage against the young girl in the short space of time which would elapse between then and my next visit, when I hoped to force Bellamy, the overseer, to take her before a magistrate and cancel the indentures.

* * * * *

The following day was the one appointed for the visit of the pious Mr. Bellamy to Madame Rendell's, and although I was much prepossessed against the man, and believed him to be as rank a hypocrite as ever took up the mask of religion, I considered that in his official capacity he could not avoid doing what was proper in the circumstances which I had laid before him.

I was resolved that he should have no excuse for neglecting the matter, and, accordingly, some time before the appointed hour I walked to George-street, in order to jog his memory on the matter, and insist upon the promised visit to Madame Rendell. I was ushered into the same evangelical-looking parlour into which I had before been shown, and the footman said, in a tone of voice, as if he feared to speak above his breath of his revered master,—

"Mr. Bellamy, sir, is at morning prayers, and cannot be disturbed for a few minutes."

"Oh, very well," said I, "I have no wish to disturb him in his devotions—I can wait."

"Thank you, sir," said the footman, as he bowed, and left the room with a demure air.

I again looked at the room, and was much amused at the parade of religion which was manifest in all the prints and books that were there. The table, too, was covered with tracts, the titles of some of which were to the full as curious as some of the tractarian productions of the Cromwell period, when evangelism was a mania, and the puritan

"Hanged his cat on a Monday,
For killing a mouse on a Sunday.
Oh! profane one!"

"People call this respectable," thought I, "and universally almost give credit for good intentions to those affected religious enthusiasts; but how often is such outward sanctity assumed to cover vices within which a heathen would blush for!"

It was full a quarter of an hour before Mr. Bellamy made his appearance; but, previous to that, a humble knock had sounded on the outer door, and a whispered discourse had taken place in the passage between somebody and the footman, at the end of which I heard the latter say,—

"Sit down a bit, he will be here soon."

Then a voice, which I recognised as that of the imperious beadle, replied,—

"Thank'e, Timmas, it's very bad it is. She's one o' our casuals, she is."—"Oh," said Thomas, "I say ——"

Then there was another whisper and a laugh, which betokened some mystery, which I could not, for the life of me, divine. A few minutes after this little episode, I heard the pompous creaking of some one's boots coming down the staircase, and then the voice of Mr. Bellamy said,—

"Oh, you are here, are you? God d—n it! what's the matter now?"

"Ah," I thought, "this is the gentleman who has just been at prayers!"

There was a great rush now of some one from the kitchen, and I heard the footman say,—

"Please there's Dr. —— waiting."

After this intimation to Mr. Bellamy I could hear his voice no more; but by the sound of feet I fancied he took the beadle into the next room to where I was. It was not long after this when the door was opened, and Mr. Bellamy appeared, looking calm and serene.

"Good morning, sir," he said; "pray be seated."—"Thank you," I said. "I have taken the liberty of calling upon you earlier than you said would be convenient, for I feel the greatest interest in the fate of the young girl whom I mentioned to you, and who, I believe, if not rescued from the abominable woman she is with, would be either sent to an early grave through harsh usage, or betrayed into a course of life full of horrors."

Mr. Bellamy gave a deep groan, and lifted up his hands as he said, in the true conventicle twang,—

"The wicked who in want of faith
With sinful thoughts do dwell,
'Midst torturing flames in brimstone lakes,
Will roll about in h—."

"Well, Mr. Bellamy," said I, "I would rather not enter into conversation with you on religious topics. The business at present in hand is the rescue of a poor orphan girl from the snares that surround her, and her restoration to peace of mind and happiness."

He turned up the whites of his eyes, and said,—

"I am a weak vessel—a very weak vessel; but what in me lays, that will I do."—"In that case, Mr. Bellamy," said I, for I was quite annoyed by his cant, "you are, being overseer of the parish, a strong vessel, and can do a great deal. It is the poor, persecuted Emma Moorsam who is a weak vessel, to whom, in comparison, you are as a great earthenware pitcher to a China tea-cup."

He looked at me very suspiciously, as if he suspected I was quizzing him, which, in fact, I was, although I kept a very grave face, and did not let him see the ghost of a smile.

"Ah," he said, "you put me much in mind of a nephew of mine, who resides, for a time, beneath my roof. You may have heard him; he wears creaking boots, has a voice very much like mine, and uses profane oaths."

Mr. Bellamy looked me very hard in the face, to see how I received this barefaced lie, and I said,—

"Indeed his voice is very much like yours, Mr. Bellamy."—"Very, very," he said. "I hope yet to open his eyes to his dreadful condition, and make him throw himself open to grace. He is very sinful."

I could scarcely forbear laughing in his face at this attempt to get over the unlucky speech to the beadle, which he felt sure I must have heard; but it was not my business to have any contention with Mr. Bellamy about his suavity or hypocrisy. All I required was, that in his official capacity he should do his duty.

"Are you ready, Mr. Bellamy, to go with me to Madame Rendell's now?"—"Yes," he replied; "I will be with you in a few moments."

He then left me alone for a few minutes, when he returned equipped for the streets, saying,—

"The distance is but short, and I have not ordered my carriage; but I will, if you object to walk."—"Don't think of such a thing," I said. "I prefer walking so short a distance."

We accordingly started, arm-in-arm, towards Madame Rendell's, and only twice or thrice on the road did Mr. Bellamy come out with any of his extemporaneous piety. I explained to him as we went my strong suspicion, amounting almost to a certainty; in fact, I was morally certain, that madame was a most questionable character, and ostensibly conducted the millinery business merely as a cloak for the worst purposes. Mr. Bellamy heard me in silence, and answered me with a profusion of groans, wondering there could be such wickedness in the world, and ascribing it all to the want of grace and faith. Thus conversing, we reached Madame Rendell's establishment, and knocked at the inner passage door. We were answered by the page, to whom Mr. Bellamy said,—

"Tell your mistress, boy, that two gentlemen require an audience of her on business of much importance."

I thought I saw a suppressed grin upon the page's face, as he flung the door open, and said,—

"Yes, sir; will you be so good as to walk in?" and he shewed us into the same waiting-room in which I had had my first interview with Madame Rendell, which had brought on her *historics*.

Mr. Bellamy said nothing, nor did I, till Madame Rendell made her appearance in a new turban, with a new bird of paradise at the top, which nodded quite as well as its predecessor had done. She drew herself up with an air of hauteur as she saw me, and exclaimed,—

"Well, sir, I am glad you have come—very glad, indeed—uncommonly glad."—"I am a man of my word, madam," said I, "and having promised to come, you might have made sure you would have the pleasure of seeing me."

"Do you know me, madam?" said Mr. Bellamy, with austere gravity.—"I believe you are Mr. Thingummy, the overseer," was Madame Rendell's response.

"My name, madam, is Bellamy, not Thingummy, and I came here at the solicitation of this gentleman, to see an apprentice of yours, who you took from the parish, and who, it is alleged, you ill-use."—"Indeed; so that's what you've come for, is it? I'm very glad to see you, both of you—oh, very!"

"You are very kind and complimentary," said I; "but, if you please, we will waste no further time in ceremonies, but at once see Emma Moorsam."

Madame Rendell gave what her servant would have called a slight *historical* laugh, as she replied, in a cracked voice,—

"I wish you may see her."

"We must see the girl," said Bellamy.—"And we shall see her," said I.

Again Madame Rendell laughed, and added immediately afterwards—

"I wish I could see her, the hussy, the wretch, the little lying baggage, the thief!"

"What do you mean," said I, "by pouring such a torrent of abuse upon the head of a poor girl who has been compelled to complain of your ill-usage?"—"Oh, that's all very fine—very fine indeed. Look here—look here, I say."

As she spoke, she dabbed down upon the tea-table a long slip of paper, on which was some writing, which she continued knocking with her hand, as she cried in a half screaming voice—

"Read that—read that."—"We can't read it, if you hold it there," I remarked, upon which she threw it towards me, and being anxious to know what it could have to do with Emma Moorsam, I took it and began its perusal.

I found it to be a sort of list, or catalogue of miscellaneous articles, and as Madame Rendell kept shouting:—"Read that—read that," I read aloud.

"Item.—Two gravy spoons. Item.—One mustard ditto. Item.—A gros-de-naples dress, and one sable boa. Item.—One chrystal ring, and one ditto garnets."—"Bless me," I said, "what has all this to do with our business here, Madame Rendell?"—"Oh, what indeed!" said Mr. Bellamy.

"Can't you guess?" said the lady, agitating her turban, fearfully. "No, indeed, I am a bad hand at conundrums."

"Then, I'll tell you," she said, raising her voice to a pitch that made me jump; "that wretched girl, who told you all manner of lies about me, has eloped—run away—left my house, taking with her all these articles, the baggage!"

"What! Emma Moorsam?"—"Yes, sir; Emma Moorsam, that you took such interest in—that you thought such a piece of injured innocence—yes, Emma Moorsam!"

These last works were screamed out so, that I instinctively drew back, for I expected nothing more or less than a demonstration with the nails of the lady upon my face.

"Oh, what wickedness there is in the world!" said Mr. Bellamy, casting up his eyes.

" ' The lack of faith's a grievous sin,
And punish'd is by fire,
What everlasting ——' "

"Pshaw!" cried I. "Cease this jargon, Mr. Bellamy, and attend to business. I do not believe one word, Madame Rendell, of all that you have said against Emma Moorsam, and I will have this affair investigated, let it cost me what time and trouble it may."

At these words of mine Madame Rendell's face assumed a tinge equal in intensity to the setting sun on a fine evening.

"You don't believe it?" she said. "Indeed, madam, I do not. I cannot, will not believe that nature works by such contraries, as to implant vice where there is every semblance of virtue."

"Then I tell you, sir, that I will have her apprehended—that I will have her transported. I will have her hung—the infamous, the vile wretch—to go and tell people lies about me and my house!"

"Madam," said I, "you seem much more angry at what Emma Moorsam should say of you and your house, than at the abstraction of the silver spoons, &c., which any one would think would give you the most uneasiness."—"My uneasiness, sir, is nothing to you," she said. "I decline any sort of conversation with you, sir,—quite decline it; and, what's more, I desire that you leave my house this moment."

"Oh, the wickedness of the world!" said Mr. Bellamy, again. "You see, doctor, how you have allowed your feelings to get the better of your judgment in this affair."—"Indeed, Mr. Bellamy," said I, "I am not sure of that, and I must have better evidence than the mere word of Madame Rendell before I give up my hopes of Emma Moorsam."

"Oh, it's all very fine—mighty fine," said Madame Rendell, with mock politeness; "but I'd have you to know, sir, that if you say anything against my character, I'll bring an action against you, I will."—"You may take what course you like," said I; "but before I leave this house, I call upon you, Mr. Bellamy, in your official capacity, to insist upon seeing Emma Moorsam, who I believe to be at the present moment in this house."

"If I thought so ——" said he.—"At least we can search," I added, as I rose. "I am determined to do so, whether you like it or not, Madame Rendell, and whether Mr. Bellamy assists me or not."

DIARY OF A PHYSICIAN.

Upon this Bellamy rose and said,—

"I dare say Madame Rendell will rather allow us to search an go away with the suspicion upon our minds which you em to intimate. What do you say, madam?"—"Oh, you e quite welcome," cried Madame Rendell, with a great toss the turban, and as tremendous nodding of the bird of radise.

Bellamy moved towards the door, muttering something out his time being precious, and that if a search was to be ade, he wished it might be done at once.

"Very well, Mr. Bellamy," said I; "my time is, I am re, as precious as yours can be, but I think we ought not leave this house without ascertaining clearly if Emma oorsam be here or not."

"Oh, search away—search away," said Madame Rendell. Pray look in all the cupboards and bandboxes—oh, dear, s—perhaps you'll find her in some needle-case or another. She then sat down, and by the playing of her fingers on the ble, and the increased vibration of the turban, I began to apprehensive she meditated some more "historics," and I cordingly got out of the room as quickly as possible, lowed, at a more demure pace, by Bellamy, who said,—

"You see, doctor, how deceitful are appearances. You supsed that young person who has now surrendered herself Satan to be an oppressed creature, when now you hear she s actually committed a most daring robbery."

"Mr. Bellamy," said I, "once for all I tell you I do not lieve one word that Madame Rendell says. There is some ystery in this affair, which I am resolved, if possible, to hom."

He spread open his hands and elevated his eyebrows, as uch as to say, "As you please; it is of no avail talking to obstinate man like you."

I then led the way, and we went over the whole house thout finding any trace of the object of our search. In t, when Madame Rendell made so very slight an opposin to my search, I gave up in my own mind any hope of ding Emma there, although I would not altogether forego e chance of doing so.

There is no manner of difficulty in searching modern uses, the places of which are all obvious, and in which ere cannot, from the contiguity of other buildings and the inness of the walls, be any hiding-places, and, consequently, less than a quarter of an hour, I felt quite satisfied that nma was not concealed anywhere there. I turned, then, Bellamy, and said—

"Well, sir, what do you propose doing now?"—"I propose thing," he said. "What would you have me do?"

"Why," added I, "the circumstances are sufficiently peliar to call for some course of action in connexion with em. Here is a young girl comes to me and complains of usage, and here is a woman, who, from her violence and ldent bad disposition, is fully capable of such conduct. ell, sir, on the very day that an inquiry was to commence, e girl mysteriously disappears. Now, Mr. Bellamy, this ry of the robbery is quite absurd, for it has no sort of conxion with the rest of the girl's conduct."

"But, sir," he replied, "there is the fact."—"The alleged t you mean, dependent altogether upon one's belief in Mame Rendell."

"Well, I can do nothing further. If you find the girl, and en come to me, I will enter again into the business, as I ve now, since the girl was apprenticed from the parish in ich I hold an official appointment. I hope she may be incent; but I have sad misgivings. I never heard that she lked in the ways of grace; and—

"'They who take the dreadful path
That sinners leads to hell,
'Mid burning coals and devil's toils,
For evermore will dwell.'

I have the honour, doctor, of wishing you a very good morning; and if you should ever feel, which I hope you will before it is too late, a yearning after grace, you will receive great spiritual consolation, and be convinced that ninety-nine out of a hundred of your fellow-creatures will be roasted to all eternity, by attending the Rev. Elias Mudpoke's pious discourses at the Little Ebenezer, in Little Britain."

He then, without waiting for any reply from me, drew on his black silk gloves, and, with a deep sigh for the sins, I presume, of the whole human race, he left me on the step of Madame Rendell's door.

That this man, Bellamy, was a hypocrite of the first order, I felt firmly convinced from his own manner, as well as from the few words it had been my lot to overhear him utter while I was waiting for him at his own house; and now, as I stood upon the step of Madame Rendell's door, a painful emotion came across my mind, that he was conniving at some desperate villany that was taking place as regarded the unfortunate Emma.

The sudden disappearance of the girl at such a juncture as this, and the evidently trumped up charge of robbery, looked sufficiently suspicious, and it appeared to me as if I was being hedged off, as it were, in this ingenious manner. My readers, however, know enough of me by this time to be aware that I am rather persevering, perhaps, I ought to say obstinate; and I made up my mind that I would not abandon Emma, although, for the life of me, just then, I could not think of any means of unravelling the mystery in which she and all connected with her were enveloped.

"What's to be done— what's to be done?" I asked myself repeatedly, as I walked slowly homewards; for I had avoided another stormy interview with Madame Rendell, which would have availed me nothing.

The question of what shall I do was much easier asked than answered; and I returned to my lodgings very much vexed and unhappy about the poor girl, whose situation, for all I knew, I had made much worse than before by my interference. But each moment that I remained in this perplexity, my suspicions of Bellamy were gaining strength. Over and over again I reconsidered every little circumstance, and every word he had said. In all, I found ample food for suspicion, but nothing of a certain and sure character to enable me to act upon.

Suddenly, then, it came to my mind, that in a circumstance which had occurred some time before I had been much struck with the calm penetration and clear-headedness, if I may be allowed the term, of a police-officer whom I had occasion to have some conversation with. His name was Eagleton; and no sooner did I think of him than I started up, and snatching my hat, I said—

"I will go and ask Eagleton's advice. He is the very man, of all others, who may offer me some valuable suggestions on the subject."

I had not the least idea of where he lived; but upon walking to the Mansion-house and making the inquiry, I was told his address in a moment, for he was a well-known man, and beginning to be much appreciated by the magistrates. From the Mansion-house, then, I walked to his house, and was lucky enough to find him at home.

"Eagleton," said I, "you recollect me?"—"Certainly, sir," he replied; "I very rarely forget any one I have seen."

"Well, then, I want you to do a kindness to one who, in all human probability, will never be able to repay you; but it is a case of real oppression, which you are just the man to unravel and set to rights."—"I shall be very happy to be of any assistance," he replied, "if you will favour me with the particulars."

I then told him distinctly and clearly the whole story, from beginning to end, and he never interrupted me once, but listened with the greatest attention. When I had concluded, his first words were—

"The robbery is all a sham."

"You think so?"—"Oh, certainly; the police have heard nothing of it, or I should have known by this time. It appears to me, now, that the girl is smuggled away somewhere, by Madame Rendell and this cousin she mentioned."

"And that cousin ——"—"Is the pious Mr. Bellamy, of course. I have met with such cases as these before."

"And the poor girl's ruin may, by this time, be accomplished."—"No," said Eagleton, "I differ with you there. That would be too serious an affair just now. You may depend that if I am right in my conjectures, and Bellamy has had her removed elsewhere, that while there is the least chance of your discovering her by any means, he will keep her uninjured, so that, if a discovery was to take place, he could not be identified in the transaction at all."

"I see what you mean," said I.

"Now," continued Eagleton, "this Bellamy, if guilty, is a most atrocious scoundrel, and shall by all means be thoroughly implicated."—"Exactly."

"The woman Rendell is, in all probability, merely in his pay, and I think our plan will be to frighten her into becoming evidence against her employer."

"But she will then escape."—"Yes, in a measure; but

then the odour of the transaction will abide by her, and she will have to be off."

"What immediate course, then, would you advise should be adopted?"—"Why, the only way it appears to me is, to keep very quiet indeed, and watch Bellamy till he thinks all danger is over, when he will visit his victim. You can leave all that to me, doctor, I will undertake that part of the business; and I would advise you to call upon Madame Rendell again, and make a fuss about Emma Moorsam, showing a great deal of chagrin at her disappearance."

"That I will do. When shall I see you again?"—"I will call upon you to-morrow evening and report progress."

I was resolved to quiet the mind of Bellamy as much as I possibly could, so as to induce him more quickly to fall into the snare that was prepared for him, and accordingly, the next morning, as soon as I could spare time, I called in George-street, and inquired for the pious gentleman.

In a very few moments he was with me, and I said,—

"You will excuse me troubling you, Mr. Bellamy, but I could not be easy in my mind concerning that poor girl, whom I really believe to be innocent, until I saw you again, and got from you your solemn assurance that you will use every endeavour to discover her, and let me know if you should be successful."

I saw his countenance change immediately from one of gloom and suspicion, which he had worn at my entrance, to pleasure and satisfaction, as he replied,—

"I solemnly pledge you my word, sir, that I will do as you desire; and, notwithstanding any little difference of opinion we may have had about this affair, I trust we give each other, in Christian charity, credit for the very best intentions that can be?"—"That is quite sufficient, Mr. Bellamy," said I; "I wish you good evening, and hope to hear from you."

He very politely came himself to the door to let me out, and every one who had seen us would have thought we were the best friends in the world.

From Bellamy's I went direct to Madame Rendell's, but what was my surprise, the moment I got into the passage, to meet the beadle with whom I had a little *fracas* at the workhouse coming out.

"Hilloa!" said I, "you here?"

He made a rush to pass me, but I dodged him from one side of the passage to the other, till he gave it up, and then in a voice of alarm, he said,—

"Wh—w—what does yer want?"—"What do you want?" said I; "you are a pretty fellow to try to get out of my way. I shouldn't wonder, now, but what you are after some iniquity."

"What me?"—"Yes, you."

"Me arter a *niquity*? I never thinks o' such things. I wonders at yer. Me arter *niquity*, indeed!"

"What brings you here?"—"I ain't agoing all for to be bullied," said the beadle, plucking up his courage; "I comes here on parochial business; my own parochial official legs brings me here."

"You are a rogue, and you know it," said I; "let me pass—get out with you."

He had no inclination to oppose my progress, but got out of the way with the greatest celerity, while I knocked at the door.

The answer to my request to see Madame Rendell was, that she was from home, so that, as I could not take the house by storm, I merely said,—

"Has Emma Moorsam been found?"—"No, she isn't," was the reply; and, with a "very well," I walked away.

* * * * *

According to appointment, I met Eagleton that evening, and he told me that Bellamy had been watched without success, for, wherever he had gone, he had not been where any suspicion could be at all excited; "but," he added, "the person I put upon him as a spy, tells me that the beadle of the parish is in such frequent connection with Bellamy, that there is every reason to believe he acts as an agent in the matter. To-morrow, therefore, we will take accurate note of his movements, and may discover something."

"And, in the meantime, you really think Emma will be safe?"—"Oh, perfectly—perfectly."

I then related to him my meeting with the beadle, which tended to confirm him in the opinion that it would be the most advisable course to follow him. Upon this understanding, then, we separated, and I was, I must own, not a little anxious and fidgetty about the non-success which had hitherto attended the exertions to save Emma Moorsam. The next evening came, and the officer was an hour behind his time in coming to me. When he did, however, his first words were,—

"Put on your hat, doctor, and come with me."

"Where to?" said I.—"To the house where Emma Moorsam is, in my opinion, kept a prisoner."

There needed no second invitation to me after this, and I at once walked out with Eagleton, who, when we got into the street, said,—

"I acted upon our arrangements, and set some one to watch the beadle, who, during the day, has been twice to Madame Rendell's, as well as several times to Bellamy's. Towards the afternoon part, however, he was seen to leave Rendell's with a bundle, and, being followed, he went towards St. John's Wood. Now my spy is perfectly acquainted with London, and is himself no better than he should be. He assures me, that he traced the beadle to a house of very questionable character. The delay in my coming to you this evening, has arisen from my going with him to see this house, to which I will now take you, and we will get into it some way or another."

I was quite delighted at the prospect of rescuing Emma, and we walked rapidly towards St. John's Wood. On our way Eagleton told me a number of most interesting and amusing anecdotes, which he had picked up in the course of his experience as an officer; some of which bore very strongly upon the circumstances of poor Emma Moorsam, although my mind was too actively engaged in thinking of what would be the result of my exertions in her behalf to permit me to pay all the attention to him that he really deserved.

It was very dark by the time we reached St. John's Wood, and after conducting me up and down several turnings, my guide paused near that dull-looking place called the South Bank, and turning to me, said,—

"Now, doctor, we are close at hand; I think the best way will be to carry things with a bold hand."—"Certainly," said I; "you will not find me averse to any measure, let it be ever so bold, which may have the effect of rescuing the girl from what must be to her an awful distressing situation."

"You are not armed, of course?"—"No," said I; "the only dangerous weapon that doctors have anything to do with is their drugs."

"Well, now," continued Eagleton, "it's just possible we may meet with some resistance, for such a house as I am about to take you to is seldom without some bullying fellows, who will attempt to intimidate. They know me pretty well, but in case we should be by any accident separated, you had better take one of my pistols, and if you have occasion to use it, I shall hear you, and soon be with you."

"I will take it," said I, as I placed the weapon in my pocket, "although I hope and trust I shall have no occasion for it, and should hesitate very much to use it, except I was seriously hurt, or opposed very much by numbers."

"That I now leave entirely to your own discretion," he said. "Come on now, doctor, we are close at hand; I will knock at the door, and the moment it is opened we will make good our entrance."

"We had better," remarked I, "have provided ourselves with a warrant for such an affair as this."

"Oh, no," he replied, "we are quite safe in acting in this business. The magistrates will always protect any one in such a matter, although a warrant would be the most regular course, I admit."

He paused now in a very dark spot, where there was a row of genteel cottage-like houses, with little gardens in front, and ornamental iron rails dividing them from the public way and from each other.

He then placed a whistle to his mouth, and blew very faintly, when from some obscure corner, I could not tell where, there stepped up a man, who said—

"Mr. E.?"—"Yes," said Eagleton; "has any one been here?"

"A woman," was the answer.

"Did you know who she was?"—"No, but she was rather big, and showily dressed. She popped in in such a moment that I could not catch a glimpse of her face."

"It is as likely to be Madame Rendell as not," whispered Eagleton to me, "but we will soon ascertain that."

As he spoke the sound of coach-wheels suddenly in the street—if street it could be called—came upon our ears, and he said—

"Let us see where this coach is going first."

DIARY OF A PHYSICIAN.

We all three drew back into the deep shadow cast by a tree, which grew from one of the gardens, some distance over the pathway.

The coach came on slowly on account of the darkness of the place, for there were no lamps, and to our surprise, when it came near where we were, a voice which I knew full well as belonging to the beadle, said—

"This here house; mind as yer drives up close to the kerb; hold unkimmon hard while I gets down. Bless yer, I would come down with a whop on no account—no, not to be made a churchwarden this blessed minute, I wouldn't."

The coach stopped close to the kerb, for there was a kerb although there was no pavement, and after a great deal of caution and numerous injunctions to the driver to hold hard, the beadle alighted from the box on which he had been sitting, to point out the precise house to the coachman.

"Well," he said, as he shook himself, "that ere's a mercy. I doesn't like getting up and down vehicles—oh, dear, no. If one was to slip, one might break one's precious neck; haccidents may happen to beadles as well as common people. We is all mere mortals, we is. Flesh is wanity, and gin is weksation, where yer can't get any on it."

The beadle had scarcely arrived at the end of these moral and philosophical reflections, when he placed his hand on the gate leading to the garden, and would have opened it, but that at the moment Eagleton laid hold of him by the collar, and said—

"Speak a word, and you are a dead man."

At the same instant he placed the muzzle of a pistol close to the cheek of the terror-struck beadle, who stood for some few moments so thoroughly bewildered that he had no power to speak or move had he been ever so much inclined to do either.

"Give the least alarm," added Eagleton, "utter so much as a whisper, except in answer to what I shall ask you, and I will blow out your brains with this pistol, which is loaded to the muzzle, as sure as you are a living beadle."

A spasmodic sort of gasp was the only answer which the

beadle could give, and then Eagleton, turning to me, said—

"Keep this man a prisoner for a moment, while I speak to the coachman."

I accordingly took hold of my old friend, the beadle, and held him tight, while Eagleton, advancing to the coach, said,

"Coachman, come down; I want to speak to you a moment."

"What do you want with me?" said the coachman.—"You will find that out when you come down," was the officer's reply. "Did you ever hear of one John Eagleton?"

"The officer?" said the coachman, in a tone which at once betrayed his alarm.—"Yes, the officer. I am that same, so if you don't please to come down, Jarvey, I shall be under the necessity of fetching you."

"I'm coming," said the coachman, as, coiled up in his voluminous great coats, he rolled off his box, and presented himself to the officer.

"What's your number?" said Eagleton.—"Nine hundred and seventy-three," said the coachman.

"How did you get here?"—"I was called off the stand in Church-street, close by the market."

"Very well. You will come to no harm if you attend to my instructions. There is my staff."—"I hope there ain't nothink wrong," said the coachman. "I didn't know nothink about it."

"Very well. All you have to do is to attend to me, and you may find it turn out a better job than you anticipated."—"I'll do anything in reason," said the coachman.

"Agreed. Then get upon your box again, and take no notice whatever of anything that occurs till I speak to you again, and I will promise you a guinea for your night's work, if you get no more."

The coachman made no further remark on the matter; after giving his hat a pull in front, he quietly got upon his box, and was as good as his word, for he looked, I verily believe, at nothing but his horses' ears for the next few minutes.

Eagleton then turned to the beadle, and said, in an abrupt tone,—

"What's your name?"—"Swabsly," replied the terrified official.

"Oh! Well, Mr. Swabsly, you may consider yourself my prisoner, and I have no doubt but I shall be able to get you transported."—"Me—me?" said the beadle; "me transported? why—why I'm a beadle."

"If you were two beadles, you shall be transported."—"Transport two beadles! Oh, gracious! what a *evolution* that would be. Parishes would take the hydrophobia, and overseers would bite the parson."

"You may hold what opinion you please," said Eagleton, "about the dignity of beadles, and such like nonsense, but you will find that we pay very little attention to such things. You have but one chance."

"Gracious! have I got a chance?" exclaimed Mr. Swabsly.—"You have, and that is, to confirm all that we already know about Emma Moorsam, in which case the Attorney-General may receive you as evidence, and forego a prosecution against you for your share in the matter."

"The 'torney-general!" exclaimed Swabsly. "Oh, goodness, you don't mean to say as a 'torney-general would come for to go to prosecute me?"—"Indeed I do, though."

"Well, then, as you knows all, I—I think as I'll confess all."—"You had better."

"I—I will. Oh, dear, what will become of me? I'm a undone beadle."—"That's as the case may be; but if you don't answer my question, I will have you locked up in the next watch-house till to morrow morning."

"What do yer want to know?"—"Is a young girl, named Emma Moorsam, in this house?"

"Ye—ye—yes."

"Against her will?"—"Ye—ye—yes."

"Who brought her here?"—"Your humble servant and Mrs. Gib—I mean Madame Rendell."

"You mean Mrs. Gibbs. We know everything, and were only testing your sincerity. Where were you going to take her in that coach?"—"Lor! do you know that too?"

"Of course we do."

"Well, then, she was a going back to Mother Gibbs's."

"Oh, indeed, and you were to escort her?"—"Yes, I was to 'scort her. Oh, dear, what will become of me?—I am a ruined beadle!"

"Why, you will be hanged some day," said Eagleton, "but not for this job. The only way, however, in which you can save yourself will be by obeying my instructions implicitly, in which case I will recommend you to mercy."—"I—I will, as I'm a sinner."

"Has Mr. Bellamy been here?"—"Mister Bellamy—the—the overseer?"

"Yes, you know well who I mean."—"Well, then, he hasn't."

"But you meant to take Emma to Madame Rendell's, in order that he might visit her? Our information is certain; you cannot deceive us."—"If so be as you knows," said the beadle, "it ain't no good for me all for to say as black's white, and deny that 'ere."

"None in the least," said Eagleton. "You would only make yourself very ridiculous, besides exposing yourself to a certain prosecution. Now, listen to me."—"Ye—ye—yes."

"You must go to the house there, as if nothing was the matter, and behave yourself in the same manner you would have done if you had not met us. Leave all else to me; and I warn you, if you attempt to give the least alarm about what has passed, you shall be prosecuted with the utmost rigour."—"Oh, I won't say a word."

"Very good. Let the coachman drive to Madame Rendell's; and whatever you do, take no notice of us, who will one of us get on the box, and the other behind."—"Ye—ye—yes."

"You fully understand now; and should any questions be asked of you by anybody concerning us, you just say that we are friends of yours, and that all is right. That is quite clear to you, I hope, Mr. Swabsly?"—"Oh, dear, yes; and you'll let me off, if so be as I does so as you tells me."—"We will."

"Won't I then. I'll confess anythink in the world, I will. Lor bless you, gentlemen, I'm a moral beadle, I is, if folks would but let me be; but there's that Master Bellamy, he's a rum un, he is; there isn't a pretty gal in our workus but he has her prenticed somewhere where he knows as all's right, and that is up to snuff, and a whole half ounce above it, and then he wisits um, he does, as true as I'm a beadle."—"Oh, indeed," said Eagleton.

"It's gospel, it is," said the beadle.—"Very well. We will talk over all that another time. Do you now go and do as you have been desired, and be sure you remember our instructions."

"Oh, won't I," said Mr. Swabsly, suddenly assuming a great excess of virtue—"we'll be down on the villains. What a horrid thing it is as wirtue shouldn't be its own reward, as the copy book says; but I'm very much afeard as it isn't—blow me!"

For the life of me I could not forbear a smile at the beadle, and the ingenious manner in which he was attempting to turn from the side of the villany he was so emphatically describing, to what he called the virtue.

"Come, come," said Eagleton, "do not lose any more time, Mr. Swabsly; we are quite convinced of your virtuous wishes and intentions."—"I'se unkimmon glad to hear it," he said; "it's like a dose o' somethink composing—it is to me—from the blessed dispensary."

He then unlatched the little iron gate, and walked with a crunching noise up the gravelled pathway to the door of the house, at which he knocked a heavy single knock.

We got out of the way, but looking, as we were, from the dark to the light, which gleamed forth from the open doorway, we could easily see every one that passed in and out.

The beadle was immediately admitted, and the door was partially closed, only without the latch being fastened, so that a narrow gleam of light from a suspended lamp in the hall came out into the garden, and made objects somewhat more distinct.

"Do you think the beadle will keep faith with us?" said I, in a whisper to Eagleton.—"Certainly I do," he said; "such men are always to be trusted when their own interests are concerned. He is acute enough to know, perfectly well, that he is safe from a prosecution, provided he keeps faith with me, for no magistrate would entertain a charge against him under the circumstances, unless he should commit now some new act, which my promises to him have preceded."

"Taking that view of the case," said I, "certainly we have everything to hope from his fears."—"Of course we have."

"And besides ——"

What I was going to say was abruptly stopped by Eagleton, who said,—

"Hush! hush! doctor, they are coming."

The door now opened, and several persons appeared in the passage, among whom I plainly perceived, and at once pointed out to the officer, the infamous Madame Rendell.

"Hush! hush!" said Eagleton; "watch them, but do not say a word."

I did watch them, and to my horror, in a few moments, I saw some heavy burthen brought into the passage, carried by two women. That it was a human body, I felt in a moment convinced, and I exclaimed, in a tone that I could not restrain,—

"Good Heavens! Eagleton, they have murdered Emma, and this is a scheme to dispose of her body."—"Hush! for God's sake, hush!" he said, "or you will ruin all. I believe you will find yourself mistaken, but if it should be so, I pray you be still till I ask you to assist me."

With great difficulty I controlled my feelings sufficiently to become a quiet spectator of what followed. The door of the house was held wide open by some one, while what, at the time, I could have taken my oath was the dead body of poor Emma, was carried out.

The beadle I could see making himself very officious indeed, and he walked before those who carried the burthen, in order to open the gate for them. "This way," I heard the voice of Madame Rendell say, "I will get in and take the head."—"What a weight she is," said one.

"They always are when they are in this state," remarked another. "Now, Gibbs, catch hold of her head. There you have her."

Madame Rendell got into the coach, and the totally insensible form of Emma, for I caught sight of her face for one fleeting moment, was handed in after her.

I thought I heard a groan or moan from the insensible girl, as she was rather roughly placed in the coach, and whispered to Eagleton,—

"For God's sake interfere, or the girl will be murdered among them."—"Have patience," he said, "for a few minutes. You may depend she will come to no harm. They have given her, I dare say, something to make her sleep, but you may depend they would not venture to do her any serious injury."

The door of the coach was then slammed, and the beadle cried,—

"All right!"

In another moment the vehicle started with myself on the box with the coachman, and Eagleton behind with the trembling beadle, who, as he told me afterwards, was, in whining accents, beseeching his merciful consideration in the event of the case coming before the magistracy.

No man could be more desperately impatient than I was for the coach to reach its place of destination, which I soon found was to Madame Rendell's. At length we turned into the street and stopped at the house. I immediately alighted from my elevated position, and Eagleton ran to me from the back of the coach, and said,—

"Let them take her into the house, doctor; we can soon follow."

We hid ourselves easily behind the horses, and then we heard the voice of Madame Rendell say,—

"Coachman—coachman—why don't you knock? Am I to be kept waiting here all night at my own door?"—"Yes," said the beadle; "why doesn't yer knock, Jarvey? You is singler inattentive, you is."

Thus urged, the coachman did knock, for in truth he had been waiting for orders from me. The door was immediately opened, and Madame Rendell, alighting from the coach, called to the beadle, saying,—

"Come, you must help me; I can't carry her in by myself."

The beadle then assisted in lifting Emma from the coach into the passage of the house, during which, Eagleton whispered to the coachman,—

"You shall be paid for your loss of time; but do not fail to be at the Marylebone Police-office in the morning by ten o'clock."

Bang went the door of Madame Rendell's house, leaving Eagleton and myself in the street.

I immediately knocked, and Swabsly, the beadle, opened the door again, and said, in a mysterious voice,—

"Second floor back—come in."

"What do you mean?"—"That's where she's tooked to."

"Now, Swabsly," said Eagleton, "is Bellamy here or not?"—"He is not; but he won't be many minutes coming, I know."

"Do you think, now," said I to Eagleton, "after the turn things have taken, there will be any necessity for doing Madame Rendell the favour of allowing her to become evidence against Bellamy? Have we not amply sufficient to ensure the punishment of both of them with the assistance of our friend the beadle?"—"Oh, punish 'em, the *willins*," said the beadle; "I hasn't no patience with 'em."

"You forget, Mr. Swabsly," said I, "how very short a time you have, as Mr. Bellamy would express it, forsaken the path of iniquity."

We were all three in the passage now, and suddenly there came a gentle double rap at the door. The beadle, with evident alarm, bustled us into the first room that was at hand, and then himself opened the street-door, for it seemed to be his post, on the occasion, to act as porter.

I heard the voice of Bellamy say sharply,—

"Is that you, Swabsly?" and the beadle replied in a whining tone, —"If you please, sir, it is me."

"All safe? —"Oh! wery, wery — unkimmon, Master Bellamy."

"And the girl?"—"Second floor front, sir."

"Well, Swabsly," remarked Bellamy, "help me off with my great coat. I think we have got the better of that d—d doctor at last."—"I rather thinks as we has, sir. Oh! there's unkimmon few comes near your worship."

"Is Gibbs up stairs?"—"Second floor front," repeated the beadle.

"Oh, very well."

"Don't yer want a light, sir?"—"No; you can shut the street door now. I can find my way."

This little bit of edifying conversation had taken place by the light that came in at the open doorway from a gas lamp, which was close at hand; and now that the door was shut, the passage was very dark.

"Sir—sir," whispered the beadle, "did you hear him?"—"Yes," said I. "Come on, Eagleton."

Without another word we ascended the staircase as softly as foot could fall, but yet not so softly as not to be heard by Bellamy, who had scarcely reached the room door indicated by the beadle; and he paused, saying,—

"Who's that? who's that?" — "Me, yer worship," said Swabsly, who had followed us.

"You! What the devil do you mean by leaving your post by the street door?"—"I'm a trying to walk in the paths of grace, if you please."

"Curse the fellow, he's drunk!" was the exclamation of Bellamy.

"What's the matter?" said Madame Rendell, opening the door of the room in which the beadle said Emma had been taken into.

A gleam of light streamed from the room, and there we all stood revealed, — Bellamy, Eagleton, myself, and the beadle.

"How do you do, Mr. Bellamy?" said I. "You see that d—d doctor is not so easily got rid of."

Madame Rendell gave a loud scream; and, as for Bellamy, he seemed perfectly stunned, and unable to say a word for several minutes.

"You are my prisoner," said Eagleton to him.

"Prisoner!" he gasped,—" prisoner! I—I have no evil intention to the girl."

"I never mentioned any girl," replied Eagleton. "You may say just whatever you like, but I shall repeat it to a magistrate."

By this time I had rushed into the room; and there, sure enough, lying upon a bed, I saw poor Emma, in the same state of insensibility that she had been in from the first. Madame Rendell had staggered back into the room, and now she was seated in the first chair she had come to, and looking as pale as death. Her guilty career she felt was at an end, and the consequences had only to come—consequences that, like some hideous spectre, almost deprived her of her reason to look upon. She looked at me for a moment or two, while I was examining the eyes of Emma, which convinced me she was suffering from the effects of opium, and then dropping on her knees, she cried,—

"Spare me—spare me, and I will confess all. Bellamy tempted me with his money. Let me escape, and I will tell all."—"That is too late now," said Eagleton, who stood in the doorway with Bellamy. "We can make no promises whatever to our prisoners."

"Oh! have mercy on me," she continued. "Bellamy only is guilty. I will tell you such a history of him, that you will shudder as even I have done—even I."

A look of demoniac rage flashed from Bellamy's eyes, as he cried,—

"Liar! 'tis false. You know it—well you know it. This is a conspiracy against me; but, with the Lord's help, I will confound it."—"For shame, sir," said I. "Do not add to your frightfully atrocious conduct the additional sin of calling upon Heaven with an untruth in your mouth. Your hypocrisy is, in my opinion, very nearly as bad as your criminality. Could you adopt no other garb than that of religion, in which to deceive your victims."

"I will tell all—I will tell all!" still cried Madame Rendell, wringing her hands.

Bellamy suddenly rushed forward, and made a blow at her that struck her to the floor; and he would have followed up his brutal attack, had not Eagleton darted after him, and placed a pair of handcuffs on him with a celerity that appeared perfectly marvellous.

"Who dares handcuff me?" he cried. "You shall dearly repent, all of you, this night's work."—"I am justified in what I have done," said Eagleton. "You are in my charge for what, at all events, is a serious misdemeanour, and you attempt violence."

From the appearance of Emma, I did not think she had taken a large dose of the narcotic. The object had, no doubt, been merely to give her so much as to enable them to bring her safely and noiselessly to the house, where God knows what her fate might have been but for our interference. I hastily wrote with my pencil, upon a leaf of my pocket-book, the name of some necessary medicines for her; and turning to the beadle, I said,—

"Go to the nearest chemist's, and get what is written for there. Be quick."—"Very good," said Swabsly; and as fast as his unwieldy carcass would enable him, he clattered down the stairs. I could do nothing for Emma now till he came back, and therefore turned my attention to Madame Rendell, who had risen from the floor, and was stanching the blood from a wound in the face that Bellamy had given her. She was muttering to herself as she did so; and I could hear her say,—

"So, it's comes to this now. Struck—struck! Well, I will have my revenge. Bellamy—Bellamy!"—"Peace, woman," he said. "Do not presume to address me."

"But I have something very particular to say. You recollect poor Jane Hargrave?"

A deadly paleness went across Bellamy's face, as he gasped,—

"What of her—what of her? She is dead."—"Yes—you deceived her by a mock marriage, assisted by me I grant. When she discovered it she fled from your roof. Her child—"

"Child! child!" cried Bellamy—"had Jane—"—"A living child—she had! What became of it for a long time I never knew till lately—now I do know."

"Woman, do you want to drive me mad?"—"What will you give to know where to find that child? Its mother you do know where to find. In the black rushing waters of the river ——"

Bellamy held up his manacled hands to Eagleton as he said—

"Take these off; I will be calm and quiet."

Eagleton immediately removed the handcuffs, and then Bellamy, covering his face with his hands, said—

"Go on—go on; if you have more to say, woman, go on." —"I have—I have. I know where your child is; I can tell you fully what became of it; what hardships it went through. The only human thing that I have heard you say you could have loved I can restore to you."

"Restore to me?"—"Yes—I can."

"And call you that having revenge upon me? I here promise, if you can restore Jane Hargrave's child to me, to pay you five hundred pounds."

Madame Rendell rose, while I think, in all my life, I never saw so thoroughly fiendish a smile upon any one's face. She glanced at Bellamy, and then burst into a high hysterical kind of laugh, as, pointing to the bed on which Emma lay, she said—

"There—there—there!"

A shriek burst from Bellamy's lips as he rose, and then cried—

"No—no—no. It cannot be."

"It can, and is," said Madame Rendell. "This girl, when an infant, was laid down at the parish workhouse door by a woman of the name of Miller. She intended to have made a market of it with you eventually, but she was transported, and only returned some weeks since to this country. During the time she was away you became overseer of the parish, and then commenced your career. Among those whom you selected for your victims has been your own child. You were attracted to her from her likeness to Jane Hargrave; you have yourself told me so."

With a deep groan, Bellamy fell on the floor—he had fainted.

* * * * *

By the next morning, Emma was perfectly recovered from the effect of the drug that had been administered to her—I had removed her to Eagleton's house, and his wife had paid her every attention.

As for Bellamy, when I found the relationship that subsisted between him and Emma, I was so much shocked at what must be his feelings, that I would have been willing to let the matter end there, and would have done so, had not Eagleton persuaded me to the contrary, by assuring me it had already gone too far, as he himself had mentioned it privately to one of the magistrates, before the most unexpected discovery had taken place.

There was therefore no resource, but for the whole party to proceed to the police office in the morning, where Swabsly, the beadle, made a full confession that Bellamy, for some years past, had, assisted by him and Mrs. Gibbs, who called herself Madame Rendell, taken advantage of his official situation to behave in the most atrocious manner. Finally, I and the officer related all we knew with regard to Emma; and, at the conclusion of the evidence, the magistrate said that since he had sat upon the bench, he had never heard so disgraceful a case.

"What have you to say to all this, Bellamy?" he asked,— "Nothing," was the answer, and that one word was expressed in a tone of such utter abandonment and despair, that it sent a chill through my blood.

"And you, Mrs. Gibbs?"—"I am willing to tell all I know," was her reply, "and I hope for mercy."

"We have quite evidence enough," said the magistrates; "I shall send the case to the sessions, and bind over all the witnesses to appear. By that time, the girl herself may be able to make some statement."

I should have informed my readers, that dreading the effect upon the delicate and debilitated frame of Emma, of coming into a court of justice against her own father, I had excused her to the magistrate, telling him that my professional opinion was, that it would be highly dangerous for her to appear in her present state.—Hence he had dispensed with her attendance.

As soon as the case was thus concluded, an attorney rose, and offered bail for Bellamy, which was taken. As for Madame Rendell, as nobody seemed inclined to become security for her, she was conveyed to prison.

Bellamy had not opened his lips, except to say that one word " Nothing!" He seemed to be labouring under a complete mental prostration. The hoots of the mob assembled outside the court he scarcely appeared to hear, but walked to his carriage like a man wandering in his sleep. The expression of his countenance was horrible—it looked like that of a corpse, while a perpetual slight movement of the lips alone undeceived as to its vitality. Scoundrel as he was, I could not but pity him in his terrible condition.

After the proceedings at the police-office, I made up my mind to tell Emma as gently as possible the whole affair, for as yet she was in ignorance of her relationship to Bellamy, and I proceeded to Eagleton's with that object. He, Eagleton, was against my letting her know so soon, but what I dreaded was that she would hear it more roughly from some one else, or accidentally come to the knowledge of it from some newspaper, when I should not be there to support her mind against the shock. Eagleton and his wife, therefore, at my request, left us alone for some time, during which I told her the whole story.

Poor Emma wept abundantly, and when I spoke of Bellamy's state of mind, she took my hand, and looking me imploringly in the face, she said,—

"Oh, sir, let me go to him, and tell him that, as I hope God may forgive me, I forgive him."

I combatted her resolution to call upon her father for a long time, but I saw it was in vain, and at last, rather than she should go without me some day, I gave a reluctant consent to go with her that afternoon.

* * * * *

Emma and I walked arm-in-arm to George-street, and upon my summons for admission, the same serious footman opened the door, and said, as usual,—

"Mr. Bellamy is at prayers, sir, but I will tell him you are here as soon as possible."—"God help him," thought I, "perhaps he really is at prayers this time."

I gave my card to the man, and we were shown into the same waiting-room I have before described. I was glad that Emma had now ample time to recover her composure, for I thought she would have fainted when she first entered the room, but after waiting half-an-hour I got a little impatient, and rung the bell.

The footman in a few moments made his appearance.

"When is Mr. Bellamy coming?" said I. "Why, sir, he went to his dressing-room, and left strict orders that he was not to be called to any one, and we were not to come near him. We expect him down every moment."

"Go to him, and I will hold you harmless," said I.

The footman went. There was a silence for some moments, and then a great scuffling noise. Some one then screamed loudly—Emma turned very pale, and I rushed into the passage. The first person I met was a sanctified-looking man, to whom I said,—

"What's the matter?"—"I cannot say," he replied. "My name is Elias Mudpoke, I am a weak vessel, and ——"

At this moment the footman almost rolled down the stairs, and when he reached the passage, he gasped,—

"M—m—master's cut his throat!"

* * * * *

Bellamy was quite dead, and poor Emma, to whom, in his will he had left everything he possessed, was laid upon a sick bed for many months.

Madame Rendell was imprisoned six months, and the last I saw of the beadle was to recognise him sweeping a crossing by the Elephant and Castle, when he told me *workuses* was not what they was, and beadles was very nearly all *flummuxed*.

THE HOPE OF THE FAMILY;

OR, A SLIGHT INDISPOSITION.

How often in families it will be found that there is some one member whom the parents, relatives, friends, and connections, all look up to; the one "par excellence," who is to do or achieve something very astonishing, and make a great figure in the world—in fact, quite the hope of the family.

Generally speaking, too, if there be real talent in this hope of the family, and if his renown be not a mere sickly reflection of the blind dotage of his or her mother, we find it associated with that fatal construction which holds existence on so slight a tenure, that an indisposition which others would successfully resist, hurries the much cherished darling, the pride and the hope of the family, into the grave.

In the course of my professional career I have been called in to many such cases. The deaths of the young are always distressing, because they are out of the ordinary course of nature, and come upon us like an accident which was not to be fairly expected; but when that young person who is carried to an early grave possesses rare affections, high intellect, and a gentle heart, which has more than commonly gained the love of all persons, the fell hand of death falls indeed heavily on many a stricken bosom; and it is hard if some bleeding heart, oppressed with deep affliction, does not soon follow the much-loved one to the silent tomb.

Our climate is particularly adapted to foster early disease in delicately-formed and highly vital natures; and it is always a sign that should be looked upon with suspicion, although by no means always a fatal one, when very early in life we see a precocity of intellect and feeling far beyond the common.

I never shall forget a scene which occurred in a family who were strangers to me, when first I was called to attend them, but with whom afterwards I had the pleasure of making and maintaining a long and lasting friendship, in consequence of having, as one of their members, a being whose soul seemed, as it were, too expansive for the mortal tenement that held it.

A medical man with whom I was acquainted, it appears, had mentioned my name to the family, the name of which was Minden, and some short time afterwards a note came to me, of which the following is a copy:—

"Mrs. Minden presents her compliments to Dr. ——, and begs the favour of a call at his convenience, to see her dear Julian, who is in delicate health, and has been for some time under the care of Mr. Paton, who mentioned Dr. —— to Mrs. Minden.

"Minden Cottage, Walworth."

From the tenor of the note, I of course concluded that it was not one of those cases in which a physician is called in as a last resource, according to the custom of people who always endeavour to get the best advice they can, when it is too late for it to be of any service. I, therefore, before I went over to Minden Cottage, called upon the practitioner who had recommended me to the family, but he was from home, and I went on until I came to the Walworth-road, where I began inquiring for Minden Cottage.

I was directed to a neat enough, small, half cottage, half villa residence, with a very pretty garden in front, and every sign of comfort about it. Upon ringing, I was promptly admitted by a smart servant girl, who took my card to her mistress, after showing me into a handsome, though small waiting-room.

I had not waited many minutes, when a pleasing-looking female about thirty, or perhaps more, entered the room, and announced herself as Mrs. Minden.

"I am much obliged to Dr. ——," she said, "for this early visit, not that there is any danger—oh, dear no—not the least."

There was a nervous earnestness about the woman as she said these words that led me to think she had a lurking suspicion there was danger, and was trying to convince herself to the contrary, if she possibly could, by assuring herself there was not—a species of mental deception exceedingly common.

"I am glad to hear you say so," I replied.

"Oh, you will find Julian very delicate—very delicate, indeed, doctor; but then, as I tell him, he don't take exercise enough, but sits alone reading, which he will do for hours together, and when he comes to anything that pleases him, he will smile in his quiet way, till—till I am ready to cry; for there is something sad as well as beautiful in his smile."

"Beyond general delicacy of constitution," said I, "has he any particular ailment?"—"No, I think not. He sometimes has a slight cold. But I think if you advise him how necessary it is to take more exercise for the benefit of his health, that it would make more impression upon him, coming from a medical gentleman, than any of his friends."—"I will do the best my judgment dictates, Mrs. Minden," said I, "you may depend."

"I will send your patient to you, doctor," she said, as she rose and left the room.

In about five minutes' time she returned with a young lad of about eighteen, I should guess. He was delicately beautiful, and although tall of his age, was far from being the awkward lout that tall boys generally are. It scarcely required a second glance from me to tell me that he was consumptive. The slight hectic upon his cheek, the melting tenderness of the full blue eye, and the veins upon the brow, which showed faintly through the thin transparent skin, all told me at once that I saw before me one of those fair flowers, to be in all probability blighted in the springtide of its beauty by that fell destroyer—consumption.

"Well, Mr. Julian," said I, "how do you do?"—"I thank you, sir," he said, in a mild, musical voice, "I am much better now. I was rather unwell yesterday."

"In any pain?"—"A little."

He pressed his hand upon his side as he spoke.

"Cough, Julian," said I.

He coughed slightly, and I could hear the peculiar after sound which indicates diseased lungs. Then he suddenly caught his breath, and for a few seconds the respiration was laboured, after which it returned to its ordinary state. I would not have taken ninety per cent. to insure Julian Minden's life for two years.

His mother at this moment entered, and I could see a look of such painful interest about her that I dreaded as much to tell her the truth as ordinarily I would have dreaded to nurture false hopes, which I always have considered extremely injudicious.

"Well, doctor," she said, "how do you find Julian?"

She caught her breath convulsively as she asked me, for I presume she saw enough seriousness in my countenance to give ample room for alarm.

"I should certainly advise," said I, evading the question as much as possible, "that he take exercise, but not allow that to go as far as fatigue."—"I like reading," said the boy, "better. If they will leave me alone, and let me get into some quiet place with a book, I am very happy."

"But," said I, "in this world we are so situated, Julian, that we cannot ourselves be happy for a long period, unless we make others so. Now, your mother enjoys little of your society when you exclude yourself in the way you mention."

He turned his soft beaming eyes upon his mother as I spoke, and when I had done, he said, gently,—

"I did not think of that, certainly."

I saw a tear in Mrs. Minden's eye as she drew him towards her, and kissed his beautiful brow. I then rose and took my hat, saying,—

"I do not think medicine necessary in this case. Light nourishing diet will do much more good than anything that can come from the apothecary's."

Julian shook hands with me, and I left the room, closely followed by his mother, who invited me into another apartment, where, offering me a chair, she looked in my face, as if to watch the slightest variation of expression, as she said,—

"Doctor ——, you—you see that it is only a slight indisposition, and Julian being delicate, makes it look more serious. You will think with me, I dare say, that my dear Julian has a cold merely, and—and is not consumptive."

She brought out this word consumptive with such an effect,

that I could see in a moment it was the bugbear of her imagination. Then she paused with such a look of fixed attention for my answer, that I scarcely ever felt in so awkward and distressing a situation before.

"Madam," I said, "it would be very wrong of me, as you have called me in professionally, to deceive you; and I must say, however reluctantly, that I do think your son Julian consumptive."

She changed colour and dropped into a chair, as she gasped, "Are you quite sure?"—"As far as human judgment can go, yes."

"Oh, my Julian! my Julian!" she cried, bursting into tears, and sobbing as if her heart would break. "Cannot you do something for him?—Cannot you cure him?—Surely—surely, doctor, something can be done. You will try, for my poor Julian's sake. You don't know him, sir—so gentle,—so affectionate—so doating—so good! Save him! save him!"—"Mrs. Minden," said I, "pray compose yourself. I do not say that your son is in any immediate danger. He is far from it, I hope; and even we medical men are, I admit, sometimes much deceived in the appearances of disease."

"Can you give me any hope?" she cried.—"We should always have hope."

"God help me! Julian—Julian—my beautiful boy—Julian!"

"Madam," said I, "you should exert your better reason. If it be the will of Heaven that your son should be taken from you, you should bear more patiently the sorrow that an Almighty hand chooses to cast towards you."

"Patience, patience!" she said. "How can you feel as I feel? Have you any one who is life and soul to you, as Julian is to me?"—"All that I can do, Mrs. Minden, I will do," said I; "and such consolation as one human being can offer another, I freely offer you."

"Forgive me, sir," she replied. "I am very ungrateful, and very unjust to you. I know I am; but when the heart is distracted, it forgets the little courtesies of life. I pray you to believe that I am not unmindful of your present kindness."

A loud knock at the street-door, at this moment, disturbed our conference, and in about a minute a servant entered the room, and said,—

"Here is Mr. Ramsay, ma'am."

I immediately rose to go, but Mrs. Minden said—

"Mr. Ramsay is Julian's uncle. He will be glad to see you, sir, for he is very fond of Julian. Show Mr. Ramsay in, Mary."

A portly man, in a moment, made his appearance at the door of the room, and Mrs. Minden, in a faltering voice—for she had not recovered from her emotion—introduced us to each other.

"Your most obedient, sir," said Mr. Ramsay, making me a very vulgar bow.

I returned his bow, but said nothing.

"Doctor —— has been to see Julian," said Mrs. Minden, "and he thinks ——"

"Yes, yes," said Mr. Ramsay, with eagerness. "Bless the dear boy! what does he think of him?"

Mrs. Minden was silent; and I did not consider myself called upon particularly to give my professional opinion to Mr. Ramsay, who, after rather an awkward pause, said to Mrs. Minden—

"Martha, I only stepped in to say how do you do. I must be off again now."—"But you have not heard Doctor ——'s opinion of Julian. He is of opinion that he is decidedly consumptive."

"God bless me!" said Mr. Ramsay, sinking into a chair with a force enough to smash it.—"Yes," sobbed Mrs. Minden. "My poor, poor Julian."

"And with his prospects, too," groaned Mr. Ramsay. Then turning to me, he added, "You must know, sir, that Julian's father was my brother—my name is Minden—that is, Ramsay Minden; but, for distinction's sake, all the family call me Mr. Ramsay—you understand?"—"Perfectly," said I.

"Well then, sir, you must know that my brother, who is dead and gone, poor fellow, left Julian four thousand pounds, which he is to have when he comes of age, to dispose of as he pleases, you must know."

"Alas, alas!" said Mrs. Minden. "He will never have his own. My poor boy will never see the age of one-and-twenty. He will drop into an early tomb, and I shall be desolate—desolate!"

"If," said Ramsay, laying a great emphasis on the "if," "we should lose poor Julian—oh dear!—the will of my brother, who is dead and gone, says that I am to have the four thousand pounds, and take care of Mrs. Minden."

Mrs. Minden leaned her head upon her hands, and burst into tears, saying—

"Oh! if we could be reduced to the most abject poverty—if Heaven would afflict me any way rather than by taking from me my Julian, I could be happy, very, very happy."

Mr. Ramsay blew a sonorous blast with his nose in his handkerchief, that he may have intended should be very fine and sympathetic, but which, in consequence, I suppose, of my not being used to it, made me jump again.

"I will call again, madam," said I, "if you will permit, in a friendly way."—"No, indeed, sir," she said. "It would be most unwarrantable in us, strangers as we are to you, to expect so much. If you will come once a week, I can manage."

"Pray, madam," said I, "say no more. I will not take any more fees of you; and if you decline seeing me in a friendly way, I really would rather not come, for this is a case in which a physician can do very little."

Mr. Ramsay groaned again, as he said—

"Martha—I beg your pardon, sir—I mean Mrs. Minden, has the interest of the four thousand pounds now to educate Julian with; and it's only three pounds seven and eightpence a-week. Then her own income arises from two houses. Sometimes they are let, and sometimes they aint; sometimes the tenants bolt without paying the rent; and when they have been enormously unlucky in their affairs, they take the fixtures with them—oh! dear."—"Hush, hush!" said Mrs. Minden.

"Upon my soul they do," said Ramsay.—"I cannot engage my mind with such things," added the mother, "when my poor Julian is in so much danger."

"Well," said Ramsay, as he rose to go, "it's only now and then I can, and then they come with quite a flash."

I rose on my feet to go, and Ramsay officiously opened the door for me, and seemed bent upon going out at the same time. In vain I tried to shoulder him off, by saying—

"Good day, sir." He would not be shaken off so easily, but remarking that he conceived he was going my way, he followed close to me into the open roadway.

When we were clear of the cottage, Ramsay said,

"I'll walk a little way with you, doctor."

My predilection for Mr. Ramsay's company was by no means great, but I did not like rudely to say—"No, you shall not,—for I prefer walking by myself;" so I let him jog on by my side as he pleased.

"Ah!" he remarked, after a pause, "poor Julian, I'm afraid, will never live to see one-and-twenty."—"The boy is certainly very unwell," said I, "but with care, although he may not recover, he yet may be preserved some time."

"Don't you think diet of very great importance in such a case as this, doctor?"—"Certainly I do."

"Then whatever you recommend should be avoided, shall be, if you will have the goodness to tell me."—"Let him avoid acids," said I, "and vegetable matter. Neither are good for him."

"Acids and vegetable matter.—Humph! Do you think a change of air would be beneficial?"—"Not if where he is at present be tolerably dry. A very humid atmosphere would be unfavourable for him, although it is not in all such cases."

"Bless me, indeed. He should not be fatigued, I think I heard you say."—"Certainly not; fatigue would be highly injurious. He should have gentle exercise."

"He shall, he shall, even if I take a walk with him myself. Do you know, doctor, he is quite the hope of the family; and it's very odd, but his mother will not believe he is consumptive. I keep on talking of Julian's slight indisposition, when upon my life I don't think myself he will see one-and-twenty."

"It is impossible to say whether he will see one-and-twenty or not; but what makes you think so much of one-and-twenty, Mr. Ramsay?"—"Who—I—oh dear, no!—that is, I want Julian, if possible, to reach one-and-twenty, so that he may have the free disposal of the four thousand pounds you know, doctor."

"Oh, indeed; well, we must see what we can do."

"Certainly. Acids and vegetables ——"—"Sir!"

"Eh!—oh, I beg your pardon, doctor, I was only calling to mind what you said Julian should avoid. I dare say, now, if he were to take acids and vegetables, he—he—never would see twenty-one."

There was a peculiar tone about this remark that I disliked extremely. It struck me very forcibly that Mr. Ramsay would be very well pleased indeed if Julian did not see twenty-one. I turned sharply round to look in his face, but he avoided my gaze immediately by saying,—

"Good morning, sir; I fear I intrude upon your very valuable time," and hurried away from my side, in the direction back again to Minden Cottage.

Well, thought I, if that uncle is not that boy's enemy, I know nothing of human nature. He would kill him if he possibly could. With what a tone he pronounced the words acids and vegetables!

I had left no prescriptions at Minden Cottage, because I intended to call on the day following, and wished to have in my mind the result of two interviews with Julian before I decided upon what course both of regimen and medicine I should recommend to be strictly adhered to in order to decrease any suffering that might arise, and if possible protract existence, if I could not save the boy altogether from the direful disease which had seized hold of him.

*   *   *   *   *

The next day then I was at Minden Cottage, at rather an early hour, and as I was rather unexpected by Mrs. Minden, I presume, I had to wait some time before I saw her. When she came into the room she thanked me warmly for my visit, adding,

"Julian is not at home. He has gone on a visit to his uncle, Mr. Ramsay, but he will be here again to-morrow."

"How far off does Mr. Ramsay live?" said I.—"He has a little place in the neighbourhood, although he resides principally in the heart of the city. He came early this morning, and so pressed me to allow Julian to go home with him, that I consented, especially as he seemed better."

"As I have come over here to see Julian," said I, "perhaps there would be no objection to my calling at Mr. Ramsay's house."—"None in the least, sir; I feared only trespassing too much upon your kindness in proposing such a thing."

"Tell me where it is, madam," said I, "and I will at once proceed there."—"I would show you myself," she said, "but am in my dishabille. Nevertheless, my servant shall point you out the house."

I bowed my assent to this arrangement, and after a little more desultory conversation, I left Minden Cottage with the servant, who pointed out to me Mr. Ramsay's little place, which was not a quarter of a mile from the Mindens.

Mr. Ramsay, who I asked for of the servant who answered my summons for admission, was declared to be at home, and when I was shown into the room in which he was, I could perceive in a moment that I was as unwelcome as unexpected.

"Doctor!" he exclaimed.—"Mr. Ramsay," said I, "I should not have intruded upon you, but I was told my patient was here, and took the liberty, with his mother's permission, of following him."

"Oh, dear, yes—bless me, of course," he said, trying to make an effort to appear suddenly very friendly. "He is here, and I am quite proud, doctor, to be honoured by your presence."

I bowed coldly, and said,

"Is Julian here?"—"Ye—ye—yes."

I followed the direction of his eyes, and lying upon a sofa, looking very pale and wan, and apparently asleep, lay Julian Minden.

"He is a little tired, I think," said Ramsay, "but was very well this morning, and he has been so full of spirits; it's been quite affecting—oh, very affecting.—You would have been surprised and thought him quite another thing, doctor."

Here Mr. Ramsay wiped his face with a disagreeable-looking blue handkerchief, and looked very nervous and fidgetty.

"Indeed," said I, as I bent over Julian, and saw in his face signs of great exhaustion; beads of perspiration were standing on his brow, and he was breathing heavily—I could have sworn he had undergone some very great fatigue indeed.

"Julian"—I said—"Julian."

He only moaned in reply.

"He—he was so very lively," said Ramsay—"oh, so uncommonly lively."

"How long has he been sleeping?"—"Oh, dear, not many minutes—we have not long come in, I could not get him home."

"Mr. Ramsay," said I, "this boy is suffering greatly from fatigue—he has walked far beyond what his state of health would warrant, and if you were his companion, I can only say, I am astonished, after what I said to you yesterday."

"To—to—me?"—"Yes, sir, to you."

"I—I—am really very sorry—has he been too far, do you really think?"—"I am not in the habit of saying what I don't think, Mr. Ramsay," said I, fixing my eyes upon him, "although I will own I do not always say on all occasions all I think."

"What—what do you mean?"—"I should imagine, sir, my words require no explanation—look at the state of this boy, he is evidently suffering from the extreme of exhaustion."

"Do—do you think a glass of wine?"—"No, Mr. Ramsay; but I caution you for the future not to take Julian Minden long walks. He cannot stand them—he will sink under it."

"You think ——"—"I know, Mr. Ramsay."

"Acids and vegetables."

"Sir?"—"Nothing—nothing:—did I speak, doctor?"

I turned from him with disgust, and placed my finger on the pulse of my patient;—it was frightfully irregular, varying from sixty to eighty-eight. As I was counting off the pulsations, Julian opened his eyes, and fixed them languidly upon me.

"Where have you been?" said I.—"Very far. Oh, I am so tired and wet."

"Wet?"—"Yes—uncle, you should have let me dry myself."

"Good God! what do you mean?" said I.

Mr. Ramsay got up, and, in his intense confusion, affected to be humming a tune, and catching a fly.

"Mr. Ramsay!" cried I.—"Eh—what—did you speak?"

"What does Julian mean by being left wet?"—"Wet—we —we—wet—oh, wet? Did you ever see such a monster blue-bottle?

"Cherry ripe, cherry ripe,
  Ripe I cry;
Full and fair ones come and buy:
  If you ask me ——"

I caught hold of his arm, and said, in a serious tone of voice,—

"Mr. Ramsay, I ask you once more for an explanation of Julian Minden's words, when he complains of being left wet?"

"We—we went for a walk, you see doctor, and bearing, you know, in mind your admirable advice, we—we—went for a walk—a walk, you know."—"Well, sir?"

"And—and Julian was so full of spirits, so lively, so—so —everything you can imagine—you know he requires to be strengthened—we want to make him hardy among us all, eh, doctor? and always bearing in mind your advice, that everything should be done, you know, to improve his constitution, and make him strong and healthy, and all that kind of thing, —we came to a pond."

"Well, sir?"—"Yes, we came to a pond—you know what I mean—a—a pond, in fact; and when we came to the pond, I said to Julian,—'there's a pond;' and Julian said,—'yes, yes,' says he, 'there's a pond;' and he was in such admirable spirits, he was a singing away,—

"Oysters, sir—oysters, sir—
Oysters, sir, I cry—
Come, buy ——"

"Psha, Mr. Ramsay," said I, "pray tell me about this pond, if you please?"—"Why—why, Julian took a fancy of bathing in it, you see, and I minded his clothes—there were a good many weeds in the pond, doctor—it's a good joke, and I dare say you'll laugh—ha! ha! ha!—when—when he got in, I cried,—'Julian, the doctor says you are to avoid the vegetables!'—ha! ha! ha!"

Ramsay's laugh was the most forced and discordant kind of noise ever I heard in my life; but when he saw my grave look, he brought it to an abrupt termination, and again wiped his face with the disagreeable looking blue handkerchief.

"So, Mr. Ramsay," I said, "it comes to this, that you took this boy, in his very precarious state of health, a long fatiguing walk, and then immersed him in a pond, leaving him to come away from it without even the chance of drying himself."

"You—you advised it yourself."

"I advised it?"—"Yes; you—you said anything should be done to give him strength."

"Upon my word, Mr. Ramsay, you give my words a very wide signification. You cannot pretend to be such an idiot, as to suppose that the course you have adopted towards this youth was other than one calculated to bring him to an early grave. Julian, tell me truly how came you to bathe in the pond?"—"Uncle Ramsay told me I was to do so, by your orders, sir."

"Then uncle Ramsay told a most atrocious falsehood."

"Don't begin to bully me," said Ramsay, in so faint a tone of voice as to be perfectly ridiculous.

"Sir," said I, "it is neither my province, nor am I induced to make any further remarks to you in your own house; but I shall this moment return to Mrs. Minden, and let her know the serious mischief that, in all probability, has been done to her son."

"Mischief? oh, nonsense! Julian is much better, I am sure. Are you not, Julian?"

The lad's answer was prefaced by a short, dry cough, as he said,—

"Indeed, uncle, I am not. I think, if you are going to my mother's, sir, I will go with you."

"I think you had better," said I; "so come along at once, for, between you and I, Julian, I think the air of your dear Uncle Ramsay's house will never agree very well with you."

"The air?"—"Yes, Julian. You don't seem quite to understand what I mean; but I have no doubt uncle Ramsay does."

Julian looked very much puzzled, first glancing at me and then at his uncle, who affected to be looking from the window, and paying no attention to what was passing in the room.

"Come, come, Julian," I cried, "I am in haste."

He took his hat from a chair on which it was laid, and lingering then a moment, he said,—

"Good day, uncle."

Ramsay started, and replied, nervously,—

"Oh, you are going, are you, Julian? Perhaps we shall see you back to dinner?"—"At which," said I, "you may be sure to have plenty of acids and vegetables. You understand me, Uncle Ramsay?"

"I—I don't know what you mean," he stammered; "you are a most incomprehensible man. I really can't understand you."—"I have a meaning which it will, perhaps, be as well for you to reflect upon. Come, Julian."

The sick lad and I left the house, and when we gained the open air, I said, seriously,—

"Now, Julian, if ever you are so imprudent as to bathe again under such circumstances as you have done this morning, your mother will soon have to mourn your death."—"My uncle persuaded me, sir."

"But, Julian, you are of an age to know better yourself. Surely you have some discretion."—"My life," he replied, "has been spent dreaming among books, and I know very little of what is real in life, I fear."

"I fear so, too; but now listen to me. Human nature, Julian, is neither so bad nor so good as you will find it in the course of your reading, for the ordinary characters of the mass of mankind are but ill adapted for the novelist, the poet, and the dramatist. They must seize upon the extremes of human character, in order to impart an interest to the production of their brains."—"I can imagine that, sir."

"Now, for example, Julian, you may read, perhaps, of an uncle who, from pecuniary considerations, would plan and execute the murder of his nephew, but in private, ordinary life, you will find the murderers very scarce—that is to say, those who would actually commit the deed; while you will find, perhaps, many who would wish the death of those who stood in the way of their own selfish desires, and who, with a refinement upon vice, would endeavour to accomplish indirectly that which their fears kept them from attempting more boldly."

The lad turned full towards me, and, fixing his deep melancholy eyes upon my face, he said,—

"Good God, sir, you don't mean to direct my mind to suspicion of Mr. Ramsay?"—"Julian, I hope to Heaven I am wrong."

"Then—then you do ——"—"I warn you of your uncle."

"My father's brother—my own near relative! Can it be possible?"—"Tell me, Julian, candidly—were you to live to twenty-one years of age, what are your prospects?"

"I understand that I come to the possession of four thousand pounds in money, besides some other property, all of which is under the management and sole control of my uncle."

"And to whom would you leave all that, were you able so to do at your pleasure?"—"To my mother, all—with the exception of my little cousin Cicely, whom I would make ample provision for. She is a dear, gentle creature, sir; you would love her as I do, and as every one does, if you knew her;—a young bird, just flushed with life, pealing to Heaven a song of joy! Dear, dear Cicely!"

A flush of colour came across his pale cheek as he thus spoke, and his eye lit up with a gleam of fire that looked like the very halo of genius.

Alas, alas, poor Julian! poor dear cousin Cicely! The cankerworm was already in the heart of the rose—the night of death was commencing!

A few moments more brought us to Mrs. Minden's door, and Julian leaned heavily upon my arm, for his temporary excitement in talking of Cicely had passed away, leaving him weaker than before.

I had some difficulty in controlling the real passion I was in, and composing myself to speak to Mrs. Minden, with anything like temper, of the proceedings of Mr. Ramsay.

"Madam," I said, "it would ill become me, a stranger, to interfere in your domestic affairs; but I have a strong opinion with regard to your son, which I will state, notwithstanding, by so doing, I may possibly be exposing myself to some disagreeable consequences."

"My son, sir? Oh, you do not think he is worse—he seemed so much better to-day."

"I will not take upon myself to say that much mischief has been done by this day's proceedings, although I cannot but admit that my fears point that way. Mr. Ramsay has done more harm to your son in a few hours than would have ensued probably in the next six months. I warn you, Mrs. Minden, of that man. He will be the death of your son if you permit him to continue as he has been acting."

"Mr. Ramsay?"—"Yes, Mr. Ramsay."

"What!—my own husband's brother!—Julian's own uncle!—One so near to him in ties of blood, and one too who has ever shown the most lively concern for his welfare! Oh, surely it cannot be possible?"—"Madam, all I can say is that it is true. It matters not to me professionally whether a knave or a fool steps between me and my patients, undoing by treachery more than the physician can ever do by the utmost exertion of the skill with which Heaven may have gifted him—the result is the same. I only state my firm conviction that one or other of those characters belongs to Mr. Ramsay. Which you choose to adopt with reference to him I leave to your own judgment."

"Gracious heavens! what has he done?"—"Julian will tell you. In the meantime I strongly urge you never to allow him to visit at his uncle's house again."

"I moved towards the door, and Mrs. Minden sprang after me. The action was quite involuntary, but she took hold of my arm, and gazing with intense emotion in my face, said,—

"Sir, sir, speak more plainly. Do you—can you mean that Mr. Ramsay would for one moment contemplate my dear Julian's death?"—"Mother, mother," said Julian, "do not imagine that. What motive could my uncle have for wishing me otherwise than well?"

"People's motives, Julian," said I, "are between themselves and their Maker. I am sure, Mrs. Minden, you don't wish me to say more than I have done. I may have already gone beyond the bounds of prudence in the warning I have given you."—"No, no, indeed you have not," she cried. "I live but for one object, and that is Julian."

"I will call again to-morrow, Mrs. Minden," I said, in a low tone. "We will talk over this matter alone if you please. I would persuade Julian now to lie down, and cover himself warmly but not too heavily; give him, likewise, a small quantity of port wine and water."

"You will come to-morrow—at what time?"—"At twelve, Mrs. Minden."

She followed me to the door with such a look of anxiety, that I said,—

"Do not distress yourself, madam; I see no worse symptoms in Julian."

"Will—will he die?" she gasped, in choking accents.—"Life and death, Mrs. Minden, are not in our hands. We are all but creatures of a day. Some of us may tarry till the evening closes gently around us, while some may, like early blighted flowers, perish in the sweet springtide of existence. Be calm, and place your trust and hope in higher hands than that of poor humanity."

My words seemed to make an impression on her, and she replied,—

"I will be patient—I will be patient, doctor; but my Julian is my life. If he were taken from me, God knows what would become of me!"—"Hush! hush!" said I. "Go to him now. He will be wondering at your absence. I will be here to-morrow."

I walked from the door, and as I leisurely strolled towards the city, my mind became filled with reflections and surmises concerning the probable end of the strange family entanglements which seemed to beset the Mindens. As far as my knowledge of their history, there scarcely seemed sufficient motive for Ramsay's conduct. True, four thousand pounds might be a considerable sum to such a man, but then it would appear that Mrs. Minden's life still stood in the way of his acquisition of it, for even were he not compelled, which in all probability he was, by his brother's will, to pay over to her the interest of that sum, even after Julian's death, he could scarcely help doing so, and Mrs. Minden's life was surely as good a one as his.

The more I thought of the matter, the more I conjectured that uncle Ramsay must have some motive, of which neither I nor Mrs. Minden knew of, for wishing Julian dead. Such motive, if he had any, could only come out in the event of such a circumstance occurring, and then I began seriously to ask myself, from a consideration of Julian's case, will he live till he is one-and-twenty, and legally capable of calling upon Ramsay to place him in possession of his own?

This was a question I found it very difficult to answer in the affirmative, although I saw as yet nothing in the case to enable me to say with anything like a positive opinion he will not.

That there was considerable disease of the lungs I could not doubt, and that Julian Minden would ultimately fall a victim to consumption, I firmly believed; but the when was a subject which was beyond my ken in that uncertain of all diseases as to the time which it takes to place its victim in the tomb.

* * * * *

I started at a rather earlier hour than the one I had named on the following morning to visit the Mindens, for I had become greatly interested in their future fortunes; moreover, there was one question which I wished to ask Mrs. Minden, and upon which I perhaps might be able to base more accurate calculations—that was the precise age of Julian—for, although I could come to a tolerable guess upon that head, yet, in consumptive subjects, patients sometimes look so much older in consequence of the too early development of the intellect, and sometimes so much younger from the air of delicacy and transparent freshness of the complexion, that the most experienced medical man might frequently be deceived.

When I came within sight of Minden Cottage, I saw some one just opening the gate leading to the garden—a second glance told me it was Ramsay, and I hung back a moment to give him leave to get fairly into the house before me. In a minute he was admitted, and then I hastened forward, for I was not sorry to meet Ramsay again, as his words and manner might afford me more ample food for speculation.

It would appear that Ramsay suspected it was I at the door, for when the servant came to admit me, he appeared with his hat in his hand, as if just coming away.

"Mr. Ramsay, don't let me disturb you," said I; "in fact, I would rather you were to remain."

"Oh, how do you do, sir?" he said, with great affected cordiality. "Mrs. Minden and I were just talking of you, and I was lamenting my little mistake of yesterday. Ah, doctor, our best feelings, as you must often have found, sometimes lead us sadly astray."

"I don't think," said I, "Mr. Ramsay, that our best feelings ever lead us very far out of the right path, or that the mischief they occasion is ever very serious."

I gave uncle Ramsay great credit for the tact with which he turned this speech to his own advantage, as he said—

"You don't know what a comfort your words are, my dear

sir. I was really afraid that Julian's walking might have done more harm."

He then preceded me into the parlour, where was Mrs. Minden.

"Martha," he said, "here is Doctor ——; how very much we are obliged to him for his friendly calls."

"How is Julian?" said I.—"He seems better this morning," replied his mother, "much better."

"I am very glad to hear you say so. Can you tell me his exact age?"—"Not one-and-twen——ahem," suddenly cried Ramsay.

"He is within one month of twenty," said Mrs. Minden.— "That's quite correct," said Ramsay. "Julian will be twenty-one on the tenth of October next year. Ah! what changes take place in a rolling, revolving year! We are all frail— very frail—and if our dear Julian should be snatched from us before he is one-and-twenty, why we must seek for consolation of the great ruler of all things—the great disposer of life and death—the great judge of ——"

I was sickened at Ramsay's abominable cant and hypocrisy, and said, interrupting him,—

"I should like to see Julian alone."

The words were scarcely out of my mouth when the door of the parlour opened, and there stood upon the threshold, hesitating whether she should enter or not, a young girl, from whose beaming and beautiful countenance I could not take my eyes for some minutes.

So much intellect—so much tenderness—so much beauty and good-temper I never saw depicted in one human face.— Her age could not be above sixteen, and there was a sweet calm childishness about her countenance that mingled delightfully with the intellect that shone in her eyes, and was proclaimed in the clear high marble brow. She was, in truth, a rare combination of infantine beauty and mental grace.

Her long hair, of a sweet sunny brown, descended as nature, who is, notwithstanding many adverse opinions, a tolerable judge of such matters, intended it should, in graceful wavy curls upon her breast and shoulders. It was not tortured into any architectural absurdity, in compliance with the dictates of the monster, fashion. Her dress was white—destitute of all ornament; and a more lovely creature, or more calculated to win all hearts, I never saw.

"Surely, surely," I thought, "the mind must be a rare and sparkling gem that has so beautiful a home." She was evidently unaware of the presence of a stranger till she opened the door, and now she stood irresolute whether to advance or retire, glancing towards Mrs. Minden, as if she wished to be directed which to do.

"Come in, Cicely," said Mrs. Minden. "This is our dear Julian's physician."—"So," thought I, "this is the Cicely— well may Julian doat upon her with all the wild enthusiasm of his poetical nature."

I bowed to her, and she returned the courtesy with much grace. Then, without taking any notice of Ramsay, she walked directly up to Mrs. Minden, and said in a very low, soft voice, slightly broken by some emotion—

"I have seen him, dear aunt—I have seen Julian. He is nobler—taller—but— dear aunt ——"

She dropped her head upon Mrs. Minden's shoulder, and burst into tears.

Mr. Ramsay blew his nose with one of his startling trumpet-like sounds, which I thought particularly annoying at the moment, and Mrs. Minden, whose own tears were mingling with Cicely's, said,—

"My dear child, what affects you so? My Cicely, why do you thus weep?"

The girl looked up from her aunt's shoulder, and fixed her beautiful eyes upon my face with such a deep melancholy scrutiny that I felt fascinated. It was that kind of gaze which very young children of delicate sensibilities and precocious intellect will often bend upon a strange face, as if they were endowed by Heaven with some rare power of reading the very soul of him or her they so minutely scrutinize.

"Cicely," said her aunt.

She startled, and a slight accession of colour visited her cheeks, as she seemed then conscious that her glance at me had been rather long—she tried to speak, but it was with great difficulty that, after several fruitless efforts, she managed to say,—

"Sir—will—will—Julian die?"

Again the uncle blew a sonorous blast with his nose, but I could see by the position of his head that he was waiting as eagerly for my answer as Cicely, whose very breathing seemed almost suspended whilst she bent forward to listen to my words.

"What human being can answer such a question with relation to time?" I said. "Miss Cicely, do not make yourself over anxious or unhappy about Julian. There is nothing at present to lead to a supposition of urgent danger. I hope he may live long to be a blessing to all who love him."

She stepped forward, and with the most natural grace in the world, took my hand, saying,—

"Thank you, sir— thank you."

"Bless my heart," said Ramsay, suddenly jumping up, "I must go. I have a very particular appointment, indeed—I must go directly."—"But, Mr. Ramsay," said I——

"Good morning, doctor—good morning, Martha. Cicely, my dear, bye, bye."

Cicely made him no answer, but turned away her face with a shudder.

"Before you go, Mr. Ramsay," said I, stepping between him and the door, "I must insist, in the presence of Mrs. Minden and this young lady, upon again warning you to refrain from trying such dangerous experiments with Julian Minden as the one you attempted but yesterday."—"I—I —I——"

"Hear me out, sir. Julian's state is delicate, and consequently precarious. Improper diet, excitement, or any great shock to the system, might prove fatal."

"Mr. Ramsay," said Cicely, "knowing this, as you did, how could you alarm Julian in the manner you have?"—"Alarm him?" said I.

"Hush—hush—hush!" said Ramsay; "don't tell—that is, I didn't—it was no matter whatever—a mere trifle."

"What was it, Miss Cicely?" said I.—"Nothing—nothing," cried Ramsay.

"Pray, sir," said I, "let the young lady answer me, if you please."—"Julian tells me he was reading in the arbour, at the bottom of the garden," said Cicely, "and in an abstracted mood, when some one fired a gun just at his ear."—"What folly!"

"Why—why, you see, I was out shooting a little early this morning," said Ramsay, "and I was coming home, and I thought, as young persons love fun and frolic, I would just fire my fowling-piece off."

"Shooting in Walworth, sir?" said I.—"Why—why, you know Woolwich marshes are free to any one, and that's where I had been."

"Cicely, what effect upon Julian did the sudden shock produce?"—"Julian is not a coward," said the girl, "but he is weak and ill, and cannot bear, as people who are strong and in good health, sudden shocks—when I went to him soon after, he was very ill indeed."

"Well, I really am very sorry," said Ramsay. "Perhaps, doctor, after all, it would be better to keep poor Julian quite serene and quiet."—"Perhaps?" said I. "Mr. Ramsay, I cannot converse with you any longer. To you, Mrs. Minden, I direct my words, and I declare, that if this man pursues, or is permitted to pursue, the system he is now acting upon, with regard to your son, he will be as much his murderer as if he had stabbed him to the heart."

"Now, really," said Ramsay, "I ——"—"Brother—brother," sobbed Mrs. Minden, "is not this dreadful for me to hear?"

"He will kill Julian if he can," said Cicely, "I know he will—Heaven knows he will. Oh, uncle Ramsay, how can you be so wicked?"—"I wicked?"

"You," said Cicely.

"What shall I do? what shall I do?" sobbed Mrs. Minden, who seemed quite unequal to the emergency of the occasion. —"I tell you, madam, what I would do," said I.

"Oh, advise her—advise her, and save us all," said Cicely, looking imploringly at me.—"I would turn uncle Ramsay out of the house."

"What me—me—me?"—"Yes, you; and then I would apply to some respectable solicitor, concerning the trust money he holds in his hands, and force from him a proper account of how and where it is invested, which I dare say he has never given you, Mrs. Minden."

"I thought not of asking accounts and vouchers from my husband's brother," she sobbed.

"I tell you what, Mr. —— a—a—curse you, what's your name?" said Ramsay to me, while his countenance was deathly pale. "I'll bring an action against you, that you may depend."

"I wish you would," said I; "for if I once drag you into a

court of justice, I will take care that your conduct shall be thoroughly sifted."

"Oh, please, ma'am, Master Julian is very bad!" cried a servant, rushing into the room at this juncture.—"My boy! my boy!" shrieked Mrs. Minden.

"He is dying," gasped Cicely.—"Get out of the way," said I to uncle Ramsay, as I rushed from the room in search of Julian.

When I got into the passage I hurried to the servant, who was at the door of the room, and cried,—

"Where is he?"—"In the arbour, sir."

"This way,—this way," said Cicely, as she took my hand and led me through a pretty greenhouse and down a flight of stone steps to a neat garden at the back of the house.

"Now, for Heaven's sake, do not alarm yourself," said I; "in all probability there is no danger. In cases such as Julian's, we have very seldom indeed any sudden fatality to mourn. Be calm, I beg of you."

She could not answer me, and her eyes were almost blinded by tears as she conducted me over a pretty grass-plot to a summer-house, overgrown with woodbine, which was at its further extremity.

The distance was very short, and upon entering the place I saw Julian seated by a table, at which he had been reading, for several books, one of which was open, lay before him. His head was leaning on his hands, and he was perfectly motionless.

"Julian!" said I, but he did not move.—"Julian!" cried Cicely, "Julian, speak."

At the sound of her voice he raised his head, and said very faintly,—

"Is that you, dear Cicely?"

I saw immediately what had occurred. He had been spitting or vomitting blood, and the ensanguined colour of his lips gave him a ghastly and terrifying appearance. Cicely flew to him with a shriek of dismay, and flung her arms round him, crying,—

"Julian, Julian, stay with me, Julian. You must not die; you must still live for me."—"Hush,—hush," said I, "my dear young lady; you will make matters worse if you do not control your feelings. Pray be calm, I implore you."

She fixed upon me a look of cold despair as she withdrew her arms from Julian, and I placed my finger upon his pulse. It was calm and regular, although very low.

"Come, come, Julian," I said, "there is not much the matter after all."—"I have been in pain," he said.

"No doubt; but you are better now."—"Much, much."

The blood he had thrown off his lungs I had no doubt had much relieved him; taking it, however, as a symptom of his disease, it was tolerably conclusive, that is, combined with others; for spitting of blood alone may occur in otherwise healthy subjects from the rupture of some small blood-vessel, and the patient live to an old age afterwards, without any return of the malady. Still, even in Julian's case, although my mind was painfully clear upon the subject of his confirmed consumptive habit, and I was quite sure he would drop into an early grave, I did not look with any alarm upon the sudden hemorrhage, but rather, provided a return of the attack did not ensue within a few days, to a partial amendment.

"You will find him better after this, Cicely," said I. "He is now suffering from weakness merely, and I have no doubt this attack has been caused by the recent excitement he has undergone at the hands of Ramsay."—"Oh! cruel, cruel," said Cicely.

"Come, now, Julian, you must walk into the house, and lie down a little. You have not so much pain now at your chest?"—"Scarcely any, sir."

"You are better, then, Julian," whispered Cicely.—"I am, indeed, my Cicely, much better. I have been reading 'Byron's Dream.' How easily and naturally the versification flows, and what sweet, tender, gushing thoughts are contained in the glowing verse!"

"You should not excite your mind too much by works of imagination," said I, "unless they be of a cheerful and lively character."—"He has been writing, too," said Cicely, as she took from the table a page of paper, on which were some verses, written in a small, delicate hand, which, by its tremulousness, betrayed the shattered state of poor Julian's nerves.

I was curious to see some production of the sufferer's mind, and I said,—

"Will you give it to me, Cicely?"

She blushed and handed it to me, saying, in a low tone,—

"You will return it when I see you again? To me it will one day be very precious, when—when ——"

She turned aside her head to weep. I knew what she would have added, and replied,—

"It shall be faithfully returned to you, Cicely; I promise you, upon my honour."

I then took Julian's arm in mine, and we walked slowly to the house. I was somewhat surprised that Mrs. Minden had not found us out in the garden yet; but I was told she had fainted, and the first person we met was Ramsay, who, holding up his hands and making a cluck-clucking noise with his mouth, which I presume he thought indicative of deep sympathy, said,—

"Poor fellow—poor fellow!—cluck—cluck—cluck. Ah! he looks very bad indeed. Have you any hopes now, doctor?"—"If you don't get out of the way," said I, "I'll knock you down, and leave you very little hopes of getting up again speedily."

I was really almost beside myself with anger at the unblushing effrontery of Ramsay. It beat everything of the sort I had ever then met with. He by no means despised my threat, however, but got out of the way quickly, and allowed us to pass without troubling us with any more of his questions or his sympathy.

"Now, Julian," I said, "go to your bed-room at once, and I will send your mother to you as soon as she is sufficiently recovered."—"Thank you, sir; you are very kind to me," he said, faintly. "I will follow your advice in all things."

"Then, Julian," said I, as I bent my mouth down to his ear, "beware of your uncle."

He gave a slight start, and then replied,—

"I am warned, I am warned; I will be careful, for the sake of my mother and Cicely."

The young girl caught the sound of her own name, and she said,—

"Did you speak to me, Julian?"—"No, dear Cicely, no, God bless you! You will be here all the day?"—"Yes, Julian."

"Then never doubt I shall be better. We shall meet again before night."

He held out his long, thin, attenuated hand, which Cicely took in hers. I saw a tear drop on it, and then Julian slowly ascended the stairs.

Cicely watched him with such a look of intense interest as he disappeared from view, that it was quite painful to see. When she could see him no more, a gasping sob came from her breast, and I expected to see her in a passion of tears; but with more self-command than under the circumstances I could have believed her capable of exercising, she controlled her feelings, saying,—

"No, no—not yet, not yet! God help me! there may come a time for tears too soon."

Ramsay was looking at me with a dark and ominous scowl, which I returned by a smile of contempt, as I said,—

"You may spare yourself the trouble, Mr. Ramsay, of bending your brows on me. I as little heed your frowns as your smiles."

I saw him tremble with passion as he replied,—

"It is time, indeed, for a man to bend his brows when he finds a physician, who is called in to prescribe for bodily ailments, prying into the concerns of a family, and endeavouring to make mischief. Curse me, sir, I thought all that had gone out with the monks and the father confessors."—"You see you are mistaken," said I, calmly.

"Oh, I see that, and my sister may be fool enough to listen to you. Any quack is sure of a welcome when people fancy they are in extremity. Oh, dear, yes."—"Mr. Ramsay, you may say just what you please in the same strain you are now proceeding in, but in the meantime your abuse will not hinder me from advising Mrs. Minden to apply to the Court of Chancery, unless you render up an immediate account of your trusteeship as regards all property belonging to Julian."

"You dare!" screamed Ramsay; "you dare advise her to harass me!"—"How can you be harassed about a trust which you are only asked to render an account of? Any one would think you had appropriated Julian's money to your own uses."

This was a random, and, perhaps, indiscreet shot of mine, but it seemed to hit Mr. Ramsay rather hard, for he positively reeled again, and had to lay hold of a corner of the cheffonier for support, as, with livid cheeks and lips, he said,—

"I'll—I'll trounce you for this; I—I will be even with you. Take care of yourself—that's all."—"Your threats I despise," said I. "I am much the stronger, and I believe much the bolder man of the two; and as for your getting any assistance in doing me an injury, I don't believe you would find any one insane enough to run the risk; so, Mr. Ramsay, I will not even throw you into the hands of the law, for I despise your threat too much."

"Do you—do you?" he cried. "Beware—that's all. Damnation!"

Mrs. Minden's mind appeared thoroughly prostrated, and she did nothing but weep during this scene. Upon the young warm heart of Cicely, however, it had a very different effect. She suddenly drew herself up to the full height of her beautiful figure, and while her eyes flashed with more lustre, and the feelings of her heart lent a glowing colour to her face, she stepped to within a few paces of Ramsay, and said,—

"Uncle Ramsay, does it become you to threaten this gentleman, who, with Heaven's help, is watching over the life of one so dear as Julian? For shame, sir! for shame! Have you no honour, no feeling? Have you no shame, that you desecrate the house of sickness and grief by your coarse threats? Go, and let us see you no more. We will find find sympathy and kindness from those whom we can claim no kindred with. Go, go, uncle Ramsay; you have exhibited a bad heart."—"You, you vile ———"

"Peace!" cried I. "You may accuse me as much as you like, but if you utter one other word disrespectful to this noble girl, as I am a living man, I'll throw you through the window."—"Hear the bully! hear the bully!" cried Ramsay, as he made a rapid retreat. "I suppose you have some needy friend a bone-setter, and wish to give him a job by assaulting me. But—but, curses on you! I'll be even with you yet. I'll ruin you—I'll ruin you yet."

I smiled.

"I dare say you want to rob the house," he added, almost foaming with rage. "You want to rob everybody! You—you blackguard, you want to seduce that young girl! You—you ———"

What other iniquitous intentions uncle Ramsay would have laid to my charge I know not, for I was so enraged at his last insinuation, that I lost, for about a minute, my presence of mind, and during that minute I am afraid I knocked uncle Ramsay's head rather hard against the doorpost, for he yelled out like a lashed hound, and just to get rid of him quietly, I was forced to give him an accelerating kick, which sent him some distance into the road.

I was a young man then, and impatient. Now that nearly sixty summers have rolled over my head, I should adopt another course; but I am dealing candidly with my readers in my revelations, and "nothing extenuate."

Cicely screamed, Mrs. Minden cried "Murder!" and I was ready in a moment to blame myself to the uttermost, lest Julian should have been disturbed. I found, however, upon proceeding up stairs, that such was not the case, to my great satisfaction.

When I came down to the parlour again, I felt it necessary to say something, and addressing Mrs. Minden, I said,—

"Madam, if it be your wish I will never again cross the threshold of your door. I have been grossly insulted by Mr. Ramsay, and, perhaps, have taken the worst means I could of resenting it; but human nature is fallible, and we cannot always control our passions. We may thank Heaven when they betray us only into an imprudence, which is my case. One thing, however, which was urged by that man is true, and that is, that I am but called in as a physician, and yet have taken upon myself to pry into your family affairs. To so much I plead guilty, and will, if you please, trouble you no more, although my sympathies are strongly interested in your truly amiable son."

Mrs. Minden looked the picture of distress, as, clasping her hands, she cried,—

"What shall I do? what shall I do?"—"Do, aunt?" said Cicely. "Can you hesitate? Let us gratefully thank this gentleman, who, although a stranger to us, has shown us more kindly sympathy than those whose duty was to feel for our sorrows. Let us tell him how truly, how fully we appreciate all that he has done for us, and for dear Julian, and let us beg him not now to desert the good work he has commenced."

"You are right, my dear Cicely," said Mrs. Minden; "but I cannot go to law with my husband's brother. While he continues, as heretofore, to make no large deductions from what we should have, I will let him be."

"That, madam," said I, "is as you please. Heaven forbid that I should be a meddler in your affairs further than your own feelings warrant me."

"You will, then, still attend on our Julian?"—"I certainly will, Mrs. Minden."

"You are very good, sir," said Cicely, so suddenly subsiding from the bold heroic girl she had shown herself to uncle Ramsay, to the gentle, confiding, timid creature she had first appeared, that I knew not which most to admire—her noble disdain of wrong and oppression, or her beautiful appreciation of, and gratitude for, intended kindness.

"My dear young lady," I said, "you may depend upon me doing all that is possible for Julian. If you and your aunt will receive me as a friend, I shall be happy to call in that capacity. I have only one hope, and that certainly is that I may not be so unfortunate as to meet Mr. Ramsay here upon any of my visits. He and I quite understand each other; and after what has passed I have no wish to come again into collision with him."

"No, no, certainly," said Mrs. Minden. "We are much obliged to you, sir. My poor, poor Julian. I will go to him now. Alas! alas! what is money to him, and what are accounts to me, when he will not be here. The sooner, then, I am laid in the grave by his side, the happier I shall be."—"And I—and I," cried Cicely, throwing herself upon her aunt's neck, and weeping bitterly.

"Now, Cicely," said I, "let me beg of you to moderate your feelings. All may yet be better than you think; I will see you and Julian again the day after to-morrow."

I had bidden Mrs. Minden and Cicely farewell, and my hand was on the lock of the room door, when I heard a step as of some one in the room above, and then a bell rang.

"That is Julian," cried Cicely.—"I will go to him," said Mrs. Minden."

In a moment she left the room, and then, before I could make any remark to Cicely, I heard her call from the top of the stairs to me,—

"Doctor, doctor, will you step up?"—"Certainly," I said. Cicely rushed to the door leading to the staircase, but I restrained her, saying,—

"There is nothing the matter; you may gather so much from the tone of your aunt's voice. Believe me, there is nothing the matter. I will return to you directly."

With these words I mounted the stairs, and, guided by Mrs. Minden, I entered a comfortable bed-chamber, where was Julian in bed. There was upon his face an expression of painful anxiety and eagerness, which I did not much like to see, unless it was in some way satisfactorily accounted for. Before I could ask a question, however, Mrs. Minden said,—

"Julian has had to rise twice, he tells me, to shut his window, and he cannot divest himself of the idea that it has been opened on each occasion by some one from the outside."

"I am quite sure of it," said Julian in an excited tone. "It was opened too quietly and deliberately to be the result of accident merely. I am not superstitious, doctor, but the window was surely opened from the outside."

"How can that be, Julian?" said I, as I examined the window, and found there was a fastening, which could, certainly, be moved from the outside, had there been any one to do it, but the impossibility of any one getting up so high without being noticed stared me in the face.

I opened the window and looked out, when, to my surprise, I saw a human head peer out from a window underneath, and then draw back with great rapidity again.

"Oh," thought I, "there is some trickery going on about this window. I will not leave this house till I know what all this means."

I made up my mind that I would watch carefully for a repetition of the opening, but before I did so I examined the fastening more particularly. It was one of those which could be opened either from the inside or the out, and the window itself was a French one, as they are called—that is to say, divided into two compartments that open like doors.

Having satisfied myself of these particulars, I descended to the parlour, and stationed myself at its window, which was immediately below that of Julian's room.

"Now, Cicely," said I, "you and I will watch how Julian's window is opened."

I had scarcely spoken when I saw something like a long stick pass the window of the parlour, and waving about as if held by some unsteady hand, proceed upwards towards Julian's in order to poke open, of course, the fastening.

"There, Cicely," said I; "some one wants to open Julian's window, in order to expose him to cold air while he sleeps, which really might kill him."

Cicely looked all amazement at the stick, and said,—

"Good Heavens, sir! who can be so wicked?"

"Who is down stairs?" said I.—"No one but Martha, the servant, I believe."

"Very well. Do you stay here while I go down to the kitchen. Should your aunt come down before I return, ask her to follow me."

So saying, I tripped down as lightly as I could, and the first object that presented itself to me was a great blousy-looking wench, leaning half out of the window, with a long clothes-prop in her hand, no doubt endeavouring to open Julian's window.

I was quite astonished for the moment, and really did not know what to do. Then I thought I should like to alarm her very much for her wickedness, and advancing slowly across the kitchen I suddenly clutched hold of her by the ear, and holding her face down close to the window-sill, so that she could not see me, I said, in an assumed growling tone,—

"So, Martha, you give the devil the trouble of coming for you before your time."

I then made a curious noise of as unearthly a character as my notions of the vulgar supernatural would allow, and gave her nose two or three hard bumps against the window-sill.

All this together had such a confounding effect upon Martha's faculties, that after two or three kicks she fainted away.

This was more than I intended, and Mrs. Minden at that moment coming into the kitchen, I pulled her in from the window, and propped her up in a chair, saying,—

"Mrs. Minden, you may well looked surprised; but the fact is your servant here, either from malice of her own, or bribery from some one, has been with a long piece of wood trying to open Julian's window. Were he, poor fellow, to catch a violent cold, I would not answer for his life seven days."

"Martha opening his window!" exclaimed Mrs. Minden. "Good Heavens! what will next occur?"—"I really don't know, madam; but I will endeavour to recover this girl, and get from her what first put such a diabolical project into her head."

By sprinkling Miss Martha's face with water I recovered her, and when she opened her eyes her first questions were,—

"Oh, where's the thingumy? Where am I? Is this down below? Oh, dear! oh, dear!"

"Martha," said I, "what's the matter?" She looked at me and at Mrs. Minden with surprise and terror in her countenance; then she said,—"Oh, I shall die of fright! There's been the old thingumy here, mum."

"The old who?"—"Scratch, mum; I saw his tail."

"Are you sure of that, Martha?"—"Oh, dear me, yes. I was just looking out of the window to see if it rained, mum, when he came with a bounce like never so many strange tom cats all at once into the kitchen, that made me faint away, mum."

"Martha," said I, "you must have been doing something very wrong, or you would never have had such a visitor. Bless me, what a smell of brimstone there is all at once. He's coming again."

Martha gave a loud scream, and said,—

"I'll tell all—I'll tell all. Oh, sir, don't leave me, and I'll confess."—"Do so—quick, or we leave you."

"Well, sir, Mr. Ramsay told me as fresh air, particularly when it rained a little mizzle, was good for Master Julian's complaint; and he says, says he, if you can poke up anythink, says he, and poke the window open, he says, and leave it open all night, says he, it will be an uncommon good thing, he says, but you mustn't say nothink to Mrs. Minden, nor Miss Cicely, he says, nor that—that—that ——"

"What, Martha? Go on."—"Why, sir, he did say 'that d—d—doctor.'"

"That d—d doctor, I suppose you mean?"—"Yes, sir."

"And what did you say to Mr. Ramsay?"—"Oh, I didn't say anything partickler."

"Well, what did you do with the guinea he gave you?"—"Guinea, sir? It wasn't but half a one."

"Indeed! Now are you not a shameful—but no matter. Mrs. Minden, I presume you will turn this person out of the house; and now that you can no longer mistake Ramsay's intentions you will forbid him coming into it again."

"What will become of me?" was Mrs. Minden's somewhat foolish answer to this, and I could not help saying, with a slight touch of asperity,

"Mrs. Minden, your first consideration as a mother should be for your son. That man, Ramsay, will kill him if he can."

Martha here got up an extemporaneous blubber, during which she asked to be allowed to stay, declaring, among other things, that she considered Julian as the apple of her eye; but I turned to Mrs. Minden, and said,—

"Madam, will you do me the favour to walk up stairs while this woman packs up what belongs to her and leaves the house, which if she does not do, I shall fetch a constable directly."—"You odious wretch," cried Martha.

"Hilloa—hilloa! Martha," said I. "Remember the old gentleman with the tail. I am afraid in your next place you won't be able to say you have no followers. Eh, Martha? Everybody don't like their house full of brimstone on your account."

Mrs. Minden stared first at me and then at Martha, in a bewildered sort of way, till I again invited her to walk up stairs, which she then did, and in a moment or two we were in the parlour, where Cicely was waiting for us in no small anxiety.

In a few words I explained to her what had occurred, and her indignation against Ramsay was as great as it could possibly be.

"Now, aunt," she said, "you must see that what this gentleman suspects is but too true. He would, indeed, murder poor Julian, and he can have no other reason for his bad conduct but to cover, by poor Julian's death, some base transactions of his own about the money that my uncle left."

"I regret to say, Cicely," said I, "that I believe from my heart you are right. Let me recommend an instant investigation into your late husband's affairs by some experienced and honest lawyer."—"I will think, I will think," said Mrs. Minden; "let me have till to-morrow."

"Far be it from me to attempt to dictate to you, madam, but I presume you will write to Mr. Ramsay, forbidding his further visits."—"Yes—yes, I will do that."

The door of the parlour was now unceremoniously opened, and Martha, equipped for the streets, made her appearance. Her face was red with passion, and with a great many oscillations of her head, she said,—

"Well, mum, I've come for my month, if so be as I am to go."—"Pay her, Cicely," said Mrs. Minden; "my purse is on the sideboard, dear."

"Oh, yes, pay her," mimicked Martha, "oh, dear me, the doctor's struck everybody now all of a heap. 'Who but me,' says he. Bless—ah, you wretch."

I laughed, which seemed to aggravate Martha dreadfully, for she turned again to me, and said, with vehemence,—

"Oh, you villain! you kills people—you know you does, all you filthy doctors. Oh, you, body-snatcher!" Then facing round to Mrs. Minden, she exclaimed—"And I tell you what, mum, I looks upon you as a poor *cretur*, and a mere female. You mean wretch—keep the key of the caddy; who wants it?—'lowance out the Flanders' brick, do—I hates you all."

Having received her month's wages, Martha gave her head a magnificent toss, and announced that she would send the carrier "to-morrow" for her things. Then she walked out of the room, banging the door behind her so as to shake the house.

I was resolved she should not do so with the street-door so I slipped after her, and when she had passed on to the step, I laid hold of the door behind, by the screw-shaped piece of iron the chain went on, and held very tight. In a moment Martha gave a tremendous pull, when, to her surprise, the door still continued some six inches or more open. Another and another pull was given, Martha having an intention of shutting herself out with a memorable bang; but I was too strong for her, and I could hear her quite out of breath with her exertions. At length she in great wonder came into the passage again, to see what could be the obstruction, when I suddenly popped from behind the door, saying,—

"You need not trouble yourself, Martha, to bang the door; we can do that ourselves if we wish it."

She was so astonished at my sudden appearance, that she gave a faint scream, and then hurried down the garden walk out of the premises.

When I returned to the parlour, I again urged Mrs. Minden to be careful of Julian, and promising to call upon him on the day after the morrow, I took my leave, being followed to the door by Cicely, who, holding out her hand to me, said, in the most charming manner,—

"We are very—very much beholden to you, sir. My aunt is much depressed in spirits, as you have seen, and wants the energy she might have under happier circumstances. She is, however, very good and kind."

"I am sure of that, Cicely," said I, as I shook hands with her; "and, if I had not been, I would take your word for much more. Hope for the best, as regards Julian, and ever bear in mind that no physician, in such cases, can say how long a patient may last. You may have him about for years, yet, possibly; at the same time, my dear girl, exert that native strength of mind which I am sure you possess, and you will disarm the worst evils that can possibly befal you in this world, of more than half their terrors. The real misfortunes of life are but very few, and those that the imagination clothes in the worst terrors are, commonly, when submitted to the test of a little clear reasoning, the least to be dreaded."

She shook my hand, and I could see a tear in her eye, as she added,—

"Thank you, sir; thank—good-bye."

Poor Cicely! She had a noble mind, but I could see that feeling would triumph over all the reasoning in the world, should she lose Julian. Time alone could mellow the remembrance of such a grief, and replace it by the tender sorrow which clings to the memory of those we love—who have passed away from us like an exhalation.

* * * * *

When I reached home, I sat down anxiously to think what could be done concerning Ramsay, and I confess I was much puzzled to know how to act, unless Mrs. Minden could pluck up a little more resolution than she had hitherto exhibited. If she did not, it was quite clear to me that Ramsay would have everything his own way, and poor Julian would be hurried to the tomb, in all probability to cover some of his, Ramsay's, defalcations in his accounts.

This was a most uncomfortable state of things; and, in fact, so strongly did I feel the necessity of something being done, that I called upon a legal friend, and stated the whole of the circumstances to him, concluding by saying,—

"Now, Weatherly (which was his name), what can be done to force this fellow to an account of his trust?"—"Nothing," he replied.

"Nothing?" cried I.—"Not a step—not a move; unless Mrs. Minden be the acting party. You see, in the first case, it is mere personal property, and there is no direct and uncontingent heir-at-law after Ramsay, otherwise that individual could petition the Court of Chancery, praying for an account. Now Mrs. Minden, as nearest relative of Julian Minden, and a person interested in the due administration of the trust, could demand accounts. If she will not, Ramsay must and will have it all his own way, till Julian is one-and-twenty, when he can take legal proceedings himself instanter."

"Humph!" said I, "that is awkward, for I don't think Mrs. Minden will ever consent to strong measures."—"Very likely," said Weatherly; "but it strikes me, doctor, that there is another aspect of this case which has not at all struck you."

"What is that?"—"Simply this; that Ramsay may have actually made away with all the trust money and property, and is now, to avoid an unpleasant exposure, and its consequences, paying the interest, or something near it, out of his current resources."

"Then if Mrs. Minden was to make a row?"—"She would be destitute."

"And Ramsay?"—"Would certainly be punished, and his goods and property seized as far as they would go to make up the sum he has so unjustly used."

"What would be his punishment?"—"He would be placed in the Fleet prison for contempt of court in not rendering an account of his trust, and there he would remain, in all probability, for the remainder of his existence."

"A poor recompence for the Mindens."—"Very; and it only shows that relations should *never*, under any circumstances, be made trustees."—"You are right, there, Weatherly," said I; "it seems that, in many cases, and with many people, a tie of consanguinity is translated to mean a licence to behave as badly as possible, without any fear of the consequences."—"To be sure."

* * * * *

After my unsatisfactory interview with my legal friend, I went home, when the first thing I saw was a letter, which was as follows:—

"My Dear ——,—If you are not particularly busy in London, Sir Charles Inchcliffe and his lady have a proposal to make to you. A similar arrangement to that you had with Lord Edenton two years ago will, I believe, be suggested. They start for Rome in a week; therefore, if you are to accompany them as travelling physician, which I would advise you, by all means, as the terms will be most liberal, there is no time to be lost.

"In haste, my dear ——, yours ever,
"J. W. WESTERN."

Here was a change in the aspect of my affairs as sudden as unexpected. Such an engagement was just what I wanted, and I at once put on my hat again, and started off to my friend Western's house, for I was really anxious on the subject, being then but a young practitioner.

* * * *

It was early spring, and nature was rapidly shaking off the shade of winter when I reached Blackwall direct from Rotterdam, which had been the last place of my temporary sojourn with the family I had accompanied from the country as travelling physician. I had been absent much longer than I had ever expected to be. A long continental tour, which appeared much to have benefited the health of some members of the family, had consumed many months, and then an accident of a trifling, but very troublesome nature, had compelled our stay at Naples for a long period.

The consequence was, that instead of being in London again as I had expected in about eight months, to resume my practice, I did not set eyes upon the white cliffs of England for a considerable time after that.

If it be delightful to wander in unknown lands, look at strange costumes, and admire the arts and genius, or laugh at the low, grotesque follies of other nations, it is still more delightful after such a sojourn among strangers to return to our own dear land, which ever grows in our esteem as we increase our distance from it.—I could well exclaim with the poet, as I stood on the land of my birth once more,—

"England, with all thy faults I love thee still;"

and it was with the most pleasurable sensations that I hurried to Broad-street in the City, to see if my old rooms were unoccupied.

My landlady welcomed me like one risen from the dead, but to my horror told me a German had possession of my apartments, adding,—

"But he's a filthy wretch, and I means to get rid of him. What do you think he does, sir?"—"I really don't know."

"Why the villain lays on his back in bed ——."—"But you know he has a right to do so; I suppose he pays for the bed?"

"Now that's always the way with you, doctor; you snap me up so—I was going to say he smokes all the while."—"Bless my heart, I suppose he is always very warm, and the superabundant caloric passes off in vapour."

"Now you know what I mean—he smokes a immense pipe, and every five minutes he spits on to the roof, as I'm a sinner; but I'll give him notice this very day—his week's up, and he must go next Tuesday."—"Very well; do you get rid of the German, and take care to have the roof whitewashed."

"You may depend, sir, upon it, and if ever I take a nasty foreigner into my house again, just tell me of it, doctor, that's all—oh, the wretches—I had a 'Merican once, and he *was* a beast." * * * *

I was attached to my old lodgings, and as the German with his pipe and all were to be turned out in a week, I took up my temporary residence at an hotel which I knew to be comfortable in its accommodation and moderate in its charges.

When the morning arrived, and the bustle of debarkation of my luggage, &c., was over, I had leisure to sit down and think of my movements for to-morrow. I unpacked my portmanteau and found my journal, which left off at my last day in Flanders, I having kept a special one for my continental our.

What a throng of old recollections came across me as I took

the well-known volume in my hand. It opened naturally where I made the last entry. It was this—

"Posted note to Mrs. Minden's, containing full instructions as to Julian's diet."

I looked no farther, but closing the book, I threw myself back in the chair with a sigh, saying,—

"Poor Julian!—Is he alive or dead? Does he still linger in life, or has the grave closed over all his hopes—all his affections?—and Cicely, too, where is she? and if the blow has fallen, how has she sustained it?"

A sudden thought struck me, and I made a hasty calculation, by which I found that Julian was within four days of the age of twenty-one, should he be still living.

"I hope Heaven has spared him," I said, "as well for the sake of those who love him as for the confusion of that scoundrel Ramsay, who has been calculating upon his decease. I must go to the Mindens the first thing in the morning. Minden Cottage shall be my first call."

I did not like to go that evening, as it was getting rather late; but I wished I had afterwards, for I got so fidgetty and anxious about Julian, as one by one there came to my mind all the little circumstances which the mob of events for the past year had temporarily obliterated from my memory, that I was compelled to take a long walk, to endeavour, by bodily fatigue, to ensure a night's repose.

This plan, however, did not succeed, for I was tormented the whole night with dreams, in which Ramsay figured in all shapes and guises. One of the most annoying of these was that I thought he held me by the nose, and that I had lost all power of resistance, and he kept saying—

"Now don't interfere with me any more, or I'll serve you in the same way again."

The morning was quite a relief when it came, and rescued my mind from all this nonsense. The sun was shining from a cloudless sky, and everything and everybody wore a gay and exhilarating aspect. Swallowing a hasty breakfast, which I nearly choked myself with, I was in such haste, I started at a good pace for Minden Cottage, resolved that, if Julian still lived, I would be a thorn in Uncle Ramsay's side, notwithstanding my dream, at which I felt very foolishly indignant.

When I came within sight of the cottage my heart beat with excitement, and I involuntarily quickened my pace, for my impatience was extreme. I rang at the garden bell, and was promptly answered by a servant, who, in reply to my eager question of—

"Does Mrs. Minden live here?" said to my ears most musically—"Yes."

"And—and"—Julian, I was going to say, when from the house, for I was close by the garden gate, I saw some one rush with great precipitancy—it was Cicely: in a moment she was by my side. Tears came in her eyes, and scarcely able to speak, she faltered—"Oh, you have come! You have come at last. Heaven has heard our prayer, and you will save him yet."

"Julian," said I, "is—is———."—"Very ill."

"And you, Cicely?" I looked in her face. She was as pale as marble. The sweet transparent freshness of health was gone. Poor Cicely was the shadow of her former self.

"You have been ill, Cicely?" I said.

"No, no; but perhaps I have made myself a little unwell from my great anxiety about Julian."

I shook my head as I took her arm within mine, and walked towards the house.

"My dear Cicely," I said, "you have been fretting immoderately, and have made yourself really ill. If you do not exert some of that strength of mind which I know you to possess, I shall have two patients instead of one."

She sighed deeply, as she said,—

"I feel much better now you are come. I have a sort of confidence I had not before, and Ramsay———"

"What of him?"—"When he found you were gone he came as usual, and my aunt was too weak to resist him. I do not, however, think he has succeeded in doing any harm to Julian, for I have watched him; and, moreover, Julian having no confidence in him, would scarcely ever speak to him."

"How is Mrs. Minden?"—"She does nothing but cry all day, and her mind seems nearly gone."

I would not press poor Cicely with any more questions, for I saw that her heart was full, so we entered the house in silence. Mrs. Minden was not in the parlour, but a man's hat and walking-stick were there. Before I had time to ask to whom they belonged, I heard the back-parlour door, which opened to the head of the kitchen stairs, creak on its hinges, and the voice of uncle Ramsay cried,—

"Kitty—Kitty, who was that?"—"I don't know, sir," said Kitty, from the kitchen.

"Oh!" said Uncle Ramsay. "Well, mind those cutlets are nicely done for my lunch—properly browned, mind."—"Yes, sir."

"Indeed," thought I, "I'll properly brown you before I'm done with you." I glanced inquiringly at Cicely, who said,—"That's the way he goes on; and from the few shillings he doles out to us, it would seem as if Julian and my aunt were living upon his charity."

"Oh, we will soon put all that right," said I. "Uncle Ramsay has had all his own way for a long time now. We must have a change."

As I spoke I opened the folding doors which led from the back parlour to the front, and there I discovered Uncle Ramsay seated low down in an easy chair, with his feet upon another, and a newspaper in his hand, propably the *Times*, for which, I was afterwards informed, he occasionally wrote leading articles on morality and religion when required.

He did not see me at first, but when he did look up, I never shall forget the look of horror and astonishment with which he regarded me.

"D———n!" said Uncle Ramsay.

"So, sir," said I, "you seem to be pretty well aware, by the word you have just used, of your ultimate destination; but if those cutlets you are so anxious about are veal, I warn you of a fit of indigestion, Uncle Ramsay."

He started to his feet as he said,—

"What—what cursed wind blew you here? How dared you come home to—to—to thwart ———."—"Go on, Uncle Ramsay."

He held by the edge of the table as, in an altered tone, he said,—

"Leave the house, sir. Leave this house. You have no business here. Leave this house directly."—I smiled as I replied,—"I shall be as often in this house as I possibly can, you may depend, sir; and I advise you to be cautious what you say or do."

"Uncle Ramsay," said Cicely, "you know this gentleman is our sincere friend, and so you hate him; but he shall come, and I thank Heaven that he has returned to his native country to protect the innocent and weak from you."

"Ah!" said Ramsay, "preach on. You have got your bully again."

"Uncle Ramsay," said I, "I'll wring your neck if you are disrespectful to this young lady. Come, Cicely, I long to see Julian."

"I'll go to my lawyer," cried Ramsay, rushing into the next room and seizing his hat,—"my lawyer—my lawyer—I'll have law and—and—revenge—revenge."

In a moment after a bang of the street door announced Uncle Ramsay's departure, and I accompanied Cicely up stairs to Julian's chamber, where she told me was likewise Mrs. Minden.

Cicely motioned me to allow her to precede me into the room, and I lingered by the door until I heard her say,—

"Julian—Julian." A low, sweet voice replied,—"Yes, dear Cicely; I am not sleeping."

"Here is your old friend, Doctor ———, come to see you."—"Indeed," said Julian, with more animation; "I am very glad—mother, do you hear?"

"Yes, my dear," said Mrs. Minden, in a despairing tone.—"Come in, sir," said Cicely; and in another moment I was by Julian's bed-side.

One glance in his face told me so eloquently what frightful ravages his disease had made since I last saw him, that I could scarcely command my voice to say—

"How are you, Julian?"

He was frightfully thin; a hectic flush was upon his cheeks, and his eyes looked preternaturally large and bright—but it was a glassy and painful brightness rather than the beaming light which flashes from a healthful vision. Before he replied to me, a short hollow cough told me that he was in the last stages of consumption. I saw the weakening moisture on his brow—I marked the awfully shattered state of the nerves, and I said to myself,—"Farewell, Julian, you will not be long among us now."

"Why," he said, in answer to my question, "I am certainly much better than I have been."

"Who has attended you, Julian?"—"Mr. Burrows; but

he has not been for these two days, so, you see, he thinks me better."

"Alas!" thought I; "he knows he can do nothing for you." —"Are you troubled much with a cough?"—"Not for these two days so much."

"Don't you think him better, sir?" said Mrs. Minden.— "If you will leave him with me," said I, "I will tell you my candid opinion before I go."

"Come, aunt, come," said Cicely, and she led Mrs. Minden from the room.

I was determined to tell Julian of his danger, at least, to some extent, and, turning to him, I said,—

"Julian, you are nearly one-and-twenty."—"I am one-and-twenty, on Saturday, sir."

"Well, Julian, the strongest and the heartiest of us have a duty to fulfil, if we leave, or think we may leave, those behind us for whom we wish to provide. You become entitled to property at one-and-twenty."—"Yes; it is in Ramsay's hands."

"I know; but, when you attain your majority, it must be in yours, you know."—"Yes, yes."

"Then, Julian, you should make a will."

He turned his large melancholy-looking eyes upon me, and said,—

"I understand you now, sir; I am dying."—"Julian, we are all dying, and who shall go first, or who last, is the will of Heaven. The counsel I now give you, I would give you were you in the most robust health."

"I thank you, sir; it shall be done. Will you take the ordering and arranging of such a matter? I will take your advice, sir; my dear Cicely shall have all,—she will take care of my mother; but, were I to leave it to the latter, her mind is so much weakened that she would be made a prey of by any designing person."—"You are right, Julian."

With a deep sigh he sunk back on the pillow, and it was some moments before I discovered that he had fainted.

I called no assistance, but quietly went about the room till I found restoratives, by the aid of which I in a little time brought him round again.

When he opened his eyes, he looked upon my face with a sad expression, and said,—

"This fainting is an imitation of death, doctor. Think you it is very like its terrible original?"

"What is called the pang of death, Julian, falls, I believe, far short of many of the pains we experience during our mortal career; but cheer up, we will not talk of such melancholy matters now. I cheerfully accept the task you have assigned me, of seeing to your will."

"Thank you, sir, thank you. Dear Cicely must not be left to the cold mercy of the world. Thank God—thank God, I have the means of placing her far above the ordinary contingencies of life."

These words were said with a fervour that much affected me, and, pressing his hand, I said,—

"To-morrow, Julian, I will be here again. Have you had any annoyance from your uncle?"

"Heaven forgive me if I wrong him," he said, in a whisper; "but I think once or twice I detected in my food some strange matters, and I have suffered dreadfully from sickness, which I could not account for, and which Mr. Burrows said must have been induced by some highly irritating matter being accidentally taken into the stomach."

"Indeed?"

"Yes; in my own mind I thought it more than an accident. I hope I am wrong; but I fear not—I fear not."

"Think no more of him, Julian. I will be here every day, and will take care that he has no hand in anything you take."

"Thank you, sir, thank you," said Julian; "your visits always leave me better than before—much better. I shall not live to thank you, sir, for all your great kindness to me, but my poor Cicely will."

"I require no thanks, Julian," said I; "but you may rely upon my promise when I tell you that I will see that Cicely's interest is properly protected."

"I know you will, I know you will," he said, faintly.

"Now, good-day, Julian," I added, "I must go now; but, be assured of seeing me again at about this time to-morrow."

He turned his face away from the light, and I thought he was about to compose himself to sleep.

"I will say no more to him to-day," I thought; "but I will go at once to my legal friend, and have a will drawn up,

leaving blanks for the bequests, and it shall go hard but I will yet prove myself one too many for dear uncle Ramsay, notwithstanding all his threats."

I had reached the door with this resolve, when I heard Julian, in a faint voice, call me back. I was by the bed-side in a moment, when, raising himself as much as he could, he fixed his eyes upon my face, with an expression I shall never forget, as he said,—

"Is there no hope—no hope?"

"Hope of what, Julian?" I said, although I guessed too well the purport of his question, and that the natural love of life was beginning, now that his case was so very hopeless, to exert its powerful sway within his breast.

"Hope of life," he added; "oh! it is hard when one is so young and so capable of loving all the dear beauties that the world presents to those who will gaze upon it with a desire to be pleased, to die. In the spring of existence, ere the mind has become conscious of its full maturity, and when, like a sweet sunny landscape, seen from afar, life is opening upon the youthful wanderer's way—it is hard, very hard to die. Oh! tell me yet that there is a hope. If no one loved me—if I looked with a cold eye upon the glorious face of Nature—if the running streams made to my eyes no pleasant melody—if I exulted not in the wild wayward beauty of the trees—if I loved not the sunshine, nor thought the pale beams of the silver moon the very extacy of romantic beauty—if I were not the worshipper of the beautiful and good that I am—if there was no Cicely—then—then I should be content to die; but now—now—God help me, I feel it here."

He pressed his hands convulsively upon his heart, and, again naming the name of Cicely, he burst into a flood of hysterical weeping that was solemn and heart-rending to hear, coming as it did from that young heart trembling on the threshold of eternity.

"Julian, Julian," I said, in a voice which must have convinced him how much I was affected by his words, "raise from the pure feelings of your own heart a better spirit. Look upon life more narrowly, and by so doing you will disarm death of its terrors. What is our mortal existence at the very longest, but a wild, fitful career of unfulfilled intentions —of ungratified aspirations. Do we not feel that there is something we would do which we cannot because the spirit that prompts us is borne down by our mortal frame? Should we not then, dearest Julian, conclude by these aspirations—these heavenward thoughts, and hopes, and feelings are the pure breathings of that immortal spirit, which, when we shall have shuffled off our mortal coil, will spread its bright pinions and ascend, a new and glorious being, to its native skies? Oh! Julian, does not your very heart expand at the thought of such a new life, ever made beautiful and bright by the sunshine of Heaven—when you may skim the blue ether of endless space from world to world—scanning new systems, and looking in the glorious light of other suns?"

"That theory is beautiful," he said; "when you come to me to-morrow, tell it me again, and I shall fancy that when my Cicely joins me in such a blissful state, I shall be very —very happy. But are you sure it is not a mere enthusiastic dream?"

"To my mind, Julian, it is no enthusiastic dream. By such contemplations and delightful fancies I have learned to look upon mortal life as a state of probation which is to fit us for a more glorious existence—an existence unfettered by the physical conditions that surround us in our earthly state."

"I will think so too," he said, as he half closed his eyes. "It would be pleasant to sleep now, and dream of such a happy state."—I pressed his hand in mine, and said—"Expect me to-morrow—expect me to-morrow, Julian."

Then I left the room, and walking gently down stairs, I entered the parlour in which were Cicely and Mrs. Minden.— The latter was weeping, but the former immediately came up to me and said eagerly—

"You will tell us the real state of Julian, doctor.—Is—is there the remotest hope?"

"Cicely," I said, "I have had an interesting conversation with Julian, and believe me he does not look upon his condition with terror—on the contrary, I believe he sets a proper, and only a proper, application upon human existence."

"Do you do so likewise?"—"I do."

She sank into a chair as she said,—"You have answered me, you have answered me." She then burst into tears. Mrs. Minden became immediately loud and frantic in her grief, and would have rushed to Julian's room if I had not interposed myself in her way, saying—

"Madam—madam—would you embitter the few remaining hours your son has yet to linger in this world by showing him such an example of grief as you present?"—"Would you have me insensible?" she said.

"Heaven forbid!—I would have you feel, and feel acutely, your loss, which must take place; but, at the same time, I would feel rationally. What effect could you suppose your frantically rushing into Julian's room, as you intended, would have had upon his weakened system and much shattered nerves?"

"Aunt, aunt," said Cicely, making a great effort to subdue her tears, "you know that I love Julian, and yet I will not show him a tear—I will not let him hear a sigh. If he must leave us, it is the will of God, and let us surrender him with hope and faith to the merciful and kindly hands of his Maker."

"My dear young lady," I said, "your feelings do you infinite honour—I will leave you now to the double task of comforting your aunt and cheering Julian, believing in my heart you to be capable of both."

*   *   *   *   *

Not having many engagements in London, in consequence of my very recent arrival, I proceeded at once to my legal friend, to whom I had before made a communication of the case of Julian, as regarded the trusteeship of his uncle Ramsay, and again opened my case by telling him how near

Julian was to one-and-twenty, and how precarious his chance of existence was until even he should reach that age.

"Well," said he, "of course we can do nothing until he, Julian, is one-and-twenty; but then he is capable of making a will. Now, what I should advise is, for you to see him on Saturday, and make up your mind, after a careful examination of his condition, whether he will last till the Monday or not. If you think he will, I should advise his will to be made early on Monday morning, in the presence of competent witnesses, which, being over his birth-day, will prevent any cavilling as to an hour or two."

"Very well," said I; "but should I suspect he may not live so long?"

"Why then we must put it off for as long a period as we can, and trust to the evidence of the hour of his birth we may be able to produce, should the validity of the will be questioned on that point."

"Then will you procure information as to the nature of the property he becomes entitled to when of age?"

"That is easy. A copy of his father's will can be got from Doctor's Commons, and then he can will away everything there is left to his uncle Ramsay in trust for him, such trust ceasing, there being no power to the contrary, when he, Julian, shall become of age."

"Exactly; where, then, on Saturday, shall I meet you?"— "I will come down to Minden Cottage, if you like."

"No," said I, "that might not be necessary; but if you will promise to be come-atable during that day, should I want you, it will do equally well, for I am sure to have some hours' notice from premonitory symptoms of Julian's approaching death."

"I will, you may depend," he said. "If you should come or send here for me, and I should be out, I shall have left word where to find me."

With this arrangement we separated, and I proceeded homewards, where I found awaiting my arrival the following letter :—

"SIR,—Lady Amelia Steventon, at present residing at the Marine Hotel, Brighton, being highly recommended to you by several families, requests me to say, that you would be conferring the greatest obligations upon her by starting for Brighton immediately upon the receipt of this note, to pay her a professional visit, and she hopes a fee of thirty guineas will be satisfactory as regards travelling expenses and professional services.   I am, sir, your obedient servant,

"Bread-street, City, London.   GEORGE LANCASTER."

"Lady Steventon," I repeated, "who is she? I never heard of her. This is very, very awkward indeed, as regards Julian; I really ——"

While I was speaking, I happened, by mere accident, to open the note, when on one of the inside blank pages, near the top, and partially smeared over, was the word—Walworth!

I positively gasped again, as I said—

"A trick of uncle Ramsay's, as I am a living man! His object is to get me out of the way. By the time I found out he hoax that had been played off upon me, and got back to London, poor Julian Minden would be a corpse. Well, of all the villains that ever I met with, this uncle Ramsay is the greatest and the most persevering in his iniquity."

I carefully perused the letter, and the thoughts of Julian and Cicely kept me awake half the night. It was a great relief to me when the grey light of morning peered into my room, and I had a fair excuse for getting up without alarming the whole house.

At a much earlier hour than I had named, I started for Minden Cottage, and a rapid walk brought me there so soon that I thought I ought hardly to intrude upon them. I, however, did so, and was gratified to hear from Cicely that Julian was no worse, but, on the contrary, appeared more cheerful in his spirit and general manner.

I ascended to his room, where I found him reading. Upon my entrance he closed the book, saying—

"I have dreamed of all you said; and from the fantastic visions of sleep, your beautiful theory of another and a happier world has gathered abundant confirmation. I do not so much shrink from death. Besides——"

He paused, and I said—

"Besides what, Julian?"—"I think I am getting better."

Here was at once a key to Julian's more satisfied state of mind. The fear of death was not so strong upon him, and, consequently, his imagination felt itself more free to philosophise upon the subject.

"I am sure I feel much better," he replied. "My thoughts are lighter, and I have not so much pain at my chest."

I looked seriously in his face, and marked the heightened hectic of his cheek, while the blue veins stood up upon his temples like threads of silk. There was, too, an expression about his eyes which told me a far different tale than that he was amusing his mind with.

It is so very common for consumptive patients to declare themselves better, even a few hours before their decease, that Julian's statement gave me no hopes whatever, although it would have been cruelty to have told him so, as I had succeeded in getting his promise to make his will, which was all that I wanted.

"Well, Julian," I said, "on Saturday you are one-and-twenty."—"Yes, I am."

"Then on that day, or on Monday, you will permit me to bring a legal friend with me about your will."

"There—there is no hurry," he said; "but still these things should be done in health rather than sickness—I am certainly much better."

"Then as this is Thursday, Julian," I said, "I don't know that I shall call upon you to-morrow; but on Saturday I shall surely be here."

Upon descending to the parlour, I found Mrs. Minden in tears, as usual; but Cicely, although she was very, very pale, was not weeping.

"Is he really better?" she said, with a hopelessness of expression that quite anticipated my answer of—"No."

"I—I thought not," she added, in a low voice. "My poor Julian."

Even as she spoke there came a rap on the street-door, and Cicely immediately said—

"That is Ramsay's knock."

"Indeed!" said I, as I thought of the letter I had received. "Will you allow me to step into the back parlour, and do not tell him I am here; I have a very special reason, indeed."

"Certainly," said Cicely.

I passed through the folding doors, which I only closed sufficiently to hide the back room from observation, but left me an ample chink, through which I could both see and hear all that passed in the parlour.

"Well, sister," he said, addressing himself to Mrs. Minden, and taking off his gloves with a self-satisfied air, "I don't see why any stranger should prevent me calling to see how Julian is."

"Oh," said Mrs. Minden, meekly, "quarrelling is very dreadful to me."—"Well, I don't want any quarrelling," said Ramsay. "Here I am; you see that fellow has not alarmed me."

"I was in hopes, sir, he had," said Cicely.—"Were you, miss impertinence," said Ramsay. "You'll do yourself no good by setting yourself up against me, I can tell you. How is Julian, sister?—I think I shall dine here to-day."

"Julian is very bad," answered Mrs. Minden, through her sobs and tears, which I had become thoroughly tired of.

"Worse?"—"Much worse, I fear."

"Oh, indeed. Then perhaps you think, after all, he may not live—till—no matter. Ah, poor boy, I'm afraid he's going. All flesh is mere grass—nothing else."

As he spoke he took off his great coat, and, hanging it across the back of a chair, on which he then sat himself, he added—

"I should be very sorry to make a disturbance here, sister; but really, if that most meddling, impertinent doctor, should come here to-day, I should feel inclined to kick him out."

"He said he would come," remarked Cicely, quietly.—"Did he, miss minx. Then I can tell you, that in my opinion he is a mere bully, and will be afraid to come to-day."

"He has always hitherto kept his word," added Cicely.—"Indeed—has he? Well, I shall dine here to-day, just to give him a chance of coming."

Ramsay sat with his back to the folding doors, so that opening them very quietly, as I did, he neither saw nor heard me. Mrs. Minden did, however, and increasing her tears, said,—

"Oh, bless me, there will be another disturbance."—"Will there," said Ramsay; "we shall see. Only let him come here again. D——n him, I——"

"What, uncle Ramsay?" said I, giving him a touch on the shoulder.

He fell off the chair as if he had received a powerful shock of electricity, and sitting on the floor, with a most ridiculous tone, as contrasted with his former one, he cried,—

"Oh, don't; I—d—didn't mean it—murder—police!"—"Uncle Ramsay," said I, calmly, "Lady Amelia Steventon is much better, and don't require my services—you understand me?"—"D——n!" he muttered.

"I see you do," added I. "Now you promised to kick me out of this house, and I am one who likes to see people keep their words. Will you do it?"—"No—no—no—I didn't mean it, upon my soul."

"Nonsense, nonsense, uncle Ramsay, you are too modest. Either you shall kick me out, or I you."—"Murder—fire! You can't kick me when I'm down. That's not fair."

"But I can lift you up, you scoundrel," said I; and suiting the action to the word, I lifted up dear uncle Ramsay, and kicked him out of the house, whence he rushed as quickly as he could, howling with rage.

Saturday morning came, and with it came to me a world of anxiety respecting Julian Minden. I resolved that no other engagement should interfere with my attendance upon him until death should drop the curtain upon his brief career. That he might live to thwart the bold, bad man, who I had no doubt had made away with a great portion of his property, I fervently and almost devoutly wished, for it would indeed have been dreadful for such a man as Ramsay to succeed in rendering destitute such a being as Cicely, who, poor girl, would have enough to struggle with in her deep grief for the loss of him to whom her young heart was knit in such endearing ties.

My nervousness during breakfast was noticed even by my landlady, who said,—

"Dear me, sir, you really seem all of a shake."—"Why," said I, "I am certainly not very well this morning."

"You not well, sir," she cried, with a look of surprise. "Well, I never!—and you a doctor, too."—"Well, suppose I am a doctor; that is no reason why I should be exempt from the ordinary evils of humanity. Doctors have nerves, I assure you."

"Yes, but, you see, it does seem odd of a doctor being ill. I'm sure I shouldn't have any confidence in a doctor that wasn't well himself, because, says you, if he can't cure himself, how can he cure other people, says you?"

"I beg your pardon," I said, "I said no such thing. It was you who said it; and astonishing as you may think it, doctors not only get ill, but they are in the habit even of dying just like other people."

"Ah, well," said my landlady, as she took up the key and left the room, "all I can say is, as it's odd to me, because what's the use of a doctor if he can't make people well, in course always beginning naturally with himself."

To this proposition I could oppose no argument, so my landlady had it all her own way. Very frequently in the course of my practice, when I have visited the houses of the poor and ignorant, I have found the same notion prevailing, that a surgeon or physician who has anything the matter with himself must be a downright idiot; and if the death of a medical man did not at once put an end to his practice, in the natural course of events, he certainly would be ruined for not taking better care of himself.

But to return to my tale.

After this little bit of argumentation with my landlady, I sallied forth to Walworth, and reached Minden Cottage in a state of excitement and anxiety such as I had very rarely experienced in my life before.

My ring was immediately answered, and to my question of "How is Julian?" I received at least the negatively satisfactory answer of, "Poor Cicely don't think he's any worse, sir."

In the parlour I met Cicely, and could see that she was agitated beyond her wont about something.

"You are unwell," I said. "Pray be ca'm, Cicely; you will produce a serious, bad effect upon your health, if you suffer your feelings to prey upon you as I fear you are doing."

"I have been talking to Julian," she said, "and he tells me you have induced him to make his will. I cannot bear the thought."

"Now, really, Cicely," said I, "you ought not to distress yourself about such a matter. Surely the making of his will by Julian, so that those whom he loves and leaves behind may be placed above the cold pressure of outward circumstances, ought not to be a subject of painful contemplation, and I think is eminently calculated to make his last moments much happier than they otherwise would be."

"I know you are right," she said; "but it does seem to me terrible to acquire anything by his death."

"Then you view the subject, Cicely, in a wrong light. You will not be acquiring anything by his death which you would not have had with more pleasure had he lived. You lose by his death, inasmuch as you lose him with whom you could indeed have enjoyed the property his father has left him."

She seemed convinced by my arguments, and after I had ascertained that Julian was alone, I went up to his room. He was sleeping, and perfectly bathed in perspiration. An awful and striking alteration had taken place in his features, which had acquired that appearance people call pinched, while a dark ring surrounded each eye. I placed my ear close to his mouth, and found his breathing most painfully irregular. I then tried the pulse—it scarcely reached forty-eight. Life was ebbing fast, and with a pang of disappointment I asked myself,—

"Will he live this day out, or will that bad man, Ramsay, after all, triumph in his villany?"

I then sat down by the bedside, and began seriously to think of the best means of protracting Julian's existence. It appeared to me that his disorder had taken a form of slow decay,—that life was gradually going,—that the circulation was each moment growing more languid, and that he would go on, with some few alternations of sleeping and waking, until, during one of his snatches of sleep, he would expire with scarce a sigh.

"I must hold up the system," I thought to myself; "I must keep him alive by stimulants until to-morrow or Monday, if possible. His end may by such means be only warded off; and as for what he takes, as far as his actual condition goes, it can be of little consequence, for no human power can save his life."

Some clouds which had been across the sun, and obscured its rays, now suddenly dissipated, and a bright gleam of golden light came through the window on to Julian's face. Before I could rise to close the blinds, Julian awoke, and heaving a deep sigh, he said,—

"The will—the will!—Oh, Cicely, Cicely, what a dream!"

"Julian," said I, "how are you this morning?"—"Oh, sir," he said, faintly, as he wiped his moist brow with his long thin hand, "is that you? I have longed to see you. Such a dream—such an awful dream!"

"Well, Julian," I said, "forget it; it was but a dream. Think nothing of it. How do you feel?"—"I scarcely know; but I have seen my father."

I was fearful at that moment that his mind was going, and that, after all, I might be foiled as regarded his will. He appeared to understand my gaze, and said,—

"I mean in my sleep, doctor,—only in my sleep. I thought he looked at me with a countenance partly of sorrow and partly of hopeful joy, and in such loving accents as cheered my heart, he said, 'Come, my Julian, come.' Then it was that I awoke. There was a warmth upon my face; it was the sunshine of my father's smile."

I let him indulge the fond conceit, and said nothing about the necessity I had had of closing the blinds, merely remarking,—

"Such visions cannot disturb you, Julian?"—"No, no," he replied. "To-day is my birthday; I am one-and-twenty, and for my dear Cicely's sake I am very glad. I remember you spoke to me of my will."

"I did, Julian, and in good time it shall be ready for your signature. Are you in any pain?"—"No, no; I am feeble, but not in pain. Do you not think me better?"

"I shall be able to tell," said I, "as the day advances; for I think I shall remain here, as I have no other calls to make."

—"You are very kind to me," he said, "very—very, and to —dear—dear—Cicely—my Cicely."

At this instant he again dropped asleep, and the cold, profuse perspiration broke out upon his brow, standing upon it as if water had been suddenly dashed there.

"He is going—he is going," thought I. "In one of these sudden, unnatural sleeps he will expire. I must prevent this occurrence."

I then walked down stairs and said to Cicely,—

"Where is your aunt?"—"She is not up," was the reply; "but I will tell her to rise if she can. I fear she is very unwell."

"Don't advise her to get up, by any means," said I; "but be so good as to tell her that I want to see her, and will come to her room."

Cicely went on my errand, and presently returned to say that Mrs. Minden would see me, and that she was in the back room on the second floor. I immediately ascended the stairs, and seeing an open door, I entered the bed chamber of Mrs. Minden.

"It is very kind of you, doctor," she said, "to visit me. I am very unwell, and shall soon follow my poor, poor boy."

Here she commenced her usual weeping to such excess, that I was compelled to say,—

"Mrs. Minden, do command yourself. I have come to ask you a particular question. Are you sure this is Julian's birthday?"—"Yes, yes, quite sure."

"At what time of the day was he born?"—She considered a moment, and then said, "Late in the evening."

This was the most unsatisfactory answer I could receive, and I thought, "Well, Julian's will cannot be made to-day, and would it be legal if made to-morrow?" That was a question I was not lawyer enough to answer, and I left Mrs. Minden's room in what I dare say she considered a very abrupt manner. When I went down stairs again I said to Cicely,—

"Is there any one about here whom I could send some distance on a message?"—"Yes," she said; "we have a lad here who can be safely trusted. But—but tell me—do you apprehend the worst—to-day?"

"No, Cicely, I do not," said I; "but we must be prepared for whatever may occur. Will you tell the lad to take this note to its address, and wait for an answer?"

I handed her a note that I had provided myself with in case I had to send for my legal friend, and in less than five minutes I had the satisfaction of seeing the boy go with it. I then said,—

"Do not be alarmed, Cicely; I will not leave Julian all day. Have you any port wine in the house?"—"Yes," she replied.

"Well, then, let a jug of half water and half port wine be kept hot, so that I can have some of it for Julian at a moment's notice."—"It shall be done," said Cicely; and then the fancied composure with which she had been speaking to me gave way—her voice broke, and tears started to her eyes.

* * * * *

In about two hours my friend the lawyer arrived at Minden Cottage. Julian had not awakened, and I left his bedside, where I had sat reading, in order to meet the attorney. I took him into the back parlour, and the moment I had closed the door, I said,—

"Julian is dying. He was born late in the day. Would his will be legal if made earlier?"—"It would be subject to cavil."

"Would it be legal if made on a Sunday?"—"Still subject to cavil, for Sunday is a *dies non*. But I think a Court of Equity would confirm the bequests in such a case."

"We must avoid litigation if we can," said I. "Will you, if I can keep Julian alive till twelve o'clock on Sunday night, be here with witnesses?"—"I will be here before that hour, so that no time shall be lost."

"Thank you," I said, and I hurried up to Julian, who I was resolved to watch narrowly.

Julian did not awaken until four o'clock, and then he showed evident symptoms of increased weakness. He looked wildly about him, and in a moaning voice said,—

"Cicely, Cicely—where is she?"—"Take this, Julian," said I, offering him a table spoonful of the warm wine and water, which I had kept hot over a lamp in the room. He swallowed the stimulant, and then sunk back on his pillow to sleep again.—I saw a flush of colour visit his cheek, and his pulse within five minutes rose fifteen degrees.

"Now," thought I, "this artificial state must be kept up; the least reaction would be his death. By such means as this I alone have the chance of spinning out Julian's life to the last thread."

I sat the whole of that night by Julian's bed-side. Four or five times he had awakened, and as often I had given him some of the wine and water. All solid food he rejected, and towards Sunday morning he was feverish, but more full of life than he had been the day before.

Such a state of things, however, I was aware could not last long, and I knew not a moment when some change might not take place which would carry him off; but I doubted not he would have been dead by then had it not been for the artificial life I had thrown into him by the wine and water.

It was about nine o'clock on Sunday morning that a knock came to the door, and I heard the detested voice of Ramsay say,—

"Is Julian dead?"—"No," said I, rushing to the door, "he's living—much better, and one-and-twenty years of of age."

"Oh, you are here are you?" he said, retreating a step. Then turning his head, he cried,—" Come on ; here he is."

Two men immediately stepped up to the door, and one of them said to me,—" You are our prisoner."

"Prisoner?" said I.—" Yes. We are Bow-street officers. We have a warrant against you on a charge of assault with intent to commit a robbery on this gentleman."

"What's all this?" said my legal friend Weatherley, at this opportune moment walking up the garden arm-in-arm with a gentleman.—" Thank God, Weatherley," cried I, "you are come! This is Uncle Ramsay, and these officers come to arrest me because I kicked him out of the house yesterday."

"They have a warrant," cried Ramsay. "D—n you, I have you now."

To my surprise I saw the two officers the moment they saw the gentleman who was with my friend, take off their hats and stand in the most respectful attitudes. My friend, seeing my amazement, said,—

"Doctor ——, this is Mr. ——, the magistrate. He granted the warrant which Ramsay applied for; but having heard from me something of what has been going on here, he came, at my request, to see to its due execution."

"Julian's life, hour by hour," said I, " depends upon my presence."

"The law must take its course," said Ramsay. "A dozen magistrates can't gainsay the warrant."

"You are quite right, sir," said the magistrate. "The law shall take its course ; but magistrates have a discretionary power. I postpone the consideration of this case for a week, taking Doctor ——'s verbal promise then to appear before me."—" I give it cheerfully," said I.

Ramsay struck the crown of his hat a furious blow, and uttered a cry of rage and disappointment more resembling in its tone that of some wild animal than a human being.

"It's a conspiracy of you all against me," he cried ; "but I will be revenged—deeply revenged! Beware of me!"

"That will do," said the magistrate. "Officers, you will take this man to the watch-house, where he can stay till to-morrow, when I will swear the peace against him, and when I have no doubt, at my request, forty-eight hours notice of bail will be required."

"Forty eight d—d devils!" cried Ramsay, trying to escape; but he was speedily captured by the officers, and borne off in triumph.

"How can I thank you, sir?" said I to the magistrate.—" My dear sir," he replied, "persevere in what you are doing for this family, and I hope you will not hesitate to apply to me in any emergency. My friend is, I believe, going to stay here."

"Yes," said Weatherley, "I shall not leave the house. The will is in my pocket, and you and I, doctor, will be its witnesses."

* * * * * *

The chimes of half-past eleven sounded painfully upon my ear on that anxious and weary Sunday evening. Julian was in one of his sleeps, and he was tossing his arms wildly about him, while faint moans proclaimed that the hour of his death was nearly come.

"He is waking," said Weatherley.—" Hush! hush!" I said ; and as I spoke Julian opened his large lustrous eyes. He made an effort to raise himself up in the bed, and motioned me to help him.

"Coming—coming, father!" he said. " I am coming."— "Drink, Julian," said I.

He mechanically swallowed some of the wine and water, and then, in a faint voice, he said,—

"Light them again—light them again."—" What, Julian, what?" I said.—" Why did you put out the lights? Where are you Cicely—Cicely—my own Cicely! God—God help me!"

"He's going," gasped I.—" Send for some of the neighbours," said Weatherley. " For the love of Heaven, let us have plenty of witnesses."

Cicely was outside the door, and hearing us talking, she came in with the exclamation on her lips of—" Julian—Julian—my Julian!"

A faint cry burst from him, and he stretched out his arms. Cicely clung to him in an agony of despair. A convulsive tremor shook all Julian's limbs. I thought another minute would be his last, and while I pressed him to take a draught from a glass of wine and water, I heard Weatherley coming up the stairs, which first apprised me he had left the room.

"A quarter to twelve," he said, in a husky whisper. "The witnesses are coming."

"Julian, Julian, speak," cried Cicely, — " speak, dear Julian."

"Cice—Cicely," he murmured. " My Cicely—dying—dying."

Weatherley spread out the will, and seized a pen. The steps of persons ascending the staircase came upon my ears, and in a moment two respectable-looking persons entered the room.

"These gentlemen," whispered my friend to me, " will witness our proceedings. We cannot in such a case as this take too many precautions."—" You are right—quite right," said I. " I pray to Heaven he may live, and yet I have my serious doubts."

"Amen to the prayer," said Weatherley.

I approached Julian, and placing my mouth close to his ear, I said,—

"Julian—Julian!"

A strange sound in his throat was the only answer I received. My instant impression was that his voice was gone, and if so all our efforts would be fruitless. I opened one of his eyes—it was opaque and lustreless. Cicely saw in my countenance my despair, and with a loud shriek she cried,—

"Julian, Julian, one word for me—for Cicely! Oh, Julian, do not, do not leave me thus!"

I saw his lips move faintly, and at the moment they did so a neighbouring clock commenced solemnly sounding the hour of twelve.

"Time, time!" cried Weatherley. "There's twelve o'clock, thank God. It's Monday morning now."

Mrs. Minden at this moment, in her night dress, rushed into the room, exclaiming wildly,—

"My boy, my boy! my Julian! What are you doing to him, all of you? Oh, save him, save him! I cannot part with him! I am dying myself, but, Julian, Julian, let the grave close over me first, my Julian, my Julian!"

She attempted to throw herself upon the bed, but I stopped her, saying firmly,—

"Mrs. Minden, moments are precious. Your own future fate, and that of Cicely, depend upon the next five minutes."

"Will he live—will he live?" she cried.—" For God's sake hold her, one of you," said I. "There is but one chance left, and that must be tried by myself."

"Aunt, aunt," said Cicely, "you hear. Oh, be ruled by our only friend."

Mrs. Minden made a faint struggle to reach the bed, and then, to my great relief, she fainted. I placed the cup of hot wine to Julian's lips with one hand, while I put the other upon his wrist. The pulsation was scarcely perceptible, and when Cicely tried to hold his head up, his neck yielded, lacking the power to support him. I knew that if I could get any of the stimulating liquid down his throat, it would either revive him temporarily, or kill him on the instant.

"Julian, drink,—drink," I cried; but he heard me not.

Another moment was not to be lost. I forced open his mouth, and poured some of the wine into it. The struggle to save himself from choking was frightful for a moment, and then he drew a more free breath, saying faintly,—

"Lights! lights!"

"You hear, gentlemen," I said. "It is past twelve o'clock, and Mr. Julian Minden speaks."—"Yes, yes," said the bewildered witnesses.

"Take, take," he gasped, "those cold fingers away from my heart!"—"Again, again!" I cried. "My hand is cold, you hear."

My hand was not touching him, but for the sake of the object I had in view, I thought I might sanctify some few little deviations from truth.

"Listen to me," said Mr. Weatherley; and then, while I gave Julian some more of the wine, he read quickly the preamble of the will, ending by saying,—

"Mr. Julian Minden, you, being now of age, hereby make your will, as herein set forth."

Julian was supported on my arm, and slowly picking the counterpane with his long thin fingers. Cicely's head was on the bed, and she was weeping most bitterly. I waved my hand before Julian's face, and saw that the sight of the eye I had not looked at was not gone; the pupil sensibly contracted and dilated.

"You can see, Julian," I whispered, "you can see?"—"Yes," he said, in a deep, strange voice.

"That will do," said Mr. Weatherley. "To whom, then, Mr. Julian Minden, do you devise all your real and personal estate?"

Julian was silent, the question evidently was incomprehensible. Upon the moment I thought of an expedient that might produce just the answer I wanted. I touched the head of Cicely, as I whispered to her,—

"For God's sake look at Julian!"

She looked up instantly. He saw her. A radiant smile played upon his face, and stretching out his arms feebly, he said,—

"My Cicely!"

Cicely clasped him in her arms, sobbing bitterly, and I said aloud,—

"You hear, gentlemen, what he says. There can be no mistake; he leaves all to Cicely. His action, too, shows there can be no error as to who he means."

Mr. Weatherley gave me one glance, as much as to say I don't know whether I am on my head or my heels, and then rapidly filled up the will as directed.

Now came the most trying question of all. Could Julian sign his will? Could he be made in any way to comprehend what it was required of him to do, and was he sufficiently master of himself to shape the letters which would form his name? Weatherley rose from the table, and said to me in a whisper,—

"All is ready; we only now want his signature. If you can obtain that, nothing more is required."—" I will try," said I. Then, addressing Julian, I said,—"You will sign your name for Cicely, Julian?—you hear me?—you will write your name? It is for Cicely."

"Oh, do not urge him—do not urge him!" said Cicely. "I shall soon die, and then what matters."—"Hush, Cicely, hush! leave all this matter to me. Julian, Julian, pray look up."

Julian looked in my face, and I began to suspect that the vision of the eye which he had seen with so much longer than I expected was gone, for he said,—

"Where is she—oh! where is she—my Cicely?"—"Here, here, Julian," cried the sobbing girl; "I am here, dear Julian."

"The pen! the pen, Weatherley!" cried I.

Weatherley handed me a pen full of ink, which I placed in Julian's hand, making vain efforts to clasp his fingers over it; and while the lawyer laid the parchment before him, I continued whispering in his ear, "Write, write, Julian—write your name for Cicely! It is for her, Julian. Make an effort, and write your name."

He clutched the pen, and seemed striving to understand and comply with my urgent request, when there came a tremendous knock and ring at the door, which lasted some moments, and awakened every echo in the house.

I sprang to the door as I cried,—

"That will kill him—that will kill him! Who dared knock in that manner at such a time as this?"—"Mr. Ramsay, sir," said the servant, opening the chamber door, when in an instant I saw Ramsay at the head of the stairs.

My first impulse was to take him by the collar and instantly turn him out of the house, but Weatherley immediately seized my arm, crying—

"Hold! hold! For God's sake commit no violence now. How on earth did that man get here?"—"If you touch me," said Ramsay, "by the Heaven that made me I will shoot you!"

He produced as he spoke a large duelling pistol, which he held threateningly at my head. Had it been on full cock I must have been shot, for Ramsay's hand shook so violently that, perhaps without intending it, he would assuredly have pulled the trigger. I was not, however, going to be taken by storm in that manner, and for the moment forgetting all else in my indignation at Ramsay, I rushed in upon him, and succeeded in clasping the wrist of the arm that held the pistol. My sudden attack was so unexpected that he fell to the floor and I above, when by some means the pistol went off with a loud report, the ball with which it was loaded hitting the dressing-glass which was near the window, and adding to the noise and confusion by the crash it made of it.

"You infernal scoundrel!" cried I, as I clutched him by the throat and knocked his head against the floor; "you would have committed murder if you could."

"Help! help!—murder!" he cried, and then he called loudly upon some one by a name which sounded like Singin, and I saw a tallow-faced looking man standing on the landing of the stairs, who said,—

"Come, come, this won't do. I take you all to witness that a murderous assault is being committed."

"Who are you?" said I, in some surprise.—"I am Mr. Ramsay's attorney," replied the villanous-looking creature. "You had better mind what you are about."

"You had better mind what you are about," said Weatherley, advancing. "I know you, Mr. Singin, and you know me. Let me add, although my language may sound rather unprofessional, that I believe a greater scoundrel than yourself is not unhung."—"Mr. Weatherley?—the devil!" exclaimed Singin.

"Now, sir, take yourself off," said Weatherley.

"No, no!" cried Ramsay, struggling to his feet, for I had let go of his throat. "Don't go, Singin; we will bring actions against them both."

"I don't mean to go," said Singin. "It was you, Mr. Weatherley, was it, that got Mr. Ramsay locked up; but he sent for me, and you quite forgot that a judge's order would release him. Oh! oh! oh! clever Weatherley, there are other professional gents who know just about as much as you do."

"Fetch a constable as quickly you can," said Weatherley to the servant girl who was lingering at the door. "Now, I warn both of you off these premises."

"Is he dead?" said Ramsay. "Tell me that, and I will go."—"If he lives," said Singin, "and makes a will, it shall be in our presence, in order that we may swear afterwards whether he was *compos mentis* or not. We know he ain't, nor hasn't been for three or four days; but you want to rob my client, all of you. It won't succeed though."

I had been positively afraid to cast my eyes towards Julian, for I entertained no manner of doubt but that he was dead; the shock of the various noises I was sure would snap the slender thread by which he held to life. My indignation against Ramsay and his rascally attorney well nigh deprived me of all self-command, and I believe I should have committed some act of great violence, had not Cicely suddenly cried,—

"Doctor, doctor! come, come! Oh Julian! Julian!"

I rushed to the side of the bed in a moment, and to my great surprise I saw Julian sitting up, pressing one hand upon his heart, while a flush of colour on his cheek, showed that some extraordinary rallying of the powers of life had taken place.

"Cicely, Cicely!" he said. "It was your voice I heard. Where are you, my Cicely?"—"Here, here, Julian," cried Cicely; "I am here."

"You are much better, Julian," said I, "and you will sign your will, for you are one-and-twenty, you know."—"No, no!" cried Ramsay.

Julian started at his voice, and immediately cried,—

"My will,—my will! It shall be all for Cicely—all for

dear Cicely! I will make my will!"—"Here, here!" cried Weatherley, "sign your name now."

He again put the pen in Julian's hand, and directing it to the proper spot on the will which lay open before him, he added,—" Write, write!"

"For Cicely," said I —" No, no," cried Ramsay. "He is mad; he knows not what he does. This is a mere trick—an infamous juggle. I take all here to witness that Julian Minden is not in a fit state to know what he is about, or to manage any of his affairs."

"Silence, fiend!" cried I. "Another word, and ——"
—"Hush, hush!" said Julian. "That is uncle Ramsay's voice which says I am mad. He has tried to drive me mad, but I am not so. I know now that I am dying. Those sobs so close to me come from the heart of my Cicely. I am not mad!"

"You hear his words, gentlemen," said I to the two witnesses. "He is perfectly master of himself. This is a most wonderful case, and Heaven has surely interfered specially to the discomfiture of the villain Ramsay."—" That's actionable," said Singin.

"To whom will you leave all your property, Julian Minden?" said Mr. Weatherley.—"To my dear Cicely," was the answer.

"Your name, your name, Julian!" I said. "The pen is in your hand. Write, write!"—In a large bold hand he wrote, "Julian Minden."

"Uncle Ramsay you are foiled."—"D———n!" cried Ramsay, as he rushed from the room with headlong speed.

"Mr. Singin," said I, "we don't want you. Do you understand a hint?"—" I will bring actions against you all," cried Singin, as he followed his iniquitous employer.

Mr. Weatherley was eagerly directing the witnesses where to sign their names, when I turned from the door and Julian was still sitting up with the pen in his hand. There was an expression of sweet serenity upon his face, and before I could reach the bed, he said, in a low voice,—

"For dear Cicely—all for dear Cicely!"—"Thank God, Julian," said I, " who has granted you strength to go through this trying scene."

"My Julian," sobbed Cicely. "Oh, he is better, doctor, look at him—he is better!" A smile played like a sunbeam across Julian's face as he said gently, "what sweet music!"

Then he sighed deeply, and lay back upon the pillow. Cicely watched his countenance for some moments in silence; then she said,—

"He is sleeping, doctor, he is sleeping."—I gently took her hand as I said,—" Come away, Cicely, come away. He is sleeping, but it is with God!"

One cry burst from her lips, and she threw herself across the body of him she had loved so fondly, and who had passed away from her so gently.

* * * * *

Julian's will was easily proved, and then came the question as to the state of the property. I and Weatherley kept so close a watch upon uncle Ramsay, that although he several times tried to leave the country, we always foiled him. A petition to the Court of Chancery obliged him to render an account of his trust, when it was found that not above one-third of what should have been Julian's came to Cicely, and that only by making Ramsay a beggar.

Then he was committed by the Court of Chancery for contempt, that is to say, for not rendering a satisfactory account, in the same way that by law a man is considered to give no account of himself, when he cannot name his home, in consequence of having none.

As for Mr. Singin, we never heard any more of him, and the last I saw of Ramsay was some years afterwards, when passing down what was then Farringdon-market, I saw his face peering through a grating some paces from the entrance of the Fleet Prison, and heard him say,—" Pray pity the poor prisoners," to induce charitable persons to place a trifle in a box that was just below, with a slit in the lid to receive coins.

Poor Cicely fell into an early grave, and was buried near to Julian. Peace be to them both! May Julian's dream of his sunny flight through endless space have been verified.

Mrs. Minden of course cried dreadfully for many months, and indeed scarcely ever left off until she married a fat old gentleman who came to lodge with her, and then he quarrelled with her so continually, that—she took to strong cordials and died.

THE MORLEYS;

OR, THE PERILS OF A NIGHT.

THAT the imagination, when unduly excited, produces more serious and irremediable evils upon the human frame than any ordinary physical causes, the experience of every medical man will testify; and my readers will, perhaps, call to mind many episodes from my "Diary," which, from time to time, have strengthened such a proposition.

What I am about to relate will, however, not only bear upon that question, as regards the phenomena of mind, but I trust it will have a more practically beneficial effect, in warning parents against a danger which is not the less great because it is hidden, or because its effect upon the most beautiful, and the most loveable, and innocent portions of the great human family, are in many melancholy instances slow and insidious.

I, of course, allude to those dear little ones, of whom, we are told in the beautiful and emphatic language of Scripture, is the kingdom of Heaven.

This danger, of which I would warn all interested—and who is not nearly or remotely?—in the young and fragile beings who are to make the generation which shall succeed us, is one purely mental; one which produces the most incalculable mischief; one which poisons every dear enjoyment of that part of existence which should be a dream of joy, a sweet, blissful, probationary state; to the innocent delight of which, in after life, we ought to be able to look back with a sigh and a smile, as a solace for the graver cares and deep disappointments of maturer existence.

Oh! if there be a glimpse of Heaven yet lingering upon earth—if there be anything living to which yet clings in sunny beauty the purity and gentleness which reigns in a happier, better world—that breathing creature is a young child, with all the pure, fresh feelings given it by God, crowding around its innocent heart, with all the sincerity, all the affection, all the love and joy which, could it be preserved, free from the plague-spot of after dissimulation, would make this world, instead of the gloomy valley of death it is, a sweet dream of beauty and love—a dear reminiscence of joy to be remembered at a happier and more enduring state with pleasurable interest.

Let me then raise my voice in defence of the small men and women, who crowd around many a heart, spreading joy around them with their innocent prattle; and let me denounce, as I would denounce the deceiver, the robber, the assassin, those who convert the dear sunshine of such minds into a teeming pit of horrors, where gaunt superstition reigns unchecked, and riots in the palace God himself has made.

Those who seek in early life to instil notions of the supernatural into a child's mind, for the purpose of subduing its energies, and stilling its small complaints by abject terror, deserve worse than the condemnation of every reflecting mind, they deserve the bitterest—the severest judgment which can be meted out to them by an offended Heaven and an outraged creation.

These remarks I have been led to by a most interesting passage in my "Diary," which, while I believe it will be as amusing as any of its predecessors, will, at the same time, I trust and hope, be of great practical benefit; and if by its means I do but rescue one dawning intellect from the ruin which has been too often made of those seeds of intellectuality which would have ripened into such glorious fruit, how amply repaid will be the physician, old as he is, and nearly done with the world and its ways, for presenting it to his indulgent readers.

I had just got through an unusually long list of poor patients one day, who visited me at my house in Broad-street, between the hours of nine and eleven, when a thundering knock at my street-door, and such an infernal jerk at my bell, that I thought the clapper had suddenly found out the perpetual motion, and never meant to leave off ringing, quite startled me and all my family.

I had walked into the back parlour, and was partaking of my usual lunch, previous to my going my daily round, when this violent application to my knocker took place.

"There," said I, laying down my sandwich I was preparing to eat; "how lucky all my poor patients are gone."—"Lucky, indeed," cried my wife, who never liked people to come for me in a hurry, as it always made her nervous after I was gone; upon which occasions, she assured me, she usually broke some of the china or the glass. "Lucky, indeed! That's always the way. Who'd be a medical man, I am sure!"—"Why, my dear," said I, "it strikes me that medical men are most useful when wanted in a hurry."

"There, now," said my wife, "contradict me as usual, and snap me up. You know, my dear, I only spoke for your sake; I have no objection to people being ill"—"Hear, hear!" cried I, "only you want them not to be in a hurry about it, and to that wish, I would cordially add another, and that is, that they should never be ill in the night."

"Ah! that's very true," said my wife, "and I have often thought it wouldn't be a bad thing to do as Mr. Bulmantle Jinkins did, when he ———."—"Please, sir, you're wanted in never such a flurry," said my servant, opening the parlour door. "Here's a young gentleman who is nearly beside hisself in the front parlour."

"A young gentleman?" said I. "I suppose it's some surgical case; tell him he's made a mistake, and that I am a physician."—"No, sir," said my servant, "I don't think it's a *scrunchical* case. He's green all over, velveteen and drab, sir."

"Is he indeed?" cried I; "that is certainly a phenomenon in medical practice; I never had a patient with green velveteen and drab."

I then walked into the parlour where the young gentleman, who was beside *hisself*, was waiting, and the first object my eyes fell upon, was a footman in green dress, smalls, and a drab coat. He looked very pale and frightened, and glanced round him every now and then, with an appearance of great dismay.

"Well, young man," said I, "what has induced you to assault my knocker so furiously?"—"Oh, sir! please sir, I come promiscuous; master and missus want you to see Algernon directly, sir."

"That's amazingly explanatory," said I; "pray, who may your master and mistress be?"—"Please, sir, Alderman Morley is my master, and Algernon is young master, sir, and that's him as they are so anxious *we* should get back to as soon as possible."

"Do you mean Alderman Morley who lives in the great house at the bottom of Threadneedle-street?" said I.—"Yes, sir," was the reply, "that's our town house; we are always there at this season of the year."

"Very well," said I; "then we can walk there at once, and on the road you can, perhaps, tell me something of the nature of Master Algernon's complaint."—"Yes, sir, oh, yes, sir!" said the footman, running after me down Broad-street, and keeping just a pace behind me, "I can do that, sir, quite stunning, as I have been in the profession myself."

"Indeed!" said I, "and what branch of the profession had the honour of you as a member?"—"Why, sir," said John, whose name, by-the-bye, was Charles, "I was in the basket-with-two-flaps-and-an-oilskin-*kiver*-on-each-side line."

"The what line?" cried I. "Oh, I see, sir," he said, with a pitying smile upon my ignorance; "you don't comprehend; afore I was a footman, I was a doctor's boy, sir, and used to carry out all sorts of nastiness, till I fell down one slippery day with never such a crush, and, as all the patients miraculously recovered, master was ruined, sir, and in course gave me the bag."

"Oh, indeed!" said I; "I am afraid, John, you are very sarcastic."—"Please, sir, my name's Charles, and as for being *sourgastriæ*, we hadn't none of that in our shop, sir. Our business *divided* itself into two great arteries. There was the mild and quiet artery, and the wild and *wicivus*—one on 'em was two penn'orth of manna, and the other was Epsom salts, made extra *wiolent*."

"An extensive and important practice," said I. "But pray what is the matter with Mr. Algernon Morley?"—"Why, sir," said John, looking as knowing as a raven peeping into a marrow-bone, "in my opinion it's a *disarrangyfication* of the disgus-ing organs. The osstilogical system, sir, doesn't seem properly to disgust its wittels."

"Charles, Charles," said I, "can it be possible that you mean digest, when you say disgust?"—"I believe you'll find it all the same," said John. "You wasn't, you know, brought up in the same shop as me, sir, and our patients might disgust their wittles, sir, without no detriment to yourn. I believe I knows a little of the *perfession*. I knows a atomy when I sees one, and I believe my Latin is as good as nobody else's. Hick jacket non nob his domino. Bono breako mendibus corpus."

Charles looked very hard in my face as he uttered these exercises, and a look of mortification came across his face, as I could not resist a very unprofessional shout of laughter.

"I—I believe I does know a little of the perfession," repeated Charles.—"So you do, Charles," said I, "and my sincere advice to you is to forget that little as quick as you can."

Charles did not seem at all to relish my advice, and, in his indignation, said nothing to me until we reached the door, at which he knocked, and to impress me more with his Latin and medical knowledge, he said,—

"Open dooro, pulverse jalap, aqua purer resurgam and seidlitz powders."

What more medical scraps Charles might have obliged me with, I know not; for the door was opened, and I escaped the scientific persecution. I was shown into a very handsome parlour, and scarcely had I time to take a seat, when from an opposite door a lady and gentleman entered, who were both evidently in a state of great mental perturbation. They looked homely, good-tempered people; and I really felt sympathy for the state of disquietude they seemed to be in.

"You are Dr. ———?" they both said in a breath.—"I am," said I.

"Then, sir," they both continued, "for your prompt attention ———" I bowed, and the lady, laying her hand on the arm of the gentleman, said, "Allow me to tell Dr. ———; I dare say his time is very precious, and you know, my dear, you are so uncommonly slow in telling a story."

"Well, Martha," said Mr. Morley, without the slightest appearance of ill-temper, "I believe you will tell it best, and I am sure we shall both be grateful to Doctor ———, if he can do anything for our poor Algernon."

"You may depend upon my utmost exertions," said I. "Pray, madam, what may be the nature of your son's complaint?" I saw tears standing in Mrs. Morley's eyes, as she said, "That, sir, we don't know; but for these two days we have thought he was going out of his senses—he does nothing but scream at nothing, that we can see; and sometimes he clings to us in so shocking a manner, as quite to terrify me and Mr. Morley. We are very unhappy about him. I am afraid he is dying, doctor, and if you can't save him, I am sure me and Mr. Morley would rather die too."

Mrs. Morley upon this burst into tears, while from the repeated and unnecessarily violent manner in which Mr. Morley used his handkerchief, I saw he was deeply affected.

"You see," added Mrs. Morley, after a moment or two, "he is the only child we ever reared from infancy, and we doat on him—quite doat on him, doctor. Don't we, Mr. Morley?"—"Yes, Martha," said Morley, as if he were half-choked. "You go on, never mind me, sir; I think I have got a cold in my head."

I was really deeply grieved to see the evident distress of this worthy couple; and I said, rather by way of saying something than for any other reason,—

"Well, Mrs. Morley, we will not despair; pray how old is your son?"—"Just turned of four," said Mrs. Morley.

"Did he ever exhibit these symptoms on any former occasion?" said I.—"Never, doctor, never; they are quite new, and have alarmed us beyond description. We don't know what to think, or how to act. Any ordinary illness we could contend against, but this, that we don't understand, quite terrifies us."—"Oh," said I, "it may pass away;" and at the moment it struck me, that Charles was not very far wrong in ascribing Algernon Morley's indisposition to a derangement of the digestive organs.

"If you will let me see him," I said, "I dare say I shall be able to give you some comforting assurance with regard to him."—"Certainly," they said, both at once; "certainly," and then, before another word could be spoken, or a movement made towards the door, so dreadful and piercing a shriek burst upon my ears, that I started and exclaimed,—

"Good God! what is that?"—"Algernon, Algernon!" said Mrs. Morley, ringing her hands. "That is the way we are terrified. God help us! God help us!"

As for poor Mr. Morley, he sat upon a sofa, looking the picture of despair; and stared from me to his wife, quite vacantly, while he twirled his thumbs, evidently unconscious of what he was doing.

"Mrs. Morley," said I, "do you intend to tell me that the scream came from your son?"—"It did—it did," she cried; "and it is not the first of the kind that has within these two days so terrified us."

"Let me see him then at once," said I.—"Yes, yes," she said, wringing her hands; "you shall see him at once, doctor; thank Heaven we have sent for you."

She immediately left the room, and I followed her, when she conducted me into a handsome apartment on the second floor, which was fitted up luxuriously as a bed-room. Standing, apparently not knowing what to do, in the middle of the floor, was a young woman; but what attracted my attention most, and immediately fixed my eyes was a young boy, of apparently about the age Mrs. Morley had described her son, huddled upon his face on a sofa, and trembling so violently, as to make the massive piece of furniture creak again.

"Algernon—Algernon," cried Mrs. Morley, "my dear Algernon, look up, here is a gentleman come to see you and make you well. Algernon, my darling—my Algernon!"

She sat down by his side on the sofa, and lifted him from the crouching position in which he had placed himself; as she did so, he put his hands over his eyes, and shrieked in the most heart-rending accents that ever I heard,—

"No, no, no! Oh, no! Oh, no!—I will sleep; not now—not now; mother—mother—mother."

He then clung to Mrs. Morley in such a frantic manner, that I am sure he must have left the indentation of his nails on her arms.

"You see, doctor, you see," she said, sobbing bitterly. "This is the way from morning to night; he will be quiet now for a little while, and then again he will scream, and we shall have a scene like this. It will—it will break my heart."

"Nay, Mrs. Morley," said I, "there is a cause for every effect, and if we can find out what occasions the excited state of your son, we shall, without question, be able to overcome it."

"These are words of comfort, sir," said Mrs. Morley, "and a mother's heart thanks you more than a tongue can tell. Algernon, my darling, look up. Here is a gentleman come to see you."

"Algernon, my dear," said I, "won't you shake hands with me, now I have come to see you? Come, Algernon, I am sure you will shake hands with me."

He slowly removed his face from his mother's bosom on which it had been hidden, and glanced, at first, at me with a shrinking terror in his looks, that was fearful to see depicted in any one so young; then, as he more carefully scanned my countenance, he seemed to feel a sensation of relief; but, before speaking a word, he lifted up both my hands and looked at them attentively; he then shook his head, and in a voice of more calmness, he said,—

"No, no; not it—not it—not it now."

Then I saw a shudder pass across him, and fixing his eyes in one corner of the room, moved his head slowly round while he surveyed every part of it; a deep-drawn sigh then came from his lips, and he kept repeating the words "No, no," in a wailing, melancholy accent, but without the terrifying vehemence with which he had formerly uttered it.

I took his small hand in mine. It was extremely feverish, and the pulse was extraordinarily high, even for so young a subject. The appearance, however, which most distressed me about the child, was a particular wildness about the eyes, which made me suspect there was some incipient brain action going on, which might terminate in inflammation of a serious character.

Such a case to a medical man who might merely view the symptoms as he saw them, would present many serious difficulties, for although the febrile state of the system might be immediately reduced by depletion, yet it might be that some local congestion was the cause of the symptoms, which we might in vain attempt to relieve, by tampering with the general circulation.

My opinion, however, was, that the case was one of nervous action, produced by some external excitement; and that to treat it as one of plethora, would destroy the subject.

There was no malformation about the head, or any general appearance in the countenance, excepting such as I have described with reference to the eyes, that would lead any professional man to predicate insanity; but, as a partial and temporary derangement of the mental structure may occur without any lesion of the brain, I resolved to be extremely careful how I treated the case.

"Algernon," I said, "are you not well?"—"Will you take it away?" he said to me; at the same time he looked at me with such deep and earnest anxiety for an answer, that I said promptly,—

"Of course I will, Algernon; certainly I will."—"For ever and ever?" he said.

"Yes, for ever and ever," said I, in a tone of firm confidence.

A smile broke like a sunbeam across his face, and his eyes lost, for a few moments, the dilated and alarmed look they formerly presented. He placed his hand in mine, with a glance of great affection, as he said,—

"It will never come again."—"Lord bless his little heart," said the young girl who was in the room, "what a pleasure it is to see him now. I was really afraid he was going to meet his blessed Saviour."

"Meet who?" said I—"The Lord of hosts," said the girl, "I am a Juggeronian."

"God bless me," said I. "What does she mean?"—"I mean," said the girl, with a conventicle twang, that sounded to me strongly like hypocrisy, "that I belong to the fold of the pious Mr. Juggers, who preaches at the Junior Bethlehem in Magg's-court."

"Susan is very religious," said Mrs. Morley, "but she is none the worse for that, you know, doctor."—"Nobody can be the worse for true religion," said I, "but cant, and hypocrisy, and fanaticism, and Juggeronians, I certainly do detest and abhor with all my soul."

Susan held up her hands, and seemed to be uttering some internal prayer, which might have been to the effect, that when I came to be roasted in a future state, the fire might be often poked, in order to do me extra brown, for my contempt of Juggeronianism.

It is a strange thing, but no less strange than true, that through a long life, I have invariably found where there was much profession, there was little practice, and that person who knew no more of religion than its forms, and if we may be allowed the expression, systematic terms, were something like one of my friend the footman's classes of medicine—wild and vicious. I took a long, steady stare at Miss Susan and I confess, I did not see much in her physiognomy to interest me.

"Mrs. Morley," I said, "we will talk about Algernon down stairs, if you please. Good bye, my dear, and mind you depend upon what I said."

"Yes, yes," said Algernon. "It will not come again—it will not come again."

"You may be assured it will not," said I. "Remember Algernon, I'm your friend, and will see you often."

He looked in my face with an air of great confidence, and then watched me to the door of the apartment with evident interest. I was grieved to see the expression of his face; it was such as might have been worn by some one left on a desolate island, and seeing slowly receding from him the vessel containing his fellow men, whose companionship he should never know again.

When I reached the parlour into which I had been first shown, the deep anxiety of the alderman and his wife to hear my opinion respecting Algernon was painfully manifest in their countenances: they almost suppressed their breathing as they looked me in my face, and seemed to hang upon every word I uttered as if it helped to make up the inevitable fiat of destiny.

"Algernon has no disease whatever," said I; "and as far as a positive ailment is concerned, you may show the physician to the door."

"Thank God!" said the alderman; then Mrs. Morley hastily added, while tears of pleasure stood in her eyes,—

"The alderman means, thank God, sir, that Algernon not ill; but as to showing you to the door, sir, I am sure we are too much obliged to you for your kindness to be otherwise than very grateful indeed."

"Yes, yes, surely," said the alderman—"surely. You are quite right, Martha, as,—as you always are, of course, my dear."

"Morning, noon, and night, doctor," continued Mrs. Morley, "you'll always be welcome to us, from a dish of tea to a cut at a sirloin; you'll be as welcome as flowers in May, won't he, my dear?"

"Oh, dear, yes, certainly,—of course," replied Mr Morley.

DIARY OF A PHYSICIAN.

"But, my good friends," said I, "while I have great pleasure in telling you that you may get rid of the physician, I regret to say that it seems to me you require the advice and assistance of a friend who is more suspicious and prying into the causes of things than yourselves. Understand me, Algernon has no disease, but still his condition is such as, to require the most careful attention and the most prompt measures."

Mr. Morley sank back into the chair again, and with a deep groan, began turning his thumbs one over the other as before, while Mrs. Morley uttered a "Gracious goodness!" and I could see the perspiration break out upon her rather shining physiognomy.

"It's the mind of Algernon," I continued, "not the body." —"Gracious! gracious!" gasped Mrs. Morley. "Do you hear that, my dear?"

The poor alderman seemed perfectly panic-stricken, and after two or three vain efforts to speak, he said,—

"You—you don't mean, doctor, that my Algernon's going to be a 'Mad Tom,' and have ratsbane put in his porridge? Don't you remember, my dear Martha, how affected we were?"

"Now, really, my love," said Mrs. Morley, "how can you be so ridiculous? I took him, doctor, to see the new little man—what's his name?—do King Lear, so ever since he thinks all mad people are Mad Toms, and have ratsbane in their porridge."

The poor bewildered alderman looked first at his wife, and then at me, in such evident perturbation of spirit, that I was grieved to the heart to see him, and could not help thinking to myself,—

"What endless misery might be brought upon these simple-minded, estimable people, by the ignorance and villany of one who is clothed, and fed, and provided with a happy home by them."

"I pray you not to be more alarmed," I said, "than there is absolute occasion for. Listen to me attentively, and I will tell you what I really think of Algernon's condition."—Yes, —yes—yes," they both said together.

"Then," said I, "Algernon has had a fright."—"A fright!" screamed Mrs. Morley. "A fright!" groaned the alderman, and at that instant, a tremendous rat-tat at the street-door made him give such a jump, that when he sat down again it was on the floor instead of the chair, and there he remained, twirling his thumbs, and looking at me with an expression of countenance that, under any other circumstances, would have been truly ludicrous.

The parlour door was flung open, and my friend the medical footman announced, in a loud voice,—

"Mr. P. Ponytowski."

"It's Peter," said Mrs. Morley, "as I am a sinner."

And in another moment, a young man, dressed in the extreme of the reigning mode, entered the apartment.

There was nothing in his countenance that one could positively dislike; nay, on the contrary, there was an expression about his mouth that was decidedly pleasant, but his sudden appearance, and his, to my mind, most extravagant attire, surprised me not a little. My first surprise, however, was nothing to that which succeeded it, for in a moment I was nearly stunned, and could have got out of the parlour window to have escaped P. Ponytowski.

His first words were to the footman, whom he bawled after as he retreated down the passage,—

"Hilloa! hilloa! Charles—you savage—you wanderer on the borders of civilization—you cannibal of words, if I may be allowed the expression, for you certainly eat them,—now, how dare you call me Ponytowski? 'Twas but last week, curse you, I made you stand on the hall mat half an hour while I bawled Poniatowski in your ears. Just let me catch you calling me Ponytowski again. Gracious powers and cerulean blasts, what's the use of my sympathising with the distressed Poles, and adopting the cognomentrical designation of Poniatowski, if it is to be degraded into the irrational verbosity of Ponytowski by an illiterate footman? Aunt, how do? So, uncle, there's a fall in stocks, is there?—How do, sir? Haven't the pleasure of knowing you, but hope you are remarkably well, and all your family. Keep moving's my motto—*nil desperandum*, and climb over house-tops. The world's a lagging planet, sir; but nature will have her own way, sir, although, if she was my aunt instead of my mother, curse me if I wouldn't play at ninepins with the spheres. Rush here, there, rush everywhere—that's my way, sir. Increase vitality, live hard and fast, make your head into a humming-top, and your heart into a high-pressure steam-engine. Keep moving—keep moving, and d—n the stationary business. Opera, ball, route, masquerade, play, pas-seul, gallopade, all's one to me, as long as they go hand over head, and keep the pot a-boiling. I ——."

"My dear Peter," cried Mrs. Morley, "how you do run on; just stop a minute to take breath. This is Doctor ——." Then, in an under tone, she added to me, "Is he not a remarkable young man?"—"Very," said I.

"Yes," said the alderman, rising to his feet, "I always feel confused for a month after he has been here."—"That's glory and delight," said Mr. Peter Poniatowski: "the very quintessence of sublime extatability. I like to be confused. They tell me there was a great confusion when I was born, and, curse me, if I haven't tried hard to keep it up ever since. People talk about being distracted by a great number of images; d—n me, I broke all my images up into small fragments, and sat in glory among the ruins. Hurrah for everything!—that's the way. Blow a cloud with the stars, and kick the moon."

"I think I had better call again," I ventured to suggest, for the hopelessness of getting in a word while Mr. Poniatowski remained at the alderman's stared me very strongly in the face.

"Never mind me," he cried; "I'm nobody, every body, and anybody—a sort of epitome of nothing, and a concatenation of everything. What's the row?"

As he looked at me I presumed he alluded to my presence as a medical man being indicative of what he called a row.

"Sir," said I, "there was no particular row until you came; but since then I must say there has been rather a disturbance. I am a medical man, called in to prescribe for Alderman Morley's son, and really Mr. Pony, or Peter, or whatever your name may be, I shall have to go away without doing so, in consequence of your extreme volubility."

"Good again," said Mr. Peter Poniatowski; "keep moving, and d—n the consequences. Never mind me—rhubarb and magnesia, senna and salts. I wish society had one tooth—you should draw it, while I stood by and saw it kick."

"Now, really, my dear Peter," said Mrs. Morley, at the same time looking at him with the most intense admiration—for I verily believe, had she ever heard of the five wonders of the world, she would have insisted on his being the sixth, and superior to the other five,—"my dear Peter, you must really be quiet. Algernon is very unwell indeed, and Doctor —— has been kind enough to come and see him. He's remarkably clever, and has a wonderful heart, though his tongue does go clack, clack, clack, from morning to night, and he wears the most extraordinary cravats in the world."

I was rather startled for a moment, for Mrs. Morley made so little alteration in her tone that this sounded like a continuous description of me, but when I looked at her I saw that she meant the last part of her speech to refer to Mr. Peter Poniatowski, who immediately said,—

"What, Algernon? You don't mean that? What's the matter with him? That's no joke. We must keep moving. Go on with the confabulation; I sha'n't say another word. I wish I had my flute—tootle, tootle."

Mr. Peter then sat down in a very extraordinary manner in a chair—that is to say, he poked one leg through the back in the most complicated manner, and looked me hard in the face as I spoke.

"I repeat," said I, "that Algernon has had a fright."—"But it isn't possible, doctor," said Mrs. Morley.

"No, no, no," said the alderman; "how can it be?"—"Keep moving," said Mr. Peter.

"I assure you it is so," said I. "His whole nervous system is now suffering from something which has greatly affected his mind, and so delicate is the mental construction at his age—so powerful is the imagination over the reason, which can only gather strength from experience, while the former is most lively in early life—that if we do not among us find out what has given him the fright I speak of, and prevent its repetition, I predict a result which I hope Heaven will ward off, but which will plunge you all in the greatest misery, and be infinitely worse than death itself."

The alderman looked the picture of terror, Mrs. Morley uttered a faint scream, and Mr. Peter Poniatowski, starting up, exclaimed,—

"Doctor, you are a sensible man. Keep moving. No, d—n it all, we'll stop now, and we won't move an inch till we find out who's frightened Algernon. D—n 'em, whoever it is; I should like to put a hundred percussion caps in their mouths, and kick them behind till they go off."

"The result I speak of," continued I, "is imbecility, if not downright insanity, and such cases, let me tell you, are the most incurable of all. I knew a family who were thrown into the deepest affliction by a foolish circumstance, which I shall relate to you.

"A boy came home from school to spend his holidays at his father's house, and having acquired, among the mischievous and ill-bred youngsters among whom he had associated, a taste for what are called practical jokes, he attempted the perpetration of one upon his youngest sister, an intelligent child of five years of age.

"He procured a human skull, and fixing it upon the end of a long stick, having previously put a small piece of taper into the head, which shone with a sickly lustre through the eyeless sockets, he stole into the bed-room of the child while she was sleeping.

"Little, then, did that happy family, in the fond security of their domestic love and their hopes of the future, dream of the awful blow of fate that was awaiting them, and of the frightful consequences which should ensue from that heedless frolic.

"The boy crept carefully into the darkened room; he laughed to himself of the fun he was about to have; and then, introducing the skull at the bottom part of the bed, he gradually pushed it upwards, without awakening the little sleeper, until it nestled apparently upon the same pillow on which she slept.

"With a scream, then, which, of itself, would have been sufficiently alarming, he awoke her."

"Keep moving, d—n it, keep moving," said Mr. Peter Poniatowski, through his clenched teeth.

"Go on," gasped Mrs. Morley.

The alderman dilated his eyes till they became nearly circular, and only uttered a deep groan, as he rotated his thumbs the other way.

"That scream," said I, with a solemnity, "was echoed by the child starting upon her elbow; she then saw the frightful companion of her couch."

"D—n it, yes," cried Peter; at the same moment he disturbed the centre of gravity of his chair, and fell with it in such a tangled manner, that to rescue him was almost equivalent to untying a difficult knot.

"Keep moving; never mind me," he cried. "Go a-head;" at the same time he kicked convulsively with the only leg he had at liberty.

"The scream," continued I, "alarmed the house; it was the knell of the fond parents' hopes for ever. They rushed into the room—the boy laughed, so did the victim of his heartless frolic; the one was the laugh of a gratified love of mischief, the other was the laugh of an idiot; her reason had fled for ever, and she is now one of the most melancholy inmates of St. Luke's."

"La—la—la—li—e—ty!" cried Mr. Peter Poniatowski, as, with a great plunge, that fractured the chair, he sprang to his feet; "tell me one thing, doctor, only one thing—it's a mere trifle."—"What is it?" said I.

"Did they make German sausages of the boy?"—"I don't think they did," said I.

"Savaloys, perhaps?" suggested Peter.—"Gracious goodness!" cried Mrs. Morley.

The alderman continued to groan, and to twirl his thumbs, looking from one to the other in such a state of bewilderment, that I could see he was quite incapable of saying anything.

"I have told you this sad history," said I, "as a fearful warning of what might ensue from a fright given to a young child; and that your Algernon is now suffering from such a source, although in a limited degree, I can safely take upon myself to state."

"What's to be done?" cried Mr. Peter Poniatowski; "what's to be done?—who shall we smother?"—"My dear Peter," said Mrs. Morley, "let us think."

"Think," cried Peter Poniatowski, "I never thought in my life. I never mean to think—it's a frightful waste of time—keep moving's the plan—thought's like an obelisk in a cross road, you are continually running against it."

"But still, my good sir," said I, "in this case I recommend not only thought, but serious thought, for the circumstances connected with Algernon are really of the most serious character."

"Certainly—certainly," said Mrs. Morley; "my dear, don't you hear the doctor says you are to think."

As she spoke, she gave the alderman an intimation that she was addressing herself to him by a poke in the side, which, as he was sitting on the extreme edge of his chair, again so far deranged his equilibrium, as to seat him on the floor, from where he had so recently risen.

"I—I am thinking," said the alderman, "I'm thinking as fast as I can."—"That's right," cried Peter; "if you think at all, think fast—whiz—pop!"

"Well," said I, "as this is an affair in which my opinion admits of no sort of delay, I think it is incumbent upon you to take some immediate steps for discovering which of your household has been tampering with the imagination of Algernon."

"I will question every one of them," said Mrs. Morley.—"Pardon me," said I, "but that will not do. Who will you get to confess such an impeachment?"

"Ah, who indeed?" cried Peter. "Did you ever hear a fellow cry stinking shrimps? Never, I'll be bound; there must be a good watch kept—leave that to me, I'm as sharp as a whole paper of needles, and you may catch the king of the weasels in a sound sleep before you see me winking."

"Well," said I, "I certainly think, if your powers of watchfulness, Mr. Peter Poniatowski, come anything near what you describe, that there will be a fair chance of finding out who is in fault in this business."

"There isn't a shadow of doubt," said Peter. "I'll creep under all the beds, and get into all the cupboards, in the short space of five minutes—keep moving—find out everything, and be down upon everybody."

"But," said I, "it appears to me something extraordinary, Mr. and Mrs. Morley, and Mr. Peter, that none of you have narrowed your suspicions to a smaller circle than would comprehend your own household."

"Goodness gracious, doctor, what do you mean?" said Mrs. Morley.—"Ah, that's the thing," said Mr. Morley, vacantly, "what's the doctor mean?"—"Keep moving—speak!" cried Mr. Peter Poniatowski, jumping upon the table.

"What do you say to Susan?" said I.—"The Juggeronian!—as I am a sinner," said Peter Poniatowski, slipping off the table with a great dab on the floor. "Keep moving—kick everybody in the eye, and sing psalms till you are in convulsions."

"But Susan is so uncommonly pious," said Mrs. Morley.—"Excuse me, Mrs. Morley," said I, with emphasis, "but I wouldn't have a Juggeronian, or any other onian, in my house, if they would pay me."

"You wouldn't?" cried Mr. Peter, springing to his feet again.—"I would not," said I.

"D——e, such a sensible fellow. Let's have a game at leap-frog. Keep moving, Mother Morley, and tuck in your tuppenny."—"It strikes me," continued I, "that if the Juggeronian is watched——"—"And be d——d to her!" interpolated Mr. Peter.

"You will find out," continued I, "that it is she, and she only, who is the cause of all the distress you are at present suffering."

"I'll get into her bed," said Peter, "no, I mean under it—that is to say, on the top of it. I'll get up the chimney, or down the chimney, I don't care which, as long as I keep moving."

"Then the latter," said I, "is the best plan, for you'll keep moving with a vengeance if you do; but if you'll really watch her with discretion, Mr. Peter Poniatowski, you will do a great deal of good."

"I will be as discreet as a file—quiet as a lamb, and slink about like a tom-cat in a strange attic. Hark—hush! D——e, shut all the doors—hush! hush! hush!"—"Good gracious!" cried Alderman Morley, "what's the matter? I don't hear anything alarming just now."—"A plot—a plot—a plot!" said Mr. Peter, mysteriously.

"What sort of a plot?" said Mr. Morley, looking about him in great wonderment.—"Uncle—uncle," cried Peter, "don't be anti-sensible: light up your brains with a wig, and think away like a hundred horse-power pop-gun. I have a plot—Algernon sleeps in the second-floor front."

"Yes, yes," said the alderman and Mrs. Morley, in a breath.—"He shakes off his diurnal cares, courts the drowsy god at night, and keeps moving."

"Yes, yes, yes," again cried the alderman and his lady.—"When Phœbus's car has gone to smash, and the fiery steeds of Apollo are gone to rack and manger, we'll all of us slink into the second-floor back; it's a spare bed-room, and there's a door opening from that to the second-floor front, which we can keep moving—no, I mean keep shut. Then we can listen to what that d——d Juggeronian says to the child; and if she behave herself well, we'll let her off easy, only frighten her after death somehow; and, if she frightens him, d——e, that's all. Have you got any oil in the house?"

"Oil, Peter?" said Mrs. Morley.—"Yes, I want a hundred gallons, and a sack of oyster shells."

"Gracious powers!" said Mrs. Morley, "what for?"—"Why, I want to scrape the Juggeronian's back-bone with the oyster-shells, and dip her now and then in the oil at a boiling temperature—keep moving—d——e, it would be a warning to her."

"I certainly think it would," said I, "a warning that would deprive the pious Mr. Juggers of one of his flock; but your plan, Mr. Peter, of watching is feasible enough; we must, however, be extremely quiet, or we shall spoil all."

"Quiet as mice, dead mice, I mean. What do you say to the plot, uncle? Ay, aunt, what do you think of it?"—"Can I suspect Susan?" said Mrs. Morley, lifting up her hands.

"Certainly, yes, nothing easier, keep moving, and try. Doctor, you are a man of the world, and regular down upon Juggeronians, and I knew an ass once that belonged to a sect they called the 'Snufflers;' when I first saw him I was struck all of a heap; he was hypocrisy from the top of his head to the toe of his boot. Then there's the 'Swiggers,' the 'Riggles of the New Connection,' and the 'Latter End Saints,' I always give 'em a kick behind, hang 'em all up in heaps—keep moving, and smother Mr. Juggers."

I took my hat then, saying,—

"There's no occasion for me to prescribe medicine to Algernon; quiet, and kind treatment, together with such conversation as shall have no effect upon his imagination, would restore him to apparent serenity, although I much doubt in my own mind whether the effects produced by having the imagination once excited in infancy are ever wholly got rid of, even in after life, when the intellect has become fully matured. I have known men of all ranks, and all grades of intellect, suffering from one depressing cause—a constitutional timidity is engendered, which follows its victim with more or less intensity to the grave. If parents would but see this subject in a proper light, they would consider it of the most vital importance to their children, and yet I will venture to say it is not thought of in one case out of a thousand; but the young mind is left to the mercy of ignorant and wretched menials, who, because they themselves have been frightened, and are so still at the supernatural, resort to that means of hushing their infant charges. They had better give them some narcotic drug, as many do, in the shape of some quack soothing syrup, for these only can destroy life, which, to my mind, is a much less crime than embittering it during a whole existence, by partially shattering that brightest portion of the intellect, the beautiful and teeming imagination."

Mr. Peter Poniatowski lay down on the hearth-rug, and kicked, exclaiming,—

"True, true, every word of it. I was frightened myself, dreadfully frightened—one thing why I keep moving so. I'll cut up that Susan, and I'll make soup for the poor with her. I'll call it soup *a la Juggers*, and flavour it with nightshade. D——e, I don't know what I'll do exactly. I should like to stand on my head, but I can never do it. Always come down with a dab—never mind, keep moving. Let us all meet to-night, and if we don't give a death-blow to Juggeronianism, my name ain't Peter Poniatowski, and I don't sympathise with the distressed Poles."

"I am quite willing," said I, "to make one of the party, if Alderman Morley thinks proper."

"Oh, certainly, sir," said Mrs. Morley, "if you will be so good, I can't say how much we shall be obliged to you. Can you, my dear?"

"Oh, dear, no," said Mr. Morley, "of course not. You all know best; I feel rather confused myself. Peter, my dear boy, when do you think you'll come again? You rather bewilder me, indeed you do; I have some idea you've been on the table, haven't you? but I really am so confused, I don't know."

"Then you should keep moving, uncle," said Peter. "Go up in a balloon with me, and come down whack in a parachute."

"Gracious goodness! I think I see myself," said Mr. Morley. "Me in a parachute! do you hear him, Martha?"

"Now, my dear," said Mrs. Morley, "don't you say another word; everything will be settled comfortably."

"Well, I'm very glad of that," said the alderman; "I like things settled. Oh, dear, yes, and particularly when they are settled comfortably; but while you are all about it—I don't often suggest anything of my own head—but if my nephew Peter could be settled too, I shall be uncommonly glad; everything goes wiggle waggle for a month after he has been here. Sometimes I think I am on the ceiling, and sometimes on the floor; it's really dreadful, quite."

"Ah! ah!" cried Peter, "that's because you don't patronise the new lights. Philosophy, fun, and frolic for me; if I could once realise a downright doubt as to whether I was on my head or my heels, I should be the happiest fellow alive."

"There he goes again," groaned the alderman, as Mr. Peter sprang upon a chair, and sat upon the back, with his feet resting on the seat.

"Name the hour," said I, "that my presence will be expected, and you shall find me here punctually."—"Come at seven," said Peter; "we'll crack a bottle first, and then be down on the Juggeronian."

These words had scarcely passed Mr. Peter Poniatowski's lips, when another of those frightful screams which I had already heard seemed to fill the house with a complete volume of sound.

Peter Poniatowski toppled backwards, chair and all—poor Mrs. Morley's rubicund countenance turned deathly pale, and Mr. Morley himself, as if he had become accustomed to the movement, and did it as a thing of course, slipped from his chair on to the floor.

"For Heaven's sake," said I, "do not alarm yourselves; leave this matter to me. By removing the cause of these attacks, which I trust we shall do to-night, we shall remove a great source of unhappiness from the house. Allow me to go to Algernon and reassure him of his safety."

"I'll go with you," said Peter. "I'll go with you—let's go and smother the Juggeronian. I'll sit down and smoke a cigar in her mouth, while you hold her heels. D—n that chair, I've nearly broken every bone in my skin; but there's one thing I'd do, if I had neither bones nor skin, and that is, keep moving."

"Come along, then," said I; "but be sure you say nothing of our plan of operations for to-night."—"Mum's the word. Did you ever hear an oyster sing a comic song?"

* * * * *

Mr. Peter Poniatowski ascended the stairs rapidly, and we entered Algernon's room without announcing ourselves; there was, however, nothing gained by that, for Miss Susan must of course have expected that Algernon's scream would bring somebody into the room.

She was standing by the side of the sofa, where was Algernon, as on the former occasion, lying on his face, and trembling violently.

"So, Susan," said I, "what made him scream now?"—"Bless his heart, sir, I can't say," responded Susan. "Something seems to tell me that he is on the threshold of a blessed eternity:

"'Where sinners great and small do dwell,
 Dabbling in brimstone flame;
But saved will Juggeronians be,
 And not among them same.

'With howls and sobs, and sighs, and shrieks,
 They'll call upon the Lord.
But all such wretches for to save,
 He surely can't afford.

'Then praised be Jugger's holy name,
 And topple not to hell,
Where those ———'"

"No more of that, if you please," said Mr. Peter; "d—e, you'd keep moving at that from morning till night, I suppose. What do you call that, I wonder? The Jugger war-song, I should presume. Cus me if an Indian, with a tomahawk, and no inexpressibles, isn't a fool to you."—"No what?" said Susan. "Oh! Mr. Ponywhiskers, how can you use such dreadful language? You are in a dreadful state."

"D—e, so shall you be before I have done with you."

I had approached Algernon, and raised him from his crouching attitude on the sofa.

"Come, come, Algernon," I said, "you promised me you would be quiet. What is there for you to be afraid of, my boy? Don't you recollect me? I came to see you a short time ago."

He opened his eyes at the sound of my voice, and, clinging to me with frantic eagerness, he said,—

"Oh! stay with me—stay with me—it won't come when you are here—stay with me—do, do stay with me."—"But you don't tell me what it is, Algernon," said I.

He shuddered, and closed his eyes, but made no reply. I did not repeat my question, for I had no wish to drive his mind back to the consideration of what had alarmed him.

"Susan," said I, "how do you account for this? You were here with him: how came he to scream in that frightful way? It is extremely odd that he should do so without some cause."

"Yes, sir, as you say," replied Susan, "it's dreadful odd; it quite gives me a turn."—"So I should think," said I.

"You may, indeed, sir," continued Susan; "and if I wasn't fortified by my religious principles, I don't know how I should fight up against it. It's a good thing to know as flesh is nothing but long, rank grass, as is continually being mowed."

"That's a curious physiological discovery, Susan," said Peter. "What do you do when there's a little trefoil and daisies among it?"—Susan cast up her eyes in holy horror, and then said, "Get behind me, Satan, I have faith above."

"Nonsense," said Peter, "your faith is in Juggers, and you know it. That's always the way with you women, you go to chapel to worship some particular person;—one of you worships the Rev. Mr. Brown, because he's, oh, dear! such a sweet man, and keeps moving. Another the Rev. Mr. Smith, because he's an angelic man, and has such loads of whiskers. Don't talk to me about above; you know nothing about it, and think nothing about it. All your Juggeronians worship Juggers, and you know it."

Susan lifted up her hands, and seemed to be uttering some internal prayer for the conversion of Mr. Peter Poniatowski to Juggeronianism, and all the advantages and privileges thereunto belonging, not the least important of which was that of being saved for everlasting, while everybody else was d—d for that same indefinite period.

"Algernon, Algernon," I said, "you need not be alarmed at anything. Your mother and father will always take care that nothing harms you; and here, too, is your cousin, Peter Poniatowski, come to see you."

"Yes—yes, I know Peter," said the boy, "he always does something funny."—"Do I, you rascal!" said Peter. "You know me well, you scoundrel! and you know I always keep moving, don't I, Algernon?"

A faint smile flushed for a moment over the face of the child, and then with a convulsive shudder he clung to me again, saying,—

"Do not leave me; oh! sir, do not leave me, or it is sure to come."

"Has he been to sleep, Susan?" said I.—"Just in a sort of dose, poor creature," said Susan, "just a matter of forty winks, and then he wakes up and calls out in that dreadful way."

"Then I am to understand," said I, "that he never screams in that way when he is awake."—"No, sir, never, except he wakes out of his sleep, poor dear."

"And have you no notion, Susan, what it is alarms him so much?"—"I a notion, sir; lor bless you, I never had a notion, all my life."

At this moment Charles, the professional footman, made his appearance at the door, and said,—

"Please, sir, missus wants to know how Algernon is?"—"Tell your mistress he is better," said I.

"Oh, I am glad to hear it, sir," said Charles; "you are quite sure, sir, the symptomatics is pungent?"—"Go along, —go along," said I.

"Calomel and magnesia, sir," said Charles; "resurgam and probono pimlico. Opium, ten drachms, and teeth extracted; sudorifics and saporifics magnum bonum."—"Now really, Charles," said I, "your medical knowledge is so astonishing, that you quite overpower me with it; go and tell your mistress that I think Algernon is better."

"I shall state," said Charles, "that his corporeal corpus is on the mendo. I like to do things professionally, sir, though I'm in neither line now; requiescat in pace, as we say in the classics; there's no knowing what we may come to. Nux womica a feeslshion, and a footman the next."—"Exactly," said I, "now be off with you."

I presume Charles had been furbishing up his medical lore in the kitchen, and had come up stairs, determined to overwhelm me with its extent; now that he went away, I felt quite convinced that I had got to the end of it, and turning to Susan, I said,—

"Well, Susan, all we can do is to keep Algernon perfectly quiet, and take care, above all things, that he is not alarmed at anything, or I will not answer for the consequences."

"Alarmed at anything, sir!" said Susan; "lor, sir, how should he be? I wouldn't have him alarmed for the king's crown; no, not to be a queen or a lady mareress."

"Well, that is right," said I; "I will call to-morrow, to see how he is."

"Thank you, sir," said Susan; "I am sure it's very kind of you, and I dare say he'll be better, bless his heart! poor dear—what a dreadful thing it is to see children suffer. I love 'em all, I do, and I do hope, Mr. Ponytowski, as, afore it's too late, you'll see the error of your ways, and repent afore you fall into the everlasting pit."

"Thank you for nothing," said Mr. Peter; "when I'm in the boxes, I never lean over too far, so I can't fall into the everlasting pit."

"Oh! how dreadful," said Susan, casting up her eyes, "to joke about such things. I hope, some day, to see you quite a large brand, snatched from the burning ——"

"Oh, you are very good," said Mr. Peter; "but if you come that at all, I beg you'll do it before I get even singed—by-the-bye, how is Mr. Juggers?"—"He's had a slight cold, sweet man," said Susan.

"Bless me!" said Peter, with an air of affected alarm; "keep moving; was it attended by a cough?"—"A slight cough," said Susan.

"D—n it, then, I hope it will choke him," said Peter. "Come along, doctor,—keep moving."

I was forced to laugh, in spite of myself, at the truly ridiculous conversation, which had been kept like a running fire from adverse ranks, between Peter Poniatowski and Susan. Two more opposite characters the world scarce ever produced, and it was really singular to reflect that there could be two such very different specimens of the same order of created things.

* * * *

In a few moments, we reached the parlour, where the alderman and his lady were listening to Charles with intense interest and wonderment at his extensive knowledge, for which I afterwards discovered they really rated him very highly, believing him to be something very little short of a medical man himself, and an amazingly clever fellow beside. When I came, however, he modestly gave way, I presume because I was actually in the profession, and he considered he had left it.

"Tell me," said Mrs. Morley—"oh! tell me, doctor, is he indeed better?"

"It is a scarcely a question I can answer," said I: "from this second interview I am only the more confirmed in my previous opinion, that Algernon has been dreadfully alarmed at something, the vivid recollection of which produces these screams—this is the more clear to me, because he does not so scream except when just awakened from sleep, when, in all probability, he dreams of that which so fully possesses his mind, and, awakening suddenly, believes it real."

"And you really think, doctor," added Mrs. Morley, "that Susan is the cause of the mischief?"—"I have seen nothing in this recent interview," I said, "to induce an alteration of that opinion."

"And I," said Mr. Peter Poniatowski, "have seen much to confirm it; who the deuce that was not radically bad would talk of burning anybody."—"Why," said I, with a smile, "you wanted to put Susan in boiling oil, and scrape her back with an oyster shell."

"Yes, but that was because she was a Juggeronian, and has frightened Algernon, two quite sufficient high crimes and misdemeanours to merit any degree of punishment that could be meted out to them; but keep moving, doctor, and let's settle all the preliminaries of our meeting for to-night. Uncle, I shall pop my legs under your mahogany to-day, and walk into your mutton."

Mr. Morley groaned, but whether it was in consequence of the continued reflections on the state of Algernon, or with horror at the threatened infliction of his nephew's company for the whole of the day, I could not tell.

Once more I took my hat, and saying—"I beg you all to be comforted, and hope for the best," I walked from the room, accompanied by Mr. Peter, who himself opened the door for me.

"Do you know, doctor," he said, "it will be the finest thing in the world if we can rid my aunt of her ridiculous notions concerning what she calls pious people. She's got a fancy in her head—and her fancies are not like mine, for they never keep moving—that anything under the name of religion, whether it is fanaticism or not, is respectable; but we'll knock that out of her to-night, and give such a blow to Juggeronianism as never was known; remember, seven o'clock, doctor, and be punctual."

"I will—I will," said I. "Good day, Mr. Poniatowski, for the present."—"Good day—good day."

* * * *

Want of punctuality was never one of my sins, and a few minutes before, by common consent, the neighbouring clocks announced the hour of seven, I arrived at the alderman's door.

In passing the window, I suppose I must have been seen, for just as I was on the point of laying hold of the knocker, the door was pulled quickly open by Mr. Peter Poniatowski, and I nearly fell into the passage.

"True as a needle to the pole," he cried; "keep moving, and come in; all's right; hush! I didn't want Charles to know you had come, so I have been on the dodge myself to let you in. The alderman's asleep with a yellow handkerchief over his head, and Mrs. Morley's with Algernon, so we've got it all to ourselves,—just slip into the back parlour, and as I have no notion of the door even being opened without Charles's assistance, here goes."

So saying, Mr. Peter gave a formidable knock at the door, and a hearty pull at the bell, when, closing the former very gently, he slipped after me into the parlour, and locked the door behind him.

In a moment we heard Charles scuffling up the kitchen stairs, then the street door was opened, and a dead silence ensued, during which it may be supposed that Charles was looking about him for the runaway knock, with great indignation. He then peeped into the front parlour, where the alderman was in a sound sleep, and muttering something about it being very extraordinary, he duly departed again to the region below.

"There now," said Mr. Poniatowski, "that's the thing, we've got it all our own way positively snug; here's a drop of Madeira that isn't at all to be objected to, if I may judge from the bottle I have already discussed, and the first toast I shall propose is 'confusion to Juggers.'"

"I have no objection to drink that," said I, and, accordingly, with great gravity and a solemn nod, we drank "confusion to Juggers."

"Has there been any more screaming?" said I.—"Just a few,' replied Mr. Peter; "they've kept moving tolerably well; we've had three; but when I thought they were coming, I covered each of my ears with a wine glass—that's what I call being too many for Juggers. In after life, when hoary Time, with a polite wish of cooling my pericranium, has pulled my hair out by the roots, I shall always call a scream a Jugger; and when I hear anything going particularly wrong, I shall ask if the domestic circle are Swiggers, Jiggers, Latter-End Saints, Wrigglers, or Juggeronians. If I get an answer in the affirmative, I shall know what to think—whiz—pop—bang, be down upon them in a minute. Doctor, your glass is empty; ' here's to all unfortunate monarchs, and may we never have the skin off our noses.' Keep moving—push the bottle, and no heel-taps—we are here to-day, and gone to-morrow; but, before I go, I'm determined to have a skinfull, and keep moving."

A low tap at the door announced that some one was approaching.

"Hush!" said Mr. Peter, "hush! that's the signal."—"What signal?" said I.

The tap was repeated twice more, and then Mr. Peter Poniatowski said,—"Oh, my prophetic soul, my aunt!" He opened the door and admitted Mrs. Morley, who, with an air of mystery, that made her extremely ridiculous, walked into the room.

"Algernon's gone to bed," she said in a low tone.—"'Tis well," said Mr. Peter; "has the drowsy god closed his eyelids—has he become decidedly somniferous?"—"I can't say, exactly," said Mrs. Morley; "but I think he is going to sleep."

"To sleep, perchance to dream," said Peter. "Ah! there's the rub. Is Susan with him."—"She is," replied Mrs. Morley, "and her duty is, of course, not to leave his room again until he is fast asleep, and that she is compelled to do, for he cries if left alone when awake."

"Very well," said Peter. "Now I think we may move."—"I am at your service," said I.

"I would rather not go myself," said Mrs. Morley; "you can tell me what you hear, and it will be quite satisfactory to me."—"No; that won't do," said Peter. "You must be thoroughly convinced that affected piety may be a cloak for great villany, and you must become, like myself and the doctor, an Anti-Juggeronian; so come you shall, aunt, and that's the long and short of it."

"Well, if I must," said Mrs. Morley, "I must; but we won't wake the alderman."—"Certainly not," said Peter; "I never wake an alderman. I could not think of such a thing. Now, come on, let's creep up stairs like North American Indians. You go first, aunt, and don't be falling down, sneezing or any of those kind of things."

"Oh, dear, no!" said Mrs. Morley, "certainly not; for, of course, if Susan should hear us, all your cleverness, my dear Peter, would go for nothing."

"So it would," said Peter, "and there would be a loss to society; by-the-bye, doctor, there are two rooms, I find, at the back of the one where Algernon sleeps, and that'll be a great convenience, as you shall see by-and-bye."

We did slink up stairs with extreme caution, and the alderman's house being by no means scantily furnished with rich carpetings, the sound of our feet could scarcely have been heard a few paces from where we were. We could hear the voices of the servants, talking in the kitchen; but no other sound disturbed the rapt stillness of the house.

"Good God! aunt," whispered Mr. Peter, "what a puffing and blowing you make; open your mouth, for Heaven's sake."

This remark amused me, for I had been perfectly aware, as we proceeded up stairs, that Mrs. Morley had been making the most extraordinary noise, by the fancied necessity for keeping her mouth shut, the consequence of which was that she was winded before she got to the first floor. There was a manifest improvement in the quiet order of things, when, in obedience to Mr. Peter's remonstrance, she condescended to breathe, in the ordinary way, and we reached the landing on the second floor without any accident.

It was a long landing, from which several doors opened, and as the staircase we ascended wound up by the back of the house, when we reached the summit we were a considerable distance from Algernon and his nurse.

Mrs. Morley opened the first door which presented itself, and she ushered us into a small apartment, in the middle of which was a table, on which burned a shaded lamp, turned down considerably, so as to produce a small light.

"This is the room," whispered Mr. Peter Poniatowski, "which is furthest off from Algernon's bed-room; the one between this and that apartment is of larger size, and all we've got to do now is to keep moving."

"Bless me, Peter, what's that?" said Mrs. Morley, as her nephew placed upon the table a mysterious looking bundle, unknown to either of us.

"That's the principal caper of all," said Mr. Peter; "that's to produce the final kick up, if we bring in a verdict of guilty against the Juggeronians."

"But, bless my heart," said I, "what is it?"—"You shall see in good time," said Peter; "all I can say is, that I have been all over the town to get it. Don't touch it on any account, aunt, for some of it is rather delicate."

"Bless us and save us, Peter, you alarm me. Is it alive?"—"Not quite," said Peter; "but I live in hopes of its producing a little kicking all ways, with the assistance of the tongs. Let me see, d—n it, I hope I have forgot nothing."

Mr. Peter then felt very anxiously in his pockets, and then, with a satisfied countenance, said,—"It is all right. Down as a hammer; wouldn't give a bad farthing for Juggeronianism after to-night. Now, doctor, you and I will creep into the next room, and holding our breath for half an hour, we'll listen like grim death to Susan."

"I think we should," said I, "long before the half hour was expired; but let us come, Mr. Peter; I am quite ready."

"I have rather done her than otherwise about the door," said Mr. Peter to me, "I have stuck a little wedge in, and it won't latch, and I have stuck another little wedge in, which keeps it close, so that when we take out that same second little wedge, which will make no noise, the door, I have ascertained, opens half an inch and two twelfths, and we can hear her like a pile of bricks."

Without making any comment on the auricular powers of a pile of bricks, I followed Mr. Peter Poniatowski into the next room, with, to tell the truth, perfect noiselessness.—The little wedge was removed, and the door did open, though a very small space, admitting a thin pencil of light from Algernon's room to the dark one in which we were keeping watch.—For some moments no sound met our ears, and then the Juggeronian said,—

"I wonder if the little wretch will go to sleep to night. How I do hate children, to be sure; they are always in everybody's way, the little beasts; he seems in a sort of dose now, ah! cus him."

At the very commencement of these operations, Mr. Peter began kicking me to such an extent, that I was compelled to give him one kick in return, as a hint not to continue that operation.—We then heard the voice of Algernon, saying,—

"Will it come again?—will it come again, Susan?"

Mr. Peter had walked away, and with incredible speed had dragged Mrs. Morley into the dark room, where, holding her ear just at the crevice of the door, she heard Susan say,—

"What ain't you asleep, you little wretch? Ah! you odious viper. I'll break every bone in your little beastly skin, and then I'll bring the devil to eat you up; he'll gnaw you into bits, you little wretch; now, mind, I'm going away. A likely thing, indeed, I'm going to be shut up here half the evening with an odious reptile like you. Now, I tell you what, Algernon, you may go to sleep, or not, just as you like; but if you dare to cry, I'll send the devil to you, that I will; you've seen him, so you had best be quiet."

"No, no, no!" cried Algernon,—"oh, no! keep him away, Susan, do keep him away!"

"Then you'll be quiet?" said Susan, in a threatening tone. "Yes—yes!" said Algernon; "I won't speak, Susan, and I won't move; I won't cry, if you keep away the devil."

Miss Susan then took the light, and walked to the door of the room leading out on the landing of the staircase; before, however, she had got so far, Algernon's fears of being alone overcame him, and he burst into a passion of tears.

"Very well," said Susan, in a tone of great anger. "Come devil—devil—devil—devil, come!"

Stifled shrieks burst from Algernon, and Mrs. Morley would have rushed into the room, but Mr. Peter Poniatowski held her fast.

"Go into the next room," he whispered to her; "and we'll come to you directly. We must know the truth of this affair, in spite of the devil."

Mrs. Morley yielded to his remonstrances, and crept into the next apartment, while Peter Poniatowski and I, placing our eyes to the chink left by the partially open door, commanded a tolerable view of Miss Susan's movements.

We saw her go to a cupboard in the room, and take from it a black veil, and a pair of black gloves; then, stooping down on to the floor, so that she was below the level of the bed, and Algernon could not see her, she placed the veil completely over her neck and face, and the gloves on her hands. Then she crept along the floor, until she came to the side of the bed, when she said in an artificial voice,—

"I'm the devil, Algernon; you little wretch! how dare you not be quiet, and let Susan go down stairs?"

Algernon trembled so excessively, that the bed shook again; and then Susan slowly and solemnly rose, presenting to his agonised vision her head with the black veil upon it, just above the edge of his bed, and working her hands, as if they had been claws.

"If you dare to scream, I'll eat you," she said; "I'm the devil—the devil—the devil—the devil!"

Here she made an indescribable noise, and pretended to claw hold of Algernon with her black hands.—He was perfectly silent, but the state of terror he was in, I could easily imagine, and could well conceive that such continual shocks to the brain would not be long in producing incurable insanity. My own feeling was to rush immediately into the room, but Peter Poniatowski detained me, whispering,—

"No don't; keep moving, but not that way. You will spoil my plan altogether; come away, now at once; we've seen and heard quite enough; pray be ruled by me."

I allowed him to lead me into the further room, where was Mrs. Morley, sitting in a state of indescribable anxiety.

"Where's my bundle—where's my bundle?" cried Peter. "Bless my heart and life! where's my bundle? Now, Mother Morley, just be so good as to follow my instructions. You must be maternally anxious, you understand—you know you are maternally anxious about Algernon. So you must go round the other way to his room, being anxious, you comprehend, to see how he is sleeping to-night; of course you'll find him awake and in a d————e stew; then you must tell Susan to remain where she is, for five minutes, while you take Algernon down stairs, remarking that you think a change of scene would amuse his mind and make him sleep better. Now, you are as clear as mud about all that, Mother Morley. When you get down stairs with Algernon you remain there; never mind what you hear or what you see. Doctor, just help me untie this bundle."

Mrs. Morley seemed instinctively to obey the directions of Mr. Peter Poniatowski, for, without demur or question, she now left the room to execute the manœuvre he had explained to her, while I was, I confess, not a little curious to know what on earth Mr. Peter's bundle could contain. I cordially assisted him to open it, for I had become quite in a fever on the subject.

When it was opened, however, I was scarcely wiser than before, for it presented to me such a curious mass of I couldn't tell what, that I looked at it in amazement, while Mr. Peter evidently enjoyed my perplexity.

"What on earth," said I, "is that?"—"Nothing on earth," said Peter.

"The devil!"—"Exactly," said Peter; "there you've hit it. I have been from one masquerade shop to another, till I have got a complete devil's dress, with what theatrical people call a practicable tail and all."

"What's that?" said I.—"One that will go wiggle waggle," said Mr. Peter. "It's made of coiled wire and a piece of whalebone up the middle."

"Ah, I understand," said I.

To my amusement and surprise then, Mr. Peter Poniatowski unfolded a complete dress, with two horns, at the top of which were receptacles for two little bits of phosphorus, which, when ignited, I could easily imagine would have a singular and spectral appearance. In fact, when Mr. Peter Poniatowski had fully attired himself, and his own eyes peeped through several circles of sparkling yellow and green tinsel, he certainly did look as good a representation of the generally received devil as I could wish to see.

"Now, Mr. Peter," said I, "what is your precise intention?"—"I want," said he, "to fight the Juggeronian with her own weapons. It's no use reasoning with her; and it's no use abusing her—discharged she'll be, as a matter of course; but then she'll go into some other family, and frighten some other child, so what will be the use? I want to prevent her, through downright fear—the only sentiment such people are entirely capable of appreciating—from acting again as she has already done."

"Well," said I, "I don't want to intercede for her, for she does deserve the utmost fright you can give her."—"And she shall have it," said Peter; "for as there is the devil to pay, I am determined to have my money's worth; so here goes—keep moving, and d—n the consequences. Come on, doctor, and you'll see the fun — it will be rather glorious, I think. I never did anything so conscientiously in my life."

"Mind you be sure," said I, "that Mrs. Morley has removed Algernon, or, in frightening the Juggeronian, you may do more mischief than we can ever again undo."

"Of that we may be well assured," said Peter. "I wonder how they are getting on."

As he spoke, he turned to the fire, in which were inserted the points of the tongs; and finding they had acquired a red heat he flourished them over his head, and walked towards Susan's room. I followed, scarcely in my own mind approving of Mr. Peter's scheme, and yet scarcely feeling either inclined or justified in opposing it.

When we reached the door, which was partly open, Susan herself was kind enough at once to put an end to our doubts as to whether Algernon was there or not, for she said,—

"So the little wretch has been taken away. I wonder what that's for. She never did that before; and I'm to wait, am I, till he's brought back, after all my trouble, too, in frightening him out of his little wretched wits. Well, I hate children, to be sure; and here's a prayer-meeting to-night at Mr. Juggers's. Sweet man! If ever there was a love, it's him. What can people mean by saying that's his child that Miss Smith had last week? What wretches there are in the world!"

Mr. Peter Poniatowski gave me a screwed-up piece of paper, saying,—

"Doctor, just be so good as to get me a light, and make my horns flare up; and mind you don't let her through this door, after I've gone into the room."

I lit the two pieces of phosphorus in Mr. Peter's horns; and with a wild, demoniac howl, he rushed into the chamber, and getting between Susan and the other door, so as effectually to preclude her escape. She stood for a moment like a statue; and I'm quite confident that none but a religious person, accustomed to think of the devil morning, noon, and night, could have stood the sudden appearance of such an apparition.

With a loud scream she fell upon her knees, and in gasping accents, she said,—

"Jug—Jug—Juggers——"—"I'm the devil, said Peter Poniatowski, in a hollow voice; "whiz—whirl."

"I know it—I know it," said Susan. "Oh, your worship, have mercy upon me!"—"Mr. Juggers's cough," said Peter, "is getting worse; and as his flock all belong to me, and he may die soon, to save trouble I'm taking a few of them off at leisure, and I'm come for you. You'd been the last, Susan, and, perhaps, have got off altogether, but I'm generally under your bed, and heard you trying to frighten Algernon Morley, which you had no right to do, as I come all that sort of business myself. Prepare to meet your fate."

He then executed a wild kind of dance round Susan, and ended by so suddenly seizing her nose by the hot tongs, that she could not escape the infliction; and, what with the pain, and her increasing terror at the supernatural visitation, she fell upon her back and fainted away.

* * * * *

Immediately upon Susan's insensibility ensuing, Peter Poniatowski had left the room, and, packing up his devil's dress again, ran down stairs, while I busied myself in recovering Susan from her trance. By a liberal supply of cold water to her face I succeeded; and, when I saw signs of returning animation, I went down stairs, leaving her to chew the cud of sweet and bitter fancy as she might.

In the parlour was assembled the family party, including Algernon, who was lying on a sofa in a more comfortable sleep than I had yet seen him.

"Here comes the doctor," cried Peter. "Now, aunt, I hope your faith in Juggeronians is gone for ever."—"It is, indeed," said Mrs. Morley; "and I begin to think that a little sound morality and practical goodness is better than psalm singing from morning till night and prayer meetings."

"That'll do," said Peter—"that'll do; that's a little bit of what I call rational religion—real piety with the chill off."

"Of course," said I, "you discharge Miss Susan?"—"Oh, dear, yes," said the alderman. "Martha has told me all about it. She called our Algernon a little wretch. Who could have believed it, and she so pious too?"

"There you go again," said Peter. "Every piece of hypocrisy which assumes most easily the appearance of what you call piety has at once a million chances to one in favour of its success. Don't let's hear anything more about piety and Juggerism. I am sure there's been a dose of it in this house."

At this moment a curious bumping noise attracted all our attentions; and upon Peter and myself going to the door to see what could occasion it, we observed Susan, with a candle in one hand, and, with the other, dragging a box, with a succession of bumps, from stair to stair.

"Hilloa, Susan!" said Mr. Peter, "what's the matter?"—"I shall not sleep another night under this roof," said Susan, trembling violently, and looking very pale; "the shocking want of faith of everybody but myself in the house has brought the devil into it."

"Susan, Susan," said Peter Poniatowski, "I do smell brimstone; and if the devil has been here, you may depend he came for the only Juggeronian in the house, and that's yourself."

"Oh, you wretch!" said Susan. "I hate you all. Give me my wages, Mr. Morley, and let me go at once."—"No," said Peter, as the alderman, who had come to the parlour door, and thrust his hand into his pocket—"no, not a penny; and if you send here for a character, Susan, we'll say we don't know what you've done exactly to deserve it; but you are so haunted by the devil, that it will be quite dangerous for any one to employ you; so march off. Open the door, Charles."

The wondering Charles, who, hearing the disturbance in the passage, had rushed up from the kitchen, held open the street-door, while Mr. Peter, seizing Susan's box, flung it with a grand crash into the street, whence she followed it of her own accord, fearful, if otherwise, she might be sent after it with too accelerated a movement. * * *

Algernon slowly, and but very slowly, recovered from the shock his nervous system received. He grew up a timid, shy youth, and was consigned to a premature grave at eighteen years of age; and I am sure that the manner in which his imagination had been played upon in infancy materially accelerated his decease.

THE LIFE POLICY;

OR, THE RESTORATION.

It was some time after I had obtained a considerable share of professional reputation, that I was applied to by one of the numerous new Life Assurance Societies which have from time to time sprung into existence, to become its consulting physician. I had to attend daily, at a particular hour, to see and report upon the state of health of any parties who might apply at the office for the purpose of insuring their lives.

Such a situation to my mind was a very onerous one, and I was glad when I obtained such full practice as to be able to give it up. I neither liked accepting nor rejecting the people in many cases, and the line of demarkation I found in some cases so troublesome to draw between a sufficiently healthy subject to warrant granting the policy, and a sufficiently diseased one to authorise its refusal, that I frequently left the examination in great annoyance and vexation.

I find, however, that my professional brethren of the present day by no means give themselves so much trouble or uneasiness, for when I was speaking to one the other day upon the subject, he said to me,—

"Between ourselves, doctor, we manage these affairs very differently now; we accept the greater number as a matter of course, or else how would the office get on?—and then what they gain largely by are the lapsed policies. People get ill, you see, and fancy there is something the matter with them, and then away they rush to insure their lives."

"Oh, indeed," said I; "that is just the contrary to what they should do."

"Exactly," said he; "but many of them get well again, or fancy so, by the time the next annual payment comes round, and then they say, 'Ah, hang this Life Assurance; I am not going to die yet, so I won't pay it.'"

"Well, but," said I, "how do you manage when you reject?"—"Oh," said he, "I'll tell you how we manage that; there comes sometimes a great rosy fellow as strong as an ox, and as healthy as a greyhound, and him we reject right off at once in a moment."

"Why so?" said I, in my innocent simplicity.—"Why," said my friend, "the porter whispers to the clerk, Doctor So-and-So has refused the most remarkably-looking healthy man that ever I saw: he must be a very clever man. Then the clerk whispers it to the actuary, and the actuary tells the directors, and all think you can see further into a mill stone than any other physician."

"Oh, well," said I, "I am very glad I have nothing to do with it."

But to return to my narrative.

* * * *

I was sitting one morning in my official room at the Life Assurance Office, when there was introduced to me a stout, good-looking man, who, bowing in the most courteous manner, said,—

"I presume, sir, you are the gentleman who is to report upon the state of my health, as I wish to effect a life assurance?"—"Yes, sir, pray sit down."

He sat down, and handed to me the document which is always sent up stairs to a physician, containing the name, age, and the amount for which the party wishes to ensure. By that I found my visitor's name was Peter Crogson, a gentleman aged thirty, and that he wished to effect an assurance upon his own life for 4,000*l.*

"You propose for a large sum, sir," said I.—"Yes," he replied; "I have an amiable family, entirely dependent upon me for support. My income is about 300*l.* a year, but it dies with me, leaving my affectionate partner, Mrs. Crogson—who, by-the-bye, always calls me Crogs for shortness—and four little Crogses, upon the merciful ways of Providence and the blasts of fate."

This was a most singular speech, and I looked very hard at Mr. Crogson, for we had several times been outrageously done by people giving us a deal of trouble for nothing. There was not, however, the slightest twinkle in Mr. Peter Crogson's eye, or the remotest twitch of the countenance by which I could gather that it was a joke, so I proceeded with my examination. Finding Mr. Peter Crogson quite sound in wind and limb, and, barring that I suspected dreadfully he now and then took a glass, or perhaps a dozen, a very unexceptionable member of society, as far as regarded the insuring of his life,—

"I think, Mr. Crogson," I said, "that we may pass you."—"A hem!" said Mr. Crogson, making the room echo again; "I have an amazing bellows."

"Why, I do think your lungs are pretty good," said I. "But pray don't do that again."—"Ah! ah!" said Mr. Crogson, almost deafening me; "I only want to convince you, doctor, what a roach I am."

"A what?" said I.—"A roach, doctor, a roach. You have heard of a person being as sound as a roach?—well, sir, that's me—head, heart, lungs, liver, and lights, altogether working in delightful harmony, like the music of the spheres, and the other tremendous works of Nature."

"Ah," said I.—"Yes, sir," continued Mr. Crogson. "You wouldn't believe it, but when myself and the little Crogses, who all take after me, bless their souls, say 'ah—hem!' the effect is tremendous."

"So I should think," said I. "I have only to hope I shall never hear you all."

"Please, sir, what's the matter?" said the porter, putting in his head.—"Nothing, I believe," said I; "but you may well ask."

"So he may," said Mr. Crogson. "I thought he'd come up, d—d if I didn't; it shows the wonderful effect of the human voice on the brute creation. There are several singular instances in somebody's travels—I think it is a Mr. Gulliver."

"Well," thought I, "this is a fool; but he may live quite as long as a wise man, for all that, and I certainly cannot reject him."

"Mr. Crogson," said I, "I shall certainly pass you, and all you now have to do is to go into the next room and show yourself to the directors."

"I am eternally obliged to you," said Mr. Crogson, "and shall never forget your great urbanity, nor the singular kind manner in which you have entered into my feelings. I have the honour, sir, to wish you an extremely good morning, and to hope, sir, that you will live long and die happy—that your latter end may be peace—that ——"

"Good morning, Mr. Crogson," said I, rising, "good morning, there's the door."—"God bless you, sir," said Mr. Crogson; "may the Almighty shower ——"

I shut the door upon Mr. Crogson, and so lost the latter part of the blessing, and in another few moments, to my great amusement, I heard him say, "Ah—hem," in the directors' room, till he made the very building shake again.

"Ah, well," I said to myself, "there's nothing the matter with him, that's quite clear. He is an eccentric; but we all have our oddities, so we should not be too hard upon a Crogson when we meet one."

I learned afterwards that his examination before the directors was considered very remarkable, but at the same time sufficiently satisfactory to induce them to grant his policy, which must have cost him something to the tune of a hundred pounds; but that was no business of mine, and the whole affair passed off very smoothly indeed, only now and then I certainly enjoyed a laugh, as I thought, at Crogson and his remarkable lungs.

* * * *

Somewhere about two months might have passed away, and in the succession of other events Mr. Crogson had quite faded from my memory, until one day, as I was sitting very comfortably and quietly in my official room at the Life Assurance Office, the actuary rushed into the room with a maniacal look.

"Gracious powers!" he said; "what do you think!"—"I don't know what to think," said I; "nor am I gracious powers."

"Well, but good God!" said he.—"No doubt of it," said I; "look around upon Nature's works, and all that sort of thing."

"Do you want to drive me mad?" he shrieked; "for I am nearly so already. I don't know but what we are ruined—done up—and consigned to the infernal regions."

"What's the matter?"—"Crogson's dead!"

"What!" cried I, with a great start; "the man with the heart and liver and lights, and with the tremendous ah?"

"Yes," said the actuary. "Here's a claim come in for four thousand pounds on account of Crogson's life policy; here have we not been in existence as a Life Assurance Office eight months when a villain, who looked so healthy that one would have sworn he would have been the last man, if the human race was becoming extinct, comes upon us plump for four thousand pounds; it's really frightful, and no mistake, upon my soul, doctor. Why didn't you see into his inside better? really it's too bad—I could almost cap myself, that I could."

"Well, but," said I, "I couldn't keep Crogson from dying. If Crogson will die, he will die, and there's an end of it."

"But it's horrid," said the actuary; "it's disgraceful— d—n it, I shouldn't wonder if the directors tore their very hair out of their heads."

"It will be a good haul for Crogson's family," said I; "the amiable Mrs. Crogson and the four little Crogsies."

"Curse his family," said the actuary; "it's my family I'm thinking of."

"Well,' said I, "it's of no use your coming and making a row with me; did they tell you what he died of?"

"No, no," was the answer. "All I know of it is, that a sanctified thief in black came into the office and asked for me. I went out to him, thinking, of course, it was somebody coming to insure, when he said, 'I merely called to inform you that Peter Crogson, Esquire, of Chilmundle Villa was dead,' and then he walked out again, leaving me, of course, nearly in a state of petrifaction. Of course I was horrified, for that infernal Crogson is the only one we have who has made an assurance to a tithe of such an amount."

"Well, then," said I, "all you have got to do is to curse Crogson's assurance."

"Don't joke," cried the actuary; "don't joke—upon my soul, I can't stand it; our banker's book will become a waste book, and our affairs will be comfortably wound up; if we wonder at Crogson's assurance, the public will wonder at ours, and we shall be set down as a party of the most elaborate swindlers that ever stepped."

"I don't like that," said I, seriously, "because my name's on the prospectus."

"Nor I don't like it," cried the actuary, "for my salary will be *non est*; we shall have to publish a pamphlet explaining that we have been in existence eight months, and that a Crogson has ruined us, to the tune of a hundred and twenty-five pounds a week to his own cheek. Curse him, my heart misgave me when he said 'Ah!' before the directors; but I didn't like to say anything, for the thief answered all the questions so well. He said a distant female relation of his lived to a hundred and seventeen, and was on intimate terms with the celebrated Henry Jenkens, who was her contemporary, and died at a hundred and thirteen, the said female relative of that damnable Crogson hemming his winding-sheet, and remarking what a thing it was to be so cut off in the flower of his days; then he said 'Ah!' till the room shook, and he gave his chest a knock that would have felled an ox; after that he leaned down and knocked his head against the table till the ink jumped out of the inkstands—'Sound as a roach there,' said he, 'sound as a roach, heart, liver, and lungs, brains, stomach, and chitterlings.' How could we doubt such a man—he seemed cast-iron, with the edges turned up with gun-metal."

The actuary said all this with such gravity, and so much real feeling upon the subject, that it had to me the most ludicrous effect, and I could not help laughing in spite of myself, although it was not a very pleasant thing to be mixed up with a life assurance society that could only protract its own existence for eight months.

"Excuse me for laughing," said I, "but really the whole

affair, although serious enough, does partake largely of the ludicrous as well. I tell you what we can do, that is, protract the payment until we are thoroughly satisfied that there is no take in in the matter; and I, as the physician to the office, will insist upon making a *post mortem* examination of Crogson."

"Ah, well," said the actuary, "I suppose that is all that can be done. We needn't pay for three months, according to the terms of the policy."

"Then during that time," said I, "there may be a great flush of prosperity in the office that may enable us to meet this demand better."

"There may," said the actuary, with a sigh; "but as far as my own judgment goes, doctor, I look upon it as a settler! It is infernally unlucky—four thousand pounds—good gracious—at one fell swoop."

"But I thought," said I, "that mathematical science, as regards life assurances, quite enabled you to provide against all such contingencies by the construction of accurate tables."

"Mathematical science be d—d!" said the actuary. "I should like to know what science would provide against a Crogson; but I must be off, for I have summoned an extraordinary meeting of the directors, and an extraordinary meeting I expect it will be; they will want your opinion, doctor, upon the matter."

"I am quite willing to attend them," said I; "but as far as my opinion goes, they have had it in the acceptance of Crogson; and I must say that so unexceptionable did he appear to me, that if just such another were to present himself here this morning, I should unhesitatingly accept him."

"Then you would unhesitatingly drive us mad," said the actuary; "for if we do withstand this cursed blow of fate we never could another such."

"Please, sir, the directors is a waiting," said the porter, popping in his head at this moment.

"Oh, poor creatures," said the actuary, as he went out of the room, "they are in a pretty frizzle? I put at the end of every one of the letters, 'P.S.—Crogson's dead.'"

It was in about a quarter of an hour that I was summoned to attend the board, and when I did so I saw about eight as miserable-looking faces as could well be imagined.

The chairman then said,—

"It has been moved and seconded that the minutes of the last meeting be confirmed, and that it be entered upon the transactions of the society, that Crogson's dead."

The directors gravely nodded their heads, and then one said to me,—

"Well, doctor, we've let ourselves in for it rather nicely—four thousand pounds; it's our general opinion that that is a sort of wind up of our affairs. By our banker's book it appears that we have three thousand seven hundred pounds cash, and what we owe in rent, &c., amounts to rather over the seven hundred, so that after being comfortably ruined, we shall be debtor to Crogson's representatives in the sum of one thousand pounds."

The rest of the directors looked very rueful at this calculation, and they all of them looked at me as if they expected I could bring the deceased Crogson to life again; however, I was determined to say nothing upon the subject until some question was fairly put to me, and that at length they did, for one of the directors said,—

"Well, doctor, what shall we do in this emergency?"

"I can't advise you," said I; "you can do whatever you like, gentlemen; Crogson's was a good life, but I should advise that a most particular inquiry be made as to the cause of his death, for it may be that he has himself vitiated the policy by suicide, a duel, or some extraordinary reckless act which we should certainly not be called upon to pay for."

"But," said the chairman, "after all, we have no official notification of the melancholy decease."

The door opened, and the porter laid a letter upon the table, on which was an ominous seal, nearly as big as a raspberry tart; moreover, the paper was edged with black, and altogether a more disagreeable-looking epistle to place before the directors of a life assurance office could not be conceived.

"Crogson," gasped the chairman.

"Crogson," groaned the other members of the board.

With a trembling hand the actuary opened the letter, and then read as follows :—

"Gentlemen,—It is with feelings of the most poignant nature, that I write to inform you of the melancholy decease, from apoplexy, of my relative, Peter Crogson, Esquire, gent., aged thirty two, and an assurer in your office for the sum of four thousand pounds, which, with his other little affairs, I am bound to see properly settled, inasmuch as the late Peter Crogson, Esquire, has left to me all and every his real and personal estate, in trust for Mrs. Amelia Orelia Cordelia Crogson, and the four infant Crogsons, for whom such assurance was effected.

"Being as I am, gentlemen, willing, and, in fact, desirous to afford you every information necessary, I have the honour to remain, gentlemen, your very obedient and most humble servant,

"Augustus Absolem Crunch,
"Attorney-at-Law, Lyon's Inn."

There were eight deep groans at the termination of this letter, from the eight directors; and the actuary, after a pause, added a ninth, which quite transcended all the others.

"Crunch!" said the chairman; "I should say we are crunched, gentlemen."

The door opened at this moment, and the office-clerk popped his head in, and said—

"Mrs. Fitzfoggrams is dead, and the Rev. Bumbleton Quicksalve has been run over."

"D—n Mrs. Fitzfoggrams!" said the chairman.—"And d—n the Rev. Bumbleton Quicksalve!" said the actuary.

"Well, gentlemen, it never rains but it pours," said I; "we are certainly in for it now; but I should propose, that Mr. Green, the actuary, and myself, visit this Mr. Crunch, and ascertain the particulars of Crogson's decease, when we can act accordingly."

"Mrs. Fitzfoggrams," said the actuary, running his finger down a column in the ledger, "wants three hundred pounds, and the Rev. — what's-his-name, curse him, five hundred."

The directors looked ghastly, and one of them suggested that the board had better abscond, in a body, to New Zealand, or to Scotland, where no civilized creature would think of looking for them.

"Well, well!" said Mr. Green, the actuary, "we must see what can be done; for my part I am in an abominable fix; but let's be off at once to this Mr. Crunch, who is so kind as to volunteer information. Come along, doctor."

"Very well," said the chairman; "I dare say the board will continue sitting till you come back."

The actuary's impatience would not permit him to walk, although I suggested, in the desperate state of the society's finances, it was advisable so to do; so we availed ourselves of the first hackney carriage we could find, and rode off to Lyon's Inn.

The curious in the localities of London, those people who go poking about into holes and corners, preferring them to the fresh and new-looking parts of the great metropolis, must have made frequent visits to Lyon's Inn, for its ancientness—if we may be allowed the term—and its dinginess must be gratifying, in no ordinary degree, to those who are fond of old places, and please their imagination when they visit them, fancying various romances and little episodes of real life, which may have been enacted within its dingy walls.

Lyon's Inn is admirably situated for such day dreams—its cold, crazy, comfortless look has a proper chilling effect upon the system; and if we wish to go to law with any one, and wish that the law should appear to that same person in all its terrors, we would employ some thief—no, we beg pardon, some lawyer—who had chambers in Lyon's Inn.

The common stairs which lead to the various chambers are worn into more hollows than the pious asses—bless us, what are we saying, we mean people—but we've got so confidential with our readers, that we may impolitely sometimes call things by their real names. Well, then, the stairs are rubbed into more hollows than the pious people have succeeded in rubbing with their knees into the stone steps leading to the shrine of Thomas a Becket at Canterbury. The banisters creak and groan as any one ascends or descends those gloomy staircases.

It took Mr. Green and myself some time deciphering the half worn-out words on the door-posts, until we came to "A. A. Crunch," which figured under a general heading, signifying that "A. A. Crunch" was to be found on the third floor. So, at the peril of our lives—for I really thought that the staircase would have come down—we ascended, and tapped at a door on which was the same name.

A solemn-looking young man opened it, and Green whispered to me—

"That's the villain that announced Crogson's death."

"Is Mr. Crunch at home," said I.—"Yes," said the same

tified young man. "Do you come about the case of 'Snitch v. Flickaway?'"

"No, we don't," said Mr. Green; "we come about that d——d thief ——."—"Hush, hush!" said I; "pray tell Mr. Crunch that two gentlemen have come from the Life Assurance-office, about Mr. Crogson's decease."

"Oh," said the sanctified-looking young man, "walk in, gentlemen; Mr. Crunch is a feeling man, and I believe he's been crying ever since."—"Ah," said Mr. Green, "some things produce different effects; I believe I have done nothing but swear ever since."

The sanctified clerk then went into an inner apartment, from whence he returned in a few moments, to say, that Mr. Crunch would be happy to see us in a minute or two, when he had a little mastered his feelings.

"Confound his feelings," muttered Green to me; "what are his feelings in comparison to mine?"

Then a little bell sounded from the inner room; and the sanctified clerk, after saying, "He's better now," opened the door for us, and ushered us into the actual presence of Mr. Crunch.

"Good morning, gentlemen," he said, "good morning. Pray be seated. Excuse my faltering speech, but the stream of anguish will keep on flowing. I knew Crog—Crog—, my feelings will only now and then permit me to pronounce all his name; so we will say, if you please, gentlemen, it is for Crog I mourn—it is for Crog I weep. I am afraid I am not resigned to the will of Providence. I ought to be—but I ain't; reason tells me that flesh is grass, and requires mowing. The scythe of death, gentlemen, is always at work, in and out, and around and about, but he should have spared Crog—he should have spared Crog."

During this speech, which was interrupted by many sighs and pats on his eye with a handkerchief, which seemed ingeniously tied up to a round ball, I had a good opportunity of looking at Mr. Crunch.

He was a thin, cadaverous-looking individual, with an abominable squint, so that it was a matter of extreme difficulty to find out whether he was looking you full in the face or out of the window. He was attired in black; and a white neckcloth, with no collar, added much to his methodistical and cadaverous look.

"Well, sir," said Green, "I am the actuary of the Life Assurance-office, and I need not say we have had the pleasure of your note, notifying the sudden and unlooked-for death of Mr. Crogson."

"Ah," said Crunch, "that's the way—one after another. When we look around us, it is quite astonishing to see how we are going; death, gentlemen, reminds me of an auctioneer that never gets tired, but goes on, morning, noon, and night, knocking down his lots."

"But, Mr. Crunch," said Green, "how came this great, strong-looking Crogson to die?"—"Ah," said Crunch, dabbing his eyes with his handkerchief, "I think I see him now."

"I wish I did," said Green.—"There he is," continued Crunch; "there he is, with his stupendous constitution, his head that was so uncommonly hard, and his chest that was stronger than any portmanteau—you recollect his head and his chest, gentlemen?"

"D—n his head and his chest," said Green, who was out of all patience.—"And how he used to talk, too, about his liver and his lights," continued Mr. Crunch, quite unheedful of the interruption; "it did one's own cockles good to hear him. It was but the last time I saw him that he said, 'Oh,' to show me what lungs he had. He had wonderful lungs. I believe, gentlemen, that that is a settled point. I believe we are all agreed upon that."

"Mr. Crunch," said Green, "this is the most business-like way of proceeding—when, where, and how did Peter Crogson die?"—"At home—eight o'clock last night—apoplexy," said Mr. Crunch, with wonderful celerity; and then he added, "gentlemen, I hope you are satisfied?"

"We hear, Mr. Crunch," said Green; "but I assure you I never was so dissatisfied in my life. This gentleman," indicating me, "is the physician of our office. Now, sir, I want to know the name of the medical man who attended Peter Crogson."—"Dr. A. K. White," said Crunch, "of No. 2, Wimpole-street, and Mr. Bennet, the surgeon, of Upper Marylebone-lane."

"Very well," said Mr. Green, "then, Mr. Crunch, just at present we won't trouble you any further."—"Don't name the trouble," said Crunch, "it's a melancholy pleasure. When do you propose settling with the distracted widow and the fatherless children?"

"We have three months allowed us," said Mr. Green, "and that you must know very well."—"Yes, my dear sir, but look at feeling—feeling," said Mr. Crunch, "look at feeling—look at the infant Crogsons deprived of the paternal support, and then look into your own heart, exclaiming, 'They shall have the money this day week! they shall have the money this day week!'"

"I won't do any such thing," said Mr. Green; "good morning, Mr. Crunch."—"God bless you," said Crunch; "mind you don't fall down stairs; take care of yourselves, gentlemen, for Heaven's sake: society has already lost a Crogs. By-the-bye, oh! good God, stop! just let me read you the epitaph I have written upon the occasion."

"'Grim death the wheel of life oft clogs,
And ruthlessly comes down on Crogs;
But lest in intellectual fogs
His memory should go to dogs,
His name be lost in envious bogs,
This stone records the loss of Crogs.'"

"D—n you," said Mr. Green, "and your epitaph too: you're an infernal, canting, hypocritical vagabond; you are driving me mad, and you know it. Come along, doctor, come along."

Mr. Green then seized me by the arm, and dragged me, with great precipitation, down the ricketty staircase, nor stopped hauling me along until we reached the street, when I said,—

"Now, Green, please to let go of my arm, or the people will think I have just picked your pocket, and you are dragging me to the nearest watchhouse."

"Yes; but wasn't that fellow enough to provoke a saint? did you ever come near such a villain? and to wind it all up, too, with his infernal epitaph, as if we cared whether Crogson was hanged, drowned, or damned."

"Well," said I, "however indifferent we may be to the future fate of Crogson, Mr. Crunch has certainly strengthened the case against the office, for the medical men he has mentioned are the most respectable members of the profession, and we are quite safe in their hands."

"Ah, well," said Green, "I shall go back to the board, and leave you to pursue the doctoring part of the business. I suppose we are regularly in for it, and no mistake. Four thousand pounds—what a haul. You can't think how I hate that man, and all his family. I fancy I see Mrs. Crogs, hypocritical wretch, rustle about in black silks, pretending to be sorry for the demise of Crogson, and all the while looking out for another husband with our money in her pocket."

"By-the-bye, Green," said I, "it ain't a bad idea. You are a widower, suppose you stick up to Mrs. Crogson."—"Stick up to the devil!" said Green.

"Why, don't you see, you might save the association from bankruptcy. Now, Green, only consider."—"Thank you, I have been married once, and had my dose. I am not going to fly in the face of Providence, after its goodness to me."

"Well, but consider how noble it is to make sacrifices. You have heard of Curtius, who leaped into a foaming gulf to save his country."—"Yes, I have, and always thought he was a confounded fool for his pains; but good morning, doctor—good morning. Four thousand pounds—four thousand devils!"

So saying, poor Mr. Green, who really appeared quite maniacal, rushed off in the direction of the city, while I, after a moment's thought, walked off to Doctor White, of Wimpole-street.

"How do you do," said I; "any apoplectic cases lately?"—"Very well, I thank you—one," said Doctor White, "a fellow of the name of Groggles, or Groggy, or Croggy, or something of that kind."

"Crogson," said I, with a groan; "last evening—Chilmundle Villa?"—"The same—you seem to know all about it."

"No," said I; "I came to inquire—he's dead, of course?"—"Oh, yes, long before I got there. I found Bennet in attendance—he had opened the temporal, and made an incision in the jugular—remarkably clear case—by-the-bye, how do you get on with your assurance society?"

"Why," said I, "White, you need not let it go any further, but we are rather getting off. I must leave you, however, to call upon Bennet, for this chap, Crogson, has let us in for four thousand pounds."

"Bless me, you don't say so?" said White.—"I have just

said so, and very sorry I am to say it; but good morning to you."

"By-the-bye," said White, "if you are passing Bartholomew's, there is a most interesting creature there now."—"Indeed."

"Yes, a good case—he has a compound fracture of the femur, and luxation of the vertebræ—depression of the left parietal bone, besides several simple fractures—but then, the beauty of it is, the case is complicated with a heart disease, and a scrofulous tendency."—"Thank you," said I, "I may call and see the interesting creature. Good morning to you."

Here was more and more confirmation of Mr. Crogson's legitimate decease—facts are stubborn things, and by the time I had called upon Bennet, who told me he had been sent for by Crogson's afflicted family, and found him dead, with decided symptoms of apoplexy, I gave up the affair as hopeless. Nevertheless, it was my duty to see the deceased Crogson, and I could not think of going back to the office until I had done so. I accordingly made what haste I could to the neighbourhood of Chelsea, where his house was situated.

Upon making inquiry for Chilmundle Villa, I was directed to a decent enough looking two-storied house, the blinds and shutters of which were scrupulously closed throughout, and round the knocker of which was tied a kid glove, which I thought was very unnecessary, considering Mr. Crogson was dead, however desirable such a course might have been, if he were labouring under a brain fever, or any disorder which required rest for a recovery. I knocked as well as I could, but it sounded remarkably like kicking an empty beer-barrel. I suppose, however, the solemn stillness of the house enabled them to hear me, for in a few moments the door was opened by an old woman, whose face was a perfect characteristic of woe.

"Is this Mr. Crogson's?" said I.—"As was, sir," she replied; "as was—this is Mr. Crogson's as was, but now as isn't."

"Is Mrs. Crogson at home?"—"She's dreadful hysterical, sir, on the parlour sofa."

"Tell her that a gentleman from the Life Assurance office wishes to see her."—"Very good, sir. Oh, dear—oh, dear, what a house this is now, and what a house it was. Did you ever see him, sir—him as is gone, I mean?"—"Yes," I said, and I added to myself, "I would to God I never had."

"Hadn't he a head and a stomach, sir?"—"Yes, yes, I know all about that—his liver and his lights, and all that sort of thing. Pray be so good as to tell Mrs. Crogson at once, that the physician of the Life Assurance office must see her."

Upon this the old woman bustled into the parlour, being careful to shut the door again, and I heard a whispered consultation taking place within; then the door was opened, and I was desired to enter, and upon availing myself of that permission, I found the room perfectly dark, with the exception of the dim rays from a rushlight, which discovered to me, lying upon a sofa, a tolerably good-looking female, of apparently about thirty years of age; she was blubbering away with extreme emotion, and it was some minutes before I could get a word out of her; when at length, however, she did speak, it was with many hysterical sobs that she said,—

"Oh, sir, nobody knows my loss but myself; there's husbands of all sorts, but none like him. No late hours—no public-houses—no gambling—no nonsense of any kind. Oh, Peter, Peter, Peter, what shall I do?"—"Madam," said I, "I have called here on a matter of business; your husband insured his life for four thousand pounds."

"Oh, have you seen him?" cried Mrs. Crogson, seizing me by the arm. "Tell me you have seen him—I have an affection for everybody who has seen him."—"I have certainly seen him," said I.

"You have, you have! Hadn't he a head and a stomach, and a voice too—did you ever hear such a voice?"—"I thought I should never leave off hearing it, madam," said I.

"And to be cut off," continued the widow; "to be so suddenly cut off; but I know the reason—I know the reason—it was all our own faults, we've nobody to blame but our ownselves."—"Indeed," said I, as a ray of hope came across me, that I should find some iniquity in the mode of Mr. Crogson's decease.

"Yes, yes; I thought it would happen some day, I knew it would."—"Oh, you knew it, madam," said I.

"Yes; we thought too much of him, and Providence snatched him away; we praised him too much, we made too much of him, and, like an early flower, a blighted lily, he's gone away with a *foof*."

"A what," said I, "ma'am?"—"An airy nothing," said Mrs. Crogson, making a motion as if she was blowing a feather from the tip of her nose, and saying *foof*, again.

"Well, madam, you will permit me to see him, I hope," I said, "for four thousand pounds are by no means a bundle of jokes."—"I leave all money matters to Crunch—the poor dear deceased is in the two pair back."

"Will anybody go with me and show me?"—"I will, sir," said the old woman, emerging from a dark corner of the room.

"Very well," said I; "I will follow you."

We duly proceeded up stairs to the second floor back, which was enveloped in the same darkness as the rest of the house. I, however, opened the window-shutters, and let the daylight into the room, which was a comfortable bed-room, the curtains of the bed in which were drawn closely. Without much ceremony, however, I unclosed them, and there, sure enough, was the unmistakeable shape of a human form, although covered over by a sheet.

"Ah!" said the old woman, "there he is, there he is,—there's poor Crogson as was—he's happy now—he's gone home. Ah! poor Crogson, wonderfully cut off he's been, sir. It was a very little while ago, sir, that he says to me, at the same time he knocked his dear head against the dining-table, 'I am as sound as a roach, and I'll insure my life for four thousand pounds.'"

By this time I had uncovered the face of the deceased, and there, sure enough, lay a dead man, who might or might not be Crogson, for all I knew, although there was by no means a greater dissimilarity between Crogson and the body I saw before me, than might have been easily and fully accounted for by the difference between a living and a dead person. I saw where the temporal artery had been opened, and where the incision had been made into the jugular. Then, all of a sudden, I recollected that in my interview with Crogson, I had remarked that his thumb nail had been split down, and presented a very perceptible mark, a mark which I well knew would have lasted him years, if ever it entirely disappeared. Here, then, was a means of at once identifying the body, or of confounding the Crogson plot, for somehow or another a conviction had been creeping across me from the very first, that all was not right. I slipped down the bed-clothes and laid hold of the hand of the corpse—there was the mark on the thumb-nail, just as I had seen it in life. Was there room for further doubt? "Ah," thought I, "it's Crogson, it's Crogson; if this life assurance had been merely for a hundred pounds, I should have had no suspicion; it's the amount that has horrified us all."

"Grandma," said a child's voice at the door, "where papa's slippers?"—"Papa's what?" cried I, in a loud voice.—"Oh, you unfeeling little wretch," said the woman, as at the same time she slammed the shutters close, and the whole room was in darkness. "So you want to play with your poor papa's slippers, do you, when you know he's going to the pit-hole—take that?"

A loud howl from the child proclaimed what "that" was, namely, a beautiful box of the ears, and then the child retired, screaming, down the stairs.

"Are you quite satisfied, sir?" said the old woman.—"Oh, I have very little to do with it," said I; "I suppose there will be an inquest?"

"Yes, sir, to-morrow; but Dr. White says, and so does Mr. Bennet, that there isn't the least occasion for a post mortar excruciation."—"Oh, very well—very well," said I. "Good day, ma'am."

* * * * * *

When I got to the corner of the street, I dare say I looked very foolish to the passers by, for I stood tapping my head for some five minutes, in deep thought as to whether the old woman had given the correct interpretation to the demand for papa's slippers or not.

"It's suspicious," I thought, "but if that isn't Crogson lying dead, who the devil is it? and the mark on the thumb too—there can be no doubt—oh, no, we are booked—we are booked—it's no use struggling against fate. I must repeat that I have seen Crogson dead, of which I should be an irrational being were I to entertain any doubt, and yet those slippers, those infernal slippers; and there did not seem the remotest disposition to apoplexy in Crogson when I saw him. Apoplexy to come on a man of a heap in less than three months! I won't say it's impossible, but it's odd, and uncommonly disagreeable in the present instance.

Full of these vague feelings and conjectures, I walked towards the city, and upon arriving at the Assurance-office, I found the board of directors still sitting, as melancholy as ever, awaiting my return.

"Well, doctor," gasped the chairman, "what news?"—"I have seen Crogson," said I.

"Is—is—is he dead?"—"Extremely dead, gentlemen. Crogson's gone, and we are dished."

Eight groans burst from the directors, and we all sat looking at each other in solemn silence for full a quarter of an hour.

*   *   *   *   *

The coroner's inquest duly took place. I attended it, and so did Green, and so likewise did Crunch; but the whole affair was so simple and straightforward, that there could not positively be two opinions on the matter.

Mr. Crunch deposed that Mrs. Crogson was his sister, and that, consequently, he (Crunch) was on the most intimate terms with the deceased. He added that he was out walking in the neighbourhood of the deceased's residence with him, and that he never knew him (Crogson) in better health and spirits. That they went on conversing upon different subjects, until Crogson complained of a slight pain in the head, upon which he (Crunch) advised him to go home, a piece of advice which Crogson attempted, by proceeding towards his own home.

"It was more by accident than any thought or impulse, gentlemen, that I looked around after I had gone some paces, and I was just in time to see Crogson stagger and fall. Several people ran to his assistance, myself among the number, and we all succeeded in carrying him home. Life, however, was extinct, and before Mr. Bennet, the eminent surgeon arrived, Crogson was no more."

Then came the medical evidence, as well as that of a person, an utter stranger, who was passing by at the time, and saw the whole circumstance. So the case was as clear as possible, and a verdict was returned of "Died by the visitation of God."

There was a curious twinkle about the eyes of Mr. Crunch after the verdict was returned, and coming up to me and Green, he said,—

"Gentlemen, is feeling to triumph, and will you pay the money to-morrow? Recollect, it's a widow's mite."—"On the last day of the three months," said Green, "if you'll duly prove the will of the deceased, and nothing happens in the meantime, you'll get the money, but not before, Mr. Crunch."

"Are we savages," said Mr. Crunch, "or are we in a state of high civilization?"—"You may answer your own questions, Mr. Crunch," said Green; "but, thank Heaven, we are not Lyon's Inn lawyer's."

Mr. Crunch walked away with a faint smile, but in a moment or two he returned, saying,—

"Gentlemen, there's another trustee named in the will, and that is likewise a gentleman in the legal profession, whose name I will now give you; but he is only to assume the trust in case of my own melancholy decease."

"And who may that be?" said Green. "Perhaps he may be a respectable man?"—"Perhaps he is," said Crunch, as he took a black-lead pencil and some papers from his pocket. From one of these he tore a small piece, and on it wrote some words, and then handed the little document triumphantly to Green, who read the following words:—

"The Lord High Chancellor of Great Britain."

"Curse his impudence," said Green; "he's quizzing us. Come along, doctor, come along."

We left the inquest-room together, and walked towards town, while Green was rolling up into a small paper pellet Mr. Crunch's important document.

"There's writing on both sides of that, Green," said I.

"Is there?" he said, as he unwrapped it, and then in a moment, to my great surprise, he cut a prodigious caper; after which he sat down on the pavement, and laughed till the street rung again, and the people rushed from all quarters to know what was the matter.

"Good God! Green," said I, "are you mad?"—"No, you devil," he cried. "No, you devil. Hurrah, fol de rol de rido. The cow jumped over the moon. Hip—hip—hip—hurrah. One cheer more."

With that he sprung to his feet again; and, taking my arm, dragged me along at a great rate; but this would not do, for we were followed by an idle crowd, who, having derived some amusement from Green's antics, thought itself much ill-used by their stopping so suddenly, so that we were obliged to get into a hackney coach, and then Green laughed so vociferously again, that I am sure the coachman must have thought him a maniac, and I his keeper.

"Green—Green," said I, in a loud voice, "be quiet."

"Come, come, Green," said the coachman, through the coach window, "lay down, sir, lay down," thinking, no doubt, that he was greatly assisting me in keeping the maniac in order.

This was too ludicrous, and I laughed aloud, and what the coachman thought then I can't say; but I noticed he made much greater speed, and seemed anxious to get rid of his fare.

"Doctor—doctor," cried Green, "you ain't half such a fool as I thought you were. Think you it's agreeable to get rid of one-half one's folly? Look at this—look at this," he continued, holding up the bit of paper within an inch of my nose; "I am green by nature as well as by name, if it ain't a four thousand pounds' note."

"Nonsense; it's a little piece of dirty writing paper."—"Read—read," cried Green.

He thrust the paper into my hand as he spoke, and on the reverse side to that on which was the astounding announcement of the Lord Chancellor, were the following words,—

"*   *   *   * all's quite right, then.

"I am, dear Crunch, yours, truly,

"September 29.   "PETER CROGSON."

I read this twice or thrice, and could see nothing in it particularly, till Green said,—

"What's to-day—I mean the day of the month?"—"Why, this is the twenty-ninth," said I.

"Then how," cried Green, in a loud voice of exultation, "could Crogson write a note to-day? Why, he's been defunct three days, doctor, and yet here comes a note to say it's all right. What do you say to that?"—"Why," said I, "I shouldn't wonder but when he wrote it he mistook the date."

"Doctor, you are an idiot," said Green, "It's no mistake at all. Peter Crogson wrote it to-day, and Peter Crogson's in the land of the living."

"It is certainly presumptive evidence," said I; "but how are we to follow it up?"

"We must hunt might and main," said Green. "We must hunt Heaven and earth, and the other place, for Crogson, and find him we must. Don't I long to see his confounded hard head again. I would give a hundred pounds down on the nail to hear him say, ' Ah!' Let's go at once to our solicitor. I mean to say this scrap of paper, combined with the little incident of the slippers you related to me, forms an ample ground-work for suspicion. I feel as certain that the office will never have to pay that four thousand pounds, as that we are now riding in this hackney-coach."

Unhappily for Mr. Green's illustration, the hind wheel came off at this moment, and it was with some difficulty that we were extricated. We were, however, near our journey's end, so that no great harm was done, and Green was so delighted with the scrap of paper, that he paid the coachman his full fare, and in a quarter of an hour more we were in the office of the company's solicitor, who was an acute, long-headed man, and one who, if he once had a clue to anything, was quite as likely to work it out well as any man I ever met with. When the circumstances were all explained to him, he said,—

"Well, gentlemen, this is amply sufficient to found an action upon; there is abundant suspicion about the whole circumstances; but we must be extremely cautious how we act, or we shall give the alarm to the enemy. Nothing but secresy and vigilance in such a case as this will produce any good result. I should recommend that the strictest watch be kept upon the house of Crogson, and that Mrs. Crogson and the family be followed wherever they may go; then, likewise, you had better put yourselves in communication with one of the most experienced of the Bow-street officers."

"That'll do—that'll do," said Green; "we shall be even with them yet."

"Offer him," continued the attorney, "a hundred pounds upon the discovery of Crogson, and then leave him alone to act as he thinks proper."

"But who," said I, "if it be not Crogson, can the dead body represent that I saw at his house, and which, unquestionably, Doctor White and Mr. Bennet were called upon to attend?"

"That is a mystery which, if Crogson be found, will unravel itself." "Of course it will," said Green; "but who shall we get to watch?"—"I have an out-door clerk," said the attorney, "who is in the habit of serving writs and subpœnas for us, and I think he would be the most likely person for such a job that ever I met with."

"The very man—the very man," cried Green. "We'll pay him well for it; d—n it, four thousand pounds is no joke."—"You can speak to him at once, if you please; he is in the house, I think."

To this Green assented, and the solicitor, ringing his hand-bell, desired the boy who answered it to send in Watkins, and in a moment Mr. Watkins came, when his master, with wonderful clearness and precision, explained to him the business, concluding with,—

"Now, Watkins, you can set about it as soon as you like: but as you cannot watch day and night yourself, you must get some assistance, and that, I dare say, you know where to pounce upon, better than I can tell you. Go to any reasonable charges and I will pay them."—"And if we succeed, Mr. Watkins," said Green, "I am sure the directors won't forget you."

"I will do my best, gentlemen," said Watkins; "and if nothing is found out, it sha'n't be my fault. Crogson is either in the house or a long way off. People generally go to one extreme or another when they are hiding."

"I believe they do," said the solicitor. "Now, off with you, Watkins, and let us have your first report at this hour to-morrow."

Thus were things put in a train for the discovery of Mr. Crogson's iniquities, although I must confess that, to my mind, the suspicion was founded altogether upon a very slender foundation, dependent as it was upon two trifling circumstances either of which were capable of the most innocent explanation; but, still, I was far from wishing to throw any damper upon Green's enthusiasm, and I rather silently, than otherwise, acquiesced in the proceedings that were thus hastily instituted in the matter.

There was another extraordinary meeting of the directors in the morning, and then, with closed doors and mysterious whispers, was the whole affair discussed and re-discussed; so solemn and serious a confabulation never, perhaps, having taken place in that house before.

Green reported that he had seen Cruchley, the celebrated Bow-street officer, and that he had undertaken the job of hunting for Crogson, saying, at the same time, that as the solicitor had placed a watch upon Mrs. Crogson, he should, himself, place one upon Crunch, so that there could be no possible communication between any of the suspected parties without its coming to our ears. The solicitor attended at this meeting, and when all this was talked of and arranged, he said,—

"Gentlemen, there is one point in the matter which might be easier come at than any other, and at the same time, if satisfactorily settled, would form a very important item in the business, and that point is, to endeavour to discover if any person, answering the description of the body which our friend, the doctor, saw at Crogson's house, has been missed lately."

"Yes," said the chairman, "some inquiry of that kind might be made."

"We seldom take up a newspaper," said Green, "without finding something of the kind; but we might advertise ourselves that such a body had been found."—"I should say so," remarked the solicitor; "let the address be to some private place, which may mystify and still keep in the dark those parties whom we do not wish to enlighten."

"That can be easily done," said Green, "and I will undertake to arrange that part of the business."—"Mr. Watkins, sir," announced the porter to the solicitor at this moment.

"Oh, my clerk, Watkins; I told him to come here, gentlemen, with his report, as I anticipated meeting you this morning. Show him up."—Mr. Watkins was accordingly introduced, and in answer to his master's questions, he said,—"I ascertained from the nearest public-house in the neighbourhood that the Crogsons had a maid-of-all-work, and that about two o'clock she came there for beer. I, therefore, kept a particular eye upon the house at that hour, and saw her emerge with a jug in her hand. It is quite needless, gentlemen, to trouble you with particulars, but I procured a good deal of information from the servant last evening, as I supped in the kitchen." The directors looked at each other, but said nothing, and Mr. Watkins continued,—"She says the Crogsons are dreadfully poor—that she can't get even her wages of them, and that many times, among them all, including Mr. Crunch, they couldn't raise the merest trifle. She added that Mrs. Crogson was a mean wretch, and always sold her own dripping; and then I brought the conversation round to the decease of Mr. Crogson, which she said she couldn't understand a bit any way, for she was quite sure he had been out all night before the day he died, and that Mr. Crunch had called in the morning, by himself, and gone away by himself, coming back a little while after, with a mob at his heels and her master on a shutter, although she certainly never saw Mr. Crogson before with a white neckcloth, black breeches, and black gaiters, but howsomdever, that was no business of her'n, as he might have put 'em on as he once put on old missus's best silk dress and beaver bonnet, to get out of the way of what he called 'his bum.'

"After tha', however, she said, she supposed the family couldn't bear him to look so unlike himself, for they put him on his bottle-green coat, with the brass buttons, his best sprig fancy cravat, his grey thingumies and Wellingtons —"

"The plot thickens," said Green, " the plot thickens."

"I certainly smell a rat," said the chairman of the board.

"I smell a whole colony of rats," said one of the directors; "as sure as eggs are eggs 'tis an attempted take in, and Crogson, with his infernal head and stomach, is as much alive as I am at this present moment."

"This information is certainly important," said the solicitor. "Did any of the family leave the house, Watkins?"

"Not one, sir; they seemed determined to keep all snug within doors, and they have kept the shutters closed scrupulously."

"Have you heard when the Crogson is to be buried?"

"The day after to-morrow, the servant tells me."

"You see, gentlemen," said Green, " there is an anxiety to get the body under ground,—that is but the fifth from the alleged death."

"Exactly," said the solicitor. "But look here, gentlemen, do you think this paragraph in the *Morning Herald* worth attention?"

We all listened attentively, while the solicitor read as follows, from the newspaper which had been laid upon the directors' table:

"MYSTERIOUS DISAPPEARANCE.—For some days the family of the Rev. Mingleton Fugs, the pastor of a respectable dissenting congregation, has been thrown into a state of alarm and consternation, in consequence of the sudden and mysterious disappearance of that gentleman. Having some years ago had an apoplectic attack, it is feared that he has fallen a victim to another, under some circumstances which have prevented the discovery of his body. The rev. gentleman started at an early hour some days since, from his residence at Paddington, to call upon a friend at Chelsea; since then he has not been heard of. His family and connections are, of course, plunged into the greatest grief. He is a stout-made well-looking man, was dressed in black, when he left home, with breeches and gaiters, and wore a white neckcloth."

The board looked at each other, and then at Mr. Watkins, when this paragraph was concluded; for the description of the missing Reverend Mingleton Fugs coincided most happily and strangely with what the servant had said regarding the singular transmogrification of Mr. Crogson's outward man.

"Hurrah! gentlemen," cried Green; "we are on the right track now— the Reverend What-is-his-name has been passed off for Crogson. There can't be a shadow of a doubt. It's a splendid do. Mr. Watkins, we are tremendously obliged to you, and there can be no doubt but we shall be even with the Crogsons this time. Virtue will be triumphant, and this glorious association will certainly not become defunct."

"I certainly have some hopes now," said the solicitor. "The thing will be to identify the body now lying at Crogson's house as that of the reverend gentleman who is missed. But that must be done without giving the alarm to the Crogsons, if possible; because, although proof of the body upon which the inquest was held is not that of Crogson would be amply sufficient to save the association from having to pay the four thousand pounds, yet it would be most desirable to find out the real Crogson, and indict him and the whole lot for a conspiracy. They richly deserve it; and the public reports of the case will do the association a great deal of good."

"But how can that be managed?" said the chairman.—"I should say, let it be quietly buried, so that the Crogsons may think they have got rid of it comfortably; then we must take into our confidence the coroner who held the inquest, and the clergyman of the church adjoining which the corpse has been interred; with their assistance, there can be no difficulty in the exhumation of the pretended Crogson, in presence of some of the relatives of this reverend gentleman who has been missed. If they identify the body, and make oath to its being their relative, that will be sufficient for us; and, at all events, the question of the four thousand pounds will have been comfortably settled; for, at the end of the three months, Mr. Crogson can be told to bring his action for the amount, and the plea we can put upon the record, in answer, will be, 'Crogson's not dead.'"—"Exactly—exactly," cried Green.

"Then," continued the solicitor, "the proving he is dead falls upon them, and there I am confident we shall defeat them. The servant girl will be an important witness to the identity of the Reverend Mingleton Fugs. We must have a verdict, and the Crogsons will, in addition to what has been paid for the life assurance, be out of pocket all the costs."

This was agreed to with acclamation; and the solicitor determined himself to call upon the missing reverend gentleman's family, while Watson was still to watch the Crogsons, and Green was to write a letter to Crunch, in order to lull suspicion, saying, that, at the termination of the three months, the society was quite ready to settle any claim that could be made upon them.

Thus were things in a fair train for the discovery of the whole conspiracy, and the head directors breathed again more freely, as, at all events, they considered that, whether Crogson was punished or not, the association was saved from bankruptcy, and themselves from disgrace.

* * * * *

'Twas a cold and tempestuous night; the air was filled with a drizzling mist, which, ever and anon, seemed gathered together by some malicious wind, which would then wait at the corner of a street for some stray passenger, and dash it all in his face, getting in between his cravat and his neck, and creeping up his very coat sleeves, in order to make him as miserable as possible.

It was true that the moon made frequent attempts to show its fair round face, but, as often as it did so, there would come a whole legion of clouds, and sweep across it, as if they had said—"Come, come, we can't have anything of that sort to-night." Now and then, too, a sparkling star peeped out from a crevice in the dun atmosphere, as if just to see what sort of night it was, and then, with a shudder, it would pop in again, no doubt to tell the other stars not to venture out on any account.

'Twas on such a night as this, so gloomy, so wild-looking, so desolate, that a party of eight persons were assembled in a little room, called the vestry, under the roof of a church, not fifty miles from Hyde-park corner.

That party of eight consisted of myself, Mr. Green, the solicitor to the assurance society, the clergyman of the aforesaid church, the coroner for Middlesex, the chairman of the board of directors, and two solemn-looking personages, one of whom was the brother of the Rev. Mingleton Fugs, and the other his eldest daughter.

There was something interesting about the young girl, even thoroughly imbued, as she seemed to be, with all the fanaticism of religion run mad. She was not beautiful—that is to say, not artistically beautiful; but there was an interesting and melancholy expression about her pale countenance, and, at the same time, an appearance of intellect in her eyes and ample brow, which procured her, involuntarily, the respect of every one there present.

She said nothing; she uttered no sigh, no complaint; but it was evident to me, as she held the black silk cloak she wore closely around her, and looked occasionally from one to the other of us, that she was suffering deeply, although she gave but little outward sign of her mental anguish.

I had spoken to her but once, and then it was to say—

"No one can regret more than myself the necessity for your appearance on this most painful occasion. Arm yourself with fortitude to bear up against it; every one here present, I am sure, feels deeply for you."

"The Lord giveth," she said, with a shudder, "and the Lord taketh away. Blessed is the name of the Lord."

I could easily see through the flimsy conventionalism of these words, which she had been taught as an antidote to all feeling, but which are about as effective when the heart is really crushed with its own agony, as would be any other cant expression.

I could see by the quiver of her lip, and by the trembling of her small hand, as she convulsively held her cloak around her, how great was the struggle to keep up even any show of outward composure, and I said to myself—

"The mere religion of terms and expressions which this girl has been taught, will not suffice to carry her through the ordeal that is approaching."

We had assembled for the exhumation of the body, in order to its identification by those near relatives of the dissenting parson, and the ultimate confusion of the Crogsons.

A better and a worse night for our purpose could not have been—better on account of the secrecy in which we wished to conduct the whole proceedings, and worse as regarded our own feelings on the melancholy errand we were upon.

"I much regret," said the clergyman, "the necessity for this extreme measure; but I do not feel myself justified, whatever may be my private feelings, in standing in the way of public justice, and therefore it is that I consent to the exhumation of this body."

"If it be identified," said the coroner, "as that of the Reverend Mingleton Fugs, it will be my duty to hold another inquest upon it."

"I should scarcely think so," said our solicitor. "The object of the inquest was, of course, to ascertain the cause of death, and that is quite settled as regards the body, whether its name, when living, was Crogson or Fugs."

"Well," said the coroner, "I have no wish to press an inquest."

"It would be better avoided, for this reason," said the solicitor—"namely, that it would certainly allow Crogson to escape from the consequences of his iniquity, by giving him warning that the plot was discovered."

"So it would—so it would," said the coroner; "if you, Mr. Elias Fugs, and Miss Patience Fugs, can identify the body, we had better just leave it quietly to its rest."

"Yes," said the solicitor, "with the understanding that you will be prepared, upon your oaths, at any time, to swear to the identity of the body."

"If the Lord will," said Elias Fugs, stretching his gaunt frame to its utmost extent, "if the Lord wills it, we will swear. We shall, of course, have our expenses."

"Certainly," said the solicitor; and then he whispered to me, "that's all right; you are sure of a man who looks to his expenses; they are the best witnesses, always. Elias Fugs is our man."

"I have come here," resumed Elias, "with the strength of grace, and full of holiness; have you any objection to the four hundred and seventy-seventh hymn?"

"The very greatest," said I. "I think all singing quite out of place here; for it's either so bad as to be execrable, or good enough to make people think more of it than they do of religion."

"Let us go," said the clergyman; "the sexton and his assistant will be waiting, and the sooner this unhappy business is settled, the better."

"So much for opinion," whispered Green to me. "I think it's a glorious hip-hip-hurrah sort of business. I think I shall propose nine cheers for Fugs, if we find it's him."

"For Heaven's sake, Green," said I, "be temperate, and let this really solemn affair go off decently. I am confident that young girl possesses feeling, if Mr. Elias does not."

We then proceeded in a body to the church-yard, the clergyman himself preceding us with a lantern, until we came to a spot close to to the wall, where, by the light of another lantern, we saw two men in their shirt sleeves, resting upon their spades, and wiping the perspiration from their brows, after digging deeply into the soil.

We gathered in a strange group round the grave's brink, and, by the light of the lanterns, one of which was placed at the foot, and the other at the head, we could dimly see the coffin, partially discoloured by the damp earth, which had been resting upon it for nearly twelve hours.

"You have reached it?" said the clergyman.—"Yes, sir," was the brief response of one of the men.—"Then raise it."

One of the men descended into the grave, to attach ropes to the handles of the coffin, while Miss Fugs, on whom I kept my eyes, crept silently to the head of the grave, and there stood with her hands clasped, so pale and wan, that she looked like some marble statue, arrayed in sombre apparel.

With a harsh grating sound the ropes passed through the handles of the coffin, and then the man ascended from the grave. The clergyman spoke in a low and tremulous voice, saying,—

"May the great God of Heaven, who reads all hearts, look with a forgiving eye upon us for thus disturbing the solemn repose of that mute form which has been consigned to his holy keeping."

The coffin was raised slowly, until it reached the surface of the grave, and then, with a heavy lurch, the men moved it on the pile of earth on the one side. There was a dead silence at that awful moment, and no one seemed capable of speaking, but all eyes were rivetted upon the movements of the sexton, who was carefully engaged in removing the screws that fastened the lid of that gloomy receptacle of the dead.

One after another they yielded, until, at length, a touch would have displaced the coffin lid, and exposed the face of the corpse; expectation was wound up to its utmost height, each one there present drew his breath short and thick, and the sexton rose, looking earnestly at the clergyman, as if for him to give the signal for exposing the face of the dead.

The whole party started suddenly, for a slight cry came from the young girl when she saw the preparations were so far completed for once more showing to the light of day the face of him who, she had every to believe, was her parent.

"Be calm—be calm," said I; "this matter will soon be over, and you'll be better pleased to know that it is really your father that sleeps here, than to be left in doubt and uncertainty regarding his fate."

She said nothing, but turned a cold stone-like gaze upon me, as if she would have said, "Do not talk to me, my feelings are too deep for the ordinary topics of conversation."

"Remove the lid," said the clergyman.

The full glare of the two lanterns was thrown upon the head part of the coffin, and the sexton sloped the lid in such a manner, that the face of the corpse was discovered.

There it lay, pale and ghastly by that light thrown across its fearful expression. The few hours which it had been placed in that cold and ghastly receptacle, seemed to have facilitated greatly the progress of decay; a clammy moisture was upon the brow, and the soft parts of the face had sunk deeply, leaving the teeth, and the more prominent portions of the bony structure, fully developed.

The girl gazed on the lifeless form for an instant, and then, with one wild shriek—a shriek that was dreadful to hear—she shrunk back, and I thought she had fainted; but such was not the case, for in a moment she spoke, and in such heart-rending accents, that it was frightful to hear her, and for long afterwards my memory was haunted in sleep by the shrieking tones of that young girl.

"'Tis he—'tis he," she cried; "I know him by the scar. Well—well. You remember the scar—he got the blow from a heathen in some island far away in the Southern Sea, where he went to preach the word of God. 'Tis he—'tis he. My father—my father! Oh, Heavens! that we should meet thus, after parting in anger!"

"Let us praise the Lord alway," said Mr. Elias.

"But will that restore me my father?" said the girl. "I have been taught to reverence Heaven, and I do reverence it; but God has given his creatures feelings which they cannot gainsay. Surely I may believe in Heaven, and still be human."

"Nay," said Elias, with a conventicle twang, "the Lord of Hosts doeth what he liketh, even as the wind bloweth when it listeth."

"Do not speak to me—do not speak to me, uncle," said the girl, "in that strain. Heaven has given me warm affections, and when they are saddened it has given me tears. Who shall tell me not to grieve for the death of my father?"

"Now, you see, Patience," said Elias, "that you ought to have consented, even as your father wished you, to give your hand to the God-fearing Barnabas Middlemast, a shining light in the connection of the United Fugs."

"Where I give my hand," said the girl, "I must give my heart. Reflection will bring me peace here."

She struck her breast as she spoke, and then, leaning her head upon her hands, she completely covered up her face, while the large tears trickled through her fingers, and her deep convulsive sobs shook her whole frame.

"Young lady," said the solicitor, "can you, at a future time, swear that this is your father's body?"—"I can," she murmured.—"And can you, Mr. Elias?"—"Ay, truly, if the scar be there, and I get my expenses," said Elias.—"Satisfy yourself, then."

Elias bent forward his ungainly form, and examined the forehead of the corpse for some moments, after which he said, with a snuffle,—

"Truly, that is the mortal receptacle of the more heavenly part of the Rev. Mingleton Fugs—the Lord willing alway; and, although the Apostle says, swear not at all, yet will I swear very much if I am paid all expenses. Come, niece Patience—come."

"Not yet," said the girl—"not yet;" then turning her eyes to the clergyman, she said,—"Sir, you will again consign to Heaven these poor remains."

"Nay," said Elias, lifting up his voice, and swinging his arms like a windmill; "we differ dreadfully from the Church of England, as by law established—ay, dreadfully; for, whereas it, by a demoniac principle called liberality, damneth not people who may differ slightly from it, we damn, with a great and tremendous damn, all who differ from us so much as a hair's breadth"

"Peace, uncle—peace," said the girl; "from this moment I will have a purer and a dearer love of Heaven than that which is taught in the howling conventicles that you admire. Holy sir," addressing the clergyman, "let me implore you, for my sake, to repeat the service for the dead over the body of my father."

"I need no imploring," said the clergyman, "to perform that office."

He took off his hat as he spoke, and we all immediately uncovered to listen to the solemn ritual for the dead.

"Nay," said Elias, "I have no objection to join in the seven-hundred-and-twenty-third Psalm, the burden of which is, 'Down to hell—down to hell, sinners great and small;' but ——"—"Mr. Elias Fugs," said I, "if you say another word, I'll knock you down."

"Do you mean with an arm of flesh," he said, "or spiritually?"—"With an arm of bone and muscle, most certainly," said I.

"Oh," said Elias, "truly I am silent, for I fight not with carnal weapons."

The clergyman then began the burial service, while deep sobs burst from the breast of the girl. When the solemn ceremony was over, the lid of the coffin was again screwed down, and, for the second time, it was lowered to the grave.

We stood by till the gloomy pit was nearly filled with earth, and then I saw the clergyman give his arm to Patience, and they walked together towards the church, while the rest of the party, with the exception of Elias, slowly followed; as for that Christian individual, he desired to be let out of the iron gates of the churchyard, whither he followed the gravediggers, muttering, as he went, what I verily believe was an elaborate curse against the whole party.

* * * * *

Here, then, was a clear case against Crogson—the life association was relieved beyond a doubt, and they would gain rather than lose by the whole transaction; but one question remained, and that was, how was Crogson to be found and punished.

The Bow-street officer could find out nothing. Mr. Crunch was perfectly exemplary in his outgoings and incomings; and as for Watkins, although he supped every night with the Crogsons' servant, and won her heart completely, she could tell him nothing more, so that affairs remained in *statu quo* for about a week, when, one day, Watkins came to say that a little circumstance had transpired of a suspicious character. It was this:—

The previous evening, while he was picking a bone with the maid of-all-work, and whispering soft nonsense in her willing ear, the family's washing came home, during the progress of which down the staircase, and safe delivery in the kitchen, he, Watkins, hid in a cupboard.

Soon after, and before he had emerged from his hiding-place, old Mrs. Crunch made her appearance in the domestic region, and, selecting from the basket of clothes two shirts, she said,—

"Susan, let these shirts be well aired, and I'll come down for them in an hour," after which she disappeared.

"Shirts," said Green—"you're sure they were not female shirts?"—"Quite," said Watkins, "I think I could make shift to know one from the other."

"Oh, very well," said Green. "What happened then?"—"Why," said Watkins, "the maid-of-all-work is rather a good-looking girl."

"You may pass over that," said I, "for it's no business of ours."—"Very well, gentlemen," said Watkins; "I was very curious to know who those shirts could be for; and as for

Susan, she was equally lost in wonder. Before, however, the old lady came down for them, I had slipped out of the house, and kept an eye upon the door, for somehow or another I had a strong suspicion the shirts would not long remain in Chilmundle Villa."

"Well, well," said Green.—"Oh, I forgot to say, Susan and I found 'P.C.' on the tail of each."

"Peter Crogson," gasped Green.—"Exactly, sir," said Watkins. "Well, then, I had not waited long in the street, when old Mrs. Crogson came out, bonneted and shawled, with a small parcel in her hand, as like what these two shirts would make as possible. She looked up the street and down the street, and round and about her, as if she were trying to scent some game; then off she set, in a very respectable old lady-like trot, in the direction of Knightsbridge.

"Like young Norval, I marked the road she took, and safely dogged her to a house in Pimlico, where, however, she remained not long; but coming out, accompanied by a little girl, she gave her some very urgent instructions in a whispered voice, which, of course, I was not near enough to hear, and then left her with the small parcel.

"Believing that that parcel contained the shirts, my object

was then to discover its destination, and I followed the girl across St. James's Park and up the Strand, until she paused at the gate of Lyon's-inn.

"I followed her into the open square, when she proceeded directly to the house in which Mr. Crunch has his chambers. Slipping up the stairs cautiously after her, I convinced myself that she knocked at his door, and then, for fear of discovery, I waited at the gate of the inn for her, satisfying myself that she came away without the parcel."

"Suspicious—uncommonly suspicious," said Green. "Did you say anything to her?"—"No; that would have been sure to have awakened suspicion at once, for it would have got round to the Crogsons, and if we put them once on their guard, he'll leave the country, and there won't be a shadow of a chance of finding him."

"That's very true," said I to Watkins. "What are we to do now, Mr. Green?"—"Why," said Green, "it looks uncommonly to me as if Crogson was concealed in Crunch's chambers."

"Likely enough," said I; "but then you see if he should not be so, and we make a demonstration there, we do more harm than good."—"There is the difficulty, gentlemen," said Watkins. "I think it will turn out that he is there; but who's to say so for a certainty?"

"True," said Green, "true; we must be cautious. Now, what would you do, Watkins?"—"Why," said Watkins, "I should first try and ascertain if Crunch slept in his chambers, and if I found that he did not, I would break into them some night, and try to see if Crogson did."

"Break into them?" said Green. "Wouldn't that sound very illegal?"—"Why, yes," said Watkins. "Crunch might bring his action, but it wouldn't be a bad thing to try."

"No, no," said Green; "we must be more cautious, Mr. Watkins—we must be more cautious. I am inclined to think with you that there is just a chance Crogson may be hidden in Crunch's chambers, and if we could certainly get anything like more evidence upon the subject, I should propose going in the broad face of day and attacking the chambers for the purpose of ferreting him out."

"Why, there again," said Watkins, "we should be illegal, for we have no right to take Crogson into custody without some process of law beforehand."

"Oh, we'd risk that," said Green.—"There is no occasion to risk it," said Watkins; "for upon a representation of the facts, we should get a warrant from any magistrate, only there again the old danger occurs, that, if he should not be there, of giving the Crogsons warning that mischief was brewing. Now, gentlemen, if you please, I have a little—just a little—scheme which I think will do."

"Let's have it," said Green; "for Heaven's sake, let us try something."—"I should propose, gentlemen, getting up a fire."

"A fire!" cried I.—"A fire!" shouted Green.—"Yes, gentlemen. I think if we all go and thoroughly surround Crunch's chambers, some of us keeping an eye on the windows, and some on the door, while we set up a simultaneous shout of 'Fire!' we shall have a good chance of Crogson making his appearance if he be in the chambers; at all events, it is worth the while."

"It might do," said Green; "and in such a quiet place, too, such a cry would rouse up everybody."—"You may depend," said Watkins, "that if a cry of 'Fire!' be raised in Lyon's-inn, there is not a soul within it but will look out of window, or rush down to the open square."

"At what hour should we do it?" said Green.—"I should advise about half an hour after the gates are shut against strangers; four or five of us will be quite sufficient. We can slink in just as the gates are about to be closed for the night, and hide about on the different staircases, until we hear St. Clement's Church give us the signal for attack; then we can each of us call out 'Fire!' three times, lustily. After which I should advise that the greatest silence be preserved while we watch Crunch's chambers."

"Will you make one, doctor?" said Green.—"I have no objection," said I.

"Very well, then. I'll get two of the directors to come with us, and that'll make five. By Jove, we'll do it to-night, and I hope we shall have luck. If we do, it will be the rarest sport that ever was."

"Let us take no notice whatever," said Watkins, "even if we should see Crogson. We can let the alarm go off, and on the next morning, by a private application to one of the magistrates, get warrants against the whole party."

"Well, then, that's all settled," said Green. "Where shall we meet,—suppose we say Somerset House?"

This Mr. Watkins and I assented to, and we fixed upon that evening for the execution of the plan.

* * * *

At the appointed hour I reashed Somerset House, but was the first of the party that arrived. The weather was far from pleasant, a general gloom hung over the sky; and although, according to all the almanacks, the moon ought to have been shining very brightly, it did not condescend to shine at all, or, at least, it wasted its sweetness on the empty air, for none of its rays reached the surface of our earth. There was, moreover, a cold and disagreeable wind whistling about the streets in a tyrannical manner, as if it wanted the thoroughfare all to itself, and was trying to blow everybody home.

To escape it I got under the archway of the ancient building, and had not to wait many minutes before Green and the two directors arrived.

"Now we are waiting for Watkins," said I.—"No, gentlemen, I am here," he said, as he suddenly emerged from the gloom further down in the archway.

"Very well, then," said Green; "here we are. Was there ever such a set of conspirators since the time of Guy Faux?"— "We had better not go in a body," said Watkins, "as we shall all get in within ten minutes."

"But now, Mr. Watkins, it strikes me that, as Lyon's-inn has but one entrance, and, consequently, one exit, the porter may prove a serious disturbance to us, by fancying we are intent upon some burglary."

"You have only to walk in with a confident air, and pop into some doorway, and I'll stay the last, as that may be the most full of risk."

One by one, then, we repaired to Lyon's-inn. Green and the two directors preceded me; and as I passed under the low archway I saw the porter take a good long stare, as if he were quite astonished at four people, neither of whom he knew, entering the peaceful precincts of Lyon's-inn within so short a period of time. He, however, said nothing, and I popped into the first doorway I came to. In a few minutes, then, somebody said—

"Hist, hist!"—"Hist!" said I.

"Doctor," said the voice of Watkins.—"Lawyer," said I.

"This way, if you please, sir;" and following him, I found the whole party congregated just within a gloomy doorway.

"Do you see those windows opposite, gentlemen," said Watkins, "in one of which is a very faint light?"—"Yes," said we.

"Well, then, that is Crunch's chambers; and it is upon that one window, and the next to it, I wish you to keep your eyes, as you all know Crogson, and I don't. I will, however, watch by his chambers' door; after hallooing "fire!" we'll all take it up, and shout 'fire!' through the key-hole, which may produce a particular effect upon Crunch's nerves."

To this we assented, and Watkins disappeared from among us.

"Well, then," said Green, "the moment we hear him cry 'fire!' we'll all take it up, and shout 'fire!' in a breath. I have brought a machine here that'll have some effect."

As Green spoke, he produced a long tin japanned speaking-trumpet from his great-coat pocket. All was silent in Lyon's-inn; it might have been a sepulchre, so still and solemn was it. The distant murmur of active life seemed to reach that old inn with subdued tones, and to pause on its threshold in order to rid itself of its jarring discord. But few lights twinkled round the small square. We heard the gates shut with a subdued clash, then the porter's footsteps died away as he retired into his lodge.

The wind had either dropped, or didn't like the trouble of coming into Lyon's-inn, for everything was there as calm as possible; and a person might have stood in dreamy contemplation in the middle of that square, forgetting, for a time, that there was a lawyer in the world to disturb the equanimity of its inhabitants.

But that calm was like the deceitful one of the ocean which precedes a storm. Loud, clear, and ear-piercing, came such a cry of "fire!—fire!" that, although we fully expected it, we all ran against each other in our momentary confusion, and Mr. Green dropped his speaking-trumpet with a heavy clatter.

"Fire!—fire!" again cried Watkins, more terrifically than before; then Green snatched up his trumpet, and the voice in which he shouted "fire!—fire!" through it, was so widely different, in its rumbling echoes, from the shrill shout of Watkins, that it sounded quite unearthly; and I could well conjecture the terrifying effect it must have had upon every one's nerves who heard it.

"Fire!—fire," cried we all, and the noise we made was truly prodigious.

The porter rushed from his lodge in a state of the wildest alarm, screaming,—"Murder! murder!—fire! Fetch the engines!—thieves!" Then tripping over the stone in the centre of the square, he fell down with a great whack, and being rather a stout man, he made no effort to get up again, but lay upon his back, making more noise than all of us put together, so that, in a moment or two, we left the whole job to him, with the exception of Green, who still continued to produce singular rumbling noises through his speaking-trumpet.

Up flew every window in Lyon's-inn, and at the one belonging to Mr. Crunch's chambers from whence the light had streamed, appeared two heads.

To identify either was impossible in the very dim light that was in the square; but fate was kind to us, for the porter had got hoarse, and was silent, so that there was a partial lull in the tempest of sound, during which—ah! what music it was to us—we heard, proceeding from one of the heads at Crunch's window, the words,—

"God bless my head and stomach—where's the fire? What lungs, liver, and lights somebody's got."

It was Crogson. We all knew it was Crogson in a moment, and Green had just got as far as the "hip, hip, hip!" through his speaking-trumpet, by way of giving a loud cheer of recognition, when I placed my hat over the other end of it, and smothered the intention.

Our object now was to get out of Lyon's-inn as quickly as possible, and leaving Watkins to take his chance, we made a rush across the square, crying,—

"Engines!—engines;—engines!—fetch the engines!"

This had the desired effect, for the porter's wife flung the gates wide open, and we gained the outer street, leaving the row to settle itself as best it might.

I have a faint reminiscence, for I did not enter this circumstance in my diary, that all of us proceeded to some hotel in the neighbourhood, and there became exceedingly jolly indeed, making speeches and drinking toasts at a great rate. I have a faint recollection of Green singing a comic song through the speaking-trumpet, and then disappearing so suddenly under the table, trumpet and all, that one could almost fancy he had gone down some trap-door.

After that I am afraid myself and the two directors became a little oblivious of what we were about. I think we walked up the Strand arm-in-arm, awakening all the peaceable inhabitants, by roaring out that we wouldn't go home till morning, a piece of gratuitous information that, I dare say, procured many a hearty curse on our heads.

Then, I believe, we vowed eternal friendship to each other, and took about half the night in seeing each other home—although, by some means, we none of us got home until broad daylight, and then we parted such attached friends that never were known, and with such shaking of hands as would have done one's heart good to see. In fact, so much did the two directors rely upon each other's friendship, that when they left off shaking hands they both fell down; and as for myself, I think some roast mutton I had had the day before must have disagreed with me, for by some means I found myself in bed, I don't know how, with my boots on.

It wasn't the wine—oh, no!—whenever is it the wine, except at a police-office, when it really has been the beer or the gin?—then people, who haven't tasted wine ten times in their lives, have always taken their extra bottle with their friends; it looks more tonish in a police report, and it costs no more.

* * * * *

It was nearly one o'clock in the day when I was aroused by somebody shaking me with great violence, and upon looking up I saw, to my momentary surprise, Green and the company's solicitor at my bed-side.

"Hilloa! hilloa! what's the matter?" I cried.—"Oh, doctor! doctor! I am surprised at you. I am very much afraid you took a drop too much last night."

"I didn't fall under the table," said I, "with a speaking trumpet in my hand. Come, come, Green, no nonsense."

"You wouldn't say it was nonsense," cried Green, "if you had the headache as I have. Now, doctor, for once in a way, give us some advice gratis. If a man once in his life—just once, you know—gets the other drop, what had he better do?"

"Oh, if it's only once," said I, "he needn't do anything; it isn't worth his while doing anything, Green."

"Confound you," said Green, "but you know it might happen again. Come now, doctor, give us something practical once in a way."

"Well, then," said I, "if you drink too much, and are sober enough to think of it, any time you do so swallow a tumbler of cold water; keep at it till you have had about a couple of quarts—half a pint at a time; and I can assure you there is not in the whole materia medica anything that will do you one tithe the benefit."

"Thank you," said Green; and proceeding to my dressing-table, he emptied the water-bottle to the last drop.

"Well, now, gentlemen," said the solicitor, "if you have settled your temperance matters, we will proceed at once to the magistrate's and get warrants against all those Crogsons, as well as Crunch. Our statement may now be a public one, for the warrants can be executed, I dare say, immediately."

We got into a hackney-coach, and soon found our way to Bow-street, where, upon the solicitor's statement of facts, and mine and Green's oath with regard to the exhumation of the Rev. Mingleton Fugs, warrants were granted for the apprehension of Crogson, his wife, Crunch, and Mrs. Crunch, we charging ourselves to show the officers where the parties could be found. By the time the proceedings at the police-office were over, the Assurance Society had assembled in great force, for there were the whole eight directors present, as well as the actuary, the solicitor, and myself, so that we formed a formidable body in aid of the two officers who were sent with us to capture Crunch and Crogson.

We sent Watkins to Chelsea, to point out to another officer Chilmundle Villa, where the other warrants were to be executed.

A most formidable party did we look, as we marched down Bow-street, Brydges-street, and so on, till we came to the gate of Lyon's-inn. The people stared after us, and made various conjectures with regard to who we were. Some declared we were the Leet Jury, and there was a general pocketing of light weights in the various shops as we passed.

Others again accused us of being the Commissioners of Pavement, and a great many people perseveringly followed us all the way we went, with an eager and restless curiosity.

The porter at Lyon's-inn was astonished at such a concourse; but we had fairly entered the iron gates before he could take any active measures to close them, and we left him staring after us with speechless wonder, while we paused not until we reached the door of Mr. Crunch's chambers.

"Now, gentlemen," said one of the officers, "some one of you who can identify the men had better accompany us up stairs, and we'll have them down in a few minutes."

"Very good," said the directors, in a body; "we'll wait here while you go, doctor."—"Agreed," said I.—"And I'll go too," said Green, "for I know them both."

Green and I then, with the two officers, ascended the ricketty staircase, while the eight directors waited below, holding, certainly, the most extraordinary meeting they had ever held.

I scarcely ever felt so much interested in the proceedings of a few minutes as I did during those which took us to reach the chambers of Mr. Crunch. Altogether, the affair had been a most agreeable little drama; and although I had tolerably well braved it out while Peter Crogson was believed to be alive, yet, of course, I could not but feel that the concern would have had a very unfavourable effect upon my future prospects in my profession, had it really turned out that I had made such a mistake as to report Peter Crogson a good life, when such was so far from being the case. This state of things being true, of course the converse held good; and Peter Crogson being alive and well, said as much for me as his being dead said against me.

When we reached the door of the chambers, I turned to the officers, and said,—

"As it is difficult to say what outlets there may be to these chambers, you had better wait here until Mr. Green and I, without creating any alarm, go in and lay hold of the prisoners."

"Exactly," was the reply. "We'll take care of the door."

They then shrunk back into a dark corner, and I knocked at the inner door of the chambers.

The door was immediately opened by Crunch's hypocritical-looking clerk, who appeared at once to recognize us, for with a pious-looking, bland smile, he said,—

"Walk in, gentlemen—walk in; Mr. Crunch is at home, and, for the present, at your service. We have a consultation at one, in Marrowfat v. Peapod; but there is a time for all things. Walk in, gentlemen—walk in."

Keeping as solemn countenances as we could, we entered the chambers, and delivering each our cards to the clerk, we desired that he would take them in to the professional gentleman, with the request that he would graciously favour us with an interview.

"Certainly, gentlemen—certainly," said the clerk. "Mr. Crunch is the most accessible gentleman in the profession. No pride—no frightful, freezing vanity—no nothing."

The rascal disappeared into the inner room, and we waited with no little glee the summons to appear before the great man, who would so soon find his air-blown castles levelled with the dust, and that he had exchanged a comfortable income, which he expected to derive from the assurance-office, for an independence most probably at the expense of government. We had not long to wait, for the clerk, in a few moments, flung open the door of Mr. Crunch's private room, and said,—

"Walk in, gentlemen, if you please; Mr. Crunch is disengaged."

We entered the room, and there sat Crunch, with an abstracted air, affecting to be deeply immersed in the consideration of some legal documents that were before him. It was quite absurd to see the look he gave us, as much as to say, "I have some dim recollection of you; but which of my important legal concerns you're come about I really can't take upon myself to say." He then referred to the two cards which were before him, and tapping his head, he said,—

"Oh! I begin to recollect something about an assurance-office; bless my heart, yes; if I am wrong, gentlemen, you will take into your kind consideration the multifariousness of my business, which I can only hope to get through but by the mercy of a mysterious Providence, which is continually bothering its creatures dreadfully."

"Mr. Crunch," said I, "we have thought that it would be better, after all, to settle this business of Mr. Peter Crogson's policy at once."

A flush of colour came across the sallow countenance of Mr. Crunch; he could not help looking for a moment the intense gratification he felt at the prospect of receiving the amount of the policy, and Green and I were quite demoniacal enough to angle with him a little longer.

"Yes," said Green; "it's no use protracting these affairs; when a settlement must be made, I always think the sooner the better."

"Yes, gentlemen—yes," gasped Crunch; "I am of your opinion—quite of your opinion; and I hope that wings of friendship and good feeling may keep on flapping for ever, between me and your office. I assure you, gentlemen, that, if any client asks me where he shall go and insure his life, I will send him to you; peace and concord will continue, and an unhappy business will be satisfactorily settled. Peter Crogson was a great man in his way—a very great man, gentlemen; and it is melancholy to look back through an extremely short vista of time, and fancy what his head, his heart, and his lungs, his lights, and his general inside were once, and what they are now. He has gone to the tomb, gentlemen; but we won't deplore him—no—no, we won't—we'll give a tear to his memory; and, whatever we think of his life and actions, gentlemen, I think we cannot but admire his *policy*. You see the joke, gentlemen, and will excuse it."

"Ah, certainly," said Mr. Green; "a joke's a joke, Mr. Crunch; every one must admire his policy; and I assure you we are not insensible to the fun of the affair, far from it—very far from it, Mr. Crunch."

"Sir," said Crunch, "you are a man of the world, and I honour you."

"I am certainly a man of the world," said Green, "as far as my opportunities will allow me; but I am really sorry, Mr. Crunch, that I can't return your compliment, for it really strikes me your acquaintance, in a little while, will be a questionable credit to me."

"Eh!" said Crunch; "what do you mean?"—"Oh, I don't mean anything," said Green; "don't say I asked you any questions; I wouldn't impede the course of justice for a thousand pounds. You're our prisoner, Mr. Crunch; and if you attempt any resistance, I'll knock you sprawling."

I ran on one side of the table, and Green on the other, so that we thought we had Mr. Crunch quite safe; but he was one too many for us, for, with a suddenness and activity that would have done credit to any harlequin on the stage, he dived under the table, emerged from the other side of it, and darted out of the room, while Green and I tumbled simultaneously over his empty chair.

"D—n it!" said Green, rubbing his head.—"Confound you," said I, "what a fool you are, Green; he has got away now, you see."

"Not exactly," said one of the officers, popping his head in at the door; "my *coujutor* has him—where's t'other?"—"I'll be hanged if I know," said Green; "all I know is, that I have knocked my head against the doctor's, and it's frightfully bruised. That Peter Crogson was born to be my bane, dead or alive—there's no mistake about it; he's a positive fiend in human shape. D—n your head, doctor, where did you get it?"

"Where's the t'other?" asked the officer; "that's what I wants to know; where's the t'other, gentlemen?"—"That's the question," said Green; "he's here, somewhere, I have no doubt, and we must have him, if a good guard is kept at the door."

"Leave us alone for that," said the officer, as he drew his little gilt-headed staff from his pocket. "I'll ferret him out, if he's here—all I wants of you is, to 'dentify him."

We never contemplated for a moment, of course, of looking in the outer or clerk's room for Peter Crogson, but commenced the search where we were conducting it with vigour and precision, but all in vain—our man was evidently not there; and, opening a door, we all then sallied into an inner apartment, a sort of *sanctum sanctorum* of the chambers, where we fully expected to find our man, with his head, and heart, and lungs, and all that kind of thing, in as blooming a state as possible; but we were doomed to another disappointment, for there he was not.

The room was a very small one, and had what is called a borrowed light, which made it a dismal-looking little den; it was scantily furnished, but had evident signs of recent occupation; a chair was placed at the table, as if somebody had jumped up from it, and on the table lay an open book of a very ominous character, for it was a legal treatise on the law as regarded conspiracies, for the purpose of fraud, and the executing or utterance of forged documents.

I recollect at the time thinking the officer as clever as a North American Indian in tracing the trail of an enemy, for, without a moment's delay, he walked up to the chair, and placing his hands upon it, he said,—

"The nest's warm, though the bird has flown; there's somebody been a sitting here not long ago; he's nigh at hand, I'll warrant."

"Then he must be in the chambers," said I, "for it's utterly impossible he could have left them."

"That's the dodge," said the officer, and he stood in the room, with his hands in his breeches pockets, and wheeling round upon his heels to take a survey of its capabilities of concealment. There was an expressive silence for some moments; then, placing his finger by the side of his nose to intimate his extreme cunning and the artfulness of the suggestion he was about to make, he said, in a deeply impressive tone of voice, "the *chimbley*."

"What! do you think he's up the chimney?" said I.— "Mum," said the officer. "What's his name? I forgets it."—"Peter Crogson," said I.

He then approached the fire-place, and looking up the chimney, he called,—

"It's no go, Peter—it's no go. Come down, my tulip. It ain't a shadow of a go." Down came a flop of soot in the officer's eye. "I told you so," he said, as, in wiping the injured organ, he gave himself a great smear down his face,— "I told you so. There's a teazer. Soot's a'most as bad as snuff in yer eye. Come, now, Peter; none of that. Climbing boys is going to be 'bolished some day, and everything's to be done with a blessed machine, as looks with utter contempt upon all the corners, something like this ere does, Peter."

Now the officer's observant eyes had discovered what I had not, namely, a very large toasting-fork in the corner of the room, and this he poked up the chimney with an energy which in about half a minute produced a singular kind of howl from up the flue.

The officer laughed at this uproariously, and put his arm up as high as he could, poking away with the toasting-fork, with remarkable glee.

"I have often heard of parliament being progued. I supposes as there is a lot on 'em, and they does it with a pitch-fork, but this ere will serve our turn."

"Murder! murder!" roared a voice up the chimney. "D—n my head and liver, what's that? God bless my lights and lungs!"

"Can't you come down, then?" said the officer. "We are not going to wait here all day for you."—"Come down be d—d!" said Peter Crogson, from the chimney. "Bless my head—I mean my tail—take away that d—d poking thing, whatever it is."

"Werry good," said the officer, giving one more terrific progue, and then withdrawing the toasting-fork; "I think I had you, then, my ancient Roman."

"Murder!" shrieked Peter Crogson, and a foot appeared, plunging desperately just above the grate. This the officer immediately laid hold of as a legal prize; and after an immense scuffling, and shouting, and hallooing, Mr. Peter Crogson, with a great many bumps of his wonderful head upon the grate and the fender, fairly landed upon the hearth-rug, accompanied by such a volley of soot, that what the officer called his 'dentity could by no means have been sworn to.

Green then threw himself into a chair, and laughed so outrageously, that I thought he was going mad; after which he danced a sort of war dance round Peter Crogson, and raised various singular shouts, such as might have struck terror into the enemies of the Greens in the ancient days.

There was something in Green's mirth quite contagious, and I laughed too, for I could not help it, while the officer threw himself into a great many singular contortions in the excess of his mirth.

At this moment, too, the comicality of the scene was considerably heightened by the door being flung open, and the eight directors appearing, with anxious countenances, to know how we were getting on.

"Hurrah!" cried Green—"hip—hip—hurrah!—we've nabbed him. How do you find yourself, Peter Crogson? How's your wonderful head?"

"What about your lungs—eh?" said I.

"Gracious powers! is that him?" said the chairman of the directors; "how's your liver, Mr. Crogson!"

"D—n you all!" said Crogson, and springing to his feet, he made a rush to bolt through the body of directors; but they all fell upon him at once, and the consequence was, they all fell down at once, Crogson being in the middle of them, while the officer, in the coolest manner imaginable, let them fight it out among them. Of course Peter Crogson was overpowered; but the directors were not aware that each of their faces was adorned with a great dab of soot.

It was rather disgraceful of me and Green, but we winked at the officer to be silent, and said nothing about it ourselves, so that they all marched back to the police-office, looking like so many public spirited gentlemen, who had been actively engaged in extinction of flues.

* * * * *

Little now remains to be told, but what the reader may himself anticipate; and they well know, that amplification is not one of the sins of their sincere friend, the physician.

Peter Crogson, wonderful head and all, was transported, and so was Crunch. Mrs. Crogson was, of course, acquitted, being supposed to have acted entirely under the direction of her husband. The mother-in-law, however, got two years' imprisonment; and, from that moment, I believe, the life-insurance society may date a long period of prosperity. It is still in existence, as one of the oldest and best offices in London; and I could mention its name, but upon applying to the actuary for his opinion, as to whether I should or not, he said,—

"My dear sir, don't, on any account; people will cough so dreadfully, and I shall be bored to death about Peter Crogson and his wonderful head."

THE NABOB;

OR, TAKEN IN AND DONE FOR.

ONE morning, among some letters which had been brought to me by an early post, I found the following, which produced in my mind some very mixed sensations. It was laughable enough for the oddity of its style, and, as I afterwards found, wonderfully characteristic of the individual who had written it. I give it to the reader entire, to make as much of it as I did at the outset, only premising, when I came to the name I did not laugh at all, for it was a hallowed one to me, as associated with one who my father on his death-bed commended to my warmest gratitude, if it should ever be my lot to meet him during my sojourn in this world.

The letter ran thus:—

"SIR,—Perhaps mistaken—don't know. Same name—rather ill—liver—d—d climate. If same—knew father. Turned doctor, eh? Come and see me—quite exhausted.
"ADOLPHUS CRUMPS.

"Alfred-place, Bedford-square."

Now, Adolphus Crumps has nothing very romantic in its sound, and there might be others of the same name besides he who had some forty years before rescued my father from peril and embarrassment, and placed him on the road to prosperity and wealth, if he never reached the goal of his wishes.

"Can it be possible," I asked myself, "that this is Adolphus Crumps that my father used to speak of with tears of gratitude in his eyes? Why, I should as soon have expected to receive a letter from Henry the Eighth, as from this man, who, to my imagination, has long ago gone down the stream of time, along with the things that have been."

It happened that I had a great many calls to make that morning, and I could not possibly get to Alfred-place before three o'clock, so that I was gnawed and tormented with curiosity for some hours although I was quite dying to see Adolphus Crumps, who, to my imagination, wore something of the aspect of an Egyptian mummy, or a gigantic fossil remain. I could not persuade myself that he was of earth, earthy. He seemed to have no business at all in the present generation, and his very existence seemed like the impertinence of some person who had become a subject of history, suddenly making his appearance and quarrelling with his biographers.

I carried the letter in my pocket, and repeatedly read it; in fact, so full was my imagination of the subject, that at one house I wrote a prescription commencing with, "Take Adolphus Crumps two ounces!" and did not discover my mistake till the lady for whom I had prescribed it asked me if it was not some extraordinary new medicine.

At length, however, I had the happiness of reaching the number in Alfred-place, from which the singular epistle had been dated, and upon desiring to see Mr. Crumps, and presenting my card, I was shown into a rather stylish front parlour, by a servant girl, who said,—

"I'll tell Mrs. Colonel Wheezle, sir, but Mr. Crumps isn't wisable."—"Very well," said I. "Let me see somebody, for my time is precious."

In a few moments a portly-looking dame, one of those great flabby women, which many men call fine, sailed into the room, and making the stiffest of all possible inclinations with her head, kept it then on a defensive tremble, as much as to say, "Mind what you are about here, for we are quite on the defensive."

"I am Doctor ——, madam," said I; "and I came to see Mr. Adolphus Crumps professionally."—"Well, sir!" said the lady, the tremulousness of the head increasing prodigiously.

"Well, madam, you are not Mr. Crumps, I presume, in disguise?"—"I can inform you, sir," said the lady, "that Mr. Crumps never was better in his life than he is now, nor half so well, thanks to a watchful Providence, sir, that keeps a finger on its creatures."

"But he sent for me," said I. "I have his own note."

"Send for you! he send for anybody! Oh, Betty Irons—oh, Betty Irons, you desperate baggage! This is the way I am to be treated, is it, by a flare-faced huzzy? Excuse my emotion, sir. Good morning; good morning, sir. I believe I say good morning?"—"I have no doubt about it, madam," said I; "but, really, this is most inexplicable conduct. I have been sent for expressly by letter, and now you seek to dismiss me with a good morning. I assure you, madam, that my mornings would be very bad mornings indeed, if I submitted to be treated in such a way."

"Will five shillings," said Mrs. Colonel Wheezle, making a great rustle in her capacious pocket, "will five shillings induce you to leave the house quietly?"—"I should say certainly not," replied I, with a laugh. "I have come to see Mr. Adolphus Crumps, and I am determined I will see him."

"You are determined, you whipper-snapper! Oh, if I was but a man—if the poor dear colonel was alive, or, Mr. Fothergill was here——"

At this moment one of the folding doors which led into the back parlour, opened, and a female, very nearly as tall as Mrs. Colonel Wheezle, but so awfully thin, that it appeared as if the latter lady could have spared stuff enough out of her own bulk to manufacture her, entered the room. With an air of the greatest assurance I ever witnessed, she pointed at me, and said,—

"Is this Doctor ——?"—"That is my name," said I.

"Then, sir, Mr. Adolphus Crumps, who has just gone to bed, presents his compliments, and says that he would rather not see you at present, but will write you a note when it is quite convenient."—"Ah!" said Mrs. Colonel Wheezle, "I am very glad, Miss Flack, that you have brought a message from dear Mr. Crumps: poor soul, I believe he would have been quite broken in upon if you hadn't."

"Certainly, mem—oh, dear, certainly," said Miss Flack; "you are quite right, mem."

At this moment a bell rung so violently, and with such a continuous peal, that Miss Flack ran against Mrs. Colonel Wheezle, and Mrs. Colonel Wheezle backed against the door with a bang that nearly shook its hinges. A great scuffle ensued, as if somebody was getting up stairs in a tremendous hurry, and in a few moments the parlour door was pushed open by the servant, who said,—

"Please mum, it wasn't my fault that the screen wasn't at the *hangle*, and Mr. Crumps is savage."

"Ah! what?" said I. "Is he out of bed?"—"Bed," said the servant; "he never goes to bed at all, but sleeps on a sofa, with *muscatel* curtains."

"Take that, Betty Irons," said Mrs. Colonel Wheezle, dealing her a blow between the shoulders, that was enough to take anybody's breath away. "You frightful baggage, you'll leave this house to-night. Now, sir," turning to me, "you've got your message, and there's the door."

"Madam," said I, "my interest in Mr. Adolphus Crumps is so great that I have made up my mind not to leave this house without seeing him."—"You made up your mind, you hideous puppy!" shrieked Mrs. Colonel Wheezle. "You think, on account of the timidity of my sex, that I am to be trampled on and drove about; but I'll let you know what's what!"

Another tremendous peal at the bell ensued, and darting past the extremely feminine lady, I made an effort to ascend the stairs; but Miss Flack, with a loud scream, laid hold of the tails of my great coat, while Mrs. Colonel Wheezle screamed "Police!" and "Murder!"

I was so resolved upon seeing if Mr. Crumps was really my father's old friend, that finding Miss Flack would not leave go of her hold, I slipped my arms out of my great-coat, and had the satisfaction of seeing her fall on the flat—that is to say, the edge of her back, in the passage.

I darted up stairs, then, like lightning, while such a din arose in the house as if Bedlam had broken loose. There was Mrs. Colonel Wheezle calling "Police!" there was Miss Flack shouting "Murder!" while Betty Irons, the maid-of-all-work, screamed "Fire!" with an energy that was enough to bring the parish engines to the spot; added to all this, there was Mr. Crumps' bell ringing away as if it had just found out the perpetual motion.

It did not take me many moments to reach the drawing-room, when the first object that presented itself to me was an immense sofa, covered all over with something of the size of a sheet, but made of muslin, beneath which I could dimly discern the outline of a human form, in which the vital principle seemed uncommonly active, for the tassel at the end of the bell-pull was introduced under the muslin, while the cord was agitated in a manner that betokened neither weakness nor patience on the part of him who pulled it.

"Mr. Crumps," cried I, "Mr. Adolphus Crumps, is that you?"—"You be d—d!" was the polite reply from beneath the muslin. "Nobody answers the bell here. I am neglected—oh, of course I've been neglected all my life. I may lie here and die, I suppose, while the wind screen is at an angle of fifty-two and the thermometer at sixty-three. Everybody's bent on my destruction. I ought to have known it—there's a draught."

"Mr. Crumps," said I, for I had no doubt but that this was my correspondent; "I am Doctor ———. You sent for me, and here I am, although I must confess I had some difficulty in getting at you."

A portion of muslin was removed, and I saw a strange-looking, old wrinkled face; the two deeply sunken eyes in which, shaded, as they were, by immense shaggy white eyebrows, were fixed upon me.

"You Doctor ———?" he growled; "it's a lie, sir. Yes, you are, though; you're like your father—no, you ain't—thank God for seeing you, sir—d—n you!"

The muslin was hastily drawn over the face again, and I fancied I could hear from underneath something that was either like a groan or a sob; but before I could decide which, the singularly old-looking face again appeared, and in a strained and cracked voice its owner said,—

"Well, I've seen you—I knew your father, boy. God bless him! he was a man of a thousand. D—n him, he would die, though, and leave me alone in the world, with nobody I care a curse about. Ha! what do you say to that?"

Over went the muslin again; and, I must confess, I was rather puzzled to know what to say. Still, as he evidently waited for my answer, I remarked,—

"I dare say, sir, my father would not have died if he could have helped it; but his last words were of Mr. Adolphus Crumps; and when my ear was close to his mouth to listen to the few inarticulate sounds he uttered with his latest breath, I heard a blessing murmured upon you; in another moment, sir, death claimed him. I clasped a corpse in my arms; but I never—never forgot that name which came softly upon my ear with my latest sigh."

"Go away—go away!" shrieked Mr. Crumps; "you want to kill me. I—I don't want to hear all that. Go away—go away. I—I am a d—d old fool, and you are an infernal villain, to—to come here, and ———"

I could hear him sobbing as if his heart would break beneath the screen which hid him from my observation: and as these papers may be looked upon somewhat in the light of my confession, I must own I was myself deeply affected.

I sat down on a chair for some time, and said nothing to him, for I was willing to allow the storm of feeling to subside in his own breast, as well as to recover myself, in some measure, before I said more upon the subject. I was pleased to fancy I had detected under the rough and uncouth exterior of Mr. Adolphus Crumps, a kindly heart, and just such a one as had been depicted to me by my father, and I congratulated myself not a little upon coming across his old and valued friend, and be enabled thus to fulfil his dying request, by talking of the grateful feelings that had haunted him to the last moment of his existence.

The sobs of the aged man—for aged did he appear—gradually decreased, until a deep silence reigned in the apartment. In a few moments, then, he uncovered his face again, when I could see the tears stand glistening in his eyes and on his furrowed cheeks.

"Young man," he said, "go away, now; I don't want to see you now. Why do you come here, speaking such words to me? Don't fancy I wept. I am iron—flint—my heart is a stone—I have not wept these fifty-five years—go away—go away. Some day, when I feel—feel quite able, I will send for you again—yet, stay a moment; let me look at you—turn your face to the light—that'll do—go away—go away—you're a doctor, I believe?"—"I am, sir," said I; "and, if I can be of any service to you, I pray command my utmost skill."

"Skill—stuff—rubbish; don't be foolish. Do you think I'd a-lived all these years if I had trusted myself ever to the wild guesses of physicians?—fortune telling is quite mathematical to your profession. Go away—go away; d—n you, how dare you be so like your father? Don't smile, now—don't attempt it—it's too—too like him."

"I will leave you, sir," said I, "with the most grateful feelings towards Heaven, for permitting me to see you. I can but echo my father's blessing upon your head. Farewell, sir, and let me indulge a hope that you will allow me again to see you shortly."—"Go to the devil."

As to being offended at anything Mr. Adolphus Crumps chose to say, I never dreamed of such a thing, being quite satisfied as to his character; and I was preparing, not to go to the devil, but to my carriage, which was waiting for me, when the drawing-room door opened with a bounce, enough to force it from its hinges, and in rushed Mrs. Colonel Wheezle, followed by Miss Flack and Betty Irons.

"Ah, my dear sir—my dear sir!" exclaimed Mrs. Colonel Wheezle, rushing to the sofa, and almost laying hold of it. "I could kill myself, I could, to think that in this house, above all others, you should be so dreadfully vexed; this villain trampled over us all, and would come up to you, though we tried all we could to quiet him; we've sent for a constable, and the ill-looking wretch will be taken into custody."

"Get off, woman—get off, woman," cried Mr. Crumps. "D—n it, do you want to smother me? So you tried to prevent the son of my oldest and best friend from coming to see me, you wretches? Ill-looking, indeed; I wish any of you were half as good-looking."

"Gracious powers!" cried Mrs. Colonel Wheezle; "I thought you told him to go to the—the—the devil?"—"Well, and if I did, what's that to you? I may alter my mind, I suppose? but that's the way I am always to be crossed, contradicted, fretted, and annoyed. He shall come when he likes, and go when he likes, and as often as he likes—he shall, and stay here all day and all night, too, and eat and drink dreadfully. I'll roll him in rupees if I like; d—n it, who'll dare to contradict me? Am I a fool or a beggar? Have I a will of my own, or haven't I? D—n you all; I know what the object is—it's to hurry me to the grave, of course, by contradiction."

Mrs. Colonel Wheezle burst into such a torrent of tears, that I quite jumped again, while Miss Flack and Betty Irons raised an accompanying howl, that reminded me strongly of the sounds I once heard from a puppy dog, with his tail cut off.

"Oh, what a woman I am—oh, what a woman I am," cried Mrs. Colonel Wheezle; "my poor foolish heart is always a getting me into scrapes. Says I to myself, Mr. Crumps shall not be disturbed—no—whoever dares to attempt it, shall walk over my mangled dead body; but, ah, ah, ah! wretched woman that I am; if I had but known that this dear, good-looking gentleman was the son of an old friend of yours, sir, I could have worshipped him; but I know I can never be forgiven; and I must look into my own bussum for consolation. Imprudent zeal is—is—is ———"

"As bad as malice," said Miss Flack. "I was making that Indian pie Mr. Crumps is so fond of."—"I—I," gasped Mrs. Colonel Wheezle. "I was knit—knit—knitting him a new pair of mittens; but now I am a lost woman ———"

"I was darning stockings," blubbered Betty Irons; "and I ain't a maid no longer."

They all three set up such a howl, that I was perfectly horrified.

"Well, well," cried Mr. Crumps, "there's an end of it—there's an end of it. I dare say, Mrs. Colonel Wheezle, you acted for the best; let's hear no more about it; hark ye, don't be making mistakes again, or by Juggernaut, I'll leave the house in a moment."

"Am I," screamed the lady, "can I be forgiven?"—"The deuce take you all," said Crumps. "Leave me alone."

Mrs. Colonel Wheezle, with a deep sigh, arranged what Betty Irons called the muscatel curtain, and then murmuring a blessing upon the head that lay beneath it, just sufficiently loud for him to hear, she moved towards the door, followed by her staff, in the shape of Miss Flack and Betty Irons.

"Good day, Mr. Crumps," said I; "I shall never intrude upon you, till you send for me."—"Stop!" said Crumps, and he stretched out one of his arms from beneath the muslin; "there's your fee."

I undid a crumpled bank note which he placed in my hand. It was for a hundred pounds.

"Mr. Crumps—Mr. Crumps, allow me really to protest——."—"Go away—go away—you rascal, go away. You want to contradict me, like the rest of them. Go away this moment; you'll make me ill among you."

I said no more, but walked down the staircase, full of wonder at my strange interview with my father's old friend.

* * * * *

It was not from any faith in what she should say, or any admiration of that extensive female, that induced me to follow Mrs. Colonel Wheezle into the front parlour, whither she invited me with such a hypocritical air of kindness, that it was more odious to me than her former discourtesy.

"My dear sir, be seated," she said. "Oh, if I could have but guessed for a moment—if I could have but guessed that you were the son of an old friend of Mr. Crumps! Only think, Miss Flack, if you could but have guessed it!"—"It was quite impossible, mem," said Miss Flack.

"Why, madam," said I, "even supposing that you could not guess who I was, I must say that, as a casual visitor to Mr. Crumps, I might have received a more courteous reception."

Mrs. Colonel Wheezle heaved a deep sigh, as she said,—

"I feel myself wandering in a vale, and trying to do my duty; to err is human, and—and—and——."—"To forgive divine, mem," said Miss Flack.

"Yes, yes. You must see, sir, that Mr. Crumps is a very peculiar gentleman. Our beds are equal to anybody's beds, but he won't sleep in them. There's nothing will satisfy him but that sofa with a small piece of muslin over it, to make what he calls a musquito curtain."—"We've no musquitos here," said Miss Flack. "I will say it, even before your face, as well as behind your back, that I never saw a musquito in this house."

"Mr. Crumps, then, I presume, is your lodger?"—"Certainly," said Mrs. Colonel Wheezle; "we never take in but one at a time."

"The difficulty," said Miss Flack, "of doing for more than one at once, would be too much for your constitution, mem. I will say it, sir, before Mrs. Colonel Wheezle's face, as well as behind her back, that from the moment she has a lodger, she becomes a West Indian negro till they goes again."—"A singular metamorphosis," said I; "I should keep the whole house to myself rather than undergo such a radical change."

"As regards to Mr. Crumps," continued Miss Flack, without noticing my interruption, "for the two months he has been here, Mrs. Colonel Wheezle has been a something between an angel out of Heaven, and a galley-slave with a chain round his leg."—"Yes," said Mrs. Colonel Wheezle, with a sigh, which seemed to shake the flooring; "I have been a gallows slave, as Miss Flack says, to Mr. Crumps. I do believe he's found out what's called the fidget. The more we try to make him comfortable, the more uncomfortable sometimes he is; and the worst of it is when he begins talking about his angles. We were quite a week finding out what he meant by it, and then he told us he meant the firescreen to be removed by degrees; but when we did move it by degrees, he abused us all for being so slow."

"And then, mem," said Miss Flack, "he keeps on telling us the right angle is the wrong angle, and said he must have forty-five degrees—that was the time, mem, he threw his chaney inkstand at me, when I just ventured to say what a time it would take to move anything forty-five times by degrees. Oh, he's like a iron chain!"—"And a roaring jungle in a tiger," said Mrs. Colonel Wheezle, "that he so often talks about; and yet, Miss Flack——"

"Ah! and yet!" said Miss Flack, casting up her eyes.—"And yet," added Mrs. Colonel Wheezle, with a ponderous sigh, "what a heart he's got."

"Shocking!" said Miss Flack.—"Miss Flack, I beg to say that I consider Mr. Crumps' heart heavenly."

"And so do I," said Miss Flack, with an assurance that ought to have made her fortune. "I said heavenly."—"He's like a dove brought up by hand," said Mrs. Colonel Wheezle, "when he likes."

"It ain't often," muttered Betty Irons, who was dusting the sideboard.

"He often declares that he never could be happy in any other house than this; for we really have studied all his little ways and fidfads. I believe we thoroughly understand his fidgets, Miss Flack?"—"Certainly we do, mem. I will say the angles is the only thing as has made rumpuses."

"This little explanation," said Mrs. Colonel Wheezle, casting an insinuating glance at me, "was quite due to you, sir. Mr. Crumps is quite a lone man, and very rich. Only think, sir, then, how frightfully he might be imposed upon, if we were to let everybody see him that came and asked for him; but you, sir, the son of an old friend, must be ever welcome. What would you please to take, sir? What have we in the house, Miss Flack?"—"I am afraid that elder wine isn't up," said Miss Flack; "but we've got some Cape that's beautiful."

"Thank you," said I; "I would rather not indulge in any such luxuries. I have been much gratified at the sight of my father's old friend, and am glad to hear that, with the exception of the angles, he is so very comfortable. Has he no relations who visit him?"—"Relations!" cried Mrs. Colonel Wheezle. "Gracious—no! We don't allow anybody—that is, nobody visits him at all."

Another of the formidable rings at the bell, such as I had previously heard, now startled the whole party into activity; and Mrs. Colonel Wheezle, crying "Excuse me, sir," disappeared as quickly as she could to answer it, and I took my leave.

* * * * *

I had no doubt at all in my own mind but that poor old Crumps was being dreadfully victimised by Mrs. Colonel Wheezle; but then, I thought to myself, he must live somewhere, and he is very aged, and no doubt full of whims and fancies, which, of course, he must pay for the gratification of; and, providing the victimising does not go too far, he is probably just as well in the hands of Mrs. Colonel Wheezle as anybody else.

That he must be very wealthy I felt convinced, or all the trouble would not be taken concerning him at his lodgings, nor would he have tendered me a hundred pounds note as a fee. From this I began naturally to think how strange it was that he should be in London, a lone man, abandoned to the tender mercies of the harpies of a lodging-house, when surely there must be living some persons who could claim kindred with him, and cheer his last days by sympathies and attentions, such as could be dictated alone by feeling.

It is quite a painful process to ransack one's memory for something which appears to be continually present, and yet continually flitting away. I knew that I had heard something from my father about Crumps' history; but for the life of me I could not recollect it; and, with a view of assisting my memory, if possible, I unpacked a heap of old letters of my father's, including the correspondence of other people with him, with the hope of finding something concerning the singular man who appeared to have sprung almost from the grave, to put me in mind of events and people that for a long time held but a dim place in my memory.

My search for a time was in vain; but, at length, I came across a letter addressed to my father, and bearing the signature of Adolphus Crumps. It was dated twenty-two years back, and seemed to have been written on the eve of the writer's departure for India. The paragraph that interested me was as follows:—

"And now, my dear ——, I can forgive Emily, and can pray for a blessing upon her head—a blessing which, alas! I fear she will much need. I think her the victim, poor girl! of one whom I really can never forgive. My brother, Alexander, is, as you know, very many years younger than myself, and I need not detail to you the frightful acts by which he succeeded in triumphing over the virtue of one who possessed those affections of mine, which will be now chilled for ever. I have forced him to marry her—she is his wife. God bless and pity her; but, so help me, Heaven! I never wish to look on his face again."

I read and re-read this paragraph, until I quite conjured up in my mind a little domestic history of the most romantic character, concerning the aged man who so long before had written it; but still it was of too vague a nature to found any proceedings upon, and I had seen quite enough of Mr. Crumps' character to warn me from asking any questions which might excite his irritability.

The following day I had occasion, professionally, to call

upon an East India director, and it struck me suddenly, as I was on the point of leaving—I thought it just possible he might, in some of his Indian connections, have heard of Crumps.

"Did you ever hear," said I, "of a Mr. Adolphus Crumps, who went to India some twenty or thirty years ago?"—"Heard of Adolphus Crumps? Of course I have; he's one of the wealthiest merchants in the East. He has a place in Calcutta like a palace; he is there now. My correspondents often speak of him."

"Indeed," said I; "I believe he is in London."—"Oh, impossible—impossible! We must have heard of it; he is the largest holder of Indian stock but one; we must have heard if he had come in any of the Company's ships."

"Well," said I, "I have some reason to believe that he is in London; but, as you say it is impossible, I suppose I must give in."

* * * * *

Two days elapsed, and I heard nothing of the nabob; but, on the morning of the third, there came a letter which beat the first one completely as to its laconic style, and the singular assortment of its sentences. It was this:—

"From Crumps'.—Supper. Half-past six—punctual. "Alfred place. To-day."

I, of course, made up my mind at once to accept this not very flattering invitation, and, punctually as the hour struck, I knocked at Mrs. Colonel Wheezle's door. Before it was opened, I took a survey of the front of the house, and saw that it was rather brilliant in the way of lighting, while a certain undeniable bustle, which proceeded from the lower regions, led me to think that preparations were being made of more than ordinary character for the supper.

I had to knock twice before I was admitted, and then Betty Irons uttered a faint scream when she saw me, and Mrs. Colonel Wheezle, rushing out of the parlour, uttered a much louder scream, while a man's voice shouted, "What the h—ll's that?" and a great coarse-looking fellow, with a mop of red hair, made his appearance, adding to his former polite inquiry,—"Who the devil are you?"

"Mrs. Colonel Wheezle," said I, as I deliberately hung up my hat in the passage, "I have come to see my friend, Mr. Crumps, and I shall certainly advise him to change his lodging if his visitors are received in this singular fashion." —"Gracious Heavens!" cried Mrs. Wheezle, backing into the parlour, "it's really him. I assure you, sir, Mr. Crumps is ill, and can't see anybody; if you will call to-morrow morning, at nine o'clock, I dare say it will do quite as well."

"What the deuce is all this?" said the big red-haired man. "Come, sir, whoever you are, troop. Your absence here will be good company."

"Cousin Futhergill, hush! hush!" said Mrs. Colonel Weezle; "this is the doctor I told you of; but, now that he knows that Mr. Crumps is asleep, he'll go away again. I am sure he'll be the very last man to disturb Mr. Crumps."—"I should think so, mem," said Miss Flack, poking her thin visage out of the parlour-door; "people should never be waked to take medicine."

"Why," said I, "it happens that I have come to supper, so that to-morrow morning wouldn't suit exactly."—"To supper!" cried Mrs. Colonel Wheezle. "Holy saints!"

"To supper!" shouted the man with the red head. "The devil!"—"Yes, to supper," said I; "and it appears to me that you must be having a bit of amusement, for I can actually scent the preparations for a most savoury meal. I have a written invitation from Mr. Crumps."

"Gracious heavens!" cried Mrs. Colonel Wheezle, "how does he send the letters out of the house?"

The bell began ringing at this moment in its usual violent style, and as it showed no disposition to leave off, I turned to the staircase, saying,—

"I know Mr. Crumps' room, and will not trouble anybody to announce me."—"D—n it, sir," cried the red-haired man, "do you fancy we are to be taken by storm this way, you infernal legacy hunter. Come down, sir, or I'll make you."

"You can try," said I, and I walked up stairs to Mr. Crumps' room, the bell still pulling all the while until I said, "How do you do, sir?" and then it ceased.

He was on the sofa as before with the gauze-work all over him, and he growled out as he stretched his hand, in which was a watch, from underneath the muslin,—

"Three minutes over time, that won't do, sir. You ought to know better."—"I do not think," said I, "that three minutes over the time is of any consequence, but the fact is I was detained down stairs for full that period."

"Three minutes of no consequence!" cried Mr. Crumps. "D—n it, sir, three moments are of consequence. Good God! haven't these people got the supper ready? there's nothing but vexation and contradiction. Just place that wind screen, which they will insist upon calling a fire screen, d—n them—at an angle of forty-five degrees from the wall."

I saw one of the deep set eyes watching me from beneath the shaggy brow as I performed the operation by guessing the angle as accurately as I could, and I suppose I did it tolerably well, for Mr. Crumps gave a grunt of satisfaction, and then added,—

"Well, sir, don't begin anything about your father. What's it to me when, where, and how he died, or what he said? Don't go fancying that I care about anybody, or ever did, or ever will. I have no feeling, sir, never had any; I hate everybody and everybody hates me—thank God."

"I should be very sorry to take you at your word, Mr. Crumps," said I, "for I feel convinced that you have a heart which ——"—"D—n it, sir, do you mean to insult me? I have no heart at all. I always used to quarrel with your father, God bless him—confound him,—on that same subject."

"As for my father, sir ——"—"Hush! hush! hush!— there now, that'll do, I know what you are going to say. Some infernal trash about his dying, and what he said, and what he didn't say. I don't want to hear it. What business had he to die at all? It's a d—d insult, and I resent it accordingly. I ain't dead. Mrs. Colonel Wheezle's a fine woman. Where the devil's the supper?"

I could perceive, from my first entrance into the room, considerable festive preparations had been made. The chandelier was lighted as well as the candelabra on the mantel-shelf, and the room altogether wore a handsome and ornamental appearance. Still I was considerably puzzled at all this being done, at the same time I had received such a very curious reception in the lower part of the house, and before anything further was said I was resolved to seek an explanation of the mystery.

"Mr. Crumps," I said, "of course I am here in accordance with your invitation, but the twice now that I have done myself the pleasure of calling upon you, I have received so very equivocal a reception from the persons with whom you live, that it has been only by force that I have been enabled to reach your apartment."

"Ah!" he said, "zeal! zeal! I expected as much; they know that I don't like to be annoyed, and of course they do all they can to keep visitors away from me. I wouldn't be found out here for a thousand pounds; they didn't know you were coming, and of course obstructed you. Never mind it. We've got a little supper party, and I allowed Mrs. Colonel Wheezle to arrange all the particulars. I believe she has invited one—some relation of her's."

"There certainly is," said I, "a man down stairs, who I cannot compliment by calling a gentleman."

Before Mr. Crumps could reply, Mrs. Colonel Wheezle entered the room.

"Oh, my dear Mr. Crumps, who could have supposed you were going to do us the favour of inviting your friend, the doctor. It took us quite by surprise, and we scarcely knew what we said to him. I believe my Cousin Futhergill was scarcely civil, under the impression that somebody was coming to interrupt you."

"Who the devil's Furthergill?" cried Crumps.—"Why, my dear Mr. Crumps, don't you recollect I mentioned to you my cousin, the young barrister? You must recollect him; he is dying to pay his respects to you."

"Well, well, Mrs. Wheezle, let him come—well, well. Hark ye, doctor, I have received from strangers more kindness and sympathy than I ever had common justice from my own relations. My own brother—but never mind about that. Mrs. Wheezle, is the supper ready?"—"Yes, my dear sir," said Mrs. Wheezle, "we've had it laid in the back drawing-room, and the Indian pickles are just placed as you desired. Oh! sir, what a pleasure it is to me, a pleasure that almost brings tears into my eyes, to fancy that you are going to enjoy yourself a little."

"Poh! poh! nonsense, I ain't a going to enjoy myself at all; I never enjoyed myself, and never shall—but come along, doctor. Now for the supper."

When he arose, which he did from the couch with apparent difficulty, I was really shocked to see the attenuated piece of mortality that he really appeared—his long white hair hung far down upon his neck, and his shaggy eye-brows actually came over to nearly his cheeks. I offered my arm, which he accepted, and we proceeded together to the back drawing-room, where a very handsome supper was certainly laid, and into which apartment there came in a moment or two, with the greatest assurance imaginable, the coarse-looking man with the red head, who had treated me so rudely in the passage.

"Mr. Crumps," said Mrs. Colonel Wheezle, "this is my Cousin Futhergill; he thinks very much of the honour of being introduced to you."

Old Mr. Crumps glanced for a moment at him from under his shaggy brows, and then muttered,—"Ill-looking thief!" which, however, Cousin Futhergill took no further notice of than by a low bow, as if some pleasant compliment had been paid to him, and then turning to me he said,—

"Upon my soul, sir, I couldn't tell who you were down stairs—I didn't know any he creature was to be here but myself. I was quite wrong, sir, and when a gentleman says that, it's all right."—" I decline the honour of your acquaintance, sir," said I, coldly and stiffly.

I heard him mutter a curse as I handed Mr. Crumps to a seat, and placed myself by his side, much mortified in my

own mind to find that he had allowed himself to be cajoled into allowing his landlady and her connexions to sit down with us at supper, during which I had hoped, never dreaming but we should be alone, to lead him to some conversation about his earlier days.

My first impulse was to leave the house, for I really shrunk from sitting down with the strange set that were there, but I did not like to leave the old man completely at their mercy; and as a feeling had begun to come over me that there was something more in the whole transaction than exactly met the eye, for the sake, then, of my father's old friend, I conquered for a time my feelings, and sat down at the same table with Mrs. Colonel Wheezle and her hateful Cousin Futhergill, who I had as much belief to be a rising young barrister as that I was the Pacha of Egypt.

Of course I had a much better opportunity of observation as regarded the appearance of Mr. Crumps now that he was up than when he lay upon the sofa, covered with what Betty Irons called the muscatel curtains, and I felt confident that he could not be long a denizen of this world. His weakness and general meagreness of appearance were perfectly remarkable; he looked like some animated mummy, whose skin and flesh, having been shrivelled up by the process of embalming, could not again recover, but preserved just sufficient vitality not to fall into decomposition. His hands were like the long claws of a bird, and, take him altogether, his appearance was rather awful, as he sat looking like a dead man among the living.

He ate of nothing save some tremendous strong pickles, which I was astonished to see him swallow with apparent ease, while a very small portion of them nearly choked me.

But little conversation took place at the supper table, although there was an attempted forced hilarity on the part of Cousin Futhergill, which soon subsided. Mrs. Colonel Wheezle was extremely fidgetty, and she and Miss Flack frequently exchanged glances of a character which led me to think that something was wrong, or some scheme had been deranged by my presence.

"They will surely," thought I, "leave me and Mr. Crumps alone after supper, and then at all hazards I will tell him my opinion of these people, who, it appears to me, are intent upon some scheme of peculation with regard to him."

This thought had scarcely passed through my mind when, with a deep sigh, the old man fell upon my shoulder, and for the moment, so corpse-like did he look, that I really thought he was dead.

"Mr. Crumps is ill," I cried, as I raised him upon one arm. "Open that door—the air of this room is too confined for him."

"D——n!" said Cousin Futhergill, "he ain't dead, is he?" — "Gracious Heavens!" said Mrs. Colonel Wheezle. "He must be put into a warm bed directly. This is the second time he's gone off in this way."

I quickly saw that he had but fainted, and pushing aside Mrs. Colonel Wheezle, I carried him into the front room, and laid him upon his sofa.

"Bring me some water," I said, "and some wine."

"The Cape or the elder?" said Miss Flack.—"Neither," said I, throwing down half a sovereign. "Get a bottle of good old port immediately; he is suffering as much from exhaustion as any other cause."

"Ah!" said Cousin Futhergill, thrusting his hands into his pockets, "he's an odd fish, I hear, and lives principally upon red-hot pickles. D—n me, I say, doctor, between you and I, he'll cut up famous. Come, now, let's understand each other. The old gentleman can't live long, and don't you think he ought to make a will? The colonel has taken care of herself."

"For God's sake!" said Mrs. Colonel Wheezle, "what are you about, Futhergill?" — "Well, well, well," cried Futhergill, "mum's the word, then,—only what's safe's safe—leave me alone for that. You know what you're about as well as most people."

"It appears to me," said I, "that Cousin Futhergill is making some indiscreet revelations. Now, I warn the whole of you that any extortion upon this weak old man will be resisted by me and many friends that I can bring around him."

With a deep groan Mr. Adolphus Crumps opened his eyes.

"Emily, Emily," he said, "where are you? What a long, long dream. My Emily, come nearer to me. Heaven must be very like your eyes. Speak to me, darling. Have I been ill or sleeping?"—"Mad as a March hare," said Cousin Futhergill.

"He means me — he means me," said Mrs. Colonel Wheezle.—"Of course he does, mem," said Miss Flack. "Your maiden name was Emily, you know, before the colonel led you to the hymeneal altar."

"Heaven bless you—Heaven bless you!" murmured Mr. Crumps. "Heaven bless you, dear, with your sweet innocent face, and beware of Alexander."—"There, mem," said Miss Flack,—"there again,—there's an allusion to your face, mem."

"Silence, silence!" cried I, "all of you; this gentleman is in a most dangerous condition. Speaking professionally, I would not answer for his life one hour from another. He must be got to bed now at once, and whatever intrigues you may have had in your mind of which he was to be the victim, cease now to attempt their execution; you will be but battling with death, which must soon put an end to his career."—"Then, if that's the case," cried Mrs. Colonel Wheezle, "I claim the care of him; he has promised me marriage, and I shall allow no one to come between me and him."

"Marriage!" cried I. "Could you, with reference to a man of his years and infirmities, dream of such a thing? Your whole scheme is now apparent; among you all you have been trying to entrap this old man into an alliance, which, of course, would give you a claim upon some portion of his fortune. I feel convinced, too, now, that you intended this night to bring your intrigues to some desperate climax. Thank Heaven, I am here to defeat you, and I warn you that any act of Mr. Crumps's, in his present state of mind, shall be disputed in a court of law, and never can hold good."

"Ha! ha! ha!" laughed Cousin Futhergill, as he threw himself into an easy chair, "very fine—very fine, doctor—all very fine, but you are just a little too late. Mrs. Colonel Wheezle has a written promise of marriage from the old gentleman, so that if he lives she can get damages of a most exemplary character. She has, likewise, a bond of twenty thousand pounds from him, payable within twelve months, if during that time he does not make her his wife. What do you say to that, doctor? I think we have got you and your old friend in a fix at last."

"Mr. Crumps, Mr. Crumps," cried I, "do you hear all that? Contradict it, for Heaven's sake; there may be some yet with kindred blood to your own in their veins, who may be made happy with a tithe of the sum these harpies say you have wasted upon them."—"All for Emily—all for Emily," murmured the old man. "God knows, it's all for Emily."

"There, mem—there, mem," chimed in Miss Flack; "the old gentleman keeps on leaving you his property perpetual."—"All this is absurd," said I, "quite absurd. You will find Mr. Crumps has connexions who will dispute every inch of ground with you."

"Let them dispute it," said Cousin Futhergill, "we will stick to our bond. Ha! ha! ha! doctor, you are too late."

"I shall now," said I, "leave Mr. Crumps in this house, while I find out some of his connexions. Upon your own heads be it if you neglect him. As his physician, I order him to be put into a warm bed, and to be given every half hour, until I see him again, a piece of crust of bread soaked in about a tea-spoonful of warm port wine. You all of you hear this,—neglect it at your peril. As for your bonds, and your written promises, they're not worth a rush, for they have either been procured by intimidation, or at some period of bodily indisposition of Mr. Crumps, when he was in an unfit state to take care of himself or his property."

With this I hurried down the staircase, and leaving the house, I precipitately threw myself into a hackney-coach, for not knowing what time I should leave Alfred-place, I had determined upon not using my own carriage. I ordered the coachman to drive me to the address of the East India director, to whom I had already spoken, although but indefinitely, concerning Mr. Crumps.

Upon reaching his house I luckily found him at home, and apologizing for the intrusion, as I had really but a very slight acquaintance with him, I related to him, as briefly and succinctly as I could, the whole of the circumstances, concluding by begging of him to assist me in rescuing the old man from the clutches of those who were evidently bent upon victimizing him to any extent that lay in their power.

"You astonish me," said the East India director, "I really thought you must be mistaken when you some time since told me that Mr. Crumps was in town, but this, of course, places it beyond a doubt. What on earth can have possessed him not to have made himself known to those who would gladly have received him in this country, and made him welcome to their houses, instead of suffering him to fall into such hands as he has?"

"Of his motives," said I, "I can be no judge: he seems a most singular character, and to do everything by contraries. Whether or not he has friends in this country I cannot say, although I should think it probable that such must be the case; but, at all events, it is a miserable thing that he should be victimized by Mrs. Colonel Wheezle and her audacious cousin, Futhergill."

"Oh, we won't despair of putting all that to rights, doctor. I am astonished we never heard at the India House of his arrival: so large a holder of stock is quite an important personage with us. I'll tell you what, doctor, we'll do; I'll go back with you at once to Alfred-place, and on the way we'll call upon my solicitor, and take him with us, when, should he be in a fit state to be removed, I think we ought to insist upon carrying him off, whether they like it or not, leaving them to take what legal remedies they think fit in the case of the bond and their promise of marriage, if they really have such."

"I am glad that you made such a suggestion," said I, "although I almost doubt if Mr. Crumps will be able to bear a removal."—"If he should not it will be very unfortunate; but let us not anticipate evil, but come along at once."

We accordingly started in Mr. Seagrove's carriage, that being the name of the director, first of all to Upper Bedford-place, where his solicitor resided, and taking him with us we proceeded to Alfred-place as quickly as possible, to the rescue of poor Mr. Adolphus Crumps from the designing persons into whose hands he had unhappily fallen.

"This written promise of marriage," said the attorney, "is scarcely to my mind, under all the circumstances, so awkward a thing as the bond, for it appears to me that a bond might be so drawn as to be available against the assets of the party should he die within the twelve months, because, of course, if he's dead he can't marry the woman."—"I cannot for one moment," said I, "believe such documents are in existence; and I hope to Heaven poor Mr. Crumps may be sane enough to give us some information upon the subject."

The distance was so short that we had very little time for consultation before we reached Alfred-place; but a new difficulty presented itself when we did get there. When we knocked the parlour window was opened, and Cousin Futhergill looked out, saying,—

"Who's there—whose there?"—"Open the door immediately," said I. "I have come again to see Mr. Crumps."

"See you d—d first," said Cousin Futhergill, as he closed the window with a slam.

We looked at each other very ruefully at this, for it seemed to be a state of things which we had no possible means of altering.

"What's to be done now?" said the attorney.—"Oh, let's go on knocking," said the East India director; "and if they won't let us in we'll break open the door."

"Fair and softly," said the attorney, "with a due submission to you. If we go on knocking at the door we make ourselves amenable to the law for creating a disturbance; and as for breaking it open, that's a very serious matter indeed, and one which I must really back out of. As a professional man, it would be indecorous to break open people's doors."—"And besides," said I, "any serious alarm might really produce the immediate death of poor old Mr. Crumps."

"Bless my heart, what are we to do?" said the East India director.—"Why," said the attorney, "if I were to give my candid opinion, I should say, to the best of my knowledge and belief, nothing."

Again the parlour window opened, and Cousin Futhergill's face appeared.

"Come, come," he said, "ain't you gone yet? We can't have improper characters loitering about Alfred-place. I shall certainly give you all into custody on suspicion of loitering about for felonious purposes if you don't be off at once."—"We are friends of Mr. Crumps'," said Mr. Seagrove, "and surely we cannot be denied admittance to him, especially in his state of health."

"You may go the devil," said Cousin Futhergill. "Mr. Crumps sends his compliments by me, and says he's rather better; and as to his having any friends, it's all moonshine."—"I am afraid you are a very great rogue," said the director.

"There, there," said the attorney, "that'll do; mind you don't say anything actionable. It's quite legal to suspect a man of being a rogue generally, but if you impute any particular roguery to him, that's actionable."

"Very good," said the director, "then I consider that fellow a scoundrel in the most general sense I can possibly use the word."

"Pray what is all this?" cried Mrs. Colonel Wheezle, appearing at the window. "Watch—police—officers—streetkeeper! take these drunken men into custody!"—"Mrs. Colonel Wheezle," cried I, "mind what you are about. I shall hold you and that red-headed rascal by your side responsible for whatever occurs to my father's old friend."

"Go home and make up some of your nasty physic," said Miss Flack.—"Rhubarb and magnesia," said Mrs. Colonel Wheezle. "Fooh! I hate the sight of him."

"Come away—come away," said the attorney; "an altercation is of no use here. They need not let us in unless they like: and it appears to me, gentlemen, that however we may wish to interfere in this transaction, it is quite out of our power"

"L n it," said the East India director, "it's very provoking. Do you mean to tell me that a man of property is to be boxed up in Alfred-place to be made a complete victim of, and that none of his friends can interfere?"—"I believe that's the law," said the attorney, "unless some one can make an affidavit that he be so imprisoned without his consent, in which case a writ of habeas corpus can be had, and he must be produced; and even then there would be difficulties, unless some one was produced who was next of kin to the party, and who could show an interest in the transaction."

We all three looked at each other with the most posed air imaginable, and the East India director was about to say something, when the street-door opened, and a bandbox was thrown out into the middle of the road, after which was projected Betty Irons, the maid-of-all-work, and bang went the door again, shut before either of us could recover from our surprise.

"Murder! murder!" shrieked Better Irons; "here's usage. Murder! thieves! I declare I didn't—I never saw such a thing. Missus's temper's enough to make small beer into winiger. I take his letter!—I never dreamed of it."

"There's a feud in the enemy's camp," said the director. "Now we shall get at something."—"Then let me go and speak to her," said I; "for, having seen me before, she's more likely to have confidence in me."

We slunk up to the railing of the next house, and allowed Betty Irons to expend her wrath upon Mrs. Colonel Wheezle's windows in the shape of two handfuls of mud, before saying anything to her, and then, when she had picked up her bandbox, and got about half way down the street, I followed her closely, and just touching her on the shoulder, I said,—

"So, Betty Irons, they've turned you out, have they?—what was that for?"—"Oh, gracious!" cried Betty, with a start, "what a turn you gave me; my blood's quite curds and whey."

"It's a very shameful thing," said I, "that a handsome girl like you should ever have been under such a mistress as Mrs. Colonel Wheezle."—"Lor, sir!" said Betty.

"Really," added I, "when first I visited Alfred-place I mistook you for the lady of the house; upon my candour, I did."—"'Evenly powers!" said Betty, "if ever there was a poor crucified martyr, I'm her; and if ever there was female dragons with fiery tales, missus is one."

"Ah!" said I, "Mrs. Colonel Wheezle certainly appears to be a very violent woman. But how came you to be turned out in so unceremonious a manner, Betty?"—"Why, sir, missus wrongfully accuses me of not behaving rightfully. Now, sir, a missus is a missus; and I always says if so be as one has a missus, one ought to do what's rightful."

"Exactly so, Betty."—"Good agin, sir. Well, missus accuses me of putting letters for old Crumps in the post, which are what brought you to supper. Now I declare solemn I didn't."

"But that seems a strange reason," said I, "for turning a servant away. It appears to me so natural a thing that a lodger may, if he likes, have a letter put in the post."—"Exactly," said Betty Irons; "but natur ain't natur exactly in Alfred-place; leastways, it ain't been since I've been maid-of-all-work there; and of all the odd missusses as is tigers afloat that ever I seed or comed near, Missus Colonel Wheezle is most worstest. She's a complete iron chain, sir, with a hextra rivet."

"Oh, indeed!—then I suppose, Betty, you are not at all sorry you have left her service?"—"Far from it, sir. It wasn't a agreeable service for no gal to be in, by no means."

"Well, Betty," said I, "I know a great many families, and it strikes me, if you are inclined to do the rightful thing as regards the old gentleman that lives in Mrs. Colonel Wheezle's house, I can get you a better situation than the one you have lost."

"Ah! poor old soul!" said Betty Irons; "he's a horrid old wretch, and yet I pities him. Missus has kept a pretty eye on him ever since he came to the house. He'll be a wictim, as sure as eggs is eggs; and in one way he deserves it, going on as he did about his angels. I told him, when he first spoke to me about such things, that I wasn't going to hear nothing improper from no single gentleman, whether he was old or young. Lor bless you, sir, missus has made up her mind to be Mrs. Crumps, and Mrs. Crumps she'll be, or else my name ain't Betty Irons."

I had no sort of doubt, along with Betty Irons, that Mrs. Colonel Wheezle had fully made up her mind to be Mrs. Crumps, and that she would not stop at a trifle in the accomplishment of that mental aspiration; but still I thought it a great point to find there was a division in the camp of the enemy, and that Betty Irons, feeling herself prodigiously aggrieved by the wrongful manner in which she had been treated, would prove of great assistance to us in spoiling the schemes of Mrs. Colonel Wheezle.

"Betty," said I, "let us fairly understand each other. Of course Mrs. Colonel Wheezle only wishes to marry the poor old man for his money, and then she would get him as quickly under ground as possible. Now, Betty, Mr. Crumps is very rich, and there can be very little doubt that somebody will be found belonging to him in London, who would make a much better use of his money than Mrs. Colonel Wheezle; now, if you will assist in every way you can to prevent the old man from being so imposed upon, you may depend upon being handsomely treated yourself, and something being done permanently to your advantage."

"Lor, sir," said Betty, "don't mention advantages. I am sure I don't want missus to marry the poor old cretur; it's quite wice in my mind; and if so be as she can be perwented I don't mind what I does."—"Very well, Betty. Then there are two gentlemen with me, those you see just a little behind, who will likewise promise you ample reward for assisting in the rescue of poor old Mr. Crumps."

I then beckoned to the attorney and Mr. Seagrove to come up, and we made quite a solemn compact with Betty that the next morning she was to go to the house for some things that were still there belonging to her, and take an opportunity of giving a note to Mr. Crumps, who, she informed us, was better, and had refused to go to bed, she having left him on the sofa with the muscatel curtain over him.

I was to write the letter, in which I intended to make a full *expose* of the designs of Mrs. Colonel Wheezle, begging him to defeat them by insisting upon leaving the house, and if any obstruction was placed in his way, to open the first floor window at twelve o'clock in the morning and show himself, when efficient assistance would be rendered him, or if he could not accomplish that, to throw some article at the window which would break a pane, and serve as a signal to me that he required help.

I then proposed to the attorney and director, that if Mr. Crumps should act in reply to the letter as I suggested, Betty Irons should be sent to obtain admittance, on pretence of having something of importance to say to Mrs. Colonel Wheezle, and when the door was opened we should make a rush and get into the house.

It was with great reluctance that the attorney consented to this arrangement, and he started a variety of legal doubts as to its propriety, anticipating actions against us all for trespass; but we overruled his objections, and having settled that point completely, the next I proposed for serious attention was to discover if Mr. Crumps had really any family connexions still in existence.

"An advertisement," said the attorney, "in one of the morning papers, would, probably, be the most direct means of ascertaining that fact, unless you think that would be giving too great a publicity to the whole affair, especially acting, as we really are, without the slightest authority from the principal person concerned."

"I am more likely," said I, "than either of you to obtain some clue to Mr. Crumps' relations, and I will endeavour to give sufficient time to-morrow to that subject."

Then, with the additional understanding that if Mr. Crumps was rescued on the succeeding day from Alfred-place he was to be taken to the director's house, until he made some determination about his own disposal, we separated, considering that, however slight it was, we certainly had made some progress towards rescuing the old man from the machinations of those by whom he was surrounded.

* * * * * *

It had occurred to me, as a piece of recollection, that my father had during his lifetime frequently mentioned Adolphus Crumps as being his near neighbour; and as of course I was well aware of the locality of the house in which my early life had been passed, I thought it possible, by making inquiries in that neighbourhood, I might get some clue as to what had become of Alexander Crumps, the brother, and Emily his wife, who appeared by the letter which was addressed to my father to have been an early love of the old man in whose fate I felt myself so much interested.

I accordingly rose at an early hour, for I felt that I had probably a very heavy day's work before me, and swallowing a hasty breakfast, I was upon the point of sallying forth, when a note was placed in my hands by my landlady, which I found to come from the East India director, conveying to me intelligence which he thought more of probably than I did.

The letter ran thus :—

"DEAR SIR,—By advices from India I have just learned something of an interesting nature concerning Mr. Adolphus Crumps. It appears that about two years ago, contrary to all his usual careful mercantile habits, he entered into a wild kind of speculation for conducting water by aqueducts and other means from Futtygunpore to Broomamundura, passing through quite a hostile district in India, and over a tremendous country. As might naturally be expected this project proved an utter failure, after Mr. Crumps had expended the bulk of his fortune upon it.

"It appears that he has sold his stock in the company, so that he is no longer what we call belonging to us. I am further informed that upon the failure of his project he took it very much to heart, sold off his splendid residence at Calcutta, and all his personal property, which must have realized, by-the-bye, something not far short of thirty thousand pounds—and then disappeared nobody knew where.

"Of course he must have come to England under an assumed name in one of the company's ships, and is now, although a rich man, certainly nothing equal to what he once was. "I am, dear sir,
"Yours, very truly,
"P. F. SEAGROVE.

"P. S. Mrs. Colonel Wheezle's bond, if enforced, would probably leave poor old Crumps in a sad condition."

"D—n Mrs. Colonel Wheezle's bond!" said I, as I thrust the letter into my pocket. "Is the remnant of a magnificent fortune to be wrenched from its possessor and legitimate usages by such an unprincipled woman as the lodging-house keeper, who has got the poor old man in her possession? No; something must and shall be done to stop her career. It would be better if he had spent it all in attempting to bring the water from what's the name of the place to Futtycum something."

In not the very best of humours, I hastened towards the street, in a house in which I had passed two-and-twenty years of my early life, and although I knew not where the Crumpses had lived, yet I trusted to find still in the neighbourhood some families who had been there during my father's lifetime, and who I knew might be able to give me every information I wanted.

Two doors from what had been my father's house I was gratified by seeing a well-worn brass plate, with the name of Williams upon it, as one familiar to my boyish days. To knock at the door was the work of a moment, but upon asking for Mr. Williams the servant gave a dead stare at me, and shaking her head, she said,—

"There's never a Mr. Williams here, sir; this is Mrs. Williams's."—"Then I wish to see Mrs. Williams," said I.

"What is that?" said an old lady, just appearing at the door of the parlour.

I knew her in a moment as a civil neighbour of my father's, with whom we had been on agreeable, if not intimate terms, for many years.

"Mrs. Williams," said I, "don't you recollect me? My name is ——."—"Bless me," she said, "are you Master ——? Well, who would have thought it? Come in; you are getting quite a great boy."

"Yes," said I, "I am Master ——; don't you think I am grown? But I have called upon you, Mrs. Williams, to know if you have heard anything of a family of the name of Crumps?"

"My dear, do you mean the Crumpses of No. 12, in the square?"—"Well, I shouldn't wonder," said I, "if I do."

"Will you take a slice of bread and butter," said Mrs. Williams, "and a glass of ginger wine? I never like giving young people anything stronger."—"No, thank you," said I; "I merely came to inquire about the Crumpses, and must be off again directly."

"Why, I am very sorry," said Mrs. Williams, "that I don't know anything about Mr. Adolphus Crumps, for, when Emily Grandison wouldn't have him, he went away to the Sandwich Islands, in the middle of Africa, and it's rather believed in the neighbourhood, that he's been eat up by a laughing hyena, or some other foreign bird."

"Oh, indeed," said I; "but hadn't he a brother Alexander?"—"Yes, he had, my dear; and it was Alexander who married Emily Grandison. But they didn't live very happy, for he took to making ducks and drakes."

"Bless my heart, a very singular occupation."—"Of his money, I mean; and, finally, he died, leaving poor Emily, with a small child, to have a great wrestle."

"A great wrestle, Mrs. Williams?"—"With the world, my dear; and so you'll find it one day, when you come on your own bottom. Children don't know what life is. It appears to me only yesterday when you were in frocks and trousers."

"But what became of Emily and her child?" inquired I, anxiously.—"Why, my dear, she had to struggle against a great deal, and at last there was a shocking seizure."

"Some disease?" said I.—"No; of her goods. We did all we could for her in the way of a subscription, but Emily was too proud-spirited, and left the neighbourhood quite abruptly; since which nothing has been heard of her—not so much as a sentence—a half word—no, nothing ——"

"Indeed!" said I. "I am sorry to hear it."—"Till two years ago," said Mrs. Williams, who certainly was about the most tantalizing teller of a story I ever met with. "Then

It appears, my dear, that she was passed — shockingly passed ——"

"Past what, Mrs. Williams?" said I. "Good God! pray tell me at once what she was past."—"To her own parish—that's this one—from somewhere ever so far in the country."

"And the child?"—"Ah! the poor child; it was dead ——"

"Dead, Mrs. Williams!"—"Nearly, with want; but it soon got better."

"But how could it have been a child, Mrs. Williams, when a number of years must have elapsed?"—"Why, you're but a boy yourself," said Mrs. Williams; "don't be presumptuous. Well, Emily herself did die, and was buried by the parish, poor thing, and the infant was in the most horrid manner put out ——"

"Then what became of it?"—"To service; and there she is now, for all I know."

"For so much information, Mrs. Williams, I am much obliged to you," said I; "and now I must bid you good morning, with many thanks."—"Good morning, my dear. Mind the crossings, and don't be playing with any rude boys on the road."

* * * * *

I went direct to the parish workhouse, and made inquiry concerning Emily Crumps and her daughter. I received a brief answer after a sort of ledger had been consulted, to the effect that Emily Crumps was dead, and her daughter had been sent to service with Mrs. Jepson, at No. 15, Arlington-street. I now considered that I had got a fair clue, and I felt exceedingly anxious to find out this orphan girl, in order that she might see her uncle before he died, and perhaps awaken his tenderest sympathies in her favour.

Arlington-street was a cold, comfortless-looking place, the houses evincing that regular aspect which proclaimed, "We have been built by contract, and we have no secrets," for any stranger might stand in the road and point out where the occupants must eat, and sleep, and drink.

My knock at the door was answered by a little shrewish-looking woman, who looked into my face with a "Well, what now?" kind of air, as if she were upon the defensive against all visitors.

"I want," said I, "Miss Emily Crumps."

"Miss who?" said the woman, with a half shriek.—"Emily Crumps," I repeated.

"Sir," she said, "my name is Miss Flowerdale, and I don't allow my servant to be called miss, or to have followers."—"Very likely, ma'am," said I; "but still I must see her; for although by unfortunate circumstances she may be your servant, it does not always follow that she is to be in adversity."

From the head of the kitchen stairs, which was visible from the passage, there came forward, attired in the most humble garments, a young girl, with whose beauty and innocence of appearance I was greatly struck. There was an expression of care upon the face, and an utter absence of that joyous look which should light the spring-tide of existence; but still misfortune could not alter the exquisite proportions of the features, nor take wholly from the deep blue eye its lustrous beauty.

"Did any one," she said, in a soft, silvery voice, while I could see her lips tremble with agitation,—"did any one really ask for me? I thought in the wide world there was no one—not one, who could mention my name with a kindly tone, and I have been wishing, much wishing, to die."

"I asked for you, Emily," said I; "and it was necessary that I should see you, in order to satisfy myself of your existence. Your father's elder brother is still alive, and my object in seeking you was to be able to ascertain with truth that you lived, and ultimately to bring you together, if possible. Wait now with patience, Emily, till I call again, and please yourself with a hope that better times are in store for you. In the meantime, Miss Flowerdale, I hope that Emily's rich friends —for rich they are—will find that you treat her with kindness."

Miss Flowerdale's eyes opened to the size of penny pieces, and Emily, whose spirits seemed in a sad state of depression, burst into tears.

It was quite useless for me to linger longer in Arlington-street, for I had said to the full as much as I was warranted in saying—perhaps more; besides, I had Betty Irons to see, in order to give her the letter to Mr. Crumps, so I at once walked away, very well pleased with my morning's work, and satisfied that when I should have an opportunity of again seeing Mr. Adolphus Crumps, I had a subject upon which to address him that I hoped would awaken the tenderness of his nature, of which I had by no means a bad opinion, from the manner in which he had received the account of my father's death, and of the last kind words he had spoken of him.

Betty Irons was waiting for me when I reached home, and I hastily added, as a postscript to my letter, that I had something to say of Emily Grandison which I was sure would deeply interest him. It was then half-past ten o'clock, and feeling that no time was to be lost, I hurried off to Mr. Seagrove's, and in his carriage we went direct to the attorney's, so that a good bit before the appointed hour of twelve we were all ready for action, and waiting eagerly the result of the letter that Betty Irons declared she would take care to place in the hands of Mr. Adolphus Crumps.

We had quite the job over again to overrule the attorney's objections to the legality of the act of forcing our way into the house in the manner we projected.

Of course we took care to go down Alfred-place as quietly as possible, meeting Betty Irons by appointment some eight or ten doors from Mrs. Colonel Wheezle's.

"Well, Betty," said I, "did you give Mr. Crumps the letter?"

"Yes, sir, I did. You must know, sir, as my best gingham was in the attic, and I wasn't going to leave that for any missus—not I; and as Miss Flack was a great deal too upper crust to bring it down herself, why, I was forced, in a way of speaking, to do so, and as I was a coming down with it I went quite a bounce into the drawing-room, and lifting up the muscatel curtain, I places one corner of the letter in his werry mouth."

"And what did he say, Betty?"

"Oh, he began swearing so dreadful that I left the room like a shot. I brought my gingham with me, but I took care to leave my pattens in the kitchen, all for an excuse to go agen; so you see, sir, if that ain't management, I doesn't know what is."

"Well done, Betty," said I. "Now wait here, all of you, and I'll give some boy a penny to walk on the other side of the way at twelve o'clock, to see if Mr. Crumps gives any signal for us to attack the house."

This was easier said than done, however, for although boys are in great abundance when not wanted, yet if one is required for any purpose, they seem all suddenly to have evaporated. It wanted five minutes to twelve, and there was no one to be seen who could perform the service we wanted. As for one of ourselves going, it would have awakened suspicion at once, and place Cousin Futhergill and Mrs. Wheezle upon their guard against the insidious attack we designed making.

Twelve o'clock struck, and affairs were getting desperate, when a low-looking man came sauntering by. A moleskin waistcoat, a fur cap, and a curious sort of belt round him proclaimed his profession to be that of a rat-catcher; and by various singular motions of a bag which he carried in his hand, there could be no doubt but that he was carrying home some of his lost captives.

"That man 'll do it for sixpence," said the director. "Just ask him to pass on the other side of the way, and come back and tell us if there is a window open or broken."

"Hi! hi!" said I; and the rat-catcher turned his head, evidently with the notion that he was being chaffed, and said,—

"Ax my sanguinary viskers. How comes you barber's clerks out so soon of a morning? You're nice 'uns, you are. How's your warious mothers?"

"My good fellow," said I, "we have no desire to insult you; on the contrary, we wish to know if you would earn sixpence, by walking on the other side of the way, and looking at No. 94, to see if there's a window open or broken in the drawing-room."

"Go it, my tulips," said the rat-catcher. "When was you born?"

"He won't believe a word we say," said the attorney. "What a witness that man would make."

"He'll believe that," said I, as I threw him the sixpence, which he immediately took up, and after biting with his teeth, to prove that it was genuine, he gave a knowing nod with his head, and said,—

"All's right, governor. I'll do it."

He then crossed the road, and performed his office very admirably, for he didn't at all appear to be looking at No. 94, but came back in a few moments to tell us of our disappointment.

"Everything is stagnation," he said. "The windows is all shut, and none of 'em broke. Werry much obliged to you for the tanner, and means to drink your blessed good healths at the werry next public-house."

At this moment a tremendous smash of a window came sharply and distinctly upon our ears, followed by another and another in rapid succession.

"Save the pieces!" said the rat-catcher. "My eye, there's a go!"

"Gracious powers!" cried Betty Irons, "there's been a scrimmage—there's been a row about the angels, I shouldn't wonder."

"Come on," cried I, "there's the signal."—"Stop a bit," said the director; "the door is not opened yet."

"True. Now, Betty, just be so good as to go for your pattens, and we will be in the house in a moment."

Betty walked up to the door, and rung the area bell; but, oh, what disappointments are in store for the best arranged schemes. A parley took place from the area, which ended in Betty's pattens being thrown into the middle of the road, so that our tremendous rush to get into the house was not at all called for, to, as I thought, the satisfaction of the attorney, who looked at us with a triumphant smile, as much as to say, "There now, you see that won't do on account of its extreme illegality."

Betty picked up her pattens, and came back to us in despair, while I and the director looked at each other like two great conquerors, who had been most unexpectedly defeated.

"I rather think," remarked Mr. Seagrove, "that Mrs. Colonel Wheezle has had some generalship from her deceased husband."—"A plague take her generalship," I cried. "It shall go hard with me if I do not eventually get into that house; although I must confess, just now I do not see exactly the way to compass that event."

"I should certainly say," remarked the solicitor, "that the best way would be to threaten them with an habeas corpus, which can be applied for on behalf of his niece, Emily Crumps, whom you found this morning."—"And, in the meanwhile," said I, "this half-superannuated old man may be cajoled or threatened into signing any documents that these people may think necessary for their own interest."

"Why," remarked the director, "the worst that can be done has been done. It appears to me, after the advices I have received from India, that in signing a bond for twenty thousand pounds, Mr. Crumps has jeopardised the whole of his fortune, and we may call him comparatively a poor man."

—"Exactly," said the attorney; "what is to be done now? A bond well executed, and properly attested, is rather a substantial antagonist."

At this moment the door of Mrs. Colonel Wheezle's house was suddenly opened to allow of the exit of Miss Flack, after which it was suddenly banged shut again without affording us the ghost of a chance of storming the garrison.

Miss Flack was attired in an extremely elaborate style, and came sailing down Alfred-place with as much superfluous dignity as ever I recollect seeing in one individual. Get out of her way we could not, because, if we had left what novelists call the friendly doorway in which we were standing, we must just have walked on before her, giving her a full opportunity of recognition, and if we remained where we were, which, by-the-bye, we did, it would have been rather an extraordinary thing for her to have passed without perceiving us. Moreover, our position was rendered conspicuous by the appearance of the rat-catcher, who having, I presume, spent the sixpence in some ardent liquor, returned to the spot to see the issue of the adventure in which he had been partially engaged, and without asking us whether it was agreeable or not, he sat down upon the step in front of us, occupying it so completely, that had we attempted to make a rush for the purpose of avoiding Miss Flack, we must have tumbled over him first.

We certainly could not blame him afterwards for the partizanship which he showed in our cause. He appeared to look upon the sixpence as the retaining fee, and to think himself compelled to do as much as possible for the annoyance of the enemy.

"Governor," he said, giving us a knowing look over his shoulders before Miss Flack arrived, "somebody has comed out of ninety-four. She's a coming full sail, like a cat in tights."—"Very well," said I. "We know."

Miss Flack at this moment reached the doorway, when her eyes fell upon my face, and her nose curled up in disdain, as she gave a toss of the head, indicative of the great contempt in which she held me. This was a proceeding which our ally, the rat-catcher, thought should be resented, and his mode of doing so was as ludicrous as it was effective.

He threw himself, in all abandonment of his line, at the feet of Miss Flack, on the pavement, and executed such an ear-piercing imitation of a puppy-dog in the agonies of death, after having been run over, that Miss Flack, with a loud scream, actually sat down on the pavement, while the rat-catcher laid hold of her ancle, crying,—

"Towrow—towrow—towrow," and a shriller sound, resembling to my ears, "pen-an'-ink—pen-an'-ink—pen-an'-ink."

We were compelled to laugh, in spite of all our efforts to preserve a decent gravity, and before Miss Flack could recover her feet, or understand what had really happened to her, the rat-catcher ran away, and disappeared round the corner, towards Tottenham-court-road.

"Murder! murder! thieves!" cried the indignant lady. "Help! help! constables! Where's the military?"

We all, then, burst into a great roar at this, and Miss Flack gathered herself to her feet, looking about in great surprise to see that no dog was lying a corpse under them. Then she darted at me a look of the most fiery indignation, and while her words came out with the spitting fury of a half uncorked bottle of gingerbeer on a hot day, she said,—

"Thief and villain—murdering monster. You beastly ogre—I'll have you taken up, that I will; you shall smart for this, you low-lived vagabond."—"Why, really, Miss Flack," said I, "your indignation seems to have outrun your discretion. I really do not know what cause of complaint you have against me—I never interfered with you in the least."

"I will have you all taken up," she cried; "I'll bring actions against you all; you shall not hear the last of this for one while to come; I'll make you all tremble when you read in the newspaper of the outrage in Alfred-place."—"Why, madam," said the director, "we've nothing to do with it. If I were to give evidence, I should certainly say, that to the best of my belief, you sat down on some dog that was passing; I don't know but what you yourself might be fined for cruelty to animals."

"Very true, very true," said the attorney; "besides, sitting down upon the pavement obstructs the thoroughfare, an illegal act under any circumstances."—"Wretches," said Miss Flack, almost intoxicated with rage; "your—your vile associates may do your worst and your best; recollect the bond—he! he! he!" and she treated us to a screaming kind of laugh, which she intended should be indicative of extreme triumph and satisfaction. "Recollect the bond, you poverty-stricken wretches. You'll rot in prison, every one of ye, while Mrs. Colonel Wheezle and I ride by in our carriage, splashing mud through the iron bars in your beastly faces;—go home, you ugly resurrectionists."

Having delivered herself of this rhapsody, Miss Flack, vibrating from top to toe with indignation, walked on, leaving Mr. Seagrove and I not a little amazed by the scene which had passed. As for the attorney, he looked rather blue, and said that he had never been so abused in his life; and that to be called a thief and a resurrectionist was quite actionable; although, certainly, any one was at liberty to call him a low-lived wretch and an ogre, as the law did not take cognizance as to whether people were low-lived wretches or ogres.

With a broad grin upon his face that showed his intense satisfaction at what had occurred, the rat-catcher now made his appearance from the other end of the street, and we could see him in the most ludicrous manner dodging behind an old gentleman, with a spencer and an immense umbrella, in order to hide himself from Miss Flack, who was some distance a-head of him.

This dodging he carried on without the least regard to the old gentleman's feelings, who after a little while became alarmed and angry at it, and turning round every few steps, and menacing, with his umbrella, the rat-catcher, threats which the latter replied to, by throwing himself into singular and convulsive attitudes, as if he were dreadfully beaten, and afraid to resist.

This went on till Miss Flack turned the corner of Alfred-place, towards Store-street, then the rat catcher made a violent rush past the old gentleman, who, in great terror, turned round and round several times, fencing in the air with his umbrella, with the impression that some diabolical attack was bout to be made upon him, and he finally sat down quite exhausted on the step of ninety-four.

One would not have laughed had it been one's own case, but I really couldn't help a positive shout at what followed. Mrs. Colonel Wheezle supposed it was one of us keeping guard on the steps of her door, and in a moment, from the second-floor window, a bason of water came slap upon the old gentleman, who, springing to his feet with the celerity of younger days, and uttering a wild kind of shout, rushed in the direction from whence he had come, and disappeared into one of the houses in North-crescent.

Alfred-place was now clear, with the exception of ourselves. Mr. Seagrove, with tears in his eyes from excessive laughing, turned to me, and said,—

"Really, doctor, this is the most amusing street I was ever in in my life. If I was sure of such scenes as these I would come here three times a week for the benefit of my digestion."—"Why, certainly," said I, " the old gentleman with the spencer is worth any money to a hypocondriac patient. I never saw anything turn out more ludicrously; and as for that rat-catcher, he seems completely to have taken an interest in our affairs—here he comes again."

The rat-catcher turned from Store-street into Alfred-place, and on coming up to us, he said,—

"Governor, she's gone into the baker's. I went in arter her, and she asked the baker if so be as he could recommend a slavey, for number ninety-four; and when she seed me, set up quite a scrimmage; she's in hystrickes now, a kicking the counter like one o'clock. I rayther think as we've given her her lunch, d——n her. Now, my dears, be quiet."

The last affectionate sentence was addressed to the bag of rats, and was accompanied by a kick, which produced the most infernal squeaking from among them that can be imagined.

"Really, my friend," said I, "you have taken a deal of trouble about us for sixpence."—"Why, that's neither here nor there," said the rat-catcher; "little accidents will happen in the quietest families, and this ere morning's vork is von as may turn out better than rat-catching. I have heard of many strange things, and never believed 'em; but now, governors, I finds as I've got a tale of my own."

"Oh! indeed," said I.—"Yes, guvernors—mutual confidence, as the proverbs say, increase suspicion. So what's the row? I axes what's the row?"

"Why, my good man," said the attorney, "you made all the row yourself, and I believe that your imitation of the death of a quadruped of the canine species, would really subject you to an action."

"What would you like to take arter that?" said the rat-catcher. "You'll want something to support nature arter that exertion."—"Come—come," said the attorney, "don't speak to me."

"Not in a whisper?" said the rat-catcher. — "There— there," said I, nudging the attorney, for it was not likely that he should be a match for our new friend in a war of words. "There, that will do. Let us hear, now, Mr. Rat-catcher, what you have to say in explanation of the great interest you take in this affair."

"There's ups and downs in life, and ins and outs, and rounds and abouts. I'm a rum 'un and always was. You guv'd me sixpence—werry good; I swallowed it—good again; and arter I had swallowed it, I said to the landlord of the public-house, 'Who lives at number ninety-four, Alfred-place?'— 'Mrs. Colonel Wheezle,' said he. 'Big,' says I. 'Yes,' said he. 'Flabby?' said I. 'Yes,' says he. 'Cast in von eye, and a mole on her chin?' says I. 'Yes,' says he. That's how, guvernors, I found out I was a domestic romance in three volumes, of the most heart-rending and thrilling character."—"Gracious powers!" said Betty Irons, lifting up her hands, " how I love romances!"

"And has your romance," I said, "anything to do with our proceedings?" — "Rayther," said the rat-catcher, "I takes it that you and Mrs. Colonel Wheezle has had some scrimmage. Now, guvernors, may I be so bold as to ax what's it about? I don't do so out of curiosity; no, guvernors, I knows as one way or t'other I shall have a finger in this ere pie, and I feels as I can be of more service to you than anybody."

There was an earnestness in the rat-catcher's manner that had its proportionate weight upon me, and I said at once,—

"Why, my friend, we have no further disposition to keep this affair a secret, than a proper reluctance to useless gossip; but since you think you can be of such service to us, I will tell you in brief, that Mrs. Colonel Wheezle keeps a lodging-house, and an old gentleman of the name of Crumps lodges with her, and she, practising upon his feebleness, has induced him to give her a written promise of marriage, and to sign a bond for twenty thousand pounds in case, within one twelve months, he should refuse to make her his wife."

The rat-catcher gave a very loud whistle, and then said,—

"You is a friend to the old 'un, and wishes to be down upon Mrs. Colonel Wheezle?"—"Certainly," said I. "I wish to save the old gentleman from her machinations."

"Werry good, I can help you there; but this here's not exact the place to make a revolution."

"A revolution! What do you mean?"—" I mean to reveal something. I thought you knew all the blessed hard words in the dictionary. To reveal things, is to make a revolution of them."

"Oh, a revelation. I understand you. Well, if you've anything to reveal, this gentleman" (pointing to the attorney) "will allow us to go to his house, and there talk over the matter."—"Lor!" said Betty Irons, "how I should like to hear. Let's go at once."

"Yes," said the rat-catcher, "we means to go at once, and you may be a werry wirtuous young woman, though, for all that, I don't mean to trust you with the secret. A burnt child goes in fear of the fire, and I've been rayther outrageously done by trusting a woman afore to-day."—"Betty Irons," said I, "you call on me in the morning. Your interest shall not be lost sight of, you may depend."

Betty was compelled to be satisfied with this, and reluctantly took leave of us, while we all adjourned, accompanied by the rat-catcher, to the attorney's offices, in Upper Bedford-place.

When we got there, he certainly made a revelation to us which was of the most extraordinary character, and which placed the whole affair between Mrs. Colonel Wheezle and Mr. Crumps in so new a light, that we were compelled to alter our line of conduct completely, for the purpose of rescuing the nabob from her insidious clutches.—The rat-catcher's narrative was as follows :—

"Guvernors," said he, "it's a matter of ten years ago since I was transported, and yet I was as innocent as a babby. I don't pretend for to set up to be more wirtuous than my neighbours, but certainly I didn't do nothing to transport me. Yet, guvernors, transported I was. The facts was these ere :—

"Guvernors, I had a wife, and a wild and wicious piece of goods she turned out. I was then in the way of business as a green grocer; but, Lord bless you, she'd a spent the arnings of Common Garden Market. She was a rum 'un, an out-and-outer. Drink like a fish, and make a fellow's home like a pocket addition of Bedlam.

"Well, guvernors, this went on, till she picked up with a cove of the name of Gill, a lankey-looking thief, with a red head. In course, I objected, and what was the consequence? Blessed if they didn't bring a lot of stolen plate into my werry bed, atween the werry mattress and the sacking, and then guved the office to the grabs to come.

"Guvernors, it wasn't of no use speechifying; the magistrates said it was a clear case, so did the judge, and so did the jewry, so they conwicted me, quite a babby unborn, and sent me across the pond for life. Gill and my wife walks into the greengrocer's shop, and they looks upon me as done brown.

"Well, guvernors, when I gets there, to the bay I means, the guvernor's house was a swarming with rats, so I let on, as I was a rum 'un at catching warmint. What's the consekens—I gets off for ten years' lagging instead of my life. Here I is, my name's Bill Wheezle—put that and that together and see what you make's on it."

"Then," cried I, "do you consider this Mrs. Colonel Wheezle to be your wife?"—"Not a doubt on it; and if I don't be even with her one of these ere days soon, may I be whalloped to death with rats' tails."

We looked on each other with amazement, and Bill Wheezle evidently enjoyed the effect he had produced by his narrative.

"Guvernors," he said, "I can prove it—the very fellow as sold Gill the swag was lagged since, and confessed to me the whole scrimmage, so that if I comes across him, I can get him conwicted by evidence as I knows where to pitch upon now in London, and no mistake."—"Then, Bill Wheezle," said I, "you'll not have to go further than 94,

Alfred-place, to find him, for there is just the sort of man you describe, calling himself Futhergill."

"The deuce there is! that settles the hash; and as for the old gentleman, he's safe enough, unless mother Wheezle wants to do a bit of bigamy."—"I don't know that," said the attorney; "it all depends upon the condition of the bond. If it should happen to be drawn up without mention of marriage at all, we may yet have the greatest difficulty in getting it from her. If, on the contrary, it mentions the payment a contingency of the refusal to marry her on the part of Mr. Crumps within twelve months, he is safe enough."

"Scarcely so," said I, "for our friend Bill Wheezle might interpose."—"I don't know that," added the attorney. "If the bond be skilfully drawn by a professional man, she may unquestionably proceed upon it. I repeat, it appears to me to be a matter still beset with difficulties."

"I begs to differ," said Bill Wheezle. "Where's the difficulty, I should like to know? Let the old gentleman marry her on conditions she gives up the bond as soon as the blessed ceremony's over, then we can have her nabbed for bigamy, and everything will be as right as ninepence."—"But, good God!" said the attorney, "we place ourselves in a very peculiar position by so doing. I very much doubt if, in this manner, we can wink at the commission of felony."

"Don't wink, then," said Bill Wheezle. "Who axed yer? Do you think I means to have no wengeance cos you have an objection to winking? I tells yer 'tis the only way of doing the business, and if you was to go on thinking for a month, and winking all the while, you couldn't find a better plan than that ere."

"Why," said I, "she amply deserves such retaliation; and really it seems to me it is she who is laying the snare for herself, and no one for her. I do certainly dread litigation concerning that bond. Why, the fortune of old Crumps, if it amounts to no more, would be frittered away among lawyers before Emily would have the remotest chance of claiming her own."

"I am very much obliged to you for your opinion of lawyers," said the attorney; "but I beg to say, we don't all of us do business in that way."

"What!" cried Bill Wheezle, catching up his bag of rats, "are you a lawyer?"—"Yes, to be sure."

"D——n my rags, here's a swindle—tooked in and done for."

So saying, Bill bolted out of the office with such speed, that he was clear off before any of us could hinder him, and we found, to our great vexation, that our principal evidence had slipped through our fingers, and that we were probably as far off as ever in obtaining justice on Mrs. Colonel Wheezle; or, at all events, we were completely at the consideration and mercy of Bill Wheezle, who might or might not communicate with us just as he thought proper.

"What's to be done now?" said Mr. Seagrove, looking very solemn.—"Ah," remarked the attorney, "that man's a desperate rogue—a most desperate rogue. I can see it in his looks."

"Why, my old friend," said Seagrove, "you must recollect he has just run away from your office because he thinks you a desperate rogue by profession. He may be a queer character, but there is a plausibility about his story that I must confess goes far towards making me believe its truth."

"And there is one point," said I, "that convinces me of its truth, which is, where he speaks of the man Gill, and describes him with quite sufficient accuracy to make us feel quite sure that Futhergill is that person. You may depend, gentlemen, that there is some, if not entire reliance to be placed upon Bill Wheezle's statement, and I am only extremely sorry he has gone from us in the manner he has. My opinion, however, is, that he will turn up again, and if so, it is very likely he might prefer arranging matters with me; therefore, pray give him my address, should he come for it; and, in the meantime, I have thought of a plan which, if carried on in connection with Bill Wheezle's own scheme, will end in justice being done to Emily Crumps as well as Mrs. Colonel Wheezle.

"And what may your scheme be, doctor," said Mr. Seagrove, "for doing justice to Miss Crumps and Mrs. Colonel Wheezle?"—"Simply this," I replied; "we hear from Bill Wheezle that Mrs. Flack's errand to the baker's in Store-street was to ask him if he knew a servant out of place who would suit Mrs. Colonel Wheezle. Now, what is to hinder Emily Crumps from leaving her present situation, calling at the baker's, inquiring for a place, and being in due course sent over to ninety-four? Once there, she could take an opportunity of declaring herself to her uncle, and, winning his heart by her simplicity and beauty, do good to herself as well as weaning him completely from Mrs. Colonel Wheezle and her blandishments."

"That would be a good plan," said Mr. Seagrove, "and one which, I have no doubt, would end in Emily being declared the old man's heiress. You say he cannot live long, and it would be some recompence to that poor girl after the sufferings she has undergone in early life, which must have been great, to find at length that fortune smiles upon her, and she's placed in the possession of affluence."

"I should rejoice," said I, "at such a consummation. It is hard to judge from first appearances, but Emily Crumps, notwithstanding her present lowly condition, appears to me eminently qualified to adorn any station in society."

"Then let us quite agree," said the attorney, "as to what is to be done regarding the old man and the bond. Is the advice of that extraordinary rat-catcher to be followed or not?"—"Why, considering all the circumstances, I should say yes," replied Mr. Seagrove. "Let us thoroughly ascertain, which we can easily do, that his name and the story of his transportation are true, and then, I should say, there is internal evidence sufficient of the fact that Mrs. Colonel Wheezle is his wife. I vote for the marriage. What say you, doctor?"—"The marriage."

"Well, gentlemen," said the attorney, "I am in a minority of one I see; but, at all events, if you like to risk it, let it be so."—"Then that is quite agreed," said I. "And now leave me to manage about Emily myself, and I shall contrive to have an interview, with old Mr. Crumps, in order thoroughly to expose to him the villany of his landlady."

* * * * *

I was compelled to make a hasty round of such patients as I was in the habit of visiting daily, so that whatever might be my impatience to see Emily and inform her of the aspect of affairs, the evening had fairly set in before I could get to Arlington-street, and it was quite dark by the time I knocked at Mrs. Flowerdale's door.

This time I was answered by Emily herself, and to my great relief I learned that Mrs. Flowerdale had gone out to tea, so that I had an uninterrupted leisure of conversing with my protegee. I told her of the early friendship that had subsisted between my father and her uncle, and then explained to her how strangely I had discovered his existence in Alfred-place, and of the conspiracy which had been entered into to rob him of the remnant of his immense property; a remnant which was a very pretty fortune in itself, and one which I told Emily ought to be hers, and should be hers if she would obey my directions implicitly.

She burst into tears at the end of my recital, and said that the mention of all these things brought to her memory her poor mother, and the dreadful sufferings she and her had gone through before they could bring their minds to apply to the parish for relief.

"I long," she said, "to see my father's brother, and would go many miles to see his face; but oh, sir, do you tell him, indeed it is not because he is the rich man that I wish to see him, it is not that I covet money; but you should be like me, sir, placed in the wide world alone, before you could dream what pleasure it was to fancy there was at last found one with whom you could claim kindred. I long to see him, sir, but oh, not from selfishness—tell him that, tell him that."

"That shall be properly explained, Emily," said I; "but there is some little management necessary before you can see your uncle. He is kept a close prisoner by the atrocious female I have mentioned to you, and there is only one way by which I think I can ensure an admittance into the house."

"Point out any plan," she said, "and I will pursue it; and yet how dare I leave this place? It is my only home, and, full of evils as it is, I dare not leave it."—"Make your mind quite easy upon that score, Emily; let the result of this adventure be what it may, I will pledge you my word that it shall not make your condition worse. Now, does Mrs. Flowerdale owe you any money?"

"Since I have lived with her," said Emily, "she has never regularly paid me what was my due. A few shillings now and then is all that I have been able to obtain from her, and then always accompanied by great abuse, as if I was actually robbing her."

"Very well, Emily; as she has dissolved the contract with you by a non-payment of your wages, you are quite at liberty to go without any notice. I should advise you certainly to pack up what belongs to you, and come away with me; should you not be successful in getting the situation in Alfred-place, I will furnish you with the means of getting a decent lodging until Mr. Crumps' friends take some means of providing for you, which at all events will do better than in a menial capacity."

I thought Emily for a moment looked distrustful of me, but it was only for a moment, and then she gave me her hand in the most artless manner imaginable, saying,—

"I will follow your direction implicitly, sir, and may Heaven reward you for your kind feeling towards one who is quite unused to the accents of friendship."

"May Heaven punish me, Emily, if I am deceiving you. So now get ready by the time I procure a coach, and in the meantime tell me where Mrs. Flowerdale is to be found, for it is necessary I should see her before you leave?"—"She is at number two, sir, in this street—you'll be sure to find her there."

"Very well. I dare say she'll come back with me, but don't you be alarmed at whatever she may do or threaten; leave me to manage her, and comfort yourself with the assurance that she can really do nothing."

Emily promised compliance with my directions, and I left

her in order to proceed to No. 2, in search of Mrs. Flowerdale.

Lights were flashing from the parlour of No. 2, and I could hear the jingle of tea-things before I knocked at the door, which was opened by a dirty, slipshod wench, who, on my asking for Miss Flowerdale, said she was in the parlour with missus.

"Then tell her," said I, "that a gentleman wishes to speak to her concerning Miss Crumps; and there is my card."

The girl took the card and carried it into the parlour, from whence, in about two minutes, spent, I presume, in spelling my name, out sallied Miss Flowerdale, accompanied by a grenadier-looking woman in a large turban, which was quite enough in itself to strike terror into the heart of a weak-minded man; but a physician sees too many curious specimens of humanity to be easily daunted by the most outrageous specimens that can be presented to him, so I took no notice of the lady at all, but addressing myself to Miss Flowerdale, I said,

"Madam, your servant, Emily Crumps, having found a near relative, will, this evening, leave your service. I come to make this announcement to you, in order that you may take measures to get some one else; at the same time I must add, that she would not have left you so unhandsomely at a moment, had you behaved with common justice to her, and paid her her wages."

"The hussy!" screamed Miss Flowerdale; "oh! you vile imposture! here's a kettle of fish! Mrs. Boodle, what do you think of this? here's a air and a grace!"

I did not stop to hear Miss Flowerdale's further laments or censures, but having given her all the notice I intended of Emily's departure, I walked away and got a coach, during which time, I suppose, Miss Flowerdale was putting on her bonnet and shawl, for just as I got the coach to her door, and was knocking for admittance, she arrived, and gave me such a whack between the shoulders as I could scarcely have believed capable of.

"Where's that hussy?" said she; "I'll have the eyes out of her head—I'll skin her alive—I'll flay her from top to toe. So, indeed, a pretty thing—vastly pretty, this—to leave my house along with one of her fellows, without so much as by your leave—but I'll let her know what's what in a twinkling."

"Indeed you'll do no such thing," said I; "for if you attempt any violence, I will give you in charge to a constable. If you feel yourself aggrieved, you have your legal remedy, Miss Flowerdale. The liberty of the subject is the liberty of the subject, and I would advise you to be very cautious how you tamper with it. Emily, where are you?"

"I am here," she said, emerging from the parlour, whither she had flown from sheer fright of Miss Flowerdale; "I am here, sir, and quite ready."

"So, you infamous baggage!" cried Miss Flowerdale; "this is the way, is it?"

"Come along, Emily," said I; and taking her at once by the arm, I led her from the house; we then drove off before Miss Flowerdale could finish her speech.

On the road to Store-street, whither I told the coachman to drive, I gave Emily full instructions as to how she should proceed when she should visit 94, Alfred-place.

"Now, Emily," I said, "this is not a regular place you are going to, so do not fancy you are doing wrong by misrepresenting yourself a little. Your own name, of course, would spoil the whole plot, so please to call yourself Jane Green. Moreover, as you'll be asked for references, give the name of Mr. Seagrove, which they don't know, and Mr. Larkins, who is an attorney, and in case any inquiry should really be made, I will prepare these gentlemen to answer favourably for you."

These names and addresses I wrote on a leaf of my pocket-book for Emily, and then I agreed with her, that should she that night be received into the house, as was very likely, considering that Mrs. Colonel Wheezle was without a servant, she should open the door for me at half-past eight o'clock, and allow me to slip up to the first floor, where Mr. Adolphus Crumps would be, doubtless, lying on his sofa, when I would explain to him whom she, Emily, was, and detail, at length, the scheme for rescuing him from his embarrassments.

This was rather a hazardous adventure I purposed plunging into, but one can dare a great deal in a right cause, and, upon the whole, I had so urgent a desire for a row with Mr. Futhergill, that I positively longed for the pleasure of knocking down such a scoundrel. At the corner of Store-street I ordered the coachman to stop, and we both got out, Emily carrying the very small bundle that contained her scanty wardrobe.

"Now you are quite prepared," said I, "to answer any question. If you are asked where you live, mention my address in the City, which they don't know, and if you possibly can, get leave to remain to-night, for if you do, I think the probability is that you may go away again in the morning, after having satisfactorily settled everything with your uncle, without being exposed to all the disagreeables of the situation, for, I suppose, they are sufficiently numerous."

"I perfectly understand," said Emily, "all that I have to do, and believe me I shall not fail for want of zeal."

I waited, not a little anxiously, while Emily went to the baker's; she returned to me in a few minutes, however, with a slip of paper, on which was written "Mrs. Colonel Wheezle, No. 94, Alfred-place;" and she told me that, upon asking the baker if he knew of any one who wanted a servant, he at once mentioned Mrs. Colonel Wheezle, and advised her to go directly, as he was quite sure she was distressed for an attendant, having lodgers in the house.

"Very well. Now, Emily," said I, "take your bundle and go; agree to whatever Mrs. Colonel Wheezle offers, and the probabilities are, of course, that you will get the situation: should you do so, and be permitted to stay at once, in about half an hour just open the kitchen window a little distance, and I will accept that as a signal that you are retained; then at half-past eight, or thereabouts, for, of course, you must choose your opportunity, let me into the house, and I will fairly introduce you to your uncle, Mr. Adolphus Crumps."

With these instructions, which Emily promised to fulfil to the very letter, she walked up to Mrs. Colonel Wheezle's house, and I had the satisfaction of seeing that, after some parley at the door, she was admitted.

Some one, at this moment, touched my arm, and upon hastily turning, I saw Bill Wheezle, the rat-catcher, who said, when he saw my face,

"I thought it was you, governor. I have seen her; it's Mrs. W., safe as the bank, and a great deal safer."

"I am very glad to see you," said I; "I had began to be afraid that you had given us the slip."

"Oh, no fear of that ere. I have seen him, too—that wagabone Gill," said Bill; "I seed um all in the parlour, when they lit the blessed chandelier, before they pulled down the blinds. 'My eyes,' thinks I, 'one of these ere days soon, I'll throw a stronger light on yer than that ere blessed thing hanging by the roof.' But mum's the word just now, governor. Mother Wheezle's no fool. She had me transported for nothink. What an out-and-out thing it will be to send her across the pond for bigamy. You manage all the matter, and you can let me know, when I calls on you some day, what church they are going to be married at—blessed if there won't be a spree. I thinks I sees Mother Wheezle, when she looks on my phisicgogomity. It's hard lines, sir, to be sarved out as I have been sarved out, and I feels it. I have been putting rats down the area all day; blessed if I ain't got a rum 'un now—I was jist a going to put him down when I seed you; there will be a little scratching and scampering to-night. Just come to this ere gash-light."

I followed Bill Wheezle to the gas-light, and then, plunging his hands in the bag he carried, he pulled out an enormous rat, which he held by a peculiar nip at the back of its head.

"There's a hanimal!" he said. "Blessed if ever I seed such viskers in my life. There's a tail, too, just for all the world like the thong of a shay whip. This ere's what I calls a cretur; and I only hopes he will find his way to Mother Wheezle's bed to-night. Just come over here, and you'll see me pop him down the area."

As I was going over at any rate, I accompanied Bill Wheezle, the rat all the while kicking and struggling and lashing its great tail about in a most frantic manner. In a moment Bill Wheezle dropped it down the area, and then the kitchen window was opened a little way.

"That's kind," said Bill Wheezle. "Blessed if he won't bolt in, in a minute, along of them thirteen others as I have dropped; them there creatures, governor, will march over the house like dragoons. Revenge is sweet, as the copy book says; cultivate your evil passions. Here goes another."

"I think that will do now, Mr. Wheezle," I said; "you had better go away now for fear of a discovery. There is my card; call upon me to-morrow morning without fail."

"You don't want the lend of half-a-crown, do you?"—"No, thank you," said I.

"Then you're luckier nor me, for I does."—"Well, here it is," I said; "but, for Heaven's sake, Mr. Wheezle, don't get drunk, for if you do you'll come here and blow the whole plan."

"You don't know me," said Bill Wheezle. "If I gets drunk I'm a safe card. I never walks till I can't stand, nor gets up till I falls under the table."

"Very well; let me see you in the morning. Now, good night, Mr. Wheezle; and I strongly advise you not to haunt this street, or you may excite suspicion; if, indeed, you are not actually seen and recognised."

"All's right," said Wheezle; "drive on." And he walked away, whistling some melody seldom heard in the drawing-rooms of St. James's.

* * * * *

It wanted nearly an hour to the time I had appointed to Emily to let me in, when Bill Wheezle left me to my own meditations in Alfred-place, and if they were of an agreeable order, as fancying I was really about to perform a singular service to my father's old friend, they were not divested of much anxiety as to the ultimate result of the affair. I did not feel disposed to go home, so I amused myself with walking about Tottenham-court-road till nearly half-past eight, and during which time many uneasy reflections crossed my mind in the shape of doubts as to the practicability of Emily's being able to let me into the house.

I revolved, too, in my mind, over and over again, what I should say to old Crumps, until I felt that I must be entirely guided by circumstances at the time, if I should succeed in getting to him.

I was standing with my back against the railings of the opposite house at half-past eight o'clock, and when a quarter of an hour after that passed away, without the door of 94 moving in the least, I began to get dreadfully impatient and fidgetty, and to blame myself for not making some bargain with Emily as to how long I was really to wait.

Then came another ten minutes, and I am afraid I swore a little. But I was suddenly aroused from my state of discomfort by seeing a rush of light through the fanlight above the door. In a moment I had crossed the road, and then the portal itself opened slowly, and Emily made her appearance. She had her finger upon her lips, and pointed to the parlour door, from which I heard noisy conversation. I understood her meaning, and stepped lightly into the passage, after which Emily closed the door with extreme caution.

"I'll bet a hundred to five," cried Futhergill, from the parlour, "that the old hunks ain't alive this day three months."

"And in that case, my dear Gill," said Mrs. Colonel Wheezle, "are you quite sure the bond's good?"

"Quite, I tell you—quite. I have had it so drawn up that, come what may, or happen what may, you must have the money—mind, that's positive."

"You're a dear creature," said Mrs. Colonel Wheezle, "that you are. I can't think, for the life of me, what he broke the windows for. It was such an extraordinary whim."

"But he's full of 'em—he's full of 'em. D—n it, don't you hear an extraordinary noise in the area?"

Emily beckoned me on, and we went the length of the passage in safety. Slowly and cautiously we began the ascent of the stairs, but we had not proceeded above three steps when we distinctly heard a hand on the lock of the parlour door.

I caught the candle out of Emily's hand, and in an instant extinguished it by clapping my hat over it, so that not the least portion of burning wick was visible.

A stream of light came from the open parlour door, and Mr. Futhergill popped his head out, saying,—

"Who's there? D—n it, I thought I heard somebody in the passage."

He then went and tried the street door, but finding it all fast he returned to the parlour, saying,—

"Oh, it's the cat, I suppose, for there's nobody there."

Bang went the door, and we were in darkness.

"Come, sir," whispered Emily, "the old gentleman is up stairs, and very unwell."

We groped our way up as well as we could, until we came to the drawing-room door, and then I said, in a cautious whisper,—

"Emily, has he seen you yet?"—"No, sir; I have been in the room, but he never turned his head."

"Were you ever reckoned like your mother?"—"Yes, when I wear my hair as she did."

"Put it so, then, for Heaven's sake. I know not how much may depend upon so trifling a circumstance as that." —"I can do so in a moment," said Emily. "It is done now."

I heard her heave a deep sigh of painful recollection, then she gently turned the handle of the door. A faint subdued light fell upon her face—I thought I had never seen anything so beautiful. In another moment we were in the room. It was but faintly illuminated by the ceiling lamp, which, although lighted, was turned on but faintly; still it was a mild, quiet light, and showed everything in the apartment clearly and distinctly. A fire was blazing in the grate, and the dancing shadow it cast upon the walls added to the picturesque appearance of the really handsome apartment. The screen, which formed such a bone of contention, was placed partially round the side of the fire-place nearest to the door, and just beyond it was the sofa, which, with its muslin covering, looked more like a bier for the dead than a place of repose for the living. A deep stillness reigned in the apartment. I felt Emily's hand tremble as it touched mine, and for a moment the awful question came across my mind of— Is the old man dead? I could not hear him breathing, and there seemed a solemnity about the room that was highly calculated to suggest the idea.

"Emily," I said, in a whisper, "remain behind the screen until I call for you; I must have some conversation with your poor old uncle first."

It was a relief to me at the moment to hear a low moan proceed from the occupant of the sofa, and then a creaking of the wood-work assured me that the old man was uneasily shifting his position.

"Thank God, he lives," I said; and advancing to his couch, I raised my voice sufficiently loud to be heard, and added,—"Mr. Crumps, do you know my voice? With some trouble and difficulty I found my way to see you. Are you better than you were, sir?"

"Who is that—who is that?" he cried, as he hastily pulled the muslin from before his eyes, showing me his countenance, so ghastly pale that I involuntarily started back a step. "Who speaks—who speaks? Are the dead crowding round me so soon?—Time enough, time enough, when I am among ye! Away with ye, away with ye."

"Nay, Mr. Crumps, I am the son of your old friend—are you not glad to see me?"

"Not now, not now—'tis a huge undertaking; but I did not know there were mountains in the way, and so I lost nearly all. Man's puny efforts could not succeed in so warring with the face of nature; but I will go to England, and there die, unknown and undegraded."

"That Indian speculation," thought I, "has turned his wits. I wish Futtygohad and the other place had been at the devil."

"There again—there again," he added, "unwelcome faces crowding round me—let me die in peace."

"Mr. Crumps," said I, "pray awaken your reason to a sense of your situation. I am no phantom form. All around you is life and reality. For my father's sake, who esteemed you highly, I have come here to tender you my best service; recollect you must have had a letter from me, and you broke some of the windows as an answering signal."

"Hush! hush!" he said, as he seized my arm with a convulsive grasp; "death is scarcely terrible to me, but still I would have it come gently, and as Heaven wills it to come to its creatures. It was hard to be so threatened as I have been in my old age; to be told I should be murdered if I dared hold further communion with you. There are times when I don't know well where I am, or what has happened, and were it not that I have had a dream, for the chance of a fulfilment of which I would fain yet linger in life, I would have told them to have mercy, to kill me. Doctor, have you heard of her?"

"What mean you?"—"Emily! Emily! my first—last— only love! It seems absurd for the old man, now tottering on the grave's brink, to use the language of that passion which is so sweet in youth—but I did love her! God knows how I did love her! I—I—dreamt, doctor, that even here she came to me, in all her purity, in all her beauty, and in all her innocence, and, bending over me, she murmured words of joy to my heart, leaving soft kisses on my furrowed cheek, as if the sweetest flower of summer had expanded its radiant blossom to the winter's wind. I felt the pressure of the velvet lips; then, doctor, then I felt that life was joy, and that moment, with a gasping sob, I implored Heaven to let me die with the sweet vision hovering near me, strewing the passage to the grave with flowers; but I awoke, and all was drear, cold, passionless, and despairing; I was again the poor, old, sorrow-stricken man, trembling upon the brink of eternity he scarcely dreads."

"Such visions, sir," said I, "I can almost believe are given by Heaven for some wise purpose. Have a better hope of the future; you may yet have many happy days—but the object of my visit, Mr. Crumps, is to call you to the present. Is it true that the bulk of your large fortune has been swallowed up in an Indian speculation?"

"You know that?" he said, with sudden energy; "it is true, and I am comparatively a poor man. I have twenty-one thousand pounds, the wreck of a fortune seven times its amount."

"I hope, Mr. Crumps, that you have taken care of that twenty-one thousand, for it appears to me very far from a contemptible wreck?"—"It is banked at Cox's," he replied; "and I shall come to want—abject, wretched want."

I could scarcely help a smile at such an idea of want, and so formidable a sum in a banker's hands.

"Now, Mr. Adolphus Crumps," said I, "believe me, for my father's sake, I have your interest truly at heart. Will you tell me candidly if you have given the woman of the house here any acknowledgment for money?"

"Money—money—I know not what you mean?"—"Why, my meaning is simply this, the woman who keeps this house, and calls herself Mrs. Colonel Wheezle, boasts of having in her possession a written promise of marriage from you, as well as a bond for twenty thousand pounds, payable within twelve months."

"'Tis false! false!" he said; "I have signed nothing here, with the exception of two papers of no importance, connected I believe with local taxation, or population returns, or something of the kind."

"Oh! then," said I, "Mr. Crumps, there's where you have been duped; those papers were, you may depend upon it, of a much more important character than you imagined."

He gave a deep groan, and closing his eyes, seemed completely to resign himself to the malignancy of his fate.

"All lost!" he murmured; "all, all lost! Oh! what a destiny is mine in my old age to feel so full a desolation. No kindred voice to speak a kind word to me, no gentle, loving hand to smooth the pillow of death; deceived by those I have trusted, robbed of the remnant of my wealth, and left to die in my despair, deserted alike by earth and Heaven."

"Nay, Mr. Crumps," I said, "you take a more gloomy view of your position than the circumstances really warrant. 'Tis true that things appear as you state, but Heaven, Mr. Crumps, has boundless mercy yet, and the evening of your life may yet be gilded by as serene a ray as ever illumined its happiest morning."

"Speak again," he said, "speak again, your words are hopeful. Moreover, they sound not strange to my ears. You remind me of your father, boy. Speak again, and I will listen. 'Tis pleasant to recall one's happy memory."

"Then, Mr. Crumps," I continued, "I have not the slightest doubt that you have been deceived, in not only signing a promise of marriage to the designing woman who is your landlady here, but I dare say she has likewise procured from you the bond for twenty thousand pounds which I mentioned to you. Now, Mr. Crumps, there is one way of completely turning the tables upon her, and catching her in her own snare. There can be no doubt but she believes you worth a great deal more than the twenty thousand pounds, and that if she were to marry you, she would, speculating upon outliving you, fancy herself much better off than with the twenty thousand. Now my advice to you is, to offer to marry her at once by special licence, and to induce her to surrender the bond to you. Tell her you will make a will bequeathing the whole of your property to her without reserve, and to satisfy her, make such a will and sign it. She will then naturally surrender to you the bond, thinking herself secure of a much larger fortune. You understand me, Mr. Crumps?"

"I think I do; but what would that avail me?"—"Everything. Mrs. Wheezle is already married. She may or may not fancy her husband dead, but certainly he is not, and he will come forward immediately you are married to her, accuse her of bigamy, and release you of all trouble concerning her, while you perceive your will becomes mere waste paper, in consequence of her marriage to you being null and void, and you having no such wife as that named in the document."

"I understand, I understand," he said. "I will adopt your advice conditionally, and if I find she has deceived me, and is in possession of such a bond as you speak of, I will carry on the plot no further than shall suffice to get it in my own possession."

"Very well," said I; "that of course, Mr. Crumps, is a matter entirely for your own consideration, and one in which no one ought to presume to direct you. And now, Mr. Crumps, let me talk to you upon another subject. You had a brother, who married one very dear to you."

"I forced him—I forced him," said the old man, with sudden energy. "I forced him to repair the wounded honour of one of God's best and brightest creations. I pray to Heaven he was penitent, as much need had he so to be. Oh, Emily! Emily! God help you."

"Mr. Crumps," I said, "did you ever hear of them since you left for India?"—"Never! never!" he replied.

"Then you must be aware that many changes have occurred since you have been absent from your native country?"

He seemed to dread what I was going to say, and raised himself partially on his couch, while he looked on my face with painful interest.

"They are both dead," I said solemnly.

He clasped his withered hands together, raised one cry, and sank back in a state of insensibility on the couch. I saw that he had fainted, but I was not so alarmed for his condition as when on the former occasion he had lapsed into a state of insensibility, for I began to think that such attacks were incidental to him.

Another cause, however, of alarm immediately ensued, for in running round the sofa hastily to ask Emily if she could get some cold water, I tumbled a chair over the bell-rope, the end of which was stretched on the sofa, and executed such a peal upon the bell, that if it didn't alarm the house it would be a mystery.

"There," said I, "I have done it now; and after all, Emily, never completed my principal object, namely, of introducing you to your uncle."

"They are coming, they are coming," said Emily. "Hark! I hear their footsteps upon the stairs. This way, sir—this way. She opened one of the folding-doors that led into the back drawing room, and we just escaped and closed it again as Mrs. Colonel Wheezle, Mr. Fothergill, Miss Flack, and somebody else I didn't know, made a wild rush into the apartment.

The folding-doors fitted badly, as they invariably do; so that there was a crevice left, which, although I could not see through, admitted a stream of light into the back room, and enabled me to hear distinctly all that passed in the room.

"What now, I wonder!" cried Mrs. Colonel Wheezle.—
"D——d if I don't think old Blue Beard's dead," said Futhergill.

"What an uncommon troublesome old man," ejaculated Miss Flack; "just as we were playing such a nice game, and thinking of turning up a trump—but it's always the way with these frumps—the time they take dying is perfectly frightful."

"Ah, the old fool," said Mrs. Colonel Wheezle, "I have really no patience with him. It's just another of his faintings. Just go and tell the gal to come up and throw a jug of cold water over him."

"Ah, he's coming to again," remarked Miss Flack; "and atween you and I, Mrs. Colonel Wheezle, the less that new gal sees on him the better. I caught her coming out of his room, and pretending to get up a snivel. Ah, she's an artful baggage, I know, by the look of her—she wants to cajole the old man out of something, of course."

"Both dead—both dead!" murmured old Crumps. "Oh, heavens! Emily dead, and I far away."

"Lor," said Mrs. Colonel Wheezle, "what does he mean now?"—"Ah, ah!" said Futhergill; "the old boy may have been a rum un in early life—he's talking of somebody he calls Emily—upon my soul it's rich. How are you, old Crumps—not quite stiff yet, eh?"

"Those soft kisses," murmured the old man—"those sweet, soft kisses."—"He's getting immoral," said Miss Flack. "What a spectacle in old age!"

"Dear fancies, come again—come again. So, Emily, dearest, you are with me still—Heaven bless you!"—"Well, I am sure!" said Mrs. Colonel Wheezle. "The idea! Emily, indeed! Some of his Indian squaws; they've squaws in India, I believe. Haven't they, Mr. Futhergill?"

"Upon my soul I don't know," said Futhergill; "but as I never was partial of overmuch to do, and am fond of money, I have always a great fancy for being an Indian idle. Ha, ha, ha!"

Nobody but himself laughed at Mr. Futhergill's joke, and Mrs. Colonel Wheezle, in a loud voice, screamed out,—

"Well, Mr. Crumps, what's been the matter now?"—"I am better," said the old man, in a calm tone of voice. "Mrs. Colonel Wheezle, I think I shall go back to India. I am used to the climate. Yes; I shall go back to India."

"Oh, indeed, Mr. Crumps, you'll go back to India!" cried the lady, in an indignant voice; "you will please to recollect, before you take any such step, that you've not only promised me marriage, in writing, Mr. Crumps, but have given me a bond for 20,000l. at twelve months' date."

"Have I?" said Crumps. "I really have no recollection of it. However, twenty thousand pounds is a very small sum out of half a million of money."—"Gracious powers!" said Miss Flack.

Mr. Futhergill whistled, and walked up and down the room, while Mrs. Colonel Wheezle repeated the words "half a million," as if she were choked with the magnitude of the amount.

"There is no one, I believe," continued the old man, "who can claim kindred with me. I think, Mrs. Colonel Wheezle, I had better give you a check at once for the twenty thousand."

"Do you want to break my heart, you dear creature?" said Mrs. Colonel Wheezle—"do you want me to fall down dead with emotions and feelings? I feel as if I could, at this present moment, go into the most violent hysterics. Oh, Mr. Crumps, what is twenty thousand pounds compared to your affections? Have you got your cheque-book in your pocket? My heart is slowly breaking. Pen and ink, Miss Flack. Mr. Futhergill, do you really think he's worth so much?"

"D——d if I don't," said Mr. Futhergill. "I saw the stars against his name at the India House; and if that isn't proof positive, I don't know what is."

"Oh, gracious!" said Mrs. Colonel Wheezle, positively gasping—"half a million!—Providence is good to us."

"Yes, yes," murmured old Crumps; "I have but a short time to live in this world; very, very few hours are numbered; it's dreadful to be a lone man with half a million of money, with no one who cares for him—no one."

"Oh, Mr. Crumps, Mr. Crumps!" cried Mrs. Colonel Wheezle, "don't say so. Look at me. Am I nobody? Do I look like nobody? Would or would it not be my pride and satisfaction, my heavenly duty, to attend upon you night and day? I—I—my feelings overpower me, but if, Mr. Crumps, you'll have me as your adoring wife, say the word, and I'm yours for ever. Oh, my poor heart, it's bursting. Why did you come here, Mr. Crumps, to steal my affection?"

Mrs. Colonel Wheezle burst into a great passion of weeping after this speech, and Miss Flack gave a sympathetic howl, while Cousin Futhergill walked to and fro in the room, saying, at intervals,—

"Upon my soul, it's affecting. D——n me if it ain't affecting!"

Mr. Crumps spoke in a low voice,—

"If," he said, "you really love me, Mrs. Colonel Wheezle, if you can sacrifice so much beauty and elegance to an old man, who, I don't think, can live a week, I must really insist upon one condition."

"Oh, name it!" said Mrs. Colonel Wheezle; "let me hear it."—"It is that you permit me to make a will, leaving you the whole of my property, without the reservation of a single pound."

"Can I consent?" said Mrs. Colonel Wheezle. "Dear friends, advise me; ought I to consent?"—"I think you ought," said Miss Flack. "Think of Mr. Crumps's happiness, mem, and do consent."—"Oh, do," said Cousin Futhergill. "Upon my soul, I think you ought."

"Won't it look selfish?"—"Selfish!" cried Miss Flack. "Good gracious! Who could accuse you of being selfish, mem?"

"My heart's bursting," said Mrs. Colonel Wheezle; "but I consent."—"Special licence to-morrow," said old Crumps, throwing himself back on the sofa.

"St. James's church," sobbed Mrs. Colonel Wheezle. "May I order some diamonds?"—"Necklace, ear-rings, bracelets, of the first water," said the old man.

"And a carriage?"—"Two."

"Heavenly powers!" said Mrs. Colonel Wheezle. "I feel as if I could sink."—"Come away, mem," said Miss Flack; "it's too much for your nerves all at once."

"In the meantime," said Mr. Crumps, "give me the bond for the paltry twenty thousand, and I'll burn it."—"At the end of a hook," said Mr. Futhergill.

"Oh, my lovely Mr. Crumps," said Mrs. Colonel Wheezle, "you shall have all your own way, everything shall be as you wish, and after the ceremony which gives me the happiness of being yours, you shall sign the will, and destroy the twenty thousand pounds bond. Will you forgive me now, and allow me to retire and compose the fluster of my spirits?"—"Be it so," said the old man; and he drew the muslin curtain over his face.

Mrs. Colonel Wheezle and her companions cast upon each other looks of astonishment and congratulation. Cousin Futhergill, with a great oath, declared his want of knowledge as to whether he was on his head or his heels, and in a few moments the whole party left the room.

* * * * *

I had been so deeply interested in the foregoing dialogue, that the time, although long, had passed as but a few minutes. It is needless to say that I was delighted with the result, and turning to Emily, I said,—

"Your uncle is in a most admirable frame of mind for carrying on this affair, and for rescuing himself from the clutches of Mrs. Colonel Wheezle. Let us not disturb him by introducing you to-night; there is no occasion, however, for you to remain in the house in a menial capacity. I have just a few words to say to Mr. Crumps, and then I will return to you, and we can leave together."

With this I repaired to the next room, where the old man lay quite in a state of exhaustion, from the long conversation he had had with Mrs. Colonel Wheezle and her coadjutors.

"Sir," said I, "you have managed this affair most admirably, and nothing can impede its success; insist upon your marriage taking place at twelve o'clock to-morrow, and in the meantime will you allow me to get you a will prepared, leaving your property to the daughter of the Emily who had your earliest affections, should such a person be in existence?"

"The daughter of my Emily!" he said. "Oh, sir, do not amuse me with a false hope. Had she a child, and is that child living?"

"Living it is," said I, "and I am not without a hope of discovering her, and bringing her before your eyes. We will meet at St. James's church to-morrow. Till then, sir, farewell, and pray believe that happier days are in store for you."

He pressed my hand, and bade me good night in a low tone, after which I again repaired to Emily, and we together crept down the staircase, and reached the street door in safety.

I waited while Emily fetched her bonnet and small bundle; in five minutes' time we were in the street, and I quite congratulated myself upon bringing Mr. Crumps' affairs to so near a successful issue.

I was unwilling to expose Emily Crumps to the dangers and disagreeables of seeking a lodging at that time of night, so I took her home to my landlady, to whom I explained sufficient of her story to give her an interest in her fate, and left her in her care, with every confidence that she would be well looked to.

It would indeed seem as if Mrs. Colonel Wheezle was quite determined that no mercy should be shown her, for she had rejected the only chance which had been left to her of escaping the consequences she projected. Had she restored the twenty thousand pounds bond to Mr. Adolphus Crumps, the denouement of the affair would have occurred much earlier, and have been of a much more satisfactory nature to her, inasmuch as, although she would have lost what she supposed the secure fruits of her villany, she would not at the same time have jeopardised her liberty, or placed herself in the extremely awkward situation of being indicted for felony, in consequence of what the law calls intermarrying with Adolphus Crump, her first husband, William Wheezle, being still alive.

I was very anxious concerning the proceedings of the morrow; and, after I had safely disposed of Emily, I went to Mr. Seagrove's attorney, and explained to him how matters now stood, at the same time I considered I had ample authority from Mr. Crumps to get a will prepared in favour of Emily, his niece, bequeathing to her the whole of his property, to the confusion of Mrs. Colonel Wheezle and her associates.

"Certainly," said the attorney, "I can draw the will from your instructions, and if carefully read over in the presence of witnesses to Mr. Crumps, and then duly signed by him, it will be a valid document; but, upon my word, doctor, you seem rather to rejoice at the prospect of a row in St. James's church to-morrow morning."

"I do, indeed," said I. "I hope that a great act of justice will be done to-morrow morning, and a church seems to me far from an inappropriate place for its perpetration, and if even people should raise their voices a little during its progress, I shall not be greatly shocked."

"Well, doctor, you've got some singular notions, and some of them not strictly legal; but, however, I certainly will be at St. James's church to-morrow, if you wish it, by twelve o'clock, and if there should be anything going on contrary to statutes, why I can but leave."

"Of course," said I; "and now I shall go to Mr. Seagrove, and solicit his attendance as a witness upon the occasion."

I easily arranged matters with Mr. Seagrove, who, not having the attorney's legal prejudices, was by no means dreadfully shocked that the denouement of the affair should come off in a church.

"You may depend upon my being there," he said; "and, what is more, I've got some news for you, which makes us in some measure independent of the rat-catcher. I have ascertained from a man in the Home-office, who knows all about convicts, that one Bill Wheezle was transported for having stolen goods in his possession; but, in consequence of good behaviour abroad, his sentence was remitted, so that he was believed to be in this country. So far, you see, the rat-catcher's tale is corroborated; and I think we have no reason at all to doubt that Mrs. Colonel Wheezle is his wife: therefore, at all events, we can rescue poor old Crumps from his disagreeable position after marriage."

"Very good. Then let us all agree," said I, "to be punctual at the church to-morrow morning; but I have no doubt, in my own mind, that Bill Wheezle will keep his word, and call upon me early, in which case I can appoint him to be there likewise, and the business can be comfortably arranged."

Thus did I consider that I had settled every preliminary necessary to Emily's interest, and the confusion of Mrs. Colonel Wheezle, who, from that day forward, would no longer be able to exercise her arts of intrigue upon single gentlemen in Alfred-place.

* * * * *

Bill Wheezle was quite in earnest, for by half-past eight o'clock on the following morning he made his appearance at my lodgings.

"Well, governor," he said, "here I is; and how does things get on? Mother Wheezle's still obstropolous, I suppose? Ah! she's a rum 'un; but she'll find as I shall be just one too many for her this time. She's a clever woman, doctor, if she took to wirtue instead of wice; but as she didn't, why she must take the consekens, and there's a end on it."

"Well, Bill," I said, "matters will come to a conclusion sooner than any of us expected; she's going to marry the old gentleman this morning, at twelve o'clock, at St. James's church."

"My eye!" said Bill; "there'll be a flare—St. James's, too; blessed if she ain't a clever woman. Does the old governor she's going to marry seem reconciled?"

"Yes, everything is arranged, and mind you are there at the hour you mentioned, as we may want you particularly."

"Down as a hammer," said Bill Wheezle; "never fear. Twelve o'clock—it's as good as done."

Bill Wheezle then walked away, and I went into the back parlour to breakfast along with my landlady and Emily Crumps. I was quite pleasurably struck by the remarkable change in the appearance of the young girl. My landlady had lent her a dress and some things belonging to her daughter, who was from home; and I could not help thinking how singular it was that, notwithstanding all her privation and state of servitude, Emily still retained that lady-like appearance which it is as impossible to deprive some persons of as it is to bestow it upon others.

She rose at my entrance into the room, and bade me good morning—at once modest and dignified.

"Emily," I said, "I am rejoiced to see you looking so well. Now be sure to-day to dress your hair in that manner which you say you have been told makes you resemble your mother. I wish your uncle, if possible, to be struck with that resemblance at first sight. There were some unhappy differences between him and your father, to which I need not more particularly allude; but, for your mother's sake, he will be inclined to look kindly upon you, and do you the justice of a near and only relative."

"I will obey your instructions in all things," she replied. "Your kindness has been too great already for me to doubt but that you are my sincere friend."

It was half-past eight o'clock exactly when Emily and I reached St. James's church. I wished to be there so early in order to make inquiry if any notice had been given to the officials of the intended marriage, and, to my great satisfaction, I found that such had been the case, for I was informed that, about half an hour previously, the rector had sent down word that he was coming to perform a marriage at twelve o'clock precisely, although they did not know the names of the parties. This was quite sufficient for me; and Emily and I walked arm-in-arm about the neighbourhood for some time, amusing ourselves by looking at some of the shops until it came to be very near twelve o'clock, when we repaired to the church, and prepared to be ready for all contingencies.

The door was open, and we accordingly entered the edifice, and upon my giving a shilling to the pew-opener, and saying we had come to see the marriage that was about to take place, and expected two gentlemen to meet us, we were shown into a pew as near the communion-table as possible, with a promise, should any gentlemen arrive, they should be shown into the same pew.

"Now, Emily," I said, "we have but to await the course of events. Your uncle must positively be married to this woman, in order to rescue his property from her clutches, or from a litigation, probably, that would quite absorb it."

These words were scarcely out of my mouth when Mr. Seagrove and his attorney arrived together, so that with the exception of Bill Wheezle, we were all assembled to proceed to active warfare against the self-subdued Mrs. Colonel Wheezle, who was no doubt congratulating herself upon the delightful prospect that was opened before her.

"Well," said Mr. Seagrove, in a low tone, "we can see all that passes here. Really this woman is running her head into a pretty noose; but she quite deserves it, and I have not the shadow of pity for her."

"I never have any pity," said the attorney, "for illegal conduct. If she will commit bigamy, she must take the consequence."

"There they come," said Mr. Seagrove, as the rattle of carriage wheels announced an arrival.

A great rush of the beadle, the clerk, and two pew-openers, took place. We heard carriage steps let down with a pompous clatter, and in a few moments the sound of persons advancing into the church announced the arrival of the bridal party.

Certainly Mrs. Colonel Wheezle was entitled to the credit of doing the thing handsomely. She was attired in a style of magnificence I can scarcely attempt to describe; her dress of fawn-coloured satin covered her ample proportions, while a perfect blaze of diamonds glittered upon her arms and chest; a robe of white lace was fastened to the top of her head by some magnificent jewel, falling in graceful folds behind her; and as she walked towards the communion table, followed by the gaping beadle and the clerk, she looked like some rather over-grown empress, dressed out for a holiday.

A few paces behind her came Miss Flack; but what was Miss Flack in comparison to the bride?—a farthing rush-light to the sun; and really her silk dress does not deserve a description. Then came a most singular sight—poor, little, old Mr. Crumps, actually in a dressing-gown and silk night-cap, had hold of the arm of Cousin Futhergill, who sported a pair of black tights, and dove-coloured waistcoat, and a light blue coat, with a profusion of basket buttons; and then came two persons apparently of the shabby genteel order; who or what they were I could not divine; but they talked together occasionally, and kept their eyes upon the bridal party, which seemed perfectly aware of their presence, and not at all put out by it. As for us, we all sunk down to the bottom of the pew, keeping our eyes only above the rails.

"What a terrible woman that seems," whispered Mr. Seagrove to me. "Who are those men, doctor, who have come with them?"—"I really don't know—for God's sake, hush! let the ceremony go off, and then we can go and congratulate the bride."

"We will, indeed, with a vengeance."—"Gentlemen, gentlemen," said the attorney, "for Heaven's sake mind you do nothing illegal. I have been looking this morning in the statute against brawling in a church, and its very first sentence is in these words ——"

"D——n the statute!" said Mr. Seagrove; "hold your tongue; there comes the clergyman."

Slowly and solemnly came the rector up the aisle; a benign and heavenly smile played around his mouth—for it was a marriage by special licence, and that the parties kept their carriages; they looked very rich, and Providence only knew how large a fee they might possibly give.

Poor Mr. Crumps was completely hidden behind the ample breadth of Mrs. Wheezle, and the top of Cousin Futhergill's red head being visible, no doubt the rector mistook him for the bridegroom, for he gave a gentle inclination of his head, and then a short cough, as much as to say, "Come along and be married, and remember the parson;" then with an extremely pious look he took his place at the communion table, and with a gentle shake of his head, which it is to be presumed dissipated from within it all earthly vanities, he cast his eyes up to one of the gallery windows and waited for the parties to be placed in their respective positions of sacrifice.

Mrs. Colonel Wheezle was led forward by Cousin Futhergill, and in all her dignity and massiveness she awaited the approach of her victim.

There was a singular look upon the face of the little old man as he placed himself at the altar, and I could see him peering round the church, from beneath his shaggy brows, as if looking for me. I wanted to reassure him, and I looked up just sufficiently for him to see my face. He lifted his hand in intimation that he recognised me; and then the clergyman, casting his eyes down from the gallery window, looked at the strange couple before him with no little degree of surprise depicted in his countenance; for the faded dressing-gown and silk night-cap of Mr. Adolphus Crumps looked very singular indeed, as contrasted with the gorgeous apparel of the bride.

However, the rector was far too well bred to show his surprise very visibly, and recollecting, probably, that he had seen quite as odd couples before at St. James's, he commenced reading the service in that conventional twang in which it is always half chanted by the clergy.

The names given were Adolphus Crumps, bachelor, and Susannah Wheezle, widow. I could see a flutter about the lady's manner as the ceremony proceeded; and her responses were spoken nervously, but that was quite excusable, poor dear creature, considering the natural anxieties, and all that sort of thing, as the novelists have it, incident to her change of life.

The ring was handed to Mr. Crumps by Cousin Futhergill, and the old man duly placed it upon the finger of his trembling spouse.

The ceremony was soon over, and Mrs. Colonel Wheezle wiped the perspiration from her face with her handkerchief, giving a very audible cough of relief, as she no doubt considered herself as the new possessor of half a million of money. She drew herself up, and looked around her with the air of a queen; and I could see her eyes quite flash with pride and vanity; never, perhaps, had a woman been so far to the top of her bent, to meet with afterwards so crushing a relapse.

There was a slight pause among the bridal party, during which the rector slightly blew his nose, and marched from the communion table; then the clerk, in the most oily tones imaginable, asked if the party would please to walk into the vestry.

"Ay, ay, of course," said old Crumps. "Who would have thought of my being a married man at my age—eugh—eugh—eugh!—really it makes one feel quite young again—eugh!"
—"I beg to congratulate you, Mr. Crumps," said Cousin Futhergill, giving him a whack on the back.

"Oh, you're very good," said the old man, dealing him a much more hearty kick of the shins than I thought him capable of. "I wish I could return the compliment—eugh—eugh."—"D—n you," said Cousin Futhergill, rubbing his shins.

"My dear," said Mrs. Colonel Wheezle, stepping up so close to the old man, that he was almost hidden in the folds of her dress, "my dear, everything has been arranged as you wished it, and the will which you insisted upon having prepared, in order that you might sign it in the vestry, is in dear Cousin Futhergill's pocket.—" Is it, indeed?" said the old man; "bless him—eugh—eugh! I long to sign it, life is so very uncertain. Half a million smoothens some of the little casualties of existence. To the vestry—to the vestry—I long to sign the will."

"D——d if he isn't the rummest old blade I ever came near," muttered Cousin Futhergill to Miss Flack.—" I am dumbfounded," said Miss Flack, "and hardly know where I am. Gracious heavens! half a million!"

"I believe you, it is gracious heavens; and it will go hard if you and I don't come in for a share of it."

The whole party now walked towards the vestry; and when they had got a little distance ahead, we left the pew, with the exception of Emily, whom I begged to remain where she was, until she should hear my voice, calling her by name.

We then walked to the vestry, the door of which was closed, but I opened it without any ceremony, and put in my head; the bridal party was there, as well as the rector and the clerk; and although I was a little uneasy at the absence of Bill Wheezle, I was resolved, whether he came or not, to rescue Mr. Crumps.

"So Mrs. Colonel Wheezle," I said, "you have got the better of me at last."

The lady gave a faint scream, and uttered the word "Wretch."

"What is the meaning of this interruption?" said the rector; "do you know, sir, where you are?"—" Certainly, sir; and I have as great a reverence for the walls of a church as I am sure you have. It is the deed, sir, and not the place, which is holy; and I mean to say, that in the marriage which has taken place here this morning, a most atrocious act has been committed. Mr. Crumps, what do you think of it yourself?"

"Eugh—eugh!" said the old man; "this lady is now Mrs. Crumps; and I am, with this gentleman's permission," pointing to the curate, "about to sign my will here, in which I shall bequeath her the whole of my property."

We had all three by this time entered the vestry, and I said,—

"Well, Mr. Crumps, if you will sign such a will, nobody can help it."—" Certainly not—eugh—eugh—give me a pen."

Cousin Futhergill laid a parchment before him, and placed a pen in his hand; then standing behind his back, he looked at me with an impudent leer, expressive of unbounded triumph. Mrs. Colonel Wheezle sat down in a chair offered her by the clerk, who looked amazed at the whole proceedings. As for the rector, he abruptly left the vestry, from which I concluded his fee had been paid.

"Eugh—eugh—this is my last will and testament. Witness it, all of you; it bequeaths the whole of the property to my wife, Susannah Crumps."

In another moment the will was signed, and witnessed by Cousin Futhergill, and the two odd-looking personages who followed the bridal party into the church. Old Crumps then handed it to Futhergill, saying,—

"And now, my good sir, give me that bond, which is of no use; I like to do things regular; let me see it destroyed."
—"It is here," said Futhergill.

"Very good—very good," said the old man. "Here, sir," turning to me, "since you have shown some anxiety about this bond, you can yourself destroy it, and be satisfied that it can be of no further service to Mrs. Colonel Wheezle, now Mrs. Crumps—eugh—eugh!"

"I will take care it is destroyed," said I. "I pity you, Mr. Crumps, for selling yourself to this artful woman. At your time of life, you should certainly have known better."—
"How dare you," cried Mrs. Colonel Wheezle, "make such remarks here? I'll have you turned out by the proper authorities. Here, beadle! beadle! beadle!"

"Do you want any rats cotched?" said Bill Wheezle, putting his head in at the door.

A shriek burst from Mrs. Colonel Wheezle, and her eyes almost started out of her head as they were fixed upon the serio-comic countenance of her real husband. Miss Flack really fainted away; and Cousin Futhergill retreated backwards until he came to the wall and could get no further.

"Right-fol-lol-diodity;" said Bill Wheezle; "rats cotched on the shortest notice—hurrah! Well, Susan, old gal, keep the pot a-biling; it's a sanguinary long lane as isn't a turning. How are you off for bigamy?"

Mrs. Colonel Wheezle gasped for utterance.

"D——n!" groaned Cousin Futhergill; and Mr. Crumps looked from one to the other with very well acted surprise.

"What is all this?" he said. "Something strange? What does it all mean?"—" Vhy, governor," said Bill Wheezle, "it means I've bowled out the rum 'un, doubled on the artful, hammered the correct tenpenny. This ere female woman as cuts such a blessed swell as never was known, is my wife—that ere vagabone, with the red hair, is her fancy chap—there's no accounting for tastes, you know—that ere's the state of the case. How do you find yourself, Mother Wheezle? Something like an old rat caught by the tail, I should say; you've upset the pan and all the fat's in the fire now, you see—right-fol-lol-diodity!"

"Then," said old Crumps, "it appears this woman is not my wife, and consequently my will is nugatory, there being no such person."—Exactly so," said I; "and behold in the vestry fire the ashes of the bond."

"It is rather warm here," said Futhergill; "I think I'll go."
—"As soon as ever you like," said Bill Wheezle; "you'll find Ned Wilks on the steps and a policeman. Ned's turned honest, and sells baked taters, so he's peached agen you about the plate robbery; so you're booked."

Cousin Futhergill sat down in a corner of the vestry-room, with his back propped up against the wall, and his face became ghastly pale, looking very extraordinary in contrast with his red hair. Mrs. Colonel Wheezle made a rush to the vestry door, but the moment she opened it she fell into the arms of a tall, thin policeman, who held her tight, saying,—

"Is this ere the female woman?"—" That's the cretur," said Bill Wheezle. "I am to be the persecutor in this ere case. Mother Wheezle, it's all up. I'll give you a few letters of recommendation when you goes abroad. They wants strong women to chew the wittles a little tender afore they eats them."

Mrs. Colonel Wheezle thought it quite prudent to faint, which she did in the arms of the tall, thin policeman, who dragged her into the church.

"It's all over?" said Mr. Crumps to me. "I feel very weary, and far from well."—" I am happy to say," was my reply, "that it is not all over, but only that part of it which has been of a disagreeable tendency. You will recollect you gave me instructions to get you a will prepared, bequeathing your property to the daughter of that Emily, the recollection of whom still clings round your heart. Will you sign that document here as you have signed the other?"

"I will—I will," he cried, "if this were my last hour upon earth I would sign such a will."

The attorney immediately produced it. It was very short, merely stating that after the payment of his just debts, he left his niece, the daughter of his brother Alexander, residuary legatee of all he possessed. In a moment he attached his signature to it, and we all three witnessed it; the two mysterious strangers then seemed all of a sudden to have found their tongues, and one of them cried,—

"But I want to know, in the middle of all this, who is to pay me for my two carriages which I trusted to Mrs. Colonel Wheezle on the representation that she was going to marry the rich Mr. Crumps, and came here to see the ceremony performed."—" And my diamonds," cried the other; "you all saw my diamonds. Who's to pay me?"

"Gentlemen," said the solicitor, "you have answered yourselves. You trusted Mrs. Colonel Wheezle; you must look to her for your money."

They both rushed in a very frantic manner from the vestry, and I afterwards heard that the one drove off with his crriage, and the other forced a restitution of his diamonds at the nearest magistrate's.

"Mr. Crumps," said I, "after the toil and trouble you've gone through you deserve a pleasurable surprise. Not only have I found your brother's daughter, but I can bring her to you here."—"Here—here!" he said, in a tone of deep emotion. "Do not trifle with me—I pray you do not."

"Not for worlds," said I; and I stepped to the vestry door, and called loudly upon Emily.

In a moment she made her appearance: the old man uttered a cry of joy as he opened his arms.

"'Tis she—'tis she," he said,—" my own, my long-lost, first, last, and only love."

Emily, in a flood of tears, fell into his arms. When we disengaged her the old man was dead.

* * * * *

Emily of course, stepped easily into the fortune of her uncle, and is at this time my happy wife. Mrs. Colonel Wheezle and Cousin Futhergill were both transported, for Miss Flack turned king's evidence, and disclosed such scenes of villany on their parts that no mercy could be shown them.

THE EXECUTION;

OR, THE MURDER AT DALSTON.

YOUNG physicians are glad to take practice whenever they can get it; and, for some years after I had obtained my diploma, I used to attend at the houses of many poor persons without expectation or thought of fee or reward, but merely for the purpose of obtaining an amount of practice which I might have waited at home for in vain.

These attendances I was not unfrequently in the habit, being young and active, of extending beyond the precincts of London, and as I resided in the city, if I had any country practice, it usually lay south or north of Bishopsgate. The singular circumstances I am going to relate occurred at the little village of Dalston, on the road to Walthamstow, but which is now scarcely a village at all, being but one of the mighty arms of the great metropolis, which has by degrees taken in within its own precincts many a rural spot which, when I was young, was quite out of town.

But to my tale. One morning I received a letter from a gentleman resident near Higham-hill, which I may as well give entire to the reader, as it in some manner explains the commencement of the singular train of events which terminated in one more singular than any of them.

The letter ran as follows:—

"DEAR SIR,—Understanding from a friend of mine that you have bestowed some attention upon a class of medical phenomena considered rare and troublesome, I have taken the liberty of addressing you, to detail to you a case which has come under my observation in this immediate neighbourhood, and to which I shall be glad to introduce you, should you be so inclined.

"I should premise that the parties are in a humble though decent sphere of life, and cannot afford to pay you for professional assistance, at all events, as you ought to be paid.

"The family consists only a mother and daughter, of the name of Renfrew. They have seen better days; but the widowed Mrs. Renfrew retired, upon the death of her husband, to Dalston, where she could live cheaply upon the small sum she had yearly.

"Everything appeared to go on comfortably for some time with them, but latterly the daughter, whose name is Harriet, has been at times affected with a species of mania, which has made its appearance, and then left her, under very peculiar circumstances.

"She will be seized suddenly with this indisposition, and for two or three days will fall into a very weak state of mind, during which she will require constant watching, and at the end of that period she will fall into a sound sleep, which will last some days, when she will recover, awakened, it is true, as if she had just come out of some great sickness, but still perfectly sane.

"A medical friend of mine who saw her—but who is now abroad, having an appointment in one of the western colonies—was decidedly of opinion that her insanity was not constitutional, but was occasioned by some cause which was shrouded in mystery, and which he was of opinion must arise from some derangement of the digestive organs, produced by some highly improper and deleterious matter being introduced into the stomach by some means.

"How this may be, I don't know, but, if you will be so good as to visit the Renfrews, you will find them at a cottage called Bute Cottage, Dalston; and I sincerely hope that you will be enabled to unravel the mystery which seems to invest this curious case, and, while you restore Harriet Renfrew to health, likewise restore her poor mother to that happiness of mind which, I am sorry to say, she has been a complete stranger to since her darling daughter has been thus afflicted in her mind.

"Sincerely apologising for thus troubling you, permit me to subscribe myself,

"Dear sir, your obedient servant,
"GEORGE ALGERNON."

This letter rather puzzled me; but I thought, as is too commonly the case, that it being written by a non-professional man, it was perhaps made more of as regarded the case it made mention of than the circumstances would warrant upon a closer inspection. I had no hesitation, however, about at once proceeding to Dalston, and, as the weather was very fine, I was rather glad than otherwise of the opportunity of a walk of a few miles, in which I could unite business with pleasant exercise.

Upon my arrival in this pretty rural village, I inquired of the first person I met, who happened to be a clod-brained fellow, if he could direct me to Bute Cottage, and the intelligent answer I got was,—

"Anan?"

"I want Bute Cottage," said I.

"Ye waunts the *Ranfraws*," he remarked, scratching his head with a vehemence which I expected every moment would bring the whole of his hair out by the roots.

"Ah! the Renfrews," said I; "I do want them."

"So I said. Well, if so be as you want the *Ranfraws*, you must *goo douon* by Hubbins' kiln, and when ye passes that, you must just rub along by Martin's cow-yard, and you'll see Raeburn's orchard a *heed*. Then ye must get on by the pond until ye *cooms* to Mark Higgles' piggery, arter which, as you——"

"Thank you—thank you, my good friend. You have been already so very explicit, that really anything else in the way of direction from you must be quite superfluous. Good day."

"Anan?" said my informant, who, I fancy, understood but little of what I had been saying to him, and stood in the middle of the road gazing after me, till I was completely out of his sight, which I very soon was, for I dived into the first cottage that presented itself, and inquired once more for Bute Cottage, the residence of Mrs. Renfrew.

In this instance I got at once an intelligent answer, and the woman of the cottage went with me a few steps, to a turn in the road, and pointed out a neat little dwelling, saying,—

"That, sir, is the Renfrews' place, poor things."

"Why poor things?" said I, for I was desirous of procuring as much information as I could concerning my patient that was to be.—"Why, sir," replied the woman, "I call them poor things because they have had sickness in their house, and the doctor, which is the worst of all calamities."

"Oh, indeed."

"Yes, sir. Poor Harriet Renfrew has had one of her strange fits of madness again this morning."

"This morning, has she?"—"Yes. Ah! poor thing, they will be the death of her, in spite of all Mr. Luke Mitchell can do for her."

"And, pray, who may Mr. Luke Mitchell be."—"He is a young man who lodges with Widow Renfrew, and, by all accounts, he's very kind to them, indeed, and pays the greatest attention to Harriet."

"What is he?"—"That, sir, I really don't know."

"Thank you for what you have told me," said I. "I feel much interested in the Renfrews, or I would not have troubled you with these questions."

I then hastened towards Bute Cottage, which I satisfactorily ascertained to be the one I was in search of, by seeing the name painted on it.

When I rang the bell, it rather struck me at the moment that I ought, perhaps, to have called on Mr. Algernon first, and got him to introduce me, as it would be rather strange for me, an utter stranger, to introduce myself; but, however, such considerations were now too late, and I resolved to wait the issue, as it would be rather undignified for an M.D. to perpetrate a runaway ring at Bute Cottage.

In a few minutes a female came to the gate with a key in her hand. At the first glance I did not take her for Mrs. Renfrew, who had been described to me as having seen better days, for this was a genuine countrywoman. She opened the gate as she asked me what I pleased to want.

"My name is Doctor ——" said I; "and my errand here is at the request of Mr. Algernon, who resides near here, to see Miss Renfrew, who I understand is very ill indeed."

"Ah, poor thing," said the woman, "that she is. This very morning she was *took agin*. Come in, sir; this way."

followed my guide into the cottage, where a very strange scene presented itself to my observation. Seated by the fireside, in an old arm-chair, was a very beautiful girl—her long auburn hair hung in disordered masses down her neck and bosom—her dress was partially in confusion, and there was an expression about her face of general excitement, which led me to expect delirium.

By her side was an elderly woman, attired in widow's weeds, who had clasped in her own both the hands of the girl, and was weeping bitterly. There could be no mistake as to these being the mother and daughter.

The woman who had unlocked the gate for me advanced towards the weeping mother, and said,—

"Mrs. Renfrew, here's a gentleman as Mr. Algernon has sent. He's some great *doctorer* from London."

The widow turned her streaming eyes towards me, and made a movement as if to rise, but I stepped towards her, saying,—

"Pray, madam, don't disturb yourself; if I can be of any service to your daughter, I shall be very happy."

"God bless you, sir," she said through her tears. "If you can restore my child, the blessing of a mother be upon you. Look at her, sir; oh, look at her!"

I did look at her, and with some surprise too, for I could not make out what kind of mental affliction she was labouring under. There seemed a good deal of muscular rigidity, and some inclination to spasmodic action, while the eyes were turned in a peculiar manner, such as is only seen in some affections of the brain.

"How long," said I, "has she been in this state?"—"Only since early this morning, sir."

"Has she been quite quiet?"—"Yes, sir."

The girl moaned now in the most piteous manner imaginable, and, in a low voice, indicative of great mental anguish, said,—

"Mother—mother! save me—save me! Oh, mother, save me! Help—help—help! The fire—oh, God, the fire!"

"That's the way she raves, sir," said the mother; "she always says something about a fire."

"That's owing to an inflammatory action going on in the brain. How long does she usually remain in this kind of condition?"—"Sometimes nearly two days, sir."

"Does she recover gradually or suddenly?"—"Very gradually, like one recovering from an illness."

"Pray, how does the attack come on?"—"With sickness."

"Are you quite certain she takes nothing of a poisonous nature?"—"Poisonous, sir!"

"Oh, I can answer for that," said the voice of a man, that made me start round, when I saw the speaker standing on the last of a flight of steps, which led to the upper rooms of the house. He was a young man, of sandy, or brick-dust complexion, and certainly nature had been rather sparing in her finer and more elegant materials when she manufactured him, for a more slovenly, ill-looking, sinister-faced rascal I never saw. "I am quite sure of that," he added; "no one can be more particular than Harriet is in what she takes."

I glanced at Mrs. Renfrew, as much as to say, "Pray, madam, who is this that takes upon himself to answer me for you?" and she said,—

"This is Mr. Mitchell, doctor; a very good friend of ours, indeed."—"Oh," said I, and, like the Irishman's parrot, that couldn't speak at all, I thought the more, for I really was sadly prepossessed against Mr. Mitchell's looks.

He came down the last stair on which he had stood, and, with a frowning look, came up to me, shaking his head, and saying,—

"A sad case, doctor, a sad case. I fear the brain is permanently affected. Alas! alas! poor Harriet, what a fate is thine."

I felt quite angry with the damnable whining, hypocritical tone in which this was uttered, and, moreover, I considered Mr. Mitchell's interference at all as a piece of impertinence which I was professionally bound to resent, and turning full upon him, I said, calmly but firmly,—

"Mr. Mitchell, as I hear that is your name, I am a physician, and, in my professional intercourse with my patients, I want no unprofessional opinion, and prefer, and insist upon communicating only with Miss Renfrew's mother, with regard to her daughter's illness, she being a far more fitting person than you, Mr. Mitchell."

So saying, I turned my back upon him, but, before I did so, I could not but catch the expression of malice and deadly hatred that came across his face as I spoke. I thought he would have taken my tolerably broad hint, and have gone, but, instead of that, he threw himself into a chair, and seemed resolved to stay me out, which I would not submit to, but, taking my hat in my hand, I said,—

"Mrs. Renfrew, it is so monstrous a thing for a male stranger to obtrude his presence with a physician and his female patient, that, unless that person leaves the room instantly, I must bid you good day."

"Mr. Mitchell, will you be so good," said the widow, "as to leave us?"—"Some folks are mighty particular," he said, with a bounce, as he rose from his chair, and sulkily left the room.

"Pray, madam, who is that?" said I.—"He lodges with us, sir; but he has been very kind. He lets us want for nothing; and, since poor Harriet's illness, we should have wanted for a good deal but for him."

"He has been brought up in rather a bad school of manners," said I.—"Why, he is rather blunt, but he means well, and is, I'm sure, a true friend to us."

"Well," said I, "that may be, but I can't have him here while I am talking to you about my patient. You must attend to my directions carefully, and I dare say we shall be able to ward off any permanent ill consequences from these attacks of illness. I will come here again to-morrow, and don't allow your daughter, even if she gets much better, to eat or drink anything but of the very simplest kind."

As I spoke, the girl made an effort to rise from the arm-chair on which she was sitting, and cried in the same voice of anguish she had before used,—

"Help, help!—murder! There—there—his hands are red!—red! Oh, save me, Andrew—Andrew! It is not you, not you, not you! Let us fly!—away! away! You shall not hold me. The fire rages—help! help!—save me from him!—him!"—"From who?" cried I, close to her ear.

She started, and pronounced the name of Luke Mitchell.

"There, you see," said I, "she is, for some cause, alarmed at that man."—"Oh, but she is mad now, sir, and Mr. Mitchell tells me that people in that state always speak ill of those they most esteem when in their proper senses."

"Mr. Mitchell has no ground whatever for such an assertion," said I. "Let go her hands, Mrs Renfrew; I will take care of her."

She rose from her chair like one walking in her sleep, and stepped across the floor, moaning as she went, and uttering some inarticulate sounds. I took care to keep close to her, for fear of accidents, but she was by no means violent, and, suddenly crossing her hands upon her breast, she commenced singing, in a sweet, plaintive voice, that was enough to bring tears into anybody's eyes to hear,—

"The wild bird sings upon the thorn,
And many an insect hum
Proclaims the day-god rising high,
But Damon does not come:—
Ah, no!
"A fickle-hearted swain is he,
His vows are false and vain!"

"Oh, God! oh, God! save me from the fire and the red hand of the murderer!"

She gave a loud scream, and I was just in time to catch her in my arms, or she would have fallen.

"Has she ever acted in this manner before?" said I, as I carried her back to the chair, and placed her in it very gently.—"Yes; she will be much better now, when she comes to herself; she breaks my heart with her snatches of old songs that I have heard her sing when she was quite a little thing."

"You must not take too gloomy a view of this case, Mrs. Renfrew. There is some mystery in it at present which I cannot fathom, but I hope to be able to do so, and then strike at the root of the mischief.'—"I hope to Heaven, sir, you may. My poor, poor Harriet!"

The mother burst into tears and sobbed so long that I had the greatest difficulty in getting her to attend to me.

"Let me advise you," I said, "to get your daughter to bed as soon as you can; she will be much better and more comfortable there than in this arm-chair."

The woman who had let me in at the gate now advanced, saying, in a kind voice,—

"Let me help her, Mrs. Renfrew."

"Where is the bed?" said I.—"Only in the next room, sir."

"Oh, then I can carry her at once. Open the door for me." I then took the young girl in my arms and carried her into the adjoining apartment, where I laid her upon the bed. "I will wait," I said, "in the next room, while you undress her, and place her comfortably in bed, and then I will see her again."

She was, I could perceive, in a state of half-syncope, and I was anxious to endeavour to recover her before I left, if it could be done without too much excitement, for in many such cases as Harriet Renfrew's, it is better to let the patients recover of themselves, than to force, as it were, the brain into action by stimulants. I accordingly retired into the next room, and, just as I entered, I saw a slight movement of the door at the bottom of the staircase, and suspecting that it was not caused merely by the air, I went towards it, and pushing it open, detected Mr. Mitchell in the act of listening to what was going on in the room from which I had excluded him.

"So, sir," I said, "you are an eaves-dropper, are you? Are you not ashamed of such conduct?"—"What's that to you?" he grumbled. "Who sent for you, I wonder? You won't get any fees here."

"I don't want any," said I, calmly, "and intend to come every day for nothing; but if you will come out into the front garden, where your cries will not disturb my patient, I will make you remember my first visit, and give you a wholesome lesson in the shape of a good kicking, which you will not forget."—"Don't bully me," he said, as he retreated up the stairs in an evident fright.

"I don't mean to bully,—I mean to kick."—"I'll have a warrant out against you."

"Then you sha'n't have it for nothing;" and I made a feint of following him up the stairs, when he disappeared with a celerity that showed the abject cowardice of his heart.

* * * * *

I sat for some time waiting a summons to the bed-room, during which I strove in my own mind to build up some hypothesis which should account for the very peculiar form of disease under which Harriet Renfrew laboured. Had I been called in suddenly to such a patient, and had been told of the attack as a sudden and quite novel seizure, I should, I confess, have assumed some vegetable narcotic poison to be the cause of all the mischief; but, in this case, there was the difficulty of its not being the first attack, and there being no sort of suspicion of poison on the mind of the mother—no apparent reason for taking it on Harriet's part; and had some noxious weed got mingled in any manner with the ordinary food of the little family, in all human probability all would have partaken of it, and, consequently, all would have been equally affected.

I was absorbed in these reflections, when the woman who was there, I presume, in the capacity of nurse and assistant, came to tell me Harriet was in bed.

"Why on earth," said I to her, "does Mrs. Renfrew keep that very disagreeable man, Mitchell, in the house? I have only just now detected him listening behind that door to all that was taking place here."—"Ah, that's like him," said the woman. "It's my opinion as he's got some design agin Harriet."

"Indeed!"—"Yes, sir. Nobody knows what he is, or how he gets a living."

"Had Harriet these attacks before he came?"—"Oh, dear, no. It was about a fortnight after he came here that she had the first, and from that time Mitchell has been so over-anxious to make everybody believe as she is going quite entirely mad, that it's quite provoking to hear him go on about it."

"He won't convince me of any such thing," said I. "But who is this Andrew that Harriet mentioned."—"Oh, sir, he is a true lover."

"A true lover?"—"Yes, sir. He's the son of Farmer Fletcher, and as good a youth as ever stepped in two shoes. He loves Miss Harriet with all his heart, I am sure."

"And what does he think of this illness?"—"Oh, it's wearing him into his grave, poor fellow. Oh, what a *puncheon* he did give Mitchell."

"Give Mitchell a *puncheon*—of rum, do you mean?"—"No, sir; I means on the head."

"Oh! a punching."—"Yes, sir. Mitchell says, says he, 'Oh! Harriet is as mad as a March hare, and she'll get worse instead of better.' Then young Fletcher he ups and says,— 'The lady you are speaking of,' he says, 'is Miss Renfrew, and take that for your evil words;' so then he gives him the *puncheon*."

"And what did Mitchell do?"—"Oh, he runned away, calling 'Murder!' but he always calls Harriet Miss Renfrew when Andrew Fletcher happens to be near at hand."

"He is a cowardly fellow: but how is Harriet now?"—"She is coming to, I think, sir. Lor, there's a ring!"

A quiet ring at the gate-bell sounded at the moment, and in about five minutes—for I waited to see who it was—the kind-hearted woman returned, ushering in a genteel-looking young man, whose appearance was as frank, manly, and prepossessing, as Mitchell's was the reverse of all those qualities.

"This is the doctor, Mr. Andrew," said the woman. From which I gathered that Andrew Fletcher, "the true lover," stood before me.—"I hope I don't intrude upon you, sir," he said, in a voice of emotion, "but I heard that poor Harriet was again afflicted. Oh, sir, if your art can restore her to what she was, the prayers, the blessings of grateful hearts will be yours."

He turned away his head to hide the tears he could not control, and I replied to him,—

"All that I can do you may depend upon my doing. The case seems to me at present involved in much mystery; but I shall be better able to judge of it when I have had some conversation with Harriet on her recovery from her present attack."—"Sir," he said, "I can never sufficiently thank you for the kind manner in which you speak. Mr. Algernon told me he would write to you, and that you would, in your generosity, he was sure, do all that could be done to alleviate poor Harriet's sufferings."

"That I will; and, if you will wait my return from the next room, we will have some conversation concerning the affair."—"I shall attend you, sir, with gratitude," he said; and I at once repaired to my patient.

She was in much the same state of torpor in which I had left her, and I made up my mind to the same simple means of recovering her. For that purpose I got Mrs. Renfrew to give me a basin of vinegar and water, and, standing a little distance from the bedside, I dashed the mixture with my hand upon her face. A slight twitching of the muscles succeeded; and, after two or three applications, she opened her eyes.

"Well, Harriet," I said, "how are you now?"—"What has happened?—where am I?—is the fire out?—Oh, God! oh, God!" was her reply.

"Have you any lemons in the house?" said I, to Mrs. Renfrew.—"Yes," she replied, producing two from a drawer.

These I squeezed into a tumbler; and, adding a little water to the juice, I offered the glass to Harriet, saying,—

"Will you drink this?—it will do you good."

She was fast relapsing into a drowsy state, and there was a heaviness about her eyes, which convinced me she was suffering from the effects of some narcotic poison, so that I anticipated the happiest effects from the citric acid (lemon juice) I was administering to her, that being the best antidote we have to narcotic poison, its effects in many cases being nearly instantaneous. She took the glass, and drank off the contents.

"Sour—sour," she cried, faintly.

"Yes," I answered; "but you will feel better, I'm sure, directly—don't you now?"

She replied to me in a much clearer voice,

"Yes, much better. Not so sick."—"Now, Mrs. Renfrew," said I, "you must get her out of bed again. I'm giving you a great deal of trouble; but I think I am finding out what is the matter. I say you must get her out of bed again, and you, with the assistance of the good woman who is here with you, must walk her up and down the room, or your garden, if you have one, at the back of the house, would be better."

"Oh, what is it, sir? Will she get better?"—"Certainly she will. You must every quarter of an hour or so give her some of the diluted lemon juice, and keep her in constant exercise. You will soon find her improving."

I was quite convinced, in my own mind, that she had, by some means, swallowed a quantity of *crude opium*, which would fully account for any symptom under which she laboured. But where did she get it? How had she taken it, and why? These were questions which puzzled me not a little to answer.

* * * * *

When I reached the front room again, I found Andrew Fletcher anxiously awaiting my coming; and his eager glance of inquiry, when he saw me, was sufficiently indicative of the deep interest he took in my report.

"There is no danger, whatever, Mr. Fletcher," said I.— "Thank Heaven!" he cried, as he clasped his hands, and a flush of colour visited for an instant his previously pale face.

"Nor," I added, "is there the slightest ground for supposing the existence of any disease. All the symptoms I have seen to-day, and that have been detailed to me, arise from mere sympathetic action on the brain, from extensive derangement of the stomach, and that has been caused by a narcotic poison."

"A poison, sir?"—"Yes, I should name opium as the drug that Harriet must have taken to produce all the mischief. How she came to take it, I cannot pretend to say, for it is not a thing likely to be about the house, nor is she such a child as to put any stray substance into her mouth. I say substance, because I think she has taken crude opium, from the sickness she has experienced, and not any extract from the drug, although I cannot go so far as to assert such to be the case. She may have taken some medical preparation of opium for all I know to a certainty."

"Good God! how could she come by it?"—"That is the question, and, what is more curious, this has not been the first time."

"Not by half a dozen, at least, sir. Although I am relieved from my worst fears, yet I am lost in terror and wonder as to how she could procure and take the poisonous drug you mention."—"So am I. There is some great mystery in the whole affair, which, some day or another, may come to light. At present she is rapidly recovering, and by to-morrow, I expect, will be quite well, when I will call and have some conversation with her on the subject."

"You are very kind, sir. I will, likewise, endeavour to unravel the mystery to the utmost of my ability, and hope to have the pleasure of meeting you here to-morrow."—"I shall be very glad to see you," said I. "Remember that citric acid is the remedy, if she should be seized in this way again, and no medical man at hand to render her assistance."

"We are deeply indebted to you, sir."

I then rose and took my leave, after seeing that Harriet was rapidly recovering. I intended to call upon Mr. Algernon before I left the neighbourhood, but I had not got many paces from the door of Bute Cottage, when I was met by no other than Mr. Mitchell himself, who with an air of great deference and humility, which sat very badly upon him, said,—

"I cannot suffer you to go, sir, without apologizing for my rudeness to you. My extreme anxiety for the recovery of Harriet Renfrew must plead my excuse. I am rough and uncouth in manner, sir, but I have beneath that, I hope, some kindly feelings, and I trust to your goodness to pardon what has occurred between us."—"Mr. Mitchell," I said, "I have now nothing to do with you or your conduct. While I am with my patient, I shall assume what command I think becomes me. Good morning, sir."

"Will you not condescend, sir, to have the extreme goodness to let me know your opinion as to what ails Harriet?"—"I have not seen enough of the case yet, sir."

"But surely you have some opinion?"—"None to communicate."

"Did I hear you use the word poison, sir? because that would be very dreadful. Mad people are uncommon artful sometimes."—"Mr. Mitchell, in one word, I decline entering into any conversation with any one on the subject. You insulted me in that cottage, and now, out of it, you have humbly begged my pardon. It is granted, and, henceforward, we are strangers as we were. I have nothing further to say to you, for I never make my patients a subject of gossip with anybody, except with professional friends with whom I am glad to consult upon their various cases."

He looked at me for a moment as if he was going to burst into a torrent of invectives; but I fancy there was to his eyes

"A something dangerous in me,"

which made him think discretion by far the better part of valour, and, without a word, he turned upon his heel and walked toward the cottage, while I went on my way to Mr. Algernon's, to whom I wished to communicate what had passed during the last two hours at the Renfrew's, in whom I had become very much interested.

I found Mr. Algernon at home, and he listened to my statement with the greatest interest. When I had concluded, he said,—

"I more than ever rejoice that I wrote to you, now that I hear what is your opinion upon the subject. I only surmised a bad medical case, but you certainly put the matter in quite a new light."—"Why, Mr. Algernon, there is a cause for both anxiety and congratulation in this matter. Anxiety concerning the manner in which poor Harriet has been made so unwell, and congratulation that it is really no disease that affects her."

"These attacks may be repeated?"—"They will, in all likelihood. It is a very ticklish matter to accuse any one; but, as a precautionary measure, I should recommend that man, Mitchell, to be sent out of the house. Can you give me any information as to who or what he is?"

"No; he is quite unknown to me; but I share with you fully your suspicions of him, and shall myself speak to Mrs. Renfrew upon the subject. If he be innocent, it cannot matter his seeking a new lodging; and, if guilty, hang the scoundrel, I think I could find it in my own heart to put a rope round his neck."—"Well, well, we must be guided by circumstances. Harriet Renfrew is just now as well as ever she was in her life, I have no sort of doubt. The removal of Mitchell may be the removal of the attacks. I shall be here to-morrow, and you may depend that I will watch this case most carefully."

"If it were not for the danger to Harriet," remarked Mr. Algernon, "it would not be a bad thing to let Mitchell remain for some time to all appearance unsuspected, and watch his actions narrowly."—"True, but there is the danger you mention—a danger of a very serious nature. I vote for his immediate dismissal."

"Then I will be guided by your opinion, and endeavour to prevail upon Mrs. Renfrew to act in accordance with it."

With this understanding we parted, and I repaired to town with my imagination full of all sorts of conjectures regarding Luke Mitchell and the Renfrews. Still, I could find no rational hypothesis by which to explain Mitchell's conduct, even supposing him to have taken some diabolical means of infusing a narcotic drug into some of the food or drink of Harriet Renfrew. The act seemed so diabolically gratuitous, that it quite bothered me to account for it, and the only conclusion I could come to was, that the principal motive of the proceeding must be one of a very powerful nature, and most likely had its foundation in one of the two great passions of humanity, avarice or jealousy.

How any discoveries were to be made with regard to the mysterious proceeding I could not tell, for there was decidedly not sufficient ground of suspicion even against Mitchell to interest the police in the matter, or, at all events, however strong my suspicions might be, I felt that if I were to detail them to any one else I had very little to say.

*   *   *   *   *   *

The following morning, at an earlier hour than I had visited the Renfrews the day before, I reached Bute Cottage, for I wished, if possible, that although my visits might be expected every day, they should not be expected at any particular hour, so that Mr. Mitchell might never know exactly when I might drop in. Mrs. Renfrew received me with a welcome that convinced me how much she appreciated my services the preceding day, and to my question, of how was Harriet, she replied,—

"As well as possible, sir. You would never have supposed anything had been the matter with her. She is quite another person to-day."—"I am glad to hear it. Has Mr. Algernon visited you?"

Before she could reply the door was opened, and Mr. Mitchell made his appearance. There sat upon his countenance a most diabolical attempt at candour, and, holding out his hand towards me, while I put mine in my pocket, he said,—

"Sir, we misunderstood each other sadly yesterday. I dare say I was wrong, and that is quite sufficient, I am sure, from one gent to another."—"Yes," said I, drily; "from one gentleman to another."

"Well, let the past be forgotten," he continued. "It would be strange, doctor, if, after all, we were to become good friends."—"Very strange, indeed," said I.

"We'll shake hands over it, and Mrs. Renfrew will warm us up a little of her elder wine."—"No, we won't, Mr. Mitchell."

"D———n, sir, you—you—"—"You may swear as much as you please, Mr. Mitchell, and yet I shall claim and exercise my right of picking my associates when and where I please. Let it suffice, once and for all, that I decline your acquaintance."

"This is insulting, sir."—"Very like."

His lips quivered with passion, and his face, as I had remarked it once before, turned of a deathlike white. He glanced round the room, as if he were looking for some deadly weapon to use against me, and then, after muttering something which I could not understand, he abruptly left the room. Poor Mrs. Renfrew looked terribly alarmed, and trembled excessively, as she looked at me imploringly.

"Madam," I said, "that man forces me to be rude in your house by addressing me. Why should he attempt, after the unequivocal manner in which I have expressed my dislike to him, to force his acquaintance upon me?"—"Oh, sir, you may depend he means well. He's blunt, and has an odd manner with him, that's all; but he means what he says, although he don't say it always in the politest manner."

"I quite differ with you, Mrs. Renfrew: Mr. Mitchell does not say what he means. I think I can distinguish between real honest bluntness, and that most abominable of all hypocrisies which assumes it for unworthy purposes."—"I don't know what to do," said Mrs. Renfrew. "There's Mr. Algernon has been here, and wishes me to give Mr. Mitchell notice to quit."

"You have done so, I hope?"—"Alas! sir, no. What can I say? He has been such a good friend to us."

"I have no right to dictate to you, Mrs. Renfrew," I said, "about your private affairs. All I will say is, that were I you I would not allow Luke Mitchell to remain in this house if he would pay me ten pounds a week for his lodging."—"But he will stay in spite of you," cried Mitchell, who had evidently been hiding behind the door to listen. "Get me out of the house if you can, d—n you! I won't go. I defy you; do your worst. Curses on you! I defy you."

"Rail on, sir," said I. "You only confirm my opinion that you are a cowardly scoundrel."—"Oh, Mr. Mitchell—Mr. Mitchell," cried Mrs. Renfrew, "don't do anything. Never mind it."

"You need be under no apprehension," said I. "He is too cowardly to resent anything, unless he saw manifestly he must have the advantage. If I were to kick him he would put up with it."

I made a movement as if to put my threat into execution, and Mr. Mitchell bolted out of the room with great celerity on the instant.

"You perceive, Mrs. Renfrew," I said, "that my estimate of the character of that man is correct. For heaven's sake get rid of him."—"We owe him so much money that I dare not," sobbed Mrs. Renfrew. "Since Harriet's illness so many expenses have arisen, all of which he has met, that I know not what to do."

"Indeed! Has he ever proposed love to Harriet?"—"Not to my knowledge. Besides, he knows that she is too much attached to Andrew Fletcher."

"Well, Mrs. Renfrew, there is a great deal of mystery in this affair from first to last. I will now see Harriet, and do you, before I go, let me have an accurate account of what you owe to this Mitchell, when I and Mr. Algernon will consult about the matter."—"I fear I cannot, sir. I have been in such a state of mind in consequence of Harriet's illness that I have not been able to keep my accounts"

"Then demand one of him immediately."

Harriet now entered the room, and if I thought her beautiful when I saw her the day before, suffering from illness, and under every disadvantage, I thought her doubly so now that I saw her with the bloom of health upon her cheeks, and intelligence beaming from every feature of her face.

"You are quite well again, now?" I said.—"Quite, sir, quite."

"Well, Harriet, in the presence of your mother, I declare my opinion that your illness proceeded from poison."—"Poison, sir!"

"Yes. Some poison, by design or accident, has been taken by you. Have you any laudanum in the house, or any preparation of opium whatever?"—"Oh, no," exclaimed Mrs. Renfrew; "nothing of the kind."

"What was the last food or drink you took previous to your attack?"—"Some mulled elder wine. Mr. Mitchell is always recommending it to mamma, and I am in a manner compelled to take some of it sometimes."

"Who prepares it?"—"Oh," said Mrs. Renfrew, "he prepares it himself; he has some particular way of doing it."

"Indeed!"—"Yes. It would quite offend him not to allow him always to get ready the hot elder wine."

"Then I fear I should offend him very much indeed. How often do you partake of the wine?"—"Only now and then. We haven't had any now for some days."

I was silent for a few moments, and then said,—

"Mrs. Renfrew, will you permit me to speak to your daughter alone for a few minutes?"—"Oh, certainly, doctor."

She left the room, and the moment she had done so, I said to Harriet,—

"Excuse, Miss Renfrew, the questions I am about to ask you, as well as the advice I am about to give you, and be assured that both are dictated by the sincerest wish to be of service to you. Has Luke Mitchell ever professed an attachment to you?"—"He has."

"And been, I presume, repulsed?"—"Most certainly. At his own urgent request, I abstained from mentioning the circumstance to my mother, and he promised that he would never again torment me with addresses I declined so positively receiving."

"I am answered, and I thank you for the candour which has dictated the answer. Now, will you promise me that the next time he brews any elder wine for you, you will take but a very small portion of it, and save the remainder for me?"—"Good Heaven!" cried Harriet, turning very pale, "a light breaks in upon my mind; he has attempted to poison me."

"Hush—hush!"—"But you mean, sir, to insinuate as much!"

"I do, Harriet; but for the present let that be quite between ourselves. Breathe the suspicion to none—not even to Andrew Fletcher."

Harriet blushed crimson at the pronunciation of the name of her lover, then, dropping into a chair, she burst into tears.

"Nay, now, Miss Renfrew," said I, "you need not distress yourself in this way. On the contrary, I think you have just cause for felicitation, seeing that we are coming at the truth as regards your illness, and that, consequently, it is very unlikely again to occur."—"You are very kind to me, sir," she sobbed; "but it is dreadful to think there should be such wickedness."

"Ah, Harriet, as you grow older, and see more of the world, you will not feel so surprised at any amount of wickedness that may come under your observation. Follow my advice, however, and I think you will find the result satisfactory?"—"I will, sir, you may depend. We have too few friends not to pay the greatest attention to any kind counsel that is offered to us."

With this understanding, then, Harriet Renfrew and I took leave of each other, after my cautioning her to say nothing of the arrangement to her mother or to Andrew Fletcher, for I feared the terror of the one and the anger of the other would effectually interfere to mar the scheme I had in view for bringing to punishment Luke Mitchell, who I now could not entertain a doubt had some extraordinary motive for producing all the confusion that had occurred among the Renfrews.

I directly went to Mr. Algernon, and told him what state the affair was now in, when he strongly urged the propriety of employing some one on whom we could rely to watch Luke Mitchell, and take a note of wheresoever he should go. To this I acceded, for I was exceedingly anxious to have him committed in any way, and it became of consequence to know how and from whom he got the poison.

Mr. Algernon had a young man in his employment as clerk and secretary, who, he assured me, would be fully competent to undertake the task of following Mitchell, and upon whose report we could with perfect safety rely; so it was finally agreed between us that he should be placed upon the secret mission, with instructions to follow Mitchell from Bute Cottage, and take particular notice of every house he should enter, and of every one he should hold any sort of communication with. This young man's name was Griffiths, and he appeared to be both intelligent and active, setting out upon his errand at once, and promising not to lose sight of Bute Cottage until Luke Mitchell, who he knew very well by sight, should emerge from it.

* * * * * *

It was towards night that I received from Mr. Algernon the following note:—

"My Dear Sir,—Griffiths followed Luke Mitchell from Dalston to London, and saw him meet a man with whom he held a long and private conference in Lincoln's Inn Gardens. Of course he could not approach near enough to them to ascertain the subject matter of their discourse, but from their manner, and the cautious way in which they met and separated, he thinks it was a meeting for some purpose of a very questionable character. They sat down for some time on a wooden seat at the end of the long walk, and Griffiths says there is ample room for any one to hide himself behind it, and so listen to their conversation should they again select such a place of meeting. To-morrow, when you come this way, we can talk of it, and perhaps arrange something. I am, my dear sir, yours very truly,

"Geo. Algernon."

I thought with Mr. Algernon, that something might be done in the way of overhearing what passed between Luke Mitchell and his mysterious friend, although I could not help regretting to myself, and it is a regret I have very, very often indulged in, that, in order to expose knavery, we are compelled to fight knaves with some of their own weapons, and to resort to tricks which otherwise would be unjustifiable and unworthy; but without going all the way with the saying of some political partizans and metaphysicians, that the end sanctifies the means, no one can hope to discover iniquity, or thoroughly protect the innocent from wicked machinations, without the exercise occasionally and cautiously, of a little trickery, which, unless in such a case sanctified by the end in view, would be quite indefensible. While I was reasoning thus, and hastily despatching my morning meal, previous to proceeding to Dalston, I was surprised almost beyond any surprise I had ever experienced in my life, at my landlady's entering my room and announcing,—

"Mr. Luke Mitchell!"—"Luke Mitchell!" I cried; "curse that fellow's perseverance. Tell him I won't see him. Turn him out. Of all the impertinent things that ever I heard of, his calling upon me is about the greatest."

"Lor, sir! is he a highwayman?"—"Worse, a great deal —worse—worse. Turn him out of the house, and if he won't go, send for a constable."

"That would save me trouble," said Mitchell himself, appearing at the doorway of my room. "I shall, unless you show me good cause to the contrary, proceed at once to a police-office to make a serious charge against Andrew Fletcher."—"You a charge against him! Has he"—I thought at the moment of the *puncheon* I had been told Andrew had given to Mitchell, and I, in my own heart, hoped he had bestowed another upon him—"has he kicked you well?"

Mitchell ground his teeth savagely, and I could see he was making great efforts to overcome his passion. He succeeded, and in a few moments added,—

"No, sir, he has not kicked me; nor do I think he will have an opportunity of so doing. Your conduct towards me has been anything but friendly—I may, indeed, say anything but courteous—notwithstanding that, I have come to warn you that probably I may want your evidence, in order to prove that Harriet Renfrew's indispositions have arisen from some narcotic poison having been administered to her."

I was so amazed at the fellow's assurance in coming to me with such words in his mouth, that for some moments I could make no reply to him. When I did speak, I endeavoured to do so as calmly as possible.

"Mr. Mitchell," I said, "I am quite ready, whenever you are, to give such evidence. Harriet Renfrew has been poisoned by a narcotic drug."—"That is quite sufficient, sir. I shall only now wait until I get a little more conclusive evidence, and then, as a friend of the family, I shall go to a magistrate, and state the circumstances which, I dare say, will produce a warrant for the apprehension of Andrew Fletcher."

"Andrew Fletcher!"—"Yes, Andrew Fletcher."

"Why, you uncompromising vagabond! how dare you carry your impudence so far as to accuse him?"—"I'd accuse you if I saw cause. Ay, or the proudest he that ever wore a head. Be careful, sir, what you say; I would advise you to be very careful. I give you the option of assisting me or not in this painful inquiry; but, at all events, my present friendly and forgiving visit ought to have its due and proper effect upon your mind."

I don't often get out of temper, but the cool impertinence of all this was too much for me, and taking Mr. Mitchell by the collar, before he could escape me, I cried to my landlady,—

"Be so good as to open the street door."

She obeyed me, and in a moment I led Mr. Mitchell along the passage.

"Murder—murder!" he cried. "Help—murder—police!"

In another moment he was sprawling in the kennel.

* * * * *

Here was a change in the aspect of affairs, with a vengeance; the suspected had become the accuser, and the innocent and manly Andrew Fletcher was charged with the production of the very circumstances which had caused him evidently the acutest feelings of uneasiness.

I hurried on my coat and hat, and started off for Dalston at a speed in accordance with the state of excitement that my recent interview with Mitchell had put me in. Long before I got there, however, I was perfectly cool and composed, and began to turn over the circumstances in my mind.

"What is the meaning of all this?" I asked myself. "When shall I find a key to this extraordinary affair? What, in the name of Heaven, is Luke Mitchell planning?"

Full of these conjectures, I arrived at Mr. Algernon's; for I wished to see him and have a consultation before I proceeded to the Renfrews. I related to him what had occurred, to which he listened with silent and unusually serious attention. When I had finished, he shook his head in a very mysterious way, much to my discomfiture, and said,—

"Ah, I expected something of this sort."—"You expected it? bless me, what do you mean?"

"I am very uneasy."—"So am I."

"I don't wonder at it. Tell me, doctor, are you a great observer of persons?"—"Tolerably so. Why do you ask?"

"Because I want to know, if you were called upon to give a description of Andrew Fletcher, what would you say?"—"What would I say? oh, I should say a thin young man of about two-and-twenty, dark brown hair, rather pale."

"And his dress?"—"Let me see—he had a black satin waistcoat."

"What cravat?"—"Cravat—cravat—oh! I recollect, it was a sort of a lavender colour with dark spots."

Mr. Algernon gave a deep groan.

"Why—what—what the devil!" cried I, "do you want to drive me mad? What's the matter now?"—"You shall hear, doctor. This affair has taken the most extraordinary and awful turn that any affair could take—you must prepare yourself for a very great surprise—a very great shock."

"Go on—go on."—"Griffiths, my young man, was going through Shoreditch last evening, when he saw Andrew Fletcher or his ghost go into a chemist's shop. You understand?"

"Well—well—What then?"—"By a presentiment that he could not resist, Griffiths followed him in, and heard him ask for half an ounce of crude opium."

"The devil!"—"Exactly—half an ounce of crude opium. What do you think of that?"

"I don't know what to think; I'm in a complete mental whirlwind, and the only thing that comes uppermost in my mind is a conviction of Fletcher's innocence."—"It's well you said conviction, for in my mind a 'conviction' will have something to do with it. Do you remember seeing a walking-stick which Fletcher had?"

"A curious knobby-looking thing?"—"Yes. Well, Griffiths doubted almost if it was Fletcher till he saw that knobby stick, and then he was convinced. What's to be done, doctor—just say now what's to be done."

"It's very easy for you to say what's to be done," said I; "I should like you to find that out yourself. I'm in a state of amazement."

"So am I; but, as Thingummy says, facts are stubborn things. How are we to get over all this evidence against poor Fletcher? There's enough to have him apprehended at once; and if so much had been found out as regarded Luke Mitchell, you know very well we should have given him into custody at once, having no further doubts of his guilt."

"We should; and yet let us pause awhile. There is some terrible mystery yet involving this whole affair—a mystery which time may unravel—but which at present appears so very inexplicable. Get Griffiths still to watch Luke Mitchell, and I am not without a hope that we shall catch him tripping. Andrew Fletcher may buy crude opium without intending it for Harriet Renfrew; nay, he may explain his purchase quite satisfactorily. Who knows but, in his deep anxiety to know if my opinion is correct, he may not be trying some experiment with the drug?"

"On himself?"—"Yes, on himself. I should say he was in that state of extreme mental affliction concerning Harriet, that he would scruple at no personal risk or sacrifice to satisfy himself that no real disease was attacking her."

"Ah, but his mental agitation which you witnessed might have been assumed."—"Then, if such were the case, he is the greatest actor the stage has produced. I never saw Garrick; but Andrew Fletcher, if he could assume the grief and interest I saw him exhibit, may well rival that hitherto unrivalled man."

"You are very confident."—"I am. Nothing short of positive, and such proof, too, as shall not leave the least loop-hole for a doubt, shall convince me that I have been deceived in Andrew Fletcher. I will myself see him, and if he tenders no explanation concerning his purchase of the opium, I will deem that to be a circumstance which greatly strengthens the suspicions against him."

"I think you would be imprudently committing yourself, doctor, by at all mentioning that he had been seen. Any explanation should come spontaneously from himself."

"It shall, or not at all. Rely upon me, he shall not be prompted to an explanation. I will now proceed at once to the Renfrews, and still hope that this affair will be wound up very differently from what its present aspect portends."

I then left Mr. Algernon, and walked hastily to Bute Cottage. My reception was, as usual, full of kindness, and I fancied Harriet looked quite well, and more blooming than ever.

"Oh, I am so much in hopes," remarked Mrs. Renfrew, "that this distressing illness will occur no more. We shall then be so very happy. We never know the value of health and peace of mind, doctor, till we are deprived by some unexpected and sad calamity of those dear possessions."

"That is true, madam," said I. "Have you seen Andrew Fletcher since I was here?"—"Oh, yes. He seldom allows an evening to pass without being here."

"Oh, indeed."—"That's his knock," said Harriet, suddenly, as a gentle rap came to the street door, and she anticipated the servant in opening it.

There were murmured a few words in the passage, and when the lovers entered the room, Harriet looked so extremely happy, that a pang of extreme sorrow crossed my heart at the remote possibility of the chosen of her heart proving unworthy of the affection she bestowed upon him.

"Oh, it cannot be," I thought. "The whole affair is too improbable—too monstrous; what motive could Andrew Fletcher have? I will never believe in his guilt, even were it forced on my mind by tenfold the circumstantial evidence which at present is in favour of the hideous supposition."

Then I fixed my eyes upon his countenance, and one more open, frank, and candid, I thought I had never beheld.

There was no possibility of mistaking the character of that face. It spoke truth and kindness from every feature.

"Good morning, Mr. Fletcher," said I.—"Good morning, sir," he replied; "you will never know, sir, how grateful I am to you, because—because I cannot find words to tell you, and it is quite impossible I should ever have a practical opportunity of convincing you of my gratitude. You have, by restoring my dear Harriet, given me a new life. God bless you, sir, and reward you."

"You need be under no further apprehensions with regard to Harriet," I said, "although crude opium is a very bad thing for any one to take."

I fixed my eyes upon his countenance as I said the words crude opium, but there was not the shadow of a change. All was respectful attention, mingled with happiness and calm serenity.

"Yes—yes, so I have heard," he replied.

"Half an ounce," I continued, "would be quite fatal."—"Yes, sir. My poor Harriet, what fiend in human shape could have placed in your way so awful a drug?"

"Awful, indeed, Mr. Fletcher. Did you ever see any crude opium?"—"Never, sir; what is it like?"

He fixed his eyes on my face with such utter unconsciousness as he spoke, that I was staggered, and changed the conversation by saying,—

"Where is your knobby stick, Mr. Fletcher? it seemed to me quite a curiosity in its way when I saw it last."—"I have left it in the passage," he said; "it is a curiosity."

Leaving the room, he entered with it in a moment, and added,—

"I have really got quite attached to the stick, and I believe I am known by it sometimes when otherwise people would scarcely recollect me."

"Indeed!"—"Yes. You perceive that some of the knobs, by the aid, and not much, either, of the imagination, appear like grotesque faces of men and animals, some of which are exceedingly highly finished."

He pointed out to me so naturally and unaffectedly some of the grotesque faces he mentioned, that I became sure it could not be a bit of acting. I longed to say to him plumply, and at once, "Andrew Fletcher, did you purchase some opium last evening in Shoreditch?" but I controlled the impulse, and made up my mind to let things for a time take their course, feeling quite clear that something or another to simplify or further mystify the matter would occur very quickly. We went on talking for some time on indifferent subjects, and I was on the point of taking my leave, when another knock came to the door, and Mrs. Renfrew said,—

"It's Mr. Mitchell. For Heaven's sake, doctor, say nothing to him. I have given him notice to quit."

"You are quite right. Do not be under any apprehension. I will be very careful."

The parlour door was opened in a moment afterwards, and Luke Mitchell made his appearance. I never shall forget the expression of his countenance. It was fearful, although the lips were parted in a smile—a smile, however, of such a peculiar character as the arch enemy of mankind might himself wear if he had just succeeded in snatching some erring soul from Heaven.

"Oh," he said. "A goodly company. Well—well. It's all the better. A good deal better. Providence acts wisely."

"Good day, Mrs. Renfrew," said I, rising. "Good day, Harriet and Mr. Fletcher, I shall see you all to-morrow."

"Nay, now, don't go, doctor," said Mitchell. "Don't think of going just yet, doctor."

I made him no answer, but commenced putting on my cloak.

"Allow me to help you," said Fletcher, and he kindly assisted me, whispering in my ear as he did so,—

"Do not heed him, sir. He is brutal; but if you will allow me to walk a little way with you, I wish to speak to you concerning a terrible suspicion that has crossed my mind."—"Certainly, put on your hat and come along."

"Why, you are not going likewise, Fletcher," cried Mitchell.—"I am."

"Ho! ho! ho! Upon my soul I can't help laughing. Ha! ha! ha! I'm subject to merriment. Now, don't go just yet, Fletcher, I advise you."—"When I ask for your advice, Mr. Mitchell," said Fletcher, "it will be time enough for you to give it. At present I want none from you."

"There you go again. How hasty you all are. Upon my word, it's absurd. You look charming to-day, Harriet."

Andrew Fletcher doubled his fist, and with one blow sent Mitchell with a thundering whack in a corner of the room.

"I warned you, Luke Mitchell," he said, "that if ever you again presumed to call Miss Renfrew by her Christian name, I would knock you down. I am a man of my word."—"D—n you all," cried Mitchell, struggling to his feet; "but I'll have my revenge, and such revenge, too, as shall make your hair stand on end. I'll see you hanged—ay, hanged, Hilloa—hilloa. Time—time. He's here. Come in. Seize the prisoner. Ha! ha! ha! Who has the laugh now? I said I would have revenge, and I, too, am a man of my word, Andrew Fletcher."

He rushed to the street-door as he spoke, and opened it, still shouting,—

"Now—now. Come on. He's here."

"Good Heaven!" cried Mrs. Renfrew, "what's the meaning of all this?"—"Is he mad?" said Fletcher.

The parlour door was flung open, and two men stood on the threshold along with Mitchell.

"There is your prisoner," cried the latter, pointing to Andrew Fletcher. "Seize him lest he make some desperate effort to escape. Seize him, I say. Seize him."—"You are our prisoner," said one of the strangers, producing a constable's staff, and laying hold of Andrew Fletcher by the wrist.

"Your prisoner?"—"Yes. I have a warrant against you on a charge of wilfully poisoning."

A shriek burst from Harriet, and she sprung forward, clasping her lover by the arm.

"No—no. He is innocent. Andrew Fletcher a poisoner! No—no, he is innocence itself."

"We can't decide upon that," said the officer. "You had better all of you accompany us to the magistrate, and then you can on oath make your statements."

Luke Mitchell threw himself into a chair, and burst into an immoderate fit of laughter.

"Ha! ha! ha!" he shouted. "Has it come to this? Oh, wise, steady Andrew Fletcher, why did you poison the girl? For shame, man; what motive could you have had?"

"Villain! liar!" cried Fletcher.—"Rail on—rail on. Ho! ho! ho! Why did you buy half an ounce of crude opium in Shoreditch? Long impunity had made you too bold, and you were seen, Andrew Fletcher."

"Hear me, all of you," said Fletcher. "As I have hopes of peace here, and mercy hereafter, I am innocent. All this is to me like a frightful dream. Oh, Harriet—Harriet!"—"Andrew—Andrew, you are innocent. Rely on that, and on Heaven. You know you are innocent."

"There's plenty of evidence, said Mitchell. "We need not trouble the young lady. The doctor here is an important witness. Officers, it would not be a bad plan to search the prisoner. Ha! ha! ha! This is glorious. How could you be so wicked, with your hypocritical face, Andrew Fletcher?"

One of the officers dived his hand into the coat pocket of the bewildered young man, and producing something wrapped in paper, he said,—

"What's this? Does any one here know what this is?"—"Show it to the doctor," cried Mitchell. "There, show it to the doctor. He's an amazingly clever man, and has come all the way from London on this business. Show it to him. He will tell you in a moment."

The officer handed the substance to me. With trembling hands I unfolded the paper. One glance was sufficient. Well did I know the drug. *It was a large lump of crude opium.*

"What is it—what is it?" roared Mitchell.—"What is it?" said Fletcher.

"Ay, sir; just give it a name," said the officer.—"Opium!" said I.

"God help me!" cried Fletcher, and he sunk on the floor in a state of utter insensibility.

* * * *

The screams of poor Harriet were awful, and she was carried out of the room in a most pitiable state of agitation. By restoratives I succeeded in producing some signs of animation within the next quarter of an hour in Andrew Fletcher, whose guilt now seemed proved past all dispute. And yet I doubted—yet I could not bring myself to believe in such a freak of nature, that she had created a being with every external appearance of virtue and honour, to give him the heart of a demon.

As for Mitchell, he seemed amazingly to enjoy the confusion he had created, and glanced at me now and then with such a devilish triumphant expression, that it took all the reason I was master of to prevent me from making an assault upon him.

"You may smile, villain as you are," I said; "but remember there is a God in Heaven, who has said, that for a season the wicked shall triumph; but only for a season. Luke Mitchell, a day of retribution will come yet."

"Go preach to old women," he replied. "I defy you and all your musty doctrines. Your own evidence will insure the conviction of Andrew Fletcher, and you have likewise an assault to answer for which you committed when I did you the favour of calling upon you."

"What has happened?" moaned Andrew Fletcher. "Good God, what has happened? Where am I now?"—"You must come with us," said one of the officers. "I suppose we must have a coach."

"Be composed, Andrew Fletcher," I said. "Although at present a cloud hangs upon your destiny, it will disappear, and all may yet be well."

"Tell me, tell me," he said, "what is it? Have I had a frightful dream? Oh, where am I now? Harriet, Harriet, has any harm come to you?"—"No," said I. "For Heaven's sake compose yourself, Mr. Fletcher. You are placed in trying circumstances. Do not give your enemies power over you by any want of nerve or resolution on your own part."

"Of what am I accused? Good God! I am quite innocent, even in thought, of any wrong. Of what am I accused?"—"Of attempted murder," said the officer. "We have a warrant against you, granted on the oath of a Mr. Mitchell, charging you with poisoning a young lady. You can say whatever you like, but bear in mind that whatever you do say will appear against or for you as the case may be."

"I am innocent."—"Say no more, Fletcher," said I; "that's quite sufficient."

Poor Harriet caught at the word sufficient as if it had cleared her lover of the charge which hung over him, and she clung to him with the most frantic eagerness.

"You are innocent, Andrew," she exclaimed. "Who could start so monstrous a supposition as that you could injure me?"—"The villain Mitchell," said Fletcher, with a shudder. "From the first moment that I saw that man a sense of evil stole over me, and a dread of him crossed my soul."—"Dread nothing, Andrew, you are innocent."

"Get a magistrate to believe it," sneered Mitchell. "It's well, Miss Renfrew, you have such a friend as I am to step between you and danger."

Harriet turned to him with flashing eyes, and she was evidently on the point of giving utterance to her scorn and contempt, when she checked herself, merely saying,

"Unworthy even of a word, reproach is wasted on such a heart."

"We cannot wait here all day," said the officer. "There's my comrade has brought a coach; so now come on."

"I will accompany you, Fletcher," said I.—"And I," cried Harriet.—"And I," said Mitchell.

"If you attempt to set your foot in the coach," said I, "you shall find cause to draw it out again very quickly."

He shrunk back, and in a few moments Andrew Fletcher, Harriet, myself, and one of the officers were in the coach. The word was given to drive to the nearest police-office, and, the other officer mounting on the box with the coachman, we started, leaving Mr. Mitchell to find his way by some other conveyance as best he might.

* * * * * * *

I need not carry the reader through a long and painful scene at the police-office. Suffice it to say that Andrew Fletcher was placed at the bar on a charge of poisoning, with intent to murder, or produce some bodily injury.

Luke Mitchell swore that going through Shoreditch on the preceding evening he saw the prisoner enter a druggist's shop, and having had his suspicions awakened by my having declared my impression that Miss Renfrew had been poisoned by some narcotic drug, (the rascal had the impudence to use my name as if we were quite intimate,) he entered the shop after Fletcher had left it, and ascertained from the chemist that he had purchased half an ounce of crude opium. He then concluded by saying,—

"Your worship, to establish this case fully, here is a host of most unwilling witnesses. God only knows what their motives were or are, but they made an endeavour to establish this very charge against me. I do honestly believe a plot was laid for my destruction, and that they are caught in their own snare. Heaven always assists the innocent and oppressed!"

"Let those witnesses come forward then," said the magistrate.

I was compelled to state that I believed Harriet Renfrew had been poisoned with crude opium, and I was likewise compelled to depose to the finding of that drug in the coat-pocket of Andrew Fletcher.

The officer proved searching the prisoner, and handing to me what I had declared to be opium.—The chemist who had been sent for, said that, to the very best of his belief, the prisoner was the man who had purchased of him the opium.—Another witness, namely, Griffiths, Mr. Algernon's clerk, I knew could likewise depose to the same fact. Who, then, could stem the torrent of evidence against poor Fletcher?

"I am innocent," he said. "I call upon Heaven to witness to my innocence. By the God that made me, I declare my innocence!"

The magistrate looked very grave, and shook his head.

"Young man," he said, "I am very sorry for you. What may be your motives I cannot pretend to say. This appears to be a most singular and distressing case. Your previous character is attested by the reluctance with which respectable witnesses give testimony against you."

"They are in connection with him," cried Mitchell. "It's a conspiracy altogether against me."

"If you say another word I shall have you turned out of the court," said the magistrate; "we cannot deal in such insinuations here. The absurdity of a young lady poisoning herself in order to materially injure you is too ridiculous. The prisoner stands fully committed for trial, and all the witnesses must be bound over to give their evidence."

"I am innocent—God of Heaven, hear me!—I am innocent," cried Fletcher.—"A jury must decide that," said the magistrate. "Remove the prisoner."

* * * * * *

With great difficulty poor Harriet was got back to Bute Cottage, and Mitchell actually had the surpassing insolence to claim his right of entry to the house likewise. The scene at home between the mother and daughter was painful in the extreme. Besides, Andrew Fletcher's father and mother were soon apprised of what had occurred, and they came to Bute Cottage in a state bordering on distraction to inquire the particulars.

"My son guilty of such an act?" said the old man. "He would sooner have cut off his right hand than injured voluntarily a hair of any one's head."—"My good sir," said I, "pray exert what patience you can. This is the most mysterious affair that ever I heard of; but still I, in common with Harriet and her mother, cling to a belief in your son's innocence."

"I am, myself," he said, "not more innocent than he." —"Believe me no pains shall be spared to establish his innocence. Be but patient, and all that can be done shall be done."

After, then, administering as much comfort in the way of hope as I could to Harriet, I repaired to Mr. Algernon's, and told him all that had occurred.

"Well," he said, when I had finished, "as I told you before I am completely staggered. Can you fight against facts?"—"No; and yet I believe in Andrew Fletcher's innocence."

"Then, doctor, you are an extraordinary man."—"Perhaps so; but will you accompany me to the chambers of some respectable attorney, and let us retain him for Fletcher?"— "With all my heart."

I could see that Mr. Algernon quite believed in Fletcher's guilt, and that what he did in the matter was more out of compliance to me than from any hope of saving the young man. However, I was, so long as I got assistance in the matter, not disposed to quarrel with any one's motives, and we went together to Lincoln's Inn, where were some respectable and intelligent attornies, to whom I was slightly known.

To the head of the firm we detailed the whole of the case, and when we had concluded the head of the firm looked very grave indeed, and remarked,—

"Gentlemen have you any doubts about this case?"—"I have," said I.

"Indeed."—"Yes; I believe still in the innocence of Andrew Fletcher."

"Well, faith is a fine thing. Of course we will undertake his defence if you like, and leave no stone unturned to

serve him; but a conviction must ensue. There is one point, however, that should be seen to. Can he prove an alibi with regard to the time he is sworn to having been seen at the chemist's in Shoreditch?"

"I don't know; but I will go to Dalston this evening myself and ascertain that. I should hope that he can. It is easy enough to place some opium in an unsuspecting man's pocket."

"Certainly," said the attorney. "If he can prove an alibi that supposition will almost follow as a thing of course."

"I wish he may prove it," said Mr. Algernon; "but I never in all my life was in such a state of doubt and botheration. All my sympathies and all my predilections go with Fletcher, and yet my reason tells me that I cannot get over the evidence of his guilt."

"I will believe him innocent," said I, "until I have abundance of proof, which I do not consider I have yet, to the contrary. In my opinion, some one ought still to be employed in closely watching Luke Mitchell."

"But what good can that do?" said Mr. Algernon.—"I don't know; but if you, sir," to the attorney, "can find me an efficient person for spying all his actions, I will pay him."

"Oh, we have always such people at hand. I will send some one to your house early to-morrow morning, and you can give him your own instructions."—"Thank you. Let it be so arranged."

With this we parted. The day was considerably advanced, but I was determined to see the parents of Andrew Fletcher, and ascertain from them if they could account for their son's time on the preceding evening, or if they knew any one who could.—I found the family in the deepest affliction, and when I explained to them my errand, the father said,—

"Alas! sir, I fear we cannot do so. My poor boy went from home yesterday evening, saying he was going for a walk. He took his favourite stick with him, and where he went I don't know at all."—" Confound that knobby stick!" thought I; "it keeps poking in as evidence on all sides."

The mother burst into a complete paroxysm of grief, exclaiming,—

"Oh, my poor, poor Andrew!—they will kill him. He is innocent, sir, indeed he is. He loved Harriet Renfrew better than he loved himself or all the world beside: he would have laid down his life to save her little finger from aching, and now they will kill him, innocent though he is."

She sobbed hysterically, and I had the greatest trouble in restoring that afflicted family to anything like a state of composure. It was only by over and over again declaring my firm conviction of the innocence of Andrew, and my determination to do all that was possible for him, that I at all succeeded in giving them any hope. I stayed a long time with them—quite long enough to become convinced that they were amiable, kind-hearted people, and more and more to believe that from such a family there could not come one guilty of the frightful crime imputed to poor Andrew.

The last coach had gone. This was vexatious, the more so as the evening was as disagreeable a one as could well be imagined, and I had no resource but to walk.

Having once come to this conclusion, I immediately set off and made my way towards town. Now, Dalston is a very pretty place in the summer, especially in fine weather, but not so pleasant when you are benighted, as I was, with the knowledge that all means of conveyance was hopeless, and the additional misery of a wet and dark night.

The wind was very keen and searching; the rain fell heavily, but was broken and dashed against the unfortunate pedestrian like so much spray, whenever the wind, which it did very often, rose with sudden violence, sweeping the avenues of trees that lined the roads with a peculiar rustling and rushing sound.

Trees are the delight of a summer landscape, but on such

occasions as that in which I was placed they were really the most disagreeable things I had to encounter; for, independent of their collecting the rain and letting it fall more heavily on you than you would experience if they were not present, they, whenever the wind shook them, rained down such a deluge of monstrous-sized drops of water as to make one really nervously agitated when one was compelled to encounter another.

The night was so dark that it rendered walking in the roadway dangerous, so that I was compelled to abide the pelting of the pitiless storm in the position the most favourable to the reception of its utmost wrath.

I, however, walked on, bad and dark as it was, never slackening my pace, save now and then when I looked up to make sure that I held my way correctly; but then I was punished by a deluge of water from some overhanging bough as it waved in the wind. This was too much to be borne without extreme resignation, but as I knew there was no help for it, I did bear with the evil, at the same moment I endeavoured by exertion to escape the earlier from it.

Cold, weary, and comfortless, then, I at last reached home, and was glad to get to bed, although my rest was disturbed all night by dreams concerning the affair at Dalston, during which all sorts of strange images floated before my bewildered imagination.

* * * * *

The morning came, as gentlemen who write novels say, and I was not a little impatient to see the cunning fellow that the attornies were to send me as a spy upon Luke Mitchell. By nine o'clock a Mr. Smith was announced, and there was introduced to me a thin, miserable-looking man, who, presenting to me the card of the attorney, said,—

"Sir, I am told you want to bowl out somebody. I'm your man. I'd find a needle in a bottle of hay, if it were requisite."

"Well, Mr. Smith, this matter won't be quite so difficult. Did you hear from Mr. Staples, the attorney, any particulars?"—"Yes, all of them. Ten shillings a-day?"

"Oh, that's your charge."—"It is. Shall I go? A day's pay in advance?"

"There it is. Do you know where to go to?"—"Bute Cottage, Dalston—one Luke Mitchell is to be bowled out. It's all right. Good morning. I shall be here at this hour to-morrow."

So saying, Mr. Smith, making a very slight bow, took his leave.—The reader may suppose I was in a tolerable state of excitement till the following morning, when Smith, abruptly as before, and punctual to a minute, made his appearance.

"Well, well," said I, " have you found out anything?"— "A little. I followed Mitchell from Dalston to town, then to Lincoln's-inn, where he met a fellow in the gardens."

"Yes—yes."—" The fellow had a knobby stick."

I gave a great jump, and in an instant a supposition flashed across my mind that Andrew Fletcher had been personated by some one in order to criminate him.

"A bit of crab," I cried,—" a curious bit of crab?"— "Yes—full of odd faces."

"The same—the same."—" They had a long conversation together, and laughed a good deal as they examined the stick. They seemed to think it a capital joke."

"Did they?"—" Indeed did they. I couldn't hear what they said exactly, but I found out who the fellow with the stick was."

"Who?"—" He's what they call out-door clerk to an attorney of the name of Paterson, in Carey-street."

"What sort of person is he?"—"Rather tall and thin; a decent enough looking young man."

"So I thought. Well, Mr. Smith, here is your day's fee. Be so good as to persevere in this business, and if it should end in the acquittal of Andrew Fletcher, a five pound note shall be at your service."

When Smith had gone I went post haste to Mr. Algernon, and dragged him off to the attorney's in Lincoln's-inn, detailing to him on the road the discovery of the stick which Smith had made, and ending by saying,—

"Now, Mr. Algernon, we have a clue to this affair. Do you not see that it is possible the whole matter might be managed so as to present just the aspect it does, and yet Andrew Fletcher be perfectly innocent? Luke Mitchell administers poison, Heaven knows why or wherefore, to Harriet Renfrew. He finds himself strongly suspected by me, and he concocts a plan for not only shifting his own guilt on to another's shoulders, but to have ample revenge on Andrew Fletcher, who, in addition to being his rival, had given him the *puncheon* I was told of. He gets a man strongly resembling Fletcher to purchase crude opium at a chemist's. He furnishes him with a walking-stick resembling Fletcher's, and then he comes forward himself as evidence of the fact."

"I see that you have got up a very good hypothesis upon the subject, doctor. I own that I have now a doubt of Andrew Fletcher's guilt, and it is a doubt of which he shall have the full benefit, for I will now join heart and hand in trying to aid him with you."

"I knew you would, Algernon. What a great gratification it will be to us both to have saved an innocent man from such an atrocious plot as that which has been got up for the destruction of poor Fletcher."

When we reached the attorney's, and detailed to them the discovery that had been made, they quite coincided with me in my opinion that there was abundant ground for suspecting the truth lay as I had surmised.

"We know something of Paterson, in Carey-street," said the head of the firm, " and he will render us every assistance, I am sure, in unravelling the business."

"It would be a capital thing," said Mr. Algernon, "if we could get the fellow who meets Mitchell to make a full confession."

"It would, indeed. I will tell you, gentlemen, how you might try it, although it would be unprofessional of us to have anything to do with such a way of proceeding."

"How?" said I.—" Why, I will arrange with Mr. Paterson to be out of the way this evening, and if you like both of you to call upon his clerk, you can try whether you can bully or coax the truth out of him."

"I am willing. What say you Algernon?"—" Yes; I will go with you."

"Very well," remarked the attorney. " You know I must be supposed to know nothing of such a plan."

"Exactly. Come along, Algernon. Do you go to Dalston, and just tell the Renfrews and the Fletchers not to despair. Meet me to-night, at seven o'clock, at the gate of Lincoln's-inn, and we will see if this out-door clerk of Paterson's is made of penetrable stuff."

"Make it past eight," said the attorney, " and then Paterson's office will be cleared of his other clerks, and this fellow, whose name is Adamson, will be there alone, for I will get Paterson to give him some paper to copy which shall detain him."—" Agreed—agreed."

I made use of rather a desperate expedient in my attempt to alarm Mr. Adamson,—an expedient which I knew was illegal, and attended with dangerous consequences; but I was so intent upon getting at the truth as regarded the affair, that I determined, for once in the way, to run a risk which I should not like to do again.

I went to Long Acre at a shop where miscellaneous property of all descriptions was sold, and purchased a constable's little brass staff, and kept it in my pocket to be produced to Adamson as a last effort should he resist all other soft inducements to a disclosure of what I firmly believed to be the truth, namely, that he made one in a conspiracy for the ruin of poor Andrew Fletcher.

* * * * *

The sonorous clock of Lincoln's-inn was pealing forth the hour of eight, when I stood at the Chancery-lane gate in anxious and momentary expectation of the appearance of Mr. Algernon, and feeling quite strong in the possession of the constable's staff I had purchased in Long Acre.

There seemed at that hour to be a general turn out from the various chambers of the inn, and many a dapper clerk hurried past me in order to get home quickly, and dress for a "sixpenny hop," or to be in good time for half-price at one of the "houses." The little fat gate porter had just begun to look at me with eyes of suspicion, and several young ladies had requested to be informed if my temper was agreeable, when, to my joy, Mr. Algernon arrived.

"I hope I have not kept you waiting?" he said.—" No; I was before the time."

"And so should I have been, for punctuality *is* one of my virtues, only I thought of a famous scheme, and it took some time to carry it into effect."

"Indeed. What was it?"—" Why, what do you think now?"

"Oh, how can I think about it?"—" Well, then, I'll tell you. I have bought a constable's staff. What do you think of that, eh?"

"The devil you have."—"Yes, I have. Here it is—a nice little brass one."

"Why so have I, and here it is."—"The devil you have."

"Yes, and a nice little brass one."

We knocked our staffs together, and simultaneously burst out laughing, to the no small surprise of the passers-by, who must have thought us two mad Bow-street officers.

"Well," I remarked, "this is an odd coincidence, but let us avoid producing them if possible; we must at once tell this Adamson that all is discovered, and that we give him an opportunity, if he likes to embrace it, of turning evidence against Mitchell."—"Exactly."

"Then, if he hold out, we must produce the staff and affect to take him into custody, which may bring him to his senses at once."

"Agreed. Do you, doctor, commence the conversation, for you are an amazingly plausible fellow, and have such a face for saying anything, whether it's true or not, that I wouldn't for the world take the job out of your hands."

"Upon my word, Algernon, you are very kind and complimentary; but, as I think you might bungle it, I will commence the conversation with Mr. Adamson. So now come along."

A few minutes' walking brought us to Paterson's chambers in Carey-street, and being, by an announcement upon the door-post, directed to the first floor, we ascended and rapped at the door. It was opened by one of those wire communications by which clerks save themselves the trouble of getting off their stools to let visitors into offices, and we found ourselves in a dimly-lighted, dingy-looking room, where sat a young man writing.

"Mr. Paterson has gone," he said. "He is never here beyond six o'clock at the very latest."—"We don't want Mr. Paterson exactly," said I.

"What do you want, then? It's over office hours."—"We want you, Mr. Adamson."

"Eh?"—"We want you, I say. Do you know one Luke Mitchell?"

I could see him turn very pale, as he gasped,—

"Do—I—know— Luke — Mitchell?"—"Yes; although your answer is of very little consequence. I have the pleasure of informing you, Mr. Adamson, that all is discovered. You understand me; the opium and knobby stick business. How do you feel, Mr. Adamson?"

"Feel be d——d!" he said. "What do you mean?"— "We mean that you and Mitchell are found out. You personated Fletcher, who, as you know, is quite innocent of the crime."

"Are you mad?"—"No; but if you neglect the opportunity you have of turning evidence against Mitchell, and so saving yourself, you will be mad. Do you understand that?" He trembled, and dropped the pen he had held in his hand, as he said,—"You—you don't know what you are talking about, nor do I. Go about your business, and leave me to mine."

"Indeed," replied I, with a smile. "Perhaps you will deny there is such a person as Harriet Renfrew."—"Who is she?"

"Have you the face to ask? Come, come, Adamson, you are a man of the world; you may have been tempted to this affair by Luke Mitchell, and now, as it's all up, you had better make the best escape out of it as can."—"Once, more," he said, "I don't know what you mean. Don't come here with your conundrums."

"So you will be obstinate?" put in Mr. Algernon. "Do you know a chemist's in Shoreditch, eh? Where did Mitchell and you buy the knobby stick, Adamson?"—"If you don't clear yourselves out of this office," he said, "I'll call in a constable."

"We won't trouble you to aggravate your voice much," remarked I, "to do that; and as I spoke I produced my constable's staff.—"You're our prisoner," cried Algernon, likewise producing his.

Adamson glanced from one to the other of us in silence for a moment; then, in a faint, weak voice, he said,—

"You—you are officers, then?"—"We are. Once more we ask you will you save yourself by turning evidence against Luke Mitchell? He has made an offer to do so as regards you, which the prosecutors have refused."

"D—n him, has he?"—"Precisely."

"Then I will: here goes. It's all a do to get hold of the property."—"Property?"

"Yes, Harriet Renfrew's property. Her cousin in Sydney has left her about twenty-five thousand pounds. Luke Mitchell knew of it, and wanted to marry her; then he——"

"Stop," cried I. "Before you go any further, Mr. Adamson, come with us to Fletcher's attorney's; there you shall receive a ratification of the promise we have given you, and be spared the trouble of telling your story twice over."

"I am your prisoner, I suppose, and must go where you may please to take me. So Mitchell would have let me in for it, would he?—d—n him!"—"Indeed he would. Come along."

In a very nervous and excited manner Adamson put on his hat, and as he did so I could not help being struck with his remarkable likeness to Andrew Fletcher,—a likeness which would have deceived Fletcher's most intimate friends as to his identity, if it were aided, as had been the case, by dress.

He walked between us, believing himself veritably in custody, till we came to Lincoln's-inn, where we had the good fortune to find the senior partner of the attornies just on the point of leaving his chambers for the night.

We accompanied him into his private room, and by the broad glare of light that was there I could see what a state of pitiable agitation Adamson was in.

"This man," said I, indicating him as I spoke, "has come to make a full and free confession of his own and Luke Mitchell's guilt in endeavouring to fix a crime of magnitude upon the innocent and maligned Andrew Fletcher, your client, sir."

"Gentlemen,—gentlemen," said Adamson, trembling excessively, "you will give me your solemn promise to let me off if I tell all the truth. I am a poor fellow, and suborned by Michell. You will not prosecute me, gentlemen?"

"I will undertake," said the attorney, "on behalf of my client, Mr. Andrew Fletcher, to subpoena you as a witness against Luke Mitchell, and so save you from the prosecution."

"Thank you, sir. You know me, perhaps, sir? I am Mr. Paterson's out-door clerk, sir."—"Tell your story. I know who you are well enough."

"Yes, sir—thank you all, gentlemen. It will be all right. Luke Mitchell is as great a scoundrel, gentlemen, as there is unhung, I assure you."

"We want no remarks, but a plain, distinct statement, which you must sign in presence of these witnesses," said the attorney. "So now, Mr. Adamson, speak slowly, and I will, if you please, write from your dictation."

"Yes, I will tell all—I will attempt to disguise nothing. You must know, gentlemen, that of course I am not so rich as I should like to be, and poor people are open to a great many temptations which rich people are not. Luke Mitchell is an old acquaintance of mine; he's a *cannibal*, gentlemen."

"A what?"—"A cannibal. He always has been a cannibal, and always will be. He hates work."

"But what do you mean by his being a cannibal?"— "Why, he lives on his family. Lots of things they have put him to, but on one excuse or another he always came home again, and lolloped about like an idle vagabond as he is. Well, gentlemen, one day I found out quite by accident that a large property had been left to Miss Harriet Renfrew."

"But how," said the solicitor, "came you by such exclusive intelligence? When large properties are left to people, it generally gets pretty well known."

"Yes, but I am very sorry to say, sir, that in *our* profession there are some people not exactly so honest as they should be."

The lawyer coughed.

"And such being the case, the fact of this large property being left to Harriet Renfrew was not divulged by the attorney who had custody of the will, because, you see, he was well bribed by the heir-at-law to suppress such a document. Destroy it he would not, as, by the occasional production of it to the said heir-at-law, he got, procured, or enforced from him divers sums, current coin of this realm, anything therein before mentioned in anywise notwithstanding——"

"None of your nonsensical jargon here," said the attorney; "all we want is a plain statement."

"Very well, gentlemen; to proceed. I by a sheer accident, which it is needless to relate, became acquainted with the fact of the existence of such a will, and instead of making a good profit—ahem!—I mean instead of proclaiming the fact to the proper parties, I, like a fool, told Luke Mitchell of it."

Here Mr. Adamson gave a deep groan, and intimated his

thorough opinion that honesty was the very best policy, *sometimes.*

"And what proceedings," said I, "did Mitchell then suggest?"—"Why, he promised me, if I kept the secret, that he would manage, by hook or by crook, to marry Miss Renfrew, and give me ultimately two thousand pounds for my information and assistance. The Renfrews had lodgings to let, and his first step was to get into the house as a lodger. Then he robbed his father of all he could lay hands on, pawned his sister's clothes, and carried on a fine game in order to get money enough to cut a dash at the Renfrews. Oh! gentlemen, you may believe me when I say that Luke Mitchell is a most thundering rogue."

"There are other thundering rogues as well as Luke Mitchell," said the attorney; "but go on."

"There are indeed. Well, in a little while he came to me to say there was a young fellow of the name of Fletcher who had been beforehand with him, and had won the affections of Harriet Renfrew. He dreaded every day that they would marry, and for some time he was quite at his wit's end to think of some scheme to stop the match. At length he came to me, and told me he had thought of a plan.

"'Adamson,' says he, 'I've got it now. The only thing which will put an effectual check upon Harriet's marriage with Fletcher, and terminate by throwing her completely in my power, will be some desperate illness on her part,—some illness which will assume a very alarming character. Now, you must go to different chemists and buy me some opium. I will take care to give it her in sufficient doses to produce great apparent indisposition.'"

"And you did so?"—"I think I did."—"Crude opium?" said I.—"Yes, that's what I bought. Mitchell had a book which related the effects of the drug, and he came to me grinning like one o'clock, some days afterwards, to say that the Renfrews were in great confusion on account of Harriet's sudden illness, and that it was quite out of the question any marriage taking place, and that he meant to persevere till he tired out Fletcher, and then, when she was weakened both in mind and body, take her himself, as if out of charity."

"After which of course the property was to be claimed?"—"Yes; some plan by fraud or force was then to be got up to get possesion of the will, and I was to have my two thousand pounds."

"A pretty pair of scoundrels you are," remarked Mr. Algernon.—"If you please, sir," said Adamson.

"Let me beg of you to make no remarks," said the attorney in a whisper to Algernon. "Go on, Mr. Adamson—go on."—"Well, matters went on in this way for some time, till a few days ago, when Mitchell came to me again, perfectly furious and raving.

"'There's an infernal doctor,' he said, 'come from London to see Harriet, and he has found out that she has had poison given her.'—'The devil he has,' says I.—'Yes,' says he; 'and he has hit upon the very thing, too. He seems one of those infernal persevering, troublesome fellows that will never leave anything alone. Curse him, if I don't mind he'll ruin me yet.'—'What's to be done?' says I.—'I don't know,' says he; 'but I wish he would break his d—d neck the next time he comes to Dalston.'—After fuming about thus for some time he went away, not being able to think of any plan of bothering the doctor. The next day he came again, and he was as pale as death, and all of a tremble.—'What's the matter now?' says I.—'The doctor suspects me,' says he. 'I overheard him; he suspects me. There is only one plan which can save us.'—'Us,' says I. 'You, you mean.'—'No,' says he, with an oath; 'whatever harm comes to me, you shall be a sharer in it. If I go down you shall, depend upon that.'—From that moment, gentlemen, I began to see clearly what a vagabond he was."

"Oh! that opened your eyes."—"Wonderfully; and yet, gentlemen, what could I do? There I was in his power; I felt like a fellow in the middle of a ditch. It was just as bad to go back as forward; so I went forward, and agreed to do just as he wished. Then he told me his plan of operations.—'It so happens, Adamson,' he said, 'that you are amazingly like Fletcher. He is a thin young man, about your height, and if you were dressed alike you might easily be mistaken for him.'—'What then?' says I.—'Why,' continued he, 'we will fix this poisoning business upon his shoulders. I will furnish you with some articles of clothing that will make your resemblance to him very great indeed, and you must go to a chemist's and purchase some crude opium, after which, if an opportunity offers, I will manage to slip it into Fletcher's pocket. If it's easy to pick a man's pocket of anything, it's surely much easier to drop something into it.'—What could I do, gentlemen—what could I say?—I was compelled to assent. Well, he brought me a cravat, which he said was like Fletcher's, and also a peculiar-looking knobby stick, that he told me he had had a hunt all over London to buy, as he was particular about its appearance. That same evening I went by his directions to Shoreditch, which lay all in his way to Dalston, and I bought half an ounce of crude opium at a chemist's there."

"Which you delivered, I presume, to Mitchell?"—"Yes."
"What occurred next?"—"I scarcely know. We met the next day again, and had a laugh over the matter. He said it had been perfectly successful, and that he had got the better of the d—d doctor at last, for Andrew Fletcher was committed for trial, and nothing could save him."

"Where was that meeting?"—"In Lincoln's-inn Gardens."
"Is that all you know of the transaction?"—"All—all."

"There is one question you must answer, and upon your answering that truly will depend not only your escape from the consequences of your foolish criminality, but likewise a handsome reward."

"What is it, sir?"—"Give us the name of the attorney who has the will which is of such importance to Harriet Renfrew."

"His name is Michaelson. He lives in Lincoln's-inn Fields."—"That will do. Now, Mr. Adamson, I will trouble you to read over and sign the minutes I have made of your present confession."

This was done, and Mr. Algernon and myself placed our names to the document as witnesses.

"Now, Mr. Adamson," said the attorney, "I will trouble you to remain here an hour or two, while we go to transact a very necessary part of this business. Your confinement shall not be of long duration. Come, gentlemen; we will leave for a brief space Mr. Adamson to his own meditations."

When we reached the square of Lincoln's-inn, the attorney said,—

"You will perceive the absolute necessity of getting possession of the will Adamson spoke of. I feared to let the scoundrel go, lest he should give the alarm to Michaelson, who is a regular black sheep of the law. That will once destroyed, and what would become of poor Harriet's claims?"—"You are quite right," said I; "but you have heard, I presume, of the real, or supposed, difficulty, of getting a lump of butter out of a dog's throat?"

"I know what you mean, but we will try force. Persuasion, I know well, would be quite thrown away. My object is now, with you two, to call upon a magistrate, and get a search warrant against Michaelson, which will enable us to find out the will, if it be really in his possession. Such a proceeding is rather irregular, but sometimes, in the law, we do irregular things, and leave folks to bring their action, if they like, as a lesser evil than the one we have evaded by the little irregularity, you see."—"Exactly. Look here."

I produced the constable's staff I had purchased, and at the same moment so did Mr. Algernon, to the great surprise of the attorney, who looked perfectly astonished.

"Why—why—dear me," he said; "how came you by these?"—"We bought them."

"But you are running some risk, give me leave to tell you, gentlemen."—"Exactly. It's a legal irregularity. We got the better of Adamson by the production of these symbols of authority, so they answered the purpose well."

"Let me advise you, then, to get rid of them again as quickly as possible; you are liable to a heavy fine."

We pocketed our staffs, and proceeded, with the attorney, to the private residence of a magistrate, with whom he was acquainted. He, the magistrate, was fortunately at home, and we stated to him the whole of the case, at the same time showing him the confession of Adamson.

"Now," said the attorney, in conclusion, "we want a search warrant against Michaelson to enable us to look for the will." — "I really, upon my word," said the magistrate, "almost think I ought not to grant it. You see it's not like searching for stolen property—I doubt my power to help you."

"Well, I had my doubts," remarked the attorney. "Yes; I have no doubt you had. You see, although I should be amazingly willing to help you, I don't see how I am to do it. If I were not a magistrate—a-hem!"

"What?" said I.—"Why, sir, I rather think I might run a little risk."

"Oh, a little legal irregularity?"

The attorney coughed, and so did the magistrate, who then added,—

"It's quite illegal to go into a man's house and tumble about all his papers in search of a will—quite—but—a-hem! It would amount to a trespass, if not a felony; but then a jury would, perhaps, look to the circumstances of a case; or, perhaps, there would be no prosecution at all. Mind, I don't advise any such violent and illegal proceedings—far, very far, from it."

"Come along, doctor," said the attorney. "Good morning, we are sorry to have troubled you."—"Oh, don't mind at, gentlemen. Do nothing illegal. Don't go and knock at a man's door, and then bounce in and find the will, leaving m to take his remedy."—"No, we won't," said the attorney.

It was not very far to Mr. Michaelson's residence, and we ought our chance all the better by his having his offices on e ground floor of the house he occupied as a dwelling.

"I don't know if I must not leave you here," remarked e attorney; "the fact is, he is very likely to know me by ght."—"Here," said I; "I will lend you my cloak; you in muffle your chin up in it, and he will scarcely be able to cognise you if he knew you ever so well?"

"I will risk it; we can but be transported."—"A pleasant ea," remarked Mr. Algernon, as he knocked at the door. Doctor, as we are in for it, we may as well use our staffs gain; we can but be hung."

"Agreed," said I, and I took from my pocket the symbol f authority which had so effectually frightened Mr. Adamson nto a confession of so much importance.

The door was opened by a footboy, with no end of sugarloaf uttons on his jacket, and in answer to my inquiry, for they ad made me spokesman, if Mr. Michaelson was within, he aid,—

"He is, sir, but he is just taking his coffee."

"Oh, indeed. Just tell him some gentlemen wish to see im on business of importance, and very much regret that hey are under the necessity of disturbing him at his coffee."

"But, sir, I cannot."

"Oh, nonsense, we must see him; is he alone?"—"Yes but——"

"Thank you; do you know what that is?"

I pushed the end of the constable's staff in the page's face, and the close contact with the little gilt crown seemed to him anything but satisfactory or pleasant. He opened his mouth so wide with horror and astonishment that I am quite sure he could have swallowed the staff with perfect ease, and staggering back against an old mop that hung in the passage, he gasped out the most expressive monosyllable, "Lor!"

"Come on," said I; and Mr. Algernon, giving his constable's staff a flourish over the page's head, ascended the staircase after me, closely followed again by the attorney, who, I could see, looked with an eye of dismay on the anti-legal proceedings he had indiscreetly allowed himself to be drawn into.

The house seemed handsomely and luxuriously furnished, and our feet sunk noiselessly into the carpet which lay upon the staircase, so that our approach was unheard by the attorney, who was enjoying his coffee and his *otium cum dignitate* in his really splendid drawing-room.

We knocked at the door, and I presume Mr. Michaelson thought it was his page, for he said, "Come in," with such a pompous tone, that it appeared the very height of condescension. We, however, quarrelled not with the manner in which the permission to go in was acceded to us, and turning the handle of the lock, we all presented ourselves before the astonished eyes of the clever practitioner.

I wished I had had time to take an accurate survey of that room, for hundreds of pounds must have been lavished upon it. It was truly superb; and there sat Michaelson, in an elegant dressing gown of velvet, sipping some coffee, and slowly cracking filberts.

"What the devil!" he cried, as he saw us; "what the devil is all this, eh?"—"You are my prisoner, Mr. Michaelson," cried I.—"And mine," said Algernon.

The nut-crackers dropped from Mr. Michaelson's hands, and he looked absolutely stupefied. Recovering, however, in a few moments, his confusion, he said,—

"There is some mistake; who do you take me for?"—"Come, come, you had better be careful," said I; "we have to search the house."

"For what, pray?"—"That we decline telling, just at present. Your keys, Mr. Michaelson."

He rung a bell violently, and we waited to see who would answer the summons. In a few moments the page appeared, and Michaelson cried out in a loud voice,—

"Run to the nearest police-station, and give my compliments to the acting inspector, requesting he will come here directly."—"If you do," said I, to the page, "we will take care to have you transported."

I had observed, from the first moment that we entered the room, there was an iron safe under a handsome sideboard, and that a massive key was in the lock of it.

"Search that safe," I said, and I strode towards it.—"If you so much as lay a finger on anything in that safe, you are a dead man," said Michaelson, and opening a drawer in the table before him with great rapidity, he took from it a pistol, and held it full at my breast.

Something at the same moment came swinging over my head, causing me involuntarily to duck. It was a huge hassock, thrown by Algernon at Michaelson, when he saw his hostile movement, and it hit him full in the face. In an instant bang went the pistol, and I then closed with him, for he might have produced another, that possibly might have done mischief, although that had not.

"Don't ill-use me," he cried; "I am your prisoner. I will give evidence against Baynes. You will find the forged bill in that iron safe."

"What the deuce does he mean?" said Mr. Algernon.—"Some other inquiry we know nothing of," suggested the attorney; "in looking for one thing we often find another. Mr. Michaelson, there is another document we must have of you."

"What is it?"—"A will, bequeathing large property to one Harriet Renfrew."

"In the iron safe," he groaned; "you will find it there. I will turn evidence in that case too."—"Very well. Then, in that case, you may very likely save yourself," said I, as, proceeding at once to the iron safe, I brought out a number of papers, one of which bore the welcome indorse of "Will of Mr. Joseph Atcherley Renfrew."

"I have it," I whispered to the attorney.—"Very good," he replied. "Then the very best thing we can do is to get ou of the house as quickly as possible. We have nothing to do with any other of Michaelson's transactions, and this one, considering the means we have been compelled adopt to get possession of this most important document, we had better back out of as quickly as may be."—"Agreed."

"You speak to him, then; he may never see you again, and he is very likely to see me often. He does not recognise me as yet, and I am very anxious that he should not."

"Mr. Michaelson," said I, "you must be aware that you stand in a very ticklish position."—"I know all about that," he replied.

"Very likely; but it may be rendered less so by a little bit of candour."—"Indeed!"

"Yes. Who are you acting for, in regard to this will of Joseph Renfrew's?"—"The heir-at-law—as great a scoundrel as ever lived."

"Very well. You and he can manage matters now as you please; you will hear that this will is proceeded upon and duly proved. Upon condition that you throw every facility in the way of the proof of it, so that Harriet may become possessed of the property that is of right hers, you will escape all proceedings against yourself."

"What!" he cried; "and—and am I not to be taken?"—"No."

"Not about Baynes's bill?"—"The less you say of that the better; we know nothing of it but what you have had the candour to state."

"The devil!"—"Good evening, Mr. Michaelson."

"I'm done—done."—"Rather so, certainly. But if you keep your own counsel you need not trouble yourself."

Leaving the lawyer perfectly aghast, we departed from his house, congratulating ourselves wonderfully upon the ease with which we had become possessed of the important document, which otherwise might have been, at a single hint of danger, thrown into Mr. Michaelson's drawing-room fire.

"What's to be done now?" remarked Mr. Algernon; "how is this Adamson to be disposed of?"—"Adamson," said the solicitor, "must be made useful in procuring the release of Andrew Fletcher."

"But that will compromise Michaelson."—"Not if he manages well. If we bring no charge against Michaelson for detaining the will, nobody else can. He is a great scoundrel, but as we have partially promised him, on consideration that he gives us what assistance he can, if called upon, an absolution for the past, we must endeavour to keep our words."

"I wish to do so," said Algernon; "but there is one who must not, on any account, escape; that one is Luke Mitchell."

"Listen to me," said the attorney. "What I propose is, that Adamson, who has acted faithfully towards us, so far as his information goes, shall be set at liberty to-night, with directions to meet us all at Bute Cottage to-morrow, in order to confound Luke Mitchell. I should like of all things to see that villain's astonishment when he perceives Adamson with us."

"Agreed," cried Algernon and myself—"agreed; at what hour shall we meet?"

"Why, seven in the evening will be most convenient for me. I think we have Adamson quite safe, for his indignation at Mitchell will be sufficient to induce him to give no warning of the coming danger; and should he feel disposed to do so, a threat that if Mitchell be not apprehended and punished on his evidence, he shall himself take all the consequences of his own written confession, will keep him faithful."

* * * * *

I felt quite easy now about Harriet Renfrew and her future fortunes. Adamson, with many protestations of thankfulness at the lenity shown him, promised to go with us, in order to apprehend Luke Mitchell, and we determined on that occasion to take a real constable with us.

The solicitor promised to procure a judge's order to have Andrew Fletcher brought up to the police office for further evidence, which would of course terminate in his discharge, such evidence being that of Adamson; and he could so time the proceeding as to enable Fletcher to accompany us to Bute Cottage, it being next to impossible that Luke Mitchell should receive any alarm of the circumstances before we should arrive and take him into custody.

All this we arranged before we parted; and for once in a way everything ran smoothly as we desired it. The judge's order was procured, and at about five o'clock Andrew Fletcher, to his intense surprise, found himself brought up again to the police office. The magistrate took the depositions in a private room, so that as little eclat as possible was given to the proceedings.

The evidence of Adamson was quite conclusive; and when he put on the cravat which had been supplied him by Mitchell, for the purpose of representing Andrew Fletcher, the likeness was so great between the two, that the magistrate remarked,—

"I rejoice very much at the turn this case has taken. It proves most emphatically how careful magistrates and juries ought to be in receiving evidence of personal identity. You are discharged, Mr. Fletcher, and as no one proffers a prosecution of Adamson, I shall leave him in the hands of you, gentlemen, only hoping that Luke Mitchell, the still greater criminal, will not be allowed to escape. I shall grant a warrant against him, and now send with you an experienced officer to apprehend him."

Fletcher was all amazement. He looked around him like a man in a dream, and it was not until I took him by the hand, and said,—

"Come, come, Fletcher. You seem quite bewildered; are you not rejoiced at the turn affairs have taken?"

"How can I thank you all?" he cried. "Oh, Harriet! Harriet! what joy will this be for you?"

"I congratulate you, sir," said the magistrate, "on your near prospect of happiness."—"I am no match," he said, "for Harriet, wealthy as she will now be. I shall leave her free, as if we had never breathed a vow."

"And if I do not very much mistake her," said I, "she will feel far greater pleasure in receiving those vows in her prosperity than ever she had in making them, when fortune wore a rougher aspect towards her."

There was no time to be lost, and we all proceeded in a coach to Dalston, an officer being seated with the coachman, armed with a warrant for the apprehension of Luke Mitchell, whose career, I congratulated myself, would soon be over, since, for what he had done, and what he had attempted to do, transportation must inevitably be his lot.

It was about half-past six, or rather later, when we reached Dalston; our drive had been a cold one—for the wind was bleak, and altogether the weather seemed in that state it so often is in our climate, when, like a spoiled child, it don't no exactly whether to laugh or to cry.

It was curious to look at Adamson and Fletcher, so identical did they seem with their similar cravats and general apparel; and Fletcher himself declared he did not wonder at the chemist in Shoreditch positively swearing to him as the man who had bought the opium.

"There has many a piece of horrible injustice been perpetrated," remarked the solicitor, "on account of such similarities of appearance, identity, and circumstantial evidence of crimes—but here we are, and we have one consolation now, that there can be no possible mistake."

"Why, we certainly," said Mr. Algernon, "have got the saddle on the right horse now."

As the day declined a heavy mass of clouds rose in the west, throwing the earth into shade much earlier than usual; night was at hand, but darkness soon enveloped the scene before the usual hour, and the wind came in moaning gusts, suddenly subduing to a dead calm.

The air was oppressive for the season, and the birds ceased their eventide song, giving out but shrill, sharp, and sudden notes, as if the weather affected them long before its approach.

The last reflection of daylight had scarcely passed away, or been absorbed by the clouds, when a streak of blue-forked lightning shot in an uncertain manner across the sky, with such distinctness, that caused many involuntarily to start and turn away in alarm.

It was many seconds ere the faintest echo of thunder reached the ears of the residents at Dalston; not long had they, however, to wait for their share of the storm that was brewing, for shortly after the whole place became the very theatre of such constant flashes of light, that well illumined the whole neighbourhood, making, for the moment, the house and gardens as plain and evident to the senses, as if you were in them. Then followed the crashing thunder—rumbling, roaring, and reverberating through the heavens with fearful violence, as if the whole universe was in commotion.

All this time the rain fell in torrents—at first it came with a few large drops, but a very few minutes sufficed for this warning, and then it suddenly fell in such torrents, that had the windows of Heaven been opened, it could scarce have exceeded it.

This was a terrible storm—a more violent one had not visited Dalston for many years; it was sudden and unexpected, and its violence bore no signs with it of any sudden termination—and for all that could be seen, it might last till that hour next day, save that its extreme violence alone gave hopes that it could not continue.

We had just succeeded in getting housed at Bute Cottage before this tremendous weather broke out in all its violence, and it was well we were so, for such perfect torrents of rain as it wound up with I thought I had never seen.

Luke Mitchell was not at home, a circumstance I was at first alarmed at, for I thought it possible he might, if in town, hear a report of what had occurred at the police-office, and take alarm; but Mrs. Renfrew assured me he had gone in the direction of Walthamstow, and had left word for something to be cooked for him, as he would be home by half-past seven at the very latest.

There was, therefore, ample time to give Harriet an explanation of all that occurred. I wish I could describe the joy that flashed in her eyes when she found that her lover was free, and untainted even by suspicion. When I had done, I called him from the adjoining room, and then she bounded towards him with a cry of joy, exclaiming—

"Andrew, Andrew! how much you must have suffered on my account."—"I have suffered much, dear Harriet," he replied; "but ere I say more, let me state that with your wealth you may well look for a higher match than the poor farmer's son. Harriet, I will love you still, but I will not blame you if now you renounce me for ever."

Her reply was interrupted by a sob, and after that, as I stood by the window, looking out at the weather, I won't swear that I didn't hear a kiss—but that's no business of mine.

* * * * *

A strolling rat-tat at the door announced a visitor.

"It's Mitchell," screamed Mrs. Renfrew. "He's got a key to the garden gate, and always knocks."

"Clear away, all of you," cried I; "let him come in here, and only see me. By-the-bye, Adamson, suppose you go up stairs to his bed-room; as he deceived others by your extraordinary likeness to Andrew Fletcher, it would be well that he should be deceived himself in turn. I will tell him Fletcher is at liberty, and do you then come down and personate him."

"As you like," said Adamson, and he ascended the staircase, while the lovers and Mrs. Renfrew, with the officer, Mr. Algernon, and the solicitor, all retired into the next room.

In another moment Mitchell, draggled with wet, and splashed from head to foot, entered the front parlour, where I stood ready to receive him. He started at sight of me, as if I had been some spectre.

"You here?" he cried. "I thought we had had enough of you."—"Yes, Mr. Mitchell," I said, "I am here;" and I spoke in a very low and humble tone. "I have come with a hope of moving your compassion for Andrew Fletcher. I think you might, by softening your evidence before a jury, yet save him."

"Ho, ho!" he laughed. "You do, do you?"—"Yes; and the more especially I think you might be so kind, taking into your consideration that he is really innocent; you know, as well as I do, that you gave the opium to Harriet Renfrew yourself, Mr. Mitchell."

"Now, confound your atrocious impudence," he cried; "you come here to intercede for a man, and libel me at the same time. If you will oblige me by saying as much as you have just now said, in the presence of witnesses, I'll trounce you nicely for it."

"Are you then so hard-hearted as to wish Andrew Fletcher to be punished for what he is innocent of?"—"If I could get him hanged, and you, too, I should be better pleased," he replied; "but I can't waste time here."

"No; you shall not, you scoundrel; Andrew Fletcher is free as air. He is in this house."

"Are you mad?"—"No; but upon a second view of the case the magistrate was of opinion that you were guilty, and he accordingly set Fletcher at liberty."

Mitchell staggered, and he held by the chair as he pronounced the name of—

"Adamson!"—"Yes," said I, "Adamson became repentant—he knew all. I rather think you will be transported, Mr. Luke Mitchell. How do you feel now?"

"Where is he?"—"Up stairs. You can attempt to plead to Andrew Fletcher for yourself, even as I pleaded to you for him. But your pleading will be in vain. The evidence against you is direct, and not circumstantial. He cannot, if he would, help you. There can be no doubt about your identity."

He said not another word, but left the room, and ascended the staircase, while I called to the officer to come and apprehend him.

We heard a door bang up stairs, and just as Mrs. Renfrew had handed the officer a light, Mitchell came down again. He was frightfully pale, and when he reached the passage he leaned his back against the wall, and laughed in a strange hysterical manner that was truly appalling.

"You are my prisoner," said the officer.—"Agreed," he cried. "Agreed. Harriet Renfrew, one word with you before I go. But a word."

Harriet appeared at the door of the back parlour.

"Wretched man," she said, "what would you say to me?" He laughed again before he spoke, and then said—"When some time since I told you I loved you, and asked you to be my wife—you refused me, and then I made a solemn declaration. Do you recollect it?"—"I do. You said I should never be Andrew Fletcher's wife. 'Twas a wicked and idle threat."

"You think so! ho, ho, ho! I will keep my word. You never shall, you never can be Andrew Fletcher's wife. I have kept my word."

"What mean you?"—"Ha, ha, ha. You look upon me as one raving, but 'tis you will rave. You are all disappointed; you thought you had laid a fine plot for me, but you are all caught in your own snare—the remembrance of me shall be a terror. Your heart, Harriet Renfrew, will bleed for this night's work; and you, turning to me—you, with all your meddling, you will find that a man, such as I am, is not to be so easily played with. I have kept my word—I have had my revenge. The scaffold awaits me, and what care I?"

"Talk to him no more, Harriet," said Andrew Fletcher, coming out of the parlour, and confronting Mitchell, suddenly; "he is unworthy you should waste a word upon him."

Mitchell uttered a loud shriek, and fell insensible on the floor of the passage.

* * * * *

This conduct of Mitchell's seemed quite inexplicable—we all looked at each other in amazement, and I could only surmise that the suddenness of the discovery of his baseness had given a shock to his mind that had quite upset it, inducing a degree of insanity upon the subject of the most earnest thoughts.

"Is he dead, sir?" said the officer to me.—"Oh, dear, no," said I, as I felt his pulse; "he will soon recover. He had better be laid on the sofa till he is better."

"Why did he utter such a cry at the sight of me?" said Andrew Fletcher. "If I had been an apparition he could not have looked more awfully terrified."

"Where is Adamson?" said Mr. Algernon.—"Up stairs to be sure," said I, "and he ought to come down. Adamson! Adamson!"—"Adamson!" cried the solicitor.

No one answered, and we all looked at each other strangely. What came across the minds of the others I don't know, but something struck me that all was not right—I seized a candle and bounded up the stairs, followed by Mr. Algernon and the solicitor.

"Adamson! Adamson!" I shouted again, when I had reached the landing. No one answered; and, pushing open the first door that presented itself, I entered the room. As I did so, I stumbled over something soft on the floor, and the candle having been placed insecurely in the candlestick, toppled over and was extinguished.

"Hilloa!" I cried. "A light! a light here, Mrs. Renfrew, if you please—a light! a light!"

It was Andrew Mitchell who brought up another candle. He held it high above his head, and stood in the door-way.

"What is the matter?" he said; "something is surely the matter."

One glance at the floor showed me that what I had fallen over was the body of some one. It lay on its face. I stooped and turned it over.

"Adamson!" cried Mr. Algernon.—"And dead!" said I.—"Dead!" echoed the solicitor.

We stood for a moment perfectly transfixed with horror. A large knife was sticking up to the hilt in Adamson's breast—he must have died instantaneously.

"Gracious Heavens!" said Andrew Fletcher; "this is horrible."—"I see it all now," cried I. "He has mistaken this wretched man for you, Fletcher. Luke Mitchell has murdered him, fancying that he was thwarting us all by your death. This awful act explains his words in the passage to Harriet Renfrew."

"And he, no doubt," added Mr. Algernon, "mistook you really for an apparition when he saw you at the parlour-door."

"What is it?" said the officer, from the passage,—"Come up here," cried I.

He ascended, and we explained to him what had occurred. He shrugged his shoulders, and whistled a long shrill note, as he said,—

"This affair grows serious. I must trouble you all now to go back with me to the police office, or at all events to a station-house, where we can charge Mitchell for the night. Is he quite dead?"—"Quite."

We descended the staircase in solemn silence, after locking up the dead body, which the officer advised should be left lying exactly where it was till the inquest. I explained to Mrs. Renfrew and Harriet what had occurred, and their consternation was very great indeed. They absolutely refused to remain in the house; and Andrew Fletcher at once offering an asylum with his parents, they hastily arrayed themselves for the open air, and, shuddering at the dreadful deed that had been so quietly perpetrated so near to them, they turned their backs for ever upon Bute Cottage, which was henceforward to have so memorable a notoriety as the scene of an atrocious murder.

As for Luke Mitchell, although he partially recovered from his state of insensibility, he seemed, from the shock his mind had experienced by the sudden sight of Andrew Fletcher in life, when he fancied he had left him a corpse, so stupefied as scarcely to comprehend his situation.

We got him into a coach with some difficulty, after the constable had put handcuffs upon him, and some of us riding while the remainder walked, we proceeded full of the most painful thoughts to the nearest police-station, where Mitchell was at once received upon the serious charge we had to bring against him, and secured for the night.

* * * * *

Our journey back to town was a very wretched one, for I blamed myself for advising Adamson to personate Andrew Fletcher—an advice which certainly had caused his death.

"But," said the solicitor, "you could have no possible notion of such a result. As well might a man blame himself for advising another to undertake a journey, if by chance the coach upsets and kills him. You should lay nothing to yourself, doctor, on such a score as the one you mention."

I still felt far from easy in my mind upon the subject; and had it not been that my object in not having Mitchell taken into custody at once, which would certainly have prevented the murder, was to try if I could find one symptom of relenting in his heart, and not for the purpose of goading him to any violence, I should have felt more uncomfortable on the subject than I did.

At the police-office in the morning the case of the murder only was entered into, as regarded Luke Mitchell, it having thrown any other charges against him completely into the shade. The evidence was quite conclusive, and he was fully committed for trial.

The sessions were close at hand, so that within a week I saw him at the bar of the Old Bailey on a charge of wilful murder. He kept a dogged silence, and refused to plead guilty or not guilty; upon which the judge ordered a plea of not guilty to be entered, and directed the trial to proceed.

There was no gainsaying the facts. The trial altogether did not last half an hour, when Luke Mitchell was condemned to death on the succeeding Monday. He was carried from the court, never having opened his lips from the moment he entered it.

I had never seen an execution—I had always shrunk from so awful a spectacle; but I was persuaded by Mr. Algernon to go with him and see Luke Mitchell hung, and I certainly consented.

"You can have no sympathy with such a man," he said, "and consequently the sight will not be so terrible to you as it otherwise would, so make up your mind and come."

*   *   *   *   *

The dawn of day was gloomy; and had it been the lightest morn the sun ever shone on, it would have been the saddest that ever broke upon an unfortunate human being; the gloomiest day that ever peeped through hills of clouds was sunshine to the free, in comparison to that which he was compelled to meet.

The clouds were heavy, dull, and almost stationary. A dense mass of vapour hung over the city, and a thick mist descended upon the streets, which rendered them wet and greasy, as it is called; difficult to walk on, on account of the constant slipping you experienced at every step you took.

The gloominess of the day increased as the volumes of vapour arose from many thousand fires, but which were unable to ascend to any great height, on account of the weight and moisture of the atmosphere, but mixed with it, and descended with it, making allthings black and dirty.

The mist now increased slowly, and in a short time took the form of a small and fine rain, which, in the course of no very great period of time, would wet any one, with not more than ordinary protection against the weather, through their clothing.

Notwithstanding the bad state of the morning, many people were abroad; the streets presented their usual occupants who traversed them at a particular period daily; and then there was the usual bustle of others who were mere passengers for the occasion. The wet and disagreeable weather in London appears never to affect London streets, for they are never deserted, be it early or late, wet or dry, gloomy or sunshine.

The shops slowly open, and the streets begin to have the appearance of something like life. The splendour of many houses, the costliness, of their goods, and the taste with which they are arranged give an appearance of gaiety that often causes the passenger to stop and forget the heavy pelting rain he may at that moment be enduring, and pause a moment to examine the riches spread out to his view.

But this was Monday morning—people were busy; they hurried to and fro in the belief that having wasted all Sunday on themselves, they must now make up for it by extra exertion; and, in consequence of this feeling, Monday mornings, in cities, are busy ones.

Yet on this morning there was an unusual haste—an excitement about Newgate which the casual passenger could scarce account for, unless he had been told that an execution was about to take place. He would then have directed his attention towards the Old Bailey, and then it would have been palpable enough.

The scaffold round the debtors' door was erected; and around its base was collected a motley crowd of the lowest and most vitiated of the London population, who make it a practice to be present at these scenes. Women, too, were there, but as the companion of some dissolute criminal who has yet escaped detection.

St. Sepulchre's had already chimed the half hour, and it wanted but a few minutes of a quarter to eight o'clock. That once chimed from that clock, and a human being would then have to meet a violent death.

The three quarters past seven chimed, and a serious and uneasy sensation was felt by some few of a more respectable (if the word can be used in connexion with people who go expressly to view the sufferings of their fellow-creatures in their last agonies) appearance, who stood apart from the throng, many of whom were evidently in liquor.

Some few of the houses in the neighbourhood had their windows opened, with people who had given a considerable sum to view the execution of the criminal; and who had put themselves to some inconvenience to come there early to gratify the morbid desire they entertained of looking upon an expiring man.

"I cannot stay here," I said to Mr. Algernon. "Come away—come away."—"Look!" he cried.

I glanced to the debtors' door of the Old Bailey; a solemn and melancholy procession issued forth. I could not withdraw my eyes from Mitchell's face; it was so awfully pale and distorted. A horrible fascination nailed me to the spot, and although I told myself at the time I would have given much to be away, yet I could not go.

Mitchell was placed on the drop. He opened his mouth to speak—but two words came from his lips—they were an awful curse. In another moment he swung in the air a corpse.

*   *   *   *   *

Andrew Fletcher and Harriet Renfrew were married within a month, before which time the whole of the property which had been bequeathed to her had been recovered. So great had been the interest excited by the murder Mitchell had committed, that the will business sank into comparative insignificance, and Mr. Michaelson escaped scot free.

Bute Cottage still remains at Dalston. It is a sad ruin, never having been occupied by a living soul since that night when the Renfrews so abruptly left it.

THE SISTERS;

OR, NOT DEAD YET.

"I should have been a dead man long ago, I tell you, doctor, if it had not been for Angelina; she is—in fact, she is everything. Innocent indeed! When I found her, I found a treasure. Ah! and I esteem her accordingly. Some of these days I'll make her Mrs. Augustus Snow. Ah! what an idea."

These words were spoken to me during a professional visit to an old gentleman of the name of Snow, residing in Woburn-place, Tavistock-square. The person he spoke of in such terms of approbation was his housekeeper, a Mrs. Angelina Puffham, who happened to be one of those masculine-looking women who are my favourite aversions; still I was not so foolish as to allow my prejudice to stand in the way of my civility to Mrs. Puffham; I had a doubt that she might be "all that fancy painted her," I mean the fancy of old Snow, and I gave her the benefit of it.

Just imagine a woman who fancies herself dignified because she is big; fine, because she is coarse; clever, because she is impertinent; and you have Mrs. Puffham. All these qualities were, however, if I may be allowed the expression, sleeked down in her intercourse with Mr. Snow, who thought her quite a paragon of a woman.

The household consisted of this Mrs. Puffham, an Irish footman, a poor draggled looking girl who was awfully snubbed by Mrs. Puffham, and a boy who was made generally useful.

I should not have taken the trouble to interest myself at

all in the affairs of Mr. Snow, had it not been that through another quarter I learnt some particulars concerning him, which induced me to be on the look-out to see if something might be done to remedy a circumstance that I looked upon with peculiar feelings of dislike. Upon mentioning to the friend who had recommended me to Mr. Snow, that I attended him very frequently, he said,—

"Did he ever talk to you of his wife?"—"His wife!" cried I; "no, he always led me to believe him a bachelor; in fact, he sometimes alludes to the probability of his marrying Mrs. Puffham, his housekeeper."

"The deuce he does!"—"I assure you, the very last time I saw him he started the notion."—"Then he must get a divorce."

"Can he?"—"I suppose so. But tell me, how do you like Mrs. Puffham?"

"That is scarcely a fair question. You should say, how don't you like Mrs. Puffham? for I don't like her at all."—"Very good. Then, to tell you a long story in a few words, Mrs. Puffham found out that Mrs. Snow was no better than she should be, and consequently Mrs. Snow was turned out of the house."

"Indeed!"—"Yes; old Snow had taken a fancy to her for her beauty, and, I believe, she married him in order to ensure the support of her aged parents."

"A sort of Auld Robin Gray business."—"Exactly. But he got a decree against her in the Ecclesiastical court, upon the testimony of Mrs. Puffham. A separation was pronounced, and I dare say, if old Snow chose to go to the expense, he could procure a divorce in due form, and marry Mrs. Puffham, or go to the devil if he liked."

"I consider those two acts as one and the same thing," said I; "in fact, of the two, I would rather go to the devil than marry Mrs. Puffham."—"Very likely, doctor."

"But what has become of the wife?"—"That I cannot tell you. Of course she has no claim at all upon Mr. Snow, since the decree of separation was pronounced, and most likely is in great poverty somewhere with her infant."

"An infant?"—"Yes, to be sure. It's a hard case, a very hard case; but as far as old Snow is concerned, I think him more weak than criminal."

"Yet," said I, "under such circumstances, weakness becomes surely a criminality."

"True; but what I meant to say was, that he has been the victim of others; for, from my heart, I do not believe in the guilt of Mrs. Snow. If she be guilty, guilt never before was arrayed in such a garb of innocence. The story was this:—That a young man, named Alfred Houghton, had paid his addresses to Mrs. Snow, before she ever saw old Snow. But poverty prevented their union. He went, by the kindness of a distant relative, to Calcutta, with an expectation of finding some lucrative employment for a few years, and then returning to claim his bride. He did get employment, but it turned out to be anything but safe, and his death appeared in an obituary published, now nearly three years back, in the India papers. Poor Harriet Hoffenden, which was Mrs. Snow's name before her marriage, took his death much to heart, and become the very shadow of her former self. Then old Snow saw her, accidentally, and became desperately enamoured of her. After a great deal of solicitation, feeling herself lost to the world, by the death of him she loved, she made a self-sacrifice, and wedded old Snow, on condition that he amply provided for her parents, and a young brother she had. This he readily consented to, and she became his wife."

"Poor girl."—"Ay, doctor, you may well say 'poor girl;' for not only has she lost the very object for which she consented to an union repugnant to her feelings, but she has been covered with what I, from my heart, consider unmerited disgrace. It appears that about a year ago, young Houghton, who, as the song says, 'had not been dead at all,' came home, not so well off as he wished, but still well enough off to claim his old sweetheart. They had a meeting; one farewell, tearful meeting; and upon that was founded the case, backed by evidence from Mrs. Puffham, against poor Mrs. Snow."

"And could not the lover exonerate her?"—"No; he had left England, and little imagines that his visit has produced such sad results."

"Well, this is a most calamitous tale, indeed!"—"It is, doctor, one of those domestic tragedies, which are, I fear, of too common occurrence."

"But have you reasoned with Snow upon the subject?"—"I have, often and often, but Mrs. Puffham, and a sister of her's, who is married to somebody, have such an overpowering influence over him, that he will listen to no one else."

"What, does she drag in her sister, too?"—"Oh, yes; the sister was collateral evidence against poor Mrs. Snow."

The particulars I had heard from my friend, naturally enough set me thinking about Mrs. Snow. I turned affairs over and over in my mind, but could come to no satisfactory conclusion as to how I could interfere to discover the truth. Besides, it was a very delicate matter to speak to the old man about at all, and I was quite in a despairing state about it, especially as I had no direct evidence to offer of the innocence of his wife, and could only have said,—

"Mr. Snow, I never saw your wife, but still I think, from what I have heard of her, she is an injured and innocent woman." Upon which, Mr. Snow might fairly have ordered the footman to show me the door.

Full of these thoughts I sat down to my bachelor's breakfast, and had got through one cup of coffee and a muffin, when my landlady announced a visitor.

"A patient?" said I.—"One o' the poor uns, sir; I knows 'em well; they is always so werry purlite, and hopes as you isn't engaged, and wipes their shoes so outrageous. Ah, I knows 'em."

"Well, but Mrs. Tweedle, we must not despise the humility of poverty, although there is always, to my mind, something very painful about it. Tell the person I will be at leisure in a few moments."

"She's a decent enough looking lady, too," remarked Mrs. Tweedle; "and to my mind looks as if she had seed better days. There's loads o' changes in this world—by-the-by, that puts me in mind of somethink."

Being put in mind of something by something she had herself said, commonly terminated my conferences with my landlady, who had a fund of goodheartedness beneath an incrustation of singularity always at command.

I hastily concluded my morning's meal, and proceeded to the front parlour, of which I had the use, as a receiving-room for my patients.

Standing near the door was the slight figure of a young female. Her dress bespoke the struggle of poverty to look respectable; that struggle which is so painful a one when quite unconnected with anything like the vanity of appearance. Her face bore that never-to-be-mistaken expression of patient suffering which is so truly sad to look upon, and the more especially so when it sits upon a countenance which, from the remains of beauty it still possesses, we will suppose has been frequently irradiated with the smiles of joy, and its fair owner petted and caressed by all around her.

Oh, what a sad and mournful change comes o'er the spirit of love's young dream frequently when least expected. We shall see some young girl, just upon that sweet dawn of womanhood when the charms of early youth are mingling with the more intellectual and acquired excellences of maturer life, petted and caressed by every one. The pet, the idol of the circle in which she moves—loved for her very caprices, indulged in every petty whim, chasing anger with a laugh, dispelling disapprobation of any outrageous fancy by a caress. How many such shall we meet with in life's pilgrimage! believing, as we cannot help believing, that such fair creatures have more than the common share of womanly gifts granted to them.

But years will pass away, and we shall see them again; we shall find that the girl so light hearted, so gay, so caressed and petted, that even the very winds of Heaven were not permitted to visit her face too roughly, has made a great venture in life, and committed to the keeping, perhaps, of one concerning whom she knew little, all her hopes of happiness in this world—she has become a wife, but, alas! in too many cases, we shall look in vain for the smiles that once have been; we shall listen in vain for the ring of merry laughter that was so sweet to hear.

Woe, woe, be to those who accept the trust of making to such beings a home of light and love, and turn it to darkness and the gloom of indifference.

I could see at a glance that my visitor could not be much over twenty. Her features were exquisitely beautiful. There was abundant intellect, too, in her fine brow and small, beautifully chiselled mouth; but the air of grief that sat upon every feature, the suppressed agony of the countenance, was most painful to look upon.

"Alas!" I thought to myself, "what history of woe is your's that it leaves such indelible traces of its presence upon your face?"

A faint flush of colour came to her cheeks as I said,— "Pray be seated," and handed a chair to her with as kind and assuring a manner as I could assume. I then, for the first time, perceived that she had a young child in her arms; and I am sure I shall be forgiven for making an uncharitable, and what turned out to be a wrong surmise, by thinking that I had some history of the betrayal of a too trusting heart to listen to.

"Compose yourself," I said. "What service can I render you? Is it yourself or your little one who is ailing?"

In a low voice, of such exquisite musical pathos that it made me start at its beauty, she said,—

"I ought to—to—apologise for intruding—I am very—very poor."—"Then now you have apologised, if apology was necessary," I said kindly, "say no more on that head, I pray you."

Something fell on the floor from her hand, and she tried to pick it up. I anticipated her. It was five shillings, rolled up in a piece of paper.

"'Tis all I have to offer," she said; "all—all"—"And do you imagine," said I, "that I am the mercenary wretch to take this of you? Good God! do you suppose I would despise myself so long as I lived for five shillings? Take them back, I beg of you; and any advice or assistance I can give you, you may depend upon receiving. Come, now, cheer up, and look upon me as a friend as well as a physician."

She tried to speak, and then burst into tears, sobbing so bitterly that for some moments I was fearful she would fall into some bad hysterical attack. By degrees, however, the storm of feeling subsided, more readily, too, because I took no notice of it, but walked to the window till it was over, or nearly so. When I heard that she had somewhat recovered, I returned to her, saying,—

"The causes why your feelings are so readily and so painfully agitated, of course I cannot know; but let me warn you against giving way to these bursts of grief; they will do you irreparable injury, you may depend."

"I have struggled hard," she said. "It is the voice of kindness only that takes me by surprise, and destroys all my resolution."

"Are you unused to kindness?"—She shook her head, saying, "I know too well what it is, not now to feel acutely its loss; but, pardon me, sir, for thus troubling you, and taking up your time; I was told that at this hour of the morning you saw poor patients, and saw them kindly, too."

"I hope I see them kindly. To be sick, and struggling with poverty, are quite evils sufficient for any one, without the addition of harshness from any quarter."—"It is my child I wish you to look at."

She unfolded a shawl that was around the infant, and showed me its face. A glance was sufficient for me; I saw it was wasting away, and that it could not live long.

"It is not so strong as it was," said the mother; "and I think it pines away daily."—"The lives of infants are very precarious," I said. "We can but hope with the best of them, that they may weather the first year or two of existence. It is only in food that we can give any directions as regards such very young children. How old is this little one?"—"About eighteen months, sir."

"Well, you must feed it on light but nutritious diet; bake some fine flour, mix it up very thin with asses' milk."—"Yes, sir; but—but———"

"But what?"—"Tell me truly, sir, I implore; do you think it will live?"

"You ask a question that no physician ought to answer— a question, too, which is in Heaven's hands alone."

She kissed the child with a despairing expression and a frantic eagerness. I could see, that from the evasive answer I had given her, she surmised how unfavourable was my opinion.

"Dear one, dear one," she sobbed, "may my last breath be mingled with your latest sigh; we are both the children of misfortune. Oh, what a cruel, cruel destiny."

"I hope you will have no scruples at calling again," said I; "your health, if I may judge from appearances, requires attention. Do you take much exercise?"—"I cannot -I cannot."

"Indeed!"—"No, sir; my utmost exertions, from morning till night, scarcely suffice to keep a roof over my head and provide food, of the commonest kind, for myself and child."

"You—you are not a widow?" I said, hesitatingly.—"No, sir; I am a wife."

"And your husband?"—A crimson flush came over her face, as, after a pause, she added, in a low, deep tone,—"Has discarded me; though Heaven knows my innocence. God help me!—God help me! I will detain you no longer, sir; the thanks of a sad heart are yours."

She moved towards the door, but I stepped between her and it, saying,—

"Nay, do not go yet. You have interested me by what you have said; tell me now frankly, is it possible for any one so disposed to afford you any efficient assistance in assuaging the terrors of your situation?"—"No—no; who can prove right when guilty machinations against it call upon Heaven, in solemn oaths, to testify to wrong?"

She drew herself up proudly as she spoke, and her eye flashed with a momentary indignation.

"Have you so suffered?" I said.—"I have—deeply—deeply suffered, and yet so innocent. But I am very, very wrong, sir, and pardon the trouble I have given you."

"Nay, before you go, at least tell me your name"—She hesitated a moment, and then said, "I am entitled to the name of Mrs. Snow."

"Snow?"—"Yes."

"What, the wife of old Snow—I beg your pardon—of Mr. Snow, in Woburn-place?"—She looked me fixedly in the face as she replied, "You know him, then; and with that knowledge you know, perhaps, how he discarded his innocent wife and child upon the false testimony of those who, for some unholy purpose, leagued themselves for her destruction."

I was so astonished at the singular circumstance of Mrs. Snow calling upon me for advice for her child at the very time when my mind was full of her sad story, that for some moments I could make her no answer; but still, when I came to reflect upon the matter, it was not so singular after all; for I was getting into good repute as a physician, and had attained some celebrity, in particular for my manner of receiving poor patients, so that many came miles to avail themselves of my advice.

"I know Mr. Snow," I said; "I am attending him professionally; and from a friend, who expressed the most favourable opinion of you, I learnt your sad history."

She sank into a chair, and again wept plentifully; during which time I was considering what really could be done to ameliorate her condition.

"Mrs. Snow," I at length said, "you are innocent?"—"As I hope and trust in Heaven!"

"Leave me your address in order that I may send to you in case I have anything to communicate; believe me, I will do all that I can to bring about a happier state of things for you. If I mistake not, your greatest enemy is Mr. Snow's housekeeper, Mrs. Puffham."

"Yes; she and her sister, a Mrs. Bennett, have, by the most awful perjuries, poisoned the ears of my husband, and driven me and my child to despair and want."

"Do not despair; I scarcely ever knew a case of deliberate wickedness that did not, sooner or later, involve its perpetrators in the most frightful consequences. Be of good cheer, Mrs. Snow, and, at all events, console yourself with the reflection, that you have friends who will exert themselves for you."

I need not recapitulate to my readers the thanks she gave me for what she called the first ray of hope that had illumined her heart for many, many months; but suffice it to say, that I parted from her with a full impression of her innocence, and a determination to do what I could to open Mr. Snow's eyes to the truth.

In such an undertaking, however, it was necessary for me to proceed with the utmost caution; for, if I were too hasty in taking his wife's part, the old gentleman might discharge me from further attendance upon him in a moment; and I had no plea of private acquaintance to urge as my excuse for meddling in his affairs.

When I made him my professional visit that day, I found him rather worse in health than I had seen him, and, of course, Mrs. Puffham was dreadfully assiduous. My object was now to make myself as intimate as I could with the old man, and after writing him a fresh prescription, I commenced talking to him of the ordinary events and circumstances of the times, intending, if possible, to draw the conversation round to some point favourable to a mention of his wife.

"Mrs. Puffham," said I, "seems very attentive to you, Mr. Snow."—"Ah! an invaluable woman," he replied; "I should soon die without her—ah!"

"So disinterested, too."—"Yes, very; I quite have to make her take her wages."

"A fine woman, too."—"Ah! if I were quite free,—ah!"

"Sir?"—"Did you ever hear of my wife?"

"I have heard you had a wife, Mr. Snow."—"Ah, and you have heard why I haven't one now, I suppose? An abandoned woman, doctor. Good God! I might have lived all my life not knowing how I was served, had it not been for Mrs. Puffham and Mrs. Bennett. They are both fine women, and so clever."—"Indeed."

"Between you and I, doctor, if it had not been for them I should never have suspected Mrs. Snow."—"Oh!"

"No; she seemed so—so very much the reverse of what she has proved to be. You would not think her capable of the conduct that has been sworn to as regards her. I—I did love her—dearly love her—but all that's passed and gone. I was an old fool, and I met the reward of my folly."

"But suppose, Mr. Snow, she had not turned out criminal?"—"Why — why then — but no matter, doctor, you have touched upon a sore place at my heart."

"Which may not be, after all, beyond cure," said I.—"Yes—quite—quite. Mrs. Snow and I have separated—separated for ever."

"But suppose you were some day to find out you had been wrong, and that your wife was really innocent."—"Pooh! pooh! doctor, don't imagine impossibilities."

"Well, well," said I, rising, for I was fearful of going too far at one conversation, "stranger things have come to pass. Good morning, Mr. Snow."—"Good morning," he said, "good—yet I— I ——"

"What, sir?"—"Nothing—nothing; good morning."

I was satisfied that I had interested him by the very idea that his wife might be innocent; and I felt a confidence in the recurrence of the conversation, from his own willingness to renew it, when we should meet again. As I was crossing the hall, the Irish footman spoke to me, saying,—

"By dad, sir, and how is the master, now? Heaven forgive the ould sinner—amen—any way."—This singular address excited my curiosity, and I said, "Why, what makes you speak in that way of your master?"—"What makes me, sir?"

"Yes, what induces you?"—"Why, sir, thin, do you think I'm a baste? Didn't the ould sinner turn the could shoulder to the mistress, pur y cretur as she was?"

"I hear he did, certainly," said I. "Are you of opinion that she was innocent?"—"Innocent is it, sir? Did you ever hear of a suckling dove in arms turning a rapparee? Innocent, sir—am I innocent?"

"I really don't know. What's your name?"—"Dennis, sir. I come of the O'Driscolls: and atween your honour and me and the post, there's an ould devil in this house o' the name of Puffham. Och, murder!"

Mrs. Puffham at this moment was seen descending the stairs, and Dennis made a precipitate retreat; I lingered a little in the hall, for I had no sort of objection to a conversation with Mrs. Puffham if she should volunteer one, considering that, possibly, during the course of it, I might hear something to confirm my strong impression of her villany.

"Oh, sir," she said, "you'll excuse that Irish lout for leaving you to open the door for yourself. I'm sure I've quite hinted to Mr. Snow, bless his heart, at least a dozen times, to discharge him."—"Why, Mrs. Puffham," said I, "we cannot expect first-rate good manners from all people."

I rather think she took this as a sidelong compliment, for she replied, "Would you like to take anything before you go, sir?"—"Thank you, madam."

She led the way into a parlour adjoining the hall, and produced from the cupboard, which I suppose contained her private stores in the drinking line, a bottle and two glasses. We very gravely inclined our heads, and I quaffed down as excellent a glass of sherry as ever I tasted.

"Oh, dear," said Mrs. Puffham, "now that we are alone, doctor, what do you really think of poor dear Snow?"—"Why, I think he keeps capital sherry."

"Yes; but I mean how is he? Do you think he'll last long, doctor?"—"It's difficult to say, Mrs. Puffham. I suppose you never hear anything of his wife?"

"His wife! the abandoned hussy! the horrid, low-lived wretch! We don't hear anything of her, and I only hope we never shall."

"Was the case against her strong, Mrs. Puffham?"—"Strong sir! horridly strong. I have no patience with her, I haven't. Oh, the hussy! I think I could tear her very eyes out."

"What a thing it is to be virtuous. I don't suppose Mr. Snow will leave her anything in his will."—"He leave her anything! I think I see him dare—that is, he won't leave her a penny piece, I'm sure."

"Ah, Mrs. Puffham, you will excuse what I am going to

say, but Mr. Snow thinks you a very handsome, fine woman."—"La, sir!"

"Yes, indeed he does; and I dare say some day he will tell you so himself. There is only one circumstance that has given me any uneasiness."

"Gracious! what's that?"—"Why, madam, the old gentleman's morals don't seem to me exactly in such good order as they ought to be."

"His what?"—"His morals, madam. Once or twice he has said to me, with a wink that is quite dreadful to see upon the face of a man of his age, 'Doctor, did you ever see Mrs. Bennett?'"

"Mrs. Bennett?"—"Yes, that is the name; and when I have answered in the negative, he has added, 'Ah,'—you know his way, Mrs. Puffham—'Ah, she is a fine woman—an angel—ah.'"

"The old wretch; why—why, Mrs. Bennett is my sister. She married a man who keeps a shop—gracious powers—the old ruffian!"

"Were you rea'ly not aware, Mrs. Puffham, of Mr. Snow's great admiration of Mrs. Bennett?"—"Aware! how should I be? She's a baggage, a frightful baggage. Oh, what treachery. There are but three sisters of us, and here have we been pulling together all our lives till now, when she's trying to set her face against me."

"Three of you, are there? What a lovely family!"—"Yes, three. My other sister drinks—that is—no, she's nervous. But I'll let Mrs. Bennett know what's what. I'll Bennett her!"

What obscure threat was intended by Bennetting Mrs. Bennett I did not pause to inquire; but, satisfied with having sown the seeds of a division in the enemy's camp, I arose, and, bidding Mrs. Puffham a very polite good morning, I left the house.

The reader must not suppose that I had no particular plan, which a quarrel between Mrs Puffham and Mrs. Bennett would help to carry out. The fact is, I had partially concocted a scheme, which, if it succeeded, would, I hoped, have not only the effect of restoring Mrs. Snow to her home and her character, but ultimately confound both the sisters, who, my fair impression was, had entered into so cruel a conspiracy for her ruin and degradation.

I went from Mr. Snow's house direct to that of the friend who had recommended me to him, and from whom I had received the particulars concerning his poor wife. By good fortune, I found him at home; and I related to him at length all that had occurred, concluding by saying,—

"Now, it appears to me that these two disgusting women, Mrs. Puffham and Mrs. Bennett, must have made a bargain together for their mutual advantage in case of Mr. Snow's death, and his leaving the bulk of his property to Puffham. If we are to get the truth from either of them, it will be by making them mutually distrustful."—"Yes; but the distrust must go a long way before it would induce a confession of perjury."

"True—it must—a very long way; but the avarice of these women must be very great, or they would never have entered into this unholy confederation. I have paved the way for exciting jealousies between them, by what I have said to Mrs. Puffham."—"Certainly, doctor, the old adage of 'When rogues fall out,' &c., is a true one."

"Exactly. I have every expectation of a row between Mrs. Puffham and Mrs. Bennett, when they shall next meet. How is Mrs. Bennett's mind to be inflamed so that she may take part in it with spirit?'—"I really don't know."

"Then I have a plan. List—oh, list!"—"Had I three ears I'd hear thee. Go on."

"Old Snow must be made doubtful about the good faith of Mrs. Puffham."—"Good."

"Or he must be made angry at anybody insinuating doubts, for that would answer the purpose as well, as he would fall readily into any plan for confounding the doubters and proving his own marvellous sagacity."—"Good again; but the how, doctor—the how?'

"Old Snow must die."—"Amen. But when old Snow is dead, his convictions cannot be of very great importance."—"But I intend him to come to life again."

"Oh."—"Yes; if we can persuade Snow to die just for a few hours, till his will is read, I think we may get up such a fracas between the Puffham and the Bennett, as may elicit some truths that will be important to Mrs. Snow."

"I begin to comprehend. Go on."—"Why, in the first place, do you know an honest, intelligent lawyer?"

"Good God, doctor! must that be part of the incantation?"—"Yes."

"Then I suppose you start with the greatest difficulty first? But it does happen that I do know such a *rara avis*, and of course he is a poor man."

"Of course. Then I want him to go to Mrs. Bennett, some time when Mr. Bennett is not in the way, and ask her her Christian name, and such other questions as, he shall tell her, will enable him to draw up a will for a gentleman in her favour. She will then press him to tell her who the gentleman is, and he must mention old Snow; adding, that he (old Snow) intends to leave her all his property, and has quarrelled dreadfully with Mrs. Puffham on the subject."—"Go on—go on"

"This, I think, will at once awaken all the cupidity and all the anger of Mrs. Bennett, so that a row between her and the Puffham will be inevitable. From that row I have great hopes."—"And so have I."

"Then we will set about it at once; and it is but fair that, in the meantime, we endeavour to lighten the load of grief which weighs so heavily upon the spirits of poor Mrs. Snow. Suppose you and I call upon her together, and tell her we are making an effort to be of service to her."—"Agreed; and we can call upon my friend, the honest attorney, as we go."

* * * * *

We found Mrs. Snow in a very miserable lodging, destitute of almost every comfort. There was a faint flush of wounded sensibility upon her face, as she said,—

"This is a poor place to receive friendly visitors in; but I have been even more wretched than I am now."

Some unfinished needlework was lying on the table, and my friend, pointing to it, said,—

"Mrs. Snow, can you procure a living at such employment?"—"By working very hard," she replied, "I can earn six shillings from Monday morning to Sunday night."

"May I ask," said I, "concerning your parents?"—"Dead, dead! They followed each other quickly to the grave. Alas! why should I mourn for them? I was deprived of the power of doing anything for them. They are happier far than I."

"Nay, do not despair," said I; "we have come to tell you, expressly, to hope; for that we, being quite convinced of your innocence, intend to make the most strenuous endeavours to show that innocence to every one."

She clasped her hands, and her eyes filled with tears, as she said,—

"And can there be room for hope?"—"Yes; ample, ample room; and for the present we have earnestly to request that you will accept from us such a loan as shall place you in a more comfortable situation than at present."

"How can I hope to repay such a loan?"—"When you are once again in your proper position in life, and clear from the unjust persecution which has reduced you to your p esent state."

I saw she could not thank us, and dreading bringing on another such violent access of feeling as she had given way to at my house, I beckoned Mr. Drummond, my friend, to come away.

Our next visit was to the attorney, who was so indiscreet as to be honest. He resided in a particularly dingy set of apartments in Gray's-inn, and opened the door for us himself, for he kept no clerk—poor soul! he could hardly keep himself.

We explained to him our business, and, upon finding that its result was likely to right an innocent person, he entered into it with great alacrity, and made so many just and pertinent remarks upon the matter, that I deeply regretted a man, with such an intellect, should be in the obscurity he evidently was.

We gave him the address of Mrs. Bennett, and left him to take his opportunity of calling upon her when Mr. Bennett should be from home—only premising that he was not to do so until we again saw him, or sent to him, with the news that we had persuaded Mr. Snow to fall into our views, and act according to our suggestions.

Mr. Drummond and I then parted, with the understanding that, while I was making my professional call, the next day, upon Mr. Snow, he should drop in, as if it were quite accidentally, and then we should see what could be done by way of inducing the old gentleman to try the experiment, which we hoped would end so beneficially to Mrs. Snow.

"Look you here, Drummond," said I; "if we make out that Snow is dead, and has left all his property to Mrs. Bennett, Mrs. Puffham will be enraged, naturally, and a quarrel concerning a division of the spoil is sure to take place."

"Exactly; and, if we achieve nothing else, we shall, probably, succeed in convincing Snow of the selfishness and worthlessness of the woman he, at present, thinks so much of."

* * * * *

The morning came, and I waited with no little share of anxiety for the hour at which I usually called in Woburn-place. At length it came, and when I knocked and rang, and was admitted by the Irish footman, he said,—

"Och! murder, doctor! we'll have a *weddin'*—a wedding, doctor! The ould sinner is going to get a *divorce* agin' the mistress."

"A divorce!"—"By dad—yes. He and Mistress Puffham, they had quite a *mal a* last night, and he promised to make her Mrs. Snow, on the word of a Christian, as soon as he could get the divorce from the mistress."

"How do you know so much, Dennis?"—"Sure, then, I ain't deaf. What's keyholes made for, anyhow?"

"Well, Dennis, I can't help it. Take my card up to your master."—"Sure, I will, sir; but ain't it a'arming, when here she comes!"

"Good morning, doctor," said Mrs. Puffham, with an air of such superadded dignity, that I could have no doubt whatever of the statement of Dennis, and could see that she already fancied herself Mrs. Snow.

"Good morning, madam."—"Pray walk into this room, sir. Would you like to take anything?"—"Thank you; I don't mind another glass of that sherry you favoured me with yesterday."

The sherry was duly produced, and I could see that Mrs. Puffham was very anxious to say something that she did not know exactly how to come out with. At last, with an affected air of intense concern, she said,—

"Ah, sir, poor Mr. Snow has taken such a strange notion into his head."—"Indeed."

"Yes, sir; he thinks he never shall be happy until he has got a divorce, by act of parliament, from his wife. Do you think he'd live till it can be got for love or money?"—"I should think he would. Perhaps he contemplates marrying again?"

Mrs. Puffham replied, with a simper, that really she didn't know, but if he did, she only hoped he would not throw himself away again upon some flighty young girl, but take some respectable middle-aged person, with stability of character, and something like an appearance. To all of which I said I hoped he would, adding,

"Your sister, Mrs. Bennett—do you know, quite between you and I, Mrs. Puffham—I cannot help thinking she has taken some opportunity of flattering the old man so as to make him think so much of her."

Fury flashed from the eyes of Mrs. Puffham as she said,—

"Do you really think so? If I were sure, oh! I'd have vengeance upon her; I'd—I'd go and tell her husband, stupid old fat fool as he is, what she was before he married her."—"That will do," thought I. "There is everything to be expected from the passions of these women."

"I'd make a nice home for her," continued Mrs. Puffham. "I'd Bennett her if I were quite sure."—"I would," said I.—"And I will—I ——" A bumper of sherry stopped further speech at the moment, and then Dennis popped his head in at the door to say,—

"Oh, then, now the master wants to see you, sir, if quite convenient, if you plase, sir."

"We shall meet again," whispered Mrs. Puffham, and I ascended to the drawing-room, where sat old Snow, looking much worse than before; in fact he was sinking every day, although by good management he might yet last a long time.

"Well, doctor," he said, "I think I'm better, rather—my mind's more composed."—"I'm glad to hear you say so, Mr. Snow."—"Yes, I have made up my mind to get divorced from my wife; then I shall marry again."

"Have you fixed your choice, sir?"—"I have; I shall marry a fine woman—Mrs. Puffham; I've promised her, too, so that's settled. I've seen my lawyer, too, and given directions about the divorce; he says it will cost nearly a thousand pounds; but I don't care—that will be settled. Ah—I don't care—ah."

"But, Mr. Snow, had not your wife a child?"—"I don't know, and I don't care. If she had it ain't mine—d—n it! —ah!"

"But, sir, since you have given me leave, by mentioning this subject yourself, to speak upon it, suppose, after you got the divorce and had married again, you were to discover that she was innocent, and had fallen a victim to a vile conspiracy, got up by designing persons, in order to grasp at your wealth, what would be your feelings then, Mr. Snow? How could you compensate your poor injured wife for the world of suffering you had inflicted upon her?"

"Pooh! pooh! doctor," he said; "facts are stubborn things. There was a fellow of the name of Houghton, an old lover of my wife's—he visited her. Mrs Bennett happened to see him come into this very house, and then she and Mrs. Puffham——but d—n it, it always makes me mad. Say no more, doctor, say no more, I'll have a divorce, and there's an end of that—ah!"

"And marry Mrs. Puffham?"—"Yes."—"Faith, then, sir," said Dennis, appearing at the door, "here's Mr. Drummond."

"Mr. Drummond—oh, show him up."—"I am glad he has come," thought I; "now for a vigorous attack upon the old man."

Drummond did his part well, for he walked into the room with the utmost gravity, and, without any salutation, he said,—

"Mr. Snow, we are old friends, and I know you will excuse the liberty I am about to take. It is to tell you, I have had a most remarkable dream, in which I thought you were dead, and had left all you possessed to Mrs. Bennett; when Mrs. Puffham, in her wild anger at not herself coming into all your property, made a confession that she and her sister had concocted the story about your wife's infidelity, and that she was perfectly innocent."

The old man turned very pale, for there was an earnestness in Drummond's manner that even had its effect upon me, for the moment.

"A—a—dream, Mr. Drummond?" he said.—"Yes, Mr. Snow, a dream. But God forbid that you should neglect the warning, and commit an injustice at which you may well tremble, and the consequences of which might even disturb, in another world, the peace of your soul."

"I—I ain't superstitious; a—dream."—"Nor am I superstitious; and yet I feel the full force of this vision; I pray you do not neglect it. But before you take any steps which cannot again be retracted, adopt some method of trying the fidelity and the truth of the accusers of your, perhaps, most innocent and injured wife."

"What—what method can I adopt?" said Snow, looking pale and agitated; "I don't know what to do."

This was exactly the point to which we wished to bring him, and Mr. Drummond looked at me significantly to go on and make the proposition with which I was prepared, and by which alone I hoped to restore Mrs. Snow to her proper position in life, that position from which she had been so recklessly and wickedly driven.

"Mr. Snow," I began, "a means has occurred to me by which you may, with very little trouble to yourself, arrive, I think, at a just opinion with regard to the accusers of your wife."—"God knows," he said, in a flurried manner, "I don't want to do anything wrong."

"Very well, sir; will you then promise, before you apply for this divorce, to adopt the means that your old friend, Mr. Drummond, and myself, have agreed to propose?"—"Yes, yes."

"Your decision will be a solace to your future existence, Mr. Snow. Have you any objection to be dead for a little while?"—"Dead, sir, dead!"

"Yes, the semblance of death is nothing. You must allow us to state that you have died suddenly. But previously you must execute a will, leaving the whole of your property, without exception, to Mrs. Bennett, the sister of your housekeeper, and one of the accusers of your wife."

"What effect will that have?—ah."—"This—that you will find by the quarrels that will arise between the sisters, their sordid disposition; and I am very much mistaken indeed, in my estimate of their character, if it does not produce such a split between them, as shall induce Mrs. Puffham to confess the truth."

Mr. Snow was silent for a few moments. Then he said, with more emotion and real feeling than I could have given him the credit of possessing,—

"My wife is either very criminal, or one of the most injured women the world ever saw. I cannot agree with you in what I see is your opinion; but you have shaken me, and I consent at once to adopt the course you have pointed out to me, or any other which is likely to place the truth beyond all dispute."

"Then, my old friend," said Drummond, taking his hand, "you will be a happier man than you have been for some time. You may depend your housekeeper, Mrs. Puffham, is a selfish woman, one who ——"

"There, there, hush!" said old Snow; "I have, contrary to my own feelings and predilections, consented to the trial you require. Let us prejudge no one, but wait the result."

"To-morrow, sir," I said, "we will call upon you again, and let us hope that your simulation of death will be but a means through which life will present to you greater charms than, perhaps, it ever has."

"Enough! enough!" he replied, faintly; "come what may, I am not long for this world. For some time past I have endeavoured to conceal from myself the fact that I was sinking, and that rapidly too. I shall outlive the experiment, I dare say, but that will be all."

After a few moments' pause, then, and just as we were rising to go, he added,—

"Have—have you seen her?"—"Your wife?" said Drummond.

"Yes."—"We have. She has suffered much; is suffering much."

He waved his hand in adieu to us, and we left the room, satisfied, to use his own words, that we had shaken, if not destroyed, his belief in the guilt of his wife.

"He looks like a dying man, doctor," remarked Mr. Drummond, when we reached the street.—"There is a remarkable change for the worse."—"I say, doctor, we ought to be very cautious. Only suppose, now, if, after this will is executed, bequeathing all his property to Mrs. Bennett, he should really die suddenly."

"That is a contingency that must be provided against," said I, "for it would, indeed, make us all look remarkably foolish; but when one comes to think of it, there can be no real necessity for having the will at all. A mere statement from a solicitor to Mrs. Puffham, that everything was left to her sister, would produce as much effect as the production of a duly signed and sealed document."—"Let that be the arrangement, then, for, upon my word, I am very suspicious that old Snow is melting away."

* * * * *

Having thus far completed our arrangements as regarded the principal difficulty, namely, getting the consent of Mr. Snow to make the experiment we wished, the attorney was duly instructed to make the attack upon Mrs. Bennett, which was so necessary a preliminary—necessary, because in making such a statement as we purposed to her, we could take care to sow the seeds of dissention between her and Mrs. Puffham, so that when they met, it should be with mutual distaste and distrust.

Mrs. Puffham would be angry, past all patience, at the arts, she would think, Mrs. Bennett must have used, in order to get a will so completely in her favour from Mr. Snow, and we intended that Mrs. Bennett should think that she had narrowly missed the losing so munificent a bequest by the opposition of her sister.

When we went to the attorney's chambers, and told him we were quite ready to proceed, he said,—

"Well, gentlemen, anticipating that you would go on in this matter, I have not been altogether idle, for I find that Mr. Bennett very frequently goes out, and that on such occasions Mrs. Bennett serves in the shop. So you see nothing will be easier than to watch for some such opportunity, and make the pleasant communication to her."

"Very good," said Drummond; "now let us clearly understand, and decide upon the exact terms of that communication."

"Above all things," said I, "do not forget fully to impress her with a notion of how strenuously her sister opposes the will, and how she has endeavoured to set Mr. Snow against Mrs. Bennett."

"That I will do, and it will have this effect. If these women have, and there can be little doubt of it, made a bargain to go shares in the fortune of Mr. Snow in the event of Mrs. Puffham getting possession of it, our proceedings will give a great blow to such an understanding, for Mrs. Bennett will think to herself, 'Why should Puffham want the money not to be left to me if she intended to give me my share fairly?' and Puffham will think, 'Why does Bennett plot and manœuvre to get the whole left to her if she did not intend to bilk me?'"

"There's truth in that," remarked Drummond; "so now let there be no time lost; for as you know, doctor, we cannot calculate upon Mr. Snow from one day to another."

Drummond seemed so firm in his opinion about the condition of Snow, that, medical man as I was, and of course more capable of judging than he, I became a little nervous about it, and joined in urging expedition.

"I will go myself, directly," said the attorney, "and I tell you what you may do, doctor. You can go into the shop and look over some goods, while I speak to Mrs. Bennett; or you may, which perhaps is better, come with me openly."

"I prefer that," said I; "perhaps I may be able to throw in a word occasionally."—"Come on, then."

"And I will wait here until your return," said Drummond, "if you have no objection to allow me, to pocket all fees that come while you are away." — "Ah," said the too honest attorney, with a sigh, "that you may do, and go to sleep at the same time."

* * * * *

We soon reached Bennett's shop; and upon peering through the window, we saw Mrs. Bennett and a lout of a boy in it.

"That's the eldest son," said the attorney.—"He's a beauty."

"Come in, doctor; she is never, I am told, in the shop when Bennett is at home."

In another moment we stood at the counter.

"Pray, madam, is your name Bennett?" said the attorney. —"Well, sir," replied Mrs. Bennett, with a confident air, and a toss of head; "what if my name is Bennett?"

"Simply, madam, that I have called upon you to request you will favour me with your Christian name."

"What is that to you?" was the answer. "It's like your impertinence —my Christian name, indeed!"—"Yes, madam —your baptismal name, perhaps I should call it."

"You are right enough there," thought I; "for Mrs. Bennett's Christian name would be difficult to find."

"And what, pray," she said, shaking her head as if she were preparing herself for a spring upon the unfortunate lawyer, "what may my Christian name be to you?"—"Do you know Mr. Snow, madam?" said the attorney, answering her question by the approved method of asking another.

The colour forsook for an instant the cheek of Mrs. Bennett, and she gasped,—

"Mr. Snow—old Mr. Snow?"—"Yes, madam, old Mr. Snow."

"Of—of Woburn-place?"—"Of Woburn-place."

"I—I do know him—a little—only a little—that is, I did know him."—"Oh; he is making his will, madam;—we are his attornies; and as he contemplates leaving you the whole of his property, without any reserve, I have taken the liberty of calling upon you for your Christian name, to prevent future litigation."

"Leave me—me his property—me!" — "Yes, you, madam."

"Crikey," said the lout of a son who was in the shop, and who had listened, open mouthed, to all that passed; "crikey, won't I smoke cigars now like a rum 'un."

"Will you," said Mr. Bennett, giving him a box on the ear that made him howl again; "I'll let you know, as long as I live, that you have no cigar money. Gracious heavens, gentlemen, is it true?"—"We have our instructions from Mr. Snow himself."

"And does he leave nothing to Mrs. Puffham?"—"Nothing."

"But I thought—dear me, I am so flurried I scarcely know what I'm saying—I thought she was to have all, as the wife was got rid of?"—"Why, madam, as regards Mrs. Puffham, she and Mr. Snow have had a serious quarrel because he avowed his intention of leaving all his property to you. But notwithstanding all she could say against you, he would do so."

"Against me?"—"Yes, madam, you don't drink, I suppose?"

"Me drink—did she say I drank?—oh, I'll have horrible vengeance!"—"That will do," thought I.

"Why," continued the attorney, "we must allow something for the natural aggravation of seeing a large fortune pass away into the hands of another."—"Ah, but she agrees —a-hem!—I'll have my revenge; never mind. It's all the better—oh, the hag!"

"Will you, then, madam, oblige me with your Christian

name?"—"Ann; my name is Ann. Oh, I'll let her see what I can do; she shall die in a kennel, or on a dunghill, before I'll help her; to say I drink, and endeavour to set old Mr. Snow against me,—what horrid perfidy!"—"Ann Bennett—very well, ma'am."

"But, sir, when you are making the will, just put in, that I am to have all the fortune for my own exclusive use, quite independent of my husband."—"You may rely upon that, madam."

"Thank you. When one is to have any advantage, one may as well have it all to oneself."—"Certainly."

"Oh, I'll—I'll be even with that hussey. I'm very much obliged to you, sir. When the old man dies, and I get all his money, I don't mind a couple of pounds for your civility." —"You are very good, madam."

"Oh, don't mention it; for Heaven's sake lose no time, but make the will at once. Dear me, how old is Mr. Snow?" —"Nearly seventy," said I.

"Then he surely cannot live long."—"I should say not."

"Well, of course the old generally go first—mind, gentlemen, make the money all for my exclusive use—for my sake; remember that; I wouldn't have that forgotten for all the world"—"You may depend it shall not, madam. We have now the honour of bidding you a very good morning."

And so we left Mrs. Bennett in her glory.

"Well," said the attorney, when we were fairly in the streets, after our visit to Mrs. Bennett; "what do you think of her, doctor?"

"Think of her? I am very sorry to be obliged to occupy my mind in thinking of her at all. I never met with such a thoroughly selfish and abominable woman—always excepting Mrs. Puffham."

"Exactly. I have heard a great deal of this Mrs. Bennett in the neighbourhood. Some people seem to know her history very well. The three sisters—that is, Bennett, Puffham, and another with whom we have nothing to do, it appears, some years since were earning a precarious living, partly by the practice of some trade, and partly by means questionable; certain it is, though, that Mrs. Puffham occupied anything but an honourable position in the establishment of Mr. Puffham, whose name she assumes. She has several children, I am told, whom she has treated in the most heartless and unfeeling manner.

"Mrs. Bennett is married to Bennett, and is considered by all her friends and connexions an exceedingly clever woman, because she has a sharp, snappish style of discourse, and half starves her husband, children, and servants, by way of economy. The eldest son, you see, is a booby. There is a daughter older still, however, who they tell me is an amiable girl, and one younger, who is a perfect Gorgon."

"Truly," remarked I, "they seem a lively, pleasant lot of people. I think, however, from all this evil we shall extract some good."

"I have no doubt. Women, when once their passions are excited, do not argue very closely upon consequences, and I am sure that the row that will ensue between Puffham and Bennett, about old Snow's property, will be sufficiently violent to induce one or other of them to speak the truth as regards his much-injured wife."

"Well, then, to-morrow be sure you remain at home, in order that I may send for you with a certainty of finding you when your presence is necessary."

"I will. When can you make your call in Woburn-place to-morrow?"

"About eleven. Then Snow must die, as we have arranged, and you, as his solicitor, must be immediately sent for to disclose what you know of his will, in case there should be any instructions therein about his funeral. You understand?"

"Yes; and I will come with all dispatch, and play my part as well as I can."

* * * * * *

I was impatient, very impatient till the morrow should come, for, to tell the truth, I began to consider time a most important object in the affair, considering how precarious a state of health Snow was really in. The only contemplation that gave me any pleasure in the affair was, that in the event of his death occuring before the morning, there was no will, so that his wife would have a legal claim upon his property, however galling it might be to her to know that he had died without declaring his belief in her innocence.

But that was a contingency which might or might not occur, and I gave up, as much as I was able, tormenting myself upon the subject, hoping that everything would come right in the end, as I had seen many much more tangled affairs do.

I could not help, however, picturing to myself all that poor Mrs. Snow must have endured. Her life seemed to have been one of unrequited sacrifices throughout, and it was sad, indeed, to reflect upon how she had given up all her heart's best affections to meet with, at the hands of a cruel destiny, such a wretched return.

I would not call upon her again, for I dreaded to awaken a stronger hope than I had of happier times, and I did not wish to say anything that would extinguish the spark I had created in her bosom of hopefulness for the future. The morrow would decide all, and either she would be welcomed home again as the wife of him who, upon the words of infamous traducers, had cast her from him, or she would be condemned to linger in her present condition, a prey to mental anguish, which those who have suffered from unmerited accusations can alone understand and appreciate.

The morrow was welcomed by me most sincerely, and I rose much earlier than was my custom, in order to get through as many of my regular morning calls as possible, before I went to Mr. Snow, for I knew not how long my presence there might be requisite.

With all my hurrying, however, I could not get to Mr. Snow's until nearly half-past eleven; and when Dennis opened the door for me, he said,—

"Oh, then, sir, the master's mighty queer he is."—"Queer, Dennis?"

"By dad, you may say that, sir. It's mighty queer he is, any way, old soul. Mrs. Puffham's been a counting the silver spoons, she has—bless her the contrary way, sir, which manes the politest curse in the world."

I went into the house, and had just said,—"Well, Dennis, I hope, notwithstanding all that, your master is not really worse," when Mrs. Puffham appeared from the parlour, with a face the colour of which at once showed she had heard what Dennis had been saying to me about her counting the silver spoons, in anticipation of old Snow's death.

For a moment she seemed scarcely able to speak for rage, and when she did, it was in a tone of such bitterness, that even Dennis made a step backwards, and looked rather astonished and alarmed.

"You thief—you low thief!" she exclaimed.

"Where is he?" cried Dennis, pretending to look about him for the individual so addressed. "A low thief is there here, Mrs. Puffham? Let me catch the vagabone."

"This day month you leave this house. Understand that —I give you a month's notice, and no character."

"Me, ma'am—do you mean me?"—"Yes, you lying scoundrel."

"A whole month? By dad, there's time to think of it, then, any way. A month—may I wear my best velveteens all that while, ma'am?"—"Doctor," half screamed Mrs. Puffham, "will you oblige me by kicking that rascal out of doors?"

"Och, murder!" cried Dennis, as he made a precipitate retreat down the kitchen stairs. "The doctor sha'n't be troubled, any way. You've got a good foot of your own, ma'am, as big as a pancake; why don't you do it yourself?— it's a ladylike employment."

Mrs. Puffham did take two steps towards the kitchen stairs, but I restrained her by saying,—

"Madam, what servants say is surely quite beneath your notice; and if you did count the spoons, I think such a proceeding was very proper, in order to guard against petty peculations."

"Yes, sir, certainly; that's the very thing, sir; but low people are always seeking for the worst motives in all things."

"Exactly. How is Mr. Snow to-day, Mrs. Puffham?"— "Ah! poor man. I very much fear he won't last long now, doctor. He's decidedly pinched."

"Pinched! who has pinched him?"—"I mean pinched up. He's beginning to look peaked. Oh, he's a going!"

"Is he, indeed?"—"Yes, sir; and, between you and me, I really think that a strong will ought to be made."—"A will, I think, ma'am, is made; but if it is not, I will to-day speak of it."

"But, sir, you said something about Mrs. Bennett, which has given me uneasiness. I assure you, though she is my own sister, she is on the whole a vile woman."—"Indeed!"

"Yes; I assure you she is an undermining kind of

woman, and she always makes the utmost ridicule of poor Mr. Snow. Oh, if he knew one half of what she has said about him, I do think he would prosecute her."

"Bless me!—you really astonish me. From the manner in which Mr. Snow spoke of her, I should almost have been led to believe that she must have come here some time when you were out of the way, and gained quite a hold of his affections."

Mrs. Puffham's face assumed quite a livid hue as she replied,—

"She come here!—she dare to venture here when I am out! I'll murder her!"—"That would be an extreme measure, indeed, Mrs. Puffham, and one I would not recommend; but I cannot conceal from you that I am quite of opinion your sister has been attempting to undermine you in the opinion of Mr. Snow."

"The vile hussey! Oh, I'll have vengeance on her! I'll let her know who I am—I'll ——" A bell rang at this moment, and Mrs. Puffham exclaimed,—"It's Mr. Snow's bell; I dare say he heard you knock, sir, and is quite impatient."

"Then I will go up to him at once." said I.

Mr. Snow looked worse, certainly. The moment I glanced at him, I said to myself, "He is going; they are all right —old Snow has not got long to live, for certain." I recognised the pinched expression of features which Mrs. Puffham had spoken of, and, in addition, I could see a restlessness of manner, which, to my mind, spoke volumes as to his condition.

"How are you this morning, sir?" I said.—"Much better than I have been for years,' was his reply—"much better; I scarcely ever felt so strong and well in my life."—"A bad sign," thought I.

"Perhaps," he continued, "the experiment we are about to try with regard to the sincerity of Mrs. Puffham, and the innocence or guilt of my wife, may have given a favourable stimulus to my constitution; I am certainly amazingly well. But do you know, doctor, it strikes me that narcotics, one of which you propose administering to me, leave behind disagreeable feelings."

"They do in many instances," I replied; "but we have preparations which contain only the sleeping principle of opium, without allowing the drug to take the after great effect upon the nervous system it frequently does."

"And yet," he added, "I think I would rather simulate death than to be thrown into one of those unnatural slumbers. I am sure I could pretend to be dead."

"Why, Mr. Snow, it is just possible that no examination would take place, and you might not be required to carry on the deception above an hour or so; but on the other hand, you see, there is no saying accurately how affairs may turn out."

"Nevertheless I cannot bring my mind to take any drug. I will affect death, if you like."

"If such is your determination, sir, so let it be. The result is in the hands of Heaven, and I sincerely hope it will lead to the triumph of innocence and virtue."

"Amen!" said the old man. "I have no other wish."

"Well, then, I think everything may be managed at once. If you will lie down on your couch here, and suffer me to tie a silk handkerchief over your face, I don't think any one will feel inclined to remove it. You must remain perfectly still; of course, the slightest movement would be fatal to the whole plan."

"Trust me," he said, as he laid himself down; "I will be a paragon of discretion. Now for the handkerchief. Good night!"

I tied a silk handkerchief loosely over his face, and he lay perfectly motionless. I rang the bell violently—in fact I took hold of the bell-rope, and kept on ringing as hard as I could, till Dennis, Mrs. Puffham, the cook, the housemaid, and the odd girl of all work, rushed into the drawing-room in a wild melee.

"Gracious powers! what's the matter?" cried Mrs. Puffham.—"Arrah, then, doctor, what's the row?" shouted Dennis.

The cook, housemaid, and odd maid of all work screamed all at once.

"Mr. Snow," said I, "is dead."

They all staggered back, as if moved by a wire that acted upon them all at once.

"Dead!" they exclaimed, in chorus.—"Yes, dead."

Mrs. Puffham separated herself from the group like the principal dancer in a ballet, and reeled to an arm-chair, into which she sat with a plump that made it creak again.

"Murder!" said Dennis. "Peace and glory to him! Would you have any objection to a dacent wake?"

"Hush, hush," said I. "Let us leave this melancholy apartment; some of you close the shutters. We can arrange down stairs what had better be done. By-the-bye, it strikes me the solicitor of Mr. Snow ought to be immediately sent for. Dennis, will you go to him? There is his address on the back of one of my cards. Get a coach and bring him back with you, if he should be at his chambers."

"I'll be there and back, sir, in no time at all," cried Dennis: and he went off with all celerity.

"Oh! doctor, doctor," said Mrs. Puffham, "what can equal my feelings now?"—"I really don't know, madam," I replied. "Mr. Snow's death is very sudden indeed; I only hope that his will may turn out a satisfactory document."

"Doctor—sir, do you think——Come into my parlour; I have something of importance to say to you."

The chamber of death, as all the household believed it, was now closed, so that Mr. Snow was left in darkness; and I accompanied Mrs. Puffham to the parlour, in which she had before treated me to some of Mr. Snow's excellent sherry. When we were there she said,—

"I need not tell you that Mr. Snow had an intention of making me his wife."—"A very judicious choice indeed," I replied.

"A-hem! You are very good, sir,—very good, sir, indeed. Well, what I wished to ask of you is this ——"

A loud shriek at this moment sounded through the house, and made me spring to my feet, while Mrs. Puffham slid off her chair, and sat down upon the floor.

"What is that?" I cried.—"Murder!" shouted Mrs. Puffham.

Then I heard a great scuffling of feet in the passage, and in another moment the parlour door was bounced open, and in rushed the cook with such headlong speed, that unless she had jumped over Mrs. Puffham, as boys do over a post in the street, she could not avoid tumbling over her, and accordingly tumble over her she did. This was a proceeding which Mrs. Puffham was not disposed to put up with quietly, and she commenced pummelling the cook violently, while the priestess of the kitchen roared murder with a power of lungs almost superhuman.

"Good Heavens!" cried I, "do be quiet, and tell me what is the cause of all this uproar?"—"I'll teach you to fall over me, and give me kicks on the head," shouted Mrs. Puffham, as she laid hold of the cook by the hair, and knocked her head against the fender; "I'll teach you to come into parlours head over heels."

"Really, Mrs. Puffham," I said, "you will murder the woman. Allow her to tell us the reason of her extraordinary conduct, if you please."—"A ghostesses!" groaned the cook.

"A what?"—"A supernatural ghostesses. Oh, dear me! I shall never be my own woman again—no, never. Oh, lauks! all the fat's in the fire. I'd rather have had the kitchen chimbley of a blaze over and over, I would. I feels as if I'd been roasted without a bit of paper on my back, to keep me from never sich a scorching."

"What has happened?"—"Oh, dear, I don't know; I feels quite overdone—overcome I means; excuse me, sir. You deals in physic, but all the physic in the world will never make me my own woman again."

"Well, but you have not told us what's the matter."—"I fells quite a bundle of matter myself. I was agoing up to my own attic—oh!"

"Really I must beg you to be more explicit."—"I feels all over explicit. I suppose as that's some doctering digression for a pain in my back—side I mean. I was agoing up to my attic all for to get a clean cap, when in course I had to pass the drawing room door. Little did I think I should get sich a basting. Look, sir, what an inspiration I am in; I'm all over dripping."

"You vile wretch!" screamed Mrs. Puffham, "if you don't explain directly the cause of this uproar, I'll send for a new policeman, and give you in charge."

"You may send, mum, for an old policeman, if you likes," said the cook; "though I happens to be aware—for I sees some things from the kitchen winder as some folks would rather I didn't. I see that you, mum, prefers a young policeman—a-hem! mum, a-hem! Cooks has eyes as well as taters."—"You wiolent wretch!"

"You may call me a wiolent wretch as much as you please,

mum. I'll make you look blue afore I've done with you, mum. What do you think of A 247?"—"I—I—good gracious, is there no one here to take the horridest vengeance for me?" exclaimed Mrs. Puffham. "I never saw A 247 in all my life."

"He's the policeman, sir," continued the infuriated cook, turning to me, "as is beating about here. Mrs. Puffham has a eye to him, and I cotched 'em once ——"—"There now, cook," said I, "that will do."

"As thick as thieves."

Mrs. Puffham took up a footstool, and threw it at the cook's head, where it made a hollow sort of sound, and then branched off, striking me on the shoulder.

"I shall leave the house," cried I, "if this behaviour is to be persevered in. Mrs. Puffham, I desire particularly that you will allow me to hear what has alarmed the cook; and you, cook, I desire to make no further remarks on Mrs. Puffham."

The cook, thus admonished, commenced her narrative as follows:—

"I was a-going up to my own attic, and in course had to pass the drawing-room door, where lays the deceased. Well,

sir, I was a thinkin' o' the shortness o' human life, which, arter all, is nothing, when I heard a coughin'."—"A coffin!"

"Yes, a coughin'. 'Gracious!' says I, and then I heard another coughin', just like old master used to cough as is dead and gone—rest his giblets—Amen!"

"Oh, you heard some one cough. Where did it proceed from?"—"From the drawing-room. I felled down the stairs immediate, and screamed immense."

"I know you did. But you must be mistaken, for Mr. Snow is dead."—"But, doctor," whispered Mrs. Puffham, "suppose, after all, he should only be in a trance."—"Nonsense, nonsense. You may satisfy yourself very soon, for in such a subject decomposition will soon commence."

"I'm sure I heard a coughin'," persisted the cook, "whether composition commences or not"—"To satisfy you, cook," said I, "I—I will go up and see the body once more."

So saying I went to the drawing-room, where I found Mr. Snow sitting up on the sofa with the handkerchief over his face.

"Well, doctor," he said, "how are you getting on?"—"I have sent for the lawyer," I replied. "But the house is full of consternation, owing to the cook, in passing the drawing-room door, hearing you cough"

"I must be more careful. I feel uncommonly well—amazingly well, doctor."—"I am rejoiced to hear it, sir. Be so good as to lie down when you hear any one coming. Even now it might have been some one else."

"Yes, yes, I will be very cautious. Tell them I am quite frightful, and they could not bear the sight of me. I wish, though, it was all over."—"So do I."

At this moment I heard the sound of wheels in the street, which stopped at the door of the house.

"That is Dennis and the attorney," I said. "Mr. Snow, I will endeavour that all explanations and statements shall take place in this room, so that you shall hear what every one has to say about the matter."—"Do so—do so."

I hurriedly left the drawing-room, and I was not a little pleased to find that not only the lawyer had come, but my friend, who had originally introduced me to Mr. Snow. I had no opportunity of speaking to them apart, for Mrs. Puffham kept very close to me; so all I could say was,—

"Gentlemen, I have the pain of informing you that our poor old friend, Snow, has gone at last."

"Ah, then, that's true for you, sir," cried Dennis. "I tould the gentleman that the ould master had gone to glory at last—rest his soul. He was an ould Christian in a good many things, and would have been in a good many more, if it hadn't been for this female, Puffham. Recollect that month's notice, ma'am, if you plase—I'm a-going."

Mrs. Puffham was too much occupied with more important matters, now that the attorney had arrived, to take further notice of Dennis than the bestowal upon him of a look which, if looks could be fatal, would have that instant put an end to his mortal career.

"For God's sake, sir," she cried, addressing the attorney, "tell me, has Mr. Snow made a will? I mean, has he properly signed it, and all that sort of thing?"—"He—has," replied the lawyer, solemnly; "I have it in my pocket."

"Yes, yes; and—and ——"—"Hush, madam, hush!—when I say that Mr. Snow's will very nearly concerns an amiable female to whom he felt himself under great obligation, and whom he admired both mentally and personally, you will quite understand me, my dear madam."

"Oh, oh," sighed Mrs. Puffham; "poor dear man. Oh, if he had but have lived, I could have lived upon bread and cheese all my life!"

"I am quite sure, madam, that you are free from any selfish longings after Mr. Snow's property, which I have the pleasure of saying is much more considerable than any one imagined."

"Goodness gracious! is it indeed? Oh, dear me, if he had left it to anybody else I should have revered his poor old memory; or if had left it to the poor of the parish I should never have repined."

"Or built arms-houses with it," put in the cook, "for deranged and parched-up cooks."

"He has done none of these things," said the lawyer; "but, consulting his judgment and his inclination, he has left all to a female in whom he had the greatest confidence, and who he told me had been of the greatest assistance to him in his domestic affairs, and taken the greatest care of his interests."

"Oh, if ever there was an angel on earth," sighed Mrs. Puffham, "it was Mr Snow. I shall never look up again."

—"And I shall never be my own woman," said the cook.

"Sir," said I, with affected solemnity to the attorney, "I think so important a document as a will ought to be read even in the presence of the deceased. Poor Mr. Snow lies above stairs; let us repair to the apartment of death, and there, if you please, you can more particularly explain the contents of the important document you have in your pocket."

"A very proper suggestion," remarked the attorney. "Let us go up stairs at once."

Mrs. Puffham seemed on the point of starting some objection, but as we all proceeded in a body to the staircase, she probably thought it useless, and followed us to the drawing-room, where Mr. Snow lay, perfectly motionless, with the handkerchief over his face.

"We need not open all the shutters," said I, as I partially unfolded one of them. "By standing here we shall have sufficient light for you to read the will by."

"Oh, ample, ample. Besides, it is a very short document indeed."

"Is it?"—"Yes; there is but one bequest in it. I cannot help thinking that some bequest ought to have been made for old servants—persons who had done their duty; and, besides, I cannot help likewise thinking that old friends ought to have had a something as a sort of *memento mori*—you understand me, doctor?"—"Yes, yes."

I could see that Mrs. Puffham was in a horrible state of fidget while the attorney was thus angling with her expectations, but she said nothing, although I felt well convinced she could at that moment have snapped his head off and eaten it.

"As I have remarked," continued the attorney, with provoking prolixity, "only one person is mentioned in the will; and it gives me sincere pleasure, before naming that person, to hear the generous and self-denying sentiments of this lady, Mrs. Puffham"

Mrs. Puffham made a sort of half bow, and then looked the very personification of impatience. The lawyer then slowly took from his pocket a parchment tied carefully with red tape, and labelled "The last Will and Testament of Abel Snow, Esq.," which he began to untie with the greatest deliberation. Suddenly then he paused, and glancing round at us, he added,—

"And yet why should I, ladies and gentlemen, trouble you with the verbiage of a legal document, when in a few words I can explain to you all that you wish to know concerning the business?"

"Ah, why indeed," said I. "Who is the lucky possessor of Mr. Snow's property?"—"A-hem!—Listen. Take a chair, Mrs. Puffham."

Mrs. Puffham sank into an easy chair, and hid her face with a cambric handkerchief.

"A-hem—a-hem! Mr. Snow, although advanced in years, and capable of knowing better ——"—"Go on," whispered I; "that's right."

"And capable of knowing better, fell in love with a female who was not in a condition to become his wife."—"Not in a condition!" cried Mrs. Puffham. "I'd have you to know, sir, that love levels all distinctions of ranks, and though a lady may be a housekeeper, she may make a capital wife for a gentleman."

"My dear madam, allow me to go on, if you please. I say, Mr. Snow, having formed this attachment to one whom he considered the finest woman in the world, has left her all his property."—"All?"—"Yes, all, without reservation—houses lands, estates, shares, money, furniture, bonds, plate—all, all, all, to her."

"I shall faint," said Mrs. Puffham. "How much does it all come to?"—"I should say nearly forty thousand pounds."

"Oh—oh—oh!"—"Be calm, madam. If you are thus excited, how much more will you be when you hear the name of the fine woman—the fortunate legatee."

"Go on," she gasped; "go on—I think I can bear it. Go on. Oh, Mr. Snow, if you had but have lived! Go on; let me hear the name. You will stay to dinner, gentlemen, if you please."—"Thank you, madam. The name of the fortunate legatee is Mrs. ANN BENNETT."

There was a pause of some moments' duration. Mrs. Puffham absolutely gasped for breath, and I feared she would go into some convulsion. She then rose from the easy chair on which she had seated herself, and stood for about half a minute glaring at the attorney as if he had been some apparition.

"Mrs. Ann Bennett?" she repeated.—"Mrs. Ann Bennett," said the attorney.

"Yes," said I, "Mrs. Ann Bennett, your sister, madam."—"Couldn't you ate her wid a grain o' salt?" cried Dennis. "Och, murder!"

Mrs. Puffham dealt him a blow on the mouth that staggered him, and then she made an attempt to seize the will, which the attorney had half in his pocket and half out. In that she was foiled, and then she seemed to awaken to all her indignation.

"She left all—she—my sister—my infamous sister?—Ha! ha! ha!—and she thinks she will enjoy it?—but she shall not. I'll have her transported—yes, transported. Oh, I—I will have revenge, if I cannot have the money. She left everything, and I nothing!—indeed. I'll have my revenge of all of you. Nothing for me! Oh, the old wretch—the old beast, that I have attended upon night and day, and made myself a slave to—the old goat! Curse him—curse him—curse you all!"

"You'd better be after sitting down, ma'am," said Dennis. "Don't you find it fatiguing swearing so on your legs, ma'am?"

She did try to sit down, but Dennis, with malice aforethought, pulled the chair a little way back, and in the midst of her passion down sat Mrs. Puffham on the carpet.

"Oh, murder!—perhaps you've hurt yourself, ma'am," cried Dennis. "Let me give you a leg up, ma'am."—"Dennis," said I, "go away. This affair is turning serious; go away now."

"You want to murder me among you, you know you do," screamed Mrs. Puffham. "Help—police—murder!"

A loud rat-tat at the door stopped her vociferations, and the attorney immediately said,—

"When Mr. Snow's footman came to my chambers and told me his master was dead, I instantly dispatched a clerk to Mrs. Bennett, who I knew was the sole legatee, requesting her presence here, in order that she might personally give her directions for the funeral of the deceased, and state what she wished done in the domestic affairs; she might wish to change the housekeeper, or some other of the domestics. I have no doubt that is her now at the door."

"Missus Bennett," cried the odd girl of all-work, flinging open the drawing-room door,—"Missus Bennett, if you pleases."

Mrs. Bennett walked into the room like an empress; she had on an enormous bonnet, with four dreadful ostrich feathers in it. Her face emulated the setting sun, and around her she held a shawl which must have cost "a matter of something," as Dennis remarked, for he would not go away, although I told him to do so. She glanced around her with an air of triumph that evidently showed that the attorney's clerk had been well tutored what to say to her.

"A—a chair," she said, in an affected lisp,—"a chair."

"Yes, ma'am," said Dennis. "Perhaps you'd like a sophy, ma'am, instead?"—"I understand," she added, when she had seated herself with a bounce,—"I understand I have been sent for."

"And I understand, and will make you understand, you had better stayed at home," cried Mrs. Puffham, making a dart at the bonnet, and demolishing it in a twinkling, in the most scientific and complete manner.

"Hurrah!" cried Dennis,—"hubbaboo—whack!" and he gave a jump nearly up to the ceiling.

"Wretch!" cried Mrs. Bennett, demolishing with one pull all Mrs. Puffham's false curls.—"Viper!" screamed Mrs. Puffham.

"Monster!"—"Beast!"

"Ladies—ladies!" cried I,—"ladies!"—"She a lady?"—"She a lady?"

"Why—why—she was only in keeping with Puffham."—"Bennett took you off the streets."

"You'll die on a dunghill."—"And you in Botany Bay."

"You hag!"—"You false——"

"Ladies—ladies!—really, upon my word, now, what is the matter?"

"I will tell all, if they hang me for it," cried Mrs. Puffham. "I'll have you transported, my lady, and old fat Bennett will be much obliged to me. Oh, you ugly wretch!"—"Ugly! you fright—you gorgon!"

Bang went Mrs. Puffham's fist in Mrs. Bennett's eye, and then Mrs. Bennett dealt Mrs. Puffham a teazer on the ear, and then we all interfered, although I was half dead with suppressed laughter, and stopped the combat from proceeding further.

"I'll tell all—I'll tell all," cried Puffham. "Mr. Snow's wife is innocent—innocent as a babe unborn; we swore against her. There, you have it, do what you like—she is innocent."

Mrs. Bennett screamed, and in an instant old Snow jumped up and rushed into the throng we made. To describe the effect his sudden appearance had is almost impossible. Puffham fainted—Bennett went into violent hysterics—Dennis raised some old Irish war cry, and capered about the room as if he had been mad.

"Send for my wife," cried Mr. Snow,—"send for her, for God's sake, and let these guilty women go. My wife—my injured wife!—I—I am dying!"

Mrs. Snow was immediately sent for, but before she came, poor old Snow was nearly insensible. She came to him and uttered his name—a spasm came across his features.

"Emily—Emily," he cried, "forgive—forgive—all yours—all yours—I leave you all—God—God bless you! It is night, Emily!"

He drew one long breath—it was his last.

* * * * *

Mrs. Puffham—I really don't know what became of Mrs. Puffham. Mrs. Bennett was till within these few years alive, but she had survived old fat Bennett, as Puffham called him, and didn't she keep in tolerable subjection the booby son who loved cigars.

As for Mrs. Snow, she is happy—very happy. She is wedded to her first love, and the last time I saw her she presented to me a little love, and when I said, "Good God! this is the fifth child you have shown me," she had the face only to laugh.

THE MYSTERIOUS PATIENT;

OR, HIS EXCELLENCY THE ——.

SOME folks think that a physician, like a family attorney, may have anything freely communicated to him without fear of censure or dread of his taking any steps to see right done against might. This feeling is particularly manifest among some of our nobility; and when I was yet acquiring a reputation that was beginning agreeably to fill my pockets with more fees than I had for years in my most sanguine slumbers dreamt of obtaining, it was gravely hinted to me by some good friends that I was doing myself no good by my meddling propensities, and that if I let things alone that were no business of mine, it would be all the better for me, and all the more agreeable to some others.

However, my disposition never would allow me to be prudent at the expense of feeling, or that kind of indignation that always took possession of me when I became cognizant of some iniquity that was being attempted to be glossed over, either with money or by trickery, or pretended sanctity; and, besides, if I had let things alone, and only minded my own business, where would have been these passages from my diary, which it has pleased me to think, now that I am in the "sere and yellow leaf," have sometimes amused an idle hour, or awakened a tender sympathy? Certainly I might have had a diary which would have convinced all the world that I had only minded my business; but then Mr. Lloyd's readers would have found no amusement in such a record as—

Jan. 10, 18—.—Called on Mr. Punchwine—decidedly better. Prescribed composing draught of gin and water, and bread pills.

Jan. 11.—Mr. Punchwine much better, and likes the composing draught amazingly, only thinks it might be made just a trifle stronger.

I think, therefore, my meddling and interfering has not been without beneficial results; and in the case which I am about to lay before my readers it will be seen that, although I lost a noble and illustrious patient, I achieved what to me was of higher importance—a triumph over one who would fain make all around him, by dint of money and assurance, assistants in his vices.

The evening of an extraordinary warm summer's day had arrived, and I had got through my routine visits, and was glad to get my coat off at home, with some prospect of getting a few degrees cooler by sitting still in a back room with an eastern aspect, when my wife came in with an expression of countenance that convinced me either something must have happened to the kitchen chimney, or that some unwelcome visitor had made his or her appearance unexpectedly.

"What is the matter?" said I.—"Oh, it's always the way," replied my wife. "Who'd marry a doctor?"

"Dear me, what have I done?"—"I don't know, but you are wanted."

"By a patient?"—"No, sir," said a servant we had with us a long while, and who considered herself privileged to say what she liked and when she liked—"no, sir, it's a impatient. He says as he can't wait no longer; he must be off."

"Oh, indeed. Give me my coat; I have no idea of a patient being off, which I suppose means dying without the doctor's assistance. Where is he?"—"He's in a thing at the door, sir."

"A what?"—"I think it's what they call a briskey. There he is, and he's rather a swearing, and the oss is a whiskin'——"

"A what?"—"His tail like nothink. You never give a body time to pronounce a sentence."

"Very well, Martha. You go and tell him I don't see patients in carriages, and that if he wants my advice, he must come into the house, and leave his horse a whiskin', as you call it."—"Very good," said Martha, and away she went, while I proceeded to the parlour, which commanded a view of the street, where, sure enough, at my door stood a carriage, something between a phaeton and a cab; but it was already so dark that I could not see who was in it.

In a few moments Martha returned to me and said,—

"If you please, sir, he won't come. He says, with quite an air and a grace, says he, 'Tell your master as he's wanted to go along o' me on an errand all for to see a sick indiwidual,' says he, 'as is some distance off,' says he."

Upon this I went to the door myself, when a voice from the interior of the carriage said,—

"Is you to go once at with me?"

The accent was decidedly foreign, and the curious manner in which the words were transposed, and thrown out of their proper places, not a little amused me.

"Who are you?" I said.—"Je suis un gentilhomme. I am—that is—I come you for to go the jeune ladi—oh! She was next week standing on the point of deccase. Will you go yesterday at once in a moment?"

I hesitated for a minute. "Shall I go or not?" I asked myself. The carriage was an unexceptionable one—the horses splendid. I could not doubt the respectability, or rather the wealth of the parties; and, moreover, I have, as the reader knows, a love of adventure, which always prompts me to see out anything that has the remotest air of mystery about it.

Hence, without another word, I stepped into the carriage, and when there I said,—

"I am quite ready. Remember, I am a physician, and it is of no use taking me to any surgical case, as I cannot attend to it."—"Oh, non, no, nein; me know well. Ah, she is she, and very bad—mal terrible. She will has some day put one foot in the grave."

Whoever my companion might me, and however defective he was in the English language, he was an admirable driver, for we set off at a great pace, turning corners in first-rate style, and passing everything on the road as cleverly as possible.

The evening was advanced, and there was no moon. Each moment, too, huge masses of clouds were getting up from the north and east, so that it was as much as I could do to see the horses' ears as we passed from one lamp-post to another. As for my companion in the carriage, I had not as yet seen him at all, for he sat so far back in the vehicle, and some curtains with which it was provided were drawn so far across the front of it, that, do all I could, I found it impossible to obtain a glimpse of his face. Moreover the carriage was so built, that when one got once fairly into it, it was very difficult to move, for the seat went so far back, and was so soft and luxurious, that one fairly sank down almost in a reclining posture, and to scramble up was next thing to impossible while the vehicle was in motion.

On we went, up one street, down another, through squares, past terraces, and round corners, all of which I was familiar with, and still there seemed no disposition to stop; so after some time I said,—

"Where are we going? I was in hopes it was not far from my own home."—"I know I don't know," was the reply.

"You don't know?"—"Certainement; I not know to tell."

"The deuce you don't! Then I will trouble you to let me out, if you please."—"No, no."

"But I insist."—"No, no."

"D—n it, sir, whoever you are, I will not allow you to whisk me along at this rate without knowing where I am going to."—"Yes; vera tru'."

"I was a fool to get in, with so poor an account of my destination."—"Vera great fool—donkey—great fool."

I made a violent effort to get out of the positive hole I had sunk into among the confounded cushions, but the more I struggled, the deeper I seemed to descend, and the faster the horses appeared to go. Then suddenly the curtains were drawn quite close, and all was darkness, while by the motion of the wheels I fancied the carriage was being turned completely round several times.

"Hilloa!" I cried; "help! help! police!"— "Sacre!" muttered my companion; "what for you make one noise?—d—n!"

"Confound your impertinence," I cried, and I made a plunge in the direction where he was sitting, but missed him. Then I heard a sharp crack of a whip, and off set the horses at a good twelve miles an hour, in what direction I had no sort of idea.

"I will not put up with this any longer," I cried. "Police! police!—help! help!—Ho, there—stop the horses!"

"Peas, peas," said my companion. "I forbid you to hold your tongue. You are all for to go to visit the young ladi who was all very bad next week. You will be paid well yesterday—never complain; all is right—complete."

"What young lady?"—"Oh, I was not telling you; she is what she is is she."

"That's explanatory," said I. "But at least you can tell me how far you are going."—"One mile—or two mile—or three mile—or less, or more—maybe—somehow."

I was confident at that moment that I heard some gate creak upon its hinges, and I was the more convinced that I had not been deceived in such a conjecture by the very different sound the wheels immediately made. They appeared to me as if passing over gravel, and our progress was certainly much slower than it had been at all from the period of our starting.

I thought to myself, "Well, after all, what but a wish for my professional assistance could have dictated this extraordinary proceeding? Perhaps after all I had better be quiet, and see where the affair will end."

With this resolve growing each moment stronger in my mind, I let myself go back among the luxurious cushions of the carriage, and made no further attempt to rescue myself from the singular circumstances in which I was placed.

"This is the great prudence," said my companion, as if he had divined my very thoughts. "It is no use at all to make one row—ha!"

"Well, I won't make a row," said I. "But since we have now come to that understanding, you will perhaps tell me how far we have to go"

"No far much at all. We shall come to the stop in one, two minute. Be much tranquil. You will see the beautiful most young ladi in all the world. You will have one good fee, and you will be blindfold soon."—"Blindfold!"

"Ah, it is most true verite."—"Nonsense. If you cannot trust me you had better never have employed me. I will not be blindfolded, and so I tell you at once. I will oppose such a process, and you will find it no easy matter, in the face of such opposition, to accomplish."

"We shall see all the things as we shall see," remarked my companion, with provoking coolness.

Then a voice, which was unquestionably English, suddenly cried,—

"Right?"—"Yes," said the Frenchman.

Another gate I heard swing upon its hinges, and the carriage immediately stopped. Still all was absolute darkness, and yet I was sure we were some distance out of town, for the sweet scent of flowers came upon my senses, and there was all that agreeable freshness in the air that came into the carriage, despite the curtains, which, after the day's splendour has gone, pervades sylvan spots of well-kept beauty.

The carriage door was now opened, and I saw at once that I was in a garden, for the impenetrable darkness in which I had been for some time enabled me to see objects quite distinctly when I no longer had anything to contend against but the very partial obscurity of a summer's night. I lost no time in scrambling out of the vehicle, and then I stood on a well kept gravel walk, but as ignorant as I could possibly be of where I was. My mysterious travelling companion then alighted, and I caught sight of his figure, although I could not see his face, in consequence of his keeping a cloak muffled up above his chin.

"Allons!" he said, taking hold of my arm.

Before then, I could stir a step, some one from behind clapped something over my head that came in an instant down to my neck, effectually obscuring my vision, and rendering me for the moment helpless. I suppose then they anticipated some opposition on my part, for I was lifted off the ground and carried rapidly along by, I was confident, the united strength of several persons. To resist would have been madness, and I would not exhaust myself by useless efforts, so I permitted them just to carry me where they pleased.

After a few moments I was conscious we were ascending a staircase, which, from the sound of the feet upon it, I conjectured to be stone, and then there was a pause of some moments' duration, and a whispered conference took place, which ended in a window being opened, as I could hear, and my being put through it. A confused glare of light came to my eyes through the covering which was over them, and then it suddenly disappeared again, as if whatever had produced the illumination had been suddenly extinguished, and I was permitted now to stand upon my feet, but my arm was held by some one. Then the covering over my head and face was suddenly jerked off, and I found myself in a room with one person, who immediately said to me,—

"I hope you have suffered no inconvenience, sir, in your coming here?"—"Do you?" I replied. "You are very kind in your inquiries, after the inconvenience I certainly have suffered. May I make the bold request of asking where I am?"

"Yes; but I dare not tell you."—"Dare not!"

"I dare not. Your professional skill has induced a certain party to send for you to attend a certain other party who is much indisposed. You will receive nothing but gentlemanly treatment, and you will be compensated at your own valuation for your time and trouble."—"Still, sir," I said, "whoever you may be, I must protest against this very strange mode of procuring my attendance upon a patient."

"There were reasons."—"There could be none. I should have been willing at any time to attend professionally upon any one, without rendering all the precautions that have been used necessary. I must say that this shall be my last visit."

"Oh, nonsense. You cannot judge of all the circumstances that have rendered this proceeding necessary. Come, now, attend to me while I give you a few particulars concerning your patient before you see her."

I made no reply, and after a slight pause he continued,—

"You will see a girl about sixteen years of age; she has been suffering three or four days from indisposition. Her intellect is a little affected at this, and she fancies that this is not her home; but her illness takes the form of excessive languor, low fever, want of appetite, and a general depression. She seems to require invigorating, and the whole system appears to want a stimulant; in fact, she is fast sinking."

"And is this her home?" said I.—"Undoubtedly. Is it one she need be ashamed of?"—"Perhaps so."

"Oh, pho! pho!—you suspect something wrong because you have been brought here rather mysteriously; but such is not the case. Make your mind perfectly easy on that score. In a few minutes I will return to conduct you to your patient."

"What is her name?" said I.—"There you must excuse me," he replied, and he immediately left the room, locking the door after him, and leaving me in nearly total darkness.

The apartment was very spacious, and decidedly handsome. From the ceiling there hung a chandelier, the lights of which were turned down, so as to afford but a faint glimmer, and yet fully sufficient to enable me to see the various costly objects with which that truly magnificent apartment was amply stored. The furniture was extremely costly, and scarce an article could be seen but what bore some marks about it that at once proclaimed it the best of its kind, and ease and elegance were the main things studied.

The carpet was evidently made for the room, since it fitted it so accurately, its rich and gorgeous pattern contrasting with the ceiling above, and the light but rich gilded mouldings that ornamented the room. The soft tread of the foot at once told you that you trod on no common manufacture, the soft light being just enough to enable you to make out its general outlines. Various reclining seats were scattered here and there, and rich tapestry hung before the windows in graceful folds, while the tables distributed about held many costly things—trifles, but trifles of value.

One feature in this room must not be forgotten, and that is, its mirrors and looking-glasses, which were superb. At every convenient space one was placed, beautifully let in, in scroll frames, in all the panels. These gave a brilliant effect to the room, which, when lighted up, was no doubt indescribable. No space was left empty and naked, and yet no overcrowding was visible; the arrangement had evidently been made by a masterly hand, and means were not lacked when such a room was designed and finished, and put in this state.

I dare say I was nearly ten minutes in this apartment alone before any one came to disturb my cogitations upon its singular richness. Then a door opened, which I had not observed, for it was painted and edged so as to resemble a picture in a very handsome and rich frame, and the same person with whom I had held the little unsatisfactory conversation I have recorded, re-entered.

"Now, sir," he said, "if you are ready, we are."—"I will follow you," said I; "but I protest against any more blindfolding."

"You need not," he said; "it is unnecessary now, quite. I was against it altogether. Come on."

I followed him from the splendid room, and we traversed several others, some of which quite equalled it in richness, although in different styles. Then we came to a marble staircase, which we ascended, and my guide, pushing open a door, entered an apartment which was so full of the odour of rare flowers, that the atmosphere of it was quite suffocating, after the contrasted coolness of the air on the staircase. We passed through that room, and then another, after which a door was opened, and a heavy silk curtain drawn on one side, when I found myself in a small octagonal apartment, well lighted, and furnished beautifully. On a sofa, near one of the windows, lay a female figure, to which my guide pointed, saying,—

"There, sir, is your patient. Don't mind what she says, for she don't know herself, but prescribe for her as quickly as you can, and charge your own fee."

There was a coarseness to my mind about the man's continual allusion to my fee, as if that would reconcile me to anything, that I was rather disposed to be angry on that ground as well as on others, and I said, in a tone of displeasure,—

"I neither solicited nor wished to be brought here; but, fee or no fee, I will do my duty."

At the sound of my voice the figure on the sofa started up, and I saw it was a very young girl, who was gazing intently upon me. I was at once struck by the expression of fearful alarm that was depicted upon her countenance. Her eyes were rapidly wandering in all directions, and she breathed short and thick, as if she lived, poor thing, in the momentary expectation of some sudden catastrophe.

No one, however, could gaze for many moments upon that face without being wonder-stricken and enchanted with its astonishing beauty. It was a form to dream of as belonging to some supremely beautiful angel, such as might be deputed by Heaven to give a welcome to some new spirit, and fill it with rich admiration of the loveliness that dwelt around the majesty of God.

It was not in feature, it was not in colour that the charm lay, but it was in the sweet harmony of all combined—the lustrous beauty of her eyes—the winning magic of her mouth —the soft small rounded chin—the infantine beauty of the brow. I certainly never had seen that young girl's equal, and for some moments I forgot the singular and unprecedented circumstances that had brought me there in a kind of reverie that came over my spirit as I gazed upon her face. And she, too, looked at me with a scrutinising eagerness, as if she would read my very soul, and was asking herself the question of "Friend or foe?" as regarded me.

"You are not well, I am told," said I.

She shuddered and turned her eyes towards a corner of the room, and there, to my astonishment, I saw a man with his arms folded across his breast, and a mask on his face. I was most indignant at the unwarrantable intrusion, and said, loudly,—

"Be you who you may, I here solemnly declare that I will not hold any conference with my patient in the presence of a third party. You shall go or I go."

A faint cry burst from the girl's lips; it was one partly of joy, partly of alarm, and she said, in a voice that I shall never forget as long as I live,—

"You are not one of them—you are not one of them! You will save me—save me!"—"D—n!" cried the disguised man, advancing. "I expected as much. George is as obstinate as h———l."

The girl sprang from the sofa, and clung to me desperately as he screamed,—

"Help me, oh, help me! Take me away! Help, for the love of God, help me! They will murder me! Keep him from me!"

Shriek followed shriek, and I was for the instant so bewildered that I knew not what to do. However, as the man with the mask was advancing, I disengaged myself as well as I could from the young girl, and, catching up the chair, I flung it at his head with all the strength I was then master of. The chair hit him, and he staggered back with a curse upon his lips. Then he drew a pistol from his pocket, and I verily believe would have fired it at me, had not the door been flung open, and several persons, who had no doubt been alarmed by the cries of the girl, rushed in to take part in the affray.

"Hold off!" I cried. "The first of you who touches me shall repent it."

My voice and determined manner awed them for a moment, and they stood irresolute for about half a minute, during which period of time the girl tightened her grasp of my arm, and cried distractedly,—

"Sir, sir, take me with you—take me with you! I have been stolen from a happy home! Save me—save me! What care I for a king———"

She had no sooner uttered the word king, than a loud voice from outside the room cried,—

"Turn him out—out!—out—turn him out!—down— down—down! Turn him out, I say!"

The men who were in the room stepped as if involuntarily on one side, and I saw a tall stout man just outside the doorway, who turned and walked away so quickly that I could not obtain the slightest view of his face. In another instant I was pounced upon by those present, and, of course, overpowered by numbers. The girl clung to me as long as she was able, and screamed terrifically until she was forcibly dragged away and held by the man with the mask, when she kept crying, in accents that went to my very heart,—

"Oh, think of me when you are gone! They have dragged me from my home. If you cannot take me with you now, come again and rescue me. They will kill me—I am dying now, and they know it. Save me—save me! I am innocent of wrong—I dare not sleep here, or eat, or drink. Save me, sir, as you hope for joy in Heaven!"—"Peace!—d—n!—peace!", cried one of the men.

He seized the girl, and forcing her down on the sofa, he held his hand over her mouth so as to stifle her cries, while the others did their best to drag me to the door, and I did my best to resist being so dragged, for I was most anxious to hear all the girl had to say. The man could not entirely stifle her voice, and she continued appealing frantically to me, saying,—

"Do not forget me—oh, do not forget me! My name is ——."—"Yes, tell me your name," cried I. "Your name—quick, quick!—your name?"

"My own name is ——."—"Speak another word, curse you," cried the man with the mask, "and I'll blow your brains out."

"My name is Frances ——"

At that moment I was by one tremendous jerk forced from the room, the door was closed, and, save one half-stifled shriek, I heard no more. I made then, despite of the numbers that opposed me, a desperate resistance, but it was a vain one, and I was dragged down the marble staircase, and before I had time to look around me, the velvet cap which had before blindfolded me was placed over my head and face, and I was lifted from the floor and carried off rapidly through the various rooms into the open air.

To struggle would have been to provoke personal injury, and I therefore abstained from so doing, although I made a vow to myself that I would leave no stone unturned to resolve the mysteries of that evening, and to rescue from the cruel thraldom that evidently oppressed her that young creature, in whose fate I felt so keen an interest. I was hurried onwards until once more I felt that I was in the beautiful, fresh, balmy air; still I was not released, and the only voice that broke the stillness was that of the infernal Frenchman who had brought me from my own house, and who I heard say,—

"Allons—d——n! Bring him vite—poke him in the carriage. Now, Peter—now, Peter."

I was hurried, still blindfolded, into the same carriage, as I guessed by the downy texture of the seats, which had conveyed me from home. In a moment the vehicle was in motion over the gravel path which I had before traversed. Then again I heard the gate opened, and I felt certain we were in some public road.

"Now," thought I, "for a chance. I may make some one hear me, and, let what will come of it, I will give my captors into custody of the first police-constable who may be attracted by my voice to come to the rescue. Gathering, then, all the breath I could, I uttered a loud shout of,—

"Police! police! police!"

I was immediately seized by one of my gaolers, and a ferocious voice said close to my ear,—

"Hark ye, sir; this is a life and death job. Repeat those cries, and, whether I like it or not, I must put a pistol bullet in your brains."

Somehow I considered this as only an idle threat, and again I cried out aloud for help, when I heard a voice inquiring,—

"Hilloa, there;—stop!—stop!—what's the matter?"—"A madman and his keeper," replied some one.

Crack went the whip, and we flew over the ground at a tremendous speed for some time. Then there was a very sudden pull up, and some whispering took place. The door of the carriage was opened, and I was dragged out and thrown upon the ground, which I felt was grass. Before I could scramble to my feet the carriage and my enemies were gone, and I was alone, with a velvet cap over my head and eyes, I knew not where.

* * * * *

My first efforts were directed to free myself from the encumbrance of the cap that was over my face, and that I quickly succeeding in doing, and then I looked about me with no little interest, in order to endeavour to ascertain where I was. The night was uncommonly dark, as I have before stated, and all I could see were the dim outlines of hedges and trees about me, and grass beneath my feet. I was evidently in the open fields somewhere—but where? That was the question—was I east, west, north, or south of London? In which direction was I to turn my face, in order to proceed homewards? Where was I even to seek a road, which, pursuing, I might eventually arrive at some house, the inhabitants of which would give me some idea of where I was?

There was not even a friendly star peeping forth to give me an idea as to the points of the compass; and, as for the moon, she had evidently given up all idea of getting up that night, or, if she was up, she had a great deal of business to transact behind the clouds.

"Well," thought I, "this is remarkably pleasant."

One! struck a clock, the low, soft sound of which was brought to my ears by a gentle breeze.

"One o'clock," I said. "The deuce! Here have I been four or five hours canted about from place to place, and now am Heaven knows where."

Then I thought I would make an effort to get into some hospitable region by walking straight forward in one direction, which surely must ultimately lead me somewhere, and so it did—that somewhere being a ditch, into which I stepped with a *sang froid* that must have astonished the frogs, and out of which I had some difficulty in scrambling. Here was an inauspicious beginning. I tried to say *nil desperandum*, but, like Macbeth's "amen," the words stuck in my throat, and then converted themselves strangely into "d——n it!"

In fact I was fairly puzzled; I wished the britska, with its downy seats,—a great deal too downy for me,—at the very devil, and I was at the point of starting off in the opposite direction to the ditch, when I saw the flash of a light at some little distance, and then heard the tramp of a horse's foot.

"Hilloa!" I cried,—"hilloa, there!"

The horse changed its pace to a canter, and a loud voice answered me with,—

"Who calls?—what's amiss?"—"Everything," said I. "Will you have the politeness to tell me where I am?"—"In the fields, I suppose."

"So do I. But what fields?"—"Tottenham Marshes."

"Oh, indeed; that's very satisfactory. Can you further oblige me by helping me out of Tottenham marshes?"—"Who are you?"

"I am Dr. ——. Who are you?"—"I am a horse patrol. I suppose you have had too much wine, eh, doctor?"

"No. I suppose you know nothing about it, eh, patrol? If you will place me in the direction towards London I shall be particularly obliged."

The man laughed, and threw the light of his lantern through the hedge, which I found was but a few feet from me, and at the foot of which ran the ditch into which I had with so much deliberation walked. By the light now afforded to me I could see to clear the ditch and fight my way through the hedge, when I found myself in a road of tolerable dimensions.

"Now, my friend," I said, "which is the way to London?"—"Straight on," he replied; "you cannot miss it. It is a straight road to Camden Town."

"And how far may it be?"—"Somewhere about four miles, I think. Good night."

"Good night."—"Pleasant this," thought I. "Four miles from Camden Town, which I fancy is the nearest point at which I can procure any conveyance." However, it was of no use grumbling over the matter, so I started at a good pace, and within an hour saw the lights of Camden Town glistening before me. I there procured a conveyance, and, weary, spiritless, and a little angry, I reached my own home about a quarter before three o'clock in the morning.

My wife was sitting up.—*Mem.* I find a great number of wives sit up when the wretch is out late; it is a kind of practical reproach upon the monster—and she insisted upon knowing all about my adventures, so that before I got any sleep I was obliged to tell her, although I closed my eyes during the narration, and nearly dropped into the arms of Morpheus.

"Well," said my wife, "I must say it's a most extraordinary affair; and if that young girl is no better than she should be, it's an awful affair."

I went fast asleep.

* * * * *

With the recovered mental and bodily activity of the morning came crowding to my mind a host of conjectures concerning my strange adventure of the preceding night. I turned the matter over and over in my mind a hundred different ways, and I blamed much my own precipitancy, which, perhaps, had prevented me from rescuing the girl from those who, to all appearance, held her in bondage. I recalled to my recollection every word she had uttered, and found abundant food for conjecture of all kinds and descriptions. Then, again, I frequently asked myself, "Was she really a little insane, or did they only say so for the purpose of throwing discredit on anything she might communicate to me?"

Really I was lost in a perfect maze of conjecture. The only rational thought I could come to on the subject was one of the most painful character, and that was, that her extraordinary beauty had tempted some wealthy libertine to take violent possession of her, and that she had made herself really ill, and alarmed them, by her resistance to his offers and rascally persuasions. This notion on the subject I communicated to my wife, and it at once awakened all her sympathies and indignation.

"I tell you what, doctor," she said; "you must not leave this matter as it is. Come, now, stir yourself, and go poking about all to-day and try and find out the house you were taken to."—"But I really don't know where to begin to poke about," said I. "If I go to the door I don't know which way to turn."

"Nonsense," said my wife. "Turn round three times, and then go straight on."—"But I might as well go straight on without turning round the three times."

"I don't know that; oh, dear!—oh! oh!"—"What's the matter?"

My wife had the *Times* newspaper in her hand, from which she immediately read aloud—

"If Frances G—— will communicate to her afflicted mother, it may save her from a broken heart. F. G.'s last communication has started awful conjecture. F. G. is implored to write."

When my wife had finished the newspaper advertisement, she laid down the time-serving, canting journal in which it appeared, and said,—

"There, now, doctor; what do you think of that? Oh, that girl's a hussey! She's been after no good, I'll be bound. A wretch, I call her!"

"Stop, stop," cried I; "don't judge hastily and harshly at the same time. I quite differ from you as to the character of the girl. What could have been the reason for all the mystery that surrounds her, and her own words to me, if she herself was a consenting party to the position in which she is now placed? I only wish if this advertisement has been inserted by the mother of the young creature I saw last night, she had put her address to it. However, it does afford some clue to the matter, if it relates to the same party."

"What can be done, though?"—"The only plan I can think of is one which I will immediately put in practice, and that is, to answer this advertisement by another requesting a meeting with this afflicted mother. At the same time I will make every exertion to discover the house to which I was conducted; and, by the bye, a thought strikes me. Being disappointed in procuring my medical assistance, some other practitioner may be employed in the same manner I was."

"Ah, but look what a load of doctors there is."—"True; but there are not many physicians with anything like a reputation, and it is among them only I think that the evidently very wealthy parties who kidnapped me will look for advice. I will go this morning among some of my professional brethren, and put them upon their guard on the subject."

I then wrote out an advertisement to the following effect:—

"If the afflicted mother who appeals to Frances G—— will send her address to M. D., at the post-office, Quebec-street, she may possibly hear something that will be of importance as regards Frances G——."

Determined to lose no time in having this inserted in the newspaper, I left home much earlier than usual, and took occasion first to pay those visits which would lead me in the direction of the newspaper-office. On the way I called on several physicians, and told them the story, advising that should such a carriage as the one which had conveyed me I knew not where to, come for them, to temporise with the matter, and have more patience than I had done, with the hope of discovering the mystery that surrounded the whole proceeding,—a mystery which I felt could conceal nothing but crime.

This was promised me in every instance, and I hoped during the day to make many such calls; why and how it was that I did not I shall now proceed to relate to my readers.

It was not quite eleven o'clock when I reached Bridge-street, Blackfriars, and turned into the little square in which is the *Times* printing-office. I had my advertisement in my hand, and was in the very act of crossing the threshold of the office door, when some one was coming quickly out. I stepped on one side to allow him to pass, and as I naturally glanced at him, I recognized in him the same man who had held a short conversation with me in the darkened room on the preceding evening, and who had annoyed me so much by his constant references as to what fee I was to have for the job I had been in a manner compelled to undertake. He knew me, and recoiled a step in evident surprise, while his face turned very pale.

"Well met," said I—"well met."

"What—what do you mean, sir?" he stammered.—"You know what I mean well enough. I say again, well met. You will find, my friend, that it is a hard matter to shake me off."

"I don't know you. You are mistaken, sir."—"You do know me. It is I, unfortunately, who am ignorant of who you are. That ignorance, however, shall not last long, for now I tell you I will follow you from here, and give you into the custody of the first constable I meet, unless you save yourself personally by a full statement and a clear explanation of the whole of the circumstances of last night."

"You give me into custody! and pray what for?"—"For imprisonment and assault."

"Oh, pho, pho! You are a madman, sir, quite a madman, I tell you. Let me pass."—"Not yet," said I; "that is to say, you may pass, but I follow you, you may depend."

Our altercation drew upon us the attention of several persons, and we were become the centre of quite a little crowd, a circumstance that gave me no uneasiness; I was so resolved not to lose sight of the man, that I cared for nothing else. He walked out, closely followed by me, and when we reached the narrow street by Apothecaries Hall, he said,—

"How can you be such a fool, sir, as to follow me in this manner? You must be mad or drunk."—"Will any one," said I, aloud, "fetch me a constable? I wish to give this man into custody."

"I am a constable," said a rough-looking personage, stepping forward. "What's he done?"—"Where's your authority?" said I, for I had my suspicions the fellow was no constable at all.

"My authority;—what's that to you?"

Then a decent-looking man, with a constable's staff, came up to me, and said,—

"What is it—what is it?"—"Oh," said I, "you are a constable? Pray take this man into your custody."

"On what charge?"—"Assault."

"I cannot, indeed; you must get a warrant. If I had seen the assault, or if you were seriously and manifestly injured, sir, I could take him."

"Then I charge him with felony. Will you take him now?"—"Certainly. You are my prisoner, my man."

"Well, I am sure!" cried the fellow, "this is a pleasant way of doing business, for a respectable shopkeeper to be taken into custody in this manner. There's my card. Come, now, you, sir, who are so very handy with your charges, will you just let us know who you are?"—"I am Dr. ——," said I. "You know me well enough."

"No, thank God, I don't; I value my health too much."

Here the crowd raised a laugh at my expense, and the tide of popular opinion seemed to be turning in favour of the prisoner, for a joke does wonders. The constable handed me the card, saying,—

"I hope you are quite sure this is the person you intend to accuse, sir?"—"I know him by his countenance, and not his card," said I, as I read the name. It was, "H. Seabrook, Tailor and Habitmaker, No. 104, Titchbourne-street."

"Now, I tell you what," said Mr. Seabrook, "I am not a very rich man, but if I don't trounce you well for this false charge, you may call me an ass."

"You persist, sir," said the constable to me, "in a charge of felony against this man?"—"I do. Let a magistrate decide the case."

These words were scarcely out of my mouth, when the fellow made a sudden halt, and, upsetting the constable, he darted down a narrow street and disappeared in a court before I could move. I attempted pursuit, but was so hemmed in by the crowd that he got much the start of me before I got into any speed, and when I and the constable reached the mouth of the court, which seemed a place of the most vile and abominable description, he said, with an air of evident chagrin,—

"He's off, sir; we might as well try to seek a needle in a bottle of hay as any one here. This place has several outlets; pursuit is quite time lost."—"Well," said I, "I am vexed indeed, for by the detention of this fellow I fully expected to unravel a mystery that I fear now is further off the clearing than ever. You don't suppose this is his correct address?"

"Extremely unlikely, sir; but I have no objection to go with you to Titchbourne-street and see"—"Very well; we may as well ascertain that fact. I shall be much obliged to you to accompany me, if you please."

We then started for Titchbourne-street, and upon making application at the house, we certainly found a tailor and draper of the name on the card, but he was a very different looking person from the man I had so opportunely met, and so very unfortunately again lost sight of. Thus was I again completely foiled, and I stood in Titchbourne street, looking, I must confess, almost bewildered.

A thought now struck me that perhaps I might satisfy myself that I was right as regarded the man I had given into custody, by making an inquiry at the newspaper-office where I had seen him. Accordingly I went back to that establishment, and, addressing the man behind the counter, I said,—

"There was a tall man here about an hour since, most likely with an advertisement having reference to a person described by the initials F. G. Will you allow me to see such advertisement?"—"No."

"But the reason of my application ——"

The man paid no more attention to me than if I had been an office-stool, so I walked away, and so there was an end of my morning's adventures as regarded any insight into the mysterious circumstances that had caused in my mind such uneasiness. I had now but the hope of learning something of the mother of the young girl, for I doubted not but the advertisement my wife had noticed bore a reference to her, and I resolved upon sending to the post-office where I had directed a communication should be left for M. D , so soon as I should see the advertisement in print. That at the very earliest could not of course be till the morrow, and patience was my only resource,—the last and hardest resource of all. With my ill success painted upon my countenance, I returned home, and reported to my wife what had occurred, when she made the consolatory remark of,—

"Well, men fancy themselves amazingly clever; but of all the foolish things in the world, to let off that fellow when you had once caught him, was the most foolish. Between you and the constable, I must say, my dear, you have made a pretty kettle of fish of it."—"Very good," said I.

* * * * *

Bang! bang! came an early postman to the door in the morning, and I triumphantly handed to my wife the following epistle from a Dr. Broughton, upon whom I had called the day before, and related the adventure in the mysterious britska:—

"DEAR SIR,—Last evening, at about nine o'clock, I was called to attend a patient, and hurried into a carriage, the amazingly soft seats of which, and the curious manner in which one tumbled down into a sort of hole when in it, put me in mind of what you informed me of when last I had the pleasure of seeing you.

"Without at all blaming you for the precipitancy which induced you to resist treatment that threw you into a justifiable resentment, I made up my mind to be sleek and civil, hoping that by so doing I should be able to arrive at the truth as regards the young girl who appears to me, as well as to you, to be suffering from some vile plot against her peace.

"I therefore made no remonstrance at all,—saw my patient, prescribed for her, pocketed a twenty guinea fee, and was very politely brought home again. To-morrow night I am to be again called for, and if you please to see me in the interim, you can make your own arrangements, and be assured of the cordial concurrence and co-operation of,

"Dear sir,
"Yours very truly,
"C. BROUGHTON."

"Hurrah!" I cried, "hurrah! Here we are now in a fair way of coming at the truth."—"A twenty guinea fee!" cried my wife; "and here I have been tormenting you for a month past to buy a chandelier for the back drawing-room, that would only cost eighteen guineas, and you said you couldn't afford it. Really, doctor, I'm rather surprised at you."

"I tell you what, my dear," said I; "if I succeed in rescuing this young girl from her persecutors, you shall have the new chandelier, and we will christen it Frances, in commemoration of the event."—"Now, there you go again, doctor. Chandelier or no chandelier, I won't be laughed at."

It was high time now for me to leave home, which I accordingly did, and hurried off to Dr. Broughton. He was at breakfast, and the moment I went in, he said,—

"Well, I have been so fortunate, as my note informed you, to see your mysterious patient."—"Your mysterious patient you mean," said I, "for I have no sort of claim to her."

"We won't fall out about the patient," said Broughton, "although doctors often do. But, to be serious, I really don't know what to think of the whole affair."—"Tell me what passed, for Heaven's sake; I am on tenter-hooks till I know all."

"Well, then, the mysterious britska came here, and I was requested to visit a patient, and promised a handsome fee. The person who spoke to me was, or affected to be, a Frenchman, and the combination of circumstances convinced me that I had got into the same train of events which had ended so uncomfortably for you. I sunk back on the down cushions as you had done, and was whirled along as you had been, I did not know where. There were the opening of gates—the sound of the wheels upon gravel—my eyes were blinded, to which I made but very slight objection, and finally I saw the patient."

"The young girl?"—"Yes."

"Was she not beautiful?"—"No description could possibly come near to giving an idea of her beauty. She made an appeal to me such as she made to you, and I flatter myself I answered it more prudently, for I knew I was watched, and my great object was to go there again, you understand?"

"Precisely. What did you say to her?"—"'I am a physician,' said I, 'and it's no use your troubling me about anything but the state of your health.' These words I said aloud, in order to throw the parties who were watching me off their guard; but I took an opportunity while examining her tongue to whisper to her,—'Be of good cheer; I will help you—hush! hush!' Upon this she could not control her sudden feeling of joy, and she uttered an involuntary 'Thank Heaven!' when in an instant a man masked came forward, saying,—

"'What is this?'—'She fancied she was dying,' said I, 'but I have assured her to the contrary.'

"I then wrote a prescription for her, and was paid twenty guineas in gold, after which I was conveyed away in the same mysterious manner in which I was brought to the place."

"And you are to go again?"—"Yes, so my guide told me, accompanied by some compliments to my discretion in the business."

"And what is your opinion?"—"Why, she is suffering from debility, arising from terror and anxiety of mind."

"Yes, yes; but of the whole affair?"—"I think she has been kidnapped by some nobleman, and now he is a little alarmed at her condition."

"So do I. I am afraid, Broughton, these things are of too frequent occurrence in London, where wealth is power. Let us do what we can towards rescuing this girl."—"I am quite at your service; any plan you may please to adopt I shall readily assist you in."

"Thank you. Will you allow me to come to your house this evening, in anticipation of the britska again calling for you?"—"Yes, of course. What will you do?"

"I will get up behind, and so ascertain where it goes to. So a great step will be gained in the affair."—"Yes, if practicable. You can try."

"I will; and now good morning. Expect me about eight." —"Good morning."

My next object was to see the newspaper of that morning, and when I did so, there, sure enough, was my advertisement, and exactly underneath it another to the following effect:—

"F. G. declines any further communication with any of her relatives, as she is perfectly happy where she is. F. G. desires that no further solicitation should be used towards her."

This confirmed me that I was right in my recognition of the man at the newspaper-office, for no doubt he, seeing the advertisement from the mother of the girl, had brought that advertisement as a mock reply to it. Still there was mine as a sort of counteraction to it, and I doubted not but I should receive some communication which would enable me personally to contradict the advertisement which was calculated to bring so much affliction to the heart of a fond mother. I gave till twelve o'clock before I myself went to the post-office where I had desired letters to be left for me, and upon saying to a woman there,—

"Madam, have you a communication here for M. D.!" she

replied, to my consternation,—"We had, sir, but it was fetched away."

"Fetched away?"—"Yes, sir—M. D."

"M. D. fetched away—a letter?"—"A letter, sir."

"Why—why—who fetched it?"—"A tall gentleman, sir, fetched it."

"The deuce!—d——n it! Thank you, madam; I am very sorry to have troubled you, but I have been taken in. Good morning, madam."

I was out-generalled as regarded my advertisement completely, and had now only the evening's proceedings to depend upon from which I could hope to do any good to the beautiful and unhappy girl of whom I had had so fleeting a view.

From the very commencement of my adventure I had become hourly more and more interested in the fate of the young creature, who, if she were really placed in the painful situation I believed she was, must indeed have suffered dreadfully. I could fancy one like she, tenderly nurtured by those who really loved her, and then, with all her gentle beauty

—all her exquisite charms of innocence, catching the roving eye of some wealthy libertine, who set all laws at defiance, human or divine, when his pleasures ran contrary to their ordination.

That such was the melancholy fate of poor Frances I fully believed, and I passed the time between my unsuccessful visit to the post-office and the evening in a state of restless impatience, which began to grow absolutely painful as the lagging hours winged their heavy flight, seeming to move on preternaturally slow, and to take a delight in my torture.

That some extensive influence and great wealth were employed to foil me, I could not doubt. It was no ordinary occupation to keep a young girl so confined in defiance of all reason and justice, and those who would undertake such an office would take care to be well paid for their pains, their danger, and their secresy, and no doubt they were, or the care that had been would not have been taken to defeat me in all my measures.

To make inquiry as to what roué nobleman had villas of pretension in the neighbourhood of the metropolis, was a hopeless task—hopeless, because there were so many of that character, unhappily, and among all how could I take upon myself to say, "Thou art the man." No; I had not a shadow of a hope upon the subject but such as arose from the possibility of my being able, undetected, to follow the britzka.

I could, however, hardly bring myself to believe that I should be allowed such an opportunity, for persons who were so active and so clever in what they had already done, were scarcely likely to expose their proceedings to such a disastrous conclusion. However, it could but be tried, and my readers may well imagine my fever of impatience till the period of that trial should arrive.

By great good luck I was called out to a patient early in the evening—I say by great good luck, because the circumstance tended in some measure to occupy my mind and withdraw it from the painful reflections which otherwise would have possessed it. The patient was a fidgetty old gentleman, who fancied he had all the complaints incidental to the human frame; consequently it took him some time to detail his symptoms, which he was exceedingly gratified at my permitting him to do at full length. In fact the process appeared to him quite reviving, and when at the conclusion I said,—

"My dear sir, I think a little stimulant would do you some good," he replied.—"Well, how very odd. I am rather fatigued with talking, and was just thinking of something. What would you advise, eh, doctor?"

"Why," said I, "if you take one bottle of port wine, and pour it into a bowl, to which add one pint of boiling water, one pint of brandy, sugar *quantum suff* ——."—"Why—why, God bless me! that would be awfully strong punch."

"Would it?—well, you can have a less quantity, taking the ingredients in proportion."—"So I will."

The old gentleman with all the disorders and I had the punch, which did us both good, for we were moderate in our potations, and when I rose to take leave of him, he said,—

"Doctor, I never felt so well in my life; I think a favourable change has taken place in my constitution."—"I'm sure there has," said I.

"Come again to-morrow evening, will you?"—"I will."

Upon reaching the street door I was annoyed to find that a most desperate wet evening had set in, and I walked but a little distance before I was compelled to stand up to avoid the pitiless storm. I look east, west, north, and south, but there were no signs of any amelioration of the weather, nor could I get my conveyance, even if it had been prudent to go to Dr. Broughton's so publicly, so I made up any mind to go through it as best I might, although with but a faint hope of seeing the mysterious britzka that night.

The rain continued to fall without intermission; a thorough wet night had some time now set in, with no hopes of amendment. The difference between a wet night in London and the country is, that in the latter there is usually some hope of amendment, and while it rains there is a cessation of all out-door employment, and all retire to the fireside.

In London, however, how different is the case; people seldom trouble themselves about the calculations of the weather; once wet in the evening, if they consider about it at all, they set it down as decidedly wet, of which they expect no mitigation; but yet the bustle of the crowded thoroughfares experiences but little diminution of the number of people who are out, save in the number of idlers who stroll about London, and who are indeed no small class.

The masses of umbrellas that float by the shop windows would to a stranger—one who had never seen such a thing before—appear strange, if not wonderful. Umbrellas in London form a moveable shelter, under which people move about in all weathers, and in many instances defying the weather. The continued shifting of the queerly-made domes form a curious sight to any one who viewed them from above, and a person looking down a street from the upper windows would imagine he was looking upon a mass of shifting mushrooms.

The night was not only wet, but uncomfortably chilly, and most of the shops were closed, and very few gave forth signs of life; the streets bore a more than usually deserted appearance, few passengers being now seen in the neighbourhood of the square. A vehicle, public or private, came dashing by, rushing across the square with unusual velocity, conveying some individual to his home or to some friend, on an errand that would admit of no excuse on account of the inclemency of the night.

The dull light of the lamps was all that now could be seen in the streets, the heavy pattering of the rain was occasionally interrupted by the solitary footfall of some passenger, and occasionally the sound of pattens might be heard with its peculiar clank. These sounds all appear to diminish as the evening grows late, and towards ten o'clock, in the squares, on a wet, chilly night, little or nothing can be seen or heard. The rain had now continued for several hours, and the streets were washed quite clean; the fronts of the houses were on one side washed by the shower, which had been dashed against its wall by the prevalent wind.

The chill blasts of the wind swept round the squares, and the rain was carried about in eddies, thus defying the usual precautions taken to guard against it, and when you came to any turning the wind either blew up or down in such a manner as completely disarranged all your previous arrangements to escape it and the rain, while you shrunk from the old encounter in a manner that at once bespoke your dread and extreme desire of avoidance.

The streets as well as the squares were tenantless: the rain fell steadily, only disturbed by the sudden gusts from the north-west, and night was fast closing in—dreariness and discomfort had it all their own way. Nearly soaked through, I reached Dr. Broughton's door—no britska was there; but then the hour had not arrived at which it might fairly be expected, so I rather congratulated myself than otherwise upon the prospect of getting a change of garments before I might be called upon once more to venture into the open streets.

The doctor was of course at home, and anxiously expecting me, although he looked so comfortable by his snug fireside that I said,—

"Well, it is really insulting of you to be so dry and warm—look at me."—"Why, bless me, you look like a drowned rat."

"Thank you, I feel like one too. Can you lend me a shirt and waistcoat, a pair of trousers, a cravat, boots, a coat, stockings, and a pair of braces?"—"Anything else?"

"No, thank you; that will do for the present."—"Very good. Come along to my dressing-room, and we will see what we can do."

I accompanied Broughton, and was soon comfortably equipped in a suit of his clothes, which really fitted me to admiration, and then we descended to the warm fireside again, when we began talking of the probable events of the evening.

"It's not very likely," said I, "you will be called upon for your professional visit to-night."—"Why, certainly," he replied, "the weather is unfavourable, particularly for an outside passenger, as you will be. I shall think of you, as I am reposing in the midst of those delicious cushions inside the britska, while you are holding on through mud and mire behind."

"Thank you; you draw an agreeable picture for me. You have only to imagine some boy crying, 'Cut, cut behind!' and the thing would be complete."—"So it would."

"Rat-tat-tat tat—bang—rat-tat—bang!" came upon the doctor's street-door, and springing to his feet, he exclaimed,—

"That's the mysterious britska, I'm sure."—"The deuce it is!" cried I.

We both ran into the front parlour, and there by the dim light in the street I saw the vehicle standing at the door, looking dark and full of mystery.

"Now, Broughton," I said, "you must delay till I get a good place behind, for I know well the speed with which your door will be left."—"Very good. You step out now and make your observations. I have only one fear."

"And what is that?"—"That there will be some one behind already."

"The deuce!"

I hurried from the house, and stepped to the back of the carriage. There was a comfortable-looking rumble behind, and I thought to myself,—

"If I can manage amid the clatter of the wheels as it starts, to get in here unnoticed, I shall do very well."

I satisfied myself that but one person had charge of the whole affair, and he, after alighting to knock at the door, had got inside again, and was holding the reins. The weather had a little abated in its severity, although it still rained briskly; but as everything is comparative, I thought nothing of the moisture now falling, in comparison with the pelting shower in which I had been so recently caught. I took a firm hold of some scroll iron work that was behind the britska, and crouching down so as to be out of observation as much as possible, I waited with all the caution of an Italian brigand or a North American Indian, for any time to clamber into the rumble.

That time was not long in coming, for Dr. Broughton, after sending out his footman, and receiving the mandate to attend upon the mysterious patient again, came out, shutting the door after him, and got into the vehicle. In an instant off we set at a hard trot. I had quite a scramble to get into the rumble, and once or twice I thought I must have given it up. However, after a great many entanglements, owing to the darkness and my ignorance of the peculiar make of the carriage, I did get in, and sat down with a feeling of great relief. Then I found I had seated myself on something rather hard, and upon getting up and feeling the seat, I found there a pair of pocket pistols in a leather bag.

"What's the meaning of this?" thought I. "Some one has surely been here and left these handy little weapons. They may be uncommonly useful to me."

By a careful investigation of the weapons I found they were loaded, and that percussion caps were upon them, so that I felt satisfied I was well armed now either for attack or for defence.

"So far so good," I thought, and scarcely had I thought so, when there was a perceptible decrease in the speed of the britska. We were just near the end of Portland-place, and as we came nearer and nearer to the left hand, the carriage gradually went slower and slower, until it stopped within an inch or two of the curb.

"Hilloa!" thought I, "what's in the wind now?"

I shrank down as low as I could in the rumble, in case the driver should get out and see me, and scarcely had I done so, when a low whistle came from the interior of the carriage, and then I saw a figure dart out from a doorway and approach the carriage.

"Right!" said a voice, and to my consternation, as the carriage rolled off again at tremendous speed, the man who had made his sudden appearance from the doorway, began climbing with great deliberation into the rumble. As his head got to a level with the seat, upon the impulse of the moment I gave it a good hard rap with the barrel of one of the pistols, saying,—

"Hilloa, friend, there is only room here for one."

A panic appeared to seize upon the man in a moment, and with a cry of alarm he let go his hold, and fell into the road with a whack that was enough to stun him. The driver apparently heard the cry, and he immediately stopped the horses. Again the whistle sounded.

"Right!" said I.

On we darted again, and I drew a long breath as we turned into the Regent's-park, leaving the real Mr. Right far behind, if he were not run over by that time. And there I was, sole tenant of the rumble, which I had maintained against all aggressors, bowling along I knew not where, at the rate of a good twelve miles an hour. I soon perceived that delay of time was an object with the driver of the britska; his object doubtless was to confuse Dr. Broughton with regard to the distance travelled over, for we went over the same ground more than once, and in some cases more than twice.

Regent's-park was not then what it is now, although the lines of road and the principal buildings were all laid out, so that the ground we travelled over in going round it, which we did, was much the same in extent as at present. It may well be supposed that I watched with no common interest all these proceedings, becoming each moment more and more convinced that some deep iniquity would be brought to light as a finale to my adventure.

After nearly half an hour of such manœuvring, the britska suddenly took a sharp turn, and then I heard the sound of the gravel under the wheels, which had before met my ears when my eyes were useless. We had turned into a long avenue leading to one of those magnificent villas that dot the surface of the park; I could smell the fresh flowers as we passed onwards, and at some places superb trees reared their heads far into the dim sky, joining their crests to others, and forming not unfrequently a leafy archway, beneath which we rolled at great speed. I should say the avenue must have been, by the time we took to traverse it, nearly half a mile in length, and then suddenly there was a pause, and looking about me as cautiously as I could, I saw that we were stopped by some gates.

Some words were uttered which I did not distinctly hear, and the gates were opened. Then I saw the driver get out of the carriage, and after him Dr. Broughton. Two or three other persons made their appearance, and I saw the doctor blindfolded as I had been. So much interested was I by what I saw, that it was not until that operation was completed that it struck me how very awkwardly I was myself situated, for in all probability a discovery that I was a stranger, would take place in a few minutes.

How was I to get out of the rumble without observation, and what chance had I, if seen, of battling successfully against the numbers that would assail me? Those men, for all I knew to the contrary, might not scruple to murder me for the purpose of hiding their iniquitous proceedings. Altogether I was certainly in a most pretty predicament. I clutched the pistols mechanically, and my only vivid sensation was to sell my life as dearly as possible.

One man held up a lantern, and I saw Dr. Broughton taken by the arm and led away. I had crouched quite down in the rumble, so that it appeared empty, and I had the intense satisfaction of hearing a man say,—

"What's become of Martin, I wonder, to-night? He was to have come in the rumble, in case of accidents."—"Drunk, I suppose, as usual," said another.

"Well, if his Excellency knew it, there would be a pretty fuss. What is there to hinder any one from getting into the rumble and coming here?"—"Not much; but there would be a d—d deal to hinder the anybody from getting back again."

"Ah, to be sure."

A large cloak was now thrown into the rumble, and completely covered me up, so that I could scarcely hear the conversation that was still maintained in a low tone by the men who were holding the horses.

I thanked my stars I was comparatively safe, although each minute that passed over me while in that really ticklish situation, appeared an age of apprehension. I could hear the wind blowing among the trees in fitful gusts, and occasionally one of the horses would tramp with impatience to be gone.

I think, upon a moderate computation of time, I was boxed up in the rumble of the britska for nearly half an hour. Dr. Broughton and I never could agree as to the length of time, a circumstance which proves the words of somebody who says somewhere,—

"Old time we measure by the busy throng
Of passing objects.—To the lone prisoner,
Counting the weary hours in donjon keep,
How sluggishly the wheel revolves. To those
Who count its progress but by sunny smiles
And mirthful cheeriness, how fleeting is the measure."

Now, Broughton was pocketing a thirty guinea fee, and I was shut up in the rumble of the mysterious britska, which made all the difference.

Nothing further was said by those who were unconsciously acting as my guards which was in any way or shape worth recording. There were repeated references to some one whom they named as his excellency, and of whom they invariably spoke in that subdued kind of deferential tone which inferiors use towards one who, even in his absence, is capable of exercising a paramount influence over their fortunes. It was always, "What would his Excellency say if he knew one thing and another thing?—what would he think?" &c., but never once did any of them forget the caution which I suppose had been carefully instilled into them not to mention any name, so that my information, gathered from being rather an unwilling listener to that dialogue, was by no means great.

The flash of a light suddenly broke upon the scene then, and I guessed that Dr. Broughton was being brought back, which turned out to be the case. I congratulated myself that my danger was nearly over, and was just considering what I should do in order by daylight to be quite certain of the place again, when a voice said,—

"Martin, Martin! where are you?"—"He did not come," replied another.

"Not come?—why, I saw him get into the rumble. Not come?—Impossible!"—"He is not here, sir."

"Now for it," thought I. "They will look in the rumble, and then comes the tug of war."—"I tell you he was in the rumble," said the first speaker, advancing and laying hold of that portion of the vehicle to look into it.

There was not a moment to be lost. I suddenly sprang up and gave him a blow in the face, which knocked him backwards, and then with one spring I cleared the rumble and alighted in safety on my feet.

"Help!—seize him!—fire! fire!—Don't let him go alive!" cried a voice.

In the darkness that reigned around, to fire at me was absurd, and yet a pistol was discharged at random by some one. As for me, I darted on as hard as I could go for about fifty yards, and was, as I fully expected, hotly pursued. A scamper of half a-mile down the avenue was no joke, especially as I was far from being a first-rate runner, so I suddenly darted on one side, and crouched down under some bushy laurels, that cast an impenetrable gloom around, and had the satisfaction of both seeing and hearing my pursuers go by me at a great rate.

I waited till they had got some distance ahead of me, and then, under cover of the evergreens, I walked on, considerably out of breath, and with a loaded pistol in each hand. Soon a silence equal to that of the grave reigned around me, and I debated with myself whether I should remain where I was for some time, advance, retreat, or take a direction at right angles with the avenue, and so endeavour to escape from my enemies, who, no doubt, would soon return from the useless chase they were now upon.

Considering all things, I thought my best plan was not to leave the avenue, for, by so doing, I might lose myself in the plantations belonging to the villa, and run a good chance of being captured. In defiance, therefore, of spiders, and all sorts of crawling things, I got into the centre of a large laurestinus, and then waited the course of events.

In about five minutes I heard footsteps returning, and the sound of voices came plainly to my ears. They belonged to my pursuers, and, as they neared me, I heard their vague conjectures as to who I was, and where I had got to with such celerity.

"He went off like the very devil," said one.—"And, besides," remarked another, "how long could he have been in the rumble, for I'm sure there was nobody there when the carriage came in."

"Perhaps, after all, it's Martin," suggested a third; "and he's popped off in that way for fear of being seen drunk."

By this time they had arrived nearly opposite to the bush in which I had found refuge, and then, he who had spoken first said,—

"Now, listen to me, all of you. Whatever it was, or whatever it was not, it concerns us all. If his excellency should hear of it, I wouldn't give a pin's head for nobody's situation. Say nothing about it to anybody. His excellency would go raving mad if he thought the carriage had been traced by any one."—"So he would—so he would; we'll keep it snug. Perhaps it was Martin, after all."

"I hope so; now, come along. D—n that girl, there is more trouble about her than we have ever had about any; ay, or half-a-dozen."—"That's true enough," remarked another; "and his excellency is as angry about her as a bear with a sore head. As for herself, if something ain't done to quiet her she'll fret herself into fiddle strings soon. Why, she's quite a atomy, compared to what she was when first she comed here."

They then passed on, and I thanked my stars I was safe at last. I let all trace of their footsteps leave my ears before I ventured to come out of the bush, and then I cautiously crept forth, and was not a little pleased to stretch myself in the free open air of the avenue. Just then I heard the rattle of the wheels, and guessed that the carriage was coming. I stepped on one side, and in a few moments it swept past me at a terrible rate.

"I wish I was in the rumble again," thought I; but it was no use wishing, for the said rumble was half-a-mile off before I could utter the aspiration.

My great object now was to get home as quick as I could, and, before I did so, take some means of accurately enabling me to know the place again in daylight. I recollected that at the road end of the avenue there was a large gate, which had stood open, and at some distance from which there was a lodge, no doubt belonging to the villa, where such mysterious events were carried on. Towards the gate, then I took my way, not with any hope of satisfactorily knowing it again by the little degree of ocular inspection I could then give, but with a resolve of taking means which could afterwards admit of no sort of doubt.

Fearful that some one might be in the lodge, I crept along with very great caution indeed, till I reached the gate. No one interrupted me, nor was any light visible, so, taking my penknife from my pocket, I carefully cut from one of the wooden bars of the gate a long slice, which I put in my pocket. Then I passed out of the avenue, and was in the inner ring of the park, to which that outer gate of the avenue immediately opened.

"So far so good," said I; "all that could be expected to be achieved by this night's adventure has been done, and the next main object of my cares shall be to seek out the mother of the unhappy young girl who is so unwilling a prisoner in yonder villa, and place all the facilities I now can in her way of recovering her child, and obtaining justice against those who have stolen her."

The round, for the purpose of confusion, which the britska had taken was immense, for the distance was really not very great from the Regent's-park to my home, which I reached within the hour, much gratified at the result of the evening's work. The pair of pistols I had in my pocket, for I thought them too important to throw away, as they might assist in the identification of some of the parties concerned in the nefarious transaction, and when I reached home my first act was carefully to examine those arms.

They were very highly finished pistols, and of considerable value, being silver mounted, and otherwise got up with great elegance. On a silver plate was engraved a crown, but, whether as indicative of the rank of its owner, or as a mere fancy ornament, I, of course, could form no opinion. However, I determined to keep the pistols until I found a proper owner, and when I should find him, I had more to say to him than "Sir, here are your pistols."—After refreshing myself at home, I hastened to Dr. Broughton's, and found him in no small degree of trepidation on my account, for he did not know what had become of me.

"Thank God!" he said, when I came in, "you are alive, and, as I suppose, unhurt. I endeavoured to learn your fate, but could not, as I was fearful of being too much apparently interested in you. How did you get away?"

I then related the particulars of my escape, and ended by saying to him,—

"So you see I had rather a narrow escape of it. But now tell me what passed with your patient, and if anything new occurred during your visit?"—"I was, as usual, conducted with great secrecy and mystery to a room, where I saw a man —the same who had previously first seen me. After a courteous salutation, he said,—

"'Your patient is better, sir, after some refreshing sleep, since you were here.'—'Oh, indeed,' I replied; 'she ought to have exercise in the fresh air.'—''That, said he, 'is impossible.'

"I was then conducted again to the room where the young girl was; her eyes brightened as she saw me, for she had no doubt remembered my friendly whisper on the preceding evening, and expected something had been done towards her release. I knew that I was watched, and, consequently, I was very careful indeed what I said to her, although I believe I succeeded in letting her know that something was being attempted in her favour; for I said, as pointedly as I could,—

"'You must have a little patience, your case is a troublesome one; but all that skill and friendship can do for you shall be done. Have but a little patience.'

"More I dared not say. She thanked me by a look which was eloquence itself, and after writing for her a prescription, containing a tonic, I took my leave."

"Did they give you another fee, Broughton?"—"Yes."

"Then you are making a tolerably good thing of it?"

"I am, indeed. Our profession would be a lucrative one with a vengeance, if we could get many such patients. However, I think I have paid my last visit. Your flight, and the disorder you have created in the whole establishment, by the surmises as to who you might be, has shocked them too much; and I was told by the mysterious driver of the mysterious britska, that he would not trouble me any more, as it was likely the whole establishment would be removed before daybreak some miles away."

"The deuce! That would be a catastrophe, indeed, that would mar all my schemes. How to find out the girl's mother I know not, without so much delay and trouble as will place her enemies on their guard. If I advertise for her, requesting her to come personally to my house, of course, they would immediately guess what was going on, and take measures to remove their victim far from the scene of action."

"If anything is to be done at all effectually," remarked Broughton, "it must be done promptly. Should you know the place again?"—"I should."

"Then what is to hinder you and I having early in the morning an interview with one of the metropolitan magistrates on the subject, and getting, as we should, immediate assistance in the release of the girl?"—"Nothing," said I; "let us agree upon that, and arrange an appointment to carry it into effect. Your humane promptitude does you great credit."

"It is a negative credit, then, for I do not consider I am entitled to any praise for not doing what would be hideously wrong."

Broughton and I then arranged that by nine the following morning we should call at the private residence of a Mr. Rushbrook, a police magistrate, and request his assistance in the matter. I took the greatest care of the piece of wood I had chipped from the gate, as by its means alone could I take upon myself positively to identify the villa where Frances was kept a prisoner.

* * * * *

Dr. Broughton breakfasted with me, and by half-past eight his chaise was at the door, and we were ready to start on our expedition.

"I have been thinking," he said, "that we ought to go first to the park, and endeavour to find out the gate, and then there will be no unnecessary delay when we procure the assistance, as most likely we shall, of an officer from the magistrate."—"Very good," said I, "let us go at once there."

Off we started, and when we got fairly into the park, we left the chaise in charge of the groom, and began looking at all the gates we came near, with a curiosity that must have much surprised the observers. For a considerable time our search was unsuccessful, and Broughton had just remarked, —"Perhaps they have found it out, doctor, and taken means to patch the gate up," when I saw one of a very handsome shape and make, which something at once struck me was that of which we had come in search.

"There," said I, as I fitted the piece I had cut off into its proper place, "this is the gate."

We looked over it, and saw the avenue, with the well-kept hedge-row on each side, formed of choice evergreens, among which were many beautiful plants, filling the air with perfume, and delighting the eye by the variety of their tints.

"This is truly a place of some pretension," remarked Broughton; "there is ample evidence here of wealth and taste."—"I am sorry to say there is," said I; "but you perceive the splinter I cut off the gate fits exactly. This is unquestionably the place."

"No doubt—let us try to ascertain who lives here."

Not far off we met a groom-looking young man, and I said,—

"My friend, can you tell me who lives in yon villa, that you can just see among the trees?"

The man shook his head.

"No, sir," he said, "I cannot; they do say a Mr. Smith keeps it; but nobody really knows who does. They say it's a fine place."—"So it seems. Thank you."

"Come on at once to a magistrate's," said Broughton. "By-the-by, these pistols may be important. Have you them with you?"—"I have."

"Did you happen to notice the maker's name?"—"Yes; they have the name of Manton on them."

"Indeed. Well, as we ought to be quite prepared before we go to the magistrate's, suppose we call upon the maker, and show him the arms?"—"Agreed."

We drove then off to the gunmaker's, and having produced the pistols to a respectable elderly man in the shop, I said,—

"Can you tell me who bought these of you?"

He took them from me and carefully examined them.

"Humph," he said, "a—a—hem!"

"Well?" said I.—"A—a—a—hem!"

"Whose pistols are these?"—"Eugh—eugh—eugh! Do you want to find their owner?"—"Yes I do."

"Leave them here then, and they shall be forwarded."—"No; I wish to know who they belong to."

"You do? Then, sir, I am sorry to appear rude, but the fact is, you must find out somewhere else."

"Why this mystery?"—"A—a—hem! That's all I can say about it. Least said, sir, is soonest mended. Take my advice; leave the pistols here, and make no further inquiries into the matter."

"No," said I, "I must certainly decline your advice.—"I don't know but I ought to detain the arms."

"You must have the power to do so," said I, as I replaced them in my pocket.

We then walked from the shop, and when we were in the street, Broughton said,—

"Well, the mystery thickens, I think. How very odd that the gunmaker should refuse to tell whose pistols these were—he must have had his instructions."—"Of course—of course. I am, however, but the more resolved, after every obstruction, to sift this matter thoroughly. Come now, at once, let us have no more delays, but proceed to a magistrate, and I finally hope that yet, before mid-day, that young girl will be free."

It was nearly ten o'clock when we reached the magistrate's private residence, and we had the mortification of hearing that he had just started for the police-court in which he was in the habit of presiding. Thither we went, after some moments' consideration, and had to wait till some night charges were disposed of, before we could be attended to. Then, however, we handed in both our cards with a request for a private interview. The magistrate smiled as he said,—

"However alarming a private interview with two physicians is generally considered, if you will accompany me to my private room, gentlemen, I shall be happy to hear any communication you have to make, trusting to you that the matter is really of a nature to require privacy."

"It is indeed," said I.—"Most certainly," said Dr. Broughton.

We then followed the magistrate from the public office to another apartment, leaving two newspaper reporters nearly in fits, and perspiring with anxiety to know what we had come about. I was spokesman on the occasion, and very soon possessed the magistrate of the whole story, concluding by saying—

"Now, sir, what we want is, authority to search the villa and rescue the girl."—"I fear," he said, "that I have hardly a case to authorise me in issuing a warrant. You see you are neither of you connexions of the girl, and all you can go upon is mere surmise. She may be a lunatic, or she may be in the hands of those who have a right to control her actions."

"But the mysterious manner, sir, of procuring medical assistance for her," said I, "speaks volumes for our view of the subject."—"True. I was only stating what I am forced to consider as a magistrate. However, gentlemen, I'll tell you what I will do. I will send an experienced officer with you, and he will endeavour to unravel the mystery. Should any obstruction be offered to him, or a satisfactory explanation of the affair not given, I shall then feel it my duty to take more energetic steps in the matter."

I then related how I had endeavoured in vain, by calling at the gunsmith's, to ascertain to whom the pistols belonged, and the magistrate expressed much surprise at that part of the affair.

"Go on your errand to the villa," said he, "and leave to me the inquiry concerning the pistols."

He then rang his bell, and desired that an officer of the name of Ratcliffe should be sent to him. When he came the whole of the matter was explained, and he was ordered to accompany us to the villa. We then left the police-office, and when we gained the street I turned to the officer, and said—

"What, now, is your candid opinion of this transaction?"—"I think you are right," he said. "The girl has been kidnapped by some nobleman."

"Do you know any of the residents in the Park villas?"—"Some. Of course we are in the habit of hearing a great many odd things. I may possibly recognize at once the villa you mention, and be able to name its owner or occupant. I think, however, we shall have a great deal of difficulty in our search."

"And so do I."

In about half an hour more we stood by the gate from which I had cut the long splinter, and made an attempt to open it without success. We were, therefore, compelled to ring a bell which connected with the lodge, and in about a minute a man came from that building, and looking at us with evident curiosity, said—

"Well, what is it?"—"Who lives here?" said the officer.—"What's that to you?"

So saying he walked back again into the lodge, and banged the door behind him.

"That's civil," remarked the officer. "I think, gentlemen, after that we may as well scale the gate."—"Agreed," said I, and we all scrambled over in a moment, a feat we had no sooner accomplished, than a bell somewhere close at hand began tolling heavily. It must have been hung in one of the trees, for we could not see it, although from its sound we were certain it was not far off. Then the lodge door opened, and the man made a rush out into the avenue, as if he were about to attack us; but the officer coolly stepped forward, and taking his staff from his pocket, he said firmly—

"At your peril, sir, make any assault upon us. Do you know who I am?"—"A—a—a constable."

"Yes. Now, perhaps, you will oblige me by telling me who lives here?"

The fellow hesitated a moment, and then he said, with affected carelessness—

"I couldn't tell who you were, nor can I guess what the devil you want here. We have no secrets. This is Mrs. Smith's villa."—"Then you may give our compliments to Mrs. Smith, and say we wish to see her."

The bell at this moment ceased tolling, and the man said—

"What names shall I announce?"—"Brown," said I.—"Green," said Dr. Broughton.—"Jones," said the officer.

The man looked at us very suspiciously, and then, muttering something to himself, the purport of which did not reach our ears, he began walking slowly up the avenue. We followed him, and when he perceived such was the fact, he turned and said—

"You will allow me to announce you first, I suppose?"—"Oh, yes, but we may as well walk on."

With a muttered curse the fellow preceded us, but at such a slow pace that we could not but imagine he had some object in delay. Suddenly then we heard the report of a gun or pistol from the direction of the villa, upon which he quickened his pace, and walked on with great alacrity.

"There is some signalling going on," remarked the officer to me. "We shall, I fear, not succeed in our errand; and remember, if we do not, our only policy is to come away, affecting to be perfectly satisfied, by which means we may throw them possibly off their guard for future operations."

We both agreed to this manifestly prudent policy, and continued to follow our guide, much to his dissatisfaction, up the long avenue. Then we reached the gate which had always been opened to admit the mysterious britska, and we looked about us—that is, Broughton and I, for the officer took the affair in a very business-like way—with no small degree of curiosity.

The grounds were full of the most elegant plants, and there was ample evidence of everything being cultivated with the most fastidious taste. We reached the door up a flight of marble steps. The hall was adorned with choice statuary and paintings, and altogether I was much charmed with "Mrs. Smith's villa."—A servant met us in the hall, and our guide said,—

"Here are some gentlemen want to see Mrs. Smith."

Then he advanced and whispered something else in the ear of the servant, who nodded, and turning to us, said—

"If you will follow me, gentlemen, Mrs. Smith will see you."

We were conducted into a handsome reception-room, where we had not waited many minutes when another door through that at which we had entered opened, and an elegantly dressed female made her appearance. She walked into the room with an expression on her face as much as to say—

"Well, gentlemen, you have taken my house by storm—what do you want?"—"Madam," said I, "we have called for the purpose of removing from here a young lady, if it should turn out that she is detained in this house against her will, and without a just pretence for such detention."

Mrs. Smith opened her eyes very wide, and turning to the officer, she said—

"Is this gentleman mad?"—"No, madam. We are given to understand that a young lady is detained here. To prevent unpleasant consequences, I strongly advise you to give her up at once."

The look of surprise upon Mrs. Smith's face was quite inimitable, and sinking into a chair, she said—

"I suppose because Mr. Smith is abroad I am to be robbed and insulted. I dislike strife and contention, and even now I give you leave to retire from this house peaceably, without a collision with my servants, if you are wise enough to avail yourselves of the offer."—"We are very much obliged to you, madam," said the officer, "but I am an officer of police, and, now that I am here, it will be more satisfactory to myself and these gentlemen to search this house before we leave it."

"Search this house!—and for what, pray?"—"A young female, supposed to be kept here contrary to her will."

"I do not know how to express my astonishment. Here must be some great mistake; there is no female on these premises with the exception of myself and servants. I will not prevent you searching the house, as you say you are an officer; but I shall immediately send for my friends, who will see that the affair is properly inquired into."—"Send for who you please, madam," said I; "what we are doing we are by no means anxious to conceal."

She rang the bell violently, and when a footman made his appearance, she said—

"Tell Thomas to saddle a horse and ride to Sir Crump Mandrake's for me, ask him to come here directly, and do you follow these persons through the house. Tell Jenkins to lock up the spoons and forks."—"Yes, madam."

"Pleasant this," remarked Broughton to me.—"Oh, never mind," said I; "we know we are in the right house; so come along."

Accompanied by the officer, and closely followed by the footman, we went from room to room, but no young lady could we see. I called aloud the name of Frances, but received no answer, and we spent nearly an hour in our useless and vexatious search.

"She has been removed," whispered I to the officer.—"I don't think that," he replied. "Further search is useless. Let us apologise to Mrs. Smith, and leave at once. Then we must get some one to watch the house."

There was no alternative but to embrace this proposition, and certainly looking rather crest-fallen, we repaired to the room in which we had left Mrs. Smith. It was empty, and upon our sending to her she sent word back that she desired particularly we would wait, in order to be given into custody when Sir Crump Mandrake should arrive. At first we thought of waiting, but thinking better of it, we laughed and went away. When we got to the lodge gate, I said to the man who was there,—

"My friend, will a five pound note induce you to assist us?"—"I don't know what you mean," he said. "Mrs. Smith lives here, and a very good mistress she is."

He then walked away, and so did we. When we had got some distance off, we held a council of war, and the officer said,—

"I don't know how it is with you, but my suspicions are considerably strengthened, and I should advise some one to be placed here to watch whoever comes in and out, and that to night we make our way through the grounds secretly, and again search the house."

As we were talking, a woman came rapidly towards us, and in an alarmed manner, she said,—

"It's all true—it's all true!—she's there—she's there! Come again—at night."

She then darted off before we could say a word, and passed through the gate up the avenue, with all the appearance of one much terrified. This circumstance confirmed us in our opinion, and we made a determination at nightfall to place a spy on the premises, and when the darkness fairly set in, to make an attack with more strength, when we hoped to discover the object of our search.

"The remainder of to-day," said the officer, "can be spent in finding the mother of the girl, which I dare say I shall be able to do. If I succeed I will bring her to your house, sir, and you can hear her story from her own lips."—"If you can accomplish that," said I, "you will have done much towards the furtherance of our plans, for then we shall not have a shadow of a doubt as to the propriety of what we are about; and, moreover, I think if the mother be produced, the magistrate will grant a warrant to take into custody any suspected parties."

"Undoubtedly he will."—"Then that is fully understood, and I shall expect, Ratcliffe, to see you in the course of the day."

"I hope so, sir."

* * * * *

About three o'clock, just as I was taking some refreshment at home, Ratcliffe, the officer, was announced. I ordered that he should be shown into the parlour, whither, in a few moments, I repaired to him, and to my great satisfaction I saw that he was not alone. A respectable widow woman accompanied him, who, the moment she saw me, exclaimed, while the tears streamed down her furrowed cheeks,—

"Oh, sir, for the love of Heaven get me back my child—my own beautiful, dear child! I am told you know where she is, sir. Oh, get her back for me! Let me see her once again, and a mother's prayers shall hallow your existence—next to Heaven shall my dearest gratitude be due to you, sir. Get me back my child—my Frances—my own dear, beautiful child!"—"Hush, hush," said I. "I am rejoiced to see you, and hope very shortly to be able to restore to your arms your daughter. Tell me, now, how you came to lose her."

"Yes, sir, I will—I will. God bless you, sir, for the pains you have already taken to get her for me. A widow's tears and prayers will do you no harm, sir. She was my only care—my only solace, and now, now I am desolate indeed—my heart will break!"—"Nay, now, be comforted. There is very reasonable expectation that she will very shortly be restored to you. But tell me at once your name, and how you came to lose her."

"I will, sir. The story is very brief. My name is Grant, and my child's name, Francis Grant. Heaven bless her!—a kinder, better heart than her's never beat in human bosom. She was all I wished her. You can judge, sir, how I loved her. Well, one day she told me she had been followed by some one who had much importuned her to meet him again, which, of course, she had indignantly refused to do. We thought nothing further of it for some days, until I had occasion to send her to a chemist's shop in the neighbourhood, and I never saw her again. Hour after hour that night, after making every possible inquiry, I waited in anxious expectation of her return, but she came not. Oh, God! I thought I should then have gone mad. The next day came, but it brought not with it my child. Then, sir, the neighbours came about me, and one advised one thing, and another advised another, till I knew not what to do. The police could give me no assistance, and so things went on till this cruel advertisement appeared in a morning paper."

She produced an advertisement which had been cut from a newspaper. It contained these words:—

"Francis G. begs to state to her mother that she is quite happy and contented, and particularly desires that no effort will be made to discover her retreat with one who loves her, and towards whom she cannot but feel the warmest sentiments of regard."

"You put no faith in that?" said I.—"Faith? No, sir. I knew my child too well. For her life's sake she could not have written such words. They did not wring my heart—they gave me no new pang, because I knew they came not from her. Oh, no—she is all goodness—all gentleness—all excellence—she never dreamt of an unkind word or action."

Mrs. Grant burst into tears, and wept bitterly for some minutes. I made no effort to stop her sorrow, but I felt much for that widowed heart, deprived of her only consolation in her beautiful child. When her tears had in some measure exhausted themselves, I said to her,—

"Be comforted. Everything that can be done shall be done to relieve your distressed condition, and restore to you your child."—"Heaven reward you—Heaven reward you!" she exclaimed.

"Have you," said I to the officer, "seen the magistrate?" —"Yes, and he has, upon Mrs. Grant's evidence, given me authority to apprehend any parties that may appear guilty in the business."

"Then let us hope to-night will restore to your afflicted heart, madam, your child, for a determined effort shall be made for her rescue."

Mrs. Grant was so urgent upon us all to allow her to be present on the occasion of our projected visit that evening to the villa, which, for want of a better name we were compelled to call Mrs. Smith's, that I at last consented, on condition that she would wait patiently by the lodge gate, and, let her hear what she would, see what she would, she was not in any manner to interfere until her daughter was brought out.

This she faithfully promised, and then Ratcliffe having duly provided a man to watch the premises, we anxiously waited till about ten o'clock before we moved towards the Regent's-park.

There were Dr. Broughton, Ratcliffe, and another officer, two young medical friends of mine, and myself, so that we made up rather a formidable party altogether, and one capable of acting efficiently, whether for attack or defence. The night was a very dark one, indeed. Huge masses of clouds had piled themselves up in the sky since sunset, and there was a strange sultriness in the air, which betokened either rain or some storm to be near at hand. As it turned out, the latter was the case; for just as we got within sight of the outer gate of the lodge, such a rattling peal of thunder shook the heavens, as I had scarcely ever seen the like.

"Hilloa!" remarked Broughton; "we shall have a rough night of it."—"Which," added the officer, "brings with it one consolation, that it will serve well to cloak our proceedings, and will enable us to make our advance to the house with the greatest ease."

"True," said I; "it's an ill wind that blows nobody good. But where is your spy, Mr. Ratcliffe?"—"The rascal ought to be here," he replied.

There came a flash of lightning that nearly blinded us. The heavens for one fleeting moment appeared in a blaze, and we involuntarily shut our eyes to avoid the terrific glare that had so suddenly broke in upon them.

"We can do nothing in this storm," I remarked. "Let us seek shelter in yon unfinished house till its violence has a little abated."

The suggestion was adopted; and it was well there was such a shelter to be had, for now the rain began to fall in torrents. The fall of the rain was fast increasing, and with it the other sounds that terrify animals as well as human beings. It might have been that the walls of the house assisted to increase the sound and violence of the force of thunder, which now rolled and came crackling and crashing through the air with an awful and tremendous sound.

The vivid and frequent flash of the lightning, as it appeared often on one side, and then on the other of the sky, and then close upon them, gave a terrific though sublime appearance to the heavy masses of clouds, which appeared to be incapable of increase. The wind blew fresh, and dashed the rain against the walls, which resisted it; and save in those places where there was no impediment, the rain did not come in, but where the walls or windows were not completed, it pelted in at a furious rate.

Still, the same wind that dashed the rain with such force against our shelter, after a time chased the storm away; the thunder was heard in a more indistinct manner, the lightning appeared not so vivid, and the pattering of the rain ceased. It was now late, but yet the light in the sky was just enough to enable us to see that the storm had quitted those parts, and passed on to another; the heavy clouds were no longer seen; and though the wind was cool and fresh, yet it brought no moisture with it.

Oh, what a relief were those long strips of light to our eyes. We immediately emerged from our hiding-place, and stood again in the open air; and there I do not hesitate to say we were repaid for all the inconvenience we had suffered, by the sweet freshness it had gained from the abundant rain that had fallen. I never in my life felt the balmy, invigorating influence of the air more strongly. Suddenly, then, Ratcliffe exclaimed,—

"Now, by Heaven! there lies my precious spy!" and pointing down the unfinished area of the house, we saw by the dim light around a human form enveloped in a large great coat, and at the same time we heard a loud snoring that would have shamed any pig in the world.

"Hilloa!" cried Ratcliffe; "hilloa, there!"—"W-w-won't you st-st-stand another pint?" growled a drunken voice from the area.

Ratcliffe was in such a rage, that had we not restrained him, I believe he would have descended, and given the fellow a good drubbing. We, however, dragged him away, and in a few moments we all stood near the lodge gate.

"It won't do to go over here," remarked Ratcliffe; "we must scale the wooden pales further on."

Scarcely were these words uttered than the sound of carriage wheels came upon our ears, and a light flashed from a window of the lodge. We all shrank back into the shadow of a large chesnut tree, that hung its boughs over the palings, and in another minute a close carriage dashed up to the gate. It was thrown open in an instant, and the vehicle quickly disappeared up the avenue.

"Now for it!" cried I, and I commenced scrambling over the wall.

The others followed me, and in less than a minute we were all, with the exception of Mrs. Grant, on the land belonging to the villa. Through the trees we could see, or fancied we could see, the lights from the windows of the villa, and with cautious footsteps, like a party of Indians on the trail of an enemy, we advanced onwards, moving aside gently the boughs of trees and shrubs that impeded our progress.

I dare say we wandered a great deal out of our way, for now and then the light in the window disappeared altogether, and we were "like vessels tempest-tost, without a rudder." However, we in about half an hour had the satisfaction of suddenly running against some iron hurdles which skirted the lawn that lay immediately in front of the house. We crossed these very quickly, and then we could perceive lights glancing strongly from several of the rooms, while a dark object was near the steps leading to the hall, which we conjectured at once to be the carriage we had seen some time before dash on with such furious speed.

"Now, sir," said Ratcliffe to me, "you have some notion, as well as Dr. Broughton here, which room in the house you saw the young girl in whom we have come to rescue."— "Certainly; if we make our way to the drawing-room, I know the apartment where I saw my patient is not far off," said Broughton.

"Then," added Ratcliffe, "everything must be done with celerity now. The search must be sudden and decisive, or we have no chance. We are enough to overcome opposition. Are you ready, gentlemen?"—"Quite ready," we said.

"Forward, then."

We were up the steps in a moment, and entered the hall, the door of which was open, and quite unguarded. Scarcely, however, had we time mentally to congratulate ourselves upon the easy entrance we had effected, when the door of an apartment opened, and the man whom I had had the fracas with at the newspaper office made his appearance. I immediately rushed forward, and collared him.

"How are you?" I said. "I thought we should meet again."—"D——n!" he cried.

"You are my prisoner," said Ratcliffe. "Give any alarm, and I'll knock you down."—"You are madmen," said the fellow; "you don't know what you are doing. You are positively running your necks into the noose. If you will take good advice you will leave this place at once. You don't know your own danger."

"It's quite enough for you," said Ratcliffe, "to know

yours. You will be so good as to come along with us."—
"Very well," said the fellow; "there is no fighting against numbers. If I must give in, I must."

Taking our prisoner with us, we ascended the staircase, after leaving one of our body as a guard upon the hall-door, to give the alarm to us in case any one should attempt to escape that way. We walked hastily, and reached the rooms on the first floor in a few seconds. One of them was very brilliantly lighted, and covers were laid for two persons at a table adorned for supper in the most costly manner. We crossed that room, and opened a door leading to another. Then I raised my voice, and cried, in a tone that echoed through the mansion,—

"Frances Grant—Frances Grant!"

A shrill scream burst upon our ears, and we dashed forward in the direction from whence it proceeded, convinced that it came from no other than the young girl herself whom we had come to seek. The tramping of feet upon the staircase met our ears, and the whole establishment seemed to be in the greatest confusion. We came to a door which was locked, and a shriek more loud and clear than the first one that had answered my call came from the other side of it.

"Allow me," cried Ratcliffe; and he sprang at the door with such force, that he burst it open, and fell sprawling in the room.

Immediately I felt some one give me a whack on the side of the head, that nearly knocked me down. All was darkness in the room we had broken into, and for some moments I was so confused that I did not know what was doing. When I recovered a little, I found that Dr. Broughton had got possession of a lamp that had been burning on the staircase, and brought it into the apartment. Our prisoner had made his escape, and the principal members of our party were grouped round a sofa. I immediately approached it, and there lay Frances Grant, dead or insensible, at the moment I could not tell which.

"Good God!" I cried, "what has happened?"—"D———n it! I don't know," cried Broughton. "Somebody made good a retreat from this room by sheer desperation, I believe."

"Then, whoever he was," said I, "you may depend he was the principal actor in this vile affair."

A very little investigation sufficed to let me see that Frances Grant had only fainted, and I said to Broughton,—

"Let us divide our force. Some of us remain here, and the rest scour the house, making prisoners of who we can."
—"Very good, cried Ratcliffe. "There can be no doubt about the matter now. I shall arrest every one I can see in the villa. Come on, gentlemen—come on."

"Hold!" said some one suddenly appearing in the doorway. "Take good advice, and go. By remaining longer here you subject yourselves to awful consequences. The owner of this place is one you dare not trifle with."—"We can talk to you by and by," said Ratcliffe, making a spring upon the man and seizing him. "We are too old birds to be taken by chaff."

Dr. Broughton had been using means for the restoration of Frances Grant, and now she had recovered sufficiently to be able to speak, when she said mournfully,—

"Oh, save me—save me—save me! They have torn me from my mother and my home!—Save me from him—save me from him!"—"Help—help!—hilloa—hilloa, there!" cried a voice from the hall, which we knew to be that of the sentinel we had placed there. For a moment we hesitated whether to remain with Frances or to obey the summons; but I cut short the difficulty by lifting her from the couch on which she lay, and crying,—

"Come on—we will take her with us! To the hall!—to the hall!—to the hall!"

She appeared to have recognized me, for she clung to me with frantic eagerness, exclaiming,—

"You have come to save me? Oh! tell me you have come to take me home again!"—"I have," said I. "You are rescued, Frances. You will be in your mother's arms again before you are a quarter of an hour older."

She burst into tears, and, still clinging to me, wept loudly and hysterically as I rushed as quickly as I could after the others to the hall, where I could hear some great contention was going on. A minute brought me there, and I said to Frances,—

"Can you stand?"—"Yes—yes," she said; "but do not leave me."

"No," I cried, as I placed her on her feet. "I am not alone here; you have friends enough now in this house to take your part."

The hall by this time was full of persons. Several carried lights, and when I reached it such a confusion of tongues was going on that it was impossible to hear what any one had to say. Mrs. Smith was there, and apparently in a great passion, loudly protesting and gesticulating, while through the inner glass doors I could perceive down the steps the top of a carriage as if waiting to carry some one away from the scene of confusion.

"Oh, she is here, is she?" cried Mrs Smith, in a momentary lull of the tumult of eloquence. "She has made up a nice story, I have no doubt; but she came here of her own accord, and I took her in for charity's sake."—"'Tis false—false!" cried Frances. "I was dragged here by force, and, oh! how frightfully have I been persecuted since I have been here!"

"Take her away!—take her away!" shouted Mrs. Smith. "I wish you joy with your bargain. You will soon find out what she is. Be off with her! It's a pity you shouldn't have her, if you wish it, especially after taking so much pains. Take her away!"—"We mean to take her away," said I; "but we mean likewise to have justice on him who would have fain been her seducer. That he possesses wealth and rank I can imagine; but such shall not screen him from public opprobrium, and the penalty attached by law to his crimes."

"You don't know what you say," cried Mrs. Smith,—"you don't know what you are talking about."

Suddenly a figure appeared at the head of the staircase; it was attired in a large cloak, that completely hid the lower part of the face. The form was tall and commanding. He spoke not, but stepped about two steps down the staircase, and then paused; some one from behind this person then said,—

"A free passage!—a free passage!"—"No," said Ratcliffe; "I must apprehend all here."

"Come this way, then. His excellency will speak to you."
—"Don't go alone," said I.

"Oh, I fear nothing," cried Ratcliffe. "I wish to know who really is the owner of this place, and by going alone I have the best chance of ascertaining. I need not take him if I once know him, for, to tell the truth, I should like further authority from a magistrate, which he can only give me after an examination on oath of the girl we have rescued. Wait for me, if you please; I will return immediately."

Ratcliffe then ascended the staircase and followed the tall, stout man into some room, for we lost sight of him. Mrs. Smith sat down in a hall chair, and smiled and nodded, as much as to say, "Now you will find yourselves in the wrong box, I rather think," while I confess I waited with no small share of curiosity the result. In about two minutes Ratcliffe came down the staircase. He was very pale, and I fancied he trembled a little.

"Now, sir," cried Mrs. Smith.—"We—we—had better let *him* pass," he said; "we—we must let *him* pass."

"Why, Ratcliffe," said I, "what's the matter with you?"
—"Hush—hush! for God's sake! Here he comes. Make way! I—I, must let him pass. For God's sake, sir, don't stop him. You must not, indeed."

"But I will."—"No, no; you would not stand in the way of ———"

"Who—who?"—"The—the—*king*."

I shrank back for a moment amazed, and *George the Fourth* passed across the hall, stepped into his carriage, and drove off.

* * * * *

Frances Grant was restored to her mother, and I must leave my readers to make their own comments upon this passage in my diary, I only vouching for its truth.

DIARY OF A PHYSICIAN.

DR. BRIGGS;
OR, THE SERVICE OF PLATE.

One of the most elaborate pieces of fraud, perhaps, that ever came under my cognizance, was that which I find recorded in my Diary, under the above title. If not instructive, I have no doubt the circumstances I have to record will be found amusing. I must premise that I had not personally so much to do with the affair as is commonly the case in my revelations; but still I was sufficiently mixed up in the matter to know all the particulars as they occurred, and, in common with others, I was made the dupe of a train of events which were conceived with wonderful skill, and carried out with amazing tact.

My readers are aware that for a considerable period of my professional career, I resided in Bread-street, in the city, and I must confess, that, taken as a whole, the citizens were always my best customers, because they looked upon the fee of a medical man as a just claim, and their business-like habits enabled them to pay it without that pang which I have found to oppress aristocratic people so frequently at parting with a sixpence, in satisfaction of a real just claim, while hundreds and thousands would be squandered on the turf, or with blacklegs and bullies in a gaming-house. Besides, the citizens, now and then, were troubled with indigestion. Real turtle is not the finest stomachic in the world.

But to my story. Among my last patients was a family of

the name of Marsh. Mr. Marsh was a gold and silversmith, in a very extensive way of business, indeed. He supplied services of plate to many of the nobility, and was a man of great repute in the good city of London, as well as the possessor of a very ample fortune. There was a large family of the Marshes, and a more amiable, pleasant set of people could not very well, or easily, be found in the aforesaid good city. I was on visiting terms with them, and used very frequently to call when I knew I was not wanted professionally; and such was the wish on the part of the Marshes to act honourably, even to the excess of justness, that, for some time, I had a great deal of difficulty to convince them that I did call as a friend, and prevent them from pushing into my hand a guinea, wrapped up in a neat piece of silver paper, as my fee for being so good as to give them a passing call.

However, we got over that in a little time, and I and the Marshes were great crónies.

One morning, about eleven o'clock, and when I was "at home" to any professional calls that might be made, a very elegant carriage drove up at my door, and a lady stepped out of it, dressed in an elaborate style of fashion. She seemed about the middle age, and by the great respect which the footman paid her on her leaving the carriage, I guessed that she must be somebody of importance. A loud rat-tat at my door convinced me that I was the individual in Bread-street who was to be favoured with so imposing a visit, and I accordingly prepared myself for the announcement of the lady.

In a few moments my servant brought in a card, on which was the name of the Hon. Lady Somerset Fitzroy.

"Show her ladyship in," said I; and much I wondered to myself what could induce her to neglect all the aristocratic practitioners of the west-end, and come to their humbler brethren in the city. My reflections, however, could not last very long, for in a few moments the lady was introduced, and I politely handed her to a seat, when, to my surprise, she burst into tears.

"Calm yourself, madam," said I. "I shall be happy to render you what professional assistance I can. Pray control your feelings, and if you can honour me so far, I beg of you to look upon me as a friend as well as a physician."

"You are very, very kind, sir," she replied; "I don't know what you will think of me for giving way to my feelings in this foolish manner, but I have come to consult you on a subject upon which I feel acutely, and which has caused me the greatest unhappiness."

"Well, madam, I hope I shall be able to render you assistance. You may depend upon my attention to your case, madam, which, from what you say, is, I suppose, one of difficulty."

"Oh, you mistake," she said; "I have not come on my own account. Thank God, I am quite well, with the exception of the mental uneasiness I feel for another."

This speech rather bothered me, and all I could say in reply to it, was,—

"Oh, indeed; very well, madam, I will hear you with great pleasure; only allow me to suggest that but little, if anything, can be done by a prudent physician, unless he sees his patient."

"It is just your opinion that I want, doctor," she said; "and when you have given that, I can take means of bringing you and your patient together."

I bowed, and the lady continued.

"My poor brother, Lord Fitzroy, is in India, and he has left under my care his only son, Markham, who is now quite a young man. Poor Markham! when his father left England, he showed so much intellect, so much real sense, that the most brilliant hopes were entertained of him, and now, alas—alas!"

"What has happened?"—"I fear that insanity is showing itself."

"Indeed!"—"Yes, sir. His manner has become strange and flighty, and from an utter disregard of money he has become most passionately attached to it, fancying that every one owes him a large sum, and until that unhappy chord in his mind is struck, you would fancy him a mild, inoffensive, quiet, intelligent, gentlemanly young man. Alas—alas! It is dreadful to think of, doctor, and, what is worse, his poor father has no idea of the dreadful truth."

"But do you not think, madam, he ought to be at once informed?"

"I do; but I have not the courage to break his heart with the intelligence. Besides, I wished, before I wrote upon the subject to my poor brother, to ascertain, if possible, what consolation I could send him as well—so I have come to you, sir, to solicit your opinion on the case; whether you think a cure could be effected, or, if such is hopeless, I trust you will not think me too troublesome, and that you will accept this fee for your kind attention."

She laid on the table before me a ten-pound note, and, as physicians never quarrel with their fees for being more than they expected, I put it in my pocket, and then replied,—

"Madam, in the first place, I advise you at once to let his lordship know the condition of his son, and, secondly, if you can let me have an interview with the young man I will bestow all the attention I can upon the case. From what you have said, it seems to me a case of monomania, which may likely be curable, more especially if taken in an early stage."

"I am greatly beholden to you, sir; you shall see him."

"Permit me, however, to add, madam, as a piece of information which you ought to have, that there are physicians who have made insanity, and all its varied precursatory symptoms, their peculiar study; and although, of course, I am much flattered by the kind preference you have given me, I think that there are other gentlemen in the profession whose opinion in cases of insanity are of more importance than mine."

"Doctor," she replied, "I know not how to thank you for so candid and gentlemanly a speech. Without resigning my intention of having the benefit of your judgment, can you name to me any gentleman in the city who has had peculiar experience in such cases?"

"Yes," said I, "there is Dr. Briggs; he scarcely has any other cases, and ranks very high in those of lunacy. You could not go to a better man."

"Doctor Briggs?"—"Yes, madam."

"I thank you, sir. Do you know Dr. Briggs personally, sir?"—"No. I have seen him, certainly. He lives in Finsbury-square; but I have no acquaintance with him whatever."

"Then you cannot favour me with a note of introduction?"

"Oh, certainly I can. One medical man can always do so as regards another. I shall have great pleasure in writing a note to Doctor Briggs."

I then wrote a short note explaining the nature of the case, and handed it to the Honourable Lady Somerset Fitzroy, who, after thanking me repeatedly, rose to go, saying,—

"It is on my poor brother's account that I feel this business so acutely. His letters from India used to give me so much pleasure, but now any expressions in them of joy or hope for the future, fill me with the most melancholy feelings. See, here, sir—here is an epistle, the last I received from him, and only this morning; it speaks of his poor boy with much tenderness."

Her ladyship handed me an open letter as she spoke, and, not to be rude, I perused some of it, and was all at once struck with a postscript that ran thus:—

"Now, my dear Ann, you must know, that we of this presidency have got up among ourselves a subscription to present a service of plate, of the value of one thousand pounds, to General Veal, who you have heard so much of. You must execute the commission for me, as the matter has been left in my hands. Be so good as to purchase and pay for, on my account, plate to that amount, of some respectable house in London."

Here, thought I, is an opportunity of saying a good word for the Marshes, and accordingly I said,—

"I see, madam, you have a commission from your brother to purchase a thousand pounds' worth of plate. If you are not fixed to a particular tradesman, it would give me great pleasure to recommend a friend of mine."

"And it will give me equal pleasure," said her ladyship, "to give him the preference, which will please me, as it will enable me to think I am, in some slight degree, repaying you for your very great kindness and disinterestedness."

"This is remarkably pleasant," thought I; and, at her ladyship's request, I wrote a note to Mr. Marsh, to the following effect:—

"My dear sir,—The bearer of this is the Honourable Lady Ann Somerset Fitzroy. She has a commission for a thousand pounds' worth of plate from her brother in India, and I have taken the liberty of recommending her to you. Believe me, my dear sir, yours very truly,

"————"

Armed, then, with her two epistles, her ladyship galloped away from my door, leaving me with a very high opinion of her, and altogether very much pleased with the whole affair.

"Dr. Briggs will be pleased," thought I; "the Marshes will be pleased, and I am pleased; so that, take it altogether, it's very pleasant indeed."

Then I thought I would call on the Marshes; but I made up my mind, after a little consideration, that I would not, because it would look like fishing for thanks for my recommendation of so good a customer.

"No," I thought; "I will not go near them now for a little time, and they will then not think me elated about being able to do them a service."

With these views and feelings, then, I studiously avoided all that day passing by the Marshes' house, although it really lay in my way to patients several times, and I quite hugged myself on my cleverness, tact, and delicacy.

So much for a beginning; and now let me tell the story, as I was but partly an actor in it, and as I gathered it together and recorded it in my Diary, as an everlasting warning to be very careful in recommendations.

* * * * *

When her ladyship left my house, she drove at once to Finsbury-square, where she found Dr. Briggs at home, and from whom I had the following very graphic particulars of the scene that ensued.

My note disarmed him of all suspicion, and he met his visitor, of course, with the most distinguished courtesy. Her ladyship detailed to him the same statements she had detailed to me, about her nephew, upon which he, of course, said what was very reasonable, namely, that he could come to no opinion upon the case unless he saw the young man.

"Then you shall certainly see him, sir, to-morrow morning," she replied, "if that will be convenient to you."

"Quite convenient, madam," said the worthy doctor.

"Then," added her ladyship, "there is one thing of which I must warn you. My poor nephew is very sensitive indeed concerning strangers, and the only way in which I can induce him to see one at all, is by making him believe that they are going to pay money to him, when he becomes immediately quite polite, and will enter agreeably enough into conversation with any one."

"Certainly, madam," said the doctor; "we often find it very necessary to humour insane patients, and even to use their particular mania as a weapon against themselves. You may rely upon my saying nothing to irritate the young man, and when you bring him to me, your best plan will be to tell him I have money for him, after which I can sound the depth of his insanity, and judge whether it be curable or not."

With a profusion of compliments, her ladyship left Dr. Briggs, after giving him, as she had given me, the liberal fee of ten pounds, with which, of course, he was very well satisfied indeed.

Her next visit was to the Marshes, and there she produced my note, which at once procured her every attention. She looked out a magnificent gold service of plate to the value of rather over the thousand pounds, saying she would herself make up the difference by a subscription of her own to the amount, for she knew how brave and distinguished an officer General Veal was, and how much he deserved such a mark of esteem. There was only one thing that just a little aroused the suspicion of the Marshes that all was not quite right, and that was that she gave no address, and said she would come for the plate herself the following morning, and have it packed in the carriage.

They said to her, on this proposition being made,—

"It is true, madam, that a thousand pounds worth of gold plate is no great weight or bulk, and might be easily packed in your chariot, but we would much rather send the articles home, and then we will unpack them at your residence, and be answerable for their safe delivery."

"You are very kind," she said; "but I shall be in the city to-morrow morning at Dr. Briggs's, in Finsbury-square, and I will call upon you."

"Very good, madam—very good; as you please."

Her ladyship then went away, but it appears the Marshes made up their minds not to part with the plate without cash down, so that they could not be possibly taken in, and, what was more, Mr. Marsh wrote to me the following note:—

"My dear Sir,—Many thanks for your kind recommendation of Lady Fitzroy. Is Dr. Briggs a respectable man, and where does he live?—Yours, very truly,

"GEORGE MARSH."

I was a little astonished at this note, and I wrote a reply to it as follows:—

"My dear Sir,—Dr. Briggs is a man ranking high in his profession, and of competent fortune. He resides in Finsbury-square.—Yours, very truly,

"————"

Then it appears Mr. Marsh, who had some suspicions, but was afraid of going too far, because he might offend where offence would be most unjustifiable, besides losing a first-rate connexion, went to Finsbury-square himself, and knocked at Dr. Briggs's door; when it was opened by the doctor's footman, he said,—

"Do you know the Honourable Lady Ann Somerset Fitzroy?"—"Let me see. She was here this morning."

"Oh! Do you know if your master is intimate with her?" —"Ask no questions," said the footman, "and you'll be told no lies. D—d if ever I heard such impudence in all my life before. Cuss me!"

"No offence," said Mr. Marsh, who was one of your homely, old-fashioned tradesmen, and he slipped half-a-crown into John's hands, which half-crown had a wonderful emollient effect, and then John volunteered a statement that he heard the lady in question say something to his master about paying money, and that she was to be there the next morning—that she gave him five shillings, and was a lady every inch.

Mr. Marsh was quite satisfied. Indeed, he got away from Dr. Briggs's house as quickly as possible, for fear he should be seen by that gentleman, and forced into an explanation that he had come there as a spy about his honourable acquaintance, the Lady Fitzroy; and when he got home, he was rather cross than otherwise to Mrs. Marsh, who had invited him to go on the errand to Finsbury-square; as for me, he had intended to have given me a call, but he was half ashamed now to do so, because he was afraid I might have taken umbrage at his letter, so home he went.

"Well, Mrs. Marsh," he said, "it's all right."—"Is it, Mr. Marsh?—are you quite sure? You know what artful hussies there are in the world."

"I know there are suspicious women—a-hem!"

"Do you mean me, Mr. George Marsh?"—"No, my dear."

"Very well, my dear; because if you do, I ——"—"But I don't. There, now, say no more about it, my love. We have had a very good customer to-day, and what is more, she has selected a service of plate that has been on hand now some years, and all our best customers have some, so that it was likely to remain for years to come."

"Very true. And now, George, we will, as this large piece of business has been done to-day, send our Samuel to college." —"Well—well, I don't mind. He's now just of a nice age, and who knows but some day he may be lord mayor, when his learning here at Oxford or Cambridge, will be of great advantage to him."

"Very true—very true."

In such like conversation, passed the evening at the Marshes, for, although they had a very good business indeed, a thousand pounds' customer seldom came, and two or three such in a few years were all that could fairly be expected at the very best.

The rapidity of the movements of the Honourable Lady Somerset Fitzroy enabled her to be more eminently successful than she would otherwise have been: a day or two's delay would have been fatal, but no such delay at all occurred, and by about eleven o'clock on the following morning she drove up to Dr. Brigg's house, in Finsbury-square.

She was of course with all due ceremony ushered into the doctor's presence, who was not at all sorry to see so good a customer again. Ten pounds made up a very good fee indeed, and no wonder the lady found herself treated with great respect, and more than common attention and civility.

"Have you, madam," he said, "brought the young man with you whom I am to see?"—"I have not, doctor," she replied; "but in order that he should not suspect he was being brought into the City for any specific purpose,—for he is dreadfully suspicious ——"

"Ah, many insane people are," interrupted the doctor.— "Exactly so. Well, sir, in order to allay, or not excite any suspicion, I have taken him first on a visit to my silversmith's, the Messrs. Marsh."

"Oh, I know them—highly respectable people."— "Yes. I have made a purchase of a service of plate for my brother in India."

"Have you indeed, madam?"—"Yes, sir; and if you will be at home, I will do myself the pleasure, within the next hour, of coming here again, and of bringing my nephew with me. You can then see him, while I take a drive round the square, as I think you had better have him all to yourself, without my being present."

"We generally do prefer that course," said the doctor.

"Then it shall be so. You will understand when I bring him who it is, and pray humour him a little, or he will get into one of his violent, ungovernable fits of passion, and no good will be done to-day at all."

"Depend upon me, madam; I will manage him with all due discretion."

"Good-morning, then, sir, for the present."— "Good-morning, madam."

The doctor attended his illustrious visitor to the door, and at it she again handed him a ten pound fee, which he received with a low bow, that brought his nose almost in contact with the door-mat.

Truly the carriage, horses and servants of the lady were all that could be desired or expected from a person of her rank and wealth. The whole equipage was faultless, and well calculated to deceive the most wary and cautious. The Marshes almost wavered in their wise resolution of insisting on the money before parting with the gold plate, and it is just possible that they would have allowed her ladyship to carry away the whole of it, and if she had said nothing about money, they would not; but an old friend of the family, who had retired from business, called early in the morning, and gave the following advice in reply to Mr. Marsh, who explained to him the circumstances.

"My old friend, this transaction appears all right enough. First, you have your friend the doctor's note concerning this lady, so you can have no doubt as to her identity; and then you have yourself ascertained that what she said with regard to Dr. Briggs is quite correct."

"Certainly I have."—"Well, then, my friend, there is but one disagreeable point of view in which you can look at the matter."

"And what may that be?"—"Simply this,—that there are swindlers and common cheats among the nobility as well as among the commonalty, and it may possibly be that this lady may be all she represents herself, and yet a terrible cheat."

"You don't say so?"—"Yes, I do. You know I was in business at the West End, and ought to know."

"So you were. But is it possible that noble people will so far sully the titles they have received from their ancestors as to do dishonourable actions?"—"The Lord have mercy upon us!" said the friend of the Marshes: "can there be such simplicity in this world in the year 18—? Is it possible?"

"Yes, but ——"—"Pshaw—hold your tongue! I tell you there is more rascality, petty trickery, roguery and swindling, ay, heartless and indefensible swindling, in the higher ranks of society, than could be ventured upon among people whose characters are of some importance to them."

The Marshes looked amazed, and the friend, who had

been in business at the West End, and knew well those of whom he was talking, continued,—

"If you let that woman you have mentioned to me have so much as a teaspoon away without the money, you deserve to lose it."—"Well, we won't, then," said Mrs. Marsh.

"Don't. If she means honestly, she will not be offended at being asked for what is fairly due. If she don't pay, why, the sooner she is offended, the better."

With this determination, then, the Marshes awaited the arrival of their good customer with no small degree of nervousness and impatience. The whole family was on the look out, and Samuel, the eldest son, who took an active part in the warehouse and general business, had put on his best clothes in order to do honour to her ladyship, who was really a handsome and fascinating woman, both in person and manners.

At length, with an aristocratic rattle and dash, the fashionable carriage drove up to the door, and Mr. Marsh rushed out to assist the lady to alight, while Samuel held the door open for her and his father.

With the most graceful condescension in the world, the lady leaned upon the arm of the goldsmith, and entered the drawing-room of his house, where was displayed the gold service.

"Oh, it looks charming!" she exclaimed. "Pack it up. I quite long to show it to some of my friends before it goes to India."—"Yes, madam, certainly."

"And, by the bye, Mr. Mask——"—"Marsh, madam—Marsh, at your service."

"Oh! Marsh. I beg your pardon; I am very bad at recollecting names indeed. Well, Mr. a—a—Mart, you will be so good as to make out a bill on a stamped receipt, and then I can pay you, and get back the money from my brother's solicitors. He is richer than I am, and can wait for a thousand pounds better."

Mr. Marsh gave a long breath of relief. Here was the difficulty solved at once; her ladyship had herself actually volunteered the payment, and there was now no occasion to go through the disagreeable ceremony of asking her for the money before she drove off with the goods.

The packing of the gold plate went on merrily, and was very soon accomplished indeed. A thousand pounds worth of gold was indeed no great bulk or burthen. Then it was stowed away in the carriage so snugly, while Mr. Marsh made out her ladyship's account. Samuel rushed here and there like a madman, and at length all was finished—the last parcel was in the carriage, and Mr. Marsh approached her ladyship with the account.

"Oh, is that—the—little bill?"—"Yes, madam."

"Thirteen hundred pounds, seventeen shillings, exactly. Dr. Briggs has the money; I left it with him, and if you, my good sir, or your handsome son will accompany me in my carriage to Finsbury-square, you can have the amount of the doctor. He is quite an oddity in his way, and insists that women should never pay bills; so being a very old friend of the family, I let him transact all business of any amount for me. It's too bad really, to give you all this trouble; but if you, sir," turning with such a bewitching smile to Samuel that he did not know for a moment whether he was on his head or his heels, "will favour me with your company in my carriage, we will go to the doctor at once."

"Ye—ye—yes," stammered Samuel; "yes, madam—my lady—if you please. I shall be honoured, my lady, very much honoured."

Then he in his agitation trod on his father's toes, and fell over a stool. Her ladyship smiled again. Who could resist that smile, so full of bewitching softness and exquisite condescension?

"Yes, yes," said the father, "my son, Samuel, will go, madam; he—he will do you the honour—I mean—I beg your pardon—you will do him the honour."

Samuel caught his hat from a peg, and was ready to go. Then her ladyship took his arm, and turning to the elder Marsh, she said,—

"Adieu, adieu, Mr. Marsh. If we never meet again, you will, I am sure, not forget——"

"Never, never!" cried Samuel for his father, "so help me, never. This way, ma'am—mind the edge of the counter. Oh, ye gods! what an anecdote. This way, this way, if you please; mind the step, and—and the scraper."

The lady hung gently upon his arm; she looked tenderly in his face, and they got into the carriage. Bang went the door, and the footman stood for orders.

"Dr. Briggs, in Finsbury-square," said the Honourable Lady Ann Somerset Fitzroy.

The footman gave that indescribable touch to his hat which only footmen can accomplish, and then Samuel fell back on the luxurious cushions of the chariot, as it started at a rattling pace for Finsbury-square.

* * * * * *

"I see it all—I see it all! Oh, my gracious providence, I see it all!"

These words were shouted by Mrs. Marsh as she rushed wildly from the back counting-house, through the glass door of which she had been a spectator of what had passed.

"Oh, Marsh, Marsh, support me! My eyes are opened now. As I am a living woman, I see it all. Oh good gracious powers! who could have thought it? Marsh, Marsh, you are a fool!"

"Good God! what's the matter?" cried Marsh.—"Hold me!—support me! Marsh, are you a brute?"

"I—I hope not."—"Our Sam—only to think of it being our Sam. Oh, dear—oh, dear!—that I should live to see with my own mortal eyes this day. It's quite plain—very plain. Why was I blind till now? Oh, dear—oh, dear!"

"Good gracious, Mrs. Marsh," cried Mr. Marsh, "what do you mean?—Are you mad?"—"No, but you are an idiot, Marsh, quite an idiot. I see it all—nobody can hoodwink me. That titled lady has seen our Sam somewhere. She loves him. He was always reckoned like his mother. She wants to make him a lord and marry him. I see it all now. She bought the plate just to scrape acquaintance with us. Didn't you see how she looked at him—how she took his arm? She loves him—I see it all. I began to smell a rat half an hour ago. Oh, Sam, Sam, you will be a great man!"

"Lor!" said Mr. Marsh, "you don't mean that?"—"I do, Mr. Marsh. Do I look like a woman who says what she don't mean?"

"No, my dear; but——"—"No buts for me, Mr. Marsh. What I say, I say; what I see, I see; and what I know, I know."

"Well, I shouldn't have thought it; but now you mention it, she did look at Sam in a sort of a kind way—I saw her do it. Really I'm quite bewildered. I don't seem to know exactly where I am. A glass of water—bless my heart and life!"

"Yes," sighed Mrs. Marsh, "Sam will be a lord or a duke; he will come in his own chariot and astonish the Smiths, the Gregories, the Browns, and the Appleyards—and I'm his mother. Oh, what a day is this! If you mind your P's and Q's, Marsh, you may be, after all, a sheriff.—What do you think of that? Who knows what we may all come to yet? Heigho—what a world is this—full of ups, and downs, and thingemties. How glad I shall be when Sammy comes home, to hear all about it,—what she said to him, and what she didn't,—whether she's had him made a lord yet, or whether she hasn't. Oh, Sammy, Sammy!"

Here Mrs. Marsh showed some sort of notion of going into hysterics, upon the strength of the sudden exaltation of Sammy to the peerage. Mr. Marsh became so alarmed that he immediately sent one of his servants to me, and so I was drawn into the affair sooner than I had intended calling upon the Marshes.

Not knowing what was the matter, for the servant who was sent to me could give no particulars very well of what had taken place in the warehouse while she was in the kitchen, I hurried as fast as I could to the house, dreading that some sad accident had occurred, as the message for me was couched in very urgent terms.

Judge of my astonishment when I arrived to find nothing the matter, but, on the contrary, Mr. and Mrs. Marsh appeared very much pleased.

"You sent for me?" said I.—"Yes, doctor," said Mr. Marsh; "but Mrs. M. is better; a little cherry brandy has recovered her. We are very much obliged to you indeed."

"That we are," chimed in Mrs. Marsh. "But now tell the truth, doctor, and shame the devil. Did you know of it beforehand?"—"Ah," said Mr. Marsh; "where did she first see Sammy?"

"Upon my word," said I, "you amaze me. Is that the only bottle of cherry brandy you have paid any attention to to-day?"—"Come, come, doctor, you know the lady you sent to us."

"I recommended a lady to purchase some plate."—"And she has, in addition to that, fallen in love with our Sammy.

She has, sir, and he will be somebody some day soon, if not to-day."

"Yes," chimed in Mrs. March, "our own Sam, you know, doctor. His fortune's made, howsomdever. He was always a handsome lad."

"Very good," said I, sitting down. "When you please to explain all this to me, I shall be quite delighted. Till then you will find me very patient indeed."

The seriousness with which I uttered these words appeared to convince them that I was really in want of information; so Mrs. Marsh had the goodness to explain matters to me in her way.

"You must know, doctor, that the lady you recommended to us came and bought a gold service of plate over a thousand pounds' value. Well, I found out that what she really came for was Sammy."

I suppose I looked the state of botheration I was really in, for Mr. Marsh now took up the story, and added,—

"Mrs. M. is of opinion, doctor, from the lady's conduct, that she was in love with our Samuel."

"Indeed! What grounds have you for such a supposition?"—"Why, she has taken him clean away."

"What, run away with Samuel? Upon my word it's the strongest case of abduction I ever heard of."—"Yes, she's taken him away in her carriage, doctor. She would have him; and I never saw a boy so nonplused in all my life."

"And what do you suppose will be the result?"—"Why, of course, she will pop the question to Sammy, and marry him. She's a lady, and, no doubt, will find means to make him a lord. There will be something that will make the Gregsons open their eyes."—"It's enough to make anybody open his or her eyes," said I. "But, however, I am much pleased that I have been at all instrumental in giving you all so much pleasure. I suppose you have been paid for the plate?"—"As good as paid," replied Mr. Marsh.

"A cheque, I suppose?"—"No; Sammy will bring back the money with him. She would have paid us here, but her scheme was evidently to get Sammy out with her in the carriage, you see, and that was how we came to suspect that she was in love with him, you understand, doctor."

"And the plate?"—"That she took with her as well. Oh, we could see she had some scheme in taking Sammy with her. He always was a handsome lad. I never shall forget his nearly falling over the footman as he stepped into the carriage—it was quite affecting, doctor. That was what quite overcame me, and made me so *sterical*."

I must own that my mind misgave me then that there was more in the matter than met the eye, and a disagreeable sensation came across my mind that the Marshes had been done. Still I could not be sure, and after a brief debate with myself, I resolved to say nothing of my suspicions, in case they should turn out unfounded; and, besides, matters had gone so far, that all the suspicions in the world could do no good. As for the lady having been attracted by Sammy, who was a great gauky-looking boy, it was rather too rich; and if she had been really so anxious to take Sammy with her as the Marshes seemed to think, I was quite sure there was some other motive in it than admiration of that youth.

I was in a perfect agony, and determined to wait till Sammy came home, for although I could not possibly be blamed for recommending a customer to a tradesman, if that tradesman, having received no sort of guarantee from me, omitted to use common caution in his dealings, yet I felt that it would be a very sore place in my mind, if ever so remotely through me the Marshes should be taken in to the tune of a thousand pounds.

By degrees I got the full particulars from them of the whole affair, and then I told them how I had become acquainted with the Honourable Lady Ann Somerset Fitzroy, concluding by saying,—

"So you see I know nothing whatever of her, and hope you did not receive her as an acquaintance of mine."

"Oh, no, no," they said. "She was a perfect lady, and Sammy at once was the object of attraction to her—they could see that. They were not blind—not they; and, besides, what they had heard at Dr. Brigg's quite satisfied them."

Now this story about Dr. Briggs made me in a perfect fever, and I was more sure than ever that there was great scheming and duplicity somewhere.

"You will notice," I said, "that the lady never mentioned to me her acquaintance with Dr. Briggs. On the contrary she professed never to have heard of him."

"To be sure," cried Mrs. Marsh; "of course what she wanted was an introduction to us, so that she might see Sammy. It's all in a nutshell, and as plain as a pikestaff, or the nose on one's face. I wonder you don't see it, doctor."

"I am afraid I do," said I.

But the Marshes would not be reasoned out of their crotchet by the indirect arguments I used, and, as I have remarked, I did not like to go too far, for fear of being wrong after all, and being set down as an alarmist without cause, so I accepted an invitation to stay to dinner, and heard with what patience I could Mrs. Marsh's felicitations upon Sammy's good fortune.

In order that my story should be fully intelligible, as it progresses, to the reader, I will proceed now to give an account of Sammy's adventures after he had left home with the elegant and accomplished Lady Ann Somerset Fitzroy. These particulars I gathered partly from his own lips, and partly from Dr. Briggs, who was most outrageously bitter, and thoroughly made a cat's-paw of in the affair, much to his after discomfiture.

Sammy was in a kind of delirium as he sat on the downy cushion of the fashionable chariot, with such a companion by his side. He was afraid to move, to speak, or even to venture a glance at the beautiful being, who he verily believed had fallen deeply in love with him; yet he declares he never for a moment forgot that business was business, and that he had to receive for his father the amount of the signed receipt, which was snugly reposing in his waistcoat pocket.

"How old are you?" asked the lady, in bewitching accents, and it might have been design, or a sudden lurch of the chariot on its exquisite springs, which brought her mouth within a hair's breadth of Sammy's.

He coloured up to the roots of his hair as he replied,—

"I—I am nineteen, madam."

The lady sighed deeply.

"Have you no *affair de cœur*, Samuel?"—"No what, ma'am? I—I believe I have——"

"No sentiment—no image enshrined in your heart of hearts, to which you pay heavenly devotion? Do you love no one Samuel?"—"Ye—yes—I—I think I do."

Here Sammy felt the receipt, and it restored him a little to everyday existence.

"Ah me!" said the lady, "what a thing to wander through life's flowery vale, with all the insignia of wealth and rank at command, and yet no kindred spirit to share with one the rapturous heart's glow, the magic bliss. Dissolved in a cloud of joys—the sweet music, delicious balls, flowers, paintings, statuary, servants, carriages, all have I, including the smiles of royalty, and yet I feel so lonely with it all."—"Yes, ma'am—yes—indeed—oh, dear!"

"Yes, Samuel, yes. Where is the heart which never loved, or felt soft passion's swell? Oh, Sam—Sam—permit me to call you Sam."—"Call me anything," said Samuel. "I'm frantic—I don't know what I'm saying. Now, if you love me, I love you—I—I ain't quite a fool. Oh, ma'am, if you will but marry me——"

"Hush!—here we are at Dr. Briggs's. Soon we shall meet again. Breathe not a word. I have two distinct incomes, and if our intended marriage was to get into the fashionable newspapers before it was really finished, I should lose one eighteen thousand a year, and we should have to do the best we could, Sam, upon the twenty-two thousand a year I get from the East India Stock. I'm afraid, Sam, you are a lady killer; I declare you have put me quite nervous. You have some money, you know, to receive of the doctor. I will leave you with him, and take a drive round the square to recover my spirits, Sam. Here we are. Be discreet."—"I—I will," said Sammy. "One—one——"

"What—good gracious!—what?"—"Kiss."

"Not for countless worlds! Are you a wretch, Sammy, or what I really took you for?"—"I am—I am anything you please."

"Hush! hush!—the footman comes."

A tremendous rat-tat at Dr. Briggs's door caused it to be opened with amazing celerity, and the lady, leaning from the window of her carriage, said,—

"If Dr. Briggs is within, will he oblige by speaking to me a moment here?"

The message was taken to the doctor, who, all civility, hurried to the side of the carriage.

"Oh, doctor, how do you do?" she said. "Here is the young man to whom you are to pay the money, you know."—

"Exactly," said the doctor, who was on his guard to humour the madman. "I will pay you, sir, if you will alight and walk into my house."

"It's—it's over a thousand pounds," stammered Sammy.—"Exactly—I know. Walk in, sir."

"It's all right," thought Sammy, as he alighted from the chariot; "it's all right."—"My dear Sam," said the lady, "I will call for you in a little time."

"She calls me dear Sam," thought Samuel. "She is quite infatuated with me. Her dear Sam!—what a slip of the tongue."—"How affectionate she is to her poor mad nephew," thought Dr. Briggs, as he heard the lady address Sammy in such sugared words.

In another moment the carriage drove off. Gradually the horses were made to go quicker and quicker, until at a good hard trot they pelted up the City-road, and turned off into a labyrinth of streets lying about Hoxton.

* * * * *

"Pray, sir, walk in, if you please," said Dr. Briggs to Sammy, who stood on the door step to catch the last glimpse of the prancing steeds that carried away from him his noble bride elect, as he believed her to be.—"Yes, yes—in a moment, sir."

"He's decidedly queer," thought the doctor, "Walk in, sir, and you shall be paid."

At these words Sammy touched his waistcoat pocket, but the receipt was gone.

"Eh—hilloa!—I was going to give you a receipt, sir," he said, "for a large sum of money, but somehow I have lost it. Where can it be?"—"Very likely, sir, you have dropped it in the carriage," said the doctor, still willing to humour his patient. "When it returns, no doubt you will find such is the case."

"But the—the money. You won't like to pay without a receipt, perhaps?"—"Oh, yes—yes, I will. That makes no difference between us. You can give me a receipt, you know, another time. What an odd delusion, to be sure."

"You are very good, sir. Do you know the amount?"—"No, but you can tell me, which will do just as well, you know. Let me beg of you to walk in. This way, if you please, sir—this way."

The doctor led the way to his parlour, where he offered Sammy a chair, who quite laughed to himself at so much out of the way civility, which he attributed entirely to the doctor having heard the honourable lady call him her dear Sam. Dr. Briggs then fixed his eyes on Sammy as he was in the habit of doing to mad people, and said,—

"It's a fine morning, sir."—"Very," said Sam, rather annoyed by the steady stare of the doctor, who imagined his perturbation to arise from insanity.

"How have you been lately?" he then said. "Do you sleep well?"—"Pretty well, thank you. I'm used to a noise, and it takes a good deal to wake me. Hammering at silver plate all day makes something of a clatter."

"Humph!" thought Briggs; "mad as a March hare. I will now touch him on the raw. Young man, you came here for some money, you fancy."—"Fancy! I know I do."

"Hush! hush, now!—be calm. Let us reason this matter over."—"It requires no reasoning. You have only to pay the amount, and then our business is settled."

"Now, now, sir, let us be calm and collected. What makes you imagine that I owe you money?"—"What makes me? Why the devil ——"

"Hush—hush—hush! Have you ever fancied you saw the devil?"—"I tell you what it is, Dr. Briggs. I am well aware what has annoyed you. The affections, sir, sometimes mislead the tongue, and you are in a rage because you heard me called by the lady who has just left, dear Sam. Pay me the money, sir—I defy you!"

"There, there, now," cried the doctor; "that's enough. Don't be violent—don't exert yourself, sir. You will make yourself very ill, indeed, if you do; and then only think of the affliction of your poor aunt."—"My aunt be d—d, sir!"

"Hush—hush!—there, now. How much money do you want? There, now—there, now—be calm—calm—calm—calm! Hush—hush!—calm—calm—calm!"—"D—n it, sir! do you take me for a restive horse, or a mad dog?" cried Sammy, jumping up. "Give me thirteen hundred and seventeen pounds, and let me go at once. I will never set foot in your house again; and let me tell you, once for all, I won't be fooled any longer. I will marry her in spite of you, and we will manage devilish well upon the twenty-two thousand dividends from the East India Stock. You may take the paltry eighteen thousand to yourself, and may they choke you—d—n it!"

"A paroxysm—quite a paroxysm," said the doctor, and he rang the bell, when two stout footmen, who were used to such affairs, came into the room.

"Hold him!" said the doctor, and poor Sammy was laid hands upon. In vain he kicked, and swore, and fought. Such conduct only produced a strait waistcoat, which was popped on him in a trice, and there he lay on a sofa, at the mercy of his opponents and Dr. Briggs, who he firmly believed intended to murder him, to prevent his marriage with the Honourable Lady Ann Somerset Fitzroy.

Hour after hour passed away, and the carriage never came back, to the great discomfiture of Dr. Briggs, who found himself encumbered with a troublesome patient, whose friends he knew not where to send to. At last it all of a sudden struck him that I knew her ladyship, and he sent one of his servants to my house, where they told him I was at Messrs. Marsh's, the silversmiths, and he came there just as a feeling of wonder, not unmixed with apprehension, was beginning to fill the minds of Mr. and Mrs. Marsh, at the long and unaccountable absence of Sammy, while my suspicions that some terrible and unexpected *denouement* was at hand had increased almost to a positive certainty.

The message to me from Dr. Briggs consisted of an earnest request that I would have the goodness to favour him with a call immediately, if I were not particularly engaged, as he could not leave his own house, or he would have come to me.

My heart sank within me, but I said nothing to the Marshes, and the message being delivered to me in the passage, whither I had gone to see the footman upon his inquiring for me, I snatched my hat from a peg, and without going back to the room where the Marshes were expecting me, I walked as hard as I could to Finsbury-square.

I was an incredibly short space of time in getting to Dr. Briggs's, and when I arrived and gave my name, I was shown into a handsome drawing-room, where I had not been five minutes, when the doctor made his appearance, and a very gentlemanly-looking man I found him. I resolved to say nothing in the way of a leading question, but to leave all explanations to him. Too soon I was convinced that my worst suspicions were about to be fully verified.

"I have taken the liberty of sending for you," he said, "to beg the favour of Lady Ann Somerset Fitzroy's address."—"I don't know it," said I.

"Why, you sent her to me."—"Yes, professionally merely. She came to me, and wanted my opinion on a case of insanity; I told her yours was much more valuable, and sent her to you. I never saw her before; I have never seen her since."

"Dear me."—"No; and now, sir, may I ask what you want her address for?"—"Why, to take away her mad nephew, to be sure."

"Indeed. Has she brought him here?"—"Yes, and was to have come back in less than half an hour; and here have I been hampered with the fellow nearly half-a-day."

"Is he mad?"—"Raving."

"The deuce he is. What form has his insanity?"—"Why, he fancies I have got to pay him thirteen hundred some odd pounds and shillings, and I have been compelled to put a strait waistcoat on him."

"Have you any objection to my seeing him?"—"None in the least. I have sent for a man to shave his head; but he is rather quiet since I have put a strong blister on his neck."

Dr. Briggs led the way to the parlour, and there upon the sofa, nearly driven mad by the treatment he had experienced, lay Sammy Marsh, with a strait waistcoat on him, and his feet tied down. Such a picture of misery I never saw in my life, and forbear laughing I really could not.

"Why—why," said Dr. Briggs, "what are you laughing at?"—"Him," said I. "Listen to me, doctor. You and I both have been made agents, unconsciously, in a swindle. This is Samuel Marsh, son of Mr. Marsh, goldsmith."

At the sound of my voice Sammy looked up, and in a loud voice cried,—

"Oh, Dr. ——, save me—save me! They want to murder me here. Go and tell my mother. Murder—murder! Help—help!"

Sammy was soon released, and I related to Dr. Briggs the whole of the affair, which almost made his hair stand on end, while Sammy wrung his hands in perfect despair.

"I'll get into the Serpentine," he said, "or I'll hang myself, I will. Oh, that I should have been such a fool!"—

"Pooh! pooh!" cried I. "Go home and tell your father what has occurred, and likewise tell him that I am taking steps to try and recover the stolen plate. Go home at once —go, go."

"Oh, sir!" cried Sammy, turning to Dr. Briggs, "how could you be such a fool as to think I was mad? You are a pretty doctor, you are."—"The deuce take you," cried Dr. Briggs. "How could I suppose you otherwise than mad when you wanted me to pay you a thousand pounds? Be off with you, or I'll have your head shaved in spite of you."

At this threat Sammy rushed away to make the best of his story at home; and very soon after, in no very enviable frame of mind, I left Dr. Briggs, resolved to devote the remainder of the day to inquiries respecting the Honourable Ann Somerset Fitzroy, but by no means clear as to the best way of setting about it.

After mature consideration with myself, I made up my mind to go to the Marshes first, for I thought it too bad that poor Sammy should be compelled to bear the whole brunt of the battle at home; and so far as Mr. and Mrs. Marsh were concerned, it was well I did so, for I found Sam dodging about the corner of the street, evidently afraid to go home minus his receipt, and minus his money.

"Why, Sam," I said, "why don't you go home?"—"I'm a desperate Samuel, sir," he said; "I think I'll make away with myself. Oh, 'tis love, 'tis love, 'tis love that makes the world go round. Why was she so beautiful?—why, eh, why? Echo answers why."

"And what else, Sam, do you expect echo to answer? unless it was an Irish one, and answered, 'I really can't tell.'"—"Oh, doctor, I'm mad in real earnest now—quite, quite mad. Oh! oh! oh!"

"Well, I think there are some grounds for your assertion; but depend upon it, Sam, no evil becomes the less by putting it off. You had better come home at once, and together we will explain to your father and mother how all this occurred."

"I don't mind going with you, sir, but I could not have faced the family by myself—no receipt and no money. Only consider, sir; ain't it enough to make one's hair stand on end?"—"Yes, it is; but come on, come on. After your father and mother once know the whole particulars, I think they cannot blame you much."

By dint of these persuasions I got Samuel to go home, and truly we found the Marshes in a great state of alarm with regard to his safety. The only consolation that Mrs. Marsh could find in the circumstances, consisted of a supposition that the Honourable Lady Ann Somerset Fitzroy, fearing opposition from her noble relatives, had posted off with Samuel to Gretna Green, and probably a letter would come from the first post town stating so much from Samuel himself. When we made our appearance together, Mrs. Marsh rushed forward, and embracing her darling, cried,—

"Oh, Sammy, Sammy, that I should live to see this day with my own two eyes! You are a married man—oh, dear! oh, dear! I may be a grandmother in nine months or less. Sammy—Sammy—Sammy!"

Mr. Marsh stood rubbing his hands together, while a dubious sort of smile played upon his face. He was evidently oppressed with doubts, and could not exactly chime in with all the maternal ecstacies of his wife. As for poor Sam himself, he looked as white as a sheet, and could not speak at all. Determined, then, to put an end to the misconstruction that was prevailing, and to come out with the worst at once, and temper it down afterwards, I said, in a clear, firm tone of voice, to the great horror of the Marshes,—

"Samuel is not married; the Honourable Lady Ann Somerset Fitzroy is a swindler; she has not paid for the plate; and the whole affair, as it at present stands, is an outrageous do."

Mrs. Marsh, with a scream, fainted away; Mr. Marsh walked backwards till he knocked his legs against a chair, upon which he sank with a deep groan, while Sammy threw himself on a sofa, and poked his head completely under one of the cushions. I could not refrain from laughing at the general consternation that prevailed, and then I added,—

"Now you know the very worst, something may be done, I think, to alleviate the circumstances. As for Sammy, I don't think he is more particularly to blame in this affair than any of you, because he, after all, with the solitary exception of allowing his pocket to be picked of the receipt for the money he was to have received, acted according to orders. Do not now, Mr. Marsh, look on the worst side of things. Let Sam come with me, and we will make an effort yet to trace the person who, with so much dishonesty, and I must say so much tact, has succeeded in robbing you of your plate."—"Gracious Heaven!" exclaimed Mr. Marsh, "what a sum to lose—over a thousand pounds."

"Do not reckon your profit on the service of plate," said I. "In estimating your actual loss, you should find out what the plate cost you—that is to say, your loss, should the affair not terminate better than it looks, is just so much, and no more, than the same that would enable you to make a similar service of plate to that now stolen from you."—"Yes, but yet only consider. You recommended her to us."

"But I did not recommend you to trust her: I did not recommend you to imagine she had fallen in love with Samuel. However, Mr. Marsh, we will not fall out upon that subject, but earnestly and rapidly do what can be done in order to have a chance of getting back your property, or punishing the guilty appropriators of it. Come along, Sam, with me, and we will take one step in the matter. Mr. Marsh, I advise you to go to the Lord Mayor, and tell your story, so that the police will be on the alert; and they may possibly find some immediate clue to the parties."

"Who would have thought it!" groaned Mr. Marsh. "Such a handsome turn out, too—footman, coachman, and all."—"No doubt it was a confederacy altogther; the servants were acting a part as well as the mistress. But I see Mrs. Marsh is recovering, so I will leave at once. Come, Sam, come."

Samuel was better pleased to leave the house than to remain in it, for he dreaded the scene that would ensue when his mother should find her tongue again, and be able to launch out eloquently regarding her hopes, fears, expectations, and disappointments. When we reached the street, I said to him,—

"Now, Sam, can you recollect the colour of the horses that were in her ladyship's carriage?"—"Yes—they were iron grey."

"And the harness?"—"Was plated."

"Very good. Now, can you describe the carriage?"—"Oh, yes; it was claret colour, fitted out with white, and the lining was crimson tabaret."

"Well, Sam, as far as I can recollect, for I had but a very transient glimpse myself of the equipage, your description is very correct. Now, I have no sort of doubt in my own mind but that the whole turn-out was hired from some coachmaker for the express purpose of carrying on this most complicated and ingenious fraud. We will get a Directory, and ascertain the names and addresses of all the coachmakers in London. Then we will hire a gig and a fast horse, and visit them all, one after the other, until we find the one who let out the carriage and horse we can describe."

"That'll do," cried Sammy, with a ray of hope lighting up his not over intellectual-looking features. "The coachmaker will surely know who hired the carriage of him, for I recollect once when I hired a chaise to take to Richmond Jemima Wilkinson, the hosier's daughter, opposite us, he would have my name and address."—"Exactly, Sam."

"We all fell down together on Barnes Common, and father had to pay six pound twelve for repairs to the chaise. Jemima was chucked on to a dunghill, and I ———"—"That will do, Sam; I can imagine all the particulars. Now for the Directory and the gig."

In the city of London both were procured with very little difficulty, and while Sammy told me the names and residences of the coachmakers, I drove, and off we set on our expedition to discover the claret-coloured carriage turned up with white, and the Honourable Lady Ann Somerset Fitzroy, who had walked off so successfully with so large a stock of plunder, and that plunder, too, of the most convertible and intrinsic value. I must confess I had very little hopes of regaining the plate, because I felt assured that such a well organized and admirably carried out scheme as that which had been put in practice to get possession of the plate must have emanated from persons who would not neglect any after precautions in duly securing their booty.

"That gold plate," I said to myself, "is no doubt by this time in a melting-pot. By to-morrow it will have assumed the shape of ingots of the precious metal, and will soon find its way among the Jew refiners and bullion merchants. Still the Honourable Lady Ann Somerset Fitzroy cannot melt herself up, and assume a different form, and at least she may be found and punished for her share in the transaction. Being a woman, too, she may be frightened, if caught, into a full confession of her accomplices, in which case there would be a chance of getting back the property, although in another shape.

London increases so rapidly, that it was not so large by many thousands of houses then as it is now; but still our search among the coach-makers was a long one, and not likely, unless we should happen to be singularly successful, to be terminated on that one day, and after some hours had been consumed unsuccessfully, Sammy began to groan, and look upon the affair as nearly hopeless altogether.

"Never despair," said I, as we turned into Long-acre. "Here is nearly a street full of coach-makers, and who knows what luck we may have."—"Nobody," groaned Sam. "I shall never hear the last of this affair, I know."

We called at the coachmakers in regular order down all one side of Long-acre, and then we proceeded up the other, when we at last found some clue to our inquiries, for upon asking at a respectable house if they had recently let a claret-coloured carriage with crimson tabaret lining, a man who was in the front warehouse replied,—

"Yes, sir, we have; but I can make more particular inquiry of the clerk."—"I shall be much obliged to you," said I, at the same time handing him my card. "The fact is, that the carriage, or at all events a carriage of the same description, has fallen into very bad hands indeed."

The man very civilly said he was very sorry, and proceeded to the counting-house. In a few minutes a young man having the appearance of a clerk made his gracious appearance—I say gracious, because he evidently thought it an act of great condescension to speak to us at all.

"What is all this about?" he cried. "What is your business, sir, eh? My time is valuable."—"Is it?" said I. "Nevertheless I must take up a small portion of it. I want to know if you have recently let for hire a claret-coloured carriage, with crimson tabaret lining?"

"I cannot say—I really don't know; I cannot be troubled with idle questions. Besides, what business is it of yours?"—"It is so much a business of mine, that after this very civil man, who might give an useful lesson to those who very probably in their conceit call themselves his superiors, has informed me that such a description of carriage has been let by you, if you will not from courtesy give me the information I require, I shall immediately go to the sitting magistrate at Bow-street, and detail to him particulars, which I am sure will induce him to send for you."

"Send for me?" said the clerk, turning pale and red by turns. "What—what do you mean, eh? How dare you speak so to me?—what have I done?"—"Nothing but refuse me information in the most uncourteous terms."

"If you recollect, Mr. Johnstone," said the man who had first answered me so civilly in the outer shop, "such a carriage was lent to a lady who you declared was a first-rate customer."—"Hold your tongue, sir!—I never made any declaration of the sort. If a carriage is let, it is entered in the books, along with the name and address of the party, and a reference."

"That is all I ask you just now," said I.—"Well, I—have—no—particular objection. You shall know, if you particularly wish it."

At this moment a respectable elderly man walked into the warehouse, and the civil workman immediately pointing to him, said,—

"This is Mr. Lee, our master, sir."—"Oh," said I, "I am very glad of it."

I found the coachmaker himself a very civil sort of man indeed. He very politely assured me he would give me any information he had in his power, and inviting me into a private room, he requested to know the causes of the inquiry. I briefly told him the story, and he then said,—

"Come with me, sir, to the counting house, and we will get all the particulars we can of the parties."

When we arrived there he said,—

"Now, Mr. Johnstone, who had that carriage?"—"Lady Ann Somerset Fitzroy, of No. 7, Curzon-street, May Fair; and the reference was Colonel Anderton, of No. 48, Manchester-square."

"You made the requisite inquiries?"—"I—I—no—I—didn't."

"Do you mean to tell me, Mr. Johnstone, that you let a carriage go without ascertaining if the parties were what they represented themselves?"—"I—I thought it was all right, sir. What's she been doing?"

"That is not the question. Mr. Johnstone, you and I must have some further conversation on this matter. For how long was the carriage taken?"—"Two days, sir, at two guineas a day, which were paid in advance."

"Then it ought to be returned."—"Yes, sir, it ought to have come in last night, but somehow it hasn't, you see, sir. Perhaps the lady wants it longer, you see, sir."

"The lady, indeed! Mr. Johnstone, this is a very loose way of doing business, and places great facilities, for a few pounds, in the hands of swindlers for carrying on their trade."

Johnstone looked rather posed at this remark of his master's, but before he could reply to it a man came into the counting-house, and, addressing the coachmaker, said,—

"If you please, sir, Lady Ann Somerset Fitzroy's footman wishes to speak to you."

Johnstone gave a groan, and the coachmaker, turning to the workman who had brought the message, said calmly, and as if nothing was the matter,—

"Tell him I shall be with him in a few moments."

When the man was gone, he turned to me, and added,—

"Now, sir, whatever plan you wish to adopt in this affair, you may depend upon my most hearty co-operation."—"I am very much obliged to you," replied I. "My plan will be to follow this footman, and ascertain accurately where he goes."

"Very good. Then I will hear his message, and then you can adopt your own course."

I went after the coachmaker sufficiently close to hear what passed, and the footman said,—

"My lady presents her compliments, sir, and says that the carriage will be returned this evening, as she has some calls to make to-day."—"Oh, certainly—that will do."

The footman touched his hat and walked away. Like young Norval, I marked the route he took, and pulling Samuel after me, got into the gig, and at a comfortable trot, followed him down Long-acre towards Soho. My gentleman went on quite in a free and easy style, as unconscious as a baby that he was followed, as Samuel remarked; but when we got to Newport-market he decidedly got the better of us, by walking up the row of butchers' stalls, where I could not take the gig.

"He'll get away," groaned Samuel.—"No, he won't," said I. "You drive round to the other end of the market, and I will follow him on foot. Can you drive, Sam?"

"I—I don't know much about it. You know I told you I drove once."—"Ah, and was upset. Be careful now."

I surrendered the rein to Samuel, and darted up the row of butchers' stalls after the footman. He went on without once looking behind him till he came to Frith-street, Soho. He paused opposite the area rails of a particular house, and I could then see that he glanced cautiously about him. My only resource was to ascend the steps of the first house I came to, and dispel his suspicions of me by knocking boldly at the door. His eyes were upon me, but the measure I had adopted appeared to satisfy him, and I had the consolation, just as the door at which I had knocked was opened to me, to see him open the area gate, and dive down as quick as possible.

"I beg your pardon," I said to the servant who opened the door to me; "I find, by the pattern of your floorcloth, that I have knocked at the wrong door." So I left her staring after me in amazement; while I passed the house the footman had entered, and found it was No. 117.

Here was important information gained, and I began to wonder where Samuel with the gig was. I walked towards Compton-street, and there I saw a crowd of people, in the centre of which was the gig. Sam had turned a corner sharply, and upset a stall crowded with fruit. Deprecating my own folly for bringing him with me, and very anxious now to get out of the neighbourhood, I rescued him on payment of one shilling for damage done, and jumping into the gig, said,—

"Now, Sam, we must go to Bow-street at once."

I drove along Compton-street fast, and when we came near to the far-famed region of the Seven Dials, my eye fell upon the face and figure of Johnstone, the coachmaker's clerk, hurrying on so rapidly, and with so much perturbation in his looks, that I was surprised, and all at once a suspicion darted across my mind that he might possibly have some guilty knowledge of the proceedings. He had not seen me, I was sure; and once again handing the whip and reins to Samuel, I jumped from the vehicle, resolved to follow Master Johnstone.

Swinging his arms, and every now and then wiping the

DIARY OF A PHYSICIAN.

perspiration from his face with a silk handkerchief, on he went till he came to Frith-street, down which he turned without a moment's pause. I increased my pace till I was within arm's length of him, and just as he slacked his pace upon nearing No. 117, I seized him by the back of his collar, and twisting him round till we were face to face, I said,—

"You are my prisoner; make any alarm, and the prosecution will show you no mercy."

I never in all my life shall forget the look of ghastly fright that was upon Johnstone's countenance. I really thought he would have died. His knees knocked against each other, his teeth chattered, and his lips became the colour of white ash.

"Come along with me," I said. "All is known, and you are safe to be transported. I pity you, but that is all I can say."

He let his feet double under him, and so I was compelled to allow him to drop on his knees, and in a half-choked, gasping tone of voice, he said,—

"Spare me! spare—have mercy upon me, and I will confess all!"—"Rise, directly," I cried. "If even you collect a crowd, you are irretrievably lost. It is just possible that if you make a full confession before a magistrate, the prosecutors may recommend you to mercy."

"I will—I will," he cried. "I will say anything—do anything—I will turn evidence, sir, against them all. They stole the plate, and I lent the carriage, you see, sir. I was to have fifty pounds—that's all; but they haven't paid me yet. The footman is my brother, and Lady Ann Somerset Fitzroy is Miss Smith. She was a super at the opera, sir. I will confess all."—"Come along—come along. To Bow-street you must come with me."

"Yes, yes. You will have mercy upon me, sir—you will, if

I confess all you wish. You see, sir, it is my dinner hour, and I thought I would go to Frith-street and warn them that there was danger, when you very properly laid hold of me. Oh, I see the error of my conduct now. I will reform, sir—indeed I will."—"You have room for improvement," said I. "But don't talk in this manner in the streets. You are attracting the eyes of every chance passenger."

"Yes, yes—thank you—I am much obliged."

But we need not pursue the ridiculous fears of Mr. Johnstone; sufficient to say, that he accompanied me to the police-office, and before the sitting magistrate made a full confession of the whole plot, stating that the plate was to be sold at once to a man named Andrews, who resided in Thames-street, and who would ship it off immediately for the Continent. The honourable lady who had acted so conspicuous a part in the affair had lodgings in Frith-street, where she was snugly living upon the produce of the plunder.

The magistrate remanded Johnstone, and sent with me two active officers to Thames-street. On the road I called upon Mr. Marsh, and had the satisfaction of finding that Samuel had returned home, as well as of giving the family some hopes of recovering their loss.

Mr. Marsh and Sam both went with us to Thames-street, so that we formed a formidable party of five persons, and finding the man Andrews at home, he was at once taken into custody. The most rigorous search was instituted in his premises, but no plate was to be found, and he declared his innocence of the whole affair. However, after some inquiries, it was ascertained that he had shipped some goods for Hamburgh, and that the vessel had dropped down the river. The assistance of the river police was at once procured from the Lord Mayor, and on board a rather suspicious-looking vessel was found, stowed in casks, the gold plate which had been so ingeniously procured from Mr. Marsh.

All this took up some time, during which I considered "her ladyship" would be perfectly safe at her lodgings; so, that when Mr. Marsh and I went back to Bow-street, in order to get a warrant for her apprehension, no difficulty was apprehended in taking her. An old practised officer was sent with us, and I own I had some curiosity to see how so really handsome and fascinating a woman would behave herself under the uncomfortable circumstances in which she was about to be placed.

"I wonder what has become of Sammy?" said Mr. Marsh, as we went in.—"I really don't know," said I; "he complained of slight indisposition while we were in the City, and I suppose he went home."

"No doubt—no doubt. Poor lad! he is unused to all these excitements. I dare say he will be ill after it."

We soon reached No. 117, Frith-street, and advancing in a body, we knocked at the door. It was opened by a decent-looking servant girl, who, in reply to the officer's request to see Miss Smith, said,—

"She is not at home; she went out a little time ago with a young gentleman, who seemed very much agitated."

"A young gentleman!" cried I. "Had he light hair and little grey eyes?"—"Yes, sir, and a blue coat."

"Gracious Heaven!" said Mr. Marsh; "it's Sammy!" and so it appeared, for although the most active search was made, no Miss Smith was to be found. The next day an advertisement appeared in a morning paper to the following effect:—

"To Mr. M., goldsmith. Sammy will return home if all is forgiven."

And Mr. Marsh put in the next day,—

"To Sammy. He is requested to return to his friends, and all will be arranged."

About twelve o'clock that day Samy slunk home. He said he could not bear to think such a sweet creature as Miss Smith should be transported, so he went and warned her of the impending danger, escorted her to a coach-office, and then hid himself and his miseries in a public-house till he heard from his father.

* * * * *

Johnstone hung himself in the new prison, Clerkenwell; Mr. Marsh got back his plate; and the only persons now who decidedly feel shy of the whole affair are Dr. Briggs and Sammy.

THE FOUNDLING;

OR, THE TWO WILLS.

I HAD a patient in Russell-square once, upon whom, his case being a very troublesome and complicated one, I used to call sometimes twice in a day, and even thrice during the twelve hours I have occasionally been to his house, in order to watch the effects of certain powerful and rarely administered medicines which I had prescribed for him.

I had not then come what my wife always called "the length of a carriage," so I used to rely upon my natural resources, i. e., my legs, to convey me to my troublesome patient; and not unfrequently, when the weather presented anything but a pleasant aspect, I was almost tempted to agree with my wife, who frequently uttered a hearty wish that that troublesome Mr. Green, my patient, would die at once, like a Christian, or get well.

But, however, Mr. Green would not be so civil, and fair day or foul day, I had to go to him, whether I liked it or not. The distance, too, was considerable, and sometimes I had to set my teeth against a north-east breeze, which was of that disagreeable, searching character that peculiarly belongs to such breezes.

It was on one of these occasions that I stayed unusually late at Mr. Green's, that is to say, it was somewhere between eleven and twelve o'clock, and had buttoned my coat up to my chin, and brought my hat as low down on my brows as possible, in order to face the north-easter, that would, in spite of all my precautions, creep down my neck, and up my coat sleeves, and round my ankles, according to the usual habit of such detestable winds, and I was at a rapid pace walking down Guildford-street, when I saw a hackney carriage slowly rumbling up from Gray's-inn-lane. It stopped at the corner of Lamb's Conduit-street, and there got from it a man and a woman, the latter of whom was carrying something that was either a child, or a bundle strongly resembling one in shape. They discharged the coach, and then stood together for some minutes, apparently engaged in earnest conversation. The streets were exceedingly thin of passengers—in fact, they were nearly about that neighbourhood quite deserted, so that my footsteps made quite a remarkable sound upon the pavement. My way lay past the couple who had got from the coach, and I heard, as I came near, the man say to the woman,—

"Hush, Cottle—hush!—somebody's coming."

They were silent as I passed them, and I could not help repeating to myself, "What an odd name—Cottle." I strolled up Lamb's Conduit-street very slowly, and after I had gone some distance something tempted me to look round, when I saw that the man and woman had crossed the road, and were standing by the gate of the Foundling Hospital. In another moment, then, they made off with such rapid steps that I was quite amazed, and watched them till they turned into the street which leads to Mecklenburgh-square, before it all of a sudden occurred to me what they had been about, and then I exclaimed,—

"As I live, they have been leaving a child at the hospital gate!"

A few moments sufficed to bring me to the spot, and there, sure enough, on the very threshold of the entrance, was a child apparently of about two years old, lying, tied neck and heels, and staring about it with a coolness and determination which under any other circumstances would have looked perfectly ludicrous.

Then I ran towards the square, but I could see no traces of the fugitives, and to pursue them without a knowledge of which direction they had turned was madness, so I slowly retraced my steps to the Foundling, picking up as I went a white handkerchief, which I was quite confident must have been dropped by the parties, for I had not seen it before, and it was a sufficiently conspicuous object; besides, no one else had passed, I was sure.

I heard, however, somebody coming down Guildford-street, the way I had first come myself after leaving Mr. Green's, and I waited till he should reach the gate of the Foundling before I took any steps as to the child. When the chance passenger did come, he turned out to be an elderly gentleman, with a stout walking-stick and a pair of blue spectacles.

"Stop, sir," said I; "here is a child which has been left here by some one."—"Keep off—keep off!" cried the old gentleman; "don't speak to me. Police!—keep off!"

"Why, what are you afraid of?" said I. "I only want you to be a witness with me that a child is deserted here."—"Keep off!" cried the old gentleman again. "You placed it there yourself—you know you did. You want to pick my pocket. Police—police!"

So saying, the old gentleman ran across the road, and kept up such a pace that he was out of sight in a few moments. I could not help laughing at his needless alarm, but I could not desert the child, and, as the most natural thing I could do, I rang the bell at the Foundling Hospital gate. I then waited for about five minutes, when hearing no symptoms of any one appearing to answer me, I rang again, and a third time I had to ring before the door was opened about a quarter of an inch, and a man's voice said,—

"What the deuce is the matter?"—"Is this the Foundling Hospital?" said I.

"Yes, to be sure."—"Very good. Then here is a foundling."

"A what?"—"A foundling. Open the door, will you."

"Curse your impudence," said the man, and opening the door, he exhibited himself to me in the undress of a kind of mongrel beadle, with a light in his hand. "Now what do you mean by knocking at this door and ringing at this bell at this time of night?"—"I have told you what I mean," said I. "This is the Foundling Hospital, and here is a foundling. Take it in. Don't you see it, stupid?"

The porter really looked staggered at what I presume he considered the extent of my impudence, and he glanced from me to the child, and from the child to me, for some moments without speaking; indeed, it is doubtful when he would have recovered sufficiently his amazement to say anything, had not I added,—

"My name is Dr. ——. I was coming past here, and saw this child left at the door. Don't stand staring there, but take it in."—"Lor," he said, "when was you born? This here may be the *Fondling* Hospital, but we has no more to do with *fondlings* nor you have. Why, you might as well expect to get into the *evenin'* service in the chapel here without paying yer *tanner*, as poke a fondling into us. I think I sees it."

"Do you mean," said I, "deliberately to tell me that you call this place the Foundling Hospital, when it is not, in fact, any such thing? I am aware perfectly that you are in the habit of charging sixpence or a shilling for admission to your chapel, and I am likewise aware that people pay it because it is considered the only theatrical performance open in London on a Sunday evening, but I have yet to learn that the very name of this place is fraudulent."

"I tell you what it is," said the man; "we is and we ain't the *Fondling* Hospital. Put that in your pipe and smoke it. Look at the board outside, and you'll see as we only takes in fondlings on the personal application of the mother on 'em."

"But how can such be foundlings?" said I.—"What's that to you? Mind yer own business, and don't be putting yer spoke into other people's *veels*."

Here he showed so strong a disposition to shut the door, that notwithstanding the reproach of putting my spoke in other peoples' wheels, I put my foot in the door-way, saying,—

"Nonsense, my friend, nonsense. This is the Foundling Hospital, and here is a foundling. How can a child with an ascertained and produceable mother be a foundling? Why, if you continue to call this place what it is not, you will some day have some legacy left to you as a foundling hospital disputed on account of such a false allegation."

"You be blowed," said the man; and as I did not wish to have my foot pinched off in defence of things by their right names, I was compelled to allow him to close the door and leave me with the child in the open street. What was I to do? Desert the child I could not. Every sentiment of compassion and sympathy prevented me from doing so, and yet I knew not what on earth I could do for it. I was in this perplexity, when a watchman came up, and to him I at once appealed, explaining the facts of the case, and concluding by saying,—

"What is to be done? The Foundling Hospital is not the Foundling Hospital, it appears, and here is a poor child deserted by those who probably should have been its natural protectors."—"By gosh, then," said the watchman, who was an Irishman, "all I can say is, sir, that I'll take it to the *workus*. It's a hard case that a great big building here calls itself the Foundling, *decaving* all the world, and then isn't the Foundling at all at all. By gosh, sir, I shouldn't at all wonder if rich people's bastards don't a mighty deal oftener get in here than poor little devils of foundlings, sir."

He then took up the child very carefully, and I gave him my name and address, after which, bidding him a good night, I went homewards, rather amazed by my adventure, and wondering who the poor little creature could be who was thus cruelly deserted to the tender mercies of a "public charity."

* * * * *

When I reached home I recounted my adventures to my wife, and produced the handkerchief which I believed to have been dropped by one of the parties who had so inhumanly left the child in the open streets. Upon examination, the initials "S. C." were found written with indelible ink at one corner, and I at once concluded that the handkerchief must have belonged to the female who was addressed by the man as "Cottle," when I first saw them near to Lamb's Conduit-street. With that meagre piece of information, however, all inquiry seemed stopped, and whatever field for conjecture might be opened, there was nothing to be got in the shape of positive information.

During the following morning I was waited on by one of the parish authorities, who made a minute of my account of the transaction, and said as he left me,—

"We have our burthens, sir, as a parish, much increased by that Foundling Hospital being situated within our boundaries. Children are deserted there by ignorant people, and as the Foundling won't take them, we are compelled to do so."

—"So I should suppose," said I. "But I tell you what, I have thought of a plan which it will only cost five shillings to try, and which I think really worth the trial."

"What is it, sir?"—"It has for its object to find out the parties who deserted the child."

"That's just what the parish would like."—"Well, we have, most likely unknown to those parties, the name of one of them—'Cottle.' I should propose that an advertisement be inserted in the newspapers, saying that if a lady of the name of S. Cottle will call upon so and so, she will hear of something to her advantage. The bait may take."

"It might, sir, and I shall suggest it to our vestry clerk, who is a very clever solicitor. It's a shame to throw children upon a parish, when the parties apparently have ample means themselves."

"How do you know about the means?"—"Why, sir, the clothing of the child was of the richest description."

"Indeed!"—"Yes, sir. Our matron says that every article was of the most exquisite quality that could be procured."

"That, then, is a feature of the case," said I, "which to my mind makes it full of a new suspicion. The child may belong to persons from whom it has been taken by this man and woman, and may now be mourned for with the greatest grief."—"Indeed it's very likely, sir."

"If such is the case, the chances of discovering the full particulars of the affair increase very much, for no one having an interest in the child will quietly put up with its loss. I shall be happy of course to co-operate in any way with the parish in bringing the truth, as regards this affair, to light."

My visitor, who was a very gentlemanly man, thanked me and walked away, leaving me more perplexed than ever as to the real circumstances which had caused the child to be deserted. There was a coarseness and vulgarity about the woman of whom I had caught so transient a gleam at the corner of Lamb's Conduit-street, which precluded the idea now that she could be the mother of a child so well apparelled, and apparently at one time so carefully tended, and my opinion of the transaction began to change its character, and I believed that the child had been abducted from its parents for some particular purpose, and that the man and woman I had seen were only agents in the transaction.

I had considerable hopes from the advertisement I advised to be inserted. In the first place, I was quite sure that some interested motive in the shape of money, had or expected, was most likely to be the stimulating cause of the man and woman risking the bringing so much trouble on their heads as might arise from the part they had taken with regard to the child. In the second place, assuming such to be the fact, the woman Cottle was not likely to look with indifference upon an advertisement which should talk of any advantages, and as for connecting it in any way with the loss of her handkerchief, such a thing was very remotely probable indeed. Therefore it was with some curiosity that the next day I watched the morning papers for the advertisement; and at length found it, to the following effect:—

"Next of Kin.—The solicitors to a large property are desirous of finding a lady, by name Cottle, and if such a one will apply to Messrs. French, Lee, and Scrubbins, No. 2, Bream's-buildings, Chancery-lane, she will hear of something greatly to her advantage."

"Very good," thought I. "Now we shall see what result is obtained from this. If it don't produce *the* Cottle, she is an uncommonly prudent woman indeed."

I fully expected all the next day to be called upon by some one connected with the parish, in order to identify Mrs. Cottle, for I had no doubt she would be taken into custody upon presenting herself at the attornies' in Bream's-buildings, and I was not disappointed. Indeed, as the sequel will show, I was terrified at my own success in the matter of the suggestion.

The day on which the advertisement appeared passed away comfortably enough, but never shall I forget the horrible morrow that succeeded it. I was taking my breakfast, and just quietly decapitating the end of an egg, when my servant announced a visiter.

"Very well," said I. "Say I shall be five minutes."—"Say ten, John," cried my wife; "I have no patience with people; they are always getting ill at all sorts of unseasonable hours. Really it's enough to aggravate a saint."

"Yes, ma'am," said John, and away he went to tell my visiter to kick his heels for ten minutes.

Now the front parlour, which was my visitors' room, was only divided from the back parlour, which was our breakfast-room, by a very thin partition indeed, so that if any one in either front or back raised his or her voice much, what he or she happened to say might be heard in the other room, whatever that might happen to be. John, I suppose, delivered his message quietly enough, but in a moment we heard a loud voice say,—

"Ten minutes!—why—why, the house will be pulled down in ten minutes!"—"Gracious goodness!" said my wife; "they are going to pull the house down, doctor, in ten minutes!"

"Hush—hush!" said I; "that must be a madman."— "Ten minutes!" repeated the visitor, still more loudly. "Give the respects of Messrs. French, Lee, and Scrubbins to him, and tell him they expect to be tossed in a blanket."

"Merciful Providence!" said my wife.—"And Dr. —— will be tossed in another," continued the man. "If he don't come to us, we must send about three hundred infuriated women to him, we must."

"Where's my smelling salts?" said my wife, faintly. "Oh! doctor, I think I see you going up and down in a blanket with three hundred infuriated females."—"I cannot wait anything like ten minutes, tell him," added the man. "I am French, Lee, and Scrubbins' managing clerk, but I can't manage a mob of mad women—d—n it! I'm nearly mad myself. I've had my very waistcoat pulled off, and I wonder, d—n me, I wonder they stopped short at my shirt and boots."

There was something so extremely ludicrous in the passion of the managing clerk that I could not forbear laughing, which my wife considered very extraordinary conduct on my part, fully believing as she did that the man in the next room was a dangerous lunatic, for she could trace at the moment no connexion between his words and the affair of the child and the Foundling Hospital.

"My dear," said I, "do not be surprised at my laughing. I see we have fallen into a fatal mistake,—that is to say, the parish and myself,—in advertising for a person of the name of Cottle so vaguely as to produce a public meeting of all the Cottles far and near. As it was my suggestion, I suppose I must go and pacify them."—"Pacify them!—Why, doctor, you know you sometimes talk of the difficulty of pacifying one woman, and how then are you to pacify three hundred?"

"Please, sir," said John, re-appearing in the breakfast room, "the gentleman says, sir, as he's lost his waistcoat already, sir, and can't wait. He comes, sir, from three hundred furious females, sir."—"Very well, John—very well. That will do."

I at once went to the front parlour, where I faced a little man with a bald head, in such a heat and state of general excitement, that he flung himself into the most extraordinary attitudes imaginable, and could scarcely articulate from anger and fright.

"Well, sir, what's the matter?" said I.—"Everything the matter," he cried. "That cursed advertisement, sir, is the matter. An immense mob of female Cottles, sir, have put in their appearance, they are now besieging the office in Bream's-buildings. Can you lend me an old hat, for one of them took mine away in the scuffle? They vow vengeance, sir, and say it's a regular do, sir. It's a Cottle insurrection. Bream's-buildings is impenetrable, and Chancery-lane blocked up."

"Dear me."—"D——n it, sir, you take it cool; but if, like me, you had to force your way through a mob of infuriated women, you would be frantic, sir. Look at me, and judge for yourself."

He turned round as he spoke, and then I saw that his coat was split up to the collar, and other depredations inflicted upon him. Suppressing as well as I could my inclination to laugh, I said,—

"Well, I really don't know what is to be done. They will go away again, I presume, when they are tired?"—"Why don't you send for a constable?" said my wife, who having heard the name of Cottle, became aware of the nature of the proceedings, and entered the front parlour.

"A constable, madam? Did you say a constable? A regiment of constables, you mean. I should like to see a constable make his appearance. They'd constable him, I'll be bound. Will you come, doctor, and identify, if you can, your Cottle?"—"It's very kind of you," said I, "to call the woman my Cottle; but out of such a number of females, I feel the utter impossibility of making any invidious distinctions. As for going, I cannot see any utility in that. Since you confess a brigade of constables would be of little service, it is not likely one physician would be of much use."

"And you won't come?"—"No."

"D—n it!—what's to be done? Here's a horrid fix. By this time I expect French, Lee, and Scrubbins are pumped upon."

"Don't you think," suggested my wife, "a fire-engine would make them go home quietly?"—"No, I don't, ma'am; I don't think a thousand hot pokers would move them. Very good, sir—you won't come. Good morning, sir—good morning. I'll go home and get into bed, that's what I'll do. Good morning, madam."

Notwithstanding I had announced to Messrs. French, Lee, and Scrubbins's managing clerk, that I could not attempt to appease the three hundred infuriated women, I had a great curiosity to know how affairs got on in Bream's-buildings, and I accordingly left home, determined, like young Norval, to hover on the outskirts of the enemy, and gather what information I could, without making myself known.

With this intent, I took a route which brought me to the back of Bream's-buildings, up some narrow wretched courts, and there I certainly saw enough to acquit the excited managing clerk of any great exaggeration as to the tumult that was raging on the spot. I dare say I could have forced my way through Bream's-buildings, but it would have been unquestionably a matter of difficulty. Such a collection of women I never saw before, and when I made my appearance, they were collected in great force round the steps of the door, from which some one was addressing them. Who the individual was I had no means of knowing, but he spoke as follows:—

"Ladies,—when I see before me such an assemblage of youth, beauty, and fashion (murmurs of approbation and a great sensation, as they say in the French Chambers); yes, ladies, beauty, youth, and fashion, I long to be among you, but imperative duties compel me to stand in this elevated position, and only look down upon you, as one might look on a sweet garden full of nature's fairest flowers, without being able to pluck one, and press it to his bosom. (Immense applause.)

"Ladies,—some wretch, some monster, some two-legged rhinoceros, or laughing hyena, put the advertisement in the newspaper, which has induced you in all your beauty and exquisite sensibility, to come here to-day. We know nothing of it, I assure you, dear ladies. At this present moment a bill is being drawn up, offering a reward of one thousand pounds to whoever can give such information as will enable us to prosecute the heartless perpetrator of a fraud which has collected together in Bream's-buildings some of the loveliest of womankind, and, for a brief space, lighted up Chancery-lane by the dazzling refulgence of beauty. (Great cheering, and cries of 'Bless you.') Therefore, ladies, under these circumstances, do not give the miscreant the triumph of seeing you here any longer, but go home, carrying with you the heart of your most devoted servant, who now addresses you. God bless you all, ladies; and may your beauty be the cheering light of many a happy home, though I fear much bloodshed will ensue among men, on your account, for who can help loving you all? Ladies, once more affectionately farewell!"

The orator bowed, and with murmurs of applause, and ejaculations of "Well, I never!" "Was there ever such a nice man?" "Oh, what a dear creature!" &c., the ladies departed, and in a quarter of an hour the alarmed locality was restored to its wonted serenity.

I never was more amused in my life than by this speech, which was so admirably adapted to its hearers that I had an involuntary respect for the talents of the man who uttered it from that moment. The coast then being clear, I ventured to proceed to the chambers of the attornies, and was at once introduced to the three partners, who were laughing ready to kill themselves in their private room. One of these, Mr. Lee, I found was the orator, and to him I said,—

"Mr. Lee, you are quite thrown away in your present position of life. I never heard a more admirable speech, or one more calculated to carry out the object for which it was spoken."

He laughed as he replied,—

"It was a great error of judgment in us to allow such an advertisement to be addressed here. It was sure to produce confusion in consequence of being placed in so vague, and, at the same time, so tempting a form."—"It appears to me," said I, "that it might have been better worded, and, moreover, personal applications should have been strictly prohibited."

"Certainly, doctor. However, one thing is pretty certain, and that is, that this proceeding will, doubtless, have the effect of putting the guilty party upon her guard."—"I fear so, indeed."

"Hilloa!" suddenly cried one of the partners, who was rapidly opening letters that had come by that morning's post, "what do you think of this?"

We were immediately all attention, and he read as follows:

"To Messrs. French, Lee, and Scrubbins.—Gentlemen,—An advertisement having appeared in a morning paper, to the effect that property was left to a female, of the name of Cottle, or that the said female might or could be placed in a position to prove herself heir-at law to property, you are requested to insert another advertisement containing more explicit information, in which case, a lady named Cottle, who, in the present very inconclusive state of the proceedings, declines troubling herself, might be induced to come forward.

"I have the honour to be, Gentlemen, with great respect,
"THE LADY'S ATTORNEY."

We looked at each other, after this letter was read, without saying anything for a few moments, and then Mr. Lee remarked,—

"That's devilish clever. No doubt this is the party we want. But she is either a very clever woman herself, or very well advised. We can just make nothing of this."—"I fear not," said one of the other partners. "But we can turn it over in our minds, and something may occur."

"Do you think," said I, "that letter was written by an attorney?"—"Yes, certainly, I do," replied Lee. "I do not mean to say, of course, that it is so, positively, but it bears evidences of such a fact. I think we may conclude that this affair is over."

"Well," said I, "it can't be helped. I regret, gentlemen, that my suggestion to the parish has been the cause of giving you so much trouble."—"Oh, that's nothing," laughed Mr. Lee. "It's over now. I am only sorry that no practical result should have followed this transaction."

* * * * *

I felt very much disappointed on the subject of the deserted child; but my ordinary avocations were sufficient to weaken any other impressions, for a physician who thinks at all has an anxious time of it, and is sure to feel deeply the responsibility of his actions; therefore, in about a week I had nearly forgotten the affair—in fact, I had made no memorandum at all about it in my diary, when a circumstance occurred that brought the whole subject on the tapis again, and afforded a most remarkable clue to parties really concerned.

A card, one morning, was handed to me, on which was the name "Mr. George E. Harrington," and the address, "Embleton Villa, Kentish Town." Underneath the name was written—"Will be much obliged by Dr. —— calling at his earliest convenience."

This was a common enough method of sending for a physician when the case was not an urgent one, and I placed the card in my pocket, with the intention of making Embleton Villa one of my morning calls. I had never heard of Mr. Harrington before; but I made no doubt, upon calling, I should have the name of some patient of mine mentioned to me who had been so kind as to say some recommendatory words of me.

It was about twelve o'clock that I reached Kentish Town, and, upon inquiry, I found that Embleton Villa was a handsome residence, situate on the high-road to Highgate, and quite through Kentish Town. When I reached it I was much struck with the noble character of the building, and could perceive in a moment that both wealth and taste must preside over its arrangements.

I rang at a gate, and soon a footman appeared, to whom I gave both my own card and the one which had been left at my house, upon which he said, respectfully,—

"Will you walk in, sir? My master has been expecting you. This way, sir, if you please."

He conducted me up a flight of stone steps, into a noble hall, and then into a waiting-room, got up with great taste and splendour, where he left me in order to take my name to his master.

The room would have sufficed to engage my attention for hours, because it was full of works of art. Rare pictures of great merit graced the walls, and statuary, too, lent the solemn magic of its presence to enhance the beauty of that apartment. There were flowers, too, in magnificent vases, which scattered their grateful odour through the atmosphere, making the place feel and look perfectly magical in its character.

"Well," I thought, "Mr. Harrington is somebody; and if this room be a specimen of his house, I should scarcely ever wish to go out of it."

Something like a sigh of envy, I am afraid, came from my bosom then, as I thought of how I had struggled against adverse fortune, and how I was then still struggling, although rising;—and then I thought of a saying of my wife's, which she had adopted from a tale she had read somewhere, which was intended to convey the moral that everybody had his share of discontent; and that had we but an opportunity of diving beneath the glittering surface of many things, which were dazzling and refulgent in their beauty, we should find a something beneath that would be a set-off against everything else, in the shape of a secret consciousness, which took beauty from the sunshine, sweetness from the music, and, like the false fruit of the lotus, altered and embittered every taste.

The tale to which I allude contains the allegorical sentence of "There is a skeleton in every house," meaning, of course, that everywhere there is some cause of discontent, so I could not help saying to myself, as I often do, when I see a great deal of apparent happiness and glitter,—

"Alas! I wonder where this person keeps his skeleton!"

Somehow, the words recurred to me very painfully at Embleton Villa, and I was rather in a contemplative and philosophical mood, when the footman returned, and said,—

"Sir, my master will be glad to see you."

I accordingly followed him; and every step I took through that superb mansion filled me with wonder, on account of the magnificence that met my eyes continually. At length I was introduced to a room which was very much darkened, and at the entrance the footman said,

"Doctor ——, if you please, sir."—"Come in," said a voice—"come in."

I entered the room, and in a moment or two, as my eyes got accustomed to the subdued light that was in the apartment, I saw, seated by a table, an old man, upon whose face there sat that irascible expression which old age and its contingent disagreeables produce upon many people who have had ill-regulated minds in early life.

"Good morning, sir," said I.—"Good morning, though I believe it is going to rain," he said. "Be seated, sir—will you take any refreshment?"

"None, I thank you, Mr. Harrington; I hope there is nothing particular the matter with you?"—"I don't know; General Eusham recommended you to me. God knows what is the matter, sir. Did you ever know grief affect the brain much?"

"Sometimes, sir."—"Only sometimes. Well, well. Did you ever know ——." Here he stopped short, and was silent for some moments, during which I said,—

"Do not distress yourself, Mr. Harrington. I pray that you will look upon me as a friend, as well as a physician, and anything you think it necessary to say to me may be as sacredly deposited in my breast as your own."

"Very well, very well," he said, in a low tone. "Did you ever know remorse, yes, remorse, that's the word, produce madness?"—"I have; and give me leave to say, I have sometimes met with cases where imagination has got up a fancied remorse all about nothing."

"Ah! you would comfort me with those words."—"They are true ones, sir."

"Well, well, be it so. When I spoke of remorse, understand me, it is not for anything that I may have done; but for things which I am sorry I left unsaid and undone. I have been placed, sir, in circumstances in which I should have been, besides more considerate, more inquiring, less easily led by interested and wicked persons, and, oh, God! what misery has been the result! I am going mad—mad!"

—"If you can accuse yourself, sir," said I, "of no sins but those of omission, or those which have arisen from errors of judgment, I think you may congratulate yourself, and such a word as remorse can surely have no sort of connection with you."

He made no reply, but leaned his head upon his hand for a few moments, during which I could perceive that he trembled from top to toe. Then suddenly he looked up, and in a strange, wild, and yet griefful manner, he said,—

"Hush—hush! Now you will hear—now you will hear. Well, Dorinda—well; you have come again to your poor, heart-broken father, with that sad, reproachful look, and your long unbound tresses floating sadly and strangely on your breast. My child, my daughter Dorinda, why do you look so on me? God help me, is there no mercy above? You see my tears; let them plead for me to my beautiful child. Mercy—mercy! Oh, God, send some accusing angel in another shape than that. Mercy—mercy—mercy!"

He fixed his eyes on vacancy, and held out his arms, as if to keep something off him; and then, bursting into tears, he laid his head upon his hands, saying,—

"Gone again—gone again! But still that old sad, reproachful look, that turns my heart to stone. Oh, God—oh, God—oh, God!"

I cannot convey to my readers the manner in which these words were uttered, although what I have here set down is the conceit and substance of them. Even I, accustomed as I was to see human nature in all its saddest, strangest aspects, was terrified at the manner of Mr. Harrington, as he looked past me, and so addressed himself to vacancy, which it was evident his disturbed brain had filled with some form which to him was one of bitterness and anguish. I thought it better to let him recover a little before I made any remark, and I sat profoundly still for about five minutes, after which he looked up, and in a saddened tone he said,—

"There—there; 'tis only once a-day. 'Tis over now. I am myself again."—"You are better, Mr. Harrington."—"Till to-morrow."

"What do you mean by till to-morrow?"—"Because to-morrow *she* will come again."

"Indeed! and who is she?"—"My daughter, Dorinda Harrington."

"And do you really suppose that you see her apparition, Mr. Harrington? I presume she is dead?"—"Yes, God bless her, she is dead; and for some purpose, which it is still in the hands of Heaven to carry out, she comes to me once in each day; as you have seen, she says nothing; but, oh! she bends upon me such sad, reproachful looks, that no words could bring to my heart so much dreadful agony."

"I beg your pardon for interrupting you," said I, "but I must say I have *seen* no such thing."

"Are you, too, deluding me, by affecting not to see that form which to my eye is so very palpable?"—"You may depend, Mr. Harrington, nobody is deluding when they say they do not see the figure which presents itself alone to your diseased imagination."

He shook his head, and I continued,—

"Your case, sir, although not a very common one, is far from being without its parallel in medical history; a diseased state of the brain, acting upon the optic nerves, will produce the effect you describe."—"But there is cause for the appearance," he argued. "A belief in apparitions has been prevalent in all ages; and, as Dr. Johnson truly remarked, many people deny it with their tongues, only to confess it with their fears."

"Which, after all," said I, "is a pompous sentence, meaning just nothing, like many other of Dr. Johnson's sayings; because people's fears arise from their superstitions, and are, of course, averse to the dictates of reason, and ———"

"Sir—sir!" he cried, suddenly, with a slight tinge of passion, "I have had all that said to me before, and I don't want it repeated. Am I going mad? That is the question. Is the fact of getting a peep beyond the confines of this world a premonitory symptom of insanity? That is the question, sir, I ask you."—"Certainly it is, then, sir."

"I thought as much. And what can be done?"—"The first thing will be to get rid of the delusion concerning the peep beyond the confines of the world."

"You will still persist in calling it a delusion?"—"Certainly."

"Very well, sir. Humph! I fear we shall not do any good. There is your fee, sir. I am much obliged to you for your call, and have the honour to bid you good morning."

I rather regretted at this moment, that I had not, for his own benefit ultimately, humoured Mr. Harrington, but he had, in the last few remarks he had made, assumed so dictatorial a tone, that, in spite of myself, I had answered him accordingly. Now he rang the bell, the pull of which was close to him, and when the footman appeared, which he did with remarkable celerity, he said,—

"Francis, tell Mrs. Cottle to lay a luncheon for this gentleman directly."—"Yes, sir."

"Cottle—Cottle," said I. "Did you say Cottle, sir?"—"Yes, I did, sir. What then?"

"Oh, nothing—nothing. Cottle—humph—Cottle."—"D—n it, sir," said Mr. Harrington, "are you mad, that you can say nothing but Cottle—Cottle—humph! Cottle?"

"No, sir," said I, rapidly forming a determination that I would stir heaven and earth to see Mrs. Cottle, and obtain a still further footing in the family of Mr. Harrington. "No, sir; the fact is, that I was at the moment engaged in deep thought upon your case, and I am now inclined to think that I have decided hastily."—"You do?"

"I do. There may be collateral circumstances connected with the matter, that may very materially influence my decision. Are you willing, Mr. Harrington, to make sufficient confidence with me as to explain the reasons you have for any feeling of remorse or dissatisfaction with yourself?"

He hesitated a moment, and then said,—

"General Eusham, who recommended you to me, spoke very highly of you, and I had an intention of telling you all."—"A determination," said I, "which I hope you will carry out, sir."

"Well, well. I think I will; but not to-day—not to day. I am free from my supernatural visitant for to-day, and I do not wish to recall images of an unpleasant nature, while I can promise myself a few hours of sweet serenity, compared with my feelings when I know not but each moment my eyes may be terrified with the sight I have in your presence seen."—"The luncheon is ready, sir," said the footman, throwing the door wide open.

"Let me see you to-morrow morning, at the same hour, or as near it as you can," said Mr. Harrington.—"I will be punctual," said I.

We shook hands, and I followed the footman from the apartment to another, where a very elegant luncheon was laid for me. I was rather hungry after my walk to Kentish Town, and I sat down with a tolerable appetite, while Francis stationed himself behind my chair, to serve me in any manner I might dictate. He brought me some delicious Bucellas from the sideboard, and I enjoyed my luncheon amazingly. I was nearly done, when the door opened, and a female, attired most sumptuously, although in mourning, sallied into the room.

I had been casting about in my mind how I could say something to Francis about Mrs. Cottle, but this sudden appearance put an abrupt stop to my reflections. The moment I looked at the woman, a strong impression came across me that it was the same person I had seen near the Foundling Hospital. There was the same great swaggering walk and bulky appearance. I could not take my eyes off her, and she said,—

"Is there anything else, sir, you would like to take?"—"No," said I. "How do you do, Mrs. a———?"

"Cottle," whispered the footman.—"Cottle," said I.

"Tolerable, thank you," she replied. "How do you find Mr. Harrington? Perhaps I should inform you he is my cousin four times removed."—"If he don't get better, madam," said I, "he will be removed once more; but I should be happy to have some conversation with you concerning him."

Mrs. Cottle hesitated a moment as I propounded my request to have some private conversation with her, concerning Mr. Harrington, and then she said,—

"Very well, sir, I'm sure I shall be very happy. Francis, you may leave."

Francis took himself off, and I fancied that Mrs. Cottle looked just a little more nervous than was necessary, as I, in compliment to her assumed cousinship to Mr. Harrington, handed her to a seat.

"Madam," said I, "I fear Mr. Harrington is not in a very satisfactory state either of mind or body. Do you know anything of those delusions about which he talks? I allude to his fancy that some apparition appears to him every day."

Mrs. Cottle shifted gradually her seat till she got her back to the light—a very suspicious sign that she was anxious to avoid too close a scrutiny of her countenance as she spoke to me, and then she replied,—

"Sir, I know, I suppose, just as much as you do on the subject; Mr. Harrington certainly has such a fancy as you mention, and, of course, I very much lament it."—"Exactly, madam. However, you must be aware that in cases where the mind is affected, we must be cautious what we say to the patient, and draw our chief inferences regarding the case from information we are able to receive from intelligent parties."

To this she made no reply, so I proceeded by saying,—

"Hence, madam, I am anxious to know if in your mind you can assign any exciting cause for this peculiar fancy on the part of your unhappy relative?"—"No—nothing very particular," replied Mrs. Cottle. "He accuses himself, I think very wrongly, of having behaved with some harshness to his daughter."

"Now dead?"—"Yes, dead; some time since."

"May I ask how long?"—"Two years about."

"Indeed, and yet a young person. What did she die of, Mrs. Cottle?"—"She died in child-birth."

"Oh! indeed; and the child?"—"He is dead too; he died about ten weeks ago, and is buried in St. George's, Hanover-square, as the registry will show. Everything was correct and legal."

"No doubt, madam—no doubt. Physicians may ask what questions they please, you know, as long as there is an object in their curiosity. May I therefore ask, if Mr. Harrington's daughter's husband is living?"—"Miss Dorinda Harrington had no husband, sir, since you must know."

"Oh! who was her reputed husband? where is he—dead or alive, eh? What did the child die of, Mrs. Cottle? You have dropped your pocket-handkerchief, madam; allow me."

I stooped to pick up her handkerchief, which she certainly dropped in the confusion induced by my asking so many questions at once. As I took it up, I looked at a mark that met my eye: there were the letters S. C. exactly fashioned as those were on the handkerchief I had picked up by the Foundling Hospital.

"Thank you, sir," she said.

Here was proof positive as to the identity of *the* Cottle; but still the whole affair was involved in very great mystery, and without answering any more queries, Mrs. Cottle rose, and making a very elaborate curtsey, said,—

"Good morning, sir," and left the room.

I felt assured that I had contracted her dislike, and that it would be in vain to expect any more information from her, so I left the house directly, and went home, resolving to weigh the circumstances in my mind with what deliberation I could, and endeavour to lay down some rules of action which could contain a promise of effects and results of a satisfactory nature. I detailed what had happened to my wife, and the advice she gave me coincided with my own notions of what should be first done.

"You ought to go to General Eusham," she said, "and very likely from him you will learn some particulars, which may materially assist in the inquiry."—"So I was thinking," said I. "The difficulty, however, appears to me, as to how far I am justified in letting the general know my suspicions of Mrs. Cottle."

"Why, you can tell the truth."—"Yes, but the truth even is not justifiable at all times, and the more especially at those times when it admits of two or three different constructions."

"Really, doctor, I don't see where you are to find your two or three different constructions."—"Why, in the first place, it is just possible, notwithstanding the strong presumptive evidence in favour of the supposition, that Mrs. Cottle may not be the person who left the child at the Foundling."

"Oh, fiddle-de-dee!"—"Very good; and then, again, I do not see why I should make myself an amateur discoverer of the mothers of stray children of any parish. It may be her own child, after all, my dear."

"Well, and if it is, ain't she a hussy, I should like to know?"—"Very true; but——"

"And ain't she an abandoned woman, and deserving of any punishment for deserting her own child, if it is her own child?"—"Very true; but——"

"And if it ain't her own child, doctor, ain't she as bad, or worse, I should like to know?"—"Very true; but——"

"Nonsense, doctor; when once you begin to refine upon doubts, and probabilities, and possibilities, you never know where to end; so just tell General Eusham everything, and hear what he has got to say about it."

Finding my wife so positive in her opinion, I did what all prudent husbands do, that is, dropped the argument, and all the while determined to do as I thought proper myself notwithstanding. I was in no humour that day to call on General Eusham, but resolved upon seeing him early in the morning, and long before it should be necessary to bend my steps towards the Highgate-road, in order to pay my arranged visit to Mr. Harrington.

Accordingly, about nine o'clock, a very unfashionable hour for a visit, but one which I knew would not put General Eusham out of the way, beheld me at his door. I sent in my card, and was in a few moments in the presence of the general, who greeted me with all the hearty frankness which characterises the soldier and the gentleman.

"General, as you have come to me for advice sometimes, now I have come to return the compliment, with one trifling omission."

"And what may that be?" he said.—"Why, I don't intend to give you any fee."

"Very good—then as the advice will be gratis, you must not grumble afterwards at the quality of it. What's the matter, a duel, or what?"—"You recommended me to Mr. Harrington."—"Colonel Harrington, you mean."

"Is he a colonel?"—"Ah, to be sure, and one of the most distinguished officers in the Anglo-Indian army; that is, he was, but he is now out of commission, and won't call himself colonel, for some eccentric whim or another."

"Of which he has a stock."—"He has, indeed, doctor. I sent you to him because you are a reasonable sort of man, and don't think much of physic or physicians."

"Thank you, general. Now, I have come to you, to ask you what you know of Colonel Harrington's history, for his mind, owing to some circumstances, appears to be very much affected indeed."—"He did not tell you, then—he said he would."

"He has promised to do so to-day; but I shall be much better prepared by hearing from another person first the main points of the story."—"Very good. Then what I know you are welcome to. He married—adored his wife, and lost her when his first child, a daughter, whom he named Dorinda, was about three or four years old. This daughter he placed at school, and then, overwhelmed with grief at the loss of his wife, he exchanged with a regiment that was about starting for India, and there he remained fourteen years, when he came back dying with impatience to see his daughter, who certainly then was the most beautiful girl I ever beheld.

"Well, sir, he was, of course, charmed and delighted with her. His affection for her amounted to an infatuation, and after remaining with her six months, he sent her back to her school, not as a scholar, but as a mere boarder and respected inmate of the house, resolving to proceed once again to India, wind up all his affairs, turn all his property into cash, sell out of the army, and come back again as soon as possible, to devote the remainder of his life to his darling child.—Well, doctor, he went, but he soon found how fallacious were human arrangements."

"Indeed, general."—"Yes. While he was away, a young fellow, by the name of Mortimer, saw his daughter, and I suppose, as a matter of course, she saw him. A mutual attachment ensued; letters, assignations, and all sorts of devilments, ending in an elopement,"

"And were they married?"—"I believe not. The colonel was written to by the school people, and he was desperate, as you may well imagine. He came home boiling with rage, and found out his daughter somehow; but she was dying. The particulars of their interview I never knew, for his feelings would never permit him to tell me. The end of it, however, was, that he took her infant child after her death home to the house you have been to, along with a Mrs. Cottle, who had been kind to his daughter, it appears, for Mortimer had deserted his poor victim."

"And that, then, is the portly lady whom I saw?"—"Yes, that is Mrs. Cottle."

"And the child?"—"Dead, dead!"

"You are quite sure?"—"Sure! Ah, to be sure I am. Seeing's believing in such cases as death, at all events."

"Oh! you saw it die?"—"No; but I saw it dead."— "Oh! very good."

"Upon my word, for a doctor, you are singularly hard of belief about any one being dead; I suppose, unless you had attended them, you can't believe in the death of any one. Eh, doctor?"—"Oh, yes, I can; thank you for the compliment all the same, general. Did you get all these particulars from Harrington?"

"Most of them."

"And the remainder?"—"From Mrs. Cottle, a very nice woman, and one who, were it not that she is rather too strait-laced in her notions, and will not allow any excuse for human frailty, would be a very respectable person indeed. She is dreadfully bitter against Mortimer."

"Has nothing been heard of him?"—"Nothing at all. He deserted his unhappy victim in a very short time after he had decoyed her from home. I understand the colonel, when he came back from India the second time, could not believe his daughter was in so much danger, and vented some very bitter reproaches against her, for which he has always blamed himself ever since."

"Well, general, it is a very unhappy story, and it has had a very unhappy effect upon Colonel Harrington, for now, from long brooding over it, he fancies that once a day the apparition of his daughter appears to him, casting on him reproachful looks, and nearly driving him to positive frenzy."

"So he has told me; and I have told you all I know on the subject. What do you think of his condition?"—"Not altogether hopeless, and yet sufficiently grave to be alarming. Has he any other relative?"—"Not one."

"Has he made his will?"—"He has; it is in my possession, as he has appointed me his principal executor. It is an odd will, because it was made during the lifetime of his daughter's child, and he had left him the whole of his property, amounting, I think, to somewhere about two hundred thousand pounds, with the exception of an annuity of two hundred a year to Mrs. Cottle. He would not destroy that will, but he came here one day, and added to the bottom these words:— 'Since my dear daughter's child is no more, I revoke that part of my will which leaves all of my property, with the exception of an annuity, to him, and desire that my executors expend the same in the foundation and endowment of an hospital, which shall be free to all applicants, the only terms of admission required being distress and sickness combined.'"

"An excellent bequest," said I. "I am greatly indebted to you, general, for the kind manner in which you have answered my, I fear, impertinent inquiries."

"Not at all—not at all; I only hope you may be able to do Colonel Harrington some good. By-the-by, don't call him colonel, or he will be frantic."—"I will be cautious. Good morning, general—good morning."

I have heard people remark, when they had to talk of things hidden and complicated, "Oh! you may depend there are wheels within wheels;" and I could not help thinking, that in this affair of Colonel Harrington and Mrs. Cottle, the wheels within the wheels were increasing greatly, so that it would be very troublesome to see which way they were working in a little while. However, by putting that and this together, as people say, I came to the conclusion, that if there were a mystery somewhere, I knew very little about it.

The time was drawing rapidly near when I ought to call upon Mr. Harrington, and I bent my steps there with such a fund of conjecture in my imagination, concerning him and his affairs, that by the time I reached Kentish Town I was well-nigh bewildered. As before, I found myself for a short time in the splendid reception room, and then was conducted by Francis to his master, who, I thought, received me with more cordiality than before, which I was pleased at; but I soon found that he was a very singular character, and that what he said was by no means to be taken as a strong indication of what he felt. He suddenly came out with—

"You need not have troubled yourself, doctor, to ask any questions of Mrs. Cottle."

I started rather at this, because it was scandalous on her part to have told him, considering his situation, and then I made answer,—

"Mr. Harrington, any questions I asked of Mrs. Cottle were dictated by a desire to do the best I could as a physician and a friend for you; and you will permit me to add, that I cannot much admire the taste of that lady, in telling you that I asked her any question at all. We were alone, and she could have no possible good motive in informing you of what took place."

"Oh, I cannot hear anything against Mrs. Cottle."—"Indeed, sir."

"No; she is a friend of mine, and has done me great service, by properly informing me of matters concerning my honour. I should never but for her, have known one half the extent of my domestic misfortunes."—"Then, sir, I don't envy her her position as your informer. 'He who is robbed, not knowing what is stolen ——'"

"Oh! pho! pho! she told me all for the best. I only throw out the hint to you, sir. Don't ask questions of anybody but of me. I will tell you all it is necessary for you to know."—"Perhaps, sir," said I, for I was a little irritated, "you are scarcely in a position to judge accurately what is necessary for me to know, and what is unnecessary."

"What's o'clock?" he said suddenly. "Hush! hush! Oh, God! she is coming—she is coming!"

He pointed directly past my head, and then at once assuming the same wild, agonised tone in which he had the day before addressed the supposed phantom, he again apostrophised it in feeling language.

"My child—my Dorinda!" he cried. "Peace, peace—oh, God! cannot you permit my children to sleep in peace? Let the grave part us yet awhile—why do you bend such looks on me? Your eyes reproach me with a bloody act! It was one of justice. Peace, peace, perturbed spirit of my child! Save me—save me!"

Again, with trembling and exhaustion he sunk his head upon his hands, and then tears, as before, came to his relief, and that proud, haughty man wept like a child. During this scene I blamed myself for being at all offended at anything he could do or say to me, and resolved to keep a strict guard on my tongue and temper, and to consider anything offensive as rather the result of disease than a matter to be resented as between man and man. As before, I waited until he had partially recovered, and then I said,—

"Mr. Harrington, I would advise you not, on such occasions as these, to be ever at home. You had better be abroad riding, or with agreeable company."—"Then it would wait for me," he groaned. "Yes, it would wait for me, till I was at home, and perhaps alone."

"You could try."—"I have tried often—often. Thank God, it is over for to-day."

"What was the vision like?"—"Like my child."

"But I mean, was it distinct or imperfect?"—"Sometimes it seems like a shadowy mist, which slowly shapes itself into her likeness—sometimes I can see the whole form, at others only the face."

"Did it ever speak to you?"—"Never—never! I think the voice would kill me."

"Do you recollect what you said yourself, Mr. Harrington?"—"No—no."

"Then I will tell you. You hinted at some deed of violence, which you had been compelled to commit."—"I am a soldier, sir."

"So I have heard, but you will excuse me if I say that what you mentioned could have no reference to any act done in your mere military capacity. Mr. Harrington, believe me, I feel sincerely for you. You may yet have many years to live,—years which I hope and trust will not be embittered to you as your life now is; all that human aid can do for you, shall be done. All I ask of you is to trust me. Tell me all, without reservation, that preys upon your mind, or tell me nothing, and bid me begone, when I will depart, leaving you my best wishes and my sincerest sympathy."

The earnestness of my words seemed to move him, and he remained silent for some few minutes, after which, in a low tone of voice, which betrayed some emotion, he said,—

"Lock the door."

I did as he desired, and then resumed my seat."

"You wish to know all?" he said.—"I do."

"Then I am a murderer."

I started.

"Yes, a murderer; but having said so much, I owe it now to myself to say much more. You shall hear my story, and from it you may yourself judge if I am not more sinned against than sinning."

I shall detail the narrative of Colonel Harrington as nearly as I possibly can in his own words. He commenced as follows:—

"Since I have made up my mind to tell you all without reservation, and since I have given myself a name which will carry with it, perhaps, more odium than I deserve, I owe it now to myself to be fully explicit.

"When I entered the army I was a young man; and not long had I been in the profession, when I saw, loved, and married the daughter of a brother officer. She was—but no matter, she is gone. She left me with one child, an infant daughter. You may judge of the nature of my own feelings when I tell you that death seemed the only release from my affliction that I could think of. I forgot that time would accomplish much for me, and I hastily exchanged into a regiment going to India, the only place where any active service was going on. I hoped to be killed, for my child was too young to have obtained any great hold of my affections; besides, it was sickly, and every one agreed that it could not possibly live.

"Well, sir, circumstances turned out in every particular different from what I anticipated. I was in many engagements during a protracted war in India, in which, with my peculiar feelings, I behaved with a recklessness that was set down to my credit as the height of courage. I was never so much as touched by a sword or shot. I seemed to have a charmed life, and I rapidly rose in the service. Thus time had begun its healing work: my grief abated, and when I had advices from England to the effect that my child was alive and likely now to live, I began to shrink from death myself as much as I had before courted it.

"It was very strange, but then I began to get hurt in almost every petty engagement I was in; not a little affair of outposts even could happen near me without my receiving some injury, although I never had a wound of a very serious character.

"Years thus passed away, and every ship from England brought me more and more favourable intelligence regarding my daughter, until at length I longed to see her; and although I had not cast eyes upon her since she was an infant, I felt

the greatest tenderness for her, and wrote to her at every opportunity. She was about sixteen years of age when the close of the war in India permitted me to proceed homewards, which I did with reputation and extensive means. I cannot describe to you my feelings when I met my child. Her beauty and gentleness, her affection, far exceeded my utmost hopes, and I was as happy as the occasional remembrance of the past would allow me to be.

"Oh, if people did but know, even in their greatest griefs, in what a blessed state they were, provided remorse did not mingle with their tears, they would soon recover from any of the inevitable evils of existence, and resignation would take the place of sighs and tears.

"Well, sir, I resolved, for my daughter's sake, upon forsaking the dangerous and precarious profession which I had once courted for its very dangers; but to do so and realise my property, it was absolutely necessary that I should go to India again. With great regret I left my child to take so long a voyage; but I left her with confidence to those in whose kind care she had been so many years, and who, you may be sure, I did not forget to reward for their trouble.

"I arrived in India; but when there, numerous delays oc-

curred, which prevented me from leaving so soon as I wished. In fact, I was delayed eight or ten months before I could make all the necessary arrangements, and feel myself free from duties and engagements in the east.—During that time I received letters from England; one from the persons in whose care I had left my daughter, informing me that she had suddenly and secretly left them; and another from Mrs. Cottle, who resided with me, stating that she had heard my daughter had eloped with a young man named Mortimer; that he had not married her, but after living with her some short time, had deserted her, actually expressing his intention of coming to India and asking me what I would pay for the honour of my child—that is to say, what large sum I meant to give to induce him, now he had effected her ruin, to marry her.

"Of course such a communication maddened me, and I delayed my departure on purpose to meet the scoundrel, if he should arrive. Mrs. Cottle likewise informed me in her letter that she had found my daughter, and given her, notwithstanding her means were limited, an asylum in her house. I sent her a thousand pounds, and then waited anxiously at Bombay for the arrival of the scoundrel Mortimer, who, I was told, had such unparalleled audacity. You may imagine the state of my feelings during that time. I was nearly mad. The former grief which had so much oppressed me was nothing to what I now suffered. I passed some days of absolute agony. A vessel was expected from England daily, but it was delayed. He whom I expected came, however. I heard afterwards that he had made his way overland with extraordinary quickness.

"One evening I was seated in my private room, when a servant came to me to say a traveller wished to see me from England.

"'Admit him,' was my brief rejoinder.

"In a few minutes a young man was ushered into my presence; he saluted me respectfully, and I said,—

"'I have not the honour of your acquaintance, sir.'—'I have come far, Colonel Harrington,' he said, 'with the hope of having the honour of your acquaintance.'

"'From where?'—'From England.'

"'Oh, indeed; and your name, my good sir?'—'Is Henry Mortimer.'

"'You came to speak to me, then, about my daughter?'—'I do sir.'

"'Then take your answer at once.'

"I drew a pistol from the drawer of a table at which I sat, and shot him through the head. His brains flew in all directions, and when my servants, alarmed by the report, entered the room, I said,—

"'Remove that thief; he has robbed me, and I, in self-defence, have shot him.'"

"Good God! colonel," said I, "and what was the result of this?"—"Such affairs are easily arranged in India," he replied; "the next day I sailed for England."

Mr Harrington's narrative had certainly now assumed, to my mind, a fearful interest. The murder he had committed was terrible, indeed, and I no longer wondered that, with such painful circumstances brooding upon his mind, he peopled vacancy with phantom forms. After a slight pause he continued,—

"During the voyage I was in a state of mind which beggars all description. I would speak to no one, but shut myself up in the cabin I had secured for myself, never once making my appearance on deck during the whole of the long, tiresome voyage. At length we reached England, and I departed to London. I sought out the house of Mrs. Cottle—my daughter was there, but she was dying. I would not believe that such was the case, but heaped invectives and reproaches on her head. She did not speak, but, pointing to her child, expired."

Mr. Harrington was silent, and I could see by the working of his countenance, that he was deeply moved.

"The child is no more?" said I.—"No more!" he repeated—"she is dead—dead!"

"And you are quite sure your daughter was not married to Mortimer?"—"Do you want to drive me mad?"—"No, no, but ——"

"Peace, peace; do not breathe to me such a supposition. I tell you such was not the case, else why my vengeance upon him? What shadow of a pretext even could I have for one harsh word to my poor Dorinda? Do not put such a hellish thought into my brain. Mrs. Cottle knows they were not married; she has assured me of it; and yet somehow my heart yearned towards my daughter's child. I loved it—yes, while it lived, I had still something to love, but now, alas! all is lost—all is lost—and I am desolate!"

I knew not what to say in the way of consolation to Colonel Harrington, but I told him I had no doubt he would feel eased in his mind, from having communicated freely to some one what had been so long secretly preying upon his imagination.

"Besides," I added, "we may think of some means yet of alleviating some of your symptoms. Did you see the child die?"—"No; it expired suddenly in the night."

"Indeed! Is Mrs. Cottle married?'—"No, she is a widow"

"And has no male acquaintance?"—"I really don't know. Why do you inquire so particularly?"

"For nothing in particular; I was thinking company might amuse you."

He shook his head despondingly, and sighed, as he said,

"I shall soon be in my grave. If I find peace there, it will be what I have sought for in vain in life"

"Have better hopes, Mr. Harrington, have better hopes. What kind of child was your daughter's?"—"A fair-haired little fellow, with blue eyes."

"A handsome child?"—"Very—very. Alas! I thought that in his happiness I might find some relief for the evils that oppressed me."

"And I hope you may," thought I, "yet, for every circumstance continues to induce in my mind a belief that Mrs. Cottle knows more about the whole affair than she would like to own, and that the child is still living."

I didn't feel disposed, or even justified, in the present stage of proceedings, to be more explicit to Colonel Harrington; but I had heard quite enough to convince me of the propriety of speaking to General Eusham more fully than I had done on my first visit. I left the house of Mr. Harrington as quickly as possible, and, hurrying over my morning calls, I took my way towards General Eusham's, and was fortunate enough to find him at home. In a short time I related to him all that had occurred concerning the affair of the foundling, and ending with the last revelation of the colonel to me that morning at his house. The general was amazed, and when I had done, he exclaimed, loudly,—

"Why, doctor, that child is Colonel Harrington's daughter's as sure as I am my mother's."—"I think so, too," said I, "but there may yet be difficulty in proving it, for I could not undertake to swear to Mrs. Cottle, you see."

"But, d—n it, doctor, what need have you to swear to her?"—"Ample, I think, general; the very identity of that child may be disputed."

"Indeed!"—"Yes, recollect its age. A child so young must be like a good number of other children; and, besides in the state of mind of Colonel Harrington, there is no knowing what whim or fancy he might take as a result of his amazing confidence in Mrs. Cottle. If the child were suddenly produced, he might repudiate it altogether, and declare it was not his daughter's, don't you see?"—"The deuce take it, so he might."

"It's very likely he would take such a cue from Mrs. Cottle, who would, of course, assert so much in a moment. It appears to me, that what must be done is, to adopt some means of proving her guilty of leaving a child destitute in the streets, and then, her character and influence being wholly gone, we can give Harrington an idea that he has been imposed upon by a sham death."—"But he saw the body, doctor."

"Very likely; how easy might the dead body of a child be got; I have had a half-a-dozen in my house at one time, that I gave two pounds a-piece for."

"You cursed brute, what did you do with them?"—"Cut them up to be sure."

"Ah, horrid! Well, well, I am of your opinion, though, so act as you think proper, and depend upon my own co operation in any way you point out."—"I am not, then, at this moment prepared to suggest a particular line of conduct. You see there is but a little weak circumstantial evidence against Mrs. Cottle, from which she would easily escape; besides, we should, by any premature step, put her upon her guard, which I am almost afraid has been done already. I would suggest, however, so certain am I that the child is the one in question, our going to the parish authorites and offering to take it away."

"Very good, I am willing. What shall we do with it?"—"Send it to some respectable parties to nurse, somewhere. I wonder if it can talk at all. How old should you say it was?"

"Oh, it cannot be two years, and I don't think it can talk at all. It is not a strong, forward child."—"Well, we will go and see it, if you please."—"Agreed."

General Eusham ordered his carriage, and we both proceeded to the workhouse where the child was. Upon explaining that we came to see a child that had become chargeable to the parish, we were at once ushered into a room, where in a few moments the beadle came to us to know the particulars of our application.

"We have come," said I, "about a child who was found some time ago near the Foundling."

"Oh, the Fondlin! wery good," said the beadle; "a—a—ahem! Are you the parents and guardians?"—"Not exactly."

"Ahem! not exactly—that's ewasive. Don't perwaricate, sir. Is you come to relieve the parish, or isn't you?"—"Come, come, no nonsense," said I; "this is General Eusham, and I am a doctor; we came to see the child. Possibly we may relieve the parish by taking it away; but we can say nothing till we see it first."

"Is you a real general?" said the beadle.—"Yes, I believe so," said General Eusham.

"No gammon—no militia?"—"No."

"You aint the city marshall?"—"No."

"Nor a lumber trooper?"—"D—n it, no. What do you mean?"

"Werry good. Give us y'r hand. You're a general and I'm a beadle; the millentary and civil authorities should always be on good terms altogether—How is you? All well at home?"—"Curse your impudence!" said General Eusham.

"Don't be obstropulous now, will you? You came to see a kid as was dropped by the Fondlin—wery good; you're a general, I'm a beadle—come on."

So saying the beadle marshalled us the way we were to go, and I succeeded in soothing the ruffled general, who was rather in a rage at the beadle's confounded impudent familiarity, as he called it. We followed our guide into a long room, on each side of which were beds, in some of which were no fewer than four or five young children. The general had not advanced many paces into the room when he paused, and exclaimed,—

"By God, it's he."—"Where?" said I.

"Here," said the beadle; "yes, it's me, I'm the beadle."—"Get out of the way," said the general, giving the beadle a push that sent him reeling some yards; and then stooping over a bed, on which a child was sitting, with great gravity in his looks, he said,—

"Well, well, who is it?"—"Tommy," said the child.

"It's he, it's he. Come along, you rascal; the sight of you will do good to somebody. What do you like best?"—"Futtyrumble," said the child.

"There's proof positive," cried the general. "Harrington taught him to say that word, which means a kind of drink he used to like in India, and which he made in this country, and used to give the child spoonfuls of."—"Tommy Futtyrumble, Tommy Futtyrumble," said the child again.

"Go it, you rascal," cried the general, "I'd swear to you now."—"D-a-m," said the child.

"There again," said General Eusham, "you hear he's swearing; that's his way of saying d—n. That's all he can say; he's got to the end of his vocabulary now; haven't you, you young villain?"—D-a-m—Futtyrumble—Tommy—Futtyrumble—d-a-m—Tommy—Tommy—Tommy—d-a-m."

"Well," said I, "it's a precocious youth, certainly."—"There never ves his ekal," said the beadle. "The wery fust thing as he says to me in the mornin is a blessed oath, and it's the last thing at night; he's been a swearing all the blessed while as he has been here."

"Oh, he's a warmint," said a woman, coming in at that moment, and just hearing the beadle, she no doubt fancying we were mere casual visiters. "That child will come to no good—a little depraved wretch."—"What," cried I, "a child of two years old depraved? Oh, for shame, woman; you ought to be ashamed of yourself."

"Ought I, sir? I'd have you to know that I'm a religious woman, sir, and a pious woman."—"Oh, then," cried the general, "that accounts for everything; I don't wonder now at your saying a child of two years old is depraved."

"Lor!" said the beadle, and if he had been a Catholic beadle he would have crossed himself.—The religious woman's face got the colour of beet-root, and she was about to make some insolent pious rejoinder, when a gentlemanly looking man walked into the ward and said, in a voice of authority,—

"What is all this?"—"Nothing particular," said the general. "There is my card; I recognise in this child the son of a dear friend; I propose taking it away with me."

"And there is my card," said I, "as further security."—"Gentlemen," said the new comer, "your names are amply sufficient guarantee for me allowing the child to go with you. If we had been aware this little fellow had so good a connection, we might have troubled you with him before."

"I understand you," said the general, "but he is none of mine."—"Oh, of course not, of course not."

"I wish he was."—"Precisely, sir, precisely."

The man laughed so provokingly that the general gave up the point, which he saw it was of no use contending, and holding the child in his arms, who kept saying "d-a-m," until it got clear of the workhouse gates, he stepped into his carriage to the surprise of his footman, who I saw wink at the coachman, who in his turn winked at John; and then the beadle, who had followed us to the gate, winked at them both, and they both winked at the beadle; so that, on the whole, I was convinced that General Eusham had the credit of being the father of the precocious Tommy whom he was taking such care of, and whose d-a-m sounded very like proof positive, since the general himself had out with two or three such little expletives during his visit to the workhouse.

General Eusham soon recovered his good humour, and laughed heartily when we reached his house with Tommy, at the honour the beadle and the other workhouse authorities had done him in fathering the child upon him.

"I ought, doctor," he said, "to have expected such a result, as a matter of course; but it is of no sort of consequence in comparison with a consideration of what we have to do as regards this child."

"Precisely," said I; "now, you are a military man, and used to all sorts of tactics—what do you suggest?"—"Let us first carefully review the state of affairs, doctor. The circumstances, if I mistake not, just amount to this and no more. Colonel Harrington, while his grandson was in life, leaves him, by will, the whole of his immense property, with the exception of an annuity to Mrs. Cottle, which in amount was very far from satisfying that lady's cupidity; she leads the child from its home, and deserts it in the public streets, and then succeeds in inducing such an alteration in the colonel's will, as shall possess her of all the property, the colonel being under an impression of the child's death. Now, the child may be restored to Harrington, but, as you say, how is he to be convinced of Cottle's guilt?'

"That is a grave question, certainly," said I. "There is no knowing by how many precautions against discovery she has fenced herself round. I am likewise convinced that Harrington's mind is rapidly wearing out his body, and that he cannot last very long. Now, certainly the affair might be left as it is, and at the death of the colonel the identity of the child might be proved, in which case the will, as it originally stood, would, no doubt, be allowed; but then Cottle would get her annuity."—"Which she shall not if I can help it. Harrington must be induced to make another will, leaving her out altogether, and you must, doctor, think of some means of convincing him of her guilt."

"Before," said I, "we proceed any further, let us be careful to ascertain, beyond doubt, if the child be illegitimate or not; and that can only be done by a diligent search for the marriage register, if such there be, of the mother and father. I have a strong impression myself, from all the circumstances, that the colonel has been awfully misled, and that his unfortunate daughter was really married to the young man, whose life he so heedlessly took."

"I always, doctor, have argued with him about the impossibility of such a girl as Dorinda leaving her home under the circumstances he supposed. A thought has entered my head. Suppose we make a desperate effort by seizing any male visitor of Mrs. Cottle's, and, assuming his guilt in the affair, try to wring the truth from him by threats. Should you again know the man who you saw with her at the Foundling?"—"Indeed I should not, and could not swear to her. But it appears to me that the will, or rather the addition at the end of it, which gives the property to Mrs. Cottle on the supposed death of the child, cannot be quite satisfactory to her; and the probability is, that she may induce Colonel Harrington to make another testamentary document, in which no mention at all may be made of the child; so that were it produced afterwards by any accident, and identified, a contingency which she surely must have an eye to, it would be penniless."

"The deuce! So she may; I will see to that. Harrington will tell me if he has done such a thing, or if she has importuned him to do so."—"Very good. You ascertain that fact one way or the other, and I will set somebody to work, looking for the marriage certificate of the colonel's daughter. When these two matters are ascertained, we can adopt some course contingent on them."

"Which course," added General Eusham, "I should recommend to be the seizing of any male visitor of Mrs. Cottle's, and frightening the truth out of him."

"But what, suppose he should be the wrong person, general?"—"Why, then, he will excuse the deed, on account of its object, which we can explain to him."

"That all will depend upon what sort of person he may happen to be; but still I am not prepared to suggest anything better, so I am forced to give into your notion with all its disadvantages. You will, of course, be aware that we subject ourselves to an action for false imprisonment for every one we take prisoner, besides failing in our object?"

"Never mind that; I will stand all pecuniary consequences. You find out if Dorinda Harrington was married or not, will you, as a first step?"—"I will; and I am only surprised that Colonel Harrington himself never made the necessary inquiries."

"I am not, doctor. The fact is, he has always had a disagreeable suspicion that such might turn out to be the fact; and after the violent course of conduct he has pursued, on a contrary supposition, it would be a dreadful thing to him to find out that he was wrong; so he won't place himself in the way of so doing, but affects thoroughly to satisfy himself with Mrs Cottle's assurance that it was not so."

"I see, I see. Well, well; he is to be both blamed and pitied, poor man; and, come what may of all these circumstances, he must suffer great uneasiness, and many compunctious visitings. It is a happiness for him that he is really so near his end; for it is quite out of the question that he should ever enjoy peace of mind in this world."

With an understanding, then, that we should meet on the morrow, to compare notes, General Eusham and I separated; both of us much pleased that we had succeeded in rescuing poor little Tommy from his rather uncomfortable quarters at the workhouse. I instantly employed an active young man to discover if such a thing was in existence as the marriage register of the colonel's daughter, and I waited for his report with considerable anxiety, for, had the child proved to be illegitimate, some very clear will in his favour would have been desirable, to the entire exclusion of Mrs. Cottle, who, of all people in the world, certainly the least deserved any consideration at the hands of Colonel Harrington.

Late in the evening my scout came to my house, and laid before me a certificate of the marriage of Henry Mortimer, gentleman, with Dorinda Harrington, spinster, which had been celebrated at Hackney Church. It was no more than I expected; and yet, when I saw it, it gave me a strange sensation to think that so much mischief, and one murder, should have ensued from the hasty temper of Colonel Harrington, who, had he but given himself time and patience to ascertain truths, instead of jumping recklessly at conclusions, and allowing himself to be misled by interested persons, would, instead of being the miserable wretch he was, have enjoyed as large a share of happiness as probably this world have afforded to any one.

Now, however, there was no hope for him; for the past was of a nature that could not be recalled. The dead could not again be brought to life, and the peace of the grave was all that poor Colonel Harrington, after making what reparation was in his power, had to look forward to. I immediately started for General Eusham's, and produced to him the important document, proving the legitimacy of Tommy, with which he was not a little pleased, and after some expressions of pleasure he added,—

"I have seen Harrington, and he assures me he has executed no other will than that which is now in my possession, and which, as he imagines, will place all he is worth into the hands of Mrs. Cottle. Of course, I said nothing to awaken in his mind any suspicions of what we are about, but I ascertained from him that she had been several times to him to induce his execution of a new will altogether, in which the name of his grandson should have no place, thus showing her fear that some day there might be a possibility of litigation under the present will."

"So far, then, so good, general. Upon consideration, I am willing to agree to your scheme of causing the apprehension of any male acquaintance of Mrs. Cottle's we can lay hold of. The question that remains to be considered is, how such a feat is to be accomplished."

"Why, in the first place," said the general, "I will accept an invitation, which has been often given me by Colonel Harrington, to remain some time at his house, to bring a bed there; and not only shall I be able to watch Mrs. Cottle, but I shall be on the spot to ascertain what visitors she may have, and, in case of any immediate necessity for action, I can send for you."—"Very good; but it is of no use your sending for me at any time but evening, as I am so constantly out otherwise."

After then having the honour of an interview with Tommy, who treated me to several "D—a—ms," I left General Eusham with an idea that the affair was at all events now in something like a satisfactorily progressing state, and that Tommy would eventually without doubt have justice done to him.

It was my duty to call again upon Mr. Harrington, and I took care not to neglect so doing; but when I had made my other visits I hastened to Kentish Town, and found him as usual sitting alone, wretched and melancholy, brooding over those matters which I felt convinced so deep and serious a contemplation of must very soon hurry him to his grave, or deprive him of his reason. He glanced at me on my entrance for a moment, as if to convince himself I was a being of flesh and blood, and not some supernatural visitant come to make his solitude terrible to him.

"Oh! doctor," he said, as he drew a long breath, "how do you do to-day? I began to think you were not coming."

"I am rather late," I replied, "in paying a professional visit; but you are so far from town, that I am compelled to go to every one of my other patients first. Do you find any improvement?"

"Can you minister to a mind diseased?"—"That can be done sometimes," said I; "and you may depend upon it, that the worst seeming circumstances always, upon careful examination, admit of some alleviation."

"There are some circumstances that will not bear thought," he added. "Such are mine. Do not talk to me. You can offer me no remedy for my heart-sickness. What I want now is for you to tell me, candidly, if the apparition that haunts me be real, or a mere fabrication of the imagination."

"Certainly the latter, Mr. Harrington; and permit me to say that I am gratified to find you sufficiently rational on the subject to admit of the doubt, for the last time I intimated so much you were angry with me for so doing."

"Heed not my anger," he said; "it is that of one who knows not what he says. I think I am all the better for a long kind letter which my old friend Eusham has sent me, in which he promises to cheer my solitude for awhile with his presence here."

"I am glad to hear it; cheerful and friendly society will do more for you than any drugs could possibly. I am, although a physician, candid enough to warn you against medicine. Now, sir, tell me, have you been, since I last saw you, visited by the apparition?"—"Yes, yes."

"Is it not strange, think you, that you do not likewise see the shade of your grandson?"—"Hush! hush! doctor. It is strange, and sometimes I am almost inclined to believe he cannot be dead on that account."

"How is your daughter dressed when she appears to you?" —"In white, as I last saw her—in white. Say no more. Things of another world, I feel assured, haunt this house; and who knows what legions of unearthly creatures may be listening to us now? I fancy, now and then, that I feel conscious of being in the presence of a crowd of people long since dead, although I cannot see them. There is a strange creeping of the blood, a mysterious shuddering feeling, comes over me at times, which makes me think I am, on such occasions, surrounded by the shades of those long since numbered with the dead."

"Indeed, Mr. Harrington, those feelings, I should explain, are from much more natural causes."

"No, no; it is as I say: I feel the truth of what I assert; there is a peculiarity in the air which occasionally rushes past me in strange sighing currents on such occasions. Even now I can fancy an active attentive group of beings, who have passed through life to immortality, listening to our words, and finding an interest as they crowd about us, close to our very faces, and in the nearness with which we approximate to truth in our conjectures, or in the wide distance from it that we are carried by our prejudices and our acquired notions from the things of this world."

There was a strange earnestness in Mr. Harrington's manner, that was irresistibly interesting and almost involuntarily I glanced around me, as if I expected to see some slight indication of the presence of those mysterious creatures of another world, with which his excited imagination peopled space.

"There, there," he cried, as he observed my movement, "you feel as I do; and if you turn your eyes very suddenly to any other direction from that in which they may have been fixed, ten to one but you catch a transient glance of some restless spirit, who has merely allowed himself to be cognisant to mortal eyes. Have you never noticed such a circumstance, as you turned suddenly—a something will seem to flit past your gaze on the moment, which you certainly have seen, but not long enough to appreciate or understand its form or shape?"

"I cannot deny," said I, "that I have at times been myself possessed of feelings similar to those you mention, but I should be sorry indeed to append your translation to them."

"Well, well, as you please—as you please. I have some hopes of a little peace from the presence of my old friend Eusham; for I began to think myself deserted by every one, excepting Mrs. Cottle; and she, I must say, does pay me attention, and do all she can to relieve me from my distresses of memory."

"Don't you think, Mr. Harrington, that it would have been better for your happiness had you not been so readily and particularly informed by Mrs. Cottle of what had taken place in England with regard to your daughter?"—"No, sir," he said, suddenly, while his countenance became distorted by sudden passion. "No, sir; I will not bear such suggestions from mortal man. They are at times whispered into my ears by fiends whom I cannot fly from, and to utter reproaches to whom would be in vain; but I will not bear them from mortal lips."

"Very well, Mr. Harrington. I am silent, but must still observe——"

"Peace, sir,—peace. Good morning to you."—"Good morning, sir."

I saw that, in his present state of mind, no steps could be

taken to prepare him for the denouement which General Eusham and myself had to bring about, so I at once left the room, hoping that, as he himself anticipated, the presence of his old friend would restore him to some degree of calmness and peace.

I had no idea of having any conversation with Mrs. Cottle; but I suppose she had began to get a little alarmed and fidgetty about what I had said to her on my last visit, and she, in quite an assumed, accidental manner, waylaid me on the staircase as I was descending to the hall.

"Oh, sir," she said, "I was not aware you were in the house; will you take any refreshment before you leave?"—"Thank you," said I; "I will, if you please."

"Be so kind, sir, as to step this way."—"Very good," thought I; "Mrs. Cottle," as I followed her into a handsome dining-room; "all's fish that comes to net in the way of information, and, if you are getting at all frightened, it is exceedingly likely that you will commit yourself in one way or another."

After ascertaining what wine was most agreeable to me, she placed some before me, with a civility quite in remarkable contrast to her former impertinent manner of behaving towards me.

"I am very much obliged to you, madam," said I; "for the distance out here is certainly great from my house."

"You are very welcome. Mr. Harrington's sad state of health, I am sorry to say, sir, prevents him from thinking of proper hospitalities. Do you find any change for the better?"—"No—no!"

"He still, then, keeps up the delusion of seeing the apparition of his daughter Dorinda?"—"He does, indeed, and he sticks to it with a pertinacity that is certainly remarkable to a degree. It is almost enough to make any one believe there was really some truth in it"

"Truth in seeing a ghost, sir—why—why, you don't mean to say that — that you believe in any such nonsense?"—"Certainly not, Mrs. Cottle; it's quite time enough for any one to believe in a ghost when he sees one. But we cannot deny that there have been very curious and authenticated instances of such things."

"Oh, rubbish—rubbish!"—"So I have been tempted myself always to exclaim; but when I was sitting with Mr. Harrington, I certainly did fancy a kind of something was in the room, although I saw nothing. There was a curious feeling in the air—a strange unearthly sort of—a—a—you understand me, Mrs. Cottle?"

"No, I don't at all."

"Humph," thought I; "Mrs. Cottle is a stronger-minded woman than I thought." Then I added aloud,—

"But what is more, I did actually hear a voice in the room."

She showed some signs of uneasiness as she said,—

"And what might the voice say, sir?"—"It said, 'not dead.'"

"Who was not dead?"—"Oh, that is left in mystery. The great evil of supernatural visitations has always appeared to me, that they required some supernatural judgment to comprehend them."

"Very true, indeed," said Mrs. Cottle. "Perhaps it was Mr. Harrington's voice you heard, lamenting that he was not dead yet; or perhaps you have a habit, as some people of not very strong intellects have, of speaking aloud without being conscious of it."

"Thank you, madam, thank you; one or other of these explanations may be the correct one; or, perhaps, it may be that there has been some desperate villany at work with regard to Mr. Harrington's domestic affairs, that, perhaps, sooner than the parties concerned in them expect, will be brought to light, to their utter confusion and shame."

Mrs. Cottle gasped again, and being quite satisfied that I had alarmed her prodigiously, and likewise had ample revenge for the impertinence of her last remark to me, I made her a very profound bow, and at once quitted the house.

I asked myself when I gained the street whether it was a wise thing or not to have annoyed Mrs. Cottle in the way I had done, and at the same time awakened her suspicions that all was not going right with her, to the extent my words must have done; but although at first I was inclined to blame myself for precipitancy, yet upon consideration I gave up that view of the subject, from a conviction that she had it not in her power to do any harm as a consequence of such suspicions of danger.

Tommy was completely out of her power; the poor victims, Mortimer and his wife, of her devilish plotting were beyond the reach of her malice; and in fact she was comparatively harmless now, having done her worst; so that when I did come calmly to reflect upon what I had said, I by no means regretted the saying it, inasmuch as she fully deserved all the mental uneasiness my words were calculated to give her.

The next day was that on which Colonel Eusham had resolved to take up his abode for a short time at Colonel Harrington's and I, of course, expected to find him there when I made my visit; but early in the morning I found a note for me from him at my house, to the effect that he would be glad if I could defer my professional visit to Harrington until the whole of my business for the day was concluded, and then, when I did pay the visit, stay for some hours.

This was an arrangement I by no means objected to; in fact, living, as Harrington did, so far out of my beaten track, it was more convenient; and accordingly, about six o'clock in the afternoon, I set off to walk the distance, with a resolution of passing the evening there, as I knew of no regular patient who was at all likely to send for me, and any chance affair I mentally made a present of to the practitioner who might live the nearest to my house. It is rare indeed that a medical man can feel himself at liberty, and when he does so it is only by absconding for a few hours from home, without telling any one where he has gone, so that he cannot be sent for. In some such a holiday state, then, I found myself as I trudged on towards Colonel Harrington's splendid mansion, revolving in my mind all the strange circumstances of his story, and the dreadful compunctious visitings which must be his when the truth should break upon his disordered mind, and he should find that he had sacrificed his daughter's husband instead of her seducer.

"Heaven help him!" I thought. "If he receive the intelligence, he must pass the remainder of his life in such wretchedness of self-reproach, that it would be the greatest mercy if he were at once to sink under the shock, and find peace and refuge in the grave from his dreadful troubles and deep anxieties."

Everything but the dreadful murder of poor Mortimer might have been got over, but that terrible act could not be extenuated, and when found to have been based upon injustice, it must assume to any mind a form of the most horrible character. I could fancy the feelings of the young man, after wandering over so many weary miles of land and ocean, to make, perhaps, his peace with the offended father of his wife, and to assure him how he would love and cherish her, and watch over her happiness, to find a deadly weapon levelled at his head, and to be hurled into eternity, as if his very name, the moment he had pronounced it, was his own death-warrant. It was indeed terrible to think of, and I no longer, after I had heard him make such a statement, wondered that the murderer's soul was troubled by strange fantasies.

"He has no resource but death now, and the mercy of Heaven hereafter," I said, half aloud; and at the moment such a dash of rain fell in my very mouth, that I was at once roused from my reverie to the consciousness of a most abominably wet night setting in.

The rain that was now falling gave no promise of cessation, for the light rain that first fell was gradually increasing till it became a settled and heavy fall. The streets soon became deserted, and scarce any one was seen in them, save the few who were exposed to it, hurrying onwards as if it had been their only wish to get through their walk, regardless of the consequences to themselves.

This part of the town was particularly cheerless and dreary, for Kentish Town and the road to Highgate are not like the centre of London, where, however the discomfort and difficulty may increase, it does not very sensibly diminish the number of persons exposed to it for many hours, but merely increases the number of cloaks, coats, and umbrellas; while here there were but few, and those few appeared to render the place more melancholy, as they came pattering along in the rain, sometimes on the pavement, and sometimes through the soft road.

The intensity of the rain by no means diminished, but rather increased than otherwise, and showed no symptoms of relaxation whatever,—a clean, straight, pouring rain, that fell thick and close, washing the pavements, and in time carrying the refuse down the road. The air itself was impregnated with moisture, and floated about heavily, and scarce a breath of wind stirred to give a direction to the shower, which fell perpendicularly to the earth from the clouds above, that seemed to stand over this part.—It may be readily believed that this was not at all calculated to increase one's comfort and good-humour; far from it, for both sensibly diminished as I proceeded on my journey.

At length, finding the rain continued so heavy, I thought it time to stand up and escape the burst of rain that now appeared to be falling; this I did under the first archway I came near, and there watched the forlorn and wretched as they passed my place of shelter.

The weather has a great effect upon the appearance and even the apparent respectability of passengers, and I was never more convinced of it than I was when I saw a young couple pass me who had been out and caught in some showy and even respectable dress, which, now that it was unsuitable to the occasion, made them look wretched, and apparently unable to purchase good and suitable garments; and, on the contrary, those who were roughly clad appeared comfortable and snug.

While reflecting on the difference of opinion, which can be changed as the light changes, I began to feel cold and comfortless myself, and also to be aware that standing up had its disadvantages, especially when one had been partially made damp from its effects before, and therefore, seeing there was no reasonable hope of its holding up, determined to go through it, and reach my destination as speedily as I could.— This I did, and soon found that I had merely changed one uncomfortable situation for another, though the latter had the good quality of being of shorter duration than the other, and through wet and mire I pursued my route.

The reader may well suppose I was in no very agreeable plight by the time I reached Colonel Harrington's, and when I rang it was some minutes before the footman seemed to think it worth his while to answer the bell, not, I suppose, imagining that anybody of any consequence would be abroad on such a night.

When he did at last condescend to let me in, he gave me that sort of stare which was easily translated into, "Well, who would have thought of seeing you!"

"Is General Eusham here?"—said I.—"Yes, sir, but—but it didn't rain when he came."

"Tell him that I have arrived, will you, and take my hat somewhere to dry."

"Shall I take your coat, sir?"—"Why, to tell the truth, you might as well take me altogether; but I dare say Eusham will procure me some dry clothes."

"Very good, sir."

In a few moments I was joined by the general, who exclaimed,—

"Hilloa! who would have expected to see you on such a night as this, doctor?"—"Now, really," said I, this is too bad. After one has come through torrents of rain to keep an engagement, and run the chance of one's death of cold, to be told, 'Oh, you were not expected,' is adding insult to injury."

"So it is—so it is. Come along, and we will go on an expedition in search of a dry coat."

By the assistance of the footman the expedition was successful, and I soon found myself equipped in one of Mr. Harrington's coats, which happened to fit me very well indeed. Then the general said to me, as we were walking towards the room in which the unhappy Harrington was sitting,—

"I intend to remain here, doctor, until some suspicious character comes to see Mrs. Cottle, and I have secured the alliance of the footman by the possession of one sovereign, and the promise of another. He is to let me know when she has any visitor, so that I can follow him at once at leaving, and frighten him as nearly as possible out of his wits."

"Well, we must arrange," said I, "exactly what we mean to say to the aforesaid visitor when we catch him."— "Oh, we will tell him he is our prisoner, and that Mrs. Cottle has confessed all, and that he had better himself confess the remainder."

"Very good," said I. "As I before stated, I am not prepared to suggest anything better, and so am willing to aid and assist in the plan you propose."—"Well, then, I'm told she has written a letter to-day, and which she would trust no one to put in the post but herself."

"Indeed!—Then there is a chance."

By this time we had reached Colonel Harrington's room, where of course further conversation on the subject was at an end, and I was gratified to see the favourable change in the spirits of Harrington which the presence of his old friend Eusham seemed to have effected. There was still a wildness about him, and a degree of fidgetty melancholy, which was painful; but he was certainly not so bad as he had been, and once or twice we succeeded in withdrawing his mind for a brief space from too close a contemplation of his domestic miseries, so that he conversed rationally and pleasantly enough, showing himself to be a man of great and varied information, as well as ability.

"About your will, Harrington," remarked General Eusham, after there had been a pause for some moments. "Do you mean to leave it in the unsatisfactory condition it is in at present?"—"Do not trouble me about it, Eusham," he replied. "Let it be, let it be. She can have everything—she is the only person in want of means who has seemed keenly to feel for my wounded honour, and besides, I cannot forget that she was kind to poor, lost, erring Dorinda. Let her have all, if on that sole consideration."

"You have such an account only from her own lips."— "True; but I saw enough beside to convince me that what she had said was true. Do not press this subject on me, general. I have forbidden Cottle herself to mention it to me, although she was so persevering last evening about it that she made me angry with her for the first time in my life."

"Oh!" thought I, "Cottle was alarmed at what I said, and that was the reason of the botheration last evening."

"Yes," continued Harrington, "she seemed half mad about something, and I was compelled to tell her that she must leave my house upon any repetition of the subject, on any grounds whatever."

General Eusham looked at me, and I at him, for we both perceived how strongly Mrs. Cottle must have felt what I said to her, before she could have been induced to commit herself so far as to become troublesome to Colonel Harrington.

At that moment we heard distinctly a ring at the bell. General Eusham made an excuse to leave the room, for he seemed to have a notion that on that evening some one would come for Mrs. Cottle; and he was not wrong, as it turned out. In about five minutes he opened the door of the room, and said,—

"Harrington, will you excuse the doctor for a little time?" —"Oh, certainly, certainly," said Harrington, and I immediately rose and followed General Eusham.

"There is a fellow here," he said. "I want you to see if you can recognise him as the one you saw with Cottle near the Foundling."—"That I could not take upon myself to do," I replied. "I had too transient a glance of him to be able to identify him. Do you intend to carry into execution with him your scheme?"

"Of course I do; come on and take a share in it. Get your hat. We will wait outside, and when the fellow comes out we will pounce upon him, and try what can be done in the way of awakening his fears."

Thus urged by General Eusham, I did get my hat, and we proceeded, notwithstanding the discomfort of the night, to the outside of the house, where we waited impatiently for the moment when Mrs. Cottle's visitor should emerge. We had not been there above a minute, when another person stopped under cover of an over-hanging tree, and appeared likewise to be determined upon waiting for some one. We were so far back in the shadow cast by the walls and trees, that we were not seen by this new arrival, who we saw was a woman, and from whom in a short time we heard deep sobs proceeding, as if she were in the greatest possible distress.

General Eusham, with a prompt humanity which had always characterised him, would have stepped forward to inquire the cause of her tears, but I restrained him, saying,—

"Let her be—let her be. Who knows but there may be some sort of connection between her and the man now speaking with Mrs. Cottle? Let him come out first, and then you can interfere."

He allowed himself to be ruled by me so far, and held back for nearly twenty minutes, during the whole of which time the female never moved from the spot, but now and then wept and wrung her hands in great bitterness of spirit. When at length the garden gate was opened, and a man emerged, she stepped up to him, and clinging to his arm, she said, in tones of exquisite earnestness and grief,—

"John, John, be advised—oh! be advised. Tell all, and

do not allow yourself to be made the slave of that dreadful woman."

"D——n! — you here?" he cried.—"Yes. You swore to me you had done with her, and that you would take an opportunity of writing to the wretched man who lives here in splendid misery to tell him all; but I suspected you, and followed you here. Oh! John, my son—my only son, wicked as you are, there must be hope above. On my knees, here, on the cold stones, I implore you to be just."

"Now, curse me," cried the fellow, "if I have not a good mind to knock you on the head."—"Oh, God!—oh, God!" cried the woman.

I held General Eusham fast, or I do believe he would have stepped forward and exterminated the fellow, who tore himself away from the grasp of this miserable, imploring mother, and walked rapidly towards town.

"Now, Eusham," I said, "who are we to attack?—the mother or the son?"—"Which do you say?"

"Pursue him, say I. You will get no information from the mother that may not be got at any time, and do not let us, if we can in any way avoid it, add to her present griefs by making her his accuser, if we can wring the truth from his own cowardly and contemptible heart." — "Come on, then—come on."

We both darted off in pursuit of the rascal, who was walking at a very rapid pace, and General Eusham said to me as we went,—

"Doctor, you must not interfere with me, but I shall not sleep to-night unless I give that fellow a thrashing. His conduct to his mother deserves it, and such men feel nothing but actual blows. They understand no other description of suffering than the purely physical, and I am resolved he shall have a taste of it."—"Well, mind you don't kill him, that's all," said I.

"Oh, I will be careful, you may depend."

By this time we had gained considerably on the ruffian, and General Eusham called out in a loud voice to him,—

"Hilloa, there,—you fellow—John—hilloa!"

The fellow at first ran on a pace or two, but then he relapsed into a very slow walk again, and allowed us to come up with him.

"Well, sir," said General Eusham, " you are my prisoner."

"What for?" he said, with all the calmness in the world. —"The affairs connected with Mr. Harrington. I may as well inform you that your accomplice, Mrs. Cottle, has confessed everything."

"Are you a madman, and is that your keeper?" pointing to me. — "Come, come, this evasion won't do. You have still an opportunity of inducing a merciful view of your case by a prosecution, if you make a confession of everything. Mrs. Cottle has admitted you were her companion when the child was deserted near the Foundling."

"I hope you will walk with me so far as will enable me to see a constable," said the fellow, "in which case I shall give you both into custody."

I saw the whole affair was a failure, and whispered to General Eusham,—

"Leave him—leave him; it won't do."—" I will," said the general, " but first here goes."

Doubling his fists, then, he gave the fellow two blows on the mouth, that sent him reeling; but he was not content with the punishment he had received, for with a yell of rage he made towards the general with a knife in his hand; but he was stopped again by two more blows, just in the same spot, which were so terribly effective, that he fell down as if he had been shot, and lay perfectly insensible.

"Hilloa! hilloa!" cried a constable, coming up; "what's all this, eh?"—"There's my card," said General Eusham. "Take that fellow into custody."

"Oh, what charge, sir?" — " Felony. I will appear against him in the morning."

"And I too," said I, "for, now I have heard his voice, I recognise him at once."

General Eusham and I hurried back towards Harrington's house, meeting, as we fully expected, on the road, the unhappy mother of the scoundrel who had already received some of the punishment due to his rascality. We immediately accosted her, and the tone and manner in which we did so appeared to have a great impression upon her. Previously to our meeting her, the general had said to me,—

"Doctor, do you speak to this poor woman; I declare I am in such a passion myself, that it is quite out of my power to do so; I am in such a rage with that scoundrel, John, confound him!"

I had no sort of difficulty in fully acquiescing in the general's opinion, that he was not in a fit state to make any conciliatory speeches, so I walked a few paces in advance, when I saw the poor moaning object of our search coming towards us, wringing her hands, and looking the picture of forlornness and misery.

"My good woman," said I, "we are in some measure acquainted with the cause of your great grief, and in asking you, as we shall do, to disclose to us the whole of it, you may believe that such a course will be more beneficial to every one, yourself and the unworthy object of your solicitude included."

She stopped and looked up in my face with a perfectly bewildered expression, and then, clasping her hands, she said, in a tone of despair,—

"Oh, spare him—spare him, gentlemen. Do not be hard upon—spare him, that he may yet repent of the evil he has done." — "Rely upon justice being tempered by mercy," said I.

At this moment the general came up, and I said to him,—

"This good woman will tell us all we wish to know. What she wishes is, that mercy should be shown to her son, and that I am sure you will readily join me in promising."— "Certainly—certainly; justice can always be done to those who are innocent, without exacting from the guilty the full meed of retribution for their great iniquities—mercy shall be shown."

The poor woman burst into a flood of tears, and, I think, had not both the general and myself assisted to support her, she must have fallen to the ground.

"Come, come," said I, "be of better cheer—all may end far more happily than you suppose. We know that Mrs. Cottle has behaved unworthily, and most inimically towards Colonel Harrington—we know, too, that your son, John, has been a party to the transaction, and an assistant to her bad proceedings. What you know with regard to all that has happened from beginning to end, you had better tell us, and rely upon our best endeavours to see justice tempered, as it should always be, with mercy."

"Tell me, gentlemen," she gasped, "oh, tell me one thing, and set my mind at rest, even if I know the worst I can possible conjecture."—" What is it? Ask your question, and I declare to you, upon my honour, that you shall be frankly answered."

"What—has—become of the—the dear child?"—"Tommy, do you mean?"—" Yes, yes."

"He is alive and well at the house of this gentleman, who rescued him from the workhouse."—" Ah, to be sure," cried General Eusham, "and they did me the honour of fathering him upon me at the same time."

"Oh, thank God—thank God!"—,"I'm very much obliged to you."

"I mean for his preservation, sir. Now, gentlemen, my mind is indeed at rest upon a subject which has long harassed it. Heaven forgive me for such a supposition, but I was possessed by a dreadful idea that that child had been murdered." —" And no wonder, too, considering that your beautiful John had a hand in the affair," said Eusham.

"Never mind that," said I. "This good woman will, I am sure, now tell us all she knows."—"I will—I will, gentlemen. Listen to me, and you shall indeed hear a sorrowful story."

We walked to and fro with her opposite Colonel Harrington's house, while in trembling accents she made to us the dreadful disclosure of circumstances which had resulted in so much misery to so many innocent persons, who else might have passed through life in joy and happiness, bound together by the tenderest bonds of mutual esteem and love.

"It is now five years ago, or rather better, gentlemen, when, by the death of my husband—rest his soul—I was left a widow with my son John, to fight my way through the world the best way I could, and that was bad enough. I took a small house in order to eke out a subsistence by letting lodgings; and one of the first persons who came as a lodger was this woman, Mrs. Cottle, who I believe, and indeed know, to be as wicked a wretch as ever lived. My son John was in an attorney's office, and she got him to write for her letters to different gentlemen, whom she said were indebted to her; but the fact is, she had been leading for many years an abandoned course of life, which she found failing her, and by threats and entreaties she was trying to wring money from those who no longer regarded her. Unhappily for me, gentlemen, she got a great influence over John, and although I say it, yet it is a melancholy truth, that he was always of a wild and a wayward disposition."

"So I should think," growled General Eusham.

"Ah! many's the blow I have had from him."—"A pretty scoundrel."

"Well—well: go on with your narration," said I.

"Yes, sir. Well, time wore on, and no money could I get from Mrs. Cottle; but one day she came home in high glee, and said to me,—

"'Mrs. Margetts,' says she, 'I have just had quite an adventure. I always told you I was distantly related to a very rich gentleman in India, and now, who should I meet but his daughter to-day, who had been at school, and ran away and got married, without her father knowing anything about it.'

"'Well,' said I, 'it's a pity the father does not know of it. What are they going to do?'

"'Why, to tell the truth,' she added, 'I have invited them to live here. They have plenty of money, and don't know where to go.'

"Well, gentlemen, to make a long story short, Mr. and Mrs. Mortimer came to my house, and a delicate, sweet, sensible creature she was, too. They had not been with me long, when Mr. Mortimer came to me one day, and said,—

"'Mrs. Margetts, I shall not be here for some time, and it is very likely a little Mortimer may be born before you again see me in this house. Mrs. Cottle will pay you for everything that is wanted for my wife; and as for me, I am going to see my father-in-law, and make my peace and Dorinda's personally with him, instead of writing.'

"I longed to warn him of what sort of woman Mrs. Cottle was; and yet as she had not done anything I could positively speak of as being absolutely wrong, I could not bring my mind to say anything upon the subject. Little did I know what wickedness she had done till some weeks afterwards, when my son John said to me,—

"'Well, mother, Cottle,'—he always called her just Cottle —'Cottle has managed matters pretty well, I think.'

"'What do you mean?' said I.

"'Just this,' he added. 'If ever you open your mouth to any one about the fact of Mrs. Mortimer being any other than a mistress instead of a wife, you will get me, perhaps, transported—perhaps hung; for I really don't know but I might be induced to murder you for spoiling sport. As for Mortimer, if ever he comes back here again it will be a very odd thing to me.'

"That was all he said; and I would not ask him any questions, although I saw there was great consultation constantly going on between Mrs. Cottle and him; while poor Mrs. Mortimer was getting weaker and weaker each day, in spite of all I could do for her.

"Well, gentlemen, my son, I should have told you, had been in a lawyer's office, and he was considered, I understand, very sharp at the business; but, all of a sudden, after a letter came one day from India to Mrs. Cottle, he left off doing anything at all, but merely walked about, spending a deal of money. Then they despised me, I suppose, too much to think it necessary to keep any terms with me, but openly lived together, and talked before me of how they made Colonel Harrington believe his daughter was not married.

"You will tell me, gentlemen, that I ought to have interfered in some way, and so I did, with my prayers and entreaties; further I dared not, for John was my son, and my only one too; and he constantly kept saying to me, that if I took any step in the matter, things would come to light that would bring him to a scaffold. Well—well, a child was born —a nice little fellow. Oh, God! you should have seen how his mother, poor young thing, wept and fondled over him, and blessed him, and laughed and cried by turns, as she looked into his sweet blue eyes, to see if he was like his father. Ah, well-a-day! gentlemen; it makes my old heart sore to think of such things; but a very short time had elapsed, indeed, when one day a carriage drew up at my house, and there got out of it a stout, military-looking gentleman, who I afterwards learned was Colonel Harrington himself, who had just arrived from India to see his daughter.

"I opened the door for him, and, looking sternly at me, he said,—

"'Are you Mrs. Cottle?'

"'No, sir,' said I.

"'Is she here—and yet, what is that to me? Is a Mrs. Mortimer here?'

"'Yes, poor young thing,' said I, 'and very bad she is too, sir.'

"'Silence, woman!' he cried, and pushing past me, he walked into the house, when Mrs. Cottle came down stairs, having heard his voice, I suppose, and made such a fuss with him, crying, and weeping, and sobbing, that anybody who didn't know her would have thought her the most tenderhearted and affectionate person that ever God Almighty put breath into.

"Well, gentlemen, then I thought, for I heard Mrs. Cottle call him Colonel Harrington, I would at once tell him all that had occurred, and assure him his daughter was the lawful wife of Mr. Mortimer; but John, I do think, guessed my intention, for he whispered in my ear,—

"'If you want to place me in the hands of the hangman, you will contradict Mrs. Cottle to Colonel Harrington.'

"A fit of trembling seized me, and I said nothing; but I could not be off hearing what passed in the house for all that, and saddened was I to hear it.

"After some talk with Mrs. Cottle, during which she told him how very kind she had been to his daughter, the colonel was shown by her into the room where lay poor Mrs. Mortimer, very unwell indeed. Poor thing! I had been thinking for some days that she never could recover; and yet, who knows, as harshness had so sudden an effect upon her, what kindness might have done. I heard her give a sort of cry of joy when she saw her father, and she said,—

"'Father—father—dear father!—where is Mortimer?—Is he with you, and have you forgiven us?'

"Then there was silence for about a minute, after which the colonel said,—

"'Shame and dishonour to my name—disgrace to me and to all who cannot escape the stigma of consanguinity to you— hear me, now, cast upon you my curse, my irrevocable curse. You are no daughter of mine, and he who induced you to wander from the path of duty, has paid the penalty of his damning crime with his life.'

"'No—no!' shrieked the poor young thing. 'No—no! Oh, God, it is not so!'

"'I swear it!' said the colonel; 'as there is a Heaven above us, I swear it—he is dead!'

"Then she gave a sort of shriek, and all was still. I could command myself no longer, but ran into the room; and oh! what a sight presented itself to my eyes. Poor Mrs. Mortimer lay on the bed with her babe in her arms, and blood was flowing from her mouth. She had burst a blood-vessel, I was told afterwards: but she never spoke again. I turned to the colonel and reproached him till he threatened to strike me, and then he went away from the house like a raging madman.

"It was some days afterwards that he took the child home to his own house, and Mrs. Cottle went with him to take care of it. My son John then laughed as he said to me,—

"'All's right now—I am now provided for. Cottle dare not call her soul her own, except by my command—she is quite at my mercy; and if I don't make her pay well for the keeping of such secrets as I know, call me a fool.'

"From that day to this, gentlemen, I have never known peace of mind. Mrs. Cottle often came to our house, and had long conversations with John, which they hardly seemed to think it worth while to keep from my ears. They appeared to imagine me either stupified, or thoroughly subdued to whatever they wished, and so I heard them one day, a short time since, decide upon putting the poor little boy, Tommy, out of the way, as they then thought the colonel would leave all he was worth to Mrs. Cottle, and John was to have an equal share when he, the colonel, should be dead, which I often heard Mrs. Cottle say would not be a very long while, as he was breaking down every day. I implored them on my knees not to do anything against the child; but they only laughed at me, and when I became more troublesome, I was struck by my own son.

"Well, gentlemen, the child was taken away, and I heard them rejoice over it; but I dreaded to think what had become of it. Heaven forgive me for charging even them in my thoughts with more evil than they had really done; but I did think they had murdered it."

"I am only surprised they did not," remarked General Eusham; "but I suppose they thought it as safe to desert it in the streets."

"No doubt, sir. I heard them talk of how they had got the dead body of another child to personate the colonel's grandson; but in my own mind I suspected such was only said to deceive me, and that the body was indeed that of poor Mrs. Mortimer's child. Thank Heaven such is not the case. I feel as if a great weight had been lifted off my breast, now that, with all his wickedness, I can, at least, tell myself that my son is not a murderer."

"And what brought you to Colonel Harrington's house to-night?" said I.

"Just this, gentlemen. There came a letter to my son from Mrs. Cottle—not that such a circumstance was unusual, or would have excited in my mind any new suspicions; but he accidentally dropped it when he went out, so that I was able to see what it was about, and its contents induced me to come after him as I did, and implore him, even at the eleventh hour, to endeavour to make some reparation for the evil he had committed, and beg the mercy of those he had injured."

"Have you that letter?"

"Yes, gentlemen. I have it with me. Here it is; you can read it if you please, and, from what it says, you will have greater faith in the truth of what I have already related to you."

She produced the letter, and General Eusham, standing under a lamp, which was near at hand, read it to me. It contained these words:—

"DEAR JOHN,—Come this evening if you can to me. I do not know what is going on; but I am afraid there is something wrong. The doctor I spoke to you about seems

inclined to be troublesome, and I think, after all, something will have to be done of a violent nature to make things safe.

"It's imprudent to say more in a letter, but you may believe that there is real danger. Come at all risks, and let us determine upon something. Have you got the W. all ready? because if H. should go suddenly, it would be immediately wanted; and, do what I can, I cannot persuade him to make a will that would, under any circumstances, suit.—Yours,
"FRANCES COTTLE."

"Humph!" said the general. "This is a precious document, indeed—what say you to it, doctor?"—"Step aside," said I; and when the general had done so, I added, "what if we repair now immediately to Harrington's, and try upon Mrs. Cottle the same plan which the cunning of John Margetts defeated. Let us tell her he has confessed all, and, as a proof, produce this letter."

"Oh, spare him—spare my son! Guilty though he is, and a terror to me as he has long been, I cannot forget that I am his mother."

"The scoundrel!" said General Eusham. "When he forgot that there was such a tie between you, you might be excused."

"No, no, no," she sobbed. "The tie from the parent to the child is much stronger than the child to the parent. Let the child forget all duty, and err ever so sinfully, the parent should never forget the sacred obligation of consanguinity. No pride—no resentments—no petty feelings of jealousies or vexations should stand in the way. A child may lose respect for a father or a mother—but the father or a mother, let the conduct of a child be what it may, surely never should turn their backs upon a child."

"I think she is right," said I.

"I'm d——d if she ain't," cried General Eusham. "Here, my good woman. Here is a five pound note for you. Go home, and, for your sake, John Margetts shall be leniently dealt with, were he the devil himself. Come along, doctor. Now for our friend Cottle."

Heaven knows what Colonel Harrington thought of our singular desertion of him, after we had come to spend the evening with him; but the fact was, that the narrative of poor Mrs. Margetts was so all engrossing, and so very important, that we never thought once of Harrington till we found ourselves again ringing the bell at his garden gate.

"He will wonder what the deuce has become of us," said General Eusham. "I think we must see him for a few moments first before we commence operations against Cottle."

—"Very good," said I. "It will perhaps be better."

We accordingly proceeded towards the apartment in which we had left our host. A large argand lamp was burning on the table, and the fire was very hollow, as if it had not been touched for some time, but no Colonel Harrington could we see.

"What has become of him?" said the general. "I don't see him, doctor."

I glanced around the room as I walked towards the fire-place, which, when I reached, I found Colonel Harrington lying before, to all appearances dead. The general saw him at the same moment, and he exclaimed,—

"Good God, doctor! suppose that fellow, John Margetts, has murdered him?"

I made no answer, but immediately lifted the colonel from the ground and placed him in an easy chair; then I saw that he had not been injured in any way, but had most probably fallen under the influence of fainting.

"He don't seem hurt," said I. "Hand me that glass of water."

"Is he dead or alive?" said the general, as he handed me the water, which I at once dashed with all my force in Colonel Harrington's face.

"Alive," I replied. "There, he moves."

The shock of the cold water produced a reaction of the vital system, and with a deep groan he opened his eyes, glaring around him in a strange and wild manner.

"How are you now, sir?" I said.

He groaned heavily, and after I had thrice repeated my question, he said,—

"It came again—it came again! Oh, horror! horror! horror!"—"Oh," remarked General Eusham, "he has had one of his ghostly visits while we have been from the house, you may depend, doctor."

"No doubt—no doubt; but do not mention it. He is in a very precarious state, and I should advise his instant removal to bed."—"I saw it—I saw it," he groaned; "it came through that window; it never came so close to me before. I shall not see another sunrise; I am a doomed man this night."

I looked painfully and anxiously in his countenance; a remarkable change had come over it, and I could not help a very strong supposition crossing my mind that in all likelihood he was quite right, and that before morning all his miseries would be over, and himself a corpse.

I rang the bell, and with the assistance of two footmen Colonel Harrington was conveyed to bed, I having desired them to say nothing whatever to Mrs. Cottle concerning their master's sudden indisposition. Then the general and I inquired where she was, and upon being informed that she was in an apartment on the second floor, which she called her own room, we resolved without any ceremony to proceed there, and leave at once with her the evidence which would put an end to her hopes and prospects, as well as probably transport the meritorious John Margetts, who we felt very anxious indeed to convict upon some secure testimony. To be sure the only distinct crime that could be laid to his charge which would involve him in legal consequences, consisted of his share in the abduction of the child from Colonel Harrington, and its desertion in the street, and that I wished to be brought home to him by the confession of Cottle, if possible; not that we meant to hold out any promise of impunity to her for her share in the atrocious transaction.

Mrs. Cottle was not a lady towards whom we felt it necessary to show any very great ceremonial deference; so after agreeing that I was to be the spokesman, for General Eusham was getting rather out of conceit of his own powers in that way, we opened the door at once, and walked into the room, to Mrs. Cottle's great consternation. She appeared to have been reading some document, which she hastily folded up and placed in her pocket, after which, drawing herself up like a great vicious-looking virago as she was, she said,—

"To what, gentlemen, am I to attribute the honour of this very unceremonious intrusion?"—"D—n it ma'am," cried General Eusham, "we don't intend it as an honour at all."

"Hush! hush!" said I; "leave all to me. Mrs. Cottle, permit me to inform you that you are found out."

She staggered as if somebody had given her a sudden blow, and then, recovering with wonderful presence of mind, she said,—

"I presume you have been drinking too much wine. I will ring for the footman to assist you to bed."—"No, madam, we are perfectly sober, and have the pleasure to inform you that John Margetts has thought proper, under certain very stringent circumstances, to make a full confession."

She was compelled to sit down, to endeavour to hide the sudden trembling that seized her as she said,—

"And pray who may John Margetts be?—what may be the nature of his confession, that you think it worth while to trouble me with it?"

I saw what she was at; she was endeavouring, before she said anything herself, to find out what he had really communicated, and so base her conduct upon what we might already have become acquainted with.

"If, Mrs. Cottle," I added, "you will look at this letter, you will find that John Margetts has not scrupled to place in our hands evidence enough to convict you. We are aware that you deceived Colonel Harrington with regard to his daughter's marriage, and we have the certificate of that marriage; we are aware that you deserted the child of Mrs. Mortimer near the Foundling Hospital, and we have that child in our own care."

"And John Margetts has told you all this?" she said.—"All, to be sure," cried General Eusham.

"Then I deny it from beginning to end."

"You do?"—"Yes, I do. The letter is a forgery."

"Mrs. Cottle," said I, "this denial will not avail you. I had hoped that you would have seen your iniquities in their proper light now, and made such reparation to Colonel Harrington as might be in your power."

A loud ring at the gate bell now met our ears, and in a moment or two a footman appeared, and said to Mrs. Cottle,—

"Here is a note for you, madam."

She took it and tore it open, but before she could read it I rescued it from her hands, for I feared it had come with some sort of warning to her from John Margetts; and such indeed was the case. The note contained these words:—

"Come down to the gate to me directly; I have just escaped from the police."

"How dare you take my letter!" cried Mrs. Cottle.—"Be easy, madam," said I; "it is from John Margetts. He is below, and ready to repeat all he has confessed before your face. Shall I send for him up?"

She shook materially, and then in a more subdued tone she said,—

"Will you promise me a protection from all ——"

Here she stopped short, as if fearful she had gone too far, and such a violent ring at some bell inside the house took place, that we each involuntarily started and turned to the door.

"It is Mr. Harrington's bell," said Mrs. Cottle.

"Then something serious is the matter," cried I; and I walked from the room, pausing but to say to the footman who brought the note to Mrs. Cottle,—

"Go to the man who brought the note, and, with the assistance of your comrades, make him prisoner; tie his hands and feet, and lay him down in the hall."

I then hastened to the chamber of Colonel Harrington, and the first glance I had of him made me recoil again on the landing, as if I had been shot, so awful, so terrible was his appearance. He was sitting up in bed; his teeth were set, his eyes fearfully distended, and staring from his head like globes of fire, while his two arms were stretched out before him, and all the fingers extended, as if to keep some dreadful object from approaching his face.

"Good God!" cried General Eusham; "how horrible!"

In a moment I recovered from my sudden panic, and went into the room again.

"Mr. Harrington, Mr. Harrington," I cried, "for God's sake lie down. Speak—speak!"

No, he moved not, spoke not. I laid hold of one of his wrists—a shudder came over me—he was dead, and fixed in that horrible attitude, his arms standing out from him stiff and inflexible as bars of iron. I could not move them to his side, and I desisted from the attempt after a moment, with a cold perspiration of terror standing on my brow, for I had never seen so terrible a sight before, although I had looked upon many a corpse. As for General Eusham, I saw him shake his head and turn on one side, as he muttered,—

"Humph! I have seen a few odd sights in India, but this beats all."

"Assist me," said I, and together we succeeded in laying the body on its back, and covering it over with the clothes; but it had a frightful and singular look, to see the bed clothing hoisted up so high above the body which lay hidden beneath.

"D—n it," remarked General Eusham, "they will have to get a packing-case made for him instead of a coffin."—"There will be no necessity," said I; "the body will soon get limp and flabby."

"Eugh!—you horrid—what the deuce do you make use of such expressions for? Well, madam, you are in at the death."

This was said to Mrs. Cottle, who, pale and trembling, just at that moment made her appearance in the doorway.

"Is he dead?" she said.—"He is," I replied. "General Eusham, send a servant to your house immediately for the colonel's will."

"I have it here in my pocket," he said. "I intended while remaining here to let my old friend know by some means or another that his grandson was alive, and so this will should have been, by his consent, destroyed."

"If, gentlemen," said Mrs. Cottle, "you will promise me impunity for the past, I will criminate John Margetts so completely in various transactions, that he shall inevitably be transported."

"But then you actually expect, I suppose, that you are to enjoy the annuity mentioned in this will?"—"No—no; I give that up. You may destroy that will entirely."

"I don't like to do that," said General Eusham.—"Then I will," she said, and snatching it suddenly from his hands, she flung it into the fire, where in a moment it was a blackened mass of cinder.

"Well, madam," said General Eusham, "the destruction of that will is your own act."

"It is. Make what you can of the past, the present, or the future. My attorney will in due time produce a neatly executed will of Colonel Harrington, which making no mention of his grandson, leaves to me the whole of his property, without reservation. With respect to what you charge me with upon the confession of John Margetts, such will have to be proved in a court of law, where perhaps he will confess nothing. Gentlemen, it strikes me very forcibly that you have been too clever by half. The letter you showed to me as having been written by me to Margetts you left with me, and although I deny its authenticity, I thought it better to destroy it. This is my house, and I demand your instant departure from it, or I will send for the police to remove you by force."

"You are an extraordinary woman," said I; "but the will you speak of shall be disputed. Colonel Harrington declared in my hearing he had made no such will."—"Which declaration," replied Mrs. Cottle, "will have no effect against a legally executed document in a court of law. I repeat, gentlemen, you have been too clever."

"Please, sir, the man in the hall is raving like a madman after Mrs. Cottle," said a footman.—"Man in the hall!" she cried. "Bring him here."

"Very good," said I; "bring him here, since such is your wish, Mrs. Cottle."

In a few moments the ruffian made his appearance along with a constable, who had been sent for by the servants to keep him quiet.

"Well, Margetts," said Mrs. Cottle, "you are welcome here. Colonel Harrington is dead, and, as you know, I am in possession of all his property by will."

Margetts looked amazed at this intimation, and then, before he could speak, I walked to the door and locked it, saying,—

"Now, here we are, all of us. I solemnly declare that neither you, Mrs. Cottle, nor you, Margetts, shall leave this room until we see this will of Colonel Harrington's which you speak of. Where is it?"—"She —" said Margetts.

"Peace!" cried Mrs. Cottle. "How dare you —"— "Oh, you have it, madam, have you," said I. "Pray let us see it."

"To destroy. Likely, indeed."—"Oh, no; you have destroyed one will, and laid yourself open to a prosecution for so doing. It is not likely in the presence of so many witnesses I would do such a thing."

"Show it to him," cried Margetts; "d—n them all, let them see it."

Mrs. Cottle took a parchment document from her pocket, and handed it to me saying,—

"I call upon all here present to witness that this is the last will of Colonel Harrington."

I opened the parchment, and after the usual legal preamble, it ran thus:—

"I give and bequeath the whole of my property, real and personal, to Mrs. Frances Cottle, my cousin, for her sole use and benefit."

"Why—why—what the devil!" cried Margetts; "does it say Cottle—Cottle?"—"Yes, indeed it does; and here I offer a thousand pounds reward to either of the parties here named as attesting witnesses for such information as shall prove this will a forgery, for ——"

"Hold your d—d tongue!" cried Margetts. "Cottle, you have put your foot in it."

"What do you mean, sir?"—"I mean that you have allowed the colonel to make a mistake in the will. You know you are my wife, and your name is Margetts. We were married by special license only last week."

"Hurrah!" cried I, "so there is no such person as Mrs. Cottle, and the will is a nullity."

Mrs Cottle looked provokingly cool, and then said,—

"Restrain your exultation and never hilloa till you are fairly out of the wood. The party who performed the marriage ceremony between me and Mr. John Margetts was not a clergyman, but an old acquaintance of mine. The fact was, he pressed me very much to wed him, and I, liking the fellow a little, affected to do so; but being aware that Colonel Harrington was about to leave me all his property, and that he might not like the match, I had it made a sham one. Moreover—a-hem!—I like to have property in my own hands; and as far as you, John Margetts, are concerned, you shall be very well provided for indeed, and your best plan, which you will easily see, is, to keep your own counsel."

"Humph!" said Margetts; "you are wrong, my dear. Never hilloa till you are out of the wood. It was night when we were married, and your particular friend was so drunk, that before you came I had him given to a constable, and the Reverend Stephen Anderton, from St. Bride's Church, performed the ceremony. It's all up now; the devil take the hindmost."

At this moment the hands of the dead body relaxed and fell to the sides. Mrs. Cottle uttered a scream, and pointing to Margetts, who made a bolt to the door to escape, cried,—

"Seize him—seize him! He forged the will. I claim the thousand pounds reward offered by you, sir. Seize John Margetts; he forged the will. I am his wife, and so escape punishment, because I acted under his direction. Give me the thousand pounds and let me go."

"Not at all," said I; "not at all. Infamous woman, you are defeated, and by your own avarice, too. Your consummate treachery and trickery has fallen upon your own head."

"D—n her!" cried Margetts; "I don't believe but she has a husband already living beside me. I admit all. The will is forged; but she made me leave blanks for the names, saying she would get the colonel, in some interval when he was not himself, to fill them up. She has filled them herself, and be hanged to her, with Cottle instead of Margetts. It's no use fighting against it; half a dozen people, at least, know of my marriage with her. I would not consent to her forging the will unless she married me, so that I could have had a claim on the whole property myself."

"Now," said I, "you will both of you have the kindness to accompany this constable to the watchhouse."—"Not yet," said Mrs. Cottle, and flying at Margetts she nearly tore his eyes out before he could be resued from her.

* * * * *

Margetts was transported, and Mrs. Cottle acquitted; what became of her, God only knows. As for Tommy, he stepped quietly into his property, and the first thing he said when he was brought home was "d—n," which General Eusham thought amazingly clever, and laughed till he cried again, prophesying great things from Tommy's precocious genius.

THE WIFE;

OR, MR. TODD'S DELINQUENCIES.

When I lived in lodgings—that is, before I was married, and before my means would enable me to keep a house, and comfortably walk into a higher rank of my profession—I rented a first floor of a Mrs. Welch, who had a very respectable house in the immediate neighbourhood of St. Thomas's Hospital, where I had some practice. She was rather a good-looking woman was Mrs. Welch, although of the showy rather than of the intellectual order, and she seemed, either from her own natural sagacity and personal observations, or from information which had been volunteered to her by some one, to be perfectly aware that she was a good-looking woman, and took care that nothing within her means should be wanting to do credit to what nature had already done for her.

Whether Mrs. Welch was a widow, or only called herself Mrs. Welch because she had reached a certain age, and thought that "Mrs." would add strength to her establishment, I don't know, for it was always made by the young men who lodged in the house a matter of debate; but there was one thing we very soon all of us found out, and that was that Mrs. Welch would have no sort of objection to become Mrs. anybody else who chose to make her an offer that way tending.

I was warned when first I went to lodge there, that Mrs. Welch would make an attack upon my heart; but that did not deter me, as I considered myself proof against all sorts of insinuations; and, moreover, Mrs. Welch was of that class of females called fine women, and I never, owing, I suppose to some defect in my tastes and perceptions of the fine, admired such, but, on the contrary, pertinaciously called them coarse women, and fixed my affection on the more delicate specimens of the softer sex. So I went to Mrs. Welch's, secure, in my opinion, against the whole artillery of her charms.

I had been not very long in the house before Mrs. Welch, of course in her ignorance of my peculiar fancies and predilections, took upon herself to invite me to tea, and no sooner did I mention the invitation to some students who lodged in the house, than they one and all told me they had passed through the same ordeal, and that it was intended as a trial by Mrs. Welch, to see if there was any chance of hooking me within the bounds of matrimony.

"Very good," said I; "let her try her best and her worst, I am proof against all sorts of spells and fascinations, and will take tea with her whenever she shall honour me with an invitation, and never fear for my liberty were she ten times what she is."

"But," said one young fellow, whose name was Wilkinson, "there is a curious circumstance connected with Mrs. Welch's tea-drinkings."—"Indeed!" said I.

"Yes," he added; "you will always find a man of the name of Todd drop in.—Into the tea?"—"Come, now, no nonsense; you know what I mean. Before the tea-drinking is over, you will find Mr. Todd will be announced."

"And who may he be?"—"That we none of us know—we should like to know, but we don't know, not one of us, who or what he is—whence he comes, and where he goes to—why he comes, and why he don't, we know nothing about; but see him you will, and a very quiet, gentlemanly, nice sort of a man you will find him!"

"Well," said I, "if before I received Mrs. Welch's invitation with indifference, I cannot do so now, for you have most decidedly awakened my curiosity; I would not stay away on any account."—"Very good—we wish you joy."

"Thank you, and as it is now five o'clock, and Mrs. Welch asked me for half-past, I shall, just in honour of the occasion, put on a white waistcoat; so good bye to you all, and to-morrow I will give an account of the tea drinking."

Mrs. Welch was magnificently dressed. Had I been the lord mayor, whether I made up my accounts or not, she could not have received me with greater eclat. A young man is always a little flattered by attentions from any woman, but Mrs. Welch was certainly a fine woman, so attentions from her ought, I suppose, to be considered as no joke at all. I was very glad I had put on the white waistcoat. She had on a crimson satin dress, with some sparkling, glittering ornaments, dingling and dangling all about, and catching the light of the two mould candles that burnt upon the table, and the two others that burnt in the lustres on the chimney-piece, in a very attractive manner.

A nice, pleasant, roaring, crackling fire was in the grate. A well-polished, handsome tea-urn, kept up a gentle, murmuring, hissing sound upon the table. There were muffins baked to a turn—crumpets soft as sucking doves. A ham, anchovies—Heaven only knows what there was not, and there sat Mrs. Welch, with such a smile, as the presiding genius of that uncommonly comfortably looking front parlour, that I could not refrain from calling into requisition my very best bow, as I ran my fingers through my hair, and bade the lady good evening.

"Upon my word, Mrs. Welch," I said, "really—a—a—you are amazingly comfortable here."

"Do you think so?"—"Indeed, I do. I never saw a more home like, happy, agreeable, comfortable sort of a fire-side in all my life, Mrs. Welch."

"Lonely," she said, with a sigh, "very lonely."—"It's a coming," thought I. "D—n it, she will make me an offer bang off at once, and I shall be under the disagreeable necessity of saying 'no, ma'am,' to a lady."

"Very lonely," she added; "ah, me, you can't think how very lonely."—"Indeed! Why you have an opportunity, madam, of seeing a great many people. I could scarcely have thought you could feel lonely?"

"The heart—the heart," said Mrs. Welch; "but no matter —pardon me, sir;" and she wiped away a real or an imaginary tear from the corner of her eye with the corner of her handkerchief—"no matter, sir. I am a poor, foolish creature, and ought not to trouble a young, good-looking gentleman, who might make any female, who really loved him, happy, with any griefs, and anxieties, and feelings."

"What a handsome ceiling lamp," said I, wishing to divert the conversation to some other topic.—"Very," said Mrs. Welch; "I gave thirty guineas for it. One must purchase handsome things sometimes—what do you think of these bracelets?"

She held out her hand to me as she spoke, and I was forced to look at a very splendid bracelet, that was on her wrist. She had a very small hand—it was very white—and —and, indeed, Mrs. Welch's hand was quite unexceptionable.

"It's very handsome," said I.

I meant the hand, and not the bracelet. She looked into my face with quite a bewitching smile, and such an amiable laugh came from her lips, that—that, in fact, I began to think there was more danger in Mrs. Welch's fascinations than I had ever calculated upon. I never have, for many years, heard so exquisite, so touching, so agreeable a laugh since I heard Mrs. Welch, occasionally, until it was my good fortune, old man as I am now, and thinking, or I ought to be thinking, I suppose, of something else than agreeable laughs, or bewitching people—until, I say, it was my good fortune to see that really enchanting actress, Mrs. Stirling; and there is, indeed, to be found the rare, musical, sweet laugh which rings upon the ears like a peal of silver bells.

For a moment I took Mrs. Welch's hand in mine, but prudence whispered to me, "Let it go—let it go," and I did, of course.

"You like it sweet?" said Mrs. Welch, as she held a piece of sugar over my cup, with the tongs.—"Not too sweet," said I, "it's apt to cloy."

She returned the sugar to the basin, and, with a sigh, remarked,—

"Ah me, what a world this is, Mr. ——. How few do we find with genuine, real hearts. Everything is so very artificial now."

Then came the laugh again—I didn't like it, and yet I did, somehow—I suppose I was getting terribly afraid, that's the truth; and when, after a little time, she added,—"Now, do you really know what I asked you to tea for?" I was on the point of making a precipitate retreat, for I fully expected an audacious declaration at once.

"No—n—n—no," I stammered. "How should I know—perhaps it was to give my opinion about the young hyson, or the favourite souchong, or—or something else."

"Ah, you man," laughed Mrs. Welch; "it was not the hyson, nor the souchong; but, it was the something else—oh, dear me." (Laughing again.)

"A-a-hem," said I, "it's getting late."

"And raining. You won't go out to-night, I know you won't—cream?"—"A little."

"Cream is so delicious, so soft, so yielding, so ——."— "Yes, yes, exactly." (The laugh again.)

I felt myself rather on the tremble, as I told myself,—

"D—n it, she will propose to me, and say 'yes' for me, and settle the when and the where without me being able to stammer out a denial."

A perspiration (it might have been owing to the tea) came out upon my brow. Mrs. Welch popped, not the question, but her foot upon mine, quite accidentally, as I had been using a hassock that was close to my chair. I gave a great jump, but she only laughed, as she cried,—

"Oh, how stupid of me! will you forgive me? I didn't see your foot." (Laugh again.) "And there now, you see, if I commit injuries, I repair them." (Laugh again.) I could have jumped out of the window.

She knelt down, and with an embroidered handkerchief she

wiped the top of my shoe, and then, resting her hands upon my knees, she looked up into my face with her bright eyes, and, while a laugh of a hundred-love power pealed from her lips, she said,—

"Pray, Goody, please to moderate the rancour of your tongue,
Why flash those sparks of fury from your eyes?
Try me, ply me, then if you deny me,
You cast me off ——"

God! how the woman sung—a voice like an angel. I was bewildered—half mad. I—I—I didn't know what to do. I —I didn't know what to say. I—I suppose I looked as like a fool as possible, while that provoking Mrs. Welch, with such a happy, d—d, no, blessed, musical laugh, kept saying,—

"Try me, ply me, then if you deny me, you cast me off to blast you never more," till I got quite frantic, and cried,—

"Mrs.—what's your name?"—"Welch, Welch, ah, me! Now I have offended you."

"Get up, will you, my dear—I mean, madam?"—"Ah, but you said 'dear.'"

"No, I didn't."—"Oh, fibs, fibs, fibs."

Then, with a laugh that, as Jonathan would say, beat the others all to immortal smash, she placed one of those provoking, soft, beautiful, child-like hands over my mouth, so that I couldn't speak—I couldn't groan—I—I couldn't move—I couldn't swear—I could only kiss it, and then she sprang to her feet, and burst into tears.

Here was a predicament. What on earth was I to do? I asked myself the question, and immediately upset my tea as a practical answer to it. I could not run away and leave her lonely—no; the artful Mrs. Welch in tears, it would be unmanly, ungentlemanly; and yet, what the deuce she was crying for, I could not make out.

"Mrs. Welch," I cried, "what is the matter?"—"Hush!" she said, stopping her tears as if by magic. "The girl with more muffins."

In marched the servant girl with such a simper upon her countenance, that I felt in a moment convinced she had been a listener to what was passing. This provoked me beyond measure; and, when she was gone, I arose, saying,—

"Mrs. Welch, all this is very extraordinary to me; I have had quite enough tea, besides breaking the cup and saucer. I must now ——"

"No, no," sobbed Mrs. Welsh. "Do not mind me. You shall not be annoyed with me any more; I could not help those tears. I do sometimes, but very rarely, weep. Old thoughts of happiness come over me: a word, a look will sometimes awaken occurrences I would fain let sleep for ever. It is very, very foolish; but I cannot help it. You looked or said something which awakened a chord of feeling, first to harmony, and then to tears. Forgive me! I will not weep again. You see, once more I can smile. Shall I sing to you—shall I laugh with you—shall I talk to you? Anything to make my peace. Come, now, you will not go now, I am sure. You will not go."

I was human nature, so I sat down again; but what a different notion had I of Mrs. Welch to that which I had first entertained. I thought her a showy, good-looking, worldly-minded woman. I found her—I was going to say, an angel —but she was, certainly, a most fascinating creature. Her voice was melody itself; her laugh—I have said already what her laugh was. The expression of her countenance; the poetry of her language; the sweetness of her manner, all conspired to make Mrs. Welch as dangerous a person as ever I met with. Although I did sit down, I quite made up my mind to get away as quickly as I could; and a most strong resolution, too, did I make, that that should be my first and last tea-drinking with Mrs. Welch and all her really fearful fascinations.

She was as good as her word, for she subdued her tears, and then, resuming her old lovely smile, she said in a sweet confidential tone of voice,—

"A woman, sir, a poor, lone woman, who has once known what it was to have around her loving and smiling faces, may be excused for giving way at some stray moments to feelings which only sleep, but never can be totally extinguished."—

"Yes, yes. Precisely," said I.

"I knew you would say yes. But I told you I had a particular motive in inviting you to tea—a motive, independent of the pleasure I expected to derive, and have not been disappointed in deriving, from your society."

"Anything in my power, madam, I—I shall be very happy, I'm sure ——"—"I want you to do me a favour."

Oh, how I wished I was out of doors.

"I have heard you talked of as a young physician of great talent—as one who, one day, would and must mount high in his profession."—"You are very complimentary, Mrs. Welch."

"Oh, no; I never compliment any one. Now, hearing so much of you, I want your medical opinion."

I breathed a little more freely.

"Your medical opinion as to a slight pain I feel about the region of the heart. I am afraid it is a heart affection. Just place your hand upon my heart."

With a very bad grace I did; and then she continued speaking with her mouth so provokingly close to mine that— that I didn't know whether to kiss her or not.

"There, now, don't you feel it beat rather irregularly, sometimes faster and sometimes slower? I am at times quite alarmed. You see what a cheat I am to get a valuable medical opinion without a fee; but I have no one to care for me, you see; so I am forced to be so cunning, you wouldn't believe—what do you think of my heart?"

Mrs. Welch's cunning, I could, upon consideration, but not just then, easily believe in. As for the state of her heart and its singular pulsations—sometimes slow, and sometimes fast, mine beat it all to nothing.

"My dear madam," I said, "I don't think there is anything the matter with your heart."

"You are sure?"—"Not quite sure; but heart diseases shew themselves far more unquestionably than this case of yours. You may, I think, depend upon there being nothing material the matter. These irregularities of heart action very often occur as phenomena of the system, without producing any known bad effects."

"Then I need not fear a sudden death?"—"Certainly not."

Her eyes filled again with tears, and she let her head drop on my breast, as she sobbed,—

"How can I thank you? How can ——."—"Mr. Todd, ma'am," announced the servant.

"D—n Mr. Todd," said I, as I with one spring got to the other end of the room, and nearly let the fascinating Mrs. Welch fall down on the floor, she had been so very confidingly resting upon me.

"Your very humble servant, sir," said a demure-looking, little man, as he stood at the door with his hat in his hand, and bowed very low. "Your very humble servant, sir. Do not let me interrupt you, I beg. I repeat, sir, I am your very humble servant."

"Oh, Todd, Todd," sighed Mrs. Welch, as she sank upon a chair.—"Yes, ma'am."

"You—have—just—come in time."—"To see me go," cried I. "Good evening, Mrs. Welch. I hope you are better; and Mr. Todd, who is an old acquaintance, will, no doubt, be better able to console you for your loneliness than I can hope to do."

"But, sir," said Todd, placing himself in the most ridiculous manner all aslant to prevent me from leaving the room. "But, sir, ——"

"Well, sir!"—"You will not go on my account, surely. A young, enterprising gentleman ——"

"Good evening, Mrs. Welch."

So saying, I took Mr. Todd by the collar, but before I could remove him an inch, he dropped at my feet, saying,—

"An assault! an assault!"

I stepped over him, and in another moment had taken my hat from a peg in the passage, and rushed from the house.

I was delighted to breathe again the clear, open air, and escape from the fascinations I had but just then quitted, and traversed the streets with as much pleasure as a schoolboy would when unexpectedly he escapes from the school. I passed rapidly along the streets—I scarce felt the earth beneath my feet; the streets passed vividly by my eyes, and I was scarce sure whither I went through the streets, or the streets, shops, and lamps, by me.

After awhile the fervour of my feelings abated, and I gradually sobered down to the exercise of common sense, and then I began to notice things about me with more coolness. I began, too, to have an indistinct notion that there was a dampness hanging round me that I had not at first noticed at all, and when I did, I could not account for it. Suddenly, however, it occurred to me that it must be rain. This was indeed the case; the pavement was all glistening and shining with the reflected light from from shops and lamps, and the troubled ocean of umbrellas convinced me of the fact.

I immediately sought out some near doorway that was protected by a portico, and sheltered myself beneath it. I passed my hand down my coat, and found it had imbibed some moisture, so that had I not discovered the fact of its raining when I did, I should have been in an unpleasant condition. The shower was sharp and heavy—people ran in various directions, to shorten the time that they would be compelled to be in it; but I thought it unwise to quit my place of shelter, seeing that, to the best of my belief, it would be but of short duration.

Already in the distance I could see the broken clouds, which, when they reached over the spot where I stood, would end the shower; the stars I could see gradually peep out from behind the mass of clouds which came riding upwards at a slow but majestic rate, but still they came, and as they neared, so the end of the shower was nigh, I was convinced. The rain fell very heavy indeed, as the last of the clouds passed over, and then a few falling drops alone came down, which decreased each moment, and the stars became distinctly visible.

By this time I had pretty well recovered my equanimity, and was able to reflect with more calmness upon the evening I had passed with Mrs. Welch. There was much in her conduct which I could not at all make out, and I thought her the most mysterious woman I had certainly ever met with. I debated within myself as to the propriety or otherwise of at once leaving such dangerous and fascinating lodgings—yet, somehow, I did not like to do so, as it would be such a confession of cowardice, and I should be unmercifully quizzed by the other students who lodged in the house. So, upon a consideration of all the circumstances, I made up my mind to go home again as if nothing was the matter, and to meet Mrs. Welch, should accident compel me to do so, with as much equanimity as I could.

Accordingly, I turned my steps towards the Borough, and very soon reached Mrs. Welch's door. For a moment I hesitated before knocking, for fear Mrs. Welch should herself open the door, and, in spite of me, drag me into the parlour to view her fascinations; but there was no other resource, and I did execute a tolerable double knock, which, with desperate duplicity, I made as unlike my usual summons for admission as possible.

The door was opened by the girl, who looked as still and demure as if nothing was the matter, and I was right glad to escape to my own room up stairs, without being again exposed to the artillery of Mrs. Welch's charms, which I really began to dread.

"Fly love, and love will follow thee," says the old adage, and so I found it, for I had scarcely been in the room ten minutes, when the girl came up to me with a note, which she laid before me silently, and then left. Upon opening it, and casting my eyes to the foot of the page, I found, to my terror, that it was from Mrs. Welch, and I almost began to doubt the prudence of reading it, so prepossessed was I now with a notion of the difficulty of escaping from her toils. Curiosity, however, got the better, as it generally does, in man, woman, or child, of all prudential reasons and suggestions, so I broke the seal, which consisted of two doves, with their mouths remarkably close together, and read the following epistle, which was duly addressed to me, and written in the lady-like Italian hand which is so much patronised:—

"Front Parlour, half-past Nine.

"MY VERY DEAR SIR,—I feel that some explanation is due to you, for the intrusion of that most odious of men, Todd, at a most interesting moment, when you were, I know, about to ask me to reciprocate those sentiments towards you, which, with all the poetry of affection, you had been just expressing.

"Oh, sir! interruption at such a time is maddening. Come to supper to-night. I write this with a determination of waiting till you come home. Let me prove to you that I detest the man who obtruded his hateful presence upon us; and at the same time I have a secret of importance to inform you of, which will, for the future, enable you, for my sake, to endure now and then the presence even of Todd.

"Believe me to be, my dear sir,
"Most sincerely yours,
"ARABELLA WELCH."

"Supper be hanged," thought I. "A likely thing, indeed. After being terrified out of my life at tea, to go to supper for the sake of undergoing a similar operation! I shall certainly not go."

With this determination I immediately wrote, and addressed to the fascinating Mrs. Welch, the following rather pithy note:—

"Front Room, Second Floor, quarter to Eleven.

"MADAM,—I regret that I cannot do myself the pleasure of supping with you, as I prefer supping in my own apartment. With respect to the man, Todd, I have no desire to see or hear anything of him. The other portions of your note are far beyond my comprehension.

"I am, madam, yours, &c.

"To Mrs. Welch."

I then rang my bell, and when the servant came, I desired her to take the note to her mistress. She was not gone above ten minutes when she came tumbling up the stairs with something very heavy, and, to my great surprise, she came into my room with an immense tray, on which were plates, dishes, knives and forks, covers, and the deuce knows all what.

"Why—why—what is all this?"

The girl set down the tray with a dab and a clatter upon my table, and then taking up a note, which was on one corner of it, she handed it to me, and immediately disappeared.

With a feeling of perfect bewilderment, I read as follows:—

"Back Parlour, five minutes to Eleven.

"MY VERY DEAR SIR,—You are quite right. I cannot sufficiently admire your prudence. We *will* sup in your room, instead of the front parlour. I will be up directly, and have ordered the things to be laid. We shall escape Todd yet.
"Yours, ever and ever,
"ARABELLA WELCH."

I jumped up, and caught hold of my hat and a great coat, resolved to rush away, and never again set foot in Mrs. Welch's house. I reached the door of my room, and was going to make a dart down the staircase, when I ran full against Mrs. Welch, who, seizing me by both arms, said,—

"Hush—hush! Mr. Wilkinson is at home. Consider that I am a woman; say nothing; come to supper; do not expose me to misconstruction—dear—dear!"

She threw herself upon my breast, and as she was a tolerable weight, I was compelled to stagger back into the room the best way I could, and place her in a chair.

"Mrs. Welch," I said, "for one moment, madam, hear me. Why, in the name of Heaven, do you persecute me in this way?"—"Persecute! Oh, Heaven!"

"Yes, madam; it amounts to a persecution, I assure you —a most abominable persecution. Tell me what I owe you, madam, and let me leave, at once, the house; I can endure it no longer."

"What you owe me, sir? Good God! do you fancy I can take money of you? No, sir. Desert me, now, if you will. Go, sir, if you can be happy, now—go, sir, at once; leave me to my own shame—to my own sorrow, I can say no more. 'Tis very, very cruel; but I will not mourn. The innocent and confiding are ever thus met by the designing and the artful. I have done with you, sir. Go at once, and thank Heaven you escape so very easily, sir."

I was more bewildered than ever at this speech. No insulted masterpiece of virtue could have spoken more to the purpose, or in a tone more likely to produce the strongest effect upon any one who loved her, I knew not what reply to make. Feeling my own entire innocence, and the manner in which I had been played upon, I began to think that some plot must be at the bottom of it all, and I got proportionately indignant.

"Madam," I said, "you know well that this scene is of your own making. From your own imagination, wholly and solely, have you drawn your fancied materials for your accusations of me. From this night I quit your house. What may have been your intention in getting up this extraordinary scene I cannot pretend to guess; but I am satisfied that you have utterly and completely failed."

"Mr. Todd," announced the servant girl; and with a cringing sort of bow, there stood, at the open door of the room, no other than Mr. Todd.

I was petrified with amazement. The plot was evidently thickening.

"What next?" I said to myself; and for some moments there was a profound silence.

Mr. Todd then beckoned in the servant girl, and closed the door of the room. Mrs. Welch pretended to weep bitterly, and I stood looking first at one and then at the other of the parties who had so oddly made free with my apartment, with something of the feeling that an amused spectator regards some scene in a drama, the plot of which he does not exactly as yet comprehend.

There was a devilish smile on the face of Mr. Todd, which seemed to promise something, and, but that my curiosity was strongly aroused by the whole affair, I believe I should have kicked him down stairs; but I really did wish to see the end of the affair, and I said nothing—did nothing, apparently much to the surprise of Mr. Todd, who fidgetted about a little, and said,—

"Very well—ve—ry well, ladies and gentlemen—very well, indeed—ve—ry well."

Still I said nothing, notwithstanding I had an appealing look from Mrs. Welsh, that was calculated to have melted the heart of a court-pensioner. I was quite obdurate, and determined that they should some of them speak first, if I waited an hour. At length Mr. Todd, unable to bear the silence patiently, broke out with—

"And so, Mrs. Welch, it is thus I find you. In a gentleman's room, about to sup with him. Pray, madam, what account do you consider I can give Captain Hanibal Welch, R.N., of this transaction?"

Mrs. Welch sobbed, and uttered the word,—

"Mercy!"

"I repeat, madam," continued Mr. Todd, "what account am I to give Captain Welch, R.N., of this transaction? I, Nicodemus Todd, of Bernard's Inn, his solicitor—his confidential friend—his family adviser—the man, to whom he said, when he went his last Indian voyage, from which, by-the-bye, he will, assuredly, return next Thursday—I say, what can I tell him—I, whom he said to,—

"'Todd,—watch my wife. She is young—she is beautiful—she has a fascinating laugh—she has amiable manners—she is virtue itself, but she is thoughtless. Todd, watch her, and if you find, or even fancy any fellow—young, middle-aged, or old, making love to her, I will, Todd, as sure as I'm a living man, blow his brains out, if I were hung for the act the next hour, Todd.'

"Such is the man, madam—a man of furious, wild, ungovernable passions, standing six feet four, without his boots, to whom I feel myself compelled to give an account of this transaction."

Here Mr. Todd paused in his oratory, and I could see his little keen grey eyes fixed on my face to see what effect it had upon me; but I could say nothing, and Mrs. Welch only continued weeping.

"I repeat," added Mr. Todd, swelling with indignation, "what shall I say to Captain Hanibal Welch, R.N.—eh? madam, will you have the kindness to answer me, or is this gentleman, who I think has got himself into a scrape, to be your mouthpiece?"

"What can I say? Oh, what can I do?" said Mrs. Welch, with a look at me.—"Just whatever you like, madam," said I.

"But, what will become of you?"—"Oh, never mind me."

"Young man—young man," said Todd, "you don't know what you are saying, when you remark 'never mind me.' A man who should, under your circumstances, insure his life, would find the policy vitiated by fraud, for to offend Captain Welch, R.N., is equivalent to suicide."—"I will run the risk."

"You—you will?"—"I will, most certainly."

"Oh, oh, dear!" cried Mrs. Welch. "But I shall be sacrificed too—I shall be murdered!"—"You will, indeed, madam," said Todd. "I don't know what can save you."

"But cannot you?" she said, imploringly. "Oh, Mr. Todd, cannot you be merciful, and keep this wretched affair from my husband's ears? You can save us both."

"My duty—my duty!" said Todd, giving his chest a blow; "duty. Bernard's Inn, madam, expects every man to do his duty."

"But you will be merciful?"—"I dare not—I dare not!"

"What will tempt you? Will gold? You shall be well paid. Believe me, you shall. I will impoverish myself to pay you."

Todd shook his head.

"Will a hundred pounds prevail upon you to keep secret that I do love this gentleman? That I have doated on him—that his very footstep on the stairs has been music in my ears? Say that a hundred pounds, Todd, will satisfy you?"

"Listen to me," said Todd, solemnly. "If Captain Hanibal Welch, R.N., hears of this affair, he will, I am quite sure, murder you, madam. I would fain spare you, and I would fain, likewise, spare this gentleman, who also will be found some day a mangled corpse. But—but, madam—and, sir—but——"

"But what, Mr. Todd?" she sobbed.—"Captain Welch pays me well. A hundred and fifty might suffice."

"Oh, thanks—thanks! Sir—sir——"

She rushed towards me and caught me in her arms, as she added, in a voice of hysterical emotion,—

"You are saved—you are saved! Your reputation would have been blasted, too, for ever by this affair, even had you escaped the captain's vengeance and it had become public. As a young medical man you would have been ruined, and all owing to me."

I got free of Mrs. Welch as well as I could, and then I said,—

"It certainly is all owing to you, madam, and I am very sorry to say it is. There is, however, one fact connected with this affair, which I beg to call your attention to, Mr. Todd."—"Name it, sir—name it."

"It simply is, that this is my apartment, and if you don't go out at the door, I will throw you out at the window."

Mr. Todd gave a great jump towards the door as he said,—

"Why, you are mad?"

"No, nor afraid. Mrs. Welch, you had better go down stairs. I am very sorry to be ungallant to a lady, but I will sup alone to-night, if you please."

"No—no. Oh, no! I will pay the money, and all will be well. Todd, I have got fifty pounds in the house—you shall have that at once and the other hundred as soon as I can possibly sell my goods to procure it. Believe me, I will pay it all. You may take my word, Mr. Todd."

"I think I may, Mrs. Welch; but if I take any money on account in this transaction my lips are sealed, because I should be as much in your power as you are in mine. I tell you what I will do now."

"Oh, what—what?"—"I will take your fifty pounds, and this gentleman's bill at three months' date."

"Yes—yes; that will do. We are saved—we are saved!"

I shook my head as I said,—

"I'm afraid that won't do, Mr. Todd—very much afraid. You don't seem disposed to go out at the door, so you must by the window. You swindling vagabond, you have dared to insult me by supposing me such a goose as to be taken in by your flimsy pretences. Come, sir. The window, if you please."

I opened the window as I spoke, and Mrs. Welch uttered a loud shriek, while Mr. Todd conveyed himself in a moment to the landing of the stairs.

"Come, sir," I added, "we will put an end to this ridiculous scene; it is not a time of night to have any more private theatricals, which I consider your conduct amounts to, so, if you please, here is the window or there is the staircase."

"I tell you what, Mr. What's-your-name," he called out, "I'll make you suffer for this. As Captain Welch's solicitor, I will immediately commence an action against you on his account, and on my own part you will find yourself in the morning forced to appear at Union-hall for an assault."

"I have not touched you."—"No; but you have put me in bodily fear."

"Well," said I, "if I must appear to answer an assault, I will not do so for nothing; so, Mr. Todd, I shall give you a sound drubbing if I can get hold of you."

This liberal promise had a perfectly electrical effect upon Mr. Todd, and he disappeared down the staircase in a twinkling, while Mrs. Welch gave various indications of an hysterical tendency, as she sat upon my sofa with her handkerchief spread nearly entirely over face.

Having thus succeeded in ridding myself of Todd, I turned to her, and although very angry with her for the part she had taken in the affair, I could not bring my mind to speak very harshly to her.

"Mrs. Welch," I said, "it is with both pain and regret that I now feel convinced you and that scoundrel, who has just left, have conspired together to make an attack upon my pocket. Had I been a weak, timid young man, I should have yielded myself wholly up to what, without any flattery, I must call your fascinations."

Mrs. Welch groaned.

"Yes, madam, your fascinations, I repeat; and I regret much that a person like yourself, so capable in every way of being the charm of all who know you, should lend yourself to the paltry trickery of a man like Todd."

She burst into tears, and they were either really genuine, or so well acted, that I felt a little unmanned by them, and could scarcely proceed; but, however, I called courage to my aid, and added, after a very short pause,—

"Madam, henceforward our acquaintance is at an end. I shall quit these apartments to-morrow, and now let me request of you, while I do remain here, to leave me the uninterrupted possession of them."

She rose without a word and walked to the door; then turning her eyes upon me, she said in a low voice of much pathos,—

"You are mistaken—you are mistaken, sir; you judge of me too harshly, much too harshly."

Then she left the room, and right glad was I to get rid of her so easily. I then sat myself down and drew a long breath, as I thought of the events of the night. There was much to annoy me and a little to alarm me. My own innocence of any wish to interfere with Mrs. Welch, or the big Captain Welch, if there were such a person, I well enough knew, and I knew likewise that innocence is but a poor barrier against the consequences in such cases of an accusation. The rascal Todd, when he had hinted at the consequences to a young medical man of an accusation of an immoral character, had spoken a home truth, and well I knew that the most absurd and improbable charge in the world against any one, however clearly it might be denied, would be believed by some people; and even the majority of society are very apt to shake their wise heads and say, "Ah, there's something in it, I dare say, after all, though it ain't exactly proved;" for there are thousands of addle-headed wretches, who, instead of giving an accused person the benefit of a doubt, will condemn him at once.

A reputation, therefore, of any professional man, sad to say, is most certainly at the mercy of any scoundrel who chooses to trump up a story against him. It is all very well to say that you may prove your innocence, but that won't suffice. It's all very well for a magistrate, or a judge, or a jury, to tell a man that he goes away from a court of justice without a stain upon his character; that will not suffice. Nay, you may indict your accuser for perjury, and get him transported, but that will not suffice. The sagacious public will shake its head and say,—

"Ah, there was a something in it."

Ten to one too, but after a year or two, when the affair is only dimly remembered, you will be made to change places with your libeller, who may have been transported, and some good folks will say, when your name suddenly is mentioned—

"Dr. —— Dr. —— Dr. ——; dear me, wasn't he transported for perjury against Jones?"

Hence people, who know anything of the world, shake their heads at all the canting nonsense about innocence supporting a man against false accusations. They know he might as well be guilty, and escape merely by some chicanery of his counsel, as be entirely innocent. The world will damn him and his prospects all the same.

"So-and-so was tried at the Old Bailey."

"But he was acquitted."

"Yes, but I dare say there was something in it."

Such is the mode by which a man may be received, and consequently I had a serious horror of Mr. Todd, who, if he chose to annoy me might do so to a ruinous extent. A young physician, only fancy, with an action of crim. con. Were he as pure as an angel out of Heaven, he is done for.

I actually trembled, and a terrible idea came across me of smothering Todd. I began to see the whole plot as plainly as possible. There was the confounded servant, no doubt, in the conspiracy. There was Todd just making his appearance twice and finding Mrs. Welch with me. There were the supper things all laid in my room. Mrs. Welch's tears—my note, which would be produced, and looked upon as emanating from some lover's quarrel; my scampering out of the house when Todd came in; my very threats to him, and his going away, leaving Mrs. Welch with me. Oh, there was plenty of evidence to make a married juryman, who stood in proper fear of his wife, shake his great stupid head, and say—

"There must be something in it."

I was really frightened, and began to think that, after all, an escape would be cheap, at the bill for a hundred pounds at a short date. Anger, dread, rage and alarm, took possession of me by turns. I could not abscond, for I had paid large medical fees at the hospitals; and, besides, a medical man can always be found, unless, like some drunken swindler, he prefers cheating his friends by the assistance of a blackguard attorney, whom I could name, out of their money to live on, instead of practising, honourably, his profession.

I was fairly bewildered, and at length, not being able to come to any rational conclusion, or to suggest to myself any mode of operations which should have the effect of rescuing me from my difficulties, I made up my mind to take the advice of some of the young men in the house, and see if, among us, we could not think of some means of getting the better of Mr. Todd.

Accordingly, I went across the landing to the room which was occupied by young Wilkinson, who, indeed, I very much wondered had not made his appearance during the row I had with Todd, when I gave him the option of the staircase or the window as a mode of exit.

I tapped at the door, and Wilkinson cried out—

"Come in."

I then at once entered his room, and found him sitting by the fire, with his feet upon the hobs of the grate, smoking a cigar, while a glass of something hot and strong looking smoked upon the chimney-piece just opposite to his mouth.

"Come in, my boy; come in," he cried. "Shut the door behind you, there's a good fellow."—"You seem to be enjoying yourself, Wilkinson."

"No, I aint, I'm only trying. Here, take a drop. Will you have a cigar?"—"Thank you, yes."

I lit a cigar, and Wilkinson having taken his feet off the hobs, and otherwise altered his position so as to afford me a good seat by the fire, I said,—

"Well, Wilkinson, didn't you hear something of a disturbance just now?"—"I did, my boy."

"Then why the deuce didn't you come to see what it was about?"—"I never interfere in family affairs."

"Family nonsense. I wish you had come; I cannot understand what on earth kept you so quiet, when you must have been aware of a riot on the very landing outside your door."—"Can't you? Ignorance is bliss, sometimes, uncommonly. Take another pull at that gin-and-water, and say no more about it."

"Why say no more about it; what the deuce possesses you, Wilkinson?"—"Nothing, my boy, nothing. Now, what, in the name of all that may be called toleration, good could I have done by coming out of my room, because you promised to kick a fellow down stairs or throw him out of the window, or something of that sort? I should only have been had up as evidence against you, you know; so don't say anything more about it."

"Well," said I, "there's something in that; but the affray has all been over now for some time, and yet you never stirred." —"No, I had my reasons."

"Indeed! May I ask what they are?"

Wilkinson took a draught of the gin-and-water, and fixed his eyes upon me all the while. Then, placing the glass again upon the chimney-piece, and drawing a long breath, said,—"No."—"Well, that's conclusive, at all events."— "Very."

"Now, Wilkinson, put joking aside, will you pay attention to what I have got to say to you?"—"Joking!"

"Are you mad likewise? Upon my word, your behaviour is very strange. I always took you for a very steady, friendly, good-tempered sort of a fellow, but to-night you seem quite the reverse, and all I can get from you are a few verbal repetitions of what I myself say. You must excuse me remarking, Wilkinson, that it's very unfriendly of you indeed."—"I'll excuse you. There, take another drink; go on, and don't mind me."

Tap, tap, came at the door, and Wilkinson cried out, "Come in;" when in came a young man, likewise lodging in the house, of the name of Scott; and before he could well seat himself and light a cigar, another tap announced the arrival of Mereweather, another student, who lodged in the first floor, so that there were now four of us assembled to do justice to Wilkinson's gin-and-water, and his really good cigars. There were a great many cordial salutations, and how are you's, until we all got seated, and then I said,—

"Well, my boys, now you are all here, I have got something to tell you, which I am glad, for the sake of saving trouble, to be able to tell you all at once."—"Very good," said they, and I proceeded.

"You know I was invited to tea by Mrs. Welch?"

Each one pulled his cigar out of his mouth, and I added,— "Well, I went."

They each gave a tap on the table with their knuckles, and, although rather annoyed at the mode in which my communication was received, I went on.

"Well, as I tell you, I went, and found Mrs. Welch a fascinating creature, and just such a woman as might be to any young man a most dangerous companion. She did all she possibly could to make me in love with her. She talked, laughed, joked, and, in short, made herself so irresistibly agreeable, that I think, even now, I shall never forget the pleasing impression she has made upon my imagination. She pretended she was fearful of a disease of the heart, and thanked me so tenderly for assuring her such was not the case, that I thought she would have devoured me. I became fairly fascinated by her."

"And then in came Todd," said Wilkinson.—"And then in came Todd," said Scott.

"And then in came Todd," repeated Mereweather; after which they all gave a tap with their knuckles against the table, as they had done before.

"Yes," said I. "And, then, as you say, in came Todd. D——n Todd, say I."—"Amen!" they all cried in chorus.

"Well, I was glad, though, that he came, and scampered off; but after that Mrs. Welch insisted upon coming to supper with me, and——"—"In came Todd again," they all repeated.

"Why, d——n it," said I, "you seem to know all about it as well as I do myself."—"Better," said Wilkinson, laying his cigar on the corner of the chimney-piece. "Gentlemen, have I your permission to make —— one of us!"

"Yes—yes—yes."

"Very good. Now listen. Mrs. Welch would come to supper with you. Then in came Todd; he threatened you with Captain Welch, R.N. You bullied. He persevered. Mrs. Welch sobbed. A compromise was offered, which, for fear of committing yourself before all your friends, and compromising, perhaps, all your professional prospects, you, after much hesitation, accepted. Mrs. Welch agrees to pay fifty pounds; you give your acceptance for a hundred, and there's the beginning of the end."

"I beg your pardon," said I. "How you became acquainted so accurately with the outline of the events as they occurred, I cannot pretend to say; but you are wrong as to the conclusion. I neither gave, nor do I intend to give, my acceptance to Todd."

"Then what do you mean to do?"—"Resist him."

"You will find the action brought against you, and be glad to compromise it for double the amount. We have been each invited to tea. We have been each fascinated. In came Todd to each of us, and—and—Todd holds each of our acceptances."

I was so astonished at this declaration, that I fairly jumped off my seat, and for some moments could not utter one word; but continued staring at them with amazement. When I did find breath to speak, I cried,—

"Why—why, you don't—you cannot mean really to tell me you have been such ninnies—such fools, as to be bullied out of your money by such a fellow as that Todd, and a designing, artful woman like Mrs. Welch! Young fellows like you, of spirit, sense, and enterprise, you don't mean it. You are joking."

"I wish we were," said Wilkinson. "It is far, very far past a joke for all of us."

"Then why did you not at once send for me?"—"Because, if you had refused the invitation to tea, there would have occurred certain consequences; and, besides, you must allow for a certain reluctance we had to mention the subject at all."

"But why do you remain here after being so jilted?"—"Because we are compelled."

They all nodded, and a silence of some minutes' duration ensued. They looked very melancholy; but I quite made up my mind they were having a bit of fun at my expense, so I said,—

"Very good, gentlemen—very good. I like a joke as well as anybody, and you have managed this very well indeed. Very good—very good; I quite admire your tact, upon my word. We'll have another cigar a-piece, and a laugh over it. I give you great credit for the joke, and I hope you will give me credit for not being such a fool as to be angry at it. Come, I will stand glasses round."

"With respect to the glasses round," said Wilkinson, "there can be, I presume, but one opinion. As to the other question, I can only answer for myself. Like you, I found the fascinations of Mrs Welch nearly irresistible. I was not afraid of the Captain Welch, R.N.; but I was afraid of the exposure of my name in a transaction which, perhaps, would have blighted my prospects for ever. My father is a struggling man, with a large family. They have all gone short to put me out in life respectably, with the hope, which, I trust, will be realised, of my assisting the younger ones. I dreaded the affair, and I gave a bill at three months, for a hundred pounds, to Todd."

"I am," said Scott, "wholly dependent on a god-father, who is a religious, prejudiced man. The knowledge that I was even accused of a liaison of this nature would have been my ruin. I, too, have given a bill for a hundred pounds, at three months, to Todd."

"My mother is a widow," said Mereweather; "I have three sisters. I gave a bill to Todd, for a hundred pounds, at three months' date."

"But—but—good God! how did you manage to pay them?"—"We didn't pay them," said Wilkinson. "Todd was merciful."

"Very, very," echoed Scott and Mereweather.—"How— how?"

"He always renews them at sixty per cent., when they become due."

"The devil, he does!"—"Yes, and we have them hanging over us continually."

"But why don't you leave?"—"Because Todd threatens a writ."

"Why—why didn't you tell me?"—"Because Todd threatens a writ."

"Then, out of you three, besides your being secured here as permanent lodgers, who dare not grumble, he gets as much money?"—"He gets nearly as forty-five pounds every three months!"

I was perfectly staggered; I no longer entertained any doubt as to the facts being just as they stated them to me. Their manner fully confirmed it; I was only amazed at the damnable ingenuity of the plot which had made the three young men the slaves of the designing rascal, Todd.

"Well," I said, "thank God I have resisted. I depend upon my uncle and aunt; Heaven only knows what effect it might have upon my fortunes if Todd finds them out, and makes a communication to them that I have formed an immoral acquaintance with my landlady."

"Find them out," cried Wilkinson; "you may depend he has done that. You had better give your bill, and trust, as we do, to paying it off some day. It's the cheapest and the best plan you can possibly adopt; we have talked it over, and we know it."

"No," said I; "no, gentlemen; if I slave, if I beg, if I eat in a debtor's prison, I will not humble to that man."

"Then we are all done for," said Scott, "for Todd, as soon as he finds we have made a confidant with one who defies him, will have revenge upon us."

"I don't think he will be such a fool," said I, "as to despoil himself of the fifteen pounds you each pay him every three months for the sake of any revenge; but depend upon me, I will not commit you; I hope to rescue you. Between now and to-morrow morning, I will adopt some resolution which shall be put in practice against the machinations of the villain Todd, you may depend."

"I wish you luck," said Mereweather; "but it's worth your considering, whether, in defying him, you are not, as a young medical man, ruining yourself."

"I will risk all that. Good night. Now I am going out to consult a friend. Good night; I think you have all of you acted very weakly, and drawn each other into the scrape; but what's done must be endured, unless it can, which I sincerely hope it may, be undone."

It was now past midnight; but as going to sleep was really quite out of the question, I made up my mind that I would take my way to the Temple, where a young friend of mine, who had very recently been called to the bar, had chambers, and slept in them. I had, in common with all who knew him, the very highest opinion of his talents; and upon his advice concerning Mr. Todd I was resolved to act, being convinced that I could pursue no sounder course than the one he should point out to me.

As I have said, it was rather an unseemly hour to call upon any one; but I wanted to be thoroughly prepared as to what I meant to do before the morning should, perhaps, renew hostilities with Mr. Todd. Besides, I knew that Mr. Croft, which was my legal friend's name, was not a very early man to go to bed, and that he would in all probability, as I had often found him, still be up, and reading in the quiet solitude of his chambers. It took some time to reach the gate opposite to Chancery-lane of the old Temple, and then I rang up the night porter, who, in not the most pleasant tones in the world, asked me who I was.

"I am going to Mr. Croft's chambers," I said.

He knew my voice, and admitted me instantly, for I had often been there before. The gates were closed, and I at once made my way to King's-bench walk, where Croft's chambers were situated. When I came home from my walk, after taking tea with Mrs. Welch, the evening had greatly improved as regards weather, and that improvement had gone on progressing; for now a lovelier night never came out of the heavens, the moon having risen high in the clear blue sky, which was studded with such myriads of stars, that it dazzled the eye to look upon them.

There is something always to my mind solemn and grand about that old Temple, even in the day-time, but more particularly at night, with such a moon shining down upon its masses of buildings. I have felt that soft, awe-inspiring feeling steal over me, as I have paced its solitary walks, which is so common to the mind of almost every one, when treading the hallowed aisles of some ancient cathedral.

In the Temple, if we linger to think of it at all, the mind is irresistibly carried back through the maze of history to that time when the ancient, chivalrous, bold, but terribly bad Templars, held it as their gorgeous and exclusive home. We fancy the echo of some armed heel treads in the paved courtyards, and that we may each moment see the gliding figure of some great scoundrel, half warrior and half priest, stealing along under some of the dark archways.

I like the old, time-hallowed Temple, and, after all, I am not sorry that the lawyers have got it; for, to tell the plain, honest truth, they do take great care of it. Moreover, they are just such a set of rogues as the old Templars used to be, so the place has not much changed. The old Templars of the feudal age made war upon the people's goods and chattels, under the mask of religion. The new Templars do the same thing under a far more understandable banner—that of justice; and both were thus alike, and arrant hypocrites; so, when I see some old lawyer skulking to his chambers, I look upon him as a kind of descendant of the old Templars, working out much the same object, namely, robbery on pretence of right.

What an apt modern representative of Sir Brian de Bois Gilbert would Sir Charles Wetherall make, if he would—perhaps he does—live in the old Temple! Yes, I certainly like the Temple amazingly. I quite lingered on my walk from the Temple-gate to King's-bench walk, so much did I admire the radiant beauty of the night. I almost forgot Mr. Todd, and what, perhaps, I was less likely to forget, even Mrs. Welch, until casting my eyes up to my friend's chamber windows, I saw a light at one of them, which at once recalled me to my senses, and told me what I had come about.

Croft was up, and reading, as usual, by the shady, pleasant light of an Argand lamp, which, after all, is worth any two of the nonsensical solars, and camphines, &c., with which the public have been so lately deluged.

"Hilloa!" he said, "who would have expected to see you at this hour? I suppose you have been to one of the theatres."—"No," said I; "but it's as good as a play."

"What is?"—"What I am gong to tell. Lend me your attentive ear, Croft, and 'be pleased to advise,' as the attornies say to you when they want your opinion."

"But they always send a fee," said Croft, drily.—"Or owe it."

"Yes—yes."—"Very good. I will place myself in the latter category, if you please; and now for the case."

I then carefully and circumstantially related to him all the circumstances with which the reader is already acquainted; and when I had concluded I paused to hear what he would say to it, for I saw by the expression of his face that he considered it as rather a serious affair.

"Humph!" he said. "This Todd is an attorney, I suppose?"—"I don't know, but it's likely enough."

"Well, as far as regards yourself, the case lies in a nutshell. You need not give a bill for a hundred pounds or a hundred farthings."

"Precisely; but what will Todd be likely to do?"—"Why, in the first place, I dare say there is no such person as Captain Welch. What Todd will do, or threaten to do, will be a private communication to your friends upon the subject; and leave you to take your remedy against him, if you think proper, when he would attempt to justify, or he will have you up for the presumed assault, and so get your name in the papers, which, if I understand rightly, would do you much harm."

"Indeed it would."—"So it is one of those awkward cases in which a victory is as bad as a defeat. Besides, you are committed not to compromise your young friends, who have already gone to all the expense and annoyance of giving the bills for quietness sake."

"Exactly."—"It is really very troublesome. You see a man gets deprived of the protection of the law when he dreads the publicity attendant upon seeking it. People will never believe but what you had a *liaison* with Mrs. Welch."

"I know they won't."—"Well, then, I tell you what I would do. Temporise with him, if you can, and if he has you up for the assault, make no defence, but appeal to the sessions. If he threatens to inform your friends that you have seduced Mrs. Welch, you had better be beforehand with him, and tell them the whole story yourself; but, if possible, get up a correspondence with him, so as to make a few days' delay, and then I will be better prepared to advise."

"But don't you think I had better leave the house?"—"No. Just stay a day or two. If, as I suspect, this Mrs. Welch and Mr. Todd are man and wife, you see, we cannot, as otherwise we might, threaten at once to indict them for conspiracy; but you must stay, in order to temporise with him: write him a note, asking specifically what he demands of you. He won't answer you in writing, I dare say, but he will come to you, when you can put him off a day or two. I will come to you as soon as I can think of any rigid line of conduct to adopt in the matter."

This was not very satisfactory, but I was compelled to put up with it, as there appeared to be no other plan, so I left Croft, and repaired home again, not getting to bed that night, all through Mrs. Welch and that abominable Todd, till somewhere fast approaching four o'clock in the morning; and then I did nothing but dream that Todd was squatting on my chest, and breaking my nose with one hand, while he flourished a bill stamp before my eyes with the other.

These disturbed visions of the night served in the morning rather as subjects of merriment than otherwise, and after partaking of a hearty breakfast, I determined to remain at home as late as I possibly could, which would be till eleven o'clock, in order to give Mr. Todd an opportunity of commencing operations. I was, besides, not a little curious to know what Mrs. Welch thought of the affair, now that she had had a whole night to con it over, but I would make no advances towards her, and never opened my lips to the servant, who, no doubt, was in the pay of Todd.

I was not left very long in suspense, either as regarded Mrs. Welch or Mr. Todd. The post brought me a note from the latter, and one from the former was pushed under my door, I expect by the lady herself, and as, in common gallantry, I could do no less than read her's first, why first I present it to my readers. It ran thus:—

"SIR,—I can easily imagine now what must be your opinion of me, after the proceedings of last night. You fancy me an intriguing woman, who has joined with the man, Todd, to cheat you. Your are right, sir, and if I may take any poor merit to myself, it will be that it was against my will I became a party in the attempted imposition. He was waiting for me in the parlour after he left your room, and when he saw me he struck me, because I had not succeeded thoroughly in ensnaring you.

"Todd is my husband. Pity me, sir, and leave this house at once. There are reasons why I cannot—dare not resist his commands—I am ever, when, as you have seen me dressed in smiles, the most wretched of women, but you, sir, I would fain spare from the fury of that bold bad man, who will persecute you relentlessly, and against whom, being his wife, I am no evidence, even if I dared come forward to expose his villanies, which God knows I dare not.

"Upon the honour of a gentleman, sir, I rely that you will destroy this letter, and I am, the unhappy,

"ARABELLA."

Mr. Todd's was in a different strain.

"Bernard's Inn.

"SIR,—This is to give notice that the circumstances connected with your seduction of Mrs. Welch are in the hands of a special pleader, in order that he may draw up a case for publication in every leading newspaper in the kingdom.

"I am, sir,
"Your most obedient and very humble servant,
"NICODEMUS HOLT TODD."

Both the letters brought me abundant food for reflection. Here was Todd's threat if a hundred pounds acceptance was not forthcoming. Here was Mrs. Welch's repentance, real or false as the case might be. I sat for about half an hour in deep thought, and then I wrote an answer to Mr. Todd to the following effect:—

"SIR,—What do you want?"

This was laconic enough certainly, but I judged it would be sufficient to produce an interview, and I had a most violent repugnance to writing more than was absolutely necessary to such a scoundrel. As regarded Mrs. Welch's letter, I felt in such great doubt concerning it, that, thinking I could not make matters worse, and that, according to the old adage, "I might as well be hung for a sheep as a lamb," I placed her note in my pocket, and walking boldly down stairs, I tapped at the parlour door.

"Come in," she said, not at all, I suppose, suspecting it was me, and in I went to her great surprise.

"Madam," I said, when I had closed the door of the room, "you are either to be pitied or blamed to excess—perhaps a little of both. Am I to believe your letter, or am I to consider it as another part of the nice little plot by which I was to have been robbed, for I can give it no milder term, of a hundred pounds?"

"Sir," she replied, and there was no mistaking now the genuineness of her words, "you may well doubt me; but I will at once, by trusting you with a secret that might destroy me, convince you that I am sincere."

"But, madam, a woman like yourself, of by no means a weak mind, might easily have resisted from the first the monstrous and illegal commands of a man whom you cannot even esteem?"—"True, sir—to my own destruction."

"Your own destruction? Surely you could have found protection from any violence of his?"

She burst into tears as she said, sobbing,—

"Sir, you will think me, perhaps, very foolish, but I cannot act towards you as I have done to others."

"Indeed! You cannot expect that I am so vain, madam, as to allow myself to be thus imposed upon?"—"'Tis gratitude speaks, sir," she said, proudly, "not love. You have, and I knew it not till the brute, Todd, told me you were the man who saved one very dear to me from death. Do you remember a poor widow named Bell, whom you lately attended, and for whom, by dint of the most untiring perseverance, you obtained a pension from the East India Company?"—"I do."

"That poor woman is my mother. God bless you, sir. I cannot longer deceive you, and this moment, if I dared, I would denounce Todd to the laws of his country, but—but ——."

"But what, madam?"—"He is my second husband."

"Well, what of that?"—"Not much alone, but the first is alive!"

"The deuce he is."—"Yes. Hush! hush! Captain Welch I had not seen for many years. Report said he was drowned, and I was mad enough, being much distressed, to marry Todd. Since then, if he knew it not before, the villain has found out that Captain Welch is living, and he threatens me with transportation if I do not yield to him the most implicit obedience. Now you know all, sir. Pity me if you can —blame if you will."

She dropped her face upon her hands and wept bitterly. I was much moved by her deep distress, and I said in a voice far from harsh,—

"Mrs. Welch, I do most sincerely pity you. From my heart, I pity you. God knows how gladly I would rescue you, if such a thing were possible, from the cruel bondage in which you are placed. I cannot, however, but think that you had better face the evil you so much dread—defy Todd. Let him accuse you of bigamy, and trust to the merciful consideration of a judge, for always in such cases the peculiar circumstances connected with them are of the greatest consequence. My life on it you would escape with some very trifling imprisonment, and recollect that by so doing you would free yourself from him who now is the cause of so much misery to you."

"Oh! if I dared—if I dared."

"Take courage and do so. Turn it over in your mind. I promise every assistance of friends and money. Take courage, Mrs. Welch—there is no evil which is not far worse in anticipation than in reality."

She wrung her hands and sobbed bitterly, saying,—

"The felon's cell—the bar—the crowd! Oh! God—could I bear it and live? No—no—no."

I forbore to press her further, for her grief affected me very much; but I spoke some kind words to her, and advised her to think the matter over, and, after some trouble, I obtained her leave to lay the case before my friend Croft for his opinion, and as soon as I did obtain leave, I scampered off again to the Temple, losing my lecture at the hospital altogether that morning.

"Well," said Croft, when I bid him good day, " you don't give me much time to think."—" Yes, I do, but I have brought some materials for thinking. Something else has happened that alters very much the complexion of the affair I mentioned to you last night."

I then showed him the letters, and related the conversation I had with Mrs. Welch.

"Humph," he said, " you are a better judge than I can be of how far Mrs. Welch is to be relied on."—" I think she has spoken the truth."

"Well, I cannot see any advantage she could possibly gain by making to you a communication of the nature you have mentioned. If the case be as she represents it, and she can produce any evidence to prove that she had reasonable grounds for believing Captain Welch was dead, I should advise her to defy Todd, and take her trial for bigamy."

"What would be the result?"—" A verdict of guilty, and about a month's imprisonment—perhaps less. The judges have immense latitude in such cases. Her first marriage being then proved, you see, she would be good evidence against Todd in any court in the kingdom. Urge her to this step if you can, for by it she, as well as you, will be freed from most, if not all your difficulties."

"I will. I have some hopes of success with her. Her feelings are strongly affected in my favour, and I think I can persuade her to act in the manner you point out."

"You know," added Croft, " there is of course still a great doubt if Todd will prosecute at all. He must have many fears about coming into a court of justice on any account. I shall give you a call in a few days, perhaps to morrow, to see this Mrs. Welch. Tell her if she will invite me to tea, I am not in the least afraid."—" I will, and it will be a hard case surely, if among us we cannot be one too many for Todd."

Back again I went to the Borough, and knocked at the door rather more gaily than usual, for I thought now I had things in a very tolerable train. Upon asking for Mrs. Welch, I found she had gone out, so I ran off at once to the hospital, and there I met likewise Scott and Mereweather, to whom I told that I was doing my best to circumvent Todd, without entering into any particulars.

"By all that's good," said Scott, " I wish you would circumvent him before to-morrow night, for my plaguy bill comes due to-morrow, and all I have in the world, unless I sell my silver-mounted flute, won't pay him his interest on a renewal."—" Throttle him if you can," said Mereweather, "for my bill comes due again next week."

"Oh! how I should like," remarked Wilkinson, " to have him here as a subject for dissection. Upon my word it would be quite a treat. My bill was due last week, and be hanged to him."

"Well, my boys," said I, " as for your bills, yourselves only are to blame for being such flats as to let him have them, but I have hopes of placing you all in such a position that you may retrieve your error, if you choose to take advantage of circumstances, and will put a bold face on the matter."

They pressed me very much to explain, but I replied to them much in the way they had once replied to me.

"Gentlemen," I said, " I have my reasons, so you must rest satisfied, as I am compelled to do, before circumstances will permit me explain matters to you. Be at home tomorrow if you all can, for I don't know but that by then some eclaircissement may take place that will be both amusing and instructive."

So saying, I left them to chew the cud of sweet and bitter fancy, while I went to fulfil several engagements that had been partially neglected, in consequence of my time being so much taken up with Mrs. Welch's affairs.

It happened to be rather late before I got home that night, so I put off till the following morning my conversation with Mrs Welch. It was a lovely morning, and the sun shone so beautifully, making everything look so gay and sparkling, that I quite shrank from going to tell that really charming woman that she had better for a time, even though it were however short, exchange her pleasant comfortable home for the gloom of a prison, whatever might be the perspective advantages. But then I thought of Mr. Todd, and I no longer relented, but with a heart of adamant, I swallowed my coffee, and said to myself,—

"It shall be done. Poor Mrs. Welch must defy the scoundrel Todd, cost her what it may, and if anything like human persuasion can induce her, she most assuredly will this day commence to do so."

I had been very surly to the servant ever she had come into the parlour with that abominable simper of her's, which had assured me that she was in the pay of Todd. Indeed, I had scarcely spoken to her, and she, finding that I suspected her, had assumed a proportionate degree of insolent disdain, to cover her apprehension and consciousness of meanness. This morning, however, I said,—

"Is your mistress below?"—" No," was the short reply.

"Is she not up yet?"—" No."

"Very good. Oh, you are a nice article," thought I; "we must see what can be done with you, by-and-bye."

When I had finished my breakfast, I went down to the parlour, but Mrs. Welch had not come down, so I left a note on the table, saying I would be back in half an hour, and I went out to take a stroll till she came down, for I can always, somehow or another, think best and arrange complicated affairs when I am taking exercise. The morning, as I have said, was beautiful in the extreme. It was one of those delightful days we sometimes have very early in the year, to give us a promise of what is to come.

The return of spring is as welcome to the busy inhabitants of London as ever it can be to those who dwell in country places. The chill and dreary time that winter appears to them is now fast passing away, and a more genial time is coming on, and nature awakens into new life her countless myriads of living and breathing creatures. The very streets appear to change, and the dull, white light, leaden-coloured sky, suddenly becomes changed to one of a brighter and more promising hue, the days lengthen, and a gentle degree of warmth is felt in the middle of the day.

In the early spring little is noticed, but no sooner do the cold nights and mornings disappear than in come all the gay flowers that nature produces, or can be forced to produce. A great trade is carried on thus, in London, and yet the greatest quantity sold, and the earliest too, are wild flowers that spring spontaneously from the fields.

The passion of Londoners for flowers is very great, and upon that passion is founded a thriving trade with gardeners, and is the means of giving many a good meal to a starving family. The shops, too, appear renovated, and spring and summer garments are displayed in the shop windows, with all the art and temptation that the shopkeeper can exert, and these are not inefficient either. Spring dresses now make a stir, and new fashions inundate the town, and people begin to talk of the approaching season, and their prospects of business.

A few rainy days now and then intervene between the fine ones, and change the aspect again; thus the time goes on alternately, between fine and bad, sunshine and rain, for some weeks, till the genial heat of the sun becomes stronger and stronger each day, and a gradual and universal rise of temperature, and with it those appearances which betoken the near approach of summer. The public promenades and walks now begin to be frequented, and those who can afford to do it quit London on every convenient opportunity, to catch a transitory glimpse of the now green fields.

Londoners take much interest in what goes on in the country—they are, as a class, exceedingly fond of rural sports, and their whole endeavours, for weeks at a time, is to enable them to spend some holiday a mile or two from home—it is the happiest moment of their lives — they see the green herbage around them, and they think they have renewed their life again, and once more sit down to hard drudging, contented and happy. Thus springs new life to the hard-working drudges of London — it is welcome to all, poor or rich, young or old.

I was much pleased with my stroll, and returned much fortified, to go through my task of persuasion, to Mrs. Welch, to be so kind as to go to Newgate on a charge of having one husband too many — pleasant but wrong, as Sir Robert might remark when he pockets the income tax.

Mrs. Welch was waiting for me in the parlour — she looked pale and agitated, as if she had passed a sleepless night, and I elt much for her; I bade her good morning, in a tone which I made as sympathising and as friendly as possible, and then I added, —

"Well, Mrs. Welch, I have seen my friend the barrister, and he wishes to know if you had any reasonable belief that your husband, Captain Welch, was dead, when you married this Todd?" — "Yes. The loss of the ship with all on board was recorded in the *Times*."

"Ah, the *Times*! Had it been in the *Herald*, or any respectable paper, it would have availed you; but the *Times* is so notorious for lies, that I'm afraid no jury would say that your seeing such a statement there could give you any grounds for believing its truth. However, don't despair, Mrs. Welch. Perhaps we may find some other evidence. After all, the *Times* may have copied it without acknowledgment from somewhere else. They are capable of any literary theft. But let me entreat of you to act independently, and tell Todd to do his worst. Depend upon it, you shall be well supported by the first talent, and you will escape easily."

"I have already," she said, "made up my mind to abide by your advice. Act as you think proper, only do stay here and protect me against his personal violence."

"Oh, we will have a warrant against him, and bind him over to keep the peace towards you; so, never fear any violence from the scoundrel. It is more than probable that when he finds you protected, and himself, for the first time, met with defiance instead of fear, he will become as cringing as he is now insolent."

"Mr. Todd," announced the servant. — "Show him in," cried I, in a sharp voice that must have been heard some doors off. "Show him in; Mr. Todd is the very man we want."

The servant was so amazed that she nearly fell down in the passage, and Todd, when he showed himself at the parlour door, looked absolutely blue from mingled rage and a arm.

"Come in, Mr. Todd," I shouted. "Be pleased, sir, to come in; you are the very man we want, sir."

"Humph! indeed!" said Todd. "Are you drunk?" — "Why, you infernal scoundrel, how dare you make such an insinuation. I drunk? You sneaking hound!"

"Come, come; no assault, sir," cried Todd. "Sarah," to the servant, "remain here, will you, as a witness, in case I'm assaulted." — "Do you imagine," said I, "that any one would commit such a slur upon his manhood as to assault a thing like you? No, Todd, there will be no assault, without you, especially, and in the presence of witnesses, give me leave to kick you out of the house."

"Humph!" said Todd, as he took off his gloves; "that's not very likely — not very likely, sir. So I find you here again with Mrs. Welch, sir. Well, I have received your note, in which you ask what I want; to which all I can reply is, that I want and must have reparation for my friend Captain Welch's honour."

"And if you don't get it, Todd?" — "You know the alternative. I should say, young man, that your coffee has been too strong this morning, for you seem all of a bluster. But you won't succeed in intimidating me; I am to be conciliated, sir, but I am not to be bullied. Mrs. Welch, I have come for your fifty pounds, if this *gentleman* is gallant enough to allow you to pay it; and, as for you, sir, you can either pay me the hundred, or give me your acceptance for it, as you please."

Mrs. Welch was about to speak, but I interrupted her, saying, —

"Allow me, madam, to manage this little affair for you. Mr. Todd, you are a very clever man — a remarkably clever man; but it unfortunately happens with most geniuses like you, that they overshoot the mark they aim at. You have gone just a little too far, Mr. Todd; and Mrs. Welch, at my advice, and at the instance of her legal adviser, Mr. Croft, of the Temple, now defies you, and dares you to do your worst. This house is her's, sir, and the sooner you leave it the better perhaps it will be for you."

Todd looked a little whiter than before, and he wiped, with a strange looking blue rag, which I suppose he called a handkerchief by courtesy, his dingy-looking face, as he said, —

"Why, you are almost as clever as I am; I quite congratulate you, sir. You fancy now you have me on the hip, nicely, and that, by getting this foolish woman to hear you silently bully me, you have done wonders. Mr. Croft, of the Temple, may be a very clever man — almost, indeed, as clever as you are; but there are such things as penal acts of parliament. I will just sketch out to you a short, and, I hope, entertaining programme of my future proceedings: Firstly, you will be brought into court by Captain Welch, on account of this affair with his wife. Secondly, I will take out a warrant for an assault; and, thirdly, I can, if I please, so punish this silly woman, for allowing herself to be led by you instead of by me, that she shall wish she had cut off her right hand before she listened to you."

"Oh, we know all that, Todd," said I. "Do what you please. You will of course have Mrs. Welch apprehended on a charge of bigamy?"

Todd gave a great jump, as he exclaimed, —

"So, so! it has come to this, has it, Mrs. Welch? You have yourself to thank now, for bringing matters to this most disagreeable conclusion. Sarah!" — "Yes, sir."

"Go and fetch a constable as quickly as you can. Mrs. Welch, I have in my pocket-book a certificate of your marriage with Captain Welch, and likewise one of your marriage with me. I wish you a pleasant voyage to Botany Bay, madam; perhaps there you will find a third husband. And, as for you, sir, if Mrs. Welch had fifty husbands, it by no means clears you or your professional character from this transaction. You understand, sir. You are out of the frying-pan into the fire, very clever young gentleman." — "But your career, Todd, is put an end to; and Mrs. Welch becomes heavy evidence against you when you are indicted for conspiracy."

"For, — for what?" — "Conspiracy. The particulars you will be informed of when you are on your trial."

"My trial! my trial! He, he, he! That won't do, young man; that won't do. Do you think I'm a fool?" — "Rather so, for you have evidently let yourself in for some disagreeable consequences."

"He, he, he! You think so? He, he, he!"

Bang came a knock at the street-door, but Sarah had gone out, and there was no one to answer it but Mrs. Welch. With tears in her eyes she rose, but I interrupted her, and walked to the door and opened it. To my great relief I found it was Mr. Croft, who had a gentlemanly-enough-looking man with him, whom he introduced to me as Mr. Plank.

"Come in," said I; "come in, Todd is here." — "Indeed," said Croft. "Well, that's lucky."

Without waiting to ask him why it was lucky, I hastily preceded him to the parlour, which I entered again just in time to see Todd with his fist raised to strike Mrs. Welch. I up with my foot, on the impulse of the moment, and sent him howling to the other end of the room.

"Murder, murder!" he cried. "He's broke my back. Oh, dear! Murder, murder. Oh! you villain; you shall rot in gaol for this." — "Mrs. Welch," said I, "th's is Mr. Croft, of the Temple."

The street-door again opened, after the rattle of Sarah's latch-key in the lock had met my ears, and in another moment she flung the parlour door open, exclaiming, —

"The constable, Mr. Todd."

A fat little publican from over the way, who was a constable, of course swaggered into the room, carrying a staff as big as himself.

"Oh," said Croft, "you are a constable, are you? You are very welcome, sir, but I really don't think we shall need you." — "I am of a different opinion," said Todd; "I give that woman, Mr. Constable, into your custody, on a charge of bigamy, which I am prepared at once to support, before the nearest sitting magistrate. What do you think of that, eh, gentlemen?"

"Not much," said Mr. Croft. "I don't believe Mrs. Welch would ever have married such a fellow as you. You are not her husband." — "Indeed. Ain't I? Just have the kindness to look at the certificate. I rather believe that it attests the marrige of Nicodemus Holt Todd to Arabella Welch, widow, and it bears date, I rather think, October the 12th, of last year."

"Well," said Mr. Croft, whose conduct I began to think very extraordinary; "so it does. I shall keep it by the side of another little document I have, which attests that upon the aforesaid twelfth of October of last year, one Ann Todd was alive and well at Bristol, she being the lawful wife of one Nicodemus Holt Todd."

Mr. Todd gave something between a shriek and a groan as Mr. Croft spoke, and then he continued to tremble so excessively that I thought he would have died.

"Come, come," cried the little fat constable publican, "I can't wait here all day. You are my prisoner, ma'am; come along if you please."—"Wait a bit," said the man who had come with Croft, as he took from his pocket a small brass constable's staff. "Mr. Todd, you are my prisoner."

"What—for?"—"Bigamy."

"But she—she—too ——"—"No!" thundered Croft. "Your marriage with Mrs. Welch was illegal, and no consequences can come to her on account of it—it is null and void, since you were not in a legal condition to marry. It is you who are called upon to answer a charge of bigamy. Mrs. Welch is free."

Todd sank on his knees, and uttered the word mercy; suddenly a ray of hope seemed to come over him, and he sprang up again, crying,—

"Why, by the same reasoning, I am free."—"No," said Croft, "no. I have a certificate here of the death of Captain Welch, on October the 1st, on board the Dreadnought, hospital ship. He had been much hurt, in consequence of a shipwreck, and expired there ere he could reach London. The Captain Welch who will arrive in the river to-day is his brother, who has been appointed to his command from being a lieutenant under him."

"The tables seem turned, Todd," said I.—"How are you, Todd?" said Wilkinson, who had just come into the room along with Scott and Mereweather, in consequence of having been asked by me to come down if they heard any contention going on.

"Todd, how are you?" said Scott.—"I'm afraid you are poorly, Todd," exclaimed Mereweather.

Todd fell flat on his back. Then he scrambled on to his knees, and, in imploring accents, said,—

"Good, kind gentlemen, oh, pray let me go. Christians, let me go. I am very poor and getting old—oh, let me go. Mrs. Welch, beg for me. Dear sir, every little legal matter you want done I'll do for you for nothing. Let me go. If you want any doubtful thing sworn to at any time, I'm your man. Only have mercy upon me, good, kind, gentlemen.

Mr. Scott, I will give you back your bill; and your's too, Mr. Wilkinson."

"And mine?" cried Mereweather.—"Oh, dear Mr. Mereweather, God bless you, I didn't see you. God bless you all. Here are the bills. I am now a ruined, broken-down, poor wretch. What is the use of prosecuting me, gentlemen?"

He produced the bills from a huge pocket-book, and the reader may well believe with what readiness they were snatched at by their respective owners.

"Oh, let the vagabond go," cried Wilkinson.—"I'm afraid, gentlemen," said the officer, "that I must not do so."

"Oh, yes, you may," said Mr. Croft. "No formal step has been taken in the matter yet; besides, his first wife is, I believe, too glad to be rid of him. Upon condition that he withdraws his name from the roll of attornies, and pays to these young gentlemen all the money he has received from them, as well as signing a document, binding upon himself not to molest Mrs. Welch, I think we may let the rascal escape."

"Oh, yes, gentlemen," he whined, "do. I consent to all. Oh, dear, yes. How very kind."—"There's a pump in the back yard," whispered Wilkinson to me.

"Really, I'm afraid," said I, with a broad grin; "you wouldn't be so barbarous?"

The word was passed to Scott and Mereweather, and before Todd knew what was going to be done, he was hoisted off his feet and carried into the back yard, yelling and screaming all the way, for he thought he was going to be thrown over the wall, perhaps, and smashed.

We all ran into the back parlour, the window of which commanded a view of the pump, and there we saw the operation performed, till Mr. Todd was thoroughly soaked, and could not gasp a single word. Then he was hauled into the passage, from whence he was kicked into the street. It was the last we saw of him, for we never troubled him to fulfil Mr. Croft's conditions.

"Really," said the officer, as he rubbed his nose with the end of his little staff, and grinned as if for a wager, "I'm afraid all this is a little irregular."

"But who am I to take up?" shouted the little fat publican, as he flourished his staff.—"Half-a-dozen of champagne," cried I.

"Coming, coming, coming," he shouted, and bustled over to execute the order with amazing rapidity.

* * * * *

Mrs. Welch was never again molested by Todd, and she kept the lodging-house for medical students many years; but she never invited any to tea, though many would have jumped at the compliment.

THE LUNATIC;

OR, MADAME DELVY'S FEELINGS.

SHORTLY after a long and fatiguing case, partly surgical and partly medical, in which I had been engaged for some months, had been brought to a successful termination, I received the following note from an eminent surgeon, now deceased, whose name I do not know that I ought at all to hesitate in using in these pages of my diary; but as hitherto I never have, for praise or for censure, invaded domestic privacy, I will abstain from doing so, merely premising that although, at the time he wrote to me the note I subjoin, he was a rising young man, he was by no means the eminent and distinguished ornament of his profession he afterwards became. The note was as follows:—

"MY DEAR SIR,

"As we have worked together so well in a case which required more of my surgical requisites than your medical skill, allow me to have the gratification of introducing you to another, where, although it is the wish of the parties that I should continue in attendance, you, as a physician, can do much more, inasmuch as it is a case lying rather without the province of a surgeon.

"If you will oblige me by a call any morning before eleven, I shall esteem it a favour, as I have flattered the parties with the happiest results from your skill and great judgment.

"Believe me to be, my dear sir,

"Yours, faithfully, ——————."

For the sake of convenience, as my tale proceeds, I shall call this surgeon Blunt; and I need not say that I felt extremely gratified by the reception of such a note from a man who was not prone to give a flattering opinion.

The next morning—for it was evening when Mr. Blunt's letter reached me—I repaired to his house, which was in Conduit-street, Bond-street, and having sent in my card, in a few moments I was ushered into his morning room.

"Good morning," he said. "I am very much obliged to you for your very prompt attention to my note, for although the case did not seem to press yesterday, when I did myself the pleasure of writing to you, it does to-day, inasmuch as I have received rather an urgent message from the parties concerned."

"Indeed," said I. "What's it all about? as we used to say after the lectures at Bartholomew's."—"And well we might say- 'What's it all about?' after some of those lectures. But, to come to the point. It is a case of lunacy, of the most extraordinary character I ever met with."

"Lunacy? Humph! Of all the troublesome afflictions in the world, these are the most troublesome."

"So you think. I suppose, then, you have not yet come across a regular hypochondriac patient?"—"Oh, yes, I have, though, and I certainly ought to have excepted such cases, if indeed they come not under the catalogue of lunatic ones."

"Aye, true enough—true enough. If a hypochondriac is not mad himself, he is enough to drive his medical attendant out of his senses. But about this case. Do you know, or did you ever hear of a Mr. Delvy?"

"Mr. Delvy? There is a member of Parliament of that name, is there not?"—"Yes; and that's the man."

"You surprise me. I have always heard him spoken of as a man of singularly clear judgment and great ability, both natural and acquired."—"And so he is."

"Then, do you mean to tell me he has gone mad?"

"Why, not exactly mad; but there are abundant symptoms to induce the gravest suspicions that something wrong is going on in the brain. He is getting subject to delusions of the oddest description, which can only be accounted for by a cerebral derangement. He fancies he sees all sorts of things, which can have no existence but in his own excited fancy, and he will describe these things to you as rationally and clearly as you or I could. Indeed, he himself has called in medical advice upon his own case."

"That is not a symptom of insanity."

"Certainly not; quite the reverse—for there is, as you know, quite a marked sensibility on the subject, even in the very earliest stages of incipient lunacy. But it was Mr. Delvy himself who sent for me, and detailed all his symptoms clearly and intelligently; so you see the case is very strangely complicated indeed."

"It is so, most truly. I never met with such an one. But I should say that it presents no bad features, and ought soon to yield."

"I scarcely hope so. He is a married man, with a most amiable wife, who, you may well suppose, is wretched enough, poor thing, under these circumstances. In fact, the whole family are in a state of the greatest affliction; and, strange to say, the only one who speaks consolation to them is Mr. Delvy himself, and yet all his strange symptoms increase instead of diminishing."

"Well, I agree with you wholly in the singularity of the case. When are you going to see him?"—"I will order my carriage and take you at once. He lives in Berkeley-square, and, from a note I have had from him, I suppose he quite expects us as soon as possible."

"Have you any objection to show me the note?"—"Certainly not. There it is."

He handed me the note, which was as unlike a letter from a madman as anything could well be. It ran thus:—

"DEAR SIR,

"Last night, I had a return of the strange symptoms I have mentioned to you, to a greater extent than before. I do not feel my general health at all affected, but should be much obliged if you could favour me with an early call, and bring with you the gentleman you have mentioned to me as having turned his attention to this class of cases.

"I am, dear sir,
"Yours, obliged,
"Berkeley-square." "A. DELVY."

"Well, Mr. Blunt," I remarked, "there is method enough in this Mr. Delvy's madness."

"So you will say too when you see him. I cannot make it out at all; and only have a fear that some paroxysms must be on the eve of happening, unless we can find some means of changing the symptoms at once. But the carriage is at the door, I perceive, and you had better come at once and judge for yourself."

In two minutes more we were going at a rattling pace, in Mr. Blunt's handsome chariot, towards Berkeley-square, where we stopped at a splendid looking house, which Blunt told me was Mr. Delvy's town mansion.

A tremendous peal at the knocker, such as only a London postman would think of achieving, soon induced the folding doors to fly open, and, the carriage steps being let down with a rattle and a dash, we found ourselves in another moment in a reception room of the really splendid mansion.

I had heard much of Mr. Delvy's wealth and the magnificent style in which he lived, and certainly, till I set foot in his house, I had no idea of the really tasteful and gorgeous nature of his home. The recollection of what we came there for struck most painfully across my mind, and I said to myself,—

"Good God! can it be that a man, surrounded by all that can make life desirable and lend the most varied charms to existence, is afflicted with so dreadful a disease as madness! How faded in his eyes must appear all this magnificence! how stale, flat, and unprofitable, must be to him all the uses of this world! With what pleasure would he exchange this family residence for the meanest hovel, provided he could carry with him his reason."

These thoughts were to me most painful ones, but they darted irresistibly through my mind, as I waited in that splendid room while our names were taken to the owner of so much magnificence.

The reception room in which we were was furnished and decorated more tastefully than fashionably. It was redundant with works of art and nature. Such a room I must confess I had not entered under that denomination before. The curtains were of the richest kind, and unique patterns; the carvings and mouldings were really superb, and to me appeared as though the owner was willing to exhibit both wealth and exuberance of taste in the fittings up of the apartments.

Rich mouldings ran along the ceiling, and appeared to descend by the corners of the room, rivetting the wainscoting, which ran shoulder-high, and then another stream of moulding ran until it met with the other side and joined again.

Pictures there were, and no lack of them either, for they hung round the entire room, save at one spot, where there hung a magnificent mirror. These pictures were various, and beautifully executed; several of them were undoubted originals, surrounded on either side by more modern works of art.

The furniture was not the less valuable and remarkable than the merely ornamental parts, but was made of the best materials and in the most costly manner. Money certainly was not stinted, and I could not help thinking that a very handsome sum indeed must have been expended in the furnishing and completing of the room. The carpets, seldom good in such a room, were such as are met with ordinarily in drawing-rooms and the saloons of the nobility. I had about ten minutes' leisure to make these few observations before we were interrupted, and Mr. Blunt had just said to me,—

"Don't you think these rich M.P.'s live in good style?"

And I had replied,—

"Style! I never saw a more magnificent room,"

When the door opened, and a lady, in an extremely elegant morning dress, entered the apartment. She seemed only to have expected to find Mr. Blunt in the room, for she drew back a step or two on seeing me, until he said,—

"Allow me the honour, madam, of introducing Dr. —— to you. Doctor, this is Madame Delvy."

I made a low bow, which the lady acknowledged by another, while I thought to myself,—

"What the deuce is she called Madame Delvy for?"—"This gentleman," added Mr. Blunt, in explanation, "comes with me this morning, at the request of Mr. Delvy, who, from my recommendation of him, is pleased to wish that he should be made acquainted with his case."

"I need not say how welcome to this afflicted house any one is," she said, "who presents us with a hope of happiness. I have had a dreadful night."

She turned away as she spoke, and I heard her sob as if her heart was breaking.

"My dear madam," said Blunt, "let me, as I have done before, implore you to keep up your spirits, and not give way in this manner to apprehensions which may, after all, turn out to be groundless."

"I have struggled hard against my fears," she replied, in a faltering voice; "but nature will have its way. Everything I could have borne, but here we are with every earthly comfort about us,—no cloud upon our hopes of years of affection—we—we were too, too happy; and now, oh, God! what a change—what a dreadful change!"

She sat down upon a sofa, and, leaning her head upon the arm of it, she burst into a paroxysm of weeping.

"Leave her alone for a few moments. She will be better for this," whispered Blunt to me, as he led me to the window. "Poor creature, she suffers dreadfully. You would scarcely credit the change in that woman since this calamity came into the house. I never saw any one feel so very acutely. Poor thing, she is truly to be pitied."—"She is, indeed," said I. "She is very young."

"Yes. Her age is not above six-and-twenty, I think. They have been only married a year, and have no child. She is passionately attached to Mr. Delvy, and if he gets worse, I really do think it will kill her, poor thing."

"It's a most melancholy thing, altogether. She seems more composed now. Shall we speak to her?"—"Yes. Come along, and say something consoling, if you can."

The lady was drying her tears as I approached, and I had

a better view of her face than before, when she had stood between me and the light. She was very beautiful, and had that very exquisitely moulded face been lit up by the animation of smiles, it would, I could see, have been most fascinating; but now there hung upon it such a cloud of dejection, that it was quite afflicting to look at her.

"Madam," I said, "the illness you deplore is one from which you should extract more hope than apprehension. I have not seen Mr. Delvy, as yet, but from what I can hear, I should say that there is every reason to believe he will entirely recover."

"Do you really think so; or are these but kind words meant to flatter me out of my grief?"—"I really think so."

"Thank Heaven! Oh, gentlemen, if you can restore my husband to what he was once, a life-time will be insufficient to express to you my gratitude. Your words give me a hope which I am almost afraid to entertain, lest it should turn out to be fallacious. I know these ideas are weak, but they are wrung from me. I cannot help it. I have but one wish if he should get worse, and that is to die."

"Do not talk so despairingly," said Blunt; "and, above all things, let me warn you, madam, against allowing Mr. Delvy to see any of these bursts of feeling. They might have the most prejudicial effect upon him."

"Trust me," she said, "I will not. Indeed, it is because I am compelled, when with him, to assume a cheerfulness I am far from feeling, that, when I am away, my heart seems ready to burst, and my tears flow in spite of all my efforts to control them."

A servant at this moment entered the room, and said, in a respectful and low voice,—

"Mr. Delvy's compliments to Mr. Blunt and Dr. ——, and he is quite disengaged now."—"Go to him at once—go to him at once," said Madame Delvy. "I will see you before you leave the house. Do not go until I have seen you again. I will wait here for you; or, possibly, I may come to his room. The blessing of God be with your efforts, gentlemen. Do not mind me, but go to him at once."

With these prayers and injunctions from the almost broken-hearted lady, whom no one could help sincerely pitying, we followed the domestic, who led us into a magnificent library, that transcended everything of the kind I had seen, and there sat Mr. Delvy, who, on our appearance, rose in the most courteous manner, saying,—

"Pray be seated, gentlemen. I am very much obliged to you, Dr. ——, for your prompt attendance."—"I only wish, sir," said I, "that my attendance upon you may produce satisfactory results."

"You are very kind, sir," he said, and his voice faltered as he spoke.

Mr. Delvy was a good-looking man, I should say over fifty years of age, so that there was a considerable disparity between the ages of him and his wife. His hair, like Hamlet's father's, was,—

"A sable silvered."

His brow was lofty and commanding, and his whole countenance was indicative of great gentleness, combined with the highest order of intelligence. The first impression one had of him was decidedly favourable, and his voice added much to it, for it was deep and melodious, and evidently capable of much modulation. A second glance at him after we were seated showed me that there was an air of great anxiety on his face, and that he was restless and fidgetty. I felt very much for him, and was glad that he commenced the conversation on his calamity himself, by saying,—

"Well, gentlemen, I don't know what's the matter with me, but, certainly, I am not getting better."—"Perhaps, Mr. Delvy," said Blunt, "if it's not taxing you too much, would you be so good as to detail to Dr. ——, yourself, the symptoms which you have already stated to me, as I would rather he formed his judgment by hearing them from your mouth than from mine."

"Certainly—certainly," he replied. "Nothing can be more reasonable." Then turning towards me, he added,—

"It is now, I think, about five weeks ago since I first began to fancy I saw things which the words of other persons convinced me had no real existence."

"Do you recollect," said I, "the first impression of that kind you had, and the circumstances connected with it?"—
"Most perfectly. I awoke one night from, as I thought, some noise in my chamber. It seemed a sort of whisper in my ear, and it started me up in a moment. I cried, 'Who's there?' but receiving no answer, I was on the point of getting out of bed, when Mrs. Delvy awoke, and asked me what was the matter. I told her, and she proposed to ring up the servants, but I would not permit her, as I began to think it must have been a dream, so I did not even get out of bed, but composing my mind as well as I could, I got to sleep again in a short time.

"How long I had been asleep I don't know; but I was awakened again in precisely the same way, by a voice, exactly in my ear, saying,—

"'Delvy—Delvy!'

"I started awake again. Mrs. Delvy was fast asleep, and, besides, the voice came from the other, or outer side of the bed, so that if she had mentioned my name in her sleep, it could not have sounded in my other ear so oddly. I remained awake about ten minutes, during which I listened with painful attention, but heard nothing, and I was about to go to sleep again, when a strange-looking light flashed before my eyes, and I saw a pale, spectral-looking face,—but nothing but a face—looking at me. It had a melancholy aspect, and I fainted; I had seen it before somewhere. Surprise, and perhaps some fear, that crept over me, kept me quiet for about a minute, and then I sprang out of bed, and rang the bell violently. The room was soon reached by some of the servants, but the face had entirely disappeared, and there the mystery remained perfectly inexplicable. Mrs. Delvy would have it that I must have been dreaming, and at last she succeeded in convincing me that such was the fact, and I felt quite ashamed of the disturbance I had made in the house upon the subject."

"And that," said I, "was the beginning of these illusions?"—"Precisely so."

"But the second was far more remarkable," said Mr. Blunt. "Will you, Mr. Delvy, detail to Dr. —— the second delusion?"—"Certainly; and what makes that more remarkable was, that it occurred in broad daylight."

"I shall thank you to detail it to me," I said, and Mr. Delvy immediately commenced.—"The second delusion, then," said Mr. Delvy, "occurred, as I tell you, in broad daylight, and in the open air, too, which renders it still more remarkable and full of mystery."

"Pray proceed," said I.

After a slight pause, he continued as follows, and I was getting not only more interested each moment, but, what was more provoking, I was getting dreadfully puzzled.

"Well, sir, that same morning after I had seen the strange face in my bedroom, Mrs. Delvy persuaded me to go out for a time, for the purpose of distracting my attention from the dream, as she would insist upon calling it, and I ordered an open carriage that I have, and which I am in the habit of driving myself, because I am fond of the exercise. The carriage holds two, and there is room for one in a rumble behind, which is usually occupied by a groom; but on that particular morning Mr. Carnaby happened to drop in, and my wife offered him the place in the rumble, which he very kindly took, so that we had no servant with us, nor did we need one, because we were only going for the drive, and not to make any calls."

I longed to ask who Mr. Carnaby was, but I thought it would sound like a very impertinent question, so I abstained, and in a moment Blunt relieved me from the difficulty, by saying,—

"Mr. Carnaby, doctor, is Madame Delvy's cousin."—
"Yes," said Mr. Delvy, "and a very gentlemanly man, indeed. He often stays for a few weeks, and we find his society enlivens us amazingly—that is, until these occurrences commenced, and since then we have thought of nothing else.

"Well, sir, I felt very well, and not at all nervous, when we started for the drive, and I put the horses to a good pace till we reached Hyde Park, when I trotted them comfortably and gently round the drive. It was morning, and, therefore, beyond a few horsemen, there was hardly any one there. Coming, however, in an opposite direction to us, I saw a carriage driving very fast, and I said to my wife,—

"'That carriage coming so quickly on belongs to Sir Nicholas Geary.'

"'What carriage?' she said.—'Why that,' said I, pointing to it, as it whirled past us.

"'I see no carriage,' said she.—'Not see a carriage! Carnaby, you saw that carriage pass us?'

"'No—no carriage has passed us yet.'

"'What! not in scarlet and white livery; two roan horses, and going very fast?'—'No, no.'

"I said nothing, but drove on till we got round near to Grosvenor-gate, when I saw the Duke of Wellington, on a white horse, come through the gate, and take the way towards Hyde Park-corner.

"'There's the duke,' I said.—'Where?' said my wife.—'Where?' cried Carnaby.

"'Why, there, on his white horse; don't you see him, going at an easy canter, towards the gate?'—'No, no,' they said; 'there is no one at all in that direction.'

"Well, gentlemen, after this, I turned the horses' heads homewards. A strange, confused feeling came over me, and I scarcely was able to drive home, so convinced was I that I was subject to delusions."

"Did any appearances show themselves that night to you in your chamber?" said I.—"My room was sometimes full of people," he replied; "at times they would appear in the costumes of ages gone by, then in modern dresses, and occasionally I would see faces resembling people I know."

"Then these appearances took the form of living persons, as well as those whom you knew to be dead?"—"Often, often. It is, of course, a delusion; and it is increasing on me to a terrible extent. Last night, strange, unearthly sounds mingled with the apparitions; I became fevered and distressed, and at length I was compelled to have a strong light in my room, when the figures vanished; but deep groans would occasionally disturb me, and whenever I tried to sleep, the voice whispered in my startled ears,—'Delvy, Delvy,' and I would start, wide awake, in a perspiration of terror and amazement. Now, gentlemen, what am I to do? My senses seem playing the fool with me, completely; I can

rely on nothing that I see, on nothing that I hear; my nerves are getting terribly shattered, and my life is becoming a complete burthen to me."

"Do not view the matter in so despairing a light, Mr. Delvy," said I; "your case is by no means uncommon or miserable. Besides, you need not fancy that it will get any worse. There are frequent instances of these spectres appearing without the disease ending in any mental derangement, and I should say that your case was precisely one of those."

"Exactly," said Blunt. "You have heard of Nicolia, the German, who saw all sorts of apparitions continually, and got cured by local depletion, thereby showing that a partially congested state of the blood-vessels of the eye and brain was the cause of the delusions."

"And in our country," said I, "we have all heard of Blake, the historical painter, who fancied he saw apparitions of all the great personages of ancient days, whose forms and likenesses he wished to transfer to his canvass."—"Indeed!"

"Yes; upon the occasion of a gentleman calling upon him he was painting an historical subject, and the gentleman observing him to pause and look vexed, he asked him what was the matter, when Blake replied,—

"'Why, I was just now sketching Henry the Fourth, and Julius Cæsar has placed himself in the way, and is talking to him, so that I cannot get one half of his costume.'"

"The strangest thing of Blake, though," said Blunt, "was how he succeeded in convincing his wife of the reality and harmlessness of these visions, to such an extent, that she conjured them up to herself by the mere force of imagination."

"Can it be possible?"—"Yes, indeed. It appears that Blake, at his death, left behind him, in the hands of his widow, a number of pictures, which were rather eagerly sought after by connoisseurs and picture dealers, and when any one called upon her, and asked the price of a particular picture, she would say,—

"'I really don't know myself; but I dare say I shall see Blake before you come again, and I will take an opportunity of asking him the price.'"

"And you think my case, then, not one for any serious apprehensions?" said Mr. Delvy.—"Certainly not for any serious apprehensions," said I; "I should advise, strongly, bleeding. As a first step in all these cases, I would remove blood from the base of the brain."

"You think that better than cupping the temples?" said Blunt.—"Yes, certainly."

But I need not fatigue my readers with a medical discussion; suffice it to say, that, upon my recommendation, Mr. Delvy was bled, and I promised to call the next day, to see if he had had any return during the night of the strange sights which so much disturbed him.

When we left him, we were shown again by the servant, who had conducted us to the library, into the waiting room, where we found Madame Delvy; she immediately flew towards me, and, in a voice of the greatest anxiety, she said,—

"You have seen him—you have seen him. Oh, tell me, sir—tell me truly—are there any hopes?"—"Abundant, madam. Mr. Delvy's mind is not at all affected, I am confident."

"But if he were to tell you he was the thief who was crucified by the side of Jesus Christ, what would you say?"

I was so staggered by this question, that for a few moments I could only stare at Madame Delvy in silent amazement, and when I recovered myself sufficiently to use my tongue, I said,—

"Do you mean, madam, that he has said such a thing to you, or have you only put it as an hypothetical case?"—"Alas! it is too true."

"Good God! that alters the case altogether."

Madame Delvy burst into tears again, and we continued looking at each other in silence for some moments.

"Speak, sir," she sobbed; "tell me again that you have some hopes. I shall die broken-hearted. Oh, this is terrible!"—"Pray compose yourself," I said. "Cases of insanity are never so bad, unless they be of very long standing, but we may entertain the most reasonable hopes of a cure. I will give the case my very best attention, you may depend; but certainly what you have last told me places the matter in a very different light."

"I hesitated," she sobbed, "whether to tell you, or not, for I dreaded to hear you say it was a bad symptom."—"Symptom!" exclaimed Blunt; "it's something more than a symptom, I think."

"Oh, no—no—no. Do not be so cruel as to deprive me of the hope this gentleman has given me. It is kinder to deceive me—far kinder. I wish I was dead. Oh, that I were dead!"

We tried all we could to comfort Madame Delvy; and then, having each of us received a very ample fee, we left the house, full of painful thoughts regarding the fate of the unhappy Mr. Delvy and his afflicted, amiable wife.

"Well," said Blunt, as the carriage dashed along, "what do you think of it, doctor?"—"It is a very sad case, indeed," I replied.

"Do you think, now, after what you have heard from Madame Delvy, that the local depletion will do any good?"—"It cannot do any harm; but, by-the-bye, why do you call her Madame Delvy?"

"Why, as I have been told, Mr. Delvy is her second husband, her first one being a Monsieur Somebody at the Opera-house."

"Oh, then, her rank in life does not equal his?"—"Oh, dear, no. There's one of your love matches. She was a poor girl, as I understand, who lost her husband within a year of her marriage to him, and on the stage she attracted the notice of Mr. Delvy, who, report says, was compelled to marry her, or leave his pursuit of her, as she held out stoutly in her virtue."

"Humph!"—"You may well say 'humph!' for Delvy's family all cut him in consequence of the marriage, and almost the only visitors he has now are parliamentary connexions and the Carnabys."

"And who are they?"—"Madame Delvy's relations. There's her mother, her sister, her cousin, John Carnaby, and God knows how many more beside. Delvy, I am told, allows them all something to live upon, and they make a pretty good thing of it among them, you may depend. But since this terrible affliction, poor Madame, or Mrs. Delvy, is much to be pitied."

"She is, indeed, poor thing. She seems a most amiable and good-hearted woman."—"She is, indeed. I firmly believe that if anything serious was to occur to her husband, it would kill her."

"Well, all we can do with such a case as this is to watch it closely. There must be a cause for every effect; and the thing will be to ascertain what functional derangement has produced these delusions in Mr. Delvy."

"True; there are so many causes of insanity. But you see as a surgeon, it is scarcely a case of mine. Will you be so good as to pay regular attention to it, and I will go only occasionally?"—"Very well. I know you are intensely occupied with your hospital practice."

"I am, indeed; I am continually operating, and you are aware that I wish to turn my attention almost exclusively to the use of the knife."—"Exactly. *Chacun a son gout*, as the French say. For my part, I should not like it."

"But you are a nervous wretch, you know."—"Most true. So I will attend upon Delvy, while you cut away at the hospitals; and here we are at your door, and I will bid you good day."

"Nay, won't you come in and have some lunch?"—"Not to-day, thank you. Good day."

"Good day, then. Let me know if any change takes place with Mr. Delvy?"—"Most certainly."

And so we parted, leaving me full of thought with regard to my new patient, and really fearing the most serious consequences that showed themselves. I got over the visits I had to make that day as quickly as possible, and then hurried home, which I reached about two o'clock, and down I sat, with all the books and cases I could collect on insanity, resolving to have a long and serious "think" on Mr. Delvy's case.

The more I thought, the more perplexed I got, and that mainly arose from the multitude of queries that arose in my mind on the subject, each of which required some definitive answer from himself to enable me to proceed with my course of reasoning upon the extraordinary case, so that by about seven o'clock in the evening I made up my mind that I would make a friendly call at Berkeley-square, and ask Mr. Delvy the questions which I considered essential.

With this determination, I wrote down on a slip of paper the questions, in order that I should forget none of them, and out I sallied, to walk the distance between my house and the magnificent and imposing mansion of Mr. Delvy. When I got into the street I found the weather anything but pleasant, so I went back for my great-coat and an umbrella, for I determined to walk, inasmuch as I thought the exercise would do me good, and, likewise, I have a habit of thinking while on my feet, and for many years past, whenever I wanted to turn anything very carefully over in my mind, I have been in the habit of taking a long walk; and the more intent I am upon the subject of my meditations, the faster I proceed, until sometimes I have suddenly found myself going along at a prodigious rate, to the astonishment of some friend or acquaintance, who has ran after me, to know what was the matter that I was posting through the streets so quickly for; so notwithstanding an east wind, some sleet, and a cold temperature, I walked from Bread-street, in the City, to Berkeley-square.

Little heeded I the inclemencies of the day, for it really was very disagreeable, more so than I at that time felt disposed to admit; indeed, in such cases, when so preoccupied with my own thoughts, the weather goes for nothing, until it should so happen that it forces itself upon my notice, by saturating my clothes with moisture, or some such palpable evidence, that I cannot entirely escape.

A walk from Bread-street to Berkeley-square is not performed without some trouble, even to a man who is thinking; nor can it be got over as easily to himself as if he were suddenly lifted up in a balloon, or a patent æriel machine, and dropped down at the precise spot, without either dislocation or fracture; but walk I did, and was compelled to suffer the inconvenience of that mode of progression.

The wind was very cold, and the air very raw and chilly; but exercise is a great enemy to cold, and I felt warm, though I could not conceal from myself the fact, that my face and my hands, despite the protection of warm gloves, were very much chilled, and the skin stiffened, so much, indeed, that the outer surface of the body was affected by the cold, and yet, beneath, all was warmth, and a good circulation kept up.

My walk was much diversified by many little odd accidents, such as running first against one person, and then against another. This I could not always avoid, for my thoughts ran on mechanically, and I sometimes forgot to take care where I ought, and was even ungallant enough to run very hard against an old lady who was turning a corner, and forced her back into the arms of a sweep, much to her chagrin and the amusement of the gentleman in black, whose attention was very remarkable, and made an impression on her, I believe, for he immediately dropped his soot bag to catch her, making a great dust about the affair. I must admit that I was glad to escape from the scene, even without apologizing.

But still, notwithstanding all my walk, I was not a bit better able to come to a conclusion respecting Mr. Delvy's case, than when I set out, because the queries I had set down on the slip of paper had as yet had no answer; so I did not regret my journey, but paused in the square to look around me for the mansion to which I had been conducted in the morning by my friend Mr. Blunt, and which I was sure I should know again, because there were some Ionic columns from the first to the second floors.

I walked completely round the square before I could convince myself that the house I recognised was the one I sought;

and at length I walked over to the iron railings of the garden, and took a long look at it to convince myself that I could not be mistaken.

But the reader will naturally ask, where was the difficulty, and I will tell him. The house was all right, and there were the Ionic columns between the windows; but the first floor was brilliantly lighted, and there came from it the sounds of music in such a lively measure, that I was astonished at any one having the audacity so to sport with Madame Delvy's feelings. It was some waltz that was being played, and now and then I fancied I heard some ringing laughter come trippingly upon the ear, and, from the flitting shadows across the blinds, I could well believe that some very merry party indeed was in that drawing-room, notwithstanding the serious and alarming affliction of the master of the house.

While I was thus staring with all my eyes, a carriage dashed up to the doorway; then, in a few moments, the sound of the music ceased, and I saw a small knot of idlers collect, to see who should be let into the carriage.

Then I crossed over the way, and mingled with the spectators. The street-door was thrown open, and a blaze of light came from the well-warmed hall, which seemed tolerably crowded with domestics. The steps of the carriage were let down, and a footman in gorgeous livery stood on each side.

"Oh, it's some heartless visitor," I thought to myself; but, in another moment, Madame Delvy appeared, leaning on the arm of a man I knew not; and immediately following, came two women, one an old fat, waddling mountain of flesh, attired in all the colours of the rainbow; and the other, thin and scraggy, with a neck like a crocus.

The whole party were in the carriage in a moment. The footman touched the rim of his gold-laced hat, and inclined his head.

"The opera!" said Madame Delvy, in an affected voice.

Bang went the door, and the carriage drove off.

The reader may well suppose me left in a state of great amazement. In fact, I was rooted to the spot, and there I remained until the idlers had all dispersed, and the door of Mr. Delvy's house was closed again.

I felt so perfectly astounded—so petrified by the whole affair—that I could almost have fancied Mr. Delvy's complaint was catching, and that I had become a victim to the infection, the appearance of Madame Delvy, and the carriage, and the corpulent old woman, and the strange, impudent-looking man, and the other female with the long, scraggy neck, being all creations of the morbid imagination, and no realities.

I rubbed my eyes, and said, "Hew! hew!" several times, till I found a butcher's boy so interested by my proceedings, that he balanced his tray of meat diagonally upon the area-railings, and was looking at me with forty-butcher's-boy power. Then I moved off, and I heard the impudent rascal saying, "Hew! hew!" until distance drowned his voice. At the time I wished it had drowned him as well, I was so in every way regularly put out.

I walked round the square about ten times, considering what it all meant, and then I resolved to knock, and ask for Mr. Delvy, which resolution I immediately put into practice; and upon the door being opened, I tendered my card, saying,—

"I want to see Mr. Delvy."—"He is not at home, sir," was the reply.

"Indeed! I thought he was too unwell to go out."—"So he was, sir; but there's a division to-night in the house of great importance, and Mr. Canning came for him himself, sir, and persuaded him to go."

"When do you expect him home?"—"Not till the house rises, sir."

"Your mistress is at home?"—"No, sir."

"Thank you; I will call to-morrow."

The man bowed me out, and held the door wide open till I was some distance from it—a custom which I like myself, as it looks significant of a welcome back again, somehow.

Now I had, indeed, ample food for reflection. That Mr. Delvy's absence from home was the reason of the mirth and the noises, and Mrs. Delvy's visit to the opera, I had no sort of doubt, and then I asked myself,—

"Is that woman, with all her fine feelings, her incoherent sentences, her floods of tears, her exalted language, and her deep heart-breaking sobs, after all playing a part?"

This was a query which came across my mind with painful interest, and I could not for some time answer it. At length I caught myself saying,—

"Yes—yes; Madame Delvy is a hypocrite, and there is, surely, at the bottom of this affair something more than meets the eye."

I turned my steps at once towards Mr. Blunt's, and by walking rapidly, I very soon found myself at his door. He was at home; and in as few words as possible I recounted to him all that had passed. He heard me silently; and, when I had finished, which I took care to do without appending any remarks of my own, he said,—

"And what conclusion do you deduce from all this?"—"I do not know," said I, "that I am warranted exactly in deducing any conclusion. All I can say is, that to my perception, the whole of the circumstances are very extraordinary."

"You are right; they are very extraordinary; and indeed, any one but a man of your own calm judgment would most probably jump at once at some very hasty conclusion indeed respecting them. But, to speak candidly, I must say I do view these proceedings of Mrs. Delvy's, or Madame Delvy's, in a very grave light. You see she's a very young woman, and you must have remarked, that when there are extremes of feeling of any kind or description whatever, there is very seldom indeed much consistency."

"Most true. I grant you your general principle. All I ask is, in this individual instance, do you think Madame Delvy's conduct merely arises from the natural levity of a buoyant constitution, which, like a spring, however much it may be compressed one moment, will fly back again to its original position?"—"Your illustration is most apt. I do think Madame Delvy to be one of those characters."

"Then you acquit her of hypocrisy?"—"Yes, of downright, essential hypocrisy I do acquit her, but not of that kind of exaggeration in the exhibition of feeling, which habit she very likely owes to her early theatrical education."

I shook my head as I replied,—

"I cannot agree with you that any theatrical, or other education can have anything to do with real feeling. A few stray expressions may escape, of a piece with some general habit, as many persons are foolishly in the custom of using superlatives, when some words of far less significant tendency would amply suffice for the expression of the sentiment they want to convey; but if you mean to tell me that Madame Delvy's tears and sobs are theatrical, I certainly call her a most abominable hypocrite, unless I don't know yet what the word hypocrisy means at all."

"Are you not rather harsh?"—"God forbid I should be so. Nothing can be farther from my intention. I always took hypocrisy to mean the assumption of some feeling which had no real home in the heart at all, or the affected violence of some sentiment which was in reality to the mind but one of limited and quiet appreciation. If madame does not feel at all the condition of her husband, she is a rank hypocrite. If she feel it but slightly, and affects to feel it acutely, still is she a hypocrite, and no theatrical habits can possibly excuse her."

"Well, well. You speak warmly, and you have half converted me. If she made herself so merry and comfortable because Delvy was out of the house, I give up her defence entirely."—"The presumption most certainly is in favour of that supposition, Mr. Blunt."

"It is, I grant. As for the people who were with her, they, I should fancy, form portions of her own family, the Carnabys."—"They may; but if I were Mr. Delvy, I would say something to these same Carnabys that would not be considered to be extracted from Lord Chesterfield."

"I have no doubt that the corpulent female you so graphically have described is Mrs. Carnaby—the scraggy one, the sister, and the man, Mrs. Delvy's cousin."—"Ah! well, it's no business of ours; only, as the lady did draw rather largely on our sympathies this morning, I was rather enraged to see her going to the opera. For the future I shall attach about as much importance to Madame Delvy's tears and sobs as I would to the groans, squeaks, and reluctant drops of water forced from an old pump with a defective sucker."

Mr. Blunt roared again with laughter, and then wiping his eyes, he said,—

"You are a funny fellow, Dr. ——, but do not take any notice of Madame Delvy, or her smiles, or her tears. As medical men, you know, if we give the matter a moment's thought, we must be aware we have nothing to do with anything, or anybody at a house but our patient."—"Precisely."

"Very good. Then leave Madame Delvy to her caprices of temper, and let her laugh, or cry, or play music, or not, as she pleases. Our business is with her husband. I think it's a pity he has gone out after that cupping."—"So do I; but I suppose he couldn't help it. And when the minister wants a vote he would drag anybody out of the grave, if they were but capable of saying, 'Ay' or 'No,' as the case might be."

"Very true. I am aware the ministry is tottering, so no doubt Delvy was urgently wanted. When shall I see you again?"—"I will endeavour to give you a call to-morrow after I have seen Mr. Delvy."

"Thank you—thank you."

I bade Mr. Blunt good night, and then returned home, for it was getting late; and I retired to rest that night in a state of great perplexity about Mr. Delvy, and Madame Delvy, and the whole of the fraternity of the Carnabys, against whom somehow I had a most terrible hatred, which savoured, on my part, rather of a prejudice that I have against anybody's wife's relations, for I had not seen enough of them to authorise me in coming to any conclusion respecting them.

* * * * *

I always take a look at the morning papers while I am at my breakfast, and judge of my surprise, when, in glancing over the parliamentary debates, I saw Mr. Delvy's name, and found that he had made a speech of five columns in length over night.

Under the very peculiar circumstances of my acquaintance with Mr. Delvy, I was of course deeply interested by any remark which had been reported as falling from his lips, and I read his whole speech through with an intent and a profound attention which I never imagined anything in the shape of a parliamentary debate could ever have awakened in my mind, for I was well enough aware, that whatever was uttered within the walls of St. Stephen's, was not intended for the ears of those who then listened to it, but to answer some purposes out of doors.

Under the peculiar circumstances, however, connected with Mr. Delvy, my interest in the parliamentary debate became absorbing, and I paused not until I had read from beginning to end all he had said, as well as all the speeches of other members who followed him, and in which there were constant allusions to what he had said, and the deductions that might be drawn from every half sentence he had uttered.

Then I looked to the "leader" of the paper, and I found it wholly occupied with an elaborate critique upon Delvy's speech, which was praised to the echo (the paper was just then ministerial), and ended with a declaration that, for the present, the ministry had been saved by Mr. Delvy.

"And is this the man," thought I, as I laid down the paper, "whom I am called upon to treat medically—to treat for insanity? Can it be possible, that upon such a man hangs the fate of a ministry? Really this whole affair becomes more and more involved each moment, and presents the strangest and most inexplicable features."

Folding up the paper and placing it in my pocket, I was about to leave the house full of deep thought. At this moment my servant entered with a note, saying,—

"Please, there's an Irish footman below, sir, and he's waiting for an answer, as well as we can understand him, sir."

"An Irish footman?"—"Yes, sir."

"Where does he come from?"—"From Mr. Delvy's, the member, sir, I believe."

"Oh, very good; tell him to wait."

I opened the letter, which I found came from no other than Madame Delvy, and if ever there was, in this world, a hypocritical concoction of villany in the shape of an epistle, I fully believed that letter to be one before I had got half through it. It lies before me now, faded by time, and I transcribe it for my readers' edification.

"Berkeley-square.

"DEAR DOCTOR,—The incoherence of this epistle will be forgiven by you, when you consider for a moment the feelings of powerful excitement under which it is written.

"Last evening an urgent note from the premier came for Mr. Delvy's attendance at the House of Commons, and despite all my earnest entreaties, my prayers, and my tears, he would go. The state of mind in which I remained during his absence watching until long past the small hours of the morning for his return, I must leave you to imagine, and proceed at once to the object of this note, which is to let you know that my worst anticipations have been realised, and that in consequence of the excitement of the parliamentary debate, poor Mr. Delvy has led a night full of dreadful horrors.

"I cannot find words to describe to you what he has suffered, and what I have suffered from sympathy. Indeed, sir, we are very much to be pitied; and I begin to have a dreadful fear that some of these days Mr. Delvy's malady will suddenly alter its character to one of great danger. Should circumstances ever compel me to adopt a course which would plunge me in the profoundest misery—namely, getting a commission of lunacy against Mr. Delvy, I feel that I can turn to no one for more friendly sympathy than yourself.

"Trusting to have the honour of seeing you shortly, believe me to be, dear sir, yours, very sincerely,

"ARABELLA DELVY.

"Be pleased to inform the bearer at what hour I may expect to see you."

* * * * *

I read this precious epistle twice, and then I walked down to the passage, where was the messenger who had brought it, and found him to be, by appearance, a raw good-humoured looking Irishman, from whom, on indifferent subjects, the truth was very likely to be extracted, with a due allowance for the talent of exaggeration, which is possessed by all his countrymen, high or low.

"You brought me a letter," I said, "from Madame Delvy."—"True, for you, sir, I did. There's no harm in that, I hope, sir?"

"None at all. Just walk into this room. Now, what's your name?"—"Dinnis O'Rourke, your honour, and not half so thirsty now, as I am now and thin."

I took Dinnis's hint, and gave him a glass of something potent, which would have driven Father Mathew into fits, after which, I said to him,—

"Now, Dinnis, how is your master?"—"Faith, sir, about five foot tin, I take it, but not so broad, in a manner o' speaking, as he might be."

"I mean, how is he in health?"—"Oh, murder; that's a good one any how, seeing you're a doctor, and I aint. But, if you must know, he's been a skrummaging agin with the mistress, rest her soul, when she gets half way to glory—if by a thundering mercy, she gets so far at all, at all."

"You have your doubts, Dinnis?"—"True for you, sir, I have."

"But what was the skrummaging about?"—"Oh, the old subject."

"But it's news to me."—"Is it, faith? Why, then, the master thinks the mistress's cousin too bould, I think."

"Indeed! Take another glass."—"It would look like scorning your honour to say no. Faith, then, this is a mighty fine drink; it goes down one's throat like a flash o' lightning, and lays in a body's stomach like a bomb shell—all of a fiz; but, as I was saying, sir, the master thinks as the mistress and her cousin are a world too thick."

"Then why don't he turn him out of the house?"—"That's the secret, sir."

"Secret?"—"Yes, surely; when the master says anything the smallest bit particular, up speaks the mistress, and, says she, 'It's mad you are, my dear; and you sees *allusions*, you do;' and then the master begins a groan like a dying Christian, and half believes it, and he half don't."

"Indeed! Well, Dinnis, that is curious; good morning to you."—"The top o' the morning to your honour, and I don't care how many times I come here any way, for though you are a doctor you keep something better than physic in that same bottle with the long neck. I believe, sir, I've had three glasses."

"Two, Dinnis, and they are quite enough; so be off with you."—"Oh, sir, wasn't I going. The blessing of all the saints wrap you up, sir, like a holy great-coat."

So saying Master Dinnis walked off, having opened my eyes to one circumstance, which, although it might not come to my mind with sufficient of the force of reality to induce absolute conviction, was still a hint of a tolerably particular nature, and one which offered, in regard to Mr. Delvy, ample materials for thinking.

I resolved at once to start away on my visit to Berkeley-square, and, in the course of an hour, I once more found myself in the unique and splendid waiting-room of the costly residence. As usual, Madame Delvy made her appearance first, and she came into the room with a theatrical kind of start as if she did not know I was there, and when she saw me she drew half back making an affectation of patting her eyes, to wipe off tears that might be there congregated.

"Oh, sir," she said, "how can I sufficiently thank you for such kind prompt attention to my note?"—"Madame," I said, "no thanks are due to me; I should have been here by this time had I not received your favour."

"Oh," she added, "how very kind. I grieve much to say, that your poor patient is much worse."

"Indeed, madam. I suppose you have seen the morning papers?"—"Yes, yes."

"You will, then, have seen what a brilliant speech was made by Mr. Delvy."—"I did. How very cunning mad people are, to be sure."

"Madam, I will be bound to say, that there was no member of the House of Commons, last night, who would not gladly have compounded for half the cunning, and put up with all the madness."

"Oh, no doubt, no doubt. How little, I dare say, they suspected that a lunatic was talking to them."—"Or ever will suspect."

"Or ever will suspect," she repeated; " but I must tell you, he passed a very bad night indeed; all his delusions visited him again, and some others which he had not before seen, which I wholly attribute to the excitement produced by the House of Commons business."

"Excitement does a good deal in such cases," I remarked; "sometimes for good, and sometimes for evil. If you please, as I have several calls to make early, I would be glad to see Mr. Delvy as soon as possible."

"He shall know you are here, sir. Oh, what a dreadful thing it would be to be reduced to the frightful alternative mentioned in my note to you, of issuing a commission to inquire into the state of mind of Mr. Delvy."

"Very. Has he ever shown any jealousy?"

Madame Delvy turned very red as I popped this home question; I looked her very hard in the face as I did so, in defiance of all good manners.

"Jealousy!" she repeated.—"Yes, madam; we generally find that feeling among the very earliest indices of insanity."

"You don't say so? It's a very delicate subject, but now you mention it, I must say that Mr. Delvy has exhibited, among his other hallucinations, some dreadfully absurd feelings of that kind, but not in a marked manner."

"Oh, not very marked?"—"Oh, dear, no, not by any means. I will let him know you are here; but let me warn you not by any means to allude to a jealous feeling existing in his mind, for I have found about him as regarded that question a greater tinge of irascibility than on any other."—"I will be most careful, madam."

"By-the-bye, doctor, excuse me for mentioning such a subject, but with regard to your fees, I will myself make your visits worth two pounds each."

Without waiting for an answer she left the room, and I certainly must confess that her last words produced anything but a disagreeable sensation in my mind. In a few minutes I was introduced to Mr. Delvy, whom I found looking pale and harassed, with an expression of anxiety upon his countenance, which I did not like at all. He welcomed me in a friendly manner, and as I had pre-arranged in my own mind what I meant to do, I cut the interview as short as possible, by saying to him,—

"Mr. Delvy, it is absolutely necessary that you, and I, and Mr. Blunt, should have a long conversation together. I hope you will look upon me as a friend as well as a physician, and so overlook the freedom I am about to take?"—"Sir," he said, "I am much obliged to you, and can only say, that any suggestions from you shall receive the most implicit obedience from me."

"Then, you will dine with me to-day?"—"I will, sir."

"You will meet no one but Mr. Blunt and myself. May I expect you at No. 10, Old Broad-street, City, at six o'clock this evening?"—"I shall most certainly be there, sir."

"Then, now permit me to wish you good morning; merely adding, for your comfort and satisfaction, that I have no doubt in the world of being able in a very short time to rid you of all your troublesome complaints."

"You give me new life," said he. "What joyful intelligence this will be to Mrs. Delvy."—"Ahem!" said I. "Remember, six o'clock."

I made what morning calls I had to make, and then took my chance of finding Mr. Blunt at home, which, although he was not, answered my purpose as well, for his servants knew where he was, and they sent for him in the course of a quarter of an hour. When he came in I said.—

"Well, Blunt, I suppose you think me a perpetual worry; but I come to see you again about Mr. Delvy."

He smiled as he replied,—

"You are one of the most indefatigable men I know, and when you do take up a subject of any kind, I am well aware you will not lay it down quietly. Has anything new happened?"—"Nothing very particular, only I want your co-operation in a little scheme."

"Ah, there you go again; and for scheming, you are the most remarkable."

"But this is a very little scheme indeed, and not very complicated. I suppose you eat dinners?"—"One at a time I do."

"Very good; then I want you to assist at the consumption of one at my house to-day."—"But, my dear fellow ——"

"I will hear no excuse, come you must."—"But ——"

"Nonsense, Delvy dines with me, and I want you most particularly; so pray look upon it as a matter of business, and come punctually at six o'clock."

"Well, I have myriads of engagements, but if I must, why I must; and now tell me what has induced you to put yourself to so much trouble?"—"Simply, that I want to try the experiment, if Mr. Delvy's delusions be local to his house in Berkeley-square, or follow him about."

"But how ——"—"Hear me out. When he comes to my house to dine, I shall persuade him to stay all night, and if, then, he sees any of his delusions, I shall believe it to be a medical case. If he do not, I shall consider that some trickery has been practised."

"But have you asked him to stay all night?"—"No, because I do not want his wife to know anything about it, or to set her fine wits to work on the subject, or she might prevent him coming; I will manage the sleeping business after he has had his dinner, and we have had our talk with him."

"Well, it is not a bad plan to find out if the disease is one depending upon imagination wholly, or some lesion of the brain, the effects of which must, of course, be manifest everywhere; you may depend upon seeing me."—"Thank you; farewell now till six."

* * * * *

To the horror of my landlady I announced that two gentlemen were going to dine with me at six o'clock, and that one of them was a member of parliament, while both of them were used to the most sumptuous dinners that were ever upon sumptuous tables.

"Gracious goodness!" she exclaimed; " we don't do it."—" But we must," said I; "and if you will only be so good as not to attempt to do anything that you are not quite sure you can do well, we shall get on most remarkably, and everything will be all right."

"I'm all of a fluster."—" Then you will make a mess of everything if you don't get out of the fluster as quick as you can."

"But it's three o'clock now."—"A quarter past, madam."

"Good God!"—" He is very good to us all."

"Now, doctor ——"—" Dinner at six," said I, and by force of arms I pushed my good-tempered landlady out of the room.

This point having been satisfactorily settled, for I knew my landlady would do the thing properly, I waited for the arrival of my visitors with some little anxiety, for as yet all concerning Mr. Delvy was but surmise, and although I had the strongest circumstantial grounds for believing that Madame Delvy was playing some deep and desperate game, yet I certainly had no direct evidence that Mr. Delvy's delusions were not as they had been reported, the veritable chimera of his imagination. Punctually at six came Mr. Blunt, and I had scarcely time to say to him,—

"Mind you second me when I ask Mr. Delvy to stay all night here," when a carriage dashed up to my door, and two footmen let down the steps with a pompous clatter to permit the wealthy M.P. to leave the vehicle, and in another moment he was in the house, and he appeared, by his manner of speaking, to be in better spirits than I had seen him for some time.

My landlady dished us up an excellent dinner, and when it had been done justice to, and the cloth was removed, as we sat with some choice wine before us, I said,—

"Now, Mr. Delvy, let me pray you to believe you are with friends, and not professional inquisitors. There is but one question I wish to ask of you, which, perhaps, should require an apologetic preface, and I trust you will not be offended."

"Ask me what you will," he said; " I declare to you that you shall be answered, fairly, fully, and frankly, and that I will not construe anything you may say into an offence."

"Very good. Are you jealous of your wife?"

I suppose the question was the one farthest from Mr.

Delvy's thoughts of any, for he changed colour, and absolutely half rose from his chair, when I plumped it out so shortly. Blunt looked rather staggered, and I waited quite quietly and patiently for an answer.

"I must say, sir," said Mr. Delvy, after a few moments' pause, "that your question is a startling and unexpected one; but I have made you my promise, on the word of a gentleman, that I will not be offended, and that I will answer all that you shall require of me. I say, therefore, in reply, that I have never had any cause to be jealous of Mrs. Delvy."

"But have you ever been jealous?"—"I have."

"Of whom?"—"Of a gentleman who is frequently at my house, a cousin of Mrs. Delvy's, which makes the matter more absurd still. At first I fancied I saw familiarities pass between them, but when I found that so many more strange sights, which had no foundation but in my own diseased imagination, came before my eyes with all the vivid appearance of reality, I discarded all thoughts dishonourable to my wife, and considered as optical delusions what I had seen on two or three occasions, upon abruptly entering some of the rooms of my house."

Blunt coughed as he said,—

"What an uncommonly comfortable feeling for a husband to have to be sure, that anything in the shape of familiarity between his wife and a cousin, is an optical delusion."—"Very," said I.

"You—you do not doubt, gentlemen?"—"Oh, not for a moment," I added; "you were very much harassed last night, were you not, Mr. Delvy, by your delusions?"

"I was indeed. There were strange sights continually in my chamber, and flashing lights and odd faces of all kinds and descriptions. I rose this morning half mad, and upon descending to the breakfast-room—by-the-bye, I was to have breakfasted in bed, by the advice of my wife—I fancied I saw her sitting in her cousin's lap. There was an odd delusion."
—"Very!"

"Very odd!"—"Very, as you say. I hear it was a delusion, and yet at the moment it had sufficient effect upon me to make me say something, I fear, very unkind."

"Do you sleep with your wife, Mr. Delvy?"—"Yes; but when my delusions begin, she is so much affected that she leaves me and sleeps alone."

"Well, sir, it's a very odd thing that you should see such delusive sights as those connected with your wife's cousin. I wonder you never sought for the evidence of other people's eyes on the subject."

"I have, and that's how I satisfied myself; Mrs. Carnaby, my wife's mother, and her sister, have both assured me they are delusions. On one occasion I thought I saw the cousin actually come out of Mrs. Delvy's bed-room, but Mrs. Carnaby swore to me he was not in the house even."

"Do you receive Mrs. Carnaby and your wife's sister as visitors?"—"Very rarely, I may say, for I have, certainly, objections to them of a very stringent character; nevertheless, they certainly do visit at my house."

"Well, Mr. Delvy, there is one point connected with your case, which is of the utmost importance, and, in order to set that at rest, will you consent to sleep here to-night?"—"If necessary, certainly; but what can be the point which can be so determined?"

"We wish to ascertain if your delusions be merely local, or if they will follow you from Berkeley-square to the city."

He shook his head as he said,—

"You will find, I fear, that the same disordered mind which conjures up such odd sights in my own bed-room, in Berkeley-square, will produce the same effects, let me lie down where I will in search of repose."

"We shall see. Let your imagination have full play. Do not make any effort to resist disagreeable impressions and feelings, and let us know in the morning what sort of a night you have passed."

Mr. Delvy promised faithfully to adhere to my instructions, and having sent a message home to the effect that the carriage need not call for him, because he was going to sleep at my house, we passed a very pleasant and a highly intellectual evening. It was about eleven o'clock at night that a note came for Mr. Delvy, and, after reading it, he handed it to me, saying,—

"I fear, doctor, that, after all, I cannot be your guest."

The note was as follows:—

"MY DEAR CHARLES,—I am very far from well. Pray come home to-night, to your own Isabella."

"From Mrs. Delvy?" said I.—"Yes. I cannot do otherwise than go home."

"Mr. Delvy, you have given me your word, as a gentleman, that you will remain here to-night; break it you can, if you like; but if you do, remember, this is our last meeting."

"But, my dear sir, you view this matter too seriously. There, I hear the carriage; nevertheless, if you insist so very particularly upon my staying ——"—"I do, most particularly."

"Very well, then, I will stay. You can send what message you please to my house. I am your prisoner."—"Very good," said I; and I sent a message back to Mrs. Delvy, to the effect that, Mr. Delvy having promised to stay with me, he could not break his word, and hoped that Mrs. Delvy would be much better by the morning.

So far had I succeeded; and, about half-past eleven o'clock Mr. Blunt left us, and Mr. Delvy was shown to the chamber I had prepared for him. I must own that I did not pass a very serene night, for I was very anxious with regard to the experiment that was being made, and several times, such was the force of imagination, that I started up, fancying I heard some sound of alarm from Mr. Delvy's bed-room. Thankful was I when the morning came, and I could find sufficient daylight to get up by—and still more thankful was I when eight o'clock came, and I thought there would be no great impropriety in rousing my guest. Accordingly, I repaired to his bed-room, and knocked at the door, when he immediately opened it himself, as he was nearly dressed.

"Good morning," said I; "how have you slept?"—"I have not slept very well," he replied; "but I saw nothing."

"You were quite free from visitations?"—"Quite. I laid awake for some hours, and tried to conjure up some of the images which were night after night my companions at home, but it was all in vain."

"Ah," said I, "like Glendower, you can call spirits from the vasty deep, but they will not come when you do call them. I shall certainly cure you, Mr. Delvy, and that I hope very shortly. I have but one favour to ask of you first, and that is, that you will manage, unknown to any one, to let me remain in your house all night."

"Oh, certainly; but why unknown to any one? Mrs. Delvy will be happy to make every preparation for your comforts."—"Nay, that's exactly what I don't wish. I don't want to be at all comfortable. Have you sufficient faith in me to order your hall-porter to admit me at any hour I please to-night, and to ask me no questions, but allow me to go where I like in your house?"

Mr. Delvy changed colour as he said,—

"Doctor, tell me frankly what you mean by all this?"—"I mean, that I think you have been hoaxed—that you are no more mad than I am."

"But—but—but—good God! who could believe so? How could it be done? And what motive ——"—"All these questions I cannot answer, sir; but I have now, in my mind, a fair conviction that you are the victim of some scheming, which might end in placing you in a lunatic asylum, if not stopped."

He clasped his hands as, in a low voice, he said,—

"You suspect my wife?"—"I do; and the cousin, and the mother, and the sister."

"This is dreadful! Can I have been such a fool? Is it possible that I can have allowed my judgment to be so wretchedly hoodwinked?"—"I cannot answer distinctly yes, to your question; but I have the strongest suspicions. May I come to your house in the manner I propose?"

"Yes, yes. This is a crisis in my existence, doctor. To-night shall make me another man. Come when you will—do what you will, so that you rescue me from the circumstances in which I am at present placed. I will take care that you shall be admitted, and free liberty given you."

"Where do you sleep?"—"On the second floor. The first door at the head of the staircase."

"Do the Carnaby family sleep in the house?"—"Most certainly not."

"Very good. How many bed-chambers are there on the same floor?"—"Only four. One is my own; and the others, with the exception of one, to which Mrs. Delvy repairs when my delusions come, are left for visitors, and very rarely used." * * * * *

All this being arranged as I considered tolerably satisfactorily, I did not think it at all necessary to trouble Mr. Blunt any more, but made up my mind that there should be something of a conclusive character at Mr. Delvy's house that night, that would either clear him of all suspicions of his wife, by proving that the delusions which he fancied he saw were really those of the imagination, or convict her as the author of them, for the purpose of carrying out her own designs, whatever they might be. It was twelve o'clock at night when I tapped gently at the door of Delvy's splendid mansion. It was opened for me instantly, and I said to the hall porter,—

"Did Mr. Delvy mention me to you?"—"Yes, sir. He said you were to be admitted, and left to go where you like."

"Very good. Have the family retired to rest?"—"They have, sir; about a quarter of an hour ago. Don't you want a light, sir?"

"No, thank you."

Slowly and carefully I ascended the staircase, until I reached the second floor, fully intending to make my way into one of the spare bed-rooms, which I trusted to good luck to be enabled to find. There was a light from the ceiling of the drawing-room; therefore, I was not quite in the dark; a circumstance that I was just congratulating myself upon, when out it went, and all I had to guide me was the dim light that came through a staircase window. My object was to find a door, which I at last succeeded in doing; but the moment I opened it, I found there was a light inside, and some one cried,—

"Who's there?"—"Nobody," said I; and I hopped away again.

I took the precaution to listen at the next door, and I heard the voice of Mr. Delvy, which let me know which was his bed-room. Just then, as I was looking about for a third door, one opened, and a man's voice said,—

"Hilloa! who's there, eh?"

I crouched down, and was unobserved; and, after muttering something about the damned cat, the fellow—whom I had seen get into the carriage on the opera night—walked across the corridor, and disappeared into a little room which seemed to me to join Mr. Delvy's bed-room. Then all was darkness again, and I stood behind a curtain, determined to wait the progress of events, and quite convinced in my own mind that something would happen soon of an interesting character.

I suppose I waited about a quarter of an hour, when I heard noises from Mr. Delvy's bed-room, and in a few moments out came Mrs. Delvy, wrapt up in a morning dress, with a candle in her hand. She walked direct to the room I had seen the cousin come out of, and, as she passed me, I heard her mutter,—

"He will have enough of them to-night, Jonas says."

Upon this hint I moved, and, making my way direct to Mr. Delvy's chamber, I glided in. There was a light burning, and he was sitting up in bed.

"Oh, doctor," he said, in a whisper, "is it you?"—"Yes—hush! Have you seen anything?"—"The light alone protects me."

On the instant, I put it out; when, on the roof of the room, appeared a strange and terrible face.

"There—there!" he whispered. "There is one of them!"

I was staggered myself for the moment, although, of course, my seeing it likewise settled the whole business.

"Hush!" I whispered; "do not speak to me."

A strange sort of howl sounded in the room, and the face at the same moment disappeared.

I crept to the door of the chamber, and opened it a little way. The cousin of Mrs. Delvy walked across the corridor, and went into the room I had previously seen her enter. I then shut the door, and, turning to Mr. Delvy, said,—

"Have you the means of getting a light?"—"Yes, certainly."

He got one in a moment, and then I added,—

"Do you use that dressing-room?"—"No; it is a mere lumber room. Yon small window looks into it."

"Come along with me."

He huddled on his clothes, and in a few moments we were in the lumber-room. There were boxes and packing-cases out of number, and I began searching them as rapidly as I could, till, in one, I found a still warm magic lantern, which I at once took out, saying,—

"Here, Mr. Delvy, is the source of your delusions. Your wife's cousin, who is, I think, at this moment with your wife ——"

He did not allow me to finish, but, catching the lantern from my hands, he darted across the corridor with it, and disappeared into the bed-room where Mrs. Delvy had gone. I heard a loud scream—volleys of oaths, and a tremendous riot. Arming myself with a large whip, which was in the lumber-room, and which was the only weapon I could get hold of, I sallied into the corridor, just in time to meet the cousin, with his face all over oil and blood, from the lamp which Mr. Delvy had used as a weapon against him. He tried to make a bolt down the stairs, but, before he could do so, I had the satisfaction of giving him a cut or two with the whip, that made him roar again. Mr. Delvy then snatched it from me, and I suspect he caught Mrs. Delvy a tolerable cut round the ankles as she, too, fled, shouting,—

"It's my mother and sister's doings—all of it! They are in the spare room."

I thought Delvy was mad now, for he suddenly said,—

"I'll clear the house of the Carnabys!"

And in he bolted to the other room, where I heard the whip going like a steam-engine, and out rushed Mrs. Carnaby and Miss Carnaby, with very scanty apparel, and flew down the staircase as if they were mad, while Mr. Delvy pursued with the whip, nor stopped until the whole four delinquents, to the absolute horror of the hall porter, had rushed into the street.

* * * *

Thus ended Mr. Delvy's lunacy. He allowed his wretched wife fifty pounds a-year, but the Carnabys he never heard of again.

THE HOUSEBREAKER;

OR, A DAUGHTER'S LOVE.

Owing, I suppose, to my giving for some years, when I first commenced medical practice, advice gratis to whoever chose to apply to me within certain hours, I attained a kind of reputation among the poor, which was as often productive of troublesome applications as of gratifying ones. Indeed, many times, without reference to time, place, or circumstances, I have been called upon to attend a gratuitous patient, as if to do so was my proper business. Once or twice, too, I have dropped into a good paying connexion by such means, and the circumstances I am about to lay before my readers were such that, I feel convinced, might have introduced me to a profitable, if not a very select or agreeable, class of friends.

One morning I had an unusual number of poor patients at my levee, and there remained several undisposed of even when the time came that summoned me to other professional duties; I was, however, always very anxious that the time of these poor people should not be wasted, and I often made some rich patient wait a little rather than send away a poor one.

Under these circumstances, I continued to see those who had been waiting some time; my servant understanding, of course, that no more were to be admitted that day. There were five patients waiting. Four of them require no remarks; but the fifth at once riveted my attention by her appearance.

She was young, and, if not eminently handsome, possessed that beaming, intelligent look about her face which is so far superior to beauty of form. At the first glance I had of her when she came into my room, I thought her about eighteen or twenty years of age, and in so doing I probably drew my conclusions more from the apparent development of intellect observable in her face than from any other circumstance. A second glance, however, served to correct the first, or, at all events, to make me doubtful if she were so old by several years.

Her figure was small and graceful, despite the shabby apparel she wore; but it was her face which riveted my attention. It was one of those sweet, child-like countenances, such as Guido might have painted, and yet it was mingled, which is rare in such countenances, with so much intelligence, that you knew not which most to admire—the cherub-like beauty of the mouth and chin, or the soul-breathing intellect which showed itself in her sparkling eyes and lofty brow.

There was, too, an expression of doubt and hesitation in her face, as if she thought her reception was an unheeded one. She looked in my face for some moments before she spoke, as if she would read my very soul ere she trusted herself to address me; but when I said, "Pray, sit down," she seemed a good deal reassured by my voice, and, like sunshine o'er a summer's cloud, there fleeted across her face a glance of feeling, and a tenderness of expression, which was beautiful to see, and much prepossessed me in her favour.

"What can be the matter with this young creature," thought I, "that she evidently thus reluctantly comes here?" but my reverie was broken in upon by her voice, which was deep for a girl's, but very soft and melodious.

"Is it true," she said, "that when chance or confidence enables physicians to become acquainted with dangerous secrets, they feel themselves bound, as men of honour, not to betray those who trust them?"

This was a most singular speech to begin with, and I began to suspect that my young visitor was something very different from what she appeared.

"I should think," I said, "that a medical man who abused the confidence which, in the course of his profession, is necessarily often placed in him, would be unworthy of the name of gentleman. The instances in which such confidence is misplaced I think are very rare indeed."

"I have heard so," she said, with a deep sigh. "I have heard that you may be trusted even with a secret involving a human life."

"I wish you would come to the point, and tell me what's the matter," I said; "you don't look unwell."—"I am quite well. It is for another I come."

"Another?"—"Yes. I have ventured, from what I have heard of you in the course of many inquiries, to come to you with a request, which, if you refuse me, I am sure you will not refuse harshly, and which, if you grant me, will entitle you to the gratitude of one who, although too poor to pay you but in words at present, may one day be able to offer a more substantial token of her appreciation of your unbought assistance."

There was evidence of mental cultivation in the girl's language, and my anxiety became excited to hear who she was.

"Any assistance that I can be of to you professionally," I said, "will give me great pleasure. My time, just now, is very valuable, and if you will either call again, or tell me as briefly as possible what you wish of me, I shall be obliged."

"To call again might be too late," she replied, with a sudden gush of anguish, which was strikingly at variance with the calmness she had hitherto displayed. "The case is urgent. I might be an orphan before I called again. Oh, God!—oh, God!"—"Calm yourself," I said; "wherefore is this transport of feeling?"

She took from her breast a small scrap of paper, and laid it down before me. On it were the words, "Ask for Jackson, No. 11, Hart-street, Covent-garden."

"What does this mean?" I said.—"He is the sufferer."

"But who may Jackson be?"—"My father—he is dying! Oh, sir, come and see him. He will die—no one else will come near him! Indeed, I—dare not ask them!"

"You dare not!"—"No, no! I have hinted at a secret! There is a dreadful one, which I think you had better know, but he must consent first. I dare not tell you now. But will you come?—oh, say you will come!"

"You must confess," I remarked "that this is an extraordinary application; as yet I know so little of the circumstances."—"I thank you, sir," she said, in a tone of deep disappointment; "I thank you. Good morning, sir."

She was about to leave immediately, taking what I had said as a kind refusal, I suppose; but as I did not intend it to be such, although I should have been glad to know more of my new patient before I went to him, I called her back, saying,—

"You are too hasty. What I wanted you to understand was, that I thought I ought to know more before I go to visit your father."

"What would you know," she exclaimed, clasping her hands, "but that he is a fellow-creature, and in want of that skilful assistance which you can give him? And yet I would rather you knew all; but without his consent I cannot tell you. If you refuse my request, he must die indeed. I will make no other attempt."

"Well, then, I will come; but I cannot tell exactly at what hour. Is he very ill, indeed?"—"Very; but we must wait."

"You may depend upon my coming as early as I can; but you must be aware that any sick person can claim in London the gratuitous medical assistance of properly appointed professional men."

"We dare not," she replied. "But you have passed your word that you will come."—"I have."

"Then I am satisfied. I have no words in which to thank you. From your own heart's sensations, when you have been deeply grateful, you can imagine mine."

Her voice shook slightly, and a tear glistened in her eye as she spoke. With a curtsey then that would not have disgraced a drawing-room, she left me, and in a few minutes more I commenced my round of professional calls for the morning, resolved to take that street in my way, as soon as I at all conveniently could.

What the mystery was which the young girl had hinted at, I had no means of guessing, although it was more than probable, from the language she used, that crime of some sort or another had something to do with it. I was, however, too much occupied to indulge in many further conjectures, and found myself at length in the immediate vicinity of the street named in the slip of paper, without having attempted to come to any decisive opinion with regard to who or what the girl could be who had called upon me.

Hart-street is not one of the most delightful of thoroughfares. It commences in Bow-street, by the side of Covent-Garden Theatre, crossing James's-street, until it merges into a horrible nest of courts and alleys lying at the back of Long Acre, itself not the most enchanting spot in London. However, I found it without any difficulty, and when I did so, it by no means prepossessed me in favour of my patient, for it was one of the most suspicious-looking houses in that very suspicious street.

The door was upon a latch merely, so that it easily opened to my touch; but who to ask for Jackson I certainly knew not; and I stood in the passage for some minutes, now and then giving a stamp with my foot to attract some one's attention before anybody appeared. At length the parlour door was opened, and a hag-like looking woman popped her head out, saying,—

"What do you want?"—"Jackson," said I.

"Oh, Jackson! Are you the physical man?"—"I am, madam, I believe, a physical man."

"A doctor?"—"And a doctor."

"Bill, Bill!"—"What's the row now?" said a gruff voice from within the room.

"Come here, will you, and look at this chap?"

I heard a stumbling about, as if somebody was making towards the door of the parlour over all the chairs and tables, and then a man's head was popped out, with a beard upon the chin of it that seemed to have been unacquainted with the razor for a month at least.

"What do you think of him?" said the woman. "Is he a plant, Bill?"—"No—too jolly green-looking for that," replied Bill; and after paying me this compliment, he drew his head in again, leaving me to make the most of it.

"Well, madam," I said, "since you have decided that I am not a vegetable production, notwithstanding my greenness, will you favour me by directing me to Jackson?"—"He's a talking French now," said the woman.

"Don't bother me," cried the man, "or I'll twist some of your d—d necks, or else do something violent."—"Quite violent enough," thought I, "the neck-twisting would be;" and then I said, aloud,—

"Will you tell me if Jackson is to be found here or not?"—"Three pair front," was the brief reply, and bang went the door of the parlour in my face.

"Three pair front," thought I to myself; "that means the front attic, I presume. Well, I promised my young friend, who called upon me this morning, that I would come to see this Jackson—so here goes."

The stairs were very dark, for either the march of bricks and mortar behind the house, or the original wisdom of our forefathers, who built it, had contrived to prevent the least ray of light from getting to the staircase. I laid hold of the banisters in order to facilitate my progress up; but when I tried to take my hand off again, my glove was nearly pulled off, so thickly lay the dirt of years there. I, therefore, stumbled up the best way I could, till I got to the landing on the second floor, which I did not reach without sundry bumps and concussions against pails, brown pans, brooms, &c., that garnished the first-floor landing, and seemed placed there on purpose to waylay any unfortunate passenger.

When I had got so far, I heard some one coming down the flight of steps immediately above, and I drew up as close to the walls as I could, to save my toes from the infliction of being trodden upon by boots which, from the noise they made, I thought to be downright hobnailers. As the man approached, whistling an air from "The Beggar's Opera," I thought it would be a good opportunity to ask for Jackson; so, when he was a few stairs from the landing where I was waiting, I said,—

"Hilloa, friend!"—"Who the devil are you?" was the polite rejoinder.

"Do you know Jackson?"—"Sink me! what do you take me for—a fool? I was born before that I can tell you. Try it on somewhere else. You'll get into the wrong crib for that fun."

"What do you mean?"—"Ax my elbow."

"Really I had no intention of giving you any offence."—"Offence be blowed! I don't know who you are, but, if you come down into the yard, I'll polish you off, or you shall me, before we are two minutes older."

"My good fellow, I have no desire to polish you, or to go through the process of polishing myself. I merely asked you a civil question, 'Do you know Jackson?' and you all at once

fly into a fury."—"Now, d—n me, if you ain't enough to provoke—what's his name?—Job, you are. Hold yer jaw, will you? I'm not a man to have fun pok'd at him, I can tell you."

So saying, and muttering besides divers threats, couched in not the most elegant language in the world, my irascible friend, whom it was too dark to see, brushed past me, and went down the staircase.

"Well, well," I said to myself, "inquiries seem not at all to be relished here, so I must just continue to ascend on a voyage of discovery for myself."

The attic stairs were darker, narrower, and steeper than any of the others, so that the ascent was not facilitated by any means. I reached the landing, though, without any disturbance, and then, of course, I ran against all sorts of minor domestic articles before I found one of the doors, and then I could not tell if it was the one I sought or another; although, of course, by the perversity of that same fate, which, if you want a knife from a collection of cutlery, makes you take up a dozen forks first, it was more than likely that I had hold of the lock of the back attic instead of the front; but we are told by philosophers that great truths are only to be arrived at by bold experiments, so I gave the lock a tremendous rattle, by way of carrying out that theory to the utmost.

Scarcely had I done so, when something from the inside was flurg against the door with a bang that was sufficient very nearly to break the panel through, and a loud voice cried in accents that might have suited some talking bear,—

"Didn't I tell you not to disturb me, you infernal thief? Just do that agin."

"Is your name Jackson?"

Bang came something else against the door.

"Is this the back attic or the front?"

Before any other missile could be sent at the door, or the infuriated individual could invent any mode of revenge for the disturbance I was giving him, there broke in upon the landing a gleam of light from an opened door, and, turning my eyes in that direction, I saw the young girl who had in the morning so urgently solicited my services, and so much awakened my curiosity.

"This way—this way," she said.

Following her light graceful figure I passed through the doorway, and found myself in a large, old-fashioned, rambling attic, utterly destitute of furniture, and presenting altogether a very cold and cheerless appearance, indeed. I had now a much better opportunity of observing the young girl, for she was without her bonnet, and her long, beautiful, dark auburn hair floated gracefully down her neck, bosom, and shoulders. There did not come a very good light through the dirty, latticed window, but still there was sufficient to assure me that whatever painful position that young creature might at present occupy, such had not always been the case; for if I had forgotten the polished language in which she had spoken to me in the morning, I could not help perceiving about her an air of elegance which never could have been acquired in Hart-street, Covent-garden.

She let me look at her for a few moments without speaking, as if she wished to make a favourable impression upon me, and if such was her motive, she certainly succeeded in it, for I felt much interest in her, as well as much curiosity to know what train of calamitous circumstances could have reduced her to the state she was in.

"You see," I said, "I am here according to my promise."

"God bless you!" she said. "Some other time I will thank you. I have thought over it since, and I know I had no right to come to you at all, or to ask you to visit him. I am now ashamed to see you."

"Oh, never mind that," I replied. "If I can be of any professional service, pray command me; and I hope, as you have much interested me, you will think me sufficiently entitled to your confidence as to tell your history."

"'Tis a very sad one."

"But it may be bettered, surely? You are very young."

"I am, in years; but, in grief, so old. Oh, so old."

"What is your age?"—"I am not seventeen."

"Your life has not always been passed in such places as this, I am sure. At one time you have been gently nurtured, and caressed by fond affections."

She covered her face with her hands, and, in a voice of great mental anguish, cried,—

"Oh, cease—cease. For the love of God and of mercy do not now conjure up to me the memory of the past. I shall break my heart, or go mad."

"Alas! alas! do you talk of the memory of the past being painful—you who are merely yet on the very threshold of existence? There must, indeed, be some great mystery connected with your fate."

"There is—there is."

"But you have not seen enough of the world yet to be a competent judge of those things which are inevitable and those which are remediable. What can have occurred to one so young as yourself that may not all be amended? You say you have known what kindness and affection are—you admit a gentle training. What, then, at your years, could cast you from your proper sphere to such a state as this?"

Before she could reply to me, a deep, hollow groan came upon my ears, and I started, for it seemed close to me, or, at all events, in the room.

The girl placed her finger on her lips, as she said, in a low voice that conveyed scarce any sound,—

"Hush—hush! He is awaking."

"Who—who?"

"My father. Hush! Behind yon curtain he has been having some uneasy slumber. Do not mind if he should seem to speak a little harshly. 'Tis the waywardness of a sick man, and may be borne with. He is not always so. You will make allowances for bodily pain. It enervates the mind, you know, and spoils the best of tempers; it—it ——"

"D——n!" said a deep, guttural voice from behind the curtain the girl had pointed out to me. "D——n everybody, and everything!"

Then there was another long, howling sort of groan, as if the preceding words had been wrung from some one impatient of long suffering.

The curtain that cut off a considerable portion of one end of the attic was composed of an old patch-work bed quilt, and of not the most elegant appearance, and now it was shaken violently by some means from the other side, while such a volley of oaths and imprecations came from the same voice that had already spoken, that I was half inclined to ascertain at once if the utterer of them was my patient, and, if so, to take my leave directly, and decline having anything whatever to do with Mr. Jackson.

Had it not been for the girl, I believe, indeed, I should have adopted such a course, but I felt deeply for the painful situation she was placed in, and I could see by the trembling of her colourless lips, as well as the general state of agitation she was in, how far she was from participating in the devilish spirit of him who should have set her so different an example. She clasped her hands, and looked at me so imploringly, as if she could read every feeling of my mind in my eyes.

"Be composed," I said. "You are not to blame for this. Go and tell him to be quiet, and I will see him."

"You—you will still see him?" she said, in faltering accents.—"For your sake, I will."

"God bless you, sir."

She passed behind the curtain, and through that frail screen I could, of course, plainly hear every word that passed between the parties.

"Father—father," she said, "peace, oh, peace."

"What for? why should I hold my peace, I should like to know, eh? It's d——d fine for those to talk of peace who ain't burnt; but I am. D——n!"—"Hush! hush!—The doctor is here."

"D——n him! why wasn't he here before?"—"You forget that he comes out of compassion, father. That he is not paid for his coming. Surely, you quite forget that, when you talk of him so thanklessly."

"I don't want him to come for nothing. Let him send in his bill; I'll pay it when suits me. Tell him I don't want him to come for nothing, and if he don't like me he may go away again, and be d——d!"

I heard the girl weeping, as she said,—

"This is too, too bad. Father, you ought to have some small degree of consideration for me. You forget what you make me suffer by this outrageous conduct."

"Outrageous, do you call it? D——n me! you'd be outrageous, too, if you were in the pain I am. As for making you suffer, if you grumble much, it sha'n't be for nothing; for I ain't so bad but I can give you a dab on the side of the head that will make you wink again."

"Not while I am here, you scoundrel!" said I, suddenly appearing before him, for I had given a pull to the curtain in my anger which brought it all down in a heap. "How dare you talk in such a manner to this young creature? I have met in my time many brutal characters, but, for unmitigated rascality, you beat them all."

He raised himself partially upon his elbow, and glared at me like an enraged tiger. Rage choked his utterance, and I had an opportunity, for about half a minute, of studying the appearance of the ruffian.

He seemed to me about forty years of age, and a more brawny, muscular looking, big ruffian I never saw in all my life. Ferocity was in every feature of his countenance, and the most skilful physiognomist, I am convinced, might have looked in vain for any redeeming expression, however faint, in that man's face. Shaggy brows, a bold, sharp, retreating forehead, corrugated with wrinkles, compressed, yet sensual looking lips, and deep set eyes, formed a *tout ensemble* which really was anything but prepossessing.

I made up my mind in a moment, that if anything was to be done with such a man, it must be by downright outfacing him—bullying him down, and thoroughly cowing him, which is much easier to do to such apparently violent characters, than to many a quiet, gentlemanly-seeming, timid man, who don't look as if he had a bit of the devil in his whole composition; but who, if once thoroughly roused, will not unfrequently give people a very disagreeable surprise.

Acting upon my opinion, then, of the bully, I took what the French call the *initiative*, and before he could recover himself from my first salutation sufficiently to speak, I again raised my voice, and while I fixed my eyes sternly in his face, I cried,—

"How dare you, you cowardly scoundrel, use such language in my presence to this young girl?"—"And who the devil may you be?" he said, in a manifestly subdued tone.

"Your superior, and I will let you know it to your cost if I have any more of your brutal insolence."—"D——n ——"

"Silence, sir. Do you fancy I came here to listen to the foul language of a ruffian like you? Silence, I say. For shame. If you had a spark of courage or manhood in you, you would blush to address a young girl in the manner you have addressed this patient creature, who, I suppose, has the misfortune to be your daughter, you blackguard."

He seemed perfectly astonished at this attack, so sudden and so utterly unexpected, too, as it was to him. He looked from the girl to me, and from me to the girl, as if undecided whether he should come out with a torrent of abuse upon one or both of us; but he was frightened, and he could not get over the impression I had made upon him. When he spoke it was in a tone which convinced me he was struggling with his fears.

"So you are a—a doctor, are you?"—"I am."

"Very good. I suppose, then, you must have it all your own way, of course. Kate, what the hell ——— "—" Once for all, Jackson," said I, "I tell you I will not have this young girl abused by you. You are quite, as you sufficiently show in every word that passes your lips, unworthy of such a daughter. She shall not be abused by you."

"I'll say what I like to my own child," he growled.—"You shall not."

"Who's to hinder me?"—"I will. Do you fancy your innocent child cannot be protected against a ruffian like you? Use another harsh expression to her in my presence, and I will soon let you know that she not only can, but shall be protected."

Again he made an evident effort to summon all his resolution to his aid, and return me some insolent reply; but again his courage failed him, and all he could say was,—

"Be off with you—be off with you. I don't want such a doctor as you. Be off with you."—"No," said I, "you understand me better now. I am called in, and I mean to remain some time. Now that you know I am not to be trifled with, what's the matter with you?"

During the whole of this dialogue the poor girl whom he had named Kate, stood in such a state of trembling and agitation that it was pitiable to see her, and had it not been that I felt so strongly the necessity of subduing the ruffianly father, I should have turned my attention to calming her fears. Now, however, that she saw I had, to all outward appearance, cooled him down, a sigh of inexpressible relief came from her lips, and she gave me a glance of thankfulness, which fully satisfied me she understood and appreciated what I had been attempting to do for her.

"Look here," said the fellow, and laying bare his right shoulder, he showed me that it was very much swollen and disfigured.

"You should have sent for a surgeon," I said, "and not a physician. This seems to me a surgical case."

The girl clasped her hands, and looking me imploringly in the face, she exclaimed,—

"Oh, sir, do what you can; I dare not go to any one else. Try your skill to aid him."

I was moved by the tears that flowed from her beautiful eyes, and to tell the truth, although I had chosen to take my degree as a physician, because I had a dislike to practical surgery, I had both studied and seen enough of it, to feel no hesitation, if the humour took me, in healing any purely surgical case.

"Well," I said, "I will try what can be done. What is this injury you have here?"—"A fall," he growled.

"Indeed!" said I, as I looked more closely. "It looks to me, my friend, much more like a gun-shot wound."—"It is," said Kate. "What madness, father, to attempt to do yourself so much injury as to deceive your medical attendant. It is a pistol-shot wound, you know it is, father."—"Have it your own way, and be d——d," he growled. "Gently, doctor; gently—oh, curses!"

"How long ago was this wound inflicted?" I asked.— "Two nights."

"And the bullet has not been extracted. How very foolish to neglect such an affair. It might cost you your life."—"His life!" cried the girl. "Is there any danger?— He is my father, although ———"

She paused, but I guessed what she would have added. I shook my head, as I said,—

"I shall be a better judge of the nature of the wound, when I have extracted the ball from it, which must be done immediately."

The bully turned pale as I took from my pocket a case of instruments, and searched for a probe.

"Will it—be—be painful?" he said.—"Certainly," said I.

"D——n—curses! All the world's against me. I'll be revenged on some one, or I'll know the reason why. Here, you Kate."—"Yes, father, yes."

"Drink—I want some drink."—"Nothing but water," I whispered to Kate, and she brought him some in a cup which she held to his lips, saying,—

"Drink, father—dear father; you will be better soon, and you will be kinder to me when you are free from pain. God bless you, father—God bless you."

He just glanced into the cup, and seeing it was water, he with one blow dashed it from her hand to the farther end of the attic, as he cried,—

"Why do you bring me water? You know I never drink it, you d——d young jade."—"Very well, Mr. Jackson," said I; "you may now lie and die, and rot, for all I care. Your shoulder will mortify, and you will be a dead man in twelve hours. I shall leave you, for such a brute is not worth seeing. Kate, you had better come away and leave him to himself. I will find some friend for you. Let him die and swear as he pleases."

"No, no," he shouted. "What do you mean? D——n! you wouldn't leave me here to die, would you?—die like a dog. Kate! you, too, where are you going? Help—murder —doctor—Kate—don't leave me, because of one wicked word or two. Kate—Kate, have some mercy upon me!"

I saw he was terribly frightened, and I said, sternly,—

"Once for all, Jackson, if I have any more of your brutality, let me assure you I will leave, and persuade your daughter to come away with me."—"But she—she wouldn't."

Kate flung herself into his arms, and was about to say that indeed she would not, when I interposed, and stopped her, by crying,—

"I would counsel her and persuade her, but there is no occasion at present if you promise to behave yourself with common propriety. Can I have some warm water?"—"Yes, yes," said the girl. I could see her trembling in every limb, she was in such a state of fearful agitation, with regard to the suffering her father was about to undergo. I stepped close to her, and whispered,—

"Do not be alarmed. The operation I am about to perform, I should hope and expect will not be a serious one. Get me warm water, and then you had better spare your feelings any unnecessary shock, by getting out of the way."— "I thank you, sir, I thank you. I will get you the water; but I should suffer more from imagination than from reality, were I to leave this room."

She then glided away for the warm water, and I took the opportunity of turning to my patient, and saying,—

"Now, tell me how you came by this wound?"

He glanced at me, for a moment or two, and then said,—

"No matter—no matter. What's the odds how and where I got it, so as I have got it?"—"You leave me, then, to put the worst construction upon this affair?"

"Put what construction you like. Curse me if you can put too bad an one."—"Indeed."

"Ay, indeed. If you must have it, 'tis a ———"—"Hush, father;—hush! for the love of Heaven," cried Kate, as she appeared with a basin of warm water. "If any revelations are to be made, leave them to me. I may, perchance, soften something in the recital; but you I know will not.—Oh, father, what would you have said?"

"Enough—enough," said I; "Kate, I would rather hear from you how this hurt was obtained."—"You promised me, sir, that all told to you would be held as sacred confidence."

"And I will keep my word. Do you intend remaining here while I endeavour to extract the bullet which I believe to be still in this wound?"

She became paler than before, as with half averted face she said,—

"Yes, yes. Let me remain here."

I need not trouble my readers with surgical details. Suffice it to say, that, after considerable trouble, I succeeded in extracting a pistol-bullet from the shoulder of the ruffianly fellow, who displayed so much cowardice during the operation, that I got more and more convinced in my general opinion that bullies are always cowards, who endeavour by sailing under the false colours of boiling courage to intimidate their adversaries.

When I had done, I dressed the wound, which, although it presented rather a bad appearance from neglect, I did not despair of curing. He sunk back on the miserable couch he occupied, and muttered such imprecations on all the world and its inhabitants, that I was glad to move away while I wiped the instruments which I had been necessitated to use.

The young girl followed me to the window, and laid her hand upon my arm as if she would have spoken, but her heart was too full, and it was not until a gush of tears had relieved her that she was able to say to me,—

"You will mention nothing of this case to any one. He is in great danger."—"Not at all," said I, "he is in no danger."

"You mistake me, sir. I do not allude to the wound. He is in personal danger."—"Oh, on his own account. Now, Kate, just tell me, will you, how he came by this really serious wound?"

She cast her eyes timidly towards the bed, and her colour went and came as she drew me, in an agitated manner, by the cuff of the coat further away from her father, who, what with the exertions he had gone through, the pain he had just suffered, and the consequent exhaustion, was in a state of half-repose. Her eyes rested on my face with a painful expression, and she spoke in a low, whispered voice of deep emotion.

"You—you ought to know," she said. "We are much beholden to you, and to refuse you entire confidence, would be now to insult your judgment, as well as your generosity. My father is—is ——"

"Take your time," I said. "Don't distress yourself, and at the same time remember that I am not one of those who confound the innocence of one with the guilt of another. Let your father be what he may, I am quite sure you are all that any one could wish you."

"You are too—too good, sir. Oh, why do I torture myself by delaying to tell you? and yet the word sticks in my throat, and I scarce dare utter it."

I inclined my head, and almost hanging upon my arm, in her intense eagerness, while her lips were so close to my face that I could feel the soft, warm breath upon my cheek, she faltered,—

"He—he is my father, sir, and that is a tie which may not be easily or lightly broken. My father you see, sir. You will bear that in mind when you feel a degree of indignation at the company you are in. I—I have no other relative in the wide world—none—none whatever. God bless you, sir, for what you have done for him. I have no words to thank you in sufficiently."

"Kate, you still shrink from telling me what your father is, and how he got his wound."—"I do, I do," she sobbed. "God help me! I do. But now you shall know. He might murder me, as he has threatened, for my placing this confidence in you; but he cannot hear me. He cannot hear me now. I—I will whisper lower still, and, perhaps, during the time you attend upon him, you may acquire some influence over him, and induce him to alter a mode of life which will drive me mad. He is—is ——"

"What, Kate?"—"A housebreaker!"

"Oh, indeed. And he has got his wound in one of his housebreaking expeditions?"—"He did—he did. Do you now despise me? Oh, tell me you do not despise me?"

"Despise you, Kate? Impossible."—"And you will save his life, if you can? You will do all that humanity and skill can suggest, ever remembering, that be he what he may, he is my father, and I am innocent. No misery—no degradation no shame can light on his head, but some heavy portion of it likewise comes on mine. Oh, God! how true it is that the sins of the parents are visited upon the children."

"Mind you don't, as religious people generally do, misconstrue that text," said I, "It don't mean, as they pretend it does, that the Almighty wreaks his vengeance upon the children on account of the sins of the father, but it does mean that a parent should be especially cautious in his mode of life, inasmuch as what distresses and degrades him must, in the natural order of things, distress and degrade those who are allied to him."

"I understand you, sir."—"Very good. Then ——"

"Hush! hush! What's that?"—"What! D—n me, what noise is that?" cried Jackson, half rising in his bed. "Who called—who called?"

Kate flew to the door, and opened it a short way, while she listened with painful attention. I, too, stepped partially on to the landing, and then I heard a voice as from the lower part of the house, cry in a strange, long, wailing sort of tone,—

"'Ware hawk! 'ware hawk!"

"What—what is that?" cried Jackson. "What does he say? D—n you all, tell me."—"''Ware hawk,'" said I.

He fell back with a shriek.

"The officers—the officers!" he said. "I am a dead man."

Such an alarm, so sudden and so utterly unexpected, was, of course, calculated to place me in an exceedingly fearful position, and while the confusion continued below stairs, my wits were in almost as much confusion above, for I was perfectly at a loss to know how to act.

The young girl seemed as much terrified as I was, and by her pale face and general demeanour of horror, I was convinced that all her presence of mind had deserted her completely. I thought once or twice that she would have fainted away, such an intense horror had taken possession of her, and on account of one who, perhaps, never had addressed to her one word of genuine affection.

Again I went to the landing-place, just outside the door, and listened attentively. All was still for a few moments; but then again came that strange cry from the lower part of the house of "Ware hawk!"—a cry which Jackson had already sufficiently explained to me to make me feel fully its disagreeable signification.

Before, then, I could make up my mind how to act, or what to do, the door of the next attic was flung open with violence, and a man, half-dressed, hurried out with a chair in his hand, as if he had been propelled by some explosive agency. The moment his eyes fell upon me, he uttered a dreadful oath, and setting down the chair, he cried,—

"It won't do. Curse me if it sha'n't be life for life. You don't take me so easy. Come on."—"I don't want to have anything to do with you," said I. "Don't put yourself in a passion about nothing."

"Then who the devil are you?"—"I am not a police-officer, which I suppose is sufficient for you just at present."

"Quite; that'll do. I suppose you are the fellow that knocked at my blessed door a little while ago?"—"Very likely; and you are the gentleman who replied to that knock with such bland courtesy?"

"I don't understand your lingo; but you can be a little useful, even if you don't know how to express yourself in a proper sort of way. Give us a leg up, and be quick about it, will you."

As he spoke, he placed the chair under a trap-door, which was in the roof, and having opened it, he waited for me to give him a leg up to ascend, which, on the spur of the moment, I confess I did, though I dare say he was a rascal who well deserved hanging; but, somehow, there is an impulsive feeling about many people which induces them to aid in an escape of any kind, without pausing to inquire into the particulars of the transaction, in order to ascertain if a great social evil is not being perpetrated by this chivalrous conduct.

"Draw the bolt agin," said my friend, who scrambled through the trap-door in the roof; "draw the bolt agin, and if you are asked for the Slashing Kiddy, give 'em an evasive answer."

This was pleasant, but I drew the bolt after the Slashing Kiddy, and was on the point of going back to Jackson, when another door opened on the landing, and a man made his appearance, with every evidence of fright upon his countenance.

"Did they say 'ware hawk,'" he cried, "or was I dreaming?"—"They did say 'ware hawk,'" said I. "Who may you be, my friend?"—"Oh, don't ask me."

To my surprise and horror, the fellow began swallowing shillings as hard and fast as if they had been grey pease.

"Good God!" I cried; "what are you about?"—"That'll do," he cried, as he gave a sort of convulsive kick to get the last one down. "If ever you take up smashing, old cock, never have a stock in trade of greater amount than you can conveniently swallow."

Before I could make any remark upon this piece of highly practical advice, Kate laid her small delicate hand upon my arm, and in despairing, imploring accents, said,—

"Come to him. Oh, sir, come to him. Save us—save us! Gracious Heaven! hark!"

From the lower part of the house came sounds of strife, and then a heavy crashing noise succeeded, as if some door had been broken open, and I involuntarily retreated into the attic along with the young girl, whose face was now as pale as monumental marble, and who trembled so excessively she could scarcely stand or speak. Jackson had huddled on some clothes, and was crouched up on the bed, looking terror personified, while what with the anguish of his mind, and his fears of capture, the perspiration stood upon his face most fearfully. All his ferocity seemed to have deserted him, and he looked the very abject villain he was—upon the point of being called upon to account for many crimes.

"Are they coming—are they coming?" he groaned. "I shall be taken—hanged like a dog! Are they coming, I say? Oh, save me, Kate—oh, save me! Ask the gentleman to say a good word for me, Kate. Kate, speak for me. You would not see me dragged to Newgate. Ask him to keep them away. I cannot help myself. I have neither means nor strength to do so. Kate—Kate, save me! Beg of him to do something for me."

"What can I do?" said I. "In such a matter as this I am powerless. How can I, an individual merely, stand between you and the laws you have offended?"

"Would you have me hung?"—"I have nothing to do with it."

"Good God! Hark! They are coming. Hark, Kate! I am a dead man—I am a dead man!"

He fell back upon the apology for a bed, and actually cried in the cowardice of his heart. I could not but feel the greatest possible contempt for such a man, and I was on the point of expressing so much, when his child, the beautiful Kate, who possessed so different a mind from her father's, threw herself at my feet, and clasping her hands, she cried,—

"Oh, sir, have mercy upon me, and save him, if you can. Remember, sir, that I am innocent, and better that he who is guilty should escape than the innocent should suffer. For my sake, I implore you, sir, to save him! This fright, and an awful one it is, may have a great effect upon him. Reformation may follow; but, sir, if you have a heart to feel for deep distress, as you have, by some kind words that have fallen from your lips, led me to suppose, you will make an effort to save him from the terrible fate that awaits him, and so save me from a misery that will kill me."

She spoke so rapidly, and with such excited, fervent tones and gestures, that had I been ever so much induced to do so, I could not have stopped her in her wild and strange appeal—strange, because I did not see that I had any power to ward off from Jackson the consequences of his criminality, or to save him, for more than a minute at the outside, from the officers who were in pursuit of him.

I was, however, much affected by the fervent appeal made to me, and when I replied to her, I was so full of emotion, that I felt nearly as much choked as the gentleman who I had seen so recently swallowing what I suppose was counterfeit money.

"Kate," I said, "as I am a living man I would aid you if I could, but how am I to do it?"

She flew to the door again and listened attentively. Then bounding back to me, she placed her hand, unconscious of the action, on my breast, as she said, in a low whisper,—

"They are coming; they are even now upon the stairs. My father will get outside the window, and lie flat along under the parapet. I will take possession of his bed; and you—you will own that you have cause to attend upon me who am sick—you understand me, sir; it will be true, too; for by this means I am sure you will save me from despair and death. You will consent; oh, say you will consent!"

"Why, really ——"—" God of Heaven! he hesitates," she sobbed, as she wrung her hands in frantic bitterness.

I could not bear that sight, and I exclaimed,—

"I will do it—quick, quick."

With an artlessness that robbed the action of the slightest impropriety, she flung her arms around my neck, as she sobbed,—

"God bless you, sir—God bless you!"

Then, turning to the trembling scoundrel, for whom she was doing, and had done so much, and who made her so sorry a return for her noble devotion, she cried,—

"Now, father—now. The window, father—the window; you will yet be saved."

He was completely cowed, and he replied,—

"Yes; thank you, sir—yes, Kate—the—the window; I shall be saved, Kate—you, you will not betray me?"—"Quick, quick," she said, "not a moment is to be lost—to the window—to the window."

With some difficulty—for to make any exertion with such a wound as he had, could not but be attended with very great pain—he was got out at the window by the joint exertions of Kate and myself, and then, by lying flat in the gutter, which was outside the parapet, he was effectually concealed from the sight of any one who might merely stand in the room.

Kate turned her beaming eyes upon me for a moment, full of thankfulness, and then she got into bed, and with great tact unloosened her beautiful long hair, so as to give an appearance of the dishabille of sickness to her face, and then all was ready for the officers, and I found myself in the unpleasant predicament of aiding and assisting in the escape from the hands of justice, of a felon who, the worst of it was, I verily believed to be as great a scoundrel as ever was born to be hung.

However, I had given my promise to Kate, and not once, by insinuating a doubt that I would keep my word, did she give me the least excuse for going back from it, which, to tell the truth, I had no sort of idea of doing at the moment, although I could not altogether blind myself to the fact that I was acting not only a very foolish part by screening Jackson, but a very wrong one as well, considering my duty to society. The arrangements were only just completed in time, and Kate had just said,—

"Thank God for this mercy," when I heard the sound of several footsteps on the stairs, and the door of the attic was in another moment flung wide open, admitting two stout men, each of whom held in his hand a small staff, such as was used by the old Bow-street runners, a race now so nearly extinct.

Their eagle eyes were in a minute cast round the room, and they seemed at once to decide that I was not the person they wanted, or even likely to want, for one of them said,—

"I don't know, sir, if we have unwarrantably intruded upon you or not, but we are in search of one Jackson, a notorious criminal, who, we had certain information, was in this house."—" No intrusion," said I. "I am Doctor ——, and this young person is one of my poor patients."

As I spoke I handed my card to the officer, who thereupon added, respectfully,—

"Then we may take your word for it, doctor, that no one is here but yourself and this young person, your patient."—"Don't take my word," said I; "look for yourselves."

"It don't require much searching," said one. "Our man is not here. May we ask if you have seen him, or any one answering the description of a tall man, with sandy whiskers?"—"This young person," said I, evading the questions as well as possible, and pointing to Kate, "does not exactly come up to such a description."

"Certainly not, sir; we are sorry to have disturbed you; our bird has taken the alarm and flown."

"What has he done?" said I.—"He broke into the house of a Mr. Harrison, an old gentleman, residing in Hanover-square, and it is supposed, but not proved, that he received a pistol shot."

"Indeed!"—"Yes; he murdered the man-servant."

"Murdered—murdered!"—" Yes; murdered."

Kate raised herself on the couch, and with a shriek, she cried,—

"No—no; not murdered. I—I did not know that. Do not say he is a murderer. Oh, God—oh, God!"

"Why, what's all this?" said the officers.—" She raves," said I; "any excitement will be her death. She raves—but are you quite certain the man you seek is a murderer?"

"A deliberate murderer, sir. He went out of his way to kill the man-servant. He smashed him with a bill-hook he found in the kitchen; and it was old Mr. Harrison who fired a pistol after him. He had a boy with him, too."—" Good God!"

"It's a bad affair. Good day, sir—a very bad affair. We had what we thought certain information that he was in this house; but we have now been in every room, and are pretty sure to the contrary, or he could not have escaped us."—" Oh, God—oh, God!" groaned Kate.

"The poor young woman, sir, seems very bad," said one of the officers.—"Her mind is much affected by family griefs," said I. "Nothing but much kindness now, and long quiet can restore her to what she once was. You will oblige me by leaving now."

The officers then took their departure. I held the door of the attic open until they had got down the staircase. I listened till I heard them leave the house, and then I closed the door again, and walked softly up to the bed on which lay Kate. Her hands were placed across her face, and she was sobbing bitterly and audibly, while I could see the tears trickling through her small fingers, and dropping silently among the tresses of her beautiful hair, which hung in disordered masses on her neck and shoulders.

It was a pitiable sight, an awful sight, to see one so young and so beautiful, so broken down by mental suffering for a parent who should have brought honour instead of dishonour upon his child. I paused for about half a minute, with the hope that the violence of her feelings would show some symptoms of subsidence; but none appeared, and I laid my hand gently upon her fair shoulder, and said,—

"Kate—Kate. Look up and speak to me."

She took her hands from before her face; oh! what an expression of speechless woe was there. She regarded me for about a moment or two in silence, and then with a shudder that pervaded her whole frame, she said,—

"It is too horrible—too horrible."

"You heard all, Kate?"—"I did, and never can forget it."

"Tell me, and call upon God to aver for you that you speak the truth—did you, or did you not, know that your father's hands were stained with the blood of a fellow creature?"

The tears gushed now from her eyes, and she clasped her hands across her breast in an attitude of prayer; she looked like some sculptured image of marvellous beauty on a tomb. In a voice soft and liquid as music from Heaven, she said,—

"As God is my judge—as I hope for mercy and joy hereafter, I knew it not."—"Enough," said I. "Kate, get up, and come away with me."

"With—with you?"—"Yes. The tie which bound you to that man is surely severed, since he has severed all ties between him and God. Come away—come away."

She half rose from the bed and clung to my arm.

"Away with you," she whispered, "and—and leave him?" —"Yes. Leave the murderer."

"Oh! that dread word—murderer; and yet, oh, God! there is another which bids me stay,—father—father. He is yet my father. Aid me, Heaven."—"This is madness, Kate. For God's sake, come away at once."

"I—I cannot think ——"—"I must leave you then. Bitterly do I regret I have lent myself to be, even to the small extent I have, the accomplice of a murderer. Farewell, Kate—farewell."

"No—no," she cried fervently, as she clung convulsively to me; "you must not leave me; I cannot look into his face again; I cannot lie down to rest now I know that he is near me. The murderer—the murderer. Oh! God."—"Then fly with me—I will denounce him. I do not ask you to do so, but leave him to the chances of his own evil destiny, which he has so horribly invoked. Kate, come away—come away at once, I implore you."

Something dark came across the window. It was Jackson who had risen, and was now attempting to enter the room from where he had been so uneasily lying. Kate pointed towards him, and with a loud scream she cried,—

"The murderer—the murderer!"

I felt her form droop, and that I was supporting her whole weight in my arms. She had fainted. A sudden thought took possession of me.

"I will save her," I cried, "from the horrors and contamination of an association with this man; despite her feelings of clinging still to him, will I save her."

I raised her from the bed, and carried her to the door, which I reached at the instant Jackson had succeeded in opening the window.

"D——n!" he cried, "leave the girl here."—"Not another moment," cried I; "scoundrel—thief—murderer; if by any means you dare from this time henceforward to disturb the peace of this young girl, I will have you apprehended for your crimes, and not even her love shall save you. I know you now."

He made a jump into the room. His eyes glared fiercely, and he drew from his pocket a pistol. I disengaged my right arm, and still supporting the inanimate form of Kate on my left, I struck him full in the face. With a yell of rage and pain he fell backwards. I seized the opportunity, and in the excitement of the moment, no more feeling the weight of Kate than if I had been carrying an infant, I dashed down the long staircase, and reached the passage in an incredibly short space of time, without meeting any one to obstruct my impetuous progress. Then a man came out from the parlour, and standing in the middle of the passage, he cried,—

"What's all this—what's all this? Hilloa! where are you coming to, my fine fellow?"—"Make way," I cried, in a voice that seemed to have stunned him, for by an involuntary movement he stepped back a pace or two. I rushed past him, and in another instant had gained the street, where I felt an immediate sense of security, whatever surprise I might produce from the singular appearance I cut with a young girl in my arms, to all appearance dead, and without a bonnet. My object was to get some conveyance immediately to my own house, and as good luck would have it, a hackney-coach passed along James-street just as I reached it, and was beginning to feel a little tired of the weight I was carrying.

I hailed the coachman, who at first seemed shy of taking such a fare; but he did draw up at length, and let down the steps.

"Help me," I said, and with his assistance I soon placed Kate in the coach, and then told him my address, and bang went the door. Some boys who had collected, and thought some prime fun was going on, gave us the salute of a parting "hurrah," and away we went.

All that I had done hitherto had been quite impulsively, but during the drive homewards I had time to think a little, and I felt much pleased that I had rescued from the terrible fate that must eventually have been hers, the young, and I was perfectly convinced innocent being I had with me, and who still remained insensible to all the changes that had taken place. I was compelled to support her all the way, or she would have fallen to the bottom of the coach, and glad was I when we drove up to my door.

"Ring and knock," said I to the coachman, "and tell the servant to come and help me out with this young lady."— "Yes, your honour."

My astonished servant assisted me with Kate, whom we at once carried upstairs to a spare bed-room I always liked to have in readiness, in case any friend or patient chose to remain with me all night, and there we laid her; and right glad was I that so far I had succeeded in rescuing her from her rascally father.

My wife, as my readers have discovered, no doubt from various circumstances recorded in other pages of my Diary, was a far better practical philanthropist than a logician, and without asking me any questions as to who or what Kate was, she set about, with the greatest alacrity, restoring her to consciousness, upon my saying that it was only an attack of syncope.

In the course of a quarter of an hour, success crowned her efforts, and, with a deep sigh, the beautiful child of the murderer opened her lustrous eyes, and gazed around her at the strange room she was in, the strange faces around her, and the strange furniture, with speechless amazement.

My wife was about to say something, but I motioned her to be silent, for I saw that Kate was not yet in a sufficiently collected state either to comprehend any question that might be put to her, or to enter into any explanation of her condition and circumstances.

After a time Kate's eyes fell upon my face, and I could see that a feeling of satisfaction crossed her countenance, as if she would have said, "Ah, now I know I am safe, although I know not where I am, for a friend is near me."

I approached the bedside, and said, in as cheerful a tone as I could assume,—

"Well, Kate, how are you now?"—"Where am I?" she said. "Oh, where am I? Where is he?"

"Never mind just at present, Kate. All's safe, and right. Will you drink this draught?"

I had prepared a composing draught, which I now handed her in a wine glass. She drank it off at once, and then lying down again upon the pillow, from which she had slightly raised her head, she at once dropped into a child-like, deep slumber.

"She'll sleep some hours now," said I to my wife; "come away, and I will tell you all about her."

This promise needed not to be repeated, and my wife followed me with great alacrity down stairs, when I detailed to her all the adventures I had had at Jackson's lodging, concluding by saying,—

"And now, my dear, have you any objection to receiving this young creature as an inmate for a time, until something can be done for her?"—"Doctor," replied my wife; "pray what do you take me for?"

"Oh, why, for Mrs. ——."—"Do you? I thought, doctor, that you imagined me an unfeeling brute, by asking me if I had any objections to a young creature, who has been rescued from perfect horror, doctor, remaining for a time under this roof, doctor."

"There, there," cried I, "that will do. Don't you go on 'doctoring' me at such a rate. I always know you are angry when you begin that sort of thing."

"And ain't it enough to make anybody angry?"—"Yes, it is."

"Ain't it enough to make a lamb in a passion?"—"Yes, it is."

"Well, then, how can you wonder at me? Let her stay, indeed; she shall stay, poor thing. I say she shall stay."— "Very good, my dear."

"And not only for a time; but altogether, if she likes

doctor. Do you hear that?"—"My dear, my auricular nerves are in perfect order."

* * * * *

Kate slept for more than four hours. I directed my servant to go up stairs every now and then and see if she were awake, and, at about the end of that period of time, she came to the parlour to say that the young lady was awake, and crying.

"Well, then, my dear," said I to my wife; "you go to her and soothe her, as you well know how, in your kind way. If she wishes to see me, of course I will come to her; but persuade her, if you can, to await until to-morrow morning for all explanations; she will be then much better able to bear them, and be in better judgment than under her present excitement, to come to correct conclusions."

My wife, accordingly, went up stairs to Kate, and, with some anxiety, I waited for the result of the interview; but as I was not sent for, I concluded that she had succeeded in inducing her to wait until the morrow. It was nearly half-an-hour before my wife came down stairs, and then she said,—

"I have persuaded her to take something to eat; she's half-starved, poor thing. She said, when I asked her to wait till the morning before any explanations were entered into, 'that if such were your wish, it was a law to her.'"

"Very good," said I. "It is far better that it should be so. Now, my dear, you read the newspapers; I do not. Do you recollect anything, lately, about a burglary and a murder?"—"Oh, dear, yes; two or three."

"But was there one in Hanover-street?"—"Ah! to be sure; at a Mr. Harrison's. The 'John' was killed."

"The who?"—"The footman. It was very interesting, and they haven't caught the man yet, you must know."

"I do know; for although I have told you all about Jackson and Kate, I have still to tell you that this Jackson is the murderer."

My wife nearly fell off her chair, but in a moment she said,—

"I don't see, though, that that makes poor Kate any the worse, though it may make her the more to be pitied. Because, you know, my dear, it's her misfortune, and not her fault, that her father has committed a murder."

"You are right; and if the world, instead, as it too commonly does, of classing the good and pure of heart with the guilty, on insufficient reasons, were to take as proper a view of such a subject, there would be much more justice done, and much fewer broken hearts to mourn over."

"The evening paper, ma'am," said the servant girl, at this moment. "It's late, ma'am; but the boy always throws it down the 'airy,' ma'am, now, and never rings, and there it lays, a wallowing in the dirt, till I go out for coals, or somethink o' that sort, you see, ma'am."

I was rather amused at the idea of the evening paper wallowing in the dirt, and I smiled as I took hold of the journal, when the first words that met my eyes were,—

"APPREHENSION OF THE MURDERER, JACKSON."

The paragraph then ran as follows:—

"We have but just time to state, that Plank, the active officer, succeeded in capturing this man, at a house, notorious as a harbour for the worst of characters, in Hart-street, Covent-garden. His examination will take place to-morrow morning at Bow-street. If the boy, who, it is said, accompanied him in his marauding expedition, be found, it is understood he will be permitted to be king's evidence against Jackson."

I handed the paper to my wife, saying,—

"There, my dear: there's news for Kate, when we come to have a long talk with her in the morning."—"News, indeed," said my wife. "Alas! poor girl—I am heart sad for her, and only hope she will have courage to bear with her great trials and misfortunes. It's a very, very terrible thing, for one so young to be so singularly situated."

"It is, indeed, and more especially one like Kate, who seems extraordinarily enough to possess an amount of education and general refinement utterly inconsistent with the character of her father, who is one of the lowest, vilest brutes I ever encountered."

In many surmises and reflections concerning poor Kate, we passed the evening; and I was very anxious to hear in the morning, from her own lips, how it was that she became so oddly situated with her father, at the same time that she must have been, at one time, so very differently circumstanced.

My wife rose early, and went to Kate's bedroom, while I dressed and hurried down stairs to the breakfast-parlour, in which, however, I had not been many minutes, when I was agreeably surprised by the entrance of Kate, who had been dressed by my wife in some of her own clothing, and persuaded to come down stairs and see me.

The moment I saw her I was enchanted with the beauty and intelligence of her looks, now that she was better personally tended, and dressed more in accordance to her mental qualifications; she flew towards me, exclaiming,—

"Oh, sir, tell me what has become of him—my father?—he, he, what else he may be—is my father still."—"Take your breakfast first," said I, "and then we will have a long talk, and a long consultation over the matter; but you shall positively take your breakfast first."

Thus urged, she said no more, until she had partaken of the morning's meal with us, after which, I said,—

"Now, Kate, commence by telling us what you yourself know of your history."

"I scarcely know where to begin," she said; "but my earliest recollection points to the school at Hammersmith, where I was so very happy with my dear playmates. I remained there until I was eleven years of age, and was taught all that could possibly be taught to me; no money was spared upon me, and a kind, good gentleman, who was so fond of me, that he would come sometimes to see me and kiss me, and cry over me, used to tell the governess that he would enable my mother to pay fully and liberally for everything I could require."

"And your father?"—"He did not come often to see me."

"You are sure he and Jackson are the same?"—"I cannot mistake," she said. "He is my father. I never recollect another bearing that title."

I felt very much disappointed, for I was in hopes that some pleasant discovery might ensue, that would free Kate from all taunts of relationship as regarded the scoundrel Jackson. Now, however, such a hope was at an end.

"Well, go on," said I. "He took you away from school, you say."

"He did, sir; and then, to my surprise, I found that we were to lead a life of poverty. He told me a great reverse had taken place in his fortunes. I had not seen him for a whole year, and he took me to a wretched place, where a woman, whom he tried to persuade me to call mother, treated me with the greatest harshness and cruelty."

"The wretch!" exclaimed my wife.—"Let her go on," said I.

"But I only wanted to remark, that no real mother could possibly ill-treat her own child—no, nor any other body's child, unless she was quite a brute, and ought to be hung." —"Very good, my dear. Now, go on, Kate."

"This lasted a considerable time, till the woman died, I believe, from some dreadful blows given by him,—my father. Then, somehow, he got still poorer, and one day he brought home a suit of boy's clothes, and ordered me to put them on. I dared not refuse him; he would have struck me to the floor if I had, so I silently, and as well as I could, attired myself in them. That night—it was a dreadful one, and I cannot forget it, or cease to tremble as it comes to my mind—he took me out on a housebreaking expedition, and made me creep through a small window, to undo the fastenings of a door for him."

"Then you are the boy who is supposed to have accompanied him on his depredating expeditions?"—"I am, sir; I am. This is the life I have been compelled to lead. What could I do?—blows upon blows visited me if I remonstrated even. I often said I would leave him; but he is my father; he is my father still."

She burst into tears, and wept bitterly.

"I much regret, Kate," said I, "that the news I have to tell you, although I think you ought to know it, is not such as will bring any consolation to you."—"News!—what news? God of Heaven! oh, tell me, sir; and yet you need not; I can read in your looks; they have taken him. He is lost—he is lost!"

"You guess rightly. He is taken; but, Kate, you must be aware, that sooner or later such must have been the result of his criminal course of life; rather, I would have you consider, that it had better happen now than later, when he had added, perhaps, largely to his catalogue of crimes, and involved you past all redemption."

She looked like a living statue of grief, with her hands clasped, and not a particle of colour in her face.

"I must go to him—I must go to him," she said.—"Not on any account," cried I. "Do not dream of such a proceeding. You cannot do him any good. On the contrary, your evidence would destroy him if it were taken."

She looked aghast at this view of the subject, and I added,—

"He will be examined this morning at Bow-street. I will take care to be there and bring you an account of all that passes. Do you remain here in peace and security, Kate. The feelings with which you regard your father, do you much honour; but you must, under the circumstances in which you are so painfully placed, endeavour to place reason as an antagonist to feeling, and reconcile yourself to things which are far beyond your control, or that of any one else, now."—
"But my father——"

"Has himself only to thank for his present position. Compose yourself, and expect me the moment the examination at the police-office is over."

I then left the room to prepare to go out, and in a few minutes my wife came to me, and said,—

"My dear, she tells me that the name of the people who kept the school at Hammersmith was Russell, and that it was called Archdale House; now, I think some inquiry ought to be made there."

"Send William, then, at once, my dear; he is a sharp lad, and you can furnish him with a note."—"I will."

In a few moments I was off, and making the best of my way to the police-office, at Bow-street, which was literally crammed with expectant listeners to the examination of the murderer when I got there, so that it took some trouble to get in, and had I not been known to the magistrates' clerk, who spied me among the crowd, and beckoned me towards him, I should have had but a sorry view of the proceedings.

After the disposal of some night charges, an unusual bustle at the door announced the entrance of Jackson, who was heavily handcuffed,—for he had, as I was afterwards told, made some desperate attempts to get away. He was awfully haggard, dirty, and wretched-looking, and such an appearance of mingled ferocity, cowardice, brutality, and meanness, I thought I never had yet encountered. His shoulder, too, had been dressed, I suppose, by the prison surgeon, for I saw it was in proper bandages, which I could not put to it in the wretched attic where I had first seen him, because I had them not.

There was a great sensation in the court, on his being placed before the magistrate, and there was some difficulty in obtaining silence; after which, Plank, the officer, stepped forward and deposed that he had paid attention to the circumstances connected with the robbery and murder at Mr. Harrison's, and had become convinced it had been planned and executed by Jackson, whom he had been on the search for now for some days, and at length from private information he had received, he succeeded in capturing him.

"Have you evidence enough to warrant a committal?" said the magistrate, "or do you want a remand?"—"A remand for a week, your worship, will be convenient," said the officer, "as I can then produce a man who saw Jackson in the neighbourhood of the house, after the robbery, trying to stop the bleeding of his shoulder, which received a bullet from a pistol fired at the burglar in the house. A silk handkerchief, too, that I understand Mr. Harrison can swear is his, was found on his person. We wish to find the boy who accompanied the prisoner on the night of the robbery."

"During the week's remand," said the magistrate, "an application can be made to the Secretary of State, for a free pardon to the boy, on condition of turning king's evidence."
—"Mr. Harrison will be here directly, your worship, and he, or his son, Mr. Algernon Harrison, may be able to identify the prisoner."

"We cannot wait," remarked the magistrate. "Those gentlemen can have liberty to see the prisoner in the New Prison, at Clerkenwell, whither he will now be taken on remand for one week, at the expiration of which time there will, doubtless, be sufficient evidence to warrant a committal for trial on the charge of murder."

This was acquiesced in, and the ruffian was about being taken from the bar, when, to my surprise and consternation, for I never could for a moment have supposed such a thing, Kate, whom I thought I had left snugly and comfortably at home at my house, rushed forward towards Jackson, and, before any one could prevent her, she clung to his manacled wrists, exclaiming,—

"Father!—father!—one word, it may be the last. Father, speak to me but a word!"

To describe the effect which so sudden an apparition, as a beautiful and interesting girl rushing up to such a man as Jackson, in such a manner, had in the crowded court, would be impossible: there was such a pushing and striving to get a look at her, and such intense curiosity and excitement on every countenance, that it was quite a remarkable sight; and even the magistrate rose from his seat, on a sudden impulse of the moment, and looked at Kate with amazement.

"Silence—silence!" cried the usher; and then the magistrate spoke, saying in a low voice,—

"Officer, who is this young person?"

She turned on the instant, and facing the magistrate, she said,—

"You wonder, sir, to see me cling to this man, now abandoned by all, and branded with the infamy of crimes I cannot, dare not attempt to deny or palliate; but—but still, sir, he is my father; yes, sir, were he ten times worse than what he is, he is still my father."

"Is it possible?"—"It is too—too true," she sobbed. "Oh, father, speak to me. Let me, for once, hear one kind word from your lips, to bear about with me in my heart as a fond remembrance; but one word, and let that be a kind, gentle one—father!—father!"

"D—n you!" said Jackson, and he raised his hand as well as he could, for the handcuffs that confined him, to strike her.

"Monster!" cried the magistrate, "monster of ingratitude, I thank God that long as I have sat here, I never found yet a man so dead to all feeling as you are."—"Curses on you all," growled Jackson.

"Cannot the generous devotion of your own child move you? Oh, shame, shame."—"Yes, yes," cried Kate; "he will yet speak to me."

"Officers, remove him," said the magistrate. "I cannot bear longer the presence of such an unmitigated ruffian. Remove him directly."

Still Kate clung to him, and the officers were fearful of hurting her by forcing her from him; but not so Jackson, who, with a yelling ferocity, cried aloud, as he struggled to free himself from her detaining grasp,—

"Break her arm. Smash her—break her d—d arm; make her leave go."—"I wish I had you all to myself," said the officer; "I'd smoothen you down a bit, my fine fellow."

"Be careful of the girl," said the magistrate.

Still she would not leave go of him, but kept saying, in agonised accents, that sent a thrill through every heart but the one, poor thing, she wished to soften,—

"One kind word, father—only one kind word, if it be the last—only one."—"Not if you were to preach for an hour," he cried. "D—n you—that's all I've got to say."

She released her hold, and I darted forward and caught her in my arms, or she would have fallen to the floor of the court, so dreadful was the shock the ruffian's words gave her.

"Oh, Kate, Kate!" I said, "why did you come here?"—"God help me!" was her brief reply.

"Bring her this way," said the magistrate; and he made her sit down near to him, and handed her himself a glass of water. Then turning to me, for his clerk had whispered to him who I was, he said, in a courteous tone,—

"Doctor, I hear you interest yourself for this poor young creature, who I can scarcely believe can be the daughter of such a ruffian as Jackson."—"It is singular, sir; but, I grieve to say, true."

"Dear me—dear me. Well, I really am very sorry. How are you, now, my dear?"— "Better—better," whispered Kate. "Oh, forgive me, gentlemen; it was the last appeal of a daughter's love. The sacred name of father came across my mind, and I ventured here. All is over now—I have no father. Alas! but in name, I never had."

Her tears flowed freely, and the magistrate was about to say something to me about her, when the clerk whispered to him, loud enough for me to hear,—

"Sir, Mr. Harrison, and his son, Major Harrison, have now come; shall they see the prisoner at once? He is only in one of the cells just outside."

"I think they had better go to the prison, Mr. Johnstone, don't you, under the circumstances?"—"As your worship pleases."

"If they particularly wish to make the attempt here to

identify him, I will not say they shall not."—" They do wish it, your worship."

"Oh, then, have him back. We must not let justice be impeded, however much we may dislike the sight again to-day, of such a scoundrel as this Jackson, who, certainly, in unfeeling rascality, transcends everything I ever came near or heard of, in all my experience."

"Then I will order the officers to bring him in again, your worship."—" Oh, certainly, certainly."

The order was immediately given. And while I leaned over Kate, and whispered in her ear,—

"Now, let me seriously advise you not to look at him again,"

The desperate, hardened ruffian, was again, apparently

much to his own surprise, brought back and placed at the bar, before the court.

Much as the scoundrel, Jackson, appeared before to have utterly abandoned all hope of bettering his condition, or else he surely would not have exhibited himself in such brutal colours, a feeling of great alarm appeared to come over him, now that he was a second time brought before the magisterial bench, and he glanced around with all the uneasy expression of some wild beast, newly caught, who does not know if he is to be fed himself, or made into food for somebody else, with a keen appetite.

I remarked the slight tremulous movement of the lip, and I rejoiced to see that the ruffian's courage was leaving him. I anticipated yet some contemptible exhibition of cowardice, such as in his own attic, in Hart-street, had followed his brutal ferocity, before the magistrate had quite done with him, or he was removed from the bar. The reader will find that I was not in such an expectation disappointed with respect to his character.

When I saw these indications of shrinking, on the part of Jackson, I was more than ever anxious that Kate should not pamper to his brutality, by speaking to him, or even casting upon him one more glance of tenderness or feeling, and I kept close to her, so that had she attempted to go towards him, I could have detained her, and, at the same time, I whispered in her ear,—

"Kate—Kate!"—" Yes," she said, softly.

"Consult your own happiness, and do not look at him again. You have done all, and, indeed, far more than any one could possibly have expected from you."

"Is he here again?"—" Yes; he is."

"Does he seem relenting?"—" Most certainly not, (here I did fib a little) most certainly not. I am quite sure, if you were even to look at him, you would draw down upon your head some more awful denunciations such as you have already had launched at you. Oh, Kate, it was ill-judged of you to come here at all. You ought have to spared yourself much pain."

"And give myself much," she whispered.

"How so?"—" By the thought which would always have haunted me, that I might, by coming here, have extracted from him one kind word."

"'Perhaps you are right," I said, "after all. But he is obdurate. Will you go now?"—" Not now. Let me stay till all is decided here."

"As you please; but remember I consider you still as under my protection, and I shall take you home again with me till something of an independent and permanent character can be done for you."

She glanced up in my face for a moment. Her eyes were filled with tears. That look spoke gratitude far more eloquently than any words could possibly have done.

"Silence!" said the usher of the court, and my attention was now directed to the prisoner, whose uneasiness appeared to be momentarily on the increase, and who grasped the wooden rail in front of him, with a nervous energy that convinced me he felt himself sinking much in spirits, and anticipated an uncomfortable climax to the scene which was about to ensue.

He looked from beneath his shaggy overhanging brows around the court, as if in vain searching for some friendly eye, or anxious to note those faces that belonged to people inimical to him. Then turning his gaze upon the magistrate, he with his sound hand slightly touched his wounded shoulder, saying,—

"It's mighty fine to drag a man about with such a hurt as this. I suppose you think yourself wonderfully humane. Why don't you send me to an hospital? Time enough, when a poor fellow gets well of a bad hurt, if ever he does, to talk to him about being identified, and robberies, and all that sort of thing."

"Your hurt does not seem bad enough to prevent the course of justice in this stage from being pursued," remarked the magistrate. "When you are committed to Newgate, you will, of course, be properly attended to by the medical officers of that establishment, and if I persevere in only remanding you to the New Prison, whither you will be taken, every assistance will be rendered to you."

"Oh, d—n!" he muttered. "You'll do as you like all of you, I know that; why don't you hang a poor fellow at once when you have made up your mind to it? There's my daughter, too, she's accommodated with what the newspapers call a seat on the bench, and she won't look at the felon, her father, though she is my own flesh and blood."

The rascal evidently now wanted Kate to make some appeal for him, and she was about hastily to rise from her seat, but I placed my hand on her shoulder, saying,—

"No—no. Be still. You can do him no good, Kate, whatever may be your intention. For Heaven's sake, do not answer him at all."

Jackson seemed aware that what I whispered to Kate was not of a nature favourable to him, and he said, in a tone of great passion,—

"I believe it's an offence in law, ain't it, to help a criminal to escape? I know it is. Take up that d——d doctor, for he did so when the officers were after me. I charge him of aiding, assisting, and comforting a felon—those are the proper words, I believe. I charge him with the offence."

"I decline taking such a charge," said the magistrate, calmly. "Officers, introduce the gentlemen who have come to identify this man at the bar."—"They are here—here, your worship."

With some difficulty, for the throng in the court was very great indeed, two gentlemen made their way forward; one might be about five-and-thirty years of age—the other was considerably his senior, and I dare say had seen at least fifty-five summers; the strong likeness between the two left no doubt on my mind that they were father and son.

Before they got quite up to the witness-box, I could see that Jackson stole a furtive glance at them, after which he evidently was making efforts to alter his physiognomical appearance, and I was both amused and surprised at his success, for he did contrive somehow, by an action of the muscles of his face to make himself look very different, and he might have succeeded in puzzling any one as to his identity, had it not been for the very marked character of his brow, which he could not by any possibility alter.

The two gentlemen at length reached the position they were to occupy while giving their evidence, and the moment the younger one of the two saw the prisoner, a loud exclamation burst from his lips, and he cried,—

"Davis—Davis! 'Tis he! Oh, Heaven! 'tis he. Villain—monstrous villain. Have I searched so long for you to find you thus?—father, it is Davis. Now aid me Heaven!"

He turned very pale, and was forced to be supported by his father, who seemed in the greatest alarm and surprise at these sudden and extraordinary exclamations.

"Herbert—Herbert!" he cried, "be calm. What is the meaning of this excessive emotion? Excuse him, your worship. He has been in a very delicate state of health for a long time past, and is not able to bear the shock of any excitements. Come away, Herbert, come away."

"No—no," said the younger Mr. Harrison. "Thank God I have come here. I identify that man as Davis, once a groom in my father's house. Some years ago he was tried and committed for a robbery against us, and condemned to imprisonment for one year."

"But," said the magistrate, "do you identify him as the party who broke into your house some time since?"—"I cannot have a doubt. The dress is the same, and he carries with him the evidence of the wound he received from me as I chased him down the staircase of the house—and in him I recognise the depredator; and now that I see his face, I know him to be Davis, the discarded servant of my father's house."

"What do you say, sir?" inquired the magistrate, turning to the elder Harrison.—"I identify the man," he replied, "as Davis, once a servant of mine; but I did not see the robber who attacked my house, as my son pursued him before I could leave my bed-room; therefore I cannot swear that this is the man."

"Nor can either of you," said Jackson, who, by-the-bye, we may as well call Davis now. "Nor can either of you. A man may get a hurt in the shoulder, otherwise than in attempting to crack your crib. As for you, Mr. Herbert Harrison, you dare not prosecute me."

"Villain!" said the younger Harrison. "I gave the evidence against you that convicted you of the heartless robbery for which you suffered twelve months' imprisonment. Why should I hesitate now to do my duty with equal boldness?"— "And I told you I would be revenged."

"Davis, Davis!" said young Harrison, stepping close to him. "Tell me, if you have any hope of heaven, or heaven's mercy, where—where have you hidden ——"

"Keep your secrets, and I'll keep mine," said Davis, with an exulting grin. "Don't you wish you may get me to speak out upon a subject that I know, to think of, makes you nearly mad. I may be bad off and disagreeably situated, but I would not change places with you now; not that I should be such a d———d ninny as to put myself into the state you have come to."

"Really," said the magistrate, "this seems to be very irrelevant to the charge. What private matters of contention there may be between you, Mr. Herbert Harrison, and the prisoner at the bar of this court, I know not, nor is this, in any respect, a proper place to discuss them. My duty is simply with the robbery you say took place at your father's house, and of which you accuse, as I understand, this man."—"I do accuse him."

"On your oath, you believe him the thief."—"I do."

"Then I remand him for a week, as the officers, I am informed, can bring other charges against him."—"At the end of the week," said Mr. Herbert Harrison, "I shall be prepared to make another charge against him, the nature of which he is well aware of."

Davis clenched his hand, and looked menacingly at Mr. Harrison, saying,—

"You dare not; you know you dare not. I defy you. I told you I would have my revenge, and I will have it yet— more amply than I have had it, although many would be well satisfied with what I have taken. Prepare your charge; I am ready at any time to meet it. You will, however, think better of the matter—I know you will; and, if you call upon me in the New Prison, I will tell you why I know you will."

Mr. Herbert Harrison turned to the magistrate, and in faltering accents said,—

"Sir, will you allow me five minutes' conversation with the prisoner in private?"—"It is a most extraordinary request," said the magistrate, "from a principal witness against him."

"It is extraordinary I own, sir, and yet ——"—"Ask him what you like now at once. This proceeding is altogether irregular, but I do not wish to thwart any wish you may have."

Mr. Herbert turned to Davis, and while every tone of his voice, and every movement of his countenance betrayed the most agonising emotion, he said,—

"Tell me of—of ——"—"I know what you mean," said Davis. "The answer is short—a thief."

"No, no."—"As you please. Believe it or not."

Mr. Herbert Harrison fainted, and was caught in the arms of some of the bystanders, or he would have fallen to the floor. A great deal of confusion took place in the court, during which the prisoner was removed, while I, as the only medical man present, was requested to be of what service I could to the insensible man, who I could see from the moment that he had first made his appearance in court, was in an extremely delicate state of health. He remained much longer totally insensible than I had ever seen any man from a mere fainting attack; but that I attributed to the very weakly state he was evidently in, which prevented the physical system from rallying so readily as it would have done in a more robust subject.

He was removed into the magistrate's private room, and because I was extremely anxious not to lose sight of Kate, for more reasons than one, I made her come with me, when I followed to attend upon Mr. Harrison.

The fact was, I saw, on looking round the court, some faces which I recognized as belonging to some of the hopeful lot I had encountered in Hart-street, and I much feared that they might make some attempt to get hold of her, fearing she would be good evidence against their, no doubt, much admired friend Mr. Davis, alias Jackson. A pretended message from him of a kind nature might have lured her away, and, consequently, I made up my mind that I would not lose sight of her for one moment, if possible. Indeed, I found her of great service in assisting me with the remedies I used to restore Mr. Harrison, and she did whatever I asked her with a readiness and a tact not at all to be expected from a young girl; but then, she had been forced upon her own resources of action early, and had had a good deal of practice, no doubt, in tending the sick couch of her suffering father.

Moreover, there was a tenderness and compassionate feeling in all she did and said, that carried with it an irresistible charm; and as she hovered, like some guardian angel, around the couch on which the calm, placid form of the sick man lay, I thought, that until then I had never thoroughly discovered how truly beautiful was Kate—I don't like to write the name —Jackson, or Davis. Alas! poor thing, that the deadening blight of such a father should cloud the joy that ought to sparkle in such a heart.

The younger Harrison, who thus lay for nearly half an hour in a state of insensibility, must have been, when the glow of health and strength was upon his cheeks, extremely handsome, and I could not help wondering what circumstances could have so shattered his constitution. That those circumstances were of a mental, and not of a physical character, I firmly believed, for there was ample evidence of acute suffering in his countenance. Even Kate, as she gazed upon his face, with a look of deep sympathy and kindness, said,—

"He is like all, sir—he has known grief."—"Indeed he has known grief, Kate," I replied; "of that I can entertain no sort of doubt. But, see! he is recovering now."

A faint sigh escaped his lips, and now the father, who had set with clasped hands, unable to do anything but look at all we were attempting for his son's recovery, started up, and, approaching the couch, leaned over it, saying, in accents of the tenderest interest and affection,—

"Herbert, my dear Herbert—my boy, Herbert! Oh, speak to me, and let me know you are better."—"Father," he replied, in a low tone.

"Thank God!" said the old man; "he speaks; he lives!" —"Your son," said I, "appears in a very indifferent state of health."

"Very indifferent, indeed, sir; very indifferent. Some overwhelming grief hangs upon his spirits which I cannot get him to disclose. I have entreated him, often and often, to tell me, but he never would; and now, a suspicion that I have for some years had, that this man Davis was in some very curious manner associated with my son's mental uneasiness, has this day been confirmed. There is some dreadful secret which I would give much to know, for I feel certain the thoughts of it are wearing my son down to the grave, and I shall soon be a childless old man, for he is my only one! Oh, sir, if you could get him to make to you a confidence of what so much oppresses him, all might yet be well!"

"My good sir," said I, "nothing shall be wanting on my part to induce such a confidence, if it can by any means be brought about. What is the age of your son?"—"He is but three-and-thirty."

"Good God! and yet his constitution is dreadfully weakened. Is there no other cause but mental depression for his very delicate state of health?"—"None whatever. Some concealed sorrow is wearing him to the grave."

"It is very sad."—"It is, indeed. What can I do—what can I think?"

"Father, father!" said Herbert, faintly; "say no more. The day will soon come when you shall know all, and knowing then, at the same time, that I shall be on the threshold of eternity, you will perhaps be able to forgive me."

"Take my forgiveness, Herbert, beforehand," cried old Harrison, "for everything and for anything. Do but unburthen your mind of what torments it so much, and I will forgive anything."—"I—I dare not."

"Young man," said I, "reflect for a moment upon what you say. You are not only destroying yourself, but all dear and near to you. Surely, surely you may calculate upon the forgiveness of your father for anything, after what he has said to you."

"Not yet—not yet," sighed Herbert. "I must see Davis first, father; he said he would be revenged upon me for being a witness against him, when he stole the plate, and attempted to convict an innocent and honest servant of the crime, by placing some of the missing articles in his box. He swore he would be revenged upon me, because I saw him do it, and swore to the fact; and bitterly has he kept his word."

"But, my son, how could you be in the power of such a man as Davis?"—"The secret—the secret!" he groaned. "I must, come what may, have an interview with him."

"Do not—do not, Herbert. Shake off all connection with such a ruffian, and entrust those who love you, and who would stir heaven and earth for your happiness, with any cause of sadness you may have weighing at your heart."

He shook his head, and, in sad tones, said,—

"I will go home, father, now. Be patient; the time will soon come, when I can bear to tell you all, and when, with the consciousness that I am going soon from you altogether, you can bear to hear me tell you."

The old man wept audibly; and then Kate, who had been an attentive auditor to all that had passed, but standing in such a position at the head of the sofa that young Harrison could not see her, quietly glided round and faced him. In the coach she had had on her a bonnet and veil, and a large cloak, which my wife I suppose, or some of my servants, had given her the use of; but now she had on neither, and her long beautiful hair hung down, in nature's own sweet disorder, on her neck and bosom, while the emotion she had felt from kindly sympathy at hearing what had passed between the father and the son, lent an air of radiant, exquisite sensibility to her countenance.

As she, with a noiseless step, glided thus from the back of the couch and faced Harrison, she might well have been taken for some sweet ministering angel, stepping between him and his wavering feelings, to speak words of peace and comfort to his agonised soul.

"Oh, sir," she said, "your father loves you. Tell him all!"

Herbert Harrison sprang to his feet, as if some powerful impulse had in a moment acted upon his whole frame. He made one step forward, with his arm extended, as he cried, with frantic accents,—

"From the dead—from the dead! Mabel—Mabel— Mabel! Oh, God, save me!"

He fell back on to the sofa, and poor Kate nearly herself fainted in my arms, so shocked and surprised was she at the extraordinary way in which the sight of her had affected the sick man.

The father became nearly frantic, for he firmly believed now that his son had really gone mad. He wrung his hands, and called upon him by name in the most heart-rending accents; while, I confess, as regards myself, I knew not what to do, or what to say, under such extremely exciting and extraordinary circumstances.

Mr. Herbert Harrison had fainted again, and from the ghastly appearance of his face, I much feared that this would be a much more serious attack of syncope than the last.

"Mr. Harrison," said I, "get him home at once. Give me your address, if you wish me to attend him, and as soon as I have taken this lady home, I will come to you. Take him home at once, for Heaven's sake, and get him to bed."—"I will, sir, I will. Come as quickly as you can. I will take him to the Tavistock Hotel."

"Good; the nearer the better. I will be with you in less than an hour. The nearest medical man can attend to him in the meantime, to whom you will explain that I am coming."

I hurried Kate into a coach, and we drove home together very quickly; but I had time, during our drive, to ask her how she thought of coming to the police-court. She wept as she answered me.

"You think I have done wrong, sir," she observed. "You speak as if you thought so; but I could not help coming. An uncontrollable impulse impelled me, and, had the sacrifice of my life, or, what is far dearer to me, the kind opinions of my only friends, been the consequence, I do not think that I could have kept away."

"Do not mistake me, Kate," I said. "The feeling which prompts you, despite every other consideration, to cling to your father, is an honourable one, and one which does credit to your heart. All I wish of you is, that you will, under the peculiar circumstances in which you are placed, control it as much as possible. It is a hard thing, I know, to say to a child, what you cannot conceal from yourself, that your father is unworthy of you."

Kate sobbed, as she laid her hand upon my arm, and said,—

"Yet, I cannot desert him wholly."—"Nor do I wish you; but let me beg that you will not make any more attempts to leave my house without my knowledge. I know more of the world than you do, and can advise you better what course to take."

"I promise, sir. You are too—too good to me."—"You fancy so, my poor girl, because you are unused to kindness; but I hope and trust that for the future such will be no stranger to you."

When I reached home I did not stay to hear the eloquent manner in which my wife explained how Kate had given her the slip, and gone she knew not where; but merely saying,—

"My dear, don't scold her. I must leave at once, but hope to return in a very short time."

So I waited for no reply, but started off as quickly as possible to the hotel, whither Mr. Harrison had been conveyed by his father, and where I had the gratification of finding that he had recovered, under the care of a medical gentleman from the immediate neighbourhood, who behaved with the greatest courtesy to me.

"What do you think of your patient, sir?" said I to him. —"Why, the fact is," he replied, "I think he wants the same sort of practitioner that was so much a desideratum with Macbeth."

"I understand you. One who could minister to a mind diseased."—"Just so. There is evidently something preying upon his spirits and wearing him down to the grave."

"I fear so, indeed."

A few moments more brought me to the bedside of Mr. Harrison, who, when he saw me, sat up, and said,—

"Thank God, you have come, sir! Thank God! I believe I am on my death-bed, and to you I feel impelled to disclose a secret which has long kept agonised possession of my heart. A curse is upon me! A solemn, awful curse is upon my head!"

There was certainly a little wildness about his manner which might almost be construed into delirium, and yet I did not feel myself so completely assured that he was wandering in his intellect as to warrant me in putting a stop to the communication he talked of making. I merely said,—

"As for curses, solemn or ludicrous, having any effect upon anybody, I wonder that you can allow your judgment to be so much stultified as to think so for a moment."— "You do not know," he replied, "what cause I have to think so. Listen—I have done an act of grievous wrong, and most grievously have I suffered for it. The time now has come when it is impossible I can keep longer a dreadful secret."

"I would much rather," said I, "if you have anything of a painful nature to communicate, that you would make a confident of your father than of me."—"He shall hear me likewise. Should there be occasion, will you plead for me to him, for he it is whom I have so grievously offended."

"Offended me!" cried the elder Harrison. "Good God, Herbert, what do you mean? To whom can you possibly allude?"—"Listen, and you shall know. The evil that men do surely brings with it in this world a terrible retribution— a retribution out of which can only spring one hope, and that is, that Heaven may be merciful hereafter on account of the suffering that has already been borne by the grieved heart of of him who has done wrong. God knows how bitterly—how severely I have repented my deep iniquity."

The medical man who had done duty for me till my arrival had left, and none were now present with Major Harrison but myself and his father, who looked petrified with astonishment and apprehension at his son. He turned to me, and in a faint whisper, said,—

"Is he mad?"—"I think not," said I.

"Then Heaven and himself only know what he can have to tell. His life has been irreproachable. Herbert—Herbert, you are labouring under some delusion! You have never caused me a pang, but in consequence of your failing health." —"Do not—do not kill me by any kind words now, father," said Herbert. "Hear what I have to say, and then—then, if you can, say 'Herbert, you are forgiven!'"

The old man trembled and sat down by the side of the bed, while his son thus commenced divulging his secret,—

"Nearly eighteen years ago, you will recollect, father, that your brother's only daughter, my cousin, Dorinda Harrison, came to reside under our roof?"—"Well do I recollect," said the father; "she was an orphan and destitute. She came to my house welcomed as would have been a child of my own. How she left it I never can forget. That has made a sear upon my heart that can never be effaced."

"I—I am going to tell you how she left it."

"You, Herbert?"—"Yes. Do not interrupt me. You shall hear all. Dorinda was beautiful, and I loved her. It so happened, though, at that time, I had some dissolute companions,—young men of talent—far more talent than honesty or honour, and with them marriage was a constant theme for scorn and contempt. I unconsciously imbibed their notions; and yet I loved my cousin too much to tear her from my heart. She was all innocence and confiding goodness—she was a creature who saw guile in no one. Child-like was she in her homely simplicity. She—she seems to me now, when I think of her, as something more than mortal."

"Go on," said the father—"go on."

"I taught her to love me—to think me something superior to all others. I won her heart completely, and she had not the heart or the wish to conceal from me how dear I was to her. She ever welcomed me with smiles—she would kiss my cheek, and call me by endearing epithets. Sweetly in her innocence would she tell me how she loved me. I was her world—what I said as an opinion, became to her an ascertained fact; no sister could love a brother with greater devotion than did Dorinda love me. She would place her soft cheek upon my breast and talk to me for hours, now and then looking up to my face with beaming eyes, like some young angel gazing at its God. She had no thought of evil— pure, holy, and beautiful was that affection, as if it came from Heaven itself. I had won her heart—yes, by kind words and gentle caresses I had made her believe me perfect, and pure and holy in my affections as she was in hers. I— I repaid all this generous, trusting confidence—oh, yes, I repaid it all—all this devotion—this heavenly affection— this child-like, beautiful, confiding affection—I—I repaid it all by—betraying her!"

The elder Harrison, who had been rocking to and fro in his chair while his son was speaking, now sprang to his feet, exclaiming,—

"Good God! why have I lived to hear this? Herbert, Herbert, why did you not kill me, ere you uttered those words? Oh, God, oh, God! has it come to this? My child, my beautiful, adopted child, my Dorinda!"

He sank on to the chair, and covering his face with his hands, the old man sobbed as if his heart would break. The colour deserted even the lips of Major Harrison, and I saw him wipe the heavy, cold perspiration from his brow, as he said, in a voice of agony which I never can forget,—

"I—I expected this—I knew it. Father—father, you have, without naming him, because ye knew not how to do so, cursed the betrayer of the adopted child of your heart; now curse him again—curse him again, and name me as you do so, for I am guilty!"

He fell back on the bed heavily, and I thought for a moment that he was dead. The old man rose, and, lifting his hands above his head, while his countenance was convulsed with agony, and his scattered grey hairs looked wild and disordered, he said,—

"The curse of God ———"

"Hold!" I cried, in a voice that rang through the apartment, "hold! what would you do, old man? He is your son. Call down from Heaven no curses;—pray rather for God's mercy on the guilty man, who now repents him of that which he has done, and shame, shame on the father who demands more of the child than God would ever demand of him."

The old man's hands dropped to his side, and he stood motionless.

"Father, father," said Herbert, faintly, "have—have you cursed me again? I deserve all—all."

The old man burst into tears, and flung himself into his son's arms.

"Herbert," he sobbed, "my—my boy—my darling boy! Herbert, Herbert, my heart is breaking!"

Deep, unbroken silence reigned in the chamber for some minutes. I retired to the window, for I felt that the feelings of both the father and son were of far too sacred a nature for any stranger to interfere with. I heard them both weeping and murmuring words of affection. I heard the father say, "God bless you, and forgive you, as I do;" and I heard the son sob hysterically, as he replied,—

"This is too much, father. All that I dared to hope was that you would not curse me."

Still I remained where I was till the younger Harrison called to me, and then I advanced towards the bed. The old man was seated on the side of it, with his son's hand in his, and, when I was near, Mr. Herbert Harrison pointed to the chair his father had recently occupied, and said,—

"A very few words, sir, if you will be seated, and condescend to hear them, will suffice to explain what mysterious connexion with this sad affair the man who calls himself Jackson has had."

I sat down, as he requested, and with a deep sigh he continued,—

"Father, you remember poor Dorinda suddenly left your house, and that you traced her to a lodging in London, where she was staying with her infant. She was dying when you saw her, and implored her to tell you the name of her seducer. She would not do so. Had you stayed another ten minutes, you would have met me."—"I only left to procure some means of conveyance to carry her to my house again."

"And when you returned, you found Dorinda a corpse, and her infant gone?"—"I did, I did."

"She expired in my arms. At first I thought of committing suicide, and I believe I should have done so had the means readily presented themselves to me, but they did not; and then the wailings of the child brought me to more rational thoughts, and I swore to endeavour to expiate my cruelty to the mother by attention to that child of dishonour. Reason took possession of me. From the moment that Dorinda breathed her last, which—she—she did, blessing me, I have never known peace. Had she lived, she should have become my wife, and the sad memory of the past might have been softened by the affection of a husband, but I was denied the power of making such atonement; she passed away to that heaven so pure and good a soul should never have left."

"And the child?" said old Mr. Harrison.

"I will tell you. I left the lodgings with it in my arms, for I was told by the people in the house that you had been there. I knew it was you by the description, and I feared to meet you. I procured a temporary nurse for it that night, and then bethought me of what I should do. After much painful, agonising reflection, I resolved to keep the matter secret from you, and I was doomed to hear you launch curses on the head of Dorinda's betrayer, while you little dreamed of the agony each word inflicted upon me."

"But of this Jackson, or whatever his real name is?" said I. "You have not spoken of him."

"I am coming to that. Being secretly fearful that my father should ever know the real criminal, I trusted this Jackson, then a groom in our family, and, as I thought, a rough, but honest, well-meaning enough fellow, to go and personate to the nurse the father of the child, to pay, with money I provided him, all necessary expenses in his own name, so that if I went, which I often did, to see the little thing, I went as a visitor merely, who felt a kindly interest in Jackson's child."

"Go on, Herbert, go on."

"In due time it grew of an age to be sent to school. It was as sweet a child as ever God gave breath to, the image of its poor sacrificed mother, her same smile, her soft, beautiful eyes, her clinging tenderness of manner."

He wrung his hands, and was for some moments so absorbed with grief that he could not speak, and, when he did resume his strange narrative, his voice was broken by sobs, which nearly made some of his words unintelligible.

"You shall hear all—you shall hear all," he said, in answer to an appealing look from his father; "I will conceal nothing from you. I confess to you as I would to Heaven." —"Do not weep, Herbert," said the old man. "You will yet be happy and forgiven. Your fault is great, but so is your repentance. You will be forgiven."

"These are words of comfort, father. God bless you for uttering them. I don't deserve them."

"But, about the child?" said I.—"Yes; my dear little Dorinda—my beautiful child. Well, Jackson, still personating its father, took it to a school I selected for it, and I called as a visitor merely, while he was recognised as the parent of the dear girl. The people of the school once remarked to me how odd it was that such a man should have such a daughter.

"Matters went on in this way for some years longer, until Jackson was detected in extensive peculations in our house. He had the insolence to ask me to screen him from the consequences of his crime, and threatened, if I did not, to reveal the fact of my having an illegitimate child at school to my father. This decided me, and I would not give way an inch to save him. He did not know who was the mother of the girl—that secret I always kept from him.

"He was prosecuted and convicted, and sentenced to twelve months' imprisonment. I thought then he would have told all he knew to my father; but he did not. He only turned to me, and said, ' My day will come. You shall repent this.' These words I considered as an idle threat, and paid no heed to them. I visited my child myself, still in my assumed character of a friend, and then I was compelled to go with my regiment to India, sorely against my inclination, as you may remember, father."

"I do—I do."

"I was away nearly three years, and I had not been returned twelve hours without rushing to the school where I had left my child, and for whose maintenance I had left an ample sum before I left England. Oh, with what delight and throbbing sensations of bliss I reached the threshold of the house which contained my treasure. It was to me a precious casket, containing the rarest jewel of my heart.

"I asked for the mistress of the school, and was shown into the same parlour in which I had so often met my beautiful girl. The lady soon appeared, and I said, eagerly,—

"'You know me, madam?'—'Yes, sir,' she replied. 'You used to come and see a young lady here.'

"'Yes—yes. Fetch her to me. I—I must see her now.'

"'Now, sir?'—'Yes—yes. Quick!'

"'Bless you, sir, she's been fetched away by her father more than two years ago.'

"In an instant I understood the full extent of my misfortune. The scoundrel I had trusted had adopted that means of being revenged upon me. The blow nearly killed me, and I looked so ghastly and so ill, that a physician was sent for. They thought that I was dying. I managed to stagger away before he came. Retribution had, indeed, begun. It is needless to say how I searched for my child. From that day till this, when my imagination conjured up a kind of vision of what she might have been, I have heard no tidings of her. God bless her, wheresoever she may be, for I shall soon be in the grave."

I was much moved by this recital, and it was with evident emotion that I said,—

"Where was the school?"—"At Hammersmith," he replied.

"And—and your child's name?"—"We named her Kate. Oh, God! that I could look upon her face before I die!"

Tears forced themselves into my eyes in spite of me. I rang the bell loudly, and said to the waiter who made his appearance,—

"Get a coach directly. Mr. Harrison, will you take a drive with me? and you, sir, likewise? I—I cannot say more just now. Come, for God's sake, come."

They both looked at me with astonishment, and thought me, I dare say, a little insane.

"Get up—dress yourself," I cried. "Quick, quick! I can take no denial. Come with me at once."

"What for, sir?"—"For—news of your child."

With a cry of joy the younger Harrison sprang from the bed, and dressed himself with tremendous rapidity.

"Tell me, now—now at once," he said. "does she live—where is she? Have you seen her? Oh! for the love of Heaven, tell me."

"The coach," announced the waiter, and I darted down stairs, followed by both father and son. In a minute we were in the coach, and I gave my directions to the driver, with an injunction to go quick, and we didn't mind doubling the fare.

The hackney-coach horses accordingly went at nearly five miles an hour—a rate of speed which, for them, was frightful. I resisted all questions till we got to my house, and then I led my guests into a parlour with folding doors, conducting into another.

"Remain here a moment," I said, "and I will bring you some one who has seen your child."

Without waiting for a reply then, I left them, and bounced into the next room, where my wife and Kate were, like a bomb-shell, as the former afterwards told me; and what astonished them more than anything was, that all I said was "oh," and then bounced out again with all my might.

The fact was, I only wanted to know if Kate was there, and seeing she was, all I had to say was "oh." When I reached the front parlour again, I said,—

"Major Harrison, you have lost your daughter; but I have one who I think will do instead. Push open those folding-doors, and take your choice of the two ladies you will find there."

He opened the door with a bewildered look. His eyes fell upon Kate; with a shriek of joy he seized her in his arms.

"Found—found—found!" he cried; "my child—my beautiful child—my own. Oh, Heaven! how have I found so much mercy!"

* * * * * *

The reader may imagine the scene that followed; how Major Harrison looked twenty years younger; how he was never tired of kissing his daughter and holding her to his heart: how he wept and laughed by turns; how far Kate had all explained to her, and hung upon the major's neck in a burst of hysterical weeping; she recollected him as her visitor at school, who used to weep over her, and say such kind words to her. As for the old man, he wanted to execute some kind of dance, I think, with my wife, he was so overjoyed. I know he knocked off the mantel-shelf ornaments in his ecstasy.

* * * * * *

Master Jackson, *alias* Forest, *alias* Smith & Co., was duly informed, in a few weeks, by one of her majesty's judges, that preparations would be made to send him to New South Wales, there to pass the remainder of his existence, with a chain round his leg; and it *sarved* him right, as the Somersetshire jury said, when a man was tossed by a bull, because he would pull its tail.

THE JUDICIAL MURDER;

OR, CIRCUMSTANTIAL EVIDENCE.

I once attended a family of great respectability of the name of Stevenson. They resided in Keppel-street, Russell-square, which was then a very fashionable locality, and not, as now, abandoned to lodging-house keepers, house-agents, doctors, and decayed solicitors. The means of the Stevensons were tolerably ample, for the "old man" as they called Mr. Stevenson, senior, had been a stock-broker, when that business was a great deal more profitable than it is at present, and he had retired some years from active business habits to enjoy himself in the bosom of his family.

Then there was Mrs. Stevenson, a very pretty and a very good-tempered dame, and a tremendous manager to boot; there were the two Miss Stevensons, and Master Andover Stevenson, a lanky sort of animal, half man half boy; and there was Charles Stevenson, an orphan nephew of Mr. Stevenson, but who, by the general kindness of the family towards him—a kindness which he fully appreciated—was made to forget his destitute state, and to feel himself quite at home in the house of such liberal and indulgent relatives.

Of course in a large family there will always be something the matter which requires to be put to rights by the family's medical man, so that I was a tolerably constant visitor of the Stevensons, and they paid me a very snug yearly account, which, to do them justice, they never seemed at all to grudge. Oh, they were quite a nice family; and although, in consequence of my being out of the profession, I have become so bold that I can afford to say, that the man who has a family doctor about him may as well call himself a family fool, yet, at the time I speak of, I would not have at all thought it prudent to broach so very dangerous a doctrine. The fact is, a family medical man is one of the luxuries of the rich, and they may as well have it as not.

These Stevensons, of course, although a very domesticated, homely family, kept servants enough to make a respectable household, and at the time my narrative, in which they cut a conspicuous figure, commences, I believe no less than five domestics, of one sort and another, found homes beneath their roof.

The Christmas of 17— came round with all its gladness and cheering influences, its hospitalities, and its merry-makings among young and old. Alas! perhaps it is because I am an old man now, and the blood does not circulate so quickly through my veins, making me view things with a jaundiced aspect, but certain it is that to me there does not seem that hearty, cordial feeling at the festive seasons of the year among all classes of people that there used to be. Long ago, as my old housekeeper sometimes says, and my wife often joins in the cry, Christmas *was* Christmas, which, I suppose, is intended to convey the fact that now Christmas is *not* Christmas; and notwithstanding I don't say much to them about it, I am rather of opinion that the march of improvement, and all that sort of thing, has obliterated some of the kindly feelings of human nature. People now are so scientific and *politico* economical—I believe that is the modern phrase—that they have not time to be abundantly social.

The different classes of society were not so placed in antagonistic positions as regards each other as we see them now. There was a healthier tone among public writers, and a healthier taste among readers; but now everything that is written, with very few exceptions, is polluted by some party purposes, and, under cover of all sorts of pretences, we have party political pamphlets foisted upon us.

For example, one Dickens, a comic writer of no mean powers, who for some time rejoiced in the *nom de literaire* of Boz, or Buz, or Phiz, or something of the sort (my readers will excuse me, being an old man, if I don't quite appreciate the wit of a name so as exactly to remember it) publishes a book, which he calls "A Goblin Story for Christmas, about Some Bells that rang an Old Year Out and a New Year In." I bought the book for some of my grandchildren, for I expected, from some little sketchy pieces I had read of the man's writing, to find in it some household homely virtues, pleasantly put into language, some amusement, and perchance a little instruction; but how was I disappointed to find this most hypocritical little work a splenetic party pamphlet, under the assumed name of "A Story for Christmas." Fie on it—fie! If this man Dickens, or whatever is his name, wanted to publish a Whig pamphlet, containing, as it is convenient for that party to make all their political tirades now contain, attacks upon the landed aristocracy, the poor law, and so on, why not do so honestly and openly? but then, perhaps, it would not have sold so well as in its present insidious disguise.

Now I cannot help thinking that such books as the one I have mentioned are very likely to disturb the cheerfulness of many a Christmas fireside, because everybody may not know enough of the chicanery of political writers, or of the little value to be attached to the rabid opinions of a splenetic individual, to treat this trash I have mentioned with the due degree of contempt it really deserves.

It is bad in design—bad in execution. The author picks out the specimens among the poor that just happen to suit his fancy; he likewise picks out the precise specimens among the rich that answer his malignant—no, that is too strong a phrase, nasty will do better—nasty purpose. He writes to create ill feelings between the rich and the poor. Alas! what an office for a public writer. In this man's creed, a rich landed proprietor must have only just intelligence sufficient to be a monster of hypocrisy and injustice. A poor man becomes completely idealized by his poverty, and in the uncongenial soil of want he must rear every virtue under Heaven.

Now, I certainly do not pretend altogether to be able to make out the causes and effects in this book of which I am gossiping, to my kind readers, whom I consider now quite as old friends, but I find that to set fire to somebody's property is the last determination expressed by one of the characters of the name of Fern, and I sincerely hope that in a second edition the author will state how he was tried, convicted, and hung for the diabolical offence. I find that an alderman advises people to consider their means before they marry, and I heartily advise the same, and, from my heart, think with him, that improvident marriages ought to be " put down." Upon the whole, this "Chimes" book chimes in with an opinion I heard once expressed of the man who wrote it, of whom some one said,—

"His writings are not liked by the higher classes, because they do not understand the allusions to which his wit refers; and, as soon as he finds that thoroughly out, he is just the man to get angry—for he has a small soul—and become a party writer, with a great affectation of consideration for the poor, and then he will fail entirely, for he is a writer of comic sketches and nothing else."

Moreover, this very man, Dickens, is a great stickler for education, and contends occasionally that all men are born by nature equal, and denies the doctrine—a harsh one, I admit —that the son of a peer is endowed with higher faculties for improvement than the son of a beggar; but yet, somehow, we find all Mr. Dickens's heroes and patterns of excellence are among the ignorant and uneducated, while those who have had the blessings of education become dreadfully selfish, and quite monsters of injustice; so that, in his heart—if he writes anything from the heart—this " Whiz" or "Boz," or whatever he used to call himself, must be a great enemy to education, since it so hardens men's hearts, making one a Sir Somebody Bowley, and another a Filer. Either this must be the case, or the badly educated man is only an accidental specimen. Is it so, Mr. What's-your-name? Why, then, so, is Trotty Veck, and some other ticket-porter, maybe, a drunken, dishonest scoundrel, while another rich baronet may be a man full of the noblest and highest feelings of humanity.

* * * * *

But to my tale.

I was on the most comfortable terms with these Stevensons, and, saving some of the little accidental derangements arising from an excess of the good things of this life, there had been nothing particularly the matter for some time. Indeed, I had not been near the house for a week, when, one morning, I was surprised by a very sudden visit from Charles, the orphan nephew, towards whom I had always a strong feeling of liking, inasmuch as I fancied I could perceive in him the germ of many admirable feelings, and the opinions he did give utterance to were all of them quite unexceptionable. I saw by his manner, when he entered my room, that something was the matter, and I cried,—

"Bless me, Mr. Stevenson, you are an early visitor; I hope no one is ill."—" Indeed, sir, I am sorry to say that there is great indisposition at my uncle's house."

"Why, what's the matter?"—" We cannot tell, sir. If you can come with me at once, my uncle and aunt will feel much obliged, for, without exception, we have all been very unwell."

"You included?"—" Yes; I have been dreadfully sick."

"Ah, you have all eaten something yesterday that has upset the bilious system; but I will walk with you."

I saw him lean on the back of a chair, and I said,—

"You don't seem well, now, Charles."—" I am not, indeed, sir. I have a dreadful feeling of exhaustion upon me. I thought this morning I should have died."

"Bless me; how do you feel now?"—" A sickness," he replied.

"Something wrong on your stomach. Stay here a few moments, and I will give you an emetic."—" No, I thank you, sir; I have been so sick, that I am quite certain my stomach is empty."

"Well, then, you must put something into it as soon as you can. Take an effervescing draught, with ten drops of laudanum in it, and you will find the sensation of sickness vanish very soon."—" I thank you, sir."

I gave him the required medicine, and he seemed much better, so that we walked away together to Keppel-street; but I was very far from being prepared for the amount of indisposition that reigned in the family. I found Mr. Stevenson lying on a sofa, looking as white as a sheet, Mrs. Stevenson in bed seriously ill, the two girls scarcely able to move, and the lanky son, who had the odd Christian name of Andover, lying on a couch, with a mouth wide open, and in such a state of exhaustion, that he looked dying.

"Why—why, what is all this?" I cried. "What's the matter with you all?"—" Sick!" gasped Mr. Stevenson.—" Sick!" said Andover, in a faint voice.

I got the same answer from the others, and then I proposed to myself to take one of them in hand first, in order to ascertain, if possible, the cause of the general malady; so, as Andover seemed the worst, I began with him, and poking him up into a sitting posture on the sofa, I said,—

"Come, now, tell me how you feel?"—" Oh, dear! oh, dear!"

"Yes, it seems oh, dear—but how are you?"—" I shall never—no, never see Matilda again! Oh, dear, oh!"

"See who?"—" The idol—the—the bright incarnation of my soul's earthly dream! Oh, Matilda! must we part? Must we bid adieu for ever? Oh, gracious! oh, murder! oh——"

"What the deuce is the matter now? Who is Matilda? Confound Matilda; think of the belly-ache."

For the life of me I could not forbear laughing, for Andover made so many grimaces, and doubled himself up into such strange forms, under the influence of intense pain in the stomachic region and intestines, that it was quite a curious sight to see him. I had heard of love living through a fever, but some one has said that sea-sickness is death to it, and now I saw that a good pain in the internals had the same effect. The twinge passed away, and with a groan Andover looked me in the face, as he said,—

"Do you think I shall die?"—" I really can't say, but I should rather think not, Andover."

"If I do die, take my heart to Matilda dear, or a lock of my hair. Tell her I love her! Tell her I doated on her, and that my last words were—oh, my bowels!"—" Really, Andover," said I, " you surprise me very much. I must decline conveying any such messages to the young lady you mention, for however much they may convey with them an air of great truthfulness, yet I doubt if they will be considered of a sufficiently romantic character. Come, now, tell me how you became so unwell?"

"I hardly know. I was dreaming of her—of the beautiful maid of my soul, when there come such a twist in my inside, that it nearly flung me out of bed."—" Indeed!"

"Yes. Then there come another, and then another, and then two together, like the ghosts of Richard the Third, and ever since then I've been dreadful! Oh, send for her to receive my dying words! Let my soul's idol see me! I never told my love, but I will now. Father, I adore her—I adore her!"—" D—n her!" groaned Mr. Stevenson. " Doctor, just cram something down Andover's throat, and then attend to me."

"I will directly. Tell me what you had to eat yesterday?" —" Boiled leg of mutton."

"What else?"—" A rice pudding—nothing else. Then we had tea, and, as we always have at this time o' the year, we had a little mulled elder wine, and then I retired to the elysium of repose to dream of her! Oh, my Matilda! the angel of my dreams! bless you! Oh, my stomach! oh! There, it's a coming again! murder! It's like a patent corkscrew in my inside!"

"But what about Matilda?"—" Don't mention her, don't. Bother Matilda! Oh! oh! The devil! Oh, murder!"

And Andover threw himself again into a variety of funny attitudes, which reminded me forcibly of a song I had heard a clown sing in a pantomime, as a chorus to which he strains his body into strange contortions, as if the notes of the music acted galvanically upon his system.

I found, upon pursuing my inquiries, that the same class of symptoms presented themselves throughout the family, and being utterly at a loss to know what it was that had so deranged them all, I prescribed what medicines I guessed might be beneficial, and after seeing that they were on the recovery, I left the house, promising to call again in the course of the day.

It happened that I could not get to the Stevensons until quite the evening; but I had been home first, and as no message had come for me, of course I considered that they found themselves better; nor was I disappointed, for I found the whole family assembled together, certainly looking rather paler than usual, but seemingly recovered from the severe, although short attack of illness they had sustained.

"Well," I said, "how do you all feel now?"—" Better,"

was the general answer; and I thought that Andover looked very foolish, probably from a recollection of the soft confession he had made concerning Matilda.

"I am glad you are over the illness," I said; "but the origin of it I suppose is as great a mystery as ever."—"Oh, quite," said Mrs. Stevenson; "a mysterious mystery, I assure you, sir! A sort of wonderful mystery! The idea of us all being so very bad at once! it was quite shocking!"

"I should suppose it was, madam. How are you, Mr. Charles?"—"Much better, sir; but weak still."

"You don't look quite the thing. By-the-bye, Andover, who is Matilda?"—"Oh!" cried Mrs. Stevenson, "you may well ask. Some hussey, I'll be bound. We never heard of her before to-day, doctor, when this boy—child, I may call him —began raving about her. Matilda, indeed! and now he won't tell us who she is, or anything about her."

"But we know something about her," said Mary, the youngest girl. "Here's some poetry about her I found on Andover's bed."—"Heaven and earth!" cried Andover; "give it to me. When I was taken ill, I hadn't time to put it away. Oh! my heart—oh! my exquisite feelings—oh! Lord Byron, and all the poets protect me—save my fond heart from this!"

"Hold your nonsense," said his father, giving him a poke with the end of a paper knife.

"Shall I read it?" said Mary with an arch look.—"Oh, do," said her sister; "who knows but it was that that made us all ill?"

"Well," said the father, "I have heard of some particular tune that was so abominable it was the death of a cow; so, on the same principle, Andover's poetry, being in the house, may have given us our indisposition."—"For God's sake, don't read it. It's unfinished," cried Andover. "It is indeed. Some other time. It's only the outpourings of a strange, bewildered fancy. Oh! my Matilda!"

"I'll Matilda you," said his mother, as she gave him a very hard knock on the crown of his head with the end of a thimble.

Andover rubbed his head and groaned, while his sister Mary, with much humour, commenced reading the outpourings of the poet's soul:—

"TO MATILDA.

Oh, ye muses, look on me,
I can ne'er be fancy free;
Because I love—oh, Heaven,
Like a rock by tempests driven.
Oh! could I, Aladdin like, *build a
Palace*, it should be for my Matilda."

"Bravo!" said I.—"Bravo, indeed," said his mother; "I never heard such rubbish in all my life."

"Then you have not heard the second verse, mamma," said Mary, with more wickedness than I thought any one with such a pretty face capable of, and she forthwith proceeded, while Andover threw himself on a couch in agony and kicked:—

"Oh, ye gods and various fishes,
New suits of clothes and savoury dishes,
They are nothing to the love I feel,
Which makes my brain and heart quite reel.
If her house was on fire, and nearly *grill'd her*,
I'd rush within, and save Matilda."

This was too much for all our gravity, and such a roar of laughter ensued that poor Andover was in despair.

"The hussey, whoever she is," said Mrs. Stevenson; "she deserves to be grilled, that she does."

At this we all laughed more than ever, until Andover gave a spring from the sofa, and catching the paper on which was written the ode to Matilda from the hands of his sister Mary, he made a wild rush from the room with it, no doubt quite in his own mind agreeing with somebody who has remarked, that no man is a prophet in his own generation, and that no man can be a poet in his own family.

I soon rose to take my leave of the Stevensons, and after bidding them all good night, and expressing my firm belief that if Andover's poetry had made them ill, it had greatly assisted, by the impulse it had given their spirits, to make them well again, I walked into the hall. The footman had his hand upon the street door to open it for me, when Charles, who had followed unknown to me, touched my arm, and said,—

"Doctor, will you spare me a few moments' conversation?"

—"Certainly."

"Come in here."

He led me into the dining-room, and shutting the door cautiously and closely, he said to me in a low tone,—

"This illness is of so mysterious a character, sir, I cannot dismiss it readily from my mind. I have a terrible—a very terrible suspicion connected with it."

"Have you indeed—what is it?"—"Nothing, in my humble opinion—but of course, sir, I defer to you in such a matter—but, I say, nothing, in my humble opinion, could have produced such general and distressing effects but poison of some kind."

"Poison!"—"Yes, doctor. I have a horrible suspicion that some attempt has been made to poison us all."

"Good God! what put such a thing into your head?"—"I cannot tell you now, because I would not for worlds, in case it should not be the fact, disturb the minds of my uncle and aunt, and my dear cousins, who have all been so good to me, and to whom I owe so much upon the subject. But I will call upon you to-morrow, if you please, and we can talk it over. It is a horrible supposition, but it has come across my mind, and since such is the case, I do not feel justified in keeping it to myself."

There was an ingenuity and a candour about Charles's manner that much pleased me. I pressed his hand as I said,—

"Come to me to-morrow morning as early as you can, and we will talk this matter over, Charles."

I then left the house, but the few words that Charles Stevenson had said to me had made a great impression on my mind—perhaps, unknown to myself even, they chimed in with a faint, distant supposition of my own upon the subject, which, when I came to think the matter over, I could easily trace to its source.

In the first place, of course, the Stevensons, to be all ill in the manner they were, must have taken something into their stomachs of a highly deleterious nature, and so far it might, although not ranking as such, be termed a poison. I and all medical men are well aware that many disturbances of the animal economy arise from the accidental admixture of matter with the ordinary food, which never can be detected. Particularly in vegetables there may be a portion of some very injurious production mingled with what is known to be pure and healthful, and so produce great evils; but these cases to excess are "few and far between," and such derangements of the digestion seldom are of any serious moment.

This illness, however, of the Stevensons had been, while it lasted, serious, and the supposition that Charles had made to me, I am quite certain he never would have made had he not had more grounds for it than he had as yet enumerated to me. Therefore it was I awaited his morning call with some degree of impatience and curiosity. It was about ten when he was announced, and we were soon seated together by my fire-side, when I said,—

"Now, Mr. Charles, let me know all that you suspect in this business?"—"Thank God, sir, I suspect nobody; but I do think that something is going on of a strange character in the house of my uncle. This is not the first time that different members of the family have been attacked by excruciating pain, accompanied with vomiting. About a fortnight since I was myself in a worse state than any of those you saw yesterday; but I made as light of it as I could— because ——"

"Because what?"—"You know, sir, how much I owe my uncle and his family. When they took me into their house I was a wretched outcast; I had neither father nor mother, and the parish must have received me had they not done so. Since then they have treated me as their own child, but now that I am old enough to know and to feel what I have cost them, I own I conceal my wants, for fear of adding to my already too large debt of gratitude, a debt I can never repay."

"Well, Charles," I said, "these are very proper feelings of yours, but you must not carry them too far. Your uncle is wealthy, very wealthy, and I am quite sure begrudges you nothing that you can possibly want. But now tell me about this poisoning business, Charles? How were your suspicions awakened?"—"By the almost simultaneous nature of the attack of illness, sir, chiefly, and by one other circumstance which has alarmed me very much."

"What is that?"—"Yesterday morning I was walking slowly down stairs, very far from well, when I fancied I saw a piece of the stair carpeting that was raised above the rest, owing to it having, as it appeared, something underneath. I don't know what prompted me to examine it, for it was likely

DIARY OF A PHYSICIAN.

to be a stray piece of mud, or something as trivial and unimportant: but I did stoop and examine the carpet, when, to my surprise, I found this piece of blue paper, doubled carefully up, and containing the small quantity of white powder you still see in it."

As he spoke he handed me a little rumpled-up piece of paper, which contained about two drachms of white powder. There was no writing upon the paper to indicate what it was, and without testing it, of course it was utterly impossible I could say.

"For the love of Heaven, sir," he cried, "tell me what that is? If harmless matter, I shall have my mind set at rest; but if of a deleterious quality, I shall be lost in conjecture of the most painful description."

"I cannot, from the mere looking at such a drug as this," said I, "tell you what it is. You see it is not labelled, nor

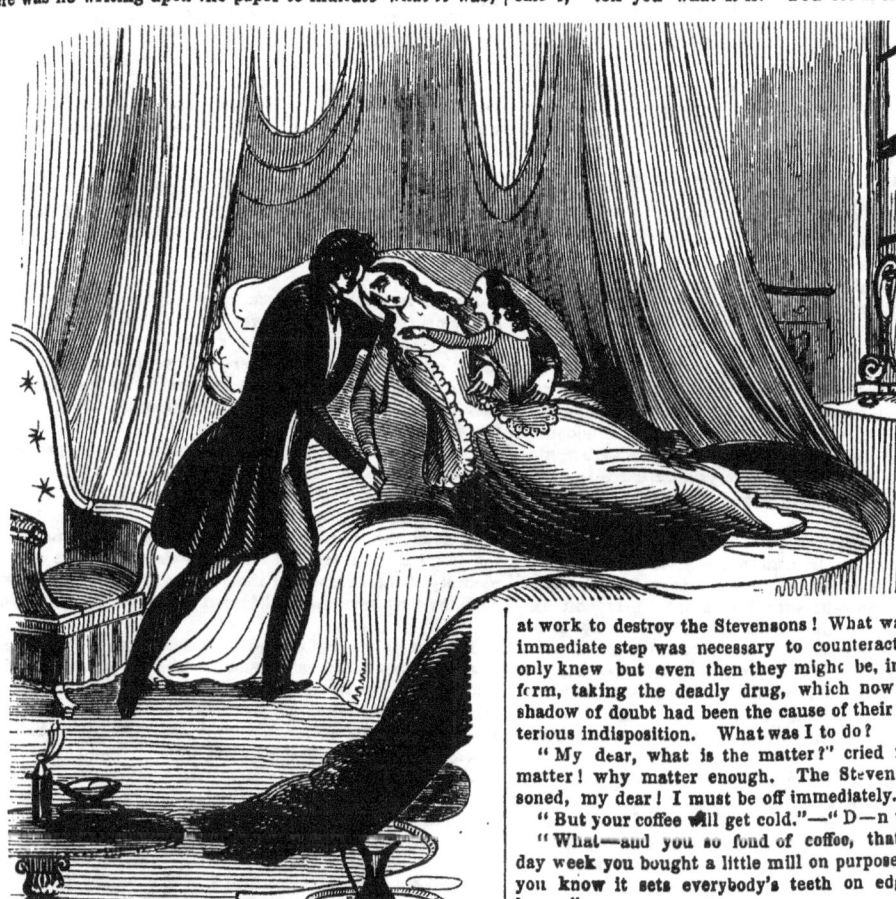

is it done up in the way that chemists do up their preparations; but come to me again to-morrow morning, when you may depend I shall have ascertained its nature and qualities."

"Thank you, sir; I shall wait with great impatience, and I hope to Heaven this will turn out a false alarm."—"Keep yourself quiet," said I. "You are making yourself as nervous as possible about this matter, when after all it may be a mere nothing. Come to me to-morrow, however, and we will have ample means of judging."

We shook hands, and he went away, leaving me more anxious and surprised than I chose to say. I took the mysterious little blue packet of white powder to an eminent chemist of my acquaintance, and requested he would do me the favour to submit it to tests during the day, and let me know as soon as possible what it was. He promised me he would, and I heard nothing of him until after my dinner, which was at five o'clock, and then my servant brought me in a small packet, which, when I opened, I found to contain some of the powder which I had placed in the hands of my friend, the chemist, along with a note, which was as follows:—

"MY DEAR ————.—The powder you placed in my hands is arsenic, in as pure a form as I have ever met with it. Believe me, my dear ————, yours truly,
"ANDREW DORTON."

Here was a stunning piece of intelligence indeed! Arsenic! Then the suspicions of Charles were verified—some fiend was at work to destroy the Stevensons! What was I to do? Some immediate step was necessary to counteract the evil. God only knew but even then they might be, in some insidious form, taking the deadly drug, which now I entertained no shadow of doubt had been the cause of their sudden and mysterious indisposition. What was I to do?

"My dear, what is the matter?" cried my wife.—"The matter! why matter enough. The Stevensons are all poisoned, my dear! I must be off immediately."

"But your coffee will get cold."—"D—n the coffee."

"What—and you so fond of coffee, that it was but this day week you bought a little mill on purpose to grind it, and you know it sets everybody's teeth on edge in the whole house."

My wife is a very good woman, but she is awfully provoking sometimes. I seized my hat, and made a rush to the street-door, when, before I could reach it, there came such a thundering knock at it that I nearly fell backwards into the dining-room again with the suddenness of the surprise and the shock.

Before there could have been time for the servant to get from the kitchen to the street-door, even had there been a junction railway between the two, the knock was repeated, and, impatient of the least delay, I flew forward and myself opened the door. A man staggered into the passage.

"What do you want?" I cried.—"Joggs," was his reply; "Joggs."

"A madman," I cried. "Get out!"—"No—no. Let me —get—a—my breath. My name's Joggs—a—I—I ah!"

"D—n your name; what do you want?"—"I've ran—all—the—the way—a—a—oh! They're all dead—by this time—oh!"

"Who—who?"—"Pisoned!"

"Who?"—"The Stevensons. I—Joggs is my name—I—oh!"

I bolted out of the door as if I had been pursued by a hundred devils, and leaving Mr. Joggs to place what construction he chose upon my behaviour, I was out of sight in a moment towards the nearest coach-stand. There I got a vehicle, and, by promising to double the fare, I induced a gallop all the way to Keppel-street, and really got there very quickly.

I sprang from the coach and knocked loudly at the door. Lights were flashing from window to window, and I could hear now and then a suppressed scream from within the house. It was some time before I could gain admission, and then a weeping servant girl, whom I had frequently noticed by her mild, inoffensive countenance, opened the door for me.

"Oh, sir!" she exclaimed, "thank God—thank God, you have come! This way, sir."

"How are they?"—"Oh, so bad! We are all dreadfully terrified."

"But, good God! why did you not send for the nearest medical advice?"—"We did, sir. The drawing-room is full of doctors."

"The devil it is!"

The drawing-room, although not full of doctors, had no less than five practitioners in it, and I announced myself, at the same time inquiring, in agitated accents, what had been done.

"Mr. Stevenson is dead," said one.—"Dead!"

"Yes. The rest of the family may recover; but the youngest girl is in a very dangerous state."

"Where are they all?"—"This way, sir."

We all proceeded up stairs, and I found that everything had been done that could be done for the sufferers, who were lying in a state of exhaustion, both from the effects of the poison and the antidotes that had been used. Mr. Stevenson was dead, and there seemed to me but faint hopes of Charles's recovery, to whom I spoke, but he was too weak to answer me much. He merely said, in a faint, low whisper,—

"Oh, God! doctor, it has come to this; we have been too late. Oh, God! oh, God!"—"Too late, indeed," said I, with a shudder. Then turning to the medical men, I added—"Gentlemen, this family has been poisoned with arsenic. Some one in this house must have administered it. No servant must be allowed to leave, and the police must be instantly appealed to."

"A magistrate has been sent for," said one, and even as he spoke I heard a carriage dash up to the door. It contained Mr. ——, the police magistrate, who was in a few moments with us. He had brought with him some trusty and experienced officers; and after we had attended carefully to the sufferers, for whom now nothing, in a medical point of view, could be done, and who, if they overcame the dreadful exhaustion they were in, would recover as the poison itself was obliterated from their system, we all repaired to the drawing-room to hold a consultation with the magistrate as to what was to be done.

"I will examine the servants at once," he said, "and any one else whom you think can throw any light on this most mysterious and inexplicable affair."—"Let me inform you," said I, "of what I knew of this affair;" and then I related all that had passed between me and Charles Stevenson concerning the poison, upon which the magistrate said,—

"If it would not be dangerous, as regards this young man's health, I should like to take his deposition first and at once."

We accordingly went up stairs to Charles's bed-side, and I said to him,—

"Charles, do you feel yourself strong enough to answer any questions that may be put to you?"—"Yes," he said, "I will try. God knows if I may live to answer them another time. Oh, what pain!"

"Poor fellow, he has suffered dreadfully," remarked one of the medical men. "I have fears of him."

"Will you be so good, sir," said the magistrate, "as to be sworn?"—"Yes—yes."

Upon a Bible he was sworn, and then, at the request of the magistrate, he repeated what had passed between us, after which there was a pause, and the magistrate said,—

"Have you anything to add to this statement?"

He sighed deeply, and then replied,—

"I grieve to say that I have."—"State it, then."

"After I left Doctor ——'s house, I could not forget the circumstance of finding the blue paper packet upon the staircase, and I had a suspicion that it must be poison. I went into the back drawing-room, and leaving the door open a little way, I made up my mind to watch any of the servants who might ascend or descend the staircase. As Providence would have it, I had not been long there, when a young girl, of the name of Martha Renton, came up. I—I saw her stoop at the spot where I had found the paper; she examined it, and then muttering some words in a tone of vexation and surprise, the precise purport of which I could not catch, she walked away."

"This is important," said the magistrate.—"I grieve to say it is," replied Charles. "I am sworn to tell the truth, but do not, oh, do not presume the guilt of that young girl.

What object could she have, gentlemen? Besides, she may have seen some derangement of the carpet, and merely stooped to place it right. I am—very faint, and can say no more—no—no more."

With a deep sigh from his nearly bloodless lips, he fell back on the pillow, and we looked at each other in horror, at the strong evidence he had given against one of the household.

"You have nothing to add?" said the magistrate.—"Nothing—nothing."

"Come away, gentlemen. Let me recommend you to the utmost discretion in this matter. We will now examine the servants, and, among them, this young girl, Martha Renton, whom he mentions, and if I see occasion, I shall have her taken into custody at once."

"Oh, Matilda!" groaned Andover, from a bed in the adjoining room, "I'm going now. Oh, Matilda, come and hear my last words."—"That boy raves," remarked one of the medical men, who had been so hurriedly called in, and knew nothing about Matilda, or Andover's predilection for the muses.

I made no remark, for I was in no humour just then to have any conversation with Andover, so we all went down to the drawing-room, which was in a very few minutes converted into a court of justice, and there all were, beneath the light of a handsome chandelier, met to consider of one of the most despicable crimes which has ever disgraced human nature—namely, poisoning.

The assassin, with his dagger, is an honourable gentleman, in comparison with the poisoner, who knows not but he may be involving many others in the destruction which he meditates against one only.

So detestable a crime, which is so much at variance with the English character, and owes its existence to the cowardly morality of the French and the Italians, ought always to meet with the very severest punishment the laws of our nation at all justify or permit.

The examination of the servants amounted to just nothing at all, for they could only depose to the alarm occasioned by the sudden sickness of the family, and to what eatables and drinkables had been taken by them for some time previous. It was agreed by them all that an unusual order had been given for some mulled elder wine, which, although the family were in the habit of taking it at night, they rarely, if ever, had ordered before in the daytime. This was proved to have been drunk hours sufficient before the sickness commenced, fully to account for it, if it, the wine, contained the poisonous matter.

The next servant examined was the young girl, Martha Renton, who was the same that had let me in, and exhibited so many symptoms of frantic grief at the serious indisposition of the family. Of course her examination excited in us all, after what Charles Stevenson had deposed, the greatest possible interest. The magistrates commenced the interrogatories, by saying,—

"How long have you been in this service?"—"Eighteen months," was the answer.

"Who mulled the wine for the family?"—"I did, sir."

"At what time?"—"About two o'clock."

"Was it unusual for them to order mulled wine at such an hour?"—"It was; but the dining-room bell was rung, and my master ordered me to bring a jug of mulled wine."

"What did you bring it in?"—"A silver tankard, which they always have ordered me to let them have the mulled wine in."

"Where is that tankard?"—"I cleaned it, and placed it in the butler's pantry again, where it is always kept."

"Where is the elder wine kept?"—"In a small cask down stairs; I drew it from there, and then mulled it."

"How do you mull it, as you call it?"—"I warm the wine, put sugar, nutmeg, and a little allspice to it."

"Nothing else?"—"No, sir—nothing else whatever."

"Have you any objection to your box being now searched?"

The girl hesitated, and a flush of colour came over her face, before she replied, faintly,—

"You—you want to search my box, sir?"—"Yes; have you any objection?"

"No—but—that is—I will go first—I—I cannot let any one go to it—and yet—I don't know that I ought to—hesitate?"—"Why do you hesitate? Don't you know that you bring upon yourself very serious suspicions by hesitating? Can you give us any reason why you do not wish your box to be searched?"

Again the colour came to the girl's cheeks, and she hesitated a moment before she replied,—

"I will tell you, gentlemen, the reason I do not wish my box to be searched. I wish I had told you at once, as the reason is one in which there is no disgrace, although, at the moment, I shrank from it for fear of a misconstruction being put upon a really innocent circumstance."

"Go on—give us your reason, if you please; but, remember, you are not bound to say anything that may prejudice yourself."—"The truth cannot prejudice me, gentlemen. In my box there is some baby linen; I am a young girl, and I did shrink from having it found there. I have sat up at night to make it when the other servants have gone to bed. My dear sister is married—she is two years older than I am, and, in the expectation of her confinement, I am assisting her to the utmost of my means. There is my key, and now, gentlemen, you know why I hesitated to have my box examined by strangers."

There was an irresistible air of candid simplicity about the girl, which made a strong impression in her favour, and I thought to myself, "If this girl is guilty, she certainly is a most accomplished actress, and would impose upon any one."

The magistrate turned to the officer, who had the keys of all the servants' trunks, and said,—

"Go and make the examination; I will wait the result."

The officer went on his errand, and we all waited with no small degree of anxiety. The servants were told they might leave the room, and they did so, looking a most disconsolate group, and wondering very much, no doubt, what it all meant. I spoke to the magistrate in a whisper, saying,—

"What do you think of this girl?"—"I don't know what to think," he said; "I am always afraid to think in so early a stage of judicial proceedings."

"You are right enough. But if she be the guilty party, I will have no faith in appearances as long as I live."—"Oh, I have had no faith in appearances for many years. A little experience of human nature, such as is to be had in a police-court, will soon stagger everybody's faith in looks or appearances."

At this moment there was a violent ring from one of the bed-room bells, and several of us ran up. Charles called to me in feeble, agitated accents,—

"For God's sake, sir, look to Andover. He has been moaning so very sadly."

I went to the boy's bed. He was dead, and must have struggled much, for the clothes were greatly deranged.

I was much shocked that thus both father and son should fall victims to this dreadful domestic tragedy. As for Charles, he sobbed as if his heart would break; and had it not have been that a dreadful accession of sickness came over him, he would have got up quite frantic, he was in such a dreadful state of despair.

I gave him what was requisite, for by this time every medicine that had a chance of doing any good was in the house, and earnestly recommended him to lay quiet, if he valued his existence, for I believed him in a very precarious condition, especially if the vomiting should continue, as that would show that the poison still remained to some extent in the system.

He promised to obey me, and I went down stairs again just as the officer, who had been entrusted with the task of searching the servants' boxes, returned with his report of the result of such examination.

Silence was commanded, and the officer said, in reply to the magistrate's question,—

"We found nothing suspicious, your worship, in any of the boxes but that of the girl called Martha Renton, and there we found three silver spoons, this diamond necklace, the duplicates of several articles, and these blue papers."

"Blue papers?" cried I.—"Yes, here they are."

"He laid upon the table some small packets. I eagerly opened one. There was a white powder. My heart sank within me; and, turning to the magistrate, I said,—

"Good God! who would have expected this?"—"You see, doctor," he said, "you must not trust to appearances. Officers, go down stairs, and take Martha Renton into custody on suspicion of murder. Bring her before me the first thing in the morning, with all the evidence you can collect. This affair grows desperately serious now."

The officers left the room. In about a minute I heard a loud shriek; it thrilled through every vein in my body, and made me feel perfectly ill. I know that Martha was arrested; and yet—even yet—a voice seemed to whisper to my heart,—

"She is innocent—she is innocent!"

It was some minutes before I could move from the sofa on which I had absolutely fallen when I heard the shriek of the young girl, who was arrested upon such ample grounds for believing her guilty of the diabolical deed, and again, as I there sat, it seemed to me as if a voice said,—

"She is innocent—condemn her not—she is innocent!"

There now ensued an awful stillness in the house. Every one in the drawing-room appeared to be listening attentively to catch any indication of another such sound as that which had just come so painfully upon our ears; but it came not, and the magistrate rose to leave, saying,—

"This is, indeed, a painful business, gentlemen. Let me see you all to-morrow morning, for it is impossible to say what evidence will become important."

One of the officers came to the door of the room.

"Please your worship," he said, "she wants to say something."—"I had much rather she would not," replied the magistrate. "Tell her that whatever she says will be repeated."

"I have, sir."—"Well, well, I am going. Request her to put off till the morning whatever she may have to say."

The magistrate walked down stairs, and I followed him; in the passage was Martha Renton. I never saw a human being stand in such an attitude of woe. Her hands were clasped—her face was of a death-like paleness—her hair had escaped from its confinement, and hung in long disordered curls down her neck and bosom—her very lips were bloodless. One of the officers had his huge, coarse hand upon her shoulder; but even he had turned aside his face, for he could not bear to look upon such exquisite misery and hopelessness as showed themselves in the countenance of that young girl.

A shudder passed through her frame, and she spoke in a tone of voice which haunted me for weeks afterwards in my dreams, it was so painfully, so exquisitely pathetic.

"Father—mother—sister, I am innocent. God, I am innocent. Save me—save me! Mother—mother!"

The officer caught her from falling; and the magistrate, in a voice of emotion, said,—

"Take her away—get a coach and take her away—remove her at once, for God's sake."

She was carried out of the house perfectly insensible. I saw her face just as she was conducted over the threshold; it looked like that of a marble statue. She was very beautiful; and now that her countenance was divested of all colour, she looked quite a different being to what she had been. I felt convinced that the preceding half hour had done the work of years upon the constitution and appearance of that young girl.

In a few more minutes she was gone. Then the magistrate stepped into his carriage, and bade me good night. I had made up my mind to remain with the surviving members of the Stevenson family. The other medical men went their way, and I was alone in that handsome drawing-room. The first act of as fearful a tragedy as it had ever been my lot to witness, was over. I leant my head upon my hands, and tried to arrange all the circumstances in my mind, so as to come to some definite conclusion; but my mind was a chaos of disjointed things, and I only increased its painful perplexity by attempting calm thought.

I rose and proceeded up stairs to see the sufferers. I found Mrs. Stevenson sleeping. She was unconscious of her double loss; the girls were better, and appeared to me only to be suffering from intense exhaustion. I commanded them to keep as quiet as possible, and then I went to Charles's room, and found him better in bodily health, but weeping bitterly.

"Come, Charles," I said, "you really must not behave in this way. It is true you have suffered a severe loss; but you must not give way so utterly and entirely to it."

"I cannot, cannot help it, sir. You do not know all the cause for affliction I have. The events of this day will crush me—I shall never look up again. I wish—oh, God! I wish that I were dead—why am I spared?—why am I spared?"

His tears flowed afresh, and he wrung his hands in the bitter agony of his spirit.

"What do you mean," said I, "by not knowing all the cause you have for affliction?"—"Martha Renton," he moaned; "I love her. I would have made her my wife as soon as I could have felt justified by my circumstances in so doing. I love her—I love her. What was it to me what she was—a poor servant in my uncle's house. What am I? dependent completely on his generosity. Sir, I love this girl, who is accused of so terrible a crime. I love her still—judge, then, what I must feel in—in being the principal evidence against her. My heart will break—it is breaking now. I would give my own life for her's. She is—she must be innocent."

"Charles," said I, "do not fancy that what you depose to is the only evidence against Martha Renton. Her box has been searched, and such damning evidence found there of her guilt, that, without your testimony at all, no one could acquit her."

"Gracious God! what was found?"—"Ample evidence of a systematic course of theft."

"Theft!—she a thief!—she? Then, where is virtue?"—"That's a very difficult question to answer, Charles; but along with such evidences were found packets of poison—arsenic, which, no doubt, produced all the illness under which you are suffering, and which has proved so dreadfully fatal to your uncle and your cousin."

"Andover—poor Andover!" sobbed Charles. "It—it—was but yesterday he shared his pocket-money with me—and now—now ——"

Charles was nearly choked by his emotion; he sobbed like a child. I never saw more grief in a man. I was myself sensibly affected.

"For God's sake, Charles," said I, "remember that there are others living who have a claim upon your care. Your aunt and your cousins have now no very near male relative but yourself; think of that, and compose yourself."

He could not answer me. He made an effort to pronounce the name Martha, and then he nearly fainted. I had considerable difficulty in bringing him round again, and then I reasoned with him, and persuaded him to lie quiet, and try to sleep, assuring him that if the sickness from which he had already suffered so much supervened again in his exhausted state, I could not answer for the consequences.

He told me faintly he did not wish to live, but still sobbing, he lay down, and I left him, much affected at the sad bodily as well as mental situation in which he was. I had, indeed, serious fears for him. The news of his attachment to Martha Renton was quite unexpected by me, and I could easily imagine what must be his feelings at having to give evidence against one who occupied a place in his heart, and such evidence, too, as placed her life in the most awful jeopardy.

Six hours or so of quietness and repose I knew would place my patients very nearly out of danger, as, after that period, it would be something extraordinary for the irritant symptoms to again show themselves. I, therefore, waited beyond that time, and then, finding that they were all sleeping, I went home, to endeavour myself to snatch a few hours' repose, before it should be necessary to appear at the police-office.

I very soon found, however, that my mind was far too actively employed in thinking over the extraordinary events that had taken place in Keppel-street to permit me to repose, and I rose, after a feverish attempt to get some sleep, at a much earlier hour than I was accustomed to leave my bed.

I dressed myself hastily, and as the morning was tolerably fine, I took a slight breakfast, and telling my wife that I should not come home until after the examination had taken place at the police-office, I determined to walk to Keppel-street first, to see how the Stevensons had passed the time I had been absent from them.

Alas! how different did that house appear from what it had been on former visits. Everything wore an air of sadness and regret. The servants were up; indeed, they told me they had not gone to bed at all. The two Miss Stevensons were sleeping; exhaustion had taken such complete possession of them, that they lay as if dead. Of course I was extremely anxious about Charles, and when I entered his bed-room, I was surprised to find him up and dressed. He was sitting in a chair by the fire side, and trembling excessively. His pale countenance sufficiently showed how much he had suffered from the effects of the poison.

"It was imprudent of you to rise, Charles," I said. "You are in by far too weak a condition to do so."—"But I must go," he said, " to speak for Martha. I must go to tell them that she is innocent—that she must be innocent—that it is contrary to all nature she should commit the crime charged against her. I must go and plead for Martha."

I shook my head as I said,—

"Charles, Charles, do not deceive yourself—a moment's thought must convince you that there are strong circumstances to form a supposition of the young girl's guilt. The evidence you yourself gave is almost conclusive."—"It was on my oath. I thought I was dying."

"You need make no excuses for speaking the truth. If she be guilty, she deserves all, and far more punishment than the laws name for her offence. You have an open, straightforward duty to perform; you have certain evidence to give upon oath, and I must say that I am amazed you do not at once, in horror of her crime, get rid of any feeling of affection you may have had for her."

"Hush! hush!" he cried; "hush! For God's sake do not try to talk me into a belief of her guilt. What if she be innocent! What if, after all, she did merely stoop to place the carpet straight on the staircase! What if some one else placed the things found in her boxes there, in order to cover his or her own guilt, by accomplishing the destruction of an innocent person? Oh, sir, such things have been done—we have read of such iniquity. I want to urge all this in Martha's favour. I cannot—cannot, as Heaven is my judge, believe her to be guilty.

"Your feelings, Charles, do you honour; but they cannot set aside facts."

"Now again, sir, listen to me. I love her, and when young men love, they are not always wise in their passion. I confess to you that some time since I made attempts upon the virtue of this young girl, which she nobly repulsed. I forced myself once even into her bedroom, but she, with a dignity and true nobility of soul I never saw excelled, resisted me. She threatened to call for aid. She triumphed in her virtue, and I was compelled to leave her, abashed at my own criminal suggestions. Now, sir, let me ask you, is such a girl the one likely to commit the dreadful crime of poisoning a whole family? Is she whose minor virtues are so great, capable of stooping to the most desperate and horrible of crimes, a crime alike denounced in the language of thundering malediction by God and man?"

"Your arguments are ingenious," said I, "and would come well from the lips of a counsel employed to defend Martha Renton; but still, facts cannot be gainsayed by any species of mere inductive reasoning. It is not a sufficient answer to direct evidence of a criminal transaction to prove that it was improbable the party should commit the crime."

When I said this to Charles Stevenson, I had no idea of the case of Mrs. Tyrwhitt, who was acquitted of a charge of theft at the Soho Bazaar, because she kept a carriage, and was well to do in the world, to the eternal disgrace of the jury on that trial.

"Do not—do not kill me," said Charles, "by destroying all hope?"—"Well, well; we will drop that portion of the subject at present. Do you really feel able to go to the police-office this morning, Charles?"

"I could not walk; but I think the strong interest I feel in the proceedings that will there ensue, will enable me to overcome the illness which otherwise I should feel too acutely to permit me to take any species of exercise."

"Well, if you think so, come. I am not aware of any particular harm you can do yourself, if you can support yourself there without fainting. I have no doubt but you have got rid of the poison, although it may be many months before you recover from its violent effects upon your system."

"But still," he urged, "can you not believe in the possibility of Martha's innocence?"—"The possibility I am certainly not prepared to dispute; but taking the evidence as it stands, her guilt amounts to far more than a possibility."

Charles sighed deeply, and by changing the subject, I sought to withdraw his mind from too close a contemplation of his wretched circumstances; for identified as were his best affections with Martha Renton, the condition in which he was placed might well be called wretched in the extreme.

I knew it would be quite ten o'clock before any of the witnesses would be required at the police office, and as I had no wish to hurry Charles away from his home, I waited until a quarter to that hour, before I would permit him to go, and then we proceeded together in a hackney-coach.

* * * * * *

To describe the scene of excitement at the police-office, and the general agitation of the whole neighbourhood, would be impossible; the news of the tragical circumstances in

Keppel-street, with such numerous additions as rumour loves to make, had spread like wildfire all over the town. We found the street almost impassable, and it was only by the assistance of constables that we could get at all inside the police-office, which itself was densely crowded in every corner.

On the magistrates' bench sat several county magistrates, and as strong a muster of members of the criminal bar as ever I saw collected together.

The mystery in which some portions of the case were involved—the, as yet, absence of all motive on the part of the accused to commit the dreadful crime—the devastating effect it had produced in the family against whom so horrible an agent as poison had been used—all conspired to bring the affair before the legal profession and the public with an intensity of interest which had rarely been paralleled.

I felt that each hour the matter was growing into vast importance. I knew that the city would ring with it. I saw at once, when I reached the police-office, that the case of poisoning in Keppel-street would become *the* topic of the day, and, turning to Charles, I said,—

"You may depend that all concerned in this affair will be made subjects of most uncomfortable notoriety. You in particular will be made much of."

He shuddered as he replied,—

"I shrink from such a notoriety. The morbid love of gossip on such matters as these astonishes me; but there is no help now. Alas! poor Martha!"

By announcing ourselves as witnesses, we got the officer to fight a way for us, and so we were presently seated on the bench, for the magistrate recognised me, and offered me a place, and I told him that Charles, in his weak state, must have one.

There were the night charges to dispose of first; and how dreadfully impatient the audience were till several drunkards were fined five shillings each, without the usual admonition from the bench, and several cases of assault were settled as summarily as possible. The last case was at length disposed of, and the magistrate's clerk, looking at the charge-sheet, pronounced the name of Martha Renton.

There was a general movement in the densely-crowded court, as if everybody was shifting his position, in order that, for some time to come, he should have no necessity for shifting it again. A great many people coughed, for fear they should want to cough during the proceedings, when it would not be near so convenient; and some blew sonorous blasts with their noses and silk handkerchief, in that artful manner which so many persons seem to consider quite fine, and, far from attempting to repress, appear to take a pride in.

A low buzz of conversation pervaded the court. The magistrate and the members of the bar, who were accommodated with seats close to him, looked anxiously towards the door, at which a slight bustle was observable.

"Silence!" cried the usher of the court.

Every tongue was mute. Several police-officers made a lane among the people from the door to the dock in which prisoners were placed. A painful suspense of about a quarter of a minute ensued, and then Martha Renton, held by the arm by an officer, was brought hurriedly into the court, and placed in the dock.

I declare I should not have known her under any other circumstances, that one night had altered her so completely. The hue of health had altogether deserted her cheeks—she looked thinner and taller—the expression of her face had completely altered from that of artless, happy simplicity, to such acute suffering, that it was agonising to look upon it. A voice from the body of the crowded court cried,—

"Sister! sister!" in wild, shrieking tones; but Martha only shuddered; and those who were near to her say she moaned,—

"The will of God be done!"

There was not one person then present who did not seem spell-bound for some seconds, in gazing upon the face of the sad criminal. There was not one heart that did not pity her —not one mind that did not wish to find her innocent of the terrible charge, which, like a thunder-cloud, ready to burst and destroy her, hung over her devoted head.

It is a common feeling, and has belonged to human nature from the world's commencement, and will adhere to it till time shall be no more, to imagine that Heaven works not by contradictions; that when virtue and beauty beam in the countenance, it must be a reflex from those feelings in the heart; that the look of innocence is incompatible with guilt; that beauty of expression cannot exist simultaneously with deformity of principle; that it is contrary to all we know of nature's doings that there should sit upon the face the god-like expression of a thousand virtues, while the heart shows such damning spots as are sufficient to hurl it to perdition.

Charity may raise its voice against this doctrine, because, if innocence is to be assumed from physiognomical expression, why may not guilt be inferred from a contrary expression? Reason may tell us that appearances are not to be trusted to. Philosophy will clamour against a prejudice for or against an accused person on such grounds, and yet then the feeling will remain, and the first sight of a prisoner produces most certainly in the mind of every one a feeling for or against the supposition of his guilt.

And perhaps there is more than cold, calculating people will please to admit in this science of physiognomy. The mind will impart expressions to the face temporarily; muscles, if continually acted upon in one direction, will acquire a corresponding development and expression. May not, then, the look of fearless, charming innocence and purity result from a heart guiltless of bad emotions? If there be a doubt, let us give virtue the advantage of it; and while we might not choose to distort a fact to the prejudice of any one whose face was repulsive with evil imaginings, let us give credit to those who present to us such a letter of introduction from nature as a candid, open, clear, and unsuspicious countenance.

Such a face had Martha Renton. There was deep grief upon it. There was terror lurking round the beautiful mouth, but there was no sign of guilt. It seemed impossible that one so gifted by nature with rare beauty should be given a heart capable of such awful emotions as must have preceded the commission of the dreadful crime of which she was so circumstantially accused.

But facts are stubborn things. I thank God, that in no sort of judicial capacity was I called upon to make a decision with regard to the guilt or innocence of that young girl! What a war of feeling and reason would I have had in my breast! She clung to the iron rail which was before her, and looked from face to face of those who, to her mind, had assembled to judge her.

"I am innocent! I am innocent!" she cried, in a shrieking voice. "I did not do it! Great Heaven, I am innocent! God knows I am innocent! Gentlemen, release me! I am nearly mad, but I am innocent of this dreadful deed!"

"Let me advise you," said the magistrate, " to be silent. A proper time will come for you to speak, should you be inclined or advised so to do; but you had far better now be silent."

"Oh, sir, why should I be silent?" she replied. "What do I wait for? I have but one answer to make to that with which I am charged. I am innocent! I can say no more. Who here would have me say less?"

"Proceed with the examination," said the magistrate.

Of course all the magistrate looked to was that he had sufficient evidence to warrant him in committing the prisoner for trial; more than that he did not wish to hear, and that there was ample testimony to warrant him in committing Martha Renton, the reader is already aware. The parties examined were myself, the medical man who had first arrived, my friend, the chemist, who had analysed one of the powders in the blue papers for me, the officer who had searched Martha Renton's box, and last, though not least, Charles Stevenson.

When it came to his turn to be examined, I thought he would have dropped. His face turned of an ashy paleness, and he trembled in every limb. Indeed he showed such evident signs of severe indisposition, that the magistrate remarked it was a pity he had been brought to the court, since he had already given his deposition, and had only to sign it, which could have been done without, in his sick state, dragging him so far.

He was permitted to sit where he was, instead of being placed in the usual place from where witnesses gave their evidence, and when asked if he had anything to add to the statement he had made, he spoke in a low tone of voice, that seemed as if each word he uttered almost choked him,—

"I—have nothing to add but my great doubt of the guilt of this young girl. Look at her, and ask yourself, sir, if she can be guilty of such an act. God forbid that I should give false testimony for or against any one, and, therefore, I cannot help saying that I saw her, according to the deposition which has been read over to me here, stoop and examine the spot on the staircase where I had previously found the blue paper, in which was contained the white powder that is sworn to be arsenic. But then, sir, let me implore you to consider that even that may be an action compatible with innocence. She may have observed a derangement of the carpet, and stooped to rectify it. Will she not herself give such an explanation?"

He looked imploringly at Martha, as if he would have said, "for God's sake adopt this suggestion." All eyes were directed to the girl, and the magistrate, who seemed as willing as any one could possibly be to give her the benefit of any doubts that might be suggested of her guilt, said,—

"Do you wish to make any remark on this witness's evidence, prisoner?"

The girl looked bewildered for a moment, and then she passed her hand across her eyes, as if she were trying to awaken herself from some dreadful dream, the strange fancies of which she felt herself the victim of, at the same time that she was conscious of their unreality.

"Say anything—say anything," she muttered. "What should I say? What—what ——"

"You can put what question you like to the witness," said the magistrate. "I think it is a pity you have no legal adviser."

"Oh, Martha—Martha," cried Charles, "you stooped to place the carpet straight. That was what you stooped for, was it not?"

"Really," remarked the magistrate, "this is very improper. I cannot permit a witness thus to suggest to a prisoner a line of defence against his sworn testimony."

"But—but, Martha," added Charles, "speak—say so."

"Great God!" exclaimed Martha, "what does all this mean? As I hope for justice here, for mercy hereafter, I have no knowledge whatever of such a circumstance occurring at all. It is said a deadly drug, wrapped in blue paper, has been found in my box. I never saw it—I never placed it there. All this to me is frightfully new. I know nothing of it. I am innocent, gentlemen."

Charles, who had risen and waited with painful anxiety for Martha's reply, now sank back in his chair with a deep groan, and everybody in court looked surprised that the prisoner had not adopted the line of defence pointed out to her, instead of trusting to a denial of a statement given on the solemn oath of another party.

"Let me seriously advise you," said the magistrate to her, "to say no more. I really wish you had a legal adviser."

As he spoke he glanced among the barristers who were accommodated with seats upon the bench, as if he would have said, "Will none of you, gentlemen, undertake the defence?"

The appeal was understood, and a young man rose, saying,—

"I shall be very happy, if retained by the prisoner, to undertake her case. If there be any attorney here who—what do you say, Mr. Bell?"

He glanced towards an attorney, whom he knew personally, and who immediately replied,—

"Please to consider our firm engaged for the prisoner. Mr. Denbigh, we will place the case in your hands."

"Then, sir," said the young barrister, "I may consider myself now as regularly acting for the prisoner?"

Poor Martha looked bewildered at all this, which she could not understand, and the magistrate, perceiving how abroad she was upon the subject, kindly said,—

"You had better leave the matter, prisoner, entirely in the hands of these gentlemen, who, you may be assured, will consult your very best interests."

"Thank God!" exclaimed Charles, "that you have now able and efficient help, Martha. There is another circumstance, too, which may place this affair in a difficult light. My uncle is embarrassed in his circumstances, and who knows what strange effect upon his brain such a state of things might have produced; and, besides ——"

"Sir," said Mr. Denbigh, "if you will mind your own business, and leave me to mind mine, it will be better for all parties. I protest against you, a witness for the prosecution, addressing the prisoner, and if such conduct be repeated, I shall demand your removal from the court."

Charles looked astonished, and the barrister, perceiving the effect he had produced, continued,—

"How dare you, sir, with unsupported evidence, come here, and with a mock sensibility pretend, after damaging my client as far as you possibly can, to shed the crocodile tears of sympathy over the ruin you would yourself produce. I say how dare you, sir, do this? I trust to be able to convince a jury that your testimony is of no value."

Charles half rose from his seat, and then he sank back into it again, saying,—

"And this is my reward!"

"Never mind," I whispered, "never mind."

"Hear me—oh! hear me!" cried Martha. "Gentlemen ——"

"Peace," cried Mr. Denbigh. "As your counsel, I advise you to say nothing. I am thoroughly convinced of your innocence, but yet I suppose you, sir," turning to the magistrate, "will consider it your duty to commit the prisoner, in which case I shall reserve the defence, which will place her innocence in a clear light, till we get before a jury."

"I certainly shall commit the prisoner for trial on the charge of wilful murder," said the magistrate. "I have amply sufficient evidence before me to justify, and, indeed, to demand such a course."

"Very good, sir."

The counsel sat down, and I could see Charles Stevenson eyeing him with a strange look. Then he leant over towards him, and said a few words in a whisper; but Mr. Denbigh, as I thought, with great coarseness and inhumanity, cried in a loud voice,—

"I don't want to be earwigged, sir, by witnesses for the prosecution. I don't believe a word of your evidence, sir. Don't speak to me, I beg."

Charles sank back again, and I said to him,—

"Charles, Charles, do not interfere. A counsel has a duty to perform to his client, which is paramount to all others. If he thinks it necessary for the defence to abuse you, you may depend upon it he will do so unsparingly."

"But it is very hard, when I would give my life to save her."—"Perhaps it is; but you see the counsel is evidently of opinion that he must attack you."

Suddenly Charles rose, and said rapidly,—

"With regard to the blue papers found in the prisoner's box, who knows but some enemy put them there?"

The counsel was on his feet in a moment, and pointing full in the face of Charles, he said, slowly and distinctly,—

"A good thought—it was you."

An extraordinary sensation was created in court by these words, and Charles seemed on the point of making some very angry reply, when the magistrate interposed.

"I cannot allow these proceedings," he said. "I must say that the indiscreet conduct of the witness, Charles Stevenson, has brought upon him these severe animadversions of counsel. The prisoner stands committed for trial."

The commitment was made out, and all the witnesses bound over to appear at the Old Bailey, after which poor Martha Renton fainted away, and was removed from the court in a state of insensibility.

A young woman clung to her as she was carried out, and sobbed bitterly—it was her sister, and although I felt strongly impelled to offer whatever services might be in my power, I dreaded rather the sort of reception I should meet with, because I too was a witness for the prosecution. However, I felt sufficiently interested in Martha to make some attempt to be of use to her. I was resolved she should have every assistance in her defence, and I went up to Mr. Bell, the attorney, and said,—

"Sir, although an unwilling witness against the prisoner, I ——"

Mr. Denbigh overheard me, and, in a loud voice, he cried,—

"It is certainly one of the strangest things in the world that the witnesses for the prosecution in this case will not leave the professional men employed for the prisoner alone. Mr. Bell, be so good as to give this gentleman his answer at once."

Mr. Bell made me a bow, and said, with marked emphasis,—

"I have the honour to bid you good morning, sir."

Then he turned upon his heel, and left me to make what I liked of it.

"Well," thought I, "perhaps they are right. They seem determined to keep no terms whatever with any one whose testimony is against the prisoner, and perhaps such a course may be wise."

"You see," said Charles to me, with more bitterness than I thought him capable of feeling, "you see that you come in for a share of the same abuse that I have been subject to."—"Well, well," I replied, "let them take their own course. God and herself only know if she be innocent or guilty."

"There will, of course," said Charles, "be more evidence on the trial. She must have purchased the poison somewhere, you know, and that has all to come out yet."—"It has, indeed. If there be any corroborative evidence of that description, it must condemn her."

"Heaven send there may not be. Oh, sir, still—still she is dear to me—I love her still."

Tears gushed to his eyes, and I could see that he was almost blinded by them as I led him from the court to the coach, which I had ordered to wait for us, in order to conduct us back to Keppel-street, when the proceedings at the police-office should be over. There was still a dense crowd waiting, for Martha Renton had not yet been removed to Newgate, and a constable was telling the people they need not wait in expectation of seeing her, for she would not be removed till night; but the sight-seers were loath to believe him, and still lingered round the office-door. As we drove to Keppel-street, I said to Charles,—

"What was that you hinted at with regard to your uncle's embarrassed circumstances?"

"Just this," he replied. "About a week ago he told me that several important speculations on the Stock Exchange had gone wrong with him, and that he had become consequently much harassed for money"

"You surprise me very much."—"It surprised me very much; but I could see that it preyed much upon my uncle's mind."

"Is Mrs. Stevenson aware of it?"—"She is not, I think. I feel myself incapable of doing so,—would you, sir, break the subject to her, and tell her you are aware my poor uncle had become embarrassed in his affairs. I should recommend her and my two cousins to retire to the quiet seclusion of some country place with the remnant of my poor uncle's fortune, for still I cannot help thinking they will have something when all his affairs are arranged."

"I sincerely hope so; but I do not like the task of being the bearer of such ill news. You, as one of the family, may do so with a much better grace."—"Alas! alas! I dread to add to their afflictions."

"And so do I, Charles."—"Well, then, sir, it is my duty, and I will do it. Oh, what days and nights of agony I shall now pass. Tell me candidly, doctor, your opinion; will she be condemned? Can anything be done to save her? Can you give me any consolation, sir, or is there no hope?"

"Truly speaking, Charles, I cannot help thinking it a very bad case, indeed; and, if I may speak my mind to you, I must say I think the course you pursued was very injudicious, notwithstanding it was dictated by the best feelings."

"Injudicious, sir?"—"Yes. You made your testimony tell doubly against the prisoner by your evident desire to screen her, and to suggest palliatives and excuses. A little consideration has convinced me of this, and afforded me a key to the anger of the counsel against you. There's no witness so dangerous as the unwilling one, who yet gives damning evidence against the accused."

"Great God," he cried, "I see it now, but I did not view it in that light before. Oh, how could I have been so foolish, so blind to the consequences of what I was about. When our feelings are much interested we feel instead of thinking; and I, with all the will to do what good I could to Martha, have most unconsciously injured her. Oh, doctor, I wish I were dead. Why did the poison spare me, and take those it did to the grave!"

"You must not," said I, "torment yourself in this way. There will be an inquest to-day, and, no doubt, your attendance will be required. You must keep up as well as you can against your afflictions, and remember you are still in very delicate health indeed. The effects of irritant poisons, such as the one you have taken, are not easily or quickly got rid of."

"I feel myself very ill; but that, sir, is nothing to the mental agony I must now endure."

We had now arrived in Keppel-street; and, as I positively declined to make the disagreeable communication respecting the late Mr. Stevenson's finances to his family, Charles said he would take an early opportunity of doing so. I found Mrs. Stevenson much better, as well as the young girls, so that there was no longer any danger; but the state of mental depression they were in I never saw equalled. It was, take it altogether, a scene in that house of the most heart-rending description. I never saw so much grief for the death of any one as was exhibited by Mrs. Stevenson and her daughters for their double loss.

They were deaf to all consolation. Nothing appeared to have any effect upon them. They answered by tears only to every word I uttered. I left Charles with them, and went home alone. The inquest was held that evening, but nothing new was elicited. A verdict of wilful murder against Martha Renton was returned; and, as she was already committed to Newgate, there the matter rested for a time.

The excitement among all classes of society seemed to be immense. The newspaper press teemed with "particulars" and "further particulars." Scarcely anything else was talked of but the approaching trial, and the diversity of opinion concerning the whole affair was most extraordinary.

I was at a party on the evening before the sessions commenced, when it was the sole subject of conversation, and I was asked over and over again to give my opinion on the various circumstances of the case, which I declined to do, alleging that as a witness I ought not to do so, upon which one of the most urgent of my questioners suddenly said,—

"At all events, although it is found that Mr. Stevenson is an insolvent, it is gratifying to know that his nephew is so well off as to be fully able to protect the family."

This speech was a great surprise to me, and I turned most anxiously to the speaker to solicit an explanation.

"Well off!" I exclaimed to the gentleman who had made what to me was so extraordinary a statement concerning Charles Stevenson. "Did you say well off, sir?"—"Yes."

"Are you sure?"—"Why, sir, I cannot tell what your notions of being well off may be. Such expressions are, of course, comparative. To my mind a man with eighty thousand pounds in the Three-and-a-Half per Cents is tolerably well off."

"Eighty—thousand?"—"Yes, that's the amount."

"But, good God, sir, you don't mean to tell me that Charles Stevenson, the nephew of Mr. Stevenson who was poisoned, has any such sum?"—"I happen to know it. I am a member of the Stock Exchange, and have made the investment for him."

"I am astonished!"—"You look so, sir."

"But—but—oh, I suppose some one has just left it him. I have not seen him for a week."—"A week! Oh, these investments have been going on for more than a year."

I was so staggered that I nearly feel off my chair; but I felt the necessity of controlling my feelings as much as possible, and leaving the party as early as I possibly could without exciting particular remark, I hurried home, in order to hold a serious consultation with myself on the words I had just heard.

It gave a strange revulsion to all my thoughts. For a time I felt quite lost in a chaos of conflicting suppositions. And yet, after all, what had the amount of Charles Stevenson's wealth to do with the main question at issue—the guilt or innocence of Martha Renton? Positively nothing, except so far as it gave me an uneasy sensation that he was not the open, candid character I took him to be. And then again, how came he by such a sum of money? That was a question easier to ask than to answer. It was one upon which I could not hazard the remotest conjecture. At one moment I thought I would go to him, and challenge him with the fact; and yet what business was it of mine? Suppose he was to reply to me, "Sir, what business have you with my financial affairs?" how foolish I should look.

I paced the room in a state of considerable mental agitation, and was still as thoroughly undecided as ever what to do, when the door opened, and my servant announced,—

"Mr. Charles Stevenson."

I started at the mention of his name, and hesitated whether to see him or not; but it was too late to deny myself to him, for with his usual familiarity with me since the terrible circumstances at Keppel-street, he walked into the parlour.

"How do you do, sir? I am happy in being so fortunate as to find you at home."—"Mr. Stevenson," I said, abruptly, for I could not temporise with him. "Mr. Stevenson, do you know a Mr. Brooke?"

That was the name of the stock-broker from whom I had my information.

"Do you mean Mr. Augustus Brooke?" he said, with a calmness that amazed me.—"I don't know," said I, "but the Mr. Brooke I mean is a member of the Stock Exchange."

"Oh, then he is my stock-broker, and you have found out my secret, doctor, at last."

"Your secret, Mr. Stevenson! Why, what on earth do

you mean?"—" Why, sir, that you have found out how lucky I have been."

"Lucky?"—" Yes. I have eighty thousand pounds in the Three-and-a-Half per Cents now."—" So I hear."

"About twelve months ago my revered uncle gave me a thousand pounds, saying,—' Charles, make the most of this in the English and foreign securities, my boy;' and I think you will own I have, sir. Oh, what a comfort it is to feel now how much I can do for my aunt and my cousins."

"But I don't understand, Charles, why you kept it a secret from them and from me."—" I wanted to surprise you, sir."

"Well, so far as that goes you have certainly succeeded; but you must have had extraordinary success to make so much money."—" I have, sir. Fortunes on the Stock Exchange are lost and won in a few hours."

"I have heard of such things," I said, coldly, for I was not half pleased with Mr. Charles.—" But the object of my visit," he said, turning the conversation, as if it was of little moment, "was to tell you that the shop at which the girl Martha purchased the arsenic has been discovered."

"Indeed!"—" Yes; I had it from one of the officers. He tells me there is ample evidence that she purchased the arsenic, and that her identity will be sworn to."

"Then she is lost."—" She is guilty!"

"God help her! I have always felt a great sympathy with that girl. I would to God some evidence of insanity would show itself in her, which would warrant the judge in saving her life."—" Insanity! She mad! She is no more mad than I am."

"I said I wished she were, as then her life might be spared; and who knows what the course of time might produce. Some chain of circumstances might prove her innocent."

"What circumstances, sir? She innocent! Impossible! Look at the evidence, sir; could anything be more complete? She will be proved to have bought the poison—some of it is found in her possession. You prove its disastrous effects; what chance can there be of that girl's innocence? Conviction of her guilt has now in my mind almost smothered the affection I had for her. Can there be a more horrible crime than poisoning?"—" There certainly cannot."

"One shudders to think of it, sir! Adieu. I merely called to let you know how complete the evidence now is against that unhappy female."

"But what imaginable motive could she have had to commit the dreadful deed?"—" To save herself from the consequences of the robberies she had committed, and of which the examination of her box bore ample proofs. Oh, her motive seems to me apparent enough, doctor. I shall never trust a fair exterior again while I live."

"Nor I, nor I."

Charles, I suppose, saw that I was in no mood for his company, and shortly afterwards he withdrew. I sat down with my hands over my face, and I think I never passed an hour of such agonising thoughts as then came over me.

There was nothing in the circumstance of Charles having eighty thousand pounds that could make Martha Renton less guilty. That I told myself over and over again, and yet, strange to say, I could not disconnect in my mind an idea of her innocence with my accidental discovery of that circumstance. I called to mind her beauty, her looks of innocence, her natural alarm when accused of the dreadful crime, her asseverations that she was guiltless, and the manner in which she had called upon Heaven to witness to that fact.

"By heavens," I cried, as I sprang to my feet, "that girl is innocent, or she is the most accomplished actress that ever trod the great stage of life. There was never her equal, and there never will be."

I now became seized with a longing to see her—I thought I should be able to come to some better judgment concerning her from her demeanour in prison; and yet, situated as I was—a witness for the prosecution, I could hardly hope that any overtures of mine would be received otherwise than with the same haughty indifference that had already characterised the counsel for the defence, who was evidently resolved to be at war with every witness who attempted to exhibit a sympathetic feeling for the prisoner.

I started off to a friend's house, and held a long consultation. He was not a man so eminently gifted with brains, that I could hope much from him in the way of conjecture or suggestion: but, then, the value of talking over a matter confidentially to some one is, that it enables us to put our own thoughts and surmises into language—that it forms something like a logical arrangement of the ideas, and frequently elucidates truths, and exposes sophisms which otherwise might have eluded observation for some time. Therefore is it that I have had a habit, whenever I found myself in any great perplexity, of talking the matter over with some one, from whom, perhaps, I expect nothing in return but secrecy. In this case, however, my friend spoke out fully and clearly, and when he had heard all I had to say, he replied,—

"The proofs of this girl's guilt are so numerous and ample, that if she be not convicted, nobody ever can be again. The evidence is direct."—" No, no," I said; "only circumstantial. Nobody saw her do the deed, you know."

"Almost. What would be your opinion if you were on the jury?"—" Don't ask me. I don't know, really. Thank God, I am exempt from serving in such a capacity."

"She will be hung."—" Do not say so. The thought is too terrible to suppose. Something may yet arise to acquit her of the dreadful charge; I pray to God it may, and can but say, that if she be guilty, never again, while I live, will I trust a face of innocence and heaven-like simplicity. You have not seen her, and can have no conception how beautiful she is."

"Yes; but people are not to poison whole families because they are beautiful."—" I admit it—I admit it. I see I can do nothing; but there has grown up somehow in my mind an invincible repugnance to Charles Stevenson. Henceforward I will hold no communication with him. His disingenuousness regarding the large amount of money he had, has given his character a shock to my mind that I cannot get over; and as a man has an undoubted right to pick and choose his own associates, I can only say that I will not have him for one of mine."

"He must be a very respectable man."—" Ah, you say so, because he has eighty thousand pounds, I suppose?"

"Well, surely that is enough to make a man respectable, is it not?"—" In the world's eyes. Adieu! adieu!"

"Good bye;—I do hope, since you feel yourself interested, that something may happen to clear this girl of the suspicions that attach to her—for myself, I can only say with you,—Thank God, I am not on the jury."—" It is an awful responsibility, and one I never would willingly run, let the case be as clear as mortal man could possibly make it."

I left my friend, and walked homeward. It was late, rather, and I walked very rapidly, for I was anxious to reach my own house, as I rather expected that I should be wanted. My friend lived some distance up Shoreditch, and my nearest way to Broad-street, or, at least, that part of it in which I lived, was to come down to a place leading from Bishopsgate, called Alderman's-walk, which is bounded on one side by the churchyard. This walk was closed at a particular hour in the evening—perhaps it is now—and a watchman was at the Bishopsgate-street end; but he used always to allow me to pass through, which to me was sometimes a great convenience. The other end was always open—it was only stopped as a thoroughfare from some whim or other.

The watchman saw me, and opened the gate, allowing me to pass on, which I did very sharply, and had proceeded half way down the walk before I saw two persons in earnest conversation in a very dark nook of the wall. Of course I should have passed on without noticing them, had not something particular attracted my attention—as I was hurrying by, I saw the man stamp with his foot, and heard him exclaim,—

"D—— you and the masquerade too; you are always harping upon that."

I staggered back apace. The voice I knew at once. It was that of Charles Stevenson—I could not be mistaken. In another moment I had stooped, so that I was completely in the shadow of the wall, and creeping as closely as I could to the conversing parties, I listened, with all the power of hearing I was master of, to what should fall from their lips.

"Very well," said the woman, in a whining sort of voice; "I won't say any more about it—but you know it was odd. For you to be going to a masquerade—where was it? I looked in all the newspapers, and there was none mentioned."—" Psha! it was a private party."

"Oh, then, that accounts for it, and for another thing beside."—" Come on, come on," said Charles.

The woman continued speaking, and they both walked on so quickly, that I could not detect what she said. I followed as closely as I could to avoid suspicion, and when they emerged into the wide open street, I was doubly cautious, for I knew that if Charles should chance to look back, he would be surprised to see me, and that I did not choose should occur. I

DIARY OF A PHYSICIAN.

hung back, therefore, and had just time to pop into a doorway, when I saw them pause and separate. Charles walked hastily towards Cornhill, and the female took an opposite direction, passing down the first street on the other side of the way.

I am not much given to hesitation; but the separation of Charles Stevenson and the young female was so sudden, that, before I could make up my mind whether to follow either of them at all, or which one, they had both disappeared, leaving me in a state of much surprise and bewilderment in the street.

I walked very slowly the remainder of the distance home, deeply revolving in my mind what I had heard; and yet, what could I make of it?—just nothing at all. Charles Stevenson had kept some secret appointment with a woman; she had upbraided him with going to some masquerade without her, and there was an end of the whole affair.

All I could say was, "Well, after all, this Charles is not the quiet, immaculate sort of young man I thought him." The circumstance might afford me another reason for cutting his acquaintance; but that was all I could, upon consideration, make of it.

There was one determination, however, which I had been hesitating about some time, that became now fixed, and that was, that I would place myself in communication with the solicitor for the defence of Martha Renton, and let him know all that accident had disclosed to me with regard to Mr. Charles Stevenson.

This step could not be taken with any degree of propriety till the following morning; but after going home, and finding I was not wanted, I started off to Keppel-street at once, for I wished very much to see Mrs. Stevenson and the two girls, in order to ascertain what they knew regarding Charles's fortune. I made good haste, for I thought I should get there before he could reach home; and when I knocked at the door, the first thing I said to the footman was,—

"Is Mr. Charles at home?"—"Yes, sir," was the reply.

"Indeed! When did he come home?"—"He has not been out, sir."

"Not out?"—"No, sir; he has been lying down for a few hours, feeling rather poorly; but I will let him know you are here, if you please, sir."

I looked hard at the footman, as I said,—

"Are you sure?"—"Oh, quite, sir. Mr. Charles is in—Ann, ain't he?" to the female servant, who at the moment came down the staircase.

"Oh, yes," she replied; "he rang for his gruel which I have just taken him. He says he is all the better for his sleep."

I felt staggered, but not convinced. I could fancy myself in the situation of a man who had seen something and sworn to it, but finds every one else who happened to be with him contradict him point blank.

"I will see Mrs. Stevenson," I said, "if it is not too late." —"The family are up, sir," said the footman.

I handed him my card. In five minutes more, I was in a small drawing-room, where were Mrs. Stevenson and her two daughters, in deep mourning. There was upon their countenances a gloom of absolute despairing grief, which it was most painful to look upon. Truly, they had felt this bereavement most deeply.

"Madam," I said, "I have many apologies to make for this interview at so late an hour."—"Do not say so, doctor; we are always glad to see you, at any time."

"You must fight up against this overwhelming sorrow—a-hem! I have to congratulate you upon Charles, at all events, being in a situation to protect you all."—"Yes," said Mrs. Stevenson, quite calmly.

"Oh, you are aware, then ——"—"Of the eighty thousand pounds? Oh, yes; he told us. We are his guests here, and in no respect can we complain of his conduct towards us.

He has compromised with the creditors, bought all the furniture at a valuation, and permits us to reside here as usual."

"For which you feel very much obliged to him, I suppose, madam?"

"How can we feel otherwise?"—"Very true. Well, then, I have nothing further to say. I came to offer you what consolation I could, and I see you know all the news I thought I was bringing to you."

"Sir," said Emma, the youngest of the girls, "I, for one, will not be dependent on the bounty of Charles; as an old friend of my poor father's, let me implore you to find me, if it be possible, some honest means of employment, by which I may free myself from this thraldom."—"Why, doctor," said Mrs. Stevenson, "Charles has made an offer to Emma, which she has rejected."

"Oh, indeed."—"She cannot love him."

"Love him, mother!" cried Emma; "how can you use the word? I despise him."—"My dear, you must be mistaken."

"No, mother. I saw him with my own eyes take down the portrait of my father, and I heard him tell the man to take it away. Does he not sneak in and out of the house at all times? Sometimes in affected mourning, and at others in the gayest dresses? Does he not shed mock tears here, and drink wine in his bed-room to such an excess as to produce intoxication? Love him, indeed! Oh, if there be not a better man in the world than Charles, our cousin, I shall glory in remaining as I am, unwed, and loving no one. I repeat, I despise him."

This was a matter in which I felt it would be impertinence for me to interfere. Mrs. Stevenson burst into tears, and the sister looked pale and frightened. I rose to take my leave, saying,—

"Ladies, I sincerely sympathise in your afflictions, and hope that time will assuage your griefs."

I left the house, still more resolved upon going to Mr. Bell, the solicitor for the defence, in the morning. I sought my own home and repose; but my thoughts were too painfully occupied with considerations regarding the unhappy girl who lay in Newgate, in all probability awaiting a dreadful doom, to allow me to sleep; and it was not until the daylight had made every object in my chamber clearly visible, that I succeeded in snatching about an hour and a half's repose, ere the usual hour of rising called me again to the bustle of existence and the struggle of real life.

My interview with Mr. Bell was short, and yet to the purpose. He at first, certainly, rather placed himself upon his defence, and adopted a show of hostility towards me; but when I said to him, in a voice of friendliness, which could not be mistaken,—

"Sir, I am only a medical witness in the case as regards Martha Renton, and the testimony I have to give is of a nature that no one can dispute; and now, with sympathy for her, I have come to tell you of matters which may lead to something affecting the credit of the principal witness."

He hesitated, and said, more mildly,—

"We are, of course, sir, grateful for anything which can assist a client. Your profession, and your position in life, of course, at once precludes the possibility of any sinister motive being imputed to you; and I assure you there was but one reason for our receiving you with unfriendly eyes, and that was, that you seemed on such very friendly terms with Charles Stevenson, whose mode of giving his evidence was of such a truly dangerous character to our client."

"Precisely," I said; "I see that; and I should not have come to you, had I still been on such intimate terms with that young man; and the reasons that I am not, may be beneficial to your client, in some way."—"Then, sir, of course, I am glad to see you."

I related to him all that had taken place as regarded my discovery of Charles's eighty thousand pounds in the funds; and then, with a reservation that I might have been mistaken, I informed him of how I believed I had seen Charles in the City, and then how I had heard he had been in bed at Keppel-street all the time, instead. He heard me with great attention, and at my conclusion he said,—

"Sir, will you accept my thanks for this communication, and at the same time excuse me from making any remarks upon it until I have consulted Mr. Denbigh, who is more qualified than I to judge of the importance of what you have detailed?"—"Certainly," said I.

Mr. Bell then very civilly bowed me out of his office, and then I was again not an inch forwarder than before in my hopes or my conjectures on the subject, which was so uppermost in my mind. I gave up, as far as I possibly could, the attempt to task my own imagination on the matter, and resolved to wait with what philosophy I could till the trial should come on, and then see what came out during the course of that most painful investigation.

I made up my mind that I would not even enter into conversation on the subject with any one. It was not long that I had to wait, for the sessions were on, and the calendar was by no means a heavy one, so that I might fairly expect shortly to know on what particular day the case was likely to come on. At length, the matter was mentioned in court, and the recorder, who was on the bench, announced that, on the following Friday, instead of the Thursday, on which it would have fallen, the trial of Martha Renton would take place.

"You know the reason of that?" said the person who told me.

"What reason?" said I.—"Why, you know, if she is found guilty, she will be hanged on the Monday, and so have the Sunday extra, you understand, to live."

I, of course, knew this arrangement well enough; but my mind had been so occupied with other things, that it had slipped my memory, and I shuddered now to think how the poor girl's fate seemed to be so dreadfully pre-arranged.

It was then Tuesday, so there was ample time for painful conjecture; and now that the exact day of trial was fixed, in what the newspapers called "The Great Poisoning Case," the popular excitement appeared to gain fresh strength, and people talked continually of Martha Renton, and of the chances of her guilt or her innocence.

Anecdotes were invented and told of her—wretched attempts at her portrait appeared in the shop windows. A thousand lies were invented every day concerning her, for the amusement and recreation of that pleasant portion of the public who have nothing better to do than to delight in the miseries of their fellow creatures.

All this, however, could not last long. The day of trial rapidly approached—it came; a dull, heavy, misty morning, ushered in that day on which the fate of Martha Renton was to be decided. Alas! what must have been her feelings as that dawn came upon her in her prison? What horrors of anticipation may have visited her in the previous night's uneasy slumbers! Oh, it was dreadful to think what a state of mind might be hers! Alas! poor Martha! if guilty, you have had your punishment already in the terrors of anticipation; if innocent, how frightful was the injustice you endured!

I, of course, had made up my mind to be at the trial, if all the world was ill, and wished to do me the honour of calling in my professional aid.

Charles Stevenson had never come near me since the time when I had treated him with a coldness about which there could be no mistake. What he thought were my thoughts I often wondered; but he knew, I suppose, that I could allege nothing against him, and so felt indifferent as to whether I were pleased or angry.

From the morning when I called upon Bell, I had felt myself on good terms with the defence of the prisoner, although I fully felt the propriety of not holding any close or marked communication with those engaged in it. The fact is, that, despite of all the astounding facts which were in array against her, I could not convince myself of her guilt, and did cling to a hope that something would yet happen of a favourable nature towards her.

* * * * *

How dense was the crowd assembled in and about the Old Bailey on that memorable morning! Barristers from all parts came wigged and gowned to hear the trial, and great was the demand for wigs and gowns by enterprising individuals, who thought that, by such means and appliances, doorkeepers would be awed into submission, and admit them at once into the body of the court, in preference to less favoured individuals. But in many cases it was evident that wisdom was not in the wig, for they failed most signally.

As regards myself, I of course, as a witness, was duly admitted; and, besides, I knew a very stout gentleman, who was under-sheriff, and he not only took care that I was not detained, but he likewise provided me a first-rate situation in the jurors' waiting-box, so that I could see everybody else very much pushed about, without receiving any great annoyance myself—not that then my mind wandered to such trivialties. Alas! I was nervous, wretched, and unhappy, at what might be the issue or that day's proceedings.

Before the judge took his seat there came a tremendous hail-storm, which dashed down with so much fury, that it threatened the demolition of every window in the place, and for many minutes made the court quite dark, so that the business was suspended, until the fury of the storm had abated.

A trial was to precede that of Martha Renton, but I was told it would not last long, and so I found was the case. It was a lady tried for shoplifting. The theft against her was fully proved by competent testimony. The conduct of her husband on the occasion was found to have been that of a man fully aware of the theft, but who wished, as the counsel remarked, to bounce the prosecution. But—but—it was proved the lady kept a carriage, and some mighty respectable people came forward and said they did not see her do the robbery, upon the principle of the man who stole the spade. Two witnesses swore they saw him steal it, but he got twenty who swore they did not see him steal it—therefore he was acquitted. The shoplifting lady was acquitted because she was well enough off to know better.

All this disgusted and annoyed me; but my feelings were soon engrossed in the great interest I now felt in what was immediately about to ensue. There was a slight bustle, and Martha Renton was placed at the bar.

Every one who has been to that most mournful of all exhibitions—the trials at the Old Bailey—is aware of the strange look that the scattered herbs have as they lie on the bar before the wretched prisoners. They look as if placed there to work him, by bringing to his mind recollections of the free air of Heaven, and the open country, with all its dear attractions, as distinguished from the lonely cell in which he had passed so many weary hours.

I recollect once an old man being placed at the bar for the murder of a gamekeeper in some poaching affray. He had been dragged from the recesses of the New Forest to a cell in Newgate. Mournful change! I saw him when he was placed at the bar take up a handful of the green herbs. The sight overcame him, and with a burst of emotion he said,—

"Be these placed her to make the old man think of home? God help them as struck this blow to my heart!"

*   *   *   *   *

My eyes were fixed upon the bar, and never while I have life shall I forget the first sight I had of the face of Martha Renton, now that she had been so long confined within these walls, and was at length dragged forth to hear the awful question, to her, of life and death.

She was plainly but neatly dressed in black; her hair was confined by a small close cap; she was of a corpselike paleness, and the slight movement of her lips seemed to me as if she were saying something to keep up her courage. I was told afterwards, by those who were near her, that she kept on saying,—

"Oh, God! oh, God! oh, God!"

They thought she was mad; but, from the first word that was spoken, she became silent, and, with her hands clutched among the herbs I have mentioned, she looked fixedly and painfully in the face of the clerk of the arraigns, as, with professional indifference and rapidity, he read the indictment.

"Guilty, or not guilty?" he cried.

Martha shuddered, as if the question had been addressed to some one else, and then the turnkey tapped here on the shoulder, and explained that she was required to answer. She flung up her hands above her head, in an attitude that I looked upon with sad interest. It was at once natural and terrible, and then, with shrieking accents, she cried,—

"Not guilty, by Heaven!"—"That will do," said her counsel, half rising.

Her hands dropped to her side, and she pronounced, in a strange, hysterical manner, the words,—

"That—will—do."

There was now a bustle at the table where the barristers sat—the crier of the court demanded silence. Several gentlemen came on to the bench from the judge's door, where already were almost all the civic dignitaries who had the right to be there. Then there was a pause, and the counsel for the prosecution slowly rose. There was a breathless silence, and thus he commenced his address to the jury:—

"Gentlemen of the jury, when an advocate, upon rising to state a case for the consideration of a jury, professes to feel most reluctant to press hard upon the unhappy person whose conduct it is his duty to animadvert upon, he is generally given credit for much more finesse than sincerity. He is generally considered, gentlemen, as in arms against the unfortunate person against whom his remarks may be directed; but God forbid, gentlemen, that this should be the case with me!

"I can imagine a counsel in a court of law fighting for a victory; but when the liberty or the life of a fellow-creature is the guerdon of triumph, I then say, God forbid, gentlemen, that the advocate should become a partizan; God forbid that he should strain a fact, or draw from a fact one unnatural sequence to the prejudice of a prisoner.

"Gentlemen, it is my painful duty to lay before you certain circumstances in the order in which it is presumed that they have occurred. I shall lay those circumstances before you dispassionately. The prisoner at the bar is accused of the murder of Mr. William Stevenson. She pleads not guilty to that charge. My task is to let you know upon what grounds she has been called upon to plead at all.

"I am instructed, gentlemen, that about two years ago Martha Renton, the prisoner at the bar, was, with a most unimpeachable character, received into the family of the late Mr. Stevenson, where, up to the present unhappy train of circumstances, she conducted herself to the satisfaction of all who were called upon to form an opinion upon her conduct.

"A very short time since a Dr. ——, who is the family medical man of the Stevensons, was called upon by a member of that family, with the news that there was much indisposition among them. That gentleman attended them, and the indisposition vanished. It vanished, although but to occur again in a far more aggravated shape. He was sent for hurriedly on the seventh day of the last month, and then he found that several medical gentlemen were already there, and that confusion and dismay were in the family of the Stevensons. These medical gentlemen, as well as Dr. ——, will be brought before you, and they will one and all depose that the symptoms of illness under which the whole of the Stevensons laboured were such as to leave no doubt in their minds that a deadly irritant poison had been administered to them.

"Yes, gentlemen, poison. I can see and translate the look of horror with which you hear the name mentioned. Poison, gentlemen, had been administered. The most dastardly, the most despicable, the meanest, most cowardly, un-English crime of poisoning, had shown itself in the peaceful bosom of a family, who had no reason to suppose they had an enemy in the world.

"The poison was there, gentlemen; some fiend in human shape—some monster, with a devilish imagination, had infused a deadly drug into that family's food! The crime was not unproductive of results. The father and son fell victims to the hellish plot! The other members of the family escaped from death, and are now, with debilitated constitutions, awaiting the issue of this sad and terrible investigation.

"One member of this family, gentlemen of the jury, is a Mr. Charles Stevenson, a nephew of the gentleman whose murder the prisoner at the bar is this day arraigned for. This Mr. Charles Stevenson had a dreadful suspicion that poison had been the medium of the family's indisposition. One day his suspicions were dreadfully confirmed.

"He was ascending the staircase, when, tucked beneath the carpet, he found a packet of white powder in a blue paper, which he took to Dr. ——, who had it analysed by an eminent chemist, who at once pronounced it to be arsenic, in as pure a state as he had ever seen it.

"Immediately upon this discovery it was, and before any steps could be taken by any of the bewildered parties, that the dreadful scene ensued which terminated in the death of two innocent persons, and the prisoner at the bar occupying the painful position in which she now is. A severe judicial inquiry, gentlemen, ensued at the house in Keppel-street, after the deaths of the parties I have mentioned to you. At that inquiry it was resolved to search the boxes of the servants—all were willing but the prisoner at the bar—she objected, but the box was searched, and some blue paper packets, identical with the one which had been previously discovered by Mr. Charles Stevenson, were there found.

"Gentlemen of the jury, these packets have been likewise found to contain arsenic in the same form as that on the staircase discovered by Mr. Charles Stevenson.

"Gentlemen of the jury, evidence will be brought before you of whom this poison was purchased, and I am instructed that the person who indiscreetly vended it is in a position to swear that it was purchased by the prisoner at the bar.

"Gentlemen, Heaven knows I have not the wish to say anything in aggravation of the circumstances. Had I the wish, it is not necessary, for such facts speak trumpet-tongued. A case more divested of technical difficulty, I never met with. The task of the counsel for the prosecution lies in a nut-shell. God help the unhappy prisoner. Should aught occur to turn from her the full tide of suspicion, who will be, in all this crowded court, more rejoiced than I?"

The counsel for the prosecution sat down, and a deathlike stillness pervaded the court. Then he glanced at some papers before him, and said,—

"Dr. ———."

It was my name, and I started up. I heard some one sobbing bitterly in the body of the court. It was the prisoner's sister.

"Silence!" said the usher, in his monotonous tones, and I stepped into the witness-box and was sworn.

I scarcely expected to have been called upon first, and yet, when I come to consider of it, it was a natural enough proceeding, for I was in a condition to depose to the first indisposition of the family of the Stevensons, and the symptoms attendant thereon. Moreover, it was by my means that the first packet of arsenic had been duly analysed and found to be that deadly drug.

All eyes were fixed upon me. At the prisoner I dared not look; I feared the glance of blank despair which I had seen upon her countenance when last I turned my eyes upon it.

From the elevated position in which I now stood, I had a better view of the court, and almost the first person upon whom my eyes rested was Charles Stevenson, with a face as white as any paper I ever saw, and his eyes rivetted upon the young girl who occupied so painful a position in that court.

At the moment, by an impulse I could not resist, I pointed towards him, and all eyes were turned to him, including even those of the judge. Not a word was spoken, but every one appeared fully aware that that miserable-looking man was in some way largely mixed up in the proceedings.

The address of the counsel, as may well be supposed, had been listened to with the attention of despair by Martha Renton, and so enchained had all her faculties been, that it was not until this moment she seemed thoroughly to comprehend that it was over. Then just as the counsel had fixed his eyes upon me, and was about to speak, she cried, in shrieking accents, that produced a most extraordinary sensation in the court and terrified many persons,—

"No—no—no—I did not do it—who dares to say I did such a deed? 'Tis false. Heaven surely will protect the innocent? Gentlemen, I could not do it—I did not dream of such a deed. What could I get by such an awful crime? God! I am innocent—I am innocent!"

The whole court was thrown into confusion. The judge rose and demanded of the officers to preserve order; several females, who had no business there, fainted; but females push in anywhere. Many persons tried to leave the court, and several voices, on the impulse of the moment, called out aloud,—

"The girl is innocent—she could not do it! Look at her—she could not do it."—"Officers," said the judge, "take these persons into custody; I will commit them."

"For God's sake, prisoner," cried Mr. Denbigh, rising, "I implore you, for your own sake, as well as for the sakes of those who have to defend you, to be still."

There was no need for such an appeal. The ebullition of feeling was over, and Martha Renton had sunk with her head on her hands on the front of the dock.

A few moments more, and order was restored. Martha Renton remained in the same attitude in which she had fallen, and the counsel for the prosecution proceeded to examine me touching what I knew of the case. The amount of that knowledge the reader is already in possession of, and, therefore, I need not pause in my narrative to recapitulate it. I was not altogether a quarter of an hour in the witness box, and the counsel for the prisoner said he had no questions to ask me.

The next witness was the chemist, who, at my request, had analysed the powder contained in the blue paper. He deposed that it was arsenic, and that he had likewise made an analysis of what was found in the prisoner's box, with a like result. Indeed he considered that both samples must have came from the same bulk.

Of him no questions were asked by the prisoner's counsel. Everything was going off rapidly and smoothly enough, until Charles Stevenson was called, and his evident state of terror and suffering led every one present to believe that something peculiar was about to happen. It would appear as if the counsel thought the perturbation of Charles might tell against the evidence he came to give, for he hastened to give an explanation of the cause, by saying,—

"Mr. Stevenson, I believe I am right in saying you were much attached to the prisoner at the bar?"—"Yes, yes," replied Charles. "Yes, yes."

"No wonder, then, that you betray much agitation at the peculiar circumstances in which you are placed; but you must conquer your feelings, and let the jury know what of your own knowledge you can state to be the cause of this lamentable affair."

Thus urged, Charles came out with the story about his suspicions, and the blue packet he found on the staircase, as well as how he had seen Martha pick it up.

There was a breathless stillness in the court while he made this statement, and everybody felt that the girl was doomed. The counsel for the prosecution sat down, and Charles was about to leave the witness-box, when Mr. Denbigh rose, and said in a loud voice,—

"Stay, sir."

He turned, and appeared on the point of making some insolent reply, but prudence restrained him, and he stood clutching the rail before him, and trying to get up a smile of composure, which sat very oddly upon his countenance.

"Now, Mr. Stevenson," said the counsel, "what position did you hold in your uncle's family?"—"Position, sir?"

"Yes, position. Remember you are upon your oath, and that I have a sacred duty to perform, and will not be tampered with, sir."—"I—I lived with them."

"On their bounty?"—"Not exactly."

"Oh, not exactly. You have money of your own?"—"I have."

"How much, and how long have you had it?"

"I throw myself upon the consideration of the court," said Charles. "What have these questions to do with the subject under examination?"

"I think," said the judge, "you will exercise a sound discretion by answering the counsel."

"I bow to your decision, of course," said Charles. "If it be necessary that my private affairs should be made public, I can say that I am in independent circumstances."

"To the tune of eighty thousand pounds, I presume," added the counsel; "and yet your uncle died insolvent; and only two years ago you were received into his house as a friendless, destitute orphan. Is all this true, sir?"—"It is true, sir."

"And very strange! Now, sir, a parade has been made in this court about your attachment to the prisoner. Pray did you ever slink into her chamber at night, uninvited?"—"I—I was there once."

"And what occurred?"—"I—I left."

"Will you swear you did not go down on your knees and beg the pardon of the prisoner, and promise better behaviour if she did not expose your conduct to your uncle?"—"On my knees?"

"Yes, sir, on your knees. Will you swear you did not make an audacious attempt upon the virtue of this young person, and then go on your knees to ask her forgiveness when you found you were foiled?"—"Have it your own way."

"No, I will have it your way. Answer my question."—"Well, I did, then. I was sorry."

"Sorry you could not succeed. No doubt you were. Pray, sir, where were you on the night of the sixteenth instant?"—"The sixteenth?"

"Yes, the sixteenth."—"I don't recollect."

"Indeed! you don't recollect? I will refresh your memory. You were in Alderman's-walk, Bishopsgate, talking with Margaret Day."

Charles Stevenson clung to the rail in front of him or he must have dropped. I saw his knees bend, and he trembled as if his last hour had come.

"Answer me, sir," cried the counsel, in those high, indignant tones, which counsel in our criminal courts know so well how to assume, and when to assume.

"Margaret Day!" gasped Charles, as if the very name was a terror to him. "Did you say Margaret Day?"—"I did."

"Well, I—I don't care about that. Hitherto I have been esteemed discreet, and—and—quiet; not at all fast; but since, because—my—my poor uncle has been murdered, it is thought necessary that my little private affairs should be—be—brought to light. I do know Margaret Day."

"Oh, you recollect now?"—"Yes—yes—of course."

"How long have you known her?"—"About a year."

"Now, sir, on your oath, state if you did or did not meet her on the night of the sixteenth instant, in Alderman's-walk?"

Charles hesitated, and then said,

"I do not keep an exact account of all my actions. An innocent, unsuspicious man, may surely be excused for not doing so; but with regard to this date of the sixteenth, on which you have stumbled, and seem to think important, it so happens that I can prove I was at home and unwell on that evening."

"You swear that?"—"I do," said Charles, more boldly. "I was in bed on that evening, suffering from a very severe cold, as well as from exhaustion consequent on the remedies I had used to rid myself of it. There is, I humbly and respectfully submit to the court, an attempt to bully me out of my evidence in this case. God knows how ready I would be to advance anything that could be of importance to the prisoner, but I am on my oath, and cannot be bullied from the truth by a hired advocate."

"Witness," said the judge, "you had better abstain from such remarks as you have just made."

Charles bowed, and the counsel said,—

"You threw in that very well, Mr. Stevenson; but the jury will see that anger at your cross-examination has extinguished the delicate sensibility with which you regarded the situation of the poor friendless girl at the bar, who is looking to Heaven and this court for that justice which she is entitled to receive, being innocent of the dreadful crime laid to her charge. Now, sir, on the night of the dreadful occurrences in Keppel-street, which laid the foundation for this painful inquiry, did you, or did you not, partake of the mulled elder wine?"—"I did."

"You swear that?"—"Most certainly. My dreadful condition afterwards attested the fact."

"Oh! you looked upon your dreadful condition, then, as an attestation of the fact?"—"It was in consequence."

"Who was taken ill first?"—"I was."

"And yet you recovered?"—"I did, as you see; but I do not think my constitution will ever recover. I am not the same man I was."

"You may have gained by the exchange, though, you know. But now, sir, I have a very serious question to ask of you. Are you a frequenter of theatres?"—"No."

"Balls, concerts, or masquerades?"—"Masquerades?"

"Yes. You know what a masquerade is, I presume?"—"I really do not know what you mean."

"Indeed, then you may stand down. But I have not done with you. Call Doctor ———."

Charles made way for me; and as I again ascended the witness-box I just caught sight of his countenance, and saw that it looked as if during his examination twenty years had passed over him.

"Were you in Alderman's-walk, Bishopsgate," I was asked, "on the evening of the 16th instant?"—"I was."

"Who did you see there?"—"Mr. Charles Stevenson and a female."

"Whom you should know again?"—"Certainly not."

"But as to his identity you are positive?"—"I am as positive as any human being can be, prone as we all are to make the most dreadful errors as to identity."—"Where did you go on that same evening?" said the counsel for the prosecution, rising.—"To Keppel-street."

"Did you find Mr. Charles Stevenson there?"—"I did."

"And seriously unwell?"—"That I cannot say."

"You may stand down."—"Call Charles Arrowsmith," said the counsel for the prosecution, and immediately a respectable-looking lad was ushered into the witness box and sworn.

"Your name is Charles Arrowsmith?" commenced the counsel.—"It is, sir."

"What are you?"—"I am assistant to Mr. Martin, chemist and druggist, residing in the Hampstead-road."

"You serve in the shop, and are acquainted with the nature of the drugs generally which make up the stock?"—"I am, sir."

"State to the jury where, to whom, and under what circumstances, you have sold arsenic lately?"

There was a breathless stillness in the court as the lad, who was not above fifteen, but very intelligent, and by his language evidently well educated, detailed the following particulars,—

"One evening, about two months ago, at twilight, and before I thought it quite dark enough to turn on the gas in the shop, my master being out, a young woman came in."

"How was she dressed?"—"In a black velvet bonnet and a plaid shawl. There was a wreath of very much faded artificial flowers in the bonnet."

"Really," said Mr. Denbigh, "this witness is amazingly precise."—"I protest against this interruption," said the other.

"I beg your pardon. Go on."—"But lest this parenthetical observation, gentlemen of the jury, which my learned friend has thought proper to make, should produce any effect upon your minds, I beg to say, that it will come out in this intelligent witness's evidence that he had more than one opportunity of noticing the dress of this female. Now, Mr. Arrowsmith, pray proceed, sir."

"She asked me for some citric acid and bicarbonate of potass, and for a small quantity of the sesqui sulphuret of arsenic."

"Pray explain to the jury what these drugs are."—"Citric acid is crystallized lemon juice; the potass is prepared with carbonic acid gas, and the sesqui sulphuret of arsenic is the drug called orpiment."

"Go on, sir."—"She likewise asked for the acetate of morphine, tincture of valerian, and a small quantity of hydrochloric acid."

"What followed?"—"I supplied her with the whole of those articles; and I made the remark to her, that it was seldom a female was so well acquainted with the systematic names of drugs, to which she replied, 'Oh, my brother is a medical man, and it is for him I want them. I have seen so much of medical matters, that it would be hard if I had not attained a little knowledge of drugs.' I wanted to light the gas, but she begged me not, saying she had weak eyes."

"She paid for the drugs then, and went away?"—"She did, sir."

"And you had, in fact, supplied her with arsenic?"—"In the form of orpiment I had. I was not forbidden to sell orpiments. People might buy active poisons at any chemists' in many shapes, if they knew what to ask for."

"Did she pay you another visit?"—"She did, sir. A few evenings afterwards, at the same hour, and when, likewise, my master was out, she came again, and that time she asked me for arsenic in the purest form we kept it. I hesitated, and she said her brother was amusing himself with experiments on the preservation of anatomical subjects, as illness prevented him from leaving home, so I supplied her."

"Is arsenic used in such preparations?"—"It is, in combination with other matters."

"Had you not been forbidden to sell arsenic in the shop?"—"I had, except to those whom I know to be in the profession; and, after she was gone, I doubted the propriety of what I had done."

"Did you mention the circumstance to your master?"—"I did; I entered the sales in the day-book, but he made no remark about it, nor did I."

"She came again?"—"Yes. It was a relief to me to see her come again, for it convinced me all was right. She had more arsenic of me—and then more on two other occasions, till I again got uneasy, and would not serve her."

"Since when you have not seen her?"—"I have not."

"Look at the prisoner at the bar, and say if that was the person." The lad looked and then he said,—"I cannot tell."

An officer stepped forward obediently to a nod from the counsel, and produced a plaid shawl and black velvet bonnet, around which was a faded wreath of flowers. The counsel held them up to the witness, and said,—"Were those the articles worn by the woman who bought of you the arsenic?"—"They are similar."

"Place them on the prisoner." They were so placed, and then the lad looked at her again.—"Very like," he said; "but I thought she was taller."

"Is your shop large?"—"No, very small."

"And this court large, comparatively, which may well account for your thinking the prisoner at the bar shorter than she who bought of you the drugs."

"Can you swear to the prisoner at the bar as being the same person whose dealings with you you have detailed to the jury?" said the judge.—"No," said the boy, "I cannot swear to it, because I am not quite sure, gentlemen."

"You deserve great credit for the manner in which you have given your evidence," said the judge.

"I most cordially," said the prosecuting counsel, "concur in that opinion; and now, Mr. Arrowsmith, look at these blue papers, and tell the jury if they are the same you wrapped the arsenic in you sold in the manner you have detailed."—"I wrapped the arsenic in white papers."—There was a sensation through the court, as if this was favourable to the accused, but the lad instantly added,—"With an outer wrapper of blue, similar to these. On the inner white paper I wrote the words—'Arsenic—Poison.'"

"But these blue papers are similar to those you used?"— "They are."

"I have no further questions to ask you. Perhaps my learned friend has."

The counsel for the defence rose and said,—

"Charles Arrowsmith, you cannot identify the prisoner at the bar as the person to whom you sold the drugs?"—"I cannot."

"Your only suspicion is in consequence of the shawl and bonnet?"—"That is all."

"Gentlemen of the jury, how many plaid shawls and black velvet bonnets could be found in London? You may go down, sir."

An officer was next called to swear that he found the shawl and bonnet produced in the prisoner's trunk at Keppel-street, as well as the blue packets of arsenic, and of him no questions were asked for the defence.

Next came Mr. Martin, the chemist, who merely deposed that he kept arsenic in his shop, but that he had not looked at his day-book, so as to notice his sales. He swore he had made an analysis of the arsenic found in the prisoner's box, and found it similar to that he kept in stock.

A Mr. Osburn was now put in the witness-box, and, in answer to questions, said,—

"I am a stock-broker—I have from time to time bought stock for Mr. Charles Stevenson. He has now about fifty thousand pounds in English securities—rather over that amount than under. I was much surprised at the insolvency of his uncle. He was always esteemed a rich man. I know nothing of the domestic affairs of the family further than that, till Mr. Charles came to me to buy stock for him, I always thought him quite dependent on his uncle for support."

The witness Arrowsmith now was recalled, and asked to fix a date to any one of the dealings with the female who had purchased arsenic of him.

He named the fourth day of the preceding month as one of those occasions, and then John Simms, a footman in the Stevensons' family, was called, and asked,—

"Was Martha Renton permitted holidays occasionally?"— "Yes, your worship, she *were*," he replied.

"Don't call me your worship, and try to speak English, will you? Do you recollect any of these occasions?"—"I are rayther forgetful, yer worship, but my *dairy* ——"

"Your what?"—"My *dairy* will show."

John took out a book from his pocket as he spoke, and the counsel said,—

"Oh, you mean your diary, do you?"—"Well, I said my dairy, didn't I?"

"Go on—go on."

John turned over several leaves, and then made a full stop, as he said,—

"Here it is."

"Can you," said the judge, "swear to the accuracy of what is put down in that book?"—"Suttenly, yer worship, suttenly."—"Very well."

"Monday, 4th," commenced John, "I believe that's the pint! Had some words with cook, cos she wanted to poke something into me which ——"

"What does he say?" said the judge. "The cook wanted to poke him?"—"He's coming, you see, to the point, my lord," said the counsel. "Go on, John Simms."

"But I wouldn't, and up said she, 'it wasn't my work,' all about cinder-sifting, to give her a clear bottom to cook on; so says I, 'make up your own back, and then poke it down,' and cook says, says she, '*warmints* is as warmint like does,' and then ——"

"I cannot understand a word of all this," said the judge.

"It's about the kitchen-fire, yer worship. Cook says ——"

"Did Martha Renton go out on the evening of the 4th of last month?" thundered the counsel.—"Ye—ye—yes; oh, yes—but ——"

"And how dressed?"—"In her plaid shawl and velvet bonnet; but cook and I—you see cook likes to preserve her ashes—but I don't, and so ——"

"Stand down—stand down."

There were very few persons indeed in the court who could stand the attack made upon their gravity by John Simms's evidence; and had not the occasion been one which was so eminently calculated to repress the least exhibition of mirth, no doubt John's "Dairy" would have produced roars of laughter.

As it was, many a covert smile might have been observed on many a mouth, and it was some moments before the counsel, who were not on the case, could acquire again the staid, serious demeanour, that became them in a court of justice, when the life of an unfortunate fellow-creature was at stake.

This examination of John Simms closed the case for the prosecution, and it was indeed a frightfully strong one. I shuddered for the fate of poor Martha Renton, who, notwithstanding all that was said against her, I could not yet believe to be guilty. I felt as if I were sitting at some heart-rending domestic drama, and seeing the innocent sacrificed without being able to change the horrible truthful denouement of the piece.

There was a slight stir and bustle in the court, now that the case against the prisoner was fairly over, and the judge retired for a few moments; a glass of water, I presume at her own request, was handed to the prisoner, who still said, faintly,—

"God help me!"

The jury I saw conversing together with serious countenances, and by the time the judge came back a general air of intense anxiety was manifest upon every countenance. Mr. Denbigh alone looked calm; his arms were folded across his breast, and he had fixed his eyes upon the ceiling, as if resolved to look at no one until the time should come for him to address the jury in behalf of his client.

The crier now called for silence, and in a few moments every sound was hushed. Expectation sat on every face except Martha's, and hers was buried in her hands.

Mr. Denbigh rose and cast an eagle glance around him. He seemed as if he had looked into every man's face individually then in court, and searched his very soul. I saw several shrink before the glance, and the jury remained in the attitudes in which he seemed to have caught them gazing at him, in a state of breathless attention.

"My Lord and Gentlemen of the Jury,—The unhappy prisoner at the bar is innocent of the crime laid to her charge; she is unhappy because she is wrongfully accused of so much atrocity. No heart can feel more sensitively than hers for the distresses and deep afflictions of the Stevenson family; but that she should be suspected to be the author or agent of those afflictions has almost driven her to the verge of madness, and quite to the confines of despair.

"It is for you, gentlemen of the jury, to rescue her from both, to restore her to herself, to restore her to sanity, to restore her to those friends who will with tears of joy receive her, and who are now plunged in affliction transcending description by the cruel circumstances in which she is placed; but she is innocent. There is a God above us, and surely truth shall prevail.

"Gentlemen, the evidence against the deceased, adduced before you with so much ingenuity this day, is of a purely circumstantial nature. There is not one positive fact to connect the prisoner with the wholesale poisoning which has filled the surviving portions of the Stevenson family with grief. It is, gentlemen, a principle in English criminal jurisprudence, that no one shall be convicted of an act upon evidence which admits of a rational explanation some other way than that which shall presume the guilt of an accused party.

"It is my duty to show you that the evidence you have heard to-day does admit of such rational explanation; and, likewise, I shall show you that this young girl's whole disposition, life, habits, and mode of action, give the lie to the charge against her. Gentlemen, she is innocent. God knows it is a fearful fight I have to wage for her, but she is innocent, and I am trebly armed.

"Gentlemen, the evidence resolves itself altogether to two heads; the one comes from Mr. Charles Stevenson; the other from Mr. George Arrowsmith. Arsenic was bought by a female of George Arrowsmith, arsenic was found in Martha Renton's box; but do not, for God's sake, gentlemen, fall into such false logic as to say, 'Martha Renton is a female, ergo, she bought the arsenic of George Arrowsmith, and placed it in her box.'

"That is the inference sought to be drawn; that it is a fair one, I deny. I do not for a moment throw doubt upon the evidence of Arrowsmith; it was given with equanimity and candour. A woman makes purchases of him, but he cannot say that woman was the prisoner, and there, gentlemen of the jury, is an end of that. A great deal has been made of this shawl and bonnet business; but are there no plaid shawls but the one worn by the prisoner? no black bonnets but of her having? Besides, Arrowsmith swears she who bought the poisons was taller than the prisoner, so that not only will he not swear that Martha Renton was the person, but he does virtually swear she was not!

"The learned counsel for the prosecution has certainly, with a vindictiveness which he should be above feeling in such a case, endeavoured to make out, that, because the chemist's shop is smaller than this court, the witness Arrowsmith made a false estimate of the height of the prisoner. Good God, gentlemen, is that the sort of suppositious evidence on which to condemn a person to death? Height, with my learned friend, is nothing in identity—locality everything. I hope, before my learned friend undertakes ever again the defence of a prisoner, he will recover from his state of mental delusion, and you may depend, gentlemen of the jury, that he will.

"Well, gentlemen, the papers of arsenic were found in the prisoner's box: but did she put them there—what evidence have we of that? none whatever—not a tittle; and so, gentlemen, in law, she did not place them there; I declare my conviction before Heaven, that, in fact, she did not place them there.

"That the Stevensons have been poisoned there can be no doubt; that the poison was arsenic, there can be no doubt; that some one placed that deadly drug in their mulled wine there is evidence to prove; but none to prove the prisoner at the bar was that person. The guilty party must have lived in the house; what so easy as to open a poor servant's box, with its common cheap lock, and place anything in it? Have we never heard of such things? Why, the trick is stale and obvious.

"But, then, there is Mr. Charles Stevenson's evidence. Gentlemen, I much wonder to what part of that person's evidence you gave credence? He deposes about this paper of poison on the staircase—what if some one had seen him find it, and he had been accused on such evidence of murder? Was even that evidence given well? Did the witness look like a witness of truth? Did he tremble or not? Did he turn pale at the mention of his money—of Margaret Day? Gentlemen of the jury, it is not fit to trust to appearances in this world, but look at the innocent, beautiful, young, gentle creature at the bar, and then look at Charles Stevenson. God forbid I should draw any inferences, but, on my soul, gentlemen, I don't believe one word of that man's evidence.

"But he has sworn to it, and suppose we reason upon it. What does it amount to? Just that Martha Renton was coming up stairs, and placed a piece of carpet straight. Is this to convict any one of murder?

"I say, gentlemen of the jury, that the poison found in this poor girl's box was placed there by the real criminal, be he or she who they may, and that if such poison be the same as was bought of the witness, Arrowsmith, it was not bought by Martha Renton, but by some one else with a plaid shawl and a black bonnet, who knew that suspicion was to be directed towards her, and took that additional mode of confirming it.

"Gentlemen, this young girl at the bar is a poor servant; a good, kind-hearted girl, but not a learned one. What, gentlemen, does she—what, I ask, can she know of sesqui sulphurets, of bicarbonates, of citric acid, of anatomical preparations, and hydro-chloric acid? Really it is too absurd to fancy for a moment the prisoner at the bar the 'learned Theban' who spoke of such things, and so lulled the suspicions of the apothecary's apprentice.

"Gentlemen of the jury, you will perceive that the evidence is, as I said at the outset of the few remarks I have made, of a purely circumstantial nature, and, for such evidence, extremely weak. The credit of the witness, Stevenson, is very much in jeopardy. He comes before you, convicted, on his own confession, of having made an atrocious attempt upon the virtue of this young girl, who resisted him heroically, and yet we are to presume she shudders at the smaller sin and commits wholesale murder. Gentlemen, where go all the probabilities of this case? If not in direct favour of the prisoner, then am I a madman, and as incapable of judging as my learned friend is of the stature of individuals.

"I shall now proceed to call evidence before you of the character of the prisoner at the bar, of her utter ignorance of sesqui sulphurets, and of the general kindly tenor of her life, which has passed in acts of far greater generosity and good feeling for others than could have been at all expected from the station in society which she occupies, and the very limited nature of her resources; and, besides, gentlemen, I have a hope of getting the witness, Margaret Day, before you, although she has disappeared for some time, to prove on oath, that she did meet Charles Stevenson on the 16th instant in Alderman's-walk, which he so stoutly denies in such positive terms."

Charles, at this moment, made an effort to leave the court, but he was so wedged in that he could not, and he gave up the attempt, striving to smile, but in such a ghastly, horrible manner, that those around him shrunk from him, shuddering, and would scarcely allow their garments to touch his.

"Margaret Day!" was shouted by the crier, and then all eyes were turned towards the witness-box, but no one made the least movement towards it. "Margaret Day!" he again cried.

There was no response, and the counsel then said,—

"As I expected, this woman is kept out of the way because her testimony would be favourable to the prisoner."

I turned my glance upon Charles Stevenson while the name was being called, and I could see that he was horribly agitated, and that when the name had been called twice without a response, he drew a long breath, as if a terrible load was taken off his heart.

A third time the crier shouted,—"Margaret Day!" and then the attempt was given up.

"Surely," said the judge, "you could have enforced the attendance of this witness?"—"No, my lord, we could not," replied the counsel. "We have seen her, and we had her positive promise; since then she has disappeared, so that we had no opportunity of binding her over to appear on this trial. Her absence, of course, says volumes in support of the fact, that her testimony is against what has been asserted by the witness, Charles Stevenson, who is her paramour, she being one of the most abandoned of characters."

Charles looked at the counsel, as if he would gladly have torn him to pieces. The witnesses now called consisted of parties who had known the prisoner from childhood—people who knew her disposition well—fellow servants, old play mates, and members of her family, the whole of whom gave her the very highest character for honesty, humanity, and the kindliest feelings that can adorn humanity.

Slowly the unhappy girl lifted her head from her hands, when she heard kindly words spoken of her in the tremulous, tearful voices of those whom she knew and loved. Her own tears flowed freely as she pronounced the well-known names to her heart of the witnesses, some of whom had come many miles to say a good word for the accused. Her fellow-servants, at Keppel-street, one and all, came forward in her favour, and John Simms offered to read many passages from his "Diary," of a favourable tendency.

All this was at length over, and the case was virtually closed. It was three o'clock when the counsel for the defence sat down, and then all eyes were directed towards the judge, who was very busy with his notes, and who coughed several times preparatory to commencing his summing up.

"Si—lence," cried the usher, and all was still. In another moment he commenced,—

"Gentlemen of the jury,—The prisoner at the bar stands charged with the murder of Mr. Stevenson, her master, by means of arsenic, administered to him according to the evidence which you have heard to-day, in mulled wine.

"Up to the present unhappy occurrence, it would appear that the prisoner had borne the most irreproachable character. It appears that Mr. Charles Stevenson, the nephew of the deceased gentleman, had his suspicions aroused that something of a mysterious character was proceeding in the family, on account of the simultaneous illness of its members, and, after that, he deposes that he found some white powder in a blue paper on the staircase, which, by competent chemical authorities, is pronounced to be arsenic. He then deposes to watching the spot where he made this discovery, and to seeing the prisoner stoop, as if to search for something, and then rise up with an appearance of disappointment.

"Of course, gentlemen of the jury, the obvious conclusion you are required by the prosecution to draw from this is, that the prisoner had placed the arsenic there, and was disappointed upon finding it removed; but that is all matter of conjecture merely, and certainly not sufficient grounds upon which to substantiate a verdict of guilty.

"After these circumstances, we find the family again taken suddenly ill, and with more fatal effects than on the previous occasion. The elder Mr. Stevenson dies, and likewise his son, Andover Stevenson, notwithstanding the exertions of medical men, no doubt of very competent skill, to save them.

"Then ensues a demi-official inquiry in the house, and the boxes of the servants are searched, in none of which, with the exception of that belonging to the prisoner at the bar, is any suspicious matter found. In her box, more arsenic is discovered, and, being submitted to a careful analysis, is found to be of a similar quality to that which was picked up on the staircase.

"After this, then, gentlemen of the jury, we have the testimony of the witness, Arrowsmith, as to the purchasing of arsenic of him by a person in a plaid shawl and a black velvet bonnet, around which is a wreath of faded flowers. This witness cannot identify the prisoner as that person. He thinks her not so tall.

"On the other hand, then, she is proved to possess garments of a similar appearance, and she is likewise proved to have been from home on the evening of the fourth of last month. There is wanting, however, a connecting link in the evidence to prove that the female in the plaid shawl, who bought the arsenic of Arrowsmith, is the prisoner at the bar. Those two circumstances of the poisoning of the Stevenson family, and the purchasing of arsenic from Arrowsmith, have no proved connection together, nor have they any necessary one, however inferential it may be, that they belonged to one and the same train of circumstances.

"Much has been said, and more hinted at, concerning a woman, by name Margaret Day. I wish we had seen that woman here, and further than that I cannot say of her.

"If the jury believe Charles Stevenson on his oath, they will, of course, give due weight to his evidence. If not, why then the prisoner must have the advantage of such non belief. It is not for me to brand a witness with perjury. You, gentlemen, saw the manner as well as I in which that young man gave his evidence, and you as well as I are aware of the singular circumstances which came out during his evidence.

"If you have any reasonable doubt of the guilt of the prisoner at the bar, you will, of course, give her the benefit of it; but if, on the other hand, you think that you have reasonable grounds for presuming her to be the person who purchased the arsenic of Arrowsmith, and you think that the discovery of the poison in her box be sufficiently confirmatory of her guilt, it will be your painful duty to pronounce a verdict accordingly.

"The counsel has suggested that the poison might have been placed in the prisoner's box by some one really guilty, who wished by such means to screen him or herself from the consequences of crime. Gentlemen of the jury, such things have been done, to the disgrace of human nature be it spoken, and you will, I am sure, give the prisoner all the benefit you can from the suggestion.

"I leave the case now in your hands, stating to you that it is one which calls for the most guarded inquiry and careful discrimination. Heaven direct you, gentlemen, in your decision, so that no injustice may be done to the innocent."

The judge ceased, and, when he had done so, you might have heard a pin drop in the court. On the whole, I considered the summing up favourable to the prisoner. That he thought the case a very strong one of circumstantial evidence, I could see; but I thought, likewise, that I could perceive he leaned very much to a merciful view of the affair, taking it as a whole in its aspect, as brought before him.

Poor Martha looked at him, while he was speaking, with a strange, bewildered gaze, as if she would have said,—

"What on earth are you talking about? Do you mean me?"

When he had finished, she dropped her head upon her hands again.

"Thank God!" I said to myself; "she does not seem to be aware that the crisis of her fate has approached so near as it now really has."

I hoped she would not look up again, at least till the verdict was announced; and what that verdict would be I never, in all the criminal trials I have attended, was in so much doubt about. Thankful, oh, most thankful, did I feel that I was not on the jury, although, had I been, I should have cut the Gordian knot of my perplexities by pronouncing unhesitatingly an acquittal.

The jury turned round in their box, and murmured for a few moments in a low tone. I could see a sanctified-looking wretch shaking his head with an expression on his Mawworm countenance, which I was quite convinced in my own mind meant guilty.

Then the foreman asked for leave to retire, and in a few moments the jury-box was empty. The judge whispered something to the lord mayor, who was on the bench, and away they went. Then the sheriff whispered to an alderman, and away they went. Some of the counsel took biscuits from their bags and covertly munched them up, while I could see, in more than one instance, men and women among the spectators taking, extremely silly, something from a very small bottle, and then trying to look about them as if they had never thought of such a thing, and would have quite disdained to eat or drink in a court of justice.

As for myself, I neither felt thirst or hunger. My whole soul was absorbed in the case, and I waited with trembling impatience for the return to court of those twelve men who held upon their breaths the fate of a fellow-creature. Dreadful power, which all may well pray to be free from! At length there was a slight bustle, and I heard several voices say, in suppressed tones,—

"They are coming—they are coming."—"Si—lence!" said the crier.

The jury, one by one, came slowly back into their box. I counted them as they came, and I strove to gather from their countenances what would soon cease to be a matter for conjecture. They looked sad and solemn, and yet there was no sternness about them, and one I thought had a half smile upon his face. The sanctified man, indeed, looked quite happy.

"She will be acquitted," I thought, as I drew a long breath—"she will be acquitted."

The judge then came in very quickly, and with rather a red face, as if he had just swallowed something in terrible haste. Then came the lord mayor, and the aldermen, and the sheriffs. Silence was once more proclaimed, and the clerk of the arraigns, in his usual monotonous voice, said,—

"Gentlemen, are you agreed upon your verdict?"—"We are."

"Do you find the prisoner at the bar guilty or not guilty?"—"GUILTY."

The awful word "Guilty" rang in my ears like a funeral knell. To say that I had flattered myself with hopes that Martha would escape would be untrue; but still, prepared as I was for the result that had now ensued—prepared as I dare say was every one in court—the word fell with a dead and sickening shock upon my heart, which made me feel for a few moments extremely faint and ill; so that judge, jury, counsel, prisoner, and crowd, flitted before my eyes like the dim phantasies of a dream, until by an effort I recovered myself, and could see what was going on.

There was a death-like stillness in the court. I glanced towards the jury; some of them were actually weeping. I looked at the prisoner. She was standing erect, but pale as death, and her arms were folded across her breast in such an attitude of sad resignation, that it was enough to move a heart of stone to look at her. I turned my eyes towards the judge; a strange-looking black skull-cap was upon his head, and I could see that he trembled very perceptibly.

"Prisoner at the bar," said he, in a deep voice, "you have been found guilty of wilful murder. Can you show any reason why the sentence of the law should not be pronounced against you?"

There was a silence as of the grave; and then Martha said, in a low, sweet voice, that thrilled through every heart,—

"Yes."

Of course all eyes were upon her; and the judge, in a voice of much emotion, said,—

"The court will hear you."—"I am innocent," she said—"I am innocent!"

Then there was a long pause; and the judge, scarcely able to speak from feeling, added,—

"Is—that—all?"—"It is all," said Martha; and her plaintive voice fell painfully upon my ears.

DIARY OF A PHYSICIAN.

The judge then clasped his hands in front of him, and leaned them on his desk, as I thought, to endeavour to suppress their trembling, and, after a few moments' silence, he said,—

"It is my most painful duty, Martha Renton, to pass upon you the sentence of the law. You have been tried by an upright, honest jury, who could have no motive of action in this most awful affair than to arrive, as far as human judgment will admit, at the truth.

"God help us all if we err. Human judgment is fallible; but if ever upon circumstantial evidence a human being is to be convicted of a crime, this is the case. I cannot help concurring in the verdict of the jury. We cannot, except on most substantial grounds, brand witnesses with perjury. I say, if we err in this case, God help us, for we are in a worse situation than you who suffer. I cannot hold out any hopes of mercy in this world. I would I could, but I cannot. My duty is a stern and a trying one, but it is straight before me, and I must not avoid it.

"Prisoner at the bar, the sentence of the law is, that you be taken back to the prison from whence you came, and thence to the place of execution, where you will be hanged

by the neck until dead. The Lord have mercy upon your soul. I ——"

Tears choked the judge's utterance, and he made a sign to have the prisoner removed. Martha had listened to the address in the same calm attitude she had fallen into after the verdict of guilty had been given; but now her fortitude gave way, and, with a shriek, she fell back into the dock in a state of insensibility.

Of course now she was immediately removed. The greatest confusion prevailed in the court, and the judge for many minutes was evidently too much affected to quell it. Finally, he left the bench, and then a tremendous rush was made to the door by persons who came to hear the trial, and now were anxious to carry away the news of how it had terminated to different quarters of the town. Among this throng I saw Charles Stevenson, looking like a ghost. I made my way up to him, and, in the excitement of the moment, I cried,—

"Charles Stevenson, if you have borne false witness against this girl, even Heaven's mercy cannot reach the amount of your great wickedness."

A groan of execration was given to him by the mob, and he shrunk back with an expression of abject fear.

"Help—help!" he said;—"officers! There is a prejudice against me. I shall be torn to pieces by the mob. As for you, sir," turning to me, "you shall pay dearly for what you have said."—"I despise your threats," said I, "as I despise yourself."

"Bring him out—bring him out!" cried several voices. "He's sworn the poor girl's life away! Bring him out!" —"You had better stay here," said one of the officers to him. "We can let you out by the governor's house in a few hours."

I heard no more, but instantly left the court, and repaired to a neighbouring hotel, where I had agreed to meet Mr. Bell, in the event of the verdict going on as it had. I threw myself into a seat, fairly exhausted, and in a few minutes he arrived, with Mr. Denbigh, the counsel, with him. They both looked pained and distressed; and Mr. Bell said, as he came up to me,—

"What's to be done now, doctor? Can you suggest any means of saving the girl, who I firmly believe to be innocent?"—"None—none," I said, mournfully, and I looked at Mr. Denbigh for his opinion.

"Gentlemen," he said, "God knows that, with a conviction of the innocence of the prisoner, I did all I could to save her. When the trial was over, the counsel for the prosecution whispered to me, 'Denbigh, my duty is now over. For God's sake, find this woman, Margaret Day, if you can.' "— "That was honest," said Mr. Bell.

"And then," continued Mr. Denbigh, "when I shook my head and said, 'But how are we to set about it?' he added, 'Do not lose sight of Charles Stevenson for a minute. Hunt him night and day. Do not let him be out of observation for a moment until Monday morning, and then it will be too late, for she will be hung, as the case stands at present.' "— "That advice shall be followed," said I, as I rose from my chair. "I will hunt him wherever he goes, I swear. He is now in Newgate."

"And will be quietly let out by the door of the governor's house," said Mr. Bell, "at eleven o'clock to-night. If you will undertake with me to watch for him, I am your companion in the enterprise."—"Thank you," I said, as I grasped his outstretched hand—"thank you. May God's blessing attend us!"

"Amen!" said Mr. Denbigh. "I will make a third, if you don't think there are too many,"—"Not at all," I cried,

—" not at all. We must only be extremely cautious not to be seen."

" Of course; and now let us, for our own sakes, as well as for the sake of the enterprise on which we are bound, take some refreshment. The court has adjourned, and I am free for to-day, as I have no case of importance now on my mind which might require study."

We had dinner at the hotel, and then we talked over the whole affair again and again, coming each time still closer to a conclusion of the innocence of Martha, although the evidence was so strongly circumstantial against her. We were all three extremely impatient for the time to arrive when we were to watch Charles Stevenson, and by about ten our impatience had increased to a pitch of perfect nervousness, which made me especially more fidgetty than ever I had been in my life before. Mr. Bell rang for a waiter, and when one came, he said,—

" Send your master here."

And, in a few minutes, the respectable master of the hotel made his appearance.

" Mr. Green," said Bell, " have you any great coats or cloaks in the house?"—" I dare say we have, sir."

" Oblige us with the loan of them, will you?"—" Certainly, sir."

The landlord retired, and in a few moments there were sent up to us some very ancient-looking coats, which were to the full shabby enough to disguise any one who had been in the habit of showing himself in respectable guise.

" Now," said Mr. Denbigh, " I think we may consider ourselves equipped for this enterprise thoroughly. There is just a chance, that, by watching this man very closely indeed, we may succeed in procuring evidence enough to induce a strong doubt in the mind of the judge of the guilt of poor Martha, and in that case the capital punishment is sure not to be inflicted upon her."

It was now getting late, and we made up our minds that we would lose nothing by not being in good time at the post we had assigned to ourselves. By a quarter past ten we sallied out from the hotel, looking as much like three conspirators as it was possible for, I hope, any three honest men to look.

" If we be not watched in our turn," remarked Mr. Bell, " by the police, on suspicion of being bad characters contemplating some felony, I shall be much surprised."—" And so shall I," added Mr. Denbigh; " but we can take measures, at all events, to prevent such an occurrence being any hindrance to us in our proceedings."

" Hindrance!" exclaimed Mr. Bell; " I think it will be of assistance. I am not at all sure that we should be able to get the assistance of any of the police in dodging Charles Stevenson; but if they dog us, and so are at hand when we want them, it will do just as well."—" Of course—of course."

In this, and such like discourse, we made our way towards the Old Bailey, and took up our station under an archway, as nearly opposite the governor's door as could be. Scarcely had we done so, than the louring aspect of the clouds began to fulfil their own prophecy, and down came rain—at first in large heavy drops, that fell like lumps of lead upon the pavement, and then in rattling streams, that made the streets smoke again with the ascending spray.

We were securely enough under cover; but how long we might be permitted to be so, we could not tell, and we began to think it highly probable that Charles Stevenson would either remain where he was, or probably ride home.

" We ought to be provided with a coach," said Mr. Bell, " for if he should send for one, see what a predicament we should be in."—" We will, at all hazards, have one," I said; and at that moment I saw a poor, miserable, half-starved looking lad, creep under the archway for shelter, with a look of humility, as much as to say,—" I believe I have no right to any shelter at all, but will try if I may be permitted to enjoy this one."

" Hilloa, my lad!" said I.—" Oh, I begs your pardon, sir," he said, " I'm a going."

" You mistake me. Here is a shilling for you ——"

" A what?"—" A shilling."

" For me?"—" Certainly."

" Oh, it's a bad 'un, of course; I ought to have thought o' that at first. Don't sell me any more jokes—I can't afford it —indeed I can't. Of course it's a bad 'un."—" Indeed it is not," said I. " All I want you to do is, to go for a coach to the nearest stand, and on the road you can satisfy yourself as to the genuineness of the coin."

I placed the shilling in his squalid-looking hand, and, after a stare of much wonderment at me for a moment, off he darted, as if he would break his neck.

" Farewell, both shilling and ragged boy," said Bell.

Mr. Denbigh laughed, but I said,—

" Gentlemen, I differ in opinion with you completely on that point. There was a something in that lad's face which convinces me he will come back."—" Very good. There is nothing like faith, doctor."

" What do you say to that?" exclaimed Mr. Denbigh, as a coach now made its way up towards the door of the governor's house, and then halted.

There now could be no doubt whatever of the prudence of providing ourselves with a vehicle, since it was clear that Charles Stevenson had taken that step.

We saw the door of the governor's house open, for, although the hackney-coach was immediately before it, yet it is reached by so high and steep a flight of steps, that it appeared above the roof of the vehicle completely. We saw some one come out, and, although we were not in a position to speak positively as to identity, we had no sort of doubt but that it was Charles Stevenson. He got into the coach in a moment, and the door was closed with the usual bang, which, by some means or another, seems to be always necessary with coach doors. Then the poor, miserable, worn-out hacks of horses, were set in motion, and the coach was off before ours made its appearance.

" There," said Mr. Bell, " we are jilted at last—we must follow on foot. Come on—come on!"

We ran up the Old Bailey, not, indeed, at a very fast pace, for the coach, after all, did not swagger along at a rate above five miles an hour, but still it was very uncomfortable to go dashing through the rain even at that rate. I felt, too, much mortified that the boy had not come, and had just made up my mind not to attempt, in the ordinary concerns of life, to carry out certain physiognomical theories of vice, when from Newgate-street there came swaggering a coach, and on the box, along with the driver and all his multitudinous coats, sat my ragged boy.

" Hurrah!" cried I; " here he is. Stop—stop, coachman!" —" Here you are, sir "

" You see that coach going down Snow-hill—we want you to follow it—you understand; you must not seem to do so, but still you must follow it."—" All's right, your honour," said the coachman.

In we got, and Mr. Bell, as well as Mr. Denbigh, each gave the boy a shilling, as some sort of recompense for the suspicions they had entertained of him, and for which we all had the satisfaction of hearing him, as he went away, mutter an opinion that we must be thieves, or we should never part with our money half so easy. How difficult it is to do a good action!

The coach in which was Charles Stevenson had nearly got to the end of Farringdon-street by the time we started, but there was no difficulty whatever in keeping it in view, and we both crawled up Holborn-hill, not twenty yards apart.

On went both vehicles to King-street, Holborn, and then I became quite convinced that all our labour was in vain, for Charles was going home to Keppel-street. I said as much to my two companions, and when we turned into Russell-square, of course there could be no longer any doubt whatever upon the subject. We stopped our coach, and satisfied—no, I mean paid, the driver—who ever yet *satisfied* the driver of a coach or cab?—and then we walked to Keppel-street, where we saw the coach just moving away from Stevenson's door.

" What's to be done now?" was the question. Here was only Friday night, and Heaven knew how long Charles might be before he again emerged from the house; perhaps not till the day of execution—perhaps not then. He might be cunning enough to feel that his best policy, most decidedly, was to be quiet—to go nowhere, see no one, and so commit himself in no way before the judicial murder, which would, unless something turned up to change materially the aspect of affairs, take place on the following Monday.

" Shall we watch him or not?" was asked, with much anxiety; and, after some time spent in discussion, I said,—

" Gentlemen, it seems to be agreed among us that if we could find this woman, Margaret Day, something would probably be got from her of a nature to shake the evidence of Charles Stevenson against that poor girl, who I am, in my own mind, convinced is the victim of the most atrocious perjury that ever emanated from human lips. We have no clue whatever to where she can be found. That Charles Stevenson does know where she is, who can doubt? That he may abstain from going near her before the execution of Martha Renton is possible; but the only chance we have is, that he may not be so prudent, or circumstances may compel him to an interview with her. Let us, then, continue to watch him, for that is our only chance."

"To-morrow morning," said Mr. Bell, "I shall advertise, offering twenty pounds reward for her."—"Good," said I; "do so; and if it succeed not in inducing her to come forward, at least it may alarm Charles Stevenson into seeking her. I am resolved to sacrifice my time until Monday morning in watching this house. Look opposite! Do you not see there is a bill in the window of 'Apartments to Let?' Could anything be more favourable? We will hire them for a week, and keep watch and ward by turns at the window, night and day. Consider, gentlemen, how great will be our reward, if we succeed in saving the life of an innocent girl, now condemned to a terrible and a disgraceful death."

With an alacrity which did them infinite credit, they both at once acceded to the proposition.

"We can, there being three of us," said Mr. Bell, "relieve guard well and handsomely; besides, I can be spared to take the advertisement I mention to a newspaper-office, while you keep watch."—"True—true; and now to take the apartments opposite."

We immediately crossed the way, and knocked at the door of the house which had the bill in the window. For the first time it then struck us all that the hour was a very odd and unseasonable one for taking apartments, but the circumstances which induced us to take them were of a nature to banish all ordinary scruples, and, accordingly, when a servant opened the door, I said,—

"We wish to see the apartments that are to let."

"The apartments, sir?"—"Yes, certainly."

"I—I will ask master, sir. It's very late—John—John!"

A boy came up from the kitchen, and the girl whispered something to him which meant as plain as possible—"Stop in the hall, in case these men steal anything," for he placed his back against the wall and kept a vigilant eye on us. The servant went up stairs, and in a few minutes she came down again, followed by a gentlemanly man, who carried a candle in his hand, and whose brows were knit suspiciously as he came in sight of the three, I must confess, rather disreputable characters who were in his hall. Moreover, Mr. Bell increased the suspicious nature of the whole affair by keeping near the street-door, and now and then peeping out in reality to watch Stevenson's house, but apparently as if to give the cue to some confederates.

"We wish to see the apartments," said I.—"At this time of night, sir?" said the master of the house, inquiringly.

"Hilloa!" cried Mr. Denbigh. "How are you, Sampson?"—"Oh! is that you, Sampson?" cried Bell.

I was amazed, and when Mr. Sampson said, with a look of consternation,—"Good God! what does all this mean?" I was inclined myself to echo his very pertinent question.

"Don't you know us?" said Mr. Bell.—"You are Mr. Bell, and you Mr. Denbigh—but—but—I suppose it's a dream?"

"Not at all, we want to take your apartments. We had no idea you lived here, but we are very glad you do, Sampson. Come into some room or another, and we will tell you all about it. Doctor, this is Mr. Sampson, whom we are all very well acquainted with, from his holding an official situation in the Exchequer. He will afford us every accommodation in our purpose."—"Most certainly," said Mr. Sampson; "walk in, gentlemen, if you please. What can I do to oblige you?"

We accompanied Mr. Sampson into the parlour, where, while I kept watch at the window upon Charles Stevenson's house, Mr. Bell and Denbigh related to him all that had occurred, and what we had decided upon doing, as the only chance of escape for the young girl who we believed to be so completely innocent of the offence of which she was so cruelly convicted.

"Make what use of my house you please," said Mr. Sampson; "I shall only be too happy if your object succeeds."

Thus, then, we were fairly established as a guard upon the door of Charles Stevenson's house, and no one could by any possibility go out or in without our observation. We took possession of the front parlour, and we agreed—that is, Mr. Denbigh and I, for Mr. Bell was forced to go out to put in the advertisement he meditated—to watch four hours each, and so relieve each other at regular intervals.

Thus we passed the whole night, and in the morning Mr. Bell, who had got a promise from the people at the *Morning Herald* office that the advertisement should appear on the Saturday morning without fail, came and said to me,—

"I have inserted the advertisement in the *Herald*, although strongly advised to put it in the *Times*; but I thought I would go to a respectable paper at once,—so the *Herald* has it."—"You are right," said I.

"And now, doctor," he added, "you can get out, if you have any urgent case to attend to."—"No," I replied; "I have made a solemn determination to see the end of this affair, and I will."

I began very much to fear that Charles Stevenson had made a determination not to move from home, for half the Saturday slipped away, and he had not made his appearance. Then we held a solemn consultation about what could be done to "unearth the fox;" but we could come to no determination beyond what we had already arrived at, namely, to watch him still closely, and to take our chance.

And so passed off the whole of the Saturday, in a most fidgetty state of expectancy. Mr. Bell had left orders with his clerks, that if any one came concerning the advertisement, they were to ask if the party knew Mr. Charles Stevenson, and, if the answer was in the negative, to take no further notice of that party; because, as he reasoned, "If *the* Margaret Day whom we want, come at all, she will have beforehand made up her mind to be explicit, and there can be no mistake."

This was reasonable enough; but no one came to his office who knew Charles Stevenson, although the confidential clerk who came on Saturday night to us at Keppel-street, said there had been at least fifty Margaret Days at the office.

Then came the Sunday, and we began really to despair—Sunday morning, Sunday afternoon, and finally Sunday evening—still Charles Stevenson had not made his appearance, and we all collected in the parlour just as the lamps were being lit, to consider again what could be done.

"I propose," said Mr. Sampson, "that the newspaper containing the advertisement be sent to him; who knows but it may alarm him, and he may leave home to see the woman Day?"—"A good thought," we all cried; "a good thought."

The newspaper was folded, and duly addressed to Mr. Charles Stevenson, and then we sent it over the way by a young gentleman who had accidentally called at Mr. Sampson's, and who was unknown to Charles's servants, so that his suspicions of being watched could not be awakened at all by the manoeuvre, which now seemed the last hope of moving him from home.

We all placed our noses very close to the glass of Mr. Sampson's parlour window, while the newspaper was taken over to Charles Stevenson's, for we had a well-grounded idea that such a move could not be wholly and utterly ineffective.

The young gentleman who gave it in of course did not immediately come across the way, lest he should be watched, but he took a round by Montague-place, and so to Keppel-street again, from Gower-street; during which time we never for a moment removed our eyes from Stevenson's door.

It was now getting very dark, but we would not have lights in the parlour, lest we should be seen; and it will be remembered that we were all personally known to Charles Stevenson. I don't think we were thus watching above twenty minutes, when Charles Stevenson's street-door opened, and out came a man enveloped in a large cloak, which covered him up entirely, with the exception of his head and face. He pulled the door after him hurriedly, and then, casting around him a nervous, shifting sort of glance, he hurried up Keppel-street, in the direction towards Tottenham-court-road.

"That's our man," cried I; and without more delay than was absolutely necessary to get out of the house, we were all three upon his track; and Mr. Sampson was following us again, for he had contracted a great interest in the matter, and was as anxious as any one could possibly be to see the end of it.

Of course we were very cautious. Mr. Denbigh, as being, perhaps, less known to Charles—for in all probability he had never seen him, but with his wig on—went first and foremost. Then I followed him, Mr. Bell followed me, and Mr. Sampson followed Mr. Bell.

I could, notwithstanding Mr. Denbeigh was before, catch a very good sight of Charles Stevenson, as he hurried along rapidly. When he reached Gower-street he paused a moment, and then turned to the left, and proceeded along Bedford-square, till he came to Russell-street. With a gesture of impatience, then, as if he had gone wrong, he walked hastily down the whole length of Russell street, to Southampton-row, which he traversed till he came to Orange-street, down which he went, and crossing Red Lion-square, Red Lion-street, &c., he appeared to be making his way as fast as he could towards the city.

I was not mistaken. He got into Smithfield, crossed it, and went up Barbican. Then he suddenly plunged down a small street to the right, which led to quite a complication of other small streets, so that we had to keep closer to him, lest by suddenly entering some house we should lose him.

He did not, after leaving Keppel-street, seem to entertain the least idea that he was being followed, for he never once looked behind him, so that, although we were very cautious, we might have been otherwise, and yet not have been discovered.

Now in some bye-street, somewhere in the neighbourhood of Whitecross-street prison, he paused, and after, apparently, a brief consideration with himself, he pulled his hat lower down over his brows, and plunged down a narrow court. The entrance to this court was an archway, so that it was very dark indeed, now that the night had fairly set in, and that night anything but a clear one, for there were some indications of similar stormy weather to what had occurred the evening previous.

Mr. Denbigh had been rapidly approaching nearer and nearer to Charles Stevenson, ever since he had turned into the throng of houses and courts which lay so thickly in that locality, so that when Charles did, with a quick movement, enter the open doorway of a common-looking house, there could be no mistake as to where he had disappeared. We were all four at the door now in a moment, where we held a council of war.

"Remember," said Mr. Denbigh, "that she whom we seek may not be here, and that if we show ourselves prematurely to Stevenson, all the trouble we have taken in this affair goes for nothing; one, and one only of us, must enter the house, and that it may not be politic to do till after he is gone. Let us get away from the door, for Heaven's sake!"

We immediately hid ourselves in different doorways, the whole of us keeping an exact watch on the one which Charles Stevenson had entered. Mr. Sampson was with me, and I said to him,—

"When he comes out, it will be necessary for some one still to follow him."—"I will do so," he said; "and depend upon me not missing him. I think, though, that two ought to go."

"Yes, yes. You are right, there might be a necessity for two. I dare say Bell will go with you."—"No," said Bell, when I went to him and proposed it. "Let Sampson go alone. I admit, that, as a matter of precaution, he should be followed, but I have the strongest possible impression that he has come here to visit this Margaret Day, and that when he leaves here he will merely go home."

"It may be so, and certainly looks most probable."—"Hush! Look there!"

A dirty slip-shod girl emerged from the door, with a jug in one hand, and a bottle in the other, which she, according to a habit of such people, partially concealed beneath a dirty apron. She ran out of the court, and presently returned with some beer, apparently, and spirits, from a neighbouring public-house, with which she paused at the doorway, in order to take toll of both, which we all saw her do; and trifling as the circumstance was, it did ultimately become of some importance.

After a good drink at the porter, and a hearty pull at the contents of the bottle, which, in all probability, was very choice Geneva, she condescended to take the liquors into the house, I, in my own mind, having no doubt but that they had been sent for by Stevenson.

A quarter of an hour, at the outside, might now have elapsed before the shadow of some one darkened the door-step, and with a hurried manner, and still enveloped in his cloak, which with great nervousness he drew closely around him, Charles Stevenson appeared. He glanced right and left, and as the distant glare of a gas lamp fell upon his face, I could see that it was ghastly pale as that of a corpse. He then darted from the court by the narrow arched entry, and I said to Mr. Sampson,—

"Now—now—follow him."

He sprang after him, and in another moment we three who were left, namely, Mr. Denbigh, Mr. Bell, and myself, stood upon the door-step of the mean, dirty-looking house, from which Charles had emerged.

"Now," I said, "we will soon ascertain, I think, if Margaret Day does or does not reside here."

Even as I spoke I raised the knocker of the door, and gave a loud rat-tat, which brought from the kitchen a woman to know what we wanted. She was of the dirtiest and lowest class; her face was begrimed with soot, and she had that haggard expression whith belongs to that unhappy class which knows nothing but poverty and wretchedness from birth to death.

"Well?" she said; "well?"—"Are you the mistress of the house?" said I,

"What if I am?"—"If you are you know the names of the people who live in it."

"I know their names? How should I know their names? They call themselves all sorts of names; but what is that to me, so long as they pay their rent?"—"Very true. But you can tell us what names they go by?"

"Well, who do you want?"—"A woman of the name of Day."

"Day? Margaret Day?"—"Yes—yes, the same."

"Three pair back. You can find the way, I dare say. What has she done, eh?—or do you come with tracts? If you do, you may as well go away again, for, to save disputes, we have no religion here."

So saying, she walked down the kitchen stairs again, leaving us in the dark passage, to go away, or stay, just as we pleased.

"We must get a light somehow," I said, and I tapped at the first door I came to, when a female voice from within cried,—

"Who's that?"—"It's I," I replied.

"And who's me?"—"I didn't say me. I want to borrow a candle of you."

"Who the deuce are you?"

The woman opened the door as I spoke, and I said,—

"Madam, I am your most humble servant, and want a candle, for which I shall be very happy to pay."—"I don't want pay, sir. There's a light."

"Come on," said I, when I had the light, and we all three ascended the staircase in search of the three pair back, where we expected to find Margaret Day.

When we reached the top of the house, which we did without the least interruption, we knocked at the first door we came to, but got no answer, and then I placed my ear to the keyhole, when I was convinced some one was moaning in the room.—I placed my hand on the lock, and opened the door, holding the candle as high above my head as possible. It was a wretched apartment; but in a moment my attention was withdrawn from everything else by seeing what appeared to be the dead body of a woman lying on the floor. I gave the candle to Denbigh, and, with the assistance of Mr. Bell, placed the female upon a wretched couch that was in the room. I felt her heart—I examined her eyes.

"What is the matter with her?" inquired Mr. Denbigh.—"She is suffering," I exclaimed, "from the operation of some powerful narcotic poison. By Heavens, gentlemen, our friend, Charles Stevenson, seems an adept in such matters. Stay by her here, both of you, till I come back."

I dashed down the staircase, and out of the house, and out of the court, to the nearest chemist's; on the road to whom it struck me—for I had seen a jug and a bottle on the table—that if the woman had been given poison to by Charles Stevenson, it had been so recently that a powerful emetic would dislodge the greater portion of it, at all events, from the stomach, where no doubt it still was.

With this view, I got the requisite medicines, and was back again within ten minutes of the time I had left. No change had taken place, except that the moaning of the woman had become fainter, and she seemed to be rapidly sinking. No time was to be lost; I got Denbigh and Bell to hold her up while I administered to her the emetic, and in a few moments she was violently sick. I had no doubt but that a quantity of morphiæ had been given to her, and I persevered with the emetic until nothing remained in her stomach, and then I gave her citric acid, and had her walked to and fro in the room until I felt quite convinced she had got rid of all the effects of the poison, except a dreadful weakness which would, of course, remain, even as a result of the powerful emetic I had given to her.

It must not be supposed that all this was accomplished

very rapidly. Indeed some hours were thus consumed, and when I looked at my watch, I was surprised to find that it was an hour past midnight before I felt that my patient could be asked a question. Then, motioning them to attend to what she should say, I commenced speaking to her.

"How are you now?"—"Better," she replied, faintly. "Oh! what is it?"

"What is your name?"—"Day—Margaret Day. Where am I?"

"In your own house, and, as to what has happened to you, you have been poisoned."—"Poisoned?—oh, God! Is this the end of all—oh, Charles, Charles, Charles! I knew the beer was wrong."

"Margaret Day," I said, solemnly, "for all I know, your hours are numbered—the life of an innocent girl hangs upon your answers to what I shall ask of you."

She wrung her hands and wept.

"I told him so—I told him so," she sobbed, "but he denied it. He swore that she was guilty, and yet the cloak and bonnet—oh! that cloak and bonnet. God help me—God help me—I see it all now. She shall not suffer—I will tell all. Oh, God—oh, God—though it kill me, I will now tell all. Gentlemen, take me where you will; I have that to tell which shall save an innocent girl. Martha Renton is innocent. Now, as if a new light from Heaven had broken in upon me, I understand it all. I think I am dying, but I will tell all."—"Right, right," cried I. "Denbigh, for God's sake, get a coach to the end of the court. Let us take her at once before a magistrate."

"I will. Is she in danger?"—"Hush! Not the least; but let us take her evidence while she is in the humour to give it. Quick, quick, or she will die!" I added aloud.

"I knew I was dying, I knew I was dying," she cried. "Only people who are dying feel as I feel now."

Denbigh was off like a shot, and to tell the truth, he executed his mission in an extraordinary short space of time, and was with us again with the news that he had a coach waiting before I thought it possible he could have procured one.

Among us we assisted Margaret Day down the staircase and into the coach. I ordered the driver to go to the private residence of the same magistrate who had taken the depositions in the drawing-room of the Stevensons' house in Keppel-street, and in another moment off we were.

It was not the most reasonable hour in the world to go to anybody's house, but the urgency of the case forbade all such considerations, and when we arrived at the magistrate's, I executed a peal upon his knocker which, I have no doubt, astonished the neighbourhood. The door, to my surprise, was immediately opened, and, in answer to my inquiry if Mr. ——, the magistrate was at home, the servant said,—

"Yes, sir, and up."—"That's all right. Take my card in, and say I come on urgent and particular business."

Fancy us all now—Bell, Denbigh, myself, and Margaret Day—in a handsome reception-room waiting for the magistrate, who soon came in and heard from me, briefly, a statement of what had occurred. I saw the look of wonder grow upon his face.

"Good God!" he said, and then he rang the bell. "Call all the servants into this room directly, and bring me a bible."

Every living soul in the house collected in that room, and a court was formed of breathless listeners. The oath was administered to Margaret Day, and the substance of her statement was to the following effect:—

"I have known Charles Stevenson for some years; he has scantily supplied me with money, and always represented himself very poor. About six months ago he gave me some money, and said he wanted me to make some purchases for him. Those purchases were a plaid shawl, and a black velvet bonnet. I bought them at a shop for the sale of second-hand female wearing apparel. I bought him, likewise, a stuff gown, and a wreath of artificial flowers for the bonnet. They were much faded. He said he was going to a masquerade, and he came to my lodging and put on the things more than once. He told me, if ever I mentioned the circumstance, that he would murder me, for it might get round to his uncle's ears, and he would then turn him adrift without a shilling. I heard of the poisoning of the Stevensons; but not thoroughly till to-night did I believe Charles did the deed. I do believe now he did it. He came to me to-night in a hurried manner, and sent out for beer and gin. After taking some I fell down, feeling very ill, and I know no more till some gentlemen questioned me."

The magistrate himself wrote down her deposition, and she signed it.

"Now gentlemen," said he, "this woman shall find an asylum in a hospital for the present, if you think her in a sufficiently bad state of health."—"It would be better," I said.

"Very good. I will leave directions to my servants concerning her; and now, as you have a coach at the door, we will use it."

"Where are you going?"

"To the Secretary of State, of course. Come along, gentlemen, if you please, and we will see what can be done."

The Home Secretary, for the time being, at the period at which the occurrences here detailed took place, lived in Spring Gardens, and thither we went at once, and knocked loudly at his door, which was opened by the astonished hall-porter, who seemed half asleep, for it was now half-past three o'clock in the morning.

"Is his lordship in?" said the magistrate.

"In—in—bed, to be sure."

"We must see him."—"Must you?"

"Yes. Take him my card—I must, and will see him."

"I—I will wake up his lordship's own man, if you like."

"Wake up who you like; but we must see his lordship."

The name on the card was not unknown to the hall-porter, and he left the hall with it, remaining away some ten minutes or so. Then he returned, followed by a man hastily dressed, who said,—

"I have orders to conduct you to his lordship, who hopes your business excuses your urgency."

To this we made no answer. It was, no doubt, uttered, but not as a message, and in either case required no reply, so we followed the "own man," as I presume he was, in silence.

We were conducted to the second-floor, and into a small, neat, dressing-room, where we were desired to sit down, and in a moment the Secretary of State came from an adjoining apartment in his night-gown and slippers. He received us very courteously, remarked that it was cold, gave a slight shiver, and then seemed to look, as much as to say, "What the devil has brought you here?"

"My lord," said the magistrate, "some important evidence has come to light, which entirely exculpates Martha Renton."

"Martha who?"

"The young woman who is condemned to death."

"Oh, oh, certainly. I am very glad."

The magistrate then read him Margaret Day's evidence, and explained how that bore upon the case, upon which his lordship said,—

"I will grant a reprieve at once on my own responsibility, and if all this can be substantiated, I will recommend a free pardon to-morrow. You may rely upon me sending to Newgate."—"Write it now, my lord," said I, "and allow me to be the messenger."

"Very good—very good. When one comes to think of it, I dare say the young woman is anxious. No doubt—no doubt."

He wrote a reprieve to the sheriff, and the moment I got hold of it, I jumped up, and cried,—

"Thank you, my lord! Come along, all of you. Come along."

I waited for no further ceremony, but was in the hall in a moment, followed by the other three. Into the coach we jumped, and bang went the door.

"Vere to now, sir?" said the coachman.—"Newgate."

"Lor!" I heard the coachman say, "what can these ere gemmen want at the Bailey?"

* * * *

When we got near the prison, we heard a strange knocking noise, which we could not at first account for, until I looked from the coach-window, and there I found an instant explanation of the phenomenon, for I saw that workmen were engaged putting up barriers, in order to keep off the crowd at the, as they thought, approaching execution.

"Look there," I said, as I pointed out those awful preparations to Mr. Bell and Mr. Denbigh. "With what very different feelings would we have looked upon such work as is now proceeding, if we were not the bearers of the document we are now possessed of."

We rang loudly at the door of the governor's house, and, after some delay, were admitted and conducted up stairs, when we found that gentleman up and dressed, and looking curiously anxious to know what had brought us there. I, without a word, placed in his hand the document we had got from the Secretary of State, and the moment his eye ran over it, he exclaimed,—

"Thank God. This ought to have gone to the sheriff's; but I will not delay for a moment the communication to the prisoner, although I go beyond my duty in making it."

I think I never felt so nervous in my life as we all walked hurriedly towards the condemned cell. I could not have spoken had my life depended upon it. The door was thrown open, and the governor entered first.

"Martha Renton," I heard him say; "thank God, I——"

From his face she gathered the purport of his tidings. Joy overcame her, and, with a loud shriek, she fell insensible on the floor of the cell.

* * * * *

Martha was removed to a comfortable bed in the governor's house; and our readers may well imagine with what feelings she recovered from her swoon of joy. She wept as if her heart would break, and then, through her tears, she smiled and thanked us all, and prayed that God might reward us, speaking all the while in such fervent accents, that all who heard her were deeply affected.

It was now nearly seven o'clock in the morning, and an enormous crowd had assembled in front of Newgate. The sheriffs had been sent for, and instant orders were given to have the barriers removed, so that the mob soon found out there was to be no execution. I stood on the steps of the governor's house, and I could not resist the impulse to shout as loudly as I could,—

"The innocence of Martha Renton is discovered!"

The huzzas with which the announcement was received shook the air, and I then felt a hand upon my arm, and one of the Bow-street runners said to me,—

"Have you a mind to come with me?"—"Where to?"

"I am going to take Charles Stevenson into custody at once. Several are going with me; and, among the rest, Mr. Bell and Mr. Denbigh."

"I will go," I said. "Where is the woman Day?"—"In the infirmary of the New Prison. She has repeated her evidence to several persons, and I have a warrant for the apprehension of Charles Stevenson for wilful murder. Take my word for it, sir, that fellow will be hanged."

We all got into a coach, and drove towards Keppel-street, for Mr. Sampson had come back to us, and told us that Charles, after leaving the house in which he thought to have left Margaret Day to die alone, had gone direct home.

Considerably less than half an hour brought us to Keppel-street. We drove right up to the door, without any attempt at concealment, and knocked loudly. The servant who answered us looked terrified, and when I said, in a loud voice,—

"Is your master within?" replied, hesitatingly,—

"Ye—yes;—but he won't see any one."

"Indeed!" said the officer. "We will see that."

Even as he spoke he bounded up stairs, and we all followed him. When we were half way up the second flight a voice from above cried,—

"What's that?—what do you want?"

It was Charles's voice, and I told the officer so, who immediately produced his staff, as he said,—

"You are my prisoner, Mr. Stevenson. Resistance is madness."

I heard a shriek and the bang of a door. The officer reached the landing, and with one blow dashed the door into splinters, and we all followed him into a bed-room. Then came a strange sound from a small dressing-room adjoining, as if some one was pouring water from a narrow-necked bottle. We went into that room in an instant. Charles Stevenson lay on the floor, with his throat cut from ear to ear, and holding a razor in his right hand. Eight o'clock at that moment struck, and, with a strange gurgling sob, he died.

* * * * *

Martha Renton, of course, received a free pardon. She is now the mother of a happy family, and some of the pleasantest hours of the old physician are spent at her fireside in Wales, where she and her husband, who are both getting in years, now reside. She married a very worthy man, and has been as happy as the crosses of the world will ever permit any one to be.

RETRIBUTION;

OR, THE REFUGEE'S DAUGHTER.

The opera season of 1798 was one of the most brilliant that had ever been known, and *habitues* of the house had been in raptures for two months. Those who are fond of operas have their fill of them; let those who detest them affect to admire them for fear of being thought unfashionable and gothic, if they please; for my own part I must confess that if the Opera House was snatched away in a whirlwind, and all the blood-suckers who squall their hour upon the stage with it, I should not be concerned at the catastrophe.

Even now, when I never go to the opera at all, for being out of practice I am more free from the prejudices of society, and can afford to indulge in my own tastes and fancies without any pecuniary sacrifice, it disgusts me to take up a newspaper, and let my eye fall upon some paragraph interlarded with bad French and meagre Italian, in which the "divine Grisi" is talked of, or the "sublime Lablache." A very ordinary woman divine, because she can produce certain sounds which every lady cannot! A fat, unwieldy, gross-looking man sublime, because he can growl a note or two lower than his compeers, and has what the profane vulgar would call a capacious bellows!

But there are two conditions of things which will always in this country make anything popular, and put John Bull into raptures at any time. There is no getting over the fact, however unpalatable it may be, that, to ensure the very highest meed of public approbation for anything, it is only to be *unintelligible* and *expensive*.

The Opera pit is eight shillings and sixpence, therefore it must be fine. If sprats were fifteen shillings a piece, we should have essays and odes written on their delicious flavour. It is astonishing what hypocrites the mass of people are in many things connected with which one would think they might, without any detriment to themselves, surely express an opinion; but what man or woman among a thousand will go to the Italian Opera, and candidly confess that it is an intolerable bore? Oh, no! they have heard of the "divine Grisi," and the "sublime Lablache," and not to admit both the divinity and the sublimity would be to draw down upon themselves an accusation of want of taste; and show me the man, woman, or child, who wouldn't, as Lord Melbourne did, on all situable occasions, give way to "enormous lying" rather than be obnoxious to such a charge.

We hope that the exceptions to the general rule are to be found among our readers—we believe that they are,—we think we have with us English hearts and English understandings, that despise the frivolity of the ballet, and 'he squalling of the emasculated vermin who fatten upon the folly of popular credulity.

Still I was occasionally at the Opera many years ago, although I never put myself to that inconvenience now. I should as soon think of going to hear Charles Kemble drone through his readings of Shakspere.

But to commence again at my starting point: the Opera season of 1798 was what in opera fashion is called a brilliant one, and the fashionable world pretended to be in raptures. Among my patients were several persons who had admissions, so that I was frequently asked to take a seat in a box, and as a physician must succumb to the feelings and the habits of society, perhaps more than any other man, I sometimes went.

It was on one of these occasions that in compliance with the pressing solicitations of a patient, I went to endure an opera, the first of a series of events occurred, which greatly interested me, and presented to me a picture of society such as I then hoped I should never see again, but which, unhappily, in my after experience I was condemned to see often. After I had got into the house, I was informed by my friend that a Signora Barronelli was to make a first appearance in a very arduous character, and that rumour had spoken rapturously of her accomplishments as a singer.

"Some Italian, I suppose," said I, listlessly, "who has

come to help John Bull to get rid of some of his superfluous cash."—"Why, to tell the truth," said my friend, "there are some ugly reports about concerning her."

"Indeed! of what nature?"—"Why, I cannot vouch for the truth of the statement, but it is said boldly by many that she is English. Mind, I do not assert it myself, by any means. One Sunday paper, and two morning journals have hinted at the fact, so you will see that it is rather a serious affair."

"Serious! What on earth do you mean? I was prepared to hear something against the *debutante*."—"And so you have."

"Oh, I beg your pardon. Upon a moment's consideration I admit that I have—I understand now. Let her have the talent of an age, and the voice of an angel, if she be found out to be English instead of Italian, of course she will fail."—"Why, yes. You see there is a feeling in favour of Italian singers here, and if she is English, I wouldn't give much for her chances of success."

"And yet here we are in England—in her native land, and she will be repudiated because she is not foreign. Now, my good sir, can you defend such a mode of proceeding?"—"Oh, it's—it's fashionable."

I said no more, for perhaps if I had said anything else, my friend might have found it rather unpalatable, and there is never any use in quarrelling with a man because he happens to be a fool.

However, in consequence of what I had heard, from being listless and uninterested on the subject of the *debutante*, I became much interested, and was extremely anxious for her appearance, in order that I might judge by her tones if she were English or Italian.

The overture was played, and a slight pause succeeded. Then came the first agitation of the curtain, like a breeze upon the ocean. Up—up, it folded slowly, and the whole expanse of that large stage was in view. There was a rustic bridge at the back, and the scene was of a Swiss character throughout. A dead stillness reigned in the house, and then across the rustic bridge there came, slowly and gracefully, a female form. A partial applause was got up, but not of sufficient extent to be very encouraging, and my friend whispered to me,—

"That is the *debutante*."—"She is very young."

"Oh, yes; she is generally agreed to be not above eighteen."—"Indeed!"

"Hush! This aria with which she commences will decide her fate. Listen! listen!"

The young girl advanced to within about four paces of the foot lights, and then, after a graceful bow to the house, she waited until a few soft notes of symphony were played by the orchestra before she began to sing. To my mind the tones were very sweet, touching, and exquisitely musical; but there was a total absence of that straining vibratory style, which is common to the Italians. The first few bars were over, and then I heard my friend say,—

"English," and a whisper ran round the house to the same effect. I heard a gentleman—no, an animal—a fop, and, of course, a fool, from a neighbouring box, say, in affected tones,—

"Pon soul! this is too bad; she is English, and that is—a—a—most shocking, really."—"Good God!" I could not help saying, "can it be possible that, because this young lady is a countrywoman of our own, she is to be condemned. Surely, surely, such cannot be the case."

"Hush!" said my friend. "For God sake, doctor, don't go on that way; you will be considered quite gothic. There, she resumes her song. Listen; really it's a pity, for she has a nice voice."

The strains ceased, and the singer was mute; a dead silence reigned in the house. Who would applaud an English girl? I rose from my seat, and, in a voice which reached to every corner of the building, I said, "Bravo!"

My friend nearly slid off his seat. There was a mighty genteel laugh in the house, one of those nasty, fashionable titters which are indulged in by people who think laughing vulgar, and that God Almighty, of course, ought not to have invented it; and then I saw the young singer drop on the stage, as if she had been shot.

Several persons ran on from the side, and carried her off. She had fainted, but even that did not arouse one generous feeling on the part of the audience. I still saw the half smile on the faces of the empty-headed coxcombs. I saw the shrug of the shoulders of the demireps, and I again heard the ominous word, " English—English!" whispered round the circle.

"This is too bad," said I, as I rose. "Excuse me, sir, but I cannot remain here any longer."

My friend muttered something about the " divine" somebody I should hear if I stayed; but I was deaf to his solicitation, and with a swelling feeling of indignation at my heart, I left the house, and was in another moment in the Opera colonnade. Then, and not till then, a sudden idea struck me, which I instantly put into execution. I went at once to the stage-door, and presented my card to the first person I met, saying,—

"Signora Barronelli has fainted, and I am to attend her. Please to take in my card."—"Certainly, sir," was the reply, and my card was taken from me."

I waited with no small degree of anxiety for more than five minutes, and then he who had taken my card, came back and said,—

"If you will follow me, sir, I will conduct you to Signora Barronelli's dressing-room."

I followed the man without a word, and after traversing several passages, he led me up a flight of stairs, and then pausing at the first door he came to, he tapped gently. The door was opened by a female, to whom the man said,—

"Here is the doctor."—"Oh, ask him to walk in. This way, sir."

I at once entered the room, which, although small, was well appointed, and extremely comfortable. What observations, however, I made concerning it were not made just then, for my whole attention was engrossed by the group that met my eyes within the precincts of that little chamber.

Upon a reclining chair sat the *debutante*, who had been so seriously convicted of the crime of being English. Her eyes were closed, her face as pale as alabaster, and she was completely motionless. At her feet knelt an elderly woman, whose look of intense grief and solicitude convinced me she could be no other than the mother of a beautiful being who had met with so very ungenerous, not to say unjust, a reception from that presumed epitome of every virtue under Heaven, " an English audience."

At some few paces distant from this group stood a gentlemanly-looking person, whose hands were clasped in a supplicating attitude, and the agonized expressions of whose countenance showed how intense an interest he had in the fate of the fair being who was, perhaps, happy in being for a time insensible. The features of this man were cast in the finest mould, and, although he was advanced in years, and his hair was, like Hamlet's father's, " a sable silvered," while care had marked more furrows on his face and brow than Time could, with all his ungentle usage, have done, yet he was handsome still.

The woman who had answered my guide's tap at the door was one of the dressers at the theatre. It was the kneeling female who first addressed me, and she cried, in passionate accents,—

"Oh, save her, sir. Save her—my child—my beautiful child. She will die—she will die!"

"Pray, madam," I said, immediately, "restrain this grief. It is uncalled-for. The young lady has fainted, I perceive, and no doubt will be well again. Be so good as to hold up her head, and give me some water in a basin."

The man sprang forward, and without a word, held up, gently and affectionately, the head of the beautiful girl, while the dresser handed me a basin with water. I dipped my hand in it, but before I splashed any upon the face of the sufferer, I saw a tear fall upon it from from the father's eye, while a half-suppressed sob testified to the deep emotion that was struggling in his breast.

"You make much of this," said I, as I dashed water upon the girl's face. "Surely you have seen a person faint before to-day. There, you see she is recovering. Open the window, some one, and let the cool air blow upon her face."

"You do not know all, sir," said the man; "I am her father."—"I presumed as much, sir; but you see she is now nearly recovered, and will be well soon."

He bent his face down towards her, and, in a gentle voice which could only have been attuned by the fondest affection, he said, in a slightly foreign accent,—

"My darling, look up. Your mother and I are with you. Felice, look up, my dear Felice. Tell me you are better, my darling child. It is your father who speaks to you."—"And your mother," said the female, rising; " we are both here, dear—we are with you."

The young girl opened her eyes slowly, and looked with a bewildered gaze around for a moment; then, in a low, alarmed voice, she said,—

"What has happened?—what was it? Something came over me like a black cloud. Oh, God, what was it?"—"You fainted on the stage," said I. "Do not be alarmed; such things have happened before, and will happen again. There is no danger. You will soon be well."

"Yes, darling," said the father; "you hear this gentleman—he is a physician, and assures you that all is well. Cheer up, my Felice, cheer up; you are well again."—"Fainted on the stage," she repeated—"a failure. I remember, now. The cold silence that followed the aria. All is over—all is over. The die is cast. Heaven help us now!"

At this moment there came a tap at the door, which, being answered by the dresser, she brought a note to the father, which he at once tore open and read. It must have contained but a very few words, for he seemed to have perused it in a moment. Then he crumpled it up in his hand, and thrust it into his pocket, as he said, in a bitter tone,—

"We will go at once—we will go at once. God forbid that we should stay in any one's way. Felice, are you well enough to go home, dear?"—"Yes, father, yes; I—I am better. Oh, God! oh, God!"

"My child—my child!" cried the mother, as she fondly clasped the sobbing girl in her arms. "Can you imagine you are not as dear to us as you ever were because you may not have succeeded on the Opera boards? You are dearer—dearer still, my darling, for how can we ever repay to you the generous attempt you have made for us? It was for us, we know. God bless you, my child. For you are our own beautiful darling still."

The girl clasped her hands, and a flush of colour came across her pale face, remaining for so brief a space, that we could hardly see it was there before it had gone again, and left her pale as a marble statue. Then, in a low, wailing tone, she said,—

"Failed—failed—failed! Oh, Heaven! and yet I sung the air. Surely the judgment was harsh and unkind."

She placed her hands over her eyes, and burst into tears, which the mother and father tried in vain to soothe.

"Let her be," I said, "she will be better now. Allow this burst of weeping to subside of its own accord; she will be all the better for it. Do not attempt to check it."

They were prevailed upon to act in accordance with my advice, and soon the tears changed to hysterical sobs, which then resolved themselves to sighs, after which, the *debutante*, who had received such cruel and chilling treatment from "an English audience," became much more composed and tranquil. I thought I might with effect now say something which would have a tendency to be agreeable to the feelings of all the parties there assembled, and, accordingly, I stepped forward, and when I saw they were all attending to me, I said,—

"Allow me before you go to speak as regards my own impression of the proceedings of to-night."—"With pleasure, sir," said the father.

"Then do not leave this house under a feeling that this young lady has not acquitted herself sufficiently well of the task she had undertaken. I was in the front of the house, and I heard and saw all that passed there. There was no adverse opinion with regard to her vocal abilities; on the contrary, I heard a favourable one expressed. The whole and sole cause why an audience of English men and women have received with cold apathy this lady, is to be found in the supposition that she is a countrywoman of their own. An impression is in the house that she is English."

"Good God!" said the father, "surely she is the more entitled to friendly regard. Myself and my wife are Genoese, although we have been now nearly nineteen years in England; our child is English, to be sure; but then we thought that as she was about to appear before an English audience, they would be well pleased to find one born in their own capital capable of equalling foreign *artistes*."

"There, my dear sir," said I, "you have shown how little you know of an enlightened British audience. Your daughter's ill success to-night is solely, I believe, attributable to the fact that when she commenced singing, her intonations convinced the audience that she was English."

"Is this possible?"—"It is true, sir, strictly true; and now you have found out John Bull in one of his eccentricities. Italian singers will alone go down, and the more insolent, unfeeling, rascally, vicious and expensive they are, the more they are thought of and patronized."

"You may be right, sir," said the father, with a sigh; "I little dreamt of such things, although, from a note I have in my pocket, I am led to believe what has occurred has been by the management here anticipated. Pray, oblige me, sir, by reading that unfeeling epistle."

He handed me the crumpled-up note which had been brought to him a few minutes before, and I found it contained the following exquisite *morceau* of literary composition :—

"M. D. De La Mortier presents *complimentary*—Please to leave as soon as *possibility* requires. Madame Sacchrina Medora de Cariabella Torre will proceed with the part since there is a great fail. The dressing-room wanted remarkable urgent."

"Who is this from?" I asked.—"The lessee of the Italian Opera."

"Indeed; it's a pity he don't keep an amanuensis."—"We must obey the mandate, and since our child has been unsuccessful in winning the suffrages of the audience, we have but to take our leave of this place for ever."

He held out his hand as he spoke, and I, thinking that he meant to shake hands with me, held out mine, when, to my mortification, I found a guinea slipped into my palm as my fee.

"No, sir," I said, "you must excuse me; I cannot take it."—"Sir?" he said proudly.—"You are mistaken," I added hurriedly, for I saw the mistake he was falling into. "My only motive for refusing this fee is, that I am not entitled to it."

"Not entitled, sir?"—"No; I was not sent for, but attended myself here, for which I have to ask your pardon. If I have been serviceable, I am much pleased, but I cannot humiliate myself by taking a fee generously tendered to me under such circumstances. I pray you take it back again, sir."

I saw his face quiver with emotion as he took back the guinea, and then he said,—

"You were one of the audience, sir?"—"I was."

"Shall I hazard a guess? Yes, if my life depended upon it, I will. It was your voice which alone gave my child an encouraging cheer."—"It was."

He grasped my hand with a force that was almost painful, as he said, in choking accents,—

"God bless you, sir—God bless you. May we hope for the honour of your acquaintance, sir?"—"If you will do me the favour of admitting me to be so," said I, "I shall have great pleasure in enrolling myself as such. I sincerely and honestly sympathise with the circumstances which have occurred to you to-night. Hope for better things, sir, for your daughter has great ability."

"Never again—never again," he said, in a dignified manner, "shall she sue to the heartless crowd which to-night has slighted her. Never again. I will beg bread for her first."—"There are other houses where the people who attend are neither so cold-hearted nor so fashionable."

"We will talk of this another time, sir. At present I am only most anxious to get home. Come, my Felice; let this be considered as but a dream. Come, my child, come."—"You have not given me your address," said I, as I presented him with a card of my own.

"I beg your pardon," he said, as he wrote upon the back of my card the required information, and handed it to me. "Is it asking of you too much to solicit the favour of a call to-morrow?"—"Not at all; I will be with you, you may depend, some time between the hours of two and four."

Having thus so unexpectedly, on my own part, and a little oddly too, made the acquaintance of the young and interesting *debutante* of the opera, my reader may well suppose that I was a little curious to ascertain, if possible, her history, and from the inquiries I was enabled to make, I learnt some very interesting particulars of the family of the Barronellis.

I was informed that he had been a man of both good family and substance at Genoa, but that owing to the political convulsions which had agitated Italy for a considerable period, he had become involved in one of those small revolutions against Austrian dominion, to which that unhappy country has been so long subject, and, as a consequence, had become so inimical to the authorities that it was dangerous to his life to remain longer in the land of his birth and his affections. With his wife he had succeeded in making, although with poor prospects for the future, the friendly shores of England, where soon after she gave birth to a daughter, who was the unfortunate Felice, the *debutante* of the opera, on the evening of the commencement of our tale.

The produce from the sale of some jewels and a few articles

DIARY OF A PHYSICIAN.

of taste and *vertu*, had for a time enabled the refugee and his family to keep around them at least some of the comforts of existence, and Barronelli had fondly hoped that long ere this resource was exhausted he should surely be able to hit upon some means of replenishing his house, and supporting his beloved wife and child.

Such expectations those who have any experience in the world know well are far more likely to be disappointed than realised, for a man may have a hundred different talents, and yet not one which is of a marketable quality, or which he can readily exchange with society for the means of subsistence.

A clever man, well educated, but knowing no one thing in particular, especially if he have, too, the habits and manners of a gentleman, is just about in the same unhappy position to get a living in London that any one can possibly be in. Moreover, poor Barronelli was a foreigner, and so in humble employments laboured under a great disadvantage, however much such a state of affairs might and would have been in his favour, could he have aspired to any high and noble occupation.

His intimacy, however, with the English language, was very great, and, of course, situated as he was, daily improved; and yet all he could get to do was occasionally some exceedingly penurious literary employment, which, from the mere fact that his wife and child were in existence, must have sufficed somehow to support them; although, had the refugee been asked how he and those two persons, who were so utterly dependent upon him, had contrived to live for the last seventeen years, he would have been actually at a loss to tell.

But people do live in London in a most mysterious manner —we see them, day by day, month by month, year by year, subsisting upon Heaven knows what, never having anything to do—no friends, no money; and yet, by some inexplicable means, they rub on, and contrive every day to get something to eat, every night somewhere to lie down in, and when their clothing becomes so desperate, that it cannot possibly be worn any longer, by some means or another, equally inexplicable with the whole affair, they get others. And such persons, after having so many hair-breadth escapes from starvation, at last come to have a reliance upon chance, and to hug themselves upon the fact occasionally, that their circumstances have become so desperate, that something or another must happen for the better.

The refugee's daughter was a weakly, small infant, but by unremitting attentions she conquered the delicacy of her original constitution, and became, about the age of sixteen, a beautiful girl, and, I need not add, the joy and pride of her parents.

The mother was an excellent musician, and had, indeed, by a little teaching occasionally, managed to assist the scanty means of the family. Partly, therefore, as a relaxation, and partly as a portion of necessary education, she had early implanted a love of that science, along with a well grounded knowledge of it, in the mind of her child.

As Felice grew up it was found that she had a beautiful voice, of quite an English character, which is so far superior to the intonations of the French and Italians, whatever the arbitrary dictates of fashion may choose to assert to the contrary.

The family were then living in Panton-street, in the immediate vicinity of the Haymarket. They were surrounded by difficulties, and being pressed by one importunate creditor, to whom they knew not what excuse to make, he it was who suggested the turning to account the vocal talents of their daughter.

"Your daughter is a good singer," he said. "Why don't you try to get her an engagement at one of the concert-rooms?"

The proposition was treated with hauteur by the Barronellis, but yet it awakened a new train of thought; and when they came to consider that they were themselves both getting in years, that there seemed to be no prospects whatever, near or remote, of their ever being permitted to return to their native country, and repossess themselves of the property which had been there confiscated, they trembled for the fate of the beautiful Felice, and became extremely anxious to provide her, before they themselves should bid adieu to the world and its cares, with some means of subsistence.

It so happened that at that time there was a composer of the name of Moriano, who was likewise a Genoese, and who had recently got a work produced at the opera, which had made for him a favourable reputation.

As a countryman, Barronelli was induced to call upon this Moriano; he took his daughter with him. The composer heard her sing, and expressed great approbation. A little intimacy sprung up between the parties, and finally Moriano had induced the lessee of the Opera to give Felice a fair chance on the boards in a new opera of his own, which he himself undertook thoroughly to prepare her for. It was but an experiment. Moriano was popular, and could not very well be refused, and hence the trial which had taken place, and ended in the manner we have described to the reader.

But, alas! it was not Felice's only misfortune that she was thoroughly English; but four days before that, on the evening of which she was to make her *debut* before a "liberal and enlightened English audience, which never fails to encourage anything," &c., &c., Moriano died, and that event altered completely the views of the lessee of the opera. Felice was no longer a *protegee* of a man with whom it was necessary to keep on good terms; and, as she did not come with an acquired continental reputation, that great authority was glad to get rid of her. Still he could find no excuse to prevent her making an appearance, and although he put up another singer in the part to be ready in case of a decided failure, Felice did appear in it, as we have seen, and was, on the sole ground of being English, condemned by the "liberal and enlightened audience."

Immediately upon this, the lessee, who was to the full, it will be understood, as liberal and enlightened as his audience, acted in the way we have shown, being extremely desirous ever to clear his premises of the persons who could not put money into his treasury, from which amiable feeling had resulted the note that had been delivered to Barronelli in the dressing-room of his daughter.

It must not be supposed that I got all these particulars easily and at once; on the contrary, they are the result of much inquiry, and I have only strung them together in their regular order, because they will enable my readers the better to understand, and fully appreciate the various circumstances which follow, and which ultimately placed the Barronelli family in so very different a position to that which they had been occupying. The results of the *debut* at the Italian Opera of Felice Barronelli had yet to develope themselves.

* * * *

I took care to keep my appointment on the morrow, and as soon as I could sufficiently free myself from numerous engagements to call an hour my own, I went directly to the address he had given me, which was in a street leading to Fitzroy-square, and remarkable for nothing but the blackened and gloomy aspect of its tall brick houses.

There are streets in London which somehow have always had, and always will have, a most gloomy and sombre appearance. The bricks of which such houses are composed, seem by general consent to get blacker than those which make the front aspect of the habitation in any other place, except one of a kindred gloomy disposition. By a like unanimity of opinion, too, the inhabitants keep their windows always in a state of uniform dustiness, which is not at all enlivened by the dull curtains that are patronised in such deadly lively localities. About Fitzroy-square, and Gower-street, such rows of melancholy-looking houses are to be found, and it was in one of them, probably from the necessity of economy, that the Barronellis resided.

It so happened, however, that at the period of my visit the sombre and subdued character of the street was much disturbed, for at the door of the house in which the Barronellis resided was a very gay modern-looking chariot, and lounging in a devil-may-care sort of attitude, between the steps and the carriage-door, was a footman, while the coachman was amusing himself by trying to hit off, with the end of his whip, a fly that was on the ear of the near horse.

There were no armorial bearings on the panels of the vehicle, nor anything to indicate titled rank on the part of the owner; and yet the whole turn-out was decidedly stylish, and quite in the modern fashion of such matters. I never for a moment suspected that the occupant of the carriage had come to see the Barronellis, and when I sent in my card I was requested to walk into a scantily-furnished room on the second floor. I was rather amazed to see a large showy-looking woman seated there, and the Barronellis in a picturesque sort of group speaking to her respectfully. The lady was saying something when I went in, which she stopped short at my appearance, and fixing a glass to her eye, she said, languidly,—

"A family connexion, I presume?"—"No, madam," said Barronelli, stepping forward to me. "Allow me to introduce you to my friend, Dr. ——. Doctor, this is Mrs. a—a——"—"Cholmondeley Morgan," said the lady. "Glad to see you, doctor. An old friend, I presume, to Barronelli."—"No, madam," he replied, "not an old friend, but a very sincere one."

"Glad to hear it. Well, as I was saying with regard to your daughter, I have quite made up my mind that she is a very talented and a very amiable young person indeed, and I very much regret the occurrences of last night at the Opera, which really were shameful in the extreme. But after all, sometimes our misfortunes are our stepping stones to the most brilliant successes. I shall patronise your daughter, most certainly."—"You are very kind, madam," said Barronelli.

"I will call occasionally for her, you understand, and take her for a carriage airing. With her musical abilities she may do herself much good, and I am convinced that she only wants properly bringing out into society to make her fortune. Now I have on Wednesday evenings a soiree at my little place in South-street. Just a few of the best people, and that will give her a charming opportunity of displaying her talents."—"Of course," said Barronelli, "we cannot but be truly grateful for so much kindness from a stranger, madam. At present I fear my child's state of health will not permit her to avail herself of it."

"Oh, it will do her good," interrupted Mrs. Morgan. "It's the very thing. She is oppressed, and in bad spirits about this failure at the Opera, and the only way to get completely over that is, by change of scene, and change of occupation, to endeavour to forget it. But of course I am a stranger to you, and I am not so foolish as to suppose you are free from all the usual suspicions which unfortunately must attach themselves to any one in London who steps out from the ordinary routine of existence even to do good. Make some inquiries about me, and then decide for yourselves if you will accept my proffered friendship or reject it. That is fair, I believe."

She smiled in rather a winning sort of way, and then rising she left the room, followed by Barronelli, who made of course a very proper and complimentary reply to her. When he returned to the room he said,—

"Doctor, what am I to think of this? Is it genuine?"—"I really cannot say. How did the lady introduce herself?"

"Merely by driving up to the door, and sending in her card. God forbid that I should cast away a friend, but these disinterested pieces of kindness so seldom happen, that when they do, it really makes one suspicious of human nature."

"Make the inquiry she herself proposes," said I. "Have you her card?"—"Yes, it is here. 'Mrs. Cholmondeley Morgan, No. 77, South-street, Grosvenor-square.'"

"All seems fair enough. There is every appearance of this lady being what she generally represents, and if so, she is certainly a good connexion for your daughter, who may make a first-rate living by teaching the art, in which she is, no doubt, a proficient."—"I have thought of that," he said, "and should prefer it to the stage. Out of evil springeth good, after all. I will make inquiries concerning this lady, and if she be the kind, generous person her behaviour would warrant us in supposing, the gratitude of all our hearts will be hers."

I was upon the point of saying that I would myself assist in making these inquiries, but I thought upon consideration that I really had much better not, for it was running a very serious responsibility indeed, although I felt sufficiently in terested in the Barronellis to determine upon asking some of my patients, who lived in the locality, if they knew of a Mrs. Cholmondeley Morgan, and what they knew of her and her position in society.

This, however, I did not say to Barronelli, but changed the conversation to inquiries about his daughter's health, and I was pleased to find that although she was a very delicate girl, yet that which I had feared, namely, that consumption was exhibiting some of its incipient traces, was not the case, and that excitement and the novelty of the circumstances by which she had been surrounded on the previous evening had robbed her of her healthful bloom, and, indeed, half her beauty, for now I thought I had never seen a more lovely creature.

She herself thanked me with much grace and sweetness for the services I had rendered her, and in doing so, she impressed me much with her amiable and gentle manner, which was beauty and truth themselves, and must have charmed any one who was not dead to all proper appreciation of grace and loveliness.

During the conversation which succeeded I gathered many of the particulars, although by no means all which I have communicated already to my readers, regarding the Barronelli family. Of course I asked no questions, but their communications were quite unreserved to me, and were all given with an amiable frankness, which was to me very delightful, because it was so very rare.

I passed an hour and a half with them very pleasantly indeed; and any one to have seen us would have thought that we were the oldest friends in the world, we were so unrestrained and easy in our conversation. Then I rose to go, and just as I did so, there came a tap on the door of the room, and Barronelli directly exclaimed,—

"That's Arthur Graham, I know. How lucky he has come to be introduced to Dr. ———. Come in."

The door opened, and an extremely good-looking young man made his appearance. He was not one of your mighty genteel, spider-looking youths with which London abounds, and who are all angles and odd corners, but he was a well-looking, frank, intelligent fellow, with a face full of thought and energy, and a well put together, compact form, although rather small. He came in with a pleasant, familiar smile upon his face, but when he caught sight of me he drew back a step, and said,—

"I was not aware you had a visitor, Mr. Barronelli; I really beg your pardon for intruding."—"No intrusion," said Barronelli. "This is Dr. ———; and allow me, Dr. ———, the pleasure of introducing you to my young friend here, Arthur Graham, who we picked up acquaintance with through lodging in the same house once for some time, and who we know to be as good a creature ———"

"Nay, now," interrupted Arthur; "nay, now, sir ———"—
"Well, well; I say no more."

"A lover," said I to myself. "Humph! So the pretty Felice is bespoke, that's quite clear."

"How are you, Felice?" said Mr. Graham.—"Very well, thank you, Arthur; how are you?"—"Oh! I am always well, you know."

"Mind you endeavour always to keep so, then; for is it not a treasure?"

These questions and answers were spoken in so cool and unembarrassed a manner by the young people, and they looked in each other's faces as they spoke with such an utter absence of all that soft confusion which hovers around the eyes of those who love and look upon the loved one, that I confess I was staggered in my judgment, and began to think that surely I must be mistaken; and yet could he help loving Felice Barronelli?

What this young man was, too, quite puzzled me. Most commonly it happens that some sort of guess can be made of what the person is to whom, for the first time, we are introduced—that is to say, we may not, of course, be such conjurors as to hit upon his profession, but we may decide upon what class of society he belongs to. Now, all I could make up my mind to concerning this young man was, that he was well educated, for he spoke the written language of his country, instead of the common colloquial one.

There are particular tones of expression—there are modes of arranging sentences which at once proclaim the scholar to those who are capable themselves of judging, and I was at no loss to come to the conclusion that Graham was an educated man. Of course I could not very well say, "Mr. Graham, what are you?" So I was left to my own surmises; and as none of them came near the truth, I need not trouble my reader with them.

"Any news?" said Barronelli, casting a peculiar look upon the young man, who said, in reply,—"Nothing particular."

"You have met?"—"Yes."

"Thank God for that, Arthur."

"I shall be certainly *de trop* here," thought I, "if I stay any longer, so I will make a merit of necessity, and go at once. There are evidently some secrets in this Barronelli family, into which, as I have no right to pry, I will not attempt to do so."

"My friend," I said, "I have made a much longer visit than I anticipated, and will now bid you good day."

"And when shall we see you again?" said Barronelli.—
"Oh, I will call in as I find time so to do, and take my chances of finding you at home, and at leisure."

I shook hands with the whole of them, including Mr. Graham, who very pointedly expressed a hope that he should have the honour of my acquaintance, to which I replied,—

"I dare say we shall meet here, and I can assure you, that from what I have seen of this very amiable family, any friend of theirs comes before me strongly recommended. I am a physician."

Now, when a man had made a pointed request to be permitted to become acquainted with me, and he knew who and what I was, I thought I was entitled from him to a similar amount of information, and hence I had, in the most delicate way I could, popped the question to him, and then I lingered a moment for his answer.

"Sir," he said, " I am a day labourer."

"A what?"—"A day labourer, sir, although the too fond partiality of my friends, now no more, intended me for something better."

I glanced at his hands—they were delicately white. I took a survey of him from top to toe—all bespoke the gentleman.

"Pray, sir," he added, as he observed my looks of surprise, "do not mistake me; I neither carry a hod nor a pickaxe; and, perhaps, I may make my calling more intelligible to you when I tell you that I am a book writer."

"An author?"—"Why, yes, sir, I believe, on occasion, I am entitled to that name."

"But," said I, "you called yourself a day labourer, as if you attached some reproach to the phrase. I should say that there are many authors who would be glad to be day labourers in their vocation. Is there not a vast amount of literary talent and industry unemployed?"—"Certainly not, sir."

"Indeed! you surprise me."—"Why, in the first place, literary talent and literary industry are very rare companions. Where they unite they afford a fair enough chance of success to a certain extent; but as I say, they seldom do. There is either the talent without the industry, or the industry without the talent; and hence, to all appearance, we see clever men and industrious men neglected and leading a miserable, half-starved existence among their fellows."

"There is sound reason in what you say, my young friend, and it is a theme which interests me much, and which I should like to pursue with you, for I see you have made it a study. Will you give me a call?"—"With pleasure, sir; and will you do me a great favour in return?"

"What is it?"—"Only to look at a lady?"

"Look at a lady?"—"Yes," said Barronelli, stepping forward. "Arthur Graham asks any one whom he in the least esteems to look at a lady for him; and he lives in the hope of identifying her at last. He has known her four years, but knows not who she is."

"That's odd enough," said I. "Will you visit me tomorrow morning, at nine?"—"I will, sir."

"Adieu, then, for the present. I have outstood some of my engagements. Adieu—adieu!"

Exactly at nine, on the following morning, as I sat at breakfast, Mr. Graham's card was brought to me. I ordered that he should be instantly admitted, and he met me with that indescribable air of frankness and ingenuousness which is so very delightful to find in man or woman, but which, alas! is sadly made war against by the conventionalities of society. I begged him to be seated, and expressed that I was very glad to see him.

"You are very good, sir," he said; "and as really a perfect stranger to me, I feel doubly grateful to you for permitting me to make this call upon you, which must be, to a certain extent, an intrusion."

"Not at all, not at all. Have you breakfasted?"—"I have,

sir. I breakfasted this morning with my kind and dear friends, the Barronellis."

"They seem an attached family."—"They are. I never knew in any family a more perfect harmony to subsist than that which I know obtains among them."

"So I thought; but you hinted, Mr. Graham, at a secret of your own, upon which you thought I might be of some service to you."

"I did, sir; and however unwarrantable it may be, and seem of me, to trouble you with my private causes of uneasiness, I feel, like the ancient mariner in Coleridge's ballad, as if I were compelled now and then to make a confidant of somebody, just to ease my heart."—"Command my services," said I, "in any way."

I was getting curious, and waited now with some anxiety for Mr. Graham to proceed, which he did profoundly enough, when he fairly commenced.

"Sir," he said, "there is a long walk from the corner of Hyde-park, among some trees, towards Kensington-gardens."—"I know it."

"Well, sir, that walk was a very favourite one of mine, and just about twelve months since I was pursuing my way down it one fine refreshing morning, when I observed, some distance in advance of me, two young ladies. They were engaged in earnest conversation, and by their dress and appearance it was quite evident that they both belonged to the most respectable class of society. They were going at about my own pace; and as I have a great aversion to the practice of dogging the footsteps of a lady, I quickened my speed, intending to pass them, and then, when I had got some distance, to resume my old pace. The fates, doctor, decreed it otherwise; for just as I was upon the point of passing them, one caught her foot in some hole, or inequality in the ground, and would have fallen, had I not supported her on the moment. As it was, she sprained her ankle, and could walk but with difficulty, so that when I offered my arm as a support, she did not refuse it, but, on the contrary, seemed grateful for it."

"Ah! I understand," said I. "I have a comprehension on the subject. You fell in love."—"I did."

"With the fair object of your tender solicitude?"—"No."

"No—no!"—"Certainly not. I never thought of such a thing for a moment, doctor; oh, dear, no."

"Why—why you told me so just now. You said you fell in love this moment."—"Ah! I did, sir; but it was you who supplied the lady. I fell in love, most truly, most deeply, and most tremendously; but it was not with the object of my tender solicitude. Oh, no, it was with her friend."

"The other one?"—"Precisely, sir. I admired the young lady who sprained her ankle, but I loved the other. I found one an admirable, sensible girl, but the other was an angel. No man could respect the young lady who sprained her ankle more than I, but, sir, I adore the other, which makes all the difference."

"Oh!" said I.—"Ah, me!" sighed Mr. Graham. "It was a year ago, as nearly as may be, a year ago. I wonder who she is?"

"You wonder who she is?"—"I do, sir. The wonder of the Egyptians, and they were a wonderful people, is nothing to equal my wonder as to who she is, what she is, where she lives, and what's her name."

"So you cannot find her?"—"Oh, yes."

"Then what, in the name of all that's enigmatical, do you mean?"—"I can find her easy enough, but I cannot find her out. That's the difficulty. I see her once a-week always, sometimes twice, but that seems to have nothing to do with it. I don't know who she is, where she comes from, what friends she has, or what is the position of life she is in."

"And you have met her fifty-two times?"—"More, by many, and all by appointment. We are affianced, our troth is plighted, but I do not know who she is; we have sworn constancy, but I don't know her; I love her—I adore her. She is beautiful—she is highly educated—she is talented—accomplished—a very angel is she—but to what bright galaxy she belongs I do not know."

"But why don't you ask her?"—"Ask her! I ask her on an average thirty times every time we meet."

"And what does she say?"—"Wait," she says, "till the beautiful month of May."

"Why don't you follow her?"—"I passed my word that I would not; and, moreover, I likewise promised that I would employ no one to dog her footsteps. The only thing I have ever ventured to attempt in the way of a discovery of who and what she is, has been now and then to let a friend, on whose discretion I could rely, see her, under a promise not to follow her from any mistaken zeal in my service. Everybody shakes his head."

"Well, Mr. Graham, it is singular. And you say you love her, and that she is all you could wish her to be?"—"She is—she is. Now, sir, what would you advise me to do?"

"To wait patiently until the beautiful month of May."—"Tortures!"

"Fiddlesticks!"—"But—but—but——"

"Psha! Mr. Graham. Have patience. It only wants a month now, or thereabouts, to the date you mention; and, after persevering for a whole year, surely you can wait a twelfth part of that time now."—"I must, I presume; but will you look at her for me? I have a sort of superstitious feeling that you will know her. Your profession, of course, carries you among all sorts of people, and you might, by recognizing her, spare me another month's vain conjecture."

"Which, were I you, I would endure. You love the lady, and the wish to remain unknown to you until the date she mentions ought to be to you a law. Let her keep her secret if she will."—"You are right—I know you are right. I have no intention for a moment of disputing that with you. You are perfectly correct in the view you take of the subject, and yet, despite all that, will you go and look at her?"

"If you wish it. There is certainly a difficulty in arguing a point with a man who tells you you are quite right, however he may adopt a directly contrary course. When and how shall I see her, Mr. Graham?"—"To-morrow, my dear sir, if you can spare the time. I know that to ask a gentleman of your avocation to do a thing of this kind is to make sometimes a serious inroad on your time. If, therefore, it is likely to be inconvenient to a great extent, put it off until some other more available opportunity."

"That I cannot calculate upon," I said. "Let it be to-morrow. At what hour?"—"I am to meet her at the Oxford-street end of the walk I have mentioned to you, and which you have remarked that you know, at twelve o'clock precisely. We shall walk slowly towards Kensington gardens."

"Then, if I start from Kensington-gardens at the same hour, we have, I presume, a very fair chance of meeting somewhere about half way?"—"My dear sir, if you can do so——"

"I admit that the hour is an inconvenient one," said I; "but unless some urgent case demands my attention, I will be there. As a physician, you know, I cannot make a positive promise as regards the disposal of my time to anybody."—"Of that I am fully aware, my dear sir; and I assure you no man can appreciate more than I do the kindness you thus show towards an utter stranger."

"Never mind that," I said. "A man is never the less estimable because one has not known him for some time, and as you are here we will tap a bottle of wine to our acquaintance, Mr. Graham."—"My dear sir," he said, and I could hear his voice shake a little as he spoke, for he was one of those grateful-hearted persons who are easily led by the soft, silken thread of kindness,—"my dear sir, I know not how to thank you."

"Don't attempt it," said I.—"I am as poor in words," he added, "as I am in pocket; but if ever I am ill, I will—no, I won't, because I could not very well afford to pay your fee; but ——"

"That will do, Mr. Graham," I said.—"But still I may be able to show my gratitude in some way. If you should ever want anything written that you have neither leisure nor inclination to trouble yourself about, allow me try it. I am used to it—from a last dying speech and confession to an epic poem, sir; I have been thoroughly drilled into the business, and but that I have had a kind, a liberal, and a noble-hearted task-master, I think that now and then I should have trembled. But, sir, the labour we delight in, as Warwickshire Will says, physics pain; not but what I know some people who physic pain to a great extent."

"That's a cut at me, I suppose?" said I.—"No, sir," he replied. "It's a cut at another, who is worth cutting at for one reason."

"What is that?"—"Because he knows the difference between a kindly jest and a bitter one."

"An abundantly good reason," said I. "You are, from what you say, happy in your business arrangements."—"I am, sir," he replied. "I serve a gentleman, and I thank God for it. Perhaps you will say you are glad I have the grace to thank God for anything; for, to tell the truth, as regards religious feeling, I am not often 'i' the vein.'"

"You depend entirely on your pen?"—"I do, sir, and work closely. Time was when I had an itch for speculation, but now I think differently.

———"'I keep my outlay, sir,
A span within my means.
    *   *   *   *
———————Better owe
A yard of land to labour, than to chance
Be debtor for a rood.'" ·

"Right," said I. (By-the-bye, I ought to mention that we were emptying a bottle of Madeira very fast.) "Right; a better rule of action could not be. One man's chance success is another's bitter distress."—"Hear, hear," exclaimed Graham. "Now, doctor, will you do me a favour—a great favour?"

"What is it?" said I. "I never make any imprudent promises."—"Will you allow me to send out for a bottle of champaigne?"

"Most decidedly not."—"Indeed! Well, I am very sorry; but you will take one with me somewhere?"

"No, I cannot. This Madeira will be *quantum suff* for me; but as regards the champaigne, we will have a bottle up."—"No, no, no, no."

"Yes, yes, yes, yes. John, bring me a bottle of champaigne."—"Yes, sir."

"Really, now, this is too bad." (John placed the wine on the table.) "My dear doctor." (John handed him a pair of nippers.) "Really now—" (bang went the cork) "D—d bad wire that."—"Indeed!"

"Yes, doctor; there's a quantity of bad wire in the market. By-the-by, they don't tie up wire; they do it up, and when they have done it up the people who buy it are *done* too. Now I know a wire-maker———"

"Do you?"—"Yes, I do, doctor. He is a trump. There is no freezing mixture in his heart, wherever else it may exist. 'Show me your company, and I'll tell you what you are.'" (The champaigne was going.)

"Why, you are as argumentative," said I, "as a Jew attorney."—"Sir," said Graham (and he seemed to grow suddenly sober), "I know a Jew attorney—a gentleman—liberal, just—full to the brim, as if his heart were an overflowing cup of good fellowship and proper feeling—generous, gifted—true in friendship—honest to all—a good fellow, sir—a clear head, and a heart exactly in the right place. Doctor, let me give you a word of advice. Don't fall into the cant of abusing a *class* because you may have happened to meet with a bad specimen. The friend you speak to may, as I can, be able to match you with such an one as shall make you shrink from wholesale sneers while you live."

    *   *   *   *   *

I have since profited by Graham's advice; but on that particular evening, I am really ashamed to say that we finished both the bottle of Madeira and the bottle of champaigne, and I recollect quite well Graham telling me a story, which I shall present to the reader as he gave it.

You must know, doctor (he said), that I have been in Ireland, and one evening there, after a few tumblers of the best whiskey that ever enlivened the hearts of man, my friend, M'Guire, felt himself all over, as he expressed himself, up to his shoulders in love with everything and everybody. I knew that this was just the happy moment to screw a multiplicity of fun from him. I began by asking him if he ever was in love, when he informed me that he had once an ardent attachment to a certain Biddy Ryan, of Ennistimon, a lady of certain considerable attractions, to whom he had been for a long time constant, and through the intervention of the priest, agreed to marry.

Paddy's consent to the arrangement was not altogether the result of his reverence's eloquence, nor indeed the justice of the case; nor was it quite owing to Biddy's black eyes and pretty lips, but rather to the soul-persuading powers of some twelve or thirteen tumblers of strong punch, which he swallowed at a merry-making in Biddy's father's house, one cold evening in December; after which he betook himself to the road homewards, where —— but we must give his story in his own words:—

"Whether it was the prospect of happiness before me, or the whiskey," said Paddy, "but so it was, I never felt a step of the road home that night, though it was every foot of five miles. When I came to a stile, or hedge, or ditch, I used to give a whoop! and ever I went; then I'd run for a hundred yards or two, flourish my stick, cry out, "Who'll say a word against Biddy Ryan?' and then over another ditch flying. Well, sure enough, I reached home at last, and wet enough I was, but I didn't care for that; I opened the door and struck a light—there was the least taste of kindling on the hearth, and I put some dry sticks into it, and some turf, and knelt down and began to blow it up.

"'Troth,' says I to myself, 'if I wor married, it isn't this way I'd be, on my knees like a sinner of a spalpeen; but when I'd come home, there 'ud be a fine fire blazin' afore me, and a clane table out afore it, and a beautiful cup of tay waiting for me—and somebody I won't mention sitting there looking at me, smilin.' — 'Don't be making a fool of yourself, Paddy M'Guire,' said a gruff voice, near the chimney.

"I jumped at him, and cried out, 'Who's that?' but there was no answer; and at last, after going round the cabin, I began to think that it was only my own voice I heard, so I knelt down again and set to blowing the fire.

"'And it's yourself, Biddy,' says I, 'that would be an ornament to a dacent cabin; and a purtier leg and foot———'— 'Be the light that shines, you're making me sick, Paddy M'Guire,' said the voice again.

"'The heavens be about us,' says I; 'what's that, and who are you at all?' for somehow I thought I knew the voice. — 'I'm your father,' says the voice.

"'My father!' said I. 'Blessed Virgin! is it the truth you're telling me?'—'The devil a word of a lie in it,' says the voice. 'Take me down, and give me an air of the fire, for the night's cowld.'

"'And where are you, father,' says I, 'if it's pleasing to you?' — 'I'm on the dressher,' says he; 'don't you see me?'

"'Sorra bit o' me. Where now?' — 'Arrah, on the second shelf, near the rowling-pin. Don't you see the green jug—that's me!'

"'Oh! the saints in Heaven be out us!' says I, 'and are you a green jug?'—'I am,' says he, 'and sure I might be worse. Tim Healy's mother is only a certain utensil, and she died two years before me.'

"'Oh, father, darling,' says I, 'I hoped you wor in glory, and you only a jug all this time!—blood and turf.' — 'Never fret about it,' says my father; 'it is the transmogrification of sowls, and we'll all be right by-and-by. Take me down I say, and put me near the fire.'

"So I up and took him down, and wiped him with a clean cloth, and put him on the hearth before the blaze.

"'Paddy,' says he, 'I'm famished with the druth. Since you took to courting, there's nothing ever goes into my mouth —haven't you a taste of something in the house?'

"I warn't long before I hated some water, and took down the bottle of whiskey and some sugar, and made a rousing jug full, as strong as the very devil.

"'Are you satisfied, father?' said I. — 'I am,' says he; 'you are a dutiful child, and here's our health, and don't be thinking of Biddy Ryan.'

"With that my father began to explain how there was never any rest nor quietness for a man after he was married —more be token if his wife was fond of talking; and that he never could take his dhrop of drink in comfort afterwards.

"'May I never,' says he, 'but I'd rather be a green jug as I am now, than live again with your mother. Sure it's not here you'd be sitting to-night, says he, 'discoursing with me, if you were married—devil a bit. Fill me,' says my father, 'and I'll tell you more.'

"And sure enough I did, and we talked away till near daylight; and then the first thing I did was to take the ould mare out of the stable, and set off to the priest, and towld him all about it, and how my father wouldn't give his consent by no means.

"'We'll not mind the marriage,' says his riverence; 'but go back and bring me your father—the jug, I mean, and we'll try and get him out of trouble—for it's trouble he's in, or he wouldn't be that way. Give me the two pounds ten,' says the priest; 'you had it for the wedding, and it will be better spent getting your father out of purgatory than sending you into it.' — 'But the green jug—my father—I cannot part with; death an age, it would be enough to kill me.'

"'Nor shall you, Pat,' said the priest; 'I will just have a few masses said over it, then you can have it home again, and we will fill it up with some of the right sort, and drink till his soul's in glory.'

"Faith, and sure enough it wasn't long till that same happened, and something else also, that I'll be after telling you another time. In the meantime, here's to your health and good-luck, and long life to enjoy it, to Biddy Ryan, and all her seed, breed, and generation," say I, " though 'tis myself that ought to have her cozy and comfortable by my side of a cowld night like this; but, God help me! 'tis the owld man that has spiled me entirely. Och—hone! 'twas a pity my father couldn't go to Heaven at once, without stopping at the half-way."

Here Paddy placed the glass on the table, gave a wild yahoo, which none but an Irishman can do, and rushed out yelling, leaping, and roaring through the country, like a madman.

"Bravo!" cried I, "bravo, Graham. Now, is not that your own?"—"No, no, no, certainly not, doctor. But I am afraid I am detaining you from your patients, doctor. I have heard a number of knocks, and will now bid you a good morning."

"I have heard the knocks, too," said I, "and so will not ask you to remain. Depend upon my punctuality to-morrow morning; I will be, precisely at twelve, in the walk by Kensington-gardens, or you may conclude that something very urgent has prevented me."—"Adieu—adieu."

I should, I must own, have been better pleased had young Graham taken Felice Barronelli to his affections than the unknown lady of Hyde-park. I thought he and Felice worthy of each other, but as for his incognita, she might be a great deal the other way, and very far from being quite an unexceptionable personage. And Felice was beautiful too; she was young, evidently of a kind and pleasant disposition; a mind richly stored, and had been gifted by partial nature with rare abilities. I wondered to myself very much how Graham could have avoided falling in love with Felice, but there is no fighting against facts. There was affection between them, but no love as a passion; and a very great pity, too, I told myself, for I am not of that school of philosophy which says, "whatever is is right."

When I came alone to consider of what Graham had told me, and of the very mysterious manner in which he had been now for so long paying his addresses to an unknown, I blamed him for being too nice in regard to not discovering the incognita of the lady; and as I suppose it is a principle of nature to suspect the worst when there is a concealment, I could not help indulging in several shakes of the head upon the subject of Graham's young lady, and what she might turn out to be.

The visit, too, of the odd-looking and odd-mannered person who kept so dashing an equipage, to the Barronelli's, gave me uneasiness. I had no right whatever to suspect her of any sinister intentions, but still I well knew that in London such beauty as Felice's was a dangerous possession; and I likewise well knew that such benevolence as the lady's who called with so much commiseration, was sufficiently rare to make it be looked upon with some suspicion.

There was certainly one circumstance in her favour. She had herself hinted at what construction might be put upon her visit, and had courted inquiry; consequently, by being at all suspected, she might be a very injured person; and as for a certain unladylike oddity of manner, it would be hard to say that a benevolent and really right-thinking person might not be so afflicted, if I may be allowed to use so strange a term.

It would, I thought, be hard indeed if young Graham were to find out that his Kensington Gardens incognito was no better, if half so good, than she should be, and poor Felice was to be led into any serious peril by the benevolent lady with the unexceptionable chariot. What a blow it would be to the family. And what right have I to be so desperately suspicious? None whatever. I might blame the world for sowing in my mind the seeds of suspicion, but I will be as cautious in permitting them to grow up too wild and straggling as I possibly can.

Having promised Graham that I would if possible take a look at his park beauty, I was anxious to redeem that pledge; and although by twelve o'clock I could not, by any possibility, have made my whole round of visits, yet I thought as I had some one to see near the top of Quebec-street, Oxford-street, I might manage to run down to Kensington Gardens and walk up again to the corner of the Edgeware-road within the magical period of time when the fair unknown was to make her gracious appearance. The inquiries I proposed making about the benevolent lady I was compelled to put off till a later period of the day, because I could not possibly tell how long they would take me.

Having thus arranged all this as well as I could, I started from my house earlier than usual to make my round of visits, and I am afraid I did not listen to the details of some hypochondriacal patients with so much patience on that morning as I was usually in the habit of calling into active exercise. One old lady, in particular, I very nearly offended completely, for when she said to me, with a serious shake of the head,—

"Doctor, a new symptom of the most dreadful character has arisen," I replied,—"Indeed; what is it madam? I expected some new symptoms."—"Did you, indeed, doctor. Well, since yesterday, at twenty minutes past six, or thereabout, the floor began to move about in waves, doctor."

"You must be mistaken, madam."—"Oh, but I saw it."

"No, madam, it's a curious delusion. You may depend, madam, the ground landlord, who is looking for the reversion of the house, would not allow such a thing."—"But, doctor——"

"Imagination, my dear madam, imagination."—"Then I begin to fear you don't understand my case, doctor."

This speech recalled me to a sense of my professional duties, and I said,—

"If it should appear again, I should say something to it, madam; of course then I should have to prescribe some conclusive remedies for it. If at the same hour to-day it begins again, we shall then know what to do."

"Very good, sir—very good."

And so, after prescribing an effervescing draught, I got over my difficulty, and was more cautious as I went on. Notwithstanding, however, all the haste I made, the clocks were striking twelve before I had finished my call in Quebec-street; and I had to make good speed to get down the Tyburn-road in anything like time, for Graham had told me that the lady was always very punctual in keeping her appointments.

I went into the park by the small gate which is close to the gardens, and then divesting myself as much as I could of all appearance of hurry, I sauntered slowly up that avenue of trees which some people just now are making such a cant about being enclosed; although, for my part, how any decent person can walk much in any of the parks or public places about the metropolis, is a mystery to me, on account of abundance of offensive particulars, with a description of which I cannot deface my pages. But to resume.

The day was a brilliant one, and although the hour was early for the haut ton, yet there was a tolerable sprinkling of equipages and equestrians in the park, as well as the usual assortment of idle, lounging blackguards and nurserymaids who come to the aforesaid, and children who are left to the care of a watchful Providence, which certainly ought not to be saddled with so much trouble when people are paid to do it.

After the haste I had made, I enjoyed my quiet, easy walk, beneath the cool branches of the trees, very much; only I began to think that, as far as regarded the object for which I had undertaken it, it would be a vain one, for I saw nothing of my new friend Graham, or of any one at all answering the description of his fair unknown devoted one.

Then passed me a butcher-boy, whistling some popular ditty; then passed me two idle-looking fellows, who were what they call "larking," which consists in hustling each other against every decent person they meet, and then declaring it was not they who did it. I had the satisfaction of making such a sudden and dead stand against one of these fellows, who was thrown with great violence against me by his companion, that he rolled in the dirt, and was nearly stunned.

On I walked, and I think I had proceeded about two-thirds of the way, and was beginning to give up the affair as a bad job, when I saw two figures coming slowly towards me. The one, of course, I recognised at a glance—it was Graham. The other, I had no doubt, was the unknown; but I was not sufficiently close to see her face. They appeared to be in deep and earnest conversation, and to be so much engrossed by each other, that they saw nothing, heard nothing, knew nothing of the world around them.

Of course, as they were making towards me, and I towards them, we made an accumulating progress, which very quickly decreased the distance between us. Without being obtrusive or particular, I kept my eyes as much upon the lady as I could. There was no mistaking the general air and manner, she was—a lady. Let her name and station be what they may, there was that about her—that indescribable charm of appearance, which showed good breeding and elegant habits. She was plainly dressed, destitute of all ornament, and yet she was "a lady every inch."

Her figure was slight, and rather, if anything, below the usual standard even of women. Till she came quite near, I had no opportunity of seeing her face, but, when she did, I thought I should have looked at it for ever.

She was very, very beautiful. There was, too, upon her countenance, the requisite charm of an excited intellect mingling secretly with her childlike symmetry of features, and delicacy of expression. At a rough guess, her age appeared to me to be about twenty. It is scarcely necessary to say that she was a complete stranger to me; I had never seen her before, nor any one like her, but I felt quite confident now that, having once seen her, I should never forget her.

Graham never looked up, so they passed on. He was too much absorbed with his companion. I dare say he forgot me and the appointment, and everything connected with it, and my sight too of him. I walked very slow, so they reached me, and I heard a soft, sweet voice—it was hers—say,—

"Yes—yes—the twenty-fourth of May."

"Would it were here," said Graham.

I heard her sigh, as if she echoed from the bottom of her heart the sentiment, and then they had passed on, and I heard no more of their conversation. When they had got, as I guessed, some considerable distance from me, I looked round. They seemed to have quickened their pace, and I watched them until, by the entwining trees, they were shaded from my sight. A seat was close at hand, and I sat down to pass five minutes in thought. My views with regard to the incognita were much altered; I had thought she might be unworthy; now I thought such a thing impossible, so much are we swayed by that most eloquent of all letters of recommendation, a beautiful and intelligent face.

"No, no," I said, "she is nothing wrong; she is innocence itself and beauty. There is a mystery, but it is one from out of which she will emerge most gloriously. I never saw such a countenance in all my life! What, in the name of Heaven, can she be? Who, in the name of all that's wonderful, can she be? If she is not virtuous, then she has no business with such a face, and well might any one who looked upon her beauty exclaim with the poet of all ages, Shakspere,—

'Oh, what a temple have those vices got,
  Which for their habitation chose out thee!'"

I was in the midst of these reflections, and had sat ten minutes on the seat, when some one touched me on the shoulder, and, hastily looking up, I saw Graham standing close to me, with an expression of animation and happiness in his face I had never before noticed in him. His eyes were brighter, and more sparkling; his whole figure seemed to be dilated, and he presented a totally different appearance from the quiet harmony of manner he usually exhibited.

"Graham!" I exclaimed.

"Yes, doctor, it's Graham. A thousand thanks for your kindness in coming here. You have seen her?"

"I have."

"Do you know her?"—"Certainly not."

"Nor any one else," he said, with a sigh. "This is an experiment I will not repeat, for I am convinced now, from experience of all sorts and conditions of people, that it is utterly useless; and yet who could ever look once upon that face and not know it again? This, to me, is most marvellous!"—"Marvellously beautiful!" said I.

"You think so—you really think so?" he said, eagerly.

"I know so, Mr. Graham. There can be but one opinion upon such a subject. She is extremely beautiful. I do not know her; and, indeed, the chances of any one knowing her must be very small, when you come to consider how long a person may live in London, and be unknown even by sight to their next door neighbours."

"True, true."

"I suppose you have made no further progress as to a discovery of who or what she is?"

"None. I urged her much, and still her reply gently given was, 'wait till the twenty-fourth of May.'"

"Then once again," I said, "let me repeat my sincere advice to do so patiently. She is entitled to so much courtesy at your hands; and the more especially as she has fixed a date, from which she has not wavered."

"I will wait, doctor, and the experiment of to day shall be the last I will make upon the subject. Nay, I will even forbear to urge her upon it at all, but continue to meet her, and to enjoy the bliss of her society without troubling her."

"A wise determination, Graham, and one which you will not repent of. And now tell me truly, have you made her thoroughly acquainted with your own position in life?"

"I have. And so fearful was I of exaggerating, that I rather, in the account I gave, decreased my means and resources."

"That I commend you in; and I must own that I wait with quite as much impatience as you do yourself for the twenty-fourth of May. In which direction are you walking?"

"In any—in any."

"Then come with me; I have a call to make in the New-road, and we can have a little gossip as we go on."

We reached the gate at Hyde-park, opposite the Edgware-road, into which I wanted to cross, but there was such a throng of carriages, that we were compelled to wait for a convenient opening.

"This is always a troublesome crossing," I had just remarked, when Graham suddenly exclaimed,—

"Good God! look there!"—"Where? where?" said I.

"By heavens, 'tis she!—'tis she! There, in that barouche! Don't you see her? There—there!"

I looked in the direction he indicated, and there, sure enough, seated in a barouche, along with a red-faced, bullying-looking, sensual-featured man, was Graham's beautiful incognita. A coronet was on the panels of the barouche, and, as it flitted past, I could see that all its appointments, as well as the servants who attended upon it, betokened great wealth.

"My God!" exclaimed Graham, "here is a surprise!"

"Did you speak, sir?" said a livery servant, who was lounging against the iron rails.

The idea suddenly struck me that I might get information from this man, and I said,—

"Are you in service in London?"—"Yes, sir."

"Then you know some of the people. Did you see a barouche pass just now with a red-faced man and a young lady in it?"—"Certainly I did, sir; don't you know 'em?"

"No; do you?"—"In course I do, sir. That was the well-known Earl of Bradstock, sir."

"And the lady?"—"His last kept woman, sir; she was a tidy one, warn't she? He's always got somebody."

Graham turned of an ashy paleness, and had to hold by the iron rails for support.

"Come, come," said I, "be a man, and congratulate yourself upon so lucky an escape—be a man, Graham. Come along with me."

He turned to the groom, who looked surprised at the effect his information had produced, and in a low, agitated voice he said,—

"My good fellow, are you sure?"

"Of course I am, sir, or else I shouldn't have said it."

"Come along, doctor, come along; God knows I loved her —what a dreadful day is this. Come along—come along. Good heavens! who would, who could have dreamt of this?"

I gave him my arm, and we crossed the road together, I feeling nearly as much bewildered by what had happened as he himself could.

"My dear fellow," I said, "be calm, and talk over this affair rationally. Tell me now, where is your next appointment with your beautiful unknown?"

"Don't call her that—don't call her that," he said; "she is too well known—don't mention her to me."

"Yes, but you must do something, you know; you will not feel disposed to allow the affair so quietly to drop?"

"No," he said, suddenly, "it shall not drop so quietly. I love her still, but it is a love which shall exhaust itself in pity; she never now can be mine, but still her mind cannot be wholly vitiated. With God's help I will yet rescue her from her present awful position. What means I have shall be placed at her disposal if she will leave her present mode of life. I will make one effort to rescue her from infamy and shame."

"Nobly spoken," said I—"nobly spoken, Graham. Carry out your intention; what if, after all, there is some mistake?"

"Oh, God, if any one could tell me that," he said, and his whole countenance became suddenly lit up with joyful emotion, "how happy should I then be."

"I do not ask you," I said, "to cherish such an idea, but still you must admit it to be possible; be, therefore, very cautious what you do, Graham."—"I will—I will. Heaven is my judge, doctor, that I would not injure her for worlds. But what mistake could there be? The man saw her, and said he knew her—oh, fatal recognition!"

"No, Graham, no, not fatal recognition; the fatality would have been all the other way. Heaven knows what inducements she may have to provide herself with a husband, and had you married her, not knowing what she was, there indeed might have been some odd day a fatal recognition. But come, now, withdraw yourself from too close a contemplation of this unhappy circumstance. Let us ascertain some further particulars concerning this Earl of Bradstock. I shall be disengaged after four o'clock to-day; suppose, now, we dine together and sally out on a double errand."

"A double errand, doctor?"—"Yes; to ascertain what we can of the Earl of Bradstock, and who is living with him, as well as to make some inquiry concerning the wonderfully benevolent lady who has taken so kind an interest in Felice Barronelli."

"We will—we will. Do you suspect her to be other than what she seems?"—"Why, to tell the honest truth, Graham, after what we have heard this morning, I could find in my heart to suspect an angel out of heaven."

"And I—and I,—God help me, and I."—"I don't wonder at it. But do not despair. Only imagine how much more, even than you ever did, you will prize the beauty and the love of your fair unknown, if she should come scathless from the dreadful suspicions that now haunt her."

"Not more—not more; I cannot love her more than I have loved her—than I love her still."—"Nay, Graham, excuse me there. We never do know fully the value of a possession until by some fortuitous course of circumstances it is in a way of being wrested from us. You are depressed now in spirits, but if you could be convinced that there was some great mistake, and that your much-loved beauty was maligned, you would feel a gush of happiness such as you have never yet known—such even, I may add, as you will never know again."

"Perhaps you are right—I cannot tell now. But I do love her, sir, surely as man never yet loved woman."

"A-hem!"

"I adore the very ground she treads on. She was to me the one bright star in all the galaxy of beauty and perfection, to fix my wondering soul for ever."—"Exactly."

"If she be unworthy, then have goodness, virtue, excellence, and every kindred quality forsaken the earth, and I shall pant to leave it too, for what to me are light, life, and all the world can offer me, without her? Oh, this dreadful sense of loneliness! Never till now did I feel it come over me in such a dread reality of pangs."—"Very good," said I. "For a man who might have been dreadfully taken in, you are about as philosophical as may be."

"But her face?"—"I grant you all about her face."

"Her hand, her small, infantine, beautiful hand—oh, how I have loved that hand?"

"I didn't see it."

"And her voice!—the harps of angels! Such dulcet melody as comes upon a pure spirit's ear when first it quaffs the breath of immortality and joy. Oh, I shall go mad! mad! mad!"—"Well, I shouldn't wonder," said I; "and, if you do, I will sign a certificate to get you into Bedlam, where you will be as comfortable, at all events, as circumstances will permit; and, on the proper days, your friends can come and see you."

"Cease! cease!"—"To be sure, I cannot promise you a billiard-table, or a violin, or a pianoforte; for, to entitle yourself to such indulgencies, you must add some great crime to the catalogue of your eccentricities."

"Come along, doctor, come along."

By the time we had dined and talked over the affair of the barouche and its occupants, Graham had got into a better frame of mind, and was more able to come to rational conclusions, than in the first flush of his disappointment.

I could, of course, well perceive that he was ill at ease, and probably he was more so than he allowed me even to see, notwithstanding an ingenuous manner about him, which made it, no doubt, difficult for him to conceal his feelings to any great extent. If, however, any man be justified in wearing a mask for a moment, it is when he makes the chivalrous and most commendable endeavour to hide his own private griefs, lest they should become a source of vexation and annoyance to his friends. This I saw that Arthur Graham was striving to do, and much I thought of him for it.

"Now, Graham," I said, "we will go out; and suppose while we are out that we endeavour to do something for the Barronellis, as well as make the necessary inquiries concerning your unknown lady, who yet you should not absolutely despair about."

"Ah, sir, have you any hope?"—"I have."

"And from what source, may I ask?"

"Certainly. I do not believe that nature works ever very enigmatically. I think that where we see a countenance full of that kind of beauty which speaks to the heart at once, and convinces us that it is made up far more of gentleness of expression and high mindedness, than of mere contour, we have every right to come to the conclusion that the disposition bears some similarity to the glorious impress of it that is on the face."

"Ah! the deadly serpent has a beautiful skin."

"Oh, pho! pho!"

"Some poisons steal over the senses exquisitely."

"I beg your pardon there—they do no such thing."

"Well, of course you know best; but, from the beginning of the world, you know ——"

"Stop. I will not listen to any illustration which commences so long ago as that. I do not mean to assert that your young lady of the park is immaculate, but I do mean to assert that even you and I should not condemn her. I have seen so many cases in which hasty conclusions have been come at, apparently upon the most well-grounded premises, that I have become doubtful now almost of what I see; vice in appearance may be virtue in reality, and what would look like the very sublimity of virtue not unfrequently turns out to be vice in an artful disguise."

"You may be right, but perhaps you allude to medical cases?"—"No, I mean moral ones."

"Well, well, it is a strange world; and the maxim of 'Never trust to appearances,' finds too frequent confirmation for it to be wholly disputed. I have but to hope, with all my heart and soul, that you are right, doctor. I shall not grudge you any amount of triumphant cheers you may feel disposed to bestow upon yourself."

"Don't," said I; "and now come along, and let us, for a moment, put you and your park incognita upon the shelf."

"The shelf—oh, I wish you could. If it were ever such a narrow shelf, I would make it do."

"No doubt; but if you go on interrupting me, I shall never get to the end of a sentence."

"Very good. Go on, go on."

"Then what I meant to say was, that you have, I am sure, the best and the kindest of feelings towards the Barronellis."

"You do me then no more than justice."

"Good. Why or wherefore you have not fallen in love with Felice Barronelli is one of those profound mysteries which I leave to some one else to unravel."—"Do."

"But I shall continue to wonder at it, whenever I have a little leisure for such an occupation. To come, however, to the point. Will you now accompany me to the neighbourhood of South-street, Grosvenor-square, to make inquiries concerning Mrs. Cholmondeley Morgan, whom we both saw at the Barronellis'?"—"Certainly I will."

"Come along, then. What is your candid opinion of the woman?"—"I don't like her."

"Nor I."

"And yet we must not judge from appearances, you know, doctor. She may be good ——"—"And great ——"

"And virtuous ——."—"And benevolent."

"Or something entirely different, doctor. Come on, and let us be diligent in our inquiries; for Barronelli, in addition to being a foreigner, and so not able to judge so well as we can in the matter, has all the anxieties of a father, about which, thank God, we you know have not."—"Amen!"

Thus discoursing, we reached the immediate neighbourhood of South-street, Grosvenor-square, and upon referring to a memorandum I had made, and finding the number of Mrs. Cholmondeley Morgan's house was 77, we walked up to it to take a look at it, not that such a process was very much calculated to enlighten us with regard to the character of the lady who there resided, but somehow or another it seemed natural for us to do so, so we did it. We were not so foolish as many people who receive a letter and sit for five minutes gazing at the outside, the postmark, the seal, and the direction, now and then exclaiming,—

"Well, I really wonder now who this can be from?" for

DIARY OF A PHYSICIAN.

such people have an opportunity of opening the letter, and we had none of opening the house, but still we did find some interest in looking at it.

Seventy-seven was a comfortable enough, aristocratic-looking house—not too large or bulky, and yet occupying space enough to be decidedly stylish. All its appointments, as far as we could see them, appeared to be quite perfect. We should liked to have seen some of the household, but in that we were disappointed, and as we did not like to be prowling about as if we meditated a burglary, we were fain to content ourselves by a good look at the house, and an unqualified approval of its personal appearance.

"This will do," said I.—"Oh, yes. Yes, it seems a respectable house enough, and we can hardly well imagine any one getting into such a house as a tenant whose character was otherwise than unexceptionable."

In all those situations at the west-end of the town, there are to be found close at hand some very retired, out-of-the-way looking public houses, where the servants are in the habit of going, and which is made a general gossipping shop for the whole neighbourhood. These public-houses are, indeed, mostly kept by men who have been servants, and who have saved enough to make the venture, or been left something by the death of a master or a mistress, which has

enabled them to enter into that line of business which of all others is the special admiration of coachmen, grooms, butlers, &c.

If these people can ever muster enough money to get into a public-house in some of those localities where they are known, they have reached the height of their ambition, as well as contriving to do very well indeed. At the bar and in the parlours of these houses the characters and the peculiarities of masters and mistresses are canvassed, and talked over with immense effect, and a new footman, or a new coachman, learns more of the neighbourhood in a week by such means than he would acquire by his own unaided powers of observation in a year.

It was for one of these houses that we looked, and at the corner of a mews we soon found one, which was quiet-looking, and apparently nearly at that time of the day deserted. Into it we went, and found a jolly looking man in the bar, with a jean jacket on, and a red face, which showed that he was not entirely accustomed to anchorite's fare. He looked at us when we came in, as if to assure himself that he knew us not, for I dare say he had few customers who were unknown to him, and civilly requested our orders.

Now, in public-houses you are always estimated according to the price of the modicum of alcohol you choose to indulge yourself with, so, if you desire to make an impression upon your host of a favourable character, you had better have brandy.

"Two glasses of brandy and water hot," said I, "and if you have no objection to join us, you may as well make it three."

Admiration twinkled in the eyes of the landlord, and he gave a kind of apoplectic chuckle, as he said,—

"Your servant, gentlemen. Great pleasure, gentlemen, indeed—very great pleasure," and he forthwith, from a private bottle, brewed the three glasses, which certainly were very good.—He looked at me when I had tasted mine, as much as to say, "That is the real article, and I hope that you know it."

I nodded, and he laughed till he nearly choked himself, and alarmed me so much that I began fumbling in my pocket for a lancet to bleed him with, in case of congestion of the brain ensuing. However, I suppose he was used to it, for he recovered, and then I said,—

"Do you know the neighbourhood well?"—"Do I know the neighbourhood?" he repeated, in a reproachful tone. "Why, haven't I lived in it seven-and-forty years?"

"Indeed! Then you ought to know it well."—"I rather think I ought. Look at the bar—look at these here bottles. Look at me."

"Yes—yes."—"Well, do I know this here bar?—do I know these bottles?—Do I know me?"

"Of course."—"Then I knows this neighbourhood; and every mortal soul as is in it, 'cepting Muley Busconobia, and him as they calls the Earl o' Piper and Flint. I don't know them."

"Indeed."—"And what's more, sir (here he drank of his brandy)—and what's more, sir, I won't know 'em.—No—no—n———o!"

"Pray, who are they?"—"You may well ask. One on 'em—the Muley one—is some fellow as has been brought over here by one of those blessed societies for the propagation o' wice, and the expression of the gospel, or something o' that ere sort, sir. He's a Turk, he is, and he com'd in here one day with a man they calls a *terpretar*, to ask me to shut up my house, cos he didn't like it all along o' getting a squint at t from his bedroom window; and when I wouldn't what do you think he said?"

"I really can't say."—" No, nor ever would—of course you can't say; and that's just why I always ask a gentleman, because he can't say—ah!"

"Oh, and a very good reason, too. But, perhaps, you will tell us what he said, and then we shall know?"—"In course you will. He made the *terpreter* tell me he hoped the 'curse of the profit' would stick to me."

"The Prophet, Mahomet, he meant."—" D——n what he meant; I told him I liked nothing better than the curse of the profit, and that it was only the curse of the loss that ever put me out of sorts."

"And what did he say?"—"He made a sort of a movement with his brown-looking paws, and wipes his feet and spits behind the door."

"What next?"—"Well, sir, I asked the *terpreter* what the devil he meant by that?—and he says, says he, 'Oh, he means that he washes his hands of you.' 'Oh,' says I, ' does he? You can tell him, then, in French, that they much need it.' Then he says he damns me in his lingo; so I damns him in good English, and I told him he might go to blazes, and away he went in a rage."

I had preserved my gravity till now; but I could hold out no longer, and I burst into a roar of laughter, which quickly found an echo in the mouth of Graham. It was really one of the most ludicrous things that I ever heard, this account which the landlord gave of his interview with the Turk.— The worthy landlord did not seem at all disconcerted at our mirth, but he joined in it most heartily; and when it had in some measure subsided, I was so much amused with him, that I was resolved to draw him out a little further, so I said—

"Well, I can easily account for your dislike to know anything of the Turk; but what objections have you to the earl you mentioned?"—" Pipe and Flint?"

"Yes. It's an odd title."—" Well, sir, I won't swear I've got it quite right, 'cos you see, sir, I won't interest myself enough in it to try."

"Indeed, why so?"—" He's a screw, sir—a Scotchman. I won't know him. He's one of those fellows, sir, as are called earls; but Scotch earls are very different things from English ones. I shouldn't wonder now, sir, but the Earls of Pipe and Flint, in their own country, don't know what a thing it is to have a pair of breeches. He's come here and brought a beggarly set with him, to try and get situations, sir, you must know; and when they were forced to employ an English coachman, they sent here to know how little I'd contract to give him half a pint of beer a day for, as he would have beer; only he wanted a pot, so he wouldn't stay with them.

"They send here, sir, for half a pint of fourpenny ale sometimes, and I wondered what they wanted it for, till somebody told me they kept it till it got sour and served for vinegar, by which, you see, sir, they saved about another halfpenny. I won't know such people, sir, and, in my humble opinion, the country will never come to much good till there's a tax on all Scotchmen."

"A tax on Scotchmen?"—" Yes, sir. They ought to be made pay enough here; that would prevent them coming from their own beggarly country, and taking the bread out of Englishmen's mouths. They are brought up, sir, to live upon next to nothing, and to think that extravagant; now, an Englishman is not, you see."

"That's true."—" You may say that, sir. I was told all about it by a Scotchman himself, who was seized with remorse, and died of it."

"A rare case that."—" Very rare, sir. He told me there were houses in London, kept by Scotchmen, where they boarded and lodged young, burly, raw-boned, fresh-caught countrymen of their own for three shillings a week till they got a situation; and whenever a situation of any sort is vacant, the usual salary of which perhaps has been twenty shillings a week, which would have been earned and spent by some Englishmen, away trots one of these Scotchmen, and offers to go for fifteen, and that's a fortune to him."

"That is mischievous."—" It is, sir, and these employers like such fellows. Brought up in that sort of way, they are cowardly, sneaking hounds, and cringe and fawn upon him, and two to one but they get somebody else turned away and offer to fill two situations at once. Take my word for it, sir, there will be too much distress among well-educated young men, unless Scotchmen are taxed, so as to make it better worth their while to remain in their own country and cut chaff without any breeches, than to come here at all, sir."

"You are quite a political economist."—" I always was, sir. A man as keeps a public-house sees something of human nature, sir. I never want to see a Scotchman within my doors, never, sir."

I now thought it high time to make my inquiries concerning Mrs. Cholmondeley Morgan, and accordingly I said,—

"Do you know No. 77, South-street?"—" In course, sir, I does."

"Who lives there?"—" Mrs. Chumley Morgan."

"Oh," said I, and I expressed no further surprise at his pronunciation of the name, because I am aware that people call Cholmondeley, Chumley; why they do so, I never could make out.—" Now she is a lady, sir, every inch."

"She is, is she."—" You may say that, sir—none of your screws there—she's about the best-hearted and kindest creature I know of in this neighbourhood. is Mrs. Chumley Morgan."

"She keeps a carriage, I believe?"—" She does, and as nice a turn-out it is as ever you'd wish to see of a fine summer's day, sir."

"Has she been long in the neighbourhood?"—" Yes, sir, seven years. She'll be going out of town I expect soon—she generally does at this season o' the year, but she's sure to do lots of good, let her go where she will."

"Then she has a character for benevolence and kindness of disposition, I suppose?"—" Nobody a better, sir. Bless her heart, many's the poor servant out o' place as she's saved from going to ruin, and got 'em into comfortable situations agin. She's always a doing some good to somebody she is— I will say that of her, though we do differ a little."

"Do you?"—" Oh, just a little; but little differences ought not to make people say a thing is as isn't."

"Upon what subject do you differ?"—" Oh, she don't bring her mind to turn as she ought to do on the public-house question—she don't approve o' public-houses, and there's an end of it; but, mind you, she never goes out of her way to do nobody any harm. Only I know as she wouldn't be sorry if there was no public-houses at all. Everybody has their faults, you know, sir."

"Very true; and she lives at 77?"—" At 77."

"The house with the green verandah?"—" The wery house."

"What do you think of this, Graham?" I said; "I should fancy we need make no more inquiries about Mrs. Cholmondeley Morgan?"—" I think we ought to be perfectly satisfied, and I move that we at once adjourn to the Barronellis', for such news as we have now for them cannot fail to be gratifying in the extreme"

"But you wish to make some inquiries concerning your fair incognita, do you not?"—" Never mind that just now; sufficient for the day is the evil thereof. I dread to hear a confirmation of my worst fears. To-morrow we'll take some steps in that business, but I have not the heart to do so now. Let us come at once to the Barronellis'; I love to look on happy faces, and the news we bring will, I think, produce such there."

Under such circumstances, and seeing what a feeling he had upon the subject, I forbore, of course, as it was his business, not mine, to press him any further, and we accordingly bade adieu to our landlord, who had afforded us half an hour's great amusement, and turned our steps towards the Barronellis'. The day was now not very young, and by the time we got there, the dead shadows of evening were beginning to confuse the outlines of all objects. The night presented every appearance of becoming a lovely one—such a one as was calculated to awaken the best of feelings, for even in town a sweet summer's eve has its beauties.

The moon, as she rises and sheds her gentle radiance upon the busy throng beneath, presents a contrast so strong, that were not the inhabitants so much occupied, they must often pause to contemplate its beauty. The many lights that stud the metropolis throw a red glow against the clouds, when the moon is hidden by the dark masses of floating vapour; but when the heavens are clear, and nothing is there to prevent her from shining in her full majesty, the artificial light of man ceases to exhibit that strength and power it does under other circumstances.

The very sphere of the lamps seems contracted below, and their light is almost useless. The silvery light of Heaven gives a degree of chaste splendour to the scene that is wholly unknown to nearly all who live in this great vortex of humanity. To witness such a sight, to enjoy and see the full extent of it, one should mount up into some old steeple, and there look around on all sides, and contemplate the scene that is presented to us.

There is every variety—every phase of forms, from the sublimest to the oddest the mind can conceive. The bell steeples of some of the churches look like mighty giants stalking above a multitude—a sea of inferior beings. There they stand, tall, dark, and threatening, as if frowning upon the much lesser beings below. Then again, some, if you turn your gaze another way, will have the moon's rays falling full upon their fronts, and producing a singular contrast, altering the very expression, losing the threatening aspect, and becoming mild and calm.

Then turn to some of the latter buildings, whose heavy projecting masses appear to have been heaved by some volcanic action from beneath, and been left there. Many glittering points, too, reflect back those rays they receive from the moon, causing a strong dissimilarity between them and many dark masses that meet the eye on every side. The masses of chimneys keep vomiting forth on every side dark vapours that contaminate and vitiate the whole atmosphere, and aid to limit the view, and check the sphere of the vision, and blacken the walls and facings that are at first raised up white, but which afterwards assume the colour known as London smoke.

Chimney-pots and cowls are of every variety and shape, presenting forms so odd and grotesque in the moonlight, that they can be likened to nothing else on earth, but remind one of the indistinct appearance of a colony of imps, or dwarfs of more than mortal life, wheeling and jumping about, carrying on their midnight gambols when unseen by mortal eyes. Yet upon all these the moonlight sheds the gentlest influence as upon other scenes oftener contemplated than such as this.

Such was the kind of evening upon which we arrived at the Barronelli's. In answer to our inquiry at the door, we learnt that the whole family were within, and a few moments sufficed then to usher us into their presence, where we were as cordially and kindly received as heart could wish.

As was to be expected, the Barronellis listened with feelings of the greatest gratification to the news which Arthur Graham and I were so well enabled to bring them of Mrs. Cholmondeley Morgan. We exactly related, as nearly as we could recollect, the precise words which the landlord of the public-house had used with regard to that lady, and then we all talked of how wrong it would have been hastily to prejudge her, because she was not exactly the sort of looking person that in our imagination answered to the high character which had been given to her.

"I should, myself, have made inquiries," said Barronelli, "but, the fact is, I have been compelled to wait at home in anticipation of a call from a countryman, whom I by no means wish to encourage as a visitor here, but who, in my absence, might, upon any coldness being shown to him, have taken upon himself to be rude."—"A specially good reason," remarked I, "for remaining at home; and, after all, I am glad that we have made these inquiries for you, as we are more likely to give a just estimate concerning the truth of the party who has answered us than you, who are not an Englishman, could possibly hope to do."

"Precisely. Then you think I may now feel quite satisfied as regards Mrs. Cholmondeley Morgan?"—"I believe, Mr. Graham," said I, "we are unanimous in that opinion?"

"Most certainly."—"Then out of evil, indeed, has sprung good, and my poor Felice, despite all the jealousies against her, and all the injustice she has met with, may perhaps still date her fortunes from her *debut* at the opera."

"I think it highly probable," remarked Graham. "Patronage of the right true-hearted quality is everything in such a case. Without it, such rare talent as Felice now possesses might remain unknown and unappreciated. If she can, through the instrumentality of this kind lady, procure a good connection among the nobility as a teacher of singing, she will do exceedingly well, for they appreciate the value of anything very much by its price, and all you have to do is to be most especially careful to place a high value upon your lessons, Felice."

The beautiful girl laughed as she said,—

"I'm afraid I shall make a poor hand at the commercial part of the affair."—"Then you must have it done for you; for it is, of course, the most important part of all."

"Very well, you shall manage that."—"Agreed. It is said the worth of anything is just as much as it will bring; but I am convinced that these affairs, which have no intrinsic value, may be made to bring much or little, according as they are well arranged or not."

"Very true, very true."—"Now, only think what a dreadful lot of humbugs make money in this great city"

"And you want me to make one of them?" laughed Felice.—"No, my dear Felice, no. That you cannot possibly be. You have high talents and accomplishments to give the delight of in exchange for gold. I cannot apply such a term to you."

"Well," said Barronelli, "doctor, have you seen Arthur's unknown lady of the park, yet?"

Graham gave a deep groan, and I said,—

"I have."

"Do you know her?"—"No."

"There, there," interposed Arthur; "I'll tell you another time, Barronelli. Just now, I cannot; my feelings will not permit me; I—I cannot mention her or think of her."—"God bless me! what has happened? Well, well, I did not mean to ask. If the subject is a disagreeable one, let it drop. What would you advise me, doctor, to do, if Mrs. Cholmondeley Morgan comes to-morrow?"

"Be polite to her, and trust her fully and implicitly. There can be no possible mistake. The inquiries we made were interested ones, and answered in the most satisfactory manner. I say, trust her."—"I will, I will."

"No," said Graham. "Really, now, when you come to think of it, how very dangerous and dreadful it is to trust a woman."

I laughed, as I cried,—

"Put no faith, just now, in what Graham says, Barronelli. He is not in a condition of mind to come to an opinion upon such a subject. I should not feel at all surprised myself if he became, as regards the fair sex, quite misanthropical."—"And enough to make me," said Graham.

"All this is, of course, a mystery to me," said Barronelli. "Shall I walk out with you, and then will you tell me about it—or is the dread secret too profound an one to be drunk in by my vulgar ears?"—"Not at all, not at all."

"Then I long to hear it."—"And when you come back," said Felice, "mamma and I will let you have no peace till we know the secret, too. Arthur, you have lost caste dreadfully. You were once upon a time the soul of gallantry and chivalric devotion, and now you ruthlessly drag from his home one of your own sex, to whom you promise to impart a secret, when, all the while you know very well that it is one of the attributed passions of us poor women to adore secrets."

"Very ably argued, but you would laugh," said Graham.

And so we all three, Graham, Barronelli, and I, left the house to take a stroll to and fro in the street, and talk over Arthur's dreadful disappointment in love. At Graham's request I stated all that had occurred, and finished by saying,—

"Now, Barronelli, what advice, under all this state of things, do you feel inclined to give to our friend Graham?"—"To meet the lady again, and say to her, 'I saw you in a carriage with such a man. What explanation have you to offer me of that strange circumstance?'"

"That's to the purpose," said I. "Do it, Graham."—"Can I?"

"Of course, you can. You have an appointment with her?"—"Oh, yes."

"Then do it. Make no inquiries upon the subject but of her. Tell her you have made none; but ask her without ambiguity for an explicit explanation. I do think, Barronelli, that the advice you have given is most sound and practicable."—"It's an awkward position to be placed in," sighed Graham. "My feelings are all at war within me, but my judgment cannot but sanction the plan you have proposed. It is the simplest. It is the best by far, because it is the simplest."

"And the simplest," said Barronelli, "because it is the best; so that place the proposition which way we will, we are sure to be quite right, you see."

"While the result may be anything but right," said Graham. "I do shrink from this matter, I own, and yet I feel that for my peace of mind it must be done. I will meet her, and I will put the question to her, as plainly as it is possible to put it. I will relate then to you both the result of this interview, and you shall give me your opinion, and guide me in what I shall further do, for when the feelings are very deeply interested we cannot think so easily as we ought, or arrive at such rational opinions as we otherwise should."

"When do you meet her?"—"On Wednesday."

"Then on that day I shall expect to see you, and believe me I wait it with all the impatience of one who feels deeply interested in your real welfare."—"I know that; I am sure of that, doctor. I thank God that in this to me serious emergency, I can count on the pure and disinterested advice of two such friends as yourself and Barronelli."

"Well, whatever we do," I said, " do not let us become complimentary to each other. I shall now bid you good night both of you, for I have yet a call to make professionally; and wishing you, Barronelli, every good fortune with Mrs. Cholmondeley Morgan, and you, Graham, a safe extrication from your embarrassments as regards your fair unknown, I say adieu."—"Good bye, good bye. I am only afraid my fair unknown may turn out to be a fair too well known."

* * * * *

There was something almost ludicrous after all in the manner of Arthur Graham's grief, about his lady love, but I think that arose more from the almost unavailing struggle he was perpetually now making to conceal the real amount of the effect which his deep disappointment had upon him. Almost all men are very sensitive about making an exhibition of their feelings in such matters, and no doubt, although he had no reason to expect ridicule from either Barronelli or myself, yet he dreaded that we should think him of so soft a nature that he should grieve for a woman who had jilted him.

Like the man in the play, no doubt he felt tempted to exclaim,—

" My lord, I ever held her form lightly,
And now she's gone I feel the same regret
I would have felt for hawk or hound, that ministered
To wayward fancy, and lent a charm to idleness.
I've done with her."

Only perhaps Arthur Graham had never happened to see or to read the play from whence we have taken the foregoing little extract, in which case, of course, he may be very well excused for not quoting it.

* * * * *

Affairs now seemed at a stand still for some little time, both as regarded Barronelli's family, and Arthur Graham's love passage; I could do no more than I had done in either case, with one little exception, and that was that I asked several people concerning the nobleman who had been named to Graham and me at Hyde-park gate, by the lounging groom, and I heard quite enough in reply to my slight inquiry to convince me that the said nobleman was not only in common parlance no better than he should be, but that it would have been a very fine thing for himself and for society at large, if he had happened to be half as good.

Of course there can be no mistake about the lady. Arthur Graham knew his idol sufficiently well to be quite certain as regarded her identity, and there then the matter appeared to rest in about as suspicious and ugly a position as it could very well assume.

It was on the Thursday morning after the succeeding Wednesday, that I received a very early visit from Arthur Graham. He was very pale; his general appearance indicative of neglect; and altogether he presented a very different appearance from that which he usually presented, which, as is said of the devil's tail, was neat, but not gaudy! I could see that something had happened very much to discompose him, and had no doubt but that the something had a relation to the fair unknown of Hyde-park. Upon the announcement of his name I was in my dressing-room, but I desired he should be shown up to me; and while I was shaving he came and sunk into a chair with a groan, that seemed to be the king of all the groans I had ever heard.

"What now?" I said, as I scraped away at my chin,— "what now, Arthur Graham?"—"It is over!" he said; "it is over!"

"Oh!"—"All is past! The dream is over! I have awakened now to cold reality! I have seen her! All is over!"

"Well, it's a good thing it's all over."—"Is it?"

"Yes, I should think so. But, now I have done shaving, you may agitate me by your agonising recital as much as you like, without my nose being in any danger. Go on, Graham, and let me hear all about it."—"If you will listen seriously, I will. If jokingly or irreverently, the recital will be lost upon you."

"I will listen," I said, " in all sober seriousness, Graham; and, believe me, that if a light expression fall from my lips, it is not dictated by any desire to undervalue your attachment."—"Very good. Now list."

"Had I three ears I'd hear thee."—"I met her in the walk leading from the gate of Hyde-park towards the gardens, as usual, and she, too, the syren, met me with her usual smile. She placed her arm within mine, and looking in my face—which, no doubt, she saw was robbed by anxiety of its usual colour—she inquired of me with such seeming tenderness what ailed me, that, had I not had such strong suspicions of her fidelity, by Heavens I could have backed her for faith and virtue, as much as I can for beauty, against a host of angels."

" Hem !"—" I had intended to be extremely cunning and polite, and had intended to sound the very depths of her duplicity or of her faith, and by degrees to make the discovery if she is worthy of such a love as I am capable of feeling or not."

"But you could not."—"As you say, I could not. When she spoke to me in such a tone—when I heard the soft music of her voice—when I felt the gentle pressure of her arm—all reflection fled from my heart, and I became a mere creature of sudden impulses; I spoke to her at once of my sad doubts —my dreadful fears; and when I saw that she turned pale and trembled, I said,—' Oh, tell me, and, as you have pity or goodness in you, tell me truly,—was it you I saw with the man I mentioned in the carriage at the corner of Hyde-park?' A mental struggle seemed to agitate her for a moment. I saw the tears standing on her long silken eyelashes; I could see her bosom heaving with emotion; but she made a strong effort, and, subduing her tears and sighs, she said,—

' ' It is true; I am the person.'

" At that moment I thought I should have dropped; a mist appeared to spread itself over my eyes, and the world seemed slipping from me. I know not how long a dreadful silence that ensued lasted, but finally I commanded myself sufficiently to say to her in distracted tones,—

"' Have you no explanation to give—no reason for the situation I saw you in, which shall restore me to serenity?'— ' None,' she said.

" ' Oh! think again—think again. Tell me I am wrong; that some most special reason, full of virtue and redolent of honour, made you for a time that man's companion.'—'Love,' she said, ' is full of faith. True love never doubts the objects of its dreams. Faith in Heaven's mercy cannot be stronger. I have no more to say, Graham. You do not love me.'

" ' Not love you? Oh, Heaven!'—' No, you do not love me. God bless and prosper you—we part for ever—farewell!'

" I seized her hand, and implored her to stay and tell me that she was innocent. The warm blood flew to her cheek, and she spoke some words of indignation. She released herself from my grasp, and left me; I could not follow her; I could only totter to a seat, and feel for a time that I had no business now in this troubling, bustling world, but that the cool, quiet repose of the grave was all I had to hope for. I was nearly maddened."

"You'd find some family vault," said I, " the coolest and the quietest, Graham, you may depend."—"Now, doctor, is this fair—is this like you?"

"Well, well, I am done. She went away?"—"Alas! she did."

"And made no re-appearance?"—" None, none; she is lost to me now for ever. What do you think of her conduct now? What is your opinion of her? Do you think her innocent? Tell me if you do, and I will search the world for her—aye, and find her, too, if she were hidden in its deepest corners."

" It is quite impossible, Graham, for me to come to any opinion upon the subject. You say she entered into no explanations; therefore, we are just left where we were. You have nothing to judge by but her manner. I own I think there is great room for doubt, and great cause for much perplexity. It is a pity you let her go."

"What could I do?"—" I wish much now that some one had been with you who could have quietly followed her without her being aware of it. Something might thus have been done in the way of inquiry; but do not despair. If she really ever loved you with that romantic feeling of real affection which she seems so full of, you have done nothing to forfeit her regard."

"True, I have done nothing."—" She talks of a faith which you are expected to have in her, without, it seems to me, feeling the same for you; or if she really love you, as her words would indicate, or is capable of loving the object upon which she places her affections at all, and she be innocent, what have you to fear? A common sense of justice will bring her to your arms again, Graham."

"Ah! could I think so!"—"I would think so. If she be innocent, you will see her again, or hear from her; if she be guilty, she was only intent upon playing her part well, and leaving you full of regrets; in which case you never will, except by accident, see her more."

"Alas! alas! never to see her more! Oh, doctor! I have been too precipitate—by far too precipitate."—"Not at all. What would she have thought of you had you concealed the circumstances of which you very properly desired an explanation? What kind of affection must it have been that could induce any man to see the object of his honourable attachment in such company, and not wish to know what combination of circumstances brought her there?"

"You reason correctly, doctor."—"Because I reason calmly; which you, who are so deeply interested, cannot."

"Then you do not think I was too hasty?"—"Not at all. The moment you saw her, before one word of welcome or affection could be uttered on either side, it was a duty you owed both to her and to yourself, to ask for an explanation. The onus of not gaining it lies upon her, not upon you; and if she has but the most ordinary powers of reflection, she must feel that you are right, and that your conduct has been unexceptionable."

"You really think so?"—"From my soul, I do. Cheer up, Graham, and, in the consciousness of having done just what was right and proper, find consolation. If she be worthy, you have not lost her; if she be otherwise, congratulate yourself that you have, for your loss is a positive gain."

"You have restored me," he said, in more cheerful tones than he had hitherto been able to command to himself. "I feel that your views of this subject are quite correct ones. I shall be now much calmer, and live upon the dear hope that she may be innocent."—"Do so," said I; "and now that you are able to talk rationally, let me tell you that, from your account of the interview you have had with her, I think there is some likelihood of a mystery in the whole affair, which, when wound up, will redound, perhaps, much to the credit of your fair unknown."

His face glowed with animation, as he exclaimed,—

"You really think so? You really think there is such a chance, doctor, of happiness for me?"—"Indeed, I really do."

"Then I will shake off this despondency which has been creeping over my spirits like a black pall, and become myself again. I have broken no faith with her, nor will I break any. I have not followed her—I have not sought to discover who or what she is—she cannot accuse me of one breach of promise to her. I have had, indeed, abundance of that trusting faith which she herself mentioned as the soul and essence of true affection. It remains for her now to shape her practice by her theory, and to have faith in me."—"Right—right."

"I will, on the days we used to meet," he added, in a sadder tone, "go to the old familiar spot, with the hope of seeing her. For some fleeting moment my eyes may be blessed with a sight of her enchanting beauty. Oh! she is all the world to me. The very sight of her is joy, and has quickened the current of my blood into a dancing measure. I doat upon her—my beautiful, beautiful love."

There was a pathos and a sincerity about the manner in which Graham uttered these words, which it is impossible to transfer to paper, but which lifted his feelings, extravagant as they seemed to be, very far above ridicule. I endeavoured now to change the subject as quickly as I could, for I felt that we had said as much upon it as was likely to be practically useful to him.

"I am anxious," I said, "to know how Felice Barronelli got on with Mrs. Cholmondeley Morgan, and if you have an hour to spare this evening we will call upon them."

"With pleasure," he said. "My time is not very intensely occupied just now, and I can take an hour or two when I please. Where shall we meet?"

"Will you come here?"—"With pleasure, if I am not, as I fear I am, a very serious hindrance to you."

"Not at all. As a professional man, of course, I should feel bound to turn you out if I had any engagement, but I have none of a particular character to-day, and if you will come here about seven this evening, we will walk to the Barronellis together, and get all the news we can."—"Agreed. I shall be punctual. It is gratifying, even in the midst of one's own misfortunes, to find that such an amiable family as the Barronellis have so fair a prospect before them as the kindness of this lady presents."

"It is," said I; "but it is not common with human nature to find gratification in misfortune from the good fortune of others. I am of opinion with somebody, I forget who now, who said that mankind always feel a sweet pleasure in each others distresses, and that when anything wrong has taken place with ourselves in any way, the most healing balm that can be applied to our wounded spirits, is to be assured that something a desperately deal worse has happened to somebody else."

We were surprised when we reached the Barronellis, to be told that the Lady Cholmondeley Morgan had never called again since the morning on which she had made so many promises, and been so kindly disposed towards patronising poor Felice, and recompensing her for the injustice which had been done to her abilities at the opera. It was not likely that such a person could be so very capricious as one moment to say what she intended to do, and the next to take a different view of the affair, without any reason for so doing.

There had been no concealment on the part of the Barronellis on any point, therefore there was nothing to find out which could have at all influenced the benevolent lady. What, then, could be the cause of her unaccountable absence, after so very particularly promising to do great things for Felice? The Barronellis, I could see, were in a fidget about it, and all I could say to console them was,—

"Perhaps as she saw, when she was here, that some suspicions were excited against her, she is resolved to wait until you have had ample time to make inquiries concerning her, and it such be her motive, it is a commendable one, with which we cannot very well find any fault."—"That may be," said Barronelli, "for aught I can say to the contrary; but still it does appear rather odd."

"Not at all, I think."

"Oh," said Felice, "you see already, dear father, what a trouble and torment this promised patronage is becoming. I have always heard that patronage is full of trouble. Let me owe what I can to my own industry, and be patronised by no one who does not feel that they get some return in full for the amount to which they patronise me."

"Felice," said I, "you are right as regards patronage in a general point of view. It is not a desirable thing even for a young person, because it gets up in the mind a reliance upon something which has nothing to do with industry, perseverance, or talent; but you must remember how cruelly you are situated as regards the art you practise. You must remember the storm of prejudice which the mere fact of your being English raised against you in an English theatre, and all you ought to owe to the patronage of such a lady as Mrs. Cholmondeley Morgan, is an opportunity of assuming your true position. Not anything extra and above your abilities, but a means of enabling you to receive their just reward. This, Felice, is the only species of patronage you require, and the only one which anybody can offer to you."

Felice thanked me, and so did the father and mother for my advice, which seemed to make a great impression on them all, Graham included, who seemed almost to forget his own woes, in the absorbing interest he took in the amiable family through whose means we had become mutually acquainted.

We were about to take our leave of the Barronellis, when suddenly the dash and rattle of a carriage in that street which was seldom or ever visited by anything higher in grade than a hackney-cab, met our ears. Simultaneously the thought appeared to come over us all that it was the carriage of Mrs. Cholmondeley Morgan, and, with the exception of Felice, who turned rather pale, we were all at the window in an instant.

Yes, it was the lady—the benevolent lady. It was Mrs. Cholmondeley Morgan. There was the faultless, aristocratic-looking equipage. There were the plainly dressed but respectable-looking servants, and in another moment the usual thundering appeal was made to the knocker, and Barronelli himself ran down stairs to welcome his kind visitor. I remained at the window, and I saw that the lady did not get out of the carriage until she saw Barronelli. She was, however, so close to the window, which was down, that I could see her face well, and until he appeared with, I suppose, a welcome smile upon his countenance, which was immediately reflected by hers, I fancied that her face wore an expression of doubt and suspicion, which the circumstances scarcely warranted.

But, however, this was no time for experiments on physiognomical expression, and what I thought at the moment passed away almost as rapidly as the expression of fear engendered it. There was a bustle upon the staircase. The door was opened, and the lady, most handsomely attired, made her appearance.

I did not like her. There was an air and manner about her that I could not like, and it required all my reflection upon what had been told me by the man who kept the public-house, to enable me to make anything approaching to a respectable bow to Mrs. Cholmondeley Morgan.

"Pray be seated, madam," said Barronelli. "Believe me, that since your last kind visit we have anxiously expected you."—"Oh, Mr. Barronelli," she replied, "you had a right to be suspicious of the intentions and of the sincerity of a perfect stranger to you. I have been, since my residence in London, the victim of so many well arranged, artfully-planned schemes of deception, that I am now the more suspicious the more plausible the party seems whom I do not know. You, in an affair of this kind, in which the welfare, the happiness, and the innocence of your child were concerned, could not be too cautious."

"Madam, you are liberal, as well as kind; it is not every one who is willing to do good at the same time that suspicion is acknowledged as a correct feeling with which to meet the first advance."—"But you ought to be suspicious. Now, tell me, without reserve, have you inquired about me, and are you satisfied?"

"Madam, such delicate inquiries as ———"—"Oh, nonsense; make full inquiries. Think of the consequences of a mistake, Mr. Barronelli. Suppose I was not the person I represented myself, now, who knows what desperate danger you might be placing your darling and beautiful child in?"

"Madam, we are more than satisfied—we are delighted and grateful."—"Well, well," said Mrs. Cholmondeley Morgan, "if you are satisfied I am. To-night, but quite early, I have a *soiree* of particular friends only—very particular friends; and if Felice can come with me now at once, she will become a little accustomed to my house, and be more at her ease than probably would be the case were she suddenly introduced."

"Her dress," interposed her mother, "is not suitable."—"Oh, we will manage all that," said Mrs. Cholmondeley Morgan. "Besides, I am the plainest person in the world, and there will be no one at my house but plain family people, although they are of a class which it is very important for Felice to know: so make no scruples, but let her come with me at once."

"I can change my dress," said Felice, falteringly.—"I tell you what we will do," said Mrs. Cholmondeley Morgan. "Felice shall go with me now, and you can send at nine o'clock to-night a servant with a parcel for her, containing what articles you like, and she can dress at my house."

This arrangement was acceded to, and Felice, trembling all the while, and with the tears, as I saw, ready to start from her eyes, got ready to accompany the benevolent lady. She kissed her father and mother with fervour, and I heard her whisper to Barronelli to come and fetch her home at an early hour. Then she shook hands with me, and with Graham, and she was ready. Mrs. Cholmondeley Morgan gave a bland smile, which I thought did not become her, and rose from the seat she had occupied.

"I have a spare bed," she said, "for Felice."—"Madam," said Barronelli, "I pray you pardon my seeming rudeness, my child has never yet slept from home. While I live, and have a home for her, she never shall."

I saw a slight frown upon Mrs. Cholmondeley Morgan's face, but she recovered in an instant, and said,—

"You are right, sir, you are quite right. I honour the sentiment you have uttered, as well as the honest frankness with which you have uttered it. Fetch her home when you please, or I will send the carriage with her, which will be better."—"Fetch me, father," said Felice.

"I will, my darling."—"Very good," said Mrs. Cholmondeley Morgan. "Make your own arrangements, and you will please me best by so doing."

It was then settled that Barronelli should fetch Felice about twelve at night, and then Mrs. Cholmondeley Morgan and her beautiful young companion descended the staircase together. I saw from the window Felice handed into the carriage. Mrs. Cholmondeley Morgan followed. The steps were folded up. Felice waved her hand, and tried to smile. Poor girl, it was a sickly effort, and then she was gone.

"Well, doctor," said Barronelli, when he reached the common sitting-room of the family again, "what do you think now?"—"Oh, think—why of course it's all right."

"Oh, of course."—"Of course," added Graham.

"Of course," said Mrs. Barronelli, as she wiped away a tear.—"And yet I don't like this Mrs. Cholmondeley Morgan," said Barronelli, after a slight pause.

"Nor I," said his wife.—"Nor I—nor I," added Graham and myself.

"We none of us like her," said Barronelli; "and yet my child—my beautiful and gentle Felice is entrusted to her care."—"Now calm yourself," said I. "You can surely rely upon the inquiries Graham and I made respecting her. There can be no room for hesitation; and only consider how insulting it would have been to this lady to say, 'Madam, we don't like your looks, and so we won't trust you, and you may go about your business, and carry your good feelings somewhere else.'"

"No—no," said Barronelli, "we could not have done that; of course we could not have done that. I dare say it's all right, but of course I cannot help feeling anxious on a subject so nearly connected with my happiness as the welfare and safety of my darling child."—"No doubt—no doubt. But look now what opportunities you have of being satisfied. You are to send at nine o'clock to South-street, and you are to go at twelve."

"True—true—doctor. I am very foolish to torment myself with such fears; I never used to be so dreadfully nervous. I will go myself to South-street with the bundle containing my Felice's clothes. I have waited on my darling too often to think it any degradation now. Wife, you can make up what is necessary, and I will satisfy my own mind by taking the things myself."—"If such is your determination," said Graham, "I will go with you."

"Will you, Graham?"—"Indeed I will."

"And I," said I. "Let us all go; and as Graham and I know the house, we can spare you some trouble, and after we have left the bundle we will go round to the original who keeps the public-house, and you shall yourself, Barronelli, hear his description of Mrs. Cholmondeley Morgan."

All this was settled in this way—we were to meet at Barronelli's house at eight o'clock, by which time I should be rid of my professional engagements for the day, and then we were to go together to South-street, Grosvenor-square, with Felice's clothes, after which we determined upon having some supper at the public-house till twelve, when we would all escort Felice home to her mother.

Barronelli was profuse in his thanks to us for the offer of our companionship, and before we parted from him he had nearly recovered his usual serenity, and expressed himself ashamed of the nervous apprehensions he had entertained of the good faith of Mrs. Cholmondeley Morgan, merely because the contour of her countenance was not one that pleased him.

* * * *

Somehow or another, the whole of that day, whenever my thoughts by chance rushed to Felice, I felt a degree of uneasiness which I could not account for, and I dare say I longed for night quite as much as even Barronelli did, who might be supposed to be deeply interested. The day too itself was a fidgetty one. A great change had taken place suddenly in the weather, which had become, as somebody somewhere says, "most insultingly hot." It so happened, too, that I had much running about to different parts of the town, and I felt it accordingly.

A hot day is, of all the atmospherical accidents that can affect human nature, the soonest felt, and the most difficult to evade or overcome; it seizes upon the system, and renders it completely enervated and incapable of any exertion, save upon the most pressing and urgent necessity. The sun sails through the heavens, not a cloud to be seen; the pure ethereal blue of heaven had not a spot on it; all was cloudless, clear, and dazzling.

The earth was hot and parched, the very pavements were too hot to bear the hand upon it, and the houses received and retained the heat, making the streets feel like so many ovens, through which the inhabitants were compelled to wander. Here and there might be seen some fat citizen waddling along, carrying his hat in his hand, while his handkerchief was in constant requisition to wipe away the streaming perspiration that troubled him.

Dusty roads and streets now render walking and breathing more uncomfortable, for clouds arise as any vehicle passes along, and it takes some time before it can subside again.

The window-blinds of all the houses exposed to the sun's rays are all let down to guard against his strength, though the windows are invariably left open. All kinds of animals, human and brute, feel the effects of this weather, especially those doomed to exertion. Scarce a horse can be seen out but his coat is reeking wet, and often white with the action of harness, or one part against another, and not unfrequently white from the mere exertion and effects of the weather.

Ladies are seen to take their walks as though they felt it not; true, they have the little silken screen, a parasol, which wards off the sun's rays, and their slow walk does not cause them so much inconvenience as it must men, who are not so guarded, and whose exertion is greater. The shops look tempting, and many are induced to become purchasers because of the cool shade and rest they offer to strollers; blinds are carefully drawn down to protect the goods from damage by the sun.

The older the day grows the more intense the heat, though certainly everything looks gay, save the animated portion of the scene, for nature pants and feels faint after the least exertion; people go home, looking red and pale at the same moment, colour being unequally distributed in their visages. Parched lips and burning throats are common enough, and the blood soon rises to fever heat, and they are fortunate who can get to the shady side of the way, and thus mitigate some of the evils they encounter.

Such was the day which I was very glad to see come to an end, which it did by presenting us with a cold wind incidental to the spring, and which seemed by its searching nature to be intent upon enabling some donkey to get up a meteorological table to convince us that we live in a temperate climate, because the mean temperature is temperate. Upon the same principle was it that a ruffian met a poor fellow once, who had had the misfortune to pass a few days in a debtor's prison, and to whom he said,—

"How do you do, friend?" and when the other said, "You must be mistaken, sir; I do not know you," he added,—

"Not know me! Why you and I have been in all the gaols in the kingdom. That is to say, you have been in one, and I have been in all the rest."

Or a man with a thousand a year might say to some poor devil with only fifty pounds,—

"You and I, Smith, are men of comfortable, moderate incomes—five hundred and twenty-five pounds per annum each —my thousand, you know, and your fifty."

This is precisely the way in which the meteorological tables are got up by the wiseacres who assure us we live in a temperate climate. Put a temperature of 90 deg. in the shade to one of 10 deg., and we have a mean of 50 deg. Oh! of course, we live in a temperate climate. Really, how long will people allow themselves to be humbugged by statistical and average tables with which big books are filled now-a-days? *   *   *   *   *

Precisely at eight o'clock I was at the Barronellis, where I found that Arthur Graham had arrived before me; for, as he said, he was so unhappy by himself about his own affairs, that it was quite a relief to be somewhere where there was some anxiety going on. Barronelli was in haste to start; and, with the bundle for Felice under his arm, he went off at a good pace with us.

"It's of course no matter," he said, "being a little early or so with the dear child's things. I should have gone an hour ago, only Graham would have me wait for you, doctor."—"I pride myself upon punctuality," said I, "and was here to a minute."

"So you were—so you were. But you know what a fidget I am in."—"Say no more—say no more."

It was about half-past eight when we reached South-street; and Graham and I at once took Barronelli up to the house of Mrs. Cholmondeley Morgan.

"A very respectable-looking house," he said.—" Very. But there are no lights anywhere," said I.

"Yes," remarked Graham; "in the kitchen. Look."

There certainly was a light in the kitchen, and that was all. The house had a very still, quiet look about it. Not a soul seemed stirring in it; and as for any appearances indicative of a music party, there were certainly none whatever. Not even a light in the passage graced the place.

"Are you sure this is the house?" said Barronelli, and I could see the bundle shake as he nervously held it.—" Quite sure. Look at the number—seventy-seven. There it is; and the little brass plate, 'Ring also,' upon it. Oh, there can be no mistake about the house."

Barronelli said no more, but obeyed the injunction to knock and ring at once, for he executed a loud rat-tat with the knocker, and a peal on the bell, which I thought would never leave off. There is, however, an end to all things, and, consequently, there was an end to the clatter of the bell, but nobody came to the door. The same odd kind of quietness reigned in the house as before. There was the gleaming light in the kitchen, but nowhere else, and suddenly, as we continued to look at it, it disappeared, and all was darkness together. Barronelli dropped the bundle, and I saw him shaking like one in an ague.

"For God's sake," I said, "do not be alarmed; let me knock. There is nothing to be alarmed at. Barronelli, compose yourself."—"My child—my Felice," he cried; "my beautiful child; where art thou?—oh, where art thou!"

"Hush! hush! We will soon make some one hear."

I raised my hand to knock again, but even as I did so I saw a faint glimmering light through the glass above the door.

"There," said I, "some one is coming."

Whoever was coming was like the celebrated Miss Long in the song, determined to take her time, for it was full a minute before the door was cautiously opened, and when it was so, we found that the chain was put slackly up as a safeguard. The wrinkled face of a dirty old woman appeared, and in her hand she held a candle, which must from its size have made one of at least forty to the pound.

"Eh?" she said. "Eh? eh? What do you say? Eh?"

I saw that she was very deaf, by her attitude, and I bawled out,—

"Is Mrs. Cholmondeley Morgan within!"—" An *organ*? Eh?"

"Morgan! Morgan!"—"Oh, sir, the morning. Very good. Have you got a card?"

"Woman," cried Barronelli, "is my child here? I want my child."

"Eh?" eh?"—" Who—occupies—this—house?" said I, with terrible distinctness.

The question reached her dulled sense of hearing, and she said,—

"Oh! oh! I ain't so deaf as people think. You want to see the house?"—" Good God!" cried Graham, "I shall knock that old hag on the head."

"Oh! oh! Some beds. Come in the morning. You must have a card. Eh? What did you say?"—" I shall go mad," cried Barronelli. "Take down the chain, woman, or you shall repent ——"

"I don't know the rent," interrupted the old woman.— "Here's a job," cried Graham, with a groan.—" I wonder if I could get my hand in and undo the chain. Old woman, will you open the door?"

"To a respectable party," said the old woman, "and for a permanency, they says as it's cheap. I don't know myself, leastways they haven't told me, and that accounts for that."— "I will get in," said Barronelli. "I am desperate—I am mad—I will get in."

Even as he spoke he commenced such a cannonade of knocks against the door, that I felt very certain the whole neighbourhood would be alarmed. The old woman swooned, and fell down in the passage. Graham and I looked on; windows were thrown open in all directions, and still Barronelli kept hammering away at No. 77, as if he had not a moment to lose in the completion of a certain number of knocks in a given period of time.

A crowd was collected, and one man stepping up, announced himself as a constable, and produced his little brazen authority with the crown at the end of it, in support of the assertion.

"I'm a constable—I'm a constable," he cried. "What's the row—eh? What is it?"—" My child—my Felice!" said Barronelli.

"What child—eh? A case of child dropping, is it?"— "No," said I. "This gentleman has reason to believe that his daughter was brought to this house. He is now refused admittance, and if you can enforce it for him he will be much your debtor."

"His daughter?"—" Yes. You look, what no doubt you are, an active, intelligent officer. Pray endeavour, if you can, to procure us admission here."

The constable bit the end of his staff and looked very wise.

"Now, stick in the mud," cried a boy in the crowd, "turn it over in your mind, and don't crumple it."—" You scoundrel!" said the active and intelligent officer; "only let me catch you. Gentlemen, I will do what I can, but you know I dare not force my way into the house."

"We are perfectly aware of that," said I. "It appears to us that there is some mistake, and if you convince the old woman who has charge of the premises that we are entitled to enter them, she will take down the chain."

Upon this hint the officer stepped up to the slightly opened door, and commenced operations by saying,—

"My good woman, what do you take these gentlemen for—eh? Look at me—what do you take me for?"—"Eh?" said the old woman. "Eh? Did you speak?"

"Did I speak? Well, that's a good un. Will you open the door?"—"A hole in the floor—eh?"

"Now this is too bad."—"Allow me," said I, and I advanced and said, in the slow, distinct tone, which is much more likely to make a deaf person hear than bawling to him or her,—

"This is a constable, who will come in with us to convince you we have no evil design. Will you let us search the house?"—"Oh, well, who do you want?"

"Mrs. Cholmondeley Morgan."—"Mrs. who? What's that you keep continually saying about an organ?"

"Did you mention the name, sir, of Mrs. Cholmondeley Morgan?" said a young man, stepping up to me.—"I did."

"Then, sir, if it be that lady you want to see, I can tell you that your labour is in vain, for she is out of town."—"Out of town?"

"Yes, sir. If you choose to call upon Mr. Stanfield, the house-agent round the corner there, he can tell you, I dare say, where she has gone to at once."

Barronelli looked bewildered, as well he might, and stared about him like a man half beside himself.

"Come, Barronelli," said I. "Let us go to this house-agent. There is some mystery in all this which requires instant clearing up."—"But my child—my dear Felice! Where is she? Where is my dear child, Felice? I want my child."

"For Heaven's sake speak low. The curiosity of a mob I am sure you do not wish to excite. Graham, take his other arm. Come—come to the house-agent's abode, Barronelli. I pray you be calm. I implore you to assume more command over yourself."—"I will—I will," he said faintly, and we all, then, proceeded to the house-agent's round the corner. He was not at home, but we found a very civil young man in his office, to whom I said,—

"Can you give us any information concerning a Mrs. Cholmondeley Morgan, who resides at No. 77, South-street?"—"Certainly," he replied. "We know the lady very well!"—"And she is—respectable?"—"Respectable, sir! There is not a more respectable, or more generally respected resident in all this neighbourhood."

"Thank God!" said Barronelli, and I saw tears start to his eyes."—"Then you see," said I, "there is only some little mystery, after all, which wants an explanation, which this gentleman, no doubt, can and will give us."

"Any information in my power, gentlemen," said the clerk, "is heartily at your service."—"Thank you," said I, as I laid my card on the desk before him. "This will show you that it is not idle curiosity which prompts us in our inquiries; we wish to know how it is that Mrs. Morgan's house appears so deserted to-night?"

"Deserted, sir? why, because it is deserted, with the exception of the person we have placed in it to mind it. We are Mrs. Cholmondeley Morgan's agents, and have had the pleasure of being so for some years past."

"Well, but where is she?"—"Out of town, sir. At Leamington."

"Leamington?" cried I.—"Leamington?" almost shrieked Barronelli.

"Yes, gentlemen. I am really not aware that there is anything so very extraordinary in a lady going to Leamington."—"Stop a bit," said I. "When did she go?"

"A month ago."—"A month?"

"Yes, I believe to the very day. Indeed I am sure, because Mrs. Major Chaplin has just left."—"Mrs. who?"

"Mrs. Major Chaplin, the lady who took the house of us for one month, furnished, at eight guineas a-week, paid in advance, and left this day; we have it now to let for another month, after which period we expect Mrs. Cholmondeley Morgan to resume her town residence."

I looked at Graham and Graham looked at me; then we both looked at Barronelli, who stood glaring at the house-agent's clerk, like some supernatural being. The whole mystery was now solved. The riddle was read; all was clear and transparent. The few last words the agent's clerk had uttered had removed a veil from before our eyes—we understood it all now. Poor Felice had been inveigled from her home, and what might be her fate we trembled to contemplate.

"Barronelli—Barronelli!" I cried, for I was terrified at his fixed, staring look. "Barronelli, rouse yourself, and meet this emergency like a man."

He fell to the ground, at once overwhelmed by the sudden stroke of fate—he became perfectly insensible, and it took me more than twenty minutes to recover him at all to consciousness. Then he looked wildly about him, and talked incoherently.

"Where is my Felice?" he cried. "Save her; oh, save her from the fire—there, there, now she hangs to the window. My child—my child! my only, beautiful child!"—"The gentleman's mad," said the agent's clerk.

"No, no," said I, "he will soon be better."—"Besides," added Graham, "what he says now relates to an actual occurrence. He is not mad."

"Where am I, and what has happened?" said Barronelli faintly now, and then before any one could answer him, he added, hastily, "I recollect, I recollect; I must have fainted at the dreadful news. Oh, my Felice, my Felice! when will these anxious eyes ever look upon your face again?"—"Soon, I hope," said I, in as cheerful a tone of voice as I could assume. "We will leave no stone unturned to find her for you. Sir," to the clerk, "can you tell us anything of this Mrs. Major Chaplin?"

"Nothing more than she came here and took the house, giving us the month's money in advance, and a respectable reference. We had no reason on earth to doubt that she was other than what she represented herself to be. We have no means of knowing where she has gone, for our connexion with her ceased entirely with her occupancy of No. 77, South-street."

"Where was her reference?" said I; "will you write it down for me?"—"With pleasure, sir."

On a slip of paper he wrote me the following name and address:—

"Mrs. Anderton, Bute Villa, Kensington."—"Thank you, thank you. Now Barronelli, will you consent to be guided by myself and Graham in this business? Believe me, we can do much more than you can. We feel strongly for you, and nothing shall deter us from an immediate search for Felice. I do now implore you to go home and calm the fears of your wife."

"Home! home without my child?"—"Nay, now listen to me. We can do more than you can. You are, of course, much excited, and far too anxious to take the best means of enabling you to be successful in a search for Felice. With all the zeal you could throw into the matter, we shall be able to throw more discretion. Let me once again implore you to go home."

"And allow me," said Graham, "to join my entreaties to the doctor's."

Barronelli rose tremblingly from the chair with which he had been accommodated, and said,—

"I yield—I yield. I know I am incapable of exertion. God assist you both. Save her, and receive the blessing of us all. My Felice! my Felice!"

We got him into a coach, and glad enough was I to see him driven off towards his home. Graham turned to me, and said, with much emotion in his tone and manner,—

"What is to be done, doctor? what is to be done?"—

"The night is yet young," said I; "let us be off to Kensington at once. We are innocently the cause of the great confidence which poor Barronelli placed in the woman who passed by the assumed name of Morgan. Let us then make it our most especial business to do all that human beings can do to restore poor Felice to her sorrowing parents."

"I devote myself heart and soul to the duty," cried Graham. "Let us go at once to Kensington and make inquiries; she shall be rescued, doctor, if I lose my life in the attempt."

We set off at a good round pace for Kensington. We were neither of us bad walkers by any means, and very soon we left Hyde-park behind us, and came upon the precincts of that little town which smacks so much of royalty, that every cats'-meat-man is a purveyor to the queen and the royal family, and every little dairy provides asses milk, a needless provision, for the royal babbies. It was half-past two o'clock when we got there, and I stopped the first decent-looking

DIARY OF A PHYSICIAN.

person I saw to ask for Bute Villa, to which I was at once directed, as if it was as well-known as the church.

"Who lives there?" said I.—"I really don't know, sir," was the reply. "It changes hands so often."

I felt very sick within me at these words, for they tended more and more to convince me that poor Felice, unfortunate Felice, had been made the victim of a deep-laid and cruel conspiracy.

Bute Villa was some distance off the main road, and situated in its own grounds. By the dim light of the night we could see that it was of gothic architecture, and altogether of rather an imposing appearance. Tall trees were in front of it, and the garden connected with the premises appeared to be extensive, and, as far as we could judge, well kept.

There were lights at several of the windows; and after a brief consultation between ourselves, which ended in an un-

derstanding that I was to be spokesman upon the occasion, I rang loudly at the bell which hung over the rather aristocratic-looking garden gate. We then waited for some time, after which we saw some one approaching with a light. It was a man in a sort of undress livery, and he stopped at the lattice work, which the upper part of the gate was composed of, and said, in rather a forbidding tone,—

"What's your business, gentlemen?"—"Is Mrs. Anderton within?" said I.

He seemed to be considering for a moment, and then he said,—

"If you will favour me with your names, gentlemen, I will go and see."—"Oh, just say two gentlemen wish to see her particularly, if you please."

I held up a crown-piece in my fingers, and the moment it caught the fellow's eye, he gave a grin, and said,—

"You have been here before, gentlemen?"—"Never mind that," said I.

"No, of course; then I'll tell her."—"Cannot you open the gate?"

"Lord bless you, no; not unless she says so. It's more than my place is worth. I sha'n't be long."—"Thank you. Very good."

I handed him the crown-piece between the bars, and off he trudged, leaving me in a state of great doubt and perplexity as to whether or not it was a do.

"Shall we see him again, Graham?" I said.—"Doubtful," said Graham.

"So I think. I wonder, now, if we could get over this gate?"

A low growl at this moment came upon our ears, and I felt certain that if we were to execute the project of getting over the garden-gate, we should most probably drop into the jaws of some dog; so the reader may at once imagine with what amazing celerity I gave up such an idea at once; for of the two, I would much rather be nabbed by a shark or an alligator, than by a dog, my horror of hydrophobia amounting to a distinct phobia of itself.

We had nothing for it now but patience, and we waited a full quarter of an hour before we again saw a light approaching the gate, and in a few moments more our friend, with the crown-piece as a retaining-fee, made his gracious appearance.

"It's awkward, gentlemen—very awkward," he said, "because some one is expected who is no joke; but you can come in on condition you will go when you are told."—"Very good," said I.

The gate was opened, and in we went.

"Down! down!" cried the man, to a huge white dog, who made his appearance, and from whom, no doubt, came the ominous growling, which had so quickly convinced me of the impropriety of getting over the garden-gate. We were led up a gravel walk, and then through a side-door, into a handsome room. The man lit two wax candles, and then left us to our own meditations.

"What do you think of all this, doctor?" said Graham.—"I don't know yet what to think," said I. "There is some mistake here, which I suspect will not turn out to be very pleasant to the parties in the house."

"But don't you think, from the nature of our reception, that this place is rather of a questionable ——"—"Hush! Some one is coming."

The door opened, and a woman entered the room. Her age might be about forty. She had been handsome—that is to say, a handsomeness of the large order of human architecture. She was elegantly dressed, and rouged up to the eyes. When she got about two steps into the apartment she paused, and, in a hesitating tone, said,—

"There must be some mistake. I do not know either of you, gentlemen."

"Madam," said I, "is your name Anderton?"—"Yes, but ——"

"That will do, madam. So far there is no mistake. We have come to make some inquiries concerning your friend, Mrs. Major Chaplin."

She started, and with an air of vexation, muttered,—

"How dreadfully stupid of Andrews!" meaning, I presume, the man who let us into the house; and then, as if to think, she said,—

"My friend, Mrs. Major Chaplin?"—"Yes, madam; your friend, Mrs. Major Chaplin. Can you tell us where that lady can be found?"

"Really, gentlemen, when you come here and call Mrs. Major Chaplin a friend of mine, you are scarcely correct. I met the lady at Brighton last season. This one, she has made use of me as a reference about some house she was taking. Beyond that I know nothing whatever of her."—"Madam," said I, "there is no use in mincing this matter. This Mrs. Major Chaplin has, by asserting herself to be another person, inveigled a young girl from her home. This young girl must and shall be recovered, and it shall go hard with all who have had a hand in the abduction of her from her home. If you can throw any facilities in the way of her recovery, you may depend upon it it will be greatly to your interest to do so."

"Indeed, sir! And pray what right have you to assume ——"—"I assume nothing. You either know where this infamous woman, Chaplain, is to be found, or you do not. If you do, I tell you it is to your interest to tell us. If you do not, it is to your interest to find out."

"This is strange language."—"It is explicit, madam."

"It is insolent, be it what else it may, and I desire that you instantly quit my house."—"Mrs. Anderton, you are getting into a very serious trouble. Save this young girl, and you shall be spared."

"Really, sir, this is one of the most ungentlemanly and unwarrantable intrusions I ever heard of. What do I know, and what am I bound to know of your Italian adventuress?"—"Italian, madam! I never mentioned Italian. Mrs. Anderton, have you ever heard the ancient and respectable proverb, that liars should have good memories? No one said Italian but yourself."

I could see the colour rise to her face through all her paint, and with much vehemence she said,—

"You mentioned her being Italian yourself."—"Nay, nay; excuse me, madam. However unpolite it may be of me to contradict a lady, I must do so. Take counsel of yourself, and believe still that your real interest lies in doing what you can to restore this young girl to her friends."

A tremendous ring at the bell of the garden gate at this moment interrupted our conference. With a look of distress she turned to the door, which in a moment was opened by the man who admitted us, and who said, with a grin,—

"He's come."—"Hush!" cried the woman. "Gentlemen, will you leave?"—"Not yet," said I.—"Whew!" whistled the man.

"I implore you to leave. Come again to-morrow morning, and you will not make your visit in vain. To remain here now is to destroy my every hope—to destroy me; perhaps, yourselves."

Another violent ring at the bell, which I thought would never leave off.

"Good God, Andrews, why don't you answer the bell?" cried Mrs. Anderton.—"I thought I had better tell you first, mum," said the man, as he left the room.

"Leave—leave at once," cried Mrs. Anderton, clasping her hands. "Let me implore you to leave at once."—"No, madam, no. Here we wait."

She threw herself into a chair and wrung her hands.

"You shall have the girl back to-morrow," she cried. "You shall, upon my sacred word. She is not here, or you should have taken her away with you. I declare to my God she is not here."

The sound of footsteps came nearer and nearer to the door of the room. I made no reply to Mrs. Anderton's appealing speeches; but kept my eyes fixed upon the entrance to the apartment. There was a slight pause, the door was flung open, and the Earl of Bradstock, the same man with the sensual, bloated face that Graham and I had seen in the barouche, along with his fair incognita, made his unexpected appearance. The woman sprung to her feet and in frantic accents, she cried,—

"It's no fault of mine. They have forced themselves here. They won't go away. I could not help it. I cannot help it. It's no fault of mine, I swear."—"D——n!" said the Earl of Bradstock, and all the fiery pimples upon his face looked more fiery than before.

"There," said the woman, turning to us, "I told you so. I told you so, but you would not be warned." As if the Earl of Bradstock saying d——n was at once a sentence without appeal. In the words of Ingoldsby I could have said,—

"Notwithstanding this terrible curse,
No one here feels a penny the worse."

But it was no time for quotations, and I said at once,—

"My Lord Bradstock, you are very welcome here. You are an hereditary legislator, and a nobleman; and, therefore, of course, you will be anxious to protect the innocent. May we claim your assistance in restoring to her distracted parents a young and innocent girl, who has been by the vilest treachery torn from their arms?"—"And let me ask you," shouted Graham, "who the young lady is with the black satin pelisse, and diamond bracelet, whom I saw in a barouche with you at Hyde-park corner?"

"You are a scoundrel!" bellowed the earl, and his great bulky form seemed to swell up like an inflated balloon. "D——n you both! Andrew—George. The dogs. Call the d——d dogs. Give me a horse-whip."

Then followed such a torrent of curses and oaths of the most diabolical character, that not only is it quite out of the question for me to record them, but I should be very sorry to leave them to the imagination of my readers. A general scene of confusion reigned throughout the house, and Graham, before I could restrain him, dashed forward, and with his fists gave the earl such a pummelling about the head and face, that down he fell with a blow that shook the villa. Mrs. Anderton screamed, dogs barked, Graham I'm afraid swore, and I seized a great candelabra to protect myself from any sudden attack that might be made against me by quadrupeds or bipeds.

"We'll search the house—we'll search the house!" shouted Graham. "Come on, doctor. Come on."

He had possessed himself of a poker, and, with a candle in the other hand, he led the way, I following him with the candelabra in my grasp, and thus we made an incursion into every room in the enemy's territory, but could find no trace of Felice Barronelli, or of Graham's fair incognita. The house had now got extremely quiet. The inmates seemed determined to let us have our own way, and when we felt satisfied that we had been everywhere, I said,—

"Now, Graham, for God's sake come away. We will get professional advice about what is to be done next, but now we have done all we could, so come away."

He followed me to the hall, and just as we were about to set foot in the garden we saw a couple of dogs standing there and licking their jaws, as if in anticipation of a mouthful or two of our animal economy.

Graham was in a desperate mood, and before I could think what to do, he rushed out with the poker and gave the dogs such whacks on the back, that they ran off howling as fast as they could, no doubt thinking that it was a madman who had got hold of the poker. Taking advantage of this circumstance we both gained the gate, and then made our way into the open lane. I threw the candelabra over the iron-railings, and Graham hurled the poker at the house like a javelin, and I suppose it did some execution, for I heard a great crash.

We walked on a little way, and then stopped to talk.

"Is this a victory or a defeat?" said Graham.—"A little

of both," I replied. "I'm glad you laid the poker over the backs of those dogs."

"Confound the dogs, I was in such a passion, that if they had been elephants, I should have served them the same way."—"I'm only surprised that they ran away."

"They generally will if you make a very furious attack upon them. They think you are downright mad already, and that it's not a bit of use biting you, and so off they go."

I could not forbear a smile at this mode of putting the question, and then I said,—

"But seriously speaking, Graham, what do you think of all this?"—"Think! what can I think but that that rascal Bradstock has taken away not only Felice Barronelli, but my own very beautiful, very—oh, d—n it! I could smash him!"

"Yes; but there is this difference between the two cases, you know, Graham. Your own—your beautiful, you know, was seated by the side of this furious, and no doubt bad earl, while Felice Barronelli was decoyed away without any consent to become acquainted with him."—"True, true."

"The coincidence is curious, I grant, and in my own mind I have no doubt but that the house we have been to is one of a very questionable character indeed, and patronized, if not wholly supported by the earl."

"No doubt—no doubt. But where is Felice—where is my incognito?"—"Two questions just now difficult to answer. Come away—come away, Graham. By remaining here we can do no good, nor at this time of night can we seek any legal assistance with effect. The whole affair must now rest till the morning. There is no other resource."

"I suppose it must be so."—"We have, however, late as it is, a duty to pay to the Barronellis; no doubt they are up and expecting us most anxiously. Let us go there at once, for suspense is worse than being told that nothing has been achieved."

"But we have a clue, doctor."—"We have, and that is something."

I placed my arm within that of Graham's, and we walked towards London. A glorious night had set in, and such floods of moonlight as enveloped every object I scarcely ever in my life had seen before.

"What a beautiful night!" I exclaimed.—"Ah!" said Graham, "it is, indeed; but it has never yet happened to me, doctor, to see with a keen perception the exquisite beauties of nature, without being, as it were, compelled to contrast them with some corroding care which was brooding at my very heart, and turning all I see to gall and bitterness. I cannot but own that all around us is beauty, but, if anything, it adds, by contrast, an additional pang here."

He struck his heart as he spoke, and I replied to him,—

"You take too mournful a view of things, Graham. Living as you do, in consequence of your profession, in a world of imagination yourself, you invest the misfortunes and the disappointments of this life, I suspect, with more importance than they justly deserve."—"Perhaps I do—perhaps I do."

"Such men as you always do."—"Yes. It is a severe tax we pay for keener perceptions than many of our fellows, that we suffer in proportion from circumstances which would press but lightly over unthinking minds, making but a transient and easily effacable impression; while on ours they carve indelible lines, which endure for ever."

"Such men as you should never marry."—"Indeed!"

"You are safe to be disappointed."—"Yes; and there comes, perchance, the fearful contest between principle and ennui."

"True. Your existence is embittered. You drag about with you a chain, the rivets of which, although they may be in your power to break, you will not."—"No more of that, doctor. I have done now with all such feelings. She whom I did love—she in whom I felt confidence and faith—has betrayed me, and my heart is closed for ever against another passion. All such feelings are now dead and entombed. I shall never—never love again—never!"

"A-hem."—"You may say a-hem as much as you like, but it's a fact, nevertheless."

"Very good—we shall see. One erring angel does not contaminate all the heavenly host."—"Oh, it's all very fine. There—there's a gorgeous scene of moonlight. Saw you ever its equal?"

There is something, indeed, spiritually beautiful about moonlight. For some time after sunset the heat of the day remains oppressive. The many thousand buildings that exist in this metropolis are so retentive of heat, and the paved streets the same, that it would appear as though pedestrians had to walk through ovens that had been; and the slightly felt evening breeze scarcely dispels this feeling, and, indeed, can scarcely be said to modify it, until the sun has gone down several hours, and darkness has enveloped the city.

This again is dispelled by the rising moon, that sheds her genial influence upon the parched and dusty street, cooling the air, and rendering the streets more comfortable and bearable to walk in, and enjoy the cool hour of the evening. The moon sails through the heavens in her majesty and beauty; her silent and effulgent light sheds its gentle rays upon the great city. This is the hour when pleasure-seekers quit their own quiet homes, and parade the fashionable thoroughfares in the metropolis, and either in the glare of the well-lighted shops parade the town, or seek the more retired and quiet parts of the city, and walk by the moonlight.

The heavens themselves are studded with stars, beautiful and resplendent—in themselves a study and a mystery that mankind will never fathom. The stars shine brightly, and give new lustre to the moon, for not only is the light it lends beautiful, but the quarter it comes from is a beautiful and interesting object for contemplation. The steeples of the churches stand up high in the heavens, and appear as though frowning with majesty. From these tall places chime the hours of night, as though some imprisoned demons stood there, to fill all the town with alarm at the passing hours.

The streets grow thin, and their frequenters quit them by groups, and the shops are mostly shut up, save some few that keep late hours; the lamps still burn, and the moon still sheds her light, but there are few up to enjoy either. I, however, have often stolen out at the quiet, still hours of the night, to look upon the giant city as it slept beneath such floods of silvery light, and if I returned home a sadder, I believe I was likewise a wiser man.

* * * * *

We reached the Barronellis, who, as we had anticipated, we found up, and most anxiously expecting us; we related to them all that had occurred, and begged of them to be patient, and to hope for the best. We promised that, the first thing in the morning, the best legal assistance should be had, and we said all we could to comfort them. Alas! what words were likely to make them feel less the loss of the light of their existence—the dear being for whom they lived—who was the only tie that bound them to the world—who had sustained them through all affliction—who had seemed to them ever like a gift from Heaven as a compensation for all the ills which evil fortune could inflict upon them.

Little indeed could we hope to do in the way of consolation to those bereaved parents, and yet we tried much, and we fancied we left them in a better and more composed frame of mind than we found them, although I had my suspicion that they assumed more calmness and resignation than they felt as a tribute to our friendship, which appeared to demand as much of them.

* * * * *

Graham and I, the first thing on the morrow, accompanied by Barronelli, whom we met by appointment, and who I could easily see had not been to rest the whole night, went to an attorney, who was as well known for his probity as for his skill in his profession. To this gentleman's private house we went, and he very kindly saw us at once, and heard with attention all we had to say. I concluded, for I was the spokesman, by saying,—

"Now, sir, we have resolved to abide entirely by your direction in this affair; what you advise we will do."

Mr. Russell nodded (Russell was his name), and then he said slowly and distinctly,—

"This is one of those affairs in which firmness and private active enterprise can always do more than the law. Not that the law does not take active cognizance of such cases—on the contrary, it does so amply; but where anything is concealed—where an offence is committed, and we cannot lay hold of the thing hidden, or of the parties whom we can prove to have hidden it, the law is inactive, for the law must have something shown to it of a tangible nature to work upon. Now in these cases, the more publicity that is given to the exertions for justice that are being made, the better chance have the guilty parties of escaping. The direct mode of operation in this affair would be, to go before a magistrate at once and lay a public information; but that I would not advise. A father has a right to claim the custody of his child, and he can take her by force, and call upon the legal authorities to assist him. There is strong suspicion against the woman, Anderson, and a magistrate would send for her—but what could we do when we had her?"

"Could she not be committed?"—"No. There is not evidence enough. Besides, you lay yourselves both open to prosecution by the Earl of Bradstock."

"Then we acted illegally?"—"Most illegally. He does not know, probably, who you are at present, and my advice is, that you do not let him know. Get hold of one of the Bow-street runners, give him a *carte blanche* as regards moderate expense, and act under his direction. Should any discovery take place, then come to me, and I will arm you at once with authority to act by getting warrants from a sitting magistrate, whose sanction we can beforehand obtain to the employment of the officer."

"This is rational advice, sir," said I, "and we thank you for it."—"I wish you all manner of success, and will now go with you, if you like, to Bow-street."

It is needless to go through every minute particular at the police-office; suffice it, that we had a private interview with a magistrate, who directed one of the most active officers on the establishment to assist us, and with him we adjourned to one of the hotels under the piazzas of Covent-garden to arrange our proceedings.

"I will soon," said the officer, "find out for you what sort of a house that villa is and who inhabits it. It seems to me, too, that the Earl of Bradstock, who is at the bottom of the whole affair, should be narrowly watched."

"And my child, sir," said Barronelli, "what do you think is the fate of my poor child?"—"I should say she was safe enough."

"Safe, and in such hands? no, ruffianly violence——"—"No; in all these cases the parties are fully aware of the great danger they run, and they will be sure to wait some time to see what sort of way the friends of the girl take the affair in. If she is unyielding, and the friends active, she is safe enough. If they found not much notice taken, there is no knowing what villany might not be practised; but, under the present circumstances, I should say, sir, your daughter was safe enough."

"God bless you," said Barronelli, and he burst into tears.—"Leave it to me for to-day," said the officer; "leave it to me. I will call upon you at what hour you please in the evening."

We agreed to leave the affair in his hands, and, with an understanding that he would call at the Barronellis as early in the evening as he could, we all separated with better hopes of a quick and satisfactory result than we had any of us entertained before.—Barronnelli seemed to lay great stress upon the officer's opinion concerning the safety of his child, and, indeed, it appeared rational enough; so that he was in a much easier frame of mind, although, of course, his anxiety must have been most intense.

I waited very anxiously for the evening, as I have no doubt so did each of us; and before it could be reasonably hoped that the officer could bring us any news, we were all assembled at the Barronellis. Alas! what a different aspect that once happy home wore now to what it had presented. All was gloom and sadness, and the half hour we had to wait before the officer came, seemed a whole day of wretchedness, so heavily, so anxiously, and so wearily had it passed away. Nobody questioned him when he came into the room, but the looks of everybody sufficiently proclaimed how very anxious they were to hear his tidings.

"I am sorry to say," he said, "that I cannot bring you much news of a satisfactory nature."

Barronelli gave a groan.

"I allude," continued the officer, "rather to the amount of my intelligence than to the matter of it."—"We could not expect," said I, "that by magic you were at once to put an end to all this trouble."

"You are more reasonable, sir, than many people we have to deal with. But to come to the point: I have been as diligent as possible in making my inquiries, the result of which are just these:—First: The house called Bute Villa, at Kensington, nobody knows anything about, although everybody is very eager to suspect everything for the worst. Secondly: The Earl of Bradstock is represented to be seriously ill at his house in Berkeley-square. Thirdly: A faint trace of a woman, who is supposed to be the sham Mrs. Morgan, has been obtained, which I have entrusted one upon whom I can depend to follow up."

"Then of my child you have learnt nothing?" said Barronelli.—"Nothing."

"God help us! God help us!"—"But you still think her safe?" said I.

"Most unquestionably; and the more so because I believe we are all of opinion that the Earl of Bradstock is at the bottom of the whole affair, and I have no doubt in the world but that he is really ill at his own house, in consequence of the punishment inflicted on him by you, Graham."—"And that may save my child," said Barronelli, as he darted a look of gratitude to Graham.

"Passion prompted," said Graham, "and jealousy. Do not, in that affair, Barronelli, give me credit for an atom of reflection or any nobler feelings. I was mad to see before me the man who had deprived me of her I loved. I was frantic to think that wealth and power should be given to such a man to be so used, and I could not resist the impulse to let him feel the weight of a pair of plebeian fists."—"You served him right," said I. "I only hope, for your own sake, that he is not seriously ill. If he were to die, there would be a pretty riot about it."

"There would, indeed," said the officer, musingly. "I think you would be in some danger, Mr. Graham—at least, at a great amount of inconvenience." — "Which I am quite willing to encounter," said Graham. "I used no weapons but those with which nature has gifted all men. I received ample provocation, and my antagonist is half as big again as I am."

"All extenuating circumstances to a jury," remarked the officer. "But now I think I have learned quite enough concerning Bute Villa to make a thorough search of it, by virtue of a warrant, a matter at once proper and justifiable."—"We searched it," said I.

"Yes; but there is a systematic mode of doing such things only known to those who make a business of it. Besides, it was night, and you were excited."—"We were, truly,"

"Very good. Now, as I do not know the young lady personally, I must have one of you with me."—"Myself—myself," cried Barronelli. "Who so proper as I to go with you on such a search?"

"Who so improper, you should say," remarked the officer. "I never like to have interested parties with me on such expeditions. He who feels the least, and knows enough, is the man for me. What has to be done must be done coolly, calmly, and systematically. I cannot have you with me, Mr. Barronelli. Your feelings are quite natural, and such as one would both wish and expect you to have, but for that very reason you are unfit to go with me."—"I submit," said Barronelli. "Do with me what you will—I submit. Only save my child, and the gratitude of a life shall not be sufficient to repay you."

"Gentlemen, will one of you come with me at seven o'clock to-morrow morning?"—-"You go, doctor," said Graham. "You have a cooller head and a less excitable temperament than I."

"Very good," said I. "I think I have, and, therefore, as in this case any mock modesty would be sadly out of place, I will go, and the more readily, too, as the earliness of the hour mentioned will suit me better than if it were late in the day."—"Then, sir," said the officer, rising, "I will meet you at half-past six, if you like, at Hyde-park gate."

"Agreed," said I.

The officer left us, and Graham and I remained some time longer with the Barronellis, attempting to calm their fears, and bring them to a better hope than they had hitherto had. When I left, Graham still remained, and as I went home a thought struck me quite accidentally, which I at once saw the importance of, and which I determined to carry out on the morrow, if possible, for it seemed to me the most likely plan of all to arrive at some facts with regard to the share that the Earl of Bradstock might have in the abduction of Felice Barronelli.

"If," I considered with myself, "it be really true that the earl is very ill, and confined to his house, of course he has medical attendance. What is there to hinder me from finding out who is his physician, and calling upon him? If that son of Esculapius be a gentleman, as most probably he is, I shall expect from him ready sympathy and assistance. If he be such a pig as to refuse it, I shall, at least, have gained a knowledge of the truth of the statement that he is really ill."

I thought this, and I think my readers will agree with me, a happy suggestion, and the more I considered it, the more likely it seemed to me to be suggestive of good results, so that I was impatient now for the next day to come, that I might go with the officer to Bute Villa, and after that ascertain what medical man was in atttendance upon the (noble?) earl.

* * * * *

The longest night, even the six months of darkness at the north pole, must go at last, and morning comes in all its exceeding freshness and beauty. I had directed myself to be called at five o'clock, and the servant was punctual in so doing. The moment I heard the tap tap at my chamber door, and the cry of—,

"It's past five, sir," I was up, for I felt sleepy, and well I knew what an insidious rascal that drowsy god is, and how glad he is to catch anybody napping when they ought to be up and doing.

It's of no use lying thinking when you have to get up; minutes fly like moments.—It must be done by a plunge—an unreflective plunge, like suicide or matrimony. It won't do to reflect upon either. Acting upon this principle I jumped up, and was half dressed by the time I was wholly awake. I swallowed a hearty breakfast, and then out I sallied, to keep my appointment with the officer at the gate of Hyde-park.

I was a little before my time, but not much, and as I judged from the habits and modes of thought of the officer, that he was a punctual man, I did not regret it, nor had I cause, for he came about five minutes before the precise time appointed. We walked on towards Kensington after some mutual compliments upon our punctuality. Alas, that it should be considered a positive virtue for a man to keep his word about an appointment. What vexation, what desperation, what degradation, and vice is produced in London by the sin, for it really amounts to one, of non-punctuality. What fortunes have been lost, what hearths have been rendered desolate, what tears have flowed, what hearts have been broken by such a cause, slight as at a first glance it would seem.

And men who call themselves in this huge city men of tact and business—fellows who bustle about, and think largely of themselves and their resources — how many of these keep themselves and everybody else in a fidget from morning till night, from want of punctuality, and its attendant virtue, system. How many whole days are somehow or another bustled through with toil and uneasiness in doing what, if rightly set about, and at the right time, would not occupy four hours.

But people will not be systematic. It is of no use arguing with them about it. The majority of persons have a mind of a slip-shod kind—a mind like a door swinging upon one hinge —it cannot do its work readily and correctly. Truly, the man who could make all London punctual, would be a greater benefactor of his species than any who has yet appeared.

Men who have the value of system in their affairs, and punctuality in all their proceedings, laugh in their sleeves at their wandering unsystematic fellows. They are as men engaged in a race who run direct to the winning post, while the others are making a hundred deviations from the path for want of tact to keep it.

If any man wins the golden hour of fame and fortune, depend upon it he has a mind well strung—an intellect which enables him to do the proper thing at the proper time. We do not mean to assert that success is invariably to crown such a man's course in life, because Dame Fortune will sometimes make a dead set at a man and conquer him. But most unhesitatingly do we assert, that no man ever became truly great without such qualities—no man wealthy, unless by an accident, without an appreciation of the value of his own time and the time of others.

My readers, I am led to believe, forgive me for occasional digressions, on the ground that they are mostly of a practical character, and, besides, I am always doing something or another at the same time, a description of which might not be so interesting or so entertaining. Thus, while I was discoursing upon punctuality, I was walking to Bute Villa at Kensington with the Bow-street officer, and by the time I got to a conclusion of the remarks I thought fit to make upon that subject, which really cannot be too often remarked upon, my readers will be so good as to suppose that the officer and I had arrived, and that our individual noses came close to the iron bars of the garden gate of that abode of mystery, caution, and, I much feared, vice.

"You have a warrant?" said I.—"Oh, yes."

"You will, however, not find it effective upon the canine race. There are dogs here."—"Are there? I shall shoot any dog who comes with a hostile look within biting distance of me."

"Then you are armed?"—"Oh, yes; we have always arms with us; we never know what desperate characters we may have to encounter. It is a principle with us, that when we have a prisoner to take, we must have him alive or dead—not that we are men in a hurry to use weapons,—we only do so when our own lives are threatened by fire-arms or superior force of numbers. But we must never be beaten off; we endeavour to get up an impression that we will only with our lives quit a prisoner."

"It is a good plan."—"It is. It invests us, you see, with a moral force we should not otherwise be able to pretend to."

"And no doubt preserves you."—"Indeed it does; we often single-handed take into custody powerful men, who yield to us from a conviction that they must murder us to get away, and that they don't choose to do; therefore, they allow themselves to be taken often without the least show of resistance. But let us ring now at this bell, and see what sort of reception we get."

The officer rang the garden-gate bell, and in a few moments the same man appeared who had before admitted me and Graham on the strength of my five-shilling piece.

The moment he saw me, he seemed to know me directly, and he set up a volley of oaths as was quite desperate to hear, and almost competed with the Earl of Bradstock, who was about the most first-rate hand at swearing I had ever encountered.

"What do you want?" he cried, when he had eased his mind by a volly of anathemas; "what do you want?"— "See," said the officer, and he exhibited his staff. "See, my man. You had better open the gate quietly."

"Here, Jowl—Jowl—Jowl!" cried the man, and in an instant one of the great dogs made his appearance. "Stay there, Jowl, and pin anybody who tries to get in."

With this instruction to Jowl, who was one of the ugliest-looking brutes ever I saw, but who seemed quite to comprehend what was expected of him, the fellow walked away, whistling, as much as to say, "Now do what you can; I don't intend to take any more notice of you."

"I will climb over the gate first," said the officer, "and as soon as you see Mr. Jowl going to lay hold of my leg, be so good as to shoot him."

He handed me a pistol as he spoke, and then commenced clambering over the gate, without a moment's hesitation.

"Is this legal?" said I.—"Oh, we do some things that are not legal, and leave the parties to take their remedy if they like."

"Very good."

He was soon on the other side of the gate, and I saw Jowl licking his great greasy-looking chops, and growling as he did so, with, I presume, the prospect of a good bite at the officer, who now put down one of his feet, upon which Jowl sprang.

The officer had top-boots on, and could not be hurt. I placed the muzzle of the pistol within two inches of Jowl's head, and then finding the heel of the officer's boot hard, Mr. Jowl very indiscreetly turned suddenly, and caught the barrel of the pistol in his mouth. I pulled the trigger, and away went the top of Mr. Jowl's skull.

"That'll do," said the officer. "Now come over; 'tis easy."—"I know there's two dogs," said I. "For God's sake, keep a look out for me."

I scrambled over, and the other dog did not put in an appearance; so we found ourselves in the garden quietly enough. We made at once for the house, the door of which was open, and so quietly had the place been carried by storm, that our appearance, I have no doubt, was as unexpected as if we had fallen from the moon.

The first room we entered we found contained the lady with whom I and Graham had had the unpleasant interview. She set up a scream when she saw us, but the officer took no more notice of it than as if she had not been there, but went as quietly to work, hunting the place through, as if we were alone.

I followed his example, and said nothing. We went from room to room, and found no one at all in the house with the exception of this woman, although there were evidences of the occupation by other parties. Trace of Felice Barronelli there was not the slightest, and we both, I think, felt a little puzzled.

"What do you think of this?" said I.—"There is something very odd about the place," said the officer. "I really cannot make it out. I sha'l go through the grounds."

He did so, but with like non-success. The garden was not large, and there was a little paddock. A villa of the same class, but which was untenanted and to let, was visible close at hand. There was no place of concealment in the grounds, and we were compelled to give up the job as useless for the present.

"We are not on the right scent somehow," said the officer. "I will place a man to watch this house day and night through. There is some mystery at the bottom of it all, which only active inquiry can possibly elucidate. We must have patience."

When we reached the garden gate again, we found the man Andrews waiting at it holding it open. He had a grin of defiance on his countenance, and when we came near, he said,—

"I hope as you have had a pleasant job. We locked up the silver spoons."—"Thank you, my friend," said the officer.

"Oh, you are vastly welcome."—"You are very kind."

"I means to be so. Good morning, gentlemen. We are going to get some steel traps to catch thieves."—"Oh, then, you will be held by the leg," said the officer.

"Shall I, spooney?"

The officer laughed, and we walked away, leaving the fellow, as was evident from his red face and the insulting epithets he launched after us, in a most thundering passion. As we went on then, I explained my plan of finding out the medical man who was attending the earl, and I had the gratification of hearing a warm approval of it by the officer, who took from his pocket a Court Guide, saying,—

"Here is some account of the Earl of Bradstock. It says he married the Lady Olivia Somerset, by whom he had one child. He is a widower now, and his title dates from the Norman Conquest. His town residence is No. 84, Berkeley-square, and I have heard what is not stated here, namely, that he is notorious for intrigues and audacious libertinisms, so much so, that his wife's relations deprived him for a long time of the custody of his own daughter."

"A pretty fellow for a father."

"You may well say that, sir; I hope, though, most sincerely, that he will get well of this illness, or it will, as I have hinted to him, involve your friend, Mr. Graham, in serious trouble."

"Well, I hope before the day is over to ascertain his actual condition."

"I trust you may; I will call at the Barronellis again as soon as I have anything to communicate worth the telling, but I am not so sanguine of bringing the affair to a hasty conclusion as I was. However, you and they may depend upon me doing my best."

We parted at the corner of Hyde-park, and I walked to Berkeley-square. It was still early, but the moment I got into the square I saw a carriage standing at one of the doors —I hastened up—it was at No. 84. At the moment the carriage steps were let down, and the hall door opening, there came out suddenly a man whom in a moment I recognized as Dr. Adamson, one of the most eminent of the faculty. I stepped up to him, and held out my hand, saying,—

"Good morning, Dr. Adamson."—"Why—why, God bless me," he cried "is it you, and out so early? How do you do? Why—why I haven't seen you for an age."

"No. Are you going home?"—"Ah, to be sure; I have not breakfasted."

"Then I will, if you please, invite myself."—"Ah, to be sure; why—why, you know you need no invitation at all, you know. Get into the carriage."

I did, and on our road to Russell-square, where Dr. Adamson resided, I told him the whole story about Felice Barronelli. The old man lifted up his hands, as he said,—

"Why—why, good gracious! I knew Bradstock was a scamp, but, of course, that's nothing to me professionally."

"Of course not."—"He has burst a small blood vessel on the lungs. Nothing of much consequence; but he is frightened, because he spits blood. He will have me make him an extra visit of a morning before my usual time. It's a five guinea fee, so you see I go."

"Oh, of course, of course. You think he will get over it?" —"Oh, dear, yes. In about a week or two he will be quite recovered again. But he must be quiet; any great excitement might produce fatal results, such as hæmorrhage on the lungs; but if he's kept quiet, he'll do well enough."

"Does he live alone?"—"Well—why—why, they say he keeps some woman or other, but really, you know, I don't know."

"Exactly. Now, Dr. Adamson, it would be very easy for you to tell him you would like to bring a professional friend with you to look at him!"—"Oh, yes, yes. Common enough."

"Will you take me?"—"Well—I—why—why, I don't see much objection; but really you know, if he's flurried, some little accident might happen."

"I will not go till you pronounce him out of danger of such a result; because, to tell the truth, I want to flurry him; so don't tell him that he is better, if you please."—"I won't—I won't. I tell you what I'll do now. You shall come with me this day week—no, let me see—yes. It's the first of May, ain't it?"

"Yes, this day week will be the first of May."—"Then— why—why, he will be well enough by then to be tossed in a blanket if necessary, and then I will take you, do you know."

I thanked the old man, who was really good-hearted, although there was much singularity about him, and I went home with him, and took a second breakfast, for my walk had given me a new appetite. After that I went to the Barronellis, and told them of all the disappointment and all the hopes. I left them in despair. I could not soothe them; one moment Barronelli was desperate, another quite prostrated with gloom. I sincerely pitied them, and it was a sad thing to have nothing to say, but patience, patience, to people situated as they were; and yet what else could be said? What was to be done but what was doing? Where were they to look for Felice? Alas! what was she, poor girl, suffering during this dreadful period of agony and suspense to all who loved her and felt an interest in her happiness?

What a world of conjecture might be conjured up of her feelings—what tears might she be shedding. How heart-broken must she feel, unless supported by that palladium of the heart, the consciousness of innocence.

* * * * *

The week had passed away—it was the first day of May, and the weather all at once became as remarkably cold and unseasonable as it had been warm and like the very height of summer for a week or two previously. The north-east winds blew keenly—the clear sky became cloudy and dreary, and many a young bud upon the trees fell an early victim to that nipping air which blew for weeks now without any intercession whatever of its severity.

The reader may imagine that I was punctual at the house of my old friend, Dr. Adamson. That is to say, he was my old friend as regarded his own age, if not as regarded the duration of our intimacy, although that has subsisted for some years.

"Is the earl well enough to be flurried?" was my first question.—"Why—why," said the old man, "I should say he was, and you may flurry and worry him as much as you like; but he thinks himself very bad, do you know—very bad, indeed."

"So much the better."—"And the women he keeps, you see——"

"Women? Are there more than one?"—"Why—why— well, I suppose so. I saw two yesterday, and they looked at each other like strange cats. A young one was good-looking, and an older one wasn't, you know."

"Oh!"—"That's it. Come along if you are ready. Come and flurry him as much as you like. This shall be my last visit. You can wait, you know, till I get my fee, and then flurry him."

"Very good."

I had taken the precaution, to guard against recognition, to be dressed very differently to what I had been when the earl and I met on the memorable evening that he got well thrashed by Graham, so that it was not likely he would know me in his own house, and under such very different circumstances.

That same evening I had told the Barronellis what I was about, and I left Graham with them. Poor Barronelli himself was in bed. He had become the very shadow of his former self, and his wife, looking the picture of misery, was only just well enough to act as his nurse and attendant. It was indeed a sad and gloomy home now, that of these poor refugees, and no one could fail to pity them, or to feel a pang of indignation against the artless abductors of their only comfort and consolation in this world,—their beautiful and innocent child.

Graham, too, had evidently suffered much—what with his

own affliction, for he still clung to a recollection of his first and only love, and his sympathy with the bereaved family, to whom he was so much attached, he had become thin and wretched, and had lost much of that flow of convivial spirits which had so frequently made him so delightful a companion, and the very soul of wit and animation.

It was really very grievous to see them. My heart bled for them, and I was more meritorious than I had proposed to myself to be in bidding them hope great things from my interview with the Earl of Bradstock, whom I was determined to awaken to some sense of feeling and of honour, if he had one spark of those commodities in his disposition.

Incited, therefore, to do my best—grieving for the Barronellis, and indignant against their enemies, I went with old Dr. Adamson to Berkeley-square. And after all we had only a suspicion against the earl. It amounted to absolutely nothing more. My perplexity of mind greatly increased as I neared the door of his magnificent mansion.

"You have, I presume, Dr. Adamson," said I, "prepared the Earl of Bradstock for my coming?"—"Yes. Why—why, I mentioned it yesterday, and told him you were a very clever man, and then he became quite eager to see you. Very eager, indeed, in a manner of speaking."

"That takes away much of the awkwardness of my interview."—"No doubt, no doubt."

"And he is tolerably well?"—"Oh, much better than he has been, no doubt. Why—why, you see, this lay-up has forced him to be circumspect in his diet, and that is everything to a great beast of a plethoric subject, such as he is, you understand."

"You give a flattering description of him."—"Why—why, you see, that's what he is. He has a face as big as your's and mine put together, and great puffy cheeks and goggling eyes; in fact, a more decided animal sort of man I never came near in all my life. He is an abomination. I can perceive that all his life he has consulted nothing but his mere sensual gratifications. He has not mind enough to fill a teaspoon—why—why, I wouldn't be such a man to be emperor of all the world."

"Nor I."—"Of course you wouldn't. He'll drop down dead some day, and—why—why, of course it will be a great pity—ahem! why, why."

"A good riddance."—"Nay, come, my dear sir. How very unprofessional. Very. Why—you know we ought to be the last people in the world to talk about sudden deaths being desirable."

"But they are in spite of all that, Dr. Adamson. Most people have a great horror of sudden death, because two large and influential classes of people have always taken especial care to get up a feeling of the sort."—"Indeed."

"Yes, doctors and parsons."—"Oh, why—why, I suppose you are right enough. That's somewhere about the truth, I reckon; but here we are; I shall take you up to his lordship's room at once."

"Is he up?"—"Oh, yes; and in a small sitting-room adjoining his bed-room. You can flurry him, you know, as much as you like."

We were announced to the earl, and in a few moments I found myself ushered with Dr. Adamson into a very handsome though somewhat small apartment, on a sofa in which sat the Earl of Bradstock, looking almost as fat and bloated as ever, but very pale.

Dr. Adamson introduced me to him, and then he said, querulously,—

"Well, am I better, or am I worse? Eh? eh?"—"Why, —why," said Adamson, "what do you think, doctor? Will you try the stethescope?"—"Yes," said I.

I placed the stethescope against the earl's chest, and listened gravely, while the expression in his face was that of ridiculous terror.

"Well, well," he said.—"Don't speak," said I.

He gave a groan.

"Now cough."—"A—hem!"

I shook my head very earnestly, and the earl groaned again.

"Why, why," said old Dr. Adamson; "what do you think, doctor, eh? What do you think?"

I shook my head again, and looked as wise as possible. The earl seemed just on the point of setting up a roar like a well caned school-boy, and his great goggling eyes, as they rolled about and glared at me, were truly ludicrous. I had immense difficulty to suppress a smile, especially when he said,—

"If you please, am I worse? Oh, am I worse? oh! oh!"

—"Your diagnosis agrees with mine," said I to Dr. Adamson. "There is considerable vascularity of the cellular tissues."

"Good God!" said the earl. "Why—why, yes," said Adamson.

"There is no doubt effusion in the left lobe?"—"I'm lost!" groaned the earl.

"Are you flurried?" said Adamson, putting on his spectacles—"Of course I am.—"Oh, very good."

"Do you think," said I, "there is any incipient ossification?"—"Well, there may be."

"Or an exostoses on the inner table of the cranium?"—"I have met with such cases."

"Then I am a dying man," said the earl.—"All human life," said I, "is short and uncertain."

"D—n other people's lives!" he cried; "it's only mine that I care about! Tell me, doctor—tell me, am I lost and done for? Oh, dear! oh, dear! I am a nobleman, too, with plenty of means. Really, can it be possible? Surely, there are remedies accessible to the rich to save?"

"My lord," said I, gravely, "have you made your will?" —"No," he cried. "What do I want with a will? D—n everybody! What do I care about anybody?"

"Have you settled your affairs? Have you done justice where you could? Have you endeavoured to repair what injuries you could? My lord, does there lie nothing heavily on your soul?"—"When I want a parson I'll send for one. D—n it," he cried, "I don't want to be preached to! I don't believe I am dying at all."

"You may recover; but I have now come from the bedside of one who will not—of one who is slowly dying of the worst of maladies, my lord."

"What the devil is that?"—"A broken heart—a broken ——"

"Oh, don't talk to me of such nonsense—I won't hear it; I don't like to hear it; and I never do anything that I don't like, so there's an end of that. Tell me at once, am I worse, or am I better?"—"Flurry him again," whispered old Adamson.—"I will."

"What do you say?"—"Listen, my lord. The case I have just left is one that nearly concerns yours, and it shows you how the mind kills the body. It will show you how much misery one bad man may inflict upon those around him by making a disgraceful use of those means which Providence has placed in his hands for better purposes."

"I will not listen."—"You shall," I cried. "You shall listen," and I raised my voice till the room echoed again. "You shall listen, or the remedies which I, and I alone, know to save you from death shall be withheld; I have but to hold up my finger, and the destroyer will be here. I could send one to this house, my lord, who could reach you, even you, hidden in its inmost recesses. Before I proceed I have one question to ask of you."

"D———n!" shouted the earl. "This in my own house?"

He sprang to his feet, and at the moment the door opened, and, to my intense surprise, the fair incognito of Graham stood upon the threshold.

A moment's reflection told me that I ought not to be so very much surprised, as I certainly had been, at the sudden apparition of the beautiful creature, who had made so deep an impression upon the mind of Graham, but who, alas! was to all appearance so unworthy of the attachment of such a heart as his.

That she should be in the Earl of Bradstock's house was unhappily to be expected. He had seen her a willing occupant of his barouche—what, then, was to prevent the likelihood of her being the companion of his leisure in his magnificent mansion? The only thing that was very sad and mournful in the business was, that she, filling the situation she there seemed to fill, should so unblushingly make her appearance before two gentlemen, perfect strangers to her.

And yet, what an air and manner she had of lofty innocence! How noble, as well as how beautiful she looked, as she stepped into the apartment, with a slightly heightened colour, and fixed her eyes upon the earl with an expression at once full of tenderness and sorrow! Truly, she was to me an enigma.

"Who sent for you?" cried the infuriated earl. "Who desired your presence here? Why do you not leave? You have many objections to stay—why do you not go at once?"

"I was not sent for," she said, with so sad an expression, and such exquisite beauty of tone, that I started to hear her. "I was not sent for—I was lingering near the door, and heard the sounds of contention—sounds, surely, all unfit for a sick chamber."

"What's that to you, eh?—what's that to you?" The young girl placed her hands before her face, and I saw the tears trickle through her fingers, as she said,—"This before strangers, too—this before others!"

"What do I care who it's before!" shouted the earl. "What is it to me who it's before, I should like to know! You were ever opposed to me—ever will be—I know that well enough. Where's Mrs. Cranberry?"—"Peace—peace! name her not before—at least, while I am under this roof. Name her not to me, nor permit me to see her!"

"Mighty fine!" cried the earl. "You thought I was dying, and, like a carrion crow, you come to the pickings. Be off—be off!"

"Gentlemen," said the girl, turning to us with an imploring look, "you are physicians. Is the earl better?"—"Why— why," began old Dr. Adamson, but I interrupted him, saying,—

"Will you allow me, Dr. Adamson, to remark, that that is a question much better answered out of the presence of a patient."—"Ah, very true—very."

"Which is as much as to say I am worse," said the earl, as he sank into his chair again. "I won't die. I—I am a nobleman, I—won't die."—"A wise determination, my lord," said I. "Will you now answer me the question I was about asking of you when this young—young person came into the room?"

"What question?"—"Where is Felice Barronelli?"

He started as if he had been shot, and his great eyes opened wider than before, as he glared at me with a mingled expression of rage and surprise.

"Where is Felice Barronelli?" cried I again. "Restore, my lord, the child to her doating parents. Your looks bespeak you guilty. I came here with strong suspicion that you were the instigator of one of the cruelest abductions of youth and innocence I had ever heard of, and these suspicions are now strengthened into certainty."

"Great God!" said the young girl, as she sank into a seat by the window.

The earl looked for a moment or so as if he were choking; then he rose and said,—

"I tell you what it is, Mr. ——, d—n you, what's your name?—if you don't get out of my house directly, I'll get my footman to kick you out. Do you understand that?"—"And despise it," said I, firmly. "Can you deny that you are concerned in the abduction of Felice Barronelli?"

"Do your worst!" he cried, almost convulsed with passion; "do your worst! Suppose I took a fancy to the girl, and chose to have her!"—"Villain!"

He gave a great, chuckling, hideous sort of laugh in my face, and added,—

"The girl was pretty, and I was at leisure. Ha! ha! Make your most of it. Ha! ha! She'll soon reconcile herself to her new prospects."

"Wretched man, have you for one moment reflected upon the dreadful consequences of your wickedness?"—"I suppose she'll go on the pave at last. Ha! ha!"

"A warrant shall teach you that justice can even overtake so bold a profligate, and so cowardly a rascal as yourself," I said.—"I shall refuse attendance," he said. "I mention no names. You can prove nothing—infer what you like, and the disconsolate parents you can inform that they may cut their throats if they like."

"My God! this is too much," said the girl, rising, with a face as pale as alabaster.—"Yes," said I to her, mournfully. "It is too much for us. Let me hope that it may yet be enough for you. You are young—you are beautiful; there is that in your countenance and manner which proclaims you a being of sensibility and intelligence. How you came to be in your present dreadful and degraded state it is not for me to inquire. But now let me implore you—let me beg of you with all my heart and soul, as I would beg of a dear child of my own, to rouse from its torpor the innate virtue which must surely be but slumbering in your breast. Oh, if you have yet left one spark of purity and innocence, let my words fan it to a flame. You shall not want friends—you shall not want words of kindness and of sympathy. There is one who loves you, in whose heart your image will for ever remain—one who weeps for you, and although you can never now be his, he will work still for you, and God knows he shall not want assistance in so doing. Turn aside, let me implore you, from the path you have chosen. You may yet be happy. Arthur Graham loved you as few have ever loved. He loved you as he would have loved an angel; he mourns for you as one fallen from her high estate, and yet he loves you still. He prays to God to bless you. He is not what he was. Grief has made ravages upon him. He will never be what he was; well I know that, with a memory of his former deep devotion, he will throw around you the shield of his honest protection. In some quiet spot, far off, you may know serenity. To see you would be too great a trial for him; but in his name I do implore you to leave this place and this mode of life for ever!"

She listened to me with fixed attention; her hands were clasped, and when I had concluded, she said, faintly,—

"And—and he would do all that?"—"He would. He is now comforting the afflicted parents of the poor girl—almost a child—who has been torn away from a happy home by that bad man's machinations."

"Her name——"—"Is Felice Barronelli."

"Felice Barronelli! I recollect that name, surely."— "She made an appearance at the Italian Opera."—"True— most true."

"What in the name of d——n is the meaning of all this?" cried the earl, as he rang the bell violently.

The young girl stepped up to him.

"Farewell for ever!" she said. "Farewell!"—"Ha! ha! you have said that before. Ha! ha!"

"You will leave him?" said I.—"I will. The struggle is severe, but I will. I have loved him."

"Loved him?"—"Yes. You pity me. Your pity is not misplaced. I love him still, yet do I love virtue better."

"Stay. Go with me from here. Have you friends?"— "A few."

"Will they receive you?"—"I think they will, sir. And I am not entirely destitute. I owe you many, many thanks, and when next we meet, I shall be able to thank you more fully."

"Emily," cried the earl, "before you go——"—"No more, no more," she said, "it is enough. The earl will live?"

"He will," said I. "Concealment is no longer necessary. He is, in fact, now convalescent."—"Then d—n you all," he cried. "Go or stay everybody who chooses. Nobody asked you to come here. Be off with you."

The girl left the room. There was the same look of lofty command about her as she did so, that she had worn when she entered it. She puzzled me completely.

"My lord," I said, turning to the earl, "immediate publicity shall now be given to the whole of these proceedings. Popular opinion and the law shall wring from you the secret where Felice Barronelli is confined."

He snapped his fingers and laughed. Then turning to a footman who had answered his ring, he said,—

"Kick the fellow down stairs, John."

"Kick, kick, my lord?"—"Yes, I'll hold you harmless. If you hesitate, take your discharge from my service at once."

John looked puzzled for a few moments, and then turning to me, he said,—

"If you please, sir, just to allow me to do what my lord wishes. It's very awkward, you see, for me, sir, for you see, sir, if I don't I shall get discharged, and you wouldn't, I'm sure, sir, like me to lose my place owing to you, sir."— "Certainly not, John," said I.

"Then, sir, you will be good enough——"—"To solve the difficulty for you, John. You are the modestest footman ever I met with."

"Thank you, sir."—"It's a pity for such a master to lose such a servant, therefore, as regards his lordship, who is the seducer of innocence, and the most bloated and detestable ruffian ever I encountered, this may suffice."

I laid my cane several times smartly across his lordship's shoulders, adding,—

"You called me by some epithets that were as false as they were insulting—take that as your reward; and, as for you, John, I'll kick you down stairs, if you please, instead of your conferring upon me that favour."

I walked to the door, and hearing something behind me, I just moved aside in time to avoid a plaster bust, which came like a cannon shot from the hands of the earl after me. As it was, it took John in the region of the stomach, and shot him down stairs with wonderful celerity.

I was not disposed for any further personal contest, so down stairs I went. Poor old Dr. Adamson had made a precipitate retreat when first the row began, and was sitting trembling

in his carriage. The earl was swearing, John was shouting murder, and by the time I reached the hall the whole household were alarmed. But before I left the house, I was doomed to encounter another acquaintance.

At the very moment that I was passing the door of one of the apartments leading from the hall, it opened, and there bounced out right into my arms a female. One glance was sufficient to enable me recognise her—it was Mrs. Cholmondeley Morgan.

"How do you do, madam?" cried I.

A scream burst from her lips.

On the impulse of the moment I twined my arms round her, lifted her off her feet, and in three strides reached the carriage door. To fling her on the top of Dr. Adamson was the work of a moment, and then I jumped after her.

"Drive to Bow-street," I cried, in a loud voice.—"Murder!" cried old Adamson.—"Fire!" shouted his footman.

Mrs. Cholmondeley Morgan screamed and fought, and before I could hinder her, or the carriage-door could be shut, she scratched old Dr. Adamson's powdered wig off his head, and nearly smothered the footman by throwing it in his face.

"Death of cold! Why—why—good God! a mad woman!" cried the old man.—"Shut the door, William, and drive to Bow-street," shouted I.

"Huff! huff! a—chew!" coughed and sneezed William, for his mouth and eyes were full of hair-powder.

I got a grip of Mrs. Morgan by her arms, and there I held her; but, unfortunately, Dr. Adamson could not get out of her way, and in the most unladylike manner he afterwards assured me that she spat in his eye.

In the midst of all this confusion we got fairly off at length. The old horses, for once in their lives, were lashed into a good hard trot. William held on behind, wiping his eyes, as if he had just met with some severe family bereavement. Mrs. Morgan swore! Yes, she swore. Old Dr. Adamson placed a silk handkerchief over his head, and crouched up in a corner on the opposite seat; and I said nothing, but held my prisoner tightly, so that escape or much mischief was out of the question.

In this order, or rather disorder, we reached Bow-street police-office; and now the job was to get Mrs. Cholmondeley Morgan out of the vehicle. The appearance, however, of the carriage attracted several officers, among whom I was much gratified to see him who was acquainted with all the circumstances of the case.

"Hilloa, Reed!" I called out. "I have got Mrs. Morgan here, and she is disposed to be violent."

He knew my voice in a moment, and sprung to the side of the carriage.

"Oh, indeed!" he said. "We will soon settle that. Now, ma'am, if you please, just slip on these bracelets."

He held up a pair of handcuffs.

"Eugh! wretches!" shrieked Mrs. Morgan; "what can one woman do against a parcel of brutes?"—"You are disposed to be quiet, then? Allow me to lead you out, madam?"

Reed, the officer, took hold of her wrist, and assisted her from the carriage; but he did not let go his hold when that operation was completed, and glaring around her like an enraged tiger, she exclaimed,—

"Oh, this is Bow-street, is it? Well, I give these two men in charge for an assault."—"Very good, ma'am," said the officer; "step inside, if you please."

"But I don't please. Who has a right to detain me? I won't step inside for you or any wretches like you."—"Very good, ma'am; we must carry you. You are our prisoner."

"Your prisoner?"—"Yes; I have had a warrant for your apprehension in my pocket now above a week. Now, madam, don't be a fool—whether your name be Morgan, or Chaplin, I don't care. You are my prisoner. We never use force here except we are obliged. When we are so obliged, we don't stop at trifles. Will you walk in?"

"Wretches!" said Mrs. Cholmondeley Morgan, alias Mrs. Major Chaplin, and alias, as I suspected, from what the earl had said, Mrs. Corberry. And in she walked, without any further trouble.

I lingered a little behind, and then I went up to the carriage-door, and, addressing the old doctor, said,—

"Doctor Adamson, I think we need scarcely trouble you any more just now."—"Oh, why—you are very good, I think, for once, and just now, as you say, why—why, I have had trouble enough."

"You know it's no business of yours."—"Oh, why—why, considering that I have rather been in the thick of it, I think——"

"Well, you have a little."—"Yes, a little. Have you any idea of what's become of my wig?"

"Really I have not."—"Thank you. That mad woman

spat in my eye, upon my life. Why, or wherefore, you made my carriage into a wild beast's den, I really cannot say."

"I will explain all to you when we meet again."—"Very good—why—why, do you know I haven't been so buffetted about and alarmed for forty years, really—my wig gone too. You say, it is not necessary I should this morning endure any more?"—"Not at all."

"Then I may go home, I suppose?"—"Yes, certainly."

"I am grateful," said the old man, with a serio-comic expression, as he leant back in his carriage—"I say ———"—"Well?"

"Let your friends have this sort of thing by turns, you know, and mind, I've had mine."—"Yes, yes. Good morning."

I entered the police-office, and for the life of me I could not help laughing to think how poor old Dr. Adamson had been let in for the adventure; but I knew well, despite all his grumbling, that he was really not at all displeased at what had occurred, and would receive me as kindly as ever, despite the loss of his wig, and the general flurry into which he had been put by the whole proceeding.

The court at Bow-street was crowded. The night charges had been disposed of, and some case of bigamy was going on, which was very quickly got rid of by the person charged with marrying two ladies being sent to Sheffield, where he committed the offence. Reed then left the court for a moment, and returned with Mrs. Cholmondeley Morgan, alias Mrs. Major Chaplin, whom he placed in the prisoner's dock with professional alacrity.

She looked firebrands at everybody, and particularly at me. Her face was inflamed with anger, and excited general curiosity, for she was in an in-door dress, as the reader may well suppose, since I had not thought it necessary, before making so sudden a capture of her, to request she would attire herself in a habit fit for the streets, or for an appearance in any public place.

The officer handed the warrant to the magistrate, who read it, and, then turning to Reed, he said,—

"Oh, this is the woman?"—"Yes, your worship. She was taken by Dr. ———, and delivered into my hands only a few minutes since."

"Are the parties prepared with evidence?"—"I think not at this moment," said Reed, "and, therefore, respectfully request your worship will remand the prisoner until to-morrow morning?"

"Very well. Have you anything to say to this, prisoner?"—"And, pray, who are you talking to?"

"To you, madam."—"Do you know who I am?"

"The warrant states two names. Perhaps you can give us your version of the matter?"—"My name is Corberry. I am housekeeper to a nobleman."

"You are charged before me as Mrs. Cholmondeley Morgan, alias Mrs. Major Chaplin, for the abduction by fraud and violence, and the unlawful detention, of Felice Barronelli."—"Greek, Greek," she said.

"Who?"—"It's all Greek to me. I never heard of such people in my life."

"Is there any one here, Reed, who can identify the prisoner?"—"Yes, your worship, there is Dr. ———."

I stepped forward, and was sworn.

"Do you know the prisoner?"—"I do."

"What is her name?"—"I have seen her now three times. Twice she named herself Mrs. Cholmondeley Morgan, which I have ascertained is an assumed name. To-day she names herself Corberry."

"You swear to her identity as the person naming herself Cholmondeley Morgan, for whom this warrant has been granted?"—"I do."

"You have no doubt?"—"None whatever; I took her into custody myself. She is the party."

"Then that will do. Mrs. Corberry, as you name yourself this morning, I have quite sufficient grounds for your detention."

"What amount of bail is required?" said a voice, rising suddenly from a side seat and addressing the magistrate.

"Do you appear for the prisoner?"—"I do."

"Very well, Mr. Hammerton."

I knew the name at once as that of an attorney in large practice, as a pleader at police-courts for prisoners, and had no doubt he had been sent by the Earl of Bradstock.

"I scarcely think," said the magistrate, "I ought to take bail."—"I submit, your worship, that the case, at the utmost, amounts but to a misdemeanour; moreover, my client is innocent of the charge, and is a most sadly ill-used woman."

"If I take bail, it will be her own recognizance in five hundred pounds, and two sureties in two hundred and fifty each."—"Very good, your worship."

"And I shall require forty-eight hours' notice of the sufficiency of the bail."—"Forty-eight hours! Why, your worship must see, that by the end of that time, precisely, the prisoner has again to appear before you."

"Very true."—"Then the bail is a mockery."

"You need not avail yourself of it unless you like. The case is a very serious one, and I cannot, consistently with my duty to the public, act otherwise as regards it than I have stated."

The solicitor looked chagrined, as he said—

"Really this looks like persecution—will your worship remand the prisoner for a week?"—"Certainly not. Here a respectable family has been for a period of time, getting on for a fortnight, in a state of agony and alarm, in consequence of this woman's conduct, and you now ask me to protract that misery for a week longer."

"But, your worship ———"—"I will not do it, sir. Let your client, if she wishes any mercy to be shown her, show contrition for what she has done by now declaring where Felice Barronelli is to be found. Then, to-morrow morning, the case might come differently before me. As it is, I shall proceed with vigour, and the full rigour that the law places in my hands."

"Will you permit me to speak to the prisoner?"—"Of course."

"You may spare yourself the trouble," said Mrs. Corberry, "I know nothing about the hussey."—"Remove the prisoner," said the magistrate, "and call the next case."

Mrs. Corberry was conducted from the court, and I saw Hammerton, the solicitor, follow her into one of the cells appropriated for the temporary accommodation of prisoners under remand, before they are removed to some one or other of the metropolitan prisons.

Affairs seemed now in tolerable train for a denouement of interest and expectation. I considered the morning's work as the most important as regarded the interests of the Barronellis, connected with the recovery of Felice, that could possibly have been achieved.

"The young girl will now be recovered," I thought, "for surely this woman, Chaplin, or Corberry, or whatever her name may be, will never sacrifice herself completely to the fancied interests of her scoundrel of an employer."

It was not likely that so much heroism was to be found in such a sphere of life, and I confidently anticipated that she would, not fancying imprisonment or its consequent entailments and disagreeables, be glad in a short time to save herself by implicating any one else.

I said so much to Reed, the officer, who replied,—

"That is precisely my view of the case, sir; I have no doubt in the world but that by to-morrow morning she will have sufficiently cooled down to see the propriety of saving herself."

"By to-morrow, you think?"

"Yes, sir. You must bear in mind that she requires some time to get over the passion she has been put in by the mode of her arrest."

"True—true."

"When she has got over that she will take a calmer view of her position, especially if anything in the shape of an overture is made to her upon the subject."

"Would you promise her a personal immunity from the consequences of her own share in the transaction?"

"That cannot be done now with any effect, because, you see, the matter is already in the hands of the magistrate, who would not and could not make himself a party to any compromise of the matter; but still every prisoner must be well aware that his or her position is bettered by conciliating the prosecutors, and by its becoming known to the judicial authorities that anything has been done to render the criminality of the proceedings of less amount."

"Exactly. Then so far, of course, I am willing, in the name of Mr. Barronelli, who will be the real prosecutor to-morrow morning, but who, I am quite sure, will sanction whatever I choose to do; I beg that Mrs. Corberry may be indulged."

"I will take care, sir, that she understands all that, and without compromising anybody. She is a desperate woman, and deserves punishment; but if she does not tell us where

Felice Barronelli is, I know not from whom we are to get the information."

"True; and time is the greatest object of all, for the sufferings of the bereaved parents are most acute, and give us a fair sample of what deep affliction must be at this very time overwhelming the poor girl herself, wherever she may be."

"Then, sir, I am glad to say, we agree entirely upon the subject. Make yourself easy, sir, and should you see the Barronellis, pray desire them to make themselves easy, for I repeat my former strong belief, that they will get their daughter back uninjured."

"Your assurance on that head, Reed, gives me faith in it, for you must be better able to come to an accurate judgment on such matters than any of us."

After this brief confabulation with the officer, I left the police-court and made the best of my way towards the Barronellis, where I hoped to bring some comfort by the news of which I was the bearer, and to prove to those afflicted people that there was an almost immediate chance of their dearly loved child being restored to them.

They were both at home, and, although I had seen them so lately, even I could not fail to be much struck with the remarkable change which incessant grief was making upon them.

I hastened to give them what relief I could.

"Cheer up," I cried. "All is not lost that is in danger. Cheer up; I do not bring you back your daughter, but I do bring you a reasonable hope that you will soon see her."

Barronelli sprang towards me, and grasped my hand.

"You have found her!" he cried, "you have found her! You know now where they have hidden my beautiful child! Oh, tell me where it is, and if she be surrounded by unheard-of obstacles to liberty, I will bear her from them all. Tell me where she is."

"Be calm, Mr. Barronelli, be calm. Exert your reason, and while you grieve for the loss of your child as becomes a father, do not forget that you are a man, and should have some moral courage."

"Alas! I have tried until my heart has nearly broken in the struggle."

"Hear me out, and I will furnish you with better materials for hope than you have yet had."

The mother wept, and the father, with a look of stern despair, listened to me; but when I came to the part of my narrative which detailed the apprehension of Mrs. Cholmondeley Morgan, his interest visibly deepened, and when I detailed to him the opinion which Reed, the officer, had expressed, that she would, before being brought before the magistrate on the following morning, endeavour to screen herself from some of the consequences of her diabolical wickedness, by telling where Felice was concealed, his feelings overcame him, and sinking into a seat he burst into tears, as in broken accents he exclaimed,—

"Thank God—thank God."

"Then there is a hope!" cried Mrs. Barronelli.—"There is, indeed," said I.

She threw herself upon her husband's neck, and wept aloud.

I could not but be sensibly affected at the scene before me, and I am not ashamed to own that a tear found its way to my own eyes as I heard the muttered words of consolation which this kindly couple spoke to each other, and saw what a great effect a hope of the early restoration of their child to their arms had upon them.

I was silent, for it was not a scene for any one to interrupt; and when they had, in some measure, got over their first gush of painful feeling, they overwhelmed me with thanks. Indeed, so profuse were they in their acknowledgments, that I was quite, in a manner of speaking, compelled to say,—

"I really must leave you if you say anything more to me in that strain. What I have done has been very little, and no more, I flatter myself, than what hundreds of my countrymen would have done under similar circumstances; for whatever may be the faults and the failings of the English as a nation, no one can attribute to them a want of feeling, or a want of that chivalric feeling which prompts them to succour distress."

"I have found more kindness here in England," said Barronelli, "than ever my own country bestowed upon me."

"May you find more still," said I. "There are bad disposed persons, of course, in all sorts of communities. But now, let me advise you to wait until to-morrow, with a patient hope that you will be gratified with still better news than that which I have been able to-day to bring you."

"We will—we will."

"That is right. I expected, by-the-bye, to find my young friend, Graham, here with you."—"He was here."

"And left?"—"Why, some one called here for him, and he went down stairs to ask who it was, and then he came up again in a moment like a madman, crying. out furiously, 'My hat! my hat! Where's my hat?' and seizing hold of it, he clapped it on his head, and was off again before we could sufficiently recover from our surprise to ask him what was the matter."

"How long ago was that?"—"Some hours now."

"And you have not seen him since?"—"We have not," was the reply.

"It's very odd. His enthusiastic temper is always getting him into some sort of adventure."—"It is; but never before did we see him in such a state of agitation."

"And yet," said Mrs. Barronelli, "there seemed to me to be something pleasurable about his excitement."—"True," said the husband; "I remarked that. It looked like the wild delirium of one who had suddenly heard some piece of news which almost took his breath away with joy."

"Indeed."—"Yes; that was the kind of feeling; and most sincerely do I hope, for his sake, that we have not mistranslated his looks and manner."—" I hope so too."

Such a ring now came at Barronelli's bell, that it said wonders for the strength of the wire which withstood the tug.

"Who can that be?" cried Barronelli.

"Let me go," said I.

"No—no; there is no occasion," said the wife. "Hark! I hear that some one has opened the street-door."

It was so. I distinctly heard the door closed, and then there was a silence of a few moments' duration; after which we heard footsteps coming up the stairs towards the apartment we were in.

Barronelli was much agitated as he said,—

"Who can that be?—who can that be?"—"Never mind," said I; "be calm."

I opened the room door, and, to my intense astonishment, for such a circumstance was the very furthest from my thoughts, there came in Graham, leading by the hand no less a personage than the young lady to whom I had read such a lecture at the earl's house, and who was, as the reader is aware, Graham's park incognita.

"My dear friends," said Graham, with much emotion,— "indeed, I may say my only friends—will you allow me to hope that until to-morrow you will permit this lady to have an asylum here?" The Barronellis stared—and well they might. "She has now no home she chooses to go to," added Graham, "and I am deeply interested in procuring one for her."

"Who—who is the lady?" gasped Mrs. Barronelli.—"My fair unknown of the park," said Graham.

"And," added I, "the young girl who, I hope, by the words I have uttered to her, I have induced to consider that recital brought with it the truest happiness."

"I always thought so, sir," she said, turning to me with so composed a countenance, that at the moment I gave her credit for a very tolerable, in one sense, and a very intolerable in another, amount of impudence.—" Indeed," I said.

"Most certainly, sir. You seem to be under an impression that my moral education must have been dreadfully neglected."

"Why," I fairly gasped, "I saw you at the earl's house only this morning, you know."—"Well, sir, I am not aware that it is any crime to have been seen by you at the Earl of Bradstock's."

I was too much astonished at this specimen of cool assurance to reply for some moments. When I did, I said,—

"Madam, allow me to congratulate you upon the possession of a degree of confidence which, under better circumstances, would have done you infinite honour, and which——"

—"Oh, pho! pho!" interrupted Graham; "if you want to congratulate anybody, congratulate me."

"Congratulate you?"—"Yes, to be sure."

"You?"—"And why not?"

"I wish to know why."—"Why, on having found my fair unknown."

"You—you have found her?"—"Exactly; and I am the happiest of men. I owe her a debt of gratitude which the duration of a life cannot repay. She has promised to become my wife, and I am nearly mad with joy."

"The deuce you are!"—"I am, indeed. The condescension, the noble-minded devotion, the more than mortal generosity, which has overlooked in me a thousand faults, fills me with grateful feelings beyond all expression."

"Very good. Then you mean to overlook, I suppose, entirely the early history of this young lady?"—"It is she who is so kind."

"Are you mad, Graham?"—"Pray, sir," said the lady, "what objection have you to urge against my marriage with Mr. Graham? You seem very much averse to it."

"Objection? Humph!"—"Yes, doctor; what objection?" cried Graham.—"I wash my hands of the whole affair," said I, for I was really provoked. "Marry whom you like, for all I care."

"Yes; but you seem as if you knew or suspected something to my prejudice, sir," said the lady, looking me in the face as coolly as possible.

"Good God! did I not see you and speak to you at the Earl of Bradstock's?"—"Well?"

"Did I not implore you to leave him?"—"Well?"

"I say well?"—"I have left him. With great grief I have felt the necessity of leaving him, and placing myself under the protection of a husband?"

"Oh, indeed."—"I tell you what it is, doctor," said Graham,—"it strikes me you are jealous."

"I jealous!"—"Yes. You evidently don't want me to marry this young lady, for some reason."

"Some reason?"—"Yes. She has certainly lived with the Earl of Bradstock."

I doubted almost the evidence of my own senses.

"Yes," said the lady.

"But what then?" added Graham; "what of that?"—"Ah, what of that?" said she.

I took up my hat and made for the door.

"It was natural," added Graham.—"I hope so," said the lady.

"D——d natural!" cried I; "and you are a confounded natural, too, Graham; so, good-bye for once and for all. We are strangers, sir."

"Why, what on earth is the matter with you?"—"Young man—young man; can you so far stultify your intellect—of what at one time I thought you had a fair share—as to fancy for one moment you can ever be happy with that young female?"—"Young female, sir! You address an earl's daughter in a strange style."

"A what?" shouted I.—"An earl's daughter, doctor. This young lady is the only child of the Earl of Bradstock. Long an alien from her father's house, in consequence of the kind of company he kept in it, she seldom saw him but by chance. One of these chances was when we saw her with him in a barouche; but hearing that he was ill, filial affection banished all scruples, and she hastened to attend upon him. You then saw her at his house."

I gasped again.

"Allow me, doctor, then," continued Graham, "before we part, as you say, to be strangers for the future, to introduce to you the Lady Emily Stuart Basingburn, the only daughter of the Earl of Bradstock."

I was bewildered, and dropped my hat from my relaxed grasp. I looked first at Graham and then at the young lady, like a man in a dream. Then she advanced towards me, and held out her hand, saying,—

"Forgive me, sir, for playing with your feelings for a time. I saw when I met you at my father's house the mistake you had fallen into, and I would not correct you. You then mentioned where Mr. Graham was to be found. I sought him here."

"And I have made so horrible a mistake?"—"You name it rightly as a mistake. Appearances were, I own, all in favour of your supposition."

"Can you ever forgive me?"—"There is nothing to forgive, sir. Mr. Graham has told me how much he values your friendship. Permit me to hope that I may be a sharer of it."

I felt the perspiration standing on my face; and Graham, seeing how much I was amazed at the unwitting mistake I had made, shook me heartily by the hand, saying,—

"Come, come, doctor, think no more of it."—"I will endeavour," said I; "but really——"—"Enough, enough."

"But what made the Lady Emily keep so strict an incognito?"—"For several reasons," she said. "In the first place, I wished to be loved for myself, and not for my rank; in the second, I could not marry without the earl's consent until I was of age, which I shall be to-morrow; and hence I always put off telling Graham who I was to some date in May."

"It's all clear enough now," said I; "and very careful indeed shall I be again before I ever trust to appearances."

"They are the most deceitful things going," said Graham.

* * * * *

My readers can easily imagine how welcome the earl's daughter was made by the Barronellis, and how happy Graham was at so delightful a termination to his many anxieties on account of his fair incognita of Hyde-park. I alone felt a degree of uneasiness in the company of the lady, on account of the injurious suspicions I had formed of her, which I was a long time shaking off.

This portion of the affair being satisfactorily settled, Graham and I were able to turn our whole attention to the affair of the Barronellis, and having invited Graham to come out with me, I said,—

"A scheme has struck me which I am inclined to think will bring this proud bad earl down a little."

"What is it?"—"I propose to go to him, and tell him that his daughter has been taken away in the same way that Felice Barronelli was, by a promiscuous acquaintance she made in Hyde-park. If he has any feeling at all, such will surely rouse it."

"Do it, doctor—do it; and I tell you what you shall do. Wait till to-morrow morning, when Lady Emily and I will be married by special licence, and then make a bargain with him that you can bring him his daughter, if he will restore Felice Barronelli."

"Good. It shall be done."

* * * * *

Graham and I managed all the proceedings very minutely. He was to be married by special licence, and quite privately, to the earl's daughter, at eleven o'clock, and at half-past eleven he was to bring her to the earl's house, and inquire for me. If then I had succeeded in making the earl give up where Felice was to be found, I was to introduce his own daughter to him as the wife of Graham; if not, I was to come down stairs, and we were all then to leave the house again at once.

By this plan I hoped to avoid the necessity of making any concession to the mock Mrs. Cholmondeley Morgan; and I dropped a note to Reed, the officer, requesting that, until he saw me, he would say nothing to her on the subject.

Everything being, then, thus duly arranged, on the following morning I left the Barronellis to go to the police-office, and make their charge against the woman Corberry, which eventually turned out to be her real name, while I went to the earl's, and Graham went to be married.

* * * * *

When I reached the door of the Earl of Bradstock's magnificent mansion, I was surprised, although it was early, to see several carriages at the door. I knocked, and when the hall-porter opened the door, I said,—

"I wish to see the earl."—"You cannot, sir. He is very ill, indeed. Nobody but a doctor can see him now, sir."

"Well, that will do. I am a doctor. Here's my card."—"Oh, then, you have come on purpose?"

"Of course I have."—"That's all right. John, show the doctor up stairs."

"Are there any other medical men with the earl?"—"Yes, sir. They are holding a consultation in the drawing-room. Shall I show you to them or to the earl?"—"To the earl, by all means."

In a few moments I was in the chamber of the vicious nobleman. It was darkened, and he was in bed. I advanced softly, and looked at him as he lay. I saw that a remarkable change had taken place in his looks. He was dying. He turned his languid eyes upon me, and said faintly,—

"Hell! hell!"

"Do you know me?" said I. He looked hard at me, and then he said,—

"Scarcely; and yet I think I have seen you somewhere. I begin to think now that I am in danger."

"I think so, too."

"Are you one of the physicians?"—"I am, my lord; and I hope a friend as well as a physician. A true friend, my lord, will tell you your true state."

He looked terrified and anxious, as he said, in a hoarse, husky voice,—

"Do—do you think there is great danger?"—"I do."

He gave a hideous groan, and tossed his arms about as if he would wrestle with the death that was coming.

"Have you settled your worldly affairs?" said I.—"What's that to you?" was the reply. "What's my worldly affairs to you, I should like to know? D—n you, I know you now."

"Do you?"—"Yes; you are the fellow who came preaching to me yesterday. Get out of my house—get out of my house!"

"When I have performed the errand which brought me here," said I, "I will, with great pleasure, get out of your house."

"Be off with you. Jackson—Jackson! D—n that valet! where is he? I want my daughter sought for."—"It is of your daughter I come to speak."

"What do you know of my daughter?"—"I almost, considering your present position, dread to afflict you with the news I bring. Your daughter, abandoned by you, who should have been her natural as well as her best protector, was compelled, it appears, to leave your house, and find an asylum where she could. Occasionally, for some time, she resided at Bute Cottage, which, I understand, belongs to you; but then you gave it into the possession of the woman who now occupies it, and your only child, because she could not sleep under the same roof with your kept mistress, was compelled to take refuge with a friend."

He was silent, but his eyes seemed to grow particularly large, and gladden as I spoke.

"During her residence about the neighbourhood of Hyde Park, she formed an acquaintance."

"Who?"—"A mere chance acquaintance. A young man who took a fancy to her. How could he know she was the daughter of an earl?"

"Go on."—"The acquaintance increased. The young man was, like some of his betters, dissolute and abandoned. He cared not what misery he brought into any family, so long as he gratified his own depraved passions. He looked to no consequences; he heeded nothing. No laws of morality restrained him—no soft emotions of humanity filled his breast. Heartless he was as a very fiend. He cared not if gloom and despair found its way to the happiest hearts in the world, so that he was successful, by fraud or force, he cared not which, in carrying out an intrigue."

"Curses!" muttered the earl.—"Ay, curses," continued I, "followed him from many an afflicted heart. Well, my lord, he cast upon your daughter the unholy eyes of passion."

"He dared not."—"But he did. This plebeian—this man sprung from the lowest dregs of society—of no rank, no honour, no conscience—but he had one quality."

"One?"—"Yes, he had money; and with that all-powerful agent he worked his way. I say he looked upon your daughter, because she was handsome, with the traitorous eyes of a deceiver."

"The villain!"—"Ay, the villain. He tried to seduce her."

"And failed. D———n! tell me he failed."—"He did."

"I knew it."—"Hold, my lord! he tried force and fraud, both. When he found persuasion of no use, he carried her off."

"My daughter! my child!"—"Yes, my lord; and no one knows where she is. He shut her up somewhere—perhaps treated her with a brutal violence, at which humanity stands aghast, and which no language can pourtray. Perhaps killed her, when he had satiated his hellish passion. Perhaps ——"

"D———n! Death! Curses!" shouted the earl, as he sprang from his bed; but I laid hands upon him, and said,— "Be calm, my lord—be calm!"

"Calm! Calm! when my child is sacrificed by a villain? Calm, when you tell me she has fallen a victim—an innocent victim to—Oh, God! this faintness."

He fell back upon the bed, and I added,—

"Yes, my lord. You ought to receive these matters calmly enough. They have happened before. Other people besides yourself, have felt the same pangs that now gnaw at your heart."

He gave a deep groan. I approached my mouth close to his ears, as I said,—

"Remember Felice Barronelli."

A shudder ran through his frame, and he said in a low voice,—

"She—she is safe!"

"Where? where?"—"I—I have never seen her since the woman Corberry got her away from her home. Never!— never!"

"And where is she?"—"At the supposed empty house at the back of Bute Cottage. I am a dying man, and my own sins are visited on my own head. Oh, my child! my Emily! Despair! despair! Oh, God! despair! Had I but one year to live again—the last year of misery and wickedness, I—I might ——"

Convulsive sobs choked his utterance, and I now heard footsteps ascending the staircase. The door was opened, and three gentlemen entered the room. I recognised them as fashionable physicians, and announced myself to them, which made them look at me with no small surprise, for they had not, of course, the least idea that I was in the house.

"You have been consulting on the earl's case, gentlemen?" said I.—"We have," said one; "and we feel it our melancholy duty to apprise his lordship, as he requested we would, should we come to such a conclusion, that his earthly career is near its termination."

The only notice the earl took of this communication was to move his hands convulsively, and mutter the words,—

"And I am childless—and I am childless!"—"My lord," I said, "listen to me."

At the moment I spoke, a servant glided into the room, and said,—

"A lady and gentleman are below, inquiring for Dr. ——. The lady is veiled, but I think she is ——"—"Hush!" said I. "Show them up at once."

The man went on his errand, and I turned to his lordship, saying,—

"At such a moment as this, I will not add one pang to those you must naturally suffer. Your daughter is safe, and the wife of an honourable man—a man of probity and intellect—a man who will make her a good husband, and ensure her happiness."

"Oh, could I see her only but for one moment."—"She is here."

"Raise me! raise me!"

We lifted him up, and he clasped his daughter to his heart. He uttered the one word, "Forgive!" and then fell back dead.

* * * * *

Mrs. Corberry, *alias* Mrs. Major Chaplin, *alias* Mrs. Cholmondeley Morgan, poor soul, declared she was ill-used; but in that opinion she was in a minority of one—she got two years' imprisonment and hard labour. What a fate for so elegant a female.

THE HOSPITAL NURSE;

OR, THE MIRACULOUS CURE.

The passage from my diary which I purpose laying before my readers under the above title, is one which I hope—but it only amounts to a hope—records events and circumstances which have now either no existence at all, or, at all events, not so prominent a one as they had at the period when the affair occurred.

If, however, in any of our metropolitan hospitals there be still abuses of the character which my reader will find in this passage from my diary recorded, I trust that so public an exposition of them will lead to some attention being paid to the subject, in a quarter or two where attention must only, by a very short space of time, precede some active interference on behalf of as helpless a class of persons in all respects, as it is possible to conceive the existence of. I mean the patients in public hospitals. Helpless in that nearly worst of all helplessness—poverty, in the first place; and, secondly, helpless on account of the circumstances which compel them to find a temporary home and medical assistance in those institutions.

Of course anything, however admirable, will have its abuses, and as there is no country on the face of the earth where so much is done in the way of public charity as in our own, of course there may be fairly expected to be a commensurate amount of abuses connected with so extended a system of active benevolence as is always at work among the rich and influential classes of England.

The poor have been taught, by selfish and interested demagogues, to believe that they are much neglected by the rich, and that little or nothing is done for them; but such is not the case. An enormous amount of good is done for them, and we are glad to be compelled to add, that a much greater amount of good is attempted to be done.

It would appear, at the first glance of such a subject, that an attempt must, in the natural order of things, be a success, except in cases were benevolence is imposed upon by impostors.

Such, however, is not the case. It must be borne in mind that the rich cannot be expected to pay for the subsistence of the poor, and hand to them as well the produce of such benevolence. No; such a state of things would be manifestly absurd. A benevolent, kind-hearted man may contribute to the funds of a hospital, but he cannot be expected to wait upon the patients.

And thus it is that so many abuses naturally and unavoidably creep into the administration of charities in England. Some persons are forced to be employed as the go-between—the medium of connexion between the alms giver and the alms receiver, and we grieve to be compelled to confess that these persons are, take them altogether as a mass, as vile, contemptible, despicable, and hypocritical scoundrels and thieves as ever stepped.

Of course there are brilliant examples to the contrary, as there always will be in all classes. When we condemn a body of people, we yet do not condemn all. There are many golden exceptions; but their virtue and disinterestedness will shine forth the brighter for any philippics cast upon their more unscrupulous brethren.

For instance, an honest lawyer is as much prized, and made as great a curiosity of, as a singing mouse, and only because lawyers, we very much fear, are not honest as a mass; and we are perfectly aware that mice, in the aggregate, do not sing like canaries. Therefore, we do not conclude we are doing harm to the really kindly-disposed and honest administrators of public bounty, by denouncing those who are not at all so disposed.

Then, again, particularly as regards hospitals for the sick, which, of course, come more under the sphere of my observations than any other class of charities, it must be borne in mind that the persons employed in them are always of necessity compelled to be taken from a low class of society.

Education and refinement make people, and especially females, revolt from the sort of employment which is entailed upon those who wait upon the sick. Affection will enable a person to go through an amazing lot of disagreeables. There are strong feelings of duty and of love, which will be fully sufficient to induce the most shrinking and timid to become courageous, and we shall find the young, the educated, and the beautiful, tending the sick chamber of a loved object fearlessly and without shrinking.

In a public establishment, however, the case is widely different. There no feelings of affection find a home. Hired service is the only service that can be there at all procured, and it is not probable that any person who could possibly avoid such a situation, would take one as nurse to persons concerning whose fate there could be no concern whatever. In one word, the nurses at the public hospitals are ignorant and low, but they still need not be brutal.

And here, before proceeding in my narrative, I must pause one moment to say a word to some of my professional brethren, and to record it as my firm conviction, that the nurses at the hospitals would not dare to treat the poor unhappy patients, as they frequently do, with brutality or neglect, were it not that the surgeons and the students treat them with the bitterest and most unfeeling contempt.

The nurses see that the daily round of the visiting-surgeon is as nearly as possible a daily farce, for, unless a case present any peculiar features, so as to make it interesting in a surgical or medical point of view, it is never looked to at all by the visiting physicians and surgeons. All is left to the house-surgeon, who, in many cases, is little better than a mere boy —at least, it was so, and we are not disposed to hazard assertions in the pages of our diary, which we are not prepared to prove. We are too old a bird to be so caught.

All is left, then, to the house-surgeon, who goes through a session of hospital practice in that capacity, and he is considered responsible for the medical treatment, if in that department, or the surgical, if attached to the accident or surgical wards.

This house-surgeon (we will speak of the accident ward of a metropolitan hospital, because there the patients are much more dependent upon their attendants than in the ordinary sick wards),—the house-surgeon, then, is assisted by one or two students, who sit up by turns, and will be house-surgeons in due time, so that, when a case comes in, they all have an opportunity of seeing it at once, although the verdict of the house-surgeon as to the nature of the injury is decisive.

And here we may remark, that it is very seldom a mistake is made at an hospital with regard to the nature of a surgical injury. There is no tenderness towards the patient to interfere with the most accurate examination. The unfortunate object of manipulation may howl, or swear, or scream, it makes no manner of difference. He is looked upon just as a machine, and nothing more.

If there be two or three present in the surgery who have a fancy to feel the *crepetus* of a broken bone, why, they indulge themselves, &c. And the nurses, finding that the medical men look upon the unhappy patients as beings destitute of all feeling, treat them accordingly.

* * * * *

And now to our tale.

I was well acquainted with a physician of the name of Plumb. He was a remarkably clever man, but very eccentric; in fact, he was quite an oddity, but, from his undoubted talent, he got into excellent practice. His temper, too, was of the fiery order, and he was apt, to use a common expression, to "flare up" upon every little provocation.

And yet I have seen him at times exercise the most wonderful control over his passions; but that was only when he saw his way clearly to some good end, for he was as truly benevolent and kindly-hearted a little man as ever drew the breath of life.

He and I became very intimate, and we used to visit each other frequently. Sometimes I called upon him of a morning, when he was seeing his poor patients, and took part with him in prescribing for them, and it was in consequence of one of these visits that the following train of circumstances occurred.

One evening I was in the reception-room, and we had already seen a number of patients, when one came in who at once interested us very much in his favour. It was a poor lad of about thirteen. He was upon crutches, which bore the stamp of what we will, for the sake of a name, call the County Hospital. With him was a respectable-looking, scrupulously clean widow-woman, in whose countenance were indelible marks of much mental suffering.

There was none of the affectation of neatness about her humble mourning. It was all evidently genuine. Her sorrow-stricken countenance showed that the blow of fate which had left her desolate had indeed fallen heavily upon her. The moment she came into the room, I could see that she was ready to drop; but as she held her pale-faced son by the hand, she made a great effort to speak, and said,—

"I—have ventured to—to hope, sir, that you will do something, sir, for my poor boy."

"Ventured to hope, have you?" cried Dr. Plumb.

She seemed terrified at his roughness of manner, which she thought was unkindness, and made a step back again, as she replied, timidly—

"If—if you are busy, sir, I will come again. I don't wish to intrude upon you, sir."

"Who the devil said you did? Ventured to hope, indeed! Do you think I'm an ogre, eh?—or a brute? Sit down and rest yourself. Intrude upon me, indeed!—venture to hope! What do you say such things here for, eh? How dare you! Of course I'll do what I can for your son."

"You are very good, sir.—"No, I ain't."

The woman looked surprised, and sat down.

"Well, ma'am," added Dr. Plumb, "what's the matter? Who's cat has kittened now, eh, ma'am?"

I said Dr. Plumb was an oddity, and he had a habit, when he asked about a case, to say "Who's cat has kittened?" but this the widow woman knew nothing of, and she looked astonished as she replied,—

"Cat kittened, sir?"—"Dr. Plumb wishes to know for what you require his professional assistance," said I. "Is it for yourself or the boy?"—"Oh, for Harry, sir, poor fellow! You wouldn't have known him again, gentlemen, had you seen him six months ago."

"And where the deuce has he been for six months?"

cried Dr. Plumb.—"For five of them, sir, in the County Hospital."

"Oh! and one with you?"—"Yes, sir."

"Well, what do you bring him here for?"—"Why, sir, he had a fall, and broke his leg, besides some of his ribs, and they said they had cured him."

"Very likely they did cure him."—"They gave him a pair of crutches, sir, and I took him home."

"Well—well?"—"Since that time, sir, he has had a pain across his loins and his back, too—a pain so very bad, that he cannot sometimes sleep at night, and it makes him very, very ill."

"Indeed! and what do they say to it at the County Hospital, eh?"—"He has not been there."

"No, no, mother!" cried the boy, with anguish on his countenance. "No, no; I dread to go there; I will never go there again, mother. Oh, do not take me there. I shudder, mother, to think of it. Never again there—never again there. I cannot, dare not go. Let me die in peace at home."

There was so much frantic eagerness about the boy, that I was astonished, and said to him, before Dr. Plumb could speak,—

"You seem, lad, to have a great dread of the hospital?"—"He has, indeed," said the mother. "He was not kindly treated. You see, sir, we are, truth to say, very poor."

"Poor!" shouted Dr. Plumb. "Why, what the devil is the hospital for but the very poor, I should like to know?"—"But, sir, we could not fee the nurses."

"Fee the nurses! Oh, nonsense! The nurses dare not take fees."—"They neglect any poor patient who cannot pay them."

"Yes, mother; and they rob one, and they get drunk at night. Oh, it is horrible to lie there, unable to move; in such a state, too, that a feather thrown upon the bed would produce a pang, and, perhaps, be tumbled down upon by a drunken woman, or wantonly hurt for mere amusement, and neglected so terribly, and sneered at—I could not have lived another week in that place, mother."

"What!" said Dr. Plumb. "Do you mean to say they do all act in that way at the County Hospital?"—"They do, sir, and then I complained."

"Ah, and quite right too."—"I complained to the house-surgeon, as he was walking along the ward."

"Ah! and what did he say?"—"He told me to be d—d, sir."

"He did? Ha! He did, did he? Ha! Very good. Let me see. The nurses neglected you, got drunk, and when you complained, you were told to be d—d."—"I was, sir."

"Very proper, indeed. What sort of food did you get?"—"Dreadful, sir. The meat, when I was put upon full diet, was like cat's meat exactly, and the stagnant beer that was brought in in a tin pail was dreadfully nauseous."

"All right. Why, doctor, the County Hospital is very well off; and, besides, if it is not, of course the number of beds ought to be reduced."—"But," said I, "there should be no excuse for unkindness on the part of the nurses."

"Certainly not. Now, my lad, what's your name?"—"Markham Russell, sir."

"Well, now, detail to me at length the conduct of the nurses in the County Hospital with you."—"Yes, sir."

The boy then gave us an account of so much roughness, so much heartlessness and brutality on the part of the nurses, that we were quite astonished. There was, certainly, no one overt act committed which could be seized hold of as a special crime, except the taking money of the patients, and that was expressly forbidden by the constitution of the hospital; but the details showed a frightful state of things for the poor patients. It showed that the nurses were in the habit of picking out favourites among the unfortunate inmates of the ward, and to them they attended almost solely, leaving the others to shift for themselves in a great measure, answering them with abuse. That drunkenness was a common vice among them. That they were continually quarrelling among themselves, heedless of the state of the patients; and that no authority could be got at to make a complaint to but the house-surgeon, and he considered it altogether beneath his notice.

"Very good—very good," said Dr. Plumb. "Now, Mrs. Russell, I consider that the symptoms of disease under which your son suffers are clearly to be attributed to causes arising from his long confinement. Here is a prescription, and here are five shillings, with which to have it made up. Come to me again this day week."

Tears started to the widow's eyes, as she said,—

"God bless you, sir—God bless you!"—"Bother!" said Dr. Plumb. "Be off with you."

He turned to me, when she had left, and said,—

"The boy is only suffering from a torpid liver. He will soon be all right again, as he can take better exercise; but what do you think of his account of how affairs are managed in the County Hospital?"—"There wants a reform there."

"There does indeed."—"But how can it be done? I dare say this boy's evidence would be disputed *in toto* if offered."—"Of course it would,"

"Then there, you see, is the great difficulty in all these cases. No one of sufficient importance to make his statement at once believed is ever likely to be in circumstances to have it to offer."

"I tell you what it is, Dr. ——. This seems very little to speak of; but only just suppose yourself at the mercy of a drunken nurse, with your leg broken, and in such a condition that a kick against your bedstead will, perhaps, produce you hours of agony."—"I can easily imagine it."

"Now, I tell you what I'll do. To-morrow, if you can spare an hour with me, I will, as a mere stranger, for I was never in the County Hospital in all my life, take the round of the medical ward. We can inquire of the patients quietly if all be as this lad has told."—"Very good. I will go with you. It shall be so."

"Meet me, then, at eleven to-morrow here, and we will go. I am certain no one knows me."—"Nor myself; for, like you, I never was within the door of the place."

With this understanding we separated, and I could not help often, in my own mind, reverting to what the boy had said of the conduct of the nurses.

I knew that in all the hospitals prayers were read by a regular chaplain, and could not help contrasting the chaplain praying for a blessing on the poor patients, the house surgeon telling them to be damned, and the nurse robbing them and getting drunk.

* * * * *

At the hour of eleven on the following morning, Dr. Plumb and I met according to the appointment we had made together, and proceeded, arm in arm, towards the County Hospital.

As he had said, it was a visiting day, and a number of people were availing themselves of the opportunity of visiting sick and disabled relatives and friends within the building. We passed in, along with others, unquestioned, and inquiring of a woman which was the way to the accident ward, we soon found ourselves within it.

The beds were all occupied, with the exception of two or three, and by most of the bedsides were sitting the friends of the sufferers, so that we had not much opportunity of speaking to the patients.

"What shall we do?" said I.

The words had hardly escaped my lips, when I heard a woman say,—

"Oh, God bless him, the dear fellow! He is, if ever there was one, an angel out of Heaven—bless him! If he was a child of my own, the dear fellow, I'm sure I could feel for him no more affection. Oh, the patient angel that he is! I call him my chickabiddy."

"Listen," said Plumb; "it's one of the nurses that ——"

I half turned, and saw a woman of that peculiar build which almost all nurses have. How they manage to be such an enormous width behind I leave to other physiologists to determine. Suffice it that I felt certain this woman was a nurse, and I soon saw she was talking to a respectable man and woman, who had come to see a youth who had sustained some accident, and was lying, pale and ghastly-looking, in bed.

I saw tears in the mother's eyes, and I heard a gingling in her pocket. Then I saw half-a-crown produced and slipped into the nurse's hand, who gave a short dry cough, such as ladies give when there is a mysterious rumbling in their insides, to which many people are subject.

"Let him go when he will, old or young," added the nurse with fervour, " he'd go bang to Heaven."

And then she moved off to another bed-side.

"What do you think of that?" said I.—"Well, I don't know what to think—wait a bit. I wonder if these people will go soon?"

We lingered, and heard the old man say,—

"George, my dear, you know we have got to take little Mary to school, so we cannot make you a long visit to-day."—"No—no," gasped the boy.

"God bless you, my dear. You will soon be well."

I could hear painfully the cracked, tremulous voice in which the father spoke. They both tenderly kissed the lad, who followed them with his sunken eye as far as he could see them, and when they were gone, he, with a deep sigh, half closed them, and took no notice of any one.

"Here's an opportunity," said I, "ready made for us. Let us ask this boy how the nurses behave to him."—"Very good. You ask him. I shall swear so infernally."

I could not forbear a smile at the reason why Dr. Plumb wished me to ask the question of the lad, and taking a hasty glance at the ticket at the head of his bed, announcing his accident, which was a fracture of the *femur*, I sat down in the chair that was by his side, and said in a low tone,—

"Are you better?" He opened his eyes, and looked at me with surprise. "I hope you are better," I said again.

He sighed deeply, as he replied,—

"Not much. If you are one of the methodist preachers, I cannot—I have not strength to listen to you."

"Methodist preachers!"—"Oh, yes; they worry me so. And I in such pain too!"

"I am not anything of the sort. I have only come here as a casual visitor, and I want in sincerity to ask you one question."

"What—what is it?"—"Are the nurses kind to you?"

He fixed his eyes upon my face for a moment, and then said,—

"Mother pays them—God knows she can ill afford it. She pays them. If she did not, God help me! God help me!"—"Indeed"

"Hush! hush! Wait—I dare not. When I am safe out, I don't mind speaking, but now look how helpless I am. Oh! don't ask me anything. Hush! hush! hush!"

He was in such great distress of mind, that I at once forbore from pressing the subject further, and, with a nod to each other, Dr. Plumb and I left the ward.

"It's all as the boy said," exclaimed Dr. Plumb. "D—n me if it ain't. And there's a great board, too, stuck over the mantelshelf, which says, 'Any nurse found to have taken any fee or gratuity from a patient, will be instantly discharged.'"—"And yet the common report is that they neglect the patients who don't pay them."—"So it seems, indeed."

"What do you mean to do?"—"I cannot imagine just now, but ——"

"What, Dr. Plumb?" exclaimed a young man, stepping up to the doctor, and holding out his hand at the same moment.

"Ah! to be sure," said Plumb. "How are you, Grey?"— "Very well. What have you been doing here?"

"Nothing particular; what have you?"—"Why, I commence my duties as house-surgeon here shortly. Green has punctured his arm with a scalpel during a dissection, and he is unwell, though he remains in."

"And who is Green?"—"Oh, he was the house-surgeon."

"I'm d—d, then, if he isn't a puppy."

"Oh, you know?"—"I have heard of him, and that's what makes me call him a puppy—a d——d puppy, too, he is, and a vagabond."

"Well, Dr. Plumb, I certainly cannot go so far with you as to call Green a vagabond. A puppy he certainly is, and a great pity is it that he is a puppy, for he has certainly some talent."—"But all submerged in his puppyism, Mr. Grey. But come, now, tell me candidly what you think of the internal regulations of the County Hospital?"

"In what respect do you mean?"—"Oh, of course, as to the treatment of the patients."

"Medical or domestic?"—"Domestic and medical both."

"Why, I believe there is nothing to find fault with in the condition of the place, that I am aware of. The medical officers, of course, do their best, and the nurses are, I know, unexceptionable."—"Indeed!"

"Oh, yes; the greatest care is taken of all that. You know the matron has the power of discharging a nurse; and as she is a most excellent woman, you may depend everything is well conducted. The nurses are most feeling women. I have seen them shed tears frequently."—"On account of gin, I suppose."

"Gin!"—"Yes. I presume they had had so much, that it was running out of their eyes."

"Now, really, Dr. Plumb."—"Now, really, Mr. Grey."

"What were you dreaming of?"—"Just this. You are a good fellow, Grey, though you are not the most artful or observant of God's creatures."

"Thank you."—"You are very welcome. Now, from what I have heard, I am inclined to believe that the nurses in the County Hospital are a gin-drinking, thievish, hypocritical set."

"You surprise me."—"I thought I should. They take money from the friends of the poor patients, and those from whom they cannot get feed are neglected."

"Oh, but that must be seen to."—"Exactly; and when a poor devil of a patient complains to the only authority he has an opportunity of complaining to, he is told to be d—d."

"By the matron?"—"The fiddlestick—the house-surgeon."

"Well, I really have always heard the patients speak in grateful terms of their treatment by the nurses. When a patient is discharged, he is brought before the board, and asked concerning the subject."

"And what does he say?"—"Oh, he says he is perfectly satisfied, and if he be very poor, we give him a few shillings for present exigencies. To be sure there was a fellow who complained of the nurses, I heard, some time ago, but upon inquiry, it was found that he was quite wrong, and an exceedingly ungrateful person, so we dismissed him with a severe reprimand."

"Oh! Upon whose evidence was this ungrateful fellow convicted of being quite wrong?"—"Upon the evidence of the patients. A deputation of the governors went solemnly into the accident ward, and said,—'Has any one here any complaints to make against anybody?' and as nobody said a word, of course they felt convinced that it was all right."

"Dr. Plumb," said I, "you seem to have taken this matter much to heart. It appears to me that there might be hit upon a plan for setting the question completely at rest."

"What plan?"—"Simply this. Here is your friend, Grey, house-surgeon. Now, what I propose is this: that he receive somebody as with a bad accident, who in reality is unhurt, and send him into the accident-ward."

"That would do," said Plumb; "that would do; but who can we get whom we could at all depend upon?"—"It would require," said Mr. Grey, shaking his head, "a person of some surgical knowledge to play the part."

"And of discretion," added I, "and such character and standing, that when he did come to give his evidence, it would be undoubted. Now, Dr. Plumb, if you could spare a little time ——"—"Who—I? I couldn't, although I should glory in it—absolutely glory in it. What a thing it would be to bowl out those nurses. I tell you what. I see my way now clearly in the matter."

"Do you?"—"Yes. You shall be the man, Dr. ——. You know how to manage, and what to say, and how to do, exactly. You shall be the man."

"Really, I ——"—"Come, come, no excuses. Recollect that none but a professional man could play the part; recollect that it requires sound discretion. You are just the fellow, with that serious-looking face of yours. You would take them in nicely. Come, now, it's a bargain."

"I really don't like it at all. It strikes me that it will be very uncomfortable indeed."

"Uncomfortable! Of course it will; it will be d——d uncomfortable, you may depend, Dr. ——; but you are just the man. You have always got your spoon in other people's broth, you know."—"Thank you. I'm really much obliged."

"Well, you'll do it. You know it won't take long. I should say you'll find everything out in about three days and nights."—"But consider the feeding."

"The feeding! Oh, you need not be uneasy on that score. You will be put upon half diet, as they call it, which means little or nothing divided by ten."—"I know it."

"You will have barley-water to drink—rice and water, with just a dash of milk in it, to eat."—"An agreeable prospect, certainly."

"Well, Mr. Grey, we'll consider that as settled. You may expect to see my dear friend, Dr. ——, brought in on a shutter."—"Upon my word, you may expect no such thing," said I. "A shutter, indeed! Do you fancy I'm going to carry the affair so far as that?"

"What do you say to a shell?"—"A shell?"

"Yes. You may be supposed to have tumbled off the parapet of a house, or something of that sort, you know, and popped into a shell, obligingly lent by the nearest undertaker, and then some one may be supposed to have had a crotchet that you are not quite dead, and to have had you brought to the County Hospital. There's a scheme for you."

"A great deal too clever for me, and too circumstantial,"

said I; "but I am not altogether so averse from endeavouring to do some good to those poor patients who come under the hands of these nurses, as absolutely to refuse the job, but you must let me do it in my own way."

"Well," said Mr. Gray, "I think between you, you are managing it very nicely: what's to become of me in the transaction?"—"You—you?"

"Yes. I shall probably be much blamed."—"Not at all

my good sir—not at all. Your motive is a good one, and that will clear you."

"Now listen to me," said I. "If Mr. Gray consents, I will come some evening in a coach with a couple of friends, who will make a show of helping me out. Then, if Mr. Gray will be alone, and have me, after a mock examination, placed in the accident-ward, I can keep the game alive for four-and-twenty hours, I think, at least."

"I don't mind that, then," said Gray. "What surgical injury will you please to have, sir?"—"Well, I am not particular; some simple fracture."

"Say, then, a simple fracture of the femur, and that is sufficiently common for no one to pay any attention to you; besides, you will not be bothered in the short time you stay with any bandages, you know."

"No; I suppose your practice is, never to put on a splint before eight-and-forty hours?"—"Not then, sometimes. We use the inclined plane here for fractures of the thigh, and sometimes we don't put on a splint for a week; of course it all depends upon the subject."

"Exactly—so be it. You may expect me to-morrow night, mind, at about seven."—"Bravo—bravo!" cried Dr. Plumb. "Come and have a bottle of sherry."

"What!" cried I, "sherry to a man who is going to be put upon half diet in the accident-ward of an hospital? Now, really——"

Mr. Gray laughed as he said,—

"I think you had better lay in a stock of all sorts of viands beforehand, doctor, for you will be most certainly starved otherwise."

"Ah, now," said I, "what an unphilosophical idea. You know that eating begets eating. If you want to eat a cow for dinner, you ought to consume a calf for breakfast. If you want to go upon half diet for a few days, begin upon three quarters first."

"You are right enough there," said Dr. Plumb; "and now, then, for the sherry."

We further arranged our scheme over a bottle of sherry, and I must confess that with my liking for adventure, the more I thought over the plan, the better pleased I was with it, and the more I felt determined to make it productive of as much good as I possibly could to the poor unfortunates who really went into the hospital with broken bones.

* * * * *

Before I retired to bed that night, I arranged in my own mind the whole particulars of the plan; and in the first place, I resolved to call very early in the morning upon a friend of mine, who was in the habit of taking a constitutional walk before breakfast, and who had often requested me to join him at sunrise some day, and see, as he expressed it, what a world and a half of good it would do me.

I accordingly ordered that I should be awakened at the first tint of dawn, and determined to walk to Islington, where my friend resided, for I intended that he should be one of the persons who were to assist me out of the coach in the evening, at the door of the hospital.

Upon his discretion in the matter, I knew I could well depend, and as for a face, he had one that was perfectly imperturbable.

Let what would occur, I felt perfectly sure no one would get a smile out of him, therefore he was just the man to assist in carrying out the plan of operations I had proposed to Dr. Plumb, but which I certainly, at the time I did so, had not an idea of being called upon to play so very important a part in.

My landlady was the most wonderful woman for calling anybody up in the world. You had nothing to do but to tell her the hour at which you wished to rise, and she was sure to tap perseveringly at your chamber-door precisely at the time. Thus I was indeed up with the lark. It was really dark, and yet I sallied out into the streets, half asleep as I felt myself.

The grey light of morning began to break through the mass of vapour that had been collecting during the night in the east, and objects became dimly visible to the eye. The street lamps were gradually losing their lustre as the daylight increased, until there was nothing but a small flame, without any apparent object, for they performed no service, and seemed visibly less than they were during the night.

The streets were empty and quiet; no sound reached the ears, save the slow, monotonous tread of the policeman on duty, who rambled onwards, devoutly wishing that his hour of duty had expired. The air was cool and sweet; the inhabitants had not yet risen to vitiate the atmosphere with the thousands upon thousands of fires that are lighted in the metropolis. The sun shone brightly, and the clouds shone in a lustre of glory and magnificence seldom equalled. They were dressed in all the gorgeous splendour of eastern colours and forms. The streets now began to show a little animation. Those who had anything to do with the various markets in the city, were arriving in carts and waggons of different kinds, bearing provisions to the various places chartered to receive them. In the summer time these places possess a very animated appearance; they are crowded, and yet scarce any accident occurs.

The chimes of the different churches were heard much more distinctly, as the streets were comparatively clear, and the atmosphere neither loaded with impurities, and the confused din of city—its never-ending streams of carriages of one kind and another.

The water-carts were at work at this early hour, and the streets are swept clean in crowded thoroughfares before the heat and bustle of the day has begun, thus preventing confusion, as well as the danger that would certainly arise in many places.

The inhabitants soon begin to traverse the streets of the metropolis—men and women, whose occupation takes them from their homes at early hours, and then the streets are scarcely without some living being traversing them, until midnight again comes round.

There are hundreds of persons in London who never saw a daybreak—slaves of luxury, who shrink from the small toil of looking upon one of nature's most beautiful phenomena; for, although the gradual retirement of the sun's light at noontide is marked by a thousand beauties, yet its dawn is a season of many delights, and well worthy the examination of any real lover of the beautiful world we inhabit.

I soon reached the house of my friend, whom I had the good fortune to catch at his door, just as he was emerging. He was quite surprised to see me, and exclaimed,—

"Is it possible! I certainly have often invited you, but I never expected you would come."

"But you see," said I, "I have. I knew that it was a difficult thing to be sure of finding you during the day, as your proceedings are rather erratic, and as I wanted to speak to you particularly, I had myself called up at this most unchristianlike hour, and here I am."

"Come along, then. When we have had a walk of about half-a-dozen miles, we will have breakfast somewhere.

'In some sweet sequestered glade,
Sacred to solitude and contemplative shade.'

There we will find a solace from the cares of life; and as we partake of some

'—— savoury messes,
Such as the neat-handed Phillis dresses,'

we will fancy ourselves transported to the groves of Arcadia, and forget the work-a-day-world, and all its disagreeables, its squabbles, its jealousies, and its ambitions."

I laughed as I said,—

"Really, my friend, you come out strongly in the poetic vein. But if you will reduce your half-dozen miles to about half the number I shall feel obliged."—"I couldn't."

"Why not?"—"My dear doctor, you know that we cannot, under half-a-dozen miles' stretch, get a sight of a green field or a tree that's worth looking at at all. Three miles, and you are still under the shadow of the cloud of smoke that hangs over London."

"But only think of the six miles back again."

"Psha! don't think of them; we have come some distance already. It is not now five o'clock; we shall accomplish it all by about ten or half-past. Come along."

I suffered myself to be persuaded, and certainly I never did enjoy a country walk more than I did that. My friend knew all the pleasant rural places and lanes which were hidden from the casual observer. We went out by Tottenham, and as we came back, I made a mental resolve that it should not be the last time I accompanied him in one of his morning rambles. Nor was it so by a great many, for he gave me quite a taste for the thing, and I became tolerably intimate during the next year with the environs of London.

It was not until my practice as a physician so much increased, that it was out of the question for me to steal so much time from repose, that I was compelled reluctantly to give up those charming excursions. A medical man in large practice, alas! is so completely the slave of his profession, that he dare not stir, and he is thankful to get a few hours' repose when he can snatch them.

On our road I arranged with my friend how we were to manage in the evening, and he promised to come to my house and bring his brother with him, so that not too many people would be let into the secret.

This was satisfactory enough, and I could not help, as we stood on an elevation which commanded a varied and picturesque view of miles upon miles of surrounding country, saying,—

"I shall awaken to-morrow morning to rather a different prospect than this, my friend."—"True, true."

"The ward of an hospital will present to me a strikingly different scene, and I shall breathe rather a different atmosphere."—"And yet, if you accomplish a work of humanity towards the poor creatures whom you are attempting to serve, the prospect will be more delightful to you than even this."

"It will—it will."—"So you see how we may find good in all situations."

So conversing we strolled into town again, and it was just half-past ten when we once more found ourselves at my friend's door.

"Now," said he, "are you any the worse?"—"The worse! I am a thousand times better."

"Are you ready for a second breakfast?"

I should have mentioned that we had made our way into a cottage, and had a delicious repast upon new milk, eggs, bacon, and bread, for which we paid our hostess so liberally, that she was astonished.

"I am ready for another breakfast," I said; "but you cannot give me one such as I have already had."

"That's true; but still we manage things pretty well here notwithstanding all that; so come in at once, and we will see what sort of an appetite our walk has bestowed upon us."

I entered his house, and found everything in the neatest order. I should mention that my friend was a bachelor. He was not a rich man, in the common sense of the term, although he was in the uncommon one; that is to say, he had not heaps of money, but as much as he wanted.

An elderly woman kept his house for him, and attended upon him. He had a good bottle of wine in his cellar, and could always spare a trifle to give away when he chose to do so.

In fact, a more happy, contented man than my friend I am quite sure could not have been found. He had the look of it in his countenance; and how he would laugh sometimes when he would hear of some one bringing himself to ruin and contempt through grasping for more than was amply sufficient for all legitimate wants.

"Such men, Dr. ——," he would say, "no one can pity.

They fully deserve all the mortification and all the contempt which accompanies them into adversity. There is no individual whom the world is so delighted to give an extra kick to as he who might have been respectable, but who threw the means away in an attempt at a greater amount of aggrandisement."

"I believe you are right."

"I know I am. And what is more, I have constantly observed that men who act in such a manner are those who carry their good fortune, if they be for a time successful, the most arrogantly to all around them. Men who fancy themselves little autocrats, who have their favourites of the day—aye, almost of the hour—and collect around them all the petty, intriguing manners of some contemptible German principality,—these are the men who then pick up some toady—some fellow who sticks to them like a vampire, and is ever ready to swear black is white and white is black at the bidding of the bloated man whom chance has for a time puffed up into a position from which he must fall from sheer want of capacity and temper to sustain. Sir, whenever I see a man of a grovelling intellect and no honesty, become by force of money suddenly important, I know that he will soon pick up some fawning hypocrite to do him lip-service; and when he does so, I know him to be a petty tyrant to the utmost of his abilities, and I know that he will fall like a stick if he went up like a rocket, and likewise I know the toady, the fawning great man's great man, will then be the first to turn coward, and kick the dead lion, whom, while living and prosperous, he declared to be a compound of every imaginable virtue."

"Bravo!" said I, "you have seen something of the world."—"I have; and what is more rare, I have profited by what I have seen."

"More rare, indeed."—"More rare, doctor; but I bore you, I am afraid, with what many people would call my misanthropy; but that is not the correct term to apply to my feelings."

"Those people," said I, "who would stigmatise you as a misanthrope, know you not as I know you, or they never would make so great a mistake concerning you. You are the very reverse character."

"Well, well; I always get morose and excited when I begin to talk of the world and its ways, so we will drop what I cannot help calling the unworthy subject."

"Agreed. Then, at seven o'clock to-night I shall see you."

"Most certainly, without fail; and I will bring with me my brother Bob; and between us we will manage to take you to the hospital somehow, doctor, where I hope you will not remain long."

"No longer than shall suffice to accomplish my purpose, you may make yourself sure of, and that a row will be the result I have a very strong impression."

Precisely at seven o'clock that evening my friend was announced to me, and came into my apartments with his brother Bob, who was to assist in carrying me to the County Hospital. Previously, however, to their arrival, I had made a few necessary preparations for the part I was about to act.

From my wardrobe I managed to select some marvellously old apparel. A threadbare coat, an old hat that had been long cast aside, a waistcoat in tatters, and round my neck I tied a not over clean red and yellow pocket handkerchief.

On the whole I certainly did not look the most respectable figure in the world, and my friend's first exclamation when he saw me thus transformed was, as he lifted up his hands,—

"What a blackguard!"—"Thank you," said I. "You mean I don't look too respectable, I suppose?"—"Respectable! Don't profane the word by mentioning it in connection with that horrible cravat."

"Oh, it's the cravat, is it?"—"It is, indeed. You are, take you altogether, remarkably shabby, but that cravat is abominable."

"That's just what I intend to be. I sincerely hope that no person could, to look at me, have the least idea that I was anything but a very poor man."

"I should, if I were in the habit of bestowing casual alms merely for appearance sake, which I am not certainly, give you a halfpenny," said brother Bob, "if I met you at the corner of a street."

"Well," said my friend, "I should act differently, Bob. If I met Dr. —— in a lonely place, I should say, 'Take my money, but spare my life,' and if I met him where I thought help was near, I should certainly call out 'Police' as loudly as I could."

"I am quite gratified," said I, "with both your opinions. I will send for a coach, and you two must make a show of helping me in. And mind when you have seen me safe in bed at the hospital, don't give a sixpence to the nurse."

"Trust us for that—we understand."

I sent for a coach, and my two friends just helped me in sufficiently to prevent the coachman from saying that there was nothing the matter, if he should speak to any person at the hospital.

"To the County Hospital," said Bob.—"Eh!" cried the coachman. "Double fare."

"What for?"—"Never takes coves to the hospital without. Get out if you won't pay."

"Imposition the first," said I. "Give him what he likes, and take his number, and we will summon him when I come out."—"Very well, charge what you like," said my friend. "Drive on."

"That's yer sort," said the coachman, as he mounted the box; "that's sensible now I calls it. When a feller must have a coach, and can't get in a passion and walk, why let him pay for it. That's my view o' that 'ere subject. Let him pay for it accordin'."

"A pretty article that," said I.—"Oh," said my friend, "he is only like the rest of the world, makes people pay for their misfortunes. I have often noticed it among birds, that if one by some chance gets disabled, the others all have a peck at him."

If I had really had a broken leg, the swinging and jolting of that abominable coach would have driven me fairly mad. As it was we made no objection, and the lumbering vehicle, with such a series of asthmatical groans and wheezes as were dreadful to hear, at length drew up at the door of the County Hospital.

"What's to pay?" said Bob, who got out first.—"Seven shillings."

"There they are. We are in too much affliction about our friend to dispute it with you, but be conscientious and take only your fare now."

The torrent of abuse that was lavished on us all upon this proposal being made was terrific, and glad I was to be helped out, and get away.

One now supported me on each side along a paved courtyard, and every person I saw I saluted with such a hideous groan, that they jumped again. We were received at the door by a porter in livery, who cried,—

"This way, this way. An accident, I suppose."—"Yes, yes."

"This way to the surgery. Let me help him—let me help. Lean on me, I'm used to it. This way, poor fellow. Are you much hurt?"—"Oh! oh! oh!"

"Bless me. Well, don't mind, you'll get well again, I'm sure. Don't mind leaning on me. There, how are you now? Come, come, you'll be comfortable when you get to bed."—

"A good fellow this," thought I. "If he is a sample of all here, Dr. Plumb will be agreeably disappointed."

In a little dingy room, which was dignified by the name of the "Surgery," was Mr. Gray alone.

"What is it?" he said, as I was led in. "God bless me!" I gave such a hideous groan that the place echoed again. "Lay him down here," he said. "There, there, gently. You can go, Robert," to the porter, "you can go. Now, my man, where are you hurt?"

My man is the recognised way of addressing all patients in public hospitals.

By this time the porter had left, and we were alone.

"All's right," said I. "Hurrah! Thus far into the bowels of the County Hospital have I ——."—"Hush," said Mr. Gray, "Green's in the next room. Be cautious."

I gave such a groan that Green, if he had been in the next house, must have heard me. I saw Mr. Gray stuff his handkerchief into his mouth to stop himself from laughing, as a pale, sallow-looking young man popped his head into the room, and said,—

"D—n me, what's this? God d—n, what an infernal row. Just cram something into that low fellow's throat."—"Oh, I'm very bad," said I.

"D—n you, I wish you were worse. Anything good, Gray?"—"No, no, only a simple fracture."

"Cuss me, if we have anything else now-a-days. Not a good case, 'pon my soul, in the d—d place—ah! really, ah! For God's sake, get him to bed; he's enough to give anybody the nightmare. I tell you what it is, my man, we won't have that infernal noise here."

I gave another groan that was as close a resemblance of

the howl of some wild beast as I could well imagine, and Mr. Green disappeared at once, closing the door with a bang.

"Really, really, you will kill me," said Gray. "Don't groan again whatever you do, or I cannot keep my countenance."—"I will groan you as gently as a sucking dove," said I; "will groan you so that Green shall say, 'Let him groan again.'"

"Very good. Now to bed, to bed."

They all three carried me horizontally along a narrow passage, and then into the accident ward.

"Is Mortimer here?" said Mr. Gray.—"Who's Mortimer, I wonder?" said my friend, in a low voice.

"We call the head nurse Mortimer," whispered Gray, "because the ward is named Mortimer's ward."

In a moment the same woman whom I had seen take the half-crown from the parents of the afflicted boy, bustled up to Mr. Gray, and said,—

"Yes, sir—yes, sir—I'm here, sir—if you please, sir—a-hem! I'm here, sir."

"Have you a bed?"—"Yes, sir. A bed, sir. Oh! dear, yes, sir. No trouble, sir."

"A fractured thigh, Mrs. Mortimer." — "Indeed, sir. Dear me, poor fellow. Oh, really, really. Very bad, sir?"

"Not very, unless it turns out so."—"Bless me, yes. Oh, dear, dear. Accidents is accidents."

I gave a low groan. "He's in great suffering, I shouldn't wonder, poor fellow. This way to number twelve—this way."

I was conducted to a bed, and my friend and his brother soon undressed me, after which an inclined plane was brought, and my leg placed in it by Gray, who then said, when he had tied a loose bandage round my foot to keep the limb in its proper place,—

"Now, my man, your cure depends upon yourself. You must keep quiet. That's all we can do with you just now." "Yes, sir," said I, with another groan. "Yes, sir."

"Mrs. Mortimer, you can use the cold lotion as usual, you know, and let me know if any change takes place."—"Yes, sir—yes, sir. Certainly, sir."

Mr. Gray went out of the ward, and my friend stooping down to me, said,—

"How do you do now, Jack?"—"Oh, better, a little," said I.

"Less pain?"—"Oh,—no. Oh!—oh!"

"I suppose it's your leg?" said Bob.—"Yes, and my eye," said I.

I saw Bob turn nearly purple in the face to keep from laughing, and then the nurse said,—

"Ah, poor fellow—a-hem. You're his friends?"—"No, ma'am," said my friend, who took his constitutional walks. "We only picked him up in the streets, and he told us his name was Jack something."

"Oh, indeed. Where do you live, my good man?"—"Nowhere," groaned I.

"Nowhere. But when you're at home, I mean, where do you live? Who are you? Where are your friends?"—"I don't live anywhere. It's a mercy to break one's leg and come here. My name is Jack. I have got no friends, and never had any."

"But—but—a-hem! Do you mean to say you've got no money?"—"Not a rap."

"Fuff—a pretty scrub!"—"A what, ma'am?"

"Oh, don't speak to me. I've no patience with gaol-birds and paupers coming here. Don't speak to me, fellow."

"Well, Jack," said my friend, "here's a shilling for you, as you say you have nothing and no friends. Where shall I put it? I see there's a little drawer here, under the head of your bed; suppose I place it there?"—"Yes," said I, in a faint voice—"yes. I thank you! Oh, dear me! Oh, my leg!"

"I suppose," said Mrs. Mortimer, "that you'll come and see him, gentlemen, sometimes, out of humanity?"—"Well, we may."

"Oh, well, then. I supposes as you know a *nuss's* place is a *nuss's* place—a-hem, gentlemen."

She held out her hand, and waggled her fingers as she spoke.

"Oh, no," said Bob. "Oh, no; we never give anything to anybody. Oh, dear me; especially to sick nurses. I suppose you are paid?"—"Oh, very good—very good! Who asked you to give nothing to nobody? I suppose, now, you mangy flea-bitten scrubs—you paupers, you will be going and saying I asked you for your dirty money: but go—go. You may go and say it to whom you like, and where you like, and how you like, you miserable wretches. You're all of a feather, I can see—get what you can; oh, you screws! Pah! I hate such a set, I do. Pah!"—"Oh, we are going directly," said Bob.

"Oh, my leg," said I—"oh, my leg!"—"Oh, drat your leg," said the nurse, "I wish it was down your throat."

My friend looked at me with a wonderfully comic expression of countenance, and then, with a nod, he took his brother by the arm, and they left me to the tender mercies of nurse Mortimer.

I had now time to look about me on the scene which the accident ward of the County Hospital presented. Truly it was one calculated to excite grave reflections.

Immediately on my right lay a stalwart man, who, by the multiplicity of bandages that were about him, one might well surmise to be a mass of injuries, one of them, as I saw by the nature of the dressings, was a broken jaw.

On my left lay one who, like myself, to all appearance, thank God, only had a broken thigh. Poor fellow! his was real, and there he lay, pale as death, and his lips quivering with the effort he made to suppress his low moans of pain, which would now and then, in spite of him, come from his lips.

Opposite lay the lad to whom I had spoken on the day previous to the present one, and whose parents had given the half-crown to nurse Mortimer.

I could hear occasionally deep sighs of anguish from some one, and now and then such a genuine groan, as made me ashamed of my mock ones—suddenly, too, one would speak, and I heard a deep-toned voice near me say,—

"Oh, good God! how long is this to last?"—"Be quiet," said some one else. "I have not slept for four nights and days now—do be quiet."—"I shall never sleep again."

"By Jasus!" said an Irishman, who had, as I afterwards heard, fallen from a scaffolding—"by Jasus! it's a mighty good thing there's sixteen of us at home any way, when the O'Callaghans gets broke to pieces in this way. I wonder, now, if ever I'll be *jined* agin. Och, murder!"

"There's that Irishman again," groaned the man who had not had any sleep for four days and four nights. "There's that dreadful Irishman again."

"Who do you call a dreadful Irishman, my friend?" cried Mr. O'Callaghan—"who do you call a dreadful Irishman?"

A groan was the only reply.

"Now, *really*," said Mrs. Mortimer, "can't you be quiet among you? If it would please God to take some of you, what a mercy it would be, surely. Oh, you are a cunning set. Now, sir—now, sir."

I was not aware that I was addressed till she exclaimed for the third time, "Now, sir," and added to it, "you with the no money and the no friends, if you please."

"Oh, you mean me," said I, with as awful a groan as I could command. "Ah—ah—what is it?"

She forced something out of a dirty-looking bottle into a dirty-looking cup, and held it towards me, saying,—

"Here's your cherry brandy."—"Cherry brandy? Oh, my leg!"

"Cuss your leg. Yes, cherry-brandy. Come, take it at once; I can't be waiting here all day upon you."—"Oh," groaned I; "you—you are very good; but I really beg to decline it; I do, indeed."

"Do you? *Will* you take it?"—"Oh, my leg! No."

"Now, of all the obstinate wretches, I *have* always remarked, that people with no friends and no money, is the vilest and the most obstinate set alive. If it pleased the Almighty to take 'em, what a good thing it would be to be sure; and why is they without friends and without money? Why is they—why is they?"

Mrs. Mortimer turned round twice, so as to take in all the beds into the space of her vision; but nobody said anything, and she continued,—

"I ask why is they? Cos they is always, of course, the most obstinatest set as ever was. Will you take your cherry-brandy?"—"No, thank you," said I—"no, thank you. You can't think how bad my leg is, and anything so strong would make it worse."

"Then die and be ———."—"D—d," cried O'Callaghan. "That's what you *mane*, Mrs. Mortimer, I know, only you are a *dale* too delicate to say so. Oh, what a jewel you are, Mrs. Mortimer."

"Who asked you to put your spoke in the wheel, Mr. Callaghan?" said Mrs. Mortimer—"who asked you for a remark, sir?"—"Faith, nobody. I came of an obstinate family, you see, like the jontleman who wouldn't take the cherry-brandy, and, perhaps, if I was asked to put my spoke in the wheel, I wouldn't."

"Will you take it?" cried Mrs. Mortimer, holding the cup to me.—"Oh, no. For the sake of my leg, I won't."

"You wretch!"—"Don't run against the bed, ma'am, whatever you do," I groaned. "You will put me to exquisite pain if you do."

"Oh, dear; we are made of glass, are we? Very good. Here's a fellow who won't take his cherry-brandy, and yet his bed mustn't be run against."

As she said this she took care to give the bedstead on which I sat a good poke.

"Oh!" cried I—"oh, God! What a pain you have put me to!"—"Serves you right," she muttered; and away she went.

"It wasn't cherry-brandy, sir," groaned the man who couldn't sleep; "it's house medicine, sir—salts and senna."

"Indeed. Oh, well, I—I won't—oh, my leg!—take it. No. What's the matter with you?"—"Oh, all my bones are broken, I think. If I was but dead—oh, if I was but dead now!"

"Dead!"—"Yes. Do you see that screen—that screen there, in the corner? Do you see it?"

"A screen? Round a bed there?" "Yes—yes. *He* is dying. Whenever they place a screen round a bed, you may know the wretched occupant is dying. It is dreadful for the living, sir. That man has been moaning, as you hear him, for four-and twenty hours."

"Has he really?"—"Yes, sir. Sorry to see a gentleman like you exposed to such things."

"A gentleman? Why do you call me a gentleman?"—"I can see it in your face. You have the well-kept face of a gentleman. You are poor, of course, but you have not always been so."

"Oh, my friend," said I, "you must not judge always by appearances, you know, in this world."—"I know it too well. Do you see yon man there, sitting up, and glaring at us?"

"Yes—yes; opposite."—"Aye; he is a madman. He cut his throat, and was brought in here raving last night. They had to tie him down on the bed, and no one slept for his wild outcries. This morning, however, he is quiet, and they have unbound him, as you perceive. They say he is an artist."

"Surely some other room than this should have been devoted to his reception. My friend and fellow-sufferer, how are you treated by the nurses?"

"Hush! hush! We—we dare not speak of that here, because we are too much exposed to injury, and when we get out, we shrink from the trouble, the mortification, and the chances after all of not being believed."—"I believe that is the case."

"It is—it is. I hope your leg is easier."—"Not a bit; it's just the same."

"You told your friend your eye was bad, did you not?"—"Yes; it is a little."

"Mortimer—oh! oh!—Mortimer," said a voice from the door of the ward, which I at once recognised as belonging to Mr. Green.—"Yes, sir—yes, sir," cried Mortimer, bounding along towards him like a round of beef on castors.

"Is that man dead yet?"—"No, sir. If you please, sir, he's alive yet."

"Oh, feel his feet, and tell me if they are any colder."—"Yes, sir. Certainly—certainly."

She made her way to the bed, round which was the screen, and I heard a feeble voice say,—

"Oh, let me be—oh, let me be. By that fatal screen I know that I am dying. All I ask is peace, peace, peace."—"Oh, you wretch!" said Mortimer; "is that your respect for Mr. Green? You ought to be ashamed of yourself. And he so kind, too, as to come hisself, and ask if you was dead. Oh, I'm ashamed of you."

"Oh, God! oh, God!" groaned the man.

"His feet, if you please, sir, are colderer," said Mrs. Mortimer.—"Oh, oh. When he is gone, let me know. Oh, he's a long time about it, Mortimer."

"Very, sir. It's a shame."—"Why, I don't know—ah, that he can help it—oh!"

"No, sir, as you say. Oh, sir, you are too good. Will you wash your hands, sir?"—"No, no; I can manage. No."

"What the deuce," said I, "does she mean, by asking him to wash his hands?"—"To free himself," said the man who couldn't sleep, "from the contamination of coming into the ward."—"Oh!"

"If you please, Mr. Green, before you go, here's No. 12 won't take his house medicine."

"Won't he? What do you mean by that, my man?"—"She has told you," said I.

"Why the devil don't you take your medicine?"—"I don't feel disposed."

"D—n you."—"Thank you, sir. It's a pleasure to talk to a gentleman."

He half turned upon his heel, and looked at me, as if he was about to make some rejoinder, but he thought better of it, and walked away.

"Oh, you wretch!" cried Mrs. Mortimer, as she placed a wet rag, with a dab, on my leg, to prevent inflammation. "Oh, you wretch! I saw what you was when you first comed in. Mr. Gray must settle you; poor Mr. Green ain't well enough, bless him."—"Oh, he'll do," groaned I; "he'll do well enough."

"Will he do well enough?"—"Yes. I'm very bad."

"And sarves you right, too. You've got a good seven weeks' job of it, I can tell you; and when the splints come to be put on you'll get a nice pull that will make you sing out above a bit; I can tell you that, too, my man."—"How kind," said I; "how kind."

I closed my eyes. It was nine o'clock, and I made up my mind to say as little more as possible, but to watch all that transpired through the coming night.

Night came, and the hospital ward was enveloped in darkness. Mrs. Mortimer took her departure, and a night nurse came on duty; a light was placed on the chimney-piece which cast a flashing radiance upon the pale faces around: all was still save now and then the recurrence of those deep sighs and moans of anguish which human nature could not repress. I feigned to be asleep.

Soon, too, I wished that I was actually wrapped in repose, for, from the man who was dying, and around whose bed was the premonitory screen, I heard at intervals, which were more painful than the sounds themselves, the deep groans of anguish that were heralding the departure of his spirit from its earthly tabernacle. It seemed to take him a full minute to collect breath enough to groan, and then when he did so, the sound was indeed horrible.

I heard a shuffling footstep approach my bedside. I half unclosed my eyes, but not sufficiently to induce any one to believe I was awake, and I saw the night nurse come up to me. She stooped and listened attentively—I breathed with regular and long inspirations to induce her to think me fast slumbering, and she did so.

"Fast as a church," she muttered, and then she stooped, and slowly and carefully opened the sliding drawer which was at the head of my bed. I heard her rattle something—it was the shilling that had been placed there—she stole it, and muttering her satisfaction as she went away, she withdrew to the other end of the ward.

"A pretty wretch!" thought I.

I heard her now conversing in low whispers to one of the patients, and presently there came wafted across my nose so strong a sensation of gin, that I could not doubt but that the night nurse was indulging in that potent and highly popular liquid.

By degrees I got accustomed to her voice, and I could hear her conversing with the favoured patient upon whom she bestowed the grace of her company during the night, or some portion of it.

"Oh, drat them all," I heard her say. "There's nurse Mortimer, too, I lead a nice life with her."—"Oh, no doubt," said a man's voice, "no doubt."

"She drinks like a fish, but I dare say you have heard as much."—"Yes, I have indeed."

"Ah, everybody has. She's a nice article, a very nice article is nurse Mortimer. Do you know somebody has told her, that I pay no attention to anybody but you all night long."—"Is it possible?"

"Indeed it is, and the old wretch threatens to discharge me. I could tell some things of her I could—robbing the patients, and one thing and another. It's really desperate; she's an old hag."

"Nurse—nurse—nurse," groaned some unfortunate man.

"Well, what now?" cried the night nurse.—"Some—some water—water—I am faint."

"Then faint away, and you'll be quiet. I suppose you think one has nothing to do but keep bringing you drink."

At this moment, I thought the man who had the screen round his bed must be dead, for he had left off groaning full ten minutes; but such was not the case, for suddenly I heard the "death rattle" in his throat, and a dreadful sound it was to hear in that ward.

"Good God!" said my neighbour, who could not sleep. "Good God! there surely might be some means devised of not horrifying the living by such a companionship with the dying as this. Surely, oh, surely, there might be some room contiguous to this into which a man, upon whom was the finger of death, might, bed and all, be wheeled without detriment to him. It is horrible to hear such sounds as that. Nurse! nurse!"

"What do you want?"—"That man is dying now."

"Well, what's that to you, I should like to know? You'll be dying yourself some day you will, you unfeeling wretch."

"Unfeeling!"—"Yes, to be sure. Don't trouble me."

"My dear," I heard the patient say who was the favourite of the night nurse. "My dear, when I get out, you shall not be exposed to all this any longer."

"Ah, you don't mean what you say."—"Upon my soul, I do. You shall be Mrs. Wilkins as sure as fate."

"Shall I though?'—"Nurse—nurse!" groaned another.

"Be quiet, will you," she cried. "I'm not going to be troubled by you as I am. Will you then, Mr. Wilkins, as you was a-saying?"—"Yes, I'll take a second floor, and make things comfortable.'

"Ah, what a man you are. Take another drop; it won't hurt you, broken ribs is nothing."—"Well, if you think so."

"Oh, it's mild. We never drink nothing here but Dradey's Death Cordial. It's a pure spirit."

I heard a sound of drinking, and the flavour of gin was wafted again over the ward. The death rattle continued in the throat of the dying man, and it appeared suddenly to have arrested the attention of the nurse, for she exclaimed,—

"Drat that man, when will he die? He's been bothering here for never so long. Howsomedever, he'll not last long, Mr. Wilkins. There's the rattles, and they is a good sign always, as you, no doubt, well knows."

"I suppose he's dying?"—"Oh, yes; a scrub. He's one of the bad bargains, and a good thing when he's gone, I can tell you. There is some cases, if you'll believe me, Mr. W., as I'd sooner see the devil come into a ward than see brought in."

"Indeed?"—"Yes; I assures you. One of 'em is a broken back; oh, it's no end of trouble, I can tell you. We calls it here a luxation of the *wurler bray*. Of course it is."

"Well, my opinion is that you know as much as any of the doctors."—"Oh, you flatterer!"

"Flatterer, be d——d," cried Mr. O'Callaghan, who, it appears, had been listening to all that passed. "If the beds here were a little flatterer it would be a good thing, but they all sink in the middle, so that if a poor fellow has a broken leg, the idea of it being mended straight is all moonshine."

"How dare you interrupt me, you wretch?"

The night nurse came towards him with a threatening aspect, and I could see, by the devious nature of her course, that the Dradey's Death Cordial had not been without its effect. "You low, Irish villain, how dare you speak to me when you ain't spoke to?"

"Oh, go to blazes."

"I will not go to blazes, or anywhere else (hiccup) to please you, you low scrub."

"Hould your tongue, you bad-mannered female, can't you. Don't you hear there's a poor fellow a-dying in the ward?"

"And what's that to you, sir?"—"Don't *rason* upon other folks by yourself. Everybody isn't such a brute as you are, you know."

What rejoinder the nurse might have made, it is impossible to say, for, at this moment, there was a trampling of feet and a number of voices. The door of the ward was opened, and I saw two persons come in with lights; after them came the hall-porter. He was very pale, and in his arms he bore a mass of what appeared bloody clothing. He passed the foot of my bed with it, and then I saw what it was. It was a young girl of about eight or ten years of age; she had been entangled in some machinery somewhere. I closed my eyes and shook like an aspen leaf.

I heard the confused murmur of voices about the ward.

"Lay her down. There—there. She's dead. No; she breathes. Yes. There—that will do—more water. A good case—no large artery is lacerated. That eye is gone."

All this was mingled with the rattle in the throat of the dying man, the groans of the others, and the screams of a boy who was nearly terrified into convulsions by the ghastly spectacle which was placed upon a bed immediately opposite to him.

I would not open my eyes, I would not hear but as little as I could, for I covered my face and ears very nearly entirely up with the bed-clothes, and thus must have elapsed nearly half-an-hour, when some one touched my shoulder.

"Who's that?" I said.—"I," said Mr. Gray, in a whisper. "How do you like it?"

"Like it—like it?"—"Hush! I will see you in the morning. Any discoveries?"

"A few."—"Very good."

"Is the young girl dead?"

"Yes—yes. There was a faint hope of her recovery, but she would have been a cripple for life; she is dead."

"Thank God! You know, Gray, I have not seen much practical surgery, and I must confess to-night has been one of horror to me."—"Never mind, it will do you good. I must away now. Good night, good night."

He walked away, and almost immediately the night-nurse staggered up to my bed, and said,—

"If you've been ear-wigging the house-surgeon I'll smash you, my child."—"Oh, my leg!" said I; "oh, my leg."

"Curse your leg. What have you been saying?"—"Nothing, if you please."

"Nothing, indeed. Nothing. Oh, such as you should always have Mr. Green to deal with; he is a gentleman, and never bemoans hisself to look to poor people. No, never; he tells 'em to be d——d at once."

"Does he, indeed?"—"Yes, he does, indeed. Oh, you sneaking ruffian."

"What for, pray?"—"Oh, I hate you, I do. I know you've been complaining, you have."

"Of my leg."

"Yes. I wish your leg was stuffed down your throat."

Away she went again to Mr. Wilkins, who I heard say,—

"Never mind, my dear; never mind. I'll take a second floor when I get well, and you and me will live in it. Never mind him."

The death-rattle had ceased. There were now two dead bodies in the accident ward. The dim grey light of morning was coming and making war with the miserable light that was on the mantelshelf. Most of the wretched sufferers had dropped into repose; some were moaning with the consciousness of pain, in their sleep, while some slept soundly, and, perchance, were watted in their dreams to happier scenes, when the smiling faces of those they loved surrounded them, and they heard the music of the voices which they were, perhaps, doomed never in this world to hear again.

Slowly, but surely, the bright morning came. A long beam of sunlight fell upon the screen which had been placed around the bed on which lay the girl's corpse. Alas! it could not rouse to life that senseless mass; never again would those lips smile—never again would those eyes reflect the life of joy. And who was she? I asked myself. Had she no friends? did no one mourn for her? did no one come to take one last lingering look at those cold remains?

Even as I asked myself the question, there came two people into the ward. The one was the hall-porter, of whose good feeling I had occasion to speak well. The other was a man about thirty years of age, whose hands were clasped, and who reeled as he came along, as if either completely heartstricken, or in a state of intoxication.

"Nurse," said the porter, "nurse. This is the girl's father. He wants to see her, and Mr. Gray says he may."

The nurse pointed to one of the screened beds, and the man tottered towards it. I cannot bring myself to describe the scene that ensued. I thought I could, but I cannot—I cannot, and my readers must excuse me. The father was carried out in about five minutes; but during that five minutes, such a world of agony had been expressed, that I was inclined to rise, and run out of the hospital.

* * * *

The night nurse was now relieved by a day one; and then, about eight o'clock, the great Mrs. Mortimer herself came into the ward. The first thing she did was to take an effervescing draught that had been ordered for one of the patients.

"It's very odd, Agnes," she said to the other nurse, "but every morning I have a kind of dizziness. It ain't from anything I take over night. Oh, no! It's the narves—it's the narves."—"And the worrit," said Agnes.

"As you say, Agnes, and the worrit. Let me think. Oh, oh!"

The thought seemed to be something concerning me, for she suddenly came up to my bedside, and said,—

"You'll have to pay me a shilling for the use of a cup and saucer."—"Oh, my leg!" said I. "Indeed."

"Yes; or else you won't have none."—"Well—but of course, as a poor man, with neither friends nor money," said I, "I shall be provided here with whatever is necessary."

"Indeed—will you?"— "Of course. This is a public charity, and I expect such matters as may be afforded me, without being compelled to fee a nurse."

"You do, do you—you scamp? Then I can tell you, you are mistaken."—"Well, so it seems. But I have a shilling in my drawer."

"Very good."

She opened the drawer, but no shilling was there, for a good reason; and from the small amount of surprise she manifested at that circumstance, I guessed that she and the night nurse had agreed upon the petty robbery, and divided the proceeds. I was upon the point of saying as much, when my attention was attracted by a strange sight at the door of the ward.

Two men came in carrying between them a great tin or sheet-iron coffin, which had evidently seen much service. They were talking as they came upon indifferent matters, and they went up to the bed in which the man had died, and disappeared behind the screen. I heard a great bump in the tin or iron coffin, which I at once concluded was the body being there placed.

I was right, for in another moment they came staggering out with their load, and carrying the coffin by two handles, covering it with an old black rag, bearing the strongest possible resemblance to the sort of thing the sweeps hang up before a chimney to prevent the soot, during the process of sweeping, from coming down into the room.—And so away they took the dead body.

The corpse of the young girl was carried off in the same style, and then I took serious thoughts with myself, as to what I should do, and I came to the conclusion that I would not endure for any longer the terrors of the accident ward of the County Hospital.

I waited until I saw Mr. Gray, to whom I communicated, in a whisper, my intention of leaving, and added,—

"Will you oblige me by sending some one to my lodgings for a suit of clothes, my gold watch and seals, a very elaborate and showy cloak I had with white lining, which I used to go to the theatres with, and sundry other articles of a showy and ornamental character, the whole of which I directed to be brought to me, packed up by a lad of the name of William, who I then kept in handsome livery to attend to the door for me during the hours I received patients. I'm afraid I was a little malicious, but I did picture to myself the enjoyment of annoying Mrs. Mortimer.—All was done as I directed, and in about an hour Mr. Gray came in and said to me, as he passed the bed,—

"William is here."—"Very good," said I. "Send him in in five minutes."

He nodded, and out he went.

"Mrs. Mortimer!" cried I. "Mrs. Mortimer—Mrs. Mortimer—Mortimer—Mortimer—Morti——mer! Hilloa! Mortimer!"

"Good God! what now?" she exclaimed. "Of all the born devils that ever was, you are the worst."

"Do you mean to tell me, ma'am," said I, "that you want a shilling of me for the use of a cup and saucer?"—"Yes, I do. What then?"

"Why, then, I have no sort of hesitation in telling you that you neglect the patients, drink gin, and abuse those who cannot pay you. That the night nurse has robbed me. That Green, the surgeon, is a brutal puppy, and that the whole system here is one of great carelessness, inhumanity, and gross mismanagement."

Mrs. Mortimer's countenance became like the setting sun in a fog, and she cried with vehemence,—

"Indeed! that's your opinion, is it? I only wonder such a mighty fine gentleman as you stick up to be, ever came here, you low, dirty, parish-brought-up scrub."—"I wouldn't, if I had known one half that I know now."

"Then why don't you go—why don't you go?" she sneered. "Ha! ha! Why don't you go?"

I saw William, who had been put up to the affair by Mr. Gray, at this moment come into the ward.

"I'm d——d," said I, "if I do stay here any longer," and up I jumped out of the bed in one moment, for I had previously loosened the bandage that bound my foot to the inclined plane. "William, help me to dress; I won't stay here another moment, William."—"Yes, sir," said William, touching his gold laced hat; "yes, sir."

"That's right, I shall not stay here another hour."

Mrs. Mortimer gave a loud scream, and retreated backwards till the bed of Mr. Wilkins stopped her, and on him she tumbled, to his great dismay. The patients looked aghast, while I dressed myself with great rapidity, William handing me each article as I wanted it.

"Not another minute will I stay here," added I, as I threw my gold watch-guard over my neck. "Not another minute, if I had twenty broken legs. William!"—"Yes, sir."

"Have you ordered the carriage?"—"Yes, sir."

"Very good. You can go now, William, and tell the coachman that the first call will be upon the Secretary of State."

Nurse Mortimer gave another scream, and rolled off Mr. Wilkins's bed.— Mr. Gray then came in, followed by my Islington friend, and his brother Bob, who overacted his part, by saying to me in a deferential voice,—

"I hope your grace has found all right here!"

There was a general commotion in the ward. Mrs. Mortimer went into hysterics, the night nurse dropped on her knees, Mr. Wilkins got completely under the bed-clothes, while O'Callaghan threw his pillow up to the ceiling with delight, and gave a shout that was perfectly unearthly.

"Has any one here," said Mr. Gray, "a complaint to make against the nurses?"—"Yes," cried a dozen voices. "Yes. Neglect, drunkenness, abuse, robbery, extortion."

"Very well; everything shall be investigated."

I threw my cloak over my shoulders, and stalked out of the ward. Within a pace of the door I met Green, who, hearing a great uproar, had come to see what was the matter.

"Mr. Green, I believe?" said I. "Yes, sir," he replied. "May I ask who I have the honour of addressing?"

"You don't recollect me, sir?"—"I have not that pleasure."

"Oh, nonsense. You told me to die and be d——d, only last night."—"I, sir! I—I!"

"Yes, certainly. Will you allow me to put on my gloves, and wait till I have done so, Mr. Green?"

"Your gloves, sir! What—what for?"—"Because, sir, when you thought I was poor and helpless, you insulted me, and now, before all the ward, here I intend to pull your nose."

He turned immediately and tried to escape, but I saluted him with a kick behind, which sent him out of the ward with greater quickness than comfort, and then I followed him, while the patients looked perfectly aghast.

* * * * * *

On the next day there was a meeting of the board of management of the County Hospital, at which the resignation of Mr. Green, as house surgeon, was accepted, and a vote of dismissal of Mrs. Mortimer and the night nurse carried unanimously. The matron received a severe reprimand that she had not better attended to her duties of seeing that the nurses were proper persons to fill so onerous an office.

The hall-porter was called in, and received the thanks of the board and a gratuity, and such a commotion was created all over the building, as I have no doubt did a world of good, and sufficed to keep everything in a much better state for years afterwards.

Reader, I will not now, because I cannot do so of my own knowledge, say that there are such abuses in any metropolitan hospital as I have stated to exist in the one I have introduced to your notice, but should there be, I hope that the number in which this passage from my Diary appears, will find its way there, and act as a warning, inducing a belief that some of these days some discovery similar to the one I have recorded may take place.

And, in conclusion, I can only say, that I have exaggerated nothing in the statement I have made, but, on the contrary, been compelled, from the very nature of the subject, to suppress some details which would place the conduct of the nurses in a worse point of view than it here appears to the reader.

THE ASYLUM;

OR, BROTHER AND SISTER.

About midway in the progress of my professional career, it occurred to me to become cognizant of a family circumstance, which, while it unhappily presents some specimens of human nature to the reader in an unfavourable light, shows a brighter picture as regards others, and may not be without some degree of practical utility.

It is certainly rather a sad thing that our experience of humanity has principally to be made up from the darker aspects in which we are compelled to view it; and in an artificial state of society, such as that which obtains in what are called civilized nations, it is to be expected that while we have got rid of some savage vices, we have at the same time repudiated some simple virtues.

It does not always follow that because mankind, or a particular section of mankind, occupying a particular locality upon the earth's surface, are much cultivated, that they should, therefore, be either feeling or moral.

Indeed there are so many inducements in life to all men to acquire that wealth, and to surround themselves with those circumstances, which they see productive of slavish respect, that the means by which such obvious advantages are obtained become but secondary considerations.

We often in society will hear a man or a family talked of as highly desirable acquaintances, for they have an income of so much per annum; but when do we ever hear any one conjecture about the means by which they procured it, from any motive higher than a selfish one to try himself and do so likewise.

No; possession is the thing in this world; and the lawyer's advice to his son when dying, although rather a severe satire, was a just one.

"Tom, my boy," he said, "whatever you do through life, mind you get money. You may get it honestly, if you can, but, Tom, mind you get it."

The only thing we object to in this anecdote is, its being foisted upon a lawyer, because lawyers are not clever enough, merely because they are lawyers, to be any greater rogues than their neighbours; and if the anecdote had simply been told of some very respectable man, who had given such advice to his son upon his death-bed, it would have been far better than merely fathering it upon a lawyer.

It is nothing new likewise to find all those feelings which are called natural ones completely placed in abeyance by such far more natural feelings as prompt men and women to be selfish. There is in some dispositions such an inherent selfishness as will outweigh every other consideration, and no sentiment of common justice will turn such persons from the path of iniquity they choose. And it is not in the statutes of the realm, or in the pages of a Newgate Calendar, or a sheriff's report, that we shall find recorded the worst crimes of which human nature is capable—far, very far, from it.

It is in the seclusion of domestic life that we shall discover heartlessness and villany far superior to anything of which the law can take cognizance—a heartlessness and villany more despicable, because more cowardly, than that which would place a man at the bar of the Old Bailey.

It is in the relations of man to man even in business that sometimes we shall find the greatest amount of hypocrisy, as well as the greatest amount of villany, and yet all on the windward side of the law.

There are no courts of honour to which such people can be subjected. As long as there are fools to be duped, there will be rogues to dupe them; and the rogue cares not for the opinion of ninety-nine men, so that he succeed in duping the hundredth, from whom he expects and anticipates advantages.

* * * * *

I was called out one evening just towards dusk, very hurriedly, to attend upon a gentleman who was taken suddenly ill at his own house in the neighbourhood of St. James's. His name was Achison; and from the urgency with which I was requested to attend to him, I guessed that something very serious must be the matter with him.

I accordingly hurried as fast as I could to the address which had been given me, and when I got there I found the whole house in a state of the greatest possible confusion.

Lights were flashing about in all directions; and any one might, I am sure, have gone in and taken hold of any article they liked, and walked out again, without interruption.

When I knocked I found that the door was not fast, for it yielded to the pressure of my hand, so I at once entered the passage.

A handsome hall lamp, which shed a brilliant light up the staircase, convinced me I had got into a house where there was every appliance to comfort which wealth could produce. I hesitated to know what to do exactly, and I was on the point of knocking again at the door in order to arouse the attention of some one, when a servant appeared from above stairs.

"Are you the doctor, sir?" he said; "are you the doctor?"—"Yes—yes."

"Oh, come up, then, sir; come up, pray, as quick as you can, if you please."

"Is it your master who is ill?" I said.—"Yes, sir, if he ain't dead."

"Dead!—why, what has occurred to him? I hope you have made no mistake in sending for me, and that this is not a surgical case, my friend?"—"I don't know, sir;—a doctor's a doctor, I suppose."

"But has your master met with an accident? Is he hurt in any way?—"Not as I know of, sir. This way, if you please."

We had reached the second floor by this time, and I was ushered into a bed-room, extremely handsome in all its appointments and fittings, in which I found a terrified group of people.

The bed was untouched, but the persons in that room were surrounding an easy chair in which sat a gentlemanly-looking young man, who was no other than Mr. Achison.

At his feet, kneeling, and with her head resting upon his knee, while her long dark hair fell in masses on the floor, was a very beautiful girl, dressed as if for some evening entertainment. In the room were likewise three or four servants the whole of whom wore expressions of consternation in their countenances.

"The doctor, ma'am," announced the footman, who had escorted me up stairs.

The young girl who was kneeling at the feet of the gentleman in the chair, immediately rose, and springing towards me, she cried in shrill, frantic accents,—

"Oh, save him, sir! save him! Take all we have! Make us poor, but save his life! Be more than skilful! God of Heaven, he will die! Save him! save him!"

"Hush!" I said, sternly, for it was imperatively necessary to stop such a flow of despair; "hush! This sort of language befits not the sick chamber. Be composed."

"Composed!"

"Affect a composure if you feel it not," I added. "Is this the gentleman to whom I have been called?"

"Yes, yes," said everybody in a breath.

The *brusque* manner I had assumed had the effect I wished and expected it to have. The young wife, for such I found she was, shrunk back, and calmed the outward demonstration of her feelings, while I advanced to the chair on which sat the gentleman, who had not yet spoken.

All that I have related occurred in a very few moments in the sick chamber, so that really no time was lost in attending to my patient.

I looked in his face, and saw that there was great anxiety and flurry visible in every feature. His eyes looked a little dilated, and unnaturally bright, while he breathed in a very peculiar and short manner, as if afraid of taking a deep inspiration.

Both his hands were pressed tightly over his heart, and from all these appearances, I had no difficulty in coming to the conclusion that all the alarm and distress arose from some sudden affection of the heart, which might or might not be of importance.

Neuralgic affections of that important organ may exist and present a train of apparently serious symptoms, without there being any actual *lesion*. Indeed so troublesome and complicated are the diagnostics of heart diseases, that the most skilful physician may be frequently deceived.

DIARY OF A PHYSICIAN.

"If you can speak, sir, without pain," I said, "do so, and tell me what you feel."

He shook his head mournfully, and I fancied that a change came over his face for the worse.

"Charles, Charles!" said his wife. "Dear Charles, speak to me."

"Hush!" I said; "hush! It's perhaps, after all, only some disturbance of the heart's action which is producing all this distress. Have you writing materials here?"—"Yes—yes."

"Then send a servant to the nearest chemists' for this directly."

Almost as I spoke I wrote a prescription, which I had found to be beneficial in such cases, and the footman was

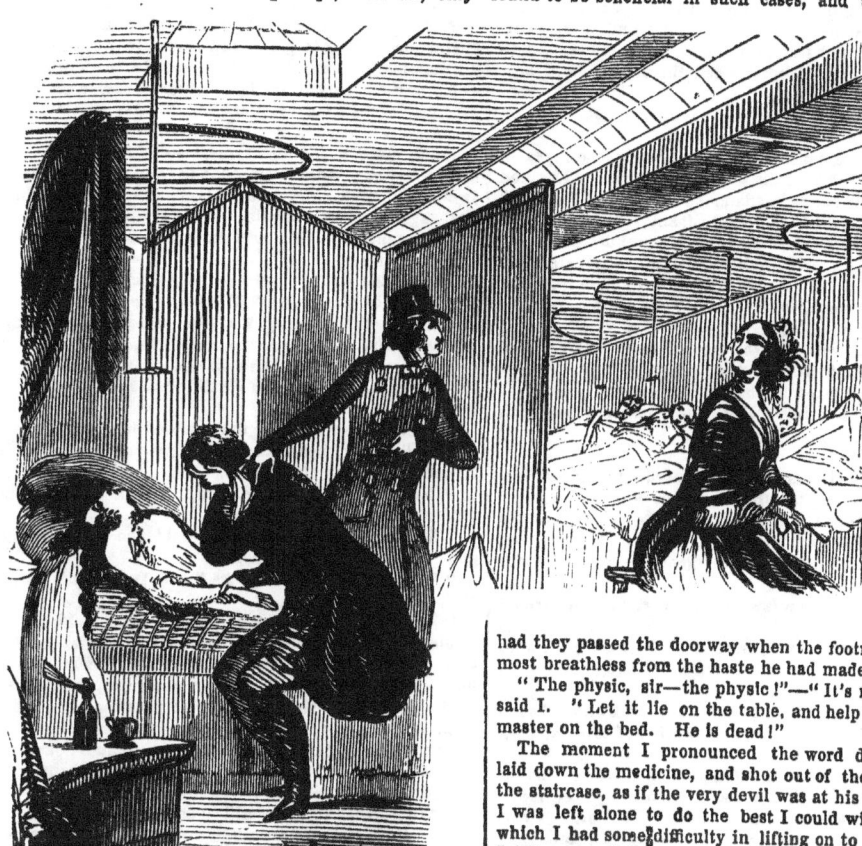

despatched with it, with an injunction to be quick in his movements.

Still Mr. Achison said nothing, and his beautiful wife—for she was very beautiful—wound one of her arms round him, while she looked in his face with an expression of such tender anxiety, that it was enough to bring tears into the eyes of any one.

"Charles," she said, "you are better? Oh, if you were a little better only! If you could speak to me!"—"Do not urge him," I said.

"No, no—I will not. He will soon be well? You are sure he will soon be well, sir?"—"I hope so, and expect so," said I. "When did this begin?"—"About half an hour since, I think, by now. He rang the bell, and when a servant came to him, he was found sitting here, precisely in the same attitude you see him."

"He has not spoken?"—"Not one word."

Suddenly now, before any one could be aware of it, the gentleman gave a gasping sob, and rose. "God! God!" he said twice, and then I was just in time to catch him, or he would have fallen on to the floor. His wife screamed aloud, and I cried to the servants,—

"Remove your mistress from this room directly."

I felt the weight in my arms of Mr. Achison grow suddenly heavier, and the head hung listlessly. He was dead! One glance at his face convinced me of that fact.

"Remove your mistress," I cried again.

She burst into a violent access of hysterics, during which the terrified servants took her from the room, and scarcely had they passed the doorway when the footman appeared, almost breathless from the haste he had made, and cried,—

"The physic, sir—the physic!"—"It's not wanted now," said I. "Let it lie on the table, and help me to place your master on the bed. He is dead!"

The moment I pronounced the word dead, the footman laid down the medicine, and shot out of the room, and down the staircase, as if the very devil was at his heels. And there I was left alone to do the best I could with the dead body, which I had some difficulty in lifting on to the bed, although I did accomplish it.

I then opened the vest, and listened attentively at the region of the heart, but there was not the least flutter of vitality. The man was quite dead. I covered the face over with a corner of the counterpane, and then I asked myself if the wife knew or not of the sudden death.

When I came to consider, I thought she did not, for her attack of hysterics was before I knew it myself, and it was not likely she would be better informed upon the subject. I much wished that I could see some responsible person about the establishment to whom I could speak, but there was no such a one, to my knowledge; therefore I left the chamber of death, and turning the key outside in the lock, I descended the staircase.

I entered a magnificent drawing-room, resplendent with works of taste. Indeed, a handsomer apartment for its dimensions I had never seen, and looking about me, I found the means of ringing a bell, which I did with considerable energy.

After three appeals of this sort, I was indulged by an answer. A young woman appeared, looking half stupified, and scarcely able to ask me what I wanted.

"Where is Mrs. Achison?" said I.—"Oh, she's a little better now, sir. We've put her into bed, sir. How's master, now, sir?"—"Dead."

The girl gave a scream.

"Why," said I, "did not the footman tell you? He knew it."—"We haven't seen him, sir."

"Well, this painful intelligence must be broken to your mistress as gently, and yet I would recommend, at the same time, as speedily as possible. You had better go and tell her."—"Who—I, sir? Lor! sir, I couldn't for the wealth of the *Hinges!*"

"Is there no relative or friend of the family who can be sent for?"—"Not as I knows on, sir. Missus has friends, but then they is foes."

"How do you make that paradoxical speech out?"—"What, sir?"

"Well, never mind. Where is your mistress? If none of you will take the task of telling her of her bereavement, I will myself, for she ought to know it most certainly, and at once, too."—"Up stairs, sir, if you please. I'll show you her room."

Preceded by the girl, I went up stairs, and was conducted into a very comfortable bed-room, where I found Mrs. Achison in that half dreamy state of intellect which follows a violent hysterical seizure. I approached the bedside, and said to her,—

"Madam, it is my painful duty to inform you that you must prepare your mind for the very worst."

She understood me, for I saw her shudder as she repeated the word "worst."—"Yes, the worst," I added. "Life and death are not in our hands, madam, but in those of Heaven."

"What do you mean?" she said; "am I in danger?"—"Not you. Can you have forgotten that your husband ——"

"No, no, no!" she cried suddenly—"no, no! He shall not die—he must not die! Let those die who are loved by no one—who have either formed no ties of fond affection, or who have outlived all such, but not Charles—not my husband. No, no; it would be too monstrous a perversion of nature."—"I grieve to disturb your belief," I said. "Bear with what calmness you may the sad intelligence ——"

She rose in the bed in which she had been laid, and with a shriek, she cried,—

"He is dead!"

I said nothing, and in another moment she was insensible.

"Now," I said to the servants, "she knows the truth. You see she has fainted. Think again, some of you, and try if you can remember any friend of the family to whom you could send in this most sad emergency."—"There's Mr. Minden," said one.

"Who is he?"—"He's a lawyer, I believe, sir, and a friend of poor master's."

"Then he's a very proper person indeed to send to; and, pray, one of you go to him at once."—"I'll go," said one; "he only lives two streets off."

While this Mr. Minden was being sent for, I ordered such matters as were necessary for the restoration of Mrs. Achison from her swoon.

This was speedily effected. The sudden shock of the intelligence of her husband's death had chained up her faculties, for, let a person be ever so prepared for a death, it certainly is, when it actually comes across the mind without any reservation of hope, a severe shock.

I was glad, however, that I had told her, for I am well aware that many people think it very kind and considerate to keep such pieces of intelligence from the living as long as possible, appearing quite to forget that the hour when the fact must be revealed is near at hand, and that then it has to be told without ambiguity, for you cannot soften down the word death by any sort of circumlocution whatever.

If, therefore, it has to be spoken, let it be spoken at once, and off-hand. It is a shock—one of the severest to which human nature, probably, is subject; while, at the same time, it is one of those which ought the soonest to yield to reflection.

In this respect death differs from many mundane misfortunes. It is at its worst at first, and the more we reflect upon it, the less fearful it becomes. There is no agony of anticipation—no anxiety—no suspense. If a beloved object has gone to the tomb, while we weep for the sufferings that heralded the event, we know that with the event the sufferings ceased, and that—

"The first sad day of nothingness
is likewise
The last of sorrow and distress."

It has always astonished me that extremely religious people make such a fuss about death; and when I have heard so much said by them of so and so going to glory, and seen the expression accompanied by so many tears sometimes, I could almost have smiled at the inconsistency of human nature, or insinuated a doubt with respect to the speaker's belief in the "going to glory" part of the business.

I recollect an extremely evangelical woman, whose husband I attended some time, but whom I afterwards lost sight of, as they went into the country; but I met her again in London, and after a remark about the weather, I said,—

"And how is your husband?"—"Gracious! don't you know?" she replied, bursting into tears. "Oh! my poor heart. He's happy now."

"Do you mean dead?"—"Yes. He's gone to the Lord."

"Well," said I, "if he's happy now, I wonder to see you crying in such a way."—"Ah," she said, "you don't know the feelings of people, doctor. He's got an immortal crown on his head now. I always cry when I think of him."

"Very good; I can't help it."

And so we find very religious people continually grudging their friends going to glory, and having immortal crowns, and all that sort of thing, which appears to me entirely wrong, and a sort of flying in the face of Providence, to use a common canting evangelical expression, if ever anything in the world was.

At all events, it's much more so than insuring your life, and we were much amused the other day to find in a twaddling publication, which is half a century behind the age, a page or two devoted to the argument that providing for your family by a life assurance was not flying in the face of Providence.

Before the servant returned who had been sent for the gentleman of the name of Minden, who had been mentioned as a friend of the family, I had succeeded in restoring poor bereaved Mrs. Achison to consciousness, and with the return of her faculties I was glad to see there came a return of the consciousness of the death that had occurred in the house.

She did not speak upon the subject, but I could see by the deep dejection of her countenance that she was fully aware of it, and that it had sunk into her heart.

"You are better now, madam," I said.—"Yes—yes, better," she replied, mournfully.

"Mr. Minden has come, sir," said the servant who had gone to fetch that gentleman.

"Thank you; where is he?"—"In the drawing-room, sir."

"Then I will go to him at once. Mrs. Achison, let me implore you not to grieve too deeply. Think rationally upon this subject. Life, at the best, is but a dream. If happy, but a short summer's day. If otherwise, a rude winter, while it lasts, and yet fleeting. We should always endeavour to make what good of it we can, and try rather to fight against its evils, than allow them to conquer; and in such cases to resolve upon not being beaten, is at once to have gained the victory."

I had no wish in the world to coax her into any conversation. I was a stranger to her, and yet a medical man feels himself more at home in a family in a short time than any one else can, and I made free to address to her these observations for her consideration.

I then proceeded down stairs, and in the drawing-room I found a little old gentleman, with a shining bald head, who received me very politely and very ceremoniously.

"Have I the honour," I said, "of speaking to Mr. Minden?" for he seemed so unlawyer-like that I could hardly believe but there was some mistake.

"Yes, sir," he said; "yes, my name is Minden."

"Sir, I have made free to send for you, in consequence of the sudden death of the gentleman of this house."

"Ah, so I was told," said Minden, shaking his head. "Dear, dear; how sudden. Poor Achison, I've known him, sir, from a boy."

"Have you, indeed?"—"I have, sir, and poor dear Emily, too. How is she?"

"Do you mean Mrs. Achison?"—"Yes, poor child; how is she?"

"She seems in a dreadful state of affliction; I am a complete stranger to the family, Mr. Minden, as you cannot have failed to perceive."

"Ah, sir; such happy prospects as they had. My heart bleeds for Emily; but I don't weep at deaths now—I have lost so many who were dear to me. You see I am getting old, too—that I—I don't now weep, although I feel the blow."

"And none the less."

"As you say, and none the less. I was intimate with Mr. Achison's father, sir, who left him a very handsome fortune, and Charles, being a prudent young man, took care of it. He has not a relative, that he knows of, in this country; and being a young man of the best feelings and principles, he married where he found virtue allied to sensibility and goodness."

"It is a sad thing when so early in life such ties get

broken."—"It is, indeed. Emily Hardy, which was Mrs. Achison's maiden name, was a poor penniless girl, sir."

"The more honour to Mr. Achison to wed her."—"True —most true. But now I very much fear that the set of harpies that will surround her, will, alas! too soon prove her destruction. I don't often call anybody names, but I cannot help calling them absolute wretches."

"Who do you mean, sir?"—"The family connexions of Mrs. Achison."

"Indeed!"—"Aye, sir; Mr. Achison has had some trouble; but, you see, being a man of means, he was able to beat them, and latterly he got rid of them pretty well; but, now that with his life a fear of him has gone, I do dread the consequences."

"Well, it is to be hoped, sir, that yourself and some other members of the family, or friends, may be able to step between Mrs. Achison and such evils; I presume she is well provided for."

"I have Mr. Achison's will in my possession, in which she is left everything without reservation."

After some further conversation with Mr. Minden, I left the house, and as I was not sent for, I did not call again until I was summoned on the inquest, which was a very short affair; as, from the symptoms, I was enabled to say conclusively that the deceased had died of ossification of the heart, and a verdict was returned in accordance with that opinion of mine.

I did not see Mrs. Achison at all, and Mr. Minden I only saw for a few moments, so that I got no news of the situation of affairs at all, and being pressed for time, I left the house as quickly as I could.   *   *   *

Six months after these occurrences, and when, indeed, in the multiplicity of events that may occur in such a period of time, I had almost forgotten all about Mr. Achison and his death, an event occurred which brought the circumstances all fresh and full to my memory.

One morning a young surgeon of my acquaintance, named Hulme, called upon me, and after some casual conversation, he said,—

"You know, doctor, I am paying great attention to a particular part in my profession in preference to any other."

"I am aware you make the diagnostics and treatment of insanity your peculiar study."

"I do."

"You could not possibly have hit upon a more important subject, or one on which you are more likely to do good, Hulme. I am very glad to find you have devoted yourself to it in the way I know you have."

"It is beset with more than due difficulties."—"I know it is. I myself, as you have often heard me say, went as far as the opportunities I could gather from my general practice would allow me into the matter, and I found the difficulties no doubt that you find."

"Of course you did, and the principal one is ———"—"The aversion which the keepers of private asylums have to the visits of any medical man but the one with whom they have made an agreement."

"Precisely; while upon such a subject of all others there should be all reasonable facilities."

"But there never will be in private asylums, which in my opinion ought not to be allowed to exist, for it is, as a matter of course, the interest of the proprietor to keep the patients instead of discharging them cured, and we have no right to look for more virtue in the keeper of a lunatic asylum than in anybody else."

"Certainly not; but what I have called upon you to-day for is, to ask you to come with me to visit an asylum, at a village called Colderhead, near Kingston."

"My dear fellow, consider the distance."—"Oh, we can get down quick. It is on this side of Kingston. I have an order to view the establishment."

"How did you get it?"—"The proprietor is in town on some business, and I accidentally sat next him at a public dinner. He got drunk, and I saw him home, with the sinister motive of getting this very order from him, and I did get it. He will be in town a week longer, so I want to take advantage of his absence, you see, to go."

"Well, I should like it."

"I knew you would."

"At what hour will you start?"

"At half-past eleven."

"It's awkward for me, but I really shouldn't like to miss it."

"Don't miss it; I'll get a horse that can go, and a cab; we will soon rattle down, and you can leave word that you are called away to a case out of town, which you know you have been often enough, and may be often enough again."

"It's done. I'll go."—"That's right; I will come for you."

Away went Hulme to make the necessary arrangements, and I waited until he came back with a cab, and a horse in it that was a good trotter.

"It's a bare fourteen miles," he said, when we were seated in the vehicle, "and I calculate we shall get down nicely by one o'clock, and then we can give the horse some hours' rest."

"Agreed."

Off we started, and on the way, as a natural consequence, considering the expedition we were bound upon, our discourse turned upon insanity, and its various complicated forms and appearances.

This was a topic very interesting in a medical point of view to both of us, and it beguiled the way extremely well for more than two-thirds of the way, and then we stopped to give the horse a quarter of an hour's rest, and some refreshment.

On we went then again, with fresh vigour, and at a better pace than we had gone at before, and by the time the clocks were striking one, my friend said,—

"There is the village. The asylum, they tell me, is a white-fronted detached house right through it."

We put up at a public-house, and then asked the way to Mr. Needham's asylum. (That was the name of the proprietor).

"You can't miss it, gentlemen," said the landlord. "It's the only house with a new white front, and besides you'll see a plate on the iron gate, with the name, Needham, on it."

"Thank you—thank you. Get us the best dinner your house can afford, and we shall be back in two hours."

Away we went, and very soon came in front of the house we sought.

"Now," said Hulme, "although we have an order to view from Needham, something else is requisite before we can view effectually. I propose that a guinea be given to the principal person he has left behind him in charge of the premises."

"Agreed—agreed."

"We will say we have a notion of setting up an asylum ourselves in another part of the country, and that such is our reason for wishing to see how it is managed. If we say we are medical men, we shall be looked upon with eyes of suspicion directly."

"Not a doubt of that. You seem to understand, Hulme, how to manage these visits."

"I have been compelled from the many difficulties I have met with to find out."

"Not a doubt of that."

Hulme rang the gate bell confidently, and in a few moments a man made his appearance. He was a rough, surly-looking fellow, of rather a peculiar aspect, and he looked at us evidently with eyes of suspicion.

Hulme placed the written order of admission in his hand, with a half-crown on the top of it, and said,—

"We bring that from Mr. Needham."

The fellow's features relaxed a little, and he said,—

"I'll show it to Mr. Atkins. We don't usually see visiters here, except it is somebody as has somebody in the place."

"Exactly. Thank you," said Hulme; "we know all about it."

Away trudged the man, and in about five minutes a stout, pompous-looking fellow came down to the gate, and said,—

"Really—really, Mr. Needham ought not to give these orders. He gave one the last time he went to town, and we had a deal of trouble—we had indeed!"

"Why," said Hulme, "we think, you see, of setting up an asylum, and as Mr. Needham pressed us very much to come down here and speak to a Mr. Atkins ———"—"My name's Atkins."

"Oh, is it? We consented; but we consider a guinea as not at all too much to pay you for the trouble. You ought certainly to have a guinea fee for every party that comes to visit here."

"Ah," said Atkins, as he at once opened the gate, "I wish I had, that's all. Everybody is not so considerate of other people's time. Really, now, when you come to consider it, we have quite enough here to do without attending to visiters, who will not be satisfied unless we tell them the reason why we do everything."

"Of course," said Hulme, as he handed him the guinea.—"Thank you, sir."

"Is your's a mixed asylum?"—"Yes; we have five females at present, and about twelve males. Lor bless you, we keeps 'em quiet enough, I can tell you."

"Do you?"—"Yes. Of course we all has our ways. We have a soothing mixture that sends 'em to sleep sometimes for two days, if they show any idea of being outrageous."

"Ah!"—"Which will you see first, gentlemen—the men or the women's ward?"

"Which you like."—"Very good. Come and see the men's, then."

He led us into a ward where there were eight lunatics; the other four he told us were not in a fit state to be allowed the liberty of coming out of their own cells. Those whom we saw seemed chiefly melancholies, and we looked into the first cell of one of the others only to look out of it quickly, for something was flung at our heads.

"Oh, you wretch!" said the keeper.—"Bow! wow! wow!" cried the man within.

"There's a nice article for you," he said, as he closed the door. "Now, the fellow in the next cell is quiet enough, only he goes on crying at such a rate, he makes the others unhappy, so we lock him up."

"What sort of discipline do you use?" I said.—"None at all. It's too much trouble. If they will be obstropolous, we lock 'em up. We had one died here in one of the lock-ups, t'other day."

"Indeed!"—"Yes, he whacked his head agin the door jist out of temper and aggravation, that he nearly knocked it off."

"The door?"—"No, his head; and one morning we found him dead."

I need not carry my readers from cell to cell of the maniacs. Suffice it to say, we saw nothing very particular to reprobate in the system adopted. The principal blame that could be attached to the proprietor of this asylum, was of a negative character; that is to say, he did not do what he ought to have done, to endeavour to restore the patients to reason. He seemed content to receive them insane, and to let them remain so, without making the least effort to adopt any curative process.

At length we had looked over the whole place, when Hulme said to Atkins,—

"By the bye, the nurse only showed us four females."

"Well, four." said Atkins.—"You said there were five."

"Did I?"—"Indeed you did, if you recollect."

"Well, so there is; but, really, we don't care to show the fifth much—she—she—you see ——" — "We don't see," said I.

"Well, if you want to see her you shall, only don't tell Needham I showed her to you."—"Oh, no—no."

"Well, then, come along; she is very mad, indeed, and we are forced to look sharp after her."—"Violent, is she?"

"Not exactly violent; but she's eternally complaining, and when we did allow her a little liberty, she made such a racket about not being mad, as if we didn't know best, that we were compelled to put her in a cell."—"Indeed!"

"Yes; that's just it. If once a lunatic gets upon that tack there's no peace, and she or he is sure to set all the others a-going upon the same tune. How pleasant then it is when anybody comes to have 'em all singing out in chorus,—'We ain't mad! We ain't mad!'"—"Very unpleasant, certainly."

"As if they knew. As if they could know better than the doctor, or we who make quite a study of the thing."

"Oh, indeed!"—"Now, you two gentlemen are reasonable people; but we have had fellows come here who have been shocked at this and shocked at t'other; and more inclined a deuced sight to believe what the mad people say, than the keepers, and there's no convincing them of anything."

"No doubt." "This way, gentlemen, if you please. She's sure to tell you she ain't mad—quite certain; but we've got a certificate, and that's enough for us, you know; and we are pretty well paid for her, too, I can tell you."

"What is her mania?"—"Oh, the old story. She is kept out of her rights and her property, and all that sort of thing; and very much oppressed she is, of course—they all are. If you take their words for it, of course they are all kept here for nothing."

Mr. Atkins led us along a narrow passage on the ground floor, until he came to another door, outside of which was a padlock.

"This is where we keeps any one as is a decided rum 'un," he said; "safe enough here, I reckon. There's no light."—"No light!"—Not a bit, till the door is opened."

"But don't you think that is calculated to aggravate the malady, rather?"—"Of course it aggravates 'em," said Atkins, mistaking my meaning. "They aggravate us, and I don't see why we shouldn't return the compliment, and aggravate them a little."

He fumbled about among a parcel of keys for some time before he found the one which opened the padlock, and then, as he did so, he nodded and smiled as he said,—

"She's as knowing as blazes. You see, she won't speak now; but I know where she is."

"Where?"—"Oh, you'll see. It will be a nice little surprise for you—you haven't an idea of the artfulness of mad people. They take in anybody."

"In what way?"—"In pretending to be sensible."

"Well; but if they can be so sensible, and continue so, how can you call them mad?"—"Just on account o' that very thing. We know they is mad on account o' that very cunning."

"And if they were not cunning or sensible, I suppose, then, they are mad, of course?"—"Exactly," said Atkins, quite gravely; "so you see we have 'em all ways," as if it were quite a desirable thing, which, no doubt, he thought it was, to prove people mad, in spite of all the evidence they could produce to the contrary.

Now he opened the door, exclaiming,—

"There, I know'd where she'd be."

A female form was kneeling exactly within the doorway, with her arms stretched out in an attitude of supplication. I took but one glance at the face, and then I absolutely reeled back, as I cried,—

"Good God! it is Mrs. Achison!"

I could not at that moment dissemble my feelings. Perhaps it would have been wiser of me to have done so. I was taken too completely by surprise, and I had uttered the name of the wretched inmate of that place before I could recall my scattered senses sufficiently to feel that it would have been better for me not to have done so so suddenly.

"You know her," exclaimed Mr. Hulme.—"I do."

"D——n!" said Atkins, and he made an attempt to close the door of the cell; but the supposed or real maniac, immediately upon hearing me pronounce her name, rushed forward and clung to me, shrieking,—

"Save me! save me!—oh, God, save me!—I am not mad—I am not mad—indeed I am not! 'Tis hard to prove sanity, but it should not be sought to be proved. Its converse requires proof, but not it. Save me—I am not mad! You pronounced my name. I do not know you; that is, I cannot name you, although I have some faint recollection of having seen you; but if you know me, you have known me in happier days. Oh, save me from despair in this horrible place. Take me with you. Do not—oh, do not, as you have a heart—leave me here. I am not mad—indeed I am not mad."

"There she goes," said Atkins;—"there she goes."

"But—but, good God," I said, "how came she here?"—"A certificate."

"But is she mad?"—"No—no—no—a million times no," she cried. "Oh! how I prayed to God that some one who knew me would come here, and now my prayer is granted. Save me! save me!"

She flung herself on to my breast, and burst into such a passion of tears as I had never heard.

"I do know you," I said.—"Yes; I am Mrs. Achison. You know me. I can tell all that has occurred. I am not mad—not mad. One day I was dragged here. I have large property; can that be the reason? Oh, let them take it all, and spare me the pang of being here."

"There she goes," said Atkins; "large property, you see."

"And you consider that," said I, "a proof of her insanity?"—"I should think so."

"But she has large property."—"You are defending me," she cried, with frantic eagerness, while with a child-like confidence, that sensibly touched me, she clung to my arm. "You sympathise with me. Oh, God has raised me up a friend at last. I am not mad; they have striven to drive me mad, but yet it has not succeeded. Ask me any questions you please. Try the powers of my mind in any way, and you will see I am not mad."

"What do you say to this, Mr. Atkins?" I said.—"She be d——d. Put her into the cell."

"Wait a bit. Mrs. Achison, what of your husband?"—"Alas, sir, he died suddenly of a disease of the heart; and then my relations came about me, and one robbed me, and another robbed me, until I was driven to resistance, and then one day, because I would sign no more acceptances, I was dragged off here."

"There, now," said Atkins, "there's artfulness. Ain't she mad now, I should like to know?"—"Good God! I have spoken the truth."

"Do you know enough of her history to corroborate all this?" said Mr. Hulme to me.—"I do, indeed."

"God bless you for those words," she sobbed. "Take me away; I will be your servant. Take me away, and let them never find me. I am not mad. Think, oh, think, sir, if I were some dear child of your own—some daughter upon whose happiness you had built all yours; and suppose some stranger found me here, and I clung to him as I cling to you, and he shook me off, consigned me again to yon cell——"

I felt a choking sensation in my throat; I twined my arms round her, and I said, in a voice that made Atkins start again,—

"You are not mad! With my life I will part with you, but not otherwise. By God's help, I will take you away from here."

Oh, I never shall forget the scream of joy with which she heard these words—how she clung to me—how she looked up so confidingly in my face and smiled—with what wild, incoherent expressions she told me I was all the world to her—how she showered down blessings on my head. I was too deeply affected for some moments to say more. Atkins looked bewildered; but quickly recovering himself, he cried, aloud,—

"Thank you for nothing. This won't do here. It's all very fine, but there will go two words to that bargain, I'm thinking."

"And who dares say him nay?" said Mr. Hulme, stepping close up to Atkins.

Hulme was full six feet high, and one of the most powerfully-built young men I ever saw. He was then in the prime of life, and a match for anybody.

Mrs. Achison seized his hand, and pressed it to her lip as she cried,—

"And you, too, will assist in saving me. Oh, joy, joy! This repays me for months of misery. I am saved!"

"Who shall stop him, sir, from taking this lady away with him if he choose to do so?" thundered Mr. Hulme.

Atkins shrunk back with conscious inferiority, but I could see ferocity gleaming from his eyes.

"Do you think we will suffer this?" he said.—"You shall suffer it."

"We have assistance here."—"Call it; and on the moment I will commence convincing you we are the stronger by smashing you."

"Smashing me!"—"Exactly. I said smash. How do you like the idea?"

"Indeed," said Atkins; and I saw he was intent upon something.

"Look out, Hulme," I cried.—"All right," he said.

In a moment Atkins grappled him, saying,—

"Perhaps you didn't expect to find one of the best wrestlers in Devonshire here, my fine fellow?"

"No," said Hulme, coolly; "nor you your master."

Even as he spoke, I saw Atkins's heels where his head ought to be; and then down he came with such a stunning thump, that I only wondered every bone in his body was not broken by the concussion.

"Don't try that again," said Mr. Hulme, as he arranged his cravat; "don't try that, my friend."—"He's in no condition to try it again," said I.

Mrs. Achison looked of a death-like paleness, and Hulme said to her,—

"Be under no apprehension. The best thing the rascal could possibly have done was to try his skill upon me. He has now had a fair fall, and is out of the field."

"And for my sake is all this?"—"Nay, think it no obligation, madam. What do you think, doctor, of shutting this fellow up here while we go?"

"A good thought. Pop him in."—"Done," said Hulme; and in he bundled the half-stunned Atkins, and closing the door, he locked the padlock, in which the key was left sticking.

"Now, come on, doctor," he said.

"Doctor!" exclaimed Mrs. Achison. "Oh, sir, now I know you. You are the medical gentleman who attended Charles on that dreadful evening."

"I am, madam; but come on now as quickly as you can; for although I do not think we have any reason to dread a collision with any one here, yet it is as well to avoid one if possible."

"Oh," she said, "need you urge me to fly quickly from this dreadful place? No, no. The very atmosphere of it is to me horrible: I feel as if I could not breathe freely within its walls. Let us fly at once."

It was not at all a difficult task to leave the house; but when we got into the garden, and were half way towards the gate, the man to whom the half-crown had been given came scampering after us, calling out,—

"Hilloa, I say—I say!"—"Well, what do you say?" asked Mr. Hulme. "Say it at once, for we are pressed for time."

"Why—why—I—I. What the devil is all this?"—"Is that what you wanted to say?"

"Why, you are taking away one of the patients."—"You see she became an impatient, so we thought we would take her from you."

"The gate is locked, Hulme," cried I.—"Is it? Then I dare say this gentleman has the key."

As he spoke, Hulme took such a grasp of the fellow's throat with his capacious hand, that I felt quite certain he could close it and strangle him if he liked.

I saw the fellow gasping and turning very red in the face. He could not speak, but he could use his hands, and he got the key from his pocket in a moment to save himself from strangulation.

"Oh," said Hulme, as he shifted his grasp from his throat to the back of his neck; "you can produce it."—"Murder!" gasped the man; "spare my life."

"Open the gate, then, and another time mind I hav'n't got to compress your wind-pipe, when you talk of what you will do and what you won't do."

The fellow opened the door as quietly as any lamb, and in another moment we passed out.

"Saved! saved!" ejaculated Mrs. Achison. "Oh, God! I am saved—I am saved!"

"Hush!" said I. "Say nothing here—attract no attention. Hulme, what shall we do?"—"Get into the cab, all three of us, and drive at once to town like a hurricane."—"Come on, then."

Mrs. Achison looked from one to the other of us, as if we had been something more than human. I dare say she did at the time think Hulme a remarkable fellow, and so indeed he was, for, although he had been commonly called among those who knew him "Gigantic Hulme," I had no idea of his actual strength, or that he possessed the skill in using it, which I was now so well pleased to see he really did.

We walked as quickly as we could to the village inn, where we had put up the horse, and the first order we gave was to have him brought out and harnessed.

"Lor, sir!" said the ostler.

"Well, what?"—"He hasn't got half through his feed."

"Never mind. He shall be recompensed in London for all losses here."—"Very good, sir."

"But the dinner?" cried the landlord, aghast, and flourishing a napkin in his hand.—"Shall be paid for," said I, "and you can eat it."

This silenced his scruples, and in about five minutes' time the horse was put in. During that period I had persuaded Mrs. Achison to take some wine-and-water, and we were just standing at the door of the inn, and seeing the reins buckled to the hand-pieces, when the landlord said, as he shaded his eyes with his hand, and looked down the road in the direction of the asylum we had so recently left,—

"Hilloa, Joe! What's all this about, eh?"—"Crowd o' people, sir," said the ostler.

I glanced in the direction, and saw the man who had been so nearly strangled by Hulme approaching rapidly with some dozen or more yokels, whom he had hired to contend with us, and no doubt rescue from us Mrs. Achison.

Hulme took but once glance in the direction whence they were coming, and then he lifted, with all the ease as if she had been a child, Mrs. Achison into the cab.

"All right," he said; "we have the start of them. Get in, doctor. Landlord, here's a five-pound note; I will send for the change to-morrow, remember."

"All's right, sir."

I was in the cab in a moment at one side, while Hulme got in at the other.

"Stop 'em—stop 'em!" cried the man who had so cunningly got the party to aid him.—"Not now," said I, loudly.

"Thieves—thieves!" he called out. "Highwaymen—stop 'em—stop 'em! Twenty pounds reward!"—"Is there, by gosh?" cried a fellow who was lounging against the door-post of the inn, and he made a dash at the horse's head.

Mr. Hulme just touched the animal under the flank, and off we set. I felt a bump as we went on, and Hulme remarked with great coolness,—

"If people will place themselves under other people's vehicles, why, you know, doctor, other people must run over them."

We went at a good ten miles an hour, and in ten minutes the village was lost in the windings of the road.

* * * * *

It was well that Hulme was a good driver, and a cool hand at a whip, or at the pace we went something might have happened. The sudden manner in which the horse had been put to, and the attempt that had been made, and frustrated, to stop him, had evidently awakened the suspicions of the creature that all was not right, and he went on at a pace which showed that alarm had something to do with it, as well as the will of the driver.

A more sagacious or quickly-observant animal than a horse, cannot be found. He will see with amazing rapidity and acuteness when anything is amiss, or if his driver look alarmed or flurried; and many a horse, if it go over a person, will feel evident anxiety and alarm for hours afterwards. A creature, too, more susceptible of attachment than the horse cannot be; and yet this noble, useful, needful animal is led so cruel a life by many persons, and the sufferings of the horse in London, through the medium of the cabs and omnibuses, forms a dark page in the history of this great city.

Most devoutly have we often wished that human ingenuity would invent some new mode of propulsion for carriages, or render available those already known, and for no other purpose do we wish it than the emancipation of the horse from his fearful labours.

"Hulme," I said, as we went on at the same serious pace we had statred at, "is not the horse alarmed?"—"Oh, yes," he said; "he has run away."

"Run away!"—"Ah, to be sure. I won't vex him by pulling him in. This cab with us in it is no load for him, you see, and we have a capital level road here for some miles. I just let him feel the rein, and when he gets tired, you may depend upon him stopping."

"Very good," said I.

Mrs. Achison had hold of the lappel of my coat with a firm grasp, and from the half-stifled, strange, gasping sob which came from her every few moments, I could judge in what a fearful state of excitement were her feelings.

I thought it best for a time to say nothing to her, but to allow these painful feelings with which she was so much oppressed to subside, in some measure, of themselves, which they would surely do in a short time.

We had gone on in this way for about five miles, when Hulme said to me,—

"We are slackening speed a little now. This horse is quite cunning enough not to hurt himself. He has, with all this hard trot, scarcely turned a hair."

"Indeed!"

"No. He is a famous creature, and will, in a few moments, be as docile as a lamb. We are coming to a gentle rise here, and my belief is, that he sees it, and is calculating upon it accordingly, and thinks upon the whole it will be better to be composed, and take things a little easier."

"You give him credit for judgment!"—"I do, indeed."

"And, I believe, deservedly so."—"I am sure of it. I have been familiar with horses from my childhood, and know pretty well what they will do, and what they will not. A more interesting study than what you might really and justly call the mind of the horse, you would be puzzled to find in the whole range of natural history."

I hoped that Mrs. Achison was attending to what we were saying, and that, by hearing us converse upon indifferent topics, she would get rid of much of the alarm which no doubt produced in her so nervous a state.

"We are going much slower," I remarked.

"Yes, I am just letting him take his own pace. Indeed, if he were to walk the remainder of the distance to town, still, from the speed we have already made, we should have done the whole distance in a short time."

"No doubt. I dare say we came at a good twelve miles an hour."

"Yes. Unless you are quite in the habit of testing it, and making accurate estimates on that subject, the speed you are driving at is of a very deceiving character. I should say that for these five miles we have traversed, we have come at the rate of at least fourteen miles an hour."

Mrs. Achison was, I thought, attending to us. At all events she did not sob so frequently as she had done before, and I could hear her breathe with greater regularity, and with deeper and more healthful inspirations.

I would not speak to her until she herself should feel sufficiently recovered to commence a conversation, and that I fully expected would now be in a very few moments.

Suddenly, however, she burst into tears. This was no bad sign, for I knew it would relieve her, and taking no notice of her weeping, I continued to hold a conversation with Hulme about horses and dogs, and other indifferent topics, in which he joined, for the same reason as myself, as we made each other understand by a glance.

Now we came on the very outskirts of the metropolis, and Mrs. Achison ceased weeping, and spoke for the first time since we had lifted her into the cab, and driven away from her pursuers.

"You must think me, both of you, weak and foolish," she said, "to give way to so much grief in appearance, when I really never, never was so happy."

"Not at all," said I; "your feelings are very natural indeed, and just what might under the circumstances have been fairly expected."

"You are kind and considerate, and you have saved me from a fate worse than death itself. Oh, had you not come down to that dreadful madhouse and rescued me, I might have lingered there in mental torture so long, that when, by some rare chance an inquiry was made concerning me, my cruel persecutors would have been able to court inquiry, by showing me as really mad, without adding that I had been driven so by confinement there."

"I fear, madam," said Mr. Hulme, "that your word contain a brief sketch of the fate of many unhappy persons who have been, from revenge or cupidity, placed in lunatic asylums."

"I am sure of it," said I. "I hear that there are some minds so constituted, that a month in a madhouse would be quite sufficient to produce symptoms there to justify their detention for life, and those minds are those of the greatest excellence, importance, and power, because they are so very nicely arranged."

"The most delicate machinery, of course," said Hulme, "is the most likely to get put out of order."

"Precisely."

"I will tell you how it was," said Mrs. Achison, "that was placed in the dreadful circumstances in which you found me to-day."

"We are just at Oxford-street," remarked Mr. Hulme "you had better delay your narrative, madam, until we are at Dr. ——'s house, when you will be quite safe, and we can attend to it with greater ease than here."

"Yes," said I, "that will be better; and then we can send for some intelligent solicitor, who will advise us what to do under the peculiar circumstances."

This was agreed to, and Hulme drove at once to my house. The horse was sent to stable, and in a quarter of an hour more Mrs. Achison had been provided with some refreshments, and Hulme and I waited with anxiety to hear what account she would give us of the circumstances that had placed her in the painful position from which we had so happily succeeded in rescuing her.

"The last time I saw you, sir," she said, turning to me "was when I was but slowly recovering from the sudden shock of my husband's death—a shock which, I may say, was much lessened by the words which you used to me upon the subject before you left, and which made a greater impression upon me than I was able at the time to say. Mr. Minden, an old friend of my husband's, was in the house, and I must say I received every kindness from him, consistently with his disposition which is, unhappily, one entirely destitute of energy, and that kind of obstinacy which is so necessary in many of the affairs of life."

"You are right," said I; "obstinacy is very essential in many of the affairs of life. It's all very well to call it firm ness, as being a polite form of speech; but we must be obstinate occasionally."

"Well, sir, perhaps from the little you saw of Mr. Minden, you became aware that he was weak?"—"I guessed so."

"Unhappily for me, then, I had no other, no better adviser, and when I came to talk with him, instead of strengthening me in the opinions and thoughts of my husband, I found him a mass of common notions and prejudices, which now I can see the dreadful evil of, but which then, overwhelmed with grief as I was, I could not at all contend against."

"What did he advise you?"—"To open my doors to my own family; those doors which my husband had been compelled to close."

"But what reason did he give you?"—"Simply, that suppose they were ever so selfish, or had behaved ever so badly, they were 'relations.'"

"Indeed!"—"My brother, too, a man possessed of every vice which it is possible to imagine of a despicable character, him did Mr. Minden defend, because he was 'my brother.'"

"And you yielded?"—"In an evil hour I did. They took possession of the house; the whole of them, and I became a mere lodger, where I should have been the mistress. The place was converted into a scene of riot and confusion from morning till night. When I threatened I could not and would not put up with it, I was abused, and finally I was struck, and actually knocked down in my own drawing-room, by my brother."

"And what did you then?"—"I went to Mr. Minden, and he said, 'really it's too bad, but it's our duty as Christians to forget and forgive, you know. There will be little differences in families. Remember, he is your brother.'"

"But," said I, "does he ever remember I am his sister?" —"Oh, well, well," he said; "go home again, and look over it; we must be considerate."

"I did go home again, and for another week I put up with ill usage. At length I could bear no more, and I declared my intention of going to some strange solicitor, and seeking redress. Within twelve hours from that time I was in the lunatic asylum from which you have rescued me."

"This is monstrous," said I. "Now, Hulme, does not this prove what I have often said to you, that a fool is a ten times worse character in society than a rogue. You can be on your guard against the latter, but you cannot against the former. Now this Minden, no doubt, was a very amiable man, and see the mischief that has occurred through making him executor of a will. The dearest and best intentions of the testator have all been frustrated."

"Exactly; but what is to be done?"—"Why, we can both vouch for the perfect sanity of Mrs. Achison, and the only plan appears to me is to send for some respectable and energetic attorney, and to give him instructions to act at once."

"What do you say, Mrs. Achison?" asked Hulme.— "Gentlemen," she said, "do as you please; you have preserved me from the most horrible fates. I throw myself entirely on your better judgments."

"Very good," said I, and at once wrote a note to a Mr. Allison, whom I knew to be an attorney of considerable attainments and skill, and who, likewise, I heard was a man of the most uncompromising character—in fact, one who never swerved from the even course of duty he laid down for himself by any such paltry prejudices or feelings as those which infest the weak muddled brain of such a man as Minden.

While we were waiting for the presence of Mr. Allison, we conversed further with Mrs. Achison, who informed us that her brother was the prime mover in all that had been done by her family; that her father and mother allowed themselves either wilfully or from stupidity to be led by him, and that from him only had she received any personal ill-usage. Indeed, when her father saw her struck by her brother, he had actually rubbed his hands together, and said he "really very much disapproved of it, and, indeed, set his face quite against such conduct."

"But what did he do to prevent it?" said I.—"Nothing."

"Indeed, I have met with such men—men who would see any iniquity practised, who would speak emphatically and loudly against even the shadow of a wrong; and yet who, at the same time, would allow it again and again to be perpetrated under their very noses, having exhausted all the energy they possessed in a wordy disapproval of such matters, and then they were done."

"And such characters are not unknown to me," said Hulme. "They are as mischievous a class as you can possibly conceive, and the great difficulty is to quarrel with them, they are so desperately plausible. The only plan with them is to pick a quarrel about anything or nothing, and be so violent that they never come near you again. Such men as those, among whom may be classed Minden, are the producers of more evil and more litigation in society than all the knaves in the world."

"I believe it," said I.

"Mr. Allison, sir," announced my servant, and I desired that he should be immediately shown in.

Mr. Allison was indeed a different man from Minden. I at once related to him the whole story of the death of Mr. Achison, and the incarceration of Mrs. Achison in a madhouse, and her rescue by us, as briefly as I could, having, at the same time, a regard for distinctness.

He listened to me throughout without one word of interruption, and when I had finished completely, he spoke,—

"There is a remedy for all that," he said. "Will you allow me, madam, to ask you a few questions?"—"Certainly, sir."

"Did you administer to your husband's will?"—"I really don't know, I left everything to Mr. Minden."

"Oh! What was the amount of property?"—"Mr. Minden told me there were about eight hundred pounds per annum."

"Have you placed your name to any papers or legal documents since your husband's death?"—"I signed two papers, which Mr. Minden told me were necessary to sign."

"Very good. Have you signed any bill, bond, or stamped paper at the request of any one?"—"No, no; I would not do that. Respect for my husband's often repeated injunction to the contrary prevented me."

"Were you asked?"—"Often, often, by my father and my brother."

"And you steadily refused."—"I did. It was the only point upon which I did fairly hold against them."

"And no mean one. I think all this may be set to rights easily enough. No doubt the brother of this lady procured a certificate of lunacy against her from two medical men, which was his authority to confine her; but she being a lunatic of property, he ought to have taken measures of another character. Now, the first thing you have to do, is to get some half dozen eminent medical men's opinion as regards Mrs. Achison's sanity."

"That we can justly procure."—"No doubt. I will not be idle in the matter, you may depend; and I dare say tomorrow you will hear from me upon the subject. Be very careful, though, of the personal safety of the lady, for an attempt may be made to move her by force."

"We will see to that," said I.

I saw Mrs. Achison turn very pale at these words, and she clasped her hands, saying,—

"Oh, save me from them—save me from them! I should die or really go mad were they once again to get possession of me."—"Be under no apprehension," said I. "You will be perfectly safe here. You have but to adopt the caution of denying yourself to anybody."

"I will see no one."—"Besides, your enemies may not be able to find out where you are at all."

"And it is not likely," added Mr. Allison, "that any public proceedings will be taken by your family to discover you, for such would at once bring about the inquiry which would defeat them and all their intentions."

"You think, then, I am safe?"—"Perfectly so."

Mr. Allison left us, and then I sent for my landlady, and made an arrangement for Mrs. Achison to stay where she was for the present, and I had a perfect reliance upon the fact of her relations having no knowledge of her place of concealment.

"I should advise, in case of any clue being got to her place of retreat," said Mr. Hulme, "that she be pleased to come to my house in a few days, which would break it completely again, and set them at fault."

"A very good plan," said I; "I hope, however, that a very few days will suffice to place you, Mrs. Achison, at perfect liberty, and out of all danger from the malice or cupidity of any one."

"I hope so, indeed," she said. "I must be indebted to you, gentlemen, for all expenses, until I have it in my power to reimburse you again."

We begged her to make herself quite easy on that score,

and then Mr. Hulme and I walked arm-in-arm from my house, when almost the first words he said to me were,—

"Suppose we walk past Mrs. Achison's house, and see what sort of aspect it bears."—"Agreed," said I.

Off we set at a brisk pace, and soon found ourselves in the street where was the handsome house to which I had gone only to see its master die before my face.

We walked along on the other side of the way, and to my surprise I saw seated in the balcony of the first floor of Mrs. Achison's house, a low-looking, ugly brute of a fellow, with that self-sufficient sort of countenance which is so destitute of real intellect, and so redolent of cunning, smoking a cigar, while at his feet was a glass containing some steaming mixed liquor.

"I'd wager a thousand pounds," I said, "that that's Mrs. Achison's brother."—"Of course it is her brother," said Hulme, "and just the brute I expected to find him."

"A brute, indeed. Look at the expression now of that fellow's great, flat-looking, hideous face."—"I'd give something," said Hulme, "for a fair excuse to horsewhip that fellow within an inch of his life. He is just the sort of man, I think, who ought to be kicked upon no provocation at all."

I laughed at Hulme's words, and I suppose the beautiful brother saw us laugh, for he called out,—

"Now, tailors, who are you laughing at?"—"Oh, that I could get at him," said Hulme. "But it's out of the question. I wonder if he has any courage."

"He courage!"—"My good sir," said Hulme to him, "we are laughing at you. We think you a brute and an idiot. Will you be so good as come down and resent the insult?"

"Come up here," said the fellow.—"Oh, we cannot; for if we were to knock at the door, you would get into some cupboard, and hide yourself. Won't you come down now?"

"I'll see you further first, you two counter jumpers."—"Ah, so I thought. You'll take good care to see us out of sight first, that you will."

At this moment an elderly-looking man appeared in the balcony, and rubbing his hands together, he said,—

"Really, now, really, I cannot but highly disapprove of this. Very much, indeed, do I disapprove of it—ahem! really I do."

"That's the father," whispered I.—"No doubt."

"Come away—come away, Hulme; we can do no good by remaining here, you know."—"Agreed,—come on; but who's this?"

A man dressed in shabby black came up to the door of the house, but before he could knock, the brother called out to him from the window, saying, angrily,—

"It's no go, I tell you. It's no go. D—n it, I told you it was no go last time you came."—"Mr. Hardy," said the man, "I only want your name to a little acceptance which ——"

"D—n your brass. Be off with you."—"Well, but you know I signed ——"

"Signed the devil. There's half a sovereign—now will you be off?"

The shabby genteel man picked up the half sovereign and walked away, saying—

"Yes, till next time I will be off. Ha! ha! He don't get rid of me and Jenkins quite so easy. We know what's what."

"Who can this be?" said I to Hulme.—"Let's follow him."—"Agreed."

We followed the shabby genteel man at a cautious distance, and he took his way towards a public-house which was not very far off, into which he at once dived, no doubt to liquify the half sovereign that had been thrown to him from the window.

We entered the house a moment or two after him, and I said to a girl who was at the bar,—

"Do you know the person who has just come in?"—"Yes, sir," she said; "do you mean Mr. Jefferson?"

"Ah, in black?"—"Oh, yes. He often comes here."

"What is he?"—"A doctor, sir."

"A doctor?"—"Yes. And they do say he's a very clever man."

Hulme whispered to me to come out, and when I did he said,—

"Don't you think it likely his claim upon Mrs. Achison's brother is for signing the certificate of lunacy?"—"Possibly."

"Probably, too, I think. I have a scheme. Come back to the public-house. Let us get into conversation with this Jefferson, and ask him to do as much for us."—"I have no objection, but you know it requires two medical men to sign a certificate of lunacy."

"I know that, but I dare say he has some obliging friend who would lend a hand in such a matter."

There seemed not only a prospect of doing Mrs. Achison's cause some good by this plan, but also a prospect of much amusement, and I at once assented to it.

We again entered the public-house, and passing into a room, on the door of which we saw the word "Parlour," we found Mr. Jefferson seated with a glass of brandy-and-water before him.

There was only one other person in the room, and that was an old gentleman who was reading a newspaper, so we walked at once up to Jefferson, and Mr. Hulme said,—

"How are you?"—"Ah!" said I. "How do you find yourself?"

He stared at us in surprise, and then he said,—

"Hang me if I know you, gentlemen, though you seem to know me both of you. Where was it—eh?"—"Never mind that, Jefferson, we want you to do a little job for us, that's all."

"Oh! you know my name, too."—"Yes, to be sure. All's safe with us. We have an order to execute, but we can't do it. Come, now, what will you charge for a certificate of lunacy against a person? What's the lowest you will do it for now, Jefferson?"

"A certificate of lunacy," said Mr. Jefferson, in a low tone. "Oh, a certificate—why, you know, there will be Smith to pay out of it as well."—"Oh, but he his not very extortionate," said I.

Jefferson laughed, and called me a funny dog, by which I guessed that the aforesaid Smith was rather inclined to be extortionate than otherwise.

"Well, then," said Hulme, "you must tell us the lowest you will do it for."—"Ten."

"Ten shillings?"—"Now, what *do* you mean by poking fun at me in that way, I should like to know? Ten guineas I mean, and of course you know I mean ten guineas."

We both got up a laugh, and Hulme said,—

"I suppose, now, you would let us have three for twenty guineas?—three in blanks, so that we might fill them up at our convenience, you know."—"Twenty-five; couldn't do it under, I assure you; and if you know anything of Dr. Smith, you will be aware of what a lion's share he always wants."

"So he does—so he does. By-the-bye, now, what did Hardy give you for the one about his sister?"—"Oh, you know of that?"

"Of course."—"Fifteen guineas, I declare."

"You took him in."—"No, no; it was really worth it, you know—an awkward case."

"Do you know where he sent her?"—"Not a bit."

"Well, that's of no consequence. He has dropped into all her money through it."—"So I understood."

"And when, Jefferson, can you let us have the certificates?"—"To-morrow, at this hour, and in this place. Cash down, you know—honour bright."

"Oh, of course—of course."—"Very good. Then it's a bargain?"

"It is—it is. And there's a guinea deposit," said Hulme.—"Ah, you know how to do business. That's the proper way to throw a light upon the affair. Now I know you'll come."

We bade Mr. Jefferson good day, and then left the public-house.

"Well," said Hulme, "what do you think of that?"—"Why, that it will save a world of trouble. We ought at once to let Mr. Allison know of this."

"So we ought, for it will enable him at once, probably, to take some active step in the affair."—"Come on, then, to his house."

Mr. Allison had his offices in the corner part of his private dwelling-house, and thither we at once repaired, and had the good fortune to find him at home.

We narrated to him what had occurred, and when we had concluded he said,—

"That at once unmasks the whole villany of the thing, gentlemen, and will be of essential service. You will be so good as to secure the three blank certificates of insanity, as their production will be essential."—"Certainly."

"There was one question I forgot to ask of Mrs. Achison;

it was, with whom did her deceased husband bank?"—"I don't know," said I, "but will ask her, and send you word."

"Thank you; it will be useful to know if the account has been at all tampered with."—"Most decidedly."

"If that has been the case, I think we ought to get a warrant at once for the apprehension of the brother; and, indeed, each moment of delay is dangerous. We don't know but even now he may have taken alarm from the intelligence of his sister's escape from the madhouse."—"We can place a watch on him."

"True; and as we must do nothing illegal, I think that will be the best plan. Leave that to me, and do you send me as quickly as you can the name of the banker; and when I have it, I will seek an interview with one of the firm, and enlist him with us."

With this understanding we left the lawyer's, and, when we got into the street, Hulme said,—

"Doctor, can you, do you think, indulge in a little freak of my own?"—"What is it?"

"Ah, there you go! You won't promise?"—"Not till I know what I promise, you may depend."

"How confoundedly prudent! Well, since you must know, we shall have three blank certificates of lunacy."—"Agreed."

"I don't want them to be wasted."—"But they must be."

"No; I propose filling up one with the name of Mrs. Achison's brother."—"Indeed!"

"Yes. Another with that of her father, and the third—ha! ha! ha! the third."—"With your own, I suppose."

"No, thank you. I should like to teach this Mr. Minden a sound practical lesson. I, therefore, propose filling up the third in his favour."—"The deuce you do!"

"Yes, I do, indeed."—"It's very hazardous and dangerous. It's doing ourselves just what we object to in others."

"I know all that."—"Besides, as Mr. Allison says, we should take care to do nothing at all illegal, you know."

"Yes, I heard him; I know all about that; but it is such a prince of a joke, that I cannot resist it. Now, I happen to know of an asylum at Chelsea, where they are not at all over nice in their treatment of lunatics. By writing to that man I could get him to send keepers, and take the three away at once, where they would have a taste of what it was to be in a lunatic asylum for a time."—"I must own," said I, "with you, that I should enjoy the joke."

"Of course you would."—"But yet it's dangerous."

"Never mind that; I'll take it all upon myself. Let them each take their remedy. I will meet you to-morrow, and we can manage it famously. Come, say the word."—"Give me till to-morrow to think."

"No; now, or never."—"Well, after all, it will serve them right. I consent; and, in consenting, I am of opinion that one may as well be hanged for a sheep as a lamb; therefore, let us have the best fun we can out of it."

"What diabolical adjuncts can you invent?"—"First of all, do you appoint the madhouse keepers to come to Mr. Minden's at a particular hour, and we will be there to see the fun."

"Agreed."—"Then, two hours afterwards, leave the others at Mrs. Achison's house, where we will manage likewise to be."

"That'll do. Oh, you are a nice article to have scruples about it! Why, I didn't myself imagine one half the fun which you have arranged."—"Why, if we are to do it, you know——"

"We ought to do it well, of course. Then we meet to-morrow; but say nothing of it to Mrs. Achison, or some feelings of compassion may induce her to spoil the plan. Do you know, by-the-bye, Mr. Minden's address?"—"Yes, I have it; for I heard it mentioned when I was attending upon the deceased Mr. Achison. Here it is."

I tore a leaf out of my pocketbook, and handed Minden's address to Hulme, who promised that he would take care to arrange everything, and who almost danced again at the prospect of the rare fun he would have on the morrow at the houses of Mrs. Achison and Mr. Minden.

I must confess that, as regarded my own feelings on this subject—although I could not conceal from myself that there was an amount of boyish imprudence about the step which Hulme had persuaded me into—I looked forward to the morrow with feelings of gratification.

"It will be a just retribution upon them all," I thought; "and as for that old fool, Minden, if he is the executor of any one else's will, I hope he will not forget the lesson he will have regarding Mrs. Achison's."

Indeed, Minden might be said to be the cause of all the mischief; for when a man has it in his power to prevent wrong from being done, and either from weakness of intellect, or wickedness, interferes not to prevent it, he may be truly enough blamed as the real cause; and Mr. Minden, who was, no doubt, an honest and well meaning man as ever lived, was just the sort of person to induce people, who were not deep or accurate thinkers, to leave him the management of matters requiring almost every quality of mind which he had not. Fatal mistake!

There are, however, hundreds of people who look only for amiability, where they ought to look for intellect, and who think a man abundantly qualified for administering a trust, because they never heard any harm of him.

Why, these harmless people are the nincompoops of society, the small-witted, half-idiotic folks, who do more mischief than all the rogues put together. And such an one was Minden; so that the more I came to reflect upon the circumstances, the more savage sort of satisfaction I felt at being able to do something which would be of such a very practical nature, that even his blunted intellect could not fail to thoroughly understand it.

"I hope they will shave the few remaining hairs he has on that stupid head of his off," I exclaimed, as I went home. "I do hope he will be most outrageously frightened."

I thought by the time I went to bed that night the scheme of Hulme's a most happy one, and just before I closed my eyes in slumber, caught myself saying,—

"Hang the illegality of the matter. Pack them off to the madhouse, and I only wish I was there myself to see each of them put into a strait waistcoat." And then I fell asleep, quite satisfied with the state of things, and anticipating much amusement for the morrow.

* * * * *

I met Mrs. Achison in the morning at breakfast, and found her, though still very anxious, much better in health and spirits than on the previous day. I had got from her the name of her husband's banker, and had the evening before forwarded it to Mr. Allison, and now I occupied myself during the morning meal in giving her assurances that all would be well, and she would speedily find herself reinstated in her own proper possessions.

"I do not," she said, "seek to punish those men who have acted so very badly against me. Let it suffice that they see I have found kind friends and protectors, and that their machinations are defeated."

"But, my good madam," I said, "although such a feeling does infinite honour to your heart, yet, permit me to say, that in all these affairs we owe something to society, as well as to ourselves, and that the mere defeat of one who attempts to do a grievous wrong is not sufficient."

"My reason sides with you," she said, "and I cannot contend the point; but let me implore you to temper justice with as much mercy as may be infused into its administration."—"Unquestionably."

"You will endeavour to spare my father and mother."—"I am in hopes that nothing but shame will fall upon them, and to that feeling I do hope and trust they are amply amenable. I cannot speak in terms too highly reprehensible of their conduct, who should have protected you from a man who is one of the most selfish I ever met with, and who evidently cares for no one, and would sacrifice anybody to his own brutal appetites."

"From a boy my brother was so," she said. "He was always of a tyrannical, desperately selfish disposition; and when, as he grew up, he began to have a taste for publichouses, he became most insufferable in the house."

"I wonder Mr. Achison never actually punished him."—"There was but one reason which prevented Mr. Achison from horsewhipping him on several occasions."

"And what was that?"—"A positive dread of having his name mingled with my brother's at a police-office."

"Well; I don't wonder at that."—"Nor I, indeed."

"And there's many a blackguard owes his impunity from chastisement to the very atrocity of his character and conduct."—"It is too true, sir—it is too true."

"Never mind. We will teach this domestic bully a lesson which he will not quickly forget, or I shall be exceedingly mistaken with regard to the powers of memory possessed by such curs as he is."

I was all impatience till the time came for seeing Mr. Hulme; but impatience, although it may appear to retard the progress of the lagging hours, never yet had the effect of hastening them, and I was compelled to be a martyr till the hour came.

I met Hulme at his own house, and I never saw such a great fellow exhibit so much glee as he did when he told me he had arranged everything with the keeper of the asylum at Chelsea.

"The best of the fun is," said he, "that I have, finding him a reasonable fellow, put him up to the joke. He is safe from all consequences, because he will have the certificates to show, and he promises me that for the expenses of the men merely, and anything else we like to add, he will shave their heads, and put strait-waistcoats on them all three quite comfortably."

"That will do."—"I believe you it will. And now for our unscrupulous friend Mr. Jefferson, at the public-house."

"But do you really mean to pay the twenty-five pounds?"—"Yes."

"It's expensive."—"Oh, but I have arranged to have him taken into custody after we leave him; we shall get that money back again."

"Very good."—"I can assure you I have left no point unprovided for, and I do anticipate a very triumphant termination to the whole business. I quite glory, too, in serving out that old fool of an executor, who has behaved so like a goose."

"Mr. Minden."—"Yes, that's the man I want to serve out."

"The head shaving won't be much to him, I think, for he is nearly destitute of that natural covering as it is."—"Never mind; the few hairs he has ought to be all the more precious to him on that account, and go they shall, so he will be forced to wear a wig."

We reached the public-house a minute or two before the hour at which we had appointed to meet Jefferson, but we found that gentleman there with another glass of brandy-and-water before him, and a benign smile upon his face.

"Good day, gents, good day," he said. "I sincerely hope I see you perfectly well, both of you."

"Very well, indeed. Have you the papers?"—"Trust me for that. Dr Smith wanted to know who they were for, but I didn't tell him."

"For the best of all possible reasons," I said, "because you don't know, Mr. Jefferson."—"True, my dear sir; true to the very letter," he said. "Smith will be glad of the money. He has been trying several swindles lately in the way of public companies, but as he has failed in all of them, he is hard up."

"Give me the documents," said Hulme.

Mr. Jefferson held out his hand, and smiled.

"Twenty-five guineas, and I decline taking a cheque. Notes or gold, if you please, gents."—"You are cautious."

"I have learned caution."—"Well, no doubt you are right. We are strangers to you, so there's the money."

Hulme placed two ten pound notes, and one five, in his hand.

"Guineas, guineas."—"Now, really"—"Oh, we said guineas."

We were compelled to give the rascal twenty-five shillings more, and then he at once handed us the certificates, with which we had nothing to do but to fill up with any names we chose.

Our object now was to leave as quickly as possible, the more particularly as a man with a red waistcoat came into the room, and took an old glance at Jefferson.

"That, I suppose, was an officer, Hulme," I said, when we reached the street.—"You are right," he said. "Come on, our friend Jefferson will find from this day forthwith his trade stopped."

"Where do we go first?"—"To Minden."

"Come on, then. What time have we?"—"It's an hour before I appointed the keeper to be at his house."

"Good. We shall have time, then, to hold a little conversation with him, which I certainly long to do."—"And so do I. I have no patience with such an obdurate old idiot. I declare I am more angry with him than I am with Mrs. Achison's brother."

"I can understand that feeling thoroughly," said I. "We make up our minds that a certain man is a rogue, and there's an end of it; but a man who pretends to honesty, and who indeed is honest, and has no wish to do any harm, and yet by an inveterate stupidity does a world of mischief, is really enough to drive anybody quite frantic."

"And such an one is Minden."—"Precisely such an one, confound him!"

We walked on, conversing in this way until we came to Mr. Minden's house. We were requested by a little brass plate under the knocker to "ring also," and we obeyed the mandate, when the door was opened by a footman.

"Is Mr. Minden at home?"—"Yes, sir."

I handed in my card, adding,—

"Say that I wish to speak with him on particular business."

We were ushered into a respectable apartment, and in a few minutes in came old Minden, looking just as I had seen him before, with his oily-looking, shiny head, and a smile upon his flabby, unmeaning countenance. He was evidently on good terms with himself on that particular day, if not always.

"How do you do, sir?" I said.—"Pray be seated. I have not the pleasure of recollecting you, sir; but be seated, gentlemen."

"Thank you. Don't you recollect, sir, my meeting you at the house of a Mrs. Achison?"—"Oh, yes, I do. My old friend Achison, who died suddenly. To be sure I do."

"Well, Mr. Minden, I have called to inquire after the welfare of poor bereaved Mrs. Achison?"—"Oh, dear—dear! Don't you know?"

"No."—"Mad—mad."

"Mad?"—"Yes. In an asylum. Placed there by the affectionate solicitude of a family, to whom so severe a blow of fate has come like a thunder-clap."

"Is it possible?"—"It is so, sir."

"But I understood from you that her family are not the sort of people to be highly approved of."—"Nor are they, sir."

"Well."—"Well; but you know the natural ties of kindred——"

"Natural fiddlesticks!" exclaimed Mr. Hulme.—"Sir," said Mr. Minden, assuming a look of heroic virtue, and speaking as if every word that came from his addle head were prophetic; "sir, I am one who looks to my church and my king, and the *Times* newspaper, sir. I am one who considers the ties—the natural ties of kindred, very strong, sir."

"So am I."—"Oh, I thought you didn't."

"I consider them so strong, that they ought to be a bar to any deceit, roguery, or ill usage, from one to another, and more especially ought they to protect the weak from being trampled on by the strong. I think that nothing can be a greater aggravation of a social offence of man against man than the fact of a relationship which ought to have acted as a safeguard, but under the cover of which so many injuries are inflicted."—"Ah, hem! That may be your opinion, sir. I am one who considers my church and my king. I can show you letters from Mrs. Achison's brother, in one of which he says that he considers the ties of relationship made by Providence."

"Indeed!"—"Yes, sir—exactly, sir; and I agree with him."

"And so excuse his bad conduct to his sister?"—"Why, sir, as I said to her, 'Remember,' says I, 'he is your brother; always remember that,' said I."

"Did she remember it?"—"Really, now, sir, I cannot descend to subtleties; as I say, I am a man who fears God and honours the king; and I do think that the ties of relationship are quite providential."

"I do neither," said I.

"Neither, sir! Do—you—you mean to say you don't fear God?"—"Not a bit. I have quite a contrary sentiment as regards the Divinity. I love and reverence—but do not fear him. As for the king, he happens to be a low sensualist, and a man destitute of all honourable principle or feeling, so I despise him instead of honouring him."

"Sir, your principles are dangerous."—"And regarding relationships," I added, "I consider them the pests of society, and acknowledge no natural tie above that which binds a parent to a child."

"Well, sir, we differ; and, as you hear Mrs. Achison is in a mad-house, I have the honour of bidding you good morning."

"But why is she in a mad-house?"—"Sir, her brother wrote me quite a plain letter, and said she was mad, and that's all I know about it."

"You are a very improper person," I said, "to be an executor of a will, or to have the interests of any one entrusted to you."—"Improper?"

"Yes, very much so."—"Who can say a word against me? Who can impeach my integrity? For forty years that I have been a professional man, who can say I ever did a dishonourable action?"

"We are quite willing to concede to you all that," said Mr. Hulme; "but, in our opinion, Mrs. Achison has been placed in a lunatic asylum by the cupidity of her brother, and she is not mad."—"Oh, no—no—no," he said; "a brother is a brother—a sacred—a—very sacred tie. I won't listen to it."

"Why, some people have been put into mad-houses for much less objects."—"Ah, for fun," said I.

"No—no—no. I won't believe it. I dare say she's mad."—"You only dare say, while she is in a cell at a lunatic asylum. Oh, for shame, Mr. Minden."

"Sir, I will not be schooled by young men."—"But you shall. Inquire into this affair, and, at least, satisfy yourself about her state?"

"No, no. I won't disunite a family. Family dissentions are very bad in the sight of Providence. A brother is a brother, you know, and I cannot interfere. Let Providence interfere."—"Now, you old fool," said Hulme.

"Come, come, sir. Come, come, I am old enough to be your grandfather."—"But, good God, does that make you any the wiser, sir?" I cried. "Are you absolutely stultified?"

"I decline holding an argument with young men who are so prejudiced as you are. You have got hold, I can easily see, of some of the dangerous doctrines of free thinking men, which are so prevalent at the present time."—"I hope," said I, "thought will ever be free."

"I decline arguing—I decline arguing."—"Why, you don't mean to insult our understandings," said Mr. Hulme, "by pretending that you have been arguing at all yet?"

"What," said I, "now, would you say if some one was to put you in a lunatic asylum?"—"Oh, impossible—impossible!"

"Not at all—not at all, my good sir. Such a thing is extremely probable."

Bang came a heavy knock at the street-door. Hulme looked at me, and I looked at Hulme. Both our looks, freely translated, said,—"There's the mad-house keeper."

"Well, gentlemen," said old Minden, "I consider our interview at an end."—"And we," said I, "consider you mad to entertain such notions as you do regarding people's relations. You have evidently a foolish impression that, because people are related to each other, they may, under cover of that accidental connexion, commit what enormities they please."

"Two men, sir," said the footman, appearing, "want you."

"Two men?"—"Yes, sir. They have come in a hackney-coach, sir, and say they must see you."

Before old Minden could make any reply, two stout, powerful fellows followed the footman into the room, and one of them said,—

"Which is Mr. Minden?"—"That is the mad old gentleman," said I, pointing to him. "There you have him."

"Eh!—eh!" exclaimed Mr. Minden; "what do you mean? Eh!—what does all this mean?"—"Come along with us," said one of the men. "You needn't make any resistance."

"Resistance?"—"Can't you go on the gallows soothing system, Bill?" said the other man. "Come on, old big wig, blow you, or we shall have to cut you into *sassingers*."

"Soothing, that," said Hulme.—"What on earth do you mean by all this?" asked old Minden, with such a bewildered look that it was really one of the most ludicrous things in the world to see him.

"If you must have an explanation," said I, "it just comes to this, that the difficulty in drawing the line of distinction between stupidity and insanity is so great, that you have been permitted to have the free use of whatever you could call your own and your personal liberty so long; but now, for fear any other misguided individual should make you an executor of a will, it has been determined to place you in an asylum."

"A lunatic asylum?"—"The man who can hold the outrageous opinion, that a young, innocent, and accomplished lady is to receive the most abominable treatment, and then excuse it all, because the villain who has behaved so badly is her brother, must be a madman."

"God bless me, I—I ——"—"Peace, sir; we are all brothers, and the finger and the eye of that Providence you are so fond of appealing to, recognises us as such. You will, therefore, on the score of the relationship, I am sure, excuse us."

"Take him away," said Hulme.—"But I won't go. Murder!—help!"

"Ah, Bill," said one of the keepers, "we was told as it would come to this."

Stepping beside old Minden, he held him in the most dextrous manner, while Bill put on a strait-waistcoat, and then, catching him up between them, they hurried him into the coach which was at the door.

"Murder! help!" he cried. "I don't think so much of relations as I did. I am altering my opinion."—"Now, don't add hypocrisy to your other vices," said Mr. Hulme. "You know you do."

"No—no—I'll interfere. I'll have Mrs. Achison brought home. I'll—I'll——"

Off went the coach with the two keepers and the supposed old madman. My attention was then turned to Mr. Minden's footman, who looked aghast and petrified at the whole proceedings.

"John," I said, "you need not be alarmed about your master; he will be back to-morrow."

"Will he, sir?"—"Assuredly."

"He don't seem to me, sir, more *madder* nor usual. He never was very bright, sir."—"But he will be all the brighter for to-day's lesson, John, you may rely on it."

John shook his head, as he said,—

"Too old, sir—he's too old! I see what the caper is—but he's too old. It's fairly in his bones, sir; you'll never do no good with him—never."—"I am inclined," said Mr. Hulme, when we reached the street, "to be of John's opinion; but, whether or no, we have certainly exercised upon old Minden no more than a measure of just retribution."

"Precisely. He fully deserves all the inconvenience and the fright he will have."—"I don't grudge him any of it, and only hope he will be sufficiently violent to justify a blister on the back of his neck, as well as his head shaved."

* * * * *

We walked hastily towards Mr. Achison's house now, and, the moment we reached it, we knocked loudly. The door was quickly opened, and we asked for Mr. Hardy.

"Which Mr. Hardy, sir?" said the woman who opened the door. "Do you mean the old gentleman?"—"Yes," said I.

"Oh,—will you walk into the parlour, sir?"

We walked in, and in a few moments there came into the room an elderly man, who looked as calm and as amiable as anybody could look.

"Your servant, gentlemen," he said.

"Have we," said I, "the pleasure of speaking to Mr. Hardy, senior?"—"Hardy is my name, sir."

"Then we have called on your daughter's account. We mean Mrs. Achison."—"Sir, I am much affected. Has anything happened to her?"

"Nothing new to you. She has been placed in a madhouse, as you know."—"Oh, poor thing! I may say my heart bleeds for her, poor thing!—a sad affair."

"But were you thoroughly convinced she was mad, sir?" —"Do you think," he said—"could you think for a moment that I would permit my daughter to be sent to a madhouse if she were not mad?"

"That is no answer, sir, to my question. Did you satisfy yourself she was mad?"—"Of course, I—I—my son, Mark, —he managed the distressing piece of business, sir. I am a martyr to my children, and I shrink from any wrong most fearfully."

"Did your son Mark ever strike Mrs. Achison?"—"Really I should very much disapprove of such conduct, and, indeed, as I said, I could not think of having it repeated. I disapprove of anything wrong."

"And you permit all sorts of wrong to go on."—"Sir!"

"You are one of those wordy people, who talk a great deal and do absolutely nothing."—"Sir!"

"I say, Mr. Hardy, your daughter is not mad, and your son Mark has had her placed in a madhouse for the sake of laying hold of her property."—"Oh, no—oh, no; I should very much disapprove of any such thing—very much, indeed. It would harm my reputation at once, I assure you, and I could not think of having such a thing repeated. You don't know me, sir, or you would feel aware of how much I disapprove of anything wrong."

"What's all this about, I should like to know?" exclaimed a big, red-faced, vulgar-looking woman, coming into the room with a bounce, which convinced me she had been listening outside the door to what was saying. "Who dares say anything against my son, Mark Hardy?"—"I do!" I exclaimed, in a voice that must have been heard in every room of the house. "I do!"

Well I knew by experience that big, bullying women were only to be cowed at once by an assumption of violence greater than their own.

"And—who—who are you?" she said, faintly.—"A friend of Mrs. Achison's," I added, "and one who has both power and determination to see her righted."

"Hit him, mother—hit him!" said a voice from the passage.

Mr. Hulme made a sudden rush outside the door, and in an instant came back again, dragging with him the brother, who, in a whining tone, cried,—

"Leave me alone, will you—leave me alone! I havn't done anything to you. Why don't you leave me alone?"— "You contemptible, sneaking hound!" said Mr. Hulme, "I am much tempted to shake your worthless life out of you.— Oh, you cowardly scoundrel!"

"Really," said the father, as he rubbed his hands together, "I very much disapprove——."—"Knock them both down, Mark—knock them both down, my dear," said the mother.

"They won't let me," exclaimed the brother. "Leave me alone, will you?"—"Not yet," said Mr. Hulme. "So you are the fellow who struck your sister. You, madam, have the disgrace of being the mother of such a cur; and you, sir, are the equally contemptible father—a man who satisfies himself, and tries to stultify his conscience, by disapproving, forsooth, of what he never attempts to put an end to, although he knows it to be an iniquity of the first water."

"Really, really," said the father, "I am at a loss to know what you want or mean."—"What we want is the restoration of Mrs. Achison to her rights—what we mean, is to enforce them."

"She is not mad," said Hulme, who had released the brother from the grasp with which he had held him.—"She is," he cried, "she is."

"You hear, gentlemen," said the father. "You hear what my son says, and he is considered very clever."—"Oh, to be sure," said the mother.

"Considered so by you, probably," said I. "The sort of intellect this young man has, is just of that amount which enables him to be thoroughly and desperately noxious. He belongs to that class of persons who must be put down."— "Oh! indeed," said Mark Hardy, who gathered a little courage from being so near the door, that if any demonstration was made against him, he could bolt out in a moment; "oh! indeed, it's all very fine, but if you do not take yourselves off, I shall send for a constable."

"I wish you would," said Mr. Hulme. "It might save us trouble. I will tell you that my own opinion is, that you and your father are both mad."—"Mad!"

"Yes, mad."—"Me mad!" cried the old man; "oh, dear, no. I very much disapprove of anything wrong."

"And yet allow wrong to be done; upon which inconsistency we pronounce you mad."—"A good joke, indeed," said the brother. "I know better how to look after number one than any mad man can possibly do."

"And you are mad," said Mr. Hulme, "because you fancy you are what you call looking out after the interests of what you call number one, when you will find in a short time that number one will land in the dirt."

We heard the rattle of wheels, which stopped at the door of the house, and then a thundering knock at the street-door announced to us the arrival of the keepers from the lunatic asylum.

There was a pause of some seconds' duration, and I could see, by the expression of the countenances of the Hardys, that some feeling of alarm had come over them, in consequence of that heavy knock at the street-door, coupled with our presence for some as yet undefined object.

The door was very quickly opened, and we heard the sound of men's voices in the hall. There was a sort of altercation for a moment, after which the parlour door was flung open and the men made their appearance.

"Well, I am sure," said Mrs. Hardy, "I suppose we are going to be all robbed and murdered, as the end of all this piece of intrusion—what do you want?"—"Not you, ma'am, just at present," said one of the men.

"Get out of the house," said Mark Hardy, who had, now that he was driven by the sudden appearance of the strange men, taken up what he considered another secure position from which to bluster, close to the folding-doors which opened into a back room.

"Yes, we means to get out of the house," said one of the keepers. "Can any one tell us which is Mr. Hardy?"—"I am he," said the father, "and I must say I very much disapprove altogether of these proceedings."

"No doubt. Which is your son, old fellow?"—"That is my son, and I must say——"

"Oh, hold your gammon. Come, now; will you both quietly get into the coach, and come away, or must we be a little persuasive—eh?"—"Into a coach?"

"Yes, it ain't far."—"Why—why—what does it all mean?" said the elder Mr. Hardy.

"Oh, are you mad?" exclaimed the younger.

The men laughed, and one said,—

"Come, now; it's only out to dinner as you're asked, with some more gentlemen. You'll be quite happy and comfortable, I can assure you, for a better, and a more quieter, and a more easy-going, steadier 'sylum' than ourn, isn't."

"Now, Dick, you have let the cat clean out o' the bag," said another of the men. "Didn't I tell you never to say the word 'sylum to 'em?"—"So you did, Joe. So you did. It slipped out unawares."

"Oh, you hidiot. You don't know what you say half your time, I believes, that I do. Come along, my two tulips. Now you knows what it is, you may as well come quietly, and at once."

"You will understand," said I, "that these men are lunatic asylum keepers, and that an impression you are both mad having gone abroad, some benevolent individuals have procured certificates of insanity against you both, and you will spend the remainder of your days in a private madhouse, while Mrs. Achison, whose perfect sanity has been satisfactorily proved, will resume housekeeping here, and quite consents to this measure, as regards you two being taken."

"We hope and trust," added Mr. Hulme, in a tone of great serenity, "that you will fully agree with us in the necessity of this step, and that you will not only find we have recommended Mrs. Achison to look after number one, but that as often as you please she will, in the politest terms, express her regret and her disapproval of the strait-waistcoats in which you will be confined."

The father sank into a chair, and waggled his hands about like the fins of some huge turbot, while the brother made an effort to escape; but the men were too sharp for him, and he was caught, and accommodated with a strait-waistcoat in a moment. He then set up a howl that might have been heard a street or two off, and cried,—

"Oh, forgive me, gentlemen, and I'll refund. Give me a ducking, or a horse-whipping, which you like; but let me go —do, pray."

"I shall faint," exclaimed the mother; "unless I have some gin directly, I shall faint."—"You will faint in the street, then," said I, "for here you don't stay another five minutes."

"Oh, you brute! I wonder, Mark, my dear, you don't knock them all down."—"Don't be a fool," was the dutiful reply.

"Come," said one of the men; "we have no time to lose, Joe; the old one looks artful. Pop a *vestcot* on him."

This was done, and old Hardy looked at me, and said,—

"Sir, may I implore the favour of being permitted to go home from hence?"

I rubbed my hands together, and said,—

"Sir, I highly disapprove of anything wrong; but beyond such expressions of disapproval, I decline interfering. I most decidedly object to its occurring again, and that's all. I hope you perfectly understand me, sir, and that I am a very moral, good sort of man, who lets any unkindness thrive around him luxuriantly. You will be in a madhouse for life, although I highly disapprove of it indeed—very highly."

"Take them away," said Hulme.

They were both bundled into the coach, and it was driven off just as another vehicle drove up to the door.

"Who can this be?" said I.

We both went into the passage, and then Mr. Hulme said,—

"This is lucky; a few minutes more, and we should have had some trouble, for this is Mrs. Achison, who, no doubt, touched with compassion, has come very injudiciously to make some terms with her relatives."

"Shall we tell her what has been done with them?"—"If we don't, the mother will."

"What a pity we did not have her out of the house first."

I went to the door of the coach in which was Mrs. Achison, and said to her,—

"Let me persuade you to go back again."—"Oh, no, no," she said. "There must surely be some feeling left in the hearts of my relations."

"For themselves, certainly; but none for you."—"I will speak to them, and, perhaps, struck with the forgiveness I shall accord to them, they may alter."

"A dangerous experiment; but come in, since such is your resolve. This is your own house."

She alighted and came into the house, when the first thing that occurred, was the mother flying at her like a tigress, and exclaiming, as she did so,—

"I'll make you feel, at all events, for what you have done. I'll tear your eyes out."—"Really, madam," said Hulme, as he suddenly placed an iron umbrella-stand in the way of Mrs. Hardy, "I am afraid you will fall over something."

Over she flew, umbrella stand and all, and down she came with a bounce in the passage that shook the house again.

"Try it again, madam," said Mr. Hulme, with imperturbable coolness; "try it again, madam. We will see now what we can do with a hall chair. Perhaps you will find that more agreeable. Get up and try it again."—"Wretches!" said Mrs. Hardy; "you want to murder me."

"Nobody touched you," said I. "If you will make charges against umbrella-stands, you must put up with the consequences of your own rashness."

"And does my own child stand by and see me used in such a manner?"—"Why, you fat lump of hypocrisy," said I, "it was to save her, whom you call your own child, from your violence, that the umbrella-stand was placed in your way; and now you have the assurance to call upon her for some sort of protection."

"Oh, mother, mother, you know that is true," said Mrs. Achison; "you know that what this gentleman says is true."
—"I knew it, I knew it," said Mrs. Hardy, gathering herself up, with a look of heroic virtue; "I knew it. My own flesh and blood turns against me. I ought to have foreseen it."

"Having set the example, you certainly ought to have foreseen it, madam," said I. "The most disgusting object in human nature is a bad mother—one who makes a favourite of one of her children, to the exclusion from her affection of another."—"And it is a remarkable circumstance," said Mr. Hulme, "and one which on such occasions I have always noticed, that the mother's favourite has been some bad dispositioned, sulky, ill-tempered brute, whom everybody else thought a positive nuisance and a pest."

"I know that," said I, "from experience. I had an elder brother who was my mother's pet, and a more despicable, brutal, ill-tempered, sulky fellow could not be. He is dead now, and I have not the hypocrisy to regret him. On the contrary, I think him a good riddance to society."

"Good," said Hulme. "Mrs. Achison, has your mother a house of her own?"—"Oh, yes, yes."

"Then let her go to it at once. Madam, there is the door."
—"No, no," cried Mrs. Achison; "I cannot."

"I wouldn't stay in the house another minute," said the mother. "My belief is, Emily, that both these fellows have got you in keeping."—"Mother?"

"Or you them. I don't know which. Perhaps they are your two bullies. I shouldn't wonder if they are. Oh, you abandoned hussy! Oh, you wretch!"—"What a delicate-minded, nice woman, Mrs. Hardy is," said Hulme, ironically.

"Very," said I.

Mrs. Achison walked into the parlour, and sitting down on the first chair she could find, she wept abundantly. The mother got her breath, and after abusing us both in some of the choicest Billingsgate I ever heard in my life, she did leave the house without her daughter making any further effort at her detention.

"Now, Mrs. Achison," I said, "you will be quite safe in remaining here."—"Where are the others?" she said.

"Do you mean your father and brother?" I said.—"Yes, yes."

"Listen to me patiently, and I will tell you. Do not allow yourself to be disturbed, for the lesson they are now learning may be the most salutary one they ever acquired."

I then related to her, clearly and distinctly, all that had occurred, concluding by saying,—

"You will not fail to perceive that a serious and wicked conspiracy is thus completely put an end to, and that the punishment which is inflicted upon the different parties is only what is richly deserved by the least culpable of them all."

"If their feelings," she said, with a shudder, "bear any similitude to mine in the place where they are taken, they will indeed be punished."—"They will not suffer so much as you did."

"Think you not?"—"Certainly not. The suffering is all mental, and such minds as their's do not possess sufficient delicacy of action to suffer one tithe of what you endured."

"When would you release them?"—"I should advise that they be kept there some days, and only released upon a warring that if they were the least troublesome to you, the law would be put in force against them for conspiring to deprive you of your property, which would be an ample ground of proceeding."

"You will let them go to-morrow under such a promise?"—"If you wish it."

"Then be it so. If they will promise never to come near me again, let them liberated. Alas! I could not have believed that ever they, selfish as I know them to be, could have behaved to me as they have."

"Why, they only took the usual licence of relatives," said I. "What else can you expect from family connexions, but one of two conditions—either great comfort and great advantages, in consequence of their being people with whom you could be on the kindest and most friendly terms, or great discomforts, annoyances, and disadvantages, from their being exactly the reverse, as too freq ently is the case."

"It would seem so, indeed."—"It is so in the majority of cases, you will find: and much to the well-being of society would it be if these imaginary ties of relationship were all abolished."

"More visiters," exclaimed Mr. Hulme, as a knock at the street-door announced some one.

The servant came into the parlour, and said,—

"I don't know who's master and who's mistress here, but there's a gentleman of the name of Allison, sir, and he's got another gentleman with him."—"Show them in," said I.

In came Mr. Allison, and closely following him a man whom there was no difficulty in seeing was a police-officer.

"Oh, gentlemen," said Mr. Allison, "I am glad to find you here, and you, too, madam. We have made some discoveries since I had the pleasure of seeing you last."

"Discoveries?" cried I.—"Yes. It appears that cheques to the amount of seven hundred pounds have been presented at your bankers, Mrs. Achison, and paid."

"Seven hundred pounds!" exclaimed Mrs. Achison. "Impossible, sir!"—"I saw the cheques."

"I never drew but one since my husband's death at all, and that was for fifty pounds."—"They have all been presented by a man bearing a descriptive resemblance to your brother, it appears, and a magistrate has issued a warrant for his apprehension for forgery."

"Oh, no—no," cried Mrs. Achison; "I will pay them all."—"It is too late, madam—it is too late. The forged cheques are in the hands of the police."

"This is more serious," said I, "than I expected. You will find him at a lunatic asylum at Chelsea."

The solicitor and the officer stared at this information, and then I told them what had been done. Mr. Allison shook his head as he said,—

"I cannot justify such a plan, and I think it was decidedly indiscreet."—"It's all one to me," said the officer; "I'm off for my man."

Away he started at once, just as Mrs. Achison, overcome by her feelings, fainted.

But very little now remains to be told. It was believed by the police that both father and son of the Hardys had a hand in the forgery, and, from the stupid supineness of Mr. Minden, he, too, was arrested. The whole three of them, therefore, had the pleasure of being taken from the madhouse to the cell of a police-court, but not before some means had been taken at the asylum to make them there feel that an asylum was not the pleasantest place in all the world. Their heads had been duly shaved, and each of them, I understand, had had a copious shower bath, while a blister was placed on the nape of each of their necks. I was told that Mr. Minden did nothing but groan and look as intelligent over the matter as some half-dead fish, while the Hardys were in a great state of anger and intense fermentation concerning the whole affair.

* * * * *

At the police-office, in the morning, they were all then placed at the bar. Mrs. Achison was summoned to attend, and unless she had chosen, which she did not, to perjure herself, she could not help fully criminating her brother. He, therefore, was committed for trial, and the father, as well as old Minden, was discharged with a suitable admonition from the bench. There was no direct evidence implicating the father, but the magistrate said to him,—

"Sir, your culpable conduct in countenancing the cruel treatment of your daughter, whom you ought to have protected, justly brings down upon you the reprehension of all honourable men; and your hypocrisy in pretending you disapproved of it, while you made no effort to hinder it, only presents your character in a far worse aspect than it would have borne otherwise."

By the unanimous opinion and consent of everybody, Mr. Minden was declared a fool, and discharged accordingly, to fear his God and honour his king, and do anything else he pleased. He looked excessively mortified, and I never heard of him again at all.

Mr. Mark Hardy was transported for life, and the judge told him that he need not expect any of the indulgencies which many convicts received, for that his crime was marked by circumstances which made it very atrocious. He did nothing but whine and cry during the progress of the trial, and beseech mercy of the court, while everybody was as much disgusted with his sycophancy and cowardice, as they were at his criminality. And that was the last I ever heard of the mother's pet and bully of the family.

There was one circumstance which puzzled us all for some time, and that was that no notice was taken, until all the proceedings became public, of the escape of Mrs. Achison from the asylum, where we had removed her by force of arms. Why this was, though, came out ultimately. Mr. Needham wanted to receive the next quarter's stipend for her use before he made known the fact of her escape, and hence he had kept the affair so very quiet.

Mr. Hulme and I took care that it should be the ruin of the establishment, for we, in our evidence against Smith and Jefferson, the two rascals who prepared the forged certificates of insanity, fully inculpated Needham and his man Atkins in a knowledge of the fact that Mrs. Achison was not mad.

Jefferson and Smith each got two years' imprisonment with hard labour, and so ended the whole transaction; Mrs. Achison soon recovering her health and spirits, and learning from what had occurred to regard even the death of her husband as not the worst evil that could possibly befall her, as I had told her.

www.ingramcontent.com/pod-product-compliance
Lightning Source LLC
Chambersburg PA
CBHW080345190426
43201CB00045B/2159